SOUTH CAROLINA

A History

The Humming Bird of South
-Carolina & Yellow Jasemin

SOUTH CAROLINA

A History

WALTER EDGAR

University of South Carolina Press

© 1998 University of South Carolina

Published in Columbia, South Carolina, by the
University of South Carolina Press

Manufactured in the United States of America

24 23 22 21 20 19 18 17 16 15   16 15 14 13 12 11 10

Library of Congress Cataloging-in-Publication Data

Edgar, Walter B., 1943–
    South Carolina : a history / Walter Edgar.
    p. cm.

    Includes bibliographical references (p.) and index.
    ISBN 1-57003-255-6
    1. South Carolina—History. I. Title.
    F269 .E34 1998
    975.7—ddc21   98-19679

ISBN-13: 978-1-57003-255-4

For BETTY

and for my students

CONTENTS

MAPS

ILLUSTRATIONS

TABLES

PREFACE

DURING the 1920s two black expatriate South Carolinians, Benjamin Brawley and Kelly Miller, expressed the view that in the history of the United States few states were as important as theirs. Brawley wrote, "The little triangle on the map known as South Carolina represents a portion of our country whose influence has been incalculable."[1] That influence, as Miller would note, could be good or bad: "South Carolina is the stormy petrel of the Union. She arouses the nation's wrath and rides upon the storm. There is not a dull period in her history."[2]

For those who know American history, few would disagree with either Brawley or Miller that, at least during certain eras of the nation's history, South Carolina and South Carolinians have played crucial roles. From its founding in 1670 until the end of Reconstruction, South Carolina was either on center stage or waiting in the wings to sally forth. However, for a century, from the end of Reconstruction until the New Deal, South Carolina slipped out of the national consciousness. Even then it was usually individual South Carolinians—not the state itself—who achieved recognition.[3]

In the post–World War II era, a state's importance is based more on its contributions to the national economy or the number of its electoral votes than on its contribution to the nation's history. Economically, South Carolina has taken the lead in several areas such as technical education and the recruiting of foreign corporations; however, its 1991 gross annual product ($66 billion) ranks twenty-seventh.[4] Although individuals from both major parties have held key leadership positions, in terms of political clout in presidential elections the state's population and eight electoral votes place it twenty-sixth. In politics as well as economics, South Carolina is in the middle or third quintile of states.

Thus, except in history books and an occasional national news story, South Carolina remains somewhat forgotten, sometimes confused with her neighbor to the north. Even those who know the state well recognize its low visibility. In *Beach Music* novelist Pat Conroy has one character, the teenaged descendant of an expatriate South Carolina family, fuss about taking South Carolina history: "I've lived all over the world and I've never heard one person mention the state's name. It's nowhere, man."[5]

Both Miller and Brawley would take exception to this adolescent's comments. They, and countless others, would argue that South Carolina is indeed somewhere. At least for the first two hundred years of its history, as Brawley noted, its influence was "incalculable." For the past century or so, while South Carolina may not have been in the forefront of national affairs, its history has been just as rich. Miller may have made his comments about the state more than seventy years ago, but they remain appropriate: "There is not a dull period in her history."

In any general history one of the first things most historians do is establish a thesis. When I wrote to fellow historians in 1992 about my plans for this history, several of them suggested what the thesis should—or should not—be. The late George C. Rogers Jr., the dean of South Carolina historians, and I discussed this topic on a number of occasions. In his syllabus for teaching South Carolina history, he had a lecture entitled "The key decade in South Carolina history, 1800–1810—South Carolinians become One People."[6] Professor Rogers used the concept of "one people" to refer to the polity of South Carolina. He observed that a summer institute for teachers I conducted had the theme "One People?: South Carolina's Cultural Memory." I used a question rather than a statement because although South Carolinians may in reality be one people—at least culturally—in the 1990s not all of the state's citizens consider that to be the case.[7] The 1810 concept of "one people" was more of an anomaly than a recurring theme.

The concept of "one people" certainly would have eluded Native Americans, Dissenters, Proprietary officials, women, backcountry settlers, Tories, blacks, Unionists, businessmen, ex-Confederates, nineteenth-century Republicans, mill workers, and sharecroppers, who at one time or another were excluded from power or marginalized. I do not believe that there ever has been any intention to create a polity of "one people" in South Carolina. I do believe, however, that throughout the state's history many different South Carolinians have sought to establish "the good order and the harmony of the whole community."[8]

The terms "good order" and "harmony of the whole community" have taken on different meanings at different times. Those terms might be interpreted one way to those responsible for creating the "good order" and "harmony of the whole community" and quite another to those who had to live in the community of the state of South Carolina under that "good order." Not all the instances of ensuring "good order" were benign. On more than one occasion "harmony" has been a misnomer. Nor has "the whole community" included all the people living in South Carolina. Nevertheless, since the first successful British settlement at Old Towne on the Ashley River, those who governed South Carolina have endeavored to promote what they envisioned as "the good order and the harmony of the whole community." If we could question the Goose Creek Men of 1706, revolutionaries of 1776, secessionists of 1860, Reconstruction legislators of 1868, Tillmanites of 1895, New Dealers of 1933, desegregationists of 1963, governmental reformers of 1992—all of them would likely reply that yes, without question, they were striving to promote "the good order and the harmony of the whole community."

ACKNOWLEDGMENTS

V. O. KEY described South Carolina politics as the politics of "friends and neigh-bors." The same could be said of those of us who teach, preserve, and write about South Carolina. As friends and neighbors we generally tend to support one another's endeavors. In working on this history I have certainly found this to be the case.

In the early 1980s I consciously began to research and plan for the writing of a new general history of South Carolina (although, as George Rogers and Barbara Bellows have reminded me, everything I have done since my graduate school days in the 1960s—both inside and outside the academy—have led to this point). In 1992 it was Charles Joyner's suggestion to the University of South Carolina Press that led to the contract for this book. During the past five years I have cursed and thanked him—depending upon how the manuscript was progressing at the time.

Along the way many individuals have generously offered their advice and coun-sel: Carol Bleser, Bill Brockington, Tom Brown, Vernon Burton, Kathy Cann, David Carlton, Allan Charles, Peter Coclanis, Thorne Compton, Ed Cox, Veronica Davis-Gerald, Chester DePratter, John Edmunds, Jim Farmer, Leland Ferguson, Lacy Ford, Horace Harmon, Flo Heyward, Darlene Clark Hine, Bill Hine, Dan Hollis, Josephine Humphreys, Rhett Jackson, Lewis Jones, Chuck Kovacik, Bob Lambert, Whitey Lander, Jim Legge, Catherine Lewis, Rus Menard, Michael Montgomery, Bobby Moss, David Rembert, Larry Rowland, Dori Sanders, Mark Smith, Stan South, Jack Sproat, Allen Stokes, Rodger Stroup, Lewis Suggs, Clyde Wilson, and John Winberry.

Among those individuals who read all or portions of the manuscript and offered suggestions were Barbara Bellows, John Bivins, Meghan Duff, John Fishel, Blease Graham, Dan Littlefield, Pete Mackey, Amy McCandless, John McCardell, and George Terry. Jim Hammond, A. V. Huff, Chaz Joyner, Alex Moore, and Debbie Roland read the entire manuscript. In addition to written comments and sugges-tions, A. V., Chaz, and Alex were willing to engage in long conversations discussing the manuscript. We did not always agree, but the debate was productive.

Local historical societies, museums, and state agencies made available their col-lections for research and suggested illustrations. Among these were Avery Research

Center for African American History and Culture, Beech Island Historical Society, Bluffton Historical Preservation Society, Broad River Basin Historical Society, Calhoun County Museum, Camden Archives and Museum, Charles Towne Landing, Charleston Library Society, Chester County Historical Society, Chesterfield County Historic Preservation Commission, Chesterfield County Historical Society, Clemson University Libraries (Political Collections), Colleton County Historical and Preservation Society, Columbia Museum of Art, Darlington County Historical Commission, Edgefield County Historical Society, Edisto Island Museum, Georgetown Public Library, Georgetown Rice Museum, Gibbes Museum of Art, Hilton Head Historical Society, Historic Aiken Foundation, Historic Beaufort Foundation, Historic Brattonsville, Historic Cheraw, Historic Columbia Foundation, Horry County Historical Society, Lee County Historical Society, Lexington County Historical Museum, Lunney Museum, McKissick Museum, Mulberry Plantation, Museum of Marion County, Newberry County Historical Society, Pendleton District Commission, Preservation Society of Charleston, Saluda County Historical Society, South Carolina Confederate Relic Room and Museum, South Carolina Department of Archives and History, South Carolina Historical Society, South Carolina House of Representatives, South Carolina Institute of Archaeology and Anthropology, South Carolina Parks, Recreation and Tourism, South Carolina Ports Authority, South Carolina Society—National Society Daughters of the American Revolution in South Carolina, South Carolina State Museum, South Caroliniana Library, State Budget and Control Board, Thomas Cooper Library (Special Collections), University of South Carolina Archives.

A number of individuals responded to questions and provided assistance in a variety of ways: Alice Appleby, Judy Bainbridge, Bob Bainbridge, Betty Barrett, Wayne Bean, Sharon Bennett, Jack Boineau, Jonathan Bové, Susan Bridwell, Faye Halfacre, Fritz Hamer, Jennifer Haynsworth, Bela Herlong, Richard Jenrette, Bill Kinney, Tom Marcil, Carolyn McMillan, Lissa and William Peterkin, Matthew Priewe, Sherman Pyatt, Wim Roefs, Sarah Spruill, Edmund Taylor, Jean Toal, and Wes Tyler.

As I traveled the state and worked in the various collections, the enthusiasm and support I received was heartwarming. Carolinians, both natives and newcomers, care passionately about this state. The South Caroliniana Library is, without question, the most user-friendly research facility in the United States, thanks to Allen Stokes and his staff: Tom Johnson, Henry Fulmer, Herb Hartsook, Beth Bilderbeck, Thelma Hayes, Mae Jones, Robin Copp, Laura Costello, and John Heiting. At the South Carolina Department of Archives and History, Rodger Stroup, Chuck Lesser, Alexia Helsley, Robert Mackintosh, Judith Andrews, and Paul Begley responded to every call upon their resources, as did Alex Moore and Stephen Hoffius at the South Carolina Historical Society. In the state there are a number of local museums and historical societies that contain real treasures (both in staff and collections) often unknown to most researchers. Some of the most interesting illustrations and historical evidence came from the following: Calhoun County Museum (Debbie Roland, director), Lexington County Museum (Horace Harmon, director), Pendleton District Commission (Donna Roper, curator), Historic Brattonsville (Wade Fairey, director). At the South Carolina State Library, Mary Bostick and Anne Schneider responded to numerous requests for information unavailable anywhere else. In North Carolina the staff at Old Salem and the Museum of Early Southern Decorative Arts in Winston-Salem, Brad Rauschenburg, Jennifer Bean, John Larson, Paula Locklair, and Sally Gantt treated me as one of their own. I would also like to thank the circulation, reference, interlibrary loan, and map library staff of the Thomas Cooper Library at the University of South Carolina for their courteous and timely assistance.

During the final year of preparing the manuscript, Bryant Sapp was my research assistant and tracked down references when my notes were incomplete. More important, he assumed the role of devil's advocate and was unafraid to challenge some of my interpretations. His candor, dedication, and ever-cheerful disposition made my task easier. Suzanne Linder helped me assemble the illustrations for the book. She also took many of the modern photographs. Her advice on the composition and quality of illustrations helped me decide which ones to include. Minhe Ji did the cartography, and Bob Lloyd made some last-minute adjustments. Alex Moore not only read the entire manuscript but, with his unerring sense of the nuances of South Carolina history and culture, was the only person whom I would trust to prepare the index. Tibby Steedly, my administrative assistant at the Institute for Southern Studies, made sure that the office ran smoothly in my absence. The University of South Carolina granted me a sabbatical leave during the 1996–1997 academic year to complete the manuscript.

Catherine Fry and Fred Kameny at the University of South Carolina Press came on board just as I was beginning to work on the final manuscript. Thanks to their encouragement and enthusiasm, I was able to produce a book that tells the story of the state without cutting any corners.

Writing local history does have its drawbacks. I have always envied colleagues who hie off to faraway places to research and write. Given the subject at hand and the local resources, leaving the state did not make much sense. However, totally separating myself from the university did. That would have been impossible had it not been for the dogged determination of my wife Betty. Few got through her telephone screen, and I was able to work undisturbed at home. As the manuscript progressed, she read it with a keen eye and never hesitated to offer her opinion.

This book is dedicated to those to whom I owe much: to my wife Betty and to my students. For thirty-one years Betty has been a partner in every endeavor I have undertaken. Without her patience and encouragement, this project would never have come to fruition. She was my muse. As for my students, despite the opinion polls, I find that teaching and learning history can still be a pleasure. For that I thank those men and women who, through the years, were both a joy and a challenge to teach. And, this being South Carolina, associations formed in the classroom have become lifelong friendships in which we share a common bond: our affection for the history of the state of South Carolina.

Walter Edgar
Columbia, South Carolina
31 August 1997

SOUTH CAROLINA

A History

Chapter One

THE LAND CALLED CHICORA

There are in this country virgin forests of oak, pine, cypress, nut- and almond-trees, amongst the branches of which riot wild vines, whose white and black grapes are not used for wine-making, for the people manufacture their drinks from other fruits. There are likewise fig-trees and other kinds of spice-plants. . . . The natives cultivate gardens in which grows an abundance of vegetables, and they take an interest in growing their orchards.

> Peter Martyr, *De Orbe Novo: The Eight Decades of Peter Martyr*

The Natives of the Country are from time immemorial ab Origine Indians, of a deep Chesnut Colour, their hair black and streight . . . ; their Eyes black and sparkling, little or no hair on their Chins, well-limb'd and featured.

> Thomas Ashe, *Carolina, or a Description of the Present State of that Country*

The Natives are somewhat Tawny. . . . They are generally very streight Bodied, and Comely in Person, and quick of Apprehension.

> John Archdale, *A New Description of the Fertile and Pleasant Province of Carolina*

*S*OUTH CAROLINA today is a "little triangle on the map" of only 31,113 square miles. In area it is the smallest of the Deep South states, and of the fifty states it is fortieth in size. That was not always the case. Three centuries ago, what is now South Carolina was part of a much larger entity, the province of Carolina.

When Charles II of England granted a second charter to eight Lords Proprietors in 1665, the boundaries of Carolina stretched from 36°30' (the southern boundary of Virginia) to 29° (about fifteen miles due south of Daytona Beach) and from the Atlantic to the Pacific. Within those boundaries were approximately 850,000 square miles of territory and all or portions of fifteen states and northern Mexico. Ironically, given its later history, the original boundaries of Carolina contained, with the exception of Virginia, most of the settled portions of what would later become the Confederate States of America (see Map 1).

The generous boundaries of 1665 soon began to be whittled down. Settlers from

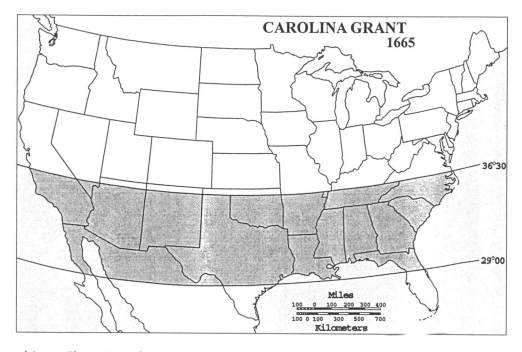

Map 1: Charter Boundaries. Based on Kovacik & Winberry, *South Carolina*

Virginia moved south into what is now North Carolina as early as 1650, a process that continued throughout much of the seventeenth century. After the establishment of Charleston as the capital of Carolina in 1670, these early North Carolina settlements were separated from those in South Carolina by rivers, swamps, and vast stretches of unsettled lands. In the section of the province "north and east of Cape Fear" a government came into being separate from that in Charleston.[1]

In 1689 Philip Ludwell received instructions from the Lords Proprietors, altering his commission from "Governor of that part of Carolina that lies North and East of Cape feare" to "Governor of Carolina," whose capital was Charleston. The Proprietors also instructed him to call for the election of delegates, by counties, to an assembly.[2]

The province of Carolina was divided into four counties: Albemarle (between the Roanoke River and the Virginia border), Craven (from the Roanoke River south to

Seewee Bay), Berkeley (from Seewee Bay to the Stono River), and Colleton (between the Stono and Combahee Rivers). Ludwell's instructions carried the proviso that if delegates from Albemarle could not attend the assembly, then its delegates would be apportioned among the other counties, with Craven's northern limits now set as "south and west of Cape Fear." He also was instructed to appoint a "deputy governor" for "North Carolina." The distance was too great, and when the first Commons House of Assembly of Carolina met, Albemarle County was not represented. Thirty years later the political division would become permanent.[3]

Political division led to boundary disputes, although the one with North Carolina was settled fairly easily. In 1735 a joint boundary commission of individuals from the two colonies met and agreed that from a point thirty miles south of the Cape Fear River a straight line would be run northwest until it reached the 35th parallel; from there a line would be run due west to the Pacific. Both colonies accepted this solution, although it was not the one that had been authorized by the British government. Surveying errors in 1737 and 1764 had the northern boundary line eleven miles south of where it should have been. Subsequently, the boundary was extended seventeen miles north of the 35th parallel and then westward to the crest of the Saluda Mountains. The last section of the boundary was a straight line from the mountains to the point where the Chattooga River crosses the 35th parallel at the South Carolina–Georgia border.[4]

In 1732 a charter was granted for the colony of Georgia with boundaries from the "northern stream" of the Savannah River south to the "southern stream" of the Altamaha River. Georgia's original southern boundary was the Altamaha because of Spain's refusal to recognize Great Britain's claims to any territory south of the river. When the Treaty of Paris in 1763 gave Britain that territory, South Carolina's governor and council acted as if South Carolina had the right to the land—based upon the original 1665 charter. They accepted petitions for 544,050 acres of land "south of the Altamaha" and issued formal grants for 92,200 acres. For his part in permitting this land rush that was contrary to the British government's plans for a "well-regulated Georgia," Gov. Thomas Boone was reprimanded. No more South Carolina grants were issued—although those that had been issued were recognized. In 1787 the two states agreed that the boundary between them would be the Savannah, Tougaloo, and Chattooga Rivers. That was fairly simple; however, the definition of what was the "northern stream" of the Savannah led to more than two centuries of friction between Georgia and South Carolina. In 1990 the United States Supreme Court awarded South Carolina 7,000 acres of water and 3,000 acres of land along the Savannah River, increasing the size of the state by four and a half square miles.[5]

When the final line was surveyed in 1815, South Carolina's boundaries were set, except for the ongoing dispute with Georgia. In 150 years what had been an empire of 850,000 square miles had been reduced to 83,825 square miles in North and South Carolina. And South Carolina's 31,113 square miles was only 37 percent of that remnant.

Today the state measures 225 miles from north to south and 285 from east to west. Although relatively small in area, South Carolina's physical landscape has magnificent variety. Geographically the state is divided into five regions: coastal zone, coastal plain, sandhills, piedmont, and Blue Ridge. Roughly bisecting the state, the fall zone runs through Aiken, Lexington, Richland, Kershaw, and Chesterfield Counties. There are three main river systems: the Pee Dee, the Santee, and the Savannah. In addition there are a number of independent streams (see Map 2).

All three of the river systems, generally flowing northwest to southeast, have their origins on the eastern slopes of the Blue Ridge Mountains in North Carolina. The Great Pee Dee, draining the northeastern quarter of the state, meanders 197 miles from the North Carolina line to the Atlantic. The Santee, with a watershed covering nearly 40 percent of the state and an average waterflow of 20,000 cubic feet per second, is South Carolina's largest river system. Most of the Savannah's basin is in Georgia, but it does drain about 15 percent of South Carolina's land area. The ACE (Ashepoo, Combahee, and Edisto Rivers) Basin, a system of independent rivers that arise in the coastal plain, drains most of the remaining 20 percent of the state. At their mouths all of South Carolina's rivers are affected by the ebb and flow of the tide.[6]

The coastal zone, extending 10 miles inland from the Atlantic and approximately 180 miles from North Carolina to Georgia, may well be the state's best-known region. It, in turn, has several distinctive subregions. The famed Grand Strand is a 60-mile stretch of sand that bows gently from the state line south to Winyah Bay. Below the Grand Strand is the Santee Delta, a 20-mile complex of marshes and streams—the largest delta on the East Coast. Beginning south of the Santee and continuing for 100 miles to the Savannah River are the sea islands.[7]

There are two types of sea islands, erosion remnant islands and active barrier islands. Erosion remnant islands, such as Lady's Island, were once part of the mainland and are relatively stable; active barrier islands, such as Daufuskie Island, are constantly changing. Generally wind and tide erode the northern ends of barrier islands and build up their southern ends. Because of the continual action of wind and tide and a two-foot rise in sea level, the landscapes of the barrier islands and the mainland coast have been altered over the past four centuries.[8]

Interspersed throughout the coastal zone are a number of natural harbors. Winyah Bay, Charleston Harbor, and Port Royal Sound serve the state's three ports. Although Charleston is South Carolina's primary port—and has been since the seventeenth century—Port Royal Sound is one of the best natural harbors on the Atlantic seaboard. Smaller bays, sounds, and inlets—such as Murrells Inlet in

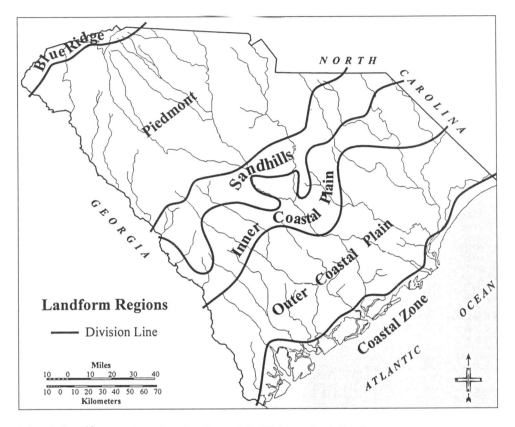

Map 2: Landform regions. Based on Kovacik & Winberry, *South Carolina*

Georgetown County, Bulls Bay in Charleston County, and St. Helena Sound in Beaufort and Colleton Counties—dot the coast.

Because of poor soil and drainage, only the southern portion of the coastal zone is well suited for agriculture. The growing season is 240 to 290 days, and annual rainfall averages forty-eight to fifty inches. In the eighteenth century the fertile freshwater swamps were used for rice cultivation. William Hilton, an early explorer, extolled the "good Soyl" of the coastal zone but thought little of the swamps: "There are great Marshes, but most as far as we saw little worth."[9]

Natural vegetation varies considerably from sea oats (*Uniola paniculata*) on ocean front dunes to live oaks (*Quercus virginiana*) and palmettos (*Sabal palmetto*) of maritime forests. In saltwater marshes cordgrass (*Spartina alterniflora*) and black rushes (*Juncus roemerianus*) predominate, while in freshwater marshes bulrushes (*Scirpus validus*) and cattails (*Typha latifolia*) are most common. In the maritime forests behind the dunes, Spanish moss (*Tillandsia usneoides*) thrives.[10]

Beginning in the sixteenth century Europeans left accounts of what they found in the land called Chicora. Based upon those records, observations made over the centuries, and modern scientific studies, it is possible to visualize South Carolina as it was in the past. It was the somewhat sinister beauty of the coastal zone, with its expanse of marshes and moss-draped trees, that almost always made an impression on observers. One person described the coast as possessing "an oppressive beauty."[11]

The coastal plain, comprising two-thirds of South Carolina, is the largest geographical region in the state.[12] It in turn is subdivided into the outer and inner coastal plains. Immediately behind the coastal zone the outer coastal plain gently rises in a series of ten terraces from sea level to an elevation of 220 feet. The terraces are the result of the ebb and flow of ancient seas. The inner coastal plain has a more rolling terrain and elevations from 220 to 300 feet.

A dozen or so rivers rise in the coastal plain, among which are the Ashley, Black, Combahee, Cooper, Edisto, and Pocotaligo. Sometimes these rivers are called "black rivers" because they appear to be the color of weak coffee. The dark color is the result of heavy concentrations of tannic acid created by the decaying leaves, branches, and roots of hardwoods.[13]

Another water feature of the coastal plain are the Carolina bays. Carolina bays are small, usually elliptical wetlands found throughout the coastal plain of the South Atlantic states from Maryland to Florida. There have been several theories advanced as to the origins of the Carolina bays, the most widespread being that they were formed by pieces of a giant meteor crashing into the earth. However, scientists have dismissed them all, and the origin of the bays still remains a mystery.[14]

Since the eighteenth century good, well-drained soils, an average annual rainfall of forty-six to fifty inches, and a growing season of 220 to 250 days have resulted in successful farming and timbering in sections of the coastal plain.[15] Eighteenth- and nineteenth-century visitors commented that in "one of the most barren districts of the State . . . [there stretches] a dreary and almost unbroken expanse of pine forest." Long leaf (*Pinus palustris*) and loblolly (*Pinus taeda*) pines were the most prevalent trees, but, depending upon the location, there were also varieties of oaks (*Quercus lævis* and *Q. margaretta*), bays (*Gordonia lasianthus* and *Magnolia virginiana*), sweet gums (*Liquidambar styraciflua*), and hickories (*Carya glabra, C. tomentosa,* and *C. pallida*). Dense stands of cane (*Arundinaria gigantea*) grew in bottomlands, and in river swamps bald cypress (*Taxodium distchum*) and water tupelo (*Nyssa aquatica*).[16]

The sandhills roughly follow the fall zone across the center of the state. When

The Port Royal area; note the local flora (palmettos, grapes, and melons) and fauna (turkeys and deer). Theodore de Bry's engraving of a drawing by Jacques le Moyne de Morgues, *Narrative of Le Moyne,* plate 5. Courtesy, South Carolinana Library.

rivers enter the region from the piedmont there is a visible difference in the topography. The crystalline rocks of the piedmont have resisted the erosion of the rivers to which the softer sedimentary rocks of the sandhills have succumbed. This erosion has created the fall zone in the state's rivers. Where the drop in elevation is swift, shoals and rapids occur. Fifty-five million years ago this region was South Carolina's seashore. The soil is relatively poor and tends to drain quickly. Thus, although the region gets an average yearly rainfall of forty-eight inches, it is ill-suited for most agricultural endeavors.[17]

Longleaf pines and turkey oaks (*Quercus laevis*) are the dominant native trees. Turkey oak barrens, stretches of exposed sand with longleaf pines and turkey oaks and not much other vegetation, reinforce the impression that the sandhills are poor land. During the summer months the sandhills are the most uncomfortable region of the state, as the characteristic white sand reflects heat.

The piedmont comprises about one-third of the area of the state. Elevation increases from three hundred feet at the fall line in the sandhills to twelve hundred feet at the foot of the Blue Ridge Mountains. It is a region of rolling hills, punctuated by numerous valleys. In the twentieth century it has been known as a land of red hills, but that was not always the case. The clay has always been there and was especially noticeable when a stream or road cut into a hill and laid bare what looked like "scarlet cheese." However, on the surface the clay originally was covered by a ten- to twelve-inch layer of rich topsoil. This was once one of the most productive regions of the state; however, more than a hundred years of poor farming practices and erosion have stripped away the topsoil, exposing the red clay subsurface.[18]

Numerous streams and rivers, tributaries to the state's primary river systems, lace the region. Among them are the Reedy, Tyger, Saluda, Pacolet, Rocky, and Keowee. Most are discolored by sediment. Even those that begin "clear and crystal-pure," such as the Keowee, become fouled by smaller, muddy streams. The region receives, on average, between forty-eight and fifty-eight inches of rain annually. Its growing season ranges from 210 to 220 days. In the past oak-hickory forests covered much of the region, and canebrakes flourished along riverbanks. In open areas there are shortleaf pines (*Pinus echinata*).[19]

The Blue Ridge is a part of the Appalachian Mountain system that was formed more than 350 million years ago. It is the state's smallest region, occupying only six hundred square miles of the northernmost portions of Oconee, Pickens, and Greenville Counties. The terrain is "rugged and truly mountainous" (although "mountainous" is a relative term), with elevations ranging from 1,400 to 3,500 feet. Mount Sassafras (3,554 feet) is the highest point in the state. Until the early twentieth century when a blight destroyed the American chestnut (*Castanea dentata*), an oak-chestnut forest covered the region. As the chestnuts died out, they were replaced by oaks, gums, and hickories. Beneath the forest canopy and along hillsides native azalea (*Rhododendron nudiflorum*) and mountain laurel (*Kalmia latifolia*) grow in abundance. With an average precipitation of seventy to eighty inches per year, the Blue Ridge has the highest measurable rainfall in the eastern United States.[20]

With the variety of topography from the mountains to the seas, one might think that South Carolina would possess a similar variety of mineral wealth. In actuality, however, the state has very little. Iron, kaolin, phosphates, granite, tin, and gold are the only minerals of commercial value. Iron and kaolin were the only minerals discovered during the colonial period, and they were not found until the 1760s.[21]

While there might not have been any mineral wealth to exploit, early written descriptions of what is now South Carolina, whether the chronicler was French or English, all have a similar theme—it was a semitropical paradise, an Eden. Observers cited as evidence the lush growth: the size of trees (especially oaks and pines); the seemingly limitless forests; the abundance of wild game, fish, and shellfish; and the healthy climate.[22]

Trees may have made the single greatest impression on Europeans. Some of the trees were familiar, but many were not. That is not surprising considering that in all of the British Isles there are but twelve types of trees; in South Carolina there are more than a hundred.[23] "This Country hath the Oak, Ash, Elm, Poplar, Beech, and the other Sorts of useful Timber that England hath, and divers sorts of lasting Timber that England hath not, as Cedar white and red, Cypress, Locust, Bay and Laurell Trees, equal to the biggest Oaks, large Mirtles, Hickery, black Wallnut, and Pynes big enough to Mast the greatest Ships, and divers other sorts, which I cannot enumerate."[24] Others commented on not only the variety and abundance of trees but their size: "Oaks of four or five sorts, all differing in leaves" that reached almost "four fathoms; in height, before you come to boughs or limbs, forty, fifty, sixty foot, and some more" and the "variety of as brave Oakes as Eye can behold, great Bodies tall and streight from 60 to 80 foot, before there be any boughs."[25]

In the forests and fields there were all sorts of wild game. White-tailed deer ranged in herds of more than a hundred from the coastal plain to the mountains. In the piedmont buffalo roamed—at least until the mid-eighteenth century. "Birds and beasts" of all sorts included turkeys, quails, passenger pigeons, beavers, panthers, squirrels, swans, geese, ducks, cranes, rabbits, raccoons, opossums, bears, foxes, and wolves. There were also "divers sorts of Birds unknowne in England," one of which was the Carolina parakeet, a colorful bird that always seemed to attract attention.[26]

"As the Earth, the Air, etc., are enrich'd and replenished with the Blessings of the Most High, the Seas and Rivers of the same bounty equally participate in the Variety of excellent and wholesome Fish which it produces." Sturgeon, catfish, striped bass, bream, jack, trout, and shad were among the freshwater fish, while flounder, eel, mullet, drum, and Spanish mackerel were found in coastal waters. Among the shellfish mentioned were crabs, prawns ("twice as large as ours in England"), and oysters. The waters could also conceal "frightful creatures" such as sharks and alligators.[27]

Just as the trees commanded attention because of their variety, their number, and their size, so too did fish, fowl, and reptiles. In South Carolina there are at least 70 species of freshwater fish, 160 species of saltwater fish, 17 species of turtles, and 43 species of snakes. And, although it is a subject of some debate, there are probably more species of birds in South Carolina than in any other state. Turkeys were reported weighing forty and fifty pounds. Flocks of passenger pigeons were so thick that they darkened the sky. Carolina parakeet flocks were also large, but the birds were not as numerous as the passenger pigeons.[28]

With the richness and diversity of its landscape, it is no wonder that South Carolina was considered a "Fertile and Pleasant Land." Most, but not all, observers thought it had a climate to match.[29] The climate of South Carolina is subtropical. Average temperatures range from 80° Fahrenheit in July to 44° in January. However, in a given month there can be wild fluctuations. The variance in temperature was something eighteenth-century Europeans noted: "Our Climate is various and uncertain to such an extraordinary Degree, that I fear not to affirm, there are no People upon Earth who, I think, can suffer greater Extreams of Heat and Cold: It is happy for us that they are not of long Duration." In verse, another observed:

"Burning heat & chilling cold / Dangerous both to young & old." The passage of frontal systems, bringing with them thunderstorms ("Boistrous winds & heavy rains"), can cause the thermometer to plunge twenty to forty degrees in a short time. Although more prevalent in spring and summer, thunderstorms can and do occur throughout the year. "The Seasons," wrote Thomas Ashe, "are regularly disposed according to Natures Laws." Although noticeable along the coast, seasonal changes are more pronounced in the area above the fall zone.[30]

Spring is spectacular in South Carolina. Dogwoods (*Cornus florida*), jessamine (*Gelsemium sempervirens*), coral honeysuckle (*Lonicera sempervirens*), bachelor buttons (*Centaurea cyanus*), cordgrass (*Spartina alterniflora*) and various magnolias (*Magnolia grandiflora, M. macrophylla,* and *M. virginiana*) brighten the fields and forests. Frontal systems sometimes spawn tornadoes, especially in the piedmont and sandhills. The last frost usually occurs in early March along the coast and in mid-April in the Blue Ridge.

Summers are hot and muggy, even along the coast where sea breezes offer some relief. Inland there is little respite from the heat. An afternoon thunderstorm might bring a drop in temperature, but it is not unusual for the humidity to climb after a storm, making the weather seem even more uncomfortable. The combination of high humidity and temperature can produce heat index readings as high as 119°. August, in particular, can be a miserable month almost anywhere in the state except on the beach or in the Blue Ridge.

October is the end of hurricane season, a five-month-long period that begins 1 June. Major storms have been recorded since the eighteenth century. In 1752 a hurricane caused considerable damage along the coast. Even more damaging in terms of loss of life and property were the hurricanes of August and October 1893, Hazel (1954), and Hugo (1989). All areas of the coast are vulnerable to tropical storms, but the area between Charleston and the Savannah River seems to be especially so.[31]

Although fall officially arrives with the autumnal equinox, the miserable, sticky dog days of summer have been known to linger into early October. In the piedmont and Blue Ridge the turning of leaves is a sign that winter is on the way. First frosts generally occur in late October in the mountains and mid-November along the coastal plain. By late November most deciduous trees have shed their leaves. Cooler temperatures and misting rain mark the onset of winter. In the piedmont and Blue Ridge winter snows are common; however, accumulations usually melt after a few days in the piedmont. Snow is less common in the sandhills and coastal plain and rare in the coastal zone.

With its relatively mild temperatures and moderate rainfall, South Carolina was considered a healthy place by early residents. John Archdale described the air as "serene and exceedingly pleasant, and very healthy in its natural Temperament." It was a healthy place before the introduction of malaria, smallpox, typhus, and yellow fever, unwelcome immigrants that came with exploration and colonization. Interestingly, after Archdale mentioned the salubrious climate of Carolina, he added that there rarely was "any Raging Sickness but what has been brought from the Southern Colonies [West Indies], by vessels coming to the Town, as the late Sickness [yellow fever] may intimate." That "raging sickness" and the other viral and vector-borne diseases transplanted to the colony had a far greater impact on natives than on those who settled in the land called Chicora.[32]

By the time of the first contact between native Americans and Europeans, human beings had been in South Carolina for nearly 14,500 years. Sometime around 13,000 B.C., during what is called the Pre-Projectile Point Horizon, the first humans entered the state. Glaciers still covered portions of the North American continent, and mammoth and great bison roamed the grasslands of the coastal zone. These first Carolinians survived by hunting and had only crude stone and bone tools. Three thousand years later, during the Paleo-Indian Horizon (near the end of the Pleistocene Era), small bands hunted big game with spears. In 1983 a fossilized elephant rib was discovered at Edisto Beach (Charleston County) with cut marks made by crude scraping tools.[33]

During the Archaic Horizon (circa 8000–1500 B.C.) changes in climate and flora resulted in the development of hardwood forests. Smaller animals such as deer, turkeys, and squirrels flourished and became food for the roving bands of hunters who no longer wandered as they once had. Semipermanent camp sites have been found all over the state, usually on forested high ground overlooking marshes, floodplains, or streams. The high ground was secure, but the forests and the lowlands provided habitats for different species, which improved the chance of success for hunters. The gathering of nuts and berries supplemented a diet of wild game and fish.[34]

The peoples of the Archaic Horizon probably migrated with the seasons from one location to another in search of food. Shellfish were an important staple in the diets of some, and the shell mounds and middens that dot the lower part of the state are testimony to centuries of seasonal occupation. Archaeological investigation of these mounds has revealed that these semimobile bands developed trade with one another. For example, tools made of chert (a quartz found only in the coastal plain) have been found all over the piedmont. Similarly, tools made of steatite (soapstone found only in the piedmont) have been found in the coastal plain.[35]

Toward the end of the Archaic Horizon (circa 2500–1000 B.C.), fiber-tempered pottery (plant fibers were infused into clay to promote the even firing of the pots) evolved along the Savannah River. The oldest-known pottery in North America was first found at Stallings Island (Columbia County, Georgia), near Aiken. Possibly, the Savannah River region was a "technological cradle of civilization." Late Archaic peoples also domesticated wild plants such as sunflowers (*Helianthus*) and sumpweed (*Iva*) and began to practice a rude agriculture.[36]

The peoples of the Woodland Horizon (circa 1000 B.C.–A.D. 1500) began to settle down. Agriculture became more important as squash (*Cucurbita*) and corn (*Zea mays*) joined the other domesticated plants in garden plots. Pottery became more sophisticated. Spears were supplemented by bows and arrows, which made hunting more effective. Archaeological evidence suggests that there were probably residential structures of some sort at several sites.[37]

About A.D. 1150 intruders, the Mississippians, entered South Carolina and built a series of settlements in river valleys along the fall zone. Although their origins are obscure, the Mississippian culture flourished in southwestern Illinois and from there spread into other parts of the continent. The newcomers were not welcome and had to build palisades to protect their villages from hostile Woodlands people.[38]

Mississippian villages generally were located on bluffs overlooking rich bottomlands. Large earthen temple mounds were the heart of the village and were surrounded by thatched-roofed wattle and daub residences. The mounds had religious significance, and the Mississippians had an elaborate social and religious hierarchy. The Mississippian chiefdom of Cofitachequi was known throughout the south Atlantic region as a rich and powerful nation. Its capital was at Mulberry Mound on the Wateree River (Kershaw County). Although Cofitachequi was still regarded as a major nation in the late seventeenth century, it had been in a state of decline for nearly a century—since the first European contact with native Carolinians.[39]

The other native South Carolinians were Woodlands people. Traditionally they were categorized by language group: Algonkian, Iroquoian, Siouan, or Muskogean. Based upon early ethnic studies, the state was neatly divided among these groups. Siouan peoples lived in the area east of the Catawba/Wateree Rivers and north of the Santee; Muskogean south of the Santee, along the coast to the Savannah; Iroquoian in the western third of the state; and Algonkian along the Savannah between Iroquoian and Muskogean territories. Over the past two decades, however, scholars have questioned the linguistic classification and history of a number of nations within the boundaries of South Carolina (see Map 3).[40]

Although some of the older assumptions are now being challenged, there are also some that have been confirmed. Iroquoian people (Cherokee) did occupy the western third of the state and Algonkian (Savannah) the area bordering the river of the same name. There was at least one Siouan nation (Catawba) in the area east of the Wateree, but the language of the remaining nations there is not known. The coastal Indians north of the Ashley River spoke a Siouan language, but those south of the river may have spoken a Muskogean one.[41]

Among the questions that cannot be answered are exactly how many Indian nations there were before the first contact with Europeans. Some older accounts list more than forty; however, the reliability of these is questionable. Some of the lists

Mississippian pottery from the Mulberry archaeological site (Cofitachiqui). Courtesy, South Carolina Institute of Archaeology and Anthropology.

may have been combined over time, resulting in duplications. Also, were Wimbee, Combahee, and Ashepoo names given to older coastal nations that had moved? The commonly accepted names of nations sometimes were what others called them, not what they called themselves. Identification, in the European sense of nationality, was foreign to them. For example, *Cherokee* may be derived from a Creek term meaning "people of another language." The Cherokee existed, of that there is no doubt, but what about the Back-Hook, Hook, Saluda, and Wappoo?[42]

By the time Europeans, especially the English, began to record information on the indigenous peoples, some of the Indian nations had ceased to exist. Disease was already a factor in the sixteenth century. When Spanish explorer Hernán de Soto entered the chiefdom of Cofitachequi in 1540 he found several villages almost depopulated by an epidemic that had ravaged the area two years previously. Whatever had killed the native population had likely been contracted by its interacting with the ill-fated Spanish colony of San Miguel de Gualdape. In 1600 one estimate placed the Indian population at about fifteen thousand. If that figure is accurate, then the Indian population prior to the first European contacts in 1521 was larger, perhaps somewhere between seventeen thousand and thirty thousand.[43]

Independence characterized the Indians' political organization. The nineteen coastal nations are not known to have lived anywhere else. They apparently maintained separate identities, and while there may have been occasional alliances, there was no confederacy. The Catawba were a confederacy in which, evidently, each con-

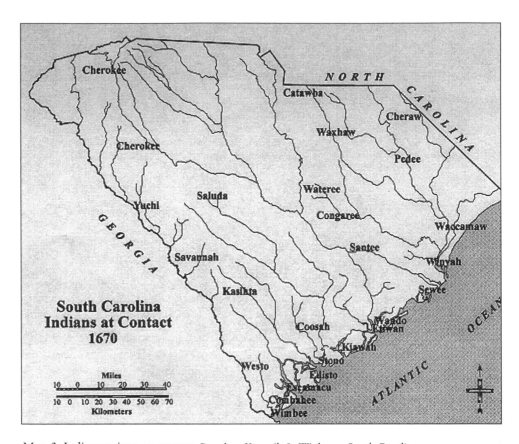

Map 3: Indian nations at contact. Based on Kovacik & Winberry, *South Carolina*

stituent nation maintained its own language and customs. These peoples had been in South Carolina for several centuries before the first European contacts.[44]

The term *Catawba* did not appear until about 1715, when Europeans began to use it to describe the group of Indian communities on the upper reaches of the Catawba River in present-day York County. Within thirty years the Indians themselves accepted the term. The Catawba were a loose grouping of often unrelated villages and peoples (such as Esau, Sugaree, Nassaw, and Cheraw) that was able to maintain its population by accepting refugees from the smaller coastal nations fleeing white settlement. External pressures from Indian enemies, especially the Iroquois, and white settlers forced these diverse peoples to create the Catawba nation. Throughout the eighteenth century the Catawba continually made adjustments brought about by war, disease, trade, settlement, and internal division—and they managed to survive.[45]

Studies of the Cherokee list their population as declining by nearly 50 percent after the first European contact in the sixteenth century. The Cherokee had been in South Carolina longer than any other nation, perhaps for several thousand years, but they were not a unified nation-state. Rather, they were "an aggregate of politically independent villages" grouped as the lower, middle, valley, and overhill towns. An example of differences within the Cherokee nation could be seen in their pottery. The pottery of the overhill towns was undecorated but had a shiny glaze made from freshwater mussels found in the Tennessee River, while that of the lower towns was noted for its stamped designs. The independent nature of the various nations was underscored by the diversity of languages they spoke.[46]

Linguistic variances were significant. Four centuries ago the four language groups spoken in South Carolina were "as different from each other as English is from Chinese." Some Indians were multilingual, and there appears to have been a lingua franca of sorts, but it has no name. While the various nations may have spoken different languages, that does not mean they were different culturally. In general, the early Carolinians had similar patterns of existence.[47]

The Indians were at home in the fields and forest. They believed in an orderly world where the forces of nature, including humans, should be in harmony. Communication with the spirits of the animal and plant worlds was common practice. When a young man killed his first animal and caught his first fish, he did not eat them. This was so as not to offend their spirits into denying him good hunting or fishing in the future. Even in the gathering of herbs, such as ginseng, there was a ritual and a prayer. Every living thing and every force in nature had a spirit. Each needed to be mollified in order to maintain the balance and harmony of the natural world.[48]

Fire was probably one of the most important elements in Indian cultural life. A Cherokee myth described how fire came into the world. When the world began, it was cold. From the heavens thunder sent lightning, which set fire to a hollow sycamore tree standing on an island. The animals knew it was there and tried to figure out how to get it to the mainland. A series of birds and reptiles tried and failed. In their failures they and their descendants were marked: the raven, black racer, and great black snake fell into the fire, which singed them black; the screech owl's red eyes were burned by hot smoke; and the great horned owl's white rings were created by burning ash. Finally, the little water spider spun thread and made a bowl for her back and successfully transported an ember, which was the ancestor of the first fire.[49]

Almost all aspects of everyday life were affected by fire. For example, it was used to girdle trees, the first stage in the clearing of new fields. Near villages fires were used to burn away brush that furnished habitats for fleas and ticks and could provide protective cover for enemies. Once or twice a year fires were set to assist with hunting, to drive game out so that it could be killed more easily. Also, firing the forests encouraged the development of secondary growth that provided cover and food for deer and fowl. The burning of stubble and debris in planted fields fertilized the soil. In order to make a dugout canoe, fire was used to soften the wood so that it could be scraped and hollowed out. Potters used fire to harden their clay wares. Over cooking fires corn was roasted or parched, bread was baked, and meat was boiled or roasted. Indians also barbecued venison, buffalo, and bear "very gradually over a slow clear fire, upon a large wood gridiron, raised two feet above the fire." Venison cooked in this fashion would keep five to six weeks. Some villages ceremoniously maintained perpetual fires.[50]

Village and town sites were usually chosen for defensive or agricultural purposes. An island, bluff, or peninsula could be more easily fortified than open terrain. In the piedmont some villages were built adjacent to the rich bottomlands of creeks and smaller streams that provided fertile soil for crops. The Cherokee generally built their towns along rivers and streams. The waterways served as avenues of trade and also as essential parts of purification rites. Coastal nations maintained inland villages for most of the year and moved to the beach for the summer months. The inland nations lived in a particular settlement until the land was exhausted.[51]

Town plans varied, but most had a community or council house at their center and a square or plaza which served as a venue for the sport that was the ancestor of lacrosse. Along the coast circular buildings were made of wattle and daub with thatched roofs woven from palmetto fronds. Further inland the Waxhaw built wooden-framed buildings covered with bark. Catawba houses were round or oval structures made from bent saplings and bark. Cherokee dwellings were plastered log structures roofed with wooden shingles. Usually fields were adjacent to the towns; however, one Edisto village was near a forest in which there were scattered cornfields and dwellings.[52]

The size of the villages ranged from perhaps an extended family to several hundred. East of the Blue Ridge Mountains in the early eighteenth century there were twenty-one hundred Cherokee living in sixteen towns. A summer town for the Edisto may have had as many as four hundred inhabitants. However, during the winter those four hundred moved inland to twelve or thirteen villages that probably consisted of extended families.[53]

Coastal Indians; note the dwelling and the dugout canoe. Theodore de Bry's engraving of a drawing by Jacques le Moyne de Morgues, *Narrative of Le Moyne*, plate 22. Courtesy, South Caroliniana Library.

The establishment of a household took place by mutual consent. Sexual promiscuity was accepted from puberty until adulthood when a man and a woman decided to become a couple. This arrangement could be broken by either party. Monogamy seemed to be the rule, although the Creeks and perhaps some of the smaller tribes north of the Santee may have practiced polygamy. Children in Indian families were treasured, and discipline was casual. In the division of labor within the family, women were responsible for child rearing.[54]

Women were also responsible for making the family's clothing, when it was used. Coastal residents generally went naked. Some may have worn animal skins, and there is record of young women wearing dresses made of Spanish moss. In the interior, clothing fashioned from animal hides and skins, especially deerskins, was the norm. Clothing worn by the Cherokee was fairly simple: moccasins, a skin covering for the midsection, and a cloak (buffalo hide for winter and feathers for summer). Catawba women wrapped cloth blankets around their waists for skirts and draped deerskin shawls over their shoulders; Catawba men wore leggings and loose shirts. Both men and women tattooed their bodies and pierced their ears and noses for ring ornaments.[55]

Providing food for the family was also primarily women's work. Along the coast women produced about 50 percent of the food supply through gardening (25 percent) and gathering (25 percent). In other regions the women produced about 75 percent (50 percent gardening and 25 percent gathering). They tended the fields, except along the coast where both men and women worked together. Indian fields were a confusion: corn, beans, squash, pumpkins, and watermelons were all planted together. This actually was an effective form of organic farming. Beans replenished the soil, and the dense foliage of beans and squash kept down weeds. Produce from the fields was supplemented by the gathering of nuts and berries. Indians did not domesticate any wild animals, probably because of their beliefs in animal spirits. Men provided the rest of the food supply through hunting and fishing.[56]

Hunting was not simply a matter of an individual's walking a short distance outside the village and shooting a deer, bear, buffalo, or turkey. It took great skill to track and kill game with a spear (hurled with great velocity by means of an atlatl) or with a bow and arrow. Hunting was done alone or, in the fall, as a communal activity. The Catawba, for example, hunted in family groups from September to March. When a village's men went on an annual hunt in the late fall after harvest, they sometimes used controlled burning to drive game into a small area so that it would be easier to kill. Hunting occurred all year, except along the coast where fall and winter were the hunting season. Fish were snared using hooks, nets, weirs, and sometimes bows and arrows. The Cherokee on occasion used walnut bark to poison small areas of streams or ponds; the poison temporarily stunned the fish for easy gathering.[57]

Hunting skill was highly regarded by all Indians. In order to enhance a male's peripheral vision, and thereby his hunting dexterity, the Etiwan and the Waxhaw practiced head deformation. With bulging eyes and flattened foreheads, these males improved their hunting prowess and their ability to attract a mate: "the prettiest Girls being always bestow'd upon the chiefest Sports-Men." Cherokee women also considered a man's hunting skills when thinking about a potential mate. Whenever there was a successful hunting or fishing expedition, there usually was feasting and celebration.[58]

The number and type of observances varied from nation to nation. The coastal nations celebrated six major feasts annually. The Catawba had a major harvest festival in the fall. For the Cherokee the busk, or green corn, feasts seem to have been the most significant. Most of these celebrations involved fasting, feasting, singing, dancing, and ritual. Some festivities had religious connotations, but it must be remembered that even when paying homage to various spirits Indians did not worship idols. Women as well as men participated in some of the rites, although certain of these were restricted to men.[59]

In some nations women played a role in government, participating in tribal council discussions. A majority of the Kussoe captains whose marks appear on an early

"Austenaco, Commander in Chief of the Cherokee Nation" in court dress. Versions of the illustration appeared in several London magazines. Courtesy, National Anthropological Archives, Smithsonian Institution.

land cession were women; the Edisto had women greet visitors; and there were women chieftains of the Ashepoo, Escamacu, and Wateree. Among the Cherokee, women were the "gatekeepers of Cherokee society" and played a significant role in decisions regarding going to war and keeping the peace. They also sat on village councils and on occasion fought as "war-women." One of the most famous native American women was the "Queen of Cofitachequi," who greeted Soto in 1540 and became a part of American folklore. Among several of the coastal nations, chieftains inherited their positions; Cherokee chieftains did not. A council representing the various villages of the nation chose a headman from the kinsmen of the previous headman.[60]

The real authority, however, lay not with the chieftain but with the village council. In council each adult in the village had a voice and a veto. No decision could ever be final, as any subject could be brought up again for debate. If a decision were agreed upon, there was no way to enforce it if a member of the village chose to ignore it. This would prove to be a major point of contention with Europeans and "peace treaties," because neither the chieftain nor the council could bind an individual member of the nation. Public opinion and the threat of public shame or ostracism, not threat of physical punishment, kept order in Indian communities.[61]

The Indian nations of South Carolina were fairly stable and were able to coexist without much difficulty until the introduction of foreign trade, technology, and disease. The incessant warfare among nations, on which Europeans almost invariably commented, was not war in the European sense. There was no attempt to eliminate a neighboring people. Rather, Indian warfare was more likely part of the natives' "eye for an eye" ethics system. Europeans frequently incited Indian warfare for their own purposes. With the arrival of Europeans, the order and harmony which were central to the world of all native Americans would eventually disappear. In their stead would be a European order based upon power.[62]

Chapter Two

SPANISH SOUTH CAROLINA

On the third day of May, the Governor [Soto] set out from Cutifachiqui; and, it being discovered that the wish of the Cacica was to leave the Christians, if she could, giving them neither guides nor tamemes, because of the outrages committed upon the inhabitants . . . the Governor ordered that she should be placed under guard and took her with him. This treatment . . . was not a proper return for the hospitable welcome he had received. . . .

About the place, from half a league to a league off, were large vacant towns, grown up in grass, that appeared as if no people had lived in them for a long time. The Indians said that, two years before, there had been a pest in the land.

> *The Narrative of the Expedition of Hernando De Soto By the*
> *Gentleman of Elvas*

*I*N SIXTEENTH-CENTURY Europe the ambitions of monarchs, fueled by religious conflict between Protestants and Roman Catholics and stoked by old-fashioned greed, led to the creation and expansion of overseas empires. Portugal and Spain both had already established empires, but it was Spain's holdings in the New World that were the envy of other nations. England, France, and the Netherlands financed intrepid explorers who made tenuous claims to vast stretches of the globe in the name of their sponsors.

Within twenty years of settlement Spain's Caribbean colonies were running short of labor. Disease and mistreatment had reduced the native population, which the Spaniards had enslaved. On the island of Española a prominent official and sugar planter, Lucas Vásquez de Ayllón, was determined to find a more reliable labor force. In 1514 Ayllón sent an agent north to explore the area beyond the Bahama Islands. On the south Atlantic coast, somewhere between present-day Georgia and Cape Fear, he made landfall and found natives much larger than those of the Caribbean. Encouraged by his agent's report, Ayllón sent out a second expedition in 1521. Unfortunately, this second expedition initiated what would become an all-too-familiar pattern of European treachery and mistreatment of the Indians.

After landing on the coast of what is now South Carolina, the Spaniards enticed some natives to come on board their ships. As soon as the Indians were on board, the ships weighed anchor and set sail for Española, where the captives were to be sold into slavery. En route one of the ships was wrecked and a number of the captives either drowned or died. Among the survivors was a young male who was given the name Francisco Chicora.

Chicora learned Spanish, became a Christian, and in 1523 accompanied Ayllón to Spain where he entertained the court with his tales of his native land: Chicora. Some of the tales the Indian related were substantiated by later observers; however, he also knew how to spin a good yarn. Among the fanciful stories he told was one of a strange people with hard tails three feet long. Because of these appendages they had to dig holes in order to sit down. Unfortunately, they subsisted solely on fish, and when the fish disappeared, the long-tailed people died out. Much of what Chicora related found its way into print in two major sixteenth-century publications. Chicora's testimony intrigued the Spanish court and helped Ayllón obtain a contract with Charles V to explore and settle the area north of today's Florida peninsula.[1]

Upon his return to the West Indies in 1525, Ayllón dispatched a scout ship. On 18 August 1525 (St. Helena's Day) the Spaniards sighted a point of land and named it and the surrounding waters Santa Elena in honor of the saint. After the scouts returned, Ayllón made plans for a major colonizing expedition, assembled a fleet of six ships, and recruited six hundred settlers. His intent to establish a permanent settlement was affirmed by the inclusion of livestock, black slaves, and missionaries. The expedition landed somewhere on the South Carolina coast in the summer of 1526 and founded the town of San Miguel de Gualdape.[2]

Ayllón's colony seemed ill-fated from the start. A ship and all its supplies were lost as it approached the coast. Francisco Chicora, acting as interpreter and guide, deserted the Spaniards at his first opportunity. The town's swampy location was unhealthy, and Ayllón was among those who came down with a fever and died in October 1526. After his death a group of malcontents mutinied, jailed his successor, and took over the colony. The mutineers then proceeded to mistreat the local Indians and slaves, who then turned on their oppressors. The Indians killed a number of colonists, and the slaves mounted the first slave rebellion in North America. The mutiny collapsed and the mutineers were executed, but the colonists' troubles did not end. They did not have enough food to get through the winter, and the only local source, the Indians, remained openly hostile. The surviving settlers decided to call it quits and return to Española. During the stormy winter voyage home, some colonists froze to death—perhaps a fitting conclusion to the grim saga of the Ayllón expedition. Of the 600 settlers who had sailed from the Caribbean in the summer of 1526, only 150 made it back safely. The failed settlement at San Miguel de Gualdape was the first European colony in what is now the United States.[3]

Although Ayllón's attempt to establish a colony was unsuccessful, Spain was still interested in exploring La Florida. In 1540 Hernán de Soto began a journey through

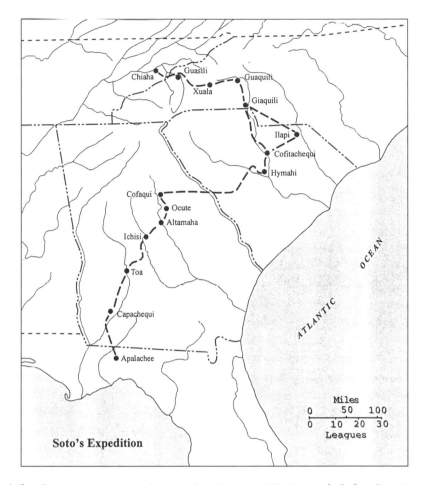

Map 4: Soto's route. Based on Hudson, Smith & DePratter, 'The Hernando DeSoto Expedition' in *Southeastern Archaeology*

the Southeast that would eventually end at the Mississippi River. His group of adventurers, some six hundred strong, crossed the Savannah River probably near Silver Bluff in Aiken County. They marched through the sandhills to the Congaree River and followed it to its junction with the Wateree. Then, turning north, the Spaniards followed the Wateree to the principal town of the chiefdom of Cofitachequi (see Map 4).[4]

When the Spaniards entered the town, they were welcomed by its ruler, whom they called the Cacica of Cofitachequi. In greeting Soto she removed a strand of pearls and placed them over his head. For two weeks Soto and his band were the

Indians' guests, but when he decided it was time to move out, he ordered the queen and some of her ladies taken hostage. The women would be guarantees against any native hostility and would also serve as guides. "This treatment," wrote one of Soto's men, "was not a proper return for the hospitable welcome." After leaving the town, the Spaniards followed the Wateree and Catawba Rivers into North Carolina and then turned west toward the mountains.[5]

The first three contacts the Indians had with Europeans all included betrayal and mistreatment. Unfortunately, these were not the worst consequences of the early Spanish presence in early South Carolina. Soto's men found Spanish artifacts, including a rosary and a cross, which probably had come from San Miguel de Gualdape. They also encountered Indian villages where the inhabitants had been killed several years earlier by an unknown disease. The epidemic, whatever it might have been, was the real legacy of the Ayllón settlement. As he marched westward, Soto left a similar one. In an unintentional, sixteenth-century version of biological warfare, nearly one-half of the Cherokee nation may have perished as a result of diseases transmitted by the Spaniards.[6]

Soto's expedition strengthened Spain's claims to the lands north of the peninsula of Florida, but it did nothing to diminish the potential for conflict with other European powers. Spain was interested in not only expanding the borders of her empire but also in protecting the wealth of the Americas that flowed back home in its treasure fleets. After rendezvousing at Havana, the fleets sailed north through the Bahama Channel and caught the prevailing westerly winds for the voyage home. A colony on Port Royal Sound, the best natural harbor on the south Atlantic coast, would provide a base to help protect the fleet (see Map 5). There was also the possibility that an overland route could be established so that the wealth of Mexico could be transported via mule caravans to an Atlantic port and then placed on ships for the voyage home. In that way the treasure ships could avoid the triple dangers of the Caribbean and the Bahama Channel: hurricanes, rival navies, and buccaneers. Conversely, if an enemy were to establish a foothold in the area, it would be a serious threat to Spain's convoys.[7]

Spain had every reason to be concerned about the claims that other nations made to what it considered its empire. Since the 1497 voyage of John Cabot, England had claimed all of eastern North America. However, it was not England that Spain viewed as the real menace; it was France. In 1524 Giovanni de Verrazano, in the employ of France, had explored the eastern seaboard as far south as the Long Bay (present-day Grand Strand). The French did not immediately exploit their claim, but they posed a potential threat to the security of the proposed overland route to Mexico, of Spain's claims to La Florida, its treasure fleet, and Caribbean colonies.[8]

In 1559 Philip II of Spain personally directed that a colony be located at what he called Punta de Santa Elena. Two years later an expedition under the command of

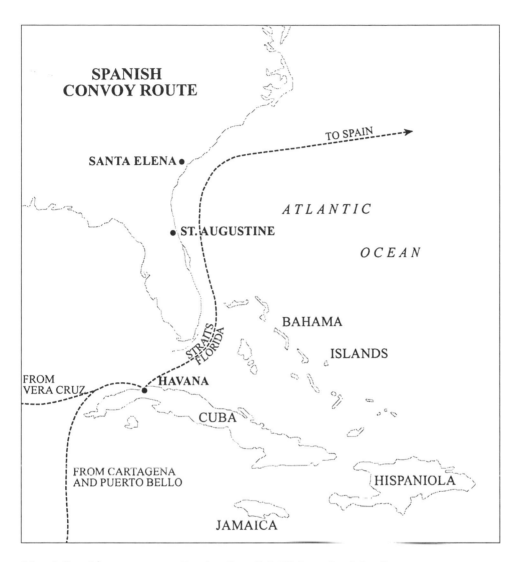

Map 5: Spanish convoy route. Based on Kovacik & Winberry, *South Carolina*

Angel de Villefañe sailed from Havana for Santa Elena. After finding Port Royal Sound and exploring several of the nearby islands, the expedition foundered. A hurricane destroyed three of the four ships in the fleet and killed twenty-six of the one hundred members of the party. Following this failure, Philip II and his advisers decided to abandon efforts to settle Santa Elena because they reasoned that there was no longer any danger from France. In this, the Spaniards were greatly mistaken.[9]

Although France and Spain were nominally at peace, there were those in France who would like nothing better than to harm Spain and its empire. One of those who felt this way was Gaspar Coligny, a French Protestant and admiral of the French navy. It was he who came up with a scheme for planting a French colony on the south Atlantic coast. The motives behind his drive for colonization were complex. Above all else Coligny was a French patriot, and the proposed colony would give his country a strong claim to new territory and undermine Spain's. As a French Protestant, a Huguenot, he believed that the colony could become a religious haven for his fellow believers. With mixed motives and the apparent blessing of the French government, Coligny implemented his plans. One of his protégés, a Norman sea captain named Jean Ribaut, was placed in charge of the enterprise.

In February 1562 Ribaut and a company of 150 men in two ships sailed for La Florida. After a voyage of more than two months, the French sighted land. For two weeks they sailed up the coast until they found a magnificent harbor they thought suitable for their colony. They named the harbor Port Royal and chose present-day Parris Island as the site for their fort. In only five days in May they felled trees and built a blockhouse, constructed bastions for cannons, and dug a moat around their fort. With overall dimensions of 160 by 130 feet, Charlesfort, as it was called, clearly was designed to be more than a military garrison. On a nearby island Ribaut had his men erect a stone column on which was carved the arms of France. In June, Ribaut and the majority of the party sailed for home. His intent was to gather new supplies and reinforcements. When he returned to France, the country was in the midst of religious civil war and his patron had more important things to consider than the outpost at Port Royal.[10]

The twenty-eight men who had remained at Charlesfort became discouraged when the anticipated supply ships did not arrive. They obtained some food from the nearby Edisto nation but not enough for their needs. The Edisto rebuffed further entreaties, claiming that their own stocks were low. A foraging party canoed up the Combahee River and obtained some corn and beans from several villages. Then disaster struck. The blockhouse, which had a thatched roof, caught fire and all supplies were lost. The Edisto rebuilt the blockhouse for the French but refused to give them any more food. The fort's commander was a martinet whose cruel treatment of his men led them to mutiny and murder him. The mutineers decided to abandon Charlesfort. They built a boat, using Spanish moss and pine rosin for caulking and

French soldiers obtaining food from Indians in the vicinity of Charlesfort. Theodore de Bry's engraving of a drawing by Jacques le Moyne de Morgues, *Narrative of Le Moyne,* plate 7. Courtesy, South Caroliniana Library.

their shirts and sheets for sails. With inadequate food and water and a clumsy, homemade craft, all but one of the survivors set sail for France. The return journey was a hell of starvation, cannibalism, and madness. Near Europe an English vessel rescued those who were left, then put some ashore in France and took others to England.

Reading the dismal tale of Ribaut's Charlesfort, it is as if the French were following a script from Ayllón's San Miguel de Gualdape. Both settlements were built in swampy locations which would have made it difficult to plant crops. The leaders who had inspired colonization were removed from the scene, Ayllón by death and Ribaut by choice. Their incompetent successors faced mutiny and death at the hands of their fellow colonists. Unprepared for the rigors of colonization, both the Spaniards and the French abandoned their efforts. And, finally, the survivors' return voyages were macabre epilogues to two ill-fated enterprises.

Spain learned about the French threat and responded with a vengeance. The governor of Cuba sent a force to extirpate the French colony. When the Spaniards arrived at Port Royal in 1564, they found Ribaut's column and removed it. They also found the young Frenchman who had remained behind to live with the Edisto, and he showed them the location of Charlesfort. The Spaniards burned what was still standing and returned to Cuba.

Meanwhile, back in France, Admiral Coligny still wanted to establish a Huguenot colony in La Florida. In 1564 a party of three hundred men in three ships set sail. After exploring the northern coast of Florida, the French built Fort Caroline on the St. John's River. Soon rumors swept through the Caribbean and back to Spain that there was a joint English-French colony of one thousand in La Florida. Philip II had no intention of permitting this challenge to go unanswered. He ordered Pedro Menéndez de Avilés to La Florida to eliminate the intruders and to establish a settlement where others had failed.[11]

Menéndez landed at the first inlet south of the St. John's and began construction of St. Augustine. In a series of maneuvers and countermaneuvers the Spaniards captured Fort Caroline and massacred most of its inhabitants. A French attempt to surprise the Spaniards at St. Augustine failed and the French surrendered, most being put to the sword. Some of the Frenchmen fled to the woods and lived with coastal Indians, and a few managed to escape either to Newfoundland or France.

Spain had successfully defended her territory and driven out her rivals, but Menéndez was still concerned. He was particularly worried about the influence of the French who remained in La Florida and might be able to rouse the Indians against the Spaniards. St. Augustine, which began as a temporary base of operations, was reinforced as a military outpost. In April 1566 Menéndez and a force of 150 soldiers sailed north with the objective of securing a firm hold on the coast as far north as Port Royal. After dealing successfully with the coastal Indians, the Spaniards began building an earthwork and palisade fort to guard the settlement of Santa Elena. When it was completed, Fort San Felipe, on the southern tip of Parris Island, was secure and had a garrison of 110. But history seemed to repeat itself. Desertion, mutiny, and inadequate supplies threatened the success of the venture, and only the timely arrival of reinforcements in July 1566 saved the enterprise. When Menéndez returned in August, he named Esteban de las Alas governor and captain-general of La Florida, and the tiny settlement of Santa Elena became the capital of La Florida.[12]

Santa Elena also became a base of operations for exploring the interior. In 1566 and 1567 Capt. Juan Pardo led two expeditions. One of his missions was to assure the Indians of Spain's friendship; another was to see if there were any wealth that could be exploited; and a third was to find and protect an overland route to Mexico. Menéndez was convinced that the mountains were only 100 leagues (about 345 miles) from Santa Elena and the mines of Mexico only 250 leagues (about 790 miles) beyond them. The first trek lasted four months and took Pardo and his men into the mountains of what is now North Carolina. The Spaniards built Fort San Juan in the foothills of the Appalachians and left a small garrison to protect Spain's

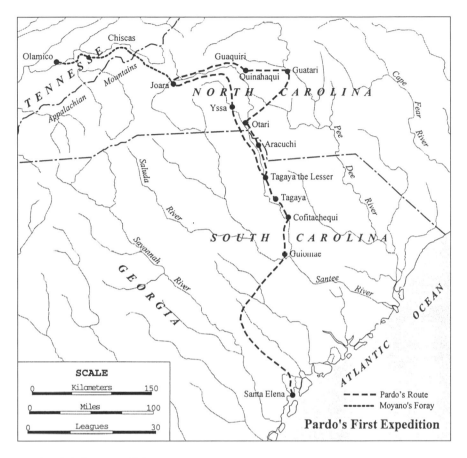

Map 6: Pardo's first expedition. Based on Hudson, *The Juan Pardo Expeditions*

interests. On Pardo's second march inland he built and garrisoned four small forts, but not much is known of the fate of those Spanish soldiers in the wilderness. It is thought that most of them were killed by Indians in retribution for the destruction of several Indian villages. Pardo and his party, however, returned safely to Santa Elena (see Map 6).[13]

As the capital of La Florida, Santa Elena was more than a military outpost. Gradually colonists arrived and built homes outside the fort. Farmers immigrated in substantial numbers, enticed by the lure of free passage, fertile land, farm animals, and a two-year subsidy. By October 1569 there were 327 men, women, and children in the town. In addition to soldiers and farmers, there were artisans (including a tailor, a blacksmith, a carpenter, and a mason), a notary, and a barber-surgeon. Entire households came from Spain to the South Carolina coast. The tailor arrived with his wife, mother-in-law, and six children; so did a doctor, his wife, three children, nephew, and three servants. Clearly Pedro Menéndez intended for Santa Elena to be an example of the Spanish maxim *poblar es conquistar* (to settle is to conquer).[14]

Although a small colonial village, Santa Elena had all the elements of a continental Spanish town. It had a highly stratified society at the top of which were Menéndez and his family. Spanish institutions were established including a *concejo* (city government), an elected *cabildo* (council), and most important of all, a Roman Catholic church. The town church, which may have been named Santa Clara, was ornately furnished.[15]

Economically, the colony appeared to be prospering. Artisans found a ready market for their wares. Settlers, with Indian assistance, traded in timber, cochineal, sarsaparilla, and deer skins. Boardinghouses and a tavern flourished. As elsewhere in the American portion of the Spanish empire, illegal trading occurred. Despite the appearance of economic self-sufficiency, the colony faced agricultural hardships. The land surrounding San Elena was poor and subject to flooding; the promised livestock never arrived; and the garrison commandeered much of whatever scraggly crops the colonists managed to coax from the sandy soil. One colonist lamented that they were "driven by hunger to the coast with their wives and children, to eat shellfish and oysters, for if they had not done so, they would have perished from hunger." In the end, it was the regular subsidy of goods and cash that supported the economy of the colony.[16]

There were other, more serious problems, however. Chronic food shortages led to regular raids against neighboring Indians. Tiring of this harassment, Indians attacked the settlement in 1570 but were repulsed. Disease was also a constant threat. The subsidy ship in 1571 brought typhus as well as supplies. The most serious problem of all was the absence of capable leadership. In 1573 las Alas, who had been unable to establish good relations with the native Carolinians, returned to Spain. He was succeeded by a series of inept, corrupt, and despotic individuals whose governance was so poor that within three years the existence of Santa Elena and all of La Florida was threatened.[17]

In the summer of 1576 the Spaniards murdered three local chieftains and terrorized nearby villagers. The Edisto and Guale nations retaliated. Soon other coastal Indian nations joined them, and general warfare erupted. Within a matter of days thirty of the fifty members of the garrison were killed. On the morning of 22 June a band of five hundred Indians attacked Santa Elena and forced the colonists to take refuge in Fort San Felipe. When the Spaniards repulsed the Indian attack, the natives retreated outside the range of the primitive Spanish firearms and waited.[18]

Inside the fort chaos reigned. Apparently a majority of the refugees were women and children, who beseeched the Spanish commander to take them to safety. Although there was more than enough ammunition and food to withstand a siege, the survivors wanted to leave. In July 1576 the colonists abandoned the settlement in which so much had been invested. As soon as the Spaniards put out to sea, the Indians torched the fort and what remained of the village.[19]

The Escamacu War, as it was called, resulted in the decimation of Spanish settlements and missions throughout La Florida. Only St. Augustine survived. Most refugees from Santa Elena fled to Cuba, but some went to St. Augustine. Despite the destruction, Spain was determined to maintain its hold on all of La Florida—and that included Santa Elena. Philip II personally decreed that Santa Elena be rebuilt and resettled.[20]

Although the Spanish monarch did not know it at the time, the French used the abandonment of Santa Elena as an opening to make another attempt to colonize the area. In December 1576 a French military colony was established in the Port Royal area. The local Indians were not any happier with the French than they had been with the Spaniards, and by the time word of its establishment reached Madrid, the colony had failed. Most of the survivors were either killed or captured by the Indians. Spanish forces hunted down and executed those living among the Indians.[21]

During the summer of 1577 local government authorities imported and erected a prefabricated wooden fortification from St. Augustine. This structure would become Fort San Marcos, a substantial wooden citadel built on a slight rise not far from the site of Fort San Felipe. Several years later, when Sir Francis Drake and other English sea dogs threatened the Spanish empire, a new, more expensive fort (with three bastions, seven cannons, and moat) was built.[22]

For several years there was only the fort, but then colonists arrived to rebuild Santa Elena. Although no longer the capital of La Florida, the second Santa Elena was more imposing than its predecessor. And unlike its successor as the capital, St. Augustine, which was simply a military outpost, it was a real town.[23]

Santa Elena prospered. By the early 1580s the town covered about fifteen acres containing forty houses, a church, and a tavern. A number of the residences were substantial, flat-roofed buildings with wattle and daub walls covered with a thick coat of oystershell mortar. The remainder probably were small, D-shaped huts of wattle and daub covered with thatched roofs that resembled the dwellings of nearby Indians. Some of the soldiers of the garrison lived in cramped quarters in the fort, while others lived in town.[24]

Of the colonists themselves, we have only fragmentary information. From archaeological evidence we know that Santa Elena was a fairly sophisticated little village that was in contact with other parts of the far-flung Spanish empire. Its residents had earthenware from Mexico, Italy, and Spain in their homes. At least a few could afford to own Chinese porcelain. However, inexpensive Indian pottery from St. Au-

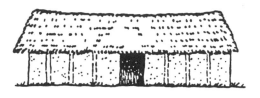

Archaeologists' renderings of Spanish dwellings at Santa Elena. Drawings by Darby Erd. Courtesy, South Carolina Institute of Archaeology and Anthropology.

Pottery and kiln from the archaeological investigation of Santa Elena. Courtesy, South Carolina Institute of Archaeology and Anthropology.

gustine or nearby natives was used by everyone. One of the more intriguing colonists was an unknown potter. His kiln has been found, and its contents seem to verify the belief that Santa Elena was meant to be a permanent settlement. He made at least twenty-one different types of clay items including cooking pots, plates, bowls, storage jars, flower pots, mugs, roof tiles, and pipe bowls.[25]

In addition to farmers and soldiers (one of whom was a barber and another a chaplain), the colonists included a tailor, a blacksmith and a tavern keeper. If the composition of the colony were anything like its predecessor, there would have been a fair number of families with children. The soldiers of the garrison came from dozens of villages and towns in Spain: from places such as Marchena, Jibraltar, Cadiz, Sevilla, Biluao, Leon, Salamanca, Toledo, and Palença. The settlers' backgrounds were probably just as diverse.[26]

The reoccupation of Santa Elena seemed to be a success. During the decade of its rebirth, farmers gained access to better land inland for their crops and cattle. This advance in the agricultural sector of the economy was possible only as long as there were no Indian problems. Success, however, was not enough to insure the colony's future. The appearance of the town and observations by settlers and visitors indicate that the second Santa Elena was flourishing. Appearances aside, subsidies continued throughout the life of the colony.[27]

In 1586 Sir Francis Drake rampaged at will through the Spanish Main, and he captured and burned St. Augustine. Philip II's ministers thought that the nation's resources were being stretched too thinly. Patrolling ships would be more effective than permanent land bases in stopping the raids on the treasure fleets and Spanish commerce. Also, in La Florida the distance between St. Augustine and Santa Elena made mutual support and defense difficult.

Local officials in La Florida, continuing the inept leadership traditions of their predecessors, ignored the advantages of the superior harbor and settlement at Santa Elena and made the decision to consolidate all of their efforts in St. Augustine. On 16 August 1587 the settlers at Santa Elena were ordered to destroy their homes and the fort and leave. Their displeasure was recorded in a lawsuit they filed against the government to recover their losses. Ironically, Philip II agreed with the arguments of the colonists who said that if Spain were to abandon Santa Elena the area would then be open to colonization by Spain's enemies.[28]

After finally succeeding in establishing a colony at Santa Elena, Spain simply abandoned it. Perhaps it was inevitable, given the inability of local officials to deal effectively with the Indians. Although Santa Elena grew, it was under constant threat from both Indian and European nations. France had made three attempts to defy Spain and plant colonies in La Florida. The Spanish reaction to the French threat had been to eradicate them as one would the weeds in a garden. The English were another matter.

Before the abandonment of Santa Elena, in 1585, the English had already made one unsuccessful attempt at colonization on Roanoke Island in present-day North Carolina. Two years later they made another attempt. It too failed, but the romance of "the lost colony" would become a part of American folklore. That did not occur with any of the French or Spanish settlements in South Carolina, although their stories are far more interesting. In spite of the fact that their existence affected the course of English settlement in the lands south of Virginia, they have been forgotten.

Traditionally, the story of sixteenth-century South Carolina ends with the observation that two names on the map, Port Royal and St. Helena, are the only reminders of the French and Spanish presence. Sometimes one or both are given credit for introducing peaches to the New World. Beyond that, silence.

The withdrawal of Spain could be interpreted as a victory for the natural order of the native population over the imperialism of Europe. After all, the Europeans had withdrawn from this portion of the south Atlantic coast after more than three decades of trying to impose their order on the wilderness and the natives of the country. Because of the resolution of the Indians in the face of Spanish coercion, Spain's attempts to colonize La Florida north of the peninsula failed. However, when the disgruntled settlers were forced to quit Santa Elena and raze it, they were unaware that they were leaving behind a legacy of their presence in South Carolina. It was a silent bequest, but its significance overshadowed all the others and it voided the apparent triumph of the Native Americans.[29]

It would be nearly a century before Europeans would again attempt to establish a colony in South Carolina. This time they would be successful—not because the English were more rugged than the French and Spaniards, but because they were the unintentional beneficiaries of the most lasting legacy of the Spanish presence in South Carolina—the deadly microbes that killed off thousands of the natives.[30]

Chapter Three

THE COLONY OF A COLONY

Barbadoes Isle inhabited by Slaves
And for one honest man ten thousand knaves
Religion to thee's a Romatick storey
Barbarity and ill got wealth thy glory. . . .
      Thomas Walduck, 12 November 1710

That we . . . do grant full and absolute power, by virtue of these presents, to them the said *Edward* Earl of *Clarendon, George* Duke of *Albemarle, William* Earl of *Craven, John* Lord *Berkeley, Anthony* Lord *Ashley,* Sir *George Carteret,* Sir *John Colleton,* and Sir *William Berkeley* . . . for the good and happy government of the said whole province . . . to ordain, make and enact, and publish any laws and constitutions whatsoever . . . according to their best discretion, by and with the advice, assent, and approbation of the freemen of the said province.
      The Second Charter of Carolina, 30 June 1665

Every freeman of *Carolina* shall have absolute power and authority over his negro slaves.
      Fundamental Constitutions of Carolina, 21 July 1669

*T*HE FAILURES AT Roanoke in the 1580s did not lead to the abandonment of England's plan to establish colonies in the New World. If those colonies threatened Spain's hegemony, then so much the better. The issuing of a proprietary charter in 1629 to Sir Robert Heath, Charles I's attorney general, certainly challenged Spain's claims to the south Atlantic coast. The southern boundary of the new colony of Carolana (named after the monarch) was the Saint Mary's River, more than 130 miles below where Santa Elena had been.

In the early 1630s Heath sponsored exploration of the coast and at least one attempt at colonization. He sent out a group of settlers who were to stop first in Virginia and then travel south into present-day North Carolina. Once they reached Virginia, they went no further. It is believed that at some point Heath intended for Carolana to be a Huguenot refuge; however, opposition from within the British gov-

Map of Barbados; nine of the eleven parish names would later be used in South Carolina. Vincent T. Harlow, *A History of Barbados, 1625–1685*, p. 335.

ernment would have stymied that plan. By the mid 1630s Heath appeared to have lost interest in the colony and signed over his rights to Henry Frederick Howard, Lord Maltravers. This young English nobleman also tried, unsuccessfully, to establish settlements in Carolana.[1]

While the Carolana charter certainly challenged the bounds of Spain's North American territory, without permanent settlement the menace was no more dangerous than the parchment on which it was written. In the Caribbean the English threat to the Spanish empire was quite another matter. English adventurers established colonies on the Lesser Antilles islands of St. Christopher, Barbados, and Nevis during the 1620s. While St. Christopher, which England shared with France, was settled first (1624), Barbados (1627) would become the cultural hearth, the model for the rest of the English West Indies—and South Carolina.[2]

On Barbados between 1640 and 1670 there evolved a powerful local culture whose institutions, with some slight alteration, would be re-created throughout the English-speaking Caribbean and along the South Carolina coast. "South Carolina and the Lower South culture that developed out of those small beginnings," writes a modern historian, "was as much the offspring of Barbados as was Jamaica or the other English Caribbean colonies." South Carolina, then, arose from a different cultural tradition than the colonies of New England and the Chesapeake. Because South Carolina's cultural heritage differs from that of other English colonies, we need to take a brief look at seventeenth-century Barbados.[3]

Barbados and the other Caribbean islands were "beyond the line" as far as the nations of Europe were concerned. That is, events that occurred south of the Tropic of Cancer or west of the prime meridian would not have any effect on European relations. In essence, the Caribbean became a no-man's-land in which possession was not just nine-tenths of the law, it was the law. Restraints of any sort, whether governmental or social, seemed to disappear. The pursuit of wealth and the pleasures it could purchase was the order of the day.[4]

During the first fifteen years of colonization, most settlers in Barbados struggled to survive. While the island might be a tropical paradise, clearing the heavy growth was tough, back-breaking work: the sort of work with which the settlers were not familiar. Once the land was cleared, the colonists planted a variety of subsistence crops. Tobacco and cotton were planted for export; however, neither brought much of a return. Barbadian tobacco, in particular, had a poor reputation back home. From the beginning Barbadian planters employed chattel labor, mostly indentured servants, in their fields. Few questioned the legality of indentures, and it became a common practice for unscrupulous labor suppliers to kidnap young men and ship them off to the island. "Barbadosed" in the seventeenth century meant the same thing as "Shanghaied" did in the nineteenth. Despite cheap labor, there was not much profit made in what some colonists called "Little England."[5]

During the 1640s sugar cane from Brazil was introduced into Barbados. Within twenty years the entire nature of the colony was dramatically altered. There seemed to be an insatiable worldwide demand for sugar as well as its by-products, rum and molasses. The price of land skyrocketed. Smaller planters were bought out and tenant farmers pushed off the land. White indentured servants were replaced by African slaves. A small, fantastically wealthy elite emerged that dominated the colony. The success of the sugar magnates in Barbados stirred the imaginations of adventurous souls at home and in other colonies. The glitter of the riches amassed by a few blinded all to the dark underside of life on the island. If ever there were a troubled paradise, it was Barbados.[6]

The society that emerged in the latter half of the seventeenth century was "individualistic, competitive, and highly materialistic." To that list should be added hedonistic. Material success, not character or honor, was the measure of an individual's worth. And how a person acquired wealth was not important. "Virginia might be the Old Dominion and Massachusetts the Bible Commonwealth, but Barbados was something more tangible: the richest colony in English America."[7]

Supplying the labor that produced this wealth were thousands of Africans. Initially the labor on the island was performed primarily by young white males. However, as white labor costs remained high and white laborers were difficult to manage, Barbadians soon turned to the Brazilian model of African slavery—especially after they took a good look at the bottom line. It was cheaper to purchase an African for life than it was to contract for a white indentured servant for four or five years. In addition, white servants were more expensive to feed, clothe, and house than blacks. The decision, then, to switch to African labor was based upon economics, not race.[8]

In 1638, before the introduction of sugar cane, two hundred enslaved Africans were only about 3 percent of the population; fourteen years later there were twenty thousand and they outnumbered whites. The rapid introduction of large numbers of Africans made the maintenance of order a primary concern of the white minority. The 1661 Barbados act "for the better ordering and governing of Negroes" carefully defined the roles of master, servant, and slave.[9]

The planter, as head of the household, had primary responsibility for preserving order. When white indentured servants were the main source of labor, they had been considered members of a planter's household, his family. That concept did not change with the introduction of African slave labor.[10]

Enslaved Africans on a sugar plantation might have been "family"; however, the black majority contributed to the general sense of unease that permeated Barbadian society. Successful planters had money, lots of it, but their lives were in constant jeopardy. In addition to the threat of servile insurrection, there were the ever-present dangers from European enemies, pirates, and disease. Given this situation, it is no wonder that carpe diem (seize the day) could have been the unofficial motto of the island.

By 1670 the Barbadian socio-economic model that would be replicated in the English West Indies and South Carolina had evolved. It was exploitative and materialistic. "They all came here in order to become rich," wrote one contemporary observer. Sugar, the major cash crop, was produced on plantations by slave labor. The demand for slave labor created a society in which blacks were 60 percent of the population. There was a highly stratified social structure, with a tremendous gap between the island's haves and have-nots. Not much attention was paid to family life or the creation of community institutions. The composition of the island's elite was ever-changing. Newcomers replaced those who chose to return home with their new wealth or died in paradise. In spite of the difficulties a society emerged in Barbados, even if perhaps an incomplete one.[11]

The interaction of English and Africans in Barbados produced a society that was "a mixture of the former and the latter but essentially distinct from both." This new creole culture that had developed in the tropics would be emulated by others and duplicated, with some modifications, by Barbadians as they left the island in search of new opportunities in such places as Jamaica and South Carolina.[12]

One Englishman who was familiar with Barbados was John Colleton, a royalist exile. When the Puritans triumphed in England, he and other monarchists had escaped to the island. There he established himself as a planter and witnessed firsthand the fortunes made from sugar. He also observed the colony's relative economic decline as sugar expanded to other English islands and the costs of production increased. In addition he was aware of the steady exodus of white colonists as the slave population increased. Where some might have seen problems and been discouraged, Colleton evidently saw opportunities.[13]

With the Restoration in 1660, Colleton returned to London to seek reward for his support of the royalist cause. Through the intervention of an old friend, John Berkeley, Baron Berkeley of Stratton and member of the Privy Council, Colleton received a knighthood and an appointment to the Council for Foreign Plantations. Membership on the council brought him into contact with Sir William Berkeley, governor of Virginia; Sir Anthony Ashley Cooper (later earl of Shaftsbury), chancellor of the Exchequer; Sir George Carteret, vice chamberlain of the household and treasurer of the navy; and Edward Hyde, earl of Clarendon, who was the king's first minister. In addition to these new and powerful acquaintances, Colleton's cousin was George Monck, duke of Albemarle.

It is probable that Colleton turned first to his cousin and his old friend, Lord Berkeley, for assistance with his scheme for a colony between Virginia and Spanish Florida. Four other fellow members of the Council for Foreign Plantations (Berkeley, Ashley Cooper, Carteret, Hyde) and William Craven, the earl of Craven, were soon party to the plan. It was a powerful group, and everyone had a claim on Charles II. Their request was successful, and on 24 March 1663 the king granted a charter for the colony of Carolina that made the eight petitioners the "true and absolute lords and proprietors" of the province. While the proprietors were interested in promoting the expansion of the empire, it is also quite evident that they were interested in making money. The charter certainly gave them every opportunity to do so.

Charles II granted the Carolina proprietors extraordinary powers, the most noted of which was the "Bishop of Durham" clause, which gave them powers normally reserved for the monarch. Among these were the rights to make war and peace, create towns and ports, grant "titles of honor," raise and maintain an army, collect taxes and customs duties, impose the death sentence ("if it shall be needful"), and issue pardons. The charter was filled with the potential for fat profits. Income might be derived from fees for the establishment of towns and fairs, taxes, and customs duties. In addition, the Lords Proprietors were given control over all "veins, mines and quarries," trade with the natives, and fishing rights, including "*whales, sturgeons,* and all other royal fishes." If certain commodities, such as "silks, wines, currants, raysons, capers, wax, almonds, oyl and olives," proved successful, they could be imported duty-free into England for seven years. Above all else, there was the land, hundreds of thousands of acres of land. It is no wonder that the Lords Proprietors, most of whom were experienced in colonial affairs, expected not only that the colony would pay for whatever administrative costs would arise, but that it would provide them with a handsome return.[14]

The first attempts to settle Carolina were in the northern portion of the province. The Lords Proprietors evidently depended upon Sir William Berkeley, who had returned to Virginia, to take the lead in encouraging colonization. A group of New

Englanders had explored the area around Cape Fear in 1662 and the following year settled there. They remained less than six months before heading back to New England. The unexplained failure of the New Englanders was a concern to the proprietors, who had hoped to attract experienced settlers from other colonies. Their disappointment was short-lived as a group of Barbadians evidenced an interest in establishing a colony in Carolina.[15]

In 1663 a group calling themselves the Barbadian Adventurers commissioned William Hilton to explore the Carolina coast. His pamphlet, published the following year, described the province in glowing terms. The Adventurers, however, could not reach an agreement with the proprietors. In January 1665 in an attempt to make Carolina even more attractive to prospective settlers, the proprietors issued a document called "Concessions and Agreements." Sir John Yeamans, one of the Adventurers, was involved in drafting the "Concessions," which would allow settlers self-government, freedom of religion, and generous land grants. In addition to the Adventurers, others were very much interested in Carolina.

A company of Barbadians, led by John Vassall, established Charles Town on the Cape Fear River. Yeamans and a rival group joined the new settlement. The colony seemed to flourish and in 1666 was reported to have a population of eight hundred. Among the settlers at Cape Fear was Robert Sandford, who had been a planter in Surinam and Barbados. In June 1666 he began a month-long exploration of the coast south of the colony. In the conclusion of his report to the Lords Proprietors he declared: "the Country which wee did search and see . . . doth for richness and fertillity of soyle, for Excellency of Rivers, havens, Creekes and sounds, for abundance of good Timber of diverse sorts, and many other requisites both to land and Sea building, and for sundry rare accomodacōns both for Navigation and Plantacōn Exceed all places that wee knowe in proporcōn of our Nacōn in the West Indies." No doubt the proprietors must have been pleased with Sandford's report that Carolina was better than the West Indies. However, the Barbadians living at Cape Fear were not as impressed with that part of the province and by the late summer of 1667 abandoned the settlement. Hostility from local Indians and lack of support from the proprietors were cited as reasons for its failure.[16]

Blaming the Lords Proprietors for not providing more assistance in the mid 1660s is unreasonable. In 1664 they had sent out to Barbados two ships with arms and ammunition to be sold "to such persons as shall desire to goe to Carolina but wante armes." They asked for and received a new charter in June 1665 that enlarged the colony's boundaries. Then, no doubt, a series of events at home had them thinking about things other than Carolina.[17]

In 1665 England became embroiled in the second naval war with Holland (1665–1667), a military and economic conflict that sorely tested the nation's mettle. Added to the tribulation of war were the twin calamities that struck the nation's capital: a visitation of bubonic plague (1665–1666) and the Great Fire (September

1666). Because of their governmental positions, several of the proprietors were preoccupied with affairs of state. Albemarle commanded the forces that maintained order in London during the plague and fire; and as an admiral of the Royal Navy, he was sometimes at sea during the war years. Shortly after the war his health failed and he withdrew from public life. He died in 1669. Clarendon, who had already accumulated many enemies, was blamed for the less-than-successful war effort that had exhausted the nation. Following dismissal by the king and impeachment by the House of Commons, he went into exile. After Clarendon's ouster Charles II tried to govern by himself without a first minister, utilizing instead a council of five ministers called the cabal. Lord Ashley was one of the five. Sir William Berkeley had returned to Virginia. Sir John Colleton died in 1666, and his heir, Sir Peter Colleton, was in Barbados. With three proprietors involved in governmental affairs and two out of the country, it is not surprising that after the initial flurry of activity between 1663 and 1665 the Lords Proprietors did not function as effectively as they might have.[18]

Suddenly in 1668 the proprietors were aroused to action, not by the urgings of the king or Council for Foreign Plantations, but by one of their own, Lord Ashley. At his instigation, six of the eight initiated action that in 1670 would result in their obtaining a grant for the Bahamas and other unnamed, unowned Caribbean islands. The proprietors believed that Carolina and the Bahamas could be mutually supportive and profitable. It has been suggested that Ashley was motivated by a near brush with death. It could also be said that he was stirred by the desire to bring glory to king and country. Or, like so many seventeenth-century Englishmen, perhaps he wanted to accumulate even more wealth. He had invested previously in the slave trade, in a Barbadian plantation, and in various overseas trading companies. There was tremendous potential for profit in Carolina. Whatever the reason, because of Ashley's actions the settlement of Carolina became a reality.[19]

On 26 April 1669 the proprietors followed Ashley's recommendations that they underwrite the cost of initial settlement. Back in 1663 each of them had contributed £75 sterling ($4,600 in 1996 dollars),[20] but since then they had contributed little or nothing. They expected Carolina to produce for them without their having to do much more. Ashley convinced them that they would have to invest money in Carolina for the colony to succeed. Each proprietor agreed to contribute £500 sterling ($36,300) and more as necessary (although they hoped that they would not be liable for more than another £200 sterling [$14,500]). There was a consensus that it would be desirable to lure experienced settlers from established colonies, especially Barbados; however, the proprietors also agreed that emigrants from the mother country should be among the first settlers of Carolina.[21]

Ashley seized the initiative and in ninety days bought and supplied three ships and induced more than one hundred English men and women to immigrate to Carolina. He commissioned Capt. Joseph West to command the enterprise. While Ashley was assembling the expedition, he and his personal secretary, John Locke, drafted

Anthony Ashley Cooper, Earl of Shaftesbury. Courtesy, South Caroliniana Library.

the first of five versions of the Fundamental Constitutions of Carolina. The document was a joint endeavor and reflects popular political thought, notably that of James Harrington's utopian *Oceana* (1656). The final document, however, was as much Locke's work as Lord Ashley's.[22]

The Fundamental Constitutions of Carolina may be one of the more misunderstood documents in colonial American history. Until well into this century, the observations of South Carolina historians Edward McCrady and David Duncan Wallace were typical. McCrady observed: "The whole scheme of the Fundamental Constitutions was visionary, crude, incomplete, and impracticable." Wallace dismissed the document as a "monstrosity of medievalism" designed to create "a form of government which would have been reactionary even for the English of that day." The settlers in Carolina would not be happy with the document and refused to ratify it or four subsequent revisions. Without the "advice, assent, and approbation of the freemen of the said province," the Fundamental Constitutions never became the basic law of Carolina. Yet a number of its provisions would be implemented de facto and be responsible for the rapid and successful development of South Carolina. Mc-

Crady, in using the term "visionary," was not far from the mark. The Fundamental Constitutions, according to Lord Ashley, was to be "the compasse [we] are to steere by." And so it would be.[23]

The Fundamental Constitutions was more than just a governmental framework; it was also a cleverly written document designed to attract settlers. In matters dealing with religious toleration, naturalized citizenship for aliens, property rights, land grants, and "titles of honor" there was something in the document to appeal to almost anyone who might be looking for a new beginning.[24]

In matters relating to religion, the Church of England would be the tax-supported church in the colony. That would satisfy hard-core Anglicans. For dissenters from the Church of England there was the promise of religious freedom to anyone who believed in God. Not only could non-Anglicans settle freely in Carolina, but seven individuals could form a "church or profession" that would be officially recognized. Religious toleration meant more than freedom to establish a congregation: "No person whatsoever shall disturb, molest, or persecute another for his speculative opinions in religion, or his way of worship." In legal matters affirmation, in lieu of an oath, was an invitation to Quakers. Not only could Huguenots worship as they wished, but upon subscribing to the Fundamental Constitutions they could become naturalized citizens. And the stipulation of a belief in God, not Christ, meant that Jews were welcome. The only religious profession not tolerated was Roman Catholicism, a view quite in keeping with the politics of Restoration England. With the exception of Rhode Island's, this was the most tolerant religious policy in English America.[25]

Scattered throughout the Fundamental Constitutions were numerous references to land, which would have been attractive to individuals in England and in the already crowded English West Indies. Baronies of 12,000 acres would be awarded in multiples to those elevated to the titles of landgrave (four baronies) or cassique (two baronies). There were property qualifications for all offices: member of parliament (500 acres), register of mesne conveyances (300 acres), and register of vital statistics (50 acres). In order to qualify as a voter, an individual had to own 50 acres. The headright system of granting land to settlers outlined in the Fundamental Constitutions and supplemented by instructions to proprietary governors was exceedingly generous. Initially the headright was 150 acres for each adult male a settler brought into the colony (including himself) and 100 acres for each adult female and any male under sixteen. Later the headright was reduced to 50 acres for all adults (including servants), and, upon completing his indenture, a servant would receive 50 acres. For enterprising individuals there was the promise of social mobility. If an individual acquired 3,000 acres, his estate could be declared a manor and he would have the rights of a lord of the manor. Even if a person agreed to become a "leetman," or perpetual serf, he would be given 10 acres when he married. On Barbados there were only about 100,000 acres of arable land, and the plantations of the wealthiest sugar magnates averaged only about 200 acres. Nearly half the landowners on the island owned less than 10 acres, and 35 percent of the families owned none at all.[26]

In addition to land, West Indian colonists were also attracted by two other provisions. All would have understood the meaning of the article that gave every freeman "absolute power and authority over his negro slaves." For wealthier planters, such as Sir John Yeamans, the chance to gain thousands of acres of land and a title, even if it be in the Carolina nobility, might have been appealing. For those at the other end of the islands' social scale, those without either land or means, those often derisively referred to as "white slaves," even the promise of ten acres in exchange for perpetual servitude could have provided old-age security in an uncertain world.[27]

Land, as Ashley and Locke envisioned it, was the basis for participation in government. An individual had to own land in order to enjoy the franchise and to hold public office, not an unusual policy at that time. However, the government described in the Fundamental Constitutions was intricately detailed, somewhat unusual, and the focus of most of the derogatory comments made about the document.[28]

A person had to have a stake in Carolina in order to participate in the political process, and the size of an individual's landholdings determined the size of his stake in society. Those with the greatest interest were, of course, the proprietors. Those next in order would have been their deputies or friends. The distribution of land reflected this order. Carolina was to be divided into provinces, and within each province there would be six counties of 480,000 acres. Within each county there would be a 12,000-acre seigniory for each proprietor, eight 12,000-acre baronies to be allocated among a landgrave and two caciques, and twenty-four 12,000-acre colonies for the rest of the settlers. Thus, within each county the proprietors and local nobility would control 40 percent of the land and the freemen of the province 60 percent.[29]

Each proprietor would have a voice in the governing of the colony. If he were to reside in Carolina, then he would participate directly; if not, then he would name a deputy to act in his stead. There was a complicated system of eight courts, each with well-defined duties (e.g., chief justice's court to hear all appeals, the admiral's court to oversee all matters related to navigation and also function as a court of admiralty, and the chamberlain's court to supervise all ceremonies, heraldry, and recording of vital statistics). The proprietors and the members of the various courts would together form a Grand Council of fifty. Among the duties of the Grand Council was to set the legislative agenda for the parliament, because no item could be discussed there without the council's prior approval. Parliament was to be a unicameral body that included the proprietors or their deputies, local nobles, and the representatives of the freemen of the province. Under such a concept the freemen could always be outvoted. Only if a proprietor questioned the constitutionality of legislation could the freemen block a measure, because any constitutional issue had to be approved by a majority of each order.[30]

Taken as a whole, though, the proprietors were trying to create a balanced form

The *Adventure,* a replica of a seventeenth-century trading vessel similar to those used by the earliest settlers in commerce with the West Indies. Courtesy, Janson Cox, Charles Towne Landing.

of government in which no one segment of society could oppress the other. They were concerned about a "numerous Democracy," as well as an arrogant aristocracy that would trample those beneath it. That was the rationale behind the convoluted governmental structure they set forth in the Fundamental Constitutions. Their fears of oppression and their desire for fairness were also the reasons that the document contained provisions for voting by secret ballot, trial by jury, and impartial jury selection. They wanted a harmonious community; therefore, attorneys and printed commentaries on the law were "absolutely prohibited."[31]

Above all else, the Fundamental Constitutions tried to create a framework for "the better settlement of the government of the said place, and establishing the interests of the Lords Proprietors with equality, and without confusion." It was not a "medieval monstrosity" whose contents were out of touch with reality, but rather a skillfully worded recruiting device that revealed its authors' knowledge about the men and women who lived in England's colonies, especially those in the Caribbean.[32]

The Fundamental Constitutions was a document designed to be all things to all people. It pleased traditionalists with its call for an ordered, aristocratic society that would curb a "numerous Democracy." For seventeenth-century Englishmen, who had learned to distrust the power of monarchy and aristocracy, there were safeguards so that "noe bodys power noe not of any of the Proprietors themselves were they there, is soe great as to be able to hurt the meanest man in the Country." Staunch Anglicans would have approved of the Church of England's being the "national religion" of Carolina. Dissenters would have been encouraged to move to a land where they could worship freely and without harassment *and* not be excluded from holding political office because of their beliefs. Most of all, the Fundamental Constitutions was attractive to those who wanted to improve themselves economically and socially. The generous land grants, the promise of upward mobility, and the creation of a Carolina nobility promised opportunities for men to rise above their stations. And for those who already owned human property, the document gave a clear indication that the highly profitable, slave-powered plantation system of the Caribbean colonies could be duplicated in Carolina.[33]

The Fundamental Constitutions might well have been a bold attempt to attract the strong, the daring, and the experienced to Carolina. However, the Fundamental Constitutions was not just a recruiting device. Those inducements to colonize were part of a framework designed to establish "the good order and the harmony of the whole community" of Carolina. That it was never ratified in South Carolina does not diminish its significance. Even in its stillborn state it had an impact on the development of the colony. This was due in part to those provisions that had a direct appeal to experienced colonists, especially those who wanted to control their own affairs. Throughout the early colonial period they picked and chose those provisions that they wanted to implement in South Carolina.

On 21 July 1669 Locke and Ashley completed the Fundamental Constitutions. Several weeks later three ships under the command of Captain West—the *Carolina,* the *Port Royal,* and the *Albemarle*—weighed anchor, but it was not until mid August that the little fleet set sail on the first leg of its journey. The permanent settlement of South Carolina was soon to become a reality.

Chapter Four

PEOPLING THE PROVINCE

The People here, generally speaking, are . . . a perfect Medley or Hotch potch . . . who have transported themselves hither from Bermudas, Jamaica, Barbados, Montserat, Antego, Nevio, New England, Pensylvania &c.

      Gideon Johnston, 20 September 1708

[T]he great quantities of Negroes that are dayly brought into this Government and the small numbers of Whites that comes amongst us, and how many are Lately Dead & gon off. How insolent and mischevious the Negroes are become. . . . for the better increasing our Number . . . it might be highly necessary if an act did provide for the Transportation of them who are not able to Transport themselves.

      Robert Gibbes, 15 May 1711

*T*HE FLEET OF three ships that sailed from England in August 1669 did not have an easy time reaching Carolina. Before it left European waters, it stopped at Kinsale in Ireland where Captain West expected to be able to take on board more settlers. Just the reverse occurred. Not only was he not able to obtain any new recruits, but some of those aboard jumped ship. In mid September the ships began an uneventful forty-day voyage from Ireland to Barbados. From late October until the end of February the colonizing party remained on the island, replenishing supplies and purchasing livestock. While on the island, as the proprietors had hoped, a number of Barbadians joined the expedition.

If the future Carolinians were aware of what had befallen earlier colonization efforts, they might have thought that history was repeating itself. While in Barbados the *Albemarle,* a thirty-ton sloop, was wrecked in a tropical storm. It was replaced by a Barbadian-built sloop, *The Three Brothers.* On 26 February 1670 the first fleet set out for Carolina. Sailing through the eastern Caribbean, it encountered a storm that caused the *Port Royal* to run aground in the Bahamas. The remaining two ships then headed for Bermuda, where another storm drove *The Three Brothers* to Virginia. Only the *Carolina,* a two-hundred-ton frigate with a majority of the settlers on board, made landfall on 15 March at Bull's Bay, thirty miles north of Charleston.[1]

The proprietors originally had planned for the first settlement to be at Port Royal. However, native Carolinians met the initial landing party, and their leader, the cacique of Kiawah, urged the English to establish their colony up the Ashley River. It has long been accepted that he did so because he thought the English would provide protection from marauding bands of Westo. After reconnoitering the Port Royal area, the settlers agreed with the cacique that the Albemarle Point site was more suitable. No doubt, providing a well-defended location for the settlers rather than protection for the Kiawah was the prime reason for choosing the site of the first settlement. Located several miles up the Ashley River on a bluff above Old Town Creek, it was on a spit of land surrounded by water on three sides. At high tide the land bridge connecting it to the mainland was only about 150 feet wide and easily defended. Most important of all, in terms of Spanish naval patrols, the settlement could not be seen from Charleston harbor.

The first group of colonists numbered about 130, most of them English men and women. There were a few from Barbados and one family from Nevis. Although there were only a handful of Barbadians in the first fleet, over the next two years about half of the white settlers and more than half of the enslaved blacks came from the island. Between 1670 and 1690 about 54 percent of the whites who immigrated to South Carolina came from Barbados. In addition, more came from the other islands in the English West Indies. In South Carolina, regardless of the island of origin, most of these settlers were called "Barbadians" (not a totally accurate appellation since settlers came from many different islands, including Bermuda and the Bahamas which were the cultural heirs to Virginia and Massachusetts, not Barbadoes).[2]

From well-nigh every island in the English Caribbean came settlers bearing names such as Beadon, Colleton, Daniel, Drayton, Fenwicke, Gibbes, Godfrey, Ladson, Middleton, Moore, Schenckingh, and Yeamans of Barbados; Amory, Parris, Pinckney, and Whaley of Jamaica; Lucas, Motte, and Perry of Antigua; Lowndes and Rawlins of Saint Christopher's; LaMotte of Grenada; and Woodward of Nevis. They were almost all of English descent, but they were not just English; they were English–West Indian.[3]

The Barbadians were seasoned by more than their exposure to and survival of diseases. Either from firsthand experience or from watching parents and relatives, they knew what was required to prosper in a colonial environment, be it political skill, economic opportunity, or plantation management. And they brought with them the Barbadian cultural model. Just as their forebears had migrated to the West Indies to make their fortunes, so these settlers now viewed South Carolina as an opportunity for their generation to improve themselves socially and economically. A majority were servants, but a substantial number were merchants or the younger sons of planting families. Eighteen of the biggest Barbadian planting families and thirty-three of the next rank, or middling planters, sent relatives or associates to South Carolina.[4]

Whether "white slaves" or scions of privilege, they had lived in a society "beyond the line." They were tough, experienced, and driven; they did not care much about how they got what they wanted. From the vantage point of the twentieth century we might think that they were ruthless rogues. Perhaps they were, but they knew what was required to succeed in the New World. There were no gentlemen adventurers here, as there were in Jamestown, lollygagging about looking for gold and pearls or planting tobacco in the streets. Whatever human faults the Barbadians may have had, no one could accuse them of being impractical.

Because they constituted the majority of the white population for the first two decades of settlement, the Barbadians set their cultural stamp on the South Carolina society that would evolve during the colonial period. There were other English settlers, from both Old and New England, but they either became acculturated to the South Carolina way of life or moved elsewhere.

An example of those who found the land and culture inhospitable were some Puritans from Massachusetts Bay. In 1695 a group from Dorchester moved to South Carolina and founded the town of Dorchester, twenty miles up the Ashley River from Charleston. Unfortunately, they selected a location with poor, sandy soil and for three generations struggled to make the land produce. By the middle of the eighteenth century they were unable to compete within the plantation economy and were out of step with their more worldly neighbors—even those who were fellow dissenters. So they decided to relocate, as a congregation, to Medway, Georgia. The New Englanders had not conformed to the Barbadian cultural model, but it had had an effect on them. Their cultural isolation as much as the sandy soil was responsible for their leaving the province.

The imprint of the English–West Indian experience is all the more amazing considering that after 1700 Barbadians made up only a fraction of the colony's inhabitants with English forebears. English men and women, regardless of origin, constituted a minority of the white population of colonial South Carolina.

The colony's diverse European population was partly due to the efforts of the Lords Proprietors. In addition to the Fundamental Constitutions, they either sponsored or encouraged the publication of fifteen promotional tracts. In doing so they were careful to remain in the background so that the pamphlets would appear to be impartial assessments of Carolina and not proprietary propaganda. A 1683 tract, published in Dublin, stressed economic opportunities and freedom of conscience. More than one-third of the pamphlets were in French and designed to attract Huguenots. In addition to promotional literature, the proprietors maintained a presence at the Carolina Coffee House in Birchin Lane, London. During the eighteenth century this tavern became a home away from home for South Carolinians. According to a 1682 newspaper account and Samuel Wilson's *An Account of the Province of Carolina,* six of the Lords Proprietors gathered every Tuesday morning at the tavern in Birchin Lane to answer questions anyone might have about immi-

Table 4.1

ORIGINS OF EUROPEAN COLONISTS

Nationality (%)	SC	NC	VA	PA	NY	Colonial Average
English	36.7	40.6	49.6	19.5	44.2	57.9
Scots	32.9	27.6	22.8	26.7	15.5	18.7
Irish	11.7	13.3	9.4	10.2	5.5	7.2
Welsh	8.8	11.6	9.5	5.9	4.8	5.8
German	5	4.7	6.3	33.3	8.2	6
Dutch	0.4	0.3	0.3	1.8	17.5	1.9
French	3.9	1.7	1.5	1.8	3.8	1.6
Swedish	0.6	0.2	0.6	0.8	0.5	0.3
Jewish[6]	—	—	—	—	—	—

U.S. Department of Commerce, Bureau of the Census, *Historical Statistics of the United States from Colonial Times to 1970* (2 parts, Washington, D.C.: U.S. Government Printing Office, 1975). Forrest McDonald and Ellen Shapiro McDonald, "The Ethnic Origins of the American People, 1790," *William and Mary Quarterly,* 3d series, 37 (April 1980): 198.

grating to Carolina. This public relations effort paid off in that it produced a small but steady stream of new settlers of various nationalities.[5]

South Carolina had one of the more heterogeneous European populations in British North America. By the time of the American Revolution there were nine European ethnic groups represented in measurable numbers. Of these, in addition to the English, the French, Scots, Irish, Germans, Welsh, and Jews maintained something of a cultural identity. The Dutch and Swedes did not.

After the English, the French were the most significant ethnic group in terms of colonial affairs, far out of all proportion to their numbers. South Carolina had the largest French population (in terms of percentage) of any of the thirteen original colonies. It was a diverse group made up of Huguenot refugees, French-speaking Swiss, and Acadians.

The first French settlers were Huguenots who were attracted to South Carolina by the promise of religious and political freedom and the availability of land. In April 1680 a group of forty-five Huguenots arrived in South Carolina aboard the *Richmond* (the Huguenot answer to the *Carolina* and the *Mayflower*). Over the next few years others immigrated as families or individuals. Then in 1685 Louis XIV revoked the Edict of Nantes that had guaranteed French Protestants the right to worship freely. Huguenots were persecuted, and thousands sought refuge in Switzerland, the

Netherlands, England, and the New World. In the decade following the revocation fifteen hundred fled to South Carolina, many of them escaping with only their lives. In 1685 after months of suffering from abuses by French soldiers, Judith Giton Manigault wrote that her family "resolved on quitting France by night . . . abandoning the house with its furniture. We contrived to hide ourselves . . . for ten days, while a search was made for us." The Gitons, via an underground railroad of Huguenot sympathizers, escaped from France and made their way eventually to England and then to South Carolina.[7]

Some Huguenots remained in Charleston, but most moved north and east along the eastern branch of the Cooper River and on to vacant lands along the Santee River, to what was then South Carolina's northern frontier. There they established themselves as planters in what would become one of the richest rice-growing areas of the colony. Until about 1720 they continued to speak and write in French and married within the Huguenot community. After that time Huguenots intermarried with the English majority in the lowcountry, joined the Church of England, and made "little effort . . . to perpetuate the remembrance of a distinct nationality." A few even Anglicized their names.[8]

While they may have become Anglicized in many ways, Huguenots and their English neighbors continued to recognize the former's heritage. The area along the Santee where they lived was known as the French Santee, and when parishes were established in the eighteenth century, one was called St. Thomas and St. Denis. The name St. Denis, with its French spelling, allegedly is derived from the site of a sixteenth-century victory by Huguenot forces led by Admiral Coligny. The French heritage was also displayed in the retention of family names: Bonneau, Cordes, DeSaussure, Deveaux, DuBose, Fort, Gaillard, Gendron, Guerard, Horry, Huger, Laurens, Legare, Manigault, Marion, Peyre, Porcher, Prioleau, Ravenel, Simons, and Timothy.[9]

Assimilation did not come easy for the Huguenots, who found themselves the objects of intense ethnic animosity. In the elections for the first Commons House of Assembly in 1692, five of the six delegates from Craven County were Huguenots. This led to an angry petition to Gov. Philip Ludwell asking him to prevent the Huguenots from taking their seats: "Shall the Frenchmen, who cannot speak our language, make our laws?" Trying to unseat the Craven delegation was not enough for some bigots. They demanded the enforcement of the more extreme provisions of England's alien laws that would have denied Huguenots the right to vote, serve on juries, or own and inherit property. Governor Ludwell ignored the protests and permitted the Huguenots to take their seats.[10]

In response to the concerns of the English majority, for election purposes Craven and Berkeley Counties were combined, thus eliminating a French-majority election district. However, by the time the Third Assembly met in 1696, there was at least one Huguenot in the Berkeley and Craven delegation.[11]

The proprietors, who had encouraged the Huguenots and other refugees to settle in South Carolina, were horrified at the emergence of this raw ethnic hatred. By word and deed they did what they could to support the Huguenots from three thousand miles away. For five years there was a great deal of ill will generated by a vocal group of narrow-minded individuals. The controversy continued to simmer until the Commons House passed its own naturalization act in 1697 granting aliens "all the rights, privileges, powers and immunities whatsoever, which any person born of English parents may, can, might, could, or of right ought to have, use and enjoy." While the act only applied to those who had petitioned for citizenship, it set a precedent for assimilation.[12]

Most subsequent French immigrants—and most others—did not have to undergo the tribulations that the Huguenots had been forced to endure during the early proprietary years. There was one notable exception, however. During the 1750s Great Britain and France were still locked in a struggle for the North American empire. For reasons of national security, the British government decided to expel French colonials from Nova Scotia. The Acadians were dispersed among the other British colonies, South Carolina receiving an allotment of 1,023. Roman Catholic, homesick, destitute, and bitter, the Acadians were scattered among the various parishes but were not well received. Neither the assembly nor parish vestries provided assistance as they should have. In Georgetown individuals came to the aid of the exiles because the parish would not. Within a year their numbers had been reduced by one third through disease or out-migration. Those who were unemployed were sold, along with their children, into indentured servitude. The story of the Acadians in South Carolina has an ending much different from that of the Huguenots.[13]

By the 1730s the Huguenots had begun to abandon their language and customs and to merge with the English majority. They were no longer as alien as they once had been. The more they became assimilated, the more successful they became. Later French immigrants settled on the frontier away from the centers of population and, for a while, clung to their own ways. Then they, too, married their neighbors whether or not they were French.[14] In Charleston no one really cared whether backwoods French or German settlers kept their "alien" culture and language. Out of sight and earshot, they were supposed to be the colony's first line of defense against the Indians.

The idea for creating townships to attract a variety of European immigrants to South Carolina originated with Col. John Barnwell, the hero of the Tuscarora War. However, it was Gov. Robert Johnson who has been most closely identified with the "Scheem . . . for Settling Townships." In 1730 he proposed to the Board of Trade a plan for the orderly settlement of the South Carolina frontier. The board, in its instructions to him, authorized the surveying of eleven townships that would ring the settled areas of South Carolina, serving as a defensive perimeter against both Indians and Spaniards. The township plan would also attract more white settlers to coun-

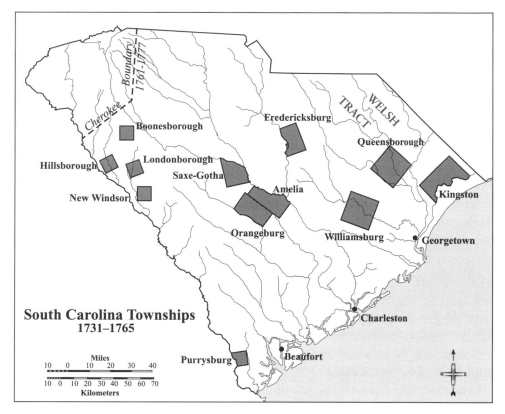

Map 7: Townships. Based on Edgar, *Biographical Directory* and Kovacik & Winberry, *South Carolina*

teract the burgeoning black population—something for which Gov. Robert Gibbes had pleaded two decades earlier.[15]

There were to be eleven townships located sixty miles inland on the colony's principal rivers from the Waccamaw River in the north to the Altamaha River in the south. Each township was to contain twenty thousand acres and stretch nearly six miles on a side. Settlers would get fifty acres for every family member, and the Commons House of Assembly agreed to provide funds for tools, transportation, and food. Quit rents, paid annually to the royal government, would be waived for ten years. Incentives and tax rebates were used to support economic development in the eighteenth century, just as they are in the twentieth. Paying for these incentives was expensive. Since one of the avowed reasons for creating the township system was to increase the white population in relationship to the black majority, it was only fitting that the funds be derived from a hefty import duty on slaves. In 1755 the headright was increased to one hundred acres for a head of household and fifty acres for each family member (including white servants and black slaves).[16]

Nine townships and one semitownship would be established in South Carolina by 1759 and another three before the end of the colonial period. The nine original townships, all with access to navigable rivers, were Purrysburg and New Windsor on the Savannah, Saxe Gotha on the Congaree, Orangeburg on the North Edisto, Amelia near the juncture of the Congaree with the Santee, Fredericksburg on the Wateree, Williamsburg on the Black, Queensborough on the Great Pee Dee, and Kingston on the Waccamaw. The semitownship was the Welsh Tract, which was laid out adjacent to Queensborough. The three townships created during the 1760s were Boonesborough on Long Cane Creek, Hillsborough at the confluence of Little River and Long Cane Creek, and Londonborough on Hard Labor Creek. All of the newer townships were on tributaries of the upper Savannah. Some of the townships originated as requests by individuals of a particular ethnic group, and others would become identified with a particular nationality (see Map 7).[17]

Two of the townships, Purrysburg and Hillsborough, were considered French settlements. During the 1720s Jean Pierre Purry, a French Swiss, had tried unsuccessfully to work out a colonization plan with the proprietors. Purry persevered and in 1730 succeeded in obtaining permission to establish a township on the lower Savannah River. Two years later a group of sixty-one immigrants arrived. Other Switzers, as they were called, followed, and by the early 1740s there may have been as many as eight hundred settlers in Purrysburg. There were also a few Germans and English, but two-thirds of the township's residents were of French descent.[18]

Hillsborough Township, on the upper reaches of the Savannah, was laid out in 1764 in response to a petition from the Reverend Jean Louis Gibert, who desired to lead a group of Huguenots to South Carolina. Gibert had great plans for the development of silk and wine culture, neither of which succeeded. The Huguenots built two small towns, which they named after French cities from whence they had come, New Bordeaux and New Rochelle. By 1765 there were nearly three hundred Huguenots in the general vicinity of New Bordeaux.[19]

The Hillsborough Township was one of four established for Protestant immigrants who entered the province in response to the Bounty Act of 1761. This legislation, a reaction to the ever-increasing black population, authorized £4 sterling ($360) per immigrant to whomever imported them into South Carolina. Upon arrival the bounty would be paid to the importer and each immigrant would get 20 shillings sterling ($90) for necessities. It was a nefarious business, one which Henry Laurens condemned as more cruel than the slave trade. Because of the complaints arising from mistreated immigrants and concerned citizens, the act lapsed in 1768. During the seven years of its existence it led to the immigration of between three and four thousand individuals, about one-fourth of whom were Germans.[20]

Prior to the Bounty Act a large group of Germans had arrived in South Carolina

The Lawrence Corley cabin, Lexington County (built circa 1771).
Courtesy, Lexington County Museum. Photograph by Suzanne C. Linder.

in July 1735, attracted by the promise of fifty acres of land. Some of the immigrants did not have sufficient funds to pay their passage and had to sell themselves or their children into indentured servitude for a period of years. When their service was up, they were not embarrassed to call themselves redemptioners. They were different from most indentured servants in that they usually came out in family groups. Nor were they destitute. Generally they had disposed of any land or other nonmovable property so that they had some small amount of capital with which to get a fresh start. Selling their children as servants was simply a means for paying the family's way to South Carolina. Those able to provide for themselves settled in Orangeburg Township, but a few went to Amelia Township.[21]

These settlers, thrust to the outer frontier, were supposed to be a buffer between the Cherokee and the prosperous rice-growing area along the coast. Shuffled off to the interior, they settled on some of the best farmland in the colony. Thrifty and industrious, the Germans of Orangeburg and Amelia turned their townships into the breadbasket of South Carolina. By the American Revolution they produced enough wheat to satisfy domestic consumption and had some left over for export.

Succeeding decades witnessed more and more German immigration. In the 1740s Saxe Gotha joined Amelia and Orangeburg as a predominantly German area. In 1752, facing an influx of fifteen hundred German settlers, the Commons House considered changing the laws that provided support for new settlers, limiting it to individuals from Great Britain. Thanks to the intervention of the Royal Council, that did not occur. Under the terms of the 1761 Bounty Act, a group of three hundred Palatine Germans was transported to Charleston. According to government officials, most of them were sick and forty-five died. The survivors were settled in Londonborough Township on Hard Labor Creek. Nearby New Windsor Township, on the Savannah River, was sparsely settled, but its population may have been as much as 50 percent German.[22]

By the end of the colonial period, Germans accounted for five percent of the white population. There were a few artisans in Charleston, but almost all the rest lived in Amelia, Orangeburg, Saxe Gotha, New Windsor, and Londonborough Townships. Except for Amelia and New Windsor, which were probably only one-third to one-half German, the others were overwhelmingly so. They retained their own customs and language in some rural areas until the early twentieth century. Even when some residents of Orangeburg converted to the Church of England in the 1750s, their German-speaking priest, the Reverend John Giessendanner, supplied them with a German edition of the *Book of Common Prayer*. Most, however, remained true to their Lutheran heritage. Among the German names found in the colonial records were Amaker, Boozer, Geiger, Harmon, Hutto, Inabinet, Kalteisen, Lever, Lorick, Rast, Sheeley, Shuler, Theüs, Wannamaker, and Ziegler.[23]

In addition to those who came into South Carolina through Charleston, there were some who came down the Great Wagon Road that ran from Harrisburg, Pennsylvania, through the Shenandoah Valley of Virginia into the piedmont of the two Carolinas. Their numbers were insignificant in comparison with the thousands of Scots-Irish who began moving into South Carolina in the 1750s.[24] The Scots-Irish who moved to the South Carolina frontier were descendants of Scots Protestants who originally settled in northern Ireland in the seventeenth century. When the Church of England began to press for conformity, the independent-minded folks now called Scots-Irish immigrated to Pennsylvania so that they could worship as they saw fit. They settled on the Pennsylvania frontier, where they came into conflict with both the Indians and the Quaker government in Philadelphia. As far as the government of Pennsylvania was concerned, the Indians were not a problem, but the Scots-Irish were. Unhappy with conditions in Pennsylvania, Scots-Irish families began to trek southward to the Carolinas.

For those who came from southeastern Pennsylvania, the journey was about 475 miles. All along the route settlers from Maryland and Virginia joined the group moving to the piedmont of the two Carolinas. They settled above the fall zone in an arc that stretched from present-day Lancaster County on the North Carolina border to Abbeville County on the Savannah River. They established settlements in the Waxhaws, an area claimed by both South and North Carolina, and along Long Cane Creek, a tributary of the Savannah. Very few, if any, sought land in townships, and none was created for them.

Bethesda Presbyterian Church, York County, founded 1769; original building burned 1780; this building dates from 1820. Photograph by Suzanne C. Linder.

By not fitting into the plan for the orderly settlement of the frontier, the Scots-Irish disrupted a process that had been in effect for a generation. The places they chose to settle also brought them into conflict with Cherokee land claims. It is no wonder, then, that their relationship with the government in Charleston was a stormy one. Part of the difficulty was due to differences in ethnicity and religion.

The Reverend Charles Woodmason, an Anglican missionary, described the Wax-haws in 1767: "This is a very fruitful Spot, thro' which the dividing Line between North and South Carolina runs—The Heads of P. D. [Peedee] River, Lynch's Creek, and many other Creeks take their Rise in this Quarter—so that a finer Body of Land is no where to be seen—But it is occupied by a Sett of the most lowest vilest Crew breathing—Scotch Irish Presbyterians from the North of Ireland." While Woodma-son's hostility might be traced to his personal difficulties with some backcountry settlers, his disdain for the Scots-Irish reflects his own ethnic and religious biases— biases that were shared, in large measure, by most white lowcountry residents.[25]

The ill will that was generated by the mass migration of Scots-Irish into the back-country was not felt by Scots-Irish who had come to South Carolina within a few years after the township plan was announced. In 1732 a group settled in Williams-burg Township, and from their angry letters it appears that they wanted the town-ship for themselves. However, grants of choice lands had been made to Charleston merchants and lawyers. With the introduction of indigo in the 1740s, Williamsburg would become the most prosperous of the townships. The Scots-Irish were a tightly knit group united by "their National Adherence to each other," family ties, and membership in the Williamsburg Presbyterian Church. Kingston was another township with a sizable Scots-Irish population. As in Williamsburg, the Presbyterian church helped strengthen the bonds of community.[26]

Whether in the townships or on the frontier, the Scots-Irish were proud of their heritage and their names: Adair, Bratton, Caldwell, Calhoun, Kuykendal, Logan, Montgomery, Moore, Ross, and Wardlaw.[27] In addition to the many Scots-Irish who came into South Carolina, there were a smaller number of Scots. There had been at least three proposals in the early 1680s to create Scottish settlements. The proprietors rejected two but approved of a plan by Henry Lord Cardross. His Stuart's Town was intended to be a haven for Presbyterians, and about 150 Scots settled in the Beaufort area on the colony's southern frontier. There they promptly tried to take over the Indian trade from Charleston and encouraged the Yamassee to raid Indian nations loyal to the Spaniards in St. Augustine. In 1686 a Spanish expedition attacked and burned the little town, then moved up the coast plundering at will. Only a hurricane stopped their planned assault on Charleston. Because of the problems that the Scots had caused, there were not many tears shed when Stuart's Town was destroyed. It was not rebuilt.[28]

With this one exception, most Scots arrived either individually or in small groups throughout the colonial period. There were three events back home that spurred Scottish immigration. The Act of Union in 1707 that created Great Britain made it possible for Scots to advance in government service, especially in the colonies. After the abortive Jacobite uprising in 1715, the English government deported a number of the rebel prisoners of war to Carolina (among them were thirteen members of the McGillivray clan). Then the defeat of the Young Pretender at the Battle of Culloden in 1746 forced many Scots to go into exile in British North America. The small number of Scots (as opposed to Scots-Irish) who came to South Carolina tended to settle in Charleston, where they went into the mercantile trade or the professions. Like the Huguenots, some intermarried with the English majority and joined the Church of England. Among those who immigrated to Carolina were individuals bearing such names as Abercromby, Allen, Buchanan, Bulloch, Deas, Kinloch, Logan, Michie, and Pringle.[29]

In some earlier histories there is confusion about who was Scottish and who was Irish. This is particularly true of Protestants from northern Ireland who, while they might have actually been Scotland-born, were sometimes referred to as Irish Protestants. Those who settled in Williamsburg and Kingston Townships were ethnically Scots. There were a considerable number of Irish in South Carolina, and their tale is not a pleasant one.[30]

In response to the Bounty Act of 1761, individuals on both sides of the Atlantic saw a way to make a profit by transporting "free poor Protestants" to South Carolina. There was a catch, however, in that to be eligible to collect the £4 sterling

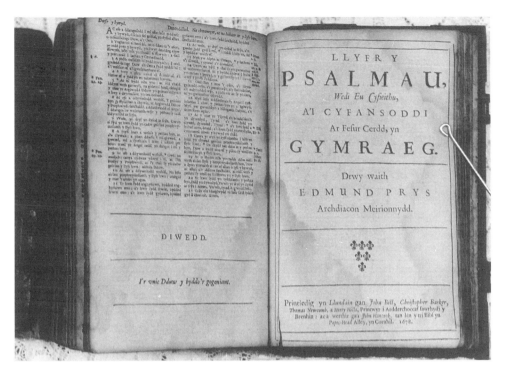

A Welsh Bible (1678) used by South Carolina Welsh Baptists in the eighteenth century. Courtesy, Darlington County Historical Commission. Photograph by Suzanne C. Linder.

($360) per person bounty, every immigrant over twelve had to take an oath that he or she was Protestant. Sometimes those who recruited the immigrants sent Roman Catholics, in which case, if they did not perjure themselves, no bounty could be collected. Sometimes those arriving in Charleston claimed that they had been kidnapped.[31]

Unscrupulous merchants and ship captains transported as many as they could under inhumane conditions that Henry Laurens compared to the better-known trafficking in human beings: "I have been largely concerned in the African trade . . . yet I never saw an instance of Cruelty in ten or twelve Years experience in that branch equal to the cruelty exercised upon those poor Irish." The sole purpose, he continued, was "to deliver as many as possible alive on Shoar upon the cheapest terms, no matter how they fared upon their Voyage nor in what condition they were landed." Because of the gross mistreatment of Irish immigrants, the government refused to pay the bounty in a number of cases.[32]

While the Bounty Act was in force (1761–1768), as many as four thousand individuals may have been shipped to South Carolina. Of these, probably three-fourths were Irish. Boonesborough Township, on Long Cane Creek, was established in 1762 specifically for Irish immigrants.[33]

In addition to the large numbers of Irish who came to South Carolina in the 1760s, individuals and families immigrated on their own. Among these were some

Irish Quakers who settled in and around Pine Tree Hill (present-day Camden). Quakers, attracted by the right to worship in their own fashion, comprised about 2.5 percent of those identified by religious belief. On the rolls of the Pine Tree Hill meeting were individuals with the names Dixon, Kelly, Millhouse, Russell, Tomlinson, and Wyly.[34]

One of the difficulties in using family names to determine ethnicity is that, particularly among those of Celtic origin, there is overlap with English and with one another.[35] There may well have been Irish as well as Scots, English, and Welsh settlers in Williamsburg and Queensborough Townships. In the latter there certainly were individuals of Welsh descent.

In November 1735 twenty-three individuals were dismissed to the Baptist Church in Charleston from the Welsh Tract Baptist Church in one of the three lower counties of Pennsylvania (present-day Delaware). The following year a group of individuals petitioned for ten thousand acres in Queensborough Township and for adjacent territory, eight miles on either side of the Pee Dee River for seventy miles.

Almost immediately Welsh Baptists began migrating to South Carolina. Some asked for grants in Queensborough, but most preferred the lands in what became known as the Welsh Tract. The Welsh Tract, like Orangeburg and Williamsburg, contained some of the best agricultural land in the colony. Within a decade the transplanted Pennsylvanians prospered as farmers of wheat, hemp, and indigo. They erected grist and saw mills. Virtually all the residents of the Welsh Tract were members of one of three Baptist congregations. By 1760 there were probably thirty-five hundred residents of the Welsh Tract, three hundred of whom were slaves. When the assembly created a new parish for the area in 1768, they acknowledged the Welsh presence by naming the parish for Saint David, patron saint of Wales.[36] Others were attracted to the fertile land of the Welsh Tract; however, the overwhelming majority of its inhabitants were Welsh, as their names indicate: Aymand, Fickling, James, Pawley, Pegues, and Wild.[37]

According to the 1931 analysis of family names in South Carolina, 0.6 percent of the white population was Swedish. That was twice the national average. There is no mention of Swedes in any of the earlier histories of South Carolina. An explanation for their presence in the colony could be that until 1655 the three lower counties of Pennsylvania had been New Sweden. Swedes might well have moved south with their fellow Pennsylvanians. In the lists of poor Protestants whose names appeared in the *South Carolina Gazette*, there is one lone Norwegian but no Swede. After the American Revolution there were Swedes in Charleston who associated with the city's German community.[38]

While not as elusive as the Swedes, South Carolinians of Dutch ancestry have been dismissed casually: "The Dutch element in South Carolina is infinitesimal." Eighteen months after the first settlement at Albemarle Point, a thirty-acre tract for a town south of the Stono River was laid out for some Dutch from New York. They soon abandoned the site and were absorbed into the general population. The origi-

Interior of Beth Elohim Syna-
gogue, Charleston. Painting by
Solomon Carvalho. Courtesy,
American Jewish Archives,
Hebrew Union College,
Cincinnati, Ohio.

nal portion of the oldest house in South Carolina, Medway, was built by John
d'Arsens, a Dutchman. Since there was regular trade between New York and
Charleston, the appearance of individuals with Dutch names is not surprising:
Gillon, Haes, Ioor, Rhett, and VanderHorst.[39]

The number of Jewish residents of colonial South Carolina was never large, probably no more than several hundred. With few exceptions they lived in Charleston.
Because of its policy of religious toleration, South Carolina attracted a sizable percentage of the Jewish residents of British North America. They were primarily
Sephardic Jews who had been expelled from Spain and Portugal, and they came to
South Carolina via the Netherlands, England, or the West Indies. A few, however,
even in the early years, were Ashkenazic, that is, from central or eastern Europe. In
1697 the names of four appear among those of Huguenots who were naturalized
under the Alien Act. One of them was Simon Valentine, "an alien of the Jewish nation," who had emigrated from Jamaica.[40]

From the beginning the small Jewish community was active in the life of the
colony. Between 1737 and 1747 there were serious discussions about creating a Jewish township, but the plan foundered when a Gentile partner in the scheme tried to
use the community's support as leverage to obtain additional lands for himself. During the 1730s a group of London Jews settled in Charleston; the remainder of those
in South Carolina immigrated either as individuals or families. In 1749 Beth Elo-

him, one of the oldest Jewish congregations in the United States, was formed and followed the ritual of a London synagogue. As late as 1820 Charleston's Jewish population, despite the small number, was the largest of any American city. Listed among the colonial records are individuals bearing such names as Avila, Cohen, DaCosta, D'Oliveria, Lindo, Salvador, and Tobias.[41]

Religious congregations such as Beth Elohim and the Welsh Neck Baptist Church were important in helping individuals maintain a sense of ethnic identity. So, too, were social and philanthropic organizations such as the St. Andrew's Society for Scots, the South Carolina Society for Huguenots, and the German Friendly Society. The Church of England served as a vehicle for assimilating non-English men and women, especially Scots and Huguenots.[42]

The maintenance of ethnic identity seems to have persevered longer in the townships and on the frontier. Among the townships, only Fredericksburg had a truly mixed population. The others were considered the provinces of particular ethnic populations. Purrysburg and Hillsborough were French; Orangeburg, Londonborough, and Saxe Gotha were German, Amelia and New Windsor between one-third and one-half German; Williamsburg and Kingston were Scots-Irish; Boonesborough was Irish; and Queensborough and the Welsh Tract were Welsh. Endogamy, marrying within the community, seemed to hold true in these areas until after the American Revolution. In the lowcountry by the 1720s Huguenots had begun to marry into the English majority. By the next decade so were Scots. In the nineteenth century most South Carolinians of European descent no longer felt constrained to marry someone from the same ethnic background.[43]

The European population of colonial South Carolina was quite an ethnic stew: English, Scots, Irish, Welsh, German, Dutch, French, Swedish, and Jewish. Those nine groups were further subdivided: the English were from Old and New England and the West Indies; the Scots from their homeland and the north of Ireland; the Germans from Baden, Württemberg, the Palatinate, other small German states, and the German-speaking cantons of Switzerland; the French from France, the French-speaking cantons of Switzerland, or Canada; and the Jews from Spain, Portugal, and central Europe. In percentages there were more French and Scots in South Carolina than in any other colony, and, except for Pennsylvania, fewer English.

The English may have made up only 36.7 percent of the total white population of South Carolina, but they were 80 percent of the white population of the lowcountry. Thus, with a powerful political and cultural center in Charleston, South Carolina's institutions and society developed with a strong English cast to them. The colony might have appeared to be English, but in this instance appearances were deceptive. It was English–West Indian. The Caribbean experience of the early settlers set the tone for the economic, social, and cultural life of the colony. Nowhere was that more in evidence than in the lowcountry, where the West Indian economic model produced a society in which blacks outnumbered whites two to one by 1720.[44]

Chapter Five

MORE LIKE A NEGRO COUNTRY

So if you will be half concern'd with us in a hundred slaves proviso you can purchase that number of very likely healthy People, Two thirds at least Men from 18 to 25 Years old, the other young Women from 14 to 18 the cost not to exceed Twenty five Pounds Sterling per head. . . . There must not be a Callabar amongst them. Gold Coast or Gambia's are best, next to them the Windward Coast are prefer'd to Angola's. . . . Pray observe that our People like tall Slaves best for our business & strong withall.

    Henry Laurens, 17 July 1755

The *Negro* Slaves . . . do all the Labour or hard Work in the Country, and are a considerable Part of the Riches of the Province. . . . They are in this Climate necessary, but very dangerous Domestics, their Number so much exceeding the Whites.

    George Milligen-Johnston, *A Short Description of the Province of South-Carolina . . . 1763*

*W*ITHIN THE FIRST year of colonization, enslaved Africans arrived in South Carolina via the West Indies. During the next twenty years of settlement, more than half of the colony's black population came from the Caribbean. A good many came with their owners, not as marketable merchandise. However, those who were shipped to the colony for sale were viewed with increasing suspicion, especially after the English West Indies began to have serious difficulties with slave revolts. In 1703, in order to prevent South Carolina's becoming a dumping ground for black troublemakers, the import duty for slaves brought from the West Indies was set at a higher rate than duty on slaves from Africa. By the end of the slave trade, probably 20 percent of South Carolina's black population had come from the West Indies and the remainder from Africa.[1]

The African slave trade, dominated by British merchants from Liverpool and London, supplied the bulk of the slaves to South Carolina. South Carolina merchants were more than willing to serve as local factors and make handsome profits. The slave trade was a tremendously profitable business for all concerned. Samuel and Joseph Wragg, Henry Laurens, and Miles Brewton all made their fortunes buy-

TO BE SOLD on Wednesday the 19th Instant, a Cargoe of about *Three Hundred* and *Fifty* choice healthy Negroes, just imported in the Ship *Loango, Thomas Dolman* Commander from the Coast of *Angola* directly, by *Benj. Savage* and Comp.

N. B. *Great regard will be had for present Pay in Rice or Currency.*

To be Sold 2 compleat Sawyers, not exceeding 24 Years of Age, apply to *John Watsone.*

Run away from on board the Snow *Molley,* lying at *Stone's* Bridge, the 3d Instant at Night, an indented Servant, named *Wm. Bridge,* aged about 19, of a short Stature, pale Complexion and low voic'd, without any Beard. and his hair off. had on a blue pea or dark Kearsey Jacket, a blue or strip'd Swan skin Wastcoat : Whoever secures him so that he may be had again, shall have 5 l. reward paid by me *John Howell.* Be it to their Peril that conceal him.

To be Sold

ON Thursday the 3d of *February* next, by *Roger Saunders* surviving Executor of the last Will and Testament of *Thomas Smith* Esq; formerly deceased, at the Plantation of said *Tho: Smith* on *Ashley* River, the personal Estate of the said *Smith,* consisting of between twenty and thirty choice Negro Slaves, most this Country born, with a Team of very good Oxen and Ox Cart, and sundry other Things : The Sale to begin at one o'Clock in the Forenoon, Credit will be given till the 1st of *May* next following, on giving such Security as will be approved of by *Roger Saunders*

A series of advertisements describing colonial laborers. The top advertisement is for the sale of 350 Angolans. Below it is a notice for a runaway white apprentice. The bottom advertisement for a plantation sale states that most of the slaves were "this Country born." *South Carolina Gazette,* 22 January 1737. Courtesy, Charleston Library Society.

ing and selling blacks. While it was a lucrative enterprise, a Charleston merchant had to do more than simply advertise a cargo of Africans for sale. A slave's country of origin and skills had a great deal to do with marketability and profit.

Early in the eighteenth century South Carolina whites noted differences in the Africans they purchased. They identified certain skills, physical appearance (to include tribal scarring), personality traits, and habits with particular regions of West Africa. As more Africans were imported, white Carolinians became even more knowledgeable about the countries whence slaves came. That made South Carolina whites different from their peers in other colonies. In Virginia, for example, the only concern was whether or not a slave were an African or a Negro (Virginia born). In South Carolina, as indicated in numerous letters and advertisements in the Charleston newspapers, whites were familiar with African ethnicity.[2]

In West Africa there is a linguistic dividing line. While no dividing line is absolute and there are exceptions, ethnic groups from the Gulf of Guinea north to the Sahara have been delineated as Sudanese, while those from the gulf south toward Angola are known as Bantu. There are physical differences as well as linguistic ones. Modern anthropological descriptions, while more scientific than Henry Laurens's,

Table 5.1

ORIGINS OF BLACK CAROLINIANS

Region	Ethnicity
Senegambia	Gambia, Mandingo, Jalonka, Bambara, Fulbe, Araba
Windward Coast	Limba, Temne, Bola, Kisi
Gold Coast	Coromantee, Fantee
Bight of Benin	Popo, Whydah, Nago, Gbari, Somba
Bight of Biafra	Ibo, Calabar
Congo-Angola	Congo, Angola, Malimbe, Wollonga, Bambona, Badongo
Guinea	Unspecified

Littlefield, *Rice and Slaves,* Table 3, 118–21; Table 11, 146–49.

are not much different from his. Bantu peoples, compared to Sudanese, are described as smaller, better proportioned, and lighter skinned, with a less protruding jaw, underdeveloped calves, and big feet. South Carolinians, as Laurens noted, preferred individuals whom we would now classify as Sudanese. Yet despite this preference, more Angolans, a Bantu people, were imported than any other.[3]

The importation of more Angolans was likely due to market circumstances. There always seemed to be a steady supply of marketable Africans from Congo-Angola because they were readily obtained and West Indian planters did not care for them. As available merchandise in a demand market (even if the merchandise were not the first choice, it was acceptable), Angolans were imported into South Carolina. By the end of the colonial period, Angolans accounted for 40 percent of the Africans imported into South Carolina. There is evidence that British slave traders understood South Carolina preferences for Gambians and did their best to obtain them. Africans from Senegambia (19.5 percent), the Windward Coast (16.3 percent), and the Gold Coast (13.3 percent), the areas that Laurens characterized as "preferr'd," totaled 49 percent.[4]

When describing countries of origin, eighteenth-century Europeans sometimes used rather loose terms such as Windward Coast, Gold Coast, and the Bight of Biafra. By the 1760s they were using more specific ethnic identifications such as Mandingo, Coromantee, Kishee, and Ibo. From seven regions of West Africa 25 individual groups or peoples have been identified (see Table 5.1).

In addition to physical characteristics, white Carolinians also ascribed personality traits and habits to particular peoples. Africans from Congo-Angola were believed to be docile, good-looking, and a bit weak in comparison to others. They were also potential runaways, a reputation they had throughout the colonial period. Counteracting these negatives were their reputed mechanical skills. Ibos were thought to be sickly, melancholy, suicidal, superstitious, and unattractive. Coromantees were brave, unforgiving, hot-tempered, and dangerous if aroused, but if loyalty could be gained they became devoted servants. Mandingos were gentle, refined, and physically attractive to Europeans; however, some whites thought they were sneaky and not to be trusted. The Popos and their neighbors were the most highly prized of all Africans imported into South Carolina: dutiful, skilled, and easy-going with a pleasant disposition and strong work ethic.[5]

White Carolinians, if given the choice, preferred their slaves to be big, strong, and black. Occasionally, as Laurens noted, there were times when any African could be disposed of for a profit: "Negroes have sold here at very exhorbitant prices all the past Summer & even down to this time. I have transmitted a Sale of a parcel of Men, refuse, aged, half blind & one dumb & deaf which made an average of £34 Sterling" ($3,100). However, as Laurens's extensive correspondence illustrates, the smart investor and the smart merchant, those who wanted to make a good profit, chose their slave cargoes carefully. They brought to the Charleston market those in demand. And the most sought after came from the Gold Coast, Senegambia, and the Windward Coast. Angolans were acceptable, but Africans from the Bight of Biafra were undesirable.[6]

During the first fifty years of settlement, there was a gradual increase in the importation of Africans as white settlers explored a variety of economic opportunities: the Indian trade, cattle ranching, naval stores, and rice. Until 1712 fewer than one hundred slaves a year were imported; in some years the number was only twenty or thirty. Also by the beginning of the eighteenth century the slave population was growing naturally at a rate of better than 5 percent a year—a rate that exceeded that of the white population.[7]

Beginning in 1712 the number of slaves imported leaped to about six hundred a year. Traditionally, the development of rice culture is cited as the reason for the increase in the colony's black population. However, rice production declined markedly after 1712 and remained stagnant until 1721. Meanwhile the production of naval stores increased, spurred by the needs of the marketplace and British bounties. Whether it was rice or naval stores, there clearly was an increased demand for inexpensive labor, African slave labor. After 1730 there is no question, however, that it was the expansion of rice production and the introduction of indigo that fueled the market for the importation of thousands of Africans. And throughout the eighteenth century there were plenty of suppliers.[8]

The process began in Africa usually within a several-hundred-mile radius of a coastal factory or trading fort. English slave traders negotiated with native rulers and merchants for their cargoes. Once selected, the unfortunate men and women were usually branded for identification purposes. Then they were loaded onto ships in which they were jammed into shelves with little headroom, sometimes not even enough in which to sit up. In these tight quarters they had to eat, sleep, and perform bodily functions. Depending upon the vessel—and the fear of insurrection—slaves might be brought up on deck for exercise. The agony of the middle passage might last as long as six weeks. One in six Africans died en route.[9]

Charleston was the most likely destination for slave ships in the North American slave trade. Between 1700 and 1775, 40 percent of the Africans imported into North America came through Charleston. Just as nineteenth- and early-twentieth-century immigrants were quarantined at Ellis Island before being allowed to enter the United States, in the eighteenth century South Carolina officials required that slaves be quarantined on Sullivan's Island in Charleston harbor. After being cleared, slaves were then auctioned off by the merchants who had imported them. In the eighteenth century sales were held onboard the slave ships or in town at places such as taverns. It was not until the nineteenth century that slave traders congregated in the neighborhood of Chalmers and State Streets and built slave marts.[10]

How did individuals endure the psychological and physical stresses of the middle passage and slavery? Strong religious convictions may account for the adjustment of some Africans. The beliefs of peoples from the Niger Delta led them to accept slavery as divine retribution. An Anglican clergyman reported that when he asked a black woman if she knew how she had become a slave, her reply was, "God would have it so & she cou'd not help it." Other ethnic groups had similar beliefs. This fatalistic approach to life helped make some sense out of what otherwise would have been an incomprehensible situation.[11]

The equally powerful Bakongo religion was held by many from Congo-Angola. They believed in Nzambi, an almighty god from whom emanated the powers of good and evil, powers that could be controlled by men with special spiritual gifts. These priests could command the spirits of the Bakongo cosmos linking mortals with the forces of the dead. Rituals were usually performed at night since then the sun was under the water, the barrier between the land of the living and the land of the dead. The cycle of day and night was a constant reminder of birth, death, and re-birth. Symbols of these beliefs, represented by circles and x marks on small earthenware bowls, have been found throughout the lowcountry, notably in rivers.[12]

While the evidence of the practice of Bakongo is widespread, there is only fragmentary evidence of one of the world's five great religions, Islam, in the lowcountry. Senegambians were the most desirable slaves, and the dominant religion of that region of Africa was Islam. There were observations of men facing east to pray five times a day and notations in plantation journals of issuing beef rations to certain individuals at hog-killing time. Otherwise, the records are silent.[13]

Other Africans adjusted to slavery in South Carolina because they had been slaves before. On the Windward Coast and in Senegambia slave labor was used in rice

Shard of a colono-ware bowl with Bakongo-style marking. Courtesy, Leland Ferguson, University of South Carolina. Photograph by Emily Short.

fields. It has been estimated that three-fourths of the population of Sierra Leone was nonfree. Having already experienced bondage, these individuals more readily adapted to slavery in South Carolina.[14]

Assimilation into South Carolina's slave culture may have been easier for earlier arrivals, most of whom came from the West Indies with their owners. The Barbadian notion that a white planter considered all persons in his household as family helped shape the initial development of institutional slavery in the colony. During the first three decades of settlement, the relationship between owner and slave was quite different from what it would become. In trying to tame the South Carolina wilderness, there was plenty of work to be done. Everyone, white and black, was a pioneer.[15]

Slaves had relatively more freedom than they would later. In fact, South Carolina did not enact a comprehensive slave code until 1696—puzzling since a majority of the colony's white population was from the English West Indies. Perhaps there was no need to pass an act "for the better ordering and governing of Negroes"—just as there had not been in Barbados until 1661. When South Carolina did get around to passing a slave code, it used a 1688 Barbadian statute that was a revised version of the 1661 original.[16]

The code defined slaves as chattel and permitted a master to discipline his property in any way he saw fit. There were extensive lists of crimes for which a slave could be punished. Capital offenses included murder, arson, rape, assault, and theft of anything of value. One of the primary purposes behind the Barbadian code was the control of the black majority. Passes were required for any slave leaving a plantation. Although South Carolina enacted virtually a duplicate of the Barbadian statute, apparently not many whites paid it much mind. Slaves were allowed to go from plantation to plantation and to the Charleston market, and they were permitted to carry weapons. This casual attitude by the white population continued as long as the black presence did not pose a threat.

Twelve years after the adoption of the Barbadian slave code, the colony had a black majority. A report by the governor and council to the proprietors noted that there had been a significant population shift in the five-year period between 1703 and 1708. The white population had increased by 7 percent to 4,080, while the black population had grown nearly 37 percent to 4,100. The small black majority of 1708 would increase until in 1720 there were two blacks for every white in South Carolina. That population ratio would remain fairly constant until the eve of the American Revolution. However, in this instance statistics alone are misleading. The colonywide black to white ratio may have been two to one, but in some of the lowcountry parishes such as St. James Goose Creek (79 percent black) and St. James Santee (74 percent black), the ratios were virtually identical to those of Barbados.[17]

The presence of such a large group of Africans was the subject of an address by Gov. Robert Gibbes to the Commons House in 1711. He was concerned about the "great quantities of negroes" that were brought in daily and the decline through death and desertion of the white population. Numbers, alone, were not the only difficulty. Gibbes noted that slaves had become "insolent and mischevious." In his remarks Gibbes was saying publicly what a number of whites were saying privately. They were plainly uneasy about the black majority and the threat it posed to the safety and security of white South Carolinians.[18]

The arming of Africans, which had been going on informally since the 1670s, made many whites nervous. In 1704, when the colony was more concerned with foreign threats, the Commons House passed a law authorizing the enlisting of "our trusty slaves" in the militia as "necessary for the safety of this Province." A 1708 report indicated that there were nineteen hundred adult males fit to bear arms, half of whom were black. In a series of colonial conflicts black Carolinians were armed and formed an integral part of South Carolina's militia. They participated in the 1702 expedition against the Spaniards in St. Augustine. When North Carolina was on the verge of being destroyed by the Tuscarora Indians, a mixed force of white and black South Carolinians and Indian allies saved the day. And when the Yamassee threatened the existence of South Carolina, hundreds of armed black Carolinians helped drive them into Florida. Given the seriousness of the Yamassee War, the role played by black Carolinians was crucial. However, in the minds of some whites the very success of black militiamen raised the specter of slave rebellion. So, too, did regular reports of uprisings in the West Indies. After 1720 white fears grew more pronounced about what the black majority might do; therefore, to prevent the unthinkable, the white minority resorted to intimidation to keep blacks in line. This was a tactic that continued throughout the eighteenth century. "Frighten the two Boys till you make them tremble," wrote Laurens in 1765, "but dont Whip them."[19]

As control of the slave population increased, so did tensions. When blacks reacted in an "insolent or mischevious" manner, whites clamped down even more. This, in turn, led to further black resistance. The colony entered into what appeared to be a never-ending spiral of action and reaction.

Overt resistance took many forms. It could be something as simple as leaving a barn door open so that livestock could escape, breaking a hoe on a rock, pretending not to understand instructions, doing something other than what was intended, or taking one's time—after all, since a slave belonged to someone for life, the job would be there tomorrow. More serious forms of resistance included assaulting an overseer or owner, poisoning, arson, and murder. The colonial records include examples of all of these. In July 1769, for example, two slaves were burned on the green in Charleston—one for procuring some poison and the other for administering it. Violence was not limited to lashing out at whites. Slave mothers sometimes induced abortions so that they would not bring children into slavery. A few committed suicide. The threat of slaves' taking their own lives was one reason that Henry Laurens urged his suppliers to obtain young Africans, fifteen to twenty years old, because they "are not accustom'd to destroy themselves like those who are Older."[20]

There were more subtle forms of resistance unrecognized by whites but just as effective: the perseverance of African folkways through the creation of a culture that was both African and American. In this regard black South Carolinians had more in common with their compatriots in the West Indies than they did with those in the other mainland colonies.[21]

Not only were blacks a majority of the population, but until 1740 a majority of them were African-born. Although no longer a majority after 1740, African-born slaves were still a high percentage of the black population until the American Revolution. When Africans arrived in South Carolina, given the patterns of importation, there was the likelihood that several individuals from the same ethnic group might end up together. In the lowcountry planters usually subdivided their large holdings into smaller working plantations with about thirty slaves each. The geography of the area created hundreds of isolated pockets where there were thirty or so blacks and rarely a white. Even when whites were present, there was little interaction with blacks. In these enclaves African folkways not only survived but thrived in a new African American culture.[22]

All peoples are ethnocentric; they are convinced that their ways of doing things are better than others. Black South Carolinians were no different. They preserved elements of their African heritage, modified by the South Carolina environment, and reared their children in a culture that was African American. The houses in which they slept, the meals they ate, the utensils they used, the songs they sang, and the stories they told—all had a decidedly West African influence even if the materials, ingredients, or subjects were of local origin. And in South Carolina they created their own language, Gullah.[23]

Coming from more than two dozen ethnic groups and speaking forty different languages, communication among slaves at first was difficult. There is evidence that some planters deliberately tried to purchase individuals from different areas so that they would not be able to communicate and therefore be less of a threat. "Whites," wrote one observer, "have no greater security than the diversity of the negroes' languages." Of necessity, black South Carolinians were forced to develop a means of communicating with one another. Initially their efforts produced a pidgin English that, with its use by the next generation of native-born black South Carolinians, became a creole language, Gullah.[24]

Gullah is a spoken, not a written, language; thus, its meaning is derived from the context of a particular conversation. Nouns and pronouns have no case; verbs have no tense; and pronouns have no gender. The structure depends entirely upon word order. For example, the statement "i kom fo wi haus" could have several meanings. The pronoun "i" could be either *he, she,* or *it;* the verb "kom" either *came* or *comes;* the preposition "fo" either *from* or *to;* and the phrase "wi haus" translates as *our house.*[25]

There is more to Gullah than just language structure. Since it is a spoken language, the way words are pronounced and the rhythm of speech are key elements. Linguistic studies have shown that most Gullah vowels are similar to those in Yoruba, a language spoken in Nigeria. The melodious lilt still heard along the coast is West African in origin.[26]

Although Gullah is a spoken language, there have been efforts to preserve it in writing. The most notable effort is that of the American Bible Society, which has translated the Gospel of Luke into contemporary Gullah. The well-known Christmas story from the second chapter begins this way: "Een dat time, Caesar Augustus been de big leada, de emperor ob de Roman people. E make a law een all de town een de wol weh e habe tority, say 'ebrybody haffa go ta town fa count by de hed and write down e nyame.' / Dis been de fus time dey count by de hed, same time Cyrenius de gobna ob Syria country. So den, ebrybody gone fa count by de hed, ta e own town weh e ole people been bon."[27] Even someone familiar with these verses would have a difficult time understanding them. To the uninitiated, the rapid-fire delivery of strange words, pronunciations, and rhythms would be virtually unintelligible. This is true today, and it was true two centuries ago. Some whites learned Gullah and became bilingual, but many simply paid no attention to "slave talk." That meant that black South Carolinians could freely communicate with one another, sometimes voicing uncomplimentary opinions of a white within earshot. With *street,* Orange, Anniseed, Clove, Lime and Tansie Waters at 40 *s.* *per* Gallon, Lemon Water at 3 *l.* Cinamon Water at 5 *l.* Citron Water at 6 *l.* fine Usquebaugh at 8 *l.* and Spirits of Wine at 3 *l.* 10 *s. per* Gallon, Bitters at 40 *s. per* Quart.

Run away on the 13th of *March* last, a Mustee Fellow named *Cyrus,* who lately belonged to Messrs. *Mulryne* and *Williams* of *Port-Royal.* Whoever secures, or brings the said Fellow to me, or to Mr. *David Brown* of *Charles-Town* Shipwright, shall have TWENTY POUNDS Reward, and the Charges allow'd by Law. And whoever gives me Information of his being employed by any Person, so that he may be convicted thereof, shall, upon such Conviction, have THIRTY POUNDS current Money paid him, by *David Linn.*

A bay stray Horse, about 13 Hands and an half high, branded WT in one on the mounting Shoulder, taken up at *Ashepoo.* The Owner may have him by applying to *J. Hutchinson.* *South-Carolina.* Whereas *John Griffin*

A runaway slave advertisement. *South Carolina Gazette,* 11 June 1747. Courtesy, Charleston Library Society.

Gullah, South Carolina's blacks had another means of evading the system, of resisting.[28]

Running away was a form of resistance that drew a great deal of attention. Not only did the slave temporarily gain freedom, but the act itself was an open threat to the institution of slavery. Fleeing was an example that could be emulated, and it showed that not all black Carolinians were going to submit to the system. During the eighteenth century the absolute numbers of runaways increased, but the percentage remained about the same, less than one-half of 1 percent of the slave population. By the 1760s there were more than one hundred runaways a year. Because there were more individuals challenging the system, notices of runaway slaves appeared with alarming frequency in the pages of Charleston's three newspapers. Just the number of notices alone would have given the impression that there was an epidemic of runaways in South Carolina.[29]

Where could runaways go? Some tried to make their way to Spanish Florida where the government promised them freedom and a safe haven if they escaped from South Carolina. Others fled to the frontier where they joined outlaw bands that plagued isolated settlements from the 1740s until after the American Revolution. On its frontiers South Carolina had more Maroon settlements of runaway slaves than any other colony. Some runaways were taken in by whites for their own financial gain, a serious issue and one addressed in all versions of the colony's slave codes. Others were able to remain at large either in Charleston or in the countryside because of the overwhelming numbers of black Carolinians.[30]

White Carolinians' preferences for slaves from certain areas of West Africa had to do with the perception that some were more likely to run away than others. Angolans, despite the large numbers imported, were considered potential runaways. So, too, were Calabars and Ibos. Recent arrivals were more apt to run away than individuals born in South Carolina. Although native-born slaves did not run away often, when they did they were more skilled at evading recapture than the newcomers.[31]

While running away was an effective way to defy white authority, the ultimate form of resistance was rebellion. After 1712 there seems to have been a constant uneasiness over the possibility of a slave revolt. With the regular flow of goods and information from the West Indies, white Carolinians were well aware that what happened there could happen here. During the eighteenth century there were two major slave rebellions during the colonial period and fears of others.

The first rebellion occurred in May and June 1720 while the colony was in an unsettled state. The proprietary regime had been overthrown in December 1719, and the new government was waiting for a response from London. The colony had just fought off an attack by the Waccamaw Indians and still feared that Spanish privateers might swoop down on Charleston. The Primus Plot was under way before whites even knew about it. On 20 May a black man named Andrew appeared before the Commons House of Assembly. What he told the members caused them to remain in session well into the night and to reconvene the next morning at seven o'clock. As the story unfolded, the legislators learned that a group of at least fourteen blacks from several plantations on the upper Ashley River intended to destroy isolated plantations, recruit more rebels, and attack Charleston. Betrayed by Andrew, they then attempted to flee to St. Augustine. Primus, a slave belonging to Andrew Percival, was considered the ringleader. The Commons House offered a reward of £20 ($380) for each of the runaways, dead or alive. It also authorized whites, blacks, and Indians to pursue Primus and his party.[32]

On 9 June, Gov. James Moore reported to the Commons House that four of the rebels had been captured and were being held at Savannah Town, an Indian trading post located on the fall line of the Savannah River. The governor urged that the runaways be executed immediately. The Commons House disagreed and decided to make an example of the participants in the Primus Plot. All were to be publicly executed in Charleston, and Primus, the leader of the group, was to be hanged alive in chains.[33]

The plot was a real threat, not just a perceived one. Its timing indicated that black Carolinians knew what was going on in the colony. The conspiracy may have been larger than originally thought because a Christ Church Parish planter received compensation for a female runaway who was killed during the crisis. A year later the Board of Trade reported to George II that the black rebels had nearly succeeded in their "revolution." Had that occurred, the result would have been "the utter extirpation of all Your Majesty's subjects in this province." During the 1720s and 1730s there were persistent rumors of slave conspiracies and servile insurrection. These plots failed to materialize because of divided leadership, the failure to recruit more than a handful of rebels, and betrayal.[34]

Throughout 1739 white South Carolinians were increasingly apprehensive about the restlessness they observed among the black population. The number of runaways increased, and whites blamed the Spaniards in St. Augustine. White Carolinians' suspicions were confirmed in March when a group of four cattle herders killed one white and wounded another, stole some horses, and fled southward. Although hotly pursued by a posse, three did reach St. Augustine where they were received with "great honours." The authorities decided to use the incident to cow the colony's black majority. Two runaways in custody were publicly executed before a group of assembled slaves, and, as reported in the *South Carolina Gazette,* one of the bodies was left hanging in chains at Hangman's Point "in sight of all Negroes passing and repassing by Water."[35]

South Carolina's enslaved Africans were not the only ones causing difficulties in 1739. During the spring and summer word reached the colony of slave unrest in Antigua, Jamaica, and St. Christopher's.[36] There seemed to be trouble everywhere. More force seemed to be the answer. The Commons House passed legislation requiring all white males to carry weapons when they attended church. The new law would go into effect 29 September 1739.

As with the Primus Plot, the Stono Rebellion seemed to occur at a time when the colony was in a weakened and threatened condition. The timing of the rebellion seems to indicate that black South Carolinians were aware of the world beyond their own plantations. Disease had taken its toll for almost twelve months. An outbreak of smallpox in late 1738 had lingered into early 1739. That was followed by a yellow fever epidemic in August that killed as many as eight or ten Charlestonians a day; among them were a number of key government officials. Not until October did the epidemic begin to abate. For some time war with Spain had been expected. It appears that news of the official declaration reached Charleston the very weekend that the rebellion began. Then there was the new law that soon would require white males to go armed to church. Thus, early September found the white population weakened by disease, threatened by war with Spain, and still unarmed on Sunday when most slaves had free time.[37]

On Sunday morning, 9 September 1739, a group of black Carolinians, many of them Angolans, met on the Stono River about twenty miles southwest of Charleston. They broke into a store at the Stono Bridge, murdered the owners, and stole arms and ammunition. The rebellion then began in earnest. Moving south on the main road, they killed whites and burned and looted houses and barns. Only two whites escaped death because they were known to be kind to their slaves. Word spread via the black grapevine and drum calls. Dozens flocked to join the growing band. If a slave did not want to participate, he was coerced so as to reduce the chances of betrayal. By noon there might have been as many as one hundred rebels heading toward St. Augustine and freedom. Late in the afternoon they stopped near Jacksonborough on the banks of the Edisto River.[38]

In a coincidence that not even Hollywood would allow, the rebels encountered Lt. Gov. William Bull on the road. Realizing instantly what was going on, he turned his horse and outran his pursuers. He then spread the alarm, and militia companies began to form. They moved toward the rebel camp and without hesitation attacked it late Sunday afternoon. The blacks returned the fire, but the whites had superior firepower. About fourteen blacks were killed in the initial skirmish, and others were captured. After a brief questioning they were executed on the spot. Some rebels tried to sneak back to their plantations undetected but failed and were shot. About two-thirds of the rebels escaped and were a real threat to the stability of the southern portions of the province.[39]

White South Carolina placed itself on virtually a war footing. Every white male carried a firearm. Key ferry crossings were placed under armed guard. Indian allies were paid to hunt for rebels. During the week of 9–16 September, perhaps as many as forty to sixty rebels were killed and executed. A thirty-man remnant of the original group was tracked down on 15 September, and after a brief fight all but a handful were killed or captured. One of the leaders escaped into the swamps and evaded pursuers for three years. Betrayed by two runaways, he was seized, tried, and hanged.[40]

The Stono Rebellion, the largest incident of its kind in British North America, resulted in the deaths of about seventy-five black and white South Carolinians. The brutality of the killings by both blacks and whites was numbing. When the rebels looted Hutchenson's store at Stono Bridge, they decapitated the storekeeper and his clerk and left their heads on the store's steps. And in the course of their rampage they cut down whites without regard to age or gender. Late on the evening of 9 September militiamen pursuing stragglers beheaded many and placed the heads on mileposts.[41]

The ruthless suppression of the Stono Rebellion did not make white South Carolinians rest any easier. Some planters living between Charleston and the Savannah decided to move their families to the capital for safety because they feared the rebels who were still at large. In December 1739 there were rumors of another slave conspiracy that had most of Charleston's white males on guard duty round the clock. Six months later an elaborate plot, "in the very Heart of the Settlements," that involved nearly two hundred slaves was uncovered. The plan called for the would-be rebels to steal weapons and march on Charleston. Exposed by one of their own, sixty-seven were tried and as many as ten executed in one day to overawe the black majority.[42]

Given the tensions in the colony, reaction of the white minority was relatively restrained and deliberate. The Commons House met for three days during the week following the Stono Rebellion, then adjourned until October. It met again briefly in October and then began a six-week session that ended in mid December. The late rebellion was not the foremost item on the legislative agenda; rather, settling long-standing constitutional disputes with the Royal Council occupied the business of the Commons House. Then late in the spring of 1740 the assembly passed three pieces of legislation that were the official response of white South Carolina to the Stono Rebellion.

Almost every white South Carolinian blamed the Spaniards in St. Augustine for inciting the colony's slave population. "We shall Live very Uneasie with our Negroes while the Spaniards continue to keep possession of St. Augustine," wrote Robert Pringle; "it is a pity our Government at home did not encourage the dislodgement of them from thence." Actually, the government had authorized Gov. James Oglethorpe of Georgia to do just that. Britain, however, would not pay for an expeditionary force; the colonials would be on their own. In January 1740 Oglethorpe turned to South Carolina. After several months of negotiations the colony furnished men, ships, supplies, and money (£10,000 sterling [$1.2 million]) to underwrite the cost of eliminating the Spanish once and for all. It was, however, a waste of money, as Oglethorpe bungled the mission.[43]

It was not until seven months after the outbreak of the rebellion that the Commons House passed any legislation related to Stono and black South Carolinians. On 5 April an act levying a prohibitive import duty of £100 currency ($1,750) a head on Africans was passed that would go into effect in July 1741. The duty had a twofold purpose. First, by doubling the price of slaves, it would effectively eliminate the importation of large numbers of new Africans. In that it was successful; only 1,562 Africans were imported during the decade of the 1740s, compared to 12,589 between 1735 and 1740. Second, those duties collected were to be used to encourage the immigration of European settlers—an attempt to reduce the size of the black majority. The duty also had an impact on the composition of the black population. By curbing the flow of new Africans of "barbarous and savage disposition," the act increased the percentage of the slave population that was South Carolina–born. Following passage of this act, the assembly adjourned.[44]

When the assembly reconvened in May, it passed one of the most far-reaching pieces of legislation in South Carolina history, the slave code of 1740. With only minor modifications, this document set forth regulations that would guide the conduct of blacks and whites until 1865. The primary purpose of the act was to prevent another Stono Rebellion, to insure the good order and harmony of the community. Not only would the behavior of slaves be more severely scrutinized, but so would that of slave owners. Any factor that might have contributed to the late rebellion was to be stopped.

Regulations governed every aspect of a slave's conduct, from prohibiting the wearing of fancy clothing to limiting what could be sold in the market. No slave was allowed to carry an "offensive weapon" without being in the company of a white person or having a ticket from his owner allowing him to do so. And, ticket or no ticket, no slave could carry a weapon of any sort from sundown Saturday until sunrise Monday. That time period coincided with what was usually free time when slaves might get together and cause trouble (although they were not supposed to get together in large groups). Sunday was a day when whites were likely to be in church and somewhat vulnerable. Fresh in the minds of the members of the assembly was Sunday morning, 9 September 1739.[45]

While too much freedom or lax enforcement of existing laws might have enabled the rebels to make their plans, the assembly recognized cause and effect. If slaves were well treated, then there would be no need for them to rise up against their masters. Since the colony could not trust all owners to do the right thing, therefore their conduct had to be regulated, too. Owners were supposed to provide sufficient food and clothing for their slaves; if they did not, then neighbors could file a complaint on behalf of the slaves—sort of an eighteenth-century neighborhood watch. The work day was set at fifteen hours from 25 March to 25 September and fourteen hours from 25 September to 25 March. Sundays were still recognized as days of rest, unless conditions warranted otherwise. These and other provisions in the code indicate that white South Carolinians understood that the mistreatment of enslaved Africans was one of the causes of their recent difficulties. Since slaves were valuable investments, owners were compensated for any that were executed by the colony—with the exception of murderers and "slaves taken in actual rebellion." This compensation clause had also been in earlier slave codes. Between 1700 and 1776 the government of South Carolina compensated owners for 215 slaves executed for the public good. That figure does not include a good many of the Stono rebels.[46]

The events of September 1739 had occurred so swiftly that a number of slaves had been killed without "the formality of a legal trial." Evidently some owners must have been thinking about suing those involved. The new law carefully declared that the danger facing those individuals fighting the rebels was so severe that they had been "obliged to put such negroes to immediate death." Therefore, all such summary executions were declared lawful.[47]

On its face, the slave code of 1740 was one of the harsher such measures passed in the colonies. However, despite the scare of the Stono Rebellion, the law was disregarded by both blacks and whites almost immediately. It is possible that black South Carolinians had greater personal freedom than blacks of any other North American colony. One of the factors that may have enabled this to occur was overwhelming black presence. While few Africans were imported into South Carolina

Table 5.2

BLACK/WHITE POPULATION OF COLONIAL SOUTH CAROLINA

	1680	1708	1720	1740	1761	1769	1775
Black (%)	200 16.6	4,100 50.1	11,800 64.5	39,000 66.1	57,000 65.5	80,000 64.0	104,000 59.8
White (%)	1,000 83.4	4,080 49.9	6,500 35.5	20,000 33.9	30,000 34.5	45,000 36.0	70,000 40.2
Total	1,200	8,180	18,300	59,000	87,000	125,000	174,000

Based on the figures found in Wallace, *History of South Carolina,* 3: Appendix IV, and Wood, *Black Majority,* 144, 146–47, 152.

during the 1740s, between 1750 and the American Revolution an additional 56,791 entered the province. Since the slave trade was cut off from 1766 to 1769 with another £100 currency ($1,200) import duty, that means that when the slave trade was open, an average of 2,500 Africans were imported annually. The result was—despite the increase in white immigration during the same period—that South Carolina was still a colony with a black majority.[48]

From grand jury presentments and contemporary accounts, it appears that as soon as the immediate threats of 1739–1740 had passed, white South Carolinians went about dealing with black South Carolinians as they saw fit. Grand juries regularly complained that slaves were able to purchase intoxicating liquors, sell any merchandise they wanted in the market, wear prohibited clothing, and openly carry weapons in Charleston. The local newspapers faithfully reported the grand juries' concerns, but seldom were any corrective actions taken.

One of the interesting aspects of slavery in South Carolina was the ability of whites to compartmentalize their fears. There was fear of the black majority in general; however, individual owners tended to believe that the black members of their family were faithful and trustworthy. Wicked and dangerous slaves belonged to someone else, someone who did not know how to deal properly with his black family.[49]

An excellent example of this compartmentalization was the pervasive fear of poisoning. In the 1740 slave code it was stated that "he or she" who administered poison would be put to death. Yet the overwhelming majority of those who did the cooking, especially in the lowcountry, were black women.

These contradictions in a society that was allegedly tightly controlled were even more apparent in the management of plantations. The stereotypical image of the master with whip in hand driving his slaves to the fields from sunrise to sunset is mostly myth created by abolitionists and Hollywood. In South Carolina the primary goal of a plantation was to produce, to make money. If slaves were mistreated or unhappy, they had innumerable opportunities for sabotage on rice and indigo plantations. That is one reason that South Carolina planters, unlike their counterparts in Virginia, tended not to meddle in the everyday affairs of their slaves. That made for a more contented workforce and also enabled black Carolinians to maintain their African heritage.[50]

While slavery in South Carolina may have been more benign than in Virginia or North Carolina, fear and intimidation were still present. Force could be and was used. If a black South Carolinian crossed a white South Carolinian, there was little doubt as to the outcome. Depending upon the seriousness of the offense, punishment could range from whipping to mutilation or death. One of the more feared punishments was being sent "off the Province," away from family and friends. In 1740 Robert Pringle got tired of Esther, a young black woman, regularly leaving his town house to visit her parents on a plantation outside Charleston. The punishment: she was shipped to Portugal. The records are silent as to any reaction by Esther's parents or friends; however, perhaps the treatment of Esther explains why Pringle was not an especially successful planter. The wise owner understood that an unhappy labor force could spell economic disaster.[51]

From records it is clear that black South Carolinians had more to say about their everyday existence than the mythmakers have told us. On lowcountry rice plantations slaves worked under the task system, which meant that once they completed a specific job they were through for the day. That free time could be spent in their own gardens, hunting, fishing, or visiting. Although the law required that there be at least one adult white male for every ten blacks on a plantation, a great many white South Carolinians ignored the law. A single white overseer on a working plantation of thirty blacks was common. Also, most planters used a black driver, an intermediary between the work force and the white owner. It was the driver's responsibility to delegate tasks and see that the day's work was completed. In some instances where there was not a white overseer on the place, drivers functioned in that capacity. The productivity of labor was the key to the success of a plantation, and black South Carolinians learned that they could turn that need to their own advantage—and they did.[52]

As the institution of slavery evolved in eighteenth-century South Carolina, the work required of an individual became a negotiated matter on plantations and in town. Sometimes black Carolinians resorted to threats to get their way. In 1763 the black chimney sweeps of Charleston refused to work unless they received an increase in pay. Although the prices were established by law, whites acceded to the sweeps' demands. Five years later Henry Laurens told a young cooper (for whom he had just paid £650 currency [$7,755]) that he was going to send him to work on a Florida plantation. The slave informed Laurens that he did not want to leave the colony and that if he were sent to Florida, he would run away. Laurens backed down, and the skilled slave in whom he had invested a great deal of money remained in South Carolina.[53]

These two incidents are illustrative of the loose manner in which the institution of slavery operated in eighteenth-century South Carolina. Blacks did not always accept what they were given. They may have been frightened and distraught on occasion, but they were also proud and resourceful. Within the system they coped as best they could. As memories of the Stono Rebellion receded, whites appeared to disregard the slave code. Rumors of slave plots in 1759 and 1766 did nothing to cause a tightening up of the system. There is an explanation for this: profit. The purpose of owning slaves was to make a return on investment. With the black majority, it was necessary to come to some sort of accommodation, especially on isolated working plantations. The lax nature of the system was likely the reason that it operated with so little trouble—and generated such enormous wealth.[54]

Enslaved Africans who became black South Carolinians not only produced wealth, they were themselves economic investments. The average price per slave during the colonial period was £30 sterling ($2,700), and skilled slaves went for as much as £200 sterling ($18,000) each. White South Carolinians treated their slaves as an investment, something that was not a West Indian tradition.[55]

In the English Caribbean the life expectancy of a slave was five to seven years. Essentially, West Indian planters depreciated their investment over that time span and had no reason to improve conditions. They literally had to work their slaves to death in order to turn a profit. South Carolina planters, on the other hand, anticipated a slave's paying for him- or herself in four or five years and then returning a profit of 16 percent to 25 percent a year, depending upon the price of rice. Even non-field hands (the young and very old) were productive in that they grew food for themselves and others. Thus, an investment of £2,000–£3,000 sterling ($173,000–$260,000) in land and slaves could produce an annual profit of £500 sterling ($43,400). While this income was not in the same league with the sugar barons of the West Indies, it was a sizable sum for its day. After all, some of Jane Austen's nineteenth-century English gentlefolk could live respectable lives with carriages and servants on incomes of less than £500 sterling ($23,000) a year when the pound had less purchasing power.[56]

Money, of course, was at the root of slavery in South Carolina. Fear may have been present from time to time, but if whites were so afraid of the black majority, why did they keep importing thousands of Africans? The answer was that greed was a more powerful stimulant than fear. After the Stono Rebellion, control by the white minority was never seriously threatened. Force played its part in that, but so did accommodation. The bottom line, after all, was the bottom line.

From its inception the Lords Proprietors had intended for South Carolina to be productive and profitable (especially for themselves). And it was (although not for the proprietors), because of the labor of black South Carolinians. In a 1756 petition to the king requesting a strengthening of defenses for South Carolina and Georgia, the following observation appeared: "Your Majestys Subjects in these provinces altho few in Number are by means of their Negroes of more Importance to Great Britain than any Colony on the Continent of an equal number of White Inhabitants."[57]

THE PROPRIETARY REGIME

Wee being willing upon all occasions to demonstrate that wee aime at nothing more than the Prosperity, ease, security & well being of the Inhabitants of our said Province, have thought fitt once more to take a review of our Fundamental Constitutions of the Government of Carolina for the future.

    The Lords Proprietors, 21 November 1682

The Proprietary-Monarchs are . . . like a Landlord to his Tenant, they have their Eyes upon the Rent; their Concern, if any, is not of Affection, but of Interest; they are Step-fathers and Strangers in the Government, and they have shown it; for their Ears have been Stopt, and shut to the Complaints of their Oppress'd People.

    Daniel Defoe, *Party-Tyranny*

THE LORDS Proprietors began their Carolina adventure with high hopes both for the utopian settlement envisioned in the Fundamental Constitutions and for the handsome profits they thought would come their way. South Carolina did survive and prosper, but it was far from an ideal community. By the 1690s money was being made in the colony, but by individual settlers and not the proprietors. The golden flood they anticipated never amounted to much more than a trickle. One of the reasons that the proprietors did not make any money had to do with the uncertain nature of the government they established and the men they sent to act in their names.

To begin with, the Fundamental Constitutions was never ratified. The royal charter required that all "laws and constitutions" be made "with the advice, assent and approbation of the freemen of the province." Not that the proprietors did not try. They produced five different versions of the document (the last in 1698) and as late as 1705 made an attempt to get the colonists' approval. The colonists' rejections of the Fundamental Constitutions frustrated and angered the proprietors. Lord Ashley and the original proprietors had seen the document as a charter that would safeguard the colonists' liberties and provide for "the better settlement of the government." The flip side was that the Fundamental Constitutions guaranteed that meaningful political and governmental authority would be retained by the proprietors—and kept out of the hands of the colonists. The determined and worldly-wise settlers of South Carolina had no intention of approving such a plan.[1]

Since the Fundamental Constitutions was never ratified, the proprietors used their instructions to a succession of governors to make their collective will known. The implementation of those instructions depended upon the strength and character of the individual governor as well as the agreement of the settlers. Therein lies the genesis for much of the factional feuding that wracked proprietary South Carolina (1670–1719). Ironically, although the Fundamental Constitutions was not the law of the land in the colony, the document nevertheless helped shape public policy and politics. Both proprietors and colonists referred to the Fundamental Constitutions when this suited their purposes.[2]

The most obvious influence of the Fundamental Constitutions was in the colony's governmental structure. The document called for a Grand Council that would have convened in England. A modified council was established in South Carolina consisting of the deputies of the eight proprietors (one of whom would be the governor) and five elected freemen. Initially this body would function as both the executive and judicial branches of government. There would be a unicameral parliament that would include proprietary deputies as well as elected representatives of the freemen of the province. Parliament could only act on issues that were proposed by the Grand Council. In this way the proprietors, through their deputies, could control the colony's legislative process.[3]

The system did not work well and contributed to internal political squabbles. Therefore, in 1692 the proprietors authorized a separate, elected body, which came to be called the Commons House of Assembly. At the same time the council's membership was limited to individuals appointed by the proprietors. In order to qualify to hold any public office or obtain a land grant in South Carolina, individuals had to take an oath to support the Fundamental Constitutions—even though this was not a legal document.[4]

Politically, within the first two years of settlement factions emerged and the colonists declined to ratify a revised version of the Fundamental Constitutions. It is easy to understand how both occurred in a small, isolated colony. Life was tenuous, and every settler was seeking economic advancement. With the tradition of the seventeenth-century Caribbean shaping the behavior of a majority of the colonists, anyone or anything that interfered with their goals (in this instance the government) was neutralized. The methods used might not have been genteel, but they were effective.

Untangling the origins of the factional or party strife that caused so many problems during the proprietary period is not easy. Who started it? Most historians tend to blame the colonists, especially the Barbadians. However, the proprietors were equally responsible. Their ad hoc decisions and instructions, based loosely on the various versions of the Fundamental Constitutions, were often contradictory. And, with few exceptions, they made unfortunate choices of men to fill the governorship. Some were corrupt; some were incompetent; some were disloyal; and some were all of the above. If that were not bad enough, at times the governor's office seemed to have a revolving door.[5]

During the forty-nine years of proprietary rule in South Carolina, there were twenty-two different gubernatorial administrations. That was an average of a little over two years per administration; however, in this instance the figures understate the instability in the office. Taken together, the administrations of Joseph West (his second, from 1674 to 1682), Nathaniel Johnson (1702–1708), and Charles Craven (1712–1716) account for more than one-third of the proprietary regime. The remaining nineteen administrations averaged less than a year and a half. Given the difficulty of transatlantic communications, it was no wonder that governors tended to act on their own or go along with the wishes of the colonists. The changing of governors alone would have caused difficulties, even in a more settled environment. However, the methods individuals used to obtain the office caused additional problems.[6]

About a year after the establishment of the first settlement at Albemarle Point, Sir John Yeamans, a Barbadian planter, arrived in the colony. He held the title of landgrave and was the deputy of the senior proprietor, Lord Berkeley. According to the rigid hierarchy of the Fundamental Constitutions, he was therefore entitled to the governorship. However, the Fundamental Constitutions had not been ratified, and the proprietors had appointed Joseph West as governor. Yeamans wanted the office and made some noises about claiming it, but the incumbent had a proprietary commission. So Yeamans campaigned among his fellow Barbadians and was elected to the colony's first parliament. That body, in turn, elected him as Speaker. As Speaker, he regularly questioned the legality of the governor's appointment and did what he could to stir up trouble.[7]

In April 1672 the proprietors recognized his claims to office, based upon the Fundamental Constitutions, and proclaimed him governor. In so doing, they replaced an able, experienced administrator with a man who was more interested in furthering his own interests than those of the proprietors. Lord Ashley observed, "If to convert all things to his private profitt be the marke of able parts Sir John is without a doubt a very judicious man."[8]

Although an unsuccessful governor, Yeamans was more politically astute than Lord Ashley gave him credit for being. The governor's successful maneuverings represented a victory for a nascent political faction. This group, which came to be called the Goose Creek Men, would give Lord Ashley and his fellow proprietors fits.

The Goose Creek Men drew their name from the area in which their original leaders lived, Goose Creek on the upper reaches of the Cooper River. The composition of the faction was intriguing. Barbadians were the largest component and supplied most of the key leaders. Joining them were most Anglicans from home, a majority of the Huguenots, and what few German Lutherans there were.[9]

Barbadian settlers formed the party and controlled its agenda. They had been among the first settlers of the colony and had come to South Carolina for one reason: to make money. In seventeenth- and eighteenth-century documents the Goose Creek Men were also referred to as the Anglican Party, the Church Party, the Barbadians, and the Anti-Proprietary Party. The latter label was certainly apt prior to 1700 when the Goose Creek Men opposed virtually every proposal the proprietors put forth. They did not do so simply to be obstinate or difficult. Rather, they saw the proprietors and their supporters in the colony as political and economic threats. They did not want any individual or the government interfering with their business pursuits, be they the illicit Indian slave trade or the equally illegal trafficking with pirates. The proprietors fumed about the machinations of these cunning politicians, and opponents of the Goose Creek Men damned Maurice Mathews, one of their early leaders, as "Metchivell Hobs and Lucifer in a Huge lump of Viperish mortality [with] a soul [as] big as a musketo."[10]

The description probably could have been applied to most Goose Creek Men. In fact, they would have gloried in it. They were Machiavellian in their political dealings. The end they sought was the control of the colony's government, and they were willing to use any means at their disposal to achieve it. The charge that they were Hobbesian probably stemmed from most of them being Anglicans and opposing the Dissenters. They were guilty of being devilish, crafty, and cunning. As pit vipers do, they often surprised their foes and paralyzed them with one swift strike. Words bounced off the seasoned political hides of the Goose Creek Men. They were men of action, and in their world actions spoke louder than words.

For the proprietors, the Barbadians were a real problem. They decided to remove Yeamans from the governorship, but he died before word reached the colony. They reappointed West as governor, and for eight years there was little factional strife. This was due partly to West's political acumen and partly to the fact that the Goose Creek Men controlled the council and parliament.[11]

If Governor West and the Goose Creek Men coexisted successfully in South Carolina, this may have been because he did little to interfere with their activities. And in a number of instances he sided with the colonists and ignored his employers' orders. One such order concerned issuing land grants so that South Carolinians would live in neatly laid out townships, like those in New England. The geography of the coastal zone helped defeat the plan, but so did land-hungry colonists who scattered as far as they dared in search of the best lands. A dispersed population was more difficult to govern and to defend against the natives of the country and European rivals.[12]

The small Indian nations that lived along the coast posed no serious threat to settlement, but it was not long before conflict arose. In 1671 the colonists engaged in their first Indian war. Responding to raids, they attacked the Kussoe nation (population two hundred) and probably the Stono (population sixty-four) as well. Some Indians were taken prisoner and sold as slaves to New England, New York, and the West Indies. Three years later the colonists were at war with the same nations. South Carolina blamed the Spaniards in St. Augustine for stirring up the Indians.[13]

Understanding the importance of having Indians as a buffer between South Carolina and the Spaniards, Lord Ashley ordered Dr. Henry Woodward to negotiate with one or more of the interior nations. In 1674 he approached the Westo and they agreed to an alliance. Woodward's efforts not only brought peace to the South Carolina frontier, but they also inaugurated the Indian trade. Colonists traded cloth, rum, and trinkets for deerskins and Indian slaves—most of whom came from nations allied with Spain. The Westo became the best-armed nation in the Southeast and roamed at will among neighboring peoples, capturing hundreds for the slave trade. For three years the Indian trade was in the hands of individual entrepreneurs. Then in 1677 the proprietors declared a seven-year monopoly for their benefit, a move that did not sit well with South Carolinians.

For the next three years there were complaints about Westo's stealing cattle or raiding the coastal nations, but there were no real difficulties. In 1680 the alliance between the Westo and the colonists broke down. Citing a Westo attack on a small coastal nation as an excuse, the colonists induced the Savannah (an Algonkin nation that had recently moved into central South Carolina) and the Creek to join in the destruction of their former allies. When the war was over, those Westo who escaped death and enslavement fled north where they joined the Iroquois.[14]

While the Westo War had produced short-term profits, it had also exposed South Carolina's southern flank. The Savannah were some protection, but they were not a large nation. Once again Woodward was sent inland to seek Indian allies and he found them: the Creek. Although they lived south and west of the Savannah River, they were still within the boundaries of the Carolina grant. Not only were the Creek a source of profitable trade, but they were also loyal and effective allies of the province until 1715.[15]

The Creek could defend South Carolina's interior borders, but there was no buffer along the coast. The remnants of the small coastal nations were not much protection. In 1684 when the Scots began their ill-fated settlement at Port Royal, they induced the Yamassee (population one thousand) to move from northern Florida to South Carolina. Unhappy with the way they were being treated by Spain and her Indian allies, the Yamassee were only too glad to immigrate. On the lands between the Combahee and Savannah Rivers, they built twelve towns.[16]

South Carolina's frontier appeared to be secure. The Yamassee and the Creek

An Election in Charleston, 1701. This eighteenth-century engraving shows the raucous nature of proprietary-era politics. Courtesy, Kendall Collection, South Caroliniana Library.

were strong enough to keep at bay any Indian nations that might be loyal to Spain. And South Carolina's trading practices soon ensnared the Indians, particularly the Creek, into a dependence upon English manufactures. For the colonists the Creek trade in deerskins and Indian slaves was a lucrative enterprise.[17]

The fortunes that were made from the Indian trade had political reverberations. The proprietors accused the colonists of fomenting the Westo War in order to gain more slaves for market. The war also effectively broke the proprietors' monopoly on the deerskin trade. After 1684 the regulation of the Indian trade was closely interwoven into the fabric of South Carolina politics. Whoever could dominate the trade would become wealthy—and that was the reason most colonists had immigrated.

The proprietors were not happy. Not only were they not making a profit out of the Carolina venture, but they also were losing money. The colonists refused to reimburse them for governmental expenses; quitrents were in abeyance until 1690; and the potential of income from the Indian trade disappeared during the Westo War.

At this point, after a decade of disappointment, the proprietors could have given up. Five of the original eight proprietors were dead, and Lord Ashley, the group's spark plug, was heavily involved in party politics at home. Instead, the proprietors began a concerted effort to recruit more settlers for the colony. More settlers would increase the potential for income, and if the right sort of people immigrated to South Carolina, there was the possibility of neutralizing the Goose Creek Men.[18]

During the 1680s the proprietors made a deliberate attempt to create a proprietary party in South Carolina. By encouraging the immigration of dissenters of all persuasions (Presbyterians, Baptists, Congregationalists, Quakers, and Huguenots), they hoped to create a group of settlers who would be loyal to them and follow their party line. Also, for a decade they did everything within their power to promote their faction.[19]

The Proprietary Party had its greatest strength in Colleton County, south of Charleston on the exposed southern frontier. The group was also known as the Dissenters because most of its members did not belong to, or were dissenters from, the Church of England. The party also included a few Anglicans, West Indians, and Huguenots. There were some older settlers, but most were newer ones attracted to South Carolina by the proprietors' promises of land and religious toleration. As the proprietors had hoped, the new colonists became loyal supporters of the regime. Just as partisan as their opponents, they used every advantage the proprietors gave them.[20]

Not content with waiting for their party to develop, the proprietors in 1682 appointed a hard-line Dissenter, Joseph Morton, as governor. They changed the Fundamental Constitutions in hopes of enticing more non-Anglicans to immigrate. They displaced Goose Creek Men from appointed positions and replaced them with Dissenters. They altered the representation in parliament so that Berkeley and Craven Counties combined would have ten members and Colleton ten; thus, the relative handful of settlers in Colleton County was given parliamentary representation equal to that of its more heavily populated neighbor. They created thirteen new landgraves, nine of whom lived in the colony; of the nine, eight were Dissenters. All of these efforts were part of a carefully orchestrated effort to undermine the political power of the Goose Creek Men.[21]

The proprietors' moves were heavy-handed, to say the least. However, in their defense, it must be said that they were acting in accordance with the preamble to the Fundamental Constitutions: "for the better settlement of the government of the said place, and establishing the interests of the Lords Proprietors with equality and without confusion." Although Dissenters occupied the governorship and controlled the council, they failed to break the strength of the Anti-Proprietary Party. An indication of that party's strength and popularity can be found in the leadership of the Commons House of Assembly. From the first session in 1692 until 1707, Goose

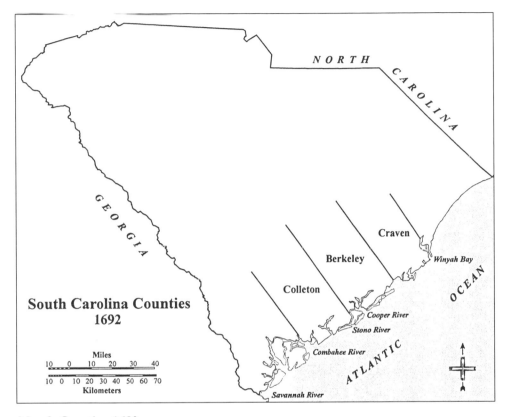

South Carolina Counties
1692

Map 8: Counties, 1692

Creek Men were elected to the position of Speaker. These men just bided their time and waited for opportunities to make life miserable for the Dissenters and their over-lords.[22]

Earlier histories have tended to paint the factional controversies in terms of good and bad. In these the worldly, expedient Goose Creek Men were the bad guys. The Dissenters, very much in the Puritan tradition of New England, wore the white hats. Never mind that they were often a contentious, self-righteous, narrow-minded, emotional, and uncompromising lot. They had a better spin doctor than their opponents, none other than Daniel Defoe. His 1706 pamphlet *Party-Tyranny*, published in London, did much to color later generations' opinions of proprietary South Carolina. When an issue is presented as Whig virtue versus Tory tyranny, the Whigs win out every time, especially on this side of the Atlantic.[23]

The factional strife in South Carolina was not much ado about nothing. By the 1690s practical governing authority had shifted to the colony. Whichever party won the political contest would win control of the government, and that had economic as well as political ramifications. Despite traditional interpretations of the Dissenters as saints and the Goose Creek Men as sinners, the former were just as rapacious as the latter.[24]

In office, Dissenters did not hesitate to use the machinery of government to line their own pockets. The most notorious of these was Joseph Blake, whose family piously appeared in the Dissenter propaganda of the early eighteenth century. An investigation by the Board of Trade discovered him to be one of the most notorious customs racketeers in colonial America: "Mr. Blake, the present Governor of this Province drives a fine Trade of seizing and condemning vessells right or wrong." The governor was able to get away with his illegal actions because he had "Judge [Joseph Morton] always on his side, and his Creatures at his back to Appraize them." Governor Blake's actions eventually resulted in a parliamentary investigation that almost cost the proprietors their charter. The proprietors' friends in South Carolina were as dangerous to their interests as their foes.[25]

The proprietors, it seemed, had an unfortunate propensity for making bad personnel decisions. The contemporary observation that they selected "very Naughty men to be their Deputys and chief in the administration" was not an unfair assessment. Instead of smoothing the troubled waters of South Carolina politics, their choices tended to roil them. The ten-year period from 1682 to 1692 illustrates that very well.[26]

That decade of turmoil opened with the proprietors' removing Joseph West. Although the colony was beginning to prosper economically, the proprietors were unhappy with the governor's inability or unwillingness to curb the Indian slave trade and the trade with pirates. His successor, Joseph Morton, was in office for two years but was no more successful. After his dismissal in April 1684, there were four separate administrations in twenty-eight months. During that time span both West and Morton were back in office for short terms. "It was," wryly commented a nineteenth-century historian, "indeed, difficult to please their Lordships." In 1686 the proprietors decided to appoint someone they were sure would follow instructions and stand up to the colonists. The man they chose was James Colleton, a Barbadian. He was the son of one of the original proprietors and brother to one of their own, Sir Peter Colleton. With those attributes they believed him to be the answer to their difficulties. They were mistaken.[27]

James Colleton was a sound administrator and soon stopped the pirate trade. However, he was politically naive and a bit greedy—something the Anti-Proprietary Party soon discovered. One of them suggested that the governor deserved a pay increase, and he thought it was a great idea. In order to pay for it, a tax would be placed on sugar and liquor. When Colleton brought the matter up before the council (which still set the legislative agenda), there were objections from his own supporters. He pressured them into agreeing and got the council to endorse the measure. When it was presented to parliament, the Goose Creek Men were waiting. They decried his greed and said that the governor "would leave no money in any mans pocket in Carolina but his owne." The tax bill was rejected and Colleton discovered that he had alienated everyone, even the members of the Proprietary Party.[28]

For the proprietors and Colleton, that was just the beginning. The proprietors wanted the 1682 version of the Fundamental Constitutions adopted, but because they gave advantages to the Dissenters, the antiproprietary majority in parliament had refused. They argued that the 1669 version, although never ratified, was the document they preferred. When the proprietors said the 1669 version was just a draft, a meaningless piece of paper, the Goose Creek Men declared all actions of the proprietors to be illegal. The royal charter, they argued, was the only basis for South Carolina law. They proclaimed themselves the defenders of liberty against the tyranny of the proprietors and their lackey, James Colleton. The governor, under instructions from the proprietors, declined to call parliament back into session. That action and his abortive attempt to declare martial law resulted in near anarchy. When the dust settled, the Goose Creek Men had engineered Colleton's ouster and the installation of Seth Sothell, a proprietor and recently deposed governor of North Carolina. This precipitated another round of intense factionalism in which at one point, in 1692, the council and the assembly could not even agree on a date for adjournment.[29]

In 1695 John Archdale, a Quaker, arrived as governor with instructions to support the various groups the proprietors had encouraged to move to South Carolina. No sooner had he landed in Charleston than members of the Proprietary Party urged him to disenfranchise the Huguenots of Craven County. Although he had been instructed to support the Huguenots, Archdale agreed and combined Berkeley and Craven Counties to dilute Huguenot voting strength (see Map 8). The Dissenters were delighted, but they had made a serious error.

In 1692 the old unicameral parliament had been discarded in favor of an elected assembly and an appointed council. Representation in what was now called the Commons House of Assembly was apportioned among the three counties. By combining the two counties, under Archdale's new arrangement, the Goose Creek Men and their allies could control twenty delegates to only ten for the Dissenters.

The Dissenters' rejection and persecution of the Huguenots is a mystery. After all, the Huguenots were Calvinists, as were many of the residents of Colleton County. When the Huguenots petitioned the Lords Proprietors for redress, the proprietors blamed the victims. Had the Huguenot representatives voted for the Fundamental Constitutions in 1692, responded the proprietors, this never would have happened.[30]

Once again the Goose Creek Men saw an opportunity in the ill-advised actions of the opposition. They decided to champion the Huguenot cause and were instrumental in the passage of the 1697 act granting them naturalized citizenship. As a consequence, most Huguenots supported the Anti-Proprietary Party. Because of local politics, the issue did not die. After elections in 1703, a Dissenter petition to the proprietors complained that "many unqualify'd Aliens" had cast their ballots as had "poor & indigent persons . . . as also several free Negroes."[31]

The Dissenters, however, were not in a position to push their case. Turnover in the holders of the proprietary shares reduced their supporters, and the Dissenters had not made a good impression on the new proprietors. During King William's War and Queen Anne's War, when England's imperial enemies threatened invasions of South Carolina, the Dissenters put narrow partisan interests over the safety and welfare of the colony. The reports from the Board of Trade in which Blake and other Dissenters were exposed as crooks did not help; nor did the investigations undertaken in both houses of Parliament. Because of Blake's and Morton's shenanigans in illegally seizing a ship, the House of Lords was considering revoking all proprietary charters. Only the energetic efforts of William Penn and the turmoil of local English politics staved off the attempt by Parliament to royalize all proprietary colonies.[32]

The 1703 protest about aliens' voting fell on deaf ears, something that did not go unnoticed in South Carolina, where the next year the Goose Creek Men passed a bill guaranteeing the right to vote to naturalized citizens. That action increased the party's voting base, as the ethnic groups who now had the franchise remembered who had given it to them.[33]

The proprietors' response to the 1703 protest must have reinforced Dissenter fears that they were in trouble. For nearly a generation they had been the Proprietary Party in South Carolina. The proprietors had encouraged them to immigrate and had supported them against the Goose Creek Men. After 1700, however, things were very different.

The changes in the proprietors' ranks resulted in a change in both leadership and philosophy. John Carteret, first earl of Granville, was now the palatine, or senior proprietor. In English politics he was a High Tory and supporter of the effort to exclude from public life those individuals who were not true members of the Church of England. In order to be eligible for any public office (this included those members of Parliament representing cities and boroughs), a person simply had to take an oath that he had received communion in the established church (not be a member). This "occasional conformity" was obedience to the law but with only minimal standards. Devout Anglicans were incensed and during the first decade of the eighteenth century tried to get Parliament to outlaw the practice.

With Granville promoting conformity in England, it should come as no surprise that he would attempt to do the same thing in Carolina. That would mean, however, a shift in proprietary allegiances. The traditional proprietary faction was the

Dissenters, and the antiproprietary faction was the Goose Creek Men. After 1700 the proprietors abandoned the Dissenters and turned to the Goose Creek Men. The elevation of James Moore Sr. to the governorship in 1700 was the first indication that the political winds were changing.

Since 1691 Moore had been the acknowledged leader of the Goose Creek Men. He was audacious and tough, perfectly suited to the rough-and-tumble of South Carolina politics. Although an opponent of the proprietors, he mollified them by paying his quit rents (and in the process avoiding a lawsuit). During the 1690s, despite his political activities, he became a proprietary deputy and a member of the council.[34]

Gov. Joseph Blake died in 1700. Under the proprietors' instructions, the council was to select a successor from the ranks of the councillors who would hold office until the proprietors either confirmed him or made another choice. When the election was first held, there were two landgraves on the council, Joseph Morton and Edmund Bellinger. Both of them were Dissenters. On the first ballot Morton was elected governor. Moore and his ally Robert Daniell objected on the grounds that Morton held a royal commission as judge of the vice-admiralty court. During the previous year the proprietors had objected to individuals' holding commissions from both them and the monarch. Moore and Daniell now raised the issue that neither of the landgraves was eligible because of a conflict of interest. The rest of the council agreed, unelected Morton, and elected Moore.[35]

The Dissenters were outraged. They railed against Moore's "unjust election" and said that he "acquired and obtained the Government of this Province by fraud, flattery & trifling exceptions." The proprietors ignored Morton's complaints. Moore was never confirmed, but Granville saw to it that he remained in the position so as to keep the non-Anglican Morton out. The message was quite clear: the Dissenters were no longer in favor.[36]

The outbreak of Queen Anne's War (1702–1713) soon gave the Dissenters something else to fuss about. Moore, despite the opposition of the Dissenters in the assembly, rammed through an appropriation to support an invasion of Spanish Florida. He assumed command of the expedition, and in September 1702 the South Carolinians captured, looted, and burned the town of St. Augustine; however they had to abandon their siege of the fort when Spanish reinforcements appeared.[37]

Moore had greater success in 1703–1704 when he led an army of fifty whites and a thousand Creek allies on a rampage through the Spanish mission settlements in central and western Florida. The missions were destroyed and hundreds of Indian prisoners sold into slavery. When Spain, with French assistance, tried to invade South Carolina in 1706, the attack was an utter failure. South Carolina's military successes (with the aid of Indian allies) severely damaged Spain's prestige and greatly enhanced England's standing among the Indians of the Southeast.[38]

The Dissenters' opposition to the St. Augustine expedition was symptomatic of

the colonists' preoccupation with internal affairs. South Carolina, as England's sur-
rogate, might be involved in a contest for empire in the Southeast, but Goose Creek
Men as well as Dissenters were locked in a power struggle that was more important
to them than the war with Spain.

Moore's election and the proprietors' refusal to undo it dealt the Dissenters a
staggering blow. Because they were a minority party, their position depended upon
the support of the proprietors. Without it, they were much like the third-world client
states of the superpowers at the end of the cold war. They had been so used to external support that they had difficulty going it alone. The Goose Creek Men had no
such problems. They had had to maneuver and survive against opposition for thirty
years. Now they were ready to eliminate their weakened rivals. The issue that they
chose—or that was chosen for them by Granville—was the establishment of the
Church of England in Carolina.[39]

The charters of 1663 and 1665, the Concessions and Agreement, and the Fundamental Constitutions all anticipated that the Church of England would be established in Carolina. Article 96 of the Fundamental Constitutions (1669) stated that
once the colony was settled, the Carolina parliament would erect churches and pay
for clergy "employed in the exercise of religion, according to the Church of England." The Anglican Church was the only one that could receive public support.
However, for nearly twenty years the proprietors had aggressively recruited non-Anglican settlers. Given that priority, it is no wonder that they had made no effort to
implement Article 96. In the early years of the eighteenth century, a new group of
proprietors altered South Carolina's political and religious landscape.[40]

Simply because he was an Anglican, Moore's election had unnerved some Dissenters. However, he was not a zealot and had been more concerned with military
adventures and, if Defoe were to be believed, lining his pockets. His successor, Sir
Nathaniel Johnson, was another matter. Like his friend Granville, Johnson was a
High Tory.[41]

Johnson assumed the governorship in June 1702, but the question of establishing the Church of England does not seem to have surfaced at all (even though conformity was occasionally a heated topic in England). He dissolved the Sixth
Assembly and called for new elections in the spring of 1703. The Seventh Assembly
of the Commons House met in April, September, and December 1703, and it was
scheduled to meet again on 10 May 1704.

The governor, however, had other plans. He called a special session, but somehow the word reached only the Anglican-dominated Berkeley and Craven delegation. They met on 26 April and on 4 May passed "An Act for the more effectual
Preservation of the Government of this Province." This legislation required all members of the Commons House of Assembly in South Carolina to swear that they conformed to the worship of the Church of England and received the Lord's Supper

St. Andrew's Church (1706–1708) is the oldest Anglican church in South Carolina. Courtesy, South Caroliniana Library.

according to the rites of the church. By a one-vote margin the Anglicans succeeded in eliminating their opponents from public office.[42]

The following fall an act was passed making the Church of England the established church in South Carolina. This act, like other South Carolina legislation, had West Indian precedents. In the West Indies, notably Jamaica, the laity controlled the church. South Carolina chose a similar path in that the Church Act provided for the creation of a commission of laymen that could remove "an immoral or imprudent clergyman" from his church.[43]

The Dissenters were desperate and were not going to give up easily. The act excluding them from the Commons House (commonly called the Exclusion Act) and the act establishing the Church of England (commonly called the Church Act) were so blatantly partisan that the Dissenters thought they could get the proprietors to disallow them. Even if they were no longer the Proprietary Party, they believed that the proprietors would agree with them that the acts violated both the royal charter and the Fundamental Constitutions. Actually, they did not violate either, since freedom to worship and the right to hold office were not the same thing.[44]

Convinced of the righteousness of their cause, the Dissenters sent John Ash and Joseph Boone to London to plead their case. Boone had a meeting with the proprietors, during which John Archdale (the former governor and now a proprietor) urged that the Exclusion Act be overturned. Granville's retort ended the discussion:

"Sir, You are of one Opinion, and I am of another, and our Lives may not be long enough to end the Controversy. I am for this Bill." Boone then engaged Daniel Defoe, who wrote *Party-Tyranny, or an Occasional Bill in Miniature; as now Practiced in Carolina*. While it made for great reading, it was nothing but political propaganda.[45]

The two acts were the centerpiece of the document, but Defoe used material supplied him to rehash a decade of Dissenter complaints: voting fraud, Moore's military campaigns, and anti-Dissenter mobs in Charleston. After cataloging the sins of the proprietors and the Goose Creek Men, Defoe sermonized that the proprietors should "Blush . . . and be asham'd for your Petty Sub-Tyrants. . . ." The blushing could just as easily have been done by the Dissenters. Defoe's shrill diatribe on the Huguenots exposed the Dissenters as little more than self-interested hypocrites, concerned only with their own welfare at the expense of others.[46]

Party-Tyranny, published in London in 1705, aroused a good deal of public sentiment. It, no doubt, made it much easier for Boone to present his case to the House of Lords. Ironically, Defoe used the lay control clause in the Church Act to argue that the act was really anti-Church of England. The House of Lords agreed that the Exclusion Act and the Church Act were arbitrary and oppressive and directed that they be set aside. The Board of Trade concurred and continued its efforts to vacate the proprietors' charter. Queen Anne, upon recommendation of the Privy Council, also directed that the acts be disallowed.[47]

The Dissenters' victory was as much a result of timing as the merits of their case. High Tories were no longer in favor, and the Whigs had done well in the 1705 elections. The changed political landscape had as much to do with the disallowance of these acts as their content. For, if lay control were illegal, why had the Jamaica statutes been approved earlier?[48]

In February 1705, unaware of events in England, the Commons House voted to repeal the Exclusion Act, but the council refused to concur. Governor Johnson dissolved the assembly because it refused to organize under the provisions of the Exclusion Act, which was still in force. A new Commons House was elected in which Anglicans had a clear majority. When it met in November 1706 the proprietors' instructions had arrived. The assembly repealed both acts and in their stead passed a new Church Act. Like its predecessor, the 1706 Church Act evidenced a West Indian connection, as the names of six of ten parishes duplicated those in Barbados. More important, the Commons House met the objections about the powers of the lay commission, and the new Church Act became law.[49]

From 1706 until 1778 the Church of England was the official church of South Carolina. Public monies paid for the construction and maintenance of its buildings and the salaries of its clergy. Later acts would make parish vestries the only local government in the province. The passage of the Church Act of 1706 did not mark the end of the politicking.

The Dissenters were a minority party, and after 1706 they began to lose members to the Anglican Party. That did not deter the die-hards; for five years they fought a losing battle. Joseph Boone and Landgrave Thomas Smith lobbied for repeal of the Church Act, and Boone convinced the proprietors to remove Johnson from office.[50]

In South Carolina, Dissenters protested by refusing to serve in the Commons House of Assembly. Eight of the ten individuals elected from Colleton County to the Twelfth Assembly in 1710 declined to serve, as did those elected in their stead. In the Thirteenth Assembly nine of ten declined, but their replacements agreed to serve. Among them was Thomas Nairne, one of the leaders of the Dissenters. His qualifying for the Commons House on 1 November 1711 signaled the end to the rancorous struggle between the Dissenters and the Goose Creek Men that had divided the colony for thirty years. While partisanship had begun to abate, it was the peril posed by the Tuscarora War that gave impetus to the new spirit of cooperation.[51]

The arrival of a new governor, Charles Craven, in 1712 was welcomed by all parties. Underscoring the new spirit of cooperation was the productiveness of the Commons House. During its four sessions in 1712 it passed forty-three and copied more than one hundred English statutes into South Carolina's code. It is interesting that an English law that was specifically rejected was one on entail (keeping an estate together); the move may have been political to thwart the proprietors, but it also enabled individuals to bequeath their worldly goods to whomever they chose. Another sign of cooperation between former foes was an act authorizing the hiring of an agent to represent the colony in England. Heretofore agents had represented partisan interests.[52]

While most of the laws enacted in 1712 were beneficial, one caused difficulties that lasted for two decades. Since 1703 the Commons House had issued bills of credit (at interest), backed by tax revenues, to pay for defense expenditures. Initially this paper currency was to be a temporary measure. By 1707 interest payments were dropped and the bills were made legal tender. There was little depreciation because of the colony's growing economy. However, in 1712 the Commons House created a land bank to back a massive new emission of paper money. Whether it was the amount of money in circulation or the abandoning of tax revenues as backing, the currency began to lose its value. By the end of the proprietary period, when even more money had been printed to pay for the colony's defense, the value of the South Carolina pound was four to one against the pound sterling. The currency question would be a headache until the 1730s.[53]

One of the reasons that South Carolina issued so much paper money between 1712 and 1719 was that the colony had to rely on its own resources for defense. The proprietors were no help whatsoever. "Neither in the infancy of the Colony or any time since," read a petition to the Board of Trade, "have they . . . soe much as contributed one penny toward the raising of forts or other fortificacions." That burden had been borne solely by the "poor inhabitants" of the province. The lack of proprietary support, coupled with the colony's being forced to fend for itself, created a situation in which South Carolinians began to question the need for the proprietors at all.[54]

In 1711, when the Tuscarora Indians attacked the North Carolina settlement at New Bern and were on the verge of annihilating that colony, New Bern asked Virginia and South Carolina for assistance. Virginia did not respond, but South Carolina sent two separate expeditions. Led by John Barnwell and James Moore Jr., a handful of white South Carolinians and hundreds of Indian allies destroyed the Tuscarora. The war cost South Carolina £4,000 currency ($75,500) and fifty-seven dead. The Tuscarora War should have been a warning to South Carolina about what would occur if the misconduct of Indian traders were not curbed. Traders' cheating and abusing the Tuscarora had been the primary cause of the war. The same things had been happening in South Carolina.[55]

Since the end of the Westo War in the 1680s, there had been sporadic attempts to regulate the Indian trade. With the establishment of the Proprietary Party, it became a partisan issue. Living on the exposed southern frontier of the colony, the Dissenters had a reason to be concerned about anything that might cause an Indian war. Also, as newcomers they were not involved in the lucrative trade and hoped that regulation might give them such an opportunity.[56]

Some early reform efforts, such as Governor Archdale's suppression of the Indian slave trade, were successful. However, the major issue was the regulation of the deerskin trade. Who would be allowed to deal with the Indians and under what terms? Who would monitor their conduct? Both of these questions dealt with money, and the Commons House discussed the issue for most of the 1690s without coming to any solutions. In 1698 it debated the question of whether "The Indjun Trade as it is now Managed be a grievance to the Settlement and Prejudicall to the Safety Theroff or Not." The trade was mismanaged and dangerous, resolved the Commons House, but nothing was done because of who controlled it.[57]

Gov. Joseph Blake, a Dissenter, and his associates (two Dissenters and three Goose Creek Men) dominated the trade and had no intention of letting anyone interfere with their profits. Following Blake's death, James Moore and Thomas Broughton assumed control of the trade. Moore was governor, and Broughton was the son-in-law of Moore's successor, Sir Nathaniel Johnson. Despite the prominence of the traders, the Commons House tackled the issue.[58]

The debate continued for seven years. Should the trade be tightly regulated but open to all? Should it be a monopoly in which the holder guaranteed to pay the colony an annual fee? If it were to be regulated, then who would control it: the Commons House or the Council? Finally, in 1707 the Commons House passed the first comprehensive act regulating South Carolina's Indian trade. A Commission of

Gov. Charles Craven and the Yamassee War. "The gruesome attack of the Indians on the English in Carolina, West Indies, on April 19, 1715 and some days after; in which action the Barbarians gruesomely tortured many human beings." Peter Schenk, Amsterdam, 1716. Courtesy, South Caroliniana Library.

the Indian Trade was created and an agent hired to live among the Indians. The act outlawed the sale of liquor to Indians and the enslavement of free Indians; it required all traders to be licensed; and it paid the governor an annual fee of £100 sterling ($6,775) in lieu of his receiving deerskins from visiting Indians, which henceforth would be sold for the benefit of the public treasury. Governor Johnson was opposed to the act, but a £400 sterling ($27,100) special appropriation induced him to approve it.[59]

The Indian Commission selected Thomas Nairne as its agent, and he took his job seriously. He prosecuted the governor's son-in-law for enslaving friendly Cherokee and stealing deerskins that belonged to the colony. Governor Johnson threw Nairne in jail and charged him with treason. Eventually Nairne was freed, but any meaningful attempt to regulate the trade was doomed. Traders multiplied, and so did their abuses. Indians were cheated, physically abused, and enslaved. As their indebtedness increased, so did pressure from English and Charleston merchants to collect, which led to further mistreatment and resentment. By 1715 the natives of the country may have owed traders and merchants as much as £100,000 sterling ($9.2 million). The Indian trade was totally out of control, and South Carolina's officials did little to correct the situation.[60]

The Yamassee, in particular, were angry. In addition to trading abuses, the government encouraged settlers to move into their lands between the Combahee and the Savannah by creating the town of Beaufort and the parish of St. Helena. In the spring of 1715 word began to filter into Charleston about an Indian conspiracy involving most of the nations with which South Carolina traded. Nairne, now back in South Carolina, was sent to the Yamassee to see what he could discover. He went to the Yamassee settlements, but he was too late. On 15 April 1715 (Good Friday) the Yamassee attacked isolated plantations near Port Royal and killed nearly one hundred settlers. By June more than 90 percent of the traders among the Indians had been killed. Among the whites killed was Nairne, who had pine splinters inserted under his skin and then lit. He died a slow, agonizing death.[61]

Settlers in outlying areas abandoned their homesteads and fled for safety near Charleston. There were almost no settlers left south of the Stono River and, except for those on a few fortified farms, not many remaining in the area between Charleston and the Santee River. A defensive perimeter with about a thirty-mile radius around the colonial capital was the only place that was even relatively secure. Governor Craven mobilized every white male and hundreds of black males to defend the colony. Despite the danger the war posed to all the southern colonies, North Carolina sent token assistance and Virginia almost none; the only meaningful support came from Massachusetts, which provided weapons. Basically, South Carolina had to go it alone. In pitched battles at Port Royal and Salkehatchie, the Yamassee were defeated and driven south of the Savannah River.[62]

The defeat of the Yamassee was not the end of the conflict, because the war was not just one nation against the settlers. All of the nations in the Southeast, with the exception of the Chickasaw and Cherokee, were united behind the leadership of the Lower Creek. The combination held because the Indians were unified in their hatred of all whites but particularly the English. A generation later whites still recalled the savagery of the Yamassee War and especially the ferocity of the Catawba warriors who laid waste to the settlements along the Santee. It was the greatest Indian alliance in colonial history with the potential to eradicate not just South Carolina but also North Carolina and Virginia. At no other time in colonial American history, not even during King Philip's or the Pequot Wars, did a colony face the danger that South Carolina did. The colonists were well aware of the threat not only to their existence but also to the empire. It was a point they made repeatedly in their meetings with imperial officials.[63]

The colony's agents met with the Board of Trade in July 1715 and pleaded for assistance since the proprietors admitted that they could (or would) not do anything. Living in a world of their own, the proprietors believed that because the Yamassee

The pirate Stede Bonnet was hanged in Charleston on 10 December 1718. Copy of an engraving from the 1725 Dutch edition of Daniel Defoe's *History of the Pirates*. Courtesy, South Caroliniana Library.

had been defeated the war was over. They ignored reports of continual raids by Creek and Yamassee and rumors of Cherokee getting ready to join in the fray. But South Carolinians knew exactly what would happen if the Cherokee joined the Indian alliance against the settlers.[64]

Governor Craven sent an expedition of three hundred men, including a company of armed slaves, to the lower Cherokee towns to ask them to ally themselves with the settlers and attack the Creek. In January 1716, after much negotiation, the Cherokee agreed and launched an attack on the Creek. The settlers now had some breathing room. With the Yamassee defeated and the Creek occupied, the smaller nations began to seek a truce. By April 1716 the worst was over; however there were numerous raids until 1718 and a few scattered ones until the mid 1720s.[65]

Devastated was a much overused and misused word in the late twentieth century. However, it was the most appropriate to describe South Carolina in 1718. The colony was devastated. One-half of the cultivated land was deserted; some of it would not be reoccupied until the 1730s. Four hundred settlers (about 6 percent of the white population) had been killed. Property loss estimates ran as high as

£236,000 sterling ($21.6 million). The defense costs alone stood at £116,000 sterling ($10.6 million), a sum more than three times the annual net value of exports over imports.[66]

The survivors of the Yamassee War realized that they had to do two things: pay for the war and prevent a recurrence. The government in Charleston accomplished both. The Indian trade was made a public corporation and private trade prohibited. A ranger company of one hundred men was to patrol the frontier on a regular basis. For an early warning against the Spaniards in St. Augustine, scout boats regularly sailed south as far as the Altamaha River. Duties were placed on liquors and slave imports to raise revenue to help pay for the cost of the war. Other acts provided for the orderly settlement of the Yamassee lands and the encouragement of white Protestant immigrants. While the colonists were in a reform mood, they passed an Election Act (1716) that made parishes, not the counties, the election districts for the colony. By so doing, they made the Commons House more representative and made it easier for voters to participate (prior to this act, all elections were held in Charleston).[67]

The colonists were aware that during the war the proprietors had refused the king's offer of financial assistance because there were strings attached. In order for the British government to provide funds for defending South Carolina, the proprietors would have had to mortgage their charter to the king. This they had rejected out of hand, putting their own monetary interests above the security of the colony and the empire. In 1715 the Commons House urged the Board of Trade to make South Carolina a royal colony. The next year, as Charles Craven was departing for London, they asked him to plead their case.[68]

Discontent with the proprietors was increasing as there seemed to be external threats on every side. The South Carolinians knew they would have to take care of these threats without any assistance from the proprietors. The French, whom many colonists blamed for brokering the Indian alliance of the Yamassee War, continued to make inroads into South Carolina's Indian trade in the west. As rumors of war between England and Spain circulated, there was the real possibility of an invasion from either Florida or Cuba. In January 1718 the colony received word that war had been declared.

While worried about what Spain might do, the colony was at the mercy of pirates driven from their Caribbean hideaways by the royal navy. Finding safe havens on North Carolina's Outer Banks, the buccaneers plundered ships sailing into and out of Charleston. In June 1718 Edward Teach (Blackbeard) captured a ship with several prominent South Carolinians aboard. He then hove to just outside the harbor and sent a messenger to the governor with an ultimatum. If the colonists did not give Teach some medical supplies, he would kill all hostages and attack the town. Blackbeard got what he wanted and sailed away.[69]

Over the next few months South Carolina prepared to eliminate the pirates' lair in North Carolina. In September, William Rhett led a small fleet into North Carolina waters and after a battle lasting more than six hours captured Stede Bonnet and a number of his crew. A Virginia expedition took care of Blackbeard. While Bonnet and his men were awaiting trial, yet another pirate ship appeared off Charleston. Again the South Carolina fleet was successful. In November and December 1718 Bonnet and forty-eight others were tried, convicted, and hanged.[70]

South Carolinians heaved a sign of relief. The Yamassee War was finally over, and the pirates had been eliminated. However, the year 1719 fulfilled the old saying that just when you think things cannot get any worse, they do. In its weakened state the colony was in no position to repel a Spanish invasion. Intelligence indicated that Spain intended to attack. It was too much. The colonists panicked. "Wee are now in the Utmost Confusion that Ever I knew the place which is 28 years," wrote Alexander Parris. "Almost everyone for selling & going off were there any purchasers." Fortunately, the Spaniards' plans were derailed by the French, who captured Pensacola, and Spain diverted the expedition to recapture its Gulf Coast outpost.[71]

Having to fend for themselves against a series of external foes, it was no wonder that South Carolinians reacted negatively to the proprietors' attempts to take a more active role in governing the colony. In sending a replacement for Craven, the proprietors selected Robert Johnson, son of Sir Nathaniel Johnson. The younger man was able and competent but tended to be a bit haughty. He got off to a rocky start when he addressed the Commons House in October 1717.

The proprietors had been livid at the assembly's requests for a royal takeover. In a condescending manner Johnson told the colonists they should be grateful for all that the proprietors had done for them. He also said that he knew more than the colonists and was therefore better able to judge what was in their interests than they. As a stunned Commons House listened, the governor announced that the price of land would be increased fourfold from £3 currency ($57) per hundred acres to £12 currency ($228). There then ensued a series of pithy exchanges between the governor and the assembly. Not much was accomplished, but the Commons House placed the governor—and the proprietors—on notice that it was not going to retreat from the assertiveness it had exhibited since 1712.[72]

The proprietors, however, were determined to rein in the colonists. In particular, they began to review laws that had been passed in South Carolina. Technically, all laws required their approval; however, they had tended to take no action at all. In response to complaints from the Board of Trade about South Carolina's monetary policies and import duties, the proprietors acted. In July 1718 they met and disallowed seven pieces of legislation, including one that was eleven years old. Among them were some of the key reforms passed by the Commons House in 1716: the new election act, the act concerning settlement on Yamassee lands, the import duties to pay for the war, and the act to encourage Protestant immigrants. They ordered Johnson to dismiss the assembly and issue a call for new elections using the pre-1716 apportionment by counties.[73]

The governor, having been in the colony for a year, had a better grasp of the situation than when he first arrived. He knew that the proprietors' instructions would lead to trouble; therefore, for a year he dissembled. He neither called for new elections nor informed the Commons House of the proprietors' veto of South Carolina laws.[74]

Johnson's inaction angered the proprietors, as did a petition from the Commons House and a majority of the council to remove Nicholas Trott as chief justice. Without bothering to investigate the matter, they rejected the petition, thanked Trott for his loyal and faithful service, and removed three of the council members who had signed the petition. The proprietors also decided to change the composition of the council and enlarge it to twelve members. They directed Johnson to call for new elections without delay and to publish their previous disallowances of South Carolina laws. They instructed the governor to include in any future act of the assembly a phrase that no law could go into effect until they personally had reviewed it. They directed that the Yamassee lands be reserved for their sole benefit. And, in a fit of pique, they ordered the land office closed; henceforth any request for a land grant would have to be sent to them for approval. The mood of the proprietors toward the colonists was one of undisguised hostility. At one meeting a proprietor was alleged to have said after hearing a report on the destruction caused by the Yamassee War: "If the inhabitants were destroyed the country might be settled by a better people." Whether or not this statement had been made, there were Carolinians who believed it had. From this point on, the colonists saw tyranny behind everything the proprietors did.[75]

In April 1719 Johnson reluctantly implemented the proprietors' instructions. He issued a call for elections to be held on 26 November 1719 in Charleston. Meanwhile, the continued rumors of a Spanish invasion forced him to attempt to raise funds for defense by public subscription, thus challenging the hard-won right of the Commons House to control public finances. His proposal, coming on the heels of the proprietors' actions, increased the antiproprietary feeling in the colony.[76]

During the summer plans for a coup materialized. We know there was planning because the colonists' actions were too well orchestrated to have been serendipitous. Parish militia musters became a means for getting the word to all parts of the province. A vague organization called the Association was formed, and almost to a man the militia agreed to join it. That meant that the plot against the government included hundreds of individuals. Despite the large number of people involved, neither the governor nor the few remaining proprietary loyalists learned of the plotting.[77]

The elections were held as scheduled on 26 November. The next evening a group of newly elected members met and agreed to ask Johnson to take over the colony in the name of the king. On 28 November they presented him a letter in which they also said that the inhabitants were "unanimously of Opinion that they would have no *Proprietors'* Government." Johnson was concerned, but Trott advised him to ignore the matter until the Commons House met in December.[78]

On 16 December 1719 the assembly met but declared itself to be a "Convention of the People." It refused to recognize the "illegal" council but would deal with the governor. Following the precedent of Parliament in the Glorious Revolution, the convention adopted a series of resolutions stating the reason for their actions. Then it went about the business of governing the colony.[79]

The governor and council were in a quandary as to what to do. The revolt was widespread and popular. Twenty-six of the thirty members elected in November were now in Charleston, and all supported the revolution. The Convention repeatedly asked Governor Johnson to accept the governorship in the name of the revolution. He rejected each offer and ordered the Convention to disperse. It refused.[80]

Sensing the possibility that the governor might try to circumvent them, the rebels ordered all public officers, in the name of the Convention, to remain at their posts. After Johnson's repeated refusals, the Convention offered the governorship to James Moore Jr., hero of both the Tuscarora and Yamassee Wars. He accepted with alacrity. Realizing that they had placed Moore in a position where he could be accused of treason, the members of the Convention vowed that they would "stand by you with our lives & Fortunes, and support you in the Honor & dignity of Government."[81]

Since spring the militia had been scheduled for a colonywide muster in Charleston on 21 December. This was also the day that Moore was to take office. Johnson sent out orders canceling the muster. However, when he entered Charleston on 21 December (only one member of the council had the courage to join him), he found all fortifications occupied and several companies in the market. In the harbor was HMS *Shoreham* with its guns trained on the town. The ship's captain, it seems, had just been named a member of the revolutionary council. The proprietary governor of South Carolina had been outmaneuvered at every step by the rebels; now he was outgunned and outmanned. He had no option but to withdraw to his plantation outside of town and write his account of the events.[82]

The revolutionaries moved swiftly to reconstitute South Carolina's government. The Convention resolved itself into the Commons House of Assembly. Moore, in consultation with the assembly, named a council, judges, and other officials. On 24 December 1719 the governor, council, and assembly drafted several petitions. One was to King George I and the other to the Board of Trade. Both carried the same message: the proprietors had forfeited their rights to govern through neglect, mismanagement, and abuse of power; therefore, for the good of the empire and the safety of the people of South Carolina, the revolution was justified and necessary. Both petitions had lengthy lists of things that the proprietary regime had done or left undone. In a letter to the Privy Council the new governor wrote that revolution was the only answer, one that followed "the Precedent of our Mother Country, the Kingdom of England, in the Late Happy Revolution." With the writing of the petitions on the 24th, the Revolution of 1719 was completed. It would be a decade before the matter was finally resolved and the royal takeover completed. However, what mattered most to South Carolinians was that the proprietors and their minions were no longer governing the colony.[83]

The revolution did not come as a shock to imperial officials. Since 1715 they had been receiving petitions from South Carolina asking that South Carolina become a royal colony. On three separate occasions Parliament had investigated the Carolina proprietors and debated bills to revoke the charter. Beginning in 1699 with Edward Randolph's report, imperial bureaucrats had argued in favor of such a move. The proprietors themselves had indicated that they wanted out, but only if the price were right.

Most earlier histories dismiss the proprietary regime as a disaster. While this view is not entirely just, it could be said that the proprietors' problems were that they got many things they wished for: experienced settlers from Barbados, Huguenot refugees, dissenters of all stripes, a proprietary party, an established church, and an end to factional politics. Some wishes went unanswered: ratification of the Fundamental Constitutions, a monopoly on the Indian trade, income from quitrents and land sales, peaceful relations with the Indians, no partisan strife, and grateful colonists.

Why did proprietary government fail in South Carolina? One of the explanations was in the nature of the proprietorship. Instead of a single proprietor, South Carolina had eight. It was a government by shareholders, and the shares changed hands during the life of the proprietary charter. By 1719 only three shares remained in the families of the original proprietors (Craven, Carteret, and Colleton). The others had been sold, some several times. In several instances trustees acted on behalf of minors. It was a situation in which informed decision-making was difficult, especially when the proprietors' trust was abused by such men as William Rhett and Nicholas Trott.[84]

It was also a situation in which the bottom line was all important—not that money had not mattered to the original eight. Even Lord Ashley, for all his public idealism, wanted to make money. (When Ashley sent Dr. Henry Woodward to explore the interior of South Carolina, he provided the explorer with a secret code so that only he would get the good news.) Several of the decisions made during and after the Yamassee War confirmed that the shareholders were interested in profits above all else: the refusal of the crown's offer of a loan to help the colonists prosecute the war; the quadrupling of the price of land; and the seizure of the Yamassee lands for themselves and their friends.[85]

For the proprietary shareholders the Carolina venture was an economic failure. The colony, however, survived. One of the reasons for its endurance might be the very neglect about which the colonists complained so incessantly.

When external foes threatened the order and stability of the colony, the colonists responded vigorously. They had twice invaded Spanish Florida, burned St. Augustine (1702), and destroyed the Indian missions (1704). They had repelled an invasion by French and Spanish forces (1706). They had twice sent expeditions to North Carolina to save that colony and put down the Tuscarora (1711, 1713). They had defeated the mightiest Indian alliance any English colony in North America faced (1715–1716). They had eliminated the pirate threats to their commerce (1718). Forced to rely on its own resources, South Carolina had become used to fending for itself. In 1699 Edward Randolph had reported to the Board of Trade: "The great improvements made in this Province is wholly owing to the Industry and labour of the Inhabitants."[86]

The attempts by the proprietors to alter the nature of the government that had evolved over forty years was just as much a threat to the order and stability of the province as the Spaniards, the Yamassee, and the pirates. The disallowance of laws passed after the Yamassee War was annoying, but the changes in the council were what most concerned the colonists. If the proprietors could unilaterally do that, might they not alter the assembly? Was the disallowance of the Election Act of 1716 the first step to something more ominous? Was the expulsion of three able councillors for opposing proprietary authority an indication that disagreement would not be tolerated?

These moves by the proprietors, especially the alteration of the size and composition of the council, "unhing'd the frame of Government." They were a threat to the order and the stability of the colony. Therefore, South Carolinians believed they had no choice but to rebel.

The Revolution of 1719 was different from many of the other colonial disturbances, such as Bacon's Rebellion in Virginia and Culpepper's Rebellion in North Carolina. It was a well-planned and well-executed coup against a legally constituted government (no matter how ill-advised its actions), not an armed conflict arising from factional disputes. At its heart was the concept that the revolution was protecting the "incontestable right" of Englishmen to be governed "by noe laws made here but what are consented to by them."[87]

In the space of a decade (1709–1719), the proprietors had succeeded in uniting the colonists. Individuals who once would have tried to undercut one another cooperated. There was no better example than Joseph Morton's voting for James Moore Jr. for governor in 1719. Nineteen years earlier their fathers had been implacable enemies. It had been, after all, the elder Moore (an unrepentant Goose Creek Man) who had engineered the unelection of the elder Morton (a hidebound Dissenter) as governor and his own election instead—an action that had precipitated another round of intense factional disputes. Now their sons were united in the cause of South Carolina against a common foe, the proprietors.

The revolutionaries of 1719 moved to stop actions they saw as endangering the good order and harmony of the community. In their revolution they appealed to the precedent of 1689. But if 1689 were a precedent for the Revolution of 1719, might not 1719 also become a precedent? William Rhett, who knew his contemporaries well, thought so. He warned an imperial official that unless the revolution were "Croped in Bud and example made of some of them they will sett up for themselves against his Majesty as well as the Proprietors."[88]

Carolina parakeet. Once this beautiful bird could be found in every part of the state; it is now extinct. Alexander Wilson, *American Ornithology* (1808). Courtesy, Rare Books and Special Collections, Thomas Cooper Library, University of South Carolina.

Bison were reported in the piedmont as late as the 1760s. Mark Catesby, *Natural History of Carolina, Florida, and the Bahama Islands* (1731–1748). Courtesy, South Caroliniana Library.

The strange-looking opossum figured frequently in early travelers' accounts.
John Lawson, *History of Carolina* (1709). Courtesy, South Caroliniana
Library.

Traditional Catawba pot by Sara Ayers (1975). Courtesy, McKissick Museum, University of South Carolina.

St. Nicholas Abbey was the seventeenth-century Barbados home of Margaret Foster Berringer, who later married Sir John Yeamans and moved to South Carolina. Courtesy, Barbados National Trust.

The architecture of St. James' Goose Creek (1708–1719), the parish church of many Barbadians, reflects European styles translated to the Caribbean and then to South Carolina. *A View of St. James' Church, Goose Creek* by Charles Fraser. Courtesy, Gibbes Museum of Art/Carolina Art Association.

The 1787 Fraktur (illuminated baptismal certificate in German Gothic script) of Maria Margareta House indicates the survival of Germanic traditions in the Carolina upcountry. Courtesy, Museum of Early Southern Decorative Arts, Winston-Salem, North Carolina.

Mulberry plantation (1715) with its slave quarters in the foreground. Recent archaeological studies suggest that the slave quarters may have been West African in design with thatched roofs. *View of Mulberry Plantation* by Thomas Coram. Courtesy, Gibbes Museum of Art/Carolina Art Association.

The Carolina herald represents the Chamberlain's Court, one of eight courts established by the Fundamental Constitutions of Carolina. This court had the responsibility for "all ceremonies, precedency, [and] heraldry." Courtesy, South Caroliniana Library.

Sir Nathaniel Johnson, proprietary governor of South Carolina (1703–1709). *Nathaniel Johnson* (circa 1645–1713) by an unknown artist. Courtesy, Gibbes Museum of Art/Carolina Art Association.

James Glen, royal governor of South Carolina (1743–1756), by an unknown artist. Courtesy of the Earl of Dalhousie.

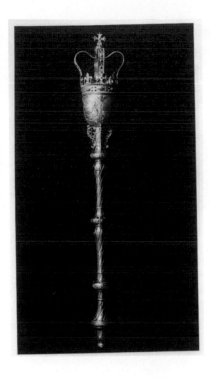

The Mace, symbol of the authority of the
South Carolina House of Representatives,
was purchased by the Commons House of
Assembly in 1756. Photograph by Bruce L.
Flashnick. Courtesy, South Carolina
House of Representatives.

Thomas Knox Gordon, the last royal chief
justice of South Carolina (1771–1775), was
also a member of the Royal Council. Courtesy, South Carolina State Museum.

Charleston, the capital city of South Carolina and the fourth largest city in colonial America, on the eve of the American Revolution. *A View of Charles Town* by Thomas Leitch, 1774. Collection of the Museum of Early Southern Decorative Arts, Winston-Salem, North Carolina.

Henriette Charlotte Chastaigner (1700–1754) by Henrietta Johnston. Courtesy, Gibbes Museum of Art/Carolina Art Association.

The Joseph Kershaw House, Camden. Built between 1777 and 1780, Kershaw's house was one of the showplaces of the backcountry. In design, it is similar to the Miles Brewton House in Charleston. Photograph by Suzanne C. Linder.

The Miles Brewton House (1769) is considered to be one of the finest colonial homes in the United States. Photograph by Rick Rhodes, Charleston, South Carolina.

An aerial view of the gardens at Middleton Place, showing the formal garden with its terraces and butterfly lakes. Courtesy, South Carolina Parks, Recreation and Tourism.

Black Carolinians at leisure. The headdresses worn by several of the participants as well as the musical instruments appear to be West African in origin. *The Old Plantation* by an unknown artist. Courtesy, Abbey Aldrich Rockefeller Folk Art Center, Williamsburg, Virginia.

Following the repeal of the Stamp Act in 1766, the Commons House of Assembly ordered a marble statue of William Pitt and placed it in the middle of the intersection of Broad and Meeting streets, Charleston. A watercolor entitled "Scene from a Theatre" from Charles Fraser's Sketchbook. Photograph, South Carolina Historical Society. Courtesy, Caroline Winthrop Weston Cohen.

Gen. Richard Richardson (1704–1780), one of the most prominent leaders in the back-country, commanded the patriot militia during the Snow Campaign. *Portrait of General Richard Richardson* by Jeremiah Theus. Courtesy of Richard Hampton Jenrette.

During the American Revolution, Francis Marion, the state's most daring partisan leader, shared his supper of sweet potatoes with a British officer. Painting by William D. Washington. Courtesy, South Caroliniana Library.

At Cowpens, American lieutenant colonel William Washington and British lieutenant colonel Banastre Tarleton came face to face as the battle was drawing to a close. *Washington and Tarleton Duel* by William Ranney. From the Collection of the State of South Carolina.

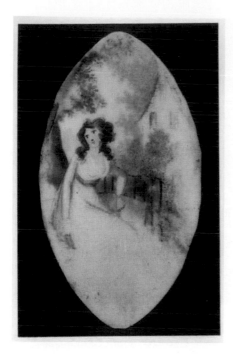

Emily Geiger, teenage heroine of the American Revolution, carried a message through enemy lines from Gen. Nathanael Greene to Thomas Sumter. Courtesy, Calhoun County Museum.

Pon Pon Chapel, built in 1754 as a chapel of ease for St. Bartholomew's Parish, Colleton County, burned in 1801. Photograph by Suzanne C. Linder.

An antebellum view of South Carolina College, now part of the University of South Carolina. *South Carolina College* by William Harrison Scarborough. Courtesy, South Caroliniana Library.

The Columbia Canal was part of an elaborate network of internal improvements undertaken by the state in the 1820s. *Congaree River near Columbia, South Carolina* by A. Grinevald. From the Collection of the Columbia Museum of Art.

Chapter Seven

TRYING ROYAL GOVERNMENT

The people, Faced . . . by absolute Necessity, and as the only means to preserve so Valuable a province to the Crown, in the Year 1720 withdrew themselves From the Confused and helpless government of the Proprietors, and absolutely renounced the same, and set up a governor under the Crown, and Immediately acquainted the Crown therewith, laying before the Crown the Necessity of this Proceeding, and humbly praying the Crown to take them under their Immediate Government.

> Sir Philip Yorke, Attorney General
> Sir Charles Talbot, Solicitor General of Great Britain, 1728

Resolved, That the Commons House of Assembly in the Province, by Laws and Statutes of Great Britain made of force in this Province, and by Acts of Assembly of this Province, and by ancient Usage and Custom, have the Rights, Powers, and Privileges in regard to introducing and passing Laws for imposing Taxes on the People of this Province as the House of Commons of Great Britain have in introducing and passing Laws on the People of England.

> The Commons House of Assembly, 28 March 1735

IN 1719 South Carolinians were willing to place themselves under the authority of the British government. They were disgusted with the bungling of the proprietary regime and the threats that it posed to their economic well-being, their freedom, and their very existence. William Rhett knew his fellow colonists well, and his comments on the revolution were remarkably prescient. The Revolution of 1719 revealed a self-determination, a self-assurance that would not tolerate much interference from outside authority, be it proprietary or royal. The colonists were determined to have their own way. Between 1721 and 1761, when the government of South Carolina was evolving, there was little or no interference from British imperial authorities. Salutary neglect enabled the colony's wealthy, aggressive elite to establish a political system that met its needs.

On Christmas Eve 1719 South Carolina's revolutionaries completed their petitions to George I and the Board of Trade. A week later the Commons House asked

Governor Moore to replace Nicholas Trott as chief justice and to appoint two new assistant judges. Besides replacing Trott, who was anathema to the rebels, the request to appoint assistant judges signaled that the revolutionaries intended to reorganize the colony's government.[1]

Although the proprietors' increase in the size of the council from eight to twelve members had "unhing'd the Constitution," Governor Moore appointed a "privy council" of twelve members. In so doing, the South Carolina council was restructured to resemble other colonial councils more closely. Also, the governor, council, and Commons House altered the manner in which a bill became law. Under the proprietary regime, after each of three readings in the house a bill was sent to the council for discussion and amendment and then returned. At Moore's suggestion, the Commons House and council adopted the British parliamentary method for the passage of bills and resolutions. Now a bill was read three times and passed in the Commons House before it was forwarded to the council. In reorganizing South Carolina government, the revolutionaries did not just toss out procedures or statutes because they had been in force under the proprietors. Rather, they kept what was useful from the old regime and only legislated what they thought absolutely necessary. Among the assembly's first actions was the revival of the legislation disallowed by the proprietors.[2]

While the revolutionary government was proceeding with the business of reform and governing, it also had to protect itself from internal and external foes. There were new rumors from the southern frontier that the Yamassee might once again attack, spurred on by the Spaniards in St. Augustine. And there were always fears of what the French might be up to in the west. Rangers and patrol boats were dispatched to provide an early warning for the colony. In May and June 1720 a slave insurrection was suppressed.[3]

As if that were not enough, former governor Johnson established what was, in essence, a government in exile—although his place of exile was only a few miles outside of Charleston. He continued to issue marriage licenses to Anglican clergy, who opposed the revolution (interestingly, Dissenter clergy opted to use only those signed by Moore). The colony suffered from drought during the spring and summer of 1720. When Moore proclaimed a day of fasting and prayer, Johnson proclaimed one to occur two days later. The former governor also probated several wills. These were small acts of resistance, but they were irritants.[4]

More serious was Johnson's encouraging proprietary officials to disregard orders from Moore or the Commons House and individuals to withhold their taxes. The revolutionaries needed to demonstrate to London that they were in charge and they had to have the revenue to operate the government. Any official who refused to join the Association against the proprietors was removed from office. Recalcitrant taxpayers found themselves facing arrest warrants issued by the Commons House. Like most revolutionaries, South Carolina's were not tolerant of any opposition; however, firing proprietary officials or jailing tax dodgers was one thing, violence quite another. The Revolution of 1719 was noteworthy in that it was a bloodless coup.[5]

In August 1720 the British government acknowledged that South Carolina was provisionally under its control and the Board of Trade agreed to appoint a governor. Francis Nicholson, a seasoned colonial administrator, was selected. Word of his appointment soon reached Charleston and emboldened Robert Johnson and William Rhett to plot a countercoup. They realized that once a royally appointed governor landed, the proprietary regime would have a difficult time reclaiming the province.

In May 1721, just before Nicholson was due to arrive, Johnson assembled several members of the old proprietary council and a rag-tag group of 120 (80 of whom were sailors from a royal warship in the harbor). They marched into Charleston and demanded that the revolutionary government surrender. Taking the moral high ground, Moore announced that his government was prepared to defend the colony in the king's name and promptly fired three cannons into Johnson's forces. After a parley during which Johnson's emissary saw official British government documents recognizing Moore's government, Johnson withdrew and agreed to stay out of politics. The putsch collapsed because it had almost no backing. Except for irreconcilable proprietary officeholders, such as Rhett and Trott, and a few disgruntled taxpayers and Anglican clergy, the white population of South Carolina endorsed the ouster of the proprietors.[6]

By moving swiftly and surely the rebels had taken the reins of government and proven to their fellow colonists and the British government that they were in control. They also were clever in the way they dealt with the British government. Their governor was the son of an individual whom imperial bureaucrats knew to be a strong supporter of the crown's interests. More significantly, for every action they took they sent London a written justification or explanation. Not only were they in charge, they presented themselves as reasonable men who had been forced to act "to prevent the utter Ruin of this Government, if not the loss of the Province, untill his Majesties Pleasure be known."[7]

With the arrival of Francis Nicholson as provisional governor, the Revolution of 1719 was history; however, it left a legacy of self-determination. South Carolinians had shown that, if need be, they could take matters into their own hands and get their way.

Although the crown had sent a governor to South Carolina, the proprietors still had a legal claim to the colony and their appointee still governed North Carolina. Their reactions to events in South Carolina were delayed and, when they came, underscored that all they were interested in was money.

The proprietors' sense of timing was as poor as their governing ability. On the heels of the South Sea Bubble scheme that ruined British investors, the proprietors entered into negotiations with three British merchants to launch a speculative venture called the Merchant Proprietors of Carolina. The Board of Trade squelched that effort immediately. Other proprietary initiatives were not so easily quashed and contributed to the instability that beset the colony during the decade of the 1720s.[8]

During Nicholson's tenure (1721–1725), the proprietors and their few remaining allies did what they could to undermine the provisional government. Trott and Rhett accused the governor of engaging in smuggling, falsehoods that the proprietors repeated in London. Nicholson was a proud man and requested leave to return home to defend his honor against the "repeated Lyes" of the proprietors. As soon as he arrived in England, the proprietors declared the governorship vacant and announced the appointment of their governor. South Carolina's agent, Francis Yonge, moved quickly to block this initiative. However, he and others were so concerned that in 1726 he published a pamphlet, *A Narrative of the Proceedings of the People of South Carolina in the Year 1719; and of the true causes and motives that induced them to renounce their obedience to the lords proprietors, as their governors, and to put themselves under the immediate government of the crown.* Two other antiproprietary pamphlets, *Liberty and Property Defended* by John Norris and *A Vindication of Francis Nicholson* by Francis Nicholson, appeared the same year. The pamphlet warfare was an indication of how seriously the South Carolinians and their friends viewed the proprietors' newfound efforts. As effective as the pamphlets might have been, the colonists were fortunate that Nicholson weighed in on their side. Not only did he champion the cause of royalization, he hired an attorney to defend himself and assist the colonists.[9]

Meanwhile, in South Carolina the political situation had deteriorated considerably. When he left, Nicholson had ignored his instructions to appoint the senior councillor (Landgrave Thomas Smith) as acting governor. Instead, he let the council elect a successor, and it chose Arthur Middleton, who had been Speaker of the Convention in 1719. Middleton simply was not up to the job. He did not work well with the Commons House, and he had to face down an attempt by Smith to seize the governorship. Middleton jailed his rival, but the militia joined those protesting the governor's high-handed actions and his refusal to deal with the economic distress facing many planters.[10]

In 1720 and 1721 new issues of paper currency were printed to help ease the shortage of circulating money. Immediately Charleston's merchants protested, and when they questioned the motives of the Commons House, twenty-eight were jailed. In 1724 Nicholson worked out a compromise to restrict the amount of paper money in circulation and to retire it gradually. The local currency also was recognized as limited legal tender. Both sides accepted the compromise, and the matter rested until 1727.[11]

South Carolina's economy was having its difficulties. The proprietors had closed the South Carolina land office in 1719 and reserved for themselves the authority for land grants. They sold or granted little land during the 1720s except to one another or their friends. The British government had removed the bounty on naval stores,

Eighteenth-century South Carolina currency was one of the most stable of the colonial currencies. This ten-pound note was issued in 1770 "in the TENTH year of his Majesty's Reign." Courtesy, South Carolina State Museum.

and a series of droughts had damaged the rice crop. Planters who had purchased slaves on credit now found themselves facing bankruptcy. They petitioned the colony's government for assistance (in the form of issuing more paper money). From the Santee River northward planters refused to pay debts or taxes and prevented the serving of papers on those who owed money. There was even a new association formed to oppose taxes.[12]

The governor and Commons House got into a wrangle over the refusal of the colony's chief justice to release Smith from prison on a writ of habeas corpus. When the Commons House did address the currency question, it could not produce a solution. Between January 1728 and January 1731 there were seven separate elections for the Commons House. One of them, the Fifth Royal Assembly, never achieved a quorum to organize. Thus, the representatives of the people were effectively out of government for three years.[13]

Ironically, the turmoil in South Carolina convinced the proprietors that they wanted to sell. After a series of legal opinions, court cases, and negotiations seven of the eight shareholders agreed to sell their interests to the crown for £2,500 sterling ($252,000) each and £5,000 sterling ($504,000) to cover incidental expenses such as former proprietary officials' salaries. On 14 May 1729 George II assented to the act formalizing the transfer of the Carolina charter from the proprietors to the king.[14]

The British government's decisions to purchase the proprietors' interests, partially restore the naval stores bounty, and permit South Carolina to ship rice directly to Portugal had a calming effect on the colony's politics, as did an agreement the newly named royal governor, Robert Johnson, worked out with London merchants to quiet the protests over the currency question. All agreed that some paper currency had to remain in circulation in South Carolina, and by the mid-1730s the colony's currency was no longer a political issue on either side of the Atlantic. For the next forty years South Carolina's currency remained relatively stable at the value of seven pounds currency to one pound sterling.[15]

The choice of Johnson as the first royal governor was an excellent one. Even though he had been the last proprietary governor, the colonists had first turned to him to be the provisional governor "untill his Majesties pleasure be known." His actions during the early 1720s had annoyed some but had not damaged the cause of the revolution. Back in London, Johnson lobbied for the position, and after the proprietors blamed him for the revolution, he assisted the colony's agents in their struggle with his former employers. His solution to the paper currency question and his proposal for the township system were examples of his experience and ability. His arrival in December 1730 coincided with a period of political quiet and economic growth. Those two factors and Johnson's adroit handling of issues reinforced South Carolinians' positive feelings for royal government.

In terms of governmental structure, most colonists hardly noticed the change. The revolutionary government and Francis Nicholson's provisional government had already realigned most of the colony's institutions with those found in other royal colonies. South Carolina had a governor, a council, an assembly, several courts, and various officials.[16]

The governor was appointed by the monarch and held his office at the royal pleasure. He had, according to James Glen (royal governor from 1743 to 1756), such "high-sounding titles" as "Governor in chief and Captain-general in and over the Province" and "Vice Admiral" of South Carolina but "little Power." One of the sources of power for any official is the power of appointment. Most public offices not elected by the Commons House were filled by British governmental patronage. The governor could appoint justices of the peace and the officers of the militia. He could also make interim appointments and suggestions for vacancies. However, all officeholders and governors knew where the real sources of power lay—with the ministry at home and with the Commons House in South Carolina. Among the powers that the governor did possess were the right to veto legislation; convene, prorogue (discontinue a session), or dismiss the Commons House; and remove judges from office (after 1750). All of South Carolina's royal governors utilized these powers, some of which had not been exercised by a British monarch since Queen Anne.[17]

By 1740 the British government paid the governor an annual salary of £800 sterling ($98,000) with an expense allowance of £300 ($37,000). Twenty years later the salary was £1,000 sterling ($84,000). The governor also received fees for issuing land grants and other documents. Depending upon the circumstances, these might range from £300 to £1,000 sterling ($25,000 to $84,000) a year. The Commons House normally supplemented the governor's salary with an annual appropriation of £500 sterling ($42,000); however, it was careful to call the appropriation a gift for services rendered the province, not a salary. When the assembly wanted to get its way, it threatened to withhold the governor's annual present. In fact, Gov. Thomas Boone did not receive what he called his "country salary" while in office. Only after he had returned to England and the Board of Trade directed South Carolina to pay him did the colony do so—and that was under special circumstances, which the Commons House duly noted.[18]

During the royal period (1730–1775) South Carolina had only six royal governors. That was a marked contrast to the proprietary period (1670–1719), during which there had been twenty-two governors. The only royal governor who served less than two and one-half years in office was Lord William Campbell, the last governor, who arrived as the American Revolution was getting under way.

For the most part, South Carolina was lucky in its first two royal governors because merit had little to do with their selection. Robert Johnson (1730–1735), son of a proprietary governor with important friends, lobbied strenuously for the position and got it. James Glen (1743–1756) became governor because of the women in his family: his sister was Sir Robert Walpole's mistress; and his wife was the illegitimate daughter of the earl of Wilmington, the president of the Privy Council. The remaining four governors, on paper, were seemingly capable men; however, their mishandling of a variety of issues helped create the climate that would lead to revolution. William Henry Lyttelton (1756–1759) was a member of the powerful Grenville family, related by marriage to William Pitt, and his older brother was chancellor of the Exchequer. Thomas Boone (1761–1764) was a descendant of the Colletons, had lived in South Carolina for several years, and had had a successful term as governor of New Jersey. Lord Charles Greville Montagu (1766–1773) was a younger son of the duke of Manchester. Lord William Campbell (1775) was the fourth son of the duke of Argyle, had married a South Carolinian, and had been governor of Nova Scotia.[19]

When there was not a royal governor present in the colony, the lieutenant governor or president of the council served in an acting capacity. Throughout the royal period only three men held these offices: Thomas Broughton, William Bull I, and William Bull II. Broughton was lieutenant governor (1730–1737) and acting governor (1735–1737). The elder Bull was president of the council (1737–1738), lieutenant governor (1738–1755), and acting governor (1737–1743). William Bull II was lieutenant governor (1759–1775) and acting governor on five separate occasions (1760–1761, 1764–1766, 1768, 1769–1771, 1773–1775). Like their British counterparts, the South Carolinians owed their positions to family connections. Broughton was Gov. Robert Johnson's brother-in-law. William Bull I was a friend and protégé of Gen. James Oglethorpe, and William Bull II got the appointment because of his father. Like the royal governors, they achieved mixed results. All three South Carolinians used membership on the royal council as a stepping-stone to the lieutenant governorship.[20]

Beginning with the "privy council" created by the revolutionary government, South Carolina's council had twelve members, as did those of most other colonies. Its members served for good behavior. In rare cases a governor could suspend a councillor; however, the suspension had to be approved in London. Until the 1750s membership on the council was highly sought after, one of the highest honors a colonial could obtain. "As the next and most Honourable Stepp in these parts is that of a Councellor," wrote John Lloyd in 1725, "I hope you will favour me with your Recommendation to be one of His Majesties Councill in the Province." He did not get the appointment in 1725 or in 1728 when he again asked English friends to help his cause. The record is silent as to Lloyd's lack of success. In some ways his failure is a puzzle because, as a Charleston merchant with strong London connections, he fit the mold of an individual likely to gain a seat.[21]

For most of the colonial period the council was exactly what Lloyd had said it was, an "Honourable Stepp in these parts." Being talented or well connected was not good enough, as Lloyd's case illustrates. Being wealthy was the most important criterion, at least for South Carolinians, to be selected for the council. A study of the forty-nine men who served from 1720 to 1763 revealed that they were very wealthy men in a wealthy society. On average they owned 7,750 acres of land and 172 slaves and had estates with a value of £9,022 sterling ($938,851).[22]

Prior to 1750 two groups dominated the membership of the council: an interrelated clan of planter families and the wealthiest Charleston merchants with strong ties to London's mercantile community. The planter clan that included the Bulls, Draytons, Fenwickes, Izards, and Middletons filled eighteen of the available forty-nine seats. Charleston merchants such as George Austin, Othniel Beale, Benjamin De La Conseillere, Alexander Vander Dussen, and Joseph Wragg held ten places. Before 1763 there were only nine placemen (or royal officials who held royal appointments to a position or "place" in the colonial administration). After the French and Indian War the British government determined that it wanted more pliable councillors. South Carolinians of stature declined to serve, and an increasing number of council seats were filled by placemen.[23]

The council fulfilled a multifunctional role in colonial government. It operated as an upper house of the assembly, an advisory body to the governor, and the Court of

Chancery. However, its dual role as an upper house and an advisory body some-times resulted in a conflict with both the Commons House and the governor. As early as 1725 the council insisted that it had the same rights and privileges as the House of Lords, an uncommon claim in colonial America. However, South Caro-lina was an uncommon place; there were no other colonial societies with the wealth or audacity to make the assertions that the South Carolinians made. There was a real problem, though. The members of the council were not peers of the realm; few even had the old proprietary titles. They were simply the first rank among equals. In 1770 Lt. Gov. William Bull actually suggested to British officials that the council be reconstituted more in the manner of the House of Lords, either becoming an hereditary office or one for life. If that were to occur, the council would be "on a more respectable footing." As a former councillor and a member of the colony's elite, Bull knew that the council had fallen in esteem. That had not always been the case. As late as 1743 the power and prestige of the council were on a par with those of the governor and the Commons House of Assembly.[24]

As the upper house of the assembly, the council had to approve bills before they could be sent to the governor for his signature. Between 1721 and 1761 the power of the council was challenged repeatedly by the Commons House of Assembly, "the representatives of the people, . . . elected by them as the house of commons in Great Britain, to be the guardians of their lives, liberties, and properties."[25]

It was to the House of Commons that South Carolina's representatives turned for authority when, in 1735, they rejected the council's amendment to an appropria-tions bill. Although the council initially demurred, it yielded to the Commons House. The issue did not end there, and in 1737 the council raised it again. For sev-eral years the two houses jockeyed back and forth. Then, in the spring of 1739 the council declared that it had the authority to amend *any* bill passed by the Commons House. The two bodies exchanged insulting messages until Lieutenant Governor Bull granted the assembly permission to adjourn.[26]

The election of a new Commons House in the fall did not alter the position of that body. When it convened in November 1739, it sent a message to the council that it was willing to work with them for the good of the colony; however, it in-sisted that its most important obligation was to preserve "that Freedom and Inde-pendence by which the Constitution of our Mother Country is to be preserved to each Branch of the Legislature."[27]

In the meantime the Stono Rebellion had occurred, the War of Jenkins' Ear had erupted, and Oglethorpe was in South Carolina seeking support for an invasion of Florida. Obviously, the colony was facing a number of serious problems, but nothing could be done until this constitutional question was resolved.

In December 1739 a compromise solution was hammered out by a conference committee of the two houses. Although called a compromise, the council in effect surrendered on almost every point. It conceded that the assembly had the authority to initiate all money bills. The council could no longer amend such bills, but it could recommend amendments to the Commons House and, as with any piece of legislation, it could reject a money bill. There were some rumblings of raising the issue again during the 1740s, but nothing substantive occurred. By 1750 it was an accepted fact that the Commons House controlled the colony's finances.[28]

The council, however, could not leave well enough alone. In 1754 and 1755 it became embroiled in another contest with the Commons House as to whether or not a certain piece of legislation were a money bill. The council said it was not and that therefore the council could amend it; the Commons House said it was and that therefore the council could not amend it. Neither side would budge. The French and their Indian allies threatened the frontier from New York to Georgia, but to South Carolinians that was not as pressing as the constitutional struggle between the two houses. Repeatedly British officials asked South Carolina to appropriate funds to help finance Gen. Edward Braddock's expedition against France's Indian allies, but to no avail.[29]

In the midst of this constitutional stalemate, a new governor arrived in Charleston. William Henry Lyttelton had instructions to stop the wrangling and get the colony behind the war effort. The governor persuaded the council to approve a new money bill, and it did so almost without a murmur.

After several council meetings it did not take Lyttelton long to pinpoint one of the sources of difficulty, councillor William Wragg. Wragg was a member of one of the colony's wealthiest merchant families and a staunch defender of the prerogatives of the crown. During the fuss with the Commons House, he wrote and published the council's view of the matter in which he asserted that neither the people of South Carolina nor their assembly had any inherent rights or privileges: all were gifts from the crown. This hard-line view of royal authority was held by few white South Carolinians. Wragg's waspish temperament did not help matters either. Having no inclination to put up with Wragg's argumentativeness, in 1756 Governor Lyttelton suspended him from the council. He convinced the Board of Trade that the colony would be ungovernable if Wragg were reinstated. In December 1757 the Privy Council formally removed William Wragg from the council of South Carolina.[30]

In the short term, Lyttelton, his successors, and the Board of Trade got a more compliant council. In the long term, the damage to the effectiveness of the council and the relationship between South Carolina's elite and the crown was ominous. The message was chillingly clear: if you were independent and disagreed with the governor (backed by the imperial bureaucracy), you would be removed. The British government had humiliated one of its most ardent defenders for doing what a councillor was supposed to do: "supporting the prerogatives of the crown in the province." In the years immediately following Wragg's dismissal, five individuals resigned from the council, something that had rarely happened previously. In 1760 Peter Taylor, Benjamin Smith, Gabriel Manigault, Ralph Izard, Henry Hyrne, and Rawlins Lowndes refused to accept even temporary appointments. Henry Laurens declined a formal appointment. In a 1764 letter to a friend, he confided the main reason: "I am & have been sorry to see that Honorable Board so much slighted as it has been at some times by certain appointments which hath reduced its character with some people almost below contempt."[31]

The "certain appointments" to which Laurens referred were council seats awarded to placemen such as Charles Shinner, Thomas Skottowe, and Egerton Leigh. For as South Carolinians declined to serve, placemen received the vacancies. With a growing number of members owing their livelihoods solely to the British government, the independence and reputation of the council became things of the past.[32]

As the council's prestige dimmed, that of the Commons House brightened. If Lyttelton and the imperial bureaucracy had been more astute, they would have realized they had made it virtually impossible for members of the colony's independent-minded elite to serve on the council. Denied that forum, South Carolina's elite focused on making the Commons House of Assembly an even stronger force in the colony's political life. Symbolic of this shift was Wragg's election to represent St. Luke's in the Commons House. He took his seat in November 1757, before his removal from the council was official. Within a few years he was an acknowledged leader of the assembly.[33]

The rise of the Commons House of Assembly paralleled the growing aspirations of South Carolina's elite. It was different from its peer groups in other colonies because it was larger (in terms of a percentage of the population) and it was far, far wealthier. A majority of the members of South Carolina's eighteenth-century elite could trace their roots back to those who had originally settled the colony. In contrast, members of Virginia's eighteenth-century elite were descended from aggressive newcomers who in the 1640s and 1650s had displaced the colony's founding political and economic elite. South Carolina's West Indian founders were made of sterner stuff.[34]

By the late 1730s the colonists had gotten past the factional disputes over religious and economic issues. With internal peace of paramount importance, an ethos evolved among the colony's elite. Based upon contemporary English political thought, their own experiences, and those of their forebears, South Carolina's elite exemplified what has been called the "country ideology." Among the chief tenets of this country ideology (which was not unique to South Carolina), was a distrust of human nature and the feeling that human beings simply could not be trusted. In order to protect their lives, freedoms, and property, people established governments. If governments functioned as they should, then the people should obey them; if they were corrupt and abused their authority, then individuals had a duty to resist. However, challenging government could lead to instability that might threaten life, liberty, and property. Therefore, in order to prevent government from getting out of hand, there needed to be checks and balances. In Great Britain the House of Commons was the protector of the people; in South Carolina the Commons House of Assembly was.[35]

In order to be free to act, to be unbeholden to anyone, and to be independent a representative had to have economic independence. He should be able and public-spirited, willing to do his duty, but above all else he should be a man of property. With a stake in society, he would naturally want to see that government operated so as to ensure the safety of the lives, freedoms, and property of the people of South Carolina. Unfortunately, even the most public-spirited individual could be corrupted, so society needed a safeguard. In South Carolina electing representatives in the parishes and voting by secret ballot provided the necessary check. Since stability was important, factions were dangerous and reflected self-interest over the public good. Partisanship, such as that which had wracked the colony intermittently for seventy years, was discouraged. By the 1750s, knowingly or unknowingly, South Carolina's lowcountry elite personified the country ideology.[36]

The elite took seriously the duty of protecting the people from tyranny and corruption. Since Governor Lyttelton and the Board of Trade made it obvious that independence and membership on the council were mutually exclusive, the council could not serve as a governmental check. Therefore, the elite turned to the Commons House of Assembly. The Wragg affair, by damaging the council, elevated the prestige of the assembly—a body which for decades had also been controlled by the colony's elite.

The South Carolina Commons House of Assembly traced its roots to the first proprietary parliament in 1671; however, it was not until 1692 that the representatives of the people sat as a separate body. That date, rather than the earlier one, marks the origin of what would become one of the most powerful assemblies in colonial America.

From 1692 until 1716 counties were the election districts for the elected body that called itself the Commons House of Assembly. Twenty and then thirty seats were apportioned among the three counties (Craven, Berkeley, and Colleton). All voting took place in Charleston, which made it easier for factions to manipulate the vote. Voting requirements were nominal; a free male with fifty acres of land could cast a ballot. Since the headright system granted fifty acres to all freemen who entered the province, South Carolina had almost universal white manhood suffrage.

One of the guiding principles behind the Fundamental Constitutions was that individuals should have a stake in society in order to participate. That applied to officeholders as well as voters. Initially the property qualification for being a member of the assembly was the same as that for voting. However, the Election Act of 1716 increased tenfold the property qualification for service in the house. As in Barbados, the parishes instead of the counties were made the election districts. Voting would be in the parishes, not in Charleston. The 1716 act was for the convenience of the colonists and to make South Carolina's elections "nearer the Methods used in *England.*" The proprietors disallowed this act and a subsequent one in 1717, but in 1721 a new Election Act was passed. As the colony developed, new parishes were created and the Commons House enlarged from thirty-six seats in 1721 to forty-eight seats in 1775. Otherwise, the Election Act, with slight modifications, established South Carolina's election procedures until the American Revolution.[37]

The act was all-inclusive and laid the foundation for the evolution of the assembly's quest for power at the expense of the governor and council. It defined a voter as a free white Christian male, twenty-one years of age, who owned fifty acres of land or paid 20 shillings currency ($25.50) in taxes and had lived in South Carolina for one year. Forty days prior to an election, the governor issued writs to the churchwardens in each parish. They, in turn, two weeks before the election announced the polling places and dates. The polls were opened for two days, and voting was by secret ballot.

In order to serve in the Commons House, an individual had to meet all the qualifications of the voter, plus he had to own five hundred acres *and* ten slaves or property worth £1,000 currency ($25,500). Initially this may have limited the pool of available candidates; however, by midcentury wealth was so widespread that probably half of the lowcountry's adult white males could qualify. Although an individual had to have been a resident of the colony for one year to qualify as a voter or candidate, there was no parish residency requirement for membership in the assembly.[38]

To safeguard the guardian of the people's liberties, the act set forth guidelines to ensure the independence of the Commons House. Elections were to be held at least every three years. If there were a disputed election, the house would be the sole judge of its own membership. Once elected, the assembly was to meet at least every six months. Nearly three decades later Governor Glen, who fancied himself a constitutional expert, complained that the secret ballot and these safeguards were unconstitutional. He and other governors were also unhappy with the control the Commons House had over key administrative officials such as the public treasurer, the comptroller, and the commissioners of Indian affairs. (Tucked into the act was the provision that any civil officer who received his salary from the colony's treasury would be elected by the assembly.)[39]

Serving in the Commons House was a duty that the colony's elite took seriously. Earlier studies have concluded that South Carolina's elite was apathetic about politics, that it spent more time with its madeira and horses than with the business of governing the colony. That simply was not true.[40]

During the 1730s and 1740s about one-fourth of those elected refused to serve.

Generally no reason was given. Likely, the economic difficulties caused by the War of Jenkins' Ear (1739–1748) contributed to the high declination rate during the 1740s. The turnover rate in most colonial assemblies was relatively high until the mid 1760s, when it declined. During the last decade before the American Revolution, the turnover rate in South Carolina's Commons House was about the same as Virginia's House of Burgesses and Massachusetts's General Court—and all were similar to the turnover in representation in the House of Commons.[41]

If a person declined to serve in the South Carolina Commons House, it might be understandable; it was likely the hardest working assembly in colonial America. Though by law it had to meet at least every six months, in practice it met more frequently. In some years the assembly was in session for a total of eight out of twelve months. While in session, it met six hours a day, six days a week. Members received no stipend—like those in Westminster and unlike other colonial assemblymen.[42]

The Commons House prided itself on conducting its affairs in the same manner as the House of Commons. In 1756 it had a magnificent mace (signifying the dignity and authority of the house) crafted by a London silversmith. Like its model, the Commons House could jail individuals for contempt. After a series of battles with the council, it asserted its right to control the colony's financial affairs. In addition to initiating money bills, the assembly adopted the policy of paying for expenses after they occurred. In that way there was never any money in the treasury for a governor to embark on projects of his own design.[43]

In its drive to be as much like the House of Commons as it could be, the Commons House of Assembly exercised more authority than its model. Without realizing it, South Carolina's assembly created a legislature that could have served as a prototype for nineteenth-century British parliamentary reformers: there were no rotten boroughs; representation was apportioned, more or less, according to population; placemen did not sit in the house; and there was universal white manhood suffrage by secret ballot.[44]

The members of the Commons House of Assembly, like their counterparts in Westminster, might have represented "the people"; however, they were anything but common folk. An analysis of representatives from fifteen parishes revealed that the parishes of St. Philip's and St. Michael's (Charleston) had the wealthiest delegations. On average, the Charlestonians had estates worth £8,883 sterling ($871,168) and owned 79 slaves. The delegation from St. George's Dorchester, with estates worth £8,691 sterling ($852,138), were the largest average slaveholders with 137. The least prosperous representatives came from the parishes on the fringes of the lowcountry. The men from Prince Frederick owned but 37 slaves, and their estates were worth only £2,153 ($211,148). However, their estates were nearly twice the net worth of free whites in the colony (£1,200 sterling [$117,686]).[45]

If the ownership of human property were taken by itself, then the wealth of the members of the Commons House was even more noticeable. Inventories of estates exist for almost half those elected to serve in the Commons House. Even by West Indian standards, more than one-half were big planters (owners of 60 or more slaves) and one-third were middling planters (owners of 20 to 59 slaves). Two individuals, Arthur Middleton and Daniel Blake, each owned in excess of 700 slaves. Of the members for whom there are records, the average number of slaves owned was 92.[46]

Not only was the wealth of South Carolina's elite impressive, so was the ability of families to maintain their wealth and prominence throughout the colonial period. The descendants of the old, established seventeenth-century families dominated the politics of most of the parishes. Between 1721 and 1775, 61 percent of the members of the Commons House were the scions of old South Carolina families. Even in places where newcomers were most likely to succeed, such as Charleston and the frontier parishes, the pre-1700 families were well represented.[47]

Family ties were important, and about 70 percent of the members had at least one close relative (father, son, brother, or in-law) who also served. In the Thirty-third Royal Assembly (1773–1775), fifty-one of the sixty-nine individuals elected had a relative who was or had been a member. If kinship patterns are extended to include relations by marriage, then the interconnectedness of the South Carolina elite became even more conspicuous. Take, for example, John Rutledge, who represented Christ Church Parish in the last royal assembly. In that assembly alone he, his relatives, and their kin accounted for 18 percent of those who served. South Carolina's elite truly were members of a vast cousinage.[48]

Not unexpectedly, more than two-thirds of the members of the assembly were planters, and until midcentury they supplied its leadership. During the last twenty-five years of colonial government, however, Charleston's merchants and attorneys took over. Economic interests united South Carolina's elite, regardless of occupation, but so did the threat posed by the colony's black majority, the Cherokee, and imperial wars with France and Spain. Harmony and agreement were essential, especially if the Commons House were to fulfill its role as the guardian of the "lives, liberties, and properties" of the people. A united front was important not just at the colonywide level; it was also essential at the local governmental level. There is no doubt that the Commons House was the most powerful assembly in the southern colonies, and there is an excellent argument that it wielded more real authority than any other in America. What set the South Carolina assembly apart from the other twelve was its control of local government.[49]

Local government in eighteenth-century South Carolina is another aspect of colonial politics that has been frequently misunderstood. One reason has been comparisons among the various colonies that attempt to invent one pattern that fits all. Politically, economically, and geographically, South Carolina was neither Virginia

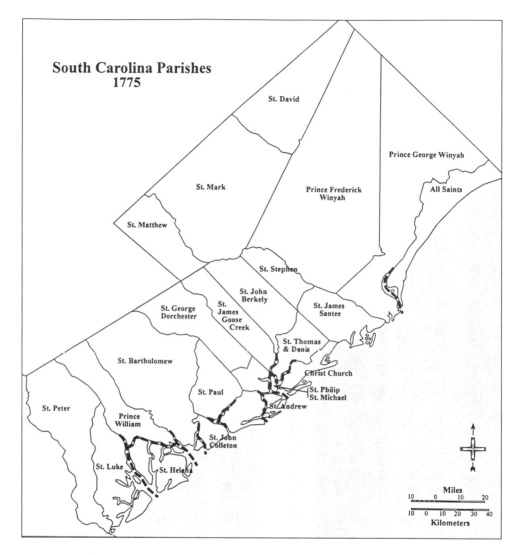

South Carolina Parishes 1775

St. David

Prince George Winyah

St. Mark

Prince Frederick Winyah

All Saints

St. Matthew

St. Stephen

St. John Berkely

St. George Dorchester

St. James Goose Creek

St. James Santee

St. Thomas & Denis

St. Bartholomew

Christ Church

St. Paul

St. Philip St. Michael

St. Peter

St. Andrew

Prince William

St. John Colleton

St. Luke

St. Helena

Miles
10 0 10 20

10 0 10 20 30 40
Kilometers

Map 9: Parishes, 1775. Based on Edgar, *Biographical Directory* and Kovacik & Winberry, *South Carolina*

nor Massachusetts. Just because there were no town meetings or county courts did not mean there was no local government. To South Carolinians, a Massachusetts town meeting would have smacked too much of "numerous democracy"; yet the franchise was far more liberal in South Carolina. Virginia needed a strong local court system because its population was widely dispersed and travel was difficult.

In South Carolina the relatively small population was concentrated in the lowcountry. Transportation by water or road to the capital was simple and convenient. Therefore, no courts were needed outside Charleston until the late 1750s. However, not everything could be done in or from Charleston. When needs arose, the Commons House responded by creating commissions to respond to local situations.[50]

The parish was the basic unit of local government in South Carolina. Following the Barbadian model, the officers of the parish had civil as well as ecclesiastical responsibilities. Initially there were ten parishes created by the Church Act of 1706. By 1775 there were twenty-one (see Map 9). Annually, on Easter Monday, voters gathered in the parish church to elect two churchwardens and seven vestrymen. Although the law stated that a person had to be a member of the Church of England to be eligible for office, non-Anglicans were elected as early as the 1720s.[51]

In all parishes the vestry was responsible for maintaining the parish church, rectory, chapels of ease, and glebe lands. If there were a parish school, it fell under the vestry's jurisdiction. Members of the vestry were also responsible for assessing residents for funds to cover the care of the poor of the parish. In rural parishes (such as St. Helena's, St. James' Goose Creek, and St. John's Berkeley) the duties were not particularly heavy, but in the two town parishes of Charleston (St. Philip's and St. Michael's), the workload was demanding.

The office of churchwarden was a testing ground for younger men, to see if they could handle civic responsibility. All wardens served as election officials for their parishes, maintained a list of eligible voters, and staffed the polls for two days. On Sundays wardens were responsible for safeguarding the weapons of worshipers. In rural parishes the duties of wardens were relatively light. In Charleston it was quite another matter since the parish operated an orphanage and a hospital. Robert Pringle wrote his brother in London that he had been elected churchwarden of St. Philip's, "an Office which is attended with some Trouble but there is no Dispensing with it here as it Comes in Course." The next year, having proven himself, Pringle moved up to the vestry. It was rare that an individual declined to take his turn. Most South Carolinians, like Pringle, did their duty when called upon to serve.[52]

Pringle's duties as churchwarden for St. Philip's were "some Trouble" because Charleston, the fourth largest city in British North America, was unincorporated. The Fundamental Constitutions had called for cities and towns to be self-governing, but it had never been ratified. There was one brief attempt to create a municipal corporation in the 1720s, but the law was disallowed by the British government.[53]

Since Charleston had no government of its own, the burden fell primarily on the shoulders of the wardens and vestry of St. Philip's parish. Even after the creation of a second city parish, St. Michael's for the area south of Broad Street, the officials of St. Philip's still had far heavier responsibilities than those of any other parish.

A city as large as Charleston had to have other officials if it were to function. So

Robert Pringle (1702–1776). Courtesy, McColl Pringle, Charleston, South Carolina.

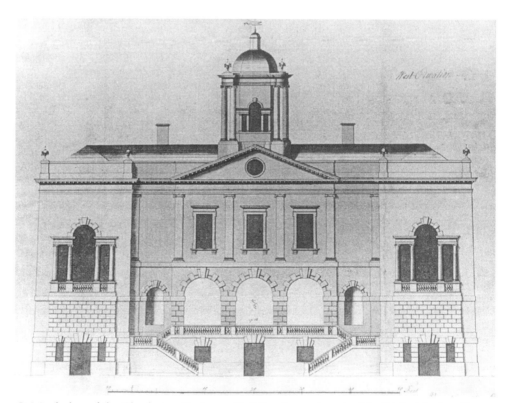

Original plan of the Charleston Exchange Building (west elevation) by Rigby Naylor. Courtesy, South Carolina Department of Archives and History.

it did: commissioners of the streets, workhouse, and market; firemasters; wood and coal measurers; and packers. Charleston's merchants dominated these offices except for the packers, which were usually chosen from among master coopers. In combination, the task of these officials was to make the port city a cleaner, safer place in which to live. The wood and coal measurers, for instance, monitored the sale of fuel to see that the people were not shortchanged. The packers inspected the packing of the colony's exports to insure quality. Initially most of these officials were named by the Commons House; however, as early as 1737 Charlestonians began to elect them annually. The Charleston commissions were unique in that the assembly permitted the voters in the city to elect them. Elsewhere in the province there were two types of commissions: self-perpetuating and special-purpose.[54]

The most important of the self-perpetuating ones were the commissions of the high roads. They were created in every parish for the purpose of maintaining the public highways. The assembly named the original members, but when any subsequent vacancy occurred, the commission filled it. Other commissions were created for special purposes such as to build a road between Mosquito Creek and the Combahee River, to prevent the spread of smallpox in Charleston, or to aid navigation into Charleston harbor.[55]

The commission system was a remarkable one in that it enabled a large number of individuals to participate in government and, at the same time, insured that governmental duties did not fall too heavily on any one individual or individuals. While it might seem to the modern reader that this was an inefficient system of government, it was not; it worked well. Especially noteworthy was the condition of the colony's public roads. Given the soil, geography, and climate, one might expect them to be poorly maintained. Just the opposite was true. John Bartram, a Philadelphia naturalist who traveled throughout the colonies, recorded that "no province in America generally has better roads." And the colony's most impressive structures—the State House, the Exchange, and St. Michael's Church—were all built by special commissions.[56]

The system of government that developed in South Carolina created hundreds of positions that had to be filled on a regular basis. In 1750 there were sixteen parishes. Annually they each elected 2 wardens and 7 vestrymen. Charleston, in addition, elected 29 men to fill the positions on its commissions. Every time the Commons House drafted a tax bill, it appointed between 51 and 65 tax assessors, inquirers, and collectors for the parishes. There were 225 places on self-perpetuating commissions. When required, there were special commissions whose membership usually was 7 or 9. Either directly or indirectly, the Commons House was responsible for the overwhelming percentage of these positions. All commissions, even the self-perpetuating ones, had to answer to the assembly. This frustrated royal governors. In 1748 Governor Glen wrote to the Board of Trade: "Thus by little and little the people have got the whole administration into their hands, and the crown is by various

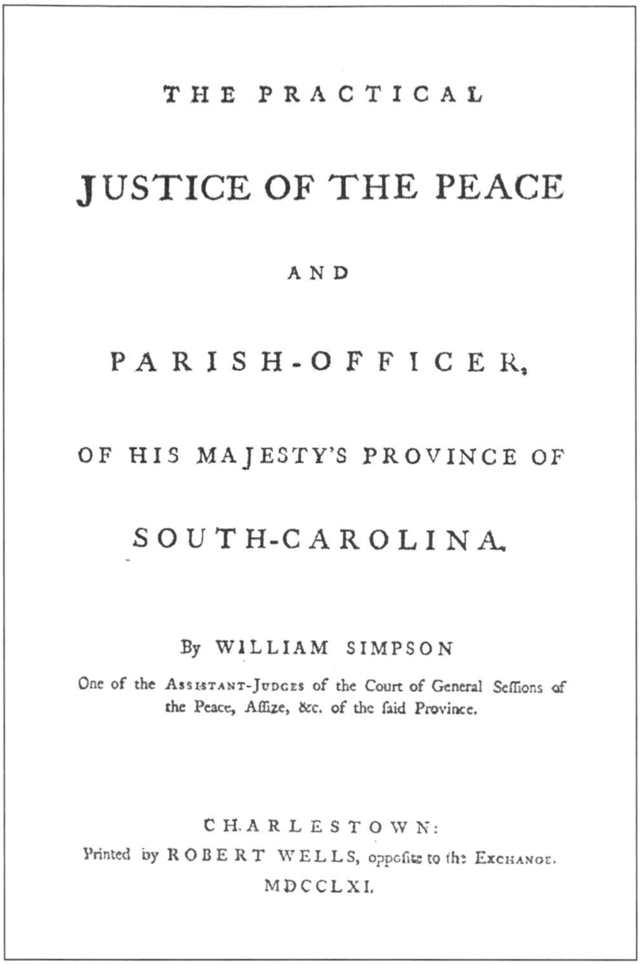

THE PRACTICAL

JUSTICE OF THE PEACE

AND

PARISH-OFFICER,

OF HIS MAJESTY'S PROVINCE OF

SOUTH-CAROLINA.

By WILLIAM SIMPSON

One of the Assistant-Judges of the Court of General Sessions of
the Peace, Assize, &c. of the said Province.

CHARLESTOWN:
Printed by ROBERT WELLS, opposite to the Exchange.
MDCCLXI.

Title page from William Simpson's *Practical Justice of the Peace*. Courtesy, South Caroliniana Library.

laws despoiled of its principal flowers and brightest jewels."[57]

The only civil offices the governor could appoint were justices of the peace. In South Carolina the position was not as significant as it was in other colonies because it had very little power. A justice's most important duty was to sit as a member of a court to determine punishments for slaves. Although Glen complained about finding men to serve, regularly between 142 and 167 accepted appointments. Some were men of modest means, but most were members of the colony's elite. In 1761 William Simpson published a manual to assist those who served: *The Practical Justice of the Peace and Parish Officer of His Majesty's Province of South Carolina*. Since the appointment as justice of the peace stemmed from the governor and the office had little authority, it was not considered as worthwhile as the commissions created by the Commons House.[58]

South Carolina's commission system was a complicated form of government and a demanding one. It required participation by a relatively large percentage of the white male population. In 1750, for example, with a white population of twenty-five thousand, there would have been a pool of approximately five thousand men. The members of the white male elite, who filled all but a handful of the offices, was even smaller—about one thousand. From that group were drawn nearly five hundred officeholders. Some individuals held more than one office, but there were a lot of positions of public trust to be filled on a regular basis. A study of those who filled many of the local offices revealed that it was the older, established parish residents who were most often chosen. The colony's governmental structure, rather than indicating a lack of interest on the part of the elite, demonstrated just the opposite. A great many men had a stake in the government of colonial South Carolina.[59]

What was the rationale for the colony's peculiar system of local government? The dispersion of authority among numerous commissions would, of course, be a check on potential corruption. The Commons House, as the guardian of the people, could keep a close watch over every aspect of local government. Therefore, the country ideology is one explanation for the commission system. Another is that the Commons House did not want to allow the development of local governments that might one day challenge its authority. That could be the explanation for the failure to incorporate Charleston, Beaufort, and Georgetown. The commissions were, in effect, extensions of the power and authority of the assembly. A third is that there really was no need for an elaborate local governmental structure on the Virginia model. Geographically, the lowcountry was a small area with excellent water and land routes to its political, social, and economic center: Charleston. While separately none of these theories fully explains the colony's government system, combined they do.[60]

By 1760 South Carolina's elite had developed a system of government responsive to its needs. The rise of the Commons House of Assembly, at the expense of the governor and council, was a measure of the growing self-confidence and aspirations of the colony's elite. So, too, was the manner in which the assembly created and dominated the colony's local government. The South Carolina government that evolved by the mid-eighteenth century was designed to maintain "the good order and harmony of the whole community."[61]

An incident involving merchant-planter Henry Laurens was indicative of the elite's sense of civic responsibility. In 1765 one of Laurens's plantations was tasked to supply slave labor to work on nearby roads. It was harvest time. Rather than asking for a delay, Laurens responded with a letter in which he expounded on the importance of placing the good of the community above individual interests; otherwise, "all regularity and good order would be destroyed." Making slightly less indigo that year was insignificant when compared to supporting "those Laws which will secure to us the property of what we do make." Those with a stake in South Carolina society did their duty when called upon.[62]

The individuals who controlled South Carolina's political life were prosperous.

As a group, they were the richest in British North America. While a majority of them were descended from the colony's seventeenth-century settlers, a sizable minority were not. Wealth was the sine qua non for admission into the class that governed South Carolina. That should come as no surprise. The earliest settlers had been imbued with the same idea their West Indian forebears had had: "They came here," wrote Father Antoine Biet on a 1654 visit to Barbados, "in order to become wealthy."[63]

Chapter Eight

TIIE RICHES OF THE PROVINCE

The great improvement made in this Province is wholly owing to the industry and labour of the Inhabitants. They have applied themselves to make such commodities as might increase the revenue of the Crown, as Cotton, Wool, Ginger, Indigo, etc. But finding them not to answer the end, they are set upon making Pitch, Tar, Turpentine, and planting rice.
    Edward Randolph, 16 March 1699

The Negro slaves are about seventy thousand; they, with a few exceptions, do all the labour or hard work in the country, and are a considerable part of the riches of the province. . . . They are in this climate necessary, but very dangerous domestics, their number so much exceeding the whites.
    George Milligen-Johnston, *A Short Description of the Province of*
        South-Carolina . . . 1763

Few countries have at any time exhibited so striking an instance of public and private prosperity as appeared in South Carolina between the years 1725 and 1775.
    David Ramsay, *The History of South Carolina*

*E*VERYONE INVOLVED in the founding of South Carolina planned on making money out of the venture. The proprietors thought the colony might develop some exotic product that would command high prices in England—much as tobacco had for Virginia. Barbadians viewed the new colony as a source of provisions for their island (so they could devote more land to sugar). Both groups, significantly, viewed South Carolina as a colony that would be oriented toward overseas, not domestic, markets. And it was in the world market that South Carolinians would make their fortunes. Although it took them a while, from the first settlement at Albemarle Point they were looking for the commodities that would bring the best returns.[1]

Among Capt. Joseph West's instructions, once he reached Barbados, were to obtain cotton and indigo seeds, ginger roots, vines, sugar cane cuttings, and olive tree sets. In detail, his employers told him how to care for the seeds and cuttings and how and when to plant them in Carolina. West was to plant his seeds in different types of soils to determine which ones were the most productive. The proprietors wanted to create, in essence, an agricultural experimental station.[2]

While finding a staple for export was important, so, too, were basic food crops. West was to plant "Indian Corne, Beanes, Pease, Turnipps, Carretts & Potatoes for Provisions." Interestingly, the proprietors instructed him to ask the natives of the country the proper time to plant the corn, beans, and peas. Also, he was to take six young sows and a boar hog from Barbados and, once in Carolina, to purchase cattle from Virginia.[3]

The proprietors and the settlers knew from the outset what they wanted to do. There were, however, several variables: land, climate, and demand. What could be produced successfully in South Carolina *and* find a niche in world markets? Above all, the product could not compete with anything produced in England. From the beginning those associated with South Carolina made rational economic decisions. If something worked, exploit it. If it did not, abandon it and try something else. In systematic fashion the colonists set out to discover the best way to make their fortunes.[4]

Even before the first rude shelter had been built at Albemarle Point, the proprietors were anticipating that there would be something to ship back to Barbados. After all, there was no sense in having the first fleet's ships return with empty cargo holds. Governor West was instructed "to helpe that of our Shippes that returnes to Barbadoes to a loading of lumber, &c." The proprietors knew from earlier reports that their province was heavily forested, and they knew that there was a market for wood products in Barbados. A year later they issued similar orders to a ship captain they sent out to the colony. Their instructions to make use of a known resource to meet a known demand was a sensible business decision.[5]

Another sound determination the original proprietors made was to ship food and other supplies to the colony during the first few years of settlement. This limited support, coupled with the experience of the Barbadians, insured that South Carolina had no starving time. Sometimes the drive of a few early settlers must have given even the profit-seeking proprietors pause. Sir John Yeamans, for example, had a successful farming enterprise and raised more food than his family (white and black) could consume. Other colonists were not as successful, and some were new arrivals. They were willing to buy Yeamans's crops; however, he knew that his surplus would bring higher prices in Barbados. Although he was Speaker of parliament and would be governor, his personal profits were more important, so he exported the food to the West Indies.[6]

Yeamans's personal ethics (if they be called such) had been learned in Barbados. There the successful pursuit of wealth, not religious mores, determined what was or was not socially acceptable behavior. The governor's fellow West Indians shared his views, and these concepts were adopted by the remainder of the colony's European settlers. If getting ahead involved exploiting the land or others, then so be it. The bottom line was what counted. Over time as new opportunities arose the methods might be altered, but the goals remained constant.[7]

During the bitter factional disputes of the late seventeenth century, the political activities of one of the leaders of the Goose Creek Men were described as Machiavellian. His economic activities were not condemned even though they, too, were Machiavellian. After all, many Dissenters had also come from Barbados and pursued mammon with as much vigor as their Anglican opponents. As Yeamans demonstrated, the ends (making a higher profit) justified the means (selling his crops to Barbados instead of to fellow colonists).

Yeamans served as a model in another way that led to the development of the colony's first major agricultural enterprise: cattle ranching. Shortly after his arrival in the summer of 1671, he sent to Virginia for one hundred head of cattle. Within a decade an observer noted that "Neat Cattle thrive and increase here exceedingly, there being perticular Planters that have already seven or eight hundred head, and will in a few years in all probability, have as many thousands." Apparently, thirty years later the prediction had come true. While the size of individual herds in the early eighteenth century is not known, in 1710 Thomas Nairne reported: "*South Carolina* abounds with black Cattle, to a Degree much beyond any other *English* colony." Some ranchers had a thousand head of cattle, and individual herds of two hundred were "very common."[8]

Cattle ranching required little capital or labor other than an initial investment in stock and perhaps a slave or two. With its mild climate and open grasslands, South Carolina was a natural cattle ranching area. The raising of cattle was something with which white Barbadians were familiar, but they were not as familiar with open-range grazing as their African slaves were. Open grazing meant that a rancher did not have to build corrals or fence pastures, but it did mean that there had to be a way to determine which stock belonged to whom. That was solved by branding. The cattle brand book in the South Carolina Department of Archives and History is one of the state's oldest existing colonial records. By law, no animal could be slaughtered unless its owner could be determined—something the brand registry made relatively simple.[9]

The raising of hogs was another effective use of resources available. Allowed to forage freely, hogs multiplied rapidly "without any charge or trouble to the Planter." Initially, like cattle ranching, it was often an individual enterprise. However, as the size of herds increased, so did the profits necessary to acquire labor for larger herds.[10]

After 1700 black labor supplanted white in herding the free-ranging swine and cattle. An indication of the extent of the cattle ranching industry in South Carolina was the number of slaves who tended the herds. In 1708 there were eighteen hundred adult male slaves in South Carolina; nearly a thousand of them were "Cattle-hunters." More than 150 years before there were cowboys and cattle drives in the

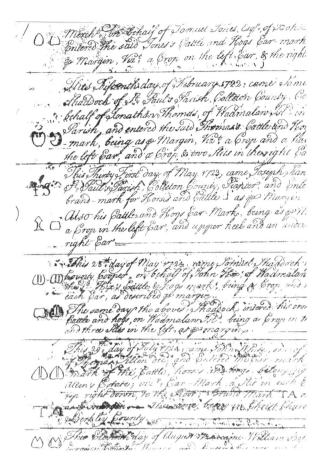

Early cattle marks or brands had to be registered with the secretary of the province. Miscellaneous Records of the Secretary of the Province, Book B (1722–1726). Courtesy, South Carolina Department of Archives and History.

American West, there were both in colonial South Carolina. Annually black "Cattle-hunters" (cowboys) rounded up their charges and drove them to cattle pens, usually a fenced area between two streams. There they were sorted and those chosen for slaughter separated from the remainder of the herd.[11]

The choice of cattle ranching was another example of a rational business decision made by the early settlers. The exotics the proprietors had planted in their agricultural experimental station were all labor-intensive. Capital and labor were in short supply, but land was plentiful. By 1682 "beefe and porke" were the two main exports of the colony. New England, Jamaica, and Barbados eagerly purchased South Carolina's salted meat exports. Recognizing this, a 1691 statute regulated the packing of meat products for export. By attempting to insure quality, South Carolina authorities hoped to maintain good returns for their ranchers. Well into the eighteenth century meat products ranked fourth among the colony's exports—behind rice, deerskins, and indigo.[12]

Between 1670 and 1700, besides ranching, colonists sought other economic opportunities. When they found them, they exploited them to the fullest. Dr. Henry Woodward was the first of a series of South Carolinians to explore the interior and report back on the opportunities for trade. He soon was followed by James Moore, Thomas Nairne, and John Barnwell—traders and explorers who created a southern frontier for the English. In New England, the middle colonies, and Virginia there were none to equal the daring or success of the South Carolina traders. While a great deal of romance has been generated about the French coureurs de bois and their success with the Indians, Woodward and his compatriots were more successful. By the early eighteenth century they had extended the colony's trading boundaries all the way to the Mississippi and, in the process, established England's claims for territory that France and Spain considered theirs.[13]

From the first year of settlement there had been some sporadic trading with the various coastal nations, but it was not until Woodward negotiated a treaty with the Westo in 1674 that the deerskin trade began in earnest. Unlike ranching, which required virtually no capital, the Indian trade did. Trade goods such as cloth, brass kettles, rum, guns, powder, and ammunition had to be purchased before individual traders could set off for the interior. For those who had the capital, the deerskin trade was a golden opportunity. John Lawson in 1709 noted that Indian traders "soonest rais'd themselves of any People I have known in Carolina." A visible example of the profits made in the trade was Mulberry (1714) on the Cooper River, the home of Thomas Broughton, one of the colony's more successful traders.[14]

Because there were fortunes to be made in the Indian trade, there was a scramble to dominate it. In 1677 the proprietors declared a monopoly for themselves. Temporarily thwarted, former traders waited for their chance. Citing Westo raids on weak coastal nations as a menace to the security of the province, the colonists enticed the Savannah to join with them in defeating the Westo. Before the proprietors realized what had happened, their monopoly along with the Westo nation was broken. The Creek and later the Cherokee became trading partners with the English. Savannah Town, an outpost on the upper Savannah River, became a major trading center.

Within a few years there were numerous complaints made by friendly Indians about the conduct of traders. The deerskin traders were a rugged lot. Theirs was a dangerous business; however, their use of alcohol and intimidation did little to help the colony's relations with its Indian neighbors. Appeals to the government in Charleston to punish crooked traders seldom accomplished much. On occasion Indians took matters into their own hands: sometimes traders were roughed up, robbed, or killed.

Seeking another option, one small coastal nation, the Sewee, decided the best solution was to avoid dealing with the South Carolina traders. They believed that by trading directly with England they would get better prices for their skins. Thinking that England was just over the horizon, they built large dugout canoes, packed them with skins, and headed out to sea. An offshore storm capsized the canoes, and the Indians drowned.[15]

Although they were frequently mistreated and cheated, the natives of the country always came back to dealing with the South Carolinians. Because of the demand for leather in England, the South Carolinians paid more for skins and offered trade goods superior to those of their Spanish and French counterparts. The Indians developed an appetite for English trade goods, some becoming dependent upon them. For Cherokee males, trade was the equivalent of war in that certain trade goods brought status or increased the status of their owners. However, Cherokee uses of such items as kettles and ceramics often differed from Europeans'. For example, iron kettles were broken up to make hoes and ceramics to make decorative items.[16]

Efforts to regulate the trade continued intermittently throughout the proprietary period. In 1691 a tax was placed on skins and an attempt made to limit the traveling of traders in the interior. This and other half-hearted measures came to naught. One of the difficulties was that frequently the colony's governors and their friends were involved. The first serious attempt to regulate the trade came in 1707 when the Commons House created the Commission of the Indian Trade and elected commissioners. Thomas Nairne was named as the commission's agent, and he was to spend most of his time among the various nations. Nairne took his job seriously, filed charges against Governor Johnson's son-in-law, and ended up in jail. Eventually he was freed, but what few restraints the 1707 statute had included (such as outlawing the sale of alcohol to Indians) were rarely enforced. South Carolina would eventually pay a steep price for its unbridled free enterprise—the Yamassee War. However, in the meantime there was money to be made.[17]

At the end of the seventeenth century South Carolina exported 64,000 deerskins. Just seven years later the figure had risen to more than 121,000. Between 1699 and 1715 a yearly average of 54,000 skins were shipped from Charleston. It was no wonder that Nairne would write: "this Province owed for a long time its Subsistence to the Indian Trade, which is now the Main Branch of Traffick."[18]

The deerskin trade brought wealth to a few, but at the same time it strengthened the colony's economic position. The profits from the trade increased the amount of local capital available for investing in other enterprises and elevated Charleston's importance as a port in the Atlantic trading world. Later South Carolina's traders would face competition from Georgia and Virginia traders, but they still managed to garner the lion's share of the southeastern deerskin trade. In 1750 the number of skins leaving Charleston totaled 150,000 and the trade accounted for 20 percent of the colony's exports.[19]

For most of the proprietary period, associated with the deerskin trade was the illicit trade in Indian slaves. One of the temporary laws the proprietors decreed explicitly forbade the practice: "Noe Indian upon any occasion or pretense whatsoever is to be made a Slave, or without his owne consent be carried out of our Country."

The proprietors' noble aims were simply ignored.[20] The enslaving of Indians was not unique to South Carolina; in practice, it occurred in all colonies (Virginia, for example, was very much involved). However, in no other colony did it become a major commercial enterprise. In 1671 the first Indian slaves, members of the Cusso nation, were shipped to the West Indies. There was a practical reason for that. In Charleston, an Indian slave fetched about one-half the price of an African. There were better prices and markets in New England and the West Indies. By 1710 perhaps as many as twelve thousand Indians had been exported to England's northern and Caribbean colonies. Another fifteen hundred to eighteen hundred remained as slaves in South Carolina where they were about 12 percent of the total slave population.[21]

Initially the coastal nations were the source of Indian slaves, but Charleston traders encouraged their customers among the Westo, Savannah, Creek, Cherokee, and Chickasaw to supply slaves as well as deerskins. Much of the Indian warfare in the Southeast in the late seventeenth and early eighteenth centuries was encouraged by South Carolina Indian traders to increase the flow of captives for the Charleston market.[22]

The proprietors regularly condemned the trade, but their officials were helpless to stop it. Some did not even try. Maurice Mathews, one of the leading figures in the trade, was the colony's surveyor general. In 1685 the proprietors removed him from office because he trafficked in Indian slaves. The other major Indian slave traders were Arthur Middleton and James Moore, both members of the council and later governor. Moore's political foes, always looking for something to damage his reputation, falsely accused him of launching an invasion of Florida solely for the purpose of gathering slaves. England and Spain were at war, and the expedition against St. Augustine was sound strategy. Besides, when it came to Indian slavery, there were lots of dirty hands. Among the possessions of Thomas Nairne's widow were five Indian slaves.[23]

Just as nefarious in the eyes of many, especially English imperial officials, was the trade with pirates. Colonists who had emigrated from the West Indies were used to dealing with them. For the first twenty-five years of the colony's existence, the freebooters were welcomed in Charleston. They spent prodigally while ashore, and their binges put much-needed hard currency into circulation. Also, most South Carolinians were eager to purchase the pirates' booty at less than market prices. Proprietary officials winked at the enterprise because the pirates were good for the colony's economy.[24]

The proprietors brought increasing pressure to bear on their appointees. Joseph West and Robert Quarry were removed from the governorship because their working relationship with the buccaneers who stopped in South Carolina was too close. Joseph Morton's conduct was also questioned. Gov. Seth Sothell brazenly reopened the trade during his governorship—just one of several actions that led to his removal. In 1694, during Landgrave Thomas Smith's governorship, the trade was suppressed. Six years later seven pirates were hanged in Charleston. While some proprietary officials, such as Smith, did their best to halt the pirate trade, it is doubtful they could have succeeded had the colonists not been willing to cooperate. With increasing prosperity in the 1690s, South Carolinians realized that safe sea lanes were more important than good deals on stolen merchandise and a few gold coins.[25]

In addition to meat products and deerskins, rice and naval stores (tar, pitch, turpentine, and masts) joined the list of South Carolina exports. Rice production increased until about 1712 when output dropped considerably and remained low until the early 1720s. The decline in rice was the result of English mercantilist policies designed to make the empire self-sufficient. In 1690 parliament levied a three-pence sterling ($12.43) per pound tax on rice imported into England and followed that two years later with a 5 percent ad valorem duty. In 1705 rice was listed as an enumerated product under the navigation acts, meaning that it had to be shipped directly to England and then reexported to the Continent.[26]

The same year rice became an enumerated product, parliament passed legislation authorizing bounties on naval stores. England's merchant marine, defended by the royal navy, was the country's economic lifeline. Naval stores were essential for national defense, but they were imported from Sweden, a source of supply that could be cut in time of war. Again, thinking in mercantilist terms, England spent hard currency for products manufactured outside the empire. If the American colonies could be encouraged to produce naval stores, then the empire could become self-sufficient in a critical area.

The bounty was substantial. Each ton of pitch and tar would generate a £4 sterling ($310) bounty and each ton of turpentine £3 sterling ($233). One of the first colonists to operate a tar kiln was Daniel Axtell, a transplanted New Englander. Between 1704 and 1706 he produced a considerable portion of the colony's tar exports. Axtell's profitable enterprise was an example of what could be done. A combination of the end of Queen Anne's War (1702–1713) and a renewal of the bounty for eleven years (1714) had a phenomenal impact on South Carolina's economy. In the year ending June 1713 the colony exported 6,617 barrels of tar and pitch. Six years later that figure had increased more than 800 percent to 52,215 barrels.[27]

The increased production was also due to the effects of the Yamassee War. The war had disrupted the deerskin trade, decimated cattle ranching, and caused the abandonment of nearly one-half the colony's cultivated lands. However, it had no impact on the seemingly endless pine forests. Turning to naval stores was not only a sensible business decision, it was the only viable option that many colonists had if they wanted to turn a profit.

One of the reasons South Carolinians were able to produce so much tar and pitch was that they used a more cost-effective method than other American colonists or the Swedes. Rather than selecting green trees from which to render tar, South Carolinians chose already fallen trees they could identify as fatwood or lightwood. Otherwise, twenty live trees might have to be felled before one with a high resin content could be found. That, to South Carolinians, seemed like a terrible waste of labor. Besides, a fatwood tree produced three times as much tar as a green one. By simultaneously reducing labor costs and increasing output, the colonists were able to maximize their profits.[28]

There were some complaints in England that the colony's tar was "hot" and damaged the very cordage it was supposed to protect. Because of the crude earthen and wooden kilns used to render the tar, sometimes the tar and pitch (the residue of the distillation process that produced turpentine) contained dirt or leaves. However, the colony's agents obtained expert testimony that its naval stores were equal to Sweden's, which were the best on the world market. In 1717 a Board of Trade report on the naval stores industry contained nary a complaint about South Carolina's products. An affirmation of the quality of the colony's tar and pitch was the demand for it in England.[29]

By 1720 South Carolina produced more naval stores for the empire than any other colony, and the value of its exports to the mother country had risen from £11,000 sterling ($887,000) in 1710 to £60,000 sterling ($6.4 million). Gov. Robert Johnson gave most of the credit for the colony's prosperity to the bounty that spurred increased production of naval stores. After 1712 the value of exports exceeded that of imports, leaving South Carolinians with money to spend on British goods and slaves. Slaves were employed in the naval stores industry and in the rice fields. After 1724, when a renewal of the bounty required that American tar and pitch be produced according to the Swedish method (with green pine trees), South Carolinians turned quickly from naval stores to what they saw as the next moneymaker: rice.[30]

The colonists made a practical business decision, one that they had made before and would make again. In 1758 a Charleston merchant reported to the Royal Society for the Encouragement of Arts, Manufactures and Commerce: "Labour Comes very High & Dear, which makes the Planters only Apply Themselves to the Planting and Raising those Commodities that will bring Them in a Certain and present Advantage & Profitt." Ranching and naval stores were no longer cost-effective. "The planting of Rice, Indigo, &c.," he continued, "Answers to Afford the Value of High Labour."[31]

That rice emerged as South Carolina's leading export in the eighteenth century was not a surprise. It was one of the crops that the proprietors thought could be grown in the swampy lands of the coastal zone. However, because of the scarcity of labor and the opportunities for immediate returns in cattle ranching and naval stores, the rice industry did not take off immediately. Once an adequate labor supply was available in the eighteenth century, rice became to South Carolina what sugar was to the West Indies and tobacco to the Chesapeake.[32]

Who introduced rice into the colony has become a subject of debate. The traditional story has a ship captain from Madagascar giving Dr. Henry Woodward some seeds from which sprang the colony's rice industry. More recent accounts of the introduction of rice credit Africans with bringing the seeds as well as the knowledge of rice culture to the colony. The proprietors and settlers also knew that rice was grown in Italy. A closer source was the Chesapeake region where rice was grown in the seventeenth century. Since the first settlers traded with Virginia for cattle and other goods, they may have obtained the first rice from there.[33]

In the seventeenth century rice was cultivated on dry land. However, in the eighteenth century most planters shifted to growing rice in freshwater inland swamps. These were relatively small areas, easily cleared. Usually a portion of the swamp was dammed to create a reservoir to provide a reliable water supply. With regular irrigation, these inland swamp fields produced higher yields and profits. In the 1730s some planters began to experiment with tidal cultivation, damming and diking lowland areas adjacent to the colony's tidal rivers and using the ebb and flow of the tides to irrigate their fields. Because of the tremendous costs involved in creating the fields for tidal cultivation, few planters utilized this method until after the American Revolution.[34]

The swamps were "the Golden Mines of *Carolina*; from them all our Rice is produced, consequently they are the Source of infinite Wealth, and will always reward the industrious and persevering Planter." It was not, however, the planter who made the swamps the colony's gold mines; it was his black laborers. In more ways than one they were "a considerable part of the riches of the province."[35]

Enslaved Africans had been part of the colony's labor force from the earliest days of settlement. Some were involved in the cultivation of rice as early as the 1690s; however, most were employed in cattle ranching and naval stores. In the 1720s white South Carolinians turned to rice, a labor-intensive crop. During the decade of the 1720s some 8,817 slaves were imported into South Carolina; more than three-fourths of these were purchased after 1724. Thus, it appears that these slaves were destined for work in the rice fields.[36]

It was evident that whites in eighteenth-century South Carolina understood the ethnic backgrounds of the Africans sold in the Charleston slave markets. They had a decided preference for individuals from known rice-growing areas such as the Windward Coast. The debate may never be settled as to who brought the first seeds; however, there can be no question as to the key role that Africans played in the production of rice.[37]

Some West Africans knew how to clear swamps, build dikes, and use the tides to irrigate fields. All understood the importance of coating the seed with clay so that it would not float when fields were flooded. When the grain ripened, they sent their children into the fields to shoo away the rice birds (bobolinks)—just as they had in

Coiled work baskets made from rushes (nineteenth century) and used on Raccoon Island, Colleton County. Courtesy, Edisto Island Museum. Photograph by James C. Linder.

A typical wooden mortar and pestle used to knock the outer husks off rice. Courtesy, Jennings-Brown House Collection, Marlboro County Historical Society.

Africa. After the rice was harvested, the grain was beaten from the stalks by flailing sticks and then large, flat fanning baskets were used to separate it from the chaff. Finally, the rice was husked using a mortar and pestle. The flailing stick, the fanning basket, and the husking of rice with mortar and pestle were all West African rice processing techniques.[38]

By the 1770s white South Carolinians assumed automatically that European procedures and ideas were superior to those from Africa. The fragmentary evidence from the seventeenth and early eighteenth centuries indicates that it was not always so. In the first fifty years of settlement, when trying to make the wilderness productive, white settlers may have been inclined to learn from their black laborers.[39]

During the colonial period increased productivity had little to do with technological advances (except in those rare instances where planters used the tidal cultivation method). Rather, it appears that economies of scale and the widespread use of the task system contributed to the increase in output. Improved transportation and port facilities and better packaging reduced costs and increased profits.[40]

One of the most important economies of scale was the size of a working plantation. As early as 1710 Thomas Nairne recommended that anyone interested in a good annual return should invest £1,000 sterling ($81,000) in a one-thousand-acre plantation with a labor force of 30 slaves. The actual number of acres in a plantation was not as important as the availability of good rice swamp. Thus, while the acreage might vary, South Carolina planters seemed to have settled on 30 to 50 slaves as the ideal size for a working plantation. Large land and slave owners broke up their holdings into smaller production units. Ralph Izard Jr., for example, owned 342 slaves. There were 10 slaves at his Charleston town house and 69 at Burton, his residence plantation. The remaining 263 were divided among five working plantations. Thomas Elliott of St. Andrew's Parish had two plantations and evenly divided his 104 slaves between them. John Ainslie of St. George's Dorchester, who raised thoroughbreds as well as rice, had 134 slaves at his residence, Windsor Hill, and working plantations in St. Paul's (51 slaves) and St. Matthew's (30 slaves).[41]

Slaves were an economic investment in South Carolina and paid for themselves in four to five years. Eighty percent of Nairne's suggested investment of £1,000 sterling ($81,000) was in human capital, so it was in the planter's interest to see that his investment survived and produced. The development of the task system on the colony's rice plantations increased productivity and profits for owners and, at the same time, enabled blacks to maintain a certain amount of control over their own lives. Under the task system, a slave was given a specific job each day, depending upon the season. Wise planters saw to it that overseers and drivers allocated chores equitably so that there would be no cause for unrest. When slaves completed their daily assignments, their time was their own. Within limits, owners appeared unconcerned as to what slaves did with their free time.[42]

As a result of economies of scale and the task system, rice production increased.

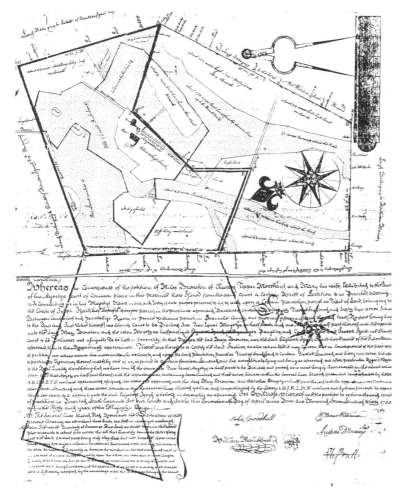

A 1760 plat of Miles Brewton's plantation in what is now Beaufort County showing indigo and inland rice fields. Court of Common Pleas, Writs of Partition, 1749–1774. Courtesy, South Carolina Department of Archives and History.

In the early eighteenth century, before the development of inland swamp fields, the average yield was 1,000 pounds of clean rice per acre; by the 1770s it was 1,500 pounds. Per worker the increase was even larger. In 1748 an average hand produced 2,250 pounds; on the eve of the American Revolution the figure had risen to 3,000–3,600 pounds. Even those slaves who were not field hands (the very young, the aged, and the infirm) were productive because they could be used to grow food crops or tend to stock and thus support themselves and others.[43]

The rate of return an individual might get from his investment depended upon the price of exports. Early in the century Nairne had estimated annual returns as great as 30 percent. A few industrious (and lucky) planters did reap proceeds as high as 33 percent, while less able ones got only 7 percent. By midcentury, however, as long as the price was "tolerable," planters reasonably might expect a return on their investments of anywhere from 16 percent to 25 percent.[44]

While returns were high, so were the costs of getting rice to market. More than half the proceeds from the sale of rice were eaten up with shipping, insurance, and handling costs. There was not much that South Carolina's planters could do about shipping fees and insurance. However, they expected the provincial government to provide the infrastructure that would make it easier to market their produce. The Commons House of Assembly responded by spending public funds on numerous projects. Commissions all across the lowcountry built roads, bridges, and ferries; cleared streams of obstructions; opened "cuts" between rivers and through swamps; and erected lighthouses and beacons. Just as important as the building of the colony's infrastructure was maintaining it—something the commission system did quite effectively. Whether by land or water, it was relatively easy and inexpensive to get produce to Charleston.[45]

Depending upon the planter, rice was transported to Charleston in either bags or casks. From there it was exported in casks of uniform size. In the 1720s rice barrels held 350 pounds of clean rice; by midcentury they held 525. Master coopers, such as Gabriel Guignard, Daniel Saylor, and Thomas Vardell, produced the barrels. Standardized sizes for the rice barrels were enforced by the city's packers. Usually these public officials were elected annually from their ranks of the city's master coopers. By enforcing standardized size and high quality in rice barrels, the packers helped with the marketing of the colony's most important export.[46]

By the early 1720s South Carolina was exporting an average of more than six million pounds of rice. A decade later that figure had increased to nearly seventeen million pounds. Over the next ten years exports rose to thirty million pounds. Then, for two decades rice production and exports stagnated. There were several reasons for this. The War of Jenkins' Ear (1739–1748) and the War of Austrian Succession (1745–1748) disrupted the colony's normal trade patterns and increased freight and insurance rates. Overproduction and low demand in England and Portugal caused prices to drop disastrously from nearly ten shillings sterling ($56.78) per hundredweight in 1738 to just a little over two shillings sterling ($12.39) in 1745 and 1746. During the 1740s few slaves were imported because of the prohibitive duty the colony imposed after the Stono Rebellion. Without an influx of additional slaves, planters could not bring many new fields into production. The amount of rice exported in 1762 was virtually the same as what had been shipped in 1742. However, in the last few years before the American Revolution, rice production more than doubled to sixty-six million pounds. Not only did production increase, but in the ten years from 1766 to 1775 prices were higher than they had ever been at any other period in the colony's history. There was good reason to call rice "Carolina gold."[47]

While rice eventually rebounded, when it was "a Verry dull Commodity all over Europe & America" during the 1740s, planters searched for other sources of revenue. Among the plants that Captain West had planted in his experimental garden at Albemarle Point was indigo. It is not clear whether he had seeds from Guatemala

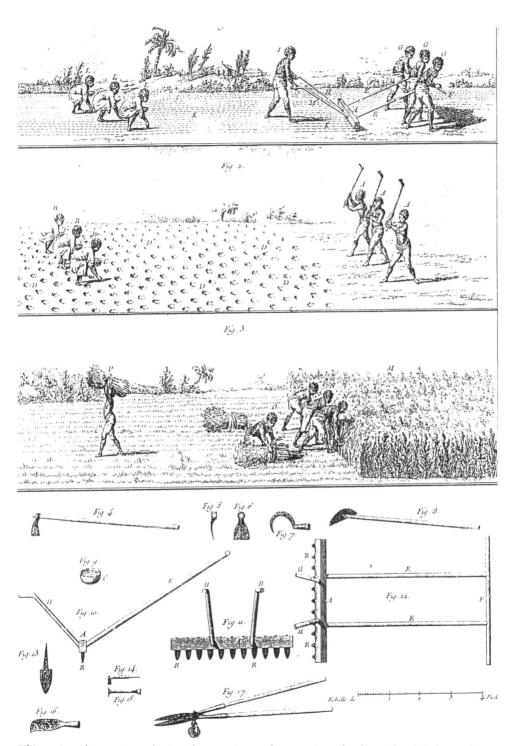

This series of engravings depicts the growing and processing of indigo. Plate IX shows the planting and harvesting of indigo and the tools necessary for its cultivation. From Beauvais de Raseau, *L'art de l'indigotier* (1770). Courtesy, South Caroliniana Library.

(*Indigfera suffruticosa* Mill.) or French (*Indigofera tinctoria* L.) indigo. There is also the possibility that he might have experimented with a native Carolina indigo (*Indigofera caroliniana* Mill.). As was the case with other exotics in the garden (notably rice and cotton), the settlers discovered that indigo would grow in South Carolina; however, the quality was not as good as that from the French and Spanish West Indies. The indigo industry also required labor and capital, both of which were in short supply. Therefore, like most of the other early experiments, indigo was discarded as a commercial venture. A few colonists, notably some Huguenots, continued to grow indigo, evidently for domestic use.[48]

The slump in the world rice markets and the disruption of sources of supply caused by the wars of the 1740s provided an opportunity for the introduction of indigo as a staple crop. Traditionally, Eliza Lucas, a young teenager, has been given the credit for reintroducing indigo into South Carolina. However, one of the individuals who helped her learn the proper way to process the plant was Andrew Deveaux, a Huguenot who had been growing it for some time. Nevertheless, Lucas's role was crucial in that her efforts alerted her fellow planters to the possibility of another staple crop. In 1739 she planted seeds her father had sent her from Antigua, and after five years of experimentation she was able to produce seventeen pounds of dye. She willingly shared her success with others, and by 1747 South Carolina exported 138,000 pounds. As was the case with cattle ranching, rice, and naval stores, it did not take South Carolinians long to exploit an economic opportunity. Then, when the war was over and rice prices rose, they just as quickly turned back to "Carolina gold." One of the reasons was that the colony's indigo had difficulty competing with the superior products of the French and Spanish West Indies. By 1752 exports had declined to only a few thousand pounds.[49]

South Carolina's agent in London, James Crockatt, urged British imperial officials to seize an opportunity to reduce indigo imports from rival empires. Crockatt made a convincing argument, and parliament passed a bounty in 1749. The bounty boosted prices artificially by about 20 percent and enabled London merchants to pay South Carolinians higher prices for their product. Even with the attraction of the bounty, planters saw better returns from rice. It was not until war erupted again that indigo became a true staple crop in South Carolina.[50]

The French and Indian War (1756–1763) made it more difficult for British textile manufacturers to get West Indian indigo, and once again there was a lucrative market for South Carolina's. This time not only did lowcountry planters turn to indigo, but so did small farmers in the backcountry. It was grown commercially as far inland as Orangeburg, Camden, and Ninety Six. Once the war ended, indigo had become a second staple to rice in the colony's economy. From 1763 until the American Revolution, the market for South Carolina indigo continued to grow despite its reputed poor quality.[51]

The poor quality probably was due to improper processing. In all stages of the

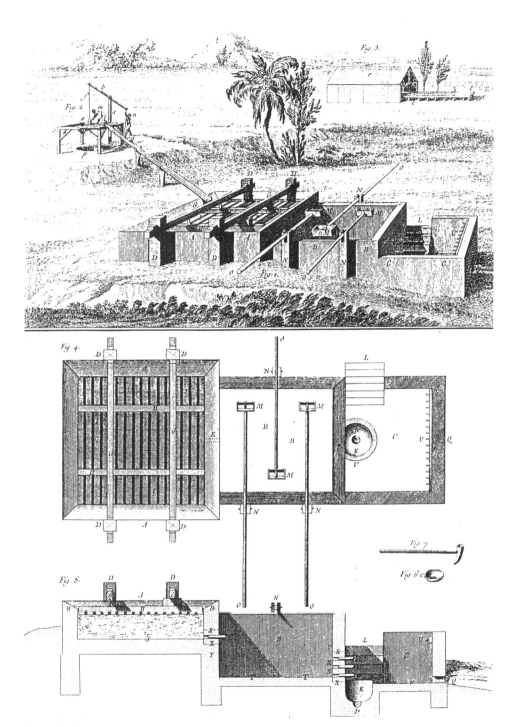

Plate IV shows the series of three vats used to process the indigo. The plants were steeped in the first vat. The liquid was then piped to the second tank where paddles agitated it until it reached the proper color. The liquid was then piped to the third tank where a mudlike substance precipitated into the bottom of the vat.

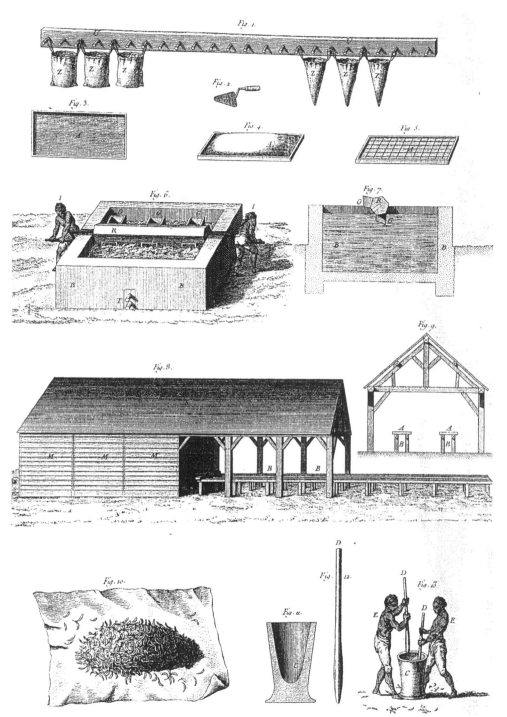

Plate V shows the final processing. The indigo mud was taken from the settler tank and placed in linen bags to drain. Afterward it was put into flat boxes to cure under sheds away from direct sunlight.

processing (harvesting, steeping, beating, settling, drying) timing was crucial. If a mistake were made, the result would be "either bad *Indigo,* or none at all." South Carolinians, unlike the French, used limewater to cause the indigo particles to precipitate out more rapidly. Some blamed this processing shortcut for the poor quality of the finished product.[52]

In 1762, in order to improve the quality of its exports, Moses Lindo was appointed as the colony's indigo inspector. For ten years he struggled in vain to fulfill his charge. Finally he resigned because he refused to approve the export of shoddy merchandise. In the London market it was automatically assumed that South Carolina indigo was of a poor grade. Some planters blamed a conspiracy by London merchants to drive down the price for their own advantage. That may have been true as a number of planters (most of them from Colleton County) were renowned for the high quality of their indigo: John Bee, James Stobo, Robert Sams, Dr. John Lining, Dr. George Mitchell, Isaac Hayne, Charles Pinckney, and John Hudson. Those who took the time and effort to produce indigo that could be "mistaken for Guatemala," received little more than those who took shortcuts. Therefore, it is hardly surprising that most producers sacrificed quality for quantity. Why not maximize production (and profits) if buyers were not going to pay for a superior product? Production skyrocketed, and in 1775 South Carolina exported in excess of one million pounds of the dye.[53]

Indigo was the only staple other than rice developed during the colonial period—not that South Carolinians did not try to find other profitable exports. Agricultural experimentation was encouraged by the Royal Society for the Encouragement of Arts, Manufactures and Commerce of London, which offered premiums or prizes for a variety of items. In 1771 the society awarded a premium of £50 sterling ($4,200) to Christopher Sherb, a German immigrant from the Neckar River in Württemberg, for his Rhenish-like wine. Sherb lived on the Broad River in Orangeburg Township where he had more than sixteen hundred vines. Lt. Gov. William Bull heard about Sherb's vineyards and interceded with the society on his behalf. The production of export-quality wine was something that colonists had long thought possible, especially since grapes (muscadines, bullises, and scuppernongs) grew wild. However, Sherb's success was an aberration.[54]

The society also offered premiums for growing mulberry trees (to feed silkworms) and hemp. Silk making was another one of those exotic industries for which there had been great hope. In the early eighteenth century some Huguenots tried to raise silkworms, but like their neighbors, they turned to more profitable pursuits. During the 1740s there was a brief revival of silk production in South Carolina (again using European immigrants), and one hundred pounds were exported annually. The industry, however, succumbed to cost-effectiveness. Labor, be it slave or free, was simply too dear.[55]

Hemp, on the other hand, was profitable. The provincial government offered a bounty of twenty shillings sterling ($105) for every hundred pounds of "Good and Merchantable Hemp" brought to Charleston for market. Hemp was a backcountry crop and, along with indigo, gave individuals a chance to accumulate capital to expand their operations.[56]

The colony's merchants and planters had correspondents all over the empire and were always on the lookout for something that might become a moneymaker. Dr. Alexander Garden, Henry Laurens, William Bull, and Hector Berringer de Beaufain either experimented with exotic plants or encouraged others to do so. Robert Pringle tried pistachios, olives, and mahogany. The pistachio seeds never germinated; the olives did not taste right; and the mahogany seedlings could not take even the mild frosts of South Carolina. His other major experiment—oranges—was briefly successful. In 1747 South Carolina exported nearly three hundred thousand oranges that were "of the Sour or Seville Kind." A hard freeze in the winter of 1747 killed the orange trees, but in the 1750s there were again some for export. After another killing winter, South Carolinians realized that the colony's climate was not tropical enough for citrus.[57]

Nonagricultural ventures included John Bartlam's potteries at Cainhoy and Charleston and William Hill's and Isaac Hayne's Aera Furnace in New Acquisition District (York County). While interesting, they had little impact on the overall economy of the province.[58]

Although there were smaller ports at Georgetown and Beaufort, Charleston was the funnel through which the colony's produce passed on its way to world markets. By the 1680s the exportation of deerskins, timber, and foodstuffs helped establish Charleston as a port in the Atlantic trading community. In the eighteenth century naval stores, rice, and indigo made South Carolina a major trading destination.[59]

Charleston's merchants were key figures in the creation of the colony's trading network. It was they who purchased a planter's crops, arranged for the freight and insurance, and negotiated with potential buyers. They also imported British manufactured goods and products from other colonies. These were then resold to smaller merchants in Beaufort, Edentown, New Brunswick, and Wilmington in North Carolina; Fredericka and Savannah in Georgia; and the South Carolina towns of Beaufort, Georgetown, Will Town, and Pine Tree Hill (Camden). After 1763 Charleston's economic hegemony extended to the Florida ports of St. Augustine, Pensacola, and Mobile.[60]

England was South Carolina's principal trading partner, and most Charleston merchants had arrangements with one or more London firms. A 1730 act of Parliament permitted the shipping of rice directly to Portugal but did not alter trade patterns much. For example, during the 1730s, even with markets in the West Indies, New England, and Portugal, South Carolina shipped nearly three-fourths of its rice directly to England. From there it was reexported to Holland and Germany. With its exports of raw materials and agricultural products and its importation of British manufactured goods, South Carolina was a model mercantilist colony. "That makes us," reported Gov. James Glen, "perhaps more Valuable to our Mother Country than any other Province on the Continent."[61]

As the value of South Carolina's exports grew, so, too, did its importance to the empire. At the beginning of the eighteenth century, the colony accounted for only about 3 percent of the value of goods exported from America to the mother country. By 1720 the figure had risen to 15 percent, and fifty years later it was 29 percent. By the 1770s, the mean value of South Carolina's exports was £343,462 sterling ($27.7 million). Not only did the colony's exports rise in real value during the colonial period, but the real cost of British imports declined. This further increased the accumulation of capital in the colony.[62]

South Carolinians used their capital to help fuel the colony's economic expansion. Individuals, churches, lodges, and charitable organizations advertised that they had money to lend at the going rate of 10 percent prior to 1748 and 8 percent afterward. In 1745 the three largest planters in St. James Goose Creek Parish (Henry Izard, James Kinloch, and Sarah Wilkinson Middleton), on average, lent out £3,500 sterling ($441,000) at interest. With its growing economy and guaranteed interest rates, the colony also attracted capital from England and the West Indies. The flood of cash available for economic development was invested primarily in land and slaves. With more land put into production and a larger labor force, South Carolina's economy was a cash cow for those fortunate enough to have a stake.[63]

In 1751 James Glen reported to the Board of Trade that five thousand had "plenty of the good things of Life"; another five thousand had "some of the Conveniencys of Life"; and ten thousand had "the Necessarys of Life"—accounting for 80 percent of the white population. There were five thousand or six thousand more who eked out a "bare subsistence." Even for those living on the margin, South Carolina was considered to be "a good poor man's country."[64]

Thomas Nairne had described how a person with a £1,000 sterling ($81,000) investment could live well. He also noted that for £100 sterling ($8,100), one could live in South Carolina with "tolerable Decency." Then, "from this small Beginning, by moderate Industry, accompanied with the Blessing of Heaven, a Man may get a competent Estate." Thomas Heyward, the founder of one of the colony's wealthiest families, fit Nairne's description perfectly. He was a hatmaker by profession but by his death in 1737 had acquired more than 500 acres and eighteen slaves. In 1771 his son, Daniel, was considered "the greatest planter in the province."[65]

Prosperity was not confined to lowcountry rice planters. Henry Laurens estimated that a small backcountry planter with nine to twelve hands planting hemp and indigo could realize an annual income of between £250 and £500 sterling ($22,000–$44,000). Many settlers in the area lived "comfortably in respect to every article necessary for the support of Life."[66]

While the South Carolina backcountry was beginning to prosper, the lowcoun-

Table 8.1

COMPARATIVE PRIVATE WEALTH

County/Area	1774 £ Sterling	1996 $
Charleston District, SC	2,337.7	194,203
Anne Arundel County, MD	660.4	54,892
Charlotte/Halifax Counties, VA	564.4	46,913
Philadelphia, PA	396.7	32,974
Suffolk County, MA	312.3	25,959
New York (hybrid)	278.0	23,108

Alice Hanson Jones, *Wealth of a Nation to Be: The American Colonies on the Eve of Revolution* (New York: Columbia University Press, 1980), 10, 170–71, 377–79.

Mr. Peter Manigault and His Friends (1750s) by George Roupell. Courtesy, Winterthur Museum.

try was already wealthy. The mean aggregate wealth per inventoried estate in the Charleston District was £2,337.7 sterling ($194,311). No other colony even came close. Anne Arundel County, Maryland, the next wealthiest population, was worth less than 30 percent of South Carolina's. By 1774 the lowcountry had more total wealth than many nations of the world today. Nowhere else in British North America did such a large percentage of the population live so well.[67]

When a tabulation was done of individuals of the ten richest men in British North America, the wealthiest was Peter Manigault of St. James Goose Creek with a net worth of £32,737.8 sterling ($2,721,185). Behind Manigault was a New Englander whose estate was worth less than one-half his. The remaining eight were all South Carolinians: Elijah Postell of St. George Dorchester, Alexander Peronneau and John Ainslie of Charleston, John Cattell of St. Andrew's, Benjamin Williamson of St. Paul's, Richard Capers of Christ Church, Dr. Archibald McNeil of St. George Dorchester, and Christopher Jenkins of St. John's Colleton.[68]

At the other end of the scale, none of the ten poorest individuals in America was from South Carolina. This is not to say that there were not any poor in the colony; there certainly were. The five thousand to six thousand that Governor Glen reported had only a "bare subsistence" were scattered throughout the province, but there was a concentration of them in Charleston. Prior to midcentury most of the "deserving poor" of the city were the elderly and infirm. During the last twenty-five years of the colonial period, the largest number of poor cases included women and small children. It was up to the churchwardens of St. Philip's to determine whether a person were sent to the hospital-workhouse, placed in the city orphanage or a foster home, apprenticed to an artisan, or provided financial assistance. During the 1760s about 2.5 percent of the city's population received some sort of public assistance. The scarcity of records makes it difficult to determine if the colony were a "good poor man's country." There were compassion and assistance for those who were deemed truly unfortunate, but little sympathy for those who failed economically.[69]

In South Carolina achievement was measured by material success. The aggressive mores brought from the West Indies might have been refined over the course of the eighteenth century, but they still formed the core of the colony's ethos. The source of a person's wealth was not important. The individual who founded a family's fortune might have dealt with pirates, sold Indian slaves, been a trader in deerskins, raised swine, run a cattle ranch, managed a Charleston mercantile establishment, or grown rice and indigo. No one, for example, shunned Miles Brewton, Henry Laurens, or William Wragg because their wealth came from the slave trade. South Carolina in the eighteenth century was an open society, one in which an individual with "moderate Industry, accompanied with the Blessing of Heaven" could build a successful enterprise upon which he could "live very handsomely."[70]

Moving into the ranks of those who had "plenty of the good things of Life" was a bit more complicated than Nairne made it out to be. External demand and world markets had a great deal to do with colonial South Carolina's economic success. So, too, did sensible business decisions. Colonists exploited whatever resources were at hand and did not hesitate to abandon a venture if there were better opportunities elsewhere. Even though colonial South Carolina was relatively small in terms of area of settlement and population, South Carolinians pursued potential sources of income with surprising alacrity and vigor. Rice production increased more than sixfold in the first decade of the eighteenth century. Naval stores exports, despite the Yamassee War, rose 800 percent in six years. During the 1720s, when rice supplanted naval stores, rice production tripled to more than 16 million pounds. Three years after Eliza Lucas successfully produced 17 pounds of indigo, the colony exported 137,000 pounds. The speed with which the colonists responded to new opportunities was greatly assisted by the labor of thousands of enslaved Africans. Because South Carolinians were willing to exploit whatever was available, make changes, and take chances, they were able to create a prosperous society that was the envy of British North America.

Chapter Nine

EVERYDAY LIFE IN COLONIAL SOUTH CAROLINA

Black and white all mixed together
Inconstant, strange, unhealthful weather
Burning heat and chilling cold
Dangerous to both young and old
Boistrous winds and heavy rains
Fevers and rheumatic pains
Agues plenty without doubt
Sores, boils, the prickly heat and gout
Musquitoes on the skin make blotches
Centipedes and large cockroaches
Frightful creatures in the water
Porpoises, sharks and alligators
Houses built on barren land
No lamps or lights, but streets of sand
Pleasant walks, if you can find 'em
Scandalous tongues, if any mind 'em
The markets dear and little money
Large potatoes, sweet as honey
Water bad, past all drinking
Men and women without thinking
Everything at a high price
But rum, hominy, and rice
Many a widow not unwilling
Many a beau not worth a shilling
Many a bargain, if you can strike it
This is Charlestowne, How do you like it?
       Captain Martin, 1769

*I*N 1769 an English sea captain described everyday life in South Carolina's capital city. What he said about Charleston applied to the remainder of the lowcountry and, with only one or two exceptions, to the backcountry as well.

The first thing that visitors, especially those from northern colonies, observed was the diversity of the population. Because they were so struck with seeing numerous black faces on Charleston's streets, observers tended to overestimate their numbers. In 1765 a Philadelphian gave the city's population as five thousand whites and twenty thousand blacks (four times the actual number). Throughout the colonial period the city's population was roughly half black and half white. The remainder of the lowcountry was another matter. In 1770 there were more than three blacks for every white; in the backcountry there were five whites for every black.[1]

South Carolina was one of the fastest growing areas in British North America thanks to the importation of thousands of enslaved Africans into the lowcountry and the migration of thousands of Scots-Irish, German, and English settlers from Pennsylvania and Virginia into the backcountry. What makes this growth all the more astonishing is that not until the 1770s did the population sustain itself naturally.[2]

There were several reasons for the inability of both black and white Carolinians to increase naturally. First, as in most colonial societies, there was a gender imbalance: more men than women among the population. For most whites it was a choice; for blacks the usual ratio was to import two males for every female. The other, more alarming reason was the tremendously high death rate.[3]

While life on the frontier was uncertain everywhere, in South Carolina death by disease made life more precarious than anywhere else in British North America. The early accounts of the province extolled the healthy nature of the air and climate. Any "raging Sickness" was believed to be the result of an infection's being brought from the tropics or intemperance. "The air of this Country," wrote John Oldmixon, "is healthy." In one respect these accounts were correct: the diseases that felled so many settlers were not indigenous; they were brought in either by the settlers themselves or by ships that stopped at Charleston. Yellow fever, malaria, smallpox, and typhus came with Europeans and Africans. So, too, did the carriers of filth and disease, the *A. aegypti* mosquito, black rat, and cockroach. All thrived in the colony's semitropical climate.[4]

Between 1670 and 1775 South Carolinians faced fifty-nine major epidemics. Yellow fever struck eighteen times, smallpox nine, and influenza four. Some years colonists had to confront multiple threats. In 1718, 1732, and 1758 South Carolinians suffered with both yellow fever and smallpox. In addition, malaria became endemic. One visitor reported that he had never seen "air so unhealthful." The colonists had "had fevers all year long from which those attacked seldom recover."[5]

While malaria, by itself, was not necessarily a killer, it could be fatal to young children and pregnant women. Malaria also weakened individuals and made them more susceptible to measles, whooping cough, and dysentery, as well as the more serious illnesses. Childhood mortality may have been as high as 80 percent. In Christ Church Parish eighty-six of the one hundred children whose baptisms were registered were buried before their twentieth birthdays. Of those who reached age twenty in St. John's Berkeley, one-third never reached forty. In Charleston between 1720 and 1750, there were 2,883 burials versus 863 baptisms. Although port city population data can be questioned (because of the high number of transients), it is interesting to note that Charleston's grim statistics mirrored those of Bridgetown, Barbados.[6]

For almost a century South Carolinians lived near their rice fields, the perfect breeding grounds for mosquitoes. Although most whites realized the swamps were unhealthy, they still chose to reside there. Robert Wells worried about his wife's visiting a John's Island plantation where "Agues and Fevers" lurked everywhere. Not until the latter part of the eighteenth century did white residents seek refuge inland at Pinopolis and Summerville or on the coast at Pawley's Island. The largest number of deaths in colonial South Carolina occurred between August and November, the sickly months.[7]

For black Carolinians, malaria and yellow fever were not as deadly as for whites. Because the final stages and harvesting of both rice and indigo occurred during the sickliest months of the year, blacks were more exposed than whites to the deadly environment. Since the eighteenth century it had been a truism that black labor was "necessary," given the climate. Modern medical research has explained why. Certain West Africans developed the sickle-cell trait that gave those who had it better resistance to malaria. In the case of yellow fever, some West Africans may have had mild cases as children. There is also the possibility that others had a genetic protection against the disease. While malaria and yellow fever might not have been as deadly for blacks as whites, the death rate for Africans was also horrible. One-third of those brought to South Carolina died within three years.[8]

"Seasoning" was something that colonists understood for both whites and blacks. Generally, it was thought that if a person survived the first sickly season, then he or she had a good chance of making it. A year or so might enable a person to adjust to the colony's climate, but given the number of diseases to which one could be exposed, "seasoning" was a cruel myth. James Moore, for example, a settler seasoned both in Barbados and South Carolina, died in either October or November 1706 (probably from yellow fever).[9]

Since the majority of the colony's Indian population lived in the piedmont away from swamps, neither malaria nor yellow fever was much of a threat to them. Smallpox, on the other hand, was another matter. It may have been introduced into South Carolina during the sixteenth century. Either smallpox or typhus may have been responsible for a great many deaths before Soto's expedition.

The 1760 smallpox epidemic was especially virulent for everyone in the colony. Instead of Europeans' infecting the Indians, in this instance the situation was reversed. The disease broke out in December 1759 among the Cherokee, who infected members of Governor Lyttelton's expeditionary force. The soldiers brought it back to Charleston where the disease spread rapidly. The city's physicians, led by Dr. Alexander Garden, advocated inoculation, but hundreds of the city's residents died, including many who had been inoculated. The *South Carolina Gazette* launched a campaign against inoculation, and in May 1760 the Commons House forbade the practice. It is estimated that of Charleston's 8,000 residents, probably 6,000 contracted the disease and 730 died. Among the Indians the results were even more staggering. Perhaps as many as one-third of the Cherokee succumbed and nearly two-thirds of the Catawba died. By late 1760 "Rum, War and Small-Pox" had reduced the Catawba to fewer than 500 souls. That meant that since the late seventeenth century, nearly nine of every ten Catawba had perished.[10]

While the settlers' death rate was nothing like that of the native population's, death was something with which South Carolinians had to deal all too frequently. Diseases and accidents left vacant places in family circles. Nothing, however, was more sorrowful than the death of children, even though it happened with sad regularity.

Couples tended to have large numbers of children. This was true whether they were members of the lowcountry elite or Scots-Irish backcountry pioneers. Henry and Eleanor Ball Laurens were married in 1750. She died twenty years later after giving birth to their twelfth child. "Poor Mrs. Laurens has been unlucky again this Year," wrote Henry in 1768. "She is confined to her Chamber (as usual once in the round of twelve Months) under the mortifying reflections which arise upon the loss of a very fine girl." Only four of the twelve Laurens children reached adulthood. Upcountry women were "burthen'd with Young Children," sometimes ten or fifteen. The mortality rate in the backcountry is not known. The population would not have suffered from malaria or yellow fever, but it would have been susceptible to smallpox and other "Epidemic Disorders, which when they happen, makes Great Havoc among them."[11]

With the colony's high infant mortality rate, the odds were against a woman's seeing more than one or two of her children reach the age of twenty—assuming, of course, that she lived that long. With malaria endemic and the threat of other diseases, pregnancy was a chancy business. Frequent pregnancies ("once in the round of twelve Months") were not unusual. Childbirth was sometimes fatal for both mother and infant. It made little difference whether a woman lived in a Charleston mansion, a backcountry log hut, or a lowcountry slave cabin. The mortality rate for females was, not unexpectedly, higher than that for males. When a person was especially long-lived, it was news. Elizabeth Wilson Baker died 13 August 1734, just five days shy of her 104th birthday. Born in Wiltshire, England, she had lived there for twenty-seven years, in Barbados for twenty-three, and in South Carolina for fifty-four. She had twelve children, twenty-five grandchildren, and forty-five great-grandchildren. On the day she died, a great-granddaughter gave birth to her only great-great-grandchild (a girl).[12]

It was not uncommon for entire families to be wiped out in a short period of

Detail from the gravestone of the three sons of Richard and Mary Savage. All three boys (ages three, five, and seven) died within the space of ten days, probably of scarlatina anginosa and a fatal croup. Photograph by Suzanne C. Linder. Used by permission, Circular Congregational Churchyard, Charleston, South Carolina.

time. The Reverend Mr. Lonsdale (rector of Prince William Parish), his wife, and his five children were all "cut off by the Endemic Fever that rages here, and not one now left." During the sickly season of 1767 Benjamin Backhouse, a Charleston tavern keeper, died in August; his daughter Eleanor in September; and his wife Catherine in October. As was the case with the Lonsdales, there were no survivors. In August 1775 Miles and Mary Izard Brewton and their two children sailed for Philadelphia. The ship was lost at sea.[13]

Given the transitory nature of life, it is not surprising that South Carolinians made out their wills, especially before they embarked on some sort of adventure. Lachlan Shaw made his in February 1761 before "going into Service against the Indians." It was proved five months later. Wills also gave individuals the chance to get the last word from beyond the grave. Elizabeth Kalteisen bequeathed her husband one shilling sterling ($2.72) only because the law said that a wife must leave her husband something. In perhaps one of the more famous wills written in the colony, Sir John Colleton left his second wife expenses to move out of Fairlawn, the family home, and a watch so that she could "make better use of the time to come than she has of time past."[14]

In addition to bequests, it was common for individuals to include their funeral plans in their wills. For much of the eighteenth century mourning was elaborate; special clothes, gloves, or rings were to be purchased for family members, pallbearers, or friends. However, by the 1760s mourning was less formal, and black crepe armbands for men and black ribbons for women were considered appropriate. Usually family members or friends of the deceased were pallbearers, but Samuel Wragg (who had made his fortune in the slave trade) named four black men who were to carry him to his grave. Coffins were made of cedar, cypress, or mahogany. A plain cypress coffin for a child cost £5 currency ($60) or less, while an adult's that was "black, full-trimmed" could cost as much as £100 currency ($1,200).[15]

Funeral services varied according to a person's religious persuasion and social rank. The Anglican burial service was brief, while a funeral at Charleston's Scots Presbyterian Church included "a sort of sermon, prayers, and singing." When Gov. Robert Johnson died in 1735, South Carolina held its first state funeral. Two companies of militia served as an honor guard, royal councillors were his pallbearers, and members of the Commons House were official mourners. Johnson was interred near the altar of St. Philip's Church. Black South Carolinians honored their dead with the same pageantry and display their ancestors had used in West Africa. Grave sites were typically marked with pieces of pottery or some personal possession of the deceased.[16]

Burial sites were scattered all over the colony. Most churches had burying grounds, but it was not unusual for families to have their own private graveyards. In the countryside slaves were sometimes buried in the white family's cemetery, but it was more usual for them to have their own. In 1746 one of the first central cemeteries in the colony was created on the outskirts of Charleston for the city's black residents.[17]

Although people died during every month of the year, the sickly season (August to November) was one of the accepted cycles in the rhythm of life and death in colonial South Carolina. The winter months (December to February) brought relief from the heat and fevers as cooler temperatures killed off the mosquitoes. Northwesterly winds brought a "purifying cold" that invigorated the populace and helped it recover "from the languid habit acquired in the warm months of June, July, August, and September." Not only did it get hot in South Carolina, but the humidity, especially in the coastal zone, coastal plain, and the sandhills, made the weather even more miserable. A visitor to Charleston noted that in late May he was "Still sauntring abt. town as much as the great heats will permit." In the backcountry at St. Mark's Church, Charles Woodmason recorded that the weather in September was "excessive sultry."[18]

Some might be able to reduce the pace of their activities, but not those in the fields and on the farms. On rice plantations fields were drained in June and were hoed constantly to keep down the weeds. The rice crop was harvested and processed in late August and early September. Indigo was cut and processed from July to September, depending upon when it had been planted. Working in the heat was made even more uncomfortable by the mud, stench, and insects, but the harvest was completed as rapidly as possible because of the danger from hurricanes.[19]

Although the colony had been hit by at least three hurricanes before the middle of the eighteenth century, the hurricane of 15 September 1752 was remembered by all who lived through it. Late in the afternoon of 14 September the wind began to blow from the northeast with ever-increasing force. By the morning of the 15th it was "irresistible." The eye of the storm crossed the coast on an incoming tide, right at Charleston harbor. The storm surge was ten feet above the highest spring tides and tossed all but one of the ships in the harbor onto Charleston's streets. The city's eight wharves were destroyed and dozens of structures swept away. Those that remained suffered heavy damage: toppled chimneys, blown-out windows and doors, and missing roofs. In the countryside for forty miles around Charleston, there was widespread damage. Barns and outbuildings were flattened, one-half the rice crop destroyed, bridges and roads washed out, and trees mowed down as if by a scythe. At least twenty-eight people were reported killed, but the total was probably much higher. While the populace was trying to clean up and rebuild, another hurricane on 30 September dealt the province a glancing blow.[20]

The Hurricane of 1752 became a part of the collective memory of the colonists. It and other weather phenomena were recorded in residents' diaries, journals, plantation books, daybooks, and letter books. Ann Ashby Manigault and Eliza Lucas Pinckney both kept journals. Robert Pringle and Henry Laurens maintained letter books with copies of their business correspondence (which often included local news) addressed to individuals throughout the Atlantic world.

The heat got a lot of attention from outsiders, but it was the occasional cold snap that fascinated locals. December 1740 with "hard frosts and Snow" was one of the coldest on record. In February 1747 the mercury dipped so low that birds fell from the air dead and in Governor Glen's kitchen a jar containing water and a live eel froze solid, even though it was in a room heated by a fireplace.[21]

Journals and diaries were just as likely to record family and social events as the weather. When the harvest was completed in the lowcountry, planters and their families moved to Charleston where many maintained second homes. The social season for the elite began in November and continued until May.

Charleston was South Carolina's economic, political, and social capital. In many ways the city was more like ancient Venice or Florence than London. Like the Italian cities, it functioned much like a city-state with a vast hinterland that included much of the present southeastern United States. Of the five great colonial cities in British North America (Boston, Philadelphia, New York, Newport, and Charleston), Charleston was the fourth in size, but it was far and away the wealthiest. Its free citizens had an average per capita worth nearly six times that of Philadelphians, seven times that of Bostonians, and eight times that of New Yorkers. In comparison with the other southern colonies, Charleston area residents were four time wealthier than those of the Chesapeake and five to ten times richer than those in North Carolina. Travelers were amazed at the city's wealth and power. When Josiah Quincy Jr. of Boston visited South Carolina in 1773, he described the city: "in grandeur, splendour of buildings, decorations, equipages, numbers, commerce, shipping, indeed in almost every thing, it far surpasses all I ever saw, or expected to see, in America."[22]

The opulent city that Quincy visited in 1773 was less than a century old. In 1679 the Lords Proprietors had decreed that Oyster Point, at the confluence of the Ashley and Cooper Rivers, was a better site for the colony's town than the settlement at Albemarle Point. Built on the Cooper River side of the peninsula, Charleston was laid out in a regular grid plan, with streets at right angles. Since the site was exposed to attack from the sea, defense was uppermost in the colonists' minds. Proprietary Charleston, a walled city complete with moat and drawbridges, was somewhat medieval in feel and look. The walls were demolished in 1718 and the grid extended across the peninsula. However, fortifications remained on the Cooper River side of town and on the neck between the two rivers. In the 1750s a massive new city wall of tabby was constructed just north of present-day Calhoun Street. Until the 1780s this was the northern boundary of the city.[23]

On the Cooper River side of town were docks, ship chandleries, and wholesale mercantile establishments. On the seaward side of Bay Street, at the foot of Broad Street, was the Exchange Building. Completed in 1771 with steps descending to the water, the Exchange was the formal entrance to the city. It was also a statement of the community's wealth and power, just as grand central railroad stations were to nineteenth- and twentieth-century American cities.[24]

Most of the buildings in the city that made such an impression on Quincy were constructed after 1740. Charleston suffered from several disastrous fires. The first in 1698 destroyed one-fourth of the early settlement. The great fire of November 1740 "Lay'd in Ashes . . . the most valuable and Tradeing part" of town. Three hundred dwellings, a great many storehouses, some wharves, and "an Immense Quantity of goods & Merchandize of all sorts." The financial losses were in the hundreds of thousands of pounds sterling. Relief for the sufferers of the fire came from other colonies and from Parliament, which appropriated £20,000 sterling ($2.4 million). After the fire the assembly enacted a building code for the city requiring brick buildings with tile or slate roofs. While not always observed, the code was partially responsible for the solid, stately appearance of the later colonial city.[25]

There were other towns in South Carolina, but Beaufort, Purrysburgh, Jacksonborough, Dorchester, Camden, and Georgetown were dismissed as "inconsiderable villages" by an eighteenth-century historian. No mention was made of the backcountry courthouse towns of Ninety Six, Cheraw, and Orangeburg. There was not much in either Ninety Six or Cheraw other than a courthouse, a jail, a store or two, and a handful of houses. Orangeburg was a "neatly laid out" town with several taverns and stores, a courthouse and jail, a number of small residences, and both a Lutheran and an Anglican church. The Circuit Court Act of 1769 did much to transform these three backcountry settlements into towns. The act also named Georgetown, Beaufort, and Camden as courthouse and jail sites; however, they were already well-established communities. Georgetown and Beaufort were trading centers and ports. Camden was an important trading link between Charleston and the backcountry of both North and South Carolina.[26]

Georgetown, founded in 1730, became an official port the next year with its own customs collector. In 1765 a British traveler described it as a "pretty little Town" on the Sampit River. Commercial activity was centered on Front Street with residences clustered nearby. The Prince George Winyah parish church was the only public building of any significance.[27]

At the opposite end of the colony's coast was Beaufort. In the last fifteen years before the Revolution, the Beaufort area was probably the fastest growing in the province. It became the center of the shipbuilding trade in the southern colonies because of the ready supply of live oaks on the nearby sea islands. The sumptuous houses built by William Elliott and Nathaniel Barnwell, rivaling most in Charleston, were indicative of the town's prosperity.[28]

Although there were settlers in the vicinity of what would become Camden by the 1730s, the oldest inland town in South Carolina was not developed until 1758. In that year Joseph Kershaw designed and laid out a modern grid plan for the town. It had a number of large trading establishments, a sawmill, a gristmill, a Quaker meetinghouse, and an Anglican church. There were a number of houses including Kershaw's fine two-story residence.[29]

Although these outlying towns were growing, they were dominated by the colony's metropolis. Politically, they were not allowed their own governments; if a problem arose, the assembly created a commission. Economically, Charleston's merchants had branches in the towns or formal business relationships with local merchants; either way, the city's merchants were in control.

In addition to these towns, here and there a country store became the magnet that attracted other commercial activity. An excellent example of this was Monck's Corner in St. John's Berkeley Parish. Beginning with one store in 1753, within twenty years it had five more as well as four "well kept taverns." Monck's Corner owed its growth to its location at the fork of the main road from Charleston. One branch went northeastward toward the Santee River and Georgetown, and the other led into the backcountry settlements along the Congaree River. The roads in the parish were well maintained by one of the colony's most effective Commissions of the High Roads.[30]

South Carolina's road network was an important part of the colony's economic infrastructure. Roads, ferries, and bridges made it possible for individuals and merchandise to travel from Charleston to all parts of the province. Except during rainy weather, the highways were "level, dry, and comfortable for driving, riding, and walking." However, even in dry weather rural roads and Charleston's unpaved, sandy streets could be "disagreeable."[31]

Horses were the most prevalent means of transportation throughout South Carolina in the eighteenth century. In the lowcountry the most common vehicle was the two-wheeled riding chair. Wealthier individuals had four-wheel carriages, and several carried "their luxury so far as to have carriages, horses, coachmen and all imported from England." Building and maintaining these fancy equipages were 148 carriage and coach makers. In 1763 Henry Laurens placed an order with Isaac King for "a neat strong carriage."[32]

Water transportation was preferred by many as being more comfortable. It certainly was more efficient for shipping rice and indigo to market. In 1768 it was estimated that there were more than 130 boats and schooners built and owned in South Carolina used in shipping "Country Produce" to Charleston. Probably three-fourths of these sailing vessels were decked and capable of carrying ten to fifty tons of freight. That meant that one of the smaller vessels could carry forty barrels of rice, and a larger one two hundred. Individual water transportation was by dugout canoe or periauger. The latter was a cypress dugout canoe that had been split down the middle and widened through the insertion of boards. Some had sails and were large enough to hold rice barrels and livestock. They might have been a bit clumsy, but they were durable means of transportation on the colony's inland waterways.[33]

News flowed with commerce. In the lowcountry Charleston served as a focal point for information from abroad and the city's hinterland. Regular mail service with the northern colonies was established in 1738. The post road ran from Charleston via Georgetown to Cape Fear in North Carolina and then northward. Overseas mail was by any ship leaving the harbor; however, in the 1760s the British postal service opened a regular packet service. Designed for speed, not cargo, the packets sailed from Falmouth for Barbados and then stopped in Jamaica, Pensacola, St. Augustine, and Charleston before heading back to England. By 1766 there were five ships in the packet service; each one made two trips on a regular schedule. The record time for the Charleston-to-Falmouth run was twenty days. If a person wanted to send mail to England, all he or she had to do was have the letter and postal fees at Peter Timothy's office on the morning of the sailing. Timothy, the secretary of the General Post Office, was also the editor of the *South Carolina Gazette*.[34]

In the 1720s the colonial government tried unsuccessfully to entice printers to immigrate to Charleston. Finally, in 1731 the assembly decided to offer a £1,000 currency ($15,000) bounty to any printer who was willing to move his press to the colony. Three responded, and in 1732 two newspapers appeared, the *South Carolina Gazette* and the *South Carolina Weekly Journal*. The editor of the *Weekly Journal* died in July 1732, and his newspaper folded. Thomas Whitmarsh's *Gazette* succeeded, but he died in September 1733, only eighteen months after arrival. With the assistance of Benjamin Franklin, Lewis Timothy assumed the editorship of the *Gazette,* and his family published it until the American Revolution. In 1765 Charles Crouch launched the *South Carolina Gazette and Country Journal,* and the following year Robert Wells began publishing the *South Carolina and American General Gazette.* In the early 1770s Charleston had three newspapers for a white population of about six thousand. Boston, in comparison, had six newspapers and a population of approximately fifteen thousand, while Philadelphia had four newspapers and a population of more than thirty thousand.[35]

The *South Carolina Gazette* was distributed throughout the Southeast, and subscriptions were available from Mobile and Pensacola in West Florida to the North Carolina/Virginia border. Sometimes the Timothys were not prompt in sending out their *Gazette* to other cities. A Georgia reader, after complaining about not receiving issues for which he had paid, commented: "Now that Timothy has a competitor he will undoubtedly see that his customers get their newspapers." In 1770 the *South Carolina and American General Gazette* also had regular subscribers in other colonies.[36]

The three newspapers were very different from one another in tone as well as content. The *South Carolina Gazette* was very much a middle-of-the-road paper. Timothy was a patriot, but the local stories he wrote, and those he included from other colonies, were somewhat restrained. Wells, on the other hand, was very much interested in the arts and literature; he was also an unabashed Tory. For example, when Henry Laurens had a run-in with royal customs officials that developed into a heated public controversy, Wells did not even report the incident to his readers; nor did he carry advertisements for the pamphlets that followed. The *South Carolina and American General Gazette* tended to be a bit on the stuffy side. The *South Carolina Gazette and Country Journal* was a stridently pro-American tabloid. It nearly always included scandalous stories about European royalty and gruesome tales from anywhere. While its competitors ignored the comings and goings of those not among the colony's elite, the *South Carolina Gazette and Country Journal* regularly published information on them in its columns.

While colonists in the Southeast were interested in Charleston's newspapers, some of the city's residents (especially merchants) wanted to read what was going on in Great Britain. Robert Pringle asked his brother, a London merchant, to send him "the most material News papers by all Conveyances," which he did.[37]

In addition to newspapers and letters, word of mouth seemed to be an effective means of letting people know what was happening. The white population was small; in 1750 there were only twenty-five thousand whites, of whom approximately ten thousand would have been adults. With Charleston as the colony's metropolis, news was disseminated fairly rapidly throughout the lowcountry—witness the speed with which the colonists plunged into new economic endeavors. Visitors were welcome everywhere as sources of news and gossip. Some lowcountry planters even posted slaves on the highway to invite travelers in for "refreshments, dinners, afternoon teas, suppers, and lodgings."[38]

When the backcountry began to fill up, intracolonial communications were not as good; however, once the circuit courts began to function in the 1770s, information seemed to get from one end of the province to the other. Grand jury presentments from the most remote courthouse town, Ninety Six, appeared in the Charleston press along with those from the city.[39]

Oral communication was fine as long as everyone spoke the same language. In South Carolina that was not always the case. Given the various ethnic origins of the colony's population (black and white), it is no wonder that one modern historian compared Charleston to Babel. There were more languages spoken there than any other place in British North America. Even when individuals spoke English, they might do so with an accent: French, Scottish, Irish, German, Dutch, Welsh, Portuguese, or West African. Some whites and blacks were multilingual.[40]

Heard everywhere was Gullah, the creole language of the black majority. Some whites spoke it but many did not, making Gullah an even more effective means of communication within the black community. The African American grapevine in South Carolina was quite effective. It is possible that because blacks were able to communicate with one another so quickly, they were able to launch the Stono Rebellion to coincide with whites' apprehensions about war with Spain.[41]

Music was an integral part of West African community life. In America songs and drums became other ways for blacks to communicate among themselves. When whites paid attention to blacks' singing, they did not pick up on the differences in tempo. When a song was sung slowly, that indicated sorrow or a lament; when the tempo was upbeat, that meant escape, freedom. Depending upon the tempo, a song could have two different meanings. Whites did understand that drums were a means of communication and usually attributed something sinister to them. Although African drums were banned by statute in 1740, they not infrequently broke the stillness of lowcountry nights and undoubtedly caused whites to remember the Stono Rebellion and shudder.[42]

By the end of the colonial period, there were seventy-five thousand black Carolinians whose labor helped make South Carolina the wealthiest colony in British North America. It is wrong, however, to think that the only hands that ever got dirty were black ones. Most of the tobacco, wheat, hemp, indigo, corn, and other products of the backcountry were raised by white farmers and their families. In Charleston and the little communities of the lowcountry, a sizable artisan class provided goods and services that were much in demand by the ever-growing elite.

In 1751 Governor Glen had calculated that the colony's wealthiest residents made up 20 percent of the population. By the 1770s the white population had doubled, with almost all of the growth occurring in the backcountry. During the same period the value of exports had nearly doubled, with most of the increase accruing to residents of the lowcountry. There were a few backcountry residents such as Moses Kirkland and Joseph Kershaw whose wealth qualified them as members of the colony's elite; however, they were the exceptions. Thus, while the growth of the low-country's white population had stagnated, its wealth had increased. Because it is not possible to assess the wealth of the majority of the colony's white population, it is difficult to determine the size (in terms of the total population) of the class Governor Glen described as enjoying "plenty of the good things of Life." It was unquestionably larger, in absolute numbers, than it had been in 1750—and it was considerably richer. South Carolina's gentry, according to George Milligen-Johnston, was "more numerous" than that of any other colony. The prosperity of South Carolina's elite trickled down to all ranks of white society.[43]

In Charleston a colonist could obtain just about any good or service that could be had in London. The city's artisans and mechanics (the terms were interchangeable in the eighteenth century) plied more than one hundred different trades. In addition to the usual ones (bakers, carpenters, glaziers, masons, painters), there were a number that reflected a market for luxury items (coach makers, artificial flower makers, fan makers, gilders, and musical instrument menders). There were shops and taverns catering to every taste. In the countryside there were blacksmiths in St. James Goose Creek and Prince William Parishes; shoemakers in Prince George Winyah, St. John's Colleton, and Christ Church; tailors in St. James Goose Creek and St. George Dorchester; a cooper in Prince George Winyah; and a peruke maker in St. Bartholomew's.[44]

There was a demand for goods and services from the general public and also from the colony's government. Carpenters, bricklayers, blacksmiths, painters, glaziers, bookbinders, upholsterers, and chimney sweeps appeared on the annual account lists. Among the more unusual listings were the purchase of three silver breastplates for Indians from John Paul Grimké, two flags for the forts from Mary Darling, and "gibbet irons, &ca. for the Negro Cain" from Nicholas Swindershine.[45]

Government contracts, at least for artisans, were not as lucrative as one might think. The Commons House did not pay its bills until the end of the year, and sometimes it either decided to pay less than what it had been billed or not at all. Thomas Gordon died between the time he completed lathing and plaster work, and the account was settled with his estate. William Edwards, a saddler, had his bill adjusted downward. Mary Clotworthy, a tavern keeper, had her small claim denied altogether. Private citizens could also be slow about payment, as the number of cases in the court of common pleas attests.[46]

Artisans, both black and white, could and indeed did prosper in eighteenth-century South Carolina. In 1734 Peter Birot advertised that he would take on as apprentices "any White Man or Negro having a mind to learn the Coopers Trade." Cooperage, important in marketing the rice crop, was a skill mastered by a fair number of black South Carolinians. They were also carpenters, bricklayers, shoemakers, blacksmiths, tailors, seamstresses, painters, wheelwrights, and silversmiths. However, by the 1750s some whites were beginning to feel the pinch of competition from blacks and got the assembly to restrict training opportunities. So many blacks became chimney sweeps that they were considered insolent and white sweeps were sought. Anne Cox, who taught "mantua-making in all its branches," advertised that she took "none but white Children."[47]

Running millinery shops and making mantuas and dresses were occupations that might be considered "typical" for an eighteenth-century woman. However, in colonial South Carolina women successfully managed plantations and a variety of businesses either through choice or necessity.[48] The role of women and property was defined by law and custom. In the eyes of the law, a woman could own her own business and property as long as she was a *feme sole* (single, widowed, or legally deeded the right to do so by her spouse). Two-thirds of all colonial legal feme sole traders lived in Charleston where they owned small shops, inns, and taverns. For example, Frances Swallow was a needleworker and milliner with a shop on the bay. In the backcountry, while some women also operated small stores, several, such as Sarah Evelyn Crawford and Mary Guess, were stock dealers in cattle, horses, and swine. Sometimes married women operated their own businesses as feme soles with the tacit, but not legal, approval of their spouses and local authorities.[49]

Once married, a woman's property usually became her husband's. The families of wealthy women sometimes resorted to marriage settlements to protect the property and interests of their womenfolk from unscrupulous spouses. One form of settlement involved the husband's compensating the wife or her heirs for the property that came with her to the marriage. Under another form of settlement a bride and her male relatives established a trust that was administered in her interests by male kinfolk. So numerous did these marriage settlements become that the secretary of the province had to create a separate record group for them.[50]

Young women in South Carolina inherited money, slaves, and land because there was no law of entail (keeping an estate together). It had been specifically excluded from the English statutes incorporated into the colony's legal code in 1712. Primogeniture (property descending to the eldest son) applied only to intestate estates. In fact, South Carolina parents tended to treat their children, male and female, generously and equitably. Death (of parents or spouse) not infrequently left women with considerable property. After midcentury marriage notices often commented on a woman's financial worth. Judith Mayrant Bull was described as "a lady of great merit and fortune"; Salley Hartley had a "handsome Fortune," Polly Butler a "considerable Fortune," Elizabeth Quash a "genteel Fortune," and Mary Elliott a "very large Fortune." Polly Golightly had a "Fortune of *Ten Thousand Pounds* Sterling" ($849,000) and Elizabeth Izard one of "*Thirty Thousand Pounds* Sterling" ($2.6 million). Not all notices concerning financial status were for women of the elite. In 1766 Mrs. Elizabeth Wingood, "an agreeable Widow Lady with a good Interest," married Andrew Hibben, a watchmaker.[51]

In a traditional society in which the husband was the breadwinner and the wife took care of the household and reared the children, the death of a spouse not infrequently led to remarriage. Stephen Bull married twice and had a child by each wife. His widow, Judith Mayrant Bull, married Robert Pringle (himself a widower) and they had three children. Companionship, not necessity, was another reason for a surviving partner's remarriage, and multiple marriages were not uncommon. Lady Mary Ainslie outlived three husbands, and John Drayton had four wives. Remarriage created interesting and complicated relationships, particularly when inheritance was involved.[52]

The death of a spouse left a woman, especially one with young children, in a precarious position. In 1741 when Captain Norberry was killed in a duel, he "left a wife and 3 or 4 children in very bad circumstances to lament his rashness." Depending upon her status, several things might occur. If she had the means, she could hire an overseer to run a plantation or someone to manage her mercantile interests in town. Because of the paternalistic nature of slavery, theoretically a black woman did not have to worry about feeding, clothing, or housing her children if she lost her mate through death or sale. The women who were left to shift for themselves were those whose husbands were subsistence farmers, artisans, or small shopkeepers. Jean Carruthers, the widow of a Charleston blacksmith, was forced to renounce the rights to administer her husband's estate to his principal creditors. Other women were able to obtain control of their deceased husbands' affairs and, in many instances, operate the businesses, which likely explains how Susannah Walker came to own a chimney-sweeping service.[53]

One of the most successful women entrepreneurs was Elizabeth Timothy, wife of the editor and publisher of the *South Carolina Gazette*. When he died in December 1738, she was a "poor afflicted widow" with "six small children and another hourly expected." She immediately assumed control of the enterprise and notified the public that she intended to make the newspaper "as entertaining and correct as possible." She did so expertly, but it was not easy. During the sickly months of September and October 1739, she buried two of her children. Nevertheless, she was an excellent businessperson and was able to buy out Benjamin Franklin's interest in the newspaper. Then, when her son Peter reached his majority in 1746, she relinquished the enterprise to him. Although she was the actual editor and publisher for seven years, her son's name appeared on the masthead.[54]

In the eighteenth century the public world was a man's world, except among the Indians. Little Carpenter, a Cherokee chieftain, attended a meeting of the Royal Council and looked around the room. Seeing no women present, he asked if "White Men as well as the Red were born of Women." His remark left his hosts speechless. White men had difficulty with the public roles of Cherokee women and seldom missed an opportunity to denigrate them. By the end of the colonial period, white Carolinians derisively referred to Cherokee women as "squaws." In "civilized" society women were expected to play subordinate roles, to support their husbands in their endeavors. During the Great Fire of 1740, while her husband was taking care of the store and its contents, Jane Allen Pringle was left to save what she could of their household effects. Eventually she was forced from her doomed home with her clothes ablaze. Henry Laurens, in gratitude for a favor done him by a business associate, promised that "Mrs. Laurens shall make you 40 Mince Pies next Christmas." Wealth and social position did not mean that women were freed from the responsibilities of assisting their husbands.[55]

When describing their wives, some colonial South Carolina males sometimes used terminology that gives us an idea about the status of women. For his wife, Pringle had "the most Tender Regard & Affection, as she makes me happy altho' but young (being but 21 years of age) is one of the Best of Wives. . . . She is," he continued, "naturally of a very Good Temper & Disposition." Upon the death of Eleanor Ball Laurens, Henry recalled that she had never complained, and he remembered her fondly as "a tender and watchful mother and faithful bosom Friend, a Wife whose constant Study was to make me happy." The marriage notice of Mrs. Sarah Field of Cheraw said that she was "endowed with every social Virtue capable of rendering the Marriage State happy."[56]

In addition to the enterprising feme sole businesswomen and the activities of women such as Elizabeth Timothy, there were glimmers that some South Carolina women were not happy with their subordinate roles. In 1743 there were poetic exchanges in the pages of the *South Carolina Gazette* concerning the status of women. In "The Ladies Complaint" a woman pleaded for equal laws for both men and women and said that if women could not have more freedom, then men should have less. A male's response to her complaint was that all her problems would be solved if she got herself a significant other.[57]

In another exchange about the roles of men and women, a woman dared to compare the plight of women to that of slaves:

> How wretched is a *Woman's* Fate,
> No happy Change her Fortune knows,
> Subject to Man in every State.
> How can she then be free from Woes? . . .
>
> Oh, cruel Pow'rs! since you've design'd
> That Man, *vain* Man! should bear the Sway;
> To a *Slave's* Fetters add a *slavish* Mind,
> That I may cheerfully your Will obey.

The reply to "Verses Written By a Young Lady" boldly stated the proper gender roles for white South Carolinians:

> The Man's to labour, toil, and sweat,
> And all his care employ,

Honour to wealth, or power to get;
'Tis Woman's to enjoy.

How happy is a woman's fate
Free from Care, free from woe,
Secure of man in every state,
Her Guardian-God below!

By the end of the colonial period some white males were beginning to think that the proper place for their mothers, sisters, wives, and daughters was the pedestal. Ideal and reality, however, did not always coincide.[58]

A woman should not have a care in the world. Then, neither should most men. The hedonism that came out with the West Indians in the seventeenth century had become ingrained into the colony's lifestyle. No other city had as frenetic a social life as Charleston. However, diversions and recreation were not limited to the port city.[59]

In rural areas fairs were held in the spring and fall at Dorchester, Ashley Ferry Town, and Childsbury. For four days rural residents bought and sold stock and enjoyed a variety of diversions such as cockfights and horse races. Horse racing was a spectator sport enjoyed by all levels of colonial society. In addition to those at the fairs, races were regularly scheduled at Ferguson's Ferry, Georgetown, and Charleston. The Georgetown Races were held the first Tuesday and Wednesday in December. Charleston's New Market Race Course sponsored the colony's premiere events, the Charles Town Plate and the Colt's Plate. Providing organizational and financial backing for the races were the Georgetown Jockey Club and the South Carolina Jockey Club. Carolinians of all classes (including slaves) attended cockfights and horse races and placed their bets, but increasingly the control of such events was in the hands of the local elite.[60]

Other organized social and cultural attractions included music and the theater. During the season, when the planters were in town, there were regularly scheduled dances about every two weeks and several balls in honor of some special occasion. Dancing was a social skill as well as exercise. For those wanting to learn the latest rage from London, there were dancing masters aplenty. Most other colonials acknowledged the grace and rhythm of South Carolinians on the dance floor.[61]

Whether at home, a club meeting, or a concert sponsored by the St. Cecilia Society, South Carolinians appreciated good music. Individuals, especially women, played the harpsichord or guitar. One of the most complete collections of music in the colony belonged to Dr. William Pillans, an apothecary. In his library were Arcangelo Corelli's concertos and other works, Carlo Marino's sonatas for violin, William McGibbon's sonatas for German flute and violin, and John Lates's sonatas for pianoforte.[62]

Since the 1730s Charlestonians had enjoyed good music, primarily by organists at

St. Philip's and St. Michael's. One organist, Peter Valton of St. Philip's, was also a skilled composer, and in 1768 subscriptions were taken to publish six of his sonatas for organ, harpsichord, and violin. The St. Cecilia Society was formed specifically to hire outstanding musicians to perform on a regular basis. Although Josiah Quincy Jr. found a number of things he did not like when he visited in 1773, he was entranced at the caliber of the musicians and the music he heard. The St. Cecilia concert he attended was held in the Long Room of Pike's tavern.[63]

In 1735 Shepherd's tavern was the scene for the colony's first theatrical season. Had Quincy been present, he would have been uncomfortable. A local wit wrote a prologue that contrasted dour New England where colonists hanged witches and "abjured Plays" with South Carolina where in "The little Time that Heaven to mortals spares" individuals saw nothing wrong with blending "Amusement with the Shades of Life."[64]

The response to the first theater season was so enthusiastic, that funds were raised to build the Dock Street Theater. As in England, seats were priced according to location. George Farquhar's comedy *The Recruiting Officer* was a frequent and popular attraction. In 1754 a new theater was built on Queen Street, and it became home in the 1760s to the American Company. Seat prices were expensive; the cheapest seats were twenty shillings currency ($12), about the daily wage of most artisans. Despite the costs, the theater appealed to all segments of the population. The 1773–1774 theatrical season was the finest in colonial America. The 188 performances included eleven of Shakespeare's plays.[65]

While some taverns offered space for large public gatherings, most were small places offering a variety of individual diversions. Many had billiard, backgammon, and card tables, and Thomas Nightingale's on the road near Charleston had a bowling alley. The main rooms of the larger taverns served as halls for dances, concerts, lectures, exhibitions, and public celebrations. A Cherokee Indian delegation was entertained at Nightingale's, and Gov. Charles Montagu's arrival feted at Dillon's. In both instances the colony paid for the food and drink.[66]

The most elegant tavern in the colony may have been at the Sign of Bacchus on the bay. Operated by Benjamin and Catherine Backhouse, the establishment featured a dining room, long room, front room, piazza, cellar, garret, and cockloft. It was splendidly furnished with mahogany furniture, much of it probably made by the city's best-known cabinetmaker, Thomas Elfe. There were nineteen beds available for lodging and, if a guest wanted to get cleaned up, a bathtub. Eighteen slaves and an Irish indentured servant staffed the Sign of Bacchus and a smaller inn "up the path."[67]

In 1763 justices of the peace issued sixty-six tavern licenses; five years later the number had more than doubled. Approximately one-half of the licensees were women. It was illegal for most skilled artisans to operate drinking establishments, but many dodged the law by having their wives obtain the licenses. Benjamin Backhouse, for example, was a blacksmith, and the tavern licenses were in Catherine's name. Since Charleston was a port, one might suspect that some of the licenses went to houses of ill repute. Every now and then the authorities cracked down and fined a woman for "keeping a disorderly house."[68]

Taverns were public establishments, but they also were meeting places for clubs. There were more private groups and clubs in eighteenth-century Charleston than in any other American city. The Beef-Steak Club and Charleston's Sons of Liberty met at Backhouse's tavern on the bay. The South Carolina Society met at Joel Poinsett's on Elliott Street. Other clubs such as the Smoaking Club, the Laughing Club, the Monday Night Club, the Segoon-Pop Club, Order of Ubiquarians, Batchelor's Society, and the Sons of St. Patrick either met in taverns or private homes. On a smaller scale, in Georgetown gentlemen gathered for drink, dinner, and conversation at either Jonathan Skrine's or Thomas Blythe's tavern.[69]

South Carolinians, regardless of class or race, did not need a tavern or an organized entertainment to have a good time. Much to the chagrin of the clergy, Sunday was a day of leisure and recreation. In the backcountry the women frolicked and the men drank, played cards, raced, hunted, and fished. In the lowcountry it was a time of "visiting and mirth" for most of the population, white and black.[70]

During the 1730s and 1740s grand jury presentments condemned the "gaming . . . and Caballing" of large gatherings of blacks in Charleston on the Sabbath. Laws were enacted requiring slaves to have tickets from their owners to be in Charleston. Laws forbade tavern keepers from selling alcohol to slaves unless owners granted permission. In spite of these laws, nothing changed. In 1773 Quincy observed that "the Sabbath is a day . . . of license, pastime and frolic for the negroes." He saw great number of them in Charleston playing such games as pitch-penny, pawpaw, and huzzle-cap. Sunday was usually a free day for the slave population, and many chose to visit family and friends on nearby plantations or in Charleston.[71] Since whites were so concerned with the black majority, why did they permit the law to be flouted so openly? Perhaps they realized that by permitting a certain amount of disorder, by allowing their slaves a limited amount of freedom, they could preserve the "good order and the harmony of the whole community."[72]

Sundays in the backcountry, according to Woodmason, were days for hunting and fishing. South Carolina males, however, really did not need a special day for outdoor recreation. Settlement of the lowcountry and the deerskin trade may have diminished some wildlife populations, but there was still "Plenty of Game" in the 1770s. While an occasional formal hunt took to the chase, most hunting and fishing were done individually or with family and friends. Occasionally such sports could be deadly. A sailor out in a periauger on the Stono River decided to poke at an alligator for sport. He fell overboard, and the news account reported that the "Alligator made a good breakfast of him." Playing with devilfish (giant manta rays) off Beaufort was a dangerous but popular sport. In 1769 a party of three hooked a ray; two were tossed from the boat and drowned, and the third was dragged two miles.[73]

The only thing that reduced outdoor activities was the weather. In South Carolina it was too hot and humid in the summer "for any kind of Diversion or Exercise, except Riding on Horseback, or in Chaises . . . in the Evenings and Mornings."[74]

Regardless of race or status, South Carolinians were a pleasure-seeking people, which led Dr. Alexander Garden to note that planters were "absolutely above every occupation but eating, drinking, lolling, smoking, and sleeping." He complained to all with whom he corresponded about the lack of intellectual curiosity in the colony. The rest of the story (which he neglected to tell) was that he was introduced to botany by the planter-politician William Bull, who gave him a copy of Linnaeus's *Fundamenta Botanica*. Perhaps Garden felt the way he did because some planters talked about subjects in which he had no interest, such as rice and slaves. In South Carolina, as in other colonies, some individuals cared little about intellectual pursuits, but others were well informed and well educated.[75]

During the colony's first century, literacy among the free population may have been higher than it would be for the next 150 years. Older histories put the literacy rate for free males in the lowcountry at better than 90 percent. Literacy rates were somewhat lower on the frontier in Williamsburg Township (80 percent) and in the German settlements along the Saluda River (71 percent). However, these astonishingly high figures are unreliable because they generally were based on comparing the number of signatures on a document with the number of marks.[76]

Those who had educations taught their children to read and write, employed private tutors, or sent them to one of the many small private schools that opened in Charleston. In education, as in so many other areas of everyday life, South Carolinians followed English practices.[77] One of the earliest references to education was in Thomas Greatbeach's will (1694), in which he bequeathed funds to continue the salary of his children's female tutor. When Richard Beresford died in 1722, he left a considerable portion of his estate for an endowment (the Beresford Bounty) to educate the poor of St. Thomas & St. Denis Parish. A century later, in 1861, the endowment was worth $71,000 ($1.2 million). There was a parish school in St. James Goose Creek in 1704, but its effectiveness and that of other parochial schools depended upon the enthusiasm of the rector or vestry. A 1712 act agreed to provide a nominal annual sum for the support of any parish school and its teacher. The latter had to be a member of the established church and approved by the vestry. Presbyterians in Williamsburg Township opted to instruct their children at home rather than let an Anglican teach them. Anglican clergy later protested that provincial officials winked at the law and permitted Dissenters to operate illegal schools.[78]

The clergy also complained that the laws governing the Provincial Library had been ignored. In 1698 a library had been established in Charleston at the instigation of Commissary Thomas Bray. Through his efforts, £300 sterling ($16,000) was raised and books purchased. To prevent books from being "embezeled, damaged, or lost," the assembly created the first library rules for any town in English America. Any inhabitant could check out a book but had first to make a deposit of three times the book's value to insure that it would be returned undamaged. The rules were not enforced, and the books in the Provincial Library and those in several parish libraries (Christ Church, St. Thomas, St. James Santee, St. James Goose Creek, and St. Paul's) disappeared. By the 1720s, save for the one at Christ Church, these church-sponsored libraries had ceased to exist.[79]

With the exception of the school in Dorchester, most parish schools went the way of the parochial libraries. The Dorchester school, created by statute in 1725, finally opened in 1757 with two substantial buildings, a schoolhouse and a residence for the schoolmaster. Although the school had an endowment of £2,600 ($37,000), it had difficulty attracting and keeping qualified teachers.[80]

Like so much else in the colony, education was centered in Charleston. By mid-century the city's schools (private and public) offered the equivalent of what we today would consider an adequate high school education. William Bull reported that there were "teachers of mathematics, arithmetic, fencing, French, drawing, dancing, music and needlework, to fit men for the busy world, and ladies for the domestic social duties of life." Unless young women had understanding parents or family friends (as did Eliza Lucas and Martha Laurens), it was difficult for them to obtain much more education. That does not mean, however, that South Carolina women were vapid clotheshorses. On the contrary, in conversation and manners they charmed visitors. One historian who seldom had anything good to say about South Carolina commented: "the glory of Carolina was its women."[81]

Women were not the only ones whose educational opportunities were limited. Not every young man should aspire to a classical education. Henry Laurens considered it a waste of time for some boys to learn the classics. "Boys," he wrote, "ought to be kept . . . to business." Young men whose parents were artisans might have the opportunity to get a rudimentary education, but not much more. The Fellowship Society (1762), founded by successful artisans, helped provide funds so that some young men could get educations. Once such a youth reached the age of twelve or fourteen, his parents usually entered into a contract with an artisan to teach him a craft. At midcentury parents paid £20 sterling ($1,900) to a master for a four-year apprenticeship; however, apprenticeships ranged from three to seven years, and fees varied accordingly. From the number and tenor of advertisements in the newspapers, apprentice/master relationships tended to be strained. In exasperation, Edward Weyman, an upholsterer, offered a reward of "Two Large Hand Fulls of Pine Shavings" to whoever returned his runaway apprentice. It was not surprising, then, that those artisans who could afford to do so purchased slaves and trained them to their trade. In 1755 the Commons House passed legislation to restrict this practice, but the law was ineffectual.[82]

Learning a skill was one of the few avenues open to some black youths. Early in the eighteenth century the St. James Goose Creek parochial school and the Charleston Free School taught white, Indian, and black children. In the aftermath of the Stono Rebellion, the Slave Code of 1740 made it illegal to teach blacks to write, but an exception was made for the Reverend Alexander Garden's school.[83]

Education is more than book learning; it also involves cultural tradition. In family groups and in the quarters after hours, West African oral traditions were passed along from one generation to the next. Among the traditions that Africans maintained was the naming of children. Sometimes black children bore the African names their parents gave them, the anglicized versions of the African names, or the English translations of the African names. It was common to name a child for the day of the week on which he or she was born. For example, a male child born on Monday might have the African name Cudjo, the shortened English version Joe, or the English translation Monday. A female child born on Friday could be Phibbi, Phoebe, or Friday. About 15–20 percent of slave names were African in origin; however, by the end of the eighteenth century many had lost their original meaning. Children were named Joe or Phoebe regardless of the day of their birth.[84]

Trickster tales were educational as well as entertaining. The hero of the tales was always small and relatively powerless (partridge, turtle, squirrel, rabbit) and used its wits to outsmart a larger, more powerful opponent (bear, fox, wolf). In the context of the telling, slaves identified themselves with the sly, small animals and their owners or overseers with the big, bad, dumb ones. The lesson was twofold: use your brains to outsmart the boss and be careful so that you do not get tricked yourself.[85]

Sons of the elite could either be educated by tutors at home, attend one of the Charleston schools, or go abroad. As his children grew up, Henry Laurens became less satisfied with the local schools. He first thought of sending his sons to Philadelphia but dismissed that possibility because of the unsatisfactory educational experiences of several South Carolina youths. In 1771 Laurens took his three sons to England where he hoped to place his eldest in college and the younger ones in preparatory schools. None of the prep schools pleased him, and he labeled Oxford a "School for Licentiousness and Debauchery." Eventually he decided to educate the boys in the more moralistic atmosphere of Calvinist Geneva.[86]

Even though Laurens and others expressed concern about the lifestyles of English college youth, South Carolinians sent their sons abroad in large numbers. In the 1770s the lowcountry of South Carolina, with a white population of only about twenty thousand, had more students in England than any other colony. Since the 1730s the sons of the colony's elite had gone abroad for either undergraduate or professional degrees. These European-educated Carolinians were joined by well-educated immigrants to create a pool of talented physicians and lawyers. Twelve individuals had medical degrees from the University of Edinburgh and five more had studied there; two had degrees from the University of Leiden (Holland). During the entire colonial period there were 166 attorneys who either were members of the Charleston Bar or served as judges. Of these, 72 (43 percent) had trained at the Inns of Court in London.[87]

An education in one of the northern colonies or abroad was expensive. Bull said that more did not attend English schools because of the cost. Laurens bemoaned the "considerable Sums of Gold and Silver (considerable in our little Province) remitted to pay for the Board and Education of our Children." Despite the complaints about cost, South Carolina parents were more willing and better able to pay than those in other colonies.[88]

Because of the costs and the necessary separation that sometimes lasted several years, there were Carolinians who wanted to establish a local college. When the Charleston Library Society was incorporated in 1755 that was one of its goals. Its founders, mostly professionals in the city, understood that learning resulted not just from formal schooling, but from "a liberal Education, together with the Use of valuable Books." The library flourished from the beginning and quickly became the center of the city's intellectual life. The society was a private organization, but basically it was open to all who were willing to pay. Its membership roster grew along with its collections. In 1770 a published catalog listed 814 titles, and several hundred more were added before the American Revolution. Funds for book purchases came from a weekly fee of five shillings currency ($3.00) and library fines. Dr. Milligen-Johnston commented that through the society, "useful and valuable Books" were made available that "would not otherwise have soon found their Way here." About two-thirds of the works listed in the catalog did not appear in the inventories of individuals' estates.[89]

Founding a college was one of the society's goals, but its efforts and those of others came to naught. South Carolinians had responded generously to appeals for funds for the colleges of New Jersey (Princeton) and Rhode Island (Brown). In the early 1770s several large bequests were left in trust with the society to support a college. In normal times such bequests would have provided the impetus for the founding of a college. After 1770, however, because of a political stalemate between the Commons House and royal officials over money matters, for all practical purposes the provincial government ceased to function. The timing was unfortunate. However, even though the Charleston Library Society did not succeed in establishing a college, its library made a significant contribution to the cultural life of colonial South Carolina.[90]

The first museum in British North America was an outgrowth of the intellectual energy generated by the Library Society. The museum was one of natural history, and its collections included specimens of South Carolina plant, animal, marine, and bird life and its soils, rocks, and minerals. It had a telescope and intended to purchase a Rittenhouse orrery, but the Revolution intervened. The museum's focus reflected the interest that a number of individuals had in the colony's natural history.

177

Carolinians were in regular contact with England through commerce and personal correspondence. Educated Englishmen, at least those associated with *The Gentleman's Magazine,* had a special interest in South Carolina, as evidenced by the number of articles about the colony that appeared in the magazine. Such learned contacts, however, had been going on since the seventeenth century.[91]

The Royal Society of London for Improving Natural Knowledge and an informal offshoot organization, the Temple Coffee House Botany Club, encouraged colonists to send home specimens and observations. The club's first contact with South Carolina was in 1678, but regular communication did not begin until the 1690s. Among the Carolinians who corresponded with the club members was Edmund Bohun, who forwarded seeds, dried plants, and "6 or 7 hundred butterflies & moths some very fine and scarce." Hannah English Williams shipped all sorts of insects, shells, and snakes along with an Indian "King's tobacco pipe and Queens Petticoat made of moss." Members of the Royal Society and the Temple Coffee House Botany Club along with Gov. Francis Nicholson sponsored the expedition of naturalist Mark Catesby (1722–1725). When he returned to England, he published *The Natural History of Carolina, Florida, and the Bahama Islands,* a magnificently illustrated work with more than two hundred color plates.[92]

South Carolina was, and is, a botanist's dream. In the colony's gardens native plant materials such as the Carolina allspice (*Calycanthus floridus*), crinum (*Crinum sp.*), passionflower (*Passiflora incarnata*), and golden glow (*Rudbeckia laciniata hortensia*) mingled with traditional European favorites such as the tulip, jonquil, hyacinth, anemone, and boxwood. Exotic plants from Asia (day lily, *Hermerocallis fulva*), Africa (cockscomb, *Celosia cristata*), and the Caribbean (spider flower, *Cleome hasslerama*) thrived in the semitropical climate. Mark Catesby, during his stay in the 1720s, transported native plants from the interior to the coast. In the late 1760s John Watson, "Gardener and Seedsman on Trott's Point," always had a fresh supply of imported bulbs and seeds. South Carolina's gardens, like its food and folkways, were a colorful hybrid of traditions.[93]

During the 1730s Charleston's medical community became the nucleus for a more organized study of South Carolina's natural history. As a group these individuals were remarkably well educated. William Bull, although not a practicing physician, was the first American to obtain a European medical degree (Leiden). He was the only native in the group that included the physicians Thomas Dale, John Lining, Lionel Chalmers, and James Killpatrick. Dale translated four medical treatises into English and corresponded with Gronovius in Leiden. Killpatrick introduced smallpox inoculation into the colony. Lining made careful observations on the colony's weather and the effect of the climate on human metabolism (his own). Chalmers was the author of several highly respected works, including *An Account of the Weather and Diseases of South Carolina* and an *Essay on Fevers* published in Charleston, London, and Riga. Modern historians of science consider his contributions to eighteenth-century medicine "impressive."[94]

When Dr. Alexander Garden, a native of Scotland, arrived in 1752, there were already individuals interested in natural history, either strictly from a scientific point of view or for its utilitarian purposes. Among these were the planters William Bull and Charles and Eliza Lucas Pinckney; merchants Robert Pringle and Henry Laurens; placeman Hector Berringer de Beaufain; and the physicians Lionel Chalmers and John Lining. When the American Philosophical Society was founded in 1760, fifteen South Carolinians were elected to membership. Yet, from the moment he landed, Garden complained to his correspondents that few white Carolinians knew or cared anything about botany. He was particularly critical of planters and thought that their slaves knew more about natural history (in terms of the medicinal properties of plants he was likely correct). Botany was his passion, but later he did turn to zoology. On a trip to the northern colonies, he met other scientists (including Cadwallader Colden, John Bartram, Benjamin Franklin, and John Clayton) and began a regular correspondence with them. He also communicated regularly with the great Swedish botanist Linnaeus, who named the gardenia in his honor. Garden's observations and specimens were of great use to others, and his achievements were recognized by his election to the Royal Society for the Encouragements of Arts Manufactures and Commerce, American Philosophical Society, Swedish Royal Society, Edinburgh Society, and Royal Society.[95]

Was Garden fair in his assessment of the lack of intellectual curiosity in colonial South Carolina? On the one hand, there probably were not as many devoted to botany as he, but then that was true of other colonies as well. On the other hand, there certainly were any number of planters and merchants interested in the practical applications of botany as seen in the continual search for new crops. One indication of the interests of nonscientists was in the works that local printers published—because they would sell—and the books that individuals had in their private libraries.

Many of the titles published were utilitarian, such as almanacs and catalogs, or partisan, such as the pamphlet warfare between Henry Laurens and Sir Egerton Leigh. Special note, however, should be made of the quality of several books first printed in South Carolina: Nicholas Trott's *Laws of South Carolina* (1736), John Wesley's *A Collection of Psalms and Hymns* (1737), John Lining's *History of Yellow Fever* (1753), Lionel Chalmers's *An Essay on Fevers* (1767), and Peter Valton's *Six Sonatas for the Harpsichord or Organ* (1768). There were also American editions of Philip Doddridge's *The Family Expositor* (1773) and George Whitefield's *A Collection of Hymns for Social Worship* (1768). Some of the titles, such as Valton's, required advance subscriptions before publication.[96]

Utilitarian and controversial publications, however, were issued in anticipation that they would sell. Beginning in 1733 almanacs appeared almost annually. Local disputes over George Whitefield's ministry, smallpox inoculation, and the Stamp Act all resulted in a spate of pamphlets. Printers found a ready market for self-help books on agriculture, law, and medicine, such as Burdon's *The Gentleman's Pocket-*

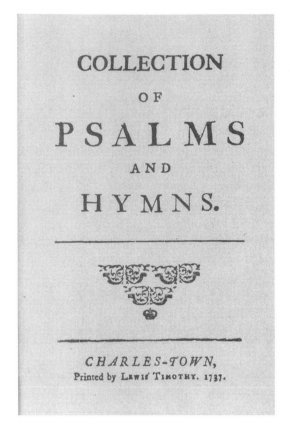

COLLECTION
OF
PSALMS
AND
HYMNS.

CHARLES-TOWN,
Printed by LEWIS TIMOTHY. 1737.

The first edition of John Wesley's hymn-book was printed in Charleston. Courtesy, Methodist Archives and History, Drew University, Madison, New Jersey.

Farrier (1734), Chapelle's *Full and Useful Instructions and Observations concerning the Culture and Manufacturing of Indigo* (1746), William Simpson's *The Practical Justice of the Peace and Parish Officer . . . of South Carolina* (1761), and John Tennent's *Everyman His Own Doctor* (1766).[97]

Booksellers, like printers, looked to the local market. The first bookstores in the colony opened during the 1730s. Prior to that time individuals either had to order books directly from Great Britain or choose from the small stock imported by Charleston merchants and shopkeepers. Of the colony's fourteen booksellers, only four remained in business for any length of time. One was Eleazer Phillips, who opened Charleston's first bookshop in 1735, and another was Robert Wells, whose "Great Stationery and Book-Store on the Bay" was the largest bookstore south of Philadelphia. English tastes and ideas reached the colony quickly. Wells advertised that he had the latest issues of English periodicals regularly put on ships sailing to Charleston.[98]

In the homes of South Carolinians, Bibles and prayer books were the most widely owned books. Bound copies of *The Spectator, The Guardian,* and *The Tatler* containing essays by Joseph Addison and Sir Richard Steele were almost as common as the Bible. From these, colonists could keep abreast of current English taste and thought. Also on many bookshelves were such practical items as Nathan Bailey's *New Universal Dictionary* and Abel Boyer's *Dictionnaire Anglais-Français*.[99]

South Carolinians' reading tastes were much the same as those of other southern colonists. The best of English literature was represented by the collected works of William Shakespeare, Alexander Pope, and Jonathan Swift as well as John Milton's *Paradise Lost* and Samuel Butler's *Hudibras*. Sets of Shakespeare were expensive, but Carolinians not only bought the books, they quoted him in their essays and flocked to see his plays. The influence of Pope, in particular, could be found in the columns of the *South Carolina Gazette*. The ultra-Whiggish *History of England* by Rapin-Thoyras, in French and English editions, was the single most popular history in the colony. Any person who expected to be able to understand the Old Testament had to have Flavius Josephus's *The History of the Jews*. The Roman poet Virgil was the most widely read classical author and was represented either by his complete works or the *Aeneid*. Although primarily either belles lettres or historical, many of these books had strong religious and/or moral overtones.[100]

Whether by category or actual number of titles, South Carolinians owned and read more religious books than they did any other. Lay readers liked the practical orthodox nature of William Burkitt's *Expository Notes . . . on the New Testament* and the simple, straightforward devotions in Richard Allestree's *Whole Duty of Man*. John Hervey's *Meditations and Contemplations* had a Calvinistic, evangelical tone and John Tillotson's sermons a practical, moral one. Tillotson was one of the most popular religious writers on both sides of the Atlantic. The most interesting aspect of the religious books found in the colony's libraries is that Dissenters owned books that were clearly Anglican, and vice versa. The diversity of religious views represented in colonial libraries indicates that the tolerance and harmony that prevailed in the lowcountry for much of the eighteenth century was not just political.[101]

In the lowcountry after the religious/political battles of the early eighteenth century, Anglicans and Dissenters got along fairly well. The absence of friction among the various denominations became an integral part of the social harmony of the Carolina lowcountry. Colonists were more concerned with the basics of Christianity (salvation and redemption) and less with sectarian doctrine. Within ten years of the passage of the Church Act of 1706, Dr. Charles Burnham wrote the bishop of London's representative that if an Anglican clergyman were not available to baptize his children, then he would get a Dissenter, noting: "I dont dout but they will git as sone to Heaven that way as the other." During the 1720s St. Helena's in Beaufort was without a rector and members turned to dissenting clergy to marry them and baptize their children.[102]

Many a lowcountry resident believed as did Dr. Burnham, and the movement between denominations was not just from Anglican to Dissenter. In open violation of the Church Act, a number of Dissenters served on parish vestries. Some individuals owned pews in both dissenting and Anglican churches. Throughout the eighteenth century there was a gradual drift of Dissenters into the Church of England so that by the time of the American Revolution, many of the old Dissenter families (Elliott, Morton, Lynch, Fenwick, and Bee) had become Anglicans.[103]

The broad-mindedness of most lowcountry residents was expressed best by William Bull. In 1770 he wrote: "I charitably hope every sect of christians will find their way to the kingdom of heaven, yet I think the Church of England best adopted to the Kingdom of England." And, he could have added, the established church was the one best suited to the Carolina lowcountry. The only limits to South Carolina's official policy of toleration were that Roman Catholics were not welcomed and African religious forms suppressed.[104]

The movement among denominations may have been facilitated by the nature of the Anglican Church in South Carolina. It was more congregational than it was episcopal. Liturgically, it was low church; members did not see the need for the taking of communion more than several times a year. The Church Act of 1706 gave the Anglican parishes the right to call their own clergy, something that dissenting churches did.[105]

The established church was always understaffed, and one of the primary reasons was the Church Act. Once a congregation called a clergyman, if he turned out badly it was difficult to get rid of him. The South Carolina solution to this problem was to hire a priest on a temporary basis for an extended period of time. If he did not work out then he could be discharged easily. It was all quite legal but probably explains why there were always clerical vacancies. There were twenty-four parishes in the colony, but it was rare to have more than fifteen pulpits filled at any one time.[106]

The Society for the Propagation of the Gospel in Foreign Parts (SPG) supported some clergy. It also sponsored several unsuccessful missions to the Indians. As early as 1745 South Carolina Anglicans urged the society to sponsor an "itinerant missionary" to minister to the needs of the backcountry. It took twenty years, but the SPG did respond with Charles Woodmason's ministry (1766–1768). While there was harmony among the various denominations in the lowcountry, in the backcountry Woodmason found sectarian rivalry rampant. With his open contempt for non-Anglicans, he exacerbated the situation.[107]

It is difficult to determine the size of the various denominations. In 1710 Calvinists (Presbyterians, Huguenots, and Congregationalists) were the largest group (45 percent), followed by Anglicans (42.5 percent), regular Baptists (10 percent), and Quakers (2.5 percent). At midcentury Governor Glen said the percentages were still valid. By the 1770s Anglicans were in a majority in the lowcountry. In the backcountry Quakers and Lutherans ministered to their own and did little proselytizing. Presbyterians did some, but Baptists made great headway among the settlers.[108]

The Scots-Irish settlers who migrated down the Great Wagon Road brought with them their Calvinist beliefs. They founded some twenty-one churches in the backcountry, some of which had sizable congregations. The Long Canes Church served five hundred families, which made it arguably the largest in the colony. Although successful at building churches, the Presbyterians were not able to obtain clergy to supply them. Only two of the twenty-one churches had ministers. The paucity of clergy hindered the Presbyterians' missionary effort, but not the Baptists'.[109]

Backcountry Baptists, influenced by the Great Awakening before migrating to South Carolina, were not dependent upon an educated clergy. They believed in letting any man preach who was called by the Holy Spirit. They also developed an effective technique for ministering to the scattered settlements in the backcountry. Once a church was established, it became the mother church for the area. For example, the Fairforest Church on Fairforest Creek (Union County) under the leadership of the Reverend Philip Mulkey organized at least nine branches before the Revolution. By 1772 this ingenious organizational plan soon resulted in twenty-four organized churches and forty-nine meetinghouses, most of which were in the backcountry.[110]

If there were no church or minister, backcountry families gathered in individual homes on Sunday evenings to sing hymns and enjoy fellowship. Sometimes their hymn singing turned into general singing, a practice that Woodmason considered blasphemous. The Anglican missionary was generally critical of dissenting congregations and often looked for motes. He also was frustrated by his own lack of progress and the obvious success of Presbyterians and Baptists.[111] When the move came to disestablish the Church of England in 1778, backcountry Baptists selected William Tennent, a Charleston Presbyterian to make the case. That he did effectively, noting that there were ninety dissenting churches and only twenty Anglican ones.[112]

In Charleston, in addition to the two Anglican churches, there were eight other congregations: a Presbyterian meeting with close ties to the Kirk of Scotland; an Independent or Congregational meeting allied with those in New England; a Baptist congregation "in Harmony with those of Pennsylvania"; a Quaker meeting associated with Pennsylvania; an Arian congregation that had withdrawn from the Baptists; a Lutheran church with a German-speaking pastor; a French Calvinist congregation that followed the Geneva form of worship; and a Jewish synagogue. The backcountry was just as diverse. There Woodmason reported that "Such a mix'd Medley of Religions is hardly any where to be found as here—not even in Philadelphia, or Amsterdam."[113]

The most important religious movement in eighteenth-century America was the Great Awakening. Although New England clergy had begun preaching repentance and rebirth in the 1730s, an Anglican clergyman, George Whitefield, has been credited with sparking the religious revival that had an impact on thousands of colonists. His preaching crusade began in Philadelphia in 1739; however, he had been in Charleston the previous year.[114]

In 1738 Whitefield, like John Wesley who had visited before him, was received cordially in Charleston. The bishop of London's representative, Commissary

Alexander Garden, permitted both men to preach from the pulpit of St. Philip's. Whitefield's second visit in January 1740 was less pleasant. The bishop of London had condemned the evangelist for violating the order of service as found in the *Book of Common Prayer*. Commissary Garden refused to let him preach in St. Philip's, but Charleston's Congregational and Huguenot churches opened their pulpits to him. He then went to Savannah before returning to South Carolina. In a sermon in Beaufort he attacked the works of Archbishop John Tillotson, saying that Tillotson "Knew no more of Christ than Mohamet." Both Whitefield and Garden resorted to personal attacks from the pulpit, and their supporters engaged in a lengthy war of words in the *South Carolina Gazette*. The dispute divided the Charleston religious community, but not along denominational lines. The city's Baptist church condemned Whitefield while the Ashley River congregation supported him. Garden ordered an ecclesiastical trial that suspended him from the ministry, but that did not stop the evangelist from preaching regularly in non-Anglican churches until the mid 1750s.[115]

Although Whitefield's preaching affected individuals and churches in most other colonies, his impact in South Carolina was limited. In the lowcountry he stirred up controversy and even made some converts among his Anglican listeners. His publication list of twenty titles that were fit for a Christian to read encouraged a Beaufort man to burn £40 ($700) worth of books not on the list. His most visible disciple was Hugh Bryan, a planter of St. Helena's parish who wrote a letter saying that the Great Fire of 1740 was an indication of God's displeasure with South Carolina. Then, even though the Stono Rebellion was still fresh in everyone's minds, Bryan began to preach to large gatherings of slaves using Exodus for his texts. Rumors circulated that he was encouraging servile insurrection. Called to task by the Commons House, he pleaded that he was innocent and that his preaching to the slaves had been inspired by Satan. Bryan's was an extreme case, but his response to the evangelist's preaching threatened the "good order and the harmony" of the lowcountry community. There is no need to look any further to see why Whitefield had less influence in South Carolina than elsewhere.[116]

Prior to Bryan's short-lived preaching to the slaves of St. Helena's Parish, there was almost no effort made to convert the black majority to Christianity. Alexander Garden, with the help of the SPG, established a school for black males in Charleston. His plan was to convert young men to Christianity, teach them to read the Bible, and then send them back to their masters to convert others. The little school operated for twenty years, and by the time of the American Revolution, Garden's plan may have been working. Baptists in the Pee Dee area made the only other real effort to bring Christianity to blacks in colonial South Carolina.[117]

Individually, usually with the encouragement of their owners, blacks began to turn to Christianity; however, Christians had to contend with strong African religious traditions. With the continued importation of slaves, new arrivals brought with them their belief in Nzambi, an almighty god from whom emanated the powers of good and evil. Some of those from Senegambia retained their Muslim faith. After conversion black Christians combined their new faith with African forms of worship. They praised the Christian God with prayer, song, and shout (a loud exultation accompanied by "polyrhythmic hand-clapping and foot-stomping") just as they would have an African deity. Christian and non-Christian alike continued to believe in a variety of spirits that tormented and threatened the living: haunts, plat-eyes, and hags.[118]

White clergy discredited the sincerity of black Christianity because of the joy and spontaneity with which they worshipped. They felt it was not "proper" and did not understand that the exuberance with which black Christians praised God was an affirmation of their faith. Some clergy questioned the depth of faith of white Carolinians because they appeared to be lackadaisical about their duties as Christians. Not partaking of the Lord's Supper as regularly as some clergy would have liked seems to have been accepted as conclusive evidence. Most of these men of the cloth, it appears, should have spent more time studying Matthew 7:1 ("Judge not, that ye be not judged"). At all levels of lowcountry society, especially among the elite, there were examples of strong religious conviction. Henry Laurens wrote a friend, "I can't help saying to you, I trust in God to direct me in this & all my designs."[119]

The men and women who lived in colonial South Carolina were religious people, but this may have been another area in which English mores influenced the behavior of many. They had a concern for the poor and were generous in their charitable giving, but they did not go to church to get stirred up. The tolerant middle way of the Church of England was well suited to the harmony of the prosperous colony. Those who attended Anglican services would have agreed with the author of *Advice to a Divine* that clergy should confine their sermons to useful and practical subjects, "for Controversy is fitter for the Chair than the Pulpit." It was advice that the Anglican clergy in South Carolina generally followed. Alexander Keith, who served both Prince George Winyah and St. Philip's, made extensive notes on *Advice to a Divine*. Samuel Quincy of St. Philip's published *Twenty Sermons* that were safe and non-controversial. Alexander Garden, who tried to silence Whitefield, was described by Governor Glen as following a path "between the dangers of deism on one side, and of enthusiasm on the other." Neither the clergy of the established church nor the majority of the lowcountry's whites to whom they ministered wanted anything to disrupt the harmony of the community.[120]

Relationships between individuals were another important element in maintaining the harmony of the community. Hospitality, making strangers welcome, was something that visitors noticed—especially in the lowcountry. "The gentlemen on this country," wrote an Englishman in 1734, "are exceeding civil to strangers." A Philadelphian described the merchant-turned-planter Benjamin Smith as "Cheerful, easy, and generous." Although wealthy and hedonistic, the colony's elite were generally "quite free from pride." In theory all white men considered their neighbors to be their equals, but in reality colonial South Carolina was a deferential society in which everyone knew his place. However, it was considered ill-mannered for a member of the elite to disparage in public those of lesser social status. When William Henry Drayton made snide, arrogant comments about Charleston's artisans, he was unceremoniously reined in by his peers. Slights, even when unintentional, were countered. When in a pamphlet Henry Laurens said that there was little difference between a "bad hearted Lawyer and a perfect Swiss," he was called to task by the Reverend John J. Zubly and sent the clergyman a written apology. Politeness, not political correctness, led Laurens to apologize. Good manners and civility were an important social glue in keeping the disparate elements of the lowcountry's white population together.[121]

On the South Carolina frontier, society was a bit rough. The Reverend Charles Woodmason, an itinerant Anglican missionary, found few people with any manners other than Joseph Kershaw of Camden. The "living and Behavior" of the "Irish Presbyterians," he wrote, were "as rude or more so than the Savages." Some were "as wild as the very Deer," and young boys "ran wild here like Indians." His own manners left something to be desired as he was openly contemptuous and disdainful of the people he was supposed to serve. When some offered him what limited hospitality they had, he rejected it out of hand as unworthy. In one of the rare recorded instances of lack of hospitality, a "Presbyterian tavern Keeper" refused to sell Woodmason meat or drink. Given the priest's prior conduct, one wonders why he was outraged.[122] In truth, what bothered Woodmason most was what he considered the loose morals of backcountry folk. He roundly condemned their drinking and fornication. However, neither was confined to those who lived beyond the fall zone.[123]

South Carolina men drank a lot. Some colonists ascribed it to the heat. Lowcountry residents could claim they inherited the habit from their West Indian forebears or the notoriously poor quality of the water. Slightly saline and sandy, it quite often caused visitors gastric distress. Backcountry settlers could blame it on the need to take the edge off the harshness of their lives. Or perhaps as they had more contact with the lowcountry, they picked up its mores. Among the Cherokee, drinking to excess was a sign of rebellion (acts committed while under the influence were forgiven) or preparation for war. The consumption of alcoholic beverages was widespread and knew no class boundaries. Women generally did not drink much alcohol, and by law it was illegal to serve slaves without the permission of their masters.[124]

There were ample supplies of just about every sort of beverage available in the colony's numerous taverns. There was a story told in Barbados about what various nationalities did upon settling a new colony: the Spaniards built a church; the Dutch a fort; and the English a tavern. In 1769 there were more than one hundred licensed taverns in Charleston, or about one for every five adult white males. Woodmason complained that "in and about Charleston the Taverns have more Visitants than the

Churches." The Reverend Charles Boschi of St. Bartholomew's reported that members left during the service for punch or water and sometimes brought it back into the church for others.[125]

Woodmason could not do anything about the conduct of lowcountry Anglicans. However, he considered it his duty to instruct the white "Savages" of the backcountry how to behave in church. His sermon "On Correct Behavior in Church" had ten rules, including be on time, do not bring dogs to church, do not drink in church, and "when the Banns [announcing an intended marriage] are published— Don't make it a Matter of Sport."[126]

The backcountry was a frontier society with few clergy, so getting married was not easy. Men and women formed relationships that were recognized by their communities, and when a clergyman came through, they got married in a religious ceremony. In the first wedding he performed, Woodmason noted: "Woman very bigg." Later he recorded that of one hundred young women he had married, only six were not pregnant. No wonder that some individuals in his makeshift congregations might make ribald asides over the announcement of a couple's impending nuptials when, in practice, they might have been living together for quite a while.[127]

What Woodmason termed licentiousness (and modern observers might call practicality) was not confined to the Scots-Irish but also applied to Germans on the frontier. In addition lowcountry whites considered blacks to be immoral. Owners tended to encourage monogamous relationships, but slave marriages were recognized only by the owner and the slave community; they had no legal status. What disturbed the clergy was the "promiscuous cohabiting" of young blacks with a variety of partners. Premarital sexual relationships were common to most West African societies, but so were stable family relationships. However, the stability of slave families was fragile.[128]

One of the causes of instability in slave families was miscegenation, or as a 1743 grand jury described it: "the too common practice of criminal conversation with negro and other slave wenches in this province." Sexual relations between whites and blacks occurred in all Britain's North American colonies. Almost everywhere such liaisons were beyond the pale. In South Carolina, as in the West Indies, miscegenation was taken rather lightly and was close to being acceptable. In no other mainland colony was the issue discussed so openly.[129]

The *South Carolina Gazette* was less than a year old when it published "The Cameleon Lover," a poem that poked fun at those who chose to have congress with "the *dark* Beauties of the *Sable* Race." When a reader objected to such behavior, the printed retort was *"Kiss black or white, why need it trouble you?"* During the 1730s interracial couples (white males and black females) cavorted openly in Charleston where there was a well-known house of ill repute that employed black prostitutes.[130]

Most relationships, however, took place more privately. If a white owner wished to force himself on a black woman he owned, there was nothing she could do.

What was sometimes called South Carolina's "secret sin" was not much of a secret. In 1773 Josiah Quincy was shocked at the casual way white men spoke of interracial affairs with "no reluctance, delicacy, or shame. . . . It is far from being uncommon to see a gentleman at dinner, and his reputed offspring a slave to the master of the table."[131]

While some white fathers may have kept their own children as slaves, others provided for them. When Josiah Harrison wrote his will in 1774, he directed that his estate be sold and put at interest "for the benefit and advantage of the Children of a Negro Woman named Willoughby." Charles Faucheraud provided a two-room house, land, and annual income for his slave woman, Bina. Bina's daughter also inherited property and an annual income of £80 currency ($926). Manumitting one's black lover or the children of an illicit union was another step that some white men took. In the colonial manumission records, one-third of those freed were mulatto children and three-fourths of all adults manumitted were women.[132]

Miscegenation was not limited to white male–black female relationships. Gideon Gibson, a free black carpenter from Virginia, moved to South Carolina and settled on the Santee River. He owned seven slaves and had a white wife. In the 1760s he was one of the acknowledged leaders of the Regulator movement. When some legislators tried to make him subject to the colony's Negro Law, his supporters pointed out that he was whiter than any Huguenot descendant in the assembly, including the Speaker, Peter Manigault. Henry Laurens defended Gibson and noted that his children, "having passed through another stage of whitewash were of fairer complexion than their prosecutor George Gabriel Powell." In the backcountry liaisons between white women and black men were not unknown. Regardless of the gender of the partners, interracial relationships produced children. An increase in the number of clergy in the backcountry seemed to have had almost no impact on the population. "There are," wrote Woodmason, "more Bastards, more Mullatoes born than before."[133]

When the lowcountry was still in its frontier stage and clergy were rare, it was not unusual to have brides appear at their weddings visibly with child. As the South Carolina frontier receded and society developed, manners and morals became more refined, more like those in Great Britain.[134] Following British, especially English, models could be both good and bad. In one of the colony's major scandals, Sir Egerton Leigh, judge of the vice-admiralty court and attorney general, had an affair with his ward who was also his wife's younger sister. Mary Barbary Peronneau deserted her husband for Gov. Thomas Boone. Sir John Colleton divorced his first wife (by an act of parliament) and married his former father-in-law's former mistress.[135]

Colleton's divorce was the only legal one in colonial South Carolina. The institution of marriage, even the promise of it, was taken seriously. When William Lennox reneged on his proposal to Mary Cooke, she sued him for breach of promise and won financial damages of £2,500 currency ($32,000) plus costs. Once married, the only way out was to die or elope. Both men and women eloped, but we know more about women's elopements because deserted spouses gave public notice that they were no longer legally responsible their wives' debts. Once the backcountry began to open up, it became a destination for those seeking to end unhappy relationships. In spite of Woodmason's disapproval, on the frontier fewer people questioned whether a man and a woman were really married.[136]

Woodmason saw lasciviousness, wantonness, adultery, and fornication everywhere. In the backcountry he blamed some of the immorality on the way young women dressed. Despite his innumerable sermons, backcountry women persisted in pinning their shifts close to their bodies "to shew the roundness of their Breasts, and slender Waists" and drawing "their Petticoat close to their Hips to shew the fineness of their Limbs."[137]

Clothing in the backcountry was simple and minimal. A shift and a short petticoat were the extent of a typical woman's wardrobe. They used bear oil in their hair and usually wore it tied up "like the Indians." Men wore frocks or shirts and long trousers. The garb of a notorious backcountry outlaw was described as "black stockings and Breeches, check Shirt, and an old Beaver hat." Children ran around "half naked." Woodmason thought that the natives of the country were better clothed than the white settlers. Like backcountry whites, lowcountry blacks and poorer whites dressed in loose clothing that was admirably suited to the colony's climate. Charleston-made deerskin breeches were sturdy and durable, appropriately tough work clothes for a mechanic or apprentice.[138]

Slaves' clothing was defined by law. The Negro Act of 1735 was concerned that blacks wore "clothes much above the condition of slaves" and concluded that they probably were stolen. When the Commons House debated the question, some legislators wanted an exemption for clothing given to slaves by their owners. That right was denied and the law then proceeded to define appropriate material for Negro clothing. The fabrics that were approved were generally coarse and/or inexpensive: osnaburg, blue and checked linen, gingham, checked cotton, duffel, and calico. During the colonial period both cloth and finished clothing were imported.[139]

Black men were issued short and long breeches and shirts or jackets; women received shifts and sometimes kerchiefs. The latter could be worn around the neck or tied up as a head covering. The plaiting of hair into cornrows tied off with string or brightly colored ribbons was a West African hairdressing technique. Shoes were issued to both men and women. In the early eighteenth century almost all shoes were imported, but toward the end of the colonial period Charleston shoemakers turned out large quantities for the local market. John and Simon Berwick advertised that they had more than one thousand pairs of "Negro shoes" for sale.[140]

While slave owners purchased minimal clothing for their slaves, they dressed themselves and their families as sumptuously as they could afford. Clothing was a status symbol, and the South Carolina elite, as had the Barbadian elite, closely followed London fashions. George Whitefield, who looked askance at much of what he found in the colony, doubted "the court-end of London" could exceed South Carolinians "in affected finery [and] gaiety of dress." In the opinion of another observer, "The Men and Women who have a Right to the Class of Gentry . . . dress with Elegance and Neatness."[141]

South Carolina women dressed far more finely than their counterparts in New England, but their hairstyles were less elaborate. In a rare concession to the climate, women felt that the towering, powdered styles favored in Boston would have wilted in the heat and humidity. Their clothes were certainly selected for style rather than comfort. Hoop petticoats were in fashion during much of the eighteenth century. Until almost the end of the colonial period they were six feet in diameter, but later they were smaller and less cumbersome. These petticoats were not undergarments, but clothing made of rich velvets, silks, and satins; frequently they were quilted, embroidered, or trimmed with fine lace. Over them were worn gowns that had plunging necklines and opened in the front to reveal the petticoats. Small waists were in vogue, and if nature did not provide one, then a stomacher (girdle) could; or perhaps whalebone stays might be stitched into the gown itself. Such styles were certainly fashionable, but in South Carolina's muggy climate they were most definitely not comfortable.[142]

Fine apparel was not limited to the elite. Catherine Backhouse, a tavern keeper and wife of a blacksmith, had an extensive wardrobe: fourteen gowns—each valued at £30 ($358) to £50 currency ($597) and sacks (loose overdresses), underpetticoats, regular petticoats, cardinals (hooded cloaks), jackets, shoes and stone buckles, hose, gloves, caps, handkerchiefs, aprons, shifts, wrappers, and various pieces of jewelry. Not only did Catherine Backhouse own a lot of clothes, they were costly.[143]

White males in South Carolina dressed just as richly and inappropriately (in terms of the climate) as did the women. Among the effects of Benjamin Backhouse were plain and ruffled shirts, silk hose, linen jackets, and a crimson velvet jacket and breeches. A Philadelphia visitor found himself in a shop where a well-dressed "gentleman with a sword by his side" sold gloves and yard goods. Sometimes a man went overboard in his attire and looked too much the dandy; he was mocked as a "macaroni" (an overdressed English fop who wore continental-style clothes).[144]

By the late 1740s there were expert tailors in Charleston capable of turning out clothes in the latest London modes. Previously some South Carolinians thought English-made clothing was finer (it certainly was more expensive). In 1739 Robert Pringle ordered from London a riding coat with horsehair buttons, a "fashionable" scarlet waistcoat trimmed with gold lace, a flannel morning gown, a broadcloth suit, and two "finest India Dimitty" jackets. A year later the merchant received his order and paid the bill of £30 sterling ($3,665), but he wrote the tailor that there was "too much wadding in the Coat for this Hot Climate." He also ordered a wig from London and asked that it be lighter gray in color than those he had ordered before because the "Sun & Heat of the Climate" tended to turn dark wigs yellow.[145]

Recognizing the effect of the weather on fashion was unusual. In the West Indies style was more important than comfort or practicality. If the surviving portraits of the elite are any indication, then that was also true in South Carolina. Dress may have been fashionably smart, but it made little sense in terms of personal hygiene and health. John Archdale blamed disease not on the air but on "carelessness in Cloathing or Intemperance." One does not have to go any further to find the causes of "Sores, boils, the prickly heat and gout."[146]

The members of the South Carolina elite overate just as they overdressed. Again, in so doing they followed a pattern of behavior set in the West Indies. Three-course dinners with fine wines were the norm for those who could afford them. The food tended to be rich and heavy and was also expensive. "The necessaries of life," wrote William Bull, "are dearer here than in England."[147]

Ironically, it was black Charlestonians who virtually monopolized the local food market by purchasing produce from country blacks and marketing it to their own advantage. There was a tremendous variety of foodstuffs available: beef, pork, poultry, game, fish, rice, potatoes, and an assortment of fruits and vegetables. The blend of cultures that would be reflected in the colony's cooking began in the marketplace where European produce (turnips, collards, cabbage, broccoli, and cauliflower) could be found alongside African (okra, cowpeas, eggplant, peanuts, and yams) and that which was native to the province (pumpkins, corn, squash, melons, and beans).[148]

Merchants imported fruit, molasses, spices, and sugar from the West Indies; wheat flour from Philadelphia; gin, beer, ale, and brandy from England; wines from Portugal, Madeira, and Europe; salted fish from New England; and rum from the West Indies and New England. These were sold both wholesale and retail to individuals and country stores.[149]

By the middle of the eighteenth century, Charleston had retail specialty shops: butchers, bakers, and confectioners. Confectioner Frederick Kreedner advertised "Sugar Plumbs, Twelfth Night Cakes, Naples-Bisket, [and] Sweet-Meats." The baking firm of Myline & Smith sold water biscuits and butter biscuits in Bedon's Alley and also baked old flour into ship biscuits. While housewives and kitchen help baked bread, there was a ready market for store-bought bread.[150]

As one of the necessaries of life, bread production was regulated by law. On the first of each month the colony's commissary general published how much a "half-crown loaf," the standard size, had to weigh. The size of a loaf fluctuated according to the price and quality of flour (white, wheaten, or household). In July 1760 a loaf of white bread had to weigh one pound, thirteen ounces and one of household bread three pounds, ten ounces. By October, after the new crop of wheat had brought more flour to market and reduced the price, the finest loaf had to weigh two pounds and the cheapest four. After South Carolina flour (from the Orangeburg area) came on the market in the late 1760s, there was a two-tier pricing system. Regardless of grade, local flour was less expensive than imported flour. Thus, in 1768 a loaf of household bread made with South Carolina flour had to weigh five pounds. Though that was a lot of bread, the price of a loaf was more than one-half the daily subsistence allowance for most of Charleston's artisans.[151]

In the kitchens of the South Carolina lowcountry European, African, and Indian cooks blended ingredients and cooking styles from around the Atlantic world into a new cuisine. Each of the elements of the colony's population was introduced to new foods and new ways of food preparation. West Africans, for example, ate little meat but in South Carolina came into contact with Europeans and Indians who consumed a great deal. Beef, pork, and salted fish along with wild game became important parts of the diet of black South Carolinians. The Cherokee planted West African and European crops (watermelons, sweet potatoes, and peaches) in their gardens. The use of clay pots in cooking was Indian. The Catawba manufactured cooking pots for sale well into the nineteenth century because it was an accepted culinary fact that an Indian clay pot was the only proper utensil in which to prepare Charleston's famed okra soup, which, in turn, was West African. Black cooks in the kitchen combined new ingredients with West African and native American ways of food preparation. The cooking of vegetables for a long time with small pieces of meat for flavor and the use of hot peppers and exotic spices found their way to white tables and into white receipt books.[152]

Corn and rice in a variety of forms became the staples in the diet of all South Carolinians. Rice was eaten boiled, as bread or pastry (after being ground into flour), and as pudding. Hoppin' John (black-eyed peas and rice) was West African, and pilaus (rice and meat) were French. Corn was eaten on the cob, stewed, or as soup; in bread, muffins, cake, grits, cornmeal mush (after being ground); and as a special vegetable, big hominy (after being soaked in lye). Of the 550 or so receipts in the first published South Carolina cookbook, corn or rice was the principal ingredient in nearly one hundred.[153]

Although there was a blending of ingredients and cooking preparation methods from three continents, what individuals got to eat was another matter. For the 20 percent of the population that enjoyed "plenty of the good things of Life" and those who enjoyed "some of the Conveniencys of Life," meals could have included roasted or boiled meat, potatoes, rice, vegetables (cooked in the West African style), bread, dessert, fruit, nuts, and wine. Eggs, butter, coffee, tea, and sugar would likely have been in the larder. Meat and imported items would have been less common for 40 percent of the population that had only the "Necessarys of Life."

Necessaries, however, were a matter of definition. Charles Woodmason was so disgusted with the "excerable" provisions and cooking methods of the backcountry that he felt "obliged to carry his "own Necessaries": biscuit, cheese, rum, sugar, chocolate, and tea or coffee. For those who barely got by, especially in the backcountry, pork and cornbread appeared on the table twice a day. Occasionally produce or game might break the monotony. Flour, milk, and eggs were rare and coffee and tea unknown luxuries. Woodmason's encounter with frontier food repeated the experience of an earlier English visitor who described the menu at a tavern outside Georgetown: "a little bumboe, which is rum, sugar, and water, and some hominy and milk and [sweet] potatoes."[154]

The weekly rations for a slave community might include rice, peas, sweet potatoes, molasses, salted fish (winter), and beef or pork (summer). Whatever food the owner or overseer distributed was supplemented by produce from the slaves' own gardens, hunting, and fishing. Breakfast and supper were eaten in the quarters and the midday meal (anywhere from noon until two) in the fields. Meals were served in wooden bowls, clay pots, or gourds. Sometimes spoons were used, but, as in West Africa, black South Carolinians mostly used their hands.[155]

European settlers still used common wooden trenchers and their hands for eating until the early years of the eighteenth century. Later these were replaced by ceramic and pewter plates, bowls, and mugs. The use of knives and spoons became widespread and the use of forks increased. When Woodmason listed the utensils he carried with him into the backcountry, he included knife, spoon, plate, and cups but no fork. Mealtime became more elaborate. Three o'clock dinner became the big meal of the day and sometimes lasted the remainder of the afternoon. In the colony's wealthier homes silver place settings and hollowware, china, and glassware were used daily—not just for special occasions.[156]

Although some household objects such as pots, pans, cooking utensils, ceramic plates, cups and mugs, pewterware, and silver were imported, South Carolina's artisans produced a wide range of items for everyday use. Some were highly wrought and decorative; others were more utilitarian. Among the most common artifacts archaeologists have found in the Carolina lowcountry are shards of colono-ware, an unglazed, low-fired pottery. In the kitchens of South Carolina plantations clay pots and bowls were used for cooking, serving, and storing food. In the early years of the settlement these common household items were obtained from the natives of the province. South Carolina Indians were expert potters, but so were Africans. Slaves in Barbados made a pottery similar to that found in South Carolina. By the 1730s, except for Catawba cooking pots, most of the colono-ware was made by black Carolinians, but the influence of Indian pottery traditions was noticeable. The use of colono-ware was more widespread in South Carolina than in any of the other southern colonies. The reason for this might have been the sheer numbers of black Carolinians or their isolation from whites. Both of these factors contributed to the continuation of strong African cultural traditions.[157]

Coiled basketry was another African tradition that found use on lowcountry rice plantations. Basket making was common to many of the peoples who ended up in the colony. Indians and many upcountry whites made woven baskets of split oak or grasses. Coiled basketry, however, was a unique West African tradition. Skilled fingers wrapped thin strips of white oak or saw palmetto around bundles of black rushes (one-third to one-half inch in diameter) to create the coils for building the baskets. Coiled baskets were built, after a fashion, much as a brickmason lays rows of bricks; each row was built upon the foundation of its predecessor. Originally basketmaking was man's work and they produced baskets in a variety of shapes and sizes. Large, flat "rice fanners" used to separate rice grains from chaff were the most familiar shape; however, it was a rare lowcountry household (white or black) that did not have one or more coiled baskets.[158]

On virtually every farm and plantation in the colony, there was someone who could knock out simple furniture or items needed for domestic or farm use. Some of these items were skillfully made and were beautiful as well as useful. Not unexpectedly, the most skilled artisans were in Charleston. One of the myths that has been perpetuated about South Carolina is that artisans had a difficult time in Charleston because of the rage for British imports and the competition from black craftsmen. Some items were imported, and black artisans did ply their crafts; however, the city attracted numerous artisans whose wares and skills were much in demand.[159]

Furniture making was one craft in which Charleston artisans more than held their own. Although older historians said that Carolinians imported most of their furniture from England, records and the examination of eighteenth-century pieces confirm that most of the surviving furniture in South Carolina was locally made. During the 1750s there were twenty-six cabinetmakers in the city. That number nearly doubled to forty-nine in the next decade. Outside the city there were joiners and cabinetmakers in Beaufort, Georgetown, and Orangeburg. The items that they made were in the latest fashion. Peter Manigault, the richest man in British North America, ordered furniture and silver that was "the plainer the better so that they are fashionable." Although he ordered imported furniture, many of his peers chose to have theirs made locally. Manigault's preference for simple but graceful furniture and silver was shared by most wealthy Carolinians. They would have turned up their noses at the old-fashioned high chests (highboys) with cabrioles from Philadelphia and New England. South Carolinians may have been flamboyant in many respects, but they preferred restrained elegance in their furniture.[160]

Among Charleston cabinetmakers, Thomas Elfe is the most widely known. He arrived in the colony about 1747 and for nearly thirty years practiced his craft. One of his account books covers the last seven years of his life. During that time his shop produced hundreds of pieces of furniture in more than thirty forms: bedsteads, double chests of drawers, desks, chairs, tables, sofas, and bookcases. Ironically, despite the documentation concerning Elfe, not a single piece can now be attributed to his shop.[161]

Inventories reveal furniture made of poplar, cypress, walnut, and pine, but mahogany was the wood of choice for fine furniture in both England and South Carolina. After Thomas Chippendale's *Gentlemen and Cabinet-maker's Director* created a new style in England, South Carolina followed suit. Chippendale's collection of "designs of household furniture" was available in local bookstores. An excellent example of a Charleston cabinetmaker's using Chippendale's *Director* is a handsome mahogany and cypress bookcase now in the Museum of Early Southern Decorative Arts. Its proportions are slightly different (the Charleston-made piece is larger), but its design model is clear. Good cabinetmakers often produced their own versions of Chippendale's designs. Certain furniture characteristics popular in an area are now used for identification. Among the characteristics identified with Charleston-made furniture are the ball and claw feet found on many Chippendale-style pieces. Called "eagle's claws," they were well rounded and had strongly projecting talons.[162]

Locally made furniture was relatively expensive. In 1772 Elfe charged £80 currency ($955) for a double chest of drawers and £100 currency ($1,193) for a library bookcase. Fine furniture was not just for the homes of the elite; Benjamin and Catherine Backhouse furnished their tavern with mahogany furniture, possibly produced in Elfe's shop.[163]

In silver, as in furniture, South Carolinians followed English tastes. Those who had fine silver displayed it. Miles Brewton, the grandson of a silversmith, had "very magnificent plate" on his sideboard. An English visitor noted that many side tables in Charleston homes were "furnished in such a manner as wou'd not disgrace a nobleman's dining room." All of the Anglican churches had communion silver; St. Michael's was described as "superb." Some silver was imported, but many handsome pieces were locally wrought.[164]

The earliest known article of southern silver was a simple chalice made by Miles Brewton in 1711 for St. Thomas's parish church. Later silver was engraved or embossed with designs. Two of the colony's best silversmiths were Alexander Petrie and Thomas You. Petrie practiced his craft for twenty years (1745–1765) and You for thirty-three (1753–1786). In addition to crafting their own work, both men imported plate, jewelry, and clocks from England. You was also a talented engraver and produced a copper plate from which an engraving of St. Michael's church was printed in London. Among the items made by Petrie and You were tankards, coffeepots, teapots, punch bowls, ladles, sugar bowls, sauceboats, sword hilts, flatware, and church silver.[165]

There never were as many silversmiths as cabinetmakers, but as a group silversmiths tended to be more prosperous. During the last two decades before the American Revolution, there were between twenty and twenty-five silversmiths working in Charleston and one each in Beaufort and Georgetown.[166]

In describing South Carolina to British imperial officials, William Bull was careful to downplay the wealth and industry of the colony. In particular, he insisted that in terms of "arts and sciences we have only such branches as serve the necessaries, the

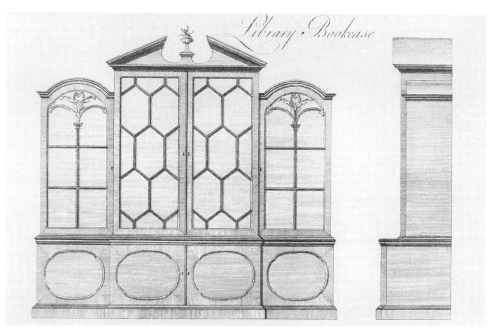

A library bookcase made in Charleston (circa 1765–1775) is similar to one depicted in Thomas Chippendale's *The Gentleman and Cabinet Maker's Director*. Collection of the Museum of Early Southern Decorative Arts, Winston-Salem, North Carolina.

conveniences and comforts of man." "The more refined," he continued, "such as serve to adorn or minister to the luxuries of life are yet little known here." The lieutenant governor's statement hinges upon the definition of "necessaries, . . . conveniences and comforts." Were mahogany furniture, silver, and coaches (all locally made) "necessaries" or were they more truly "the luxuries of life"? Perhaps Bull was playing the inferior colonial to his British superiors. Or, as a South Carolinian and an official of the empire, maybe he was trying to downplay local accomplishments. The colony was prosperous, and Charleston artisans were turning out luxury items. However, to tout direct competition with British craftsmen would not have been prudent. Bull knew well that British officials were looking for an excuse to tighten up on the colonies.[167]

In describing dwellings, Bull said: "Our houses are plain, but convenient." An English visitor was somewhat more impressed with the "many large handsome modern brick houses" that lined Charleston's streets; about half of the city's residences, he noted, were wooden, and most were "good sized."[168]

Two distinct house forms, the famed Charleston single house and the English manor–style double house, became fairly standard by midcentury. The single house, with its gable end to the street, was two or three stories high. Usually a piazza or side porch ran along the side of the house. The earlier ones were only one story, but later in the century two-story porches became popular. A house was generally built along one property line to permit a garden. Entrance to the property was either through a door set into the street side of the first-floor piazza or a garden gate. The front door was in the middle of the house, facing the garden. Generally, there were two rooms and a stair hall per floor. Double houses, usually square, were entered directly from the street. The central stair hall was flanked by two rooms on each side. The drawing room, the most important room in the house, generally was on the second floor in both single and double houses.[169]

The origins of South Carolina house forms, particularly the single house, have been debated for years. A 1657 history of Barbados used the terms *single* and *double house* in the same way that Carolinians did; however, there is not much additional evidence. Others claim that the single house with piazza is either West Indian or Afro-Caribbean. There may well be a West Indian connection, but in a view of Charleston painted before the Great Fire of 1740 there are wooden and iron balconies but no piazzas. Single houses with piazzas are wonderfully suited for the climate by allowing breezes to circulate, something that would not have been possible with row houses, a more typical English urban design.[170]

While form did not change, there was a difference between those houses constructed prior to 1760 and those built afterward. Older residences were only about two feet above the ground while newer ones were raised well above grade. This allowed for an English basement for storage, protection from storm floods, and elevation to catch sea breezes. Interior ornamentation and decoration depended upon

A silver coffeepot (circa 1750–1760) by Alexander Petrie. Collection of the Museum of Early Southern Decorative Arts, Winston-Salem, North Carolina.

An engraving of St. Michael's Church, Charleston, by Thomas You. Courtesy, South Carolina Historical Society.

the owner's taste, pocketbook, and time of construction. Earlier dwellings had simple moldings and mantles; those built after 1760 tended to be more ornately finished.[171]

The Miles Brewton house on King Street is acknowledged as "one of the finest colonial town houses in America." Built at a cost of £8,000 sterling ($684,000), it reflected the height of English fashion. The vaulted ceiling in the "grandest hall" Josiah Quincy had ever seen was covered with painted blue paper edged with gold papier-mâché borders. This style of interior decoration had just become popular in London the year the house was completed (1769).[172]

Fine interiors were not limited to the elite. In 1772 John Fullerton, a carpenter and contractor, built a wooden three-story single house on Legare Street. The mantle in the second floor parlor was decorated with fretwork purchased from Thomas Elfe.[173]

Charleston lots were narrow but deep. Arranged along the property line behind the main house were outbuildings such as a kitchen, servants' quarters, washhouse, and stable. One type of outbuilding seldom mentioned was a privy (although nineteenth-century Charleston had thousands). Chamber pots were widely used and emptied into the open sewers that ran down most city streets. For those who had the money and wanted to conceal this "necessary," Thomas Elfe made closestools with pewter pans.[174]

Rural residences ranged from simple raised wooden cottages to elaborate brick mansions with matching dependencies. Floor plans tended to follow English styles with a central hall flanked by two rooms. Since most planters spent a significant amount of time in Charleston, it is not surprising that they might have finer homes in the city than on their plantations. There were, however, numerous showplaces such as Peter Manigault's Silk Hope, John Drayton's Drayton Hall, Henry Middleton's Middleton Place, Ralph Izard's The Elms, Joseph Blake's Newington, and Joseph Allston's The Oaks.[175]

Surrounding these homes were formal gardens. The oak alley leading from the highway to the plantation house (often associated with the lower South and Hollywood films) was found in colonial South Carolina. Middleton Place, with its formal terraces descending to the Ashley River and its butterfly-shaped lakes, is the finest remaining example of a colonial garden. There were town gardens too. Some, such as Henry Laurens's brick-walled garden (600 feet by 450 feet) were elaborate and contained plants from around the world. He employed John Watson, an English gardener, to maintain his grounds.[176]

Located away from the big house on lowcountry plantations were the quarters. For a good portion of the colonial period enslaved Africans were responsible for building their own dwellings. As in West Africa, the houses were small because most activity was communal and took place outdoors. The houses, made from either wattle and daub or clumps of clay laid like bricks, had steep thatched roofs. The only

Plan of a four-room house with central hall by Henry D. Boykin II. *Camden: Homes & Heritage.* Courtesy, Henry D. Boykin II.

Plan of a Charleston single house by Henry D. Boykin II. *Camden: Homes & Heritage.* Courtesy, Henry D. Boykin II.

opening was a door; there were no windows. Earlier houses did not have chimneys, but later ones had chimneys of sticks and clay. The small structures (ten feet by ten feet) with their thick walls and natural floors kept the cool evening air inside and the hot midday sun out. In winter a fire could heat each small space. Colonial slave houses in South Carolina were more like those in West Africa than those anywhere else in the United States.[177]

Housing on the frontier evolved from crude, temporary shelters to finished housing. Settlers threw up houses made out of branches covered with dirt, which provided little protection from the elements. When it rained, the sandy roofs dissolved and those inside were covered with wet grit. In Williamsburg County these dirt houses were called "potato houses." More typical were dirt-floored, single-room cabins with open fireplaces made of sticks and clay. Roofs were made either of split logs or bark. Some cabins were not fully enclosed, and even those that were could be breezy. Clay was sometimes used as chinking between logs but seldom beyond head height. Woodmason was offended by everyone sleeping together in a common room: "The People all new Settlers . . . Live in Logg Cabbins like Hogs." Later either frame or hewn-log houses with wooden shingle roofs replaced the first homesteads. As individuals improved their conditions, they built better housing. Joseph Kershaw's Georgian-style house in Camden would have fit in with Charleston dwellings.[178]

Kershaw's house on Pine Tree Hill in Camden, as did Miles Brewton's on King Street in Charleston, made a statement. It spoke of wealth and privilege, of an owner who with skill and luck had prospered, who had in the closing words of Captain Martin's poem, found "many a bargain." Lowcountry whites, unlike residents in other colonies, were not concerned about having money or using it. While New Englanders, Virginians, and Pennsylvanians were concerned about the moral decay brought by prosperity and yearned for the good old days when life was simpler and purer, Carolinians did not believe that affluence led to a decline in morality. From the outset the influence of the West Indies had produced a society in the Carolina lowcountry in which the acquisition and enjoyment of wealth were not only accepted, but encouraged and applauded. Joseph Kershaw's Camden mansion was an omen that backcountry whites would emulate the lowcountry lifestyle if they had the means.[179]

The homes of Kershaw and Brewton made another statement: they said that English taste and English fashion were important. In architecture, dress, and furniture South Carolina's elite copied the styles of the mother country. Their government, manners, morals, educational system, and religion were based upon English models. They read English books and magazines. Some modern historians see these facts as evidence that South Carolinians were simply a consumer society that bought whatever they wanted directly from England.[180]

While it is true that a variety of items were ordered from English merchants, most of the furniture and clothing "in the latest English fashion" were made in South

Plan of a one-room house by Henry D. Boykin II. *Camden: Homes & Heritage.* Courtesy, Henry D. Boykin II.

Carolina. Everything looked English, but appearances were deceiving. The composition of the colony's population and environment were major factors in modifying English models. Single houses were built with English architectural details, but their floor plans and piazzas were unique to South Carolina. One of the most famous pieces of southern American furniture, a library bookcase (in the Heyward-Washington House), looks at first glance to be English with its matched veneers and bookcase doors. However, a closer examination reveals that the bookcase in design and detail is unmistakably Germanic and likely the work of a German cabinetmaker, Martin Pfeninger. The cabinetmaker used mahogany for the exterior but Carolina cypress in some of the interior construction. This piece of furniture is a visible reminder of the colony's rich ethnic mix—what appears to be English but is not.[181]

Everyday life in colonial South Carolina reflected the collision and blending of cultures: European, West African, and Indian. These cultures not only interacted with one another and were changed, but all had to deal with the reality of the environment. French and German cabinetmakers interpreted English styles and produced furniture scaled to fit local residences. Black Carolinians made coiled baskets in the West African tradition but used New World materials. Indian corn became a staple in the diets of all Carolinians, and West African sweet potatoes quickly made their way to frontier gardens. Blacks worshipped their new Judeo-Christian God in West African style. Lowcountry whites spoke English with a lilt that has been characterized as "high Gullah." The examples are virtually limitless.[182]

All residents, regardless of ethnic heritage, shared one common bond: the ever-present threat of death. As in the Caribbean, the response was the open pursuit of pleasure, and the hedonism of the original West Indian settlers became the accepted standard of behavior for all. The unashamed pursuit of wealth and the open enjoyment of the pleasures it could buy set South Carolinians apart from other British colonists. They may well have been the only colonial society to produce a new cultural identity.[183]

Lowcountry whites were proud of their "little world," and we need to remember how little it actually was (only about 15 percent of the population). Nevertheless, the small lowcountry elite had an impact on the remaining 85 percent of the population because of its wealth and power. By example and authority it shaped the lives of the rest of the population. The elite was proud of its accomplishments. In addressing a grand jury, Judge Robert Pringle boasted of the transformation of the wilderness into the "most opulent and flourishing colony on the British Continent in America." Yet members of the elite knew the limits of their success. They knew that Charleston was not London; they knew that as wealthy as they were, they were not in the same league with the British aristocracy. They also understood the colony's dangers. Nevertheless, they were content with their "little world." While studying abroad, Peter Manigault wrote to his mother: "What can induce any one to change Carolina for England I cant imagine unless it be for the sake of their Health." Twenty years later, at the age of forty-two, the wealthiest individual in British North America died in England where he had gone to try to recover from the fevers that ravaged his body.[184]

THREATS

Foreign and Domestic

Resolved, That His Majesty's subjects in this province are entitled to all inherent rights and liberties of his natural born subjects within the Kingdom of Great Britain. . . .
That the only representatives of the people of this province are persons chosen therein by themselves, and that no taxes ever have been, or can be constitutionally imposed upon them but by the Legislature of this province.
>   Resolution of the Commons House of Assembly, 29 October 1765

We are *Free-Men*—British Subjects—Not Born *Slaves*—We contribute our Proportion in all Public Taxations and discharge our Duty to the Public, equally with our Fellow Provincials Ye[t] We do not participate with them in the Rights and Benefits which they Enjoy, tho' equally Entituled to them. . . . We may be deem'd too bold in saying "That the present Constitution of this Province is very defective, and become a Burden, rather than being beneficial to the Back-Inhabitants."
>   "The Remonstrance presented to the Commons House of Assembly by the Upper
>   Inhabitants," 7 November 1767

Since the Cessation of the Cherokee War . . . these back settlements have been in a state of anarchy, disorder, and confusion.
>   Petition to the Commons House of Assembly, 5 July 1769

WHEN PETER MANIGAULT wrote his mother in 1753, the "little world" of the Carolina lowcountry elite was secure, orderly, and prosperous. Religious and partisan squabbles were a thing of the past. The elite, and indeed the entire white population of the lowcountry, acted as one in the face of the black majority. Neither Manigault nor his peers could have foreseen the events of the next quarter century. From within and without the colony came challenges to the authority of the elite that disrupted and redefined the meaning of "the good order and harmony of the whole community."

The first disruptions came from within, from the Carolina frontier, the backcountry. In the eighteenth century the territory more than fifty miles inland was referred to as the backcountry. In St. George Dorchester Parish there was a place known as Parish End, about fifty miles from Charleston. For some lowcountry residents it might as well have been called World's End as few knew, or cared, about anything outside their "little world."[1]

Beginning in the 1740s, frontier families from Pennsylvania and Virginia had begun moving south to the Carolinas. Some came to escape the threat of Indian warfare and others to take advantage of the colony's generous land policy. Because the settlers in the backcountry entered South Carolina through the back door, their settlements were not westward extensions of the lowcountry. Although some individuals in the lowcountry had contact with the backcountry settlements, for the most part the two sections were isolated from one another. In the backcountry there were few roads and no schools or courts. If a person wanted to register a deed, prove a will, swear out a warrant, or file a lawsuit, a trip to Charleston was necessary. Estimates on travel times to the provincial capital (on horseback and under optimum conditions) ranged from ten days to two weeks from Long Canes to a week or so from Ninety Six or Camden. Travel by wagon took more than twice as long.[2]

The only government that backcountry settlers experienced was an occasional justice of the peace and the tax assessor. The colony had a uniform tax policy, which meant that the hardscrabble farms of the backcountry were taxed at the same rate per acre as the more productive and valuable rice plantations along the coast. Lowcountry legislators did organize backcountry males into militia units, but that was as much for the lowcountry's protection against the possibility of a slave revolt as it was for the backcountry's defense against the Cherokee. In the 1750s backcountry society was unstable and unorganized. The Cherokee War would cause it to become dysfunctional.[3]

For more than a half-century the French had used their colonies on the Gulf Coast as bases from which they could compete with Carolina for the deerskin trade of the interior. They also made a concerted effort to subvert the various alliances that the English (through Carolina) had with the Indian nations of the Southeast, especially the Cherokee. The Cherokee, upset with broken promises by the English, began to listen to French blandishments. The English had promised to build and garrison forts in Cherokee territory to help protect them from their hereditary enemies, the Creek. Fort Prince George was built near the lower Cherokee town of Keowee in 1753. Four years later Fort Loudoun was completed over the mountains in eastern Tennessee. Even though the English kept their promises and built the forts, some Cherokee viewed them more as a threat to Cherokee sovereignty than as protection from the Creek.[4]

The outbreak of the Great War for the Empire (French and Indian War) officially was declared in 1756, but it had begun two years earlier on the Virginia frontier with George Washington's defeat at Fort Necessity. In 1755 Virginia militia killed several Cherokee warriors who had deserted General Braddock's ill-fated expedition against the French at Fort Duquesne. The murder of Indian warriors by their erstwhile allies and the inability of the English in South Carolina to keep all their promises led to talk of war in Cherokee country. Gov. William Henry Lyttelton sent presents to the Cherokee, but they were not mollified and there were isolated attacks along the frontier of both Carolinas. Having made a fiasco of dealings with the Commons House and Council, the governor decided that military glory would rescue his reputation. In 1759 he organized an expeditionary force of about thirteen hundred militia and marched into the backcountry. Miserably cold, wet weather and an outbreak of smallpox and measles caused hundreds to desert. Nevertheless, Lyttelton got the Cherokee to agree to a treaty in late December and several weeks later returned to Charleston in triumph. Under the terms of the treaty Cherokee hostages had to remain in Fort Prince George until those responsible for the earlier raids were turned over to the British garrison. While some chieftains may have signed a treaty, they could not bind the entire Cherokee nation, and there was open talk of war.[5]

Rumors of potential Indian attacks spurred frontier settlers to abandon their homes for safer settlements nearer the coast. In February 1760 a Cherokee war party attacked a refugee wagon train mired in a swamp near Long Cane Creek. Among those killed and mutilated was Catherine Montgomery Calhoun (the grandmother of John C. Calhoun). Within days the war touched communities as far east as Saxe Gotha and Orangeburg. The Ninety Six–Long Canes settlements and those between the Tyger and Enoree Rivers were particularly exposed. Lachlan Shaw of Augusta wrote that "if I was to give one hundred Guineas to a person to Cross the Country [from here] to Orangeburgh, I could not get any person to Undertake it." Brutality and treachery were common on both sides. The garrison at Fort Prince George massacred the hostages in its care. The Cherokee promised safe passage to the surrounded garrison at Fort Loudoun and as soon as the garrison left the fort cut down all but one.[6]

There was chaos all along the frontier. By the hundreds, settlers crowded into makeshift forts where disease and corruption were as deadly as the Indians. The assembly appropriated £5,000 sterling ($420,000) for refugee relief, but the individuals who commanded the private forts embezzled funds and supplies. They also extorted high prices for limited foodstuffs from the helpless men and women supposedly under their protection. Outside the forts militiamen and others helped themselves to abandoned property, setting a pattern that would plague the backcountry for a decade.[7]

The Commons House asked for British troops, and in April 1760 Col. Archibald Montgomery and twelve hundred Scots highlanders arrived. Marching inland, they were ambushed by the Cherokee; Montgomery decided, after burning some villages and crops, to return to Charleston and announce that the Cherokee had been defeated. Montgomery's retreat no doubt confirmed Henry Laurens's opinion that the war should be fought with colonials because British soldiers were "frightened out of their wits at the sight of Indians." Neither the colonists nor the Cherokee were fooled by Montgomery's pronouncements, and the war dragged on. The winter of 1760–1761 was unusually cold with lots of snow, making conditions miserable for both the Indians and the refugees.[8]

A second British expeditionary force, under the command of James Grant, was organized in 1761. Composed of British regulars and a provincial regiment, it launched its attack on the Cherokee in March. In June at the Battle of Etchohih, near the town of Estatoe, the Cherokee were routed. Grant's troops burned villages and fields, chopped down orchards, and killed cattle. He boasted that he had driven five thousand Cherokee into the mountains to starve. In September 1761 the Indians sued for peace and an unpopular treaty was hammered out. Throughout the campaign there had been friction between British regulars and the provincials. When the force returned to Charleston, a spate of pamphlets attacked Grant's integrity and courage. The British commander was openly insulted on the streets of the city and ended up fighting a duel with Thomas Middleton, who had commanded the provincial regiment.[9]

The Cherokee had been subdued and no longer posed a danger to the colony, although there were still problems in the backcountry. However, these problems were of no real import to members of the lowcountry elite as they were more concerned with the threats they now faced from imperial officials.[10]

Gov. Thomas Boone arrived in South Carolina in December 1761. As a descendant of the Colleton clan, he was welcomed by Carolinians as "one of us." However, his instructions from the Board of Trade directed him to obtain a revision of the Election Act of 1721 that would reduce the power of the Commons House. His predecessor had been given the same charge but because of the war had let the matter slide. Boone, bent on proving his mettle to the imperial bureaucracy, wasted no time in raising the question. When the assembly refused to act, he waited for an opportune moment to force the issue.[11]

In April 1762 there was a vacancy in the delegation for St. Paul's, and Christopher Gadsden was the overwhelming choice of the voters. The House certified the election, although technically, the wardens had not followed the exact letter of the law. Boone refused to administer the oath of office to Gadsden and dissolved the assembly for violating the Election Act. New elections were held, and the colony's voters, sensing a challenge to the assembly's right to determine its own elections, reelected all but ten of the members of the earlier assembly. Gadsden was returned with an "almost unanimous vote."[12]

The new assembly decided to investigate the Gadsden election controversy and resolved not to do any more business until the governor apologized and acknowledged his mistakes. He indignantly refused to do either. For the last year of the French and Indian War (1762–1763), the government of South Carolina did no public business because of the struggle between the governor and the Commons House. In an attempt to curry favor with wealthy locals, the governor made large grants of land "south of the Altamaha River." Although willing to accept the grants, few rallied to the governor's defense. In May 1764 Boone sailed for London where he was admonished by the Board of Trade for acting in an undignified manner with "more Zeal than prudence." The Gadsden election controversy was not a prelude to the American Revolution, but those who gained experience in resisting imperial authority would be among the colony's leaders for the next two decades.[13]

Boone's unsuccessful attempt to check the authority of the Commons House was just one imperial initiative. The Board of Trade had decided as early as 1748 that the colonies needed to be brought into line, but the war had forced the delay of such plans. The Peace of Paris was signed in February 1763. Imperial authorities were unhappy with all the colonies, and South Carolina came in for some specific criticism. Not many South Carolinians had joined the British forces, and some merchants had traded with the enemy. Overlooked was the colony's nearly £10,000 sterling ($850,000) contribution to the war effort, a financial burden that resulted in the highest per capita tax rate in British North America.[14]

One of the first actions of the British government after the war was to prevent another major conflict on the frontier, to separate colonists from Indians. Imperial authorities, such as Colonel Montgomery, had thought the settlers more at fault than the Indians for the hostilities on the frontier. The Proclamation Line, issued in 1763, ran down the ridge of the Appalachian Mountains; colonists were to stay east of the line. While the proclamation line irritated land speculators in other colonies, there was little reaction in South Carolina. The treaty ending the Cherokee War had pushed the Cherokee into the western corner of the colony, but they were still east of the mountains.[15]

That was the last treaty that South Carolina negotiated with an Indian nation. Indian policy, after the war, would no longer be left to individual colonies. It was now the responsibility of the imperial bureaucracy represented by two superintendents for Indian affairs, one for the northern colonies and one for the southern. A South Carolinian, John Stuart, was named superintendent for the southern department. In December 1763, at Augusta, he negotiated a treaty with representatives of all southeastern tribes. The eastern boundary of the Cherokee nation was confirmed, and by 1767 blazed trees marked the boundary. The Treaty of Augusta also established a 225-square-mile reservation for the Catawba. The Catawba, pressured by white settlements and reduced in numbers by disease and strife with other Indian nations, wanted the reservation for protection. When the boundaries were drawn, the Catawba reservation contained the traditional homeland of the nation where Sugar and Twelve Mile Creeks joined the Catawba River.[16]

More important than the Indian problem were the costs associated with the successful prosecution of the war. With taxes already alarmingly high in Britain, the government was determined to make the colonists help pay not only for the war but for the costs of maintaining and defending the empire. The Sugar Act (1764) was designed to raise revenue by levying duties on European luxuries such as Madeira. Other trade legislation passed at the same time granted special concessions to South Carolina's rice trade. When the new trade regulations reached the colony there was little reaction because things did not seem to change. Besides, those who could afford to import Madeira and luxury fabrics could afford to pay the duty.[17]

Clearly, though, the British government was not going to stop with the Sugar Act. When George Grenville, the king's first minister, presented his plan for a stamp tax to all of the colonies' agents, they protested. In strong language the Commons House instructed the colony's agent to lobby against the proposal. In February 1765 Parliament passed the Stamp Act with little opposition. Scheduled to go into effect on 1 November 1765, the act required revenue stamps be obtained for all paper items including newspapers, legal documents, books, dice, and playing cards. If the ministry had set out to craft a tax that hit all segments of the population, it could not have done a better job. Attorneys, printers, merchants, tavern keepers, and artisans—all urban dwellers would be affected. The tax would be especially burdensome to a master mechanic, who had to pay £7 currency ($91), about one-half a week's wages, to certify an apprenticeship agreement.[18]

As in other colonies, when the word reached South Carolina, the reaction was instantaneous and overwhelmingly negative. There were letters, essays, and poems in the local papers (pro and con) about the act. The editors of the *South Carolina Gazette* and the *South Carolina Gazette and Country Journal* supported the colonists' opposition to the act, while Robert Wells and his *South Carolina and American General Gazette* backed imperial authority. In July, after the Commons House had elected delegates (Christopher Gadsden, John Rutledge, and Thomas Lynch) to the Stamp Act Congress, Wells wrote to a friend: "I wish to be under the direction of the British Parliament and not our little Provincial Senate aping the grandest Assembly in the World." Had the newspaperman risked putting such a statement into print, he would have been run out of town.[19]

Charleston in October 1765 was the scene of the worst rioting and disorders since the Revolution of 1719. The city's Sons of Liberty, influenced by Gadsden, took to the streets to demonstrate in favor of the "rights of Englishmen" and to harass anyone suspected of supporting the Stamp Act. Tensions increased throughout the month as the deadline for the implementation of the Stamp Act approached. When the stamps arrived in the harbor on 18 October, William Bull, now the acting governor, ordered them secured first in Fort Johnson and later on a British warship. Mobs roamed the streets. The day after the stamps arrived, the Sons of Liberty erected a tall gallows at the intersection of Broad and Church Streets; hanging from it was an effigy of a stamp collector. Prominently displayed was a banner that read "Liberty and No Stamp Act" and a warning against anyone's tampering with the

The last issue of the *South-Carolina Gazette* (31 October 1765) before the Stamp Act went into effect; note the reference to "PRINTING-WORK that does not require STAMPS." Courtesy, Charleston Library Society.

display. No one dared. For nine days a mob of more than two thousand did what it wanted; royal officials were impotent. Two stamp officials lived in Charleston, Caleb Lloyd and George Saxby. Both took refuge behind the walls of Fort Johnson. Mobs ruled the streets and searched the home of any one, such as Henry Laurens, whom they suspected of supporting the Stamp Act. To the tolling of the bells of St. Michael's, a funeral procession carrying a coffin labeled "American Liberty" was carried through the city and buried with great ceremony. On 28 October the stamp officers came ashore in a boat flying the Union Jack with the word "Liberty" emblazoned upon it. To a cheering throng of seven thousand they announced they had resigned their offices and would not sell the stamps.[20]

British officials, fearful of what might happen if they used stamps, shut down the government. All public offices, the courts, and the port of Charleston were closed. Heightening the tensions were rumors of a Christmas slave rebellion. It did not occur, but a group of Catawba was employed to track down runaways in the swamps. The Commons House met and appointed a committee, chaired by Christopher Gadsden, to draft the assembly's official response to the crisis. The committee reported out a petition to the king with eighteen attached resolves. Although similar to the resolutions of the Stamp Act Congress, South Carolina's resolutions were much more forceful: "in taxing ourselves and making Laws for our own internal government . . . we can by no means allow our Provincial legislatures to be subordinate to any legislative power on earth." The assembly adopted the report with only one dissenting vote (William Wragg's).[21]

There was considerable pressure on Bull to reopen the port and the courts without stamped clearances, but the acting governor was adamant. When word came that northern ports had opened, the clamor became greater. Finally, in late February 1766, ships were allowed to clear port with a permit for which they paid the customs collector an amount equal to what the stamps would have cost. In March 1766 Bull appointed three new assistant judges to the courts; they joined with the other assistant to outvote Chief Justice Charles Shinner. In the case of *Jordan* v. *Law* they ruled that to delay justice for any reason (even an act of Parliament requiring stamps) was a violation of the Magna Carta and ordered the clerk to record their decision. When he refused, they fined him and requested that he be removed from office. The courts were still at an impasse when word arrived of the act's repeal.[22]

The news reached Charleston on 3 May 1766, and two days later there was a grand illumination. The word on the city's streets was that any unlit house would be defaced. As darkness fell, candles twinkled in almost every window in every house in town, including those of the chief justice and most other royal officials. The Commons House voted £1,000 sterling ($82,000) for a marble statue of William Pitt in gratitude for his efforts to get the act repealed and also commissioned portraits of its Stamp Act Congress delegates to be hung in the State House. Clergy preached special sermons; the Reverend J. J. Zubly's *A Sermon upon the Repeal of the Stamp Act* was available from the offices of the *South Carolina Gazette*.[23]

With the exception of Gadsden and a few Sons of Liberty, few people paid attention to the Declaratory Act that accompanied the repeal. Most coastal residents were more concerned with the impact of the Currency Act of 1764, which declared that colonial currency no longer had to be accepted as legal tender. As the money supply shrank, the colony's prosperity hit a bump. For the rest of the decade times were difficult, especially for Charleston's artisans and mechanics, who were in no mood to accept the import duties imposed by the Townshend Act on glass, lead, paint, paper, and tea. At this time the colony's merchants were more concerned about the arbitrary actions of Charleston's customs officials, and the entire lowcountry was beginning to realize that there were serious problems in the backcountry.[24]

Given the scope of the lawlessness that resulted in the first organized vigilante movement in the colonies, it is astounding that more people in the lowcountry were not aware of what was happening in the backcountry, although some individuals, including Chief Justice Charles Shinner and Charles Woodmason, were. In October 1766, a full year before the provincial government took any official note of the lawlessness that was threatening to destroy the backcountry settlements, Woodmason accused the assembly of refusing to create backcountry parishes, even though population growth warranted it, because new parishes might "lessen the Town Interest." Whether or not that was a fair assessment, it is true that there were serious problems in the backcountry and the provincial government did nothing to solve them.[25]

The Indians were no longer the threat they once had been, but the law-abiding settlers were beset by "Virginia crackers and rebels." The frontier in America had always attracted a certain lawless element, but the further rending of the meager social fabric that existed in the Carolina backcountry seemed to serve as a magnet for even more ne'er-do-wells. During the war even decent citizens had taken to appropriating property when an owner was not in sight, perhaps justifying such actions by assuming that the owner was either dead or might not return. This breakdown of respect for property rights continued after the war. Squatters, poachers, and thieves were a real problem, but organized gangs of outlaws posed even greater threats.[26]

The crime problem in the Carolina backcountry was part of a larger pattern of lawlessness on the frontier from northern Georgia to western Pennsylvania. The gangs were an assortment of genuine criminals and individuals who had turned to this way of life during the Cherokee War. Among the gang leaders were Winslow Driggers and Edward Gibson from the Pee Dee area, and Govey and George Black, who had been landowners along the Wateree River. The bandit gangs were democratic, and runaway slaves and Indians figured prominently in reports of gang activities. Gibson, one of the acknowledged bandit leaders, was a mulatto. Just as the gangs were open to all, they did not discriminate when it came to their victims.[27]

During the summer of 1766 a crime wave swept over the backcountry. Gangs terrorized the Dutch Fork and Saxe Gotha settlements. Anyone thought to have money or valuables was tortured until he revealed the whereabouts of his cache. Hot coals or pokers to feet and various other parts of the anatomy were common. Women and girls (as young as ten) were raped and kidnapped. Decent folks were either cowed into silence or coerced into assisting the gangs. Country store owners and tavern keepers were especially vulnerable. If they did not cooperate, their buildings likely would be burned with them inside. After a few examples of those who tried to resist became known, many reluctantly cooperated in the fencing of stolen goods. Attempts to track down the bandits resulted in violent retribution. The militia in the Camden area was afraid to go after the outlaws for fear of retaliation.[28]

Only a handful of outlaws were captured and sent to Charleston for trial; six were convicted, but five were pardoned by Governor Montagu, who wanted to begin his administration by showing clemency. It was a misguided gesture and one not appreciated by the law-abiding citizens of the backcountry. If the government in Charleston were not going to protect honest citizens, then who could blame them for taking matters into their own hands?[29]

The summer of 1767 began where the previous one had ended. Outlaws acted as if they owned the backcountry. Then, spontaneously in community after community, individuals reacted. If the government would not restore order, then they would. They turned on the bandits, burning their hideouts and whipping those they caught. The gangs responded in kind, and open hostilities broke out between those who wanted to build communities and those who wanted to destroy them. Reports filtered down to Charleston of what was occurring, and the governor acted. On 6 October 1767 he considered the nascent vigilantes to be nothing better than an unruly mob and ordered them to disperse. His proclamation was ignored but was an indication of how out of touch the provincial government was with the territory that lay beyond Parish End.

By the end of October the separate resistance groups had coalesced to form what were termed the Regulators. Although Governor Montagu condemned them as "licentious Spirits," the Regulators represented the substantial citizens of the backcountry. It is uncertain exactly how many men participated in the movement, but there were probably three thousand to six thousand at various times, with an active nucleus of about five hundred. Many of them were small planters who owned several hundred acres they tilled with the help of their families. They worked hard and resented those who did not. They were men of property and their leaders were slave owners. Rather than one commander-in-chief, the movement had regional captains: Claudius Pegues of Cheraw; Henry Hunter and Charles Woodmason of Camden; Moses Kirkland of lower Saluda; Barnaby Pope of the area between the Broad and Catawba Rivers; Gideon Gibson of Mars Bluff; James Mayson of Ninety Six; and William Wofford of the area between the Tyger and Enoree Rivers.[30]

What the Regulators wanted above all else was law and order. They yearned for the "good order and harmony" of their communities. Nowhere was this desire more striking than in the petition submitted to the Commons House on 7 November 1767. Written by Charles Woodmason, it listed twenty-three requests. Among them were pleas for courts, courthouses, jails, and schools—institutions that would help bring order and stability to the backcountry. Initially it was tabled by the Commons House because most members of the assembly knew its author, a man who had supported the Stamp Act. Also, the petition contained gratuitous insults aimed at Charleston attorneys and the purchase of the Pitt statue. After the representatives of the Regulators apologized for offending the dignity of the assembly, it went to work. Within two weeks the assembly authorized two companies of rangers (in effect deputizing Regulators) to restore order to the frontier settlements. An act creating circuit courts took a bit longer, but in April 1768 it passed.

The most immediate result of the Regulator movement was the success of the ranger companies. These mounted units, paid by the colony, moved swiftly from the Savannah River to Virginia in pursuit of outlaws. They hanged sixteen in North Carolina and flogged numerous others. The most notorious bandits were sent to Charleston for trial, and this time those convicted were punished either by hanging or branding. By March 1768 the outlaws had been defeated, but the Regulators were not finished.[31]

The outlaw bands, the most serious threat to the lives of the law-abiding folk, had been suppressed. However, there were still "Rogues, and other Idle, worthless, vagrant People" who posed a danger to property. These "baser sort of people" stole fruit from orchards and corn from fields. They were lazy and immoral. They were disgraces to their communities and needed to be disciplined. And that is precisely

High Hills Baptist Church, Sumter County, was formed in 1770. This early-nineteenth-century structure replaced the original, which burned. Photograph by Suzanne C. Linder.

what the Regulators set out to do. In June 1768 Regulators from all parts of the backcountry met in a congress at the Congarees (near present-day Columbia) where they adopted the Plan of Regulation to deal with the "baser sort of people." Again, they could have been justified in their actions because South Carolina was the only southern colony without a vagrancy law and there still were no courts operating in the backcountry.[32]

The Regulators were now in complete control of the colony from fifty miles inland all the way to Cherokee territory. For nearly three years they effectively cut off the backcountry from the lowcountry. The Plan of Regulation was the only law. Assuming the powers of government, the Regulators intervened in family life, disciplined wayward husbands, and enforced debt collection. The only writs they permitted the provost marshal to serve were for debts. "The Country," wrote Woodmason, "was purged of all Villains. The Whores were whipped & drove off. The Magistrates & Constabls associated with the Rogues, Silenc'd & inhibited. Tranquility reigned. Industry was restor'd." Eventually all that did occur, but not without difficulty.[33]

With no one to challenge their authority, some Regulators took advantage of the opportunity to settle old scores. Punishments became cruel and unusual. Flogging to excess became a sadistic entertainment rather than a punishment for wrongdoing. When victims of this treatment resorted to the courts, the former champions of law and order resorted to violence. The deputy provost marshal was kidnapped and other officials physically assaulted. Several were shot. At Mars Bluff the militia not only refused to assist the provost marshal of South Carolina but threatened him. William Bull, as acting governor, issued two proclamations in August 1768: the first ordered the suppression of the Regulators, and the second was a pardon for anyone who from that date onward kept the peace. The Regulators ignored the proclamations and the provincial government did nothing, conceding control of the backcountry to the Regulators.[34]

With the "baser sort" cowed, the Regulators determined to right a grievance not addressed fully by the assembly: representation in the Commons House. There were three backcountry parishes: St. Mark's (established 1757), St. Matthew's (1765, 1768), and St. David's (1768). However, they gave the colony's white majority only three of the forty-eight seats in the assembly. Elections were scheduled for 4–5 October 1768, and backcountry voters trekked more than a hundred miles to cast their ballots in three lowcountry parishes. The wardens of St. Bartholomew's refused to let them vote. In St. Paul's they were allowed to vote, but their ballots did not affect the outcome. In St. James Goose Creek they overwhelmed the local voters, and the backcountry slate of Moses Kirkland, Aaron Loocock, and Tacitus Gaillard carried the day. When questioned as to why they let this occur, the wardens from Goose Creek said that they "favoured the Liberty of the Subject and the right of voting." The following year, in Prince William Parish, Patrick Calhoun led a group of men from Long Canes to the polls and was elected.[35]

The triumph of the backcountry at the polls in 1768 was short-lived. After being in session for only five days, Governor Montagu dissolved the Commons House for considering the Massachusetts Circular Letter protesting the Townshend Duties. Backcountry needs were caught up in the clash between the lowcountry elite and imperial authorities as well when the Circuit Court Act of 1768 was disallowed by the Board of Trade because it included a provision that judges would be appointed for good behavior, not his majesty's pleasure. Upon being notified of the disallowance, the Commons House reluctantly gave in to imperial authorities and passed a new Circuit Court Act (1769) that met earlier objections. It also authorized the spending of £7,000 currency ($83,500) for land, courthouses, and jails in Beaufort, Camden, Cheraw, Georgetown, Orangeburg, and Ninety Six.[36]

The circuit courts did not begin functioning until 1772, so until then all legal matters still had to be initiated in Charleston. That was inconvenient, but not as dangerous as the unchecked rule of the Regulators. By 1768 the Regulators had begun to lose their hold on the backcountry population. Those truly interested in law and order were concerned about the capricious and arbitrary manner in which punishments were meted out. When solid citizens such as John Musgrove, a substantial planter along the Saluda River, and Jonathan Gilbert, a justice of the peace from Beaverdam Creek, complained, they were harassed and assaulted. Soon an unlikely alliance emerged between some of the most prosperous residents of the backcountry and the "lower sort." The former simply wanted the rule of law, while the latter thirsted for revenge.[37]

Assuming positions as leaders of the opposition, Musgrove and Gilbert began to chip away at influence of the Regulators. The two men traveled to Charleston where they described the situation to the governor and council. As a result, several prominent Regulators lost their positions as justices of the peace. The governor asked for volunteers from lowcountry militia units to help bring the Regulators into line; since almost no one responded to the governor's request, Musgrove and Gilbert knew they would have to raise their own armed force. They recruited Joseph Coffell of Orangeburg, and he assembled a motley band to go after the Regulators. Styling themselves the Moderators, they soon had a band of about six hundred spoiling for a fight. In late March 1769 the Moderators and an equal-sized band of Regulators camped near the junction of the Bush and Saluda Rivers. It looked as if there would be a bloody battle, but Richard Richardson of the High Hills of the Santee and William Thomson of Orangeburg, two of the most respected men in the backcountry, talked both groups into agreeing to a truce and going home.[38]

Although there was sporadic activity for the next few years, essentially the Regulator movement was over and there was no longer a need for the Moderators. The original objectives of the Regulators had been achieved; the outlaws had been eliminated and the "lower sort" had been taught a lesson. The backcountry had been made safe for the development of a plantation economy. The Regulators' concern for order had struck a responsive chord with the lowcountry elite, who saw in the racially mixed outlaw bands a potential threat to the stability of their "little world." The Moderators, too, had attained their goal of serving as a brake on a vigilante movement that had spun out of control. Governor Montagu's issuing a general pardon for most of the Regulators in 1771 brought formal closure to a turbulent decade in the Carolina backcountry.[39]

The lowcountry elite had addressed some of the concerns of the backcountry, but the tensions between the sections had only been lessened, not eliminated. Issues raised in 1767 would continue to plague the relationships between the more populous backcountry and the wealthier lowcountry until the early nineteenth century. Temporarily satisfied with their partial loaf, backcountry planters put their energies into agriculture instead of politics. The lowcountry elite was relieved not to have the distraction of the backcountry as it faced what it considered the primary threat to its hegemony: imperial prerogative.

In 1767 only South Carolina's artisans and mechanics had seen any danger in the Townshend Duties. The colony's merchants were more concerned about the seizure of coastal trading vessels by crooked customs officials. Under the Navigation Acts, a ship was supposed to have customs papers properly filed every time it left port. In the coastal trade, small vessels from plantations frequently entered Charleston without them because there were no customs officials available. However, a new crew

Walnut Grove (1765), Spartanburg County, is an example of the homes built by the rising planter class of the backcountry. Photograph by Suzanne C. Linder.

of customs officials decided to enforce the law without regard to practicality or reason (and to enrich themselves with the profits made from seized ships and cargo). They made the mistake of seizing two vessels belonging to Henry Laurens, who promptly took them to court.

When the case came before the vice admiralty judge, Egerton Leigh, he tried to work out a compromise by releasing one vessel and letting the collector keep the other. His decision was sloppily done and opened the door for Laurens to file a successful damage suit against the customs official, George Roupell. In that case Leigh, who was also attorney general, served as Roupell's defense attorney. Roupell then seized another of Laurens's ships and hinted that if Laurens renounced the damage award, he would release the ship. In the vice admiralty court Leigh ruled that while there may have been grounds for seizing the vessel, he was releasing it because of Roupell's scheming. Laurens was outraged at his mistreatment by imperial officials and wrote four pamphlets setting forth the case and exposing the vulnerability of Americans to customs racketeers and vice admiralty courts where there was a judge and no jury. Leigh responded with a vitriolic pamphlet attacking Laurens personally. In private correspondence Laurens described the character of the customs officials as similar to the "Miscreants who were driven out of the Temple by Jesus with a Scourge of small Cords." The Laurens-Leigh controversy of 1767–1768 turned the conservative Laurens into a defender of American liberty, and several of his pamphlets were circulated widely throughout the colonies as documentation of imperial tyranny.[40]

Anti-imperial feelings were already running high when the Massachusetts Circular Letter arrived in November 1768. Despite warnings from Governor Montagu, the Commons House voted to take up consideration of the letter and he dissolved the assembly. New elections were held, but Montagu did not call the assembly into session until 15 June 1769. By that time most of the members of the Commons House had signed a nonimportation agreement that they would boycott British imports. A committee of thirty-nine (equally divided among planters, merchants, and artisans) was created to implement the agreements. Force and intimidation were used to get most lowcountry residents to comply, but among the holdouts were William Wragg and William Henry Drayton.[41]

The committee that enforced the nonimportation successfully for more than a year was the first of a number of extralegal bodies that appeared in the last six years before the American Revolution. Governors could prorogue and dissolve assemblies and imperial officials disallow acts of the Commons House, but none of them had any authority over the committees and other revolutionary organizations that began to function somewhat as a shadow government.

In December 1769 the Commons House voted to send £1,500 sterling ($130,000) to the Society for the Support of the Bill of Rights in England—a fancy title for a fund set up to cover the legal expenses of John Wilkes, a British politician. Wilkes was a scoundrel but became a hero when the government jailed him for criticizing the king's speech opening Parliament. The assembly's unilateral action and the appropriation of such a large sum (nearly 10 percent of the total raised) for a public enemy of the government caused an uproar in London.

The Wilkes Fund Controversy lasted for five years during which both the Commons House and imperial officials were willing to shut down the government rather than yield what each considered to be a crucial constitutional question: the authority of the representatives of the people of South Carolina to appropriate funds as they saw fit. The Commons House in a series of reports and resolutions affirmed its position. The ministry in London insisted that governor and council had to concur *and* that the assembly could only appropriate funds for local purposes. The constitutional issue was very real: the inherent rights of Englishmen and their elected representatives in assembly versus limited authority granted (and hence revocable) by the British government to colonial assemblies. The situation was complicated by the ill-advised actions of the colony's council and governor.[42]

Charles Greville Montagu, whose previous colonial administrative experience looked good on paper, continued to make one mistake after another. In the space of eighteen months he dissolved the assembly four times. At one time he thought he might get a more pliable Commons House if it met in Beaufort. Instead, his actions fueled suspicions that he and his imperial masters were up to no good. When the council tried to force the Commons House to pass a bill renewing the general duty law, councillors John Drayton and William Henry Drayton protested and had their dissents published in the *South Carolina Gazette*. The council ordered the printer, Thomas Powell, arrested for contempt, but he was ably defended by Edward Rutledge. The Commons House promptly condemned the council's actions and instructed its agent to seek the removal of the councillors responsible for jailing Powell; it also sought Montagu's recall.[43]

In the other twelve colonies, local issues were secondary to the general issues of parliamentary taxation and imperial policy. In South Carolina a series of local issues contributed to the onset of the revolution, and the Wilkes Fund Controversy was as important as parliamentary taxation in convincing the elite that if it wanted to control the political destiny of South Carolina, revolution was the only answer.[44]

Imperial officials underestimated the resolve of the South Carolinians. The colony's elite was determined that it would not knuckle under to the "unjust and unconstitutional measures of an Arbitrary and Oppressive Ministry." For all practical purposes, royal government in South Carolina ceased in 1771 (the last year any legislation was passed), four years earlier than in other colonies.[45]

The Wilkes Fund Controversy was still boiling when news arrived of the Tea Act granting a monopoly to the British East India Company and its colonial agents. The tea would be less expensive than smuggled Dutch tea, but the colonists would have to pay the only one of the Townshend Duties still in place (a three-pence [$1.00] per-pound levy). It was another miscalculation on the part of the British government. In New York and Philadelphia, after local agents resigned, the tea was returned to England. In Boston there was the well-known Tea Party.

In Charleston news of the arrival of the ship *London* with 257 chests of tea led to the calling of a Mass Meeting on 3 December 1773 to protest the importation of the tea. At the meeting the consignees of the East India Company announced they would not accept the tea; all present agreed not to purchase or use tea and established a committee to encourage others to do likewise. As with the Non-Importation Association of 1769 (a boycott of British goods to protest the Townshend Duties), intimidation and peer pressure were used to get people to cooperate. Even though the meeting resolved that the tea would not be unloaded, several weeks later it was and was stored in the basement of the Exchange. There it remained until 1776 when it was sold to purchase war matériel for the state of South Carolina.[46]

The significance of the Mass Meeting lay not in its response to the Tea Act, but in its laying the groundwork for an independent government in South Carolina. The Mass Meeting established the General Committee to enforce its resolutions and the nonimportation agreement at subsequent gatherings. When word arrived of the parliamentary response to the Boston Tea Party, South Carolina already had in place an organization that could react.

The Intolerable Acts were designed to punish the citizens of Boston and Massachusetts. The Boston Port Act closed the port until the costs of destroyed tea and its duties had been paid. The Massachusetts Government Act altered the colony's charter and reduced the power of the town meetings. The Impartial Administration of Justice Act provided that any royal official accused of a crime could be sent to Great Britain or to another colony for trial. The Quartering Act authorized British military commanders to appropriate private residences to house their troops. In all of these British acts, many Carolinians saw threats to their liberty.

Thinking of their own recent tangle with the ministry over the Wilkes Fund, Carolinians realized that what happened to Boston and Massachusetts could happen to Charleston and South Carolina. The closing of the port would destroy the colony's economy. The alteration of the Massachusetts charter was a clear message that all colonial governments were subordinate to Parliament, a constitutional position 180 degrees from that of South Carolina's Commons House. Had the Impartial Administration of Justice Act been in effect in 1767, would George Roupell have been tried in Charleston? During the French and Indian War, South Carolina had constructed barracks in Charleston to avoid having troops quartered in individual homes, but what if there were not sufficient room or the local British commander decided to station soldiers in Beaufort or Georgetown? Given their recent experiences with inept and venal royal officials and the struggle with the British government over the power and authority of the Commons House, South Carolinians were inclined to imagine the worst.

When the Boston town meeting asked for assistance and the New York assembly suggested an intercolonial congress, the General Committee was ready. It issued a call for the General Meeting of delegates from all corners of the province to meet in Charleston on 6 July 1774. For the first time, the backcountry had something more than token representation. After adopting a series of resolutions, the General Meeting on 7 July elected five delegates to the First Continental Congress: Christopher Gadsden, Thomas Lynch, Edward Rutledge, John Rutledge, and Henry Middleton.

As a group, the delegates were representative of the interconnected world of the lowcountry elite and its growing disenchantment with imperial authority. All were South Carolina natives from that portion of the population that had "plenty of the good things of Life." Gadsden was a merchant-planter; Lynch and Middleton were planters; the Rutledges were attorneys and, in addition, John was a land speculator. The Rutledges were brothers, and Middleton was Edward Rutledge's father-in-law. All had served in the Commons House of Assembly. Each had protested against what he viewed as unjust actions by royal officials. Gadsden, Lynch, and John Rutledge had been delegates to the Stamp Act Congress. Edward Rutledge had defended the publisher of the *South Carolina Gazette*. Middleton had been the only member of the council to vote to open the port of Charleston without stamps; later he had resigned from the council and joined the Nonimportation Association.[47]

It was a strong, talented delegation that South Carolina sent to the First Conti-

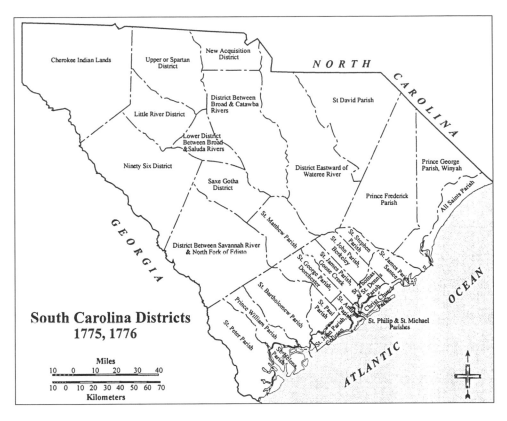

Map 10: Election districts, 1775, 1776. Based on Edgar, *Biographical Directory*

nental Congress in Philadelphia. Gadsden and Lynch, more radical than the other three, openly advocated strong measures. The Rutledges and Middleton were more cautious, but the radicals controlled the congress. A number of petitions, declarations, and resolutions proclaimed that Americans had the same rights as Englishmen and condemned a long list of what were seen as governmental abuses of power. Congress created the Continental Association to implement a boycott of British goods and an agreement not to export colonial products to Great Britain. South Carolina, more than any other colony, produced enumerated commodities that were supposed to be shipped to Britain. Therefore, the delegation felt that the colony was being asked to make more of a financial sacrifice than the others. All but Gadsden threatened to bolt the meeting. The other colonies yielded to South Carolina's demands, and a compromise was worked out that permitted Carolina to export rice but not indigo. For the first time, but certainly not the last, South Carolina's threats of disruption forced the union of colonies (states) to accede to its wishes.[48]

In South Carolina the General Meeting elected a Committee of 99 (15 artisans, 15 merchants, and 69 planters) to act for it. Among those elected were Peter Timothy, Daniel Cannon, Joshua Lockwood, and Edward Weyman (artisans); Miles Brewton, David Deas, George Abbot Hall, and Roger Smith (merchants); and Elias Horry Jr., William Thomson, James Ravenel, and Benjamin Singleton (planters). This committee quickly became the de facto government of South Carolina. There were still royal officials in Charleston, but the majority of the city's residents responded to the Committee of 99, not the king's appointees. The Commons House fully supported the actions of the General Meeting and appropriated funds to cover the expenses of the delegates to the Continental Congress.[49]

The General Meeting received the delegates' report from Philadelphia with some grumbling about preferences being given to rice magnates. Nevertheless, the delegation was reelected to the Second Continental Congress. The Secret Committee was chosen and given the mission to secure arms and ammunition. The association was rigorously enforced by committees in every crossroads. When the Charleston committee voted to let a merchant import thoroughbred horses he had been using in England, public opinion forced a reversed decision. In November 1774 the General Meeting called for elections of 187 delegates to a Provincial Congress. Representation was apportioned almost inversely to the white population. The lowcountry with less than 40 percent of the white population got 132 seats, and the backcountry with more than 60 percent got only 55 (see Map 10).[50]

When the Provincial Congress met in Charleston on 11 January 1775, forty of the forty-eight members of the last royal assembly were among its members. Over the next nine months the Provincial Congress and its various committees moved to consolidate their hold on the colony. In April the Secret Committee confiscated official government mail from the regular packet boat. In letters to the governors of the southern colonies, British officials revealed their intentions to use military force against the colonies. Shortly thereafter, under cover of darkness, the Secret Committee confiscated sixteen hundred pounds of gunpowder, eight hundred muskets, and two hundred cutlasses from the colony's powder magazines and the State House. In May came news of the battles at Lexington and Concord and rumors that British authorities intended to induce the Cherokee to attack the frontier and incite lowcountry slaves to rebel. Realizing the potential dangers, congress voted to raise a force of three regiments (five hundred men in each), issue £1,000,000 currency ($12.5 million) to support its operations, and create a Council of Safety with unlimited authority. A slim majority of congress approved these actions. South Carolinians were far from united in taking steps that meant an armed confrontation with Great Britain.[51]

Not everyone was ready to make the break with the empire in the summer of

1775, but few associated with the revolutionary government were in any mood to tolerate dissent. Those who disagreed with congress and the association were dealt with harshly. William Wragg, for instance, was banished to his plantation and, after hostilities began, exiled abroad. Thomas Jeremiah, a free black harbor pilot (and slave owner), was hanged after being accused of plotting a slave insurrection and saying he would aid British forces. Minor imperial functionaries were tarred and feathered; others fled. While those favoring strong measures were able to cow their lowcountry opponents, the backcountry was another matter.[52]

The backcountry was a source of real concern. After all, many of its residents had a bigger beef with the provincial government in Charleston than they did with the British. Even when the lowcountry-dominated congress included the back-country, the lowcountry looked out for its interests first. One of the three regiments was to be a mounted ranger unit in the backcountry under the command of Col. William Thomson of Orangeburg. The other two were created to safeguard the lowcountry.[53]

Individuals who supported the Provincial Congress sent troubling reports of rising opposition to its actions. Thomas Fletchall of the District Between the Broad and Saluda, one of the more prominent men in the backcountry, openly declared: "I am resolved, and do utterly refuse to take up arms against my King." A counterassociation, proposed by Joseph Robinson of New Acquisition District, garnered widespread support. After troops of the new backcountry regiment took powder and supplies from Fort Charlotte, an abandoned outpost on the upper Savannah River, they were captured by loyalists who liberated the powder. Gov. William Campbell was in regular contact with backcountry loyalists and urged them to stand firm. In an attempt to convert the backcountry to its side, congress sent a persuasive group of individuals: William Henry Drayton, chairman of the Secret Committee; Oliver Hart, a Baptist clergyman; William Tennent, a Presbyterian minister; Joseph Kershaw of Camden; and Richard Richardson of the High Hills.[54]

The group's first meeting was at McLaurin's Store in the Dutch Fork area of Saxe Gotha. It went poorly, and Drayton recorded in his journal that the German settlers were "not with us." However, he might have noted that they were not against the congress either; they just wanted to be left alone. That meeting was something of an omen for the entire mission. The group found a warmer reception at Lawson's Fork on the Pacolet River but a hostile one at Thicketty Creek. Turning from reason to intimidation, Drayton ordered the arrest of several prominent Nonassociators (as they called themselves because they refused to join the Nonimportation Association) and the burning of their homes. He then asked for a parley with the opposition; the result on 16 September 1775 was the Treaty of Ninety Six. Basically, the Nonassociators agreed that they would remain neutral in the contest between congress and Great Britain. In return, they received some vague assurances that the Council of Safety would not molest them. While Drayton and his team were trying to get the

A fifty-pound note issued by the Commons House of Assembly to cover expenses of the Provincial Congress, 1 June 1775. The reverse of the note contained the motto "For the Public Good." Courtesy, South Carolina State Museum.

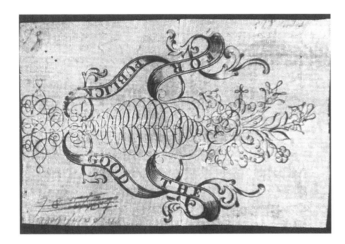

backcountry to side with congress, the Council of Safety considered arresting Lord William Campbell, the last royal governor.[55]

Campbell had arrived in Charleston on 18 June 1775. Fifteen years earlier he might have been a good choice for governor. He was married to a South Carolinian, Sarah Izard, and had had experience as a colonial administrator. Normally the arrival of a royal governor was the signal for pageantry and celebration. Campbell, however, was met on the steps of the Exchange by a handful of nervous placemen and "sullen silence." He received a delegation from the Provincial Congress but did not recognize it as a legitimate body. A meeting with the Commons House accomplished nothing. The members of the Thirty-third (and last) Royal Assembly scolded the governor as the minion of a government that had repeatedly ignored the petitions of the American people. In July, as one of its last acts, the Commons House gave its approval to the Provincial Congress's issuing of paper currency. Then it simply faded out of existence. On 15 September, Campbell officially dissolved it and fled for his life to a British warship in the harbor. Royal government, which had been so eagerly sought in 1719, had been driven from the colony for the same reason it had been welcomed: for the good order and the harmony of the whole community.[56]

There was a major difference, however, between the Revolution of 1719 and the beginnings of the American Revolution in South Carolina in 1775. In the earlier revolution there had been almost total agreement that the proprietary regime had to go. In 1775 there was considerable disagreement in congress, on the Council of Safety, and among the general population about breaking ties with Great Britain. The rents that had begun to appear in the social fabric of South Carolina in the 1760s and 1770s would not be mended until the first decade of the nineteenth century. From the outbreak of the Cherokee War in 1759 until the Great Compromise of 1808, there was neither good order nor harmony in South Carolina and no such thing as a whole community.

Chapter Eleven

THE AMERICAN REVOLUTION

Left mainly to her own resources, it was through the depths of wretchedness that her sons were to bring her back to her place in the republic . . . having suffered more, and dared more, and achieved more than the men of any other State.

George Bancroft, *History of the United States* (1857)

WHEN LORD WILLIAM CAMPBELL slunk out of Charleston in September 1775, it was an ignominious end to formal British rule. It was also a statement of failure. The success of the revolutionary movement in South Carolina was very much in doubt in 1775. Campbell had been in contact with backcountry loyalists since his arrival. Yet, instead of heading for the backcountry to rally support for the crown, he opted for a warship in Charleston harbor. In so doing, he abandoned the loyalists to their own fates and handed the patriots a victory. The only government in South Carolina now was the revolutionary Provincial Congress, and it moved to suppress any opposition.[1]

Not all backcountry Tories were willing to abide by the Treaty of Ninety Six. Robert Cunningham of Saluda River openly defied congress, was arrested, and was imprisoned in Charleston. This and other hostile actions by congressional forces resulted in renewed tensions in the backcountry. Both loyalist and patriot militia units mobilized. In November 1775 at Ninety Six there was a skirmish, and the first blood of the Revolution in South Carolina was shed. In retaliation, Col. Richard Richardson raised a force of more than four thousand and in December marched through the upper piedmont. He defeated the loyalist militia and tracked down the remaining Tories on the Reedy River and captured them. The Snow Campaign (so called because of the more than fifteen inches of snow and sleet on the ground) silenced the backcountry opposition to the Provincial Congress.[2]

The new year began with the Provincial Congress in control of all of South Carolina. The backcountry was now quiet, and the British warships had left Charleston harbor. In March 1776 South Carolina became the first southern colony and the second of the thirteen to draft a state constitution. The Constitution of 1776 was clearly a temporary document designed to provide a governmental framework "until an accommodation of the unhappy differences between Great Britain and America can be obtained." In it South Carolina is still referred to as a colony. The constitution was a legislative enactment and was not ratified by the people. On the morning of 26 March 1776 the last session of the Provincial Congress declared itself adjourned, and in the afternoon the same men convened themselves as the First General Assembly of South Carolina.

The House of Representatives, as had been the Commons House, was the most powerful branch of government. The new legislature was bicameral, but the house elected the upper chamber (Legislative Council) from its own membership. All money bills were to originate in the House of Representatives. Jointly the two chambers elected the president of South Carolina and other statewide officers. The chief executive had a great deal of power, including an absolute veto and the power to make war and peace (with the consent of both houses). Given the colony's disputes with governors Lyttelton, Boone, and Montagu, it was somewhat surprising that members of the Provincial Congress were willing to grant the executive so much authority. Perhaps they trusted one of their own more than royal appointees. In the elections that followed the convening of the First General Assembly, John Rutledge was elected president and Henry Laurens vice president.[3]

South Carolina's government was concerned with the defense of the province—and with good reason. There were incessant rumors that the British intended to attack Charleston and incite the Cherokee to strike the frontier. On 28 June a British fleet with eleven ships and an invasion force of twenty-nine hundred regulars and marines launched an ill-planned assault on the unfinished palmetto log and sand fort on Sullivan's Island. Leading the South Carolina forces were Col. William Moultrie and Col. William Thomson. Landing on Long Island (Isle of Palms), the British intended to wade across Breach Inlet and attack the fort from the rear; however, the depth of the inlet and its riptides were insurmountable barriers. When the British tried a small amphibious landing, Thomson's forces drove them off with deadly marksmanship. Then the invading force watched impotently from Long Island as the battle unfolded. The fort's construction rendered the heavy fire from the fleet ineffective as cannon balls either bounced off the spongy logs or buried themselves harmlessly in the sand. Three ships ran aground and one was destroyed by its crew to prevent capture. At the end of the day the British withdrew in disarray. American casualties were light in what was a tremendous victory over both the British army and navy.[4]

There were a number of local heroes, but none more celebrated than an enlisted man, Sgt. William Jasper. During the battle a shot destroyed the pole from which flew the new militia flag (indigo blue with a white crescent moon in the upper-left-hand corner). Jasper grabbed a gun sponger, attached the flag to it, and mounted it on the bastion closest to the enemy. In a public ceremony President Rutledge took off his own sword and presented it to the sergeant.[5]

The Battle at Sullivan's Island gave a psychological boost to the revolutionary

Col. William Thomson by an unknown artist. Courtesy, Gibbes Museum of Art/Carolina Art Association.

Sgt. William Jasper on the ramparts of the palmetto log fort on Sullivan's Island, 28 June 1776. "Centennial Album" (1875). Courtesy, South Caroliniana Library.

cause in South Carolina. It provided a new symbol for the state (the palmetto tree) and inspired the design of the state seal (on the front an upright palmetto [South Carolina] stands over an uprooted oak [royal navy]). It also gave the upper hand to those who favored a more resolute course of action.

The British fleet remained off Charleston until August. Its presence, and the urging of northern nations, spurred the Cherokee and some Tories (painted as Indians) to launch a series of raids in July. A number of white Carolinians had been waiting for an excuse to drive the Cherokee from South Carolina. The response was immediate and brutal. Col. Andrew Williamson led backcountry militia units against the Indians, destroyed most of their towns east of the mountains, and then joined with the North Carolina militia to do the same in that state and Georgia. Captured warriors were sold into slavery. In a short time the Cherokee were routed and sued for peace. In 1777 they signed a treaty giving up all their lands in South Carolina (most of present-day Anderson, Greenville, Oconee, and Pickens Counties). For the remainder of the war the Cherokee were not a factor. The Catawba early on sided with the colonists. They joined militia units and tracked down Tories and runaway slaves.[6]

While the backcountry was dealing with the Cherokee, news arrived on 2 August of the Declaration of Independence. Four of the state's five delegates in Philadelphia had signed the document: Thomas Heyward Jr., Thomas Lynch Jr., Arthur Middleton, and Edward Rutledge. Thomas Lynch Sr., the fifth delegate, had had a stroke and was paralyzed. On the engrossed copy of the Declaration, there was a space left among the South Carolina delegates for him to sign, but he never recovered and died on his way home.

On 5 August 1776 President John Rutledge made the formal announcement of independence a time of public celebration. There was a procession and the city's troops paraded near the Liberty Tree. The document was read at three separate locations in the city. One of the participants in the ceremonies was Vice President Henry Laurens. His private reaction was anything but jubilant: "In truth, I wept that day, as I had done for the melancholy catastrophe which caused me to put on black clothes—the death of a son—and felt much more pain."[7]

The General Assembly convened in September and announced its pleasure with the dissolution of ties with Great Britain. That, however, may have been the high tide of revolutionary fervor for a while. After the twin threats of invasion and Indian war had been defeated, the state entered a two-year period of calm that bordered on apathy. When elections were held for the Second General Assembly later in the fall of 1776, voter turnout was dismal even though the new assembly would be drafting a permanent constitution.[8]

The framing of a new constitution was necessary to replace the temporary one of 1776 because "the United Colonies of America have since been constituted as independent states and the political connection heretofore subsisting between them and Great Britain entirely dissolved." Disestablishment of the Anglican Church was the most hotly debated issue. An impassioned address by the Reverend William Tennent and the support of Christopher Gadsden and Charles Cotesworth Pinckney helped carry the day. An effort to maintain a limited sort of establishment lost by only ten votes, but the question of disestablishment passed unanimously. By early spring the General Assembly completed its draft of the proposed constitution and then set it aside for nearly a year so that members could get their constituents' reactions. Copies were printed and distributed across the state.

The document was skewed to benefit the lowcountry elite. The backcountry was allocated only 64/202 seats in the new House of Representatives. Property and residential qualifications (£10,000 [$41,000] and ten years) for governor and lieutenant governor seemed tailored to exclude even rising backcountry planters. Each parish or district got one senator, except that the city of Charleston (with two parishes) received two. One of the most outspoken critics of the constitution (after the fact) was Christopher Gadsden. He complained that a few conniving individuals had seen to it that the document had "as high a tincture of aristocracy as possible." His observations would be shared by others. This constitution and its 1790 successor would cause tremendous discontent among Charleston's old Sons of Liberty and the rising planters of the backcountry. Less controversial were the reduction of the executive to a figurehead and guarantees that a person could not be "deprived of his life, liberty or property, but by the judgment of his peers, or by the law of the land" and that "liberty of the press" would be "inviolably preserved." In March 1778 it was adopted by the legislature as the new basic law of the state of South Carolina.[9]

There was little fanfare or celebration over the adoption of the new constitution, even though it underscored the break with Great Britain. Maintaining zeal for the Revolution was difficult. In Charleston there were sporadic displays of enthusiasm, but then only on special occasions. Palmetto Day (28 June in honor of the Battle of Sullivan's Island) and the Fourth of July were celebrated with great fanfare. The first anniversary of the Declaration of Independence was especially festive. At sunrise the city's church bells began to peal. Then there was a military parade followed by a seventy-six-gun salute. In the afternoon President Rutledge hosted a "most elegant entertainment" that featured thirteen toasts (each one punctuated by a thirteen-gun salute). As darkness fell and a crescent moon rose over the city, there were fireworks and a grand illumination. The third anniversary in 1779 was also marked "with great demonstrations of joy."[10]

Having a good time did not translate into active support of the Revolution. So many legislators absented themselves that it was difficult for the General Assembly to meet a quorum. "An Act Enforcing an Assurance of Allegience & Fidelity to the State" requiring a loyalty oath and prescribing severe penalties for any who refused was largely ignored—even after the deadline for taking it was extended.[11]

A more ominous indication of the lack of enthusiasm for the Revolution was the decline in enlistments. In 1776 more than two thousand South Carolinians had enlisted as Continentals or regulars, but by 1778 there were only a handful still in service. In order to fill its quotas for the Continental army, the General Assembly decreed that "all idle, lewd, disorderly men," beggars, deserters, and night hunters attracting deer by fire would be sentenced to active duty. Volunteers would receive a bonus of one hundred acres in the lands ceded by the Cherokee. The following year, with few volunteers signing up, the legislature added $500 cash ($812) to the land bonus. Inflation was so bad that before the year was out, the cash bonus was increased to $2,000 ($1,427) at 10 percent interest. And in 1780 "An Act to Procure Recruits and Prevent Deserters" authorized a bonus of one slave for each year of service. Nothing worked.[12]

In 1778 the militia law was revised so that one-third of the militia could be slaves (although to be used only in support roles as engineers and sailors). After the war Gov. Charles Pinckney noted that "To their hands were owing the erection of the greatest part of the fortifications raised for the protection of our country . . . particularly Fort Moultrie." Some black Carolinians did play more than support roles. There were black soldiers in Francis Marion's partisan band and in militia units at Cowpens and King's Mountain. On both sides blacks were effectively used as messengers and spies. In the General Assembly, Col. John Laurens's proposals to arm slaves were overwhelmingly defeated. The British, however, had no qualms about arming black South Carolinians and created a unit known as the Black Carolina Corps. Arming slaves might have seemed like a sensible move to British officials, but it was just one of a series of incredibly ignorant errors they made between 1778 and 1782.[13]

The two years of nonwar ended late in the fall of 1778 when British troops landed in Georgia and captured Savannah (see Map 11). With a base of operations, the British now could execute their "southern strategy" to roll up the southern colonies one by one. Throughout 1779 the British made a series of probing attacks against South Carolina. In February, Gen. William Moultrie's command repelled an amphibious assault at Port Royal and Col. Andrew Pickens's backcountry militia defeated a large Tory unit at Kettle Creek, Georgia. By June, however, a British army was at the walls of Charleston. Sensing a possible encirclement by American forces that outnumbered his three to one, the British commander, Gen. Augustine Prévost, withdrew toward Georgia. In September a French fleet arrived, and the following month the allies launched a bloody and unsuccessful frontal attack on entrenched British positions at Savannah. After the battle the French fleet sailed away leaving the Americans to fend for themselves.

Although the year ended with the British still in Georgia, South Carolinians received a taste of what was to come. During their campaign the enemy had carried

Map 11: The American Revolution in South Carolina. Based on Don Higginbotham, *The War of American Independence: Military Attitudes, Policies, and Practice, 1763–1789* in Louis Morton, gen. ed., The Macmillan Wars of the United States (New York: The Macmillan Company, 1971)

away with them most things of value: horses, silver, furniture, and slaves. What was not stolen was wantonly destroyed. In addition to those slaves carried away as prizes of war, hundreds more flocked to British camps seeking their freedom.[14]

The new year did not look promising for the Americans in the South. The already thin ranks of the Continentals had been further depleted at Savannah. Although Washington and Congress agreed to send reinforcements, only a fraction of them arrived. Virginia and North Carolina promised to send militia units. Benjamin Lincoln, the commander of American forces, always seemed to count the number of soldiers who might someday be in his command rather than those actually present for duty. Under pressure from South Carolina political leaders, he let himself be convinced (although it did not take too much argument) that he should move his army behind the walls of Charleston. In effect, he trapped his army on the peninsula between the Ashley and Cooper Rivers—not a wise decision. He made no attempt to take advantage of the swampy terrain in and around the city, territory with which many of his troops were familiar.

Leading the British forces was Sir Henry Clinton, who was determined not to repeat the fiasco of June 1776. He brought a large, well-supplied army of eleven thousand to South Carolina. His task was made a great deal easier by Lincoln's strategic mistake. In February 1780 Clinton's army landed thirty miles south of Charleston. By the end of March, Clinton had begun a land siege and the royal navy a blockade by sea. Lincoln's army was trapped. Siege guns lobbed heated cannonballs into the city, causing fires. Lincoln offered to surrender the city if he could withdraw his army. Not only did the British reject the offer, but Christopher Gadsden and the remaining civil authorities opposed both surrender and evacuation. Gadsden's son-in-law went so far as to threaten to open the city gates to the British and to fire on the Continentals if they tried to leave town. Thus, General Lincoln's incompetence was compounded by that of civilians.[15]

On 13 April, Gov. John Rutledge and several members of his council slipped out of the city so that state government could continue to function. Two months earlier he had been granted extraordinary powers by the General Assembly to prosecute the war "'till ten days after their next session." His escape was none too soon as the next day Clinton's forces cut off all escape routes from the city. After mid April it was not a question of whether Charleston would capitulate but when. On 12 May 1780 Lincoln surrendered his army of more than fifty-five hundred men to Clinton. It was the largest surrender in the annals of the United States Army until Corregidor. When word of the fall of Charleston reached interior garrisons, they too surrendered: Andrew Williamson and Andrew Pickens at Ninety Six and Joseph Kershaw at Camden.[16]

Clinton had conquered an "opulent, populous, and very important colony," but then he and his subordinates made a number of blunders that would lead to the undoing of his victory. Under the terms of surrender (which applied to civilians as well as military), adult males were paroled. They agreed they would not take up arms against the British, and in turn they would not be molested. That suited many South Carolinians, who simply wanted to be left alone. However, in early June the British commander abrogated the parole of most Carolinians and issued a proclamation that they must now swear a new oath of allegiance that included the phrase "that whenever I shall be thereunto required, I will be ready to maintain and defend the same against all persons whatsoever." If they took the oath, Carolinians could be placed in the position of taking up arms against their countrymen—something most were loath to do. He then announced the confiscation of the estates of leading revolutionaries and looked the other way as his army plundered the lowcountry. Encouraged, Tories went on a campaign of retribution. Each of these events drove men into the rebel camp.[17]

The revolutionary slogan "Liberty or Death" was cast into this iron fireback, manufactured by the Aera Furnace, York County (1778). Collection of the Museum of Early Southern Decorative Arts, Winston-Salem, North Carolina.

To solidify his hold on the province, Clinton dispatched units to capture Augusta, Ninety Six, and Camden. He then left the province for New York, placing Lord Cornwallis in command. Cornwallis ordered his men to "take the most *vigorous* measures to *extinguish the rebellion.*" As they moved into the interior, the British troops followed orders. Executions were common, and the soldiers harassed and mistreated everyone. One commander declared that Presbyterian meetinghouses were "sedition shops" and ordered them burned; another exhumed and abused Richard Richardson's body. Rather than cowing the populace, these deliberately wanton acts roused them. "Brutality, fear, and the resultant social disorganization," observed historians of twentieth-century warfare, "can work only for the guerrillas, no matter who initiates them." That was also true in the eighteenth century. Near Nelson's Ferry, the British burned Thomas Sumter's home—a big mistake.[18]

Taking the destruction of his home personally, Sumter began to rally backcountry residents to join him in an independent force. Whatever his military shortcomings (and they were many), Sumter was the only organized opposition in the summer of 1780. He became a rallying point, an important symbol. When it looked as if there were no hope for the Whig (American) cause, Thomas Sumter energized South Carolina's resistance. He led a series of successful raids against British supply lines, but had mixed results in attacking British forces. On 6 August at Hanging Rock (Lancaster County) his men ambushed a loyalist militia unit and decimated it. That was a bright spot for the Americans, but the remainder of the month was gloomy.[19]

On 15–16 August, Gen. Horatio Gates led an ill-prepared and exhausted command against fortified British positions at Camden. The British carried the day, and

Gates jumped on his horse and did not stop until he reached Charlotte some sixty miles away. Two days later Sumter was surprised at Fishing Creek (Chester County) and his forces smashed by Banastre Tarleton's Legion. Upon learning of the American defeats at Camden and Fishing Creek, the French foreign minister made an overture to the British that the war cease immediately and that South Carolina remain British territory.[20]

Then things began to unravel for the British. Gates's army had been beaten at Camden, but its presence gave renewed hope to backcountry Whigs. In addition to Sumter, other leaders emerged to wage guerrilla warfare: Francis Marion in the northeastern quarter of the state from the Pee Dee River to the coast, Andrew Pickens in the upper Savannah River Valley, and William Harden in the Beaufort area. Marion, whose ragged band of black and white volunteers had been laughed at by Gates and his Continentals, made his presence felt almost immediately. At Nelson's Ferry (Clarendon County), Black Mingo (Williamsburg County), and Tearcoat Swamp (Williamsburg County) he ambushed British detachments and disappeared into the swamps. Nearly 150 years and six thousand miles removed from the swamps of South Carolina, a Chinese partisan put into words what Marion practiced so successfully: "In guerrilla warfare, select the tactic of seeming to come from the east and attacking from the west; avoid the solid, attack the hollow; attack; withdraw; deliver a lightning blow; seek a lightning decision."[21]

One measure of the success of a military leader is how he is regarded by his foes. Tarleton, probably one of the most effective British officers in South Carolina, reportedly said: "Come let us go back and we will find the gamecock [Sumter]. But as for this damned fox [Marion], the devil himself could not catch him!" Within six months of having taken the field, Cornwallis wrote that because of Marion, "there was scarce an inhabitant . . . that was not in arms against us."[22]

While Marion was disrupting British lines of communication in the lower part of the state, a force of Tory militia and British regulars under Maj. Patrick Ferguson was marching through the backcountry threatening all who did not cooperate, even those who lived over the mountains. Instead of being frightened, the settlers decided that Ferguson needed to be stopped. Hundreds of men from both Carolinas mobilized, and the British began to retreat eastward. At King's Mountain (York County), Ferguson decided to make a stand and suffered a humiliating defeat. His troops were mostly armed with smoothbore muskets, which were ineffective in shooting downhill, while the backcountry men had rifles. It was no contest. Even after the British tried to surrender, they were cut down as their cries for "Quarter" (mercy) were drowned out by replies of "Tarleton's Quarter" (massacre). More than one thousand British soldiers were killed, wounded, or captured. The defeat at King's Mountain so unnerved Cornwallis that he delayed a planned invasion of North Carolina.[23]

The situation deteriorated throughout the remainder of the year as partisan bands struck at will against isolated outposts and supply trains. In November, Sumter redeemed himself with victories at Fish Dam Ford (Chester County) and Blackstocks (Union County). In December, Gen. Nathanael Greene appeared with a new Continental army. It was a turning point of the war. Well-read in military tactics and seasoned by five years of service with Washington, Greene devised a strategy for defeating the British that today is called "mobile war." Unlike most regular military men who disliked and dismissed partisan warfare, Greene coordinated their efforts with his own and kept the British off balance. By trading space for time, he planned a war of attrition that would eventually destroy the enemy.[24]

Shortly after his arrival in the state Greene divided his forces, sending a large detachment under Col. Daniel Morgan toward Ninety Six (Greenwood County). In seizing the initiative, Greene forced Cornwallis to respond to him. As he had hoped, the British divided their army. A detachment under Banastre Tarleton was sent to pursue Morgan while the main force would shadow Greene. On 17 January 1781 Morgan made a stand on the Broad River in Spartan District at Hiram Saunders's cow pens (from which the engagement took its name, Cowpens). Morgan's battle plan for what would be called today a "defense in depth" was daring and innovative.[25]

Since militia normally ran when faced with a charge from British regulars, Morgan built that into his plan. After firing, the militia feigned fright but withdrew in an orderly fashion behind the main lines. The British responded, as anticipated, and rushed forward to rout the Americans. Instead of firing at the backs of fleeing militia, they found themselves facing the gun barrels and bayonets of Continentals. Cavalry forces attacked them from the rear. It was a rout, but not of the Americans. The British broke ranks, and nearly one thousand were either killed or captured. At Cowpens, for the first time in the Revolution, an American army defeated a force of mostly British regulars.[26]

It had been a bad five months for the British. In mid August 1780, after Camden and Fishing Creek, their plan to roll up the southern states seemed to be working. Then came Marion's and Sumter's victories, King's Mountain, and Cowpens. The events in South Carolina had turned the tide in the Americans' favor, but the war had not yet been won.

After Cowpens, Morgan moved swiftly into North Carolina to rejoin Greene's main army with Cornwallis right behind him. Both armies moved rapidly, sometimes covering as much as thirty miles in a single day. Eventually, after racing to the Dan River, Greene doubled back to Guilford Court House where, on 15 March 1781, he made a stand. His battle plan was a copy of Morgan's at Cowpens, except that it was not as successful. When the fighting was over, the British held the field of battle, but they had suffered heavy casualties, losses they could ill afford. Needing supplies, Cornwallis withdrew to Wilmington and from there marched north to Virginia.[27]

Early in April, Greene notified George Washington that he was "determined to carry the war immediately into South Carolina." On 5 April he headed south. Facing him was a combined regular-loyalist force of about eight thousand stationed in Charleston and various outposts from Georgetown to Ninety Six. The British may have controlled the strong points, but the countryside belonged to the partisans. With Greene's army to keep the main British force occupied, the partisans picked off the British garrisons one by one: Fort Watson (Clarendon County), Fort Motte (Calhoun County), Orangeburg, Fort Granby (Lexington County), Fort Galphin (Aiken County), Georgetown, and Monck's Corner (Berkeley County). Without a fight, the British abandoned Dorchester on the Ashley River above Charleston.[28]

Greene's army fought three major battles during the spring and summer of 1781. In April the British won the battle at Hobkirk's Hill (Kershaw County) but decided to withdraw their garrison from Camden. At Ninety Six, Greene conducted an unsuccessful siege of the fort, but the British evacuated the post in June. After resting his men in the High Hills of the Santee for the remainder of the summer, Greene moved toward the coast. At Eutaw Springs (Orangeburg County), on 5 September, Greene's army initially carried the day. Then the hungry and nearly naked men (some had placed Spanish moss between their skin and their equipment to prevent chafing) broke into the main British camp and became a drunken, disorderly mob. The British counterattacked and at the end of the day drove the Americans back. But once again the British had suffered irreplaceable losses.[29]

There were other battles after Eutaw Springs, but none of any strategic significance. On 14 November 1782 the last of the 137 battles fought in South Carolina and the last battle of the American Revolution occurred on Johns Island (Charleston County).[30]

From the fall of Charleston in May 1780 until the end of 1781, civilian government in free South Carolina existed in the person of Gov. John Rutledge. His proclamations were a continual reminder, despite British successes in the field, that South Carolinians had not given up. More important was his success in persuading the Continental Congress to support the war effort in the state. The "capital" of the state was wherever he was, and on several occasions he barely escaped capture.

Meanwhile, in occupied Charleston the British did not establish civilian government, although Lt. Gov. William Bull and other former royal officials had returned. The military commandants of Charleston appointed a Board of Police (mostly former royal officials) to perform quasi-judicial functions and give them advice. The board's authority was unclear, and before the end of the occupation many of its actions had been undercut by British officials. In the eyes of South Carolina patriots, its members were collaborators who were involved with the implementation of a variety of punitive actions.[31]

As opposition to the occupation mounted outside Charleston, the British imposed increasingly harsh policies on those who had once opposed them. One of the first, in

August 1780, was the deportation of sixty-five parolees to St. Augustine where they were imprisoned. Among them were Peter Fayssoux, William Hasell Gibbes, Thomas Heyward, and Edward Weyman. Later the exiles were exchanged but forbidden to return home and their wives and children ordered to leave South Carolina. Many went to Philadelphia, where by the end of 1781 there were about five hundred South Carolina exiles. In September 1780 Cornwallis ordered the sequestration of more than one hundred estates belonging to individuals identified as revolutionaries, including Isaac DaCosta, Christopher Gadsden, Michael Kalteisen, Henry Laurens, Francis Marion, Peter Horry, Charles Cotesworth Pinckney, and John Rutledge. One year after the capture of Charleston, all parolees were confined to their homes and then jailed as "Inveterate Enemies" of Great Britain.[32]

British authorities harassed anyone they suspected of not being loyal. Women were jailed "for some trifle or another" (evidently for being saucy to some members of the government of occupation). When Elizabeth Allston Gibbes petitioned the Board of Police for compensation for her home's having been appropriated, she was verbally abused. In a futile attempt to force South Carolinians into submission, British authorities took an increasingly hard line; this tactic backfired. Eliza Yonge Wilkinson, a Charleston resident, wrote: "Do the Britons imagine that they will conquer America by such actions? If they do, they will find themselves much mistaken. . . . We may be led, but we never will be driven!"[33]

By the summer of 1781 British authorities were getting anxious. Defections thinned the already slim ranks of Tory militia units. Individuals who had taken parole flocked to partisan bands or Greene's army. When Col. Isaac Hayne was captured south of Charleston, the British decided to make an example of him. After a brief hearing by a military court of enquiry, the South Carolinian was sentenced to death for accepting parole and then taking up arms against the king. The *Royal Gazette* reported the story with some smugness that on 4 August 1781 "Mr. Isaac Hayne" had been "executed as a Traitor." Initially the execution chilled the military ardor of some South Carolinians. A number who, like Hayne, had agreed to parole and then rejoined revolutionary forces quit their units and went home. Greene issued a proclamation stating that he would retaliate, and after Eutaw Springs he had enough British officers as prisoners to insure that there would be no further executions.[34]

The revocation of paroles, the exile of entire families, and the execution of Isaac Hayne were acts of desperation borne of frustration. The British had expected thousands of loyalists to rise up and join their army once they captured Charleston. Many did, but their loyalty was shaky. Some families were honestly divided, with some supporting the Revolution and others remaining loyal to the king. Others, especially those with property and wealth, were a bit more pragmatic; preservation of the family's fortune was more important than any cause, British or American. When several hundred South Carolinians signed a congratulatory address to the victors after the fall of Charleston, neither British nor Americans considered it an indication of loyalty. The British simply did not know who was a loyalist and who was not.[35]

Determining who was a Tory (and therefore should be punished) was the main business of the Fourth General Assembly that convened in January 1782. Because the British still occupied Charleston, the legislature met in Jacksonborough on the Edisto River. After nearly six weeks of debate, the legislature passed one act identifying 238 individuals whose betrayal of South Carolina was to be punished by banishment and the confiscation of their estates. A second act identified 47 whose actions were less objectionable; their estates were to be amerced (assessed) at 12 percent of the appraised value. A conditional amnesty act provided for the pardoning of others who had betrayed the state to a lesser degree after they paid a fine amounting to 10 percent of their estates. Almost immediately efforts were made either to reduce certain individuals' punishments or to get them stricken from the list altogether. Over the next four years fifteen separate bills reduced the punishments of about two-thirds of those initially singled out. Both Christopher Gadsden and Francis Marion disapproved of the amercement acts, but the most outspoken opponent was Aedanus Burke, a lowcountry lawyer. The acts would, he said, "give more loose to malice, avarice, or revenge; commit more injustice and glaring partiality and . . . would fix disgrace on the very name of a republic." He was absolutely correct, but the mood of the General Assembly, especially of the representatives from the backcountry, was to punish the sunshine patriots and traitors of the lowcountry.[36]

The 1782 acts punished only a small fraction of the twelve thousand to fifteen thousand who assisted the British. Given the nature of the conflict, many of them at one time or another may have aided the American cause. Most loyalists lived in the backcountry. Whether from the lowcountry or the backcountry, the overwhelming majority of South Carolina loyalists had been in the state only a short while, generally less than fifteen years. Those in the backcountry (primarily German or Scots-Irish) had either emigrated directly from their native lands or the colonies of Virginia, Pennsylvania, or Maryland. In the lowcountry, whether artisan or merchant, many were Scots. Among those who remained faithful to Great Britain were John Wells, publisher of the *South Carolina and American General Gazette;* Jannet Cumming, a midwife; Moses Kirkland, a backcountry planter; Robert Frogg, a tailor; and Violet and Boston King, a free black couple. They constituted a cross section of the population.[37]

By the time the Jacksonborough Assembly met to decide their fates, a good many of the state's Tories were living in Charleston. Except for an occasional foray in search of food, the British did not venture outside their lines. Where once they had controlled the entire state, now only the Charleston peninsula and James Island still flew the Union Jack. Before the year was out, that territory too would once again be American.

In July 1782 the British quit Savannah. Two months later a British fleet sailed into Charleston harbor and plans were made to evacuate the remaining British troops and the forty-two hundred loyalists who wanted to leave the state. The loyalist refugees notified British officials that they wanted to take seventy-two hundred slaves and other property with them. Robert Frogg, for example, dismantled his house for shipment. Eventually more than three hundred ships were necessary to effect the evacuation. Initially a good many refugees went to East Florida, but that became Spanish territory after the war, so the refugees moved on to other locations. About one thousand refugees and their twenty-two hundred slaves went to the Bahamas and another three thousand to other "States of America." The remaining five thousand expatriate Carolinians either settled in Nova Scotia, New Brunswick, St. Lucia, Jamaica, or Great Britain or filtered across the mountains to the frontier. When the commission established by Parliament made its awards to loyalists who had suffered losses because of the Revolution, South Carolina had the largest number of successful applications except for New York.[38]

On 14 December 1782 the last British troops left Charleston and, block by block, the city was turned over to Gen. Nathanael Greene's Continental troops. It was an orderly transition. At three o'clock in the afternoon Greene escorted Gov. John Mathewes and other officials into the city. For South Carolina the war was over.

It would take a while for news to reach the state that the preliminary treaty had been signed in Paris on 30 November. Henry Laurens, former president of the Continental Congress, participated in the negotiations with John Adams, Benjamin Franklin, and John Jay. It was nearly another year (23 September 1783) before the definitive treaty ending the war was signed, but for South Carolina that was just a formality.

With the removal of British troops in December 1782, South Carolinians were once again in control of their own affairs, thanks in no small measure to Gen. Nathanael Greene. Earlier histories have presented a bitter debate over who "won" the war in South Carolina and given all the credit to the partisans, dismissing Greene as a mere opportunist, or worse. Recent military historians have understood that it took both the Continentals and the partisans to liberate the state. However, that would not have been possible if the commander of the regular army had not appreciated and supported guerrilla operations. In April 1781 the British had controlled all of the state, but by the end of the year they had withdrawn all their forces to a small perimeter around Charleston. Greene never won a tactical battle in South Carolina, but he achieved his goals of destroying the British army and winning the war. Mao Tse-tung could not have designed a more perfect campaign of mobile war.[39]

For the most part, though, South Carolina has forgotten Greene. When the new state capital was laid out in Columbia and the streets were named for Revolutionary War heroes, Benjamin Lincoln and Horatio Gates were honored, but not Nathanael Greene. Among those honored, quite appropriately, was Francis Marion. In fact, in nineteenth-century America, Marion emerged as a national hero of the Revolution.

Parson Mason Weems took a manuscript by Peter Horry and converted it into a popular biography, *The Life of General Francis Marion* (1824). Like his earlier *Life and Memorable Actions of George Washington* (circa 1800), this revolutionary folktale was a tremendous success. New Englander William Cullen Bryant immortalized the man and his partisans in the "Song of Marion's Men," which opened with the following stanza:

> Our band is few but true and tried,
> Our leader frank and bold;
> The British soldier trembles
> When Marion's Name is told.
> Our fortress is the good greenwood,
> Our tent the cypress-tree;
> We know the forest round us,
> As seamen know the sea.
> We know its walls of Thorny vines,
> Its glades of reedy grass,
> Its safe and silent islands
> Within the dark morass.

The war was fought and won by lots of unsung heroes, men who chose to take up arms because of some perceived deprivation. It is fashionable today to say that the lowcountry elite led South Carolina into rebellion because they felt snubbed by the British or that their personal political ambitions could not be fulfilled. As important as the elite was in challenging imperial authority, it needed the support of Charleston's artisans and mechanics, who were more concerned about the impact of imperial trade regulations on their livelihoods. The war may have begun and ended in Charleston; however, it was not won there. It was won in the backcountry.[40]

What were the deprivations that led John Adair of Chester District to join up in 1779 and fight in fourteen battles from Cowpens to Eutaw Springs? Or Francis Whelchel Sr. of Union District, who was at both King's Mountain and Cowpens? Or John Hampton of Newberry District, who spent three years in uniform, much of that time with Sumter? Or Edward Harris of Richland District, who fought at Savannah, Cowpens, and Eutaw Springs? Or Jeremiah Files of Abbeville District, who fought with Pickens from 1780 until the end of the war? These men were not upset with royal officials over having their aspirations thwarted. Only Hampton fit the profile of a rising backcountry planter who might have seen participation in the Revolution as an opportunity to improve his status. Since they were members of the militia and not regulars, it is probable that some blundering British soldier such as Patrick Ferguson or an overly zealous Tory militiaman such as William "Bloody Bill" Cunningham threatened their families or their neighbors. No doubt they shared the sentiments of William Moultrie, who in 1781 said he would continue to fight so long as his country was "still deluged with blood and overrun by British troops, who exercise the most savage cruelties."[41]

The women of South Carolina also took sides. Only one woman, Margaret Colleton, was named in the confiscation acts. Margaret Reynolds of Ninety Six had been a nurse at a refugee hospital in occupied Charleston, and Eleanor Lester had operated a cheap tavern. Both women were Tories and chose exile in 1782. Interestingly, the General Assembly tended to consider women more as victims than perpetrators despite the well-known assistance that several women gave the American cause. Rebecca Brewton Motte's providing a bow and arrows so that Marion's forces could set fire to her own home was the stuff of legend. So, too, were Emily Geiger's carrying a message from Greene to Sumter, Mary Dillard's warning Sumter of Tarleton's approach before Blackstocks, and Rebekah Couturier's alerting Marion to a British ambush. Several of the stories, such as those of Martha Robinson Bratton of York District and Ann Kennedy of Broad River, dealt with their refusing to betray partisans even when threatened or tortured. The news of such occurrences became widely known and reinforced the resolve of those fighting the British.[42]

The war in the backcountry left a great deal of bitterness. It would take more than a peace treaty to blot out the memory of Tarleton's Quarter and Sumter's Law, which led to indiscriminate murder and looting. Examples of the former were the massacre of the Dugan brothers (they were ambushed by a band of Tories, tied up, and literally hacked to death with a sword) and the murder in cold blood of a small partisan band at Hayes's Station by Bloody Bill Cunningham. Both of these atrocities happened in Newberry District. On the American side, Sumter's infamous "Law" was simply a justification for looting the countryside. Since there was no money to pay his men, he authorized the appropriation of property belonging to alleged Tories. For example, in December 1780 he gave a receipt to a Colonel Goodwyn for a slave, horse, saddle and bridle, cutlass, and nineteen silver dollars ($209) "for the use of the public." He would neither return the items nor compensate Goodwyn "Unless it should appear when a full investigation can be made that Col. Goodwyn's conduct has been nowise injurious to the liberties of America." Goodwyn and countless others were guilty until proven innocent. In early 1782 Governor Rutledge repudiated Sumter's Law and the general retired.[43]

Despite the bloody nature of the war in the backcountry, when it came time to punish Tories, only a handful of the area's loyalists were named in the confiscation and amercement acts. Among those who were forbidden to return to South Carolina were the cousins Robert and William Cunningham, who settled in the Bahamas. Given their activities during the Revolution, they probably would not have been safe at home. The Cunninghams were not the only Tories who were personae non gratae in their home districts. In Ninety Six, which had the greatest concentration of loyalists in South Carolina, there were reprisals. After a court freed Matthew Love, one of the participants in the massacre at Hayes's Station, he was lynched by a mob. In

Rebecca Motte and Francis Marion, May 1781. Cecil Hartley, *The Life of Francis Marion* (1866). Courtesy, South Caroliniana Library.

other backcountry districts former Tories were run out of town or killed by "Whigs with long memories." In Charleston most members of the elite who had either been pro-British or played both sides were welcomed back with little recrimination. This easy reconciliation would lead to difficulties and class conflict in the decade after the war.[44]

Reconciliation probably was the most sensible response after seven years of warfare. It had been more than a decade since the Wilkes Fund Controversy had unhinged royal government. South Carolina very much needed good order and harmony in 1782. From Ninety Six to Charleston the countryside was in ruins. The damage was more apparent in the lowcountry, but the backcountry too had suffered. Homes, farm buildings, and mills had been burned. Fields had been abandoned and were overgrown. Horses and livestock had been taken by one side or the other. There were thirty thousand fewer slaves in the state than there had been in 1775. In addition to those carried away in the loyalist evacuation, about twenty-five thousand were stolen by the British. With the dissolution of the ties with Great Britain, South Carolina lost its primary trading partner and the indigo bounty. The state's economy was in a shambles.

Not only were the means of production either damaged or destroyed, but individuals and the state faced huge debts. In prosecuting the war South Carolina, with a white population of less than one hundred thousand, had spent about $5.4 million ($89.2 million) in supporting the country's war effort. In spite of the difficulties facing the state, it had regularly met its financial obligations to the Continental Congress and in 1783 was the only one of the thirteen states to pay its requisition in full.[45]

The financial losses were nothing compared to the personal ones. In 1783 a visitor noted the large number of widows in Charleston, but there were far more in the backcountry. "In District No. 96 alone (and I know this from good authority) there are twelve hundred widows." Given that constant, grim reminder of the war, it is remarkable that the majority of South Carolinians had so little time for hate. When something untoward occurred, such as the hanging of Matthew Love in Ninety Six, Judge Aedanus Burke blamed the victim, not the mob. It was unfortunate that a person as infamous as Love would be "so infatuated as to return among the Citizens, and thus prevent the restoration of the public tranquility."[46]

Old enemies might be grudgingly accepted back into their communities; however, South Carolina after the Revolution was anything but a tranquil place. Economic difficulties and political problems kept the pot stirred. The artisans and mechanics of Charleston and the residents of the backcountry had been crucial to the success of the Revolution. They knew it, but their aspirations were thwarted by the old colonial elite that reasserted itself and acted as if it were the 1760s instead of the 1780s. For another generation the state would be bitterly divided against itself. There was neither good order nor harmony and absolutely no sense of community.

Chapter Twelve

QUEST FOR ORDER

The empire of the laws is subverted throughout the state, except within the city of Charleston, and its environs: as beyond that, no officer of justice dare serve a writ, or levy an execution.

Columbian Herald, 26 October 1785

Great abuses in government, like great rivers, arise from small beginnings. They are easily checked at first, but encreasing imperceptibly in their progress, they at length become too powerful for opposition. Thus corruption crept into the British government; and thus your liberties will be gradually undermined, unless you speedily apply a remedy to the dangerous malady under which our constitution labours.

Appius [Robert Goodloe Harper], *Appius to the Citizens of South-Carolina*

Whereas, The proper education of youth contributes greatly to the prosperity of society, and ought always to be an object of legislative attention; and whereas, the establishment of a college in a central part of the State, where all of its youth may be educated, will highly promote instruction, the good order and the harmony of the whole community.

"An Act to Establish a College at Columbia," 19 December 1801

*T*HE NATURE of the warfare in South Carolina had left the state in disarray. The heaviest fighting had taken place outside Charleston in the backcountry and in the vicinity of Beaufort and Georgetown. Both patriots and loyalists had torched their opponents' homes and barns and carried off everything of value. The only real inland town, Camden, had been almost completely destroyed. Joseph Kershaw's mills, probably the most extensive commercial operation in the backcountry, had been burned to the ground. As late as five years after the Peace of Paris, residents of Winton (Barnwell) County talked about their farms "just immurging from the ruins & devastations of the late unnatural war." About the same time, in Lancaster County, a judge addressed the grand jury and discussed "the terrible inroads which the disorders of war have created."[1]

In addition to the physical damage caused by the fighting, there was a great deal of social instability. New settlers continued to flood into the backcountry in great numbers, and among them were outlaws and thieves. It was the 1760s all over again. Bandits assaulted travelers and robbed isolated homesteads. It was so bad in Ninety Six District that Aedanus Burke reported: "No man has security for even a worthless plow horse. . . . As to Trade and commerce it is at an end in that District unless the Government take some measures for extirpating the outlyers."[2]

The end of the war did not bring prosperity. South Carolinians still owed large sums of money to British merchants, but that did not stop them from going further into debt. Within a few years they had amassed new debts of £1.5 million sterling ($103.4 million). Even if the state's agricultural sector had rebounded immediately, such a large debt would have been difficult to carry. Unfortunately, there were three bad rice harvests in a row. Between 1783 and 1785 South Carolina exported an average of fewer than 50,000 barrels of rice annually. In 1773 and 1774 the average had been 129,000.[3]

Credit had been too easy, and South Carolinians, especially lowcountry rice planters, had borrowed heavily to purchase thousands of slaves to replace those lost during the war. Henry Laurens wrote that "debtors are here the great majority." Aedanus Burke blamed it all on the British, who had "seduced us to contract" debts that could not be paid. He described British merchants as "harpies" who preyed on unfortunate (and foolish) South Carolinians. When British firms tried to obtain repayments, they met with little success. In August 1784 several major London commercial houses failed; the next year many more declared bankruptcy.[4]

There was no money in South Carolina. The closing of the British West Indies to American commerce cut off a major rice market and the primary source of hard currency. An indication of the economic difficulties in which all Carolinians, not just rice planters, found themselves can be found in the tax returns for the mid 1780s. In 1784 the District Eastward of the Wateree paid £1,252 sterling ($82,100) in taxes, and in 1785 only £127 ($8,750). The returns from St. Bartholomew's Parish went from £2,500 ($164,000) to £136 ($9,375), and St. Paul's from £3,600 ($236,000) to zero.[5]

Frightened and angry debtors thumbed their noses at the law. In 1784 in Camden, Hezekiah Maham, upon being served with a writ, forced the sheriff's deputy to eat it and three others. The following year debtors closed Camden's courts to prevent foreclosures. In Cheraw, a county where judges were "no great favorites," the people banded together to prevent sheriff's sales. Judge Aedanus Burke had all of his clothing stolen while on the circuit, and Judge Thomas Waties was pelted with mud and cow manure while on the way to open court. The most violent action took place in Winton (Barnwell) County, where the posted notices of sales were ripped down by a mob that later returned to trash the courthouse and set it afire.[6]

There was disorder in Charleston as well. Almost as soon as the war was over, those who had been less than loyal to the American cause returned home with little or no punishment. Following in their wake were the British merchants who soon controlled a sizable share of the city's commerce. The easy acceptance of both these groups angered those who had fought and suffered during the war, especially artisans and mechanics. Tory toughs sometimes roughed up those who complained about their presence. Under the leadership of Alexander Gillon, artisans and local merchants formed the Marine Anti-Britannic Society. The organization published virulent tracts and did what it could to make Tories and British merchants feel unwelcome. Throughout 1783 there were riots in the streets of Charleston that sometimes took on the color of class conflict as the mob denounced the state's elite as well as Tories.[7]

The state government was slow to respond, but eventually it did. In August 1783 it incorporated the city of Charleston, which turned over local government to the city's residents. The election of several artisans to city council helped calm the tense situation there. So, too, did a 1785 gubernatorial decree ordering Tory exiles from other states and individuals who had been banished from South Carolina (but returned anyway) to leave. In the backcountry ranger companies were ordered out to help eliminate the bandits.[8]

In 1784 a long-standing grievance was addressed when the General Assembly reformed the land tax, replacing a uniform rate with one based upon assessed value. The Sheriff's Sale Act of 1785 (sometimes called the Pine Barren Act) benefited all debtors by allowing them to offer their creditors land in lieu of cash. Suddenly creditors were faced with either extending debts or having to accept marginal lands located anywhere in the state as payment (hence the Pine Barren Act). In the same year the General Assembly also issued £100,000 sterling ($6.9 million) in paper currency in the form of loans ranging from £30 ($2,070) to £250 ($17,230). The loans, secured by land or silver, carried an interest rate of 7 percent. Many of the loans went to lowcountry planters, but backcountrymen such as Wade Hampton of Richland County were able to obtain them. Although initially the loans were to be repaid in five years, in 1800 there were notes for £58,067 ($3,101,182) still in circulation. The currency could be used to pay taxes but was not legal tender for debts. This limited amount of paper in circulation helped pump some life back into the economy as most citizens accepted it in the course of business.[9]

The Sheriff's Sale Act was allowed to lapse in 1787 and was replaced by an Installment Act that postponed until 1790 the final payments on all debts contracted before 1 March 1787. Beginning in 1788 debtors were to make three annual payments. Coupled with the Installment Act was a three-year moratorium (1787–1790) on the foreign slave trade that was extended repeatedly until 1803. Lowcountry debtors wanted to remove temptation in the form of imported Africans, while backcountry residents, many of them aspiring planters, favored keeping the trade open.[10]

Although not related to the economic crisis, the General Assembly passed legislation in 1785 and 1786 that was aimed at reducing tensions between the backcountry and the lowcountry. With a growing population, representatives from the portions of the state beyond the parishes were increasingly restive with the dominance of state government by the lowcountry elite. In what would be the first of several political hush puppies tossed to the backcountry, counties and county courts (one of the demands of the Regulators) were created in 1785. The following year, after a great deal of wrangling, the legislature voted to move the capital from Charleston to a new town that would be built on the banks of the Congaree, Columbia. It was a decision against which some members of the lowcountry elite fought a determined rear-guard action.

During the course of the debate in the state senate, Arnoldus Vanderhorst of Christ Church Parish snidely suggested that the new capital in the wilderness be called the "Town of Refuge" because it was beyond the pale of the law. To this, John Lewis Gervais of Saxe Gotha riposted that he hoped the oppressed of every land might find refuge under the wings of Columbia. Columbia, a symbolic representation of the new nation, won out over Washington as the name for the new capital.[11]

Temporarily pacifying the backcountry and interfering with the sanctity of contracts to relieve debtors were conscious decisions made by the state's leadership in an attempt to restore the good order and harmony of the community. It is likely that the Pine Barren Act helped avert more serious problems such as those that wracked western Massachusetts in the 1780s. "The eight years of war," wrote David Ramsay, "were followed by eight years of disorganization, which produced such an amount of civil distress as diminished with some their respect for liberty and independence."[12]

In Philadelphia, Charles Pinckney, one of the state's delegates to the Confederation Congress, was concerned about what appeared to be a collapse of respect for the national government. He chaired a congressional committee that recommended seven amendments to strengthen the Articles of Confederation. When New Jersey threatened to withdraw its financial support from the national government in 1786, he was one of three members of Congress sent to persuade that state not to withhold its funds. In his remarks to the New Jersey legislature, Pinckney suggested that it "urge the calling of a general convention of the states for the purpose of increasing the powers of the federal government and rendering it more adequate for the ends for which it was instituted." When the call for a convention was issued, however, it came from an intercolonial gathering in Annapolis.[13]

The South Carolina General Assembly responded by electing five men to what would be called the Constitutional Convention: Pierce Butler, Henry Laurens, Charles Pinckney, Charles Cotesworth Pinckney, and John Rutledge. "Charleston and the surrounding parishes were represented at Philadelphia," observed one modern historian; "South Carolina was not." While unrepresentative of the state as a whole, it was nevertheless a talented group of individuals. Because of ill health Laurens did not attend, but the other four (all lawyer-planters) did and made their pres-

Charles Pinckney (1757–1824).
Courtesy, South Caroliniana
Library.

ence felt. Delegates from the northern states sometimes referred to the Carolinians as "nabobs" or "bashaws" (pashas) because of their wealth and bearing.[14]

In the convention it was clear from the beginning that the South Carolinians favored an aristocratic republic. After all, that was what they were trying to create in South Carolina. Nowhere was that more apparent than in discussions on representation. Butler and the Pinckneys voiced opposition to the popular election of the House of Representatives. C. C. Pinckney argued that "In South Carolina the inhabitants are so sparse that four or five thousand men cannot be brought together for a vote." Charles Pinckney urged property qualifications for all federal office-holders.[15]

While Charles Pinckney and the other members of the South Carolina delegation wanted a stronger central, or national, government to insure "their state's place in the sun (and for their place in the state)," they would brook no interference with the state's domestic institutions. Their places and their fortunes rested upon an agricultural export economy powered by African labor. Any attempt to strike at the heart of the state's economic well-being would determine, as Rutledge bluntly put it, "whether the southern states shall or shall not be parties to the Union." C. C. Pinckney said that "South Carolina and Georgia can not do without slaves," and

Charles Pinckney gave a moral and historical defense of the institution of slavery.[16]

Any national navigation act also posed a potential threat to the state's economy. In a foreshadowing of the state's concern about being in a minority within the union, Charles Pinckney proposed that any navigation acts be passed only with the approval of three-fourths of the states.[17]

While the delegates' comments on slavery have attracted attention for more than two centuries, defending the institution was neither their primary purpose nor their principal contribution in Philadelphia. In a study of the fifty-five men in the convention, all delegates were ranked in one of eight categories from "principals" to "inexplicable disappointments." James Madison and George Washington were among the four ranked "principals." Behind them were eleven "influential" delegates; three of them were from South Carolina, the two Pinckneys and John Rutledge. Pierce Butler fell into the third tier as a "very useful" member of the convention. Rutledge served on five committees and was the key member of the committee of detail that produced the draft of the Constitution. Charles Cotesworth Pinckney served on the committee that crafted the compromise over the slave trade and navigation acts. Charles Pinckney spoke more than one hundred times and proposed a successful amendment to Article VI: "no religious test shall ever be required as a qualification to any office or public trust under the authority of the United States." And it was Butler who proposed the idea of having the Constitution go into effect once ratified by nine of the thirteen states. When South Carolina's delegates spoke, the rest of the convention listened.[18]

The convention adjourned in September, and the South Carolinians returned home where they lobbied for the ratification of the document. The General Assembly voted (76–75) for the state's ratification convention to meet in Charleston in May 1788. The vote on the location of the convention was a harbinger of the sectional conflict that would plague the state for another generation. Lowcountry legislators simply were not going to give up power or advantage without a fight. Aedanus Burke, an opponent of ratification, would later claim that one of the main reasons the Constitution was ratified was that the convention was held in Charleston "where there are not fifty inhabitants who are not friendly to it. The merchants and leading men kept open houses for the back and low country members during the whole time the Convention sat." What Burke did not say, however, was that as a member of the General Assembly, he had voted in favor of holding the convention in Charleston.[19]

Burke and Rawlins Lowndes were the recognized leaders of the antifederalist forces in South Carolina, but Lowndes was not a member of the ratification convention. The old revolutionary feared that the northeastern states would dominate the new government and that South Carolina would become "the backcountry" of the United States. His choice of words was ironic because it was the state's backcountry that was most opposed to ratification.[20]

Aedanus Burke (1743–1802). Courtesy, the Hibernian Society, Charleston, South Carolina.

Many observers assumed that ratification was a foregone conclusion, given "the ascendancy" of the lowcountry elite in the General Assembly and in the convention. Apportionment in both was rigged to give the white minority in the lowcountry an overwhelming advantage. Each lowcountry vote carried as much weight as six from the backcountry. The views of the two sections of the state were about as far apart as Charleston was from Caesar's Head.[21]

Despite the odds, those opposed to ratification presented their case in the press and within the convention. Basically the antifederalists had three concerns: (1) Congress would have the authority to close the external slave trade in 1808; (2) a national navigation law would benefit northeastern shipping interests and would therefore cost South Carolinians more than if they had free access to cheaper British ships; and (3) the state's debtor relief legislation (such as the Installment Act and the issuing of paper currency) would be illegal because they violated the sanctity of contracts. All were economic issues and reflected the hopes and desires of the rising backcountry planter class. The backcountry already had to deal with a government in Charleston that was unresponsive and disinclined to support its interests; another one even more removed and more powerful was certainly not desired. Each of the objections was answered with reasoned responses from lowcountry delegates. Charles Pinckney and John Rutledge were especially effective in putting a positive spin on the new Constitution.[22]

In the convention Thomas Sumter tried to derail the ratification process by proposing that the convention adjourn until the fall (in so doing he hoped that the antifederalist forces would have time to rally). His motion was defeated 89–135.

The vote on ratification was not even close (149–73). The three coastal centers (Beaufort, Charleston, and Georgetown) voted 99–1 in favor of ratification, but the other lowcountry parishes were divided, with 22 voting yes and 15 no. In the backcountry there were more than twice as many no votes (57) as there were yes votes (28). The leading supporters of ratification were the Charleston merchants, lawyers, and lowcountry rice planters. The more economically prosperous the area of the state, the more likely it was to support the new Constitution. Before the ratification convention adjourned, it recommended several amendments that included the states' unequivocally keeping control of all election procedures for national offices; the states' retaining all powers not specifically given to the central government; and prohibiting direct taxes except in the case of extreme exigency.[23]

When the ratification of the Constitution was announced, there were celebrations not only in Charleston and the lowcountry but also in Camden. Burke reported that in the backcountry "in some places the people had a coffin painted black, which, borne in funeral procession, was solemnly buried, as an emblem of the dissolution and interment of publick liberty." Eighty percent of the backcountry folk, he claimed, despised the document, and he lashed out at the power of the lowcountry elite. Some scholars have questioned Burke's accuracy, but there can be no doubt that backcountry opposition to the Constitution was deeply held and long remembered. Despite their hard feelings, though, most adopted Burke's attitude that everyone would "be obliged to take it, as we take our wives, 'for better, for worse.'"[24]

When the voters of South Carolina elected their representatives to the first Congress of the United States, two of the five members were outsiders; they were not members of the lowcountry elite: Thomas Sumter (Camden) and Aedanus Burke (Beaufort-Orangeburg). The remaining members of the delegation were Thomas Tudor Tucker (Ninety Six), Daniel Huger (Georgetown-Cheraw), and William Loughton Smith (Charleston). Burke and Sumter had also been among the more active opponents of ratification. John F. Grimké referred to the delegation as a "black list," and Timothy Ford lamented that South Carolina would not have "as much respectability on the floor of Congress as this state could have been entitled." The congressional elections were an indication to the lowcountry elite that when the state's voters had the opportunity, they looked after their own interests. The lowcountry elite's ascendancy was not as secure as it once had been.[25]

In Congress the South Carolina elite could not control events either. Hardly had the first session opened than a group of Philadelphia Quakers petitioned Congress to clarify the ambiguity in the Constitution concerning slavery and the slave trade. Both Smith and Burke denounced the petitions and those who wrote them. In his remarks Burke noted that he was not an advocate of slavery but that he was "an advocate for the protection of the property, the order, and the tranquility" of South Carolina. Burke's rough manner and sometimes intemperate style of speaking amused Smith and the silk-stocking crowd of the nascent Federalist Party. They were not amused, however, when Burke launched a verbal assault on Alexander Hamilton that almost resulted in a duel.[26]

There was no provision in the Constitution for political parties; however, it was not long before differences over the powers of the new government evolved into the Federalist and Jeffersonian-Republican Parties. Most of the lowcountry elite who had supported the ratification of the Constitution became Federalists. William Loughton Smith, described as a "Federalist's Federalist," was Alexander Hamilton's spokesman in the House of Representatives. He supported the secretary of the treasury's plans for funding the national debt, assumption of state debts, and the creation of a national bank. He, like many others in his party, tended to be pro-British.[27]

Among the leaders of the Federalist Party in South Carolina were two signers of the Constitution, John Rutledge and Charles Cotesworth Pinckney. Rutledge was appointed an associate justice of the United State Supreme Court and nominated, but not confirmed, as chief justice. Pinckney was minister (ambassador) to France and the party's nominee for vice president (1800) and president (1804, 1808). His brother Thomas was the party's nominee for vice president (1796) and minister to Great Britain and Spain. Smith was rewarded with being named one of the first directors of the Bank of the United States and minister to Portugal and Turkey.[28]

Initially the Jeffersonian-Republicans were not as well organized as the Federalists. The party's strength came from the backcountry and from those who opposed ratification and the rapprochement with Great Britain. However, two of the state's signers of the Constitution, Charles Pinckney and Pierce Butler, both members of the lowcountry elite, deserted the Federalists and cast their lots with the Jeffersonians. By breaking ranks, these two men became social and political pariahs, traitors to their class. Pinckney was denounced as "Blackguard Charlie," a man who fed his ego by riding around Charleston in a big carriage "to receive the grateful tribute of bows from the sans culotte & other low fellows." South Carolina Jeffersonian-Republicans did not fare as well as their Federalist peers when it came to reaping the rewards of partisan politics. Charles Pinckney's appointment as minister to Spain was their only political plum.[29]

For a decade the Federalists were a real power in South Carolina and South Carolina Federalists were powers within the national party. There were various local factions, but most of the lowcountry elite rallied to elect their men to Congress and the General Assembly. The Jay Treaty (1795) with Great Britain, however, divided the party in South Carolina. John Rutledge and others denounced it as demeaning and unworthy of an independent nation. In Congress, Sen. Jacob Read provided the crucial vote necessary for ratification and then discovered that it would be safer for him to remain out of the state for six months. Because Rutledge opposed the treaty, the Federalist-dominated senate rejected his nomination as chief justice.[30]

The party received a temporary boost in popularity when C. C. Pinckney, as one of three American commissioners named to restore diplomatic relations with France, responded to a French request for a bribe with "No! No! Not a sixpence." Robert Goodloe Harper (whose views on the apportionment of the General Assembly were anathema to most of the lowcountry elite) transmogrified Pinckney's reply into "Millions for defense but not one cent for tribute." The new phrase was picked up by the popular press, and Pinckney became something of a national hero in what was called the XYZ Affair. In the midst of preparing for war with France, the Federalists passed the Alien and Sedition Acts, and their popularity plummeted in South Carolina as they were now seen as a party that threatened basic American liberties.[31]

The declining power of the Federalists was illustrated by their failure in 1796 to carry the state for John Adams and Thomas Pinckney. Although there was a brief Federalist revival in 1798, the ticket of Adams and C. C. Pinckney lost in 1800; that defeat, wrote a die-hard South Carolina Federalist, "ends our hopes and the hopes of the federal party in America." When the election was thrown into the House of Representatives, the lame-duck Federalist congressmen voted for Aaron Burr and thus ensured the enmity of a majority of the state's electorate. By 1804 no Federalist represented the state in Congress and only a handful remained in the legislature. For the remainder of the period before the Civil War, organized political parties would be almost completely absent from South Carolina.[32]

The lowcountry elite had a difficult time dealing with the changing political scene. Among themselves they referred to backcountry Jeffersonians as "yahoos" and "a parcel of illiterate second rate fellows" and those in the lowcountry as "demagogues and blockheads." Such class-ridden comments would have been denounced by their forebears as foolish snobbery and reflected their desperation. They were particularly incensed about the relocation of the capital to Columbia. When the state found itself needing to write a new constitution in 1790 to conform with the new federal one, the old animosities resurfaced. William L. Smith said that having the capital in the interior would "shed a malignant influence on all the proceedings of the Legislature." The real issue was, of course, power. Ralph Izard had written to Thomas Jefferson that with the capital located in the interior the backcountry's influence would increase fourfold. The backcountry's strength would not have been increased by reapportionment, but by better attendance from the backcountry and lower attendance from the lowcountry. Although the General Assembly had voted in 1786 to build a new capital in Richland County, it was a struggle to get the legislators to agree to hold the constitutional convention in Columbia.[33]

The Constitution of 1790 was remarkable in that there were few concessions granted to the burgeoning backcountry. The apportionment of the convention delegates (the same as the legislative apportionment) was skewed in favor of the lowcountry parishes, and a majority of those delegates saw little need to make any concessions. After all, they had the votes.[34]

The first South Carolina State House (1786–1865). Courtesy, South Caroliniana Library.

The state was divided into twenty-two counties (each county had a court), but the lowcountry parishes continued to be the election districts for representation in the House of Representatives. The size of the house was reduced from 208 to 124, and proportionally the backcountry received a small boost in representation. Each parish or county was allotted one senator, but that meant that the city of Charleston (St. Philip's and St. Michael's Parishes) got two. Property qualifications for holding public office were increased. In order to be a member of the House of Representatives an individual had to own five hundred acres of land *and* ten slaves or have real estate holdings worth £150 sterling ($11,000) free of debt; state senators had to have holdings of £300 sterling ($22,000) and governors £1,500 sterling ($110,000). Yeoman farmers seldom qualified for the General Assembly.

Columbia was confirmed as the state capital; however, the governor only had to be in the capital while the legislature was in session. Moreover, there would be two state treasurers, one in Columbia and one in Charleston. The secretary of state and the surveyor general had to maintain two offices, one in Columbia and one in Charleston; the official could reside in the city of his choice and a deputy in the other. And the state's highest court (Court of Appeals) had to hold sessions in both places.

The justification for partitioning the state into an Upper Division (the judicial districts of Camden, Cheraw, Ninety Six, and Orangeburg) and a Lower Division (the judicial districts of Beaufort, Charleston, and Georgetown) was "for the better conveniency of the citizens, in the upper and lower parts of the state" (see Map 12). Interestingly, the General Assembly only became concerned about the "better

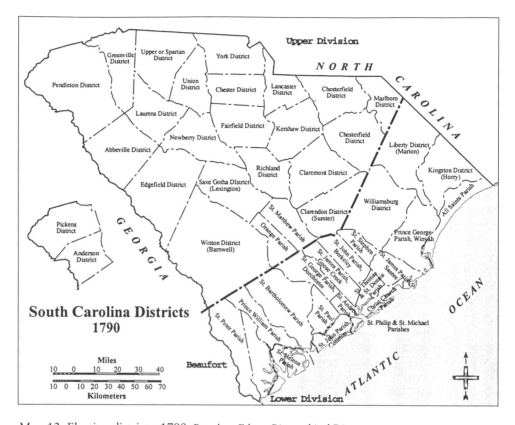

Map 12: Election districts, 1790. Based on Edgar, *Biographical Directory*

conveniency of the citizens" when the capital was moved to Columbia. Until 1790 the lowcountry elite had thought nothing of inconveniencing the backcountry. During the debate over the location of the capital, Edward Rutledge of Charleston could not understand why backcountry legislators were using travel time as a justification for Columbia over Charleston. Since they had to travel goodly distances anyway, "the additional fatigue of riding 50 or 60 miles farther was not an object worthy of consideration."[35]

The major issue, a more equitable apportionment of the House of Representatives to reflect the growth of the backcountry, was virtually ignored. Efforts to have the house apportioned according to population and a provision for regular reapportionment were handily defeated. With the Constitution of 1790, many lowcountry politicians were pleased with themselves. They thought they had restored order to the state and that they had things under control. They were mistaken.[36]

Members of the backcountry leadership, many of whom were now substantial planters, were not willing to accept second-class citizenship. Nor were their constituents. In 1794 a group met in Columbia to form the Representative Reform Association. Among its founders were Wade Hampton of Richland County, William Falconer of Chesterfield, Robert Goodloe Harper of Ninety Six, John Kershaw of Camden, and Ephraim Ramsay of Abbeville. The association quickly established committees throughout the backcountry.[37]

Harper, using the pseudonym Appius, published a pamphlet, *An Address to the People of South-Carolina, by the General Committee of the Representative Reform Association at Columbia,* in which he chronicled the inequities of the current apportionment of the General Assembly. "A state in which one-fifth of the people [29,000 whites] can make laws to bind the other four fifths [120,000 whites]," he wrote, "cannot be free." Charleston District with only about 11 percent of the population elected 39 percent of the members of the House of Representatives and 35 percent of the senate. St. Stephen's Parish, with a white population of 226, had three representatives and one senator; so did Edgefield (9,785) and Pendleton (8,731) Counties. One vote in St. Stephen's, the least populous parish, was worth forty-three votes in Edgefield County and thirty-eight in Pendleton.[38]

Acknowledging that the lowcountry paid more taxes than did the backcountry (£28,081 [$1,969,215] versus £8,390 [$588,359]), Harper said that if property should be represented as well as people in the General Assembly, then changes still needed to be made. The lowcountry's tax contributions were only three times greater than the backcountry's, while the population differential was five to one in favor of the backcountry.[39]

The pamphlet recognized the differences between the two sections of the state. In comparing the two, the lowcountry was found wanting. It was the stagnant portion of the state; its population had grown very little, no doubt due to the "sickliness of the climate." In the upstate, by contrast, Pendleton County had gone from being "entirely a desert" in 1786 to a "fertile country increasing in the number of inhabitants" (8,731). The backcountry preferred low taxes, "a very frugal, civil establishment," and was self-sufficient. The lowcountry was extravagant, favored "numerous offices . . . and an expensive government" and had to import virtually everything it consumed. The contrast that disturbed the lowcountry the most was the last one: "One wishes for slaves; the other would be better without them." Unintentionally Harper had pushed the button of every lowcountry legislator. Even his choice of a classical name, Appius (the Roman official who supported the cause of the plebeians and made it possible for former slaves to vote and be elected to the senate), must have given some pause.[40]

The responses were immediate, blunt, and intemperate. Lowcountry politicians conjured up visions of slave revolts in the West Indies and the Whiskey Rebellion in western Pennsylvania. They also tried to paint the reformers as extremists who wished to abolish slavery. In their writings and their public comments, the low-countrymen also exhibited a penchant for trying to put the backcountry in its proper (subordinate) place.[41]

The association sparked a petition drive that inundated the General Assembly. Forced to take up the matter of reapportionment, the house defeated it 58–53. Charles Cotesworth Pinckney wrote that the legislative session had "not been so stormy as I expected, and the Appian plan is for the present defeated." Realizing Harper's error in mentioning that the backcountry would be better off without slavery, new appeals stressed the large number of slave holders in the backcountry, especially in what was termed the middle districts (St. Matthew's and Orange Parishes; Saxe Gotha [Lexington], Winton [Barnwell], Clarendon, Claremont [Sumter], Kershaw, Darlington, Marlboro, Chesterfield, and Richland Counties). As an aside, it was noted that *every* member of the General Assembly from the backcountry was a slave owner. The general tenor of those pressing for reform was calm but insistent:

> Be just on your part; be candid and wise. Human life is a system of compromises and compensations. None of us can procure and retain all that our self-love would prompt us to wish; but we all find ourselves obliged to make sacrifices to submit to deprivations. They ought to be mutual. We have given up much of that to which we think ourselves entitled; do you, in turn, acquiesce, and acquiesce with cheerfulness and with alacrity, in our reasonable and modest requisitions? We shall then accept as a boon what we might claim as a right.

If the lowcountry were willing to compromise, then "the wounds of our country" would be healed and "the source of our differences forever dried up." Reform of the patently unfair representation in the General Assembly would restore to South Carolina the good order and harmony that had been absent in the body politic for nearly forty years.[42]

Lowcountry legislators were unmoved. They were convinced that the backcountry was hostile to slavery. There were other indications that this was so besides Harper's pamphlet. Many of the leading men in the backcountry warmly supported the French Revolution. Citizen Edmond Genêt, the envoy of the French Republic, landed in Charleston in April 1793. His arrival stoked the already warm feelings that many Carolinians, especially backcountry residents, had for republican France. There were republican societies, the wearing of tricolor cockades, and expressions of liberty, equality, and fraternity. The lowcountry elite was concerned about where all of this French radicalism might lead. The slave rebellion in the French colony of

Saint Domingue had been raging since 1791 when the island's assembly had begged South Carolina for assistance. After describing the arson and mayhem, the French colonists noted that "Principles destructive of our properties have brought flames into our cities and armed our very slaves against us—Philosophy in general the comfort of men brings to us despair." Saint Dominguan refugees in Charleston provided personal accounts of the horrors of servile insurrection. When the French government recognized the slaves' revolution in the fall of 1793, the lowcountry establishment was truly alarmed.[43]

Every time the lowcountry looked at the backcountry, it seemed to see antislavery agitation everywhere, even in the churches. In the postwar years Charles Woodmason had finally gotten his wish: the backcountry population became churchgoers. The only problem, at least for the lowcountry, was that there was evidence of antislavery activity in the three evangelical denominations (Methodist, Presbyterian, and Baptist) to which most backcountry residents belonged. Also, there was a strong Quaker presence in Kershaw, Laurens, Newberry, and Union Counties. The Methodist General Conference decreed in 1784 that owning slaves was an offense serious enough to justify expulsion from the church and in 1800 directed all Methodist clergy to sell any slaves they might own. Individual Presbyterian clergy were outspokenly opposed to slavery. The Cedar Springs Baptist Church (Spartanburg County) debated "whether or not it is agreeable to the gospel to hold Negroes in Slavery."[44]

Faced with French republicanism and Saint Domingue, antislavery evangelicals and Appius's observations, it was no wonder that the lowcountry, with its black majority population (78,000 blacks to 29,000 whites) was not enthusiastic about increasing the backcountry's power in the General Assembly (see Map 13). Reform efforts failed in 1796, and sectional bitterness festered like an unlanced boil.

The 1800 census bore out Harper's comment about population growth in the two sections of the state. There were only about 4,800 more white residents in the lowcountry in 1800 than there had been in 1790. In contrast, the backcountry population had increased by nearly 42,000 whites from 120,000 to 161,800. The decline of the Federalist Party and the linkages between lowcountry Jeffersonians and leading inland planters such as Robert Anderson, Andrew Pickens, and John Ewing Colhoun of Pendleton District; Robert Hunter of Laurens; and Wade Hampton of Richland made the possibility of reform more and more likely. In order to ameliorate what was certainly a losing situation, the lowcountry decided to toss another hush puppy to the backcountry: a publicly funded college in Columbia. Their reasoning was that they knew "the power of the State was thence forward to be in the upper country, and we desired our future rulers to be educated men."[45]

While the lowcountry elite had its agenda, the backcountry was not certain that it wanted a college. Even after the act creating it was passed in 1801, petitions from Laurens and Union Districts asked that it be repealed, but they were buried in com-

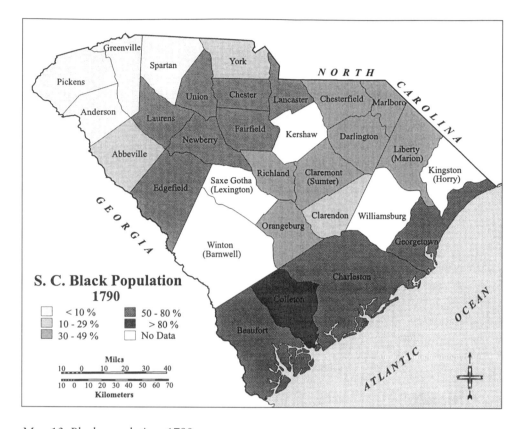

Map 13: Black population, 1790

mittee. The supporters of the college had high hopes that it would help unify the state. In his 1801 address to the General Assembly, Gov. John Drayton proposed the creation of the college where "the friendships of young men would thence be promoted and strengthened throughout the State and our political union be much adanced thereby."[46]

On the fiftieth anniversary of the opening of the college, the *Charleston Courier* proclaimed that South Carolina College had fulfilled the hopes of its founders: "It has effaced sectional lines of state division that once threatened to become permanent and it has moulded and shaped the whole population of the State into a spirit of unity and concord, rarely exemplified elsewhere." Nonalumni complained that public office in South Carolina had become virtually closed to anyone who had not graduated from the college. In 1835 eight of the state's nine representatives in Congress, the governor, and one U.S. senator were all alumni; nineteen years later four of six representatives, the governor, both senators, three of the state's four law chancellors, and five of six judges were graduates. Of the twenty-one governors of the state between 1824 and 1865, twelve (57 percent) were alumni; so too were 40 percent of the antebellum legislators. In an editorial the *Charleston Mercury* credited the college with helping create unity and harmony within the state.[47]

The plaudits were a half-century away, however, and in 1801 backcountry legislators were still seeking political parity for their section. According to Pierce Butler, South Carolina could become "One family" by agreeing to constitutional reform and supporting the Jeffersonian-Republican Party. The policies of the latter were, he insisted, "the best insurance against social disorder."[48]

By 1804 the Republicans were firmly in control of state government, but in that year an effort to address the apportionment issue passed the house but failed in the senate. The mood of the lowcountry was slowly changing. The backcountry's infatuation with republican France had cooled with the XYZ Affair. By 1805 the Methodists had dropped their official disapproval of slave ownership from the denomination's *Discipline;* the antislavery Presbyterian clergy had moved to Ohio; and a larger percentage of Baptist clergy than laity owned slaves. In the early years of the nineteenth century, many backcountry Quakers abandoned South Carolina for the Midwest. Most important of all to lowcountry rice planters, the number of slaves in the backcountry had increased considerably (nearly 60 percent) between 1790 and 1800. At the beginning of the nineteenth century, one-third of South Carolina's slave population (48,981 of 146,151) resided in the middle and western districts. Middlecountry planters in the General Assembly frequently voted with the lowcountry rather than the upcountry.[49]

The surprising champion of reapportionment was not a backcountry figure, but Joseph Alston, a wealthy rice planter from Prince George Winyah Parish. He argued that the existing apportionment of the legislature was arbitrary, and while he personally thought that legislative seats should be apportioned according to the white population, he had no objection to the representation of taxable wealth. The result was what came to be known as the Compromise of 1808. In June 1808 a special session of the General Assembly passed an amendment to the constitution with only two dissenting votes. Under the constitution of 1790 the amendment had to be ratified in the succeeding session of the General Assembly, and in December 1808 it was.[50]

The House of Representatives (124 members) was to be apportioned according to the number of white inhabitants and "the amount of all taxes raised by the legislature." There was to be one representative for every 1/62 of the population and one representative for every 1/62 of taxes collected. The first apportionment using the new scheme would be made in 1809, and every ten years thereafter there would be a reapportionment. Each parish and district was to have one senator.

At first blush it appeared that the backcountry had gained control of the House of Representatives while the lowcountry still controlled the senate. The sharing of power between the lowcountry and the backcountry was cited by Calhoun in *The Discourse on the Constitution and Government of the United States* as an example of the concurrent majority principle in action. Each section of the state had enough power to prevent the other from ramming a measure through unilaterally; there had to be a consensus. What was true in 1810, however, was no longer valid by 1830 because the commonality of interests of the black belt districts and parishes over-rode the old sectional divisions.[51]

Looking strictly at the Lower Division and Upper Division as the two sections of the state, in the house the Lower Division had fifty-four seats and the Upper Division had seventy; in the senate the Lower Division had twenty-two seats and the Upper Division twenty-three. However, these legal divisions no longer reflected demo-graphic reality. The black belt parishes and districts (those with a black population of 50 percent or more) had just two fewer seats in the house than did white belt dis-tricts, and in the senate the black belt had twenty-six senators, the white belt nine-teen. Between 1810 and 1860 the number (and power) of the black belt counties continued to increase until by 1860 they controlled 93/124 house seats and 36/46 senate seats.[52] Of the white majority districts in 1860, all were at least 30 percent black except for Pickens (about 22 percent). What appeared to be a triumph for the backcountry in 1808 was illusory. The real victors were the lowcountry planters as their worldview eventually became that of the rest of the state. Even in the white sands of Kingston (Horry) District or the mountains of Pickens District, slaves were a significant presence.[53]

In 1809 another amendment to the constitution passed the General Assembly for the first time and was ratified the following year. It eliminated property qualifica-tions for voting: "Every white man of the age of twenty one years . . . being a citizen of this State . . . shall have a right to vote." South Carolina thus became the first state to have universal white manhood suffrage. John C. Calhoun, the chair of the legislative committee that drew up the amendment, rode that notoriety into the U.S. House of Representatives.[54]

Why had the lowcountry caved in after a generation of unremitting resistance? There were some who feared the threat of civil disorder in the early nineteenth century. The intransigence of lowcountry legislators (many of them die-hard Feder-alists) and the arbitrary nature of the legislature's apportionment had caused the sore on the body politic to become even more inflamed. By working out the com-promise, the lowcountry responded to the 1790s petition of representation reform-ers, granted a boon to the backcountry, and avoided the backcountry's seizing what

Table 12.1

EXPANDING POWER OF THE BLACK BELT

SENATE	1810	1820	1830	1840	1850	1860
Lower Division	22	22	22	22	22	22
Upper Division	23	23	23	23	23	24
Black Belt	26	26	29	33	35	36
White Belt	19	19	16	12	10	10

HOUSE	1810	1820	1830	1840	1850	1860
Lower Division	54	52	47	47	48	47
Upper Division	70	72	77	77	76	77
Black Belt	61	61	69	83	94	93
White Belt	63	63	55	41	30	31

was its right. The boil was lanced and the healing process, the knitting of the state into a whole community, begun.[55]

For nearly two generations, since the outbreak of the Cherokee War in 1759, there had been little order or harmony and almost no sense of community in South Carolina. The little world of the lowcountry elite was no longer all of South Carolina as it had been before 1750; the populous backcountry (or upcountry, as it was more frequently called after 1790) clamored for a meaningful share of power. Relinquishing some of the power they had held for so long could not have come easily for lowcountry legislators who, even on the eve of the Civil War, considered upcountry folk lacking in "polish, refinement, and delicacy." That the lowcountry elite did so with hardly a murmur (only two dissenting votes) was due neither to magnanimity nor justice.[56]

Since the 1760s there had been business ties between backcountry settlements and the coast. Backcountry planters had the same aspirations as did their lowcountry counterparts, but until the 1790s they lacked a staple crop. Tobacco, hemp, and indigo were tried and found wanting. Then came short staple cotton and Eli Whitney's improved design for a cotton gin, which gave backcountry planters a staple upon which to build an agricultural export economy. South Carolina produced 69,840 pounds of cotton in 1790 and a decade later 20 million. Cotton did not begin the process of creating a planter class beyond Parish End, but it certainly enhanced the fortunes of those who were already planters and gave others a boost from the ranks of the yeomanry into that of the planters. Staple agriculture required more labor, and as cotton production spread inland across the districts of the middle country and upcountry, so did slavery.[57]

The reform of the apportionment of the General Assembly was the culmination of a number of grudging concessions by the lowcountry to accommodate the upcountry: the reform of the land tax (1785), creation of counties and county courts (1785), removal of the capital to Columbia (1786), chartering of South Carolina College (1801), election of James Burchell Richardson of Clarendon as the first non-Charleston governor (1802), changing the election of sheriffs from the General Assembly to the district level (1806). Then the Compromise of 1808 helped bring into being what one historian has termed "the first solid South Carolina."[58]

The upcountry reformers were good prophets about what would transpire once the question of representation was settled. "The wounds of our country [will] be healed, the sources of our differences forever dried up, and our public prosperity and happiness be fixed on a basis broad as our soil."[59]

Chapter Thirteen

TO RAISE SOMETHING FOR SALE

In the husbandry of Carolina, two objects are particularly kept in view by the planters and farmers. The first is to raise something for sale; and the second is to procure provisions for family concerns.

> John Drayton, *A View of South-Carolina*

The clear profits on one crop planted in cotton . . . will purchase the fee simple of the land. Two, three, or four will in like manner pay for the negroes who make it.

> David Ramsay, *History of South Carolina*

Cotton is falling, falling never to rise again.

> James Henry Hammond, 3 July 1841

Since the discovery that cotton would mature in South Carolina, she has reaped a golden harvest; but it is feared it has proved a curse rather than a blessing. . . . Cotton has been to South Carolina what the Mines of Mexico were to Spain, it has produced us such an abundant supply of all the luxuries and elegancies of life, with so little exertion on our part that we have become enervated, unfitted for other and more laborious pursuits, and unprepared to meet the state of things which sooner or later must come about.

> William Gregg, *Essays on Domestic Industry*

Cotton *is* King.

> James Henry Hammond, 4 March 1858

*I*N 1784 Henry Laurens described the frenzied activity of lowcountry residents' attempts to rebuild the economic cornucopia that had brought fabulous wealth to so many before the American Revolution. "All are busy in their respective vocations," he wrote, "covering as fast as they can the marks of British cruelty, by new Buildings, Inclosures, and other Improvements, and recovering their former State of happiness and Prosperity." Everyone was "anxious in the pursuit" of restoring his own fortunes. Laurens also could just as easily have been describing the farmers and planters of the backcountry. They, too, were furiously trying to recover from "the marks of British cruelty."[1]

In the generation after the Revolution, the backcountry would recover from the ravages of war and pass through a stage of development that the lowcountry had experienced in the middle of the eighteenth century. There were differences, of course, but they were "in degree rather than kind." Across the state individuals looked to the production of staple crops for world markets as the quickest and surest way to prosperity. Their single-mindedness would shape the state's economy and tie its future and well-being to market forces beyond their control.[2]

Rice and indigo had been the twin engines of the lowcountry's economic express for more than a generation. Both were planted after the war, but within a decade indigo was discarded—a victim of international competition. With independence, the British bounty that had inflated the incomes of many a Carolina planter was gone. The loss of the bounty in itself was not enough to discourage the production of indigo. In fact, production continued to rise in the decade after the war and began to approach the record levels of the 1770s. In 1794 South Carolina exported 715,000 pounds, most of it to Great Britain. Two years later almost no indigo was exported. The state's indigo survived the loss of the bounty, the competition from the French and Spanish West Indies, and even its wretched reputation for poor quality. However, when all three of these factors were combined with a flooding of the market by inexpensive, high-quality indigo from India, South Carolina's indigo was driven from the market.[3]

The state's indigo planters took the loss of their international market in stride. In the lowcountry those who remained concentrated on rice production, and in the backcountry they turned to cotton.

Rice had been a staple export for nearly a century; however, most of it had been produced on inland swamps, which limited the size of fields and potential profits. In the 1760s and 1770s a few planters had begun to experiment with the tidal cultivation of rice. However, tidal cultivation required a good deal of labor and capital, and most rice planters were simply content to reap the returns from their existing fields.[4]

The widespread destruction caused by the war evidently led a number of rice planters to reconsider their reluctance to change the way they planted. Since they had to rebuild anyway, why not try tidal cultivation? No doubt, the success of the Heyward brothers (James and Nathaniel) along the Combahee River changed a few minds too. When the Heywards built their rice dikes, some of their fellow planters laughed at them and their dams. The Heywards, however, had the last laugh as they produced twelve hundred to fifteen hundred pounds of rice per acre with the new method as opposed to six hundred to one thousand pounds by the older one. More important, given the cost of labor, one slave could produce three thousand to thirty-six hundred pounds of rice in tidal fields (five or six times the per slave yield from inland swamps).[5]

The change to tidal cultivation altered the rice-producing areas of the lowcountry. Inland swamp plantations were simply abandoned. In St. Paul's there had been 128 before the Revolution; afterward there were only eight. In 1843 Edmund Ruffun observed that "for a long time the Ashley river plantations were the most highly appreciated & productive lands in the colony. Now these lands are almost left untilled. . . . & the whole presents a melancholy scene of abandonment, desolation, & ruin." About the only use made of these former inland swamp rice plantations was to supply lumber for the Charleston market.[6]

The tides affected all of the lowcountry's rivers for thirty to thirty-five miles inland, but not all lowcountry tidal rivers were good for rice production. Some were too brackish, a complete mix of salt- and freshwater. Those that were suitable carried a sheet of freshwater on top of the saltwater. It was that top layer of freshwater that provided irrigation for the successful tidal cultivation of rice along the Santee, Waccamaw, Black, Great Pee Dee, Little Pee Dee, Edisto, Ashepoo, Combahee, and Savannah Rivers and, to a lesser extent, the Ashley and Cooper.

In order to harness the tides to irrigate fields and, at the same time, to protect fields from freshets and flooding, dikes or dams had to be erected along the riverbanks. A typical earthen dike might be twelve to fifteen feet thick at the bottom, three feet wide at the top, and rise to a height of five feet. Its sides were sloped to prevent erosion. On the inside of the bank was a ditch for drainage. Irrigation trenches or canals provided water to the fields, which were separated from one another by smaller earthen banks. Rice trunks, ingenious devices consisting of cypress boxes with hinged gates at either end, ran through the base of the dikes and controlled the flow of the tides. Samuel Porcher's rice fields along the Santee River were an engineering marvel. Begun in 1817 and completed in 1841, his main dike stretched for four and a quarter miles along the river and enclosed a total of fourteen hundred acres. Because of the levels of the river, his dikes were eight to fourteen feet high with bases that ranged from thirty-five to sixty feet thick.[7]

Rice dikes were built using only hand tools, primarily picks and shovels. Even today many old dikes still stand along the banks of lowcountry rivers, a tribute to the skill of the individuals who erected them. In almost all instances the dikes were built by enslaved Africans; however, in the 1840s William A. Carson, a planter on the Cooper River, hired Irish laborers to increase the size of his holdings.[8]

Behind the dikes were the rice fields. Once these had been swamps thick with cypress, tupelo, and sweet gum trees. Slaves, using axes, crosscut saws, hoes, and shovels, cut the trees and cleared the land. The land itself was an obstacle with which to contend. Frequently it was anything but solid, and it was not unusual for workers to be up to their knees in muck. Snakes and alligators were constant companions.

Once the dikes were built and the fields cleared, they were ready for planting. Almost the entire process of cultivating and harvesting rice was hand labor. After the fields were drained and dried out in the winter, the stubble of the previous crop was ploughed under. Mules or oxen, wearing special shoes that looked like miniature

Rice trunk on the Matthews Canal, Bear Island plantation, Colleton County. Photograph by Suzanne C. Linder.

snowshoes to keep them from sinking into the muck, pulled the plows. In March the fields were plowed again and the clods broken by hoes. In April the seeds, coated with clay to keep them from floating, were sown. Then the fields were flooded for three to seven days for the sprout flow. After the fields were drained, they were hoed. The fields were next totally submerged for several days to kill weeds and insects; then the water level was reduced to about one half the plants' height and maintained for three weeks for the stretch flow. After the plants had stretched, or grown, the fields were drained and over another three-week period were hoed two or three times. In mid July the harvest or lay-by flow flooded the fields for two months. The water might be changed to keep it fresh, but the fields were never allowed to dry out. In September the fields were drained and harvested by hand using a rice hook.[9]

After drying in the fields for several days, the sheaves of rice were transported to the farmyard where they were threshed and fanned by hand. The final stages of processing rice for market, removing the husk and polishing the grains, required a great deal of skill because if rice grains were broken their value was greatly reduced. In the eighteenth century rice was husked and polished using a wooden mortar and pestle. The first rice mills linked mortars and pestles together to rods that were powered by horses. Later the tides and steam were used for power sources, but the principle remained the same. By 1860 most mills could also thresh the grain.[10]

Georgetown District (the parishes of All Saints Waccamaw and Prince George Winyah) was the leading rice-producing area in the United States. In 1850 South Carolina produced 104,759,672 pounds of rice (74.6 percent of the nation's output); Georgetown District produced 46,765,040 (44.6 percent of South Carolina's total and 33.3 percent of the nation's). Ninety-eight percent of the county's rice came from the plantations of ninety-one planters who produced at least 100,000 pounds each. In 1860 a dozen planters (among them Plowden Charles Jennet Weston, John Izard Middleton, Frederick Wentworth Ford, and William Algernon Alston) produced more than one million pounds each. Rice planting in Georgetown County was big business. There were no small producers.[11]

What was true for Georgetown County was pretty much true of the rest of the state's rice-growing areas. An 1853–1854 survey of rice production in the United States listed 559 planters who produced more than 20,000 pounds of rice annually. Of these, 446 (79.8 percent) were from South Carolina. Economies of scale may have been one of the reasons for the large increase in total production. In the 1770s South Carolina exported 66 million pounds of rice; in 1860 it produced nearly twice that amount, 117 million pounds. The slave population of the lowcountry in 1860 was almost twice what it had been in 1770, but for some reason the yield per slave was nearly 150 pounds less.[12]

In the world markets South Carolina rice faced competition from other states (Georgia, North Carolina, and Louisiana) and the colonies of European empires (Brazil, Java, and Burma). In 1839 the state produced 75 percent of the nation's rice; twenty years later its share had declined to 63.6 percent. Georgia, with rich tidal fields along the Altamaha River, was the main competitor. By the 1830s Javanese rice had taken the northern European market away from the Americans; Burma eventually would become the world's major rice exporter. In 1838 East Indian rice could be purchased more cheaply in Charleston than rice grown along the rivers that flowed by the port. The threat of having its local market invaded by cheap foreign rice caused South Carolina politicians to lobby for rice's being placed on the nation's enumerated list. They were successful, and in 1846, little more than a decade after the Nullification Crisis of 1832–1833 (during which the state denounced all tariffs as unconstitutional and threatened to leave the union), U.S. tariff walls were raised to protect South Carolina rice from foreign competitors.[13]

Although few realized it at the time, 1820 marked the end of the lowcountry's golden age. An imperceptible decline set in that could be seen in per capita rice production figures and in the area's demographics. During the 1830s there was a population decline in the rice-producing parishes, and in 1860 there were fewer slaves than there had been in 1830. In 1860 the per capita wealth of Georgetown District's free population was $4,038.10 ($73,345), second in the state to Sumter's $4,467.28 ($81,141) and barely ahead of Fairfield's $4,009 ($72,817). Those figures confirmed the anecdotal evidence that had been accumulating since the 1790s: cotton was the wave of the future. That may have been the case at the time; however, like rice, cotton prosperity depended upon the fickleness of world markets.[14]

For many South Carolina farmers and planters, cotton seemed like a gift from heaven, especially to those who had relied on indigo, tobacco, and wheat. By 1796 indigo had ceased to be a staple crop and was grown only for domestic use. The production of tobacco, a crop introduced into the state by immigrants from Virginia, increased after the Revolution. In 1783 upcountry growers exported 643 hogsheads of tobacco; sixteen years later they exported 9,646, a fifteenfold increase. However, the state's tobacco suffered from many of the same drawbacks as indigo: relatively low yields, poor quality, and strong competition. By the 1790s upcountry tobacco growers turned to wheat. That, too, proved to be a dead end as an export staple. The overproduction of wheat glutted the local markets, prices dropped, and farmers turned to other crops. By 1808 the mills at Camden closed because there was not enough wheat being grown to justify their continued operation. Cotton had become the major crop of two-thirds of the state.[15]

Cotton had been known to South Carolinians since the days of the Lords Proprietors. In the 1740s the Commons House had authorized a bounty for its production. As early as 1754 small amounts were exported; however, it was grown primarily for domestic consumption. Most of the prerevolutionary experimentation was with sea island cotton, also known as black seed or long staple cotton.[16]

In the 1780s Kinsey Burden of St. Paul's Parish began to experiment with sea island cotton as a possible staple export crop (after his death his widow continued the experiments). With its long, silky fiber and smooth black seeds, it was relatively easy to separate the seeds from the fiber or lint by hand. Because of the nature of the plants and the soil (they seemed to thrive only in the coastal zone and outer coastal plain), sea island cotton was grown along the southern coast from the Santee River to the Savannah. Its territory reached into the interior along the Combahee, Edisto, Cooper, and Santee Rivers; however, not much sea island cotton was grown commercially beyond the old colonial parish boundaries.[17]

Short staple cotton, also called upland or green seed cotton, became the plant that would transform South Carolina and the American South. It was known before the 1790s, but the rough seed stuck to the short fibers and made it difficult and time-consuming to produce lint. That meant that the use of slave labor was cost-prohibitive just as it had been for the ill-fated silk industry. The invention of a workable cotton gin in 1793 made the growing and processing of upland cotton cost-effective.

Eli Whitney, a transplanted New Englander living in Georgia, perfected his gin in 1793 and received a federal patent the next year. He tried unsuccessfully to monopolize the process and charged exorbitant rates (40 percent of the ginned cotton) to those who availed themselves of his invention. Soon blacksmiths in Georgia and

South Carolina were making local versions of Whitney's gin and even improving upon his model. In 1802 the state of South Carolina granted him a patent and paid him $50,000 ($704,000) to let state residents make their own gins. The inventor got into a dispute with state authorities, who revoked their patent only to reinstate it in 1804. The actions of governments, both state and federal, were inconsequential. With the potential for profits to be made from selling cotton to Great Britain's growing textile industry, Carolinians made their own gins, patent or no patent.[18]

Unlike rice, which required a tremendous capital investment, cotton needed only land and a few tools: for planting, a plow and hoes; and for the processing, a gin and baler. Not every farmer had a gin and baler, and many used those on neighboring farms or plantations, paying with a certain small percentage of the ginned cotton. Cotton was practically the perfect crop for upcountry yeoman farmers. It gave them the chance to produce a staple for cash and with the profits to purchase slaves and become planters. It also gave landless whites who were tenants the chance to become landowners. The only limit on cotton production was harvesting. On average, an individual could pick fifty to eighty pounds per day.[19]

Short staple cotton was planted for export after 1794. In 1799 the first large crops were harvested in Richland District. Production had spread to Edgefield three years later and by 1804 as far inland as Spartanburg. Before 1810 the districts of the lower Piedmont (Abbeville, Chester, Edgefield, Fairfield, Laurens, Newberry, and Union) were major producers of cotton. Almost all of the 94,000 pounds of cotton exported in 1794 was sea island cotton. Just six years later, in 1800, South Carolina exported 20 million pounds of cotton, most of it short staple. Ten years later the state produced 50 million pounds. One of the few areas of the state that was not a part of the cotton belt was Greenville District, where as late as 1840 only about 115,000 pounds were produced. The old indigo planters of the 1740s would have been pleased and astonished at the rapidity with which upcountry farmers and planters abandoned indigo, tobacco, and wheat for cotton—pleased because a rational decision had been made to pursue a profitable staple crop, and astonished because the phenomenal increases in production dwarfed their earlier efforts.[20]

Wade Hampton of Richland District made one of the first great cotton fortunes. He earned $75,000 ($920,000) from his initial crop in 1799 and within a decade had an annual return of about $150,000 ($1,840,000). By his death in 1835 he was one of the wealthiest individuals in the American South. His was one of the major success stories, but it was not the only one.[21]

The first cotton boom (1794–1819) enriched almost all who planted cotton. A standard measure of an individual's wealth was the number of slaves owned. In 1790 James Burchill Richardson of Clarendon District was a minor; when he died in 1836 he owned 395 slaves. In 1790 Jacob Wannamaker of Orangeburg District owned no slaves; in 1830 he had 69. Thomas Harllee of Marion District had 2

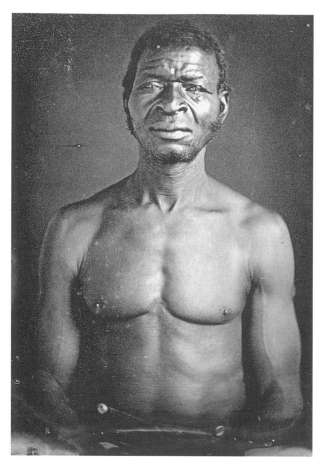

Jack, an African-born slave, on the plantation of B. F. Taylor, Richland County. The daguerreotype was taken in 1850 by J. T. Zealey for Louis Agassiz of Harvard. Courtesy, Peabody Museum, Harvard University.

slaves in 1790 and 29 in 1827. Further upstate William Pettus of York had no slaves in 1790, but at his death in 1818 he owned 19. In Abbeville District the number of slave owners in 1800 was 603; by 1820 the number had nearly doubled to 1,148. In 1800 nearly 25 percent of the families in the upcountry owned slaves, but twenty years later 40 percent did. The first boom alone enabled 4,000 upcountrymen to become slave owners (see Map 14).[22]

Among those who prospered from the first cotton boom was William Ellison, a free black gin maker of Sumter District, who used the profits from his shop to purchase land and slaves. By 1860 he owned 63, more than any other black person in South Carolina and more slaves than 90 percent of the nation's white slaveholders.[23]

As the case of William Ellison indicates, cotton brought prosperity not just to those who planted it, but also to those who were involved in its processing and marketing. Charleston remained the state's primary market, but there were important interior trading centers at Columbia, Camden, Hamburg, and Cheraw. Just north of Columbia's city limits was "Cotton Town," where merchants established

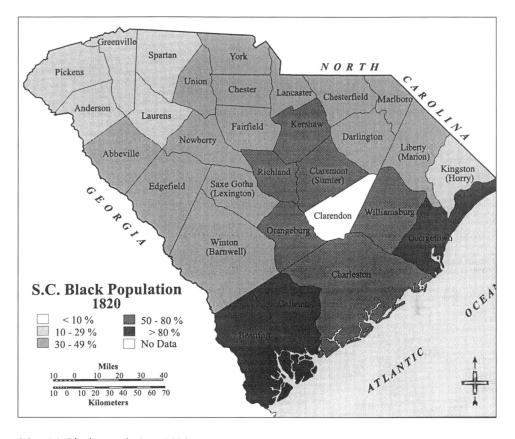

Map 14: Black population, 1820

warehouses and stores to cater to those who produced the staple. Cotton was the "community's life blood," and the prosperity of an area rose and fell with the cotton market.[24]

Between 1794 and 1860 there were two boom periods during which the price of cotton and the value of land and slaves rose significantly. The first boom began in the 1790s and, though interrupted by Thomas Jefferson's embargo and the War of 1812, continued until the Panic of 1819 plunged the nation's economy into a depression. Cotton had commanded 30.8¢ ($3.66) per pound in 1818 but dropped to 12¢ ($1.73) in 1823; from 1826 until 1832 it averaged about 9¢ ($1.46). Individu-

This Sumter County residence (circa 1800) was the home of Gov. Stephen D. Miller, Mary Boykin Miller Chesnut, and, after 1835, William Ellison and his family. Courtesy of Granger McKoy. Photograph by Suzanne C. Linder.

als who had purchased land and slaves at inflated prices found themselves in economic difficulty. Deflation doubled the real dollar value of debts. Ezekiel Noble of Abbeville District was forced to sell much of what he owned, including his household furnishings, to settle his debts. All he had left was "a fine house . . . and nothing in it."[25]

For about five years (1832–1837) there was a brief period of moderately rising cotton prices. In February 1837 cotton brought 18¢ ($2.84) a pound. Then came the Panic of 1837, and by May cotton was selling for 8¢ ($1.26) a pound. The value of a prime field hand dropped even more precipitously from $1,500 ($23,700) to $400 ($6,320). "Every day, I look forward to the future with more anxiety," wrote James Henry Hammond of Edgefield District. In 1841 he averred that the state's cotton growers lost money when the price dipped below 8¢ ($1.39). Low prices were compounded by a severe drought in 1845. Food crops withered in the fields and many a farmer could not feed his family. It is no wonder that the out-migration to the richer lands of the lower South accelerated.[26]

In the late 1840s another period of prosperity began that lasted until 1860. Cotton prices averaged 10¢ ($1.76) a pound. While prices were lower than they had been in the 1830s, the increase in output more than made up for the price differential. In 1850 the state produced 300,091 bales (150,450,000 pounds), more than twice what it had in 1834. A decade later the figure increased to 353,412 bales

(176,706,000 pounds). The thirteen counties of the upcountry accounted for 46 percent of the state's production in 1850 but only 42 percent in 1860. The rich lands of the inner coastal plain had the highest yields, and Sumter District in 1860 had the highest free per capita wealth in the state.[27]

Despite the continued expansion of cotton farming, the state's output could not keep pace with other southern states. In 1821 South Carolina was the leading cotton producing state in the nation—as it had been since the 1790s. The 1850 crop was three times larger than the 1820 one, yet South Carolina ranked fourth behind Alabama, Georgia, and Mississippi. A decade later the state had slipped to seventh as Mississippi, Alabama, Louisiana, Georgia, Arkansas, and Texas all produced more.[28]

The increase in cotton acreage during the nineteenth century had several harmful side effects. One of the most damaging was the destruction of the land, or "land butchery," as some have termed it. Cotton robbed the soil of its nutrients, and when yields declined too much, fields were abandoned rather than fertilized. "Nature has been so kind to the soil of this state, and adapted it to such early, and productive vegetation, that the exertions of the cultivator are not called forth," wrote John Drayton. "Hence, all the art of manuring and rotation of crops, have hitherto been little attended to," he continued, "and when one piece of land has been exhausted by culture, another has been cleared of woods for similar purposes." When Edmund Ruffin, a champion of fertilizing fields and scientific farming, visited the state he could not understand what he considered the wasteful agricultural practices of all but a few. During the decades before the Civil War the American South experienced the worst land erosion in its history.[29]

There was a reason, however, for the practice of farming land without the use of fertilizers until it no longer was productive and then abandoning it: profit. Labor was expensive and in short supply; land was not. It was not cost-effective to waste a valuable slave's time having him fertilize fields. The object of the state's farmers and planters (like their peers elsewhere in the country) was to get as much production from each hand as possible.[30]

A second unfortunate consequence of increased cotton production was the gradual abandoning of subsistence farming for cash crops. For much of the early nineteenth century, upcountry planters and farmers practiced "safety-first" farming; that is, they first decided how much land to put into food crops to feed all on the place and then what would be planted in cotton. Farmers of fewer than fifty acres of improved land, especially tenants (about 12–20 percent of all upcountry farmers), generally planted more cotton than corn in an attempt to get ahead. In 1850 probably three fourths of the upcountry's farms were self-sufficient, but in 1860 barely one half were. The production of corn and meat declined as cotton increased. In 1860 in Richland District, the yields for all crops were lower than they had been a decade earlier; however, the 50 percent drop in corn production and the decline in cattle

(27 percent) and sheep and swine (40 percent) were indications that many had forsaken "safety-first" farming.[31]

A third result of the state's love affair with cotton was the continual out-migration of its white and black residents. In Alabama planters could make as much as three times the amount of cotton per acre as those in South Carolina. The lure of the West led James Henry Hammond to lament in 1841 that almost all of his childhood and college friends had left the state. At times he wished that he were "comfortably settled in some western wild, surrounded by rich lands." It was an option that he had considered on several occasions. In fact, he had visited southern Georgia and northern Florida in search of new opportunities. He had even invested in a Texas land company. However, Hammond decided not to leave the state. Others, such as Wade Hampton and Andrew Pickens Jr., opted for a middle course. Both invested in richer lands to the west: Hampton in Louisiana and Pickens in Alabama. Hampton's son, Wade Jr., increased the non–South Carolina holdings he had inherited, purchasing land in Georgia, Mississippi, and Texas. They, however, were the exceptions as thousands of South Carolinians left the state after the War of 1812 opened up new and more fertile land for settlement.[32]

The *Camden Journal* reported in 1835 that "the old and the young are preparing to emigrate, and the inquiry is not whether you are going, but when do you go." As many as eight hundred residents left the middle districts in one week, and the newspaper said that there were three hundred in a single caravan. "The whole country about the Wateree and Congaree," bemoaned the *Journal*, was "breaking up and moving en masse to the west." The census figures reveal that the Kershaw District newspaper was not engaging in journalistic hyperbole. The out-migration was considerable and left those who remained feeling uncertain about the future.[33]

Between 1820 and 1860 nearly 200,000 whites (about one half those born in the state) lived somewhere else. By 1850 there were 50,000 Carolinians in Georgia, 45,000 in Alabama, and 26,000 in Mississippi. Among them were John Alexander of Greenville District, Archibald Odom of Marion, and William Pope of St. Luke's Parish, who immigrated to Georgia; John Ramsay Witherspoon of Christ Church Parish, George Bowie of Abbeville, John Joel Chappell of Richland, John Archer Elmore of Laurens, James G. Spann of Sumter, and Wilson Nesbitt of Williamsburg, who went to Alabama; John Ford of Marion and John Halbert of Pendleton, who relocated to Mississippi; and Dominick Augustin Hall of Charleston, who became a resident of Louisiana. Every one of these individuals had been a member of the South Carolina General Assembly. In 1854, of the twelve alumni of the South Carolina College who were governors, seven served their native state and five were elected elsewhere. The state lost many of its best and brightest.[34]

The black out-migration was almost as large. James Henry Hammond estimated in 1840 that due to out-migration, the state's slave population (335,334) was 83,000 fewer than it should have been. In the half-century before the Civil War, perhaps as

Table 13.1

THE POPULATION OF THE COTTON SOUTH

State	1800	1820	1830	1860
Alabama	—	127,901	309,527	964,201
Arkansas	—	14,273	30,338	435,450
Florida	—	—	34,370	140,424
Georgia	162,686	340,989	516,823	1,057,286
Louisiana	—	153,407	215,739	708,002
Mississippi	—	75,448	136,621	791,305
South Carolina	345,591	502,741	581,185	703,708
Texas	—	—	—	604,215

Dodd and Dodd, *Historical Statistics,* 2, 6, 14, 18, 26, 34, 46.

many as 179,000 black Carolinians went west with their owners.[35]

While the state's overall population grew, the rate of population increase was not steady, especially after 1820. In the lowcountry, for example, there were not as many black Carolinians in 1860 as there had been in 1830. The black population of Charleston declined 25 percent between 1850 and 1860. Also during the 1850s, in Richland District there was an out-migration of large landowners and their slaves, and the number of farms declined from 543 to 203. There were fewer whites in Newberry in 1860 than there had been in 1790. Between 1830 and 1850 Abbeville, Chester, Fairfield, Laurens, and Union each had a decrease in white population.[36]

In 1830 South Carolina had the largest population of the states in the cotton South. Thirty years later it ranked fifth, behind Louisiana, Georgia, Alabama, and Mississippi.[37]

The loss of enterprising citizens to the lower South and the butchery of the land were of concern to a number of South Carolinians, especially those who belonged to the various agricultural societies. In 1785 a group of lowcountry planters formed the South Carolina Society for Promoting and Improving Agriculture and Other Rural Concerns. The group was seeking alternatives to rice and indigo and offered premiums for the raising of peanuts, rhubarb, castor beans, hops, madder (a red dyestuff), figs, and merino sheep. By 1839 there was a State Agricultural Society and about a dozen local farmers' clubs or agricultural societies scattered across the state. Eventually almost every district would boast one of these organizations.[38]

Among the more active groups in the state were the Pendleton Farmers' Society (Pendleton District), the Beech Island Farmers' Club (Edgefield District), and the

The Pendleton Farmers' Society building (1826). Courtesy, Pendleton District Commission.

Black Oak and Strawberry Agricultural Societies (St. John's Berkeley Parish). These were not gatherings of yeoman farmers but rather of the leading planters in their respective communities. A survey of the membership of the Pendleton group revealed that on average its members owned nearly twelve hundred acres and most owned more than ten slaves. "The improvement of agriculture" was the stated purpose of all four organizations. The use of better plowing, rotation of crops, and fertilizer were debated and endorsed by all. In 1843, at the behest of several agricultural societies and with the active support of Gov. James Henry Hammond, the General Assembly appropriated funds to bring Edmund Ruffin of Virginia, a proponent of agricultural reform, to the state.[39]

The Virginian discovered considerable marl beds (a clay deposit rich in calcium carbonate) that could be used for fertilizer. A few lowcountry planters were already using manures (as all fertilizers were called), but he found little interest at a meeting of the Black Oak Agricultural Society or elsewhere in South Carolina. An 1856 debate at the Beech Island Farmers' Club captured the sentiments of most South Carolina farmers and planters on the question of agricultural reform: "Like the Christian religion," said Dr. H. R. Cook, "everybody agrees that it is good, but few endorse it."[40]

Similarly, a number of Carolinians agreed that the development of manufactur-

Reedy River Falls, Greenville. Courtesy, South Caroliniana Library.

ing plants (especially textile mills) might be a good idea, but not many were willing to provide the necessary financial or political support. All of the state's leading industries during the antebellum period were related to the field and forest: flour mills, gristmills, lumber, turpentine distilleries, and rice mills. With the exception of several turpentine distilleries and rice mills, these were small family enterprises. Jacob Geiger invested $1,000 ($17,500) in his water-powered gristmill in Richland District that he ran with the assistance of only one employee. Vardry McBee in Greenville, on the other hand, employed ten workers in what was one of the larger mills in the state.[41]

There were several other moderately sized manufacturing operations. Three nineteenth-century iron companies struggled to make a go in competition with larger eastern manufacturers. The most successful of these was the South Carolina Manufacturing Company of Spartanburg District, which had plants in Hurricane Shoals and Cowpens. In Edgefield District alkaline-glaze pottery manufacturing developed on a commercial scale. There were five thriving establishments in 1850, employing white journeymen and slave labor. Among them was Dave, a slave, whose stoneware often was inscribed with verse: "Dave belongs to Mr. Miles / wher the oven bakes & the pot biles." Edgefield pots with their characteristic olive green or black-brown glazes were prized for their utility as well as their beauty. By the 1850s there was considerable capital investment in carriage-making plants in Abbeville, Edgefield, Greenville, and Richland Districts. One factory in Columbia turned out more than 150 vehicles a year.[42]

Charleston was the state's leading manufacturing center. By the 1850s Charleston's factories turned out umbrellas, cordage, hats, organs, stained glass, railway cars, furniture, crockery, silverware, carriages, wagons, bricks, saddlery, tinware, and sails. There were also gristmills, rice mills, turpentine distilleries, and boat works. In 1849 the South Carolina Institute for the Promotion of Art, Mechanical Ingenuity, and Industry began holding annual fairs to showcase South Carolina-made goods. Interestingly, on the eve of the Civil War the cultural center of the lowcountry planters was the third largest manufacturing center in the American South, after Richmond and New Orleans.[43]

Missing from Charleston was a textile mill, although one had operated there briefly (1847–1852). The failed Charleston Cotton Manufacturing Company was one of a small number of textile mills that were established in South Carolina before 1860. Among the pioneer textile manufacturers were David R. Williams of Society Hill (Darlington District), William Bates of Batesville (Greenville District), and Dr. James Bivings (Spartanburg District). There was a flurry of textile-mill building in the 1840s. William Gregg of Graniteville (Edgefield District) was the state's most outspoken proponent and most successful antebellum textile manufacturer. His Graniteville Company had sufficient capital and was well managed. Poor management and bad luck plagued other efforts. For example, fires destroyed mills in Lexington, Bennettsville, and Camden.[44]

In 1860 the state's eighteen textile factories were all located above the fall zone. Most were small operations that had difficulty competing with New England manufacturers. On average, these small mills operated fewer than 1,000 spindles and had a capital investment of $27,000 ($490,000). The Graniteville Company had 9,245 spindles and a capital base of $360,000 ($6.4 million), which enabled it to hold its own with northern competitors.[45]

Despite the success of Gregg and a few other manufacturers, there was in general an antibusiness climate in antebellum South Carolina. The concept of a white working class in a slave society made some people uneasy. How could a person be independent if he worked for someone else? During the 1840s, when cotton prices slumped, slaves were used in the mills, but when cotton boomed again in the 1850s slaves went back to the fields where their labor was more profitable. The expectations of Gregg and others to create a working force of young white women (as had New England mills) failed miserably. Textile owners then recruited white families but usually employed only women and children; adult males had to find employment elsewhere.[46]

Factory labor was sometimes held out as a salvation for those who could not support themselves any other way. When Reuben Reid of Big Rabun Creek in Laurens District died in 1837, he left a widow and five children. Following the advice of neighbors, the widow moved to Greenville and sought work for herself and her two older children (a boy thirteen and a girl eleven) in a cotton factory.[47]

Working in a factory might have been the only option for Mrs. Reid, but for other white South Carolinians, especially adult males, there was not much incentive for such work. Wages were low–with the exception of North Carolina the lowest in

Graniteville Cotton Mill, Graniteville. *DeBow's Review,* March 1851. Courtesy, Gregg-Graniteville Library, University of South Carolina–Aiken.

the South. In 1850 the average annual wage in a textile mill was $126 ($2,435); in other industries it was $161 ($3,111), a difference of 27 percent. White labor was scarce, and what was available tended to gravitate to more lucrative opportunities planting cotton or building the state's rapidly expanding railroad network. In 1860 there were only 891 individuals employed in South Carolina textile factories, a decline of 12.5 percent from a decade earlier.[48]

Despite the success of some manufacturing enterprises, there remained a general attitude in the state that industry was a danger to South Carolina's way of life. The person responsible for developing and promoting this point of view was John C. Calhoun, the undisputed political leader in the state from 1824 until his death in 1850. Gregg boldly attacked "Mr. Calhoun, our great oracle," and his political lieutenants in print for their opposition to industrialization: "Those who are disposed to agitate the State and prepare the minds of the people for resisting the laws of Congress, and particularly those who look for so direful a calamity as the dissolution of our Union, should, above all others, be most anxious so to diversify the industrial pursuits of South Carolina, as to render her independent of all other countries." However, this did little to persuade them to change their minds.[49]

State government, where the influence of Calhoun was strongly felt, was less enthusiastic than the state's newspaper editors about industrialization. When Gregg and his associates asked for a charter for the Graniteville Company from the General Assembly in 1845, the request was reported out negatively from the house committee on incorporations. Eventually the committee's decision was reversed, but not without a struggle. It passed the state senate more easily, and the Graniteville Company was chartered. In 1848 the South Carolina House of Representatives refused to establish a standing committee on commerce, manufacturing, and mechanical industry. Given this antimanufacturing climate, it is no wonder that Gregg had plans to seek a charter from the Georgia legislature if his efforts failed in South Carolina. While there was hostility toward industry, there was widespread political and financial support for banks and various transportation schemes.[50]

In 1786 the Santee Canal Company was formed to cut a canal from the Santee River to the headwaters of the Cooper and thus make it easier to transport crops from the middle- and upcountry to Charleston. The company's board of directors reflected the economic unification of the state that was taking place: Thomas Sumter, Wade Hampton, and John Chesnut from the backcountry served with lowcountry-men Aedanus Burke, John Rutledge, Ralph Izard, and William Moultrie. Izard understood the unhappiness of the residents of the "back parts" in not being able to "bring their produce to market upon moderate terms." The canal would do just that, bring prosperity to the backcountry, and within a generation create "an united and happy people." The Santee Canal Company was one of five private canal companies chartered by the state before 1800. The other four never got off the ground, and the Santee Canal had a checkered career (during the drought of 1816–1817 it ran dry) and was in disuse by 1840. A decade later the legislature revoked the company's charter.[51]

In the last decade of the eighteenth century, the General Assembly established commissions to improve the state's transportation network. For Greenville one of the most important was the "waggon road over the Western Mountains" that linked the upcountry with the growing settlements in Tennessee. The major push for internal improvements, as roads and canals were called, came in the years after the War of 1812.[52]

In 1818 the General Assembly authorized a Board of Internal Improvements to oversee a $1 million ($11.9 million) program of roads and canals. It was a tremendous special appropriation, four times the normal annual budget of $250,000 ($3 million). Caught up in politics and the economic downturn after the Panic of 1819, the internal improvements program was not successful.

The state's canal system, in particular, was a disaster. The plan called for eight canals. There were to be four on the Catawba and Wateree Rivers above Camden at Wateree, Rocky Mount, Landsford, and Fishing Creek. The Columbia and Lockhart canals would open up navigation on the Broad River for 110 miles above Columbia. Two canals on the Saluda River, the Saluda and Dreher, would enable boat traffic to reach Laurens and Abbeville. All eight were built, and the system's supporters bragged that every district in the state, except for Greenville, could be reached by water. Despite the twenty-five miles of canals and fifty-nine locks, poor routes were selected because of politics, and the public did not use the canals. As a result not enough revenue was collected to pay the lockkeepers' salaries. By 1838 six of the eight had been abandoned.[53]

Inland navigation might have been successful if the state had heeded the recommendations of its engineer, Robert Mills. In two pamphlets, *Inland Navigation* and *Internal Improvements,* he argued that too much money had been spent upstate on canals that had been built piecemeal without any regard to a system. His plan would have improved navigation between Columbia and Charleston, with possible extension into the Alleghenies.[54]

The state road that was built as a toll road fared little better. Beginning in Charleston, it followed a route that skirted present-day Holly Hill, Cameron, and St. Matthews to Columbia; from the capital it went up the western side of the Broad River to the Enoree River; the road crossed the Enoree and then went over Saluda Mountain in Greenville District. The lower portion of the road, from Columbia to Charleston, was completed in 1829. It, like the canals, was a failure. Residents refused to pay what they considered exorbitant tolls and instead used the rutted and ill-kept local roads. Later, when it became a free road, it was heavily traveled.[55]

Although burned by the $1 million ($11.9 million) or more spent on roads and canals, South Carolinians and their state government did not abandon efforts to improve the state's transportation network. Early on the state evidenced an interest in railroads. In 1827 the South Carolina Canal and Railroad Company was chartered by the state, and in six years it laid 136 miles of track from the Charleston city limits to Hamburg (Edgefield District). When it was completed, it was the longest railroad in the world. In 1835 the trip was scheduled to take eleven and one-half hours with seven stops en route, and the price of a one-way ticket was $6.75 ($115.66). Charlestonians, in particular, thought that the railroad would boost the city's economy. Eventually it would, but not until after the city lifted restrictions on steam engines within the city limits.[56]

The South Carolina Canal and Railroad Company eventually became the South Carolina Railroad Company with the state as a major stockholder. Using its stock in the railroad company and its banking subsidiary, the Southwestern Railroad Bank, the state created a revolving fund that spurred the construction of 703 miles of track during the 1850s. By 1860 there were eleven railroads operating in the state, and all districts except Lancaster were linked by rail to Columbia or Charleston. In total mileage the state trailed Virginia and Georgia, but on the basis of miles of track per one thousand square miles South Carolina ranked second only to Virginia. The only signal failure was the inability of the Blue Ridge Railroad to complete the tunnel through Stump House Mountain.[57]

The development of a railroad network brought economic benefits to towns across the state, just as their promoters had hoped they would. In Anderson, for example, property values increased fourfold between 1848 and 1860 after the town became a major stop on the Greenville and Columbia Railroad. Before the Charlotte and South Carolina Railroad ran through eastern York District in 1851, Rock Hill did not exist. Once tracks could run to Charleston's docks, more cotton was shipped to the port by rail. In 1855 there were 164,619 more bales shipped by rail to Charleston than there had been just five years earlier. Rail transportation also made it possible in 1858 for South Carolina peaches to reach the New York market for the first time.[58]

Banking was another sector of the economy in which the state was a major factor. In 1812 the Bank of the State of South Carolina was chartered as a quasi-public agency owned solely by the state. Headquartered in Charleston, it eventually had branches in Abbeville, Camden, Columbia, and Georgetown and agencies (just a representative to seek business, not a full-service branch bank) in Chester, Clinton, Laurens, Marion, Newberry, Spartanburg, Sumter, and Yorkville. It also had out-of-state agencies in Charlotte, Liverpool, London, New Orleans, and New York. Well managed and politically powerful, the Bank of the State fulfilled its mission as a fiscal agent for the state, a source of additional state revenue (during the 1850s its profits were more than $3 million [$55.6 million]), and supporter of the state's commercial interests.[59]

In addition to the Bank of the State, there were sixteen successful privately owned banks, six of which were chartered during the 1850s. Although there were banks in Camden, Cheraw, Chester, Columbia, Georgetown, Hamburg, Newberry, and Winnsboro, nearly three fourths of the private banking capital in the state was located in Charleston. All of these banks, as well as the Bank of the State, issued paper currency that circulated not only in South Carolina but as far west as Alabama and Mississippi. Private banknotes were issued in denominations ranging from $5 to $100. Only the Bank of the State could issue smaller ones. These banknotes and the banks that issued them enhanced the growing commercial activity of the prosperous 1850s.[60]

Although the 1850s were a prosperous period, there were warning signs that South Carolina's economic well-being was illusory. Nowhere was that more in evidence than in Charleston. In the eighteenth century it had been the principal entrepôt for the Southeast, with Savannah, Pensacola, Mobile, and the North Carolina ports its satellites. Now Charleston was no longer on the direct trade route from Europe; it had become a satellite of New York, Boston, and Philadelphia. In the South, New Orleans and Mobile easily surpassed Charleston in trade, and Savannah was threatening to overtake it. Despite the advantage of new railroad connections (which should have brought about a population increase), the city actually lost residents during the decade.[61]

There were danger signals elsewhere as well. Land butchery increased as more land was planted in cotton. From all sections of the state out-migration continued apace. There were fewer black Carolinians in the lowcountry in 1860 than there had been in 1830. On his travels outside Charleston, Ruffin wrote that "the country appears like the former residence of a people who have all gone away, leaving their land tenantless." The surplus capital of the lowcountry was not invested there but instead went into western lands or manufacturing ventures such as the Graniteville

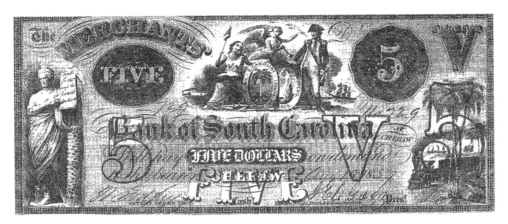

Five-dollar banknote issued by the Merchants' Bank of South Carolina (Cheraw), 1857. Note Hiram Powers's statue of John C. Calhoun in the lower left corner; it was destroyed in Columbia, 17 February 1865. Courtesy, South Caroliniana Library.

Company. According to one modern economic historian, most rice planters had negative returns on their investments in land and slaves after 1820.[62]

Many of the signs that the state's economy was not as healthy as it appeared were obscured by others that shouted progress and prosperity. During the last decade before the Civil War almost every indicator of wealth increased: personal property and real estate values, bank deposits, and exports. There was a good deal of wealth in South Carolina despite its continued decline in relation to the states of the lower South. The average free per capita wealth in 1860 was an incredible $2,017 ($36,635). When slaves are included as persons, the per capita wealth was $864 ($15,693), well above the national average of $608 ($11,043). South Carolina ranked third in the country, behind Mississippi and Louisiana. By comparison, the wealthiest nonslave state, Connecticut, had a per capita wealth of $774 ($14,058). In 1860 there were thirty districts in South Carolina, every one of which, with the sole exception of Horry District, had a free per capita wealth that exceeded the national average. Even if the wealth were on strictly a per capita basis, only four districts (Georgetown, Chesterfield, Pickens, and Horry) would fall below the national average.[63]

There was a direct correlation between slave ownership and wealth. The ten richest districts were better than 60 percent black; the ten least prosperous districts had an all-white majority. Most of the accumulated wealth of white South Carolinians was in human property. Conservatively, it has been estimated that 60 percent of a slave owner's wealth was in slaves and 33 percent in land and buildings; however, a more accurate appraisal might be that two-thirds of a slave owner's wealth was in slaves. When slave ownership as an economic investment is compared to nonslave owners, the numbers are stunning. If a person owned as few as three slaves, he or

Table 13.2

THE WEALTH OF SOUTH CAROLINA, 1860

District	Free Per Capita Wealth, 1996$	Per Capita Wealth, 1996$	Percentage Black
Sumter	$81,140	$24,384	71.3
Georgetown	$73,345	$10,708	85.9
Fairfield	$72,817	$21,659	71.2
Beaufort	$72,272	$13,591	83.3
Newberry	$63,410	$21,818	66.5
Colleton	$63,236	$14,496	77.9
Clarendon	$51,329	$17,718	66.6
Richland	$50,405	$20,104	62.5
Abbeville	$47,771	$17,815	64.4
Orangeburg	$47,250	$15,813	67.4
Edgefield	$44,146	$17,517	60.8
Kershaw	$43,859	$17,579	61.4
Chester	$43,469	$17,400	60.8
Marlboro	$40,464	$17,931	56.8
Barnwell	$40,233	$17,460	58.7
Williamsburg	$38,748	$13,183	66.5
Laurens	$36,541	$16,323	55.9
Charleston	$35,219	$16,483	58.4
Darlington	$35,137	$14,641	58.6
Union	$34,376	$15,057	55.8
York	$26,943	$14,433	47.3
Marion	$26,644	$14,132	48.1
Lancaster	$24,145	$12,580	48.7
Anderson	$22,114	$13,968	37.5
Greenville	$21,749	$15,745	33.2
Lexington	$20,454	$12,337	40.1
Chesterfield	$16,941	$10,275	37.9
Spartanburg	$15,926	$10,050	31.1
Pickens	$15,926	$ 9,484	21.9
Horry	$ 6,072	$ 4,383	30.1

Coclanis and Ford, "The South Carolina Economy," 98–99. Ford and Coclanis, "Ranking—1860 . . . Free Population" and "Ranking—1860 . . . Total Population," tables compiled by Lacy K. Ford and Peter A. Coclanis. Wallace, *History of South Carolina,* 3: 504.

she had a greater capital investment than the average nonslaveholder did in all other forms of wealth combined. As high as they were, the South Carolina figures, especially for the lowcountry, may be understated. In 1860, while the average price of a slave in the American South was $900–$1,200 ($16,350–$21,800) and the price of a prime field hand $1,600 ($29,100), for some reason the values in the Carolina lowcountry were only $600–$625 ($10,900–$11,350) for an average slave and $1,200–$1,500 ($21,800–$27,250) for a prime field hand. On a per capita basis, free South Carolinians (white and black) were still among the wealthier residents of the United States, but in 1860 they were not as well off as their forebears had been in 1774.[64]

On the eve of the American Civil War, South Carolinians continued the economic pattern established more than 150 years earlier: an agricultural economy based upon staple crops produced for world markets by enslaved black labor. What would have happened to the state's economy had there been no Civil War is a matter of conjecture. There were warning signs, and had been since 1820, that all was not well; however, the state's economic decline was relative. Compared to the rest of the free population of the United States in 1860, the average free South Carolinian (white and black) was better off financially than most other Americans.

Chapter Fourteen

A VISIT TO ANTEBELLUM SOUTH CAROLINA

It will be seen that the number of slaves greatly surpasses that of the free whites; indeed this state has begun to suffer the inconveniences of slavery to such a degree, that measures of security have been adopted through fear, which at once are painful to humanity, and violate the rights of property. . . . This state of things, relating to slavery in South Carolina, is the more painful, because it is strongly contrasted with the character of the inhabitants of the state. The Carolinians are particularly distinguished by the improvements of their minds, the elegance of their manners, their politeness and hospitality to strangers.

Auguste Lavasseur, *Lafayette in America, in 1824 and 1825*

*A*FTER THE AMERICAN REVOLUTION it became fashionable for both Americans and Europeans to tour the new United States and to publish their travel accounts. Nearly one hundred of these accounts relate visitors' impressions of antebellum South Carolina. Whereas most colonial visitors sailed into Charleston and rarely ventured much beyond its environs, these later travelers generally came overland and saw at least the middlecountry as well as the lowcountry. From reading a number of these travel accounts, a pattern emerges.[1]

Any town encountered got at least a mention. So, too, did points of interest (especially in Columbia and Charleston), religion, education, intellectual life, morality, recreation, and entertainment. It was a rare visitor who did not go to a plantation and describe both the big house and the quarters. Encounters with slaves or free persons of color were noted. Although there were some visitors who, because of their antipathy to slavery, were hostile witnesses, more were simply curious. With its highly visible black majority, South Carolina was different. There was not an aspect of everyday life that was not affected by the peculiar institution. The Reverend James H. Thornwell, a Presbyterian clergyman and president of the South Carolina College, rightly observed, "slavery is implicated in every fibre of southern society."[2]

Antebellum South Carolina was a rural society. In 1860 there were only five towns in the state with populations of more than 1,500: Charleston (40,522), Columbia (8,052), Georgetown (1,720), Camden (1,621), and Greenville (1,518). Most of the courthouse towns were like Marion, "a pleasant little village," with a courthouse, several churches, a school, and about twenty houses. Beaufort was "a picturesque town composed of an assemblage of villas, the summer residences of numerous planters." Newberry, with a new college, was served by two railroads and supported two weekly newspapers. Anderson changed so much between 1847 and 1857 that a former resident said he "knew not where to find any place or any person."[3]

By the 1850s Columbia was the largest inland town in the two Carolinas, but it was smaller than Augusta, Atlanta, or Columbus in Georgia. Although Richland District had a black majority, Columbia did not. As the state capital, a major cotton market, and a railroad center, Columbia prospered. Three rail lines connected the capital with Charleston, Greenville, and Charlotte. The *Daily South Carolinian,* the *Daily Southern Guardian,* and the *Daily Carolina Times* competed fiercely for readers (the three papers also appeared in triweekly and weekly editions).[4]

The city's prosperity was reflected in private residences and public buildings. Raised classic revival cottages were everywhere; in fact, because they were so common they were often referred to as "Columbia cottages." With twelve- to fourteen-foot ceilings, pitched roofs, and lots of windows, they were well suited for Columbia's muggy climate. The style was used by members of the elite (for example, the home of Louisa Susannah Cheves and David J. McCord on Pendleton Street) and the city's small free black population (the home of Cecilia Mann and William Simons on Richland Street, for instance). Probably the most imposing house in town was James Henry Hammond's mansion. Surrounded on all four sides by two-story columns and furnished with the latest fashions from New York, it was designed to make a social statement. Some contemporary observers thought it looked more like a bank or a church.[5]

By midcentury Baptists, Episcopalians, Lutherans, Methodists, Presbyterians, and Roman Catholics had built substantial houses of worship. There was also a Hebrew Benevolent Society. There were only a few black Episcopalians, but in 1841, 360 of the 405 members of the First Baptist Church were black. First Presbyterian and Washington Street Methodist had separate meetinghouses for their black members; after 1865 they would become separate congregations (Ladson Presbyterian and Bethel African Methodist Episcopal).[6]

A visitor usually attended the church of his or her choice, but almost all wanted to see the Lunatic Asylum. Designed by Robert Mills and located on the outskirts of town, the Greek Revival structure was quite a tourist attraction. South Carolina was in the vanguard of the treatment of the mentally ill. It was the first state in the lower South (and only the third in the country) to operate a state-supported facility. The Lunatic Asylum was a place for the treatment, not the warehousing, of the insane.[7]

Another tourist destination was the campus of the South Carolina College, only two blocks from the State House. With its Federal style buildings flanking an open lawn, the college predated Jefferson's plan for the University of Virginia by two

The Mills Building at the South Carolina State Hospital, Columbia. Courtesy, South Caroliniana Library.

decades. The college had the first separate library building in the country, and in 1850, with 18,500 volumes, its collection was larger than those of either Princeton or Columbia. The college's faculty, many of them European-educated, were often as much an attraction as the sylvan campus.[8]

Visitors generally commented on the beauty of Sidney Park below Assembly Street and the Pride of India (chinaberry) trees that lined Columbia's wide streets. The town had about it, wrote one visitor, "an air of neatness and elegance." Although the town's waterworks had been built in 1820, it was still considered something of an engineering marvel and gave the community a regular, healthy water supply, something Charleston sorely lacked. That city's water, drawn from cisterns and shallow wells, was "for the most part undrinkable."[9]

Charleston was the largest city in the state, and in 1860, like Columbia, it had a white majority (58 percent). Ten years earlier its population had been 53 percent black, but a decade of black out-migration combined with white in-migration (mostly working-class Irish and German) resulted in a dramatic demographic change. Nearly 20 percent (3,237) of the black population were free persons of color. With its large class of working poor, its population was more like that of many northern cities. Socially and politically it was a city divided against itself. Said William Gilmore Simms, "There are two very distinct cities in Charleston—the old and the new—representing rival communities." In reality, though, there were more

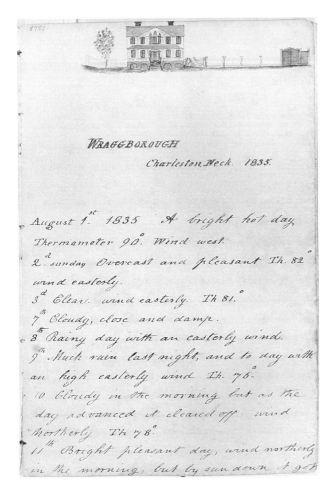

A page from the diary of Charles Heyward (1802–1865). The drawing at the top of the page is of his Charleston town house in Wraggborough. Courtesy, South Caroliniana Library.

than just two "Charlestons" because Simms never considered the worlds of working whites, free blacks, or slaves.[10]

Even though it was a city in relative decline, Charleston was still a place that visitors found appealing. Its handsome homes, churches, public buildings, and lush gardens drew favorable comments from even the most jaundiced travelers.[11]

After the American Revolution architectural styles changed, but the basic designs of the city's homes did not. Federal- and Classical Revival-style single and double houses blended in with their older, colonial neighbors. Interior details, however, reflected new, popular tastes in terms of moldings, fireplaces, and stairways. Piazzas still looked out over walled gardens, many of which now included imports from the Orient such as azaleas, camellia japonicas, and wisteria. Accenting the houses and garden walls were marvelous wrought-iron balconies, railings, fences, and gates produced by the city's skilled blacksmiths.[12]

While it was easy to select the most imposing home in Columbia, in Charleston there were (and are today) so many examples that the choice was a matter of personal taste. From the Federal period, the Blacklock House (1800) on Bull Street and the Joseph Manigault (circa 1802) and Nathaniel Russell (circa 1809) Houses on Meeting Street are structures of national importance. None of the city's Classical Revival residences ranks as highly with preservationists or architectural historians. However, on East Battery the Louis DeSaussure House (circa 1850), the William Roper House (1838), the William Ravenel House (1845), and the Edmonston-Alston House (circa 1828) give modern visitors an excellent sampling of antebellum architecture.[13]

Although Charleston's antebellum residences might not have been in the same league as their colonial and federal antecedents, its early Classical Revival public buildings were magnificent. Robert Mills, a native Charlestonian and the country's first professional architect, designed a number of these landmark structures—among them the First Baptist Church (1822) and the Fireproof Building (1822). For a brief period during the 1830s, after fires in 1835 and 1838 had destroyed significant portions of the city, Charlestonians flirted with the idea that from the ashes would rise a city that was "more solid and beautiful than ever . . . 'the Queen of the South.'" The Charleston Hotel (1838) with fourteen Corinthian columns marching across its facade and the Hibernian Society Hall (1839) with its Ionic portico reflected the civic aspirations of the community. To a lesser degree, so did the Doric temple plan for the new sanctuary of Beth Elohim (1840). Unfortunately, the dreams voiced in the toast at the dedication of the Hibernian Society Hall died with the Panic of 1839, and thereafter Charlestonians settled for structures that were not quite as grand as those built prior to 1840.[14]

Charleston was a city of churches. Their spires dominated the city's skyline. In the years after the American Revolution, there was an increase in church attendance and public piety. That was true for the rest of the state as well. The Second Great Awakening swept the upstate in 1802 and had a tremendous influence on the Baptists, Methodists, and Presbyterians. For example, in three years (1802–1805) the number of Methodists in the state doubled and thirty-five new upcountry Baptist congregations were organized. In 1799 only about 8 percent of the white population of the upcountry belonged to a church; by 1810 the number had nearly tripled to 23 percent.[15]

The camp meeting, often a week-long revival, was the means by which the gospel spread to so many so rapidly. Initially the meetings were interdenominational with Baptist, Methodist, and Presbyterian clergy preaching to upwards of five thousand souls. The ecumenical spirit did not last long, however, as both Presbyterians and Baptists pulled out. By the 1820s camp meetings were identified with the Methodist Church and became an important aspect of that denomination's church life.[16]

The Episcopal Church in the early nineteenth century began a mission effort of its own. Using the old colonial Society for the Propagation of the Gospel in Foreign Parts as a model, it created the Protestant Episcopal Society for the Advancement of Christianity in South Carolina (1810). Its first major undertaking was establishing a church in Columbia. Lowcountry Episcopalians considered such a move essential because Columbia was the state capital and the home of the South Carolina College. It was important for lowcountry collegians to be able to worship God "after the manner of their Fathers." Thus, the church became another means to help bring together the two sections of the state.[17]

Interestingly, the Episcopal Church, which tended to avoid emotionalism, was as affected by the revivalism of the 1830s as were the state's Baptists and Methodists. In Beaufort hundreds crowded old St. Helena's Church as well as the Beaufort Baptist Church for revivals. Among those converted was Richard Fuller, who became one of the country's leading Baptist clergymen, and Stephen Elliott, who became the Episcopal bishop of Georgia. In Newberry the revival was responsible for the construction of churches in the courthouse town. Shaped-note singing (each note was shaped differently so that individuals without any musical knowledge could be taught to sing) was a key factor in upcountry revivals. William "Singing Billy" Walker of Union District published *Southern Harmony* (1835), which helped thousands learn to carry a tune in praise of the Lord.[18]

During the 1830s a good many white South Carolinians decided it was their Christian duty to proselytize black Carolinians. Lowcountry Episcopalians built fifty chapels (thirteen alone in the small parish of All Saints Waccamaw), primarily for the use of slaves. Despite the law, it was not unusual for owners to permit all-black religious gatherings on their plantations. In Charleston, Calvary Episcopal became the subject of controversy, but its backers persevered and it flourished. So, too, did Zion Presbyterian, which by 1860 was one of the largest congregations in the city. Statewide the Methodists supported twenty-four missions to the slaves. Episcopalians and Methodists published catechisms for teaching black Carolinians, which posed an interesting question: Since it was illegal to teach slaves to read, how could they use a catechism or read the Bible? In the 1830s and 1840s devout Christian whites from Abbeville, Chester, and Sumter petitioned the General Assembly to repeal the portions of the 1834 law forbidding the teaching of slaves to read. Evangelism among the slave population resulted in large numbers of black Carolinians becoming Christians.[19]

On the eve of the Civil War there were more black Methodists than there were whites (46,740 to 37,095). In the Episcopal Diocese of South Carolina there were six more white Episcopalians than there were black (2,979 to 2,973). Some individual congregations were overwhelmingly black. At All Saints Episcopal in Georgetown District 254 out of 290 members were black, and at Euhaw Baptist in Beaufort District 458 out of 482 members were. Across the lowcountry and middlecountry there were other predominantly black congregations: Swift Creek Baptist in Kershaw District (995/1301), the Methodist church in Darlington (230/317), James Island Presbyterian in Charleston District (143/177), and Salem, Black River

Presbyterian in Sumter District (149/194). What is noticeable, however, is that Episcopalians were the owners of the largest number of slaves, yet that did not translate into church membership.[20]

While denominations, congregations, and individual members endeavored to spread the gospel to black South Carolinians, there was little opposition to the institution of slavery. In the late eighteenth century some Methodists, Presbyterians, and Baptists had wrestled with the issue; however, by the early nineteenth century the struggle was over. The Quakers of the middlecountry, who did not alter their opposition, opted to leave the state. Between 1802 and 1807 about one hundred members of the Bush River meeting in Newberry District migrated to Ohio. A few remained, but in 1822 the meeting was "laid down" and its trustees advised either to lease or sell its property.[21]

Throughout the antebellum period prominent clergy of every denomination voiced support for the state and its domestic institutions. Presbyterian clergyman James H. Thornwell and Roman Catholic bishop John England found biblical sanctions for slavery. In his pamphlet *Domestic Slavery Considered as a Social Institution* Baptist minister Richard Fuller not only cited Scripture but quoted George Whitefield: "As to the lawfulness of owning slaves, I have no doubt." In 1859 the *Southern Episcopalian*, published in Charleston, editorialized that slavery was "a necessary element towards the composition of a high and stable civilization—as a thing good in itself."[22]

Many clergy, such as Thornwell, linked support for slavery with support of traditional patriarchal families. He yoked abolitionism with women's rights and other northern reform movements that threatened to disrupt what he saw as the God-ordained order of things. From his reading of Scriptures, the Presbyterian divine found "masters exhorted in the same connection with husbands, parents, magistrates"; the flip side of that equation was "slaves exhorted in the same connection with wives, children, subjects." South Carolina native Angelina Grimké's 1838 appearance before a Massachusetts legislative committee was seen in her home state as proof positive of the connection between abolitionism and feminism. The same outside forces that endangered slavery also endangered a man's control over his family and, thereby, his place in society. A yeoman farmer might not be a slaveholder, but he could understand a threat to his role as head of his household. This message was preached almost ceaselessly in churches of all denominations. All Yankee isms were threats to the good order and harmony of the community of South Carolina.[23]

Louisa Susannah Cheves McCord, one of the brightest individuals in antebellum South Carolina, vigorously defended the established social order. In biting essays she brutalized northern and English abolitionists. She was especially critical of women who did not faithfully adhere "to the laws of God and nature." A woman's place was in the home; she should not yield to the temptation of the "forbidden fruit" of fame. Ambition was unnatural in a woman and should be avoided at all costs. While much of her criticism was meant for northern feminists (whom she mocked unmer-

Louisa Susannah Cheves McCord
(1810–1879). Courtesy, Georgia
Historical Society.

cifully), she also condemned the "ballroom belle"—because by flouting herself, she forgot "duty, conscience, and heart, in the love of notoriety."[24]

McCord was one of a number of well-educated women in antebellum South Carolina. She was widely read and published essays in the *Southern Quarterly Review,* yet she maintained a low profile, generally signing her pieces with her initials, L. S. M. She was a talented essayist, and more than one editor sought to entice her into writing for his magazine. Her views were not unique; both Mary Moragne of Abbeville District and Caroline Howard Gilman of Charleston felt the same way. Gilman, however much she might have wanted to avoid the public spotlight, did receive some recognition as the editor of the *Rose Bud,* a young woman's magazine, and the author of such works as *Recollections of a Southern Matron* and *Love's Progress.* Both of these books were published in the North, and surely some South Carolina women must have whispered that Gilman was *not* a native but rather was from Boston. However, in her personal life the author conducted herself as a proper southern matron.[25]

European visitors sometimes were taken aback by the conventions of South Carolina society. At a dance one observed that "the ladies were planted firmly along the walls, in the coldest formality, while the gentlemen . . . stood in close column near the door." At a dinner party in Columbia there were only three women present (two ladies of the household and the visitor) and thirteen men, which led the visitor to conclude that "women are just looked upon as house-keepers." At another party the same visitor later had "as tough an argument regarding slavery with some ladies as ever . . . had on any subject with gentlemen." South Carolina women may have been "house-keepers," but when forced to do so, they could be ardent defenders of their society and its institutions. While there is not much discussion of slavery in southern women's letters and diaries (most were silent on the subject), the silence most likely indicates assent.[26]

In the late 1840s, because of the conduct of northern female radicals, the public role of women was under increasing scrutiny. Questions were raised about such long-standing legal and social customs as feme sole traders, especially of married women operating businesses. South Carolina women were forced to pull back from the energetic role they had played in dealing with the less fortunate. For nearly half a century, particularly in Charleston, women had been active in providing succor for the poor.[27]

There were numerous benevolent associations in the port city, some private, some public. According to Robert Mills, his hometown had more charitable institutions, in proportion to the population, than any other city in the country. Whether or not that was true, in 1826 there were an impressive number of benevolent organizations (fifty-one) in Charleston. One of the most successful and effective was the Ladies Benevolent Society, which by 1861 had an endowment that yielded $4,000 ($68,500) a year. Led by dedicated women such as Sarah Russell Dehon and Mary Smith Grimké, the society was no tea-and-crumpets circle of do-gooders. The women not only raised money for Charleston's growing indigent population (white and free black), but went into the city's squalid slums, assessed family needs, and then delivered the aid. They did what few individuals in any part of the country would do. From the perch of her safe middle-class world in the North, Angelina Grimké dismissed the efforts of her friends and relatives; however, they did more than just talk about a cause.[28]

The Ladies Benevolent Society was concerned primarily with the plight of white workingwomen. By 1848 about 13 percent of the white labor force was female. Economically these workingwomen, many of them single mothers (widows or the spouses of seamen) were terribly vulnerable. In many ways their lives were not much different from those of slaves except that slaves were provided food, clothing, housing, and, most of the time, medical care. Margaret Ryan, a young widow with two small children, was one of Charleston's many working poor. She earned 25¢–30¢ ($4.45–$5.34) each 12- to 14-hour day doing needlework; in contrast, a field hand on an upcountry plantation could earn 50¢ ($9.90) for the same amount of time on Sunday hiring himself out to chop cotton. Although men recognized the difficulties facing workingwomen, most, like Thomas Cooper, concluded that it was a woman's problem. And Charleston's women were more than willing to step forward.[29]

There were several public institutions in Charleston. The poor house was the last refuge for the city's paupers, most of whom were disabled as the result of poverty or disease. Many were alcoholics. Heavy drinking among the working class was not unique to the city, but it was so widespread as to attract attention from visitors.[30]

The Orphan House was one of the city's great success stories. Built in the 1790s, it was generously supported by Charleston's elite. Carefully nondenominational, the Orphan House provided a safe, structured environment for abandoned, orphaned, or needy children. Parents who were unable to care for their own could place them in the care of the city. So could a poor man, but a poor woman had to get men to endorse her request. Depending upon their abilities, the "children of the city" were either apprenticed to tradespeople or given the opportunity for a high school or college education.[31]

Charlestonians were benevolent, both as individuals and as a corporate community. In addition to the various private organizations, the city annually appropriated $12,000 ($218,000) for poor relief. That was a marked contrast with Nashville, Tennessee, which begrudged its poor even $500 ($9,100) of taxpayers' funds.[32]

In other South Carolina communities there were private organizations that assisted the poor. Beaufort had male and female benevolent societies, and Georgetown had a Ladies Benevolent Society. When Micajah A. Clark returned to Anderson District to visit, he found some aged relatives "much broken, looking quite feeble. The two old people with scarcely the comforts of life . . . living in an old field, land worn out. House likewise." Most individuals looked to their churches for some assistance; a few sought the aid of wealthier neighbors. Public assistance was limited in most districts, and private acts of charity frequently were resented by proud yeoman farmers and their wives. The social safety net in antebellum South Carolina was weak, and many, such as Clark's relatives, fell through.[33]

Similarly, the state did not provide much funding for public education. In 1811 the General Assembly enacted legislation authorizing public schools in every district of the state. There were to be as many schools per district as there were members of the legislature. Appropriations would also be based upon legislative apportionment. Thus, the wealthy lowcountry parishes were authorized more schools and state funding relative to the white population to be educated than the more populous middlecountry and upcountry districts. Even so, in 1860 only about half the state's white children were in school—probably because the free schools were stigmatized as schools for the poor and were treated as such by the men who operated them. In Richland District, school commissioner John Bryce said that except in Columbia, the funds expended on public schools were wasted.[34]

Another Richland school commissioner, Robert W. Gibbes, believed in the 1840s that the problem was not wasting money but underfunding. He estimated that perhaps as many as 850 poor children in the district needed to be educated, yet only about 175 were in school. He considered the district's annual expenditure of $1.41 ($25.86) per child grossly inadequate. In Newberry District in 1857 the annual expenditure per child was $4.09 ($70.75) for about ten weeks in the classroom.[35]

Children of parents with means attended private schools or were tutored at home.

For example, the Palmers of South Santee sent their daughters to Miss Murden's Seminary for Young Ladies in Charleston, Josiah O'Bear's in Winnsboro, and Barhamville in Columbia and their sons to Willington Academy in Abbeville District and Mount Zion Academy in Winnsboro.[36]

There were private schools in every district. The education they provided varied with the school's head. Good instructors were difficult to obtain, and the life of these academies was often fleeting. When Micajah Clark returned to Anderson District and visited the location of his old academy, all he found was "occasionally a brick bat, or a rise in the ground showed there was once a chimney there" where twenty years earlier had stood a flourishing school with eighty-five students. In 1830 Richland School, a male academy, briefly attracted students from as far away as Louisiana and Pennsylvania; however, by 1835 it had closed its doors. Throughout the antebellum period Saint David's Academy in Society Hill and Mount Zion Academy in Winnsboro educated primarily the elite of their respective districts. In 1860 there were 227 private "Academies and other schools" in South Carolina.[37]

Some schools, such as Madame Ann Mason Talvande's French School for Young Ladies in Charleston and Moses Waddel's Willington Academy in Abbeville District, enjoyed regional reputations. At Madame Talvande's, Mary Boykin Miller, Elizabeth Waties Allston, and Susan DuPont Petigru studied languages, literature, art, and music; they also trained for their roles as future wives of the South's elite. A list of the alumni of Waddel's Academy includes some of the most noted figures of antebellum South Carolina. John C. Calhoun, Augustus Baldwin Longstreet, James L. Petigru, Preston Brooks, and William Porcher Miles all mastered the school's rigorous regimen. Students were required to be at their books from sunrise until 9:00 p.m. Bright pupils were expected to memorize as many as 1,000 lines a day from the works of Homer, Virgil, and other classical writers, while less gifted ones struggled with their task of 150 lines.[38]

The lack of education for the majority of South Carolina's white children was a matter of concern to several governors. James H. Hammond declared that the state's system of public education was "a disgrace to an enlightened people" and recommended the creation of schools in every district to train teachers. The legislature ignored his proposal. Visitors, especially those from Europe and New England, were quick to comment on the inadequate school system.[39]

In the last decade before secession, a true public school system did develop in Charleston. In the 1850s Christopher Memminger became aware of the growing white working class in Charleston and persuaded his peers to support a public school system modeled after the best ones in the North. In 1856 the Charleston city schools began operation with eleven schools and 600 students; three years later there were 2,786 students. It was a classless system in which children of the elite went to school with those from the city's poorest working families. There is no doubt that Memminger and his allies in Charleston were sincere in wanting a good public school system; however, when the city's elite felt threatened by outside forces (as it did in the 1830s and 1850s), it increased support for nonslaveholding whites. That was also true on the state level, where the appropriations for schools were doubled during the 1850s.[40]

When it came to educating its black population, South Carolina had some of the most stringent laws in the nation outlawing the teaching of blacks, slave or free. In the aftermath of the Nullification Crisis, several schools for free black children in Charleston were forced to shut down. One of them was Daniel Payne's. Payne, a free person of color, operated his school for six years with the support of white clergy of all denominations. In 1835 he closed his school and left for the North. Another victim was the school operated by the city's Roman Catholics. Bishop John England agreed to close the school, but only if those operated by other denominations also closed. Later, despite the law, schools for free black children in Charleston reopened. In 1859 a white slaveholder confirmed the ineffectiveness of the law. Every day he observed "crowds of black children . . . on their way to school, with satchels well filled with books."[41]

Throughout the state individuals ignored the law and taught their slaves. In Chester a Presbyterian clergyman reported that nearly all of the twenty-three slaves who were members of his church could read. Christian duty was the main impetus behind the teaching of slaves. Mary Miller Chesnut noted in her diary that most of her house servants could read: "I have taught several myself." White Carolinians who educated their slaves did so knowing that they were violating the law, but also that they were relatively safe from prosecution. In protesting the law, John Belton O'Neall asked rhetorically: "Who would tolerate an indictment against his son or daughter for teaching a favorite slave to read?" Despite the penalties, it is estimated that perhaps 5 percent of the state's black population had some acquaintance with reading and writing.[42]

Only about half of the state's white children received any elementary education at all in 1860. Of these, only those enrolled in the Charleston schools (about 10 percent of the total) obtained anything like a real education. For the great majority of South Carolina's children, elementary and secondary education was inadequate at best and nonexistent at worst. Higher education, though, was much stronger in South Carolina. The South Carolina College, although it had some lean years, prospered. There were lots of "colleges" in the American South, and most were little more than grammar schools; however, the college in Columbia was one of the region's few real institutions of higher education. It attracted an internationally renowned faculty that included such notables as political economists Thomas Cooper and Francis Lieber and natural scientists John and Joseph LeConte. Stephen Elliott and James H. Thornwell were professors of sacred literature. Augustus B. Longstreet, author of *Georgia Scenes,* was the college's eighth president. Although some prominent alumni, such as Gov. James H. Hammond, wanted the college to create a special school to teach the latest technological and agricultural developments, its classical curriculum remained unchanged. As president, Thornwell spurned all such reform efforts. The college stood, he declared, as a bulwark for "the preservation of the established order" in South Carolina.[43]

For most of the nineteenth century the South Carolina College had a virtual monopoly on higher education in the state. The College of Charleston (chartered 1785), which had never been much more than an elementary school, closed in 1836; it reopened in 1838 as a municipal college, supported by the taxpayers of Charleston. Beaufort College (1795), with generous financial backing from local supporters, had an auspicious beginning; however, it quickly became just a preparatory school, albeit an excellent one.[44]

Beginning in the 1830s the South Carolina College came under increasing criticism from religious denominations, especially Presbyterians. Founded in 1801, the college reflected the secular spirit of Jeffersonian America. Thomas Cooper—a friend of Jefferson, member of the college faculty, and later its president—was an outspoken deist. Although not alone in his views, he was the most visible and vocal. As such, he became a lightning rod for outraged churchmen. In the 1830s pressure was brought to bear on the board of trustees to dismiss the controversial president. They held a hearing, and Cooper was acquitted of all charges against him; however, it was a Pyrrhic victory for both him and the college. The increasing number of Baptists, Methodists, and Presbyterians in the state were clearly unhappy with the secular tone of the institution.[45]

One option open to them was establishing their own denominational colleges. In 1839 the state's Associate Reformed Presbyterian Church founded Erskine College, but friends of the South Carolina College in the General Assembly blocked the efforts of the new college to obtain a charter. The absence of state recognition did not stop the little school in Due West from becoming the first four-year denominational college in South Carolina. During the 1850s a combination of the perception that the South Carolina College was an irreligious institution and a school for the "privileged class" led to the chartering of a number of denominational schools. Erskine finally received its charter in 1850. In the same year South Carolina's Baptists obtained a charter for Furman College. Later the state's Methodists received a charter for Wofford College (1851) and Lutherans one for Newberry College (1856). All of these were schools for males. The denominations also established separate colleges for women: Greenville Female Baptist College opened in 1855, Columbia Female College (Methodist) in 1859, and Due West Female College (Associate Reformed Presbyterian) in 1860. Some of these institutions had had earlier incarnations as secondary schools before being chartered as colleges.[46]

In their respective towns, these colleges served as stimuli to local intellectual life. Nowhere was that more true than in Columbia. Educated townspeople and the college faculty formed a lively cultural community. Robert Wilson Gibbes, Wade Hampton II, John L. Manning, and John Smith Preston were art collectors and pa-

William Gilmore Simms (1806–1870). Courtesy, South Caroliniana Library.

trons. Gibbes, Hampton, and Preston were patrons of James DeVeaux and Hiram Powers. With the financial support of Columbia's art patrons, both DeVeaux and Powers were able to further their studies abroad. DeVeaux, a native Charlestonian, is known today primarily for his portraits of upcountry Carolinians. Powers, a Vermonter, became one of the country's best-known antebellum sculptors. Among his surviving works in South Carolina are a bust of William Campbell Preston, a mantlepiece in the Hampton-Preston Mansion, and the font in Trinity Episcopal Cathedral—all in Columbia.[47]

When James H. Hammond complained that a group of Columbia men (including Gibbes, Hampton, and Preston) did not appreciate the art he had purchased in Europe, it was not a reflection upon his visitors but upon his own tastes. With the exception of three portraits, most of the paintings in his ornate home were second-rate (or worse) copies of European masterpieces, items he had picked up in the flea markets of Florence and Rome. No wonder many of his visitors, several of whom were serious collectors, viewed Hammond's paintings "with the apathy of Indians."[48]

Hammond might have been ignorant in artistic matters, but according to Edmund Ruffin, he had the "most powerful" mind in the South. However, he always felt his genius was unappreciated. William Gilmore Simms was another southerner who felt undervalued. For several decades the two men commiserated with one another about their talents' being ignored. Simms, however, had an advantage over Hammond: in

Charleston he was the leading figure in what has been called the Charleston School, a literary outpouring in the last decade or so before the war.[49]

Charleston in the 1840s and 1850s had a vibrant intellectual life, but the city's cultural community was not as sophisticated in 1860 as it had been a century earlier. Nevertheless, it was vital and active, if more insular and less diverse. Whereas eighteenth-century Charleston had prided itself on being a city of the empire and the world, the nineteenth-century city aspired only to be the cultural capital of the American South. As citizens of the empire Carolinians, like the moon, had absorbed and reflected much of their culture from the sun of London. As nineteenth-century southerners Charlestonians were creators, not just consumers, of culture, but their horizons were much more limited.[50]

William Gilmore Simms, a native of the city, was also its most renowned author. Determined to make a living as a professional writer, he wrote what appeared to be a never-ending stream of essays, reviews, poems, histories, and novels. In 1856 *Ballou's Pictorial* predicted that his novels, set in eighteenth-century South Carolina, would be read with interest "while the works of authors, now more popular, will have passed from the public recollections." Students today, however, are more likely to read James Fenimore Cooper's *Last of the Mohicans* or Herman Melville's *Moby-Dick* than they are Simms's *Woodcraft* or *The Partisan*.[51]

Along with Simms, Paul Hamilton Hayne, Henry Timrod, and William J. Grayson were the leading figures in the Charleston School. *Russell's Magazine*, edited by Hayne, was an outlet for their essays, reviews, and poetry. The last in a series of literary journals published in Charleston, the magazine took its name from John Russell's bookstore on King Street. The back room at Russell's was the place where authors and the city's educated elite met. Although there were innumerable gatherings in the city where erudition and wit were prized, there was no salon (such as the salon over which Octavia Walton LeVert presided in Mobile) that attracted traveling notables.[52]

The city's elite admitted bright, talented men of humble origins to their parlors and into various literary and debating societies, but they did not necessarily welcome new ideas. Order, tradition, and stability were more prized than originality. Thus, Isaac Harby, a young Jewish intellectual; John England, an Irish Roman Catholic; and John Bachman and Henry Timrod, both German Lutherans, could mingle with the likes of James L. Petigru, Mitchell King, Henry L. Pinckney, Hugh S. Legaré, and John J. Pringle. Men such as Simms, who desperately wanted to be able to make a living from their creative endeavors, resented these "amateurs" who made their money at the law or some other profession and dabbled in the arts as an avocation rather than a vocation. But in antebellum South Carolina either one chose that route or went elsewhere.[53]

Since the late eighteenth century some of South Carolina's more promising creative talents had been choosing the latter. Washington Allston was one of the state's first cultural expatriates. In order to pursue art as a profession, he sold his inheritance to finance his study and travels. Isaac Harby, unhappy with the pressures to create for a regional rather than a national audience, opted to move to New York. In 1830, after a decade of working for the state (during which time he designed sixteen district courthouses and twelve jails), financial necessity prompted Robert Mills to accept a position with the federal government in Washington.[54]

The artists and writers who remained in South Carolina turned their backs on what they viewed as an increasingly hostile contemporary world. Like the society from which they sprang, they looked to the glories of the state's colonial past for inspiration. Whereas David Ramsay's *History of South-Carolina from its First Settlement in 1670 to 1808* reflected the nationalism of the postrevolutionary period, the 1860 edition of William Gilmore Simms's *History of South Carolina* stressed sectional differences and magnified the role of the South in the American Revolution. In a letter to an editor Simms explained that in his novels his goal was not just creating a story. "I am really," he wrote, "revising history." After the war Hayne observed that Simms loved South Carolina and that "he upheld and vindicated her historic fame." The essays, reviews, poems, and stories of the Charleston School in the 1850s were but the culmination of a process that had begun during the economic decline of the late 1820s.[55]

In addition to holding up the state's past glories for the edification of its people, South Carolina's literati used their energies in defending the South. Unquestionably, the members of the Charleston School believed in South Carolina and her "domestic institutions"; however, when it came to attracting readers for southern journals and magazines, there had to be a strong political component. As Simms lamented in the April 1853 issue of the *Southern Quarterly Review:* "No periodical can well succeed in the South, which does not include the *political* constituent. The mind of the South is active chiefly in the direction of politics. . . . The only reading people of the South are those to whom politics is the bread of life."[56]

In 1855 the lawyer-poet William J. Grayson published *The Hireling and the Slave* in response to the criticism of the South in Harriet Beecher Stowe's *Uncle Tom's Cabin.* A pastoral poem in heroic couplets, it is a celebration of the superiority of the agricultural society of the South and a condemnation of the industrialized societies of Great Britain and the North. Although Charleston failed to become the economic "Queen of the South," it did become the region's cultural capital. And there is no more eloquent testimony to its claim as the chief exponent of the southern way of life than Grayson's elegant, old-fashioned verse.[57]

While clergy and writers tended to think of their fields in terms of southernness, South Carolina's naturalists did not. They may have investigated local flora, fauna, or geology, but they placed their investigations in the context of the international scientific community. In the decade before the war there were more than twice as many members of the American Association for the Advancement of Science from

Devil Fishing, from William Elliott's *Carolina Sports by Land and Water*, 1859. Courtesy, South Caroliniana Library.

South Carolina than from any other southern state. There had been a long tradition of gentlemen-scientists in the state. Unlike poets and intellectuals, who felt neglected by the general public, naturalists were appreciated because their work was seen as useful.[58]

John James Audubon was in the state in the 1830s and did a great deal of the field work for his *The Birds of America* here. The Reverend John Bachman of Charleston assisted him in his work, and the two formed a lifelong friendship. They later collaborated on *Viviparous Quadrupeds of North America* (1845–1849), a three-volume work for which Bachman wrote the text and Audubon did the illustrations. Among other scientific works of note that came out of antebellum South Carolina were Stephen Elliott's two-volume *Sketch of the Botany of South Carolina and Georgia* (1811, 1824) and Robert Mills's *Atlas of the State of South Carolina* (1825) and *Statistics of South Carolina* (1826).[59]

Carolina Sports by Land and Water (1846, 1859) by William Elliott contains some natural history, but among the sports stories the author intended "to place the institution of slavery in the South on its true basis, that exigency of climate." The semitropical landscape of the Carolina lowcountry serves as a backdrop for the sporting pleasure of local planters as they harpoon manta rays; fish for drum, sheepshead, and bass; and hunt deer. Fishing and hunting remained popular pastimes and a source of food for all South Carolinians.[60]

Hunting was one of several recreational activities that continued from the eighteenth century. Horse racing continued but became more organized. The South

Carolina Jockey Club's annual races in Charleston not only provided entertainment but served as a common meeting ground for the elite from across the state. Middle-country planters such as Wade Hampton II and Richard Singleton of Richland District and James B. Richardson of Sumter owned some of the finest horseflesh in the South. But, as out-of-state visitors discovered, the races attracted all segments of the population and, on occasion, the crowds could become unruly.[61]

In Greenville and Spartanburg sale days (the first Monday of each month) and court days (October) attracted large crowds to town. So, too, did political campaigns, especially near election day. Candidates treated voters to generous supplies of food and drink. In 1806 it was reported that Elias Earle, a member of congress campaigning for reelection in Greenville, "presided over the Whiskey jugs himself." When William J. Grayson lost his bid for reelection to Congress, he blamed it on his refusal to ask for support or dispense whiskey. Issues, however, did matter. When Calhoun's anointed candidate lost a congressional race in 1838, he blamed it on the victor's successfully presenting his case at militia musters.[62]

The militia in South Carolina, through the patrol system, was responsible for helping insure the good order and harmony of the community. At the beginning of the nineteenth century the state developed one of the most complex militia systems in the country. It was top-heavy with high-ranking officers, but by 1825 there were fewer men of the ranks. The out-migration of whites to the lower South and the increase in the black population resulted in the smallest ratio of militiamen to the total population (1 to 19) of any state in the Union. In Ohio, by comparison, every fifth resident was enrolled in the militia.[63]

The militia also served a social function. Early-nineteenth-century banquets on the Fourth of July or Washington's Birthday sometimes turned into drinking bouts with too many toasts. However, by the 1850s the Sons of Temperance became a real force in Greenville, Charleston, and Columbia. In the capital city public celebrations became rather dry affairs.[64]

Militia units also sponsored dances for visiting dignitaries and in celebration of George Washington's Birthday. European visitors observed that Carolinians "danced in the manner of the tedious German quadrilles" and were too proper to waltz. Europeans were often surprised at the stiff formality between men and women. The social behavior of white Carolinians—whether at a dance or on the plantation—was an important component of an orderly society and was regulated by the family, the church, and the community.[65]

South Carolina society was based upon deference. The leading men of a community, be they lowcountry rice planters whose forebears emigrated from Barbados in the seventeenth century or upcountry cotton merchant-politicians whose fathers might have been tenant farmers, expected those beneath them in the social order to defer to them. In turn, the elite were careful to treat all white men with courtesy, especially if one had political ambitions. Since 1810 South Carolina had had universal white male suffrage. Voter turnout was generally heavy, especially in upcountry districts, for much of the antebellum period. Incumbency was no guarantee of reelection (which may have been why Elias Earle had such a heavy hand with the jug). For example, in 1818 only 20 percent of sitting legislators were reelected.[66]

When deference was not forthcoming, members of the elite were often shocked. Eliza Carolina Burgwin Clitherall of Colleton District was caustically told by the widow of a yeoman farmer that her daughter was just as good as Clitherall's children. In 1831 William Elliott of St. Helena's Parish resigned his seat in the South Carolina Senate because the parish's voters favored nullification and he did not. After resigning he dashed off a pamphlet complaining that the common people had "shown poor grace and judgment not to follow the local squire whose family leadership has not heretofore been questioned."[67]

Elliott's resignation was probably more than just a temper tantrum; it was also a matter of principle, a matter of honor. And he was not the only Beaufort District politician to do so. Robert Barnwell Rhett resigned his newly won seat in the U.S. Senate because the South Carolina Convention of 1852 refused to adopt any radical measures of opposition to the federal government. Elliott and Rhett did what few politicians ever do: voluntarily give up office over principle.[68]

Much has been made about the "Code of Honor" that prevailed in the state between 1783 and 1860. Despite opposition from church leaders and such influential groups as the Society of the Cincinnati, dueling was more common in South Carolina than in most southern states. Duels were fought for a variety of reasons, often with tragic results. During the presidential electioneering of the early 1820s, Calhoun's protégé George McDuffie was crippled for life after a duel with one of William H. Crawford's supporters. Greenville newspaper editor Turner Bynum, a Nullifier, was killed by Benjamin F. Perry, a Unionist. A South Carolina College student, James G. Adams of Richland District, died as the result of a quarrel with his best friend, A. Govan Roach of Colleton District, over a plate of fish in the student dining hall. Some men made their reputations as dueling champions. Gov. James Hamilton Jr. fought and wounded fourteen men who had offended him. John Lyde Wilson, governor of South Carolina (1822–1824), published *The Code of Honor* (1838), which became the standard guide for southern duelists.[69]

Dueling reinforced status, as only social equals could give or receive a challenge. Common folk, such as those William Elliott decried, settled matters in their own way. At the Charleston races in 1828 a fistfight between two individuals soon turned into a general melee, which was put down by a whip-wielding track official.[70]

In terms of regulating personal morality and conduct, South Carolina law did little other than prohibit divorce. Attempts to pass legislation concerning adultery failed in 1844, 1856, and 1860. The double standard was at least tolerated, if not accepted. Brothels operated openly in Charleston and Columbia. A white man's sexual mores were considered his own business. It was left up to the churches to punish a person for sexual misconduct.[71]

Baptist and Methodist churches were among those denominations most likely to discipline their members. Adultery, premarital sex, fornication, and spousal abuse and neglect were among the transgressions dealt with by individual congregations. In 1826 the Edgefield Baptist Church, for example, questioned Mrs. Harriet Caldwell as to why her child had been born so soon after her marriage. When John Kelly, a wealthy member of the Gum Branch Baptist Church (Darlington District), denounced his wife, Lenore, for leaving him, the congregation appointed a committee to investigate the matter. Even though it discovered that David had "committed a crime of uncommon terpitude," the committee decided that both husband and wife should be excluded from the fellowship of the church. The patently unfair decision was later overturned by a local church council that directed Lenore be restored to fellowship.[72]

Interracial sexual relations, primarily between white men and black women, knew no class lines. A European visitor in Columbia reported that a white coachman had protected his "sable Dulcinea" from arrest. James H. Hammond was so smitten with the twelve-year-old daughter of his mulatto mistress that when his wife followed through on a threat to leave him unless he sold the young woman, he refused. Catherine Elizabeth Fitzsimons Hammond's decision to move out was an unusual one. Most white women either simply ignored or endured their spouses' relationships with slave women. Sometimes that must have been difficult as family resemblances were often unmistakable. "The mulattoes one sees in every family exactly resemble the white children," wrote Mary Chesnut, "and every lady tells you who is the father of all the mulatto children in everybody's household, but those in her own she seems to think drop from the clouds, or pretends to think so." One Georgetown planter employed his illegitimate mulatto children to serve his dining room table.[73]

These relationships were sometimes voluntary, but most were not. Arthur Augustus Simkins of Edgefield District compelled his slave Charlotte to sit naked on a pile of manure until she yielded to his unwanted advances. How much resistance could Louisa, Hammond's twelve-year-old slave, mount? The offspring of interracial liaisons posed problems for antebellum planters. Prior to 1800 a slave could be freed by his or her master. Manumission was made more difficult in 1800 and 1820; in 1841 the legislature closed all loopholes, making it impossible to free an enslaved person in South Carolina. Before the 1841 act William Farr of Union District bequeathed half of his $60,000 ($947,000) estate to a neighbor as trustee for the care of his mulatto mistress and their child. White relatives unsuccessfully contested the will. The same Georgetown planter who used his children as household servants also sent some to market to be sold. Hammond and his son Harry evidently shared the same mistress, who bore the Hammonds, *père et fils*, several children. In a letter to Harry the former governor said it would be cruel and inhumane to send the children north to be freed. "Nor," he wrote, "would I like that any but my own blood should own as slaves my own blood. . . . Slavery in the family will be their happiest earthly condition."[74]

South Carolina's free persons of color lived in a society in which they were neither slave nor truly free. In 1790 there were 1,801 free blacks in the state; in 1860 there were 9,914, one-third of whom lived in Charleston. One of the sticky issues surrounding the free black population was that over time some of them had passed for white. Antebellum South Carolina, unlike most other southern states, did not prohibit interracial marriages nor define who was black and who was white. Instead, after several court cases, there seemed to be a consensus that determining a person's racial status was up to local communities. Physical appearance counted more than did actual percentage of African blood. That, however, could cause difficulties. In the 1780s Henry Laurens had remarked that Gideon Gibson of Mars Bluff had a fairer complexion than did most white Carolinians of Huguenot descent. In a celebrated case from Kershaw District, Elijah Bass was more than seven-eighths white and was married to a white woman, but the local jury and tax collector ruled that he was a free person of color. The Court of Appeals agreed.[75]

Free persons of color between the ages of sixteen and sixty had to pay an annual capitation tax of $2.00 ($36) and register with the local court. The tax was a means of keeping tabs on the district's free black population. In the aftermath of the Denmark Vesey Plot, all free blacks were required to obtain a "respectable" white guardian who would agree to serve. Between 1820 and 1841 a number of masters "freed" their slaves by deeding them to friends who served as trustees who nominally "owned" the slaves and administered the property for their benefit. Legal challenges to such arrangements led the General Assembly in 1841 to forbid manumissions and outlaw any future trust arrangements. During times of political and social turmoil, such as the summer of 1860, white trustees and guardians often failed to honor their obligations.[76]

On the shifting sands of an uncertain status, free persons of color in South Carolina led remarkably successful lives. As much as possible they tried to fit into their communities. In rural areas they were yeoman farmers and planters and a small percentage were slaveholders. In 1830 one-fourth of black slaveholders owned more than ten slaves, and two black owners in Colleton District, Justus Angel and Mistress L. Horry, each owned eighty-four slaves. In 1840 about 5.5 percent of free blacks (454) owned slaves; in 1860 less than 2 percent (171) did. In 1860 there were black masters in fourteen of the state's twenty-five districts. Most were small slaveholders: Benjamin Robert in Anderson had two, as did Sarah Bower in Lexington. Among the larger black slaveholders were William Ellison of Sumter District (sixty-three) and Daria Thomas of Union (twenty-one). Of the 171 black slaveholders in 1860, 137 lived in Charleston. On the eve of the Civil War the city's black taxpayers owned real and slave property worth a bit more than $1.5 million ($27.2 million).

Nancy Weston Grimké, although technically a slave, lived as a free person of color in antebellum Charleston. Courtesy, Moorland-Spingarn Research Center, Howard University.

Maria Weston, for example, owned fourteen slaves and $40,075 ($728,000) in real estate.[77]

William Ellison, of Stateburg (Sumter District), may have been one of the most successful free black entrepreneurs in South Carolina. Whereas most of Charleston's successful free blacks were involved in skilled trades, Ellison succeeded as a cotton planter in a white man's world. As a youth in Fairfield District, he had been apprenticed to a local gin maker. After Ellison learned the trade his master let him work on his own, and in 1816, at the age of twenty-six, he was able to purchase his freedom. Ellison moved to Stateburg where he established himself first as a gin maker and then as a planter. By 1860 he owned nine hundred acres of land, sixty-three slaves, a pew in the Episcopal Church of the Holy Cross, and the plantation home of former governor Stephen D. Miller. His total wealth, which he under-reported to the census takers, was officially $61,250 ($1.1 million). In 1860, of the

26,701 slaveholders in South Carolina, only 1,646 owned more than fifty slaves; in the fifteen slave states only 13,770 did. William Ellison was one of the larger slaveholders in the United States.[78]

The idea of black masters has long been a controversial one. While some free blacks purchased their loved ones (whom they could not free after 1841), others owned slaves for economic reasons. Among the explanations given for the decline in black slaveholders and the number of slaves they owned were the liquidation of slaveholders' estates, outmigration of free persons of color, the refusal of owners to report slave ownership to census takers, and the sale of surplus slaves.[79]

In Charleston in 1860 nearly three-fourths of the free black population were mulattoes or lighter-skinned persons of color. There was a color line within the black community, a line between enslaved blacks and free persons of color and between light-skinned free persons and those who were darker. Except for New Orleans, Charleston had the largest brown elite in the South. For self-preservation in a hostile white world, members of the city's brown elite tried to distance themselves as much as possible from the slave population. Jehu Jones, who operated the city's most fashionable hotel on Broad Street, disdained the company of even light-skinned free persons. Intermarriage along color lines reinforced the differences between black slaves and the brown elite. The brown elite created its own social, cultural, and charitable organizations that were modeled on those of the white elite, such as the Brown Fellowship Society, the Friendly Moralist Society, Christian Benevolent Society, and Clionian Debating Society. Although free blacks attended church at either Zion Presbyterian or Calvary Episcopal, many could be found in the balconies of the city's predominantly white Episcopal churches. They lived in the same neighborhoods with whites who often patronized their businesses. When South Carolina seceded, eighty-two members of the city's brown elite signed an address to the governor that made clear where they stood: "We are by birth citizens of South Carolina, in our veins is the blood of the white race in some half, in others more, our attachments are with you." They then vowed that they would "offer up our lives, and all that is dear to us" in the defense of South Carolina.[80]

Yet, no matter how hard they tried, the state's free persons of color could never overcome the pigment in their skin. Laws forbade them to leave the state unless it was a permanent move. One free black confided to a visitor that he was a prisoner in South Carolina. In 1859 Edward Moore from York District proposed that any free blacks who did not leave the state by 1 March 1860 be sold into slavery. Christopher Memminger of Charleston helped defeat this and two other related bills. During the summer of 1860, when the state was beset by political and social turmoil, white guardians looked the other way as free blacks were illegally mistreated and detained. Poor free blacks were reenslaved. Panic gripped Charleston's free black community. The city's white working class united behind several candidates for the General Assembly, such as James M. Eason, who sponsored legislation

Table 14.1

OWNERS OF FIFTY OR MORE SLAVES, 1860

	50–99	100–199	200–299	300–499	500–999	1000+
ALL	11,403	2,039	230	84	14	1
SC	1,197	363	56	22	7	1
SC %	10.5	17.8	24.3	26.2	50	100

Manuscript Census for South Carolina, 1860, SCD AH. Inter-University Consortium for Political and Social Research Study 00003.

that would bar free blacks from any trade or occupation except day laborer or domestic service. The bill failed, but it had attracted support from upcountry planters. In this atmosphere hundreds of free blacks fled the state for the North, Canada, or Haiti, selling their property at a loss to whites all too willing to take advantage of the situation (not unlike the Japanese Americans in California in 1941–1942). A group of refugees arriving in Philadelphia in December 1860 said that 780 free persons of color had fled Charleston during the previous six months. Writing to Henry Ellison at Stateburg, James M. Johnson quoted a friend as saying "it is plain now all must go."[81]

Free blacks who abandoned their homes and livelihoods did so because they feared enslavement. Although bills calling for the enslavement of free blacks and curtailing their economic opportunities had been defeated, the debates in the legislature had been chilling. Free persons of color knew all too well the condition of slaves in South Carolina society.[82]

By 1860, with almost one-half of its white families (45.8 percent) owning slaves, South Carolina had the highest percentage of slaveholders in the nation. It is generally accepted that the ownership of twenty or more slaves placed an individual in the planter class. In the South only about 12 percent of slaveholders fell into that category; in South Carolina about 20 percent did. At the time of the Civil War the only American who owned more than a thousand slaves was Plowden Charles Jennet Weston of Georgetown District. At least seven lowcountry planters owned more than five hundred slaves, and seventeen owned more than three hundred; five middlecountry planters in Richland, Sumter, and Fairfield also owned more than three hundred. However, nearly 61 percent of the state's slaveholders (16,199) owned fewer than ten slaves, and about 14 percent had just one.[83]

The popular perception that most large slave owners lived in the lowcountry while most of the small slaveholders lived in the upcountry is not supported by the

Slave Auction, Charleston, 1856. *Illustrated London News*. Courtesy, South Caroliniana Library.

figures. A majority of the largest slaveholders did live in the three coastal districts (Beaufort, Charleston, and Georgetown); however, there were owners of more than one hundred slaves in every district in the state except Anderson. Conversely, not all nonslaveholders and small slaveholders lived in upcountry districts. In 1860 more than one-half of the white families (323 out of 578) in St. Peter's Parish (Beaufort District) owned no slaves. However, slavery was more widespread in South Carolina than in any other state. It was a rare white person who did not come into contact with a black person who was someone's property.[84]

Property, slave, chattel, stock, head—all were nonhuman terms for black human beings in nineteenth-century South Carolina. A. P. McElveen, a white slave trader who purchased slaves in Sumter District and shipped them to the Charleston slave market, used such terms as "ten head" and "pore stock" in referring to slaves. Sylvia Cannon, who grew up a slave in Darlington District, recalled seeing slave traders' coffles pass: "I see slaves when they be travelling like hogs to Darlington. Some of them be women folks looking like they going to get down, they so heavy [with child]." When Charles Ball, a Chesapeake slave, was brought into the state for sale, he noticed a tremendous difference in the condition of slaves on cotton plantations. As the coffle to which he was chained moved upstate he noted: "It was manifest, that I was now in a country, where the life of a black man was no more regarded than that of an ox." Ball considered slavery on South Carolina's cotton plantations

The Driver (Solomon of Landovery plantation, Colleton County). Basil Hall, *Forty
Etchings, from Sketches Made with the
Camera Lucida in North America in 1827
and 1828.* Courtesy, Rare Books and Special Collections, Thomas Cooper Library,
University of South Carolina.

to be much harsher than on the tobacco plantations of Virginia and Maryland. Yet
the middlecountry and upcountry were settled in the main by people from the Middle Atlantic, and the institution of slavery in those sections of the state more closely
resembled slavery in the Chesapeake than it did slavery in the lowcountry.[85]

In the lowcountry the task system continued to be used effectively on both rice
and sea island cotton plantations. The basic task unit was one-fourth acre, but tasks
were assigned to a variety of plantation operations including cutting timber and
making fence poles. If tasks were completed by early afternoon, then slaves had off
time either to work for themselves or just loaf. If an energetic slave did a two-day
task in one, then he or she had a full day off. By using off time to work for themselves slaves were able to accumulate property. One of the unwritten laws of the
lowcountry was that a slave's off time was inviolable.[86]

On many rice plantations black drivers ran plantations for their white owners.
Not only was this a violation of the law, but it was also a contradiction of the institution itself. Were not only whites capable of disciplining and managing the workforce? The law required that a white overseer be employed, but it was frequently
ignored. Plantation owners generally had more trust in their black slave drivers than
they did in white overseers. Charles Cotesworth Pinckney commented that Ralph
Izard's most productive plantations "where you make the most to the hand and really a good Crop, there is no overseer but only a Black Driver." Although not unique

to South Carolina, the practice of employing black slave drivers was more common here than anywhere else. When European visitors stopped at William Skirving's plantation on the Combahee River, they were shocked and amazed that a black man, Solomon, was totally in charge not only of the fields but of the house as well. While not unique to the lowcountry, such a situation would have been rare beyond Parish End.[87]

Upcountry cotton planters employed the gang labor system that they had used in Virginia. Under the gang system slaves worked in the fields under the supervision of an overseer or driver. There were few breaks and all hands were expected to work the entire day. The gang system was more brutal than the task system and was a constant source of friction and hostility. Even after middlecountry and upcountry planters became familiar with the lowcountry's method of dealing with slave labor, they continued to use gangs. On some upstate plantations, because the hilly terrain made the supervision of gangs difficult, a modified form of the task system evolved.[88]

On farms and plantations where there were fewer than ten slaves, owners and their families worked side-by-side with their field hands—at least some of the time. David Golightly Harris of Spartanburg District owned five slaves in 1850 and ten in 1860. Although he was a slaveholder, he did not lollygag on his piazza playing lord of the manor. He did whatever needed to be done, whether that meant plowing fields, cutting wheat, digging potatoes, setting out peach trees, or repairing the chimney on the "negro house." In 1860 there were 16,199 South Carolinians who owned from 1 to 9 slaves. Thus, the work experiences of the 63,590 black Carolinians they owned were different from those of the more than 270,000 (65+ percent) who labored on large cotton or rice plantations.[89]

By the 1830s southern planters were looking for more efficient and orderly ways to manage their plantations. They wanted to be modern without introducing any of the dreaded reforms from the North that might upset the stability and order of their communities. The device they turned to was the clock. By regulating work hours and meal and rest periods, they could make their field hands more productive. Increased productivity per hand, not per acre, was a much-desired goal. A clock was "at once an engine for economic efficiency and a tool of social discipline." Since slaves did not own timepieces, time was communicated through the use of bells, horns, and whistles. Slaves became used to clock time in addition to traditional time measurements of sunrise, noon, and sunset. One South Carolina slave recalled that the midday meal was always served at "half-past eleven."[90]

The daily schedule for most slaves on cotton plantations began with being awakened before sunrise so that they could be working in the fields at first light. After working for several hours, they usually had breakfast about 8:00 A.M. The time for dinner, the midday meal, varied from 11:30 A.M. until 1:00 P.M. The midday break might be forty-five minutes to an hour or more. It usually was longer during the hot

In 1828 Basil Hall drew these slave cabins on Nathaniel Heyward's Whitehall plantation, Colleton County. *Slave Cottages West of Charleston,* from Hall, B. ms. no. 65, Manuscripts Department, Lilly Library, Indiana University, Bloomington, Indiana.

summer months. After the break work continued until dark. After returning to their quarters, slaves ate a light supper.[91]

Although work times varied, all slaves worked Monday through Friday. They worked from sunrise to sunset on cotton plantations and from sunrise until completion of the assigned task on rice plantations. Occasionally some cotton planters required work at night. A Union District slave remembers that "we picked cotton by de light of de moon." Most rice and some cotton planters gave their slaves Saturday afternoons off, but others required full days' work. Except on an occasional upcountry plantation, Sundays were generally days of rest. Few owners were as generous with off time as Plowden C. J. Weston of Georgetown District, who gave his slaves a half day every Saturday, every Sunday, and eight to ten holidays per year. Christmas was a universal holiday, and many owners also gave their slaves the two days after Christmas off. On 28 December 1857 David Harris wrote: "To day our Christmas is out and I put the hands to work on the fish-pond. They do not like to go to work so soon but they have to do it." Almost without exception, Christmas was a time for eating, drinking, and making merry.[92]

While some former slaves remembered "good food and a lot of it," more remembered monotonous diets of corn (cornbread, ash cake, mush, hominy, or grits), molasses, and whatever vegetables and meat they were able to provide for themselves. Slaves from the Pee Dee recalled being able to drink all the buttermilk they wanted, but as was common everywhere, any meats or vegetables were usually supplied by the slaves themselves. Charles Ball reported that breakfast and dinner consisted of a three-quarter-pound loaf of cornbread and water; supper was a cold meal, eaten in the quarters after dark.[93]

Slave quarters in the nineteenth century, especially in the middle- and upcountry, generally were different from eighteenth-century slave housing. Slave dwellings dur-

Slave cabin, Brattonsville, York County. This brick building is a reconstruction of one of eight such cabins that originally flanked the main house. Courtesy Historic Brattonsville. Photograph by Suzanne C. Linder.

ing the colonial period were West African in design and construction: small square wattle and daub buildings with dirt floors, a smoke vent in the roof, no windows, and a low door opening. Sarah Grimké declared that slaves were "wretchedly sheltered and lodged" in 12-by-14-foot dwellings. She was not the only critic of slavery to report on the small size of slave dwellings. Actually, by West African standards, a 168-square-foot house was larger than normal; more typical dimensions were 64, 81, and 100 square feet. It is quite possible that later slave rows or quarters of neat clapboard houses were built in response to abolitionist criticism; while well meaning, the artificial styles forced on black Carolinians robbed them of one of their West African cultural traditions. (However, West African practices of having a swept communal yard and using paling fences for livestock continued.)[94]

From the narratives taken in the 1930s, a pattern emerges of two types of slave housing: log and pole (wattle and daub). House size and the use of wattle and daub construction both continued the West African housing traditions. Some houses had one room and others had two. Most had chimneys, and double houses usually shared a single flue. Peter Clifton of Fairfield District said he was raised in a "log house with a plank floor and a wooden chimney that was always catching a fire." One- and two-room log cabins, some with plank floors and some with dirt floors, were found on other cotton plantations. Chimneys usually were made of sticks and mud. Pole houses were more commonly found in the middlecountry. In Clarendon District, Gable Locklier lived in a "two room pole house dat have a wood floor," and in Darlington, Sylvia Cannon lived in a "one-room pole house what was daubed with dirt." One European visitor described the slave quarters on a lowcountry rice plantation as "uncommonly neat and comfortable." Such an observation was seldom made about slave housing in the middle- or upcountry.[95]

The quarters, or "the street," were the center of black community and family life. Owners realized it was to their advantage to encourage stable slave family life. They were in favor of "marriages," though these were not recognized by law even if performed by white clergy. Slaves living as families also meant the probability of reproduction, a return on investment in human property. Slaves who had families were less likely to run away or cause trouble. Stability, control, and profit were among the benefits of owners' encouraging the establishment of slave families.[96]

The institution of slavery, however, denied male slaves the opportunity to be the true heads of their families. Shelter, clothing, food, and working conditions were all dictated by the owner. A man could not protect his wife or daughters from unwanted advances by overseers or owners. Every member of the family was subject to being disciplined, and children saw their parents whipped and vice versa. The community and parents carefully taught children at an early age how to survive in a world where a misspoken word could mean trouble. Nevertheless, in spite of all the obstacles, black men and women created nurturing family units in which to rear their children.[97]

The greatest threat to slave family life—and the most feared—was the break up of families through sale. Even in All Saints Waccamaw Parish, where slavery may have been more benign than almost anywhere else in the South, the possibility of family separation was ominously omnipresent. In South Carolina the district courts were an integral part of the credit system and conducted one-half of all slave sales in the state. Court sales were about the business of getting top dollar, and slave owners knew that individual sales brought higher prices than group sales. "If I would separate them," wrote Nathaniel Coggeshall of Darlington District, "I could get more." James Henry Hammond calculated that individuals brought about 10 percent more than those purchased as a family or group.[98]

When reading the proslavery polemics of the 1840s and 1850s and comparing them with the slave narratives, it becomes apparent that few white Carolinians had any real concept of what life was like under slavery. "The negro," wrote Louisa McCord in her critique of *Uncle Tom's Cabin,* "left to himself, does not dream of liberty." She, like most whites, misinterpreted the happy darkies who always had a smile and a "yessuh, Boss" as being satisfied with their condition. Of course, they were not. Pompey, a Georgetown District slave, told an English visitor that he wanted to live in England. When asked why, the reply was "All free dar, suh!"[99]

Being a slave meant constantly walking on eggshells, living in dread of making a misstep that could lead to being punished. Deprivation of food or privileges were mild forms of chastisement. Whipping was a universal punishment and no respecter of age or gender. Cruelty was not uncommon; for example, a Charleston woman had her maid's ears slit for petty theft. In reality the punishment was whatever the master or mistress dictated; they literally had life and death control over the lives of human beings subject to their caprice.[100]

Among the few who realized that a slave's cheerful countenance might mask something else was Keziah Goodwyn Hopkins Brevard of Richland District. In her diary Brevard made frequent references to feeling uneasy amid the slaves on her plantation. She recorded anxious moments in which she feared servile insurrection, arson, and poisoning. "Many an hour," she wrote in her diary, "have I laid awake in my life thinking of our danger." In Beaufort District, Robert W. Barnwell said that there was nothing "so cruel as fear." Often isolated on their plantations, amid a large number of black slaves, South Carolina whites sometimes found life in the big house a bit unsettling.[101]

The big house has been the source of much mythmaking over the past century. For example, Keziah Goodwyn Hopkins Brevard's home in lower Richland County reflected the economic cycles of the middlecountry. The original house, built in 1815 (probably with money from the first cotton boom), was a story-and-a-half cottage with four rooms and a central hall. During the second cotton boom of the 1850s, the young widow made major alterations to the earlier structure. She reoriented the entrance to the house by adding a two-story Classical Revival entrance, complete with double porches and columns. A new, wide central hall was flanked by large rooms with thirteen-foot ceilings. While her remodeled home was somewhat fancier than before, it was not a grand mansion; however, Milford in Sumter District and Kensington in Richland District, also built during the 1850s, were.[102]

Matthew Richard Singleton, the owner of Kensington, also opted to embellish an older home. He had his upcountry Georgian dwelling cut in half, which then became wings for a grand twelve-thousand-square-foot, twenty-nine-room house. While most South Carolinians in the 1850s were either building homes in Classical Revival or Colonial styles, he chose something altogether different: Renaissance Revival. It was quite a showplace and would have been very much at home on the Mississippi River Road or in Natchez.[103]

Although there were great plantation houses in virtually every district, most plantation homes, even of large slave owners, tended to be functional. There might be columns and the homes might be spacious, but they were seldom palatial. The "great plainness" of Thomas Taylor's home astonished visitors. Another traveler wrote, "Instead of princely mansions . . . one sees nothing but low, piazza'd domicils." What he described could have been one of several house types found in antebellum South Carolina: the one-room house, the two-room hall and parlor, or the four rooms and central hall. Regardless of form, all of these buildings had porches. These wooden dwellings were a step or two above the pioneer stage; however, there were many poorer residents who still lived in log cabins or pole (wattle and daub) houses. Rude rural housing for whites may have reflected their Celtic ancestry.[104]

One of the most ubiquitous housing styles in the middle- and upcountry was

The McConnell Cabin (circa 1820), originally built in McConnellsville (York County). Courtesy, Historic Brattonsville. Photograph by Suzanne C. Linder.

what is variously called upcountry Georgian or central passage plan. Typically, the house was a wooden two-story structure with a one-story shed porch supported by square pillars (sometimes hewn from a solid piece of timber). The floor plan featured a room on either side of a central hall. The stairs in the hall led to a second story with two rooms. If there were a rear shed porch, it might be enclosed for additional living space. Chimneys usually were located at either gable end but sometimes, as in Kershaw District, at the rear of the house. Excellent examples are the Berly House in Lexington and Tanglewood in Camden.[105]

Although there were professional architects and builders in Charleston, the majority of the dwellings in the state were built by their first occupants, local carpenters, or slave labor. Sometimes, as was the case with Kensington, a professional architectural firm designed the house but it was built by skilled slaves. Not only did Singleton's slaves build the house, but they planed the cypress and pine lumber used in its construction. The black Carolinians whose skills created in brick, wood, plaster, and ironwork many of the state's beautiful nineteenth-century structures felt a real pride of ownership in their creations.[106]

One of the ironies in building spacious plantation homes is that a large number were occupied for only part of the year. The summer months were deadly in the lowcountry and only a little less so in the middlecountry. Even upcountry districts such as Abbeville and Chester experienced outbreaks of malaria. "I would as soon

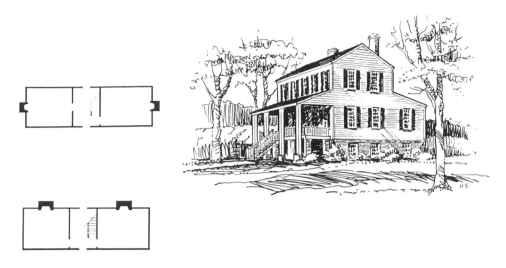

Plan of an upcountry Georgian or Carolina "I" house by Henry D. Boykin II. *Camden: Homes & Heritage.* Courtesy, Henry D. Boykin II.

stand fifty feet from the best Kentucky rifleman and be shot at by the hour, as to spend a night on my plantation in summer," stated one lowcountry planter. Yellow fever continued to be an unwelcome visitor; there were severe outbreaks and many deaths in 1817, 1838, 1849, and 1854. The 1854 epidemic affected not only Charleston but also Beaufort and Georgetown. And thanks to modern technology (the railroad), Charlestonians fleeing the pestilence spread the fever inland to Blackville, Hamburg, and Aiken. Charleston was an unhealthy city. With no municipal water supply, open sewers, and growing slums, it is not surprising that diseases caused by filth cropped up regularly. Cholera was a major health concern, and in 1849 nearly 80 percent of the city's population (about thirty-four thousand) came down with dysentery. In the 1840s one out of every four white children died before his fifth birthday and one of every five black infants before her first.[107]

By the eighteenth century those South Carolinians who could afford to leave Charleston or their lowcountry plantations during the unhealthy season had begun to do so. They had a variety of options. There were beach communities at Edisto, Sullivan's Island, and Pawley's Island, but the premiere lowcountry resort was Beaufort. Inland there were "pineland villages" such as Plantersville and Summerville. Some lowcountry residents such as John S. Palmer simply built their own homes in pine forests away from rivers and swamps. A number built summer homes in Greenville and Pendleton Districts, and a few created a South Carolina colony at Flat Rock, North Carolina. There were other out-of-state destinations, including Saratoga Springs in New York, where William J. Grayson complained that the town was dusty, accommodations uncomfortable, and everything overpriced. A wealthy group of Carolinians (including the Richard Singletons, Wade Hamptons, and Lawrence Mannings) chose White Sulphur and Salt Sulphur Springs in Virginia, where they dominated the social whirl.[108]

In the state spas or springs developed not only as places to take the waters but also as summer resorts. Spartanburg District had two of the more famous ones, Limestone Springs and Glenn Springs. Both opened hotels in the 1830s, but by the 1850s Glenn Springs had eclipsed its nearby rival and become a major tourist destination. The hotel's register in the 1840s and 1850s reads like the blue book of South Carolina society. In addition to a large hotel, there were individual cottages, a race course, and an Episcopal church. The waters at Glenn Springs were sulphurous and unpleasant, so those who actually wanted to drink mineral waters or bathe in them frequented the smaller springs: Cherokee and Pacolet (Spartanburg District) and Chick (Greenville District).[109]

Improved transportation helped make it easier and more convenient to get to the different resorts. One visitor commented that not only were the state's railroads as good as those in the North, but they were "as well, if not better managed." Railroads served all districts except Lancaster. By 1860 there were two trains daily from Columbia to Charleston and Charlotte and one to Greenville. The trip by express train between Charleston and Columbia took seven and one-half hours. The railroads, with their schedules, helped to make Carolinians more time-conscious. Instead of having the midday meal around noon, there were specific times. Travelers usually found dinner scheduled at 2:00, although it could be as late as 4:30. When Micajah Clark returned in 1857 to visit his relatives in Anderson District, he made the journey by rail. In his diary he made specific notations as to time: "Left Augusta 20 minutes after nine o'clock a.m.," "got to Columbia 10 minutes after six p.m.," and "Passed Frog Level 20 minutes before 12."[110]

The steam-powered locomotives helped link South Carolinians more closely with national and international markets. Tropical fruit was regularly imported from Cuba and began to find its way to inland towns. Individuals and merchants could more easily make bulk purchases of household goods from northern firms. The impact of northern marketing was obvious on holidays. Valentine's Day, which was not mentioned in the eighteenth century, became a popular observance. James H. Hammond mentioned Valentine's Day in his wooing of a "dear sweet girl" from Charleston," and David Harris noted it in his journal. The commercialization of Christmas, which so many bemoan today, had already begun. Santa Claus was expected in rural Spartanburg District, and in Columbia newspapers promoted Christmas sales: "Bargains! Bargains! Presents for Christmas: Cheap, Elegant and Useful." In 1860, with newspapers published in every district except Horry and Marlboro, fashions and fads were widely disseminated. The telegraph linked Charleston and Columbia with the rest of the nation, so news could be transmitted quickly. Greenville did not get telegraph service until after the Civil War.[111]

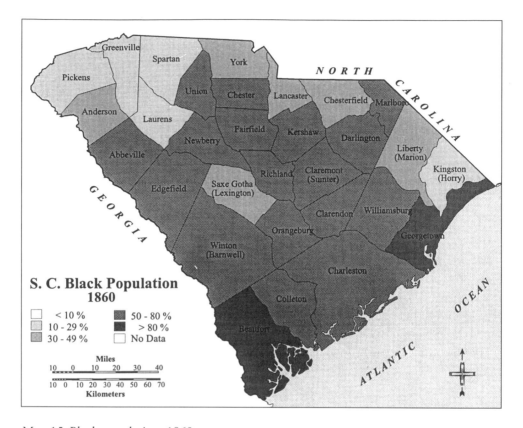

Map 15: Black population, 1860

Improved communications and transportation did not necessarily translate into lower costs for goods and services. The cost of living was higher in the Southeast than in New England or the Middle Atlantic states. Living costs may have been one of the contributing factors to the continued exodus of native white Carolinians in search of better opportunities. Charleston's growing immigrant population was highly mobile. In 1860 about 70 percent of the Irish families listed in the 1850 census had moved elsewhere.[112]

More than merely statistics, the composition of the state's population was one of the significant differences between South Carolina in 1860 and the state in 1775. In the eighteenth century immigrants had flocked to South Carolina, seemingly a land of milk and honey; on the eve of the Civil War natives and newcomers alike abandoned it for more promising opportunities elsewhere. The population of Charleston, the citadel of the lowcountry elite, was becoming more and more like that of northern cities. Statewide, however, the white population was more homogeneous. In 1775 a majority of the white population had been born elsewhere; in 1860 nearly 95 percent were native South Carolinians. The black population also was overwhelmingly native born, but the percentage probably was not as high due to the continued purchase of slaves from the upper South.[113]

There was a black majority in 1860 as there had been in 1775, but the distribution of that population was significantly different. In 1775 the black population was concentrated in the lowcountry parishes; by 1860 the black belt comprised all but ten of the state's thirty districts. And in those districts that had white majorities, black Carolinians were a sizable and visible presence (see Map 15).

The reality of the black majority and the homogeneity of the white population led to a closed society. There was a political correctness in antebellum South Carolina unequaled in twentieth-century America. Even when the issue was one with which many whites disagreed, such as the reopening of the African slave trade, men remained silent. In the 1850s William C. Preston wrote that Columbians were "under a reign of terror and the public mind exists in a panic."[114]

There were a number of similarities between the South Carolina of 1860 and the state of 1775; there were also differences, but many were more a matter of degree. However, an important change had taken place in the nineteenth century. Charleston had become a closed city; then the remainder of the state followed its lead, and South Carolina became a closed society. Whereas colonial South Carolina had welcomed new people and new ideas as vital to its growth and development, antebellum South Carolina, especially after 1835, viewed them as potential threats to its way of life.

Chapter Fifteen

CALCULATING THE VALUE OF THE UNION

Our Federal Union—It must be preserved.
  Andrew Jackson, 13 April 1830

The Union—next to our liberty most dear; may we all remember that it can only be preserved by respecting the rights of the states and distributing equally the benefits and burdens of the Union.
  John C. Calhoun, 13 April 1830

The Union, such as the majority have made it, is a foul monster, which those who worship, after seeing its deformity are worthy of their chains.
  George McDuffie, 19 May 1831

I have, Senators, believed from the first that the agitation of the subject of slavery will, if not prevented by some timely and effective measure, end in disunion.
  John C. Calhoun, 4 March 1850

I am for a rational and successful defense by the union of the South, which will redress our wrongs, secure our rights, and preserve the Union of the States.
  Benjamin F. Perry, 11 December 1850

We, the people of the State of South Carolina in Convention assembled, do declare and ordain . . . that the union now subsisting between South Carolina and the other States, under the name of the "United States of America" is hereby dissolved.
  Ordinance of Secession, 20 December 1860

*T*HE DEFEAT of the British at the Battle of New Orleans was a glorious ending to what had been several miserable years. The embargo of 1807 (which prohibited all American exports and forbade the importation of certain British goods) and the War of 1812 caused South Carolina's economy to come almost to a halt. With peace in 1815, however, the cotton boom resumed and prices skyrocketed to 30.8¢

($3.66) a pound. Along with the rest of the nation, the state and its leaders were in an expansive mood. The Federalist Party, tarred with treason because of the anti-war and pro-British sentiments of many of its leaders, faded out of existence. In South Carolina almost everyone was a National Republican (as the party of Thomas Jefferson was now called), but there was no common political philosophy. The "Era of Good Feelings" had begun.[1]

In 1800 Jefferson had said, "We are all republicans—we are all federalists." Wade Hampton of Richland, as were many of his fellow citizens, was a bit of both. According to Edward Hooker, Hampton considered himself a Republican but was a man with "many notions and sentiments which are more characteristic of federalism." And Hampton did not "hesitate to condemn, openly and unequivocally, some measures of the republican party." Some Carolinians, however, tended to be more one than the other. U.S. senator William Smith of Spartanburg District was an old-fashioned states' rights Jeffersonian, while Rep. John C. Calhoun of Abbeville was an outspoken nationalist. Calhoun's nationalism led the *Richmond Enquirer* to label him an "ultra-politician of the federal school."[2]

In Congress, Calhoun and Langdon Cheves were ardent War Hawks who advocated war with Great Britain and, after the war, a strong national government. Cheves served as Speaker of the House of Representatives for the last year of the war (1814–1815). Calhoun endorsed the Tariff of 1816, supported federal funding for internal improvements such as roads and canals, and sponsored the bill that created the Second Bank of the United States. In the waning hours of the Fourteenth Congress, a New York congressman rose to thank the gentleman from South Carolina "for the judicious, independent, and national course which he has pursued . . . for the last two years." Within a few months President James Monroe would appoint Calhoun as secretary of war.[3]

For nearly another decade Calhoun and his allies continued not only to advocate a vigorous central government but to deprecate the idea of states' rights. In part the secretary of war was motivated by his desire to improve the nation's defenses, and that meant increasing expenditures for fortifications, the army, and roads. According to George McDuffie, a Calhoun protégé, the only individuals who promoted states' rights were "Ambitious men of inferior talents" who could not distinguish themselves on the national scene; therefore, they sought "to increase the power and consequence of the State governments, the theatres in which they expect to acquire distinction." McDuffie's views were shared by most of the up-and-coming political figures in the state.[4]

There were, however, those within South Carolina and in Washington who disagreed with the nationalism of the Monroe administration. Calhoun's carefully developed plans for a professional, standing army and fortifications received a severe jolt in 1821. After the Panic of 1819 Congress became more economy-minded and gutted his proposals. There was more than just saving the taxpayers' dollars involved. One of the declared contenders for the next presidential contest (1824) was

Secretary of the Treasury William H. Crawford of Georgia, an old-fashioned states' rights Republican. His friends in Congress seized upon the army appropriation to embarrass the administration and tarnish the reputation of the secretary of war, who was considered one of the rising stars on the national political scene and a potential rival for the White House.[5]

In December 1821 Calhoun announced that he would be a candidate for president. The remaining three years of the Monroe administration were shadowed by the contest among five candidates. In addition to Crawford and Calhoun these were John Quincy Adams of Massachusetts, the secretary of state; Henry Clay of Kentucky, the Speaker of the House of Representatives; and Andrew Jackson of Tennessee, hero of the Battle of New Orleans and U.S. senator. It was a vicious campaign. Calhoun's followers slung muck and manure along with the rest. At one point McDuffie fought a duel with one of Crawford's supporters that left McDuffie crippled for life. The race left festering political wounds. Crawford's supporters, including Sen. William Smith from South Carolina, did not forget, and for many years they never missed an opportunity to snipe at Calhoun. While theirs was a personal vendetta, it had ramifications not only for the man but for the state.[6]

Although Calhoun had a strong national organization, his campaign soon hit some rough spots. There were no national party conventions in those days, and individuals were nominated by state legislatures or congressional caucuses. The South Carolina General Assembly placed the name of William Lowndes, not Calhoun, in nomination. That hurt Calhoun, but the secretary of war suffered the first real defeat of his career when his forces in Pennsylvania switched to Jackson. They nominated the South Carolinian for the vice presidency. With that, the campaign that had begun with great promise was over and he settled for second place. At age forty there would be other opportunities. His age, his ambition, and his politics all contributed to his defeat; however, he and others also grossly underestimated the candidacy of Andrew Jackson.[7]

While Calhoun and his allies were preoccupied with presidential politics, the voters back home were beginning to be concerned with other matters. The economic shocks caused by the collapse of cotton prices were soon joined by a series of events that raised white fears about the state's black population. The 1820 census revealed that for the first time since the American Revolution, South Carolina had a black majority (see Map 14). The debate over the admission of Missouri to the Union made slavery a national issue. Then in 1822 the Denmark Vesey Plot dredged up historical memories of the Stono Rebellion and more recent ones of Haiti.

Since the 1750s the in-migration of thousands of settlers down the Great Wagon Road into the middle- and upcountry had transformed what had been a black majority (59.7 percent) in 1775 into a white majority (56 percent) in 1790, a significant swing in demographics. There were only about four thousand more black Carolinians in 1790 than there had been in 1775, while the white population had practically doubled. The black/white ratio in 1800 was the same as that of 1790.

Table 15.1

SOUTH CAROLINA POPULATION, 1790–1850

	1790	1800	1810	1820	1830	1840	1850
B	108,895	149,336	200,919	265,301	323,332	335,314	393,944
W	140,178	196,255	214,196	237,400	257,863	259,084	274,563

Dodd and Dodd, *Historical Statistics*, 46.

Then the demographic tide turned. In the 1840s Robert Barnwell Rhett would lament that "Every census has added to the power of the nonslaveholding states and diminished that of the South." His comments could be paraphrased to say that every census increased proportionally the number of black Carolinians and decreased that of whites. By 1820 South Carolina, for the first time in more than a generation, had a black majority, and with each succeeding census that black majority increased. In 1850 the state's population was 58.9 percent black.[8]

Against this backdrop of an increasing black population, the debate over the admission of Missouri caused a great deal of anxiety in South Carolina, especially in the predominantly black lowcountry parishes. In Washington, Charles Pinckney, as the only founding father in the House of Representatives, made an impassioned speech. He argued that it had never been the intent of the delegates in Philadelphia to allow the federal government to interfere in any way with the institution of slavery. In the larger scheme of things he believed that the compromise itself was unimportant. The crucial issue was, he said, "keeping the hands of Congress from touching the question of slavery." However, he was a minority voice, even in South Carolina. Most of the remainder of the state's delegation were satisfied with the compromise that admitted Missouri as a slave state and Maine as a free state, and drew a line (36°30') above which would be free territory. As secretary of war, Calhoun did not participate in the discussion, but he did support the compromise. It would "settle forever," he commented, a "question which has so deeply agitated this country." In the cabinet he convinced President Monroe that Congress *did* have the authority to regulate slavery in the territories. To the would-be presidential candidate, the constitutional issues were insignificant when compared with quieting the "agitation" over slavery. Pinckney was disconsolate and viewed the Missouri Compromise not as a compromise at all, but as a defeat for the South. In South Carolina the Missouri debate was deliberately downplayed by the Charleston press.[9]

Living among blacks as a minority was not anything new to lowcountry rice planters, but it was new to cotton planters in the middlecountry districts. Reported incidents of slave unrest were unsettling. There had been slave plots discovered and thwarted in Columbia (1805) and Camden (1816) and at Ashepoo (1816). Because of the latter two, the state had passed a law forbidding the importation of slaves from other states. In 1819 the law was repealed as totally unenforceable. In its stead a new patrol law was enacted that was designed to keep the slave population in line. Then late in the spring of 1822 lowcountry whites were rocked by the news of a purported slave rebellion.[10]

On 30 May a house servant reported to his master that he had been approached to join in a planned slave uprising. When arrested, the accused black man confessed and implicated three others, including a valued house servant of Gov. Thomas Bennett. All three vigorously denied the accusation and proclaimed their innocence. The authorities let them go, convinced that their prisoner was lying. There was, however, a plot afoot. Organized by a free black man, Denmark Vesey, it may have involved hundreds of black Carolinians in and around Charleston.[11]

Vesey, who had been born a slave, had been allowed by his master to hire his labor out to others. With some of the money he earned he bought lottery tickets, and in 1800 he won enough money to purchase his freedom. He then established himself in Charleston as a carpenter where he was respected but not especially well liked by his fellow black Charlestonians. There were allegations that he used sorcery, and one of his closest associates was a well-known shaman named Gullah Jack. Vesey was a Sunday School teacher in the local African Methodist Episcopal Church. According to the testimony of Rolla, a slave, Vesey exhorted his followers by reading passages from the Bible, especially Exodus.[12]

Because of the activities by authorities, Vesey and his lieutenants moved the date of the rebellion from 14 July to 16 June. Then, less than seventy-two hours before the rebels planned to strike, they were again betrayed. This time James Hamilton Jr., the city's intendent (mayor), and Gov. Thomas Bennett reacted in alarm. The militia was called out, and on 17 June the city council appointed a special tribunal of five citizens to conduct a trial. Over the space of five weeks charges were brought against 117 black Carolinians, but there was only sufficient evidence to try seventy-nine. Of these, thirty-five were sentenced to death and thirty-seven sold out of state because they were deemed dangerous to the safety and order of the community.[13]

Not until Vesey was convicted on 28 June did the local press report to a horrified white community the rebels' plans. The court, in pronouncing sentence on Vesey, found him guilty of a plot that would "trample on all laws, human and divine; to riot in blood, outrage, rapine . . . and conflagration, and to introduce anarchy and confusion in their most horrid forms." Because he had planned to disrupt the order and harmony of the community, his life was "a just and necessary sacrifice, at the shrine of indignant Justice." Vesey was hanged on 2 July, and four weeks later there was a mass execution of twenty-two convicted conspirators.[14]

Denmark Vesey went to the gallows protesting his innocence. Some white Charlestonians, notably associate justice of the U.S. Supreme Court William Johnson, questioned the fairness of the trials. In print he described how mass hysteria had swept over parts of Edgefield District a few years earlier and innocent slaves had been hanged. The reaction of the press and Charleston's white community were instantaneous and hostile. According to one Charlestonian, had the plot succeeded, the results would have been "unparalleled, even exceeding, if possible, the Demons of St. Domingo." Johnson issued something of an apology for questioning the actions of his fellow Charlestonians, but he may have been closer to the truth than he knew. There are arguments that there was no plot at all and that it was manufactured by local authorities as a control measure, to "strike terror into the heart of every slave."[15]

There were several immediate responses to the Vesey Plot. The African Methodist Episcopal Church was closed and the building demolished. The General Assembly in December 1822 passed the Seamen's Act, designed to prevent free black sailors from associating with local slaves. If a ship docked in Charleston with a free black seaman on board, he would be housed in the city jail while the ship was in port. If the vessel's captain did not pay for his room and board, then the captain would be arrested and, if convicted, fined $1,000 ($12,900) and the free black seaman could be sold into slavery. This act and a subsequent one in 1823 both violated treaties that had been ratified by the federal government. The law of the land was ignored despite protests from abroad and the nation's capital.[16]

Following the Vesey Plot there seemed to be one incident after another, most of them external and all of them threatening to undermine the order and harmony of South Carolina society. The Ohio legislature adopted a series of resolutions, endorsed by eight other northern states, condemning slavery as a national evil and calling for gradual emancipation (1824). In Washington, Sen. Rufus King of New York proposed that proceeds from the sale of public lands be used to purchase slaves (1825). President Adams's request to send delegates to a Pan-American congress in Panama was defeated by southerners because there would be delegates from Haiti present and the San Domingan revolution might be discussed (1826). A series of costly, suspicious fires destroyed hundreds of thousands of dollars worth of property in downtown Charleston (1826). The American Colonization Society petitioned Congress for governmental funding of its efforts to transport freed slaves back to Africa (1827). Northern Congressmen almost blocked payment to a petitioner for property damaged during the War of 1812 because the property was a slave (1829). There was a slave plot in Georgetown that was thwarted at the last minute, but for more than a year one of the state's most heavily black districts was on edge (1829–1830). William Lloyd Garrison began publication of the abolitionist newspaper *The Liberator* (1831). These events caused concern, but none aroused fears as much as did the outbreak of servile insurrection in Virginia.[17]

The Nat Turner Revolt (1831) caused panic throughout the South, including South Carolina. False alarms spread about possible copy-cat rebellions, and vigilance groups formed. In addition to the constant rumors, real stories of earlier slave crimes recirculated: in Marion District a slave murdered his master; in Lancaster a slave killed his master's daughter; in Charleston a slave knifed two white men before he was apprehended. Then in 1832 a black cook in Sumter District poisoned the food at a Fourth of July celebration that left several dead and two hundred dangerously ill. White southerners, especially South Carolinians, were beginning to find their social situation incomprehensible. Some agreed with Robert J. Turnbull, who blamed the beginning of slave unrest on the Missouri Compromise debates. In taking stock of their world, they first began to question the value of the Union, and a few even began to think in terms of forming a southern nation.[18]

During the decade of the 1820s a number of factors came together that led South Carolinians to calculate the value of the Union. First, there was the economic distress caused by the Panic of 1819, the fluctuation of world markets, and the competition from the newer (and richer) cotton lands of the lower South. Second there was uneasiness over the agitation of the slavery issues because slaveholding had increased throughout the state and because of the apparent restiveness of the overwhelming black majority in the lowcountry parishes. The tariff, which South Carolinians related to both the economic and slavery questions, was the issue that ignited the debate. It also was an issue to which other Americans could relate, as not even other southerners were ready to endorse slavery openly. In 1830 Calhoun said that he considered the tariff "as the occasion, rather than the real cause of the present unhappy state of things." What should be of concern to southerners was the danger to "the peculiar domestick institutions of the Southern States."[19]

The Tariff of 1824 was clearly a protectionist measure. Southerners believed that it discriminated against them because they were an agricultural region and had to import manufactured goods. Higher tariffs meant that Great Britain would export less to the United States and not be able to import as much southern cotton. By 1824 George McDuffie, among others, had shed his nationalism and was a fervent opponent of the tariff. In speech after speech he told struggling cotton planters that the tariff was responsible for their misery.[20]

In response, in 1825 the General Assembly adopted resolutions denying that Congress had the authority to promote internal improvements and declaring protective tariffs unconstitutional. Their passage was a public rebuke of Calhoun and his lieutenants, who were reminded later that they had "acted with too great liberality—to say the least of it" with regard to internal improvements and protective tariffs.[21]

The legislature's relatively mild response to what was a growing crisis of confidence in the nature of the Union did not address the issue that troubled more and more white Carolinians. If Congress had the authority to pass protective tariffs, were there no limits as to what it could do? Were South Carolina and her "peculiar and local institutions" safe? An increasing number thought not. In 1825 Whitemarsh Seabrook, a St. John's Colleton Parish planter, addressed the issue squarely in a pamphlet in which he listed the attacks by the North on the South and its domestic institutions. "The tenure by which we hold our slaves," he wrote, "is daily becoming less secure, and more the subject of acrimonious animadversion." The following year, during the debates over the Pan-American Congress, Robert Y. Hayne stated that the southern states would never allow "any interference, whatever, in their domestic concerns." If federal authorities ever made an attempt to do so, the southern states would consider themselves as "driven from the Union."[22]

During the summer of 1827 radical spokesmen captured the headlines in the state's newspapers. In Charleston, Robert J. Turnbull published a series of essays in the *Charleston Mercury* denouncing the tyranny of the federal government and reminding his readers that any discussion of slavery was a threat to the security and harmony of the state. The essays were later published as a pamphlet, *The Crisis,* that would become the handbook for nullification and resistance. In Columbia, Thomas Cooper, president of the South Carolina College, gave an oration that attracted national attention: "I have said, that we shall "ere long be compelled to calculate the value of our union; and to enquire of what use to us is this most unequal alliance? By which the south has always been the loser, and the north always the gainer? . . . The question, however, is fast approaching to the alternative, of submission or separation." Although a goodly number of Carolinians thought that Cooper might have exaggerated a bit, the passage of the Tariff of 1828 gave validity to his observation that "the south has always been the loser, and the north always the gainer."[23]

Ironically, what was termed the "Tariff of Abominations" passed because Calhoun and his followers in Congress supported it. As part of the political maneuvering designed to help elect Andrew Jackson president in 1828, his supporters in Congress came up with a plan for presenting a tariff with outrageously high rates on raw materials (which western producers wanted but New England manufacturing interests opposed) as well as manufactured items. They anticipated that the House of Representatives would pass the measure but that New England's senators would block it. That did not occur. Adroitly New England senators restructured some of the rates to make the tariff more palatable to their constituents and voted for it. Import duties increased 30 to 50 percent. McDuffie had warned his fellow South Carolinians about "fighting the devil with fire," but they had ignored his advice and been burned badly. South Carolinians went ballistic when the Tariff of 1828 was enacted.[24]

National politics were not as important to South Carolina's voters as they were to Calhoun. The state's growing radicalism was dangerous to his political ambitions. In 1828 Andrew Jackson was nominated for president and Calhoun renominated for vice president. It was widely believed that the aging hero of New Orleans would serve only one term and that the South Carolinian would be his heir apparent. However, if South Carolina continued talking about disunion, then there was little chance that Calhoun would get the nomination. He urged restraint but was unable to get

McDuffie, Cooper, and others to tone down their rhetoric. There was a real danger that he might lose his home base. At the urging of his friends in the state, in November 1828 he wrote what would become the *South Carolina Exposition and Protest*. There was no author's name on the document that was considered by the legislature in December 1828, but from the time it was made public, most knowledgeable Americans attributed it to the vice president.[25]

In the *South Carolina Exposition and Protest* Calhoun addressed several constitutional issues. The tariffs were a danger to the republic because they were an example of the tyranny of majority rule. He rejected the idea of national sovereignty and said that the founding fathers had insisted upon the sharing of power by both state and national governments. There were "general powers, expressly delegated to the General Government" and "peculiar and local powers reserved to the States." Sovereignty rested with the "people of the several States" that created the Union. If there were a constitutional dispute between a state and the national government, then the Supreme Court was not the proper arbiter because it was a creature of the national government. It was left to each state to be the judge of disputes between itself and the general government. However, the constitutionality of an issue (such as the tariff) was not to be judged by the legislature, but by "a convention especially called for the purpose." If the convention judged the tariff, for example, to be unconstitutional, then it had the authority, nay the duty, to nullify (veto) it. Much of the political theory in the document drew upon the precedents of the Virginia and Kentucky resolutions of 1798. However, the last step, the nullification of a federal law, was Calhoun's own idea for peacefully solving the problem.[26]

The South Carolina House of Representatives considered a committee report that altered Calhoun's draft a bit. It agreed to publish five thousand copies, passed a strongly worded protest on the tariff, but did not adopt the committee report. Nor, when radicals pushed for a convention, could they even come close to obtaining the necessary two-thirds vote. The legislature's relatively moderate stance pleased Calhoun, but the state's radicals were most unhappy.[27]

In March 1829 when Calhoun was sworn in as Jackson's vice president, he was convinced that he could manage things back in South Carolina and solidify his role in Washington as Jackson's successor. He believed that if the radicals gained control and nullified the tariff, he could persuade the president to go along. Unfortunately, Calhoun misjudged the temper of the South Carolina electorate, the skill of his political rivals, and Andrew Jackson. Within two years Calhoun's stature as a potential presidential candidate would be diminished and, whether fairly or unfairly, he would be viewed primarily as a sectional spokesman.[28]

During 1829 Calhoun's relationship with the president began to deteriorate. Floride Colhoun Calhoun refused to recognize socially Margaret O'Neill Timberlake Eaton, the wife of Secretary of War John H. Eaton. Mrs. Eaton was a woman with a shady reputation, and Mrs. Calhoun shunned her. Eaton was Jackson's closest personal friend in Washington, and Eaton and his wife complained to the president about the Calhouns' conduct. When others in Washington society did the same, Secretary of State Martin Van Buren used the issue to drive a wedge between the president and the vice president.[29]

The question of the Union further served to alienate the two men. When Sen. Samuel A. Foote of Connecticut proposed that the sale of western lands be limited, southern senators rushed to defend the West. They compared the damage the Foote Resolution would do to the West with what the tariffs had done to the South. Sen. Robert Y. Hayne of South Carolina and Daniel Webster of Massachusetts engaged in a historic debate that came to involve the nature of the Union. Webster accused Hayne of supporting the "Carolina Doctrine" of nullification, which he equated with disunion. Hayne was a polished public speaker, but he was not John C. Calhoun, and Webster's ringing phrase "Liberty and Union, now and forever, one and inseparable" found receptive audiences in all sections of the country. Several months later, in April 1830, in his toast at a Jefferson Day dinner, President Jackson made it quite clear that on the question of the Union he stood with Webster. Vice President Calhoun responded in defense of the "Carolina Doctrine," but the challenge had been issued.[30]

The vice president, personally and politically, was on the defensive. His old enemies, the supporters of William H. Crawford, made sure that Jackson learned that during the Monroe administration it had been Calhoun, not Crawford, who had wanted to court-martial him for disobeying orders. It was a matter of interpretation, and neither Calhoun nor Jackson would admit to error. When Jackson pressed for an explanation, Calhoun responded with a nine-thousand-word epistle (plus enclosures) justifying his position. The president's response was chilling: *et tu, Brute.* Despite the rift, mutual friends almost succeeded in negotiating a reconciliation. Then one of Calhoun's supporters published all the correspondence between the two (thinking that Jackson had given his approval when, in reality, the president had not even seen it because John Eaton withheld it from him). Calhoun always maintained that the letters vindicated his conduct, but that did not stop his being cast into political outer darkness.[31]

Throughout his trials in Washington, Calhoun continually counseled those favoring nullification in South Carolina to go slowly. He did not want anything to damage his still faint presidential hopes. However, the radicals were becoming increasingly vocal, demanding action rather than words. As one visitor to the lowcountry reported in 1830, "Many openly avow that they not only think it time to calculate the value of the Union—but that they *have calculated* it—and with them it has been found wanting."[32]

In 1830 two groups emerged in the state, each with a single issue agenda: the Union. Nullifiers, as the radicals came to be known, wanted to call a convention to nullify the tariff and let the rest of the nation know where South Carolina stood. Their opponents, the Unionists, opposed the rashness of the Nullifiers and argued that the best interests of the state would be served by working within the system.

Each was convinced that its position was correct and would insure the good order and harmony of the whole community.[33]

For nearly two years there was an unceasing campaign to gain control of the General Assembly. The issue divided families, alienated friends, and severed business and professional relationships. "The State," according to William J. Grayson of Beaufort District, "became for a time a great talking and eating machine. The appetites and lungs of the conflicting parties never failed." The States' Rights and Free Trade Society, the Nullifiers' support organization, sponsored more than three hundred dinners, meetings, and debates in eighteen months. The Unionists, while not as well organized, hosted their share of gatherings. The Nullifiers had the better orators and better organization. Among their leaders were Robert J. Turnbull, William Harper, Robert Barnwell Rhett, Francis W. Pickens, James Hamilton Jr., Henry L. Pinckney, James H. Hammond, Waddy Thompson, and Robert Y. Hayne. The Unionists could not always agree among themselves as to the best strategy. Their leadership included James L. Petigru, Joel R. Poinsett, William Drayton, Henry Middleton, Daniel E. Huger, John B. O'Neall, and William J. Grayson. The Nullifiers attracted men who had been outside the state's power structure but who saw the opportunity to become part of it. Unionist James L. Petigru snidely referred to the "nullies" as "little men . . . crowing on their own dunghill." His comments were indicative of the tenor of the campaigning.[34]

By the summer of 1831 the Nullifiers wanted to know where John C. Calhoun stood. He continued to equivocate in public because he still harbored presidential ambitions. However, his silence was no longer acceptable to many. If he did not come out publicly behind nullification, then he faced the threat of political retaliation. In July he wrote and published an essay in which he announced his support for and adherence to the doctrine of nullification. Forced to reveal his hand, Calhoun, in turn, forced the voters of the state to make a decision.[35]

The electioneering for the legislature in 1832 was fierce. Insults were hurled by both sides. The Unionists, who were the conservatives, likened the Nullifiers to the Jacobins of the French Revolution and predicted bloodshed and civil war if nullification led to secession. Nullifiers branded their opponents "submissionists" who lacked the courage to stand up for their state. In private correspondence Calhoun wrote that "The hope of the country now rests in our gallant little state. Let every Carolinian do his duty." Opposing mobs in Charleston roughed up those with whom they disagreed. In Spartanburg, Calhoun was hanged in effigy. In Greenville, Unionist editor Benjamin F. Perry of the *Greenville Mountaineer* killed Nullifier editor Turner Bynum of *The Sentinel* in a duel. Gov. James Hamilton Jr. turned his 1832 inspections of militia units into Nullifier rallies. The actual voting, especially in the lowcountry, was marred by bribery and fraud on both sides. In the upcountry the turnout was heavy; in York District 95 percent of eligible voters went to the polls, and in Laurens 99 percent voted.[36]

The State Rights and
Union Ticket, 1832.
Courtesy, South Caro-
lina Historical Society.

The Nullifiers swamped their opponents, capturing 80 percent of the seats in the house and 75 percent of those in the senate. Statewide they won 59 percent of the vote. However, despite those impressive totals, a change of just sixty-seven votes in Charleston would have given the Unionists the city's delegation and prevented the Nullifiers' having the two-thirds majority necessary to call a convention. The man most responsible for engineering the Nullifiers' smashing victory was Gov. James Hamilton Jr.[37]

No sooner were the results of the election in than the governor summoned a special session of the General Assembly. Its sole order of business was to issue a call for the election of delegates to a convention to meet in Columbia in November. On 24 November 1832 the delegates declared the tariffs of 1828 and 1832 to be "null, void, and no law, nor binding upon this State, its officers or citizens." After 1 February 1833 state and federal officials were forbidden from collecting tariffs. Appeals to the federal courts were prohibited. If there were any attempt made "to coerce this State," then the people of South Carolina "will forthwith proceed to organize a separate government."[38]

The state's leadership fully believed that it could nullify the tariffs and that the president would do nothing. After all, had not the state's seamen's acts for nearly a decade effectively nullified treaties that were supposed to be the law of the land? And had not the president permitted Georgia to thumb its nose at a Supreme Court decision that also was supposed to be national law? Jackson's annual message to Congress (4 December) appeared conciliatory. That, however, was simply a subterfuge. The president ordered additional federal troops and revenue cutters to Charleston and issued a proclamation in which he admonished the "Fellow-citizens of my native State" on the unwise and dangerous course of action they were pursuing. Nullification was *incompatible with the existence of the Union . . . and destructive of the great object for which it was formed.* As to the threat of secession, "Disunion by armed force is *treason.*"[39]

South Carolinians were stunned by the militant tone of the president's proclamation, but the Nullifiers prepared to defend the state. In the governor's call to arms, more men volunteered than had voted for Nullifier legislative candidates. Unionists also began to organize their own units and were supplied with five thousand muskets by the president. The General Assembly elected Hayne as governor and Calhoun, who would shortly resign as vice president, as U.S. senator. The next several months were tense as South Carolina remained defiant. But she was alone; not a single southern state rallied to her cause. The Mississippi legislature accused South Carolina of acting "with a reckless precipitancy (originating, we would willingly believe in delusion)." Nullification, said Mississippians, was "a heresy, fatal to the existence of the Union." Even less complimentary was the reaction of a Tennessean who said that if Old Hickory would give two weeks' notice, a sufficient number of men could be assembled "to stand in the Saluda Mountains and piss enough . . . to float the whole nullifying crew of South Carolina into the Atlantic Ocean."[40]

When he left for Washington to assume his seat in the Senate, Calhoun had once again advised caution and moderation. He intended to find a way to negotiate the state off the limb upon which it found itself—before some South Carolina hotspurs sawed it off. A public meeting in Charleston (which did not have the authority to do so) agreed to postpone the implementation of the Nullification Ordinance. In cooperation with Henry Clay, Calhoun forged a compromise on the tariff. Once passed, the rates would gradually be reduced until in 1842 they would return to approximately the level they had been in 1816. Jackson submitted legislation that authorized the president to use the army and navy to enforce the laws of the land.

Calhoun fought the passage of what would become the Force Act, but the administration rammed it through. Fifteen senators, nearly one-third of that body, joined Calhoun in abstaining.[41]

Governor Hamilton called the Nullification Convention back into session, and on 11 March 1833 it repealed the Ordinance of Nullification but then proceeded to nullify the Force Act. The president and the remainder of the country ignored South Carolina's last gesture of defiance.

Who won in 1832–1833? The more ardent Nullifiers such as Cooper and Rhett (who were really secessionists) were bitterly disappointed. "I fear that there is no longer hope or liberty for the South, under a Union, by which all self-government is taken away," said Rhett. "A people, owning slaves are mad, or worse than mad, who do not hold their destinies in their own hands." He and his associates viewed the compromise as a defeat, while the more moderate Nullifiers such as James Hamilton Jr. regarded it as a great victory for South Carolina. While the closet secessionists were losers because they did not disrupt the Union in 1833, almost everyone else was a winner. Andrew Jackson had preserved the Union. Henry Clay had, once again, crafted a successful compromise. Although John C. Calhoun had been tossed out of the Democratic Party, by staring down a popular president and causing him to blink, he had solidified his base in South Carolina.[42]

There were several legacies of the nullification controversy. The first was the state's acquiring a reputation for rashness that lingered for a generation. Even other southern states thought it prudent to keep South Carolina at arm's length. Daniel Wallace of Union District was upset to discover in Mississippi that there was a great deal of "prejudice against South Carolina, on account of the Doctrines of 1832." James Hamilton Jr. reported that "Georgia came to dislike us . . . more than the people of Massachusetts." The second, and more disturbing, consequence was "the great divisions and animosities" within the state that took a decade to heal. There was not much internal harmony in South Carolina between 1830 and 1840.[43]

The victorious Nullifiers were determined to crush their opponents. They might be in favor of minority rights on a national level, but within South Carolina they insisted on total adherence to their party line. The legislature debated imprisoning Unionists for treason but settled on a test oath that put loyalty to South Carolina above loyalty to the United States. The South Carolina Court of Appeals ruled in June 1834 that the oath was unconstitutional; however, a modified version was later incorporated into the state constitution that was vague enough that both Nullifiers and Unionists could interpret it according to their own beliefs.[44]

The test oath was but one example of the attempt to create harmony and stability in South Carolina by suppressing dissent. Unionists were hounded from office. Some, such as William Drayton, chose to leave the state; others, such as Joel R. Poinsett, withdrew from public life. The 1834 decision of the Court of Appeals had outraged the Nullifiers, in part because a majority of the justices were Unionists; when the court upheld an act of Congress in 1835, it was abolished and not reconstituted until 1859. The vindictiveness of the Nullifiers was due primarily to the vicious campaigning between 1830 and 1832. The wounds were "too recent," wrote John B. Grimball of St. Paul's Parish. "However desirable it may be that harmony and good fellowship be restored, it is much too soon for union men to come forward for office." Although Calhoun counseled moderation throughout the 1830s, he viewed those who did not support nullification as men who had not done their duty.[45]

After 1834 Calhoun believed his own effectiveness, as the chief defender of South Carolina and the South, depended upon a united South Carolina. There is no question that for the remainder of his life he had a majority of the state's voters on his side. Henry Laurens Pinckney, former editor of the *Charleston Mercury* and a member of Congress, was the first to learn that it did not pay to disagree with Calhoun. In presenting the so-called "Gag Rule" to the U.S. House of Representatives, there was an implication that Congress had the authority to regulate slavery in the District of Columbia. Such an admission was political heresy, and Pinckney was defeated for reelection. James H. Hammond, Francis W. Pickens, and Robert Barnwell Rhett, among others in public life, found their ambitions or careers curtailed because Calhoun thought it best. Even if he reversed himself on a matter of party or principle (as he did with Van Buren's subtreasury plan in 1838 or internal improvements for the Mississippi River Valley in 1845), his lieutenants were expected to follow suit unquestioningly. When Robert Barnwell Rhett decided that Calhoun was too cautious and conservative and organized the "Bluffton Movement" (1844) calling for immediate secession, it got nowhere. Only after Calhoun's death did many realize the stabilizing (some would say stultifying) role the statesman had played in South Carolina politics. Benjamin F. Perry was less charitable: "Calhoun was absolute in South Carolina. . . . He thought for the state and crushed out all independence of thought below him." Yet, without the support of the voters he would not have been able to dominate the state as he did.[46]

Political parties were dangerous to the unity and harmony of the state and something to be avoided. Repeatedly Calhoun thwarted efforts to have the governor and presidential electors chosen by the people, rather than the General Assembly, because he feared that popular election would lead to the formation of parties. By 1860 South Carolina was the only state in the Union that did not allow the people to elect their governor or vote for presidential electors. When it looked as if the Whig Party might attract a following, Calhoun saw to it that the effort came to naught. Nominally, most South Carolinians were Democrats, but their allegiance to the national party was always tentative—following the lead of the man from Fort Hill. On several occasions the state refused to send delegates to the Democratic National Convention and cast its electoral votes for noncandidates as a protest against the nominees and platforms of the major parties.[47]

The absence of parties in South Carolina did not make state government impossible. In fact, without the strictures of party loyalty, it was relatively easy to get the legislature to act in concert. Continuing a tradition of legislative dominance begun in the eighteenth century, the General Assembly of South Carolina retained all meaningful governmental authority. Writing in 1850, former governor James Henry Hammond noted that the "Legislature has all power. The Executive has none. The people have none beyond electing members of the legislature." With the exception of sheriffs, probate judges, tax collectors and commissioners, and commissioners for the poor, the General Assembly elected almost all other local officials. The legislature was not only controlled but dominated by planters. In no other southern state were planters a majority or was there such a high percentage of slaveholders (80 percent). The commonality of interests and the prodding of Calhoun made possible the political rehabilitation of the state's Unionists. In 1840 John P. Richardson of Sumter District, a wealthy slaveholder and leading Unionist, was elected governor with Calhoun's blessing.[48]

Reconciliation was accompanied by an increase in sensitivity to any criticism of slavery. Regardless of status, anyone who deviated from the state's nineteenth-century version of political correctness was condemned. Henry Laurens Pinckney, son of one of the state's founding fathers, was labeled a "traitor and a bastard" for introducing the "Gag Rule." As one modern historian put it, the "campaign to create a monolithic society was relentless." The ever more vocal criticism of the state's "domestick institutions" by northern abolitionists made it all the more imperative that South Carolina present a united front to the rest of the nation.[49]

Among the most vigorous critics of slavery were two expatriate South Carolinians, Sarah and Angelina Grimké. Born to wealthy slave-owning parents, they became Quakers and renounced their inheritance. In pamphlets addressed to the "Clergy of the Southern States" and the "Christian Women of the South," each of the sisters used Scripture to buttress her attacks on slavery. The institution was doomed because a righteous, angry Jehovah was on the side of the abolitionists. "There is no Doubt," wrote Angelina, that "there will be a most terrible over turning at the South in a few years, such cruelty and wrong, must be visited with Divine vengance soon." Not many in the state got the chance to read these or any other abolitionist tracts. Since 1835 postmasters in Charleston and across the state had been removing what they considered to be inflammatory materials from the mails.[50]

By the 1840s the abolitionist movement was gaining adherents in every northern state. Following Calhoun's lead, after 1837 white southerners no longer apologized for the institution. Instead they defended it vigorously as a "positive good." "On the inviolability of the institution," said Langdon Cheves in 1844, "which is threatened and assailed, depends, not our prosperity alone, but every blessing under heaven, which we enjoy." To guard against potential trouble at home, state-supported military schools were created in Columbia (Arsenal Academy) and Charleston (The Citadel) so that the state would have a trained military force to use in case of servile insurrection. The unceasing clamor over the issue of slavery, especially in Congress, had white Carolinians on edge.[51]

Benjamin Franklin Perry (1805–1886).
Courtesy, South Caroliniana Library.

Beginning in 1844 a series of events caused even such devout Unionists such as Perry to question their attachment to the Union. The "Gag Rule" in the House of Representatives was repealed by the votes of northern congressmen. Then came the Senate's rejection of the annexation treaty with Texas. Negotiated by Calhoun, President John Tyler's secretary of state, Texas was seen as the salvation of the South. As Texas was a slave state, its admission to the Union would help maintain the balance between free and slave states in the Senate. Expansion became an issue in the 1844 campaign, and it was as if Pandora's Box had been opened. Manifest Destiny, the divine right of the United States to occupy the North American continent, captured the imaginations of Americans on both sides of the Mason-Dixon Line. Just before the end of Tyler's administration, Calhoun managed to get Texas admitted to the Union by a joint resolution of Congress. He feared, however, that expansionist fever might result in war with Mexico and that would, in turn, lead to a national debate as to whether or not slavery would be allowed in the territory won in the war. In this, as in so many other matters, his foresight was uncannily accurate.[52]

In August 1846 an obscure Pennsylvania congressman, David Wilmot, introduced an amendment to the appropriations bill that would prohibit slavery in any territory acquired from Mexico. South Carolina's leadership had not wanted the Mexican War. They knew that most of the territory that might be gained would be unsuitable for plantation slavery. They were especially concerned about the drive to annex all of the Mexican Republic. With the inevitable national debate over slavery in the territories and the potential for nonslaveholding territory adjacent to Texas, they viewed the efforts to annex Mexico as "a threat to the state's social order." But there was a principle involved: if the blood and treasure of the South had been expended in fighting the war, then southerners should not be denied the right to take their property with them into what had been Mexican territory.[53]

The men of the Palmetto Regiment fought bravely in Mexico as a unit of the United States Army. The first flag atop the heights of the Mexican citadel at Chapultepec was the palmetto flag of the South Carolinians. Of the 1,048 who joined the unit, 441 died—a death rate of 42 percent, three times that of the army as a whole.[54]

While the men of the Palmetto Regiment were fighting and dying as American soldiers, many in South Carolina openly calculated the value of the Union. Across the state, in public gatherings and in private correspondence, there was almost unanimity on the reaction to the Wilmot Proviso. One of the state's most outspoken Unionists, Benjamin F. Perry said that "any interference, on the part of the Federal Government, with our Slave property, will be the cause of an immediate dissolution of this great and hitherto glorious Union." The debate was not limited to denunciations of the Wilmot Proviso. Perry and others raised the specter of abolitionists' "wanting to place the Southern Slave on an equality . . . with the white man." Freed slaves would be allowed to vote, sit on juries, and "meet with the white man as his equal . . . to intermarry with his children, and form one society and one family!"[55]

Committees were organized to protect local citizens from abolitionist plots and northern agents fomenting rebellion. In May 1849 representatives of twenty-nine local committees met in Columbia and established a Central Committee of Vigilance and Safety that determined it would be a quasi-official advisory body to the governor. Community vigilance paid off in Spartanburg, where an abolitionist provocateur and copies of an abolitionist pamphlet were discovered. These incidents fed the paranoia that gripped the state.[56]

Events in Washington did not help matters. In 1849 President Zachary Taylor, a Louisiana slaveholder, made it clear that he would press for the admission of California to the Union. California would be a free state, and its admission would upset the balance in the Senate between slave and free states. For the last year of his life John C. Calhoun would try desperately to convince southern politicians that the region's only hope lay in a southern party and that the admission of California as a free state would lead to disunion.[57]

On 4 March 1850 a dying Calhoun was assisted into the Senate. Since he was physically unable to deliver his own speech, Sen. James Mason of Virginia read it for him. In reviewing the history of the republic and his perception of how it had been changed, he urged the nation to alter its course before it was torn asunder. "The cords which bound these states together in one common union" were breaking, and he cited as evidence the division of the Baptists and Methodists into northern and southern churches. Those cords that had not yet snapped had been "greatly weakened" because of the unceasing debate about slavery. Only if agitation over slavery ceased, all western territories were opened to slavery, and the Constitution were amended to give the South a veto to protect its interests could the Union be saved.[58]

Calhoun's speech reflected a lifetime of reading and thought. During the last two years of his life he refined his ideas on how best to protect the South's interests within the Union. The results were two significant works on political theory and history, *A Disquisition on Government* and *A Discourse on the Constitution and Government of the United States*. In a republic, he argued, a numerical majority tends to become corrupt and act in its own interests rather than those of the entire nation. Therefore, a concurrent majority (such as South Carolina had created in 1808 with the compromise between the lowcountry and the upcountry) was the only way to insure that the rights of minority interests could be protected. The creation of a dual executive, one from the North and one from the South, with each having a veto over congressional legislation, was one way to protect the South's interests.[59]

John Caldwell Calhoun did not live to see his prediction of disunion transpire. He died in Washington on 31 March 1850 and, after a state funeral, was laid to rest in St. Philip's churchyard in Charleston. While he lived he kept in check the more radical politicians in the state and region. After his death no statesman had the stature to calm the radicals bent on creating an independent southern nation.[60]

In June 1850 a southern convention assembled in Nashville to orchestrate a united southern response to the proposed Compromise of 1850. Only nine slave states were represented, and the mood was conciliatory. The president of the convention said that its purpose was to rectify the "violations of the constitution . . . and to perpetuate the Union, not destroy it." In such an atmosphere South Carolina's radicals were not especially welcome. A majority of the delegation, prodded by Langdon Cheves, James H. Hammond, and Robert W. Barnwell, opted for a strategy of moderation over the objections of Francis W. Pickens and Robert B. Rhett. Every effort was made to keep Rhett out of the picture because his intemperate speeches calling for disunion, widely reported in the nation's newspapers, had been denounced throughout the South. The Nashville Convention passed a series of timid resolutions but left the door open for a second convention after Congress had acted.[61]

In Washington the state's delegation fought a losing action against the various pieces of legislation that comprised the Compromise of 1850. Few members of Congress listened; South Carolina's radicals had painted themselves into a corner. A North Carolina congressman said that it was futile to alter anything as "No arrangement which can or will be made will satisfy South Carolina." By September 1850

Robert Barnwell Rhett
(1800–1876). Courtesy, South
Caroliniana Library.

the Compromise of 1850 was law. Calhoun had warned the nation, but his warning went unheeded; as in the case of Mexico, he had foreseen what would occur. James H. Hammond spoke for most South Carolinians when he declared that the Compromise of 1850 was not a compromise at all, but a defeat for the South. He feared that it was only a matter of time, with free states in the majority, before there would be enough votes to abolish slavery "and reduce us to the condition of Hayti." The *Laurensville Herald* editorialized "that we must give up the Union or give up slavery." Thundered Edward B. Bryan of St. John's Colleton, "*Give us slavery or give us death.*"[62]

A rump convention reconvened in Nashville in November 1850, but its extremist rhetoric and resolutions were ignored everywhere but in South Carolina. The state's radicals, led by hotheads such as Robert B. Rhett, Francis W. Pickens, and Maxcy Gregg, demanded that the state secede from the Union whether or not other southern states joined South Carolina. Although the most vocal and best-organized faction in the state, the radicals were just one of three. Their main opponents were cooperationists who believed that while secession and the formation of a southern nation were ideal, solitary secession was suicidal. They remembered the results of isolation in 1832–1833 and did not want to see a recurrence. They were not a cohesive group but rather a coalition of individuals (such as James R. Bratton, James L. Orr, and Preston Brooks) whose opinions sometimes clashed. The third faction, the unionists, had declined in numbers since the 1830s; however, Benjamin F. Perry, James L. Petigru, and John B. O'Neall still could be counted on to oppose secession. Like the cooperationists, not all unionists agreed. A few were diehards, but some would go along with secession if slavery were threatened. On one issue all three factions agreed: the institution of slavery was essential to the well-being of the state of South Carolina.[63]

When the General Assembly met in December 1850, radicals had majorities in both the house and senate and elected one of their own, John H. Means of Fairfield District, governor and Robert B. Rhett to the U.S. Senate. The legislature authorized a $350,000 ($6.8 million) appropriation to purchase weapons and munitions to be used to defend the state. That large sum, greater than the annual budget for 1850, necessitated a 50 percent increase in all state taxes.[64]

On the question of secession, the legislature took several steps that would carry the state to the brink. First, it issued a call for a Southern Convention to meet in Montgomery, Alabama, in January 1852. Meanwhile, elections would be held in February 1851 for a state convention that would meet in April 1852 to decide South Carolina's course of action. Elections were also set for October 1851 to chose delegates to the Montgomery convention.

The radicals won about two-thirds of the seats in the February elections for the state convention that was still more than a year away. Their success was probably due to light voter participation. Turnout was low across the state, and in Horry District the polls did not even open. Meanwhile, the reaction of the rest of the southern states to South Carolina's call for a convention was less enthusiastic. Once again the radicals had yelled "Charge!" and galloped off on their steeds, only to look back and see that no other southern state was following the "mighty warriors of Palmettodom."[65]

Silence or condemnation from the rest of the South did not deter the radicals. They took control of most of the local Southern Rights Associations as cooperationists either dropped out or were ignored. In May 1851, 442 delegates from thirty-nine associations gathered in Charleston. The Beaufort association's statement of principle contained the following:

> We, the people of Beaufort District, in this our primary assembly, do declare: That we believe that Abolitionism, in common with Socialism, Communism, and Agrarianism, is the natural fruit of a spirit of infidelity. . . . That we regard domestic slavery as the great safeguard of political freedom. . . .
>
> Therefore it is now the solemn duty of the Southern States to sever the formal tie that binds us to a Union already practically sundered, and to unite in a slaveholding Confederacy, maintaining as a fundamental principle, the perpetual recognition of that institution.

There was not a delegate in Charleston who would have disagreed.[66]

The cooperationists, having been bloodied in the February elections, decided to make the October canvass a referendum on separate state action. They held two statewide meetings and, for once, organized their efforts. Unionists threw in their lot with the cooperationists. The radicals dared not back down from the challenge. Throughout the summer and fall of 1851 the campaigning was continuous and brutal. The state's newspapers took sides: the *Mercury* (Charleston) and the *Advertiser* (Edgefield) supported the radicals, while the *Daily South Carolinian* (Columbia), *Courier* (Charleston), and *Miscellany* (Yorkville) advocated cooperation.[67]

The cooperationist camp was relentless in painting the radicals as madmen who, like Samson, threatened to bring down the temple of South Carolina. In the aftermath of the election, Rhett and company would whine that they lost because "alarms and falsehoods were covertly disseminated among the more ignorant class." Actually, given what Hammond called the "reckless & excited ignorance" of pronouncements by leading radicals, all cooperationists had to do was quote them accurately. When it appeared that Charleston was leaning toward the cooperationists, Edmund Bellinger of Barnwell District remarked, "The experiment of Moscow [burned during Napoleon's invasion of Russia] ought to be repeated." And there were rumors, apparently true, that Rhett was involved in some sort of plot to capture United States facilities in Charleston to try to force an armed confrontation and thereby boost the sagging radical campaign.[68]

As the summer of 1851 ended, it became clear that no other southern state was interested in following South Carolina's lead. Most accepted the compromise, although some did so grudgingly. The radicals found themselves, for once, facing a united opposition that was willing to talk tough—and sometimes a bit personal and nasty. Rhett received the supreme insult of being accused of having been born in North Carolina. It was not true, but by responding with a published genealogy he made himself a laughingstock among the state's old elite. In the upcountry the cooperationists openly played upon sectional animosity, class antagonism, and fear that secession would bring civil war. The *Southern Patriot* (Greenville) was relentless in linking secession to "the barons of the low country." "Your rulers," it chided, "are about to plunge you into the vortex of revolution." The newspaper also argued that if secession were legal for a state, then it was legal for districts and therefore Greenville reserved the right to secede from South Carolina and join North Carolina.[69]

In desperation the radicals resorted to skulduggery to try to slow their opponents' momentum. They published advertisements and sent out flyers scheduling conflicting rallies. They sent bullyboys to disrupt cooperationist gatherings. Nothing worked. When South Carolina's voters went to the polls in October, they cast their ballots for the cooperationist-unionist alliance in overwhelming numbers. Unlike the February elections in which only a small percentage of the voters had cast their ballots, turnout was heavy in all districts. The cooperationists swept Charleston and the up-country districts. Of the state's twenty-nine districts, the cooperationists carried twenty-one. They had clear-cut majorities in all ten white majority districts and ten of nineteen black majority districts, but triumphed in Edgefield by *one* vote, 939–938. The radicals took the lowcountry parishes and the middlecountry black majority districts. In St. Thomas Parish, for example, the radicals received every vote. The final tally was 25,062 to 17,617. Those opposed to separate state action won 58 percent of the vote, a landslide.[70]

When the state convention met in April 1852, the radicals were shut out of the very meeting they had orchestrated. Rhett and Gregg were given short shrift and not even allowed to address the secessionist caucus. The convention adopted an ordinance reconfirming the state's right to secede in response to illegal or oppressive actions by the federal government; however, it was deemed not advisable for South Carolina to do so in April 1852. In disgust, Rhett resigned his senate seat.[71]

After five years of rancorous and emotional debate (1847–1852), the first secession crisis was over. "Secession is dead," pronounced one of the leaders of the Southern Rights Association in October 1851, even before the April convention interred the corpse of separate state action. For the time being it was; however, South Carolina had traveled far down the road toward leaving the Union. The next journey, over terrain previously explored, would be easier and not seem quite as foreboding.[72]

The state's more responsible leaders, including radicals such as Governor Means, realized that as a people South Carolinians needed peace and harmony. The body politic had been bitterly divided over the question of secession. Other issues raised during the summer and fall of 1852 would not go away.

During the 1850s unsuccessful attempts to change the method of legislative apportionment raised the specter of sectional conflict. The only concession the black belt districts were willing to toss to the white majority in the upcountry was the division of Pendleton District into Anderson and Pickens Districts. Even after the division the inequities were glaring. The two new districts with a white population of 24,295 now had seven representatives and two senators while the two lowcountry districts of Charleston and Colleton with a white population of 26,795 had thirty-two representatives and thirteen senators. Such was the legacy of the Compromise of 1808, an agreement that Calhoun had blessed as being almost on a par with holy writ. It would not be undone before 1860 because legislators realized the "common internal racial and external political danger" the state faced.[73]

An unreal sense of calm, akin to that in the eye of a hurricane, descended upon the state. The disputes over apportionment and the popular election of governor and presidential electors did not generate the hostility and animosity they once had. South Carolinians were emotionally drained from the struggles of the first secession crisis. And they did not perceive any untoward actions in Washington. In fact, just the opposite occurred. President Franklin Pierce, although a New Englander, was prosouthern in his policies. Congress passed the Kansas-Nebraska Act (1854), which would let the people of the states created out of the territory decide for themselves whether or not they would be slave or free states. In effect, the act repealed the Missouri Compromise, which had set northern limits on slavery. Southerners rejoiced. Kansas could be a slave state.[74]

Across South Carolina thousands of dollars were raised and men volunteered to go west to assist proslavery settlers. Fifty residents of Edgefield District agreed to emigrate and so did twenty from Chester. In Darlington, A. J. Hoale and Betty Brunson married and moved to Kansas (eighteen months later they were back home). Companies of armed Carolinians from Sumter and Beaufort shipped out for Kansas. In May 1856 the Beaufort company, the "South Carolina Bloodhounds," participated in the proslavery forces' raid on the free-soil capital at Lawrence, seized the Free State Hotel, and raised over it the palmetto flag. The violence escalated with John Brown's retaliatory raid, and "Bleeding Kansas" became a symbol of the struggle between North and South.[75]

In speech after speech northern members of Congress denounced the deteriorating situation in the West, but none more so than Sen. Charles Sumner of Massachusetts. On 19 May 1856 he damned those who supported slavery in Kansas and made a vicious verbal attack on South Carolina's senator A. P. Butler and the state itself. Sumner mocked the aged South Carolinian's unfortunate habit of expectorating when he spoke and said that although Butler considered himself a knight, he had "chosen a mistress to whom he has made his vows, and who, though ugly to others, is lovely to him; though polluted in the sight of the world, is chaste in his sight—I mean the harlot slavery." It was such a mean-spirited speech that even some of Sumner's constituents were appalled.[76]

Congressman Preston Brooks of Edgefield District, a cousin of Butler's, was irate. He decided that since Sumner was a social inferior, he would not challenge him to a duel; rather, he would cane the man who had insulted a kinsman and Mother Carolina. Three days later Brooks, accompanied by South Carolina congressman Lawrence M. Keitt, entered the Senate chamber and beat Sumner senseless. The Brooks-Sumner affair made Sumner a martyr in the North and Brooks a hero in the South. The Carolinian later wrote that "fragments of the stick are begged as sacred relics." The *Edgefield Advertiser* editorialized that "our Representative did exactly right; and we are sure that the people will commend him highly for it," which they did. Admirers from all over the South sent him canes, silver loving cups, and pledges of financial support for legal fees. Special meetings in South Carolina towns adopted laudatory addresses. The outpouring of southern support further exacerbated sectional feelings.[77]

Meanwhile, in Washington the House of Representatives voted to expel Brooks

The Brooks-Sumner Affair. *Southern Chivalry—Argument versus Club's,* lithograph by J. L. Magee. Courtesy, the Print Collection, Miriam and Ira D. Wallach Division of Art, Prints and Photographs, the New York Public Library; Astor, Lenox and Tilden Foundations.

and censure Keitt. Although the House did not have the necessary two-thirds vote to oust Brooks, he took the majority vote as an act of censure and resigned his seat. So, too, did Keitt. Special elections were set for the summer. There was no opposition, but the press wanted a good turnout. The real issue, said the *Sumter Watchman,* was "between Massachusetts and South Carolina—it is North and South—it is Abolitionism and Slavery!" In July nearly eight thousand voters in Brooks's congressional district went to the polls to show their support; the congressman received every vote save one, a blank ballot. Keitt was also reelected with ease.[78]

In the midst of the Brooks-Sumner brouhaha, for the first time in decades, South Carolina sent delegates to the National Democratic Party convention. Even though the state had cast its electoral votes for Democrats most of the time, it had avoided any formal participation in the party. Pickens, Orr, and other supporters of the national party were convinced that they could best protect South Carolina's interests by working within the party. They were disgusted with Rhett and the Southern Rights Democrats with their "loudly professed provincial patriotism." Hammond viewed the state's radicals and their fiery rhetoric as little more than "*recruiting sergeants* for Seward [and the Republican Party]."[79]

For a while it looked as if the strategy of Pickens, Orr, et al. would succeed. Orr was elected Speaker of the House of Representatives in 1857. Unfortunately, a series of events inflamed public opinion on both sides of the Mason Dixon Line as the nation began to lurch toward disunion. The Republican Party, with its opposition to the expansion of slavery in the territories, made a strong showing in its first national election (1856). Gov. James H. Adams recommended the reopening of the for-eign slave trade to give more nonslaveholders the opportunity to become masters, which kindled a fierce debate in the South (1856). The Supreme Court ruled in the Dred Scott Case that the Missouri Compromise was unconstitutional (1857). South-erners were elated—Calhoun had been right all along. Slavery followed the flag. James H. Hammond, now one of South Carolina's senators, delivered a speech (1858) in which he said that the North "dare not make war on cotton. No power on earth dares make war on it. Cotton *is* King." Later in the same speech he asserted that every society had its "mud-sills" and the South's were slaves. Eighteen months later (1859) John Brown launched his raid on Harpers Ferry, Virginia.[80]

South Carolina and the rest of the South reacted in fear and panic over the abo-litionist-financed expedition to incite servile insurrection. The radicals reacted swiftly to what they viewed as a godsend. Newspapers fueled the panic by conjecturing if this were but the first of a series of attempts to bring race war to the South. A map found in Brown's possession had mysterious X's on it, but some papers superim-posed census figures over the marks and determined that the state's most heavily black majority districts were intended targets. Cooperationists and unionists were quick to proclaim their support of the state and its "domestic institution of African slavery," even if that meant disunion.[81]

Immediately vigilante committees appeared in almost every community in South Carolina. Anyone from the North or any stranger just passing though was suspect. Individuals were beaten, interrogated, tarred and feathered, and forced to leave the state. When the General Assembly met in December 1858, it passed several laws de-signed to discourage outsiders from traveling through South Carolina. One required traveling salesmen to purchase special licenses, post $3,000 ($55,000) bonds, and obtain references from two South Carolinians; another levied a $100 ($1,835) daily fee on circuses. It became unlawful to make available to slaves anything (especially reading material) that might demoralize them and make them unhappy with their lot.[82]

In this post-John Brown atmosphere South Carolinians chose a group of moder-ates to attend the Democratic national convention that would be held in May 1860 in Charleston. When the convention refused to adopt a plank requiring Congress to pass legislation protecting slavery in the territories, the Alabama delegation (led by former South Carolinian William L. Yancey) walked out. Seven other states of the lower South, including South Carolina, joined the exodus. Later in the summer the National Democrats reconvened in Baltimore and Southern Democrats in Rich-mond. Between the conventions a new slate of delegates was elected and the radi-cals seized control. In Richmond, with Rhett among the delegates, the South Carolinians' reception was underwhelming. The National Democrats nominated Stephen A. Douglas. All of the protesting states except South Carolina had gone from Richmond to Baltimore to seek to be reinstated in the party. When they were rejected, they held a rump convention and nominated John C. Breckenridge. With the Democrats divided and a third party candidate, John Bell, in the race, it was obvious to most that the Republicans would win the 1860 election.[83]

In South Carolina the radicals thought they were in control, but behind the scenes a group of conservatives were plotting. They were determined that when the state seceded (and most of them had come to accept that as inevitable) South Carolina would not be alone as it had been in 1832–1833. To assure this they felt that they, not Rhett and his hotheads, had to be in charge. In September the 1860 Association was formed in Charleston with William D. Porter as its president. Its membership was drawn from the state's elite and included individuals with a variety of views, but most were old cooperationists. They believed that the only way they could create a unified South Carolina was to adopt the radicals' position that the election of Abraham Lincoln would mean that South Carolina would secede. Hammond argued in vain that using Lincoln's election, a nonconstitutional issue, as the basis for secession would make the state, once again, look foolish. During the fall of 1860 most moderates in the state accepted the premise that if Lincoln were elected, then separate state action was justified. Unanimity was more important than standing up for principles.[84]

Since its founding in 1854 South Carolinians had viewed the Republican Party as anathema. States Rights Gist of Union District described it "as a fungus which will continue to grow and ultimately elect a President." To H. Perkins Hoyt of Laurens, it was "that foul, God-defying party." The Reverend Richard Furman of Greenville told his white audiences that if Lincoln were to be elected, "every negro in South Carolina and every other Southern State will be his own master; nay, more than that, will be the equal of everyone of you. If you are tame enough to submit, abolition preachers will be at hand to consummate the marriage of your daughters to black husbands." Congressman John D. Ashmore voiced similar sentiments. The equation was simple: the election of Lincoln equals the victory of abolitionism, which adds up to Africanization.[85]

Newspapers throughout the state seemed to be in competition with one another as to which one could print the latest reported atrocity committed by a slave somewhere in the South or the direst prediction of what would follow Lincoln's election. The *Keowee Courier* (Pickens District) said that the goal of the Republican Party was "to bring the negro into equality, contact, and rivalry with the laboring white," and the *Camden Weekly Journal* said that the victory of Lincoln and abolition would mean that the "races would flow together." The message got through. In lower Richland District, Keziah Goodwyn Hopkins Brevard wrote in her diary after learning of Lincoln's election: "The die is cast. 'Caesar' has past the Rubicon.' We now have to act. God be with us in my prayer and let us all be willing to die rather than free our slaves." Later she wrote, "I do not go for mixing the two races."[86]

The October legislative elections were surprisingly quiet. Sectionalism was sel-

South Carolina Congressmen Resign. Top: Lawrence M. Keitt, John McQueen, Milledge L. Bonham. Middle: James Chesnut, James H. Hammond. Bottom: William W. Boyce, John D. Ashmore, William P. Miles. *Harper's Weekly,* 22 December 1860. Courtesy, South Caroliniana Library.

dom an issue, but when it was, radicals usually lost. The General Assembly met in Columbia on 6 November to choose the state's presidential electors. Then, rather than adjourning, it waited until the results of the election were known. Within twenty-four hours South Carolinians' worst fears were confirmed: Lincoln had been elected. In Charleston federal district judge Andrew G. Magrath ripped off his robes, announced his resignation from the bench, and walked out of the courtroom. His actions electrified the state because he had long been an opponent of separate action. In Washington the state's congressional delegation resigned. In Columbia the legislature called for elections to a state convention to be held in Columbia on 17 December.[87]

Delegates to the Secession Convention assembled in Columbia, with preliminary sessions held in the First Baptist Church. The momentum for secession, now that the moment had arrived to make a decision, began to falter. It had become clear during the fall that no other southern state would take the first step. The old fears about the state's being isolated resurfaced. Columbia was no hotbed of secession, and its most prominent citizen, Wade Hampton, was less than enthusiastic about disunion. Rumors circulated that smallpox had broken out in the capital and that the convention should be moved to Charleston. There may have been one case in the city, but by moving to Charleston those favoring secession would be in a locale more hospitable to their ideas. With prosecession fever running high and excited crowds

Secession Notice, Columbia, 21 December 1860. Courtesy, Calhoun County Museum.

thronging the streets, 169 South Carolinians met in Institute Hall in Charleston to decide the fate of their state and the nation. The pressure for action, united action, was intense. On 20 December 1860 all 169 voted for the state to secede.[88]

Louis Grimball wrote that South Carolinians had not left the Union for *"mere abstract principle."* As the victims of northern oppression, Carolinians had taken the action to save "all that we hold most dear—our Property—our institutions— our Honor." Arthur P. Hayne, in a letter to President James Buchanan, was more specific: "Slavery with us is no abstraction—but a *great* and *vital fact*. Without it our every comfort would be taken from us. . . . *Nothing short of separation from the Union can save us."*[89]

South Carolinians left the Union in order to preserve, protect, and defend themselves, their families, their homes, and the good order and harmony of their community from the horrors they feared a Republican administration and abolition would bring: race war, economic disaster, political subjugation, and social equality. With freedom, the state's black majority would turn on its former masters and butcher them, as had occurred in Haiti. Not only would South Carolinians' capital investments in slaves be lost, but without slavery blacks would not be an effective labor force; therefore, the value of agricultural land, buildings, and machinery would decline. Working-class whites and yeoman farmers would have to compete with free blacks in the labor market. If black Carolinians were given the right to vote, their numbers would overwhelm the white minority in two-thirds of the state's thirty districts. Any statewide elections would be controlled by the black majority. Social equality would bring with it the possibility of racial amalgamation. In the aftermath of the war that followed secession, some of the worst nightmares of many a white South Carolinian would come true.[90]

Since the 1820s South Carolinians had been calculating the value of the Union. With each passing year, more and more found the Union wanting in the balance, a threat to the order and harmony of the state. In the wake of the nullification controversy, when an English visitor to Columbia asked a group of young men if they were not Americans, one replied: "If you ask *me,* if I am an American, my answer is No, sir, I am a South Carolinian." Pondering this reply, the visitor mused: "If the children of these Nullifiers are brought up in the same opinions, which they are very likely to be, here are fine elements for future disunion." And so it came to be. A decade after the death of John C. Calhoun, white South Carolinians made their final calculation as to the value of the Union.[91]

Chapter Sixteen

THE CIVIL WAR

Part I, 1860–1865

I fear that we will have a long Civil, Bloody war, and perhaps an inserections among the slave. The Lord save us from such as horrid war.
> David Golightly Harris, 22 February 1861

Two battles will close the war and our independence will be acknowledged. Great Britain and France will offer their mediation and the Yankees will gladly accept it and make peace.
> States Rights Gist, 17 May 1861

I am very sorry to hear of the death of some our men . . . but we may expect to loos a great many of our men and god only knows how many but we have to whip the yankees, let it cost what it may in men or money.
> Alsey Neves, 20 June 1862

I was sent to Columbia, where I was when the hour of liberty was proclaimed to me, in 1865. This was the year of jubilee, the year which my father had spoken of in the dark days of slavery.
> Jacob Stroyer, *My Life in the South*

We are scattered—stunned—the remnant of heart left alive with us, filled with brotherly hate. . . . Such a hue and cry—whose fault? Everybody blames somebody else. Only the dead heroes left stiff and stark on the battlefield escape.
> Mary Boykin Miller Chesnut, 16 May 1865

*T*HE PASSAGE of the Ordinance of Secession touched off celebrations by white Carolinians in every community. In Columbia the *Tri-Weekly Southern Guardian* editorialized on 25 December 1860 that "Additional zest is given to the enjoyment of this day, in the fact, that within a week, South Carolina has declared her independence." Readers were urged to say special prayers of thanks on Christmas for the reality of secession, "the great blessing just vouchsafed to us as Carolinians." In honor of the signers of the Ordinance of Secession, George O. Robinson composed "The Palmetto State Song," the first piece of Confederate sheet music.[1]

The reaction to those who had opposed secession was mixed. In Charleston, James L. Petigru steadfastly refused to forsake his unionism and remarked that "South Carolina is too small to be a Republic, and too large to be an insane asylum." His old comrade in the state's factional battles, Benjamin F. Perry of Greenville, resigned himself to secession and said that since Carolinians were "now all going to the devil . . . I will go with them." In the armed forces of the United States, all but a handful of Carolinians resigned their commissions and hurried home to serve their state.[2]

The Secession Convention, once it had passed the Ordinance of Secession, set about drafting two other documents, the "Declaration of the Immediate Causes Which Induce and Justify the Secession of South Carolina from the Federal Union" and "The Address of the People of South Carolina . . . to the People of the Slave-holding States of the United States." The "Declaration" rested its case squarely on the threats to slavery. While that upset some delegates, Lawrence M. Keitt said that slavery was "the great central point from which we are now proceeding." Ironically, the "Address," drafted by Robert B. Rhett, was more temperate. It was a restatement of South Carolina's views on the destruction of the Constitution by the North and the dangers facing the South as a minority section, and it concluded with an invitation to form "a Confederacy of Slaveholding States." The calmer tone of the "Address" was matched by the convention's choice of well-known moderates, such as James L. Orr and John L. Manning, to carry its messages to the other seven states of the cotton South.[3]

Keeping the radicals out of power was also the goal of many in the General Assembly. When the assembly met to elect a governor in 1860, Judge David L. Wardlaw wrote to a friend in Columbia: "For God's sake and the sake of our beloved state don't let Rhett be elected governor." He was not; Francis W. Pickens, now considered a moderate, was chosen. Mary Boykin Miller Chesnut was, perhaps, more observant than the state's legislators when she said that the new governor was "a fire-eater down to the ground." Pickens was just one of many South Carolinians who had undergone political transmogrifications of one sort or another in the decade before secession. James H. Hammond, the avid secessionist of 1850, was viewed as dangerously conservative by 1860. Regardless of label—conservative, moderate, radical—one must remember their South Carolina context. A "moderate" South Carolinian in 1860, such as Pickens, would likely have been a radical in most other Southern states.[4]

Those in control of the secession movement were trying to do everything in their power to present an image of calm and reason. Having quietly divorced the state from the Union, the convention now turned to trying to come to an agreement on

James and Mary Boykin Miller Chesnut. Courtesy, Mulberry plantation, Camden, South Carolina.

community property—the federal installations in and around Charleston. Three commissioners were selected to go to Washington to negotiate with the federal government.[5]

In the nation's capital William H. Trescot of Beaufort District, the acting secretary of state, was an ally of the men who controlled South Carolina's convention. He and the other Southern members of President James Buchanan's administration worked diligently (their Republican successors would say treasonously) to make secession a quick, peaceful process. For nearly two months they successfully kept the president from forcing a confrontation with South Carolina. By the time Buchanan finally decided to do something, it was too late; secession was a fait accompli.[6]

The indecisiveness of the president and the moderation of South Carolina's conservatives were overcome by events. The state's commissioners arrived in Washington on 26 December 1860; that evening, under cover of darkness, Maj. Robert Anderson, commander of the federal garrison in Charleston, moved his men by boat from Fort Moultrie on Sullivan's Island to Fort Sumter in Charleston Harbor. Governor Pickens viewed this as a hostile act and ordered the seizure of Fort Moultrie, Castle Pinckney, the arsenal, the customhouse, and the post office. The negotiations collapsed with heated charges and countercharges of broken promises. The *Charleston Courier* said that Anderson's move to Fort Sumter had "achieved the unenviable distinction of opening civil war between American citizens by an act of gross breach of faith." To both North and South, Fort Sumter became a symbol of the United States of America; the North intended to preserve Sumter and the South to eradicate it. The *Courier* was wrong when it said that the war began 26 December 1860, but realistic Northerners and Southerners realized that it was only a matter of time.[7]

By 1 February 1861 the other six states of the lower South had seceded and elected delegates to answer South Carolina's call for a Southern convention. On 4 February the convention held its opening session in Montgomery; four days later it had formed a provisional government of the Confederate States of America. The state's delegates reflected the tight control that the 1860 Association had on the secession convention. With the exception of Rhett and Keitt, the remaining six delegates were cooperationists of 1852: Barnwell, C. G. Memminger, James Chesnut Jr., T. J. Withers, W. W. Boyce, and William P. Miles. Rhett very much wanted to play a leading role in the new Confederate nation he had helped birth; however, his fellow Carolinians quashed any hopes he had of being president, or even a member of the cabinet. A majority of the delegation voted for Jefferson Davis. There would be one South Carolina place in the cabinet, and Davis asked Barnwell to be secretary of state. Barnwell demurred because the delegation wanted Memminger to be secretary of the treasury.[8]

Just as Rhett and other Southern hotspurs (notably W. L. Yancey of Alabama) were passed over for leadership positions in the new government, so, too, were South Carolina's wishes ignored during the writing of the new nation's constitution—even though Rhett was chairman of the committee that drafted the document. He and his fellow Carolinians wanted provisions included that (1) guaranteed the right of secession; (2) forbade appeals from state courts to Confederate courts; (3) counted each slave as a full, rather than three-fifths, person for congressional apportionment (thus giving the state a considerable boost in representation); (4) directed that presidential electors be chosen by legislatures; and (5) limited the Confederacy to slaveholding states. In addition they wanted stricken a provision prohibiting the reopening of the slave trade. The only item on which the Carolinians were even partially successful was the admission of nonslaveholding states by approval of a two-thirds vote in both house and senate of the Confederate Congress. When the constitution was presented to South Carolina's convention for ratification, there was heated debate. Some delegates found it "imperfect and objectionable." Rhett and others proposed amendments be made before the state ratified the document. Although most of the sessions were closed, some votes are known, and the unanimity of 20 December had disappeared. Not until 3 April 1861 did South Carolina ratify the constitution (by a vote of 138 to 21), just nine days before the first shots of the war were fired at Fort Sumter.[9]

After the breakdown of negotiations over the forts in late December, President Buchanan resolved to resupply the garrison at Fort Sumter. On 9 January 1861, as the *Star of the West* approached the harbor, it was driven off by cannon fire from a battery manned by Citadel cadets. Buchanan made no further attempts, and there the matter stood until March when the Confederate government assumed control of the military forces in Charleston and Lincoln was inaugurated. On 12 April, Anderson was given an ultimatum to surrender immediately. He refused, and several hours later, at about 4:30 A.M., Charlestonians were roused from their beds with the opening salvos of the conflict that they and their fellow South Carolinians referred to as the "civil war."[10]

After thirty-four hours of steady bombardment, Anderson surrendered Fort Sumter on 14 April. In the North, Lincoln issued a call for 75,000 volunteers, and that triggered the secession of the four states of the upper South. In South Carolina a carnival-like atmosphere prevailed as "all the agreeable people in the South" descended upon Charleston as soon as the shooting started.[11]

South Carolina had been on a war footing since December 1860 when the General Assembly passed the first of a number of acts creating a military establishment. Although it envisioned a volunteer force, the legislature authorized the governor to draft for units that did not fill their monthly quotas. Thus, a state that prided itself on individualism was willing to resort to coercion, if need be, to defend itself. Once the fighting started, the state was divided into ten districts. The Georgetown military district had difficulty meeting its quota, probably because some men were having second thoughts. "The war is assuming a rather ugly appearance," wrote David Harris in 1862. "The people are becoming alarmed. I think that war is not the game of fun that they did at the commencement." Nonetheless, most adult males shared Harris's view that "The time has come for all such as me to go to the feild & do our part for the defence of our Country. . . . Every-one should do his part."[12]

It is probable that as many as 60,000 South Carolinians fought for the Confederacy, but multiple enlistments and South Carolinians' enlisting in North Carolina units (because of bonuses) make figures uncertain. In 1860 there were only 60,000 white males of military age (eighteen to forty-five) in the state. In January 1864 a report from the Confederate conscription office said that 60,127 had responded to their country's call. There can be no question that participation was extraordinarily high. For example, the early draft laws permitted the hiring of substitutes; 7,050 Georgians and 15,000 Virginians paid someone else to fight and die for them, whereas only 791 South Carolinians did. However, South Carolina had more categories of exemptions from military duty than any other state—the most galling of which was the "twenty-nigger" exemption, which excused from service an overseer or owner on plantations with twenty or more slaves.[13]

Lancaster, an upcountry white majority district, provided an interesting glimpse of the state's support for the Confederacy. In 1860 there were 1,100 males of military age. By April 1863 another 124 were eligible for service when the area conscription officer made his report. There were 67 exemptions (26 of whom were overseers), and 35 men were medically unfit. Only 25 eligibles were not accounted

Pvt. Felix Glausier of Dorn's Mines,
Abbeville County; Company K, 15th
South Carolina Volunteer Infantry.
Courtesy, South Carolina Confederate
Relic Room and Museum.

Capt. Richard Smallwood DesPortes
of Winnsboro, Fairfield County;
Company G, 2d South Carolina
Regiment. Courtesy, South Carolina
Confederate Relic Room and Museum.

for, just 2 percent of the population. Thus, approximately 88 percent of the district's white males were in uniform.[14]

South Carolina units participated in virtually every major battle of the war (including Manassas, Sharpsburg, Gettysburg, Petersburg, Cold Harbor, Pittsburg Landing, Chickamauga, and Atlanta) and surrendered with Lee at Appomattox and Johnston at Durham Station. The details of the military campaigns in the Virginia and western theaters of the war were, for the most part, news stories to those on the home front. Except for the coast, much of the state was insulated from contact with the enemy until the last few months of the war.[15]

Within a month after the fall of Fort Sumter, Lincoln proclaimed a naval blockade and there were Union ships off Charleston. The South Carolina coast, with its numerous inlets, bays, and islands, created difficulties for the Confederate forces charged with defending the state. Charleston's defenses were strengthened, and slave labor was put to work building earthenwork forts at the entrances to Beaufort and Georgetown.[16]

Federal officials knew that in order to support the blockade they needed a supply base somewhere on the Southern coast. After considering three alternatives—two of which were Bull's Bay and Port Royal in South Carolina—the decision was made to seize Port Royal. On 7 November 1861 the fleet sailed into Port Royal Sound. The first shots were fired at 9:00 A.M. The Confederate fortifications were no match for the heavier, more numerous federal guns, and about noon the decision was made to evacuate Fort Walker on Hilton Head Island. By midafternoon the United States flag was flying over Fort Walker.[17]

A number of planters had been watching the battle and rushed to their homes to gather what they could. Those who tried to get their slaves to leave with them met almost universal refusal. Black Carolinians knew full well the meaning of what they would for generations call the "Day of the Big Gun Shoot." Beaufort's white residents boarded a steamboat and fled to Charleston. When Union forces finally entered the town on 9 November, they discovered slaves occupying their masters' homes. Looting and destruction had been widespread and, initially, Union troops joined in.

Within a matter of hours the old order disappeared under fire from the federal fleet and the defiance of black Carolinians. It was a chilling preview of what was to be. Beaufortonians in exile told tales that gave pause to the state's white minority. Mary Chesnut reported that John DeSaussure "was in a state of abject fright because the negroes show such exultation at the enemies making good their entrance at Port Royal." Her sister-in-law and aunt, "two of the very kindest and most considerate of slave-owners, aver that the joy of their negroes at the fall of Port Royal is loud and open." The resistance of Beaufort's slaves and their actions following the Union victory confirmed the secret fears of many whites. Chesnut, however, noted no changes in her own slaves. "Their faces," she wrote, "are as unreadable as the sphinx."[18]

The capture of Port Royal gave the Union not only a supply base for its blockade, but one from which it could harass the interior of South Carolina. The speed and ease of the Union victory at Port Royal caused alarm all along the coast. In Charleston government officials feared the city would fall in thirty days. Robert E. Lee, the commander of the Department of South Carolina and Georgia, was gloomy about the prospects of defending the state. There were no reinforcements available from Richmond; South Carolina would have to defend itself.[19]

Governor Pickens had been doing what he could to improve South Carolina's military preparedness, but unfortunately his personality alienated those who would have been his allies. Then came the disaster at Port Royal, the threat of further invasion, and the Great Charleston Fire. On 11–12 December 1861 a conflagration swept through the port city that destroyed 540 acres of buildings, including such landmarks as St. Andrew's Hall, Institute Hall, the Circular Congregational Church, and the Roman Catholic Cathedral of St. John and St. Finbar. The order of the community seemed to be unraveling. Although the governor was not at fault, he became an easy scapegoat.[20]

On 14 December, David F. Jamison, the president of the Secession Convention, called members of the convention back into session to deal with the "perils which now threaten the State." Since there was almost no public confidence in the governor or the legislature, the convention created an executive council of five (governor, lieutenant governor, and three members elected by the convention) and gave it virtually unlimited powers.[21]

"The Convention . . . must try and provide for the public safety. . . . The actions taken may surprise many," wrote John S. Palmer of St. Stephen's Parish, "but we feel bound to do the best." For twelve months, from December 1861 to December 1862, South Carolina had two governments: a governor and legislature elected under the constitution of 1790 and an executive council chosen by the Convention of the People. The real power lay with the council.[22]

In order to improve the state's war preparedness, the council passed a number of measures that impinged on the rights of individuals. In March 1862 a draft was implemented so that the state could fill its troop quotas from Richmond. The state was divided into four districts, each of which was to furnish 750 slaves per month for building fortifications. Cotton exports were forbidden unless the profits were bonded to purchase war materiel. Martial law was proclaimed along the coast, and for a time passports were required to enter and leave Charleston and Columbia. The distillation of grains into liquor was outlawed unless an individual had a government contract. Taverns near military encampments and installations were closed. One order in council (later withdrawn) decreed that an inventory be taken of all privately owned gold and silver with the idea that it might be melted down into coinage "if such shall be deemed necessary." Also, both the council and the convention held many of their sessions in secret. The Confederacy was a revolutionary experience, and just as South Carolina led the Southern states out of the Union, so it was in the vanguard of sacrificing the cherished Southern principle of individual independence on the altar of wartime necessity.[23]

Opposition developed almost immediately. In March 1862 Mary Chesnut compared the infighting between the council and its detractors in Columbia to the squabbling between Jefferson Davis and the Confederate Congress in Richmond. "We are so busy fighting each other," she wrote, "We forget everything out of sight. . . . Never mind the Yankees."[24]

Chesnut was right. South Carolinians expended a tremendous amount of energy in either defending or opposing the council and its creator, the convention. Its supporters, relying on Calhoun's theories, said the convention represented the sovereign will of the people. Its voice and actions were theirs. The council's opponents said that the convention had been called into existence only to determine the state's relationship with the Union; therefore, its continued existence and its creature, the council, were illegal. Public support for the council and the convention disappeared under a rising tide of criticism of the "odious despotism" and "Lilliputian Lincolnism" of the "usurpers."[25]

In September 1862 the convention reassembled, reviewed the work of the council, and voted to go out of existence on 17 December 1862. It would be up to the General Assembly to decide the council's fate. When the legislature met in December, members and Governor Pickens wasted little time. The council was abolished; a resolution censuring the convention for unconstitutional actions passed; and all measures promulgated by the council (except for contracts) were declared null and void.[26]

History has not been kind to the Executive Council of South Carolina. However, the council did what it was supposed to do. As a result of its actions, the state was much better prepared to fight a protracted war. Its conscription policy resulted in a flurry of volunteering, and the state met its quotas. The council directed that coastal fortifications be built with impressed slave labor; purchased war matériel abroad that was shipped back via blockade runners; encouraged war-related industries such as foundries and a niter works; built the *Chicora*, a warship, to defend the coast; and appropriated state funds to purchase rolling stock and build railroad sidings for military purposes. Its actions were revolutionary and, to some, arbitrary. Yet the council, like the Confederate government, realized that the exigencies of war called for strong measures. Before the war's end, the same General Assembly of South Carolina that condemned the actions of the council passed legislation limiting the amount of cotton a person could plant and directing that one-tenth of a farmer's produce be delivered to designated collection points.[27]

The Confederacy was anything but a loose federation of states. Congress enacted laws that created not only a centralized government but one that has been labeled the first modern experiment in state socialism. Jefferson Davis, as president, was a lightning rod for irate South Carolinians. James H. Hammond was convinced that

"The Yankees would not stand from Lincoln what we do from Davis." Robert B. Rhett and his *Charleston Mercury* were virulently anti-Davis from the beginning of the Confederacy. However, after losses in the West in 1862–1863, other newspapers joined the anti-Davis chorus. By 1864 the only newspaper in South Carolina that even bothered to defend the president was the *Charleston Courier*.[28]

The earliest rumors of an anti-Davis faction in the Confederate Congress centered around members of the South Carolina delegation. Congressman Lawrence M. Keitt said that "to be a patriot, you must hate Davis." By 1862, with the exception of Sen. Robert W. Barnwell, the entire delegation was in the anti-Davis camp. Those in Richmond had their position regularly reinforced by letters from home. In March 1862 Hammond wrote William W. Boyce: "Impeach Jeff Davis for incompetency & call a convention of the States." The election of Andrew G. Magrath as governor in 1864 was widely interpreted as a victory for the state's anti-Davis faction.[29]

There was opposition in South Carolina to some of the policies of the Confederate government. Although the *Lancaster Ledger* condemned conscription as "anti-republican," most Carolinians accepted it—at first. By 1863, though, draft dodging and desertion posed significant problems. In Sumter and Barnwell districts individual deserters stole at will from isolated plantations. Armed bands of draft dodgers and deserters preyed upon the countryside in Clarendon, Marion, Horry, Greenville, Pickens, and Spartanburg Districts. When the 16th South Carolina was shipped from Charleston to Mississippi, its ranks were decimated by men who slipped home to upcountry districts. In the "Dark Corner" of upper Greenville District, few men volunteered for Confederate service and conscription officials entered the area at their own peril.[30]

Resistance to the Confederacy's economic policies, although less violent, was more widespread. The impressment of slaves and provisions was highly unpopular. In 1863 the Confederacy passed a graduated income tax and a tax in-kind on agricultural produce requiring farmers to give up 10 percent annually to the government. The General Assembly passed resolutions of protest. James H. Hammond simply refused to cooperate with government officials when it came to the labor of his slaves or the produce of his plantation. When finally forced to do so in 1864, he claimed that he had been cheated. In Spartanburg District, Emily Harris wrote: "I received warning to send a fourth of our slave labor to the coast immediately. . . . I've sent my husband and that is enough for me to do." In contrast, when Lewis Wesley Rast of Lexington harvested his crop, he made the notation "Wheat belonging to the Government."[31]

Governmental intrusion into the daily lives of South Carolinians brought home the truth that the war would not be over in a few weeks, as did Union activity along the coast. In 1862 the Confederacy abandoned the forts defending Georgetown in order to concentrate its limited forces around Charleston. Discovering that the port was undefended, Union ships sailed into the harbor and took possession. As at Beau-

Robert Smalls (1839–1915) served as a second lieutenant in Company B, 33rd Regiment, United States Colored Troops. Courtesy, South Caroliniana Library.

fort, planters fled inland. For a few months Union gunboats sailed as far as thirty-five miles up the Waccamaw River, "committing great depredations . . . such as burning barns, stealing negroes and rice, etc." Until the end of the war, however, federal forces did no more than use the harbor as a safe anchorage. Even so, the fleet was a magnet for black Carolinians. Not even the hanging of six slaves trying to reach the ships stopped the exodus.[32]

Shortly after the Union success at Georgetown, a black harbor pilot, Robert Smalls, absconded from Charleston with the steamer *Planter* and made it safely to the blockading fleet. His escape made him a hero in the North, and he was rewarded with a military commission and command of the *Planter*. Smalls supplied the Union forces with valuable information about torpedo fields and the absence of Confederate defenses on the southern end of James and Morris Islands. In early June a six-thousand-man army landed on James Island. Although outnumbered twelve to one, on 16 June the Confederates defeated the invaders at the Battle of Secessionville. The enemy withdrew, but of the five hundred Confederate defenders (many of them Charlestonians), two hundred were casualties. "The war," said James L. Petigru, "begins to make itself felt very near to us."[33]

A year later the Yankees were back. An April 1863 naval attack on Fort Sumter was unsuccessful, but in July they began a campaign to capture Battery Wagner on Morris Island. On 10 July the first attack was repulsed. Then on 18 July a massive frontal assault across open terrain was carried over the battery's parapet. White

Union raid on the Combahee River, June 1863. *Harper's Weekly,* 4 July 1863. Courtesy, South Carolina Department of Archives and History.

South Carolinians were horrified and enraged to see black soldiers of the 54th Massachusetts in the thick of the fight and mounted a savage counterattack. Union casualties were heavy, and the assault was not repeated; instead, a fifty-day siege began. Under fierce bombardment, the Confederates reluctantly, but successfully, evacuated Battery Wagner and Morris Island on 7 September.[34]

The defeat at Battery Wagner, coming on the heels of Gettysburg and Vicksburg and a Union raid up the Combahee River deep into Confederate South Carolina, severely damaged civilian morale. It also placed control of the entrance to the harbor in enemy hands. Union gun emplacements on Morris Island, in coordination with the blockading fleet, commanded access to Charleston Harbor. The city's reign as the Confederacy's leading blockade-running port was over, and most Charleston firms shifted their operations to Wilmington, North Carolina. Union batteries reduced Fort Sumter to rubble. On 22 August the last gun in the fort was silenced, but Sumter was not surrendered until 1865.[35]

Also on the 22 August large Union guns began shelling Charleston as far north as Calhoun Street. Banks, hospitals, and government offices all moved north of Calhoun. The Orphan House was closed and the orphans evacuated to Orangeburg. For those residents who remained in the lower portions of the city, the frenetic social whirl of the first two years was replaced by constant dread. Alice Gaillard Palmer wrote that "we all have been made to feel quiet anxious. Our house was struck on

Saturday." The bombardment lasted 587 days, and by the time Charleston surrendered in February 1865, much of the second largest city in the Confederacy was a ghost town.[36]

The disruption of community life in Charleston was severe, but no aspect of South Carolina society was more drastically changed than the institution of slavery. When Union forces occupied Beaufort and the sea islands in the fall of 1861, they found thousands of black Carolinians who had refused to leave with their owners. Unsure as to what to do with the property of rebels, slaves and the sea island cotton in the fields were declared "contraband of war."[37]

In Washington, Secretary of the Treasury Salmon P. Chase championed a plan that would be called the Port Royal Experiment, a cooperative endeavor between private philanthropy and the federal government. An organization called the Educational Commission was formed in Boston with its primary mission being "the industrial, social, intellectual, moral and religious elevation of persons released from Slavery in the course of the War for the Union." Supported by wealthy abolitionists, the Educational Commission recruited teachers and missionaries to go to South Carolina. The commission's backers were convinced that the black contrabands, with their help, would prove to a doubting white Northern public that persons of African descent would work for a living and that they would fight for their freedom.[38]

Although there were difficulties, the black men and women of Port Royal—as much on their own as with Northern white assistance—demonstrated that the answer to both questions was yes. Whether as a hired laborer or an independent landowner, freedmen demonstrated their willingness to work as paid wage labor. They flocked to the schools with a thirst for education that amazed and gratified their teachers. In November 1862 the 1st South Carolina Volunteers (later the 33rd Infantry Regiment, U.S. Colored Troops) was mustered at Beaufort, one of the first black units in the United States Army and one of three black regiments raised in the state. In a little over a year the freedmen made Port Royal "a showcase for freedom."[39]

The Port Royal Experiment, however, was not a complete success. Land was seized by federal tax commissioners under several wartime statutes, but in March 1863 the government decided to retain much of it and sold most of the rest to private Northern investors. Only a small portion ended up in the hands of former slaves. Members of the Educational Commission moved into abandoned plantation homes to oversee the continued planting of sea island cotton and to establish schools. They also assumed, all too easily, the paternalistic roles vacated by the former slaves' previous owners. A few, who decided to become colonial-style entrepreneurs, exploited their newly free labor force. Union soldiers regularly mistreated black Carolinians. In the sale of lands the former slaves were led to believe that they could preempt forty acres of land, but the plan was never implemented. By 1864 black Carolinians at Port Royal trusted few Northern whites.[40]

On 22 September 1862 Abraham Lincoln announced that on 1 January 1863 he would issue the Emancipation Proclamation. Federally occupied portions of Louisiana and Virginia were exempt from its provisions, but South Carolina was not. On 1 January thousands of black Carolinians gathered at Camp Saxton, a Union military post. There the Reverend William H. Brisbane (a native of St. Peter's Parish who had moved to Ohio and freed his slaves) read the president's proclamation. Beyond federal lines there was little immediate impact, but black Carolinians were simply biding their time. That time came when Union armies swept into South Carolina in 1865 and tens of thousands of black Carolinians let their feet speak for them.[41]

What had been viewed as a mutual, trusting relationship between master and slave disappeared early in the war. Beaufort District planters who tried to evacuate their slaves after the fall of Port Royal were interested only in prime field hands; the elderly and disabled were to be left for the Yankees. In 1862 when Mary Chesnut told her husband that her maid complained about the lack of food, his reply was "Tell her to go to the devil—she or anybody else on the plantation who is dissatisfied. Let them go. It is bother enough to feed and clothe them now." For the most part blacks concealed their feelings, but whites wondered what they were really thinking. Chesnut reassured herself in her diary that her slaves were trustworthy and loyal; however, even her optimism was clouded by occasional doubts. She wrote that Dick, the family butler, "scents freedom in the air. . . . He is the first negro that I have felt a change in."[42]

As the war progressed dislocation, privation, and distrust undermined black-white relationships, especially the personal bond between master and slave. When white owners went off to war, wives and overseers were left in charge. While they managed to keep agricultural operations going, it was not easy. Women complained of difficulty with field hands. "The negroes are becoming so impudent and disrespectful," wrote Emily Harris. Many owners, especially those who had moved inland from the coast, found themselves with too many idle hands. They resorted to hiring out their slaves to strangers to keep them occupied and to bring in ready cash.[43]

The absence of adult white males on plantations was compounded by the lack of men to patrol rural highways. In Clarendon District one man noted that he was the only adult white male in a neighborhood containing five hundred slaves. There were reported slave uprisings in Anderson, Chesterfield, Darlington, and Sumter Districts. In Lancaster three black insurrectionists were sentenced "to be hung by the Neck until they are dead! dead! dead!!!" From the records it is not clear how serious any of these slave rebellions were, but the fear of them was very real. There was also a breakdown in civil authority as district courts ceased to function. Rules and regulations were more difficult to enforce, and black Carolinians used every opportunity to increase their abilities to control their lives.[44]

Concern about the loyalty of their slaves was just one of the many difficulties that the white women of South Carolina faced on the home front. By 1863 the effects of the blockade and a wartime economy were beginning to make life difficult for most Carolinians, with the exception of the state's wealthiest citizens. Efforts to break the blockade with new weapons of war such as the submarines *David* and *Hunley* were isolated successes; however, neither of these technological advances in warfare had any real impact on a blockade that was slowly strangling the Confederacy.[45]

Simple everyday items such as cloth, thread, and needles were in short supply. Coffee, flour, and sugar disappeared from most tables. South Carolina women became experts at recycling old clothing, paper, and metal. Recipes substituted molasses for sugar and eggs for meat. The wardrobe that Emma LeConte, a Columbia teenager, had in January 1865 was not atypical. Her underwear was made from "coarse, unbleached homespun, such as we gave the negroes formerly." She knit her stockings herself, and her shoes were "heavy calfskin." Six dresses hung in her closet (two calicoes, one homespun, one woolen, and two old, prewar silks). Genuine shortages were exacerbated by hoarding and speculation. For example, in Columbia flour and sugar had been virtually unavailable for months before Sherman's entry into the city on 17 February 1865. Yet before Union troops entered the city, locals broke into the stores on Main Street and found ample supplies of corn, sugar, and flour. Local merchants were as much the enemy as the Yankees. "Speculators and extortionists are starving us," wrote LeConte.[46]

The discomfort and privation that LeConte felt occurred at the end of the war; however, a great many South Carolinians were in distress as early as June 1861. Private charity and churches did what they could, but it was not enough. The *Lancaster Ledger* reported that the families of some of the district's soldiers were in need and urged its readers to contribute for their support. By 1863 Lancaster merchants were refusing to accept Confederate currency and speculators caused the prices of what was available to rise to unheard of heights. The problems there and in other districts were becoming critical. With its large class of working poor, the port city would seem to have been a good candidate for urban unrest. But because Charleston already had a well-established system of public assistance, it provided relief for two thousand indigents and managed to avoid the bread riots that rocked Richmond and Savannah.[47]

When the legislature met in December 1863, it passed special taxes to aid in the relief of soldiers' families. The State Board of Relief distributed grain, salt, and cloth to eligible individuals. In Greenville, Sale Days (the first Monday of each month) became Draw Days, on which hundreds of district residents obtained corn. During the last year of the war 1,000 residents of Pickens District were on charity and 3,500 dependents of soldiers received some sort of public assistance. In Lancaster 1,267 were officially destitute; across South Carolina the figure was 54,652 (19 percent of the 1860 white population).[48]

Inflation made life difficult for the families of the thousands of enlisted men who fought for the Confederacy. When David Harris went off to war, his words probably spoke for a majority of his fellow South Carolinians in uniform:

> I am called into servise. One of my hands is demanded by the Government. A tenth of all
> I make is taken for the Government. I am taxed upon all I sell, or have to sell, and still
> have to buy at these extravagent prices while the Government only gives me eleven dollars
> per month. But money is very plenty, by far too plenty. Every man, woman, child & negro
> has their pocket full. It is hard upon those who have nothing to sell, Hard upon the
> Soildiers' wive & widow who have nothing but children & they do not seem to bring
> much of a price at present.

Eleven dollars per month—that is what the Confederate States of America paid its private soldiers. (In terms of purchasing power in 1996 dollars, a private's pay declined from $197.81 in January 1861 to $3.43 in January 1865.) In October 1863 a young soldier's wife had written to a Columbia newspaper that she did not know how she could make it through the winter on her husband's army salary with wood costing $34 ($33) a cord. Before the war a cord of wood would have been priced at $1 ($18). Prices rose steadily during the war. By 1865 the 10 percent monthly increase in the general price index resulted in a level that was ninety-two times higher than the prewar base. All Carolinians by 1864 were feeling the effects of inflation and the blockade. In order to make ends meet Mary Chesnut sold eggs and butter that brought her $200 ($85) a month—but, she commented: "In what? In Confederate money."[49]

Despite the difficulties they faced, those who remained at home sacrificed what they had to support the men at the front. Two statewide organizations, the South Carolina Hospital Aid Association and the Central Association for the Relief of South Carolina Soldiers, were formed early in the war in support of South Carolinians fighting in Virginia. The former established a chain of six hospitals (eighteen hundred beds) and a central supply depot in Richmond. The latter collected food, clothing, and comfort items that were shipped to Richmond every Wednesday until almost the end of the war.[50]

In communities across the state there were women's organizations that collected food and clothing, assisted soldiers' families, staffed hospitals, and operated soldiers' rests (a nineteenth-century version of the USO). Among the various soldier-support organizations were the Aiken Relief Association, Ladies Relief Association of Spartanburg, Greenville Ladies' Aid Association, and Charleston Soldiers Relief Association. The most famous of these was the Wayside Hospital in Columbia, which was managed entirely by the women of the city, much to the chagrin of Confederate bureaucrats. Volunteers worked in shifts, tending soldiers and preparing three hundred meals a day. More than seventy-five thousand soldiers received assistance of some kind during the hospital's existence (1862–1865). Among the women who spearheaded these various efforts were Mary Amarintha Yates Snowden in Charleston, Mary Ann Wilks Duncan in Greenville, and Susan Hampton Preston in Columbia.[51]

Reports of distant battles and their attendant casualty lists reached Charleston and Columbia via the telegraph. From there the news was carried by train to other towns in the state. In Greenville, Dr. Edward T. Buist went to the railroad station and there read aloud to anxious crowds the names of those killed in action. For aged parents, wives, children, and sweethearts the lengthening casualty lists were numbing. By 1864 reactions to news of deaths indicate that the white population was in something akin to a state of shock: "Day after day we read the death roll. Someone holds up her hands. 'Oh, here is another of our friends killed. He was such a good fellow.'"[52]

The letters that families received from the front reinforced what they were hearing and seeing back home. After Spotsylvania, Private Francis Asbury Wayne Jr. of the 1st South Carolina described to his mother the carnage in graphic detail: "I fought almost ankle deep in the blood & brains of our killed & wounded. . . . Sergt. Force of our Co. was killed just by me & his blood & Brains poured on my right leg & shoe. Such is war, *in reality*." After being transferred from Charleston to Virginia, William C. Leak wrote his wife and children: "I will tell you that this thing called war is an awful affair." Similar letters received at home made it obvious that the war was not about parades and flags. It was about hunger, exhaustion, loneliness, fear, and death. Stoically South Carolina women persevered. Many would have seconded the sentiments of Emily Harris upon hearing from her husband: "He is in low spirits. I am very sorry for him, I can only help him by trying to do my duty at home." Letters from loved ones in uniform were welcome, no matter how distressing the contents.[53]

After the Union victories at Gettysburg, Vicksburg, and Battery Wagner and the raid up the Combahee River, most Carolinians realized that their cause was lost. In caring for wounded soldiers at railroad stops across the state, the women of South Carolina came face to face with the brutality of the war—much as their descendants would in the 1960s with televised reports of the Vietnam War on the evening news. Yet for another eighteen months they soldiered on doggedly. However, under pressure from increasingly grim news from the front and the deteriorating situation at home, South Carolina's social fabric began to rend along class and sectional lines.

The idea that it was a "rich man's war and a poor man's fight" surfaced during the first year of the war, but it did not become a serious problem until after 1863. The inequities of the draft and the impact of inflation and food shortages all fell on those least able to help themselves. Middle-class and yeoman whites reacted bitterly against the elite they blamed for leading them into war. A group of South Carolinians who deserted to the enemy on James Island in 1863 reported that their officers did not treat them properly: "We are compared to niggers." How else could they feel when members of Charleston's elite hoped that the war would kill off the mem-

Map 16: Sherman's march through South Carolina. Based on B. H. Liddell-Hart, *Sherman: Soldier-Realist-American* (New York: Frederick A. Praeger, Publisher, 1958) and James McPherson, ed., *The Atlas of the Civil War* (New York: Macmillan USA, 1994)

bers of the city's working poor and the Confederacy paid a slave owner $11 per month for the use of a slave's labor—the same as a white private? Upcountry folk were irate at the open, frivolous social scenes in Charleston and Columbia when in one upcountry village there were eight war widows, the eldest of whom was only twenty-eight.[54]

The animosity sometimes turned personal and violent. In Spartanburg in 1863 James H. Carlisle, the secretary of the Secession Convention, overheard the barbed comment "There's one of the fellows got us into this trouble." In Marion District, Alfred W. Bethea, a member of the convention, was killed by a band of armed deserters. In November 1864 Wade Hampton's Columbia home was robbed and antiwar graffiti painted on the walls. With William Tecumseh Sherman and his troops marching on Columbia, Col. A. R. Taylor issued orders for members of the 23d South Carolina Militia to appear at the courthouse or face arrest. He received anonymous death threats and warnings that if he implemented the order his house would be burned down. Law and order in Charleston and Columbia were only words. South Carolina's war-ravaged society was on the verge of collapse.[55]

As 1864 ended, Sherman was in Savannah poised to enter South Carolina, but the state's leadership seemed incapacitated by the threat. Edward McCrady of Charleston was "sorely troubled at the levity of our Legislature in these momentous times. It seems to me like the recklessness of sailors when shipwreck seems inevitable." There was continual bickering between state officials and Confederate military authorities. The Richmond government sent Gen. Wade Hampton and some cavalry as a show of support, but nothing more. Neighboring Georgia refused to send its troops across the Savannah, just as South Carolina had refused to help defend Atlanta.[56]

With a force of fewer than twenty thousand effective soldiers (many of them sixteen to seventeen years old and others over fifty), Gen. P. G. T. Beauregard had to decide where to place his troops. He finally apportioned them among Charleston, Augusta, and Columbia. The undermanned, ill-equipped, divided Confederate army was no match for Sherman's sixty thousand well-seasoned veterans.

On 1 February 1865 the Union army crossed the Savannah River into South Carolina. Except for battles at Rivers Bridge (Barnwell District) and Aiken, there was little resistance other than sniping and rearguard action. The federal juggernaut overwhelmed the Confederates at Rivers Bridge, but at Aiken, Gen. Joseph Wheeler's cavalry routed the Yankees and sent them scuttling back to Sherman's main force. As the Union army marched toward Columbia, it left in its wake a swath of destruction thirty miles wide. The towns of Robertville, Hardeeville, Gillisonville, Grahamville, McPhersonville, Springfield, Hickory Hill, Purrysburg, Lawtonville, Barnwell, Blackville, Midway, Orangeburg, and Lexington were looted and torched. So, too, were most farms and plantations. On 15 February, Sherman reached the Congaree River (see Map 16).[57]

The situation in refugee-swollen Columbia was totally out of control. The city's population in 1860 had been eight thousand; in 1865 it was three times that. Every building in the city was filled to capacity with women, children, and the elderly. Friends from the coast had sent their valuables—silver, furniture, paintings, books, wine, and the bells of St. Michael's—for safekeeping. The vaults of the city's seventeen banks were crammed with securities, gold, silver, and jewelry. Everyone thought that Columbia was one of the safest places in the Confederacy.[58]

Union Forces enter Cheraw (Chesterfield County), 3 March 1865. *Frank Leslie's Illustrated Newspaper*, 8 April 1865. Courtesy, South Caroliniana Library.

Thousands fled the city via the Charlotte railroad and any other available conveyance. Looting became general, and an explosion at the South Carolina Railway Depot killed thirty. General Beauregard ordered that cotton be taken from warehouses and burned to keep it from falling into Union hands. Confederate forces evacuated the city on the morning of 17 February 1865. Shortly thereafter Mayor Thomas Jefferson Goodwyn rode out to surrender the city to the advancing Union forces. When the tired and hungry bluecoats entered the city, they were greeted by civilians ladling out copious quantities of whiskey. Before he evacuated the city, Hampton had countermanded Beauregard's order about burning the cotton, but some had been set afire anyway.[59]

Broken cotton bales, wooden roofs, drunken soldiers, and gusting winds were a recipe for disaster. By dusk the occupying army was a drunken mob and fires had broken out in several parts of the city. Some citizens were protected in their homes by Union guards, but others were driven into the streets by abusive soldiers. It was a night of terror, likened to Dante's *Inferno*. Something akin to a firestorm devoured over thirty-six square blocks, about one-third of the city. When dawn broke, dazed Columbians could see nothing but a forest of broken chimneys and piles of rubble. The business district and portions of the best residential areas were gone, but miraculously not a single Columbian had been killed. On 20 February, Sherman's army left Columbia and marched toward North Carolina, inflicting similar damage on portions of Winnsboro, Camden, Rocky Mount, Hanging Rock, Chester, Cheraw, and Florence.[60]

Charleston also surrendered on 17 February 1865, and like Columbia, it was the scene of looting and disorder. There were fires throughout the city, and explosions at the Northeastern Railroad Depot killed 100–150. Most of the occupying troops were men from the 21st United States Colored Regiment, and as they entered the city, black Charlestonians greeted them with joy.[61]

Georgetown was occupied on 25 February. In April, using it as a base, Gen. Edward H. Potter began a raid that carried him as far inland as Sumter District. There he destroyed most of the South's surviving railroad locomotives and rolling stock and fifty-one thousand bales of cotton. When he returned to the coast, some five thousand black Carolinians followed him.[62]

Lee surrendered at Appomattox on 9 April 1865 and Johnston at Durham Station on 26 April. The war was over, but there was one last military action. In early May, Union cavalry under the command of Maj. Gen. George Stoneman conducted a raid through the upcountry towns of Spartanburg and Greenville in search of Jefferson Davis. The last cabinet meeting of the Confederate States of America was held in Abbeville on 2 May, but Davis was already in Georgia when Stoneman entered South Carolina.

Men in gray reacted differently to the war's end. At Appomattox neither Lt. William G. Hinson nor Brig. Gen. Martin W. Gary of the 7th South Carolina Cavalry could believe what was happening. Gary cursed while his hardened veterans wept. David Harris had been sent home to get another horse and was cut off from his unit. On 21 April the news reached Spartanburg of Lee's capitulation and Johnston's impending surrender. "At least, I am relieved from the army at present. . . . I am now going back to work instead of to war. I think I will like it best."[63]

Not many white South Carolinians, especially women, were as philosophical as Harris. Four years of desperate struggle and sacrifice had not brought victory. Many held a deep-seated resentment against their enemies whom they variously characterized as "fiends," "vandals," "despots," "tyrants," "ruffians," and "Huns." No one expressed the animosity the vanquished felt more forcefully than Emma LeConte: "A sea rolls between them and us—a sea of blood. Smoking houses, outraged women, murdered fathers, brothers, and husbands forbid such a union. Reunion! Great Heavens! How we hate them with the whole strength and depth of our souls!"[64]

The war that had been inevitable once South Carolina seceded in December 1860 had come home with a fury. Major portions of Charleston, Columbia, and twenty-one villages lay in ruins. The state's war debt was $2,621,740 ($24.3 million), but that did not include losses of its investment in the Bank of South Carolina or various railroad stocks. With emancipation, the $296,870,400 ($5.4 billion) capital invested in human property, nearly one-half the state's total wealth in 1860, was gone. By 1867 land values had declined 60 percent. In terms of livestock (horses, cattle, mules, sheep, swine, and milk cows), the state suffered greater losses than any other Southern state. The state's leaders, said William J. Grayson, had misled the people

Columbia after the fire of 17 February 1865. Courtesy, South Caroliniana Library.

"to plunge into the volcanic fires of revolution and war," promising them that "not a drop of blood would be spilled; that no man's flocks, or herds, or negroes, or houses, or lands would be plundered or destroyed."[65]

As staggering as the property losses were, the toll in human lives was even greater. After the state seceded, South Carolina's leaders stated repeatedly that there would be no war. In 1860 there were 60,000 men of military age (eighteen to forty-five). Actual recorded deaths total 18,666, and there are indications that the total may have been as high as 21,146. That means that the equivalent of between 31 percent and 35 percent of South Carolina's 1860 young adult white male population died in the war. (In contrast, only 4,129, or 1.05 percent, of the state's male population perished in World War II.) While one in every nineteen white Southerners died in the Civil War, one in every fourteen or fifteen white South Carolinians were killed.[66]

Some communities were hit harder than others as units were recruited by towns and districts. Of the 1,001 men from Lancaster District, 282 did not return home. The Georgetown Rifle Guards went to war with 125 men on the rolls; only 10 of them survived unscathed. Maxcy Gregg's Brigade suffered 1,279 killed and 3,735 wounded. Of the 26 Confederate units that suffered at least a 50 percent casualty rate in a single action, 6 were from South Carolina: the 17th and 23d South Carolina at Manassas, 1st South Carolina Rifles at Gaines' Mill, 1st and 12th South Carolina at Second Manassas, and 7th South Carolina at Sharpsburg. A Darlington District family, the James Kellys, had six sons in uniform, but only two got back unharmed; one was known to have died and another was disabled. The remaining two, said a sister, "we never heard from again" (recent records reveal that both died— one in battle and another in a prisoner-of-war camp).[67]

South Carolina lost a generation of young men in the war that its leaders swore would never take place. Of those who returned, hundreds were permanently disabled. Among those who survived and their families, surely some must have thought about the bitter irony of Francis W. Pickens's November 1860 oratory as he urged the state to secede: "I would be willing to appeal to the god of battles—if need be, cover the state with ruin, conflagration and blood rather than submit."[68]

Three times in a century and a half South Carolina's elite led its people into a revolution to preserve the order and harmony of their community: 1719, 1775, 1860. Keenly aware of their heritage, the men of 1860 knew that their forebears had succeeded by daring the odds, by being willing to take risks. In 1860 they gambled on their future and that of their children—and lost. The good order and harmony of the society they sought to protect and preserve had disappeared even before Appomattox. South Carolinians were willing to sacrifice cherished principles (independence, property rights, republicanism) in order to preserve their society. Some, such as James H. Hammond and William H. Trescot, condemned the trampling "on private rights in order to meet public ends," but in the maelstrom of war their protests were not heard. The revolution that Carolinians launched in 1860 assumed a life of its own, one they could not control. It ended, not in victory as had those of 1719 and 1775, but, as Joel R. Poinsett had feared it would, in "defeat and humiliation."[69]

Chapter Seventeen

THE CIVIL WAR

Part II, 1865–1877

For us the war was not ended. We had met the enemy in the field and lost our fight, but now we were threatened with a servile war, a war in which the negro savage backed by the U.S. and the intelligent white scoundrel as his leader was our enemy.

Thomas Lowndes Pinckney, "Reminiscences"

The slaves in South Carolina having been emancipated by the action of the United States authorities, neither slavery nor involuntary servitude . . . shall ever be re-established in this State.

Article IX, Section 11, Constitution of 1865

The general interest of both the white man and the negro requires that he should be kept as near to . . . the condition of slavery as possible, and as far from the condition of the white man as practicable.

Edmund Rhett, 14 October 1865

It is a patent fact that, as colored men, we have been cheated out of our rights for two centuries. . . . Nearly all the white inhabitants of the State are ready at any moment to deprive us of these rights, and not a loop-hole should be left that would permit them to do it constitutionally.

Francis L. Cardozo, 13 February 1868

We do not mean to threaten resistance by arms. But the white people of our State will never submit to negro rule. We may have to pass under the yoke you have authorized, but by moral agencies, by political organization, by every peaceful means left us, we will keep up this contest until we have regained the heritage of political control handed down to us by our honored ancestry.

The Respectful Remonstrance . . . of the White People of South Carolina (1868)

WAR COMES in many forms, and armed combat is just one of them. White South Carolinians may have taken off their uniforms in 1865, but they did not stop fighting for the right to control their own affairs and restore order and harmony to their community.

The study of people's warfare, or insurgency, is much in vogue in the post-cold war world. Until the 1970s little attention had been paid to the American Revolution in South Carolina as an almost textbook model for partisan warfare. Similarly, studies of Reconstruction in South Carolina have focused on why Reconstruction failed. Not until recently has there been a modern study on how the white minority triumphed. White South Carolinians were able to regain control of the state because they mounted an insurgency against what they viewed as an alien government imposed upon them by a conquering foe. From 1865 until 1877 they successfully prosecuted what today would be called an insurgency, or a people's war, to accomplish what they had failed to do through secession and civil war.[1]

No sooner had Sherman left the state than whites made it plain that they were going to try to do things their way. Gov. Andrew Magrath called for a special session of the General Assembly to convene in Greenville on 25 April, but only a few legislators responded. In the spirit of John Rutledge, Magrath issued proclamations trying to rally the people. His actions attracted the attention of the commander of the federal garrison in Charleston, who ordered him to desist. He refused and on 25 May was arrested and imprisoned in Fort Pulaski, Georgia.[2]

There were federal troops along the coast at Beaufort, Charleston, and Georgetown. On 14 April 1865, the anniversary of the surrender of Fort Sumter, Robert Anderson (now a major general) raised the flag he had lowered four years earlier. A band played "The Battle Cry of Freedom," and more than three thousand black Carolinians in the huge crowd (including Robert Smalls and the son of Denmark Vesey) cheered lustily. In mid to late May detachments of federal troops occupied the rest of the state.[3]

In Columbia and the other towns left in Sherman's wake, feeding and housing were primary concerns. From Charlotte, Augusta, Greenville, Chester, and Sumter food and supplies were sent by wagon to the stricken capital city. Individuals who had refugeed from the coast began to filter home, and so did soldiers. "The troops are coming home," wrote Emma LeConte. "One meets long-absent, familiar faces on the streets, and congregations once almost strictly feminine are now mingled with returned soldiers." Then came the shocking reality of occupation, of learning that an army commander's word was law. In June the commander of the Columbia garrison ordered the Reverend Peter J. Shand, rector of Trinity Episcopal Church, to pray for the president of the United States (now Andrew Johnson)—as prescribed in the denomination's *Book of Common Prayer*. When the aged cleric demurred, the officer let it be known that a member of his staff would be present the following Sunday. LeConte described the scene: "At the first words the congregation rose from their knees. Mr. Shand hurried through it as if the words choked him, and at the end not one *amen* was heard throughout the Church." Earlier, St. Paul's Episcopal Church in Charleston had been closed because its rector had refused to say the prayer.[4]

These incidents should have been signals that local decisions could be overturned, but somehow many whites figured that nothing had really changed, that even slavery would continue. In late May, Robert W. Shand of Union District wrote his father: "Is it true that the negroes are freed?" In September, Francis W. Pickens of Edgefield was one of several individuals who were concerned that there were "men taking the ground that slavery was not & could not be abolished, & swearing they would never submit to it &c."[5]

Between February and June 1865 most black Carolinians learned that they were free. In May, it became army policy to announce that emancipation was a reality. Wherever Union soldiers went the word spread through the black population like wildfire. Some planters tried to ignore the realities of war and defeat and keep their slaves in bondage. One notable exception was Pickens, who called together his more than 270 slaves and told them they were free. He then announced that he would henceforth pay them for their labor. In Spartanburg District emancipation was proclaimed on 5 June. David Harris did not believe that it would have much effect, but the next day one of his field hands was gone. A month later another one disappeared. It was not until 15 August that Harris informed his remaining hands that they were free. One left immediately, but the "others wisely concluded they would remain until New years day."[6]

Just as three of David Harris's slaves slipped away quietly, so, too, did many other black Carolinians. In the rice-growing parishes the desertion was tremendous. By 1867 forty-five of fifty-one plantations on the Cooper River were idle. Generally those blacks who came into closest contact with their white owners (domestics, artisans, or hands on small plantations such as Harris's) were among the first to leave. Patience Johnson, a Laurens District house servant, declined her owner's offer of wages: "I must go, if I stay here I'll never know I am free." The very act of walking out was a visible manifestation of freedom. Thousands went to Charleston, where the white majority of six thousand in 1860 became a black majority of four thousand in 1870. About 10 percent of South Carolina's black population immigrated to Florida, Arkansas, and Louisiana where wages were higher. A handful abandoned the United States and settled in Liberia.[7]

Although many black Carolinians took off at the first news of emancipation, their freedom jaunts seldom lasted more than a few months, and some were as short as a day or so. Economic necessity forced some to reappear on their former owners' back doorsteps, but so, too, did attachment to the land. Black Carolinians had a sense of place as strong as whites'. By the spring of 1866 the majority of former slaves were living either on the plantation where they had previously labored or somewhere in the neighborhood.[8]

White Carolinians were unhappy with the idea of emancipation as a matter of principle. For the first time in their lives elite white men and women found themselves having to do manual labor. In March 1865 Malvina Gist wished she "had been taught to cook instead of how to play the piano. A practical knowledge of the preparation of food products would stand me in better stead at this juncture." Emma Holmes lamented that her brother Willie had to haul "rails on his shoulders to make a fence" and live in an old "negro house" where his wife Maria Broughton Scriven Holmes did the cooking. The family of Thomas J. Withers had been accustomed to the "greatest luxury," but the family circumstances were "so reduced" that the nineteen-year-old heir had to cut the family's daily wood supply. Holmes resented having to do housework because it tired her out and left her "no time for reading or exercise."[9]

The desertion of their slaves was a real blow to whites' egos and to their perceptions of the institution. "If they were content, happy, and attached to their masters," wrote Augustin L. Taveau of Charleston, "why did they desert him in the moment of need and flock to an enemy, whom they did not know?" Taveau concluded that he and his fellow whites had been living under a delusion. Emma Holmes described in detail the loyalty of one freed person because "Such faithfulness 'among so faithful few' deserved to be recorded."[10]

Lack of loyalty, combined with long-held racial beliefs, caused whites to become irritated with the behavior of freed persons, especially in the first year of emancipation. Black Carolinians were now free to dress anyway they chose, to travel, to walk on sidewalks without yielding to whites, to ride in horses and carriages, to own weapons, and to celebrate "their" holidays—the Fourth of July and New Year's Day (Emancipation Day). Black males got drunk, swore, and fought in public. In schools Northern teachers taught young black children to sing "Marching Through Georgia" and "John Brown's Body." On the streets and in conversations black Carolinians referred to whites as "Rebels." Wrote an early-twentieth-century black historian, "This was not diplomatic to say the least."[11]

In the first flush of freedom some blacks exhibited no hostility at all toward whites, but others were insolent, sassy, and rude. There were clashes over contracts, working conditions, and wages. In Edgefield and Barnwell Districts planters conspired to keep wages artificially low. Only the threat of the removal of those districts' labor forces to other areas caused the planters to treat their workers fairly. In some areas former slaves who refused to agree to contracts with their former owners were whipped or murdered. More than one landowner agreed with a Laurens District planter who said that workers were to "leave their freedom over the fence when they came in his yard." That attitude did not go down well with most former slaves, who wanted to set their own work schedules. In the end it was the Freedmen's Bureau (much maligned by white Carolinians) that cajoled or coerced black Carolinians to sign their contracts. And workers tended to honor those agreements.[12]

Blacks wanted to rent land outright, but whites were reluctant to do so, at least initially. Most contracts for labor involved some sort of sharecropping arrangement. In return for one-third to three-fourths of the cotton a tenant raised, he got to farm a plot of land that seldom exceeded fifty acres. In rice-producing areas, where labor was available, work was almost always for cash wages. A variation was the "two day system" whereby an individual received a plot of land (usually for food crops) by working for the landowner two days a week. Lowcountry blacks, long used to negotiating their own terms, continued to do so whether planting rice or digging phosphates. One of the interesting legacies of the task system was that the region had the South's highest percentage of landowners and the lowest percentage of sharecroppers.[13]

Laborers tested landowners and landowners tested laborers as each sought an advantage. On some plantations there was not enough work available for those who sought employment. Sometimes owners refused to renew contracts with difficult individuals. When one lowcountry planter "turned off his negroes because they would not work," his house was burned down and he was shot at during the night. Such incidents fueled whites' fears.[14]

Throughout 1865 the state's white minority lived in dread of another Haiti. That led some whites to take harsh actions, but then they lived in fear of retribution. Grace B. Elmore thought that there was a "bitter feeling & sharp antagonism between the two races." Whites were absolutely convinced that a race war would begin on the Fourth of July 1865. When that did not occur, Christmas 1865 and New Year's Day 1866 became the target dates. Even though there was considerable violence directed by whites against blacks, black Carolinians also attacked whites. In 1865 and 1866 there were racial disturbances in Abbeville, Charleston, Marion, and Orangeburg. Unfortunately for South Carolina, racist thuggery was an equal opportunity employer.[15]

Whites' animosity toward blacks was palpable. Emma Holmes considered black Carolinians "the curse that clogs us at every step." When David Harris told his slaves that they were free, he asked them to leave. When only one did, he was glad that she had and "would feel relieved if the others would go. For the negroes now, with the yankees to back them in their meanness, are worse than nothing." White Carolinians drew lines and forbade interaction that once was commonplace, such as permitting their children to play with blacks. Casual contact was seen as the first step on the road to miscegenation. Black Carolinians reacted to white hostility by separating themselves as much as possible from the world of their former owners. By so doing they also made another statement of their freedom.[16]

There was hardly a phase of life in which freed persons did not choose to sunder their connections with the world of whites. On plantations they opted to move away from the slave quarters either by building new houses or literally moving their cabins. They wanted their homes to be out of sight of the white men's houses. When offered the rare opportunity to send their children to integrated schools, most opted instead for all black ones. Except in Charleston's brothels (the most color-blind places in the state), social interaction was kept to a minimum.[17]

The most obvious withdrawal occurred in the churches. Prior to 1860 the state's denominations had thousands of black members. There were almost as many black Episcopalians as white, and a majority of Methodists were black. After the war the efforts of missionaries from Northern churches and blacks' desires to control their own services led to the creation of all-black denominations. Northern branches of the Baptist, Methodist, and Presbyterian Churches attracted black members, as did two black denominations, the African Methodist Episcopal Church and the African Methodist Episcopal Church (Zion). Denominational membership rolls reveal a black exodus of biblical proportions. In 1860 there were 46,640 black Methodists and 2,973 black Episcopalians; in 1876 there were but 421 and 262, respectively.[18]

By the end of Reconstruction there were a great many more black Christians worshipping in their own churches than there had been slaves attending church with their owners. In less than a decade membership for the predominantly black churches grew impressively: Colored Baptist Educational, Missionary, and Sunday School Convention, 100,000; African Methodist Episcopal Church, 44,000; South Carolina Conference of the Northern Methodist Episcopal Church, 26,000; African Methodist Episcopal Church (Zion), 46,000; and Northern Presbyterian Church, "several thousand." Before the war only 85,000 black Carolinians were on denominational rolls; by 1877 more than 218,000 were. Three Charleston churches—Emanuel (AME), Zion (Northern Presbyterian), and Centenary (Northern Methodist)—were among the largest congregations, black or white, in the state.[19]

The state's white Baptists and Methodists tried to keep their black members, but if blacks insisted on leaving, there was little that they could do. In Darlington a group asked for and received a dismissal from Antioch Baptist and formed a congregation called New Hopewell. Several Baptist and Presbyterian congregations remained affiliated with Southern denominations. Only in the Episcopal Church were blacks officially made unwelcome and, in some instances, literally forced out of churches where they had worshiped for years. In 1876 the Episcopal Diocese of South Carolina refused to allow St. Mark's, Charleston, (a black congregation) to be represented in the annual convention because it feared that to do so would lead to social equality and miscegenation. In 1875 the Reformed Episcopal Church entered the state and made an appeal directly to black Carolinians.[20]

Even before the first year of emancipation ended, black Carolinians found their freedom being limited. Part of that limitation, though, was self-imposed by blacks' distancing themselves as much as possible from contact with whites. Some did it out of a desire to remove themselves and their families from any reminders of slavery. In parts of the state separation was also a matter of self-protection and a way to avoid violence. It was probably the only effective way for the newly freed men and women to respond to discrimination. The withdrawal of blacks into their own communities, while giving them freedom from white supervision, tended to increase white anxiety. And as black churches became centers of political activity, whites felt that their suspicions were confirmed.[21]

It was against this backdrop of emancipation and racial tension that presidential Reconstruction began in South Carolina. On 30 June 1865 President Andrew Johnson appointed Benjamin Franklin Perry of Greenville the provisional governor of South Carolina and gave him the authority to reorganize state government and prepare South Carolina for readmission to the Union. Perry wasted no time as he wanted the state restored to the Union as quickly as possible. He called for elections to a constitutional convention to meet in Columbia in September 1865.

When the delegates assembled in Columbia's First Baptist Church, an observer would have thought he or she was taking a trip in a time machine. The state's antebellum elite dominated the proceedings in the very same location where the first sessions of the Secession Convention had been held. Under prodding from Perry, the convention reluctantly repealed the Ordinance of Secession (although the president had said they must declare it null and void) and acknowledged that slavery no longer existed. The wording, however, was an omen: "The slaves in South Carolina having been emancipated by the action of the United States authorities." Even so, there were eight delegates who voted no, the most outspoken of whom was Alfred P. Aldrich of Barnwell District.[22]

The constitution of 1865 recognized that slavery had been abolished, but not much else. In the political sphere it removed property qualifications for office, allowed the people to elect the governor directly, made districts the basis for house and senate elections (the lowcountry parishes were eliminated), and gave the governor veto power. Continuing a tradition of letting the voters have as little to say as possible about their government, the constitution was not submitted to them for ratification. President Johnson approved the constitution, and elections were held. James L. Orr of Anderson was elected governor. The men elected to the legislature and congress, like Orr, were members of the prewar elite.[23]

The General Assembly met in special session in Columbia in October 1865 on the campus of the South Carolina College—the house in the chapel and the senate in the library. Both bodies organized themselves, and the house chose A. P. Aldrich as its Speaker. The only action of the session was to ratify the Thirteenth Amendment abolishing slavery.[24]

The regular session that met in December passed what became known as the "Black Codes," white South Carolina's plan for Reconstruction. The codes were actually three separate statutes. One said that "The Statutes and regulations concerning slaves are now inapplicable to persons of color; and although such persons are not entitled to social and political equality with white persons," they did have the right to buy and sell property, make contracts, sue and be sued, and be protected in their persons and property under the law. For the first time in its history, the state defined who was a person of color (seven-eighths black) and prohibited interracial marriages. Travel was limited; freed persons were forbidden to engage in trades unless they paid exorbitant license fees; and a "judicial ghetto" was created in a system of district courts in which only blacks would be tried. No person of color could own a weapon without written permission of the district court judge (unless he were a landowner, and then he could have a hunting piece). If a freed person signed a labor contract, then he or she could not "be absent from the premises without the permission of the master." The terms *master* and *servant* were used throughout the codes as the General Assembly did everything it could to re-create the institution of slavery under another guise.[25]

One of the reasons for the codes, argued Perry, was that President Johnson had insisted that freedmen be given legal protection before a state could be readmitted to the Union. Prevailing racial attitudes considered black Carolinians to be little more developed than children; they were incapable of taking care of themselves. Therefore, according to Perry, the codes *did* protect the freedmen by making white Carolinians their legal guardians. James Chesnut and others, including Edmund Rhett, while not disagreeing with the idea behind the codes, thought their consideration in the fall of 1865 incredibly ill-timed. Rhett was convinced (correctly) that the passage of the codes would enrage the Radical Republicans and make it more difficult for the state to be readmitted to the Union. Chesnut argued that the safest course was to "repeal all laws enacted for negroes and leave the emancipated negroes and the white man on the same footing before the law." Their advice went unheeded, and Rhett's prediction proved to be accurate.[26]

At the same time the General Assembly was enacting the Black Codes, Congress was meeting. President Johnson had permitted South Carolina and the other Southern states to go their own way, but the mood of Congress was quite different. When the clerk of the House of Representatives did not read the names of the members from the former Confederate states at the opening session, there was a strong message that reconstruction of the South did not mean the return of the ancien régime.

In South Carolina the federal reaction to the Black Codes was swift. Within ten days after the General Assembly adjourned, Gen. Daniel E. Sickles, the new commander of the Department of South Carolina, declared them invalid. He further proclaimed that the laws of the state had to apply equally to all Carolinians. The state's leadership, still betting its future on President Johnson, continued to misread events in the nation's capital.

Between the president's obstinacy and his ineptness, Radical Republicans gradually gained the upper hand. In March 1866 they overrode his veto of the Civil Rights Act, which prohibited states from discriminating against their citizens on the basis of color. In June, Congress passed the Fourteenth Amendment, defining citizenship and guaranteeing all Americans equal protection under the law. The amendment was then sent to the states for ratification. Johnson made the 1866 congressional elections a referendum on which Reconstruction would prevail—his or the Radicals'. In November, Northern voters gave the Radicals an overwhelming victory with a veto-proof congress. Somehow, though, the message did not get through to Columbia.[27]

South Carolina responded to national events as if the year were still 1856, not 1866. A special session of the legislature in September 1866 tinkered with the Black Codes by eliminating references to race. Thus, it met the letter of the law of the Civil Rights Act and insured that cases would not be transferred from state to federal courts. Comments made to Northern visitors, however, left the impression that Carolinians wanted no part of rejoining the United States, "that a large majority, probably nine-tenths, of the [white] people of South Carolina, are opposed to the [U.S.] government, and look to their connection with it as the greatest calamity which could befall South Carolina."[28]

Actions spoke even more loudly than words. In many districts, especially in the upcountry, patrols once more roamed rural roads. Violence and intimidation by paramilitary groups were openly tolerated as white Carolinians tried to reconstruct as much of their pre-1860 order as they could. In December 1866, less than a month after the Radicals' triumph at the polls, the General Assembly convened. At the opening session Governor Orr denounced the Fourteenth Amendment by saying that few people in history had "been required to concede more to their conquerors than the people of the South." By a vote of 95 to 1 in the house and an unrecorded, but overwhelmingly negative vote in the senate, the legislature refused to ratify the Fourteenth Amendment. South Carolina was not alone, as all other Southern states did the same. There were some Carolinians, however, who saw the issue more clearly. Christopher W. Dudley of Marlboro District wrote Orr that he was afraid South Carolinians, by their recalcitrance, were actually inviting their own destruction.[29]

The first and second Reconstruction Acts, passed by Congress in March 1867, overturned presidential Reconstruction. With the exception of Tennessee, the act ruled that no state governments existed in the South. In their stead five military districts were created. South and North Carolina comprised the Second Military District, and General Sickles was named its commander. Requirements were established for a state's readmission to the Union: voter rolls opened to all male citizens, elections held for a constitutional convention based upon universal male suffrage, a new constitution written (including the guarantee of universal male suffrage) and submitted to the people for approval, the Fourteenth Amendment ratified, and *all* military organizations disbanded.

It would be an understatement to say that white Carolinians were in a state of shock. They ranted; they raved; they resisted. After General Sickles ruled that any taxpayer or voter was eligible to serve on jury, Judge A. P. Aldrich refused to seat black jurors and was removed from the bench. In the rest of the South whites adopted the strategy of trying to elect as many delegates as they could to their constitutional conventions so as to have some influence on the resulting documents. South Carolinians devised a totally different strategy. The second Reconstruction Act required that a *majority of the registered voters* cast their ballots in favor of a constitutional convention. Whites registered in large numbers and then boycotted the election, hoping to prevent the required majority and thereby blocking the constitutional convention. In the fall of 1867 there were 128,000 registered voters in South Carolina. On 19–20 November 1867, 56,000 voters (44 percent) stayed home. The convention passed only because 85 percent of registered black voters turned out and voted yes. The boycott had almost worked; however, because it failed, native white Carolinians had virtually no say in the writing of the state's constitution of 1868.[30]

On 14 January 1868 the constitutional convention opened in Charleston. There were 124 delegates, 73 of whom were black (closely reflecting the percentage of the black population). Of the 51 white delegates, 36 were native-born and 15 were Northern interlopers. Local whites who cooperated with the Reconstruction regime were openly derided as scalawags, and nonnatives were referred to as carpetbaggers.[31]

The constitutional convention of 1868 was remarkable, not only because of the composition of its membership but in what it accomplished. Using the Ohio Constitution as a model, in sixty days delegates crafted a document that was designed to create a new order in South Carolina based upon equal opportunity. Suspicious of white Carolinians, Francis L. Cardozo of Charleston argued that "not a loop-hole should be left" that would allow them to deprive blacks of their newly-won rights. In addition to voting rights, educational opportunities were to be available to all South Carolinians "without regard to race and color." The state's black leaders were much more conscious and supportive of the need for public education than their white predecessors had been. Said Jonathan J. Wright, "Where there is no education, vice thrives, and the people sink deeper and deeper into misery."[32]

In terms of local governmental authority, the constitution reversed a two-hundred-year tradition of centralized control in the General Assembly. Districts became counties, but the change was more than just a name (see Map 17). A three-man county board of commissioners with budgetary and taxing authority was to be elected by local voters.[33]

In many respects South Carolina's 1868 constitution was a model document. However, because it had been written predominantly by blacks, the state's white citizens refused to acknowledge it as theirs. They overwhelmingly agreed with Henry D. Green of Sumter County, who said he had no intention of obeying what was now the legal, fundamental law of the state because it was "a *negro constitution, of a negro government, establishing negro equality.*" The state's white press was unanimous in its condemnation of what it called the "Africanization" of South Carolina, and there were petitions to Congress. All, of course, were to no avail. White reactions to the convention and the constitution were the opening salvos in an unrelenting nine-year war to overthrow the Reconstruction regime. A government that is not seen as legitimate by a significant portion of its people is vulnerable to insurgency.[34]

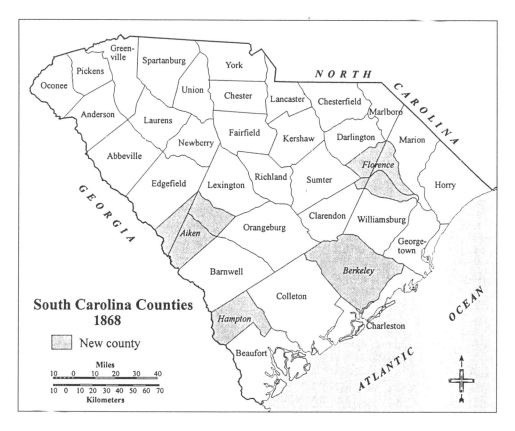

Map 17: Counties, 1868. Based on Edgar, *Biographical Directory*

The constitution was ratified by the voters of the state, and elections were held for all state offices. The newly organized Republican Party triumphed in every corner of the state. From governor to town councils, almost every officeholder was a member of the party of Lincoln. Robert K. Scott, a white Republican from Ohio who had been head of the Freedmen's Bureau in South Carolina, was elected governor. The new secretary of state was Francis L. Cardozo, a Charleston native, who became the first person of color to win a statewide office. In the General Assembly 109 of 124 members of the house (75 black, 34 white) and 25 of the 32 members of the senate (10 black, 15 white) were Republicans.[35]

The 1868 election was just the beginning. As black Carolinians began to flex their political muscles within the Republican Party, they obtained an even greater share of state offices. In December 1870 Joseph H. Rainey of Georgetown became the first black member of the U.S. House of Representatives. During Reconstruction six of the fifteen black Americans serving in Congress were from South Carolina. Persons of color occupied the offices of lieutenant governor, adjutant general, and secretary of state from 1870 to 1877 and state treasurer from 1872 to 1877. Jonathan J. Wright was one of three justices of the state supreme court (1870–1877). Had it not been for carpetbagger "Honest John" J. Patterson's buying a U.S. Senate seat in 1872, it is likely that the state would have had a black senator, Robert Brown Elliott of Beaufort. At the county office level blacks were not nearly as successful as whites continued to be elected sheriffs, clerks of court, and county treasurers.[36]

Blacks achieved greater political power in South Carolina than in any other Southern state. Between 1867 and 1876 there were 487 elections for state or federal offices. Of these, black Carolinians won 255 (52 percent). The real basis for black power was not in congress or statewide elected offices, but in the General Assembly. In the legislature the percentage of black members increased from 54 percent in 1868 to 61 percent in 1872, the high tide of black electoral success. In 1872, 81 out of 124 members of the house and 16 out of 33 members of the senate were black. With an actual black majority in the house and, with white Republicans, an effective one in the senate, black Carolinians were elected Speaker of the house (1872–1876) and president pro tempore of the senate (1872–1877). They chaired two-thirds of the committees, including most key ones.[37]

White Carolinians reacted to the rise of black Carolinians to power with growing horror. In the press and in private correspondence they wrote that civilization itself was in peril, that the black majority was out to turn South Carolina into "a new Liberia." "South Carolina is Polandized—aye worse than that—*Africanized,*" shrieked an editorial in the *Edgefield Advertiser.* Whites, native and visitor, often mocked those who now ruled the state by using racist and animal imagery. Louisa McCord described the 1868 legislature to her daughter as the "crow-congress," "monkey show," and "menagerie." Some of the most unflattering descriptions of black Carolinians came not from locals but from Northern reporters such as Edward King and James S. Pike.[38]

Denigrating and dismissing black officeholders as illiterate, venal, propertyless rogues is one of the most enduring myths of Reconstruction. Most black legislators (87 percent) were literate; more than three-fourths were property owners and taxpayers. A majority were middle-class artisans, farmers, and shopkeepers—not former field hands. At least one in four had been free persons of color before the war. Contemporary whites and their descendants either refused to acknowledge or deliberately distorted the accomplishments of the state's black leaders. In *Reconstruction in South Carolina* (1905) Cardozo, one of the state's most prominent black officials, was described as "a mulatto preacher, a man of some ability and alleged culture." Cardozo, a Charleston-born free person of color, studied at Glasgow, London, and

The General Assembly of South Carolina (1876). *Leslie's Illustrated Newspaper,* 16 December 1876. Courtesy, South Caroliniana Library.

Edinburgh and was an ordained Presbyterian clergyman.[39]

Of one charge, political inexperience, black Carolinians were guilty. Not only had they been excluded from the body politic before 1867, but once they had access to power there was considerable turnover in office. For example, some 61 percent of the members of the General Assembly were one-termers. Thus, in the House of Representatives in every session there was a group of individuals who had to learn the ropes. However, the inexperience of black voters and black politicians was not much different from that of upcountry whites during the first twenty-five years of universal white male suffrage (1810–1835). During that period it was not unusual for voters to oust 50 to 60 percent of incumbents. In fact, at no time were a majority reelected, and in 1818 only 20 percent were. There was, however, one big difference between antebellum upcountry white politicians and Reconstruction-era black politicians: the latter were thrust immediately into positions of leadership and power seldom open to the former.[40]

In the General Assembly the state's black leaders worked to establish their version of the "good order and harmony of the entire community" on the twin pillars of public education and public equality. Education, as Jonathan J. Wright had reminded the delegates to the 1868 constitutional convention, was "the foundation of all good government." Public equality was a radical idea only in that it meant civil and political equality for blacks as well as whites. It was nothing more than the antebellum republican ideal applied to all citizens, not just whites. That, of course, is what made it radical.[41]

In pushing for public equality, black Carolinians *were not* espousing social equality. In 1870 Martin Delaney, a proud black Charlestonian, said, "I don't believe in social equality; there is no such thing." In the halls of Congress, South Carolina congressman Richard H. Cain spoke eloquently for the passage of a federal civil rights act: "We do not want any discrimination to be made. I do not ask for any legislation for the colored people of this country that is not applied to the white people of this country. All that we seek is equal laws, equal legislation, and equal rights throughout the length and breadth of this land." It is doubtful that even a few white Carolinians read these remarks in the *Charleston Daily Republican* or in any of the thirty-seven other Republican newspapers of the state. But if they had, they would not have believed them. Had not the Republican legislature repealed the 1865 law forbidding interracial marriages? Did not Governor Franklin J. Moses Jr. host integrated social functions in his Columbia residence (the former home of the Hamptons and Prestons)? And the center of Republican society in the state capital was the salon presided over by the Rollin sisters, descendants of Charleston's antebellum brown elite. If anyone wanted to do state business, it was wise to pay a social call on the "Misses Rollin." To whites, political equality had already led to public equality, and they had no doubts that would lead to social equality.[42]

White Carolinians were adamantly opposed to both. One of the antebellum rationales for slavery, according to Charleston native James D. B. DeBow, was to insure that "little children of both races shall [never] be mixed in the classes and benches of the schoolhouse and [never] embrace each other filially in its outside sports." Such contact would lead to miscegenation and the amalgamation of the races. The 1868 constitution, ratification of the Fourteenth and Fifteenth Amendments, and subsequent state legislation dealing with public schools and public accommodations appeared to whites to be giant leaps toward social equality and racial intermarriage. Whites might use the term *Africanization* to describe state government, but for them its meaning went much deeper, to the very quick of their beings.[43]

To the average white Carolinian, there was no need to provide education for most blacks (especially if funded by white tax dollars). After all, were not most just field hands? If there were to be any schooling, it should be rudimentary, and there should be absolutely no mixing of white and black children in the same schools. When Charleston placed black and white children in the same school (on separate floors but with the same playground), the white community's angry outcry quickly brought about separate schools. With the exception of one integrated school in Kershaw County and several in Richland County, the remainder of the state's public schools were segregated. The establishment of a universal, publicly funded system of education was one of the major success stories of Reconstruction. Not only were black children being given the opportunity for schooling for the first time, but so were many whites.[44]

South Carolina congressman Robert B. Elliott's support of civil rights legislation was the centerpiece of this circa 1890 celebration of the contributions of black Americans titled *The Shackle Broken—By the Genius of Freedom.* Courtesy, Amistad Foundation Collection at the Wadsworth Atheneum, Hartford, Connecticut.

Not all black Carolinians patronized the public schools. Some preferred to send their children to private schools that generally were funded by Northern churches or philanthropists. During and after Reconstruction these schools provided education and training for the state's black leadership. Among these private schools were Avery Normal Institute and Wallingford Academy in Charleston; Howard School in Columbia; Mather Academy in Camden; Schofield Normal and Industrial Institute in Aiken; Brewer Normal, Industrial, and Agricultural Institute in Greenwood; Penn Normal and Industrial School on St. Helena's Island; and Brainard Institute in Chester. The state's first black college was Claflin, founded in 1869 in Orangeburg by Northern Methodists. Three years later the state began funding the South Carolina Agricultural College and Mechanics Institute as a department of Claflin.[15]

The South Carolina College, which had closed during the war, was rechartered as the University of South Carolina in 1865 and by 1867 had ten schools including

A school for black children conducted at Zion Presbyterian Church, Charleston. *Harper's,* 15 December 1866. Courtesy, South Caroliniana Library.

engineering, law, and medicine. Funding was minimal, and student enrollments were low. The 1868 constitution clearly stated that all educational institutions funded by the state would be "open to all the children and the youths of the State, without regard to race and color." With the appointment of two black trustees in 1869, the enrollment of black students seemed imminent. Several faculty resigned, and enrollments dwindled. In 1873 Henry E. Hayne, the secretary of state, became the first black student to enroll. The few white students still on campus withdrew, and the remaining members of the faculty either resigned or were dismissed. Among the new faculty hired was Richard D. Greener, the first black graduate of Harvard and a distinguished professor of philosophy and the university's librarian. By 1875 there were 233 students enrolled, but only 130 were taking college-level work; the others were in the preparatory department. The University of South Carolina was the only Southern state university open to black students, and in 1875 the student body was 90 percent black. White Carolinians considered the integration of the University of South Carolina at all levels (trustees, faculty, and students) one of the most heinous acts of Reconstruction.[46]

In 1867 black taxpayers in Columbia protested being denied access to publicly funded institutions such as the almshouse and the orphanage. At about the same time black Charlestonians protested not being allowed to ride on the city's street railway system. When denied access, they conducted one of the first recorded sit-in demonstrations. The military government then ordered officials in both cities to open the contested facilities to black Carolinians.[47]

The General Assembly in 1868 passed an antidiscrimination act that opened, at least on paper, all public accommodations to all citizens. Across the state some black Carolinians pressed for and achieved access to restaurants, bars, and saloons. When they were rebuffed, they filed suit. Numerous individuals were charged with violating the act, but there were no recorded convictions. At the Exchange Hotel in Columbia blacks could eat in the hotel's famous dining room but not relax in its billiards room because it was a "private club." Nor was it likely that they could rent a room. Hotels seem to have been one of the few public accommodations that remained segregated. In both Columbia and Charleston there were incidents in theaters when black patrons sat in front rows on the main floor and not in those in the rear or balcony. However, white Charlestonians loved the theater so much that they did not boycott it even though black Charlestonians sat wherever they wanted. It was ironic that the state's black leadership advocated equal access to public accommodations but permitted segregation in all state facilities (including the asylum and the penitentiary) except the university.[48]

When the integration of the university was coupled with other efforts of black Carolinians to obtain public equality, white Carolinians reacted by withdrawing from those segments of public life where they might have to interact with blacks. They refused to have anything to do with what they now called the "Radical University" or the School for the Deaf and Blind. In Charleston whites would not ride integrated streetcars. And, almost to a man, they refused to join integrated militia units (and all were, by law). When native whites had to deal with local governmental officials, they invariably dealt with a white Republican regardless of the office he held.[49]

The most noticeable retreat by whites was in state politics. Except for halfhearted efforts in support of reform Republican candidates in the elections of 1870 and 1874, whites simply took a walk. The state Republican Party never seriously considered trying to become a "big tent" under which whites and blacks could gather. It was without question the party of black Carolinians and was determined to strengthen its hold on the state. Republicans did what they could to dilute or eliminate white voting strength through gerrymandering districts and election fraud. Between the reality of the state's black majority and the Republicans' political machinations, few whites thought it worth the effort to vote. A number gave up on South Carolina and immigrated westward to Arkansas, Texas, and California. One émigré wrote home that he had rather "make terms with the Wild Comanches" of Arkansas "than with the hourds of Radicals" in South Carolina.[50]

While the state's black leadership enacted legislation to insure that black Carolinians had the legal right to public equality, as a rule most did not exercise that right. They wanted to put as much distance as possible between themselves and whites, and vice versa. In addition to voluntary segregation, there was segregation by class. For example, anyone could purchase a railroad ticket, but few black Carolinians could afford to travel first class. Most integrated public accommodations were in Charleston and Columbia. Elsewhere de facto segregation existed in South Carolina a generation before there was de jure segregation. Attitudes, habits, traditions, and fears of both black and white Carolinians created a color line, leading to the creation of two separate communities, one black and one white.[51]

From 1868 to 1877 the black community had the authority of government in its hands and did its best to insure that blacks' aims of public education and public equality would become permanent fixtures of the state's social landscape. The white community, though, had the power, but it took them a while to begin wielding it. As outraged as whites were on social issues, it was economic ones that opened up the way for statewide action and the eventual overthrow of Reconstruction.

Regarding taxes and what many regarded as wasteful spending, the state's white press in a seemingly endless litany decried the tax burden placed on the white population and the graft and corruption of the various Republican administrations. New programs, especially the public school system, were expensive. Taxes were raised. It was the deliberate policy of the state Republican Party to give its voters what they wanted and needed most. If that meant placing higher taxes on white landowners, so be it. The pre-1860 tax code was rewritten and all real and personal property taxed at a uniform rate. The tax burden was transferred from merchants and shopkeepers to landowners. State taxes were not particularly onerous; however, local ones could be, and often were, manipulated by corrupt Republican officeholders. One carpetbagger cynically declared that it was the policy of the Republican Party to drive white taxpayers "to the wall by taxation." In that, the radical regime was ruthlessly effective. In 1873, 270,000 acres of land were seized for taxes; the following year the total was 500,000 acres. Losing one's land was bad enough, but to have it confiscated for taxes to support the spendthrift government in Columbia was intolerable to many.[52]

The decade after the Civil War witnessed a lapse of public ethics across the United States. Graft and corruption knew neither race nor party label, but in South Carolina the Republican Party was in power, and its membership was overwhelmingly black. Republicans may have had a difficult time governing South Carolina, but they certainly had no trouble looting it. Official malfeasance, misconduct, and chicanery reached their zenith (or nadir) between 1872 and 1874. It was a sordid record unmatched by any other Southern state during Reconstruction.[53]

The administration of Robert K. Scott was so corrupt that a group of Republican legislators tried to impeach him and state treasurer Niles G. Parker in 1872. The effort failed after the governor bribed enough legislators (probably with state funds) to get off scot-free. Native South Carolinian Franklin J. Moses Jr. succeeded Scott and carried graft and corruption to new levels.[54]

In 1878 a joint legislative committee published a nine-volume compilation of what it termed "public frauds" perpetrated by the state's Reconstruction government. While the committee was selective in its findings, later historians have corroborated the magnitude of the raid on the state treasury. During one session $125,000 ($1.54 million) was spent on wine and whiskey. Furnishings purchased for the State House ended up in legislators' homes. The state printing bill soared from $21,000 ($223,000) in 1868 to $450,000 ($5.7 million) in 1873.[55]

The state's bonded indebtedness was double what it should have been. The New York firm handling the sale of South Carolina securities got governors Scott and Moses to issue twice as many bonds as the General Assembly had authorized. For example, in 1868 the legislature passed a bond issue of $1 million to reestablish the state's credit, but $2 million in bonds (guaranteed by the public credit of the state) were sold to investors. The same was true of state bonds to finance the completion of the ill-fated Blue Ridge Railroad. The "ring" of individuals involved in these bond schemes was not limited to Republican officeholders. When a taxpayers' convention met in Columbia in 1871, a New York brokerage house hired former Confederate generals Martin W. Gary and Matthew C. Butler of Edgefield County to convince delegates that there was nothing wrong with the state's finances. It is doubtful that either "first class gentleman" told his fellow taxpayers that he would receive a percentage of the profits when the value of the state's bonds rose (as they were expected to do once the taxpayers' convention blessed them). Gary was also a major player in the Blue Ridge Railroad "ring." When a reporter for the *Charleston Daily Courier* began to do some investigative reporting on the bond and railroad "rings," he was fired.[56]

White Carolinians might have denounced corruption, but they were not opposed to sticking their hands in the till or dealing with Republican officials. The administration of Charleston's Democratic mayor John A. Wagener was so graft-ridden that local white conservatives joined with reform Republicans to oust him and elect a Republican. Throughout the state there were "closet" or "economic scalawags," stalwart white Democrats who were willing to deal with Republicans (black or white) as long as their money was green. Charleston businessmen joined with carpetbaggers to obtain mining rights to phosphate deposits in the lowcountry; this cost them $40,000 ($463,000) in bribes, but their companies reaped enormous profits. Although these men placed economics above politics, they did not suffer from loss of caste or influence as did scalawags who joined the Republican Party.[57]

Corruption was the Achilles' heel of the Republican Party and Reconstruction in South Carolina. It led to divisions within the state and national parties. It gave opponents of Reconstruction a powerful weapon which they used effectively in the Northern press and in Washington. Sadly, corruption undermined programs designed to help black Carolinians get ahead. The widely praised public school system was hampered at the local level by school commissioners who squandered funds.

Corruption in the state militia kept it from becoming the effective military force that the Reconstruction government desperately needed to combat insurgency.[58]

One program that worked in spite of mismanagement was the South Carolina Land Commission. Created in 1869, it immediately became the center of controversy, but by 1872 the commission had been reformed. The South Carolina Land Commission purchased tracts of land and resold them to small farmers for modest sums at interest. The impetus for such an agency was the desire of freedmen to own their own land, to be independent. By 1877 some two thousand small farmers, most of them black, had purchased commission lands. Today in Greenwood County residents in the Promised Land Community live on land their forebears purchased from the South Carolina Land Commission. No other Southern state was as successful in making land affordable for its former slaves.[59]

Although not state-run, the Freedmen's Bureau was disliked by more white Carolinians than any other program. Convinced that it was staffed by flaming abolitionists bent on inciting a race war, whites denounced it at every turn. Yet had it not been for the bureau and other federal relief efforts, thousands of South Carolinians (black and white) probably would have starved to death in the three years after the war. In Charleston in June 1865 at least 20,000 persons were receiving rations. The following year 10,000 were reported destitute in Richland County. In Greenville nearly one-half of aid recipients were white and 63 percent were children. Assistance, except for orphans, elderly, and disabled, was a loan, not a grant. By the time it closed its doors in 1872, the Freedman's Bureau had provided medical aid to 175,000 Carolinians and issued three million rations.[60]

The Freedmen's Bureau only handled the truly destitute, but almost all South Carolinians, black and white, had a difficult time in the decade after the war. "The war," wrote Charlestonian John Berkeley Grimball, "has ruined us." The children of William Ellison of Stateburg had property valued at about $8,000 ($106,000); their father's holdings in 1860 had been worth more than ten times that figure. In Greenville, Peter Cauble, a successful entrepreneur, had been worth $100,000 ($1.8 million) in 1860; in 1865 he had only $3,000–4,000 ($28,000–$37,000) in assets and tremendous debts, and five years later he was insolvent. In the year after the war Greenville's economy was so bad that locals referred to the once-bustling community as "Slow-Hole."[61]

Agricultural statistics from 1870, when compared with those a decade earlier, tell a grim tale. More than 1.5 million acres of land were fallow. Sixty percent of the value of livestock (swine, cattle, horses, mules, milk cows, sheep) had disappeared as had the animals themselves. Barns, fences, and outbuildings had been destroyed along with big houses.[62]

The war had dealt South Carolina's economy a staggering blow, and the national depression that began in 1873 eradicated what little economic recovery there had been. The impact on Charleston, the state's most prosperous community, was telling. In 1873–1874 nearly one hundred firms closed their doors. Among them was the local branch of the National Freedmen's Savings Bank, and fifty-three hundred black Carolinians and two hundred whites lost their savings. Along Bay Street fine mansions were chopped up into tenements or converted into boardinghouses or brothels. Sections of the old city south of Broad began a half-century slide into some of the state's most squalid slums.[63]

Interest rates were outrageous. Rural suppliers of capital had to get their money from Charleston or New York at 12 to 36 percent interest per year. Small town merchants charged higher prices for goods bought on credit. If a customer paid cash for fertilizer, it cost him $70 ($765) a ton, but if he opted to pay for it at the end of the season, "carrying it" for eight months, then the price was $110 ($1,359). In the upcountry it cost 20 to 50 percent more to purchase an item on credit than to pay cash for it. In Marion County in 1872 interest rates were calculated to be 1.5 percent a month.[64]

Economic distress fueled the righteous rage that white Carolinians now directed at the Reconstruction regime. The key issue was power, not corruption. However, the shameless behavior of Republican officeholders gave white Carolinians a moral weapon and an acceptable political cover for a new phase in their war to regain control of the state.[65]

One of the primary responsibilities of any government is to protect its citizens and maintain order. But Reconstruction government in South Carolina was not able to do this for its Republican constituents, especially black Carolinians. Within a year after the war a federal officer reported that the town of Edgefield was "inhabited by thieves, murderers, and disloyal men" who terrorized "the loyal population," which "the Civil law is powerless to protect." Not all the fault lay with officials in Columbia; their sponsors in Washington must also share the blame. However, both were either incapable or unwilling to deal effectively with the white insurgency that eventually toppled the Washington-backed regime.[66]

White Carolinians never accepted as legitimate the government of South Carolina based on the 1868 constitution. Unlike modern insurgencies that have to convince their constituents that the existing government is illegitimate, those opposed to Reconstruction in South Carolina did not have to do much persuading. What the insurgents in South Carolina did do, though, was to show the regime's supporters that it could not protect them.[67]

In 1868 almost all white Carolinians began to withdraw from public life and tried to distance themselves as much as possible from representatives of the Reconstruction regime. At the same time they began an unrelenting campaign against that regime and the Republican Party. During the course of their people's war, they used methods with which twentieth-century insurgents are quite familiar: propaganda, economic retaliation, harassment, intimidation, assault, assassination, and murder.[68]

After the ratification of the 1868 constitution and the election of the first Reconstruction legislature, the U.S. Army began to withdraw from South Carolina. By October there were only 881 troops in the entire state. Law enforcement was now the responsibility of newly elected officials who could not rely on the state militia because there was none (all military units had been disbanded in 1867). Almost immediately there were reports of scattered violence across the state. Republican Party members, local officials, and members of the General Assembly were attacked. Representatives from Abbeville and Kershaw Counties were murdered, and an Orangeburg County senator was assassinated while speaking in Abbeville. The attacks were not coordinated but rather the work of individual dens of the Ku Klux Klan (KKK) formed to neutralize the Union League, the successful grassroots organization of the Republican Party. In 1868 the KKK began to spread throughout the twelve western counties of the upcountry where there were fewer black residents.[69]

South Carolina government officials appeared helpless in the face of determined resistance. In 1868 they confronted the same dilemma that the British had in 1780: Who was the enemy? Obviously, the insurgents were white, but the white community erected a barrier of silence as impenetrable as a Carolina canebrake and refused to cooperate with law-enforcement officials. Local courts were filled with incompetent political appointees, which made it difficult to prosecute the few cases that could be tried. When a black person was willing to press charges or testify, the retribution was swift. If economic intimidation did not work (loss of labor contract, home, or credit), then physical violence usually did. Terrorizing the civilian population is one of the most effective weapons available to insurgents; anyone identified as a government supporter, and any family member, is a potential target. And in South Carolina no one was safe: women, children, and the elderly were all victims of KKK attacks.[70]

The terrorism that wracked the upstate in the fall of 1868 had several unforeseen consequences. First, Governor Scott sent a message to Wade Hampton that if he did not speak out against the violence, the long-feared race war might erupt. Hampton responded with an address that appeared in the state's newspapers appealing for the "preservation of order." There was always the possibility that any more outrages might lead to federal intervention. Almost overnight the KKK went underground, and for eighteen months the state was relatively peaceful. The Republican governor got the peace he sought, but he demonstrated to friends and enemies that Wade Hampton and the white community, not he, had the real power in South Carolina.[71]

The second unexpected result (at least for the white community) was the creation of a state militia. In 1869, in order to protect black Carolinians, a new state militia was authorized. Since native whites refused to join, it was virtually all-black. By late 1870 there were one hundred thousand militiamen in South Carolina. One of the more persistent myths, even perpetrated by twentieth-century historians, is that the KKK was formed to protect white Carolinians against the black militia and to oust the corrupt Reconstruction government. The KKK first appeared in the state in 1868 and was terrorizing upcountry black Carolinians nearly two years before the militia was organized or Republican officials decided to treat the state treasury as their per-

Ku Klux Klan: A Night Raid of the Ku Klux Klan. Courtesy, Corbis-Bettmann.

sonal slush fund. As militia units appeared in communities, black Carolinians become more assertive. The Klan found that intimidation was no longer the weapon it once had been, especially when blacks responded to force with force.[72]

For about eighteen months, thanks to Hampton's plea, Scott's veiled threat, and the black militia, there was almost no Klan activity. Then in 1870 violence exploded and never fully abated until the Republican regime collapsed in 1877. In order to demonstrate its authority, a government threatened by insurgency must have a "well-disciplined, highly professional, motivated security force." That was not the case with the South Carolina militia. Although some individuals were highly motivated, the spoils system that weakened so many other Reconstruction programs corrupted the militia as well. Even in areas where units were well disciplined and well led, the state's Republican governors usually held them back from confrontation with armed whites to avoid bloodshed. However, this reluctance to let militia units defend themselves and their communities undermined their effectiveness.[73]

By the fall of 1870 South Carolina witnessed terrorism on a scale previously unknown. Although Klan activity was centered in the upstate (especially Laurens, Chester, and Spartanburg Counties), violence occurred everywhere. In Williamsburg County, S. A. Swails reported that "you cannot speak without a guard if you are a Republican." The failure of state or federal officials to crack down only encouraged the insurgents. In Laurensville more than two thousand armed whites seized the town and murdered nine Republicans, including a state legislator, the probate judge, and a constable. In York County nearly 80 percent of white males rode with the Klan. From November 1870 to September 1871 the York Klan scheduled weekly night rides that established a level of brutality seldom seen in the United States: eleven black Carolinians were murdered, six hundred whipped, and black schools and churches burned. Blacks retaliated with a favorite weapon from antebellum days: arson. Although the state's leading white citizens publicly distanced themselves from the Klan, few raised a hand or voice to stop the outrages. The Klan's actions were brutally effective. Republican party officials and officeholders began resigning in considerable numbers.[74]

Governor Scott, under intense pressure from black legislators, sent repeated messages to Washington requesting military assistance. On his own initiative he asked for help from the white establishment. In March 1871 he met with seventeen leading men and worked out a deal. Scott agreed to disband certain upstate militia units and to replace some local officials. In return the whites said that they would do everything in their power to bring peace to the upcountry. It was peace at any price; however, it was also a realistic assessment of the situation in the state's twelve western counties. Local officials were powerless, and the militia was outnumbered and outgunned. This 1871 deal, like the 1868 Hampton letter, made it quite clear who really controlled the state. Scott and the Republicans had authority—they were the de jure government. But the leaders of the white community were the de facto government of South Carolina—they had the power.[75]

During March the federal government finally decided to act and sent additional troops to South Carolina. However, without the president's declaring martial law or giving new instructions to the army, the soldiers were only a potential threat, not a real one. Even with the increased force, the federal military presence amounted to only nine hundred soldiers for the entire state. Within twenty-four hours more armed whites than that could assemble in almost any county in the state. The half-hearted response of Washington to the insurgency in South Carolina was a test of its resolve, which both whites and blacks saw as weak.[76]

In April, Congress passed the Ku Klux Klan Act, but it was action, not legislation, that was needed. Finally, in May, President Ulysses S. Grant issued a proclamation that threatened more federal intervention if violence did not abate. Faced with armed resistance in almost every Southern state, Washington opted to make an example of one (South Carolina) in the hopes that the others would be cowed. Even before the president acted, white leaders (whether in response to the deal with Governor Scott or the fear that more violence would be counterproductive) called off the Klan. Nevertheless, Washington proceeded with its plan to root out the insurgents in South Carolina.[77]

On 12 October 1871 the president issued another proclamation calling for all armed groups to disband and within five days turn in their weapons and disguises. On 17 October he suspended the writ of habeas corpus in nine upcountry counties that were declared to be in rebellion: Chester, Chesterfield, Fairfield, Lancaster, Laurens, Marion, Newberry, Spartanburg, and York. The inclusion of Marion was an error, and the order was later corrected; Marion was dropped and Union included. Fearing that they might be hanged, hundreds of Klansmen surrendered to authorities. The three key upcountry leaders (J. Bank Lyles of Spartanburg and James Avery and J. Rufus Bratton of York) fled the state. The trials in Columbia accomplished little. Federal prosecutors were overwhelmed by the task, by the fact that many of the alleged crimes had occurred before the passage of the Ku Klux Klan Act, and by the talented out-of-state defense attorneys hired by the white community to defend the accused. The example that the federal government had hoped to make of South Carolina was a dreadful failure. By mid 1872 about 1,300 individuals had been indicted but only 158 cases disposed of (23 convictions, 67 guilty pleas, 38 acquittals, and 30 cases dismissed); there were still more than 1,000 cases pending.[78]

Although the last thing that white Carolinians had wanted to do was provoke federal intervention, once it occurred they realized they had nothing to fear. Instead of suppressing the white insurgency, the feeble federal show of force encouraged it. Even while the KKK trials were under way and before the drawdown of army troops in 1873, insurgents terrorized Republicans in Abbeville, Laurens, Newberry, and Union Counties. It was a direct challenge that went unanswered. As one modern historian has bluntly concluded: "Republicans—at the state and federal levels—dealt in bluff, while conservatives dealt in blood."[79]

In November 1872, upon learning of Franklin J. Moses Jr.'s election as governor, Wade Hampton said that it was time for white Southerners to "dedicate themselves to the redemption of the South." The insurgency in South Carolina now came out in the open and proceeded on several fronts. Whites organized rifle, saber, and gun clubs. Terrorism continued unchecked. The white community won the propaganda war by successfully manipulating the Northern press. Northern reporters (many of whom had racial prejudices) tended to talk only with native white Carolinians. They portrayed a "prostrate state" in the hands of Philistines—or worse. In May 1871 a reporter for the *New York Herald* quoted a white Charlestonian on events in South Carolina: "We have all around us negro national guards armed and equipped by the Legislature and Governor at our expense. . . . Regiment after regiment is organized with nigger colonels. The Lieutenant Governor of our State is a Nigger; there are seventy-four niggers in the State Legislature who cannot read or write. . . . We are taxed until we can't draw breath, and . . . you . . . ask me what our boys are forming rifle clubs so suddenly for?" It made no difference that much of the statement was untrue. The *Herald* reporter believed that it was, and so did much of the Northern public. Between 1865 and 1874 *Harper's Weekly* published innumerable illustrations about the South. In 1865 the black Southerner was depicted as a wounded war hero, but by 1874 he was a clownlike member of the South Carolina General Assembly.[80]

The second taxpayers' convention met in 1874 to protest the egregious excesses of the Moses administration. This time there was no whitewash. The convention

401

adopted a number of resolutions and prepared an address to Congress detailing the "schemes of public plunder" that were sapping the financial well-being of the state. The South Carolina Republican Party responded with a lengthy address of its own to Congress refuting, point by point, almost all the taxpayers' charges except one: the Republicans admitted that bribery was rampant but excused it by saying that everybody did it.[81]

By 1875 whites were getting even bolder. After Mississippi used paramilitary groups to overthrow its Republican government, the state's white newspapers published glowing accounts of "The Mississippi Plan." "Why not here?" they editorialized.

Had the Republican Party in South Carolina been united it might have been able to withstand, at least for a few more years, the assault of the white community. South Carolina was not Mississippi; the black majority here was far larger and much more politically powerful. However, the party was divided between reformers who desired honest, effective government and regulars who were interested primarily in the spoils of office.

Daniel H. Chamberlain, although elected governor by the regular faction, turned reformer. He and his allies in the General Assembly reduced taxes, printing costs, and the militia; equalized property assessments; restructured the state's finances; and began an investigation into some of the shady financial dealings of the early 1870s. In cooperation with men such as Francis W. Dawson, editor of the *Charleston News and Courier,* he pursued a fusion policy of working with members of the white community. He removed Republicans from office and in their stead appointed white Democrats, much to the dismay of party regulars. Nor were they happy with his downsizing of the militia because it took black Carolinians off the state payroll and also left them vulnerable to white assaults.[82]

Chamberlain's fusion policy seemed to be working until it was derailed by the General Assembly in December 1875. While the governor was out of town, the legislature elected Franklin J. Moses Jr., the infamous scalawag , and William J. Whipper, a black legislator, to circuit judgeships. Although the governor blocked both appointments, the election convinced whites that reform Republicanism was an oxymoron. Fusion and cooperation were irreparably damaged. In the white community those who favored a policy of "straightout" voting only for Democrats began to gain the ascendancy.[83]

The Democratic Party organized from the state executive committee down to the precinct level and geared up for a statewide campaign. Wade Hampton, a representative of the best traditions of antebellum South Carolina and a military hero, was the party's choice for governor. Not all members of the party agreed with the general because his stand on racial issues was relatively mild. He urged the recruiting of black members, but there was little response from black Carolinians to the party that espoused denying them the right to vote. He also disagreed with Martin W.

Gary of Edgefield, an advocate of force and violence. Hampton championed what he called "force without violence," that is, the various white military clubs should parade through communities in a show of force but not attack Republicans.[84]

The hopes for a peaceful campaign ended in July with an incident that occurred in Hamburg, a predominantly black town in Aiken County. The commander of the town's militia company harassed some white travelers, who continued to the nearest white community. They filed charges against him, and he filed countercharges. Hundreds of armed whites descended on Hamburg, and in the ensuing skirmish one white and one black were killed. After the black militia surrendered, six of them were murdered in cold blood. Southern newspapers, including the *Charleston News and Courier*, condemned the senseless barbarity of the self-appointed regulators. The Hamburg massacre galvanized the white community and killed any hope for fusion. It also exposed, once again, the inability of the Republican regime to defend its own.[85]

After Hamburg the straight-outs (those who opposed cooperation with the Republicans and favored voting a straight Democrat ticket), under the leadership of Alexander C. Haskell and Martin W. Gary, gained control of the Democratic Party machinery. Hampton may have wanted a peaceful campaign, but it was out of his hands. Gary's "No. 1 Plan for the Campaign," a thirty-three-point guide for loyal Democrats to follow, detailed how Republican voters could be neutralized. Reminiscences of the 1876 election, such as Alfred B. Williams's *Hampton and His Red Shirts* and William A. Sheppard's *Red Shirts Remembered,* read like military, not political, memoirs. Haskell and Gary directed the campaign with ruthless military precision, disrupting Republican rallies and intimidating black voters.[86]

There were further armed confrontations in Charleston, Ellenton (Aiken County), and Cainhoy (Charleston County). After the Ellenton riots whites executed thirty to fifty blacks they had captured, including Rep. Simon P. Coker of Barnwell County. At Cainhoy a group of black Republicans responded to white attackers and forced them to flee. Hampton condemned both incidents but could not control the excesses of his followers. Governor Chamberlain appealed to Washington for assistance, and President Grant sent more than eleven hundred troops to South Carolina and ordered all gun clubs disbanded. In an open show of defiance, many reported to the governor that they had obeyed the president's order when they clearly had no intention of doing so. The Allendale Rifle Club became the Allendale Mounted Baseball Club, and the Columbia Flying Artillery announced that it had reorganized itself as the Columbia Musical Club with Four Twelve Pounder Flutes.[87]

In September, Hampton began a triumphal tour of the state. Everywhere he went he was accompanied by hundreds of mounted men clad in red shirts. At Sumter, when he entered the town square, he found a lone woman lying on the ground with a sash identifying her as "South Carolina." He dismounted, strode across the square, and raised her up. The crowd's response was electric. The tableau became a fixture of the campaign, and the reaction of white Carolinians everywhere was something akin to religious ecstasy. Wade Hampton was the savior of white South Carolina.[88]

Republicans, encouraged by the late show of force from Washington and fearful of what might happen if they lost, were united in their determination to maintain their hold on the state. It was the first time since 1868 that the party had not been riven by factionalism. One was neither a regular nor a reformer, just a Republican. And like their opponents, Republicans were willing to use any tactic necessary to win.[89]

With federal soldiers present, there was little violence on election day, but they were not responsible for preventing voting irregularities. When the initial tallies were reported in Columbia, Hampton led Chamberlain 92,261 to 91,127. There were immediate cries of fraud from both camps, but especially from the Republicans. Gary and his men had been too successful in Edgefield and Laurens Counties where Hampton and the Democratic slate received more votes than there were registered voters of both parties. The Republican-controlled election commissions in those counties declared the totals fraudulent. Because of the irregularities, under the 1868 constitution the General Assembly would elect the governor. The contested Democratic legislative delegations from Edgefield and Laurens obtained certificates of election from the state supreme court and the Republicans from the state election commission. There was maneuvering by both parties as legislators journeyed to Columbia in late November.[90]

Governor Chamberlain tricked the local federal military commander into stationing two companies of soldiers in the State House and directed them to admit only individuals with commissions from the election commission or the secretary of state. The reaction of white Carolinians brought the state to the brink of a confrontation with the U.S. Army. Once again Wade Hampton stepped in and demonstrated who really controlled the state. He addressed the angry crowd surrounding the State House and asked them to disperse, which they did. Then the Democrats withdrew from the House of Representatives, organized themselves as the official South Carolina House, and elected William H. Wallace of Union County as Speaker. The Republicans, meeting in the State House, did the same and elected E. W. M. Mackey of Charleston as their Speaker. The South Carolina Senate had a Republican majority and organized without any difficulty.[91]

On 6 December 1876 the General Assembly elected Daniel H. Chamberlain governor, and he was inaugurated on 7 December. At a rally that same day, the usually mild-mannered Wade Hampton delivered an address full of fire in which he declared: "The people have elected me Governor, and, by the Eternal God, I will be Governor or we shall have a military governor." A week later he took the oath of office. For the next four months South Carolina would have rival houses and governors, each claiming to be the legitimate government of the state. However, as had been demonstrated time and again during Reconstruction, authority and power in

Dual Speakers: Edward W. M. Mackey (Republican) and William H. Wallace (Democrat) both occupied the Speaker's desk after the disputed election of 1876. *Leslie's Illustrated Newspaper,* 4 December 1876.

South Carolina were not one and the same thing.[92]

It takes money to run any government, and white taxpayers refused to pay their taxes. However, at Hampton's request, they voluntarily contributed one-tenth of their previous year's tax liability to his government. If a state agency head wanted to operate, he had to go to the Hampton government. Chamberlain's treasury was empty. Some black taxpayers gave their money to Hampton's tax collectors. Steady defections from the Republican camp to the Democrats drained what remaining vitality the Chamberlain government had left. The Reconstruction regime in South Carolina had lost what little authority and legitimacy it had. No one paid Chamberlain's government any taxes or any mind. It continued to exist only because of the life support system supplied by federal troops.[93]

While Carolinians were preoccupied with their own election problems, the nation did not know who had been elected president of the United States in November 1876. Samuel Tilden, the Democratic nominee, had 184 electoral votes, one shy of victory. There were 22 disputed votes, including 7 from South Carolina. A congressionally-chosen commission awarded all the disputed votes to Rutherford B. Hayes, the Republican candidate. During all the wheeling and dealing in Washington, white Carolinians kept a low profile and concentrated on consolidating their hold on the state. Hampton and his supporters waged a successful propaganda campaign in well-reasoned correspondence with President Grant, Tilden, and Hayes. Both he and Chamberlain visited with Hayes after he was inaugurated, and it was evident to the president who controlled South Carolina. No doubt Hayes agreed with his predecessor's analysis that "the whole army of the United States would be inadequate to enforce the authority of Governor Chamberlain." On 3 April 1877 the president pulled the plug on South Carolina's Reconstruction regime and issued the order for the remaining military units to withdraw.[94]

One week later federal troops began to leave South Carolina. An embittered Chamberlain issued a proclamation to the Republican Party faithful saying that the government of the United States had abandoned them. On 11 April 1877, at the stroke of noon, he and his staff quietly vacated their offices in the State House. The second phase of the Civil War in South Carolina was over. Those who had lost in 1865 triumphed in 1877.[95]

This alkaline-glazed stoneware jug with slip decoration was manufactured (circa 1840) by the Phoenix Factory in Edgefield County. Collection of the Museum of Early Southern Decorative Arts, Winston-Salem, North Carolina.

A View of Brattonsville in York District (circa 1840) reflects the growing prosperity of the upcountry. The Bratton family's original log house (circa 1776–1780) in the left foreground has been covered with clapboards and a newer residence (1824) built with the profits from the first cotton boom is in the right background. The painting is attributed to Martha Bratton (1825–1908). Private collection.

The Roper House (1838) on East Battery in Charleston is an excellent example of a single house built in nineteenth-century high style. Photograph by Suzanne C. Linder. Courtesy of Richard Hampton Jenrette.

Wavering Place (circa 1855) in lower Richland County was built during the flush times of the second cotton boom. Courtesy, Julian Adams, M.D. Photograph by Suzanne C. Linder.

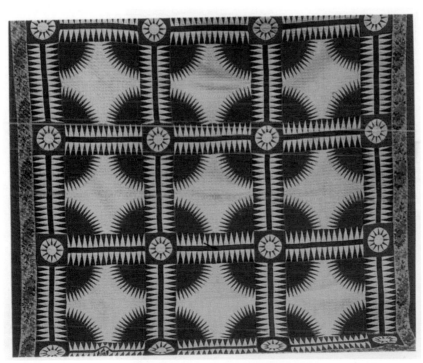

A Crown of Thorns–design quilt (circa 1850–1855) from the Dutch Fork area of Lexington County. Courtesy, Lexington County Museum.

The young woman in this portrait is "Ruth," a character from Charleston novelist Caroline Gilman's novel *Love's Progress. Ruth* by Charles Fraser. Private collection. Courtesy, Museum of Early Southern Decorative Arts, Winston-Salem, North Carolina.

John C. Calhoun (circa 1811), as a new member of Congress. *John C. Calhoun* by Charles B. King. Courtesy, South Carolina State Museum.

The Palmetto Regiment storming the heights of Chapultepec near Mexico City. The first American flag to fly over the captured Mexican capital was the palmetto flag of the regiment. *The Palmetto Regiment* by an unknown artist. Courtesy, South Caroliniana Library.

BUILT FROM THE RUINS.

The Secession Banner that hung in Institute Hall, Charleston, during the South Carolina Secession Convention. Courtesy, South Carolina Historical Society.

Flag of the 6th Regiment, South Carolina Volunteer Infantry, Chester County. Photograph by Scott Coleman. Courtesy, Chester County Historical Society.

Emma LeConte (1848–1901) was a teenager when she recorded the events in Columbia, 1864–1865. Courtesy of Carolyn S. McMillan.

Richard Greener (1844–1922), the first black graduate of Harvard University, was professor of philosophy and librarian of the University of South Carolina (1873–1877). *Richard Greener* by Larry Francis Lebby. Courtesy, South Caroliniana Library.

The Confederate Monument on the State House grounds, Columbia. Photograph by Suzanne C. Linder.

Wade Hampton III, governor of South Carolina (1876–1878) and U.S. senator (1878–1890). Courtesy, South Caroliniana Library.

This cover illustration from the English magazine *Puck* mocked the 1895 constitution provision that made counties liable for $2,000 ($36,000) to the heirs of any lynching victim. Courtesy, South Caroliniana Library.

Tillman Hall, Clemson University, the oldest building on the campus, is named for Benjamin Ryan Tillman. Courtesy of Dave Dryden, Publications and Marketing, Clemson University.

The Plantation Street by Alice Ravenel Huger Smith. Smith's watercolors were just one example of the cultural vitality of the Charleston Renaissance. Courtesy, Gibbes Museum of Art/Carolina Art Association.

Rainbow Row was one of the early successful preservation efforts in Charleston. Photograph by Rick Rhodes, Charleston, South Carolina.

Justice as Protector and Avenger, Aiken County Courthouse. This WPA mural by Stefan Hirsch was so controversial when it was painted that a local judge ordered curtains hung to hide it. Courtesy, South Carolina State Museum.

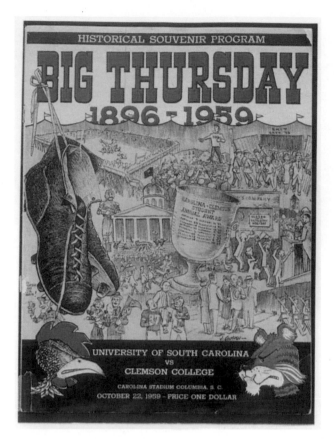

The cover of the program for the last Big Thursday football game at the South Carolina State Fair between Clemson College and the University of South Carolina (22 October 1959). Courtesy, University Archives, University of South Carolina.

The punch bowl from the battleship *South Carolina* silver service was part of a 1908 gift of the people of South Carolina to the U.S. Navy. It was returned to the state when the *South Carolina* was decommissioned after World War II. Photograph by Doug Alverson. Courtesy, South Carolina Society—National Society Daughters of the American Revolution in South Carolina and the Governor's Mansion.

The Congaree Swamp National Monument (Richland County) is the sole remaining large tract of virgin bottomland in the Southeast. Photograph by Elizabeth Dozier Steedly.

The Wedding, 1988. Oil on Masonite 48" by 48" by Jonathan Green. In his colorful paintings Green, a native of Gardens Corner (Beaufort County), captures the spirit of the sea islands. Courtesy, Jonathan Green Studios.

Myrtle Beach and the Grand Strand are the state's number one tourist attraction. Courtesy, South Carolina Parks, Recreation and Tourism.

Harbortown on Hilton Head Island. Courtesy, Hilton Head Island Chamber of Commerce.

When Union Camp Corporation built a multi-million-dollar paper mill, it also restored Kensington plantation. The old and the new South Carolina coexist peacefully in lower Richland County. Photograph by Fred Martin. Courtesy, Union Camp Corporation.

RETURN OF THE OLD ORDER

I have come to the conclusion that you have made up your mind that this is the white man's land and must forever remain so. . . . Whilst I know that if the men you have nominated had their way, none of our rights would be endangered, yet what guarantee have I that their opinion will be regarded?

James Davis, 5 October 1876

Let the Stranger, Who May in Future Times Read This Inscription Recognize That There Were Men Whom Power Could Not Corrupt, Whom Death Could Not Terrify, Whom Defeat Could Not Dishonor, And Let Their Virtues Plead For Just Judgment Of the Cause in Which They Perished.

Confederate Monument, Columbia, 13 May 1879

THE ELECTION of 1876 publicly confirmed what had been the political reality in South Carolina since the early 1870s: Wade Hampton and the white minority effectively controlled the state. Hampton and others elected to state offices were members of the elite that had governed the state before the Civil War. Other than ousting the carpetbaggers and undoing as much of Reconstruction as they could, the Conservatives (as they styled themselves) really had no stated political agenda. However, they had an unstated one. Politically and socially they intended to re-create as much as possible the world of antebellum South Carolina, a world in which they and their kind held sway.[1]

It was a fragile world, like Humpty Dumpty, that they were trying to put back together again. Many, including Hampton, had lost almost everything in the war. The newly elected governor had even suffered the indignity of having his possessions sold at public auction to meet his creditors' demands. That, however, was unimportant. He was Wade Hampton, and his chief lieutenants were, to a man, former Confederate generals: John Bratton of Fairfield County, Matthew C. Butler of Edgefield, Johnson Hagood of Barnwell, Joseph B. Kershaw and John D. Kennedy of Kershaw, and Samuel McGowan of Abbeville. They were older men who had come of age before the war. The overwhelming majority (85 percent) of the Conservative leadership had attended a college in the state, and most of them were alumni of the

South Carolina College. Agriculture and land were still more important to them than commerce, although they were no longer as antibusiness as they had been before the war. Indeed, several prominent Bourbons—Alexander and John Haskell, Joseph W. Barnwell, and William H. Brawley—were the corporate counsels for railroads. If they had had any political party affiliation, they were Democrats. [2]

The men who overthrew Reconstruction regimes in the American South were variously called Conservatives, Bourbons (for the French royalists who resumed power after Napoleon and acted as if nothing had changed), or Redeemers (for having redeemed their states from the clutches of Reconstruction). Except in South Carolina, few styled themselves Democrats until the 1880s. South Carolina's Bourbons were different from those in other southern states. Elsewhere younger men led the effort to oust the carpetbaggers. Many were former Whigs and probusiness with few, if any, ties to the land. Nor were they members of their states' antebellum elites but rather were a new class of leaders. South Carolina went with those who had proven themselves tried and true.[3]

As former Confederate officers and scions of some of the state's older families, South Carolina Bourbons did not expect to be questioned or challenged. They were used to giving and taking orders. Their lack of concern with anything other than the present was obvious. However, few called them to question. In private, though, some of their peers were distressed. In 1878 Wilmot DeSaussure observed that "those who are legislating do not look to the future." The only policy that he could discern was "present expediency."[4]

It is difficult to point to any one reason for the way the Bourbons governed South Carolina. Perhaps it was because they were old men; perhaps it was because they were tired. For sixteen years they had fought to control the destiny of their state. In 1877 they had finally won—but then had to face a difficult two-year period of consolidating their power.

When Hampton assumed the governorship, Richard Gleaves, the Republican aspirant for lieutenant governor, resigned his position. William D. Simpson, the Democratic candidate, claimed the office and as presiding officer of the senate helped undo a Republican majority of six. He swore in Democrats for disputed seats. Those new senators, coupled with Republican resignations, left the senate evenly divided (15–15); however, since the lieutenant governor cast the tie-breaking vote on any measure, the Democrats effectively had control. Before the legislature reconvened in the fall of 1877, ten more Republicans had resigned and the Democrats had a comfortable majority.[5]

Members of the Wallace House of Representatives, which had been recognized by the South Carolina Supreme Court as the legitimate house, demanded that all members of the Mackey house appear before them and take an oath that absolved them of contempt. All fifty-five members of the Mackey house appeared, but not all took the oath. Through expulsion, resignation, and chicanery the Republican membership of the House of Representatives was reduced to thirty-seven.[6]

Old Newberry County Courthouse (1852); the bas-relief in the pediment was added in 1879 and reflects local white sentiment about Reconstruction. It depicts an uprooted palmetto tree (state of South Carolina) tied up by a federal eagle (federal government) while a gamecock (white Carolinian) struts defiantly. Photograph by Suzanne C. Linder.

With legislative majorities in both houses, it was an easy matter to go after Republican judges. Supreme court justice Jonathan Wright resigned to avoid an impeachment trial for alleged public drunkenness (a test that few legislators could have passed). When the attorney general asked the state supreme court for an opinion on the validity of the Reconstruction elections of circuit judges, the supreme court declared that the state's circuit judges had been elected illegally and must resign. Under pressure from Governor Hampton, two Republican judges were elected, but the other six seats went to good Democrats.[7]

Eliminating Republican officeholders was just the beginning. The Democrats were determined to prove to the world that they had saved the state from fraud, vice, and corruption. A special legislative committee made an exhaustive investigation and produced reams of allegations of fraud. The committee's widely publicized reports were designed more as party propaganda than anything else. Reforms begun by the Chamberlain administration were somehow overlooked—as was the connivance of prominent Democrats in various unsavory state bond and railroad stock deals. If the state had been looted as badly as the Bourbons claimed, why were just twenty-five individuals indicted? Of these, only four were brought to trial and convicted. And Hampton pardoned them after cutting a deal with federal officials to drop election fraud charges against South Carolina Democrats. However, the primary pur-

The First Baptist Church building on Edisto Island housed a black congregation after the Civil War. Photograph by Suzanne C. Linder.

pose of the legislative committee was to blacken the reputation of those who governed the state from 1868 to 1877 so that Reconstruction in South Carolina would become synonymous with graft and corruption. In that, the committee succeeded.[8]

It had been the intention of Hampton and his circle to consolidate and honor the state's debts. However, between the special committee's reports and the intransigence of Martin W. Gary, now the senator from Edgefield County, that was not possible. Gary wanted to repudiate virtually all of the state debt. He launched a vicious personal attack on Hampton and the consolidation effort. Finally, a compromise was worked out whereby a special bond court was created to determine the legality of all state bonds. A little over $1 million ($12.6 million) worth were repudiated, but $4.5 million ($56.7 million) in bonds were validated. In addition to honoring some of the Reconstruction government's debts, the Bourbons left in place several key pieces of legislation. Among these were the crop lien law and a tax exemption designed to encourage economic development.[9]

The state's first lien law had been passed in 1866. It was replaced by an 1868 statute that gave lenders (usually country store owners and merchants) first priority for debt repayment and allowed only those individuals who controlled their own crops to take out liens. Thus, tenant farmers could, but sharecroppers could not, obtain credit via a lien on their crops. In 1874 the law was amended to give the landowner first claim on the crop (if certain conditions were met). During their first year in power the Bourbons passed legislation to eliminate the lien law, on 1 January 1878. The impact on the state's farmers who could not get credit any other way was instantaneous, and in March 1878 a new lien law passed that opened up credit in time for spring planting. The 1878 statute was even more favorable to landowners than the old one had been. As onerous as the crop lien was to many, the state's agricultural sector could not have functioned without it. By 1881 the crops on more than 75 percent of South Carolina's farms were encumbered by liens.[10]

The modification of the lien law in favor of landowners and the passage of a law enabling townships (a Reconstruction subdivision of counties) to require the fencing of livestock were indicators that the Bourbons' primary allegiance was to landowners. By 1878 Abbeville, Anderson, Laurens, Newberry, and Union Counties required fences countywide.[11]

South Carolina's Bourbons were not antibusiness, but they were more cautious in their support of economic and commercial development than their peers in other southern states. They did not give away the state's timber resources, an activity that caused public scandals in Louisiana, Mississippi, and Florida and made any carpetbagger swindle seem mild in comparison. They created a state railroad commission and, for a brief time, gave it power to regulate rates. In 1885 they repealed the ten-year tax exemption granted to individuals or corporations who invested in manufacturing. The following year they enacted the state's first general incorporation law; prior to 1886 companies had to seek special legislation granting them charters. South Carolina's rulers were willing to tolerate business, but they had no intention of surrendering control of the state to commercial interests.[12]

In the same fashion, Wade Hampton and his lieutenants were tolerant when it came to racial matters—as long as black Carolinians did not threaten the white minority's control of state government. Hampton credited his election to the seventeen thousand black Carolinians who had cast their ballots for him. The governor, in speeches at home and in the North, talked of racial harmony and political fair play. He appointed eighty-six black Carolinians to office and forced his party to elect a white Republican as chief justice of the state supreme court. The funding for black and white schools was nearly equal. Since funding was based on student population, the Bourbons actually spent more money annually educating black children than they did educating whites.[13]

In counties, especially those in the middle- and lowcountry that had black majorities, political accommodation of a sort was reached. In Orangeburg County black Democrats regularly named one member of the legislative delegation and one of the county commissioners. As late as 1888 St. Matthews Democrats placed a black man on the ticket for local office. Until the late 1880s the black majority in Beaufort was too powerful and too well organized to consider sharing power with whites; however, by the end of the decade the county's white minority had negotiated a fusion plan with the black majority to share offices. So, too, did blacks and whites in Berkeley County. Charleston's reform-minded fusion government was ousted in 1877.[14]

The most successful fusion plan was that in Georgetown County (black population 82 percent). Republicans and Democrats decided to share offices in town elections in 1879 and the following year in county elections. Each party nominated candidates for specific offices, and the other party agreed not to nominate anyone to oppose them. Thus Democrats nominated the sheriff, clerk of court, two county commissioners, and one state representative, and Republicans nominated the state senator, one representative, probate judge, school commissioner, and one county commissioner. With the exception of one white Republican probate judge, all the other Republican officeholders were black. White Georgetonians honored Wade Hampton's pledge to the black community, and the black community was willing to assert itself. The Georgetown plan worked successfully (albeit grudgingly on the part of whites) until 1900 when a race riot ended biracial government. In 1881 the *News and Courier* approved of the Bourbons' policy of toleration: "Far from the Democratic leaders in South Carolina being determined to maintain the 'color line' they have worked assiduously and patiently to obliterate it."[15]

The Bourbons' policy of toleration infuriated the Negrophobic Gary. In addition, he was bitter that Wade Hampton thwarted his bids for the U.S. Senate and the governorship. Gary believed that he, not Hampton, was the real hero of 1876 and that his, Gary's, fraud and violence won the election—not the seventeen thousand black Democratic voters Hampton credited with the victory. The Edgefield senator never missed an opportunity to try to embarrass the governor and his friends or to limit the political and civil rights of black Carolinians. His effective opposition to the political allies of the "elegant, smooth mannered, oily tongued bondholders, bond speculators, banks and members of financial boards" forced the Bourbons to compromise on debt consolidation and agree to a usury law limiting legal interest at 7 percent. However, it was his outspoken and unrelenting attacks on the status of black Carolinians that helped undermine the Bourbons' policy of racial tolerance.[16]

In 1878 Hampton won reelection as governor with the support of the overwhelming majority of the state's voters, black and white. The state's Republicans came close to endorsing his candidacy. They did not, nor did they nominate anyone to oppose him. Of the 169,763 votes cast, Hampton received 169,550 and the remainder were scattered among a number of noncandidates. As soon as the General Assembly met, the governor was elected to the U.S. Senate and was effectively removed as an active force in South Carolina politics. With the exception of blocking Gary's run for the governorship in 1880, Hampton simply let matters back home take their own course. N. G. Gonzales, the Washington reporter for the *News and Courier,* in 1882 described the state's venerated hero as a has-been clinging to office. Hampton had neither the inclination nor the energy to lead South Carolina.[17]

Traditionally, historians have absolved Hampton and blamed others for South Carolina's abandoning racial moderation, but the first step at disenfranchising black Carolinians occurred while he was still governor. In 1877 the General Assembly passed a new election law that redrew precinct boundaries and considerably reduced the number of polling places, especially in black majority counties. In a number of instances black voters were required to travel more than eight hours to cast their ballots. The 1878 elections were marked by more fraud, intimidation, and violence. Hampton lectured black Carolinians on the dangers of making race a political issue. Translated, that meant that if they voted for Republican candidates they made race an issue. On the other hand, "bloc voting by . . . whites became an accepted policy."[18]

The white minority was determined to make it as difficult as possible for black Carolinians to participate in the political process. One of the primary reasons was not that black politicians had been inept but that they had been effective, especially in the last four years of Reconstruction. The other reason was the overwhelming black presence from the mountains to the sea. The 1880 census revealed that South Carolina had the highest percentage of black citizens of any state in the country (60.7 percent). Only Anderson, Chesterfield, Greenville, Horry, Lexington, Oconee, Pickens, and Spartanburg Counties had white majorities—and each of these counties was more than 25 percent black.[19]

One of the justifications for the conduct of white Democrats in the post-Reconstruction period was that since black Republicans had introduced political shenanigans into South Carolina, it was permissible for white Democrats to imitate them. Wilmot DeSaussure noted the irony. "It was but two or three years since the Democratic Party denounced the Republicans for districting congressional districts in such a manner as would ensure majorities, and yet we are proposing to go through the same kind of legerdemain for state politics." However, his was a minority opinion.[20]

The organization of the South Carolina Democratic Party made it easy to limit meaningful black participation in the political process. At the local level there were Democratic clubs that elected delegates to the county convention. The county convention, in turn, elected delegates to the state convention, which met twice during election years. The spring convention set the rules for the upcoming election, and the convention in the summer nominated state officers, elected the state executive committee, and amended the party's constitution. Each level of the organization was autonomous. In 1876, for example, Pickens County instituted a primary for the nomination of local candidates, and Abbeville, Anderson, Fairfield, and Sumter Counties followed suit in 1878.[21]

In 1878, at Gary's insistence, the Edgefield County Democratic convention banned blacks from participating in its deliberations or voting in party primaries. The convention also refused to recognize black Democratic clubs. The reactions to the Edgefield convention's actions were virtually all negative. Newspapers across the state were unusually harsh. The *Newberry Herald* condemned the action as an indication of a "half-civilized people." Yet within five years a campaign to eliminate black voters by any and all means had gathered considerable momentum.[22]

One of the state's urbane Bourbons, Edward McCrady Jr. of Charleston, was the chief architect of what would come to be called the "Eight Box Law." Opposed to violence and fraud, the Charleston legislator argued that only literate citizens should be allowed to vote. A strict literacy test found little support in the General Assembly (even though it would eliminate 83 percent of South Carolina's black voters) because it would disenfranchise 20 percent of the state's white voters. By 1882 McCrady had gathered enough support in the legislature to pass the Eight Box Law. The statute drew its popular name from the requirement that there be eight separate ballot boxes for different offices (a voter had to be able to read to know where to place his ballot; he could ask help from a poll manager, but if a ballot were placed in the incorrect box, it was invalid). The law's less well known provisions called for the reregistration of all voters by 1 June 1882. If an eligible voter did not reregister, then he was *forever* barred from voting. Upon registering, a voter received a certificate containing his name, address, and place of employment. If there were any change—even if he moved within the same precinct—he had to pay to get another certificate. Local registration officials were given carte blanche to determine a voter's eligibility. If an official refused to register a voter, there was an elaborate appeals process designed to frustrate the poor and uneducated.[23]

During the debate on the bill in the state senate, Thomas E. Miller of Beaufort called the hands of the bill's supporters. He claimed that all the lofty phrases about protecting the voters of the state and the sanctity of the ballot box were "a libel on our intelligence." Like other black legislators, he knew full well what the Eight Box Law would mean to black Carolinians. Samuel A. Melton, the U.S. attorney in South Carolina, estimated that three-fourths of the state's black voters were disenfranchised by the new law's reregistration requirements. Not content with that, polling managers were brazen in their abuse of office. (One of their favorite stunts was to rearrange the order of the eight boxes to confuse the unwary voter.) Melton brought suit in federal court against poll managers who had violated blacks' right to vote but failed to get any convictions. At the urging of Gov. Hugh S. Thompson, the legislature appropriated $10,000 ($148,000) to pay the legal fees of any polling official against whom a suit was brought.[24]

After the passage of the Eight Box Law and the defense of polling officials, county Democratic conventions and clubs that once had condemned the Edgefield County convention now followed its lead. In 1884 Barnwell County refused to let black Democrats vote in its primary. Two years later the Fifth Congressional District banned black voters from party contests. And in 1888 Laurens agreed to allow any black resident to vote, *provided* he could produce five white voters to testify that he had cast his ballot for Wade Hampton in 1876. In Williamsburg a few blacks were per-

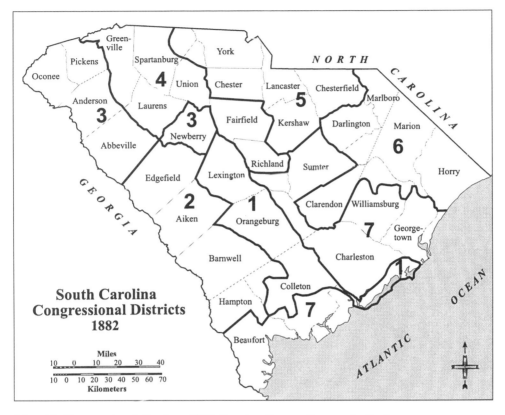

Map 18: Congressional districts, 1882. Based on Cooper, *Conservative Regime*

mitted to vote, "but," wrote the county's historian, "the spirit of South Carolina has been and is that only whites shall cast ballots." In 1876 more than ninety-one thousand black Carolinians had voted; by 1888 not quite fourteen thousand did (fewer than had voted for Hampton in 1876). In 1872 there had been ninety-six black legislators; by 1890 there were only seven.[25]

In 1882, the same year that tens of thousands of black Carolinians were disenfranchised, the legislature gerrymandered the state's congressional districts to cram as many black voters as possible into one district (the Seventh). Designed by Samuel Dibble of Orangeburg, a former legislator, the district looked like a Rorschach test. It began on the banks of the Savannah River and meandered up the coast (excluding the city of Charleston) to Winyah Bay in Georgetown County; it then moved inland to include lower Richland and Sumter Counties. Also included were all or portions of Berkeley, Charleston, Clarendon, Colleton, Orangeburg, and Williamsburg Counties (see Map 18). Even with the Dibble plan, five of the state's seven congressional districts had black majorities in 1882; only the Third and Fourth Districts in the upper piedmont had slim white majorities. However, after 1882 only the Seventh (or Black) District elected a black congressman. George Washington Murray of Rembert (Sumter County), the state's last nineteenth-century black congressman, was defeated for reelection in 1896.[26]

The state's remaining black voters posed no threat to the resurrected white government of the Bourbons. In consolidating their position, white Carolinians did to black Carolinians (at least politically) what had been done to them during Reconstruction. Interestingly, blacks in the post-Reconstruction period responded as whites had earlier. A few switched parties and there were black Democratic officeholders (for example, George M. Mears of Charleston and Aaron Simmons of Orangeburg). However, most black Carolinians, like whites before them, seemed resigned to their fate. After 1878 the Republican Party did not even nominate a candidate for governor. It remained barely viable as a patronage party as Republican presidents appointed loyal party members to such posts as postmasters and customs officials.[27]

Neither the elimination nor the withdrawal of blacks from political life protected them from acts of violence. In 1882 there were six lynchings in the state. If a white woman accused a black man of rape, his life was forfeit. The *Newberry Herald* considered rape a crime too serious to merit the niceties of a legal trial; "summary punishment" was justified. Sometimes accused murderers met the same fates. The *News and Courier* agreed that lynching was necessary to protect the virtue of the state's white women and the sanctity of white homes. Only E. B. Raggsdale, the editor of the *Winnsboro News and Herald,* condemned lynching as "a bold declaration that law is irretrievably impotent in South Carolina." He was correct, of course, especially for a society that paid considerable homage to order and harmony.[28]

The reactions of white Carolinians, notably women, to lynchings is telling. White women lionized common thugs if they were brought to trial. After a black man was lynched in Clarendon County in 1880, Elizabeth Porcher Palmer wrote that she hoped it would "have a good effect." The effect she meant was described in greater detail by the *News and Courier* after a Barnwell mob stormed the county jail in 1889 and murdered eight black prisoners: "The condition on the part of the whites is one of absolute safety; on the part of the blacks it is one of utter demoralization. The former is a consequence of the latter."[29]

Occasionally black Carolinians raised their voices in protest, but not often. Those who spoke out too loudly or defended accused blacks sometimes found themselves in danger. On rare occasions blacks took the law into their own hands. In 1888 when a black Pickens County mob lynched a white man for raping a young black girl, they were brought to trial. The jury, however, could not agree on a verdict, and the accused went free.[30]

Violence was not limited to racial matters. In 1877 a mob closed polling places in Union County to prevent the passage of a fencing law. P. P. Hamer, editor of the *Pee Dee Index* (Marion), was roughed up and tossed down a flight of stairs by editors of the rival *Marion Star* for an uncomplimentary editorial. Francis W. Dawson, editor of the *News and Courier*, took it upon himself to cane a local physician who had been dallying with the Dawsons' French maid. The doctor shot and killed Dawson, claimed self-defense, and was acquitted in a sensational trial.[31]

Dawson had long been a champion of antidueling legislation, but not until the 5 July 1880 duel in which Ellerbe B. C. Cash killed William M. Shannon did the state finally act. The incident upset Shannon's neighbors so much that Cash barely escaped being lynched. Under public pressure the General Assembly outlawed dueling and made participation in a duel a disqualification for holding public office. A. Smith Gibbes of Pendleton was one of a group of old-fashioned Carolinians who thought the practice should continue—especially in the case of "cowardly" newspaper editors and lawyers. The threat of a duel often forced such "miserable cattle" to apologize for their damaging remarks.[32]

Outlawing dueling did not diminish personal violence. After 1877 homicide in South Carolina increased at an alarming rate. By 1890 the state had three times as many murders as did all the New England states combined (with a population four times as large). The white minority, not the black majority, was responsible for the largest share of the killings. And as often as not their victims were fellow whites.[33]

Why was South Carolina so violent? The *Aiken Journal and Review* blamed whiskey and pistols. No doubt, easy access to both aided and abetted those with murderous intent. However, violence was one of the legacies of Civil War and Reconstruction, especially of the insurgency (1868–1877) mounted by the state's white minority against the Reconstruction regime. During a regular war men take up arms in support of a legitimate government; however, an insurgency, by its very nature, "makes a virtue of defying authority and violence rules." Under such conditions it is difficult to rebuild a stable society. South Carolina, with its bloody statistics, could be "Exhibit A" to the social dysfunction caused by an insurgency.[34]

Just as violence created a certain societal tension, so, too, did race relations. During Reconstruction black Carolinians had withdrawn from contact with whites in almost every phase of community life. Legally, public equality was reinforced by the state's Civil Rights Act, which remained on the books until 1889 (six years after the U.S. Supreme Court declared the federal Civil Rights Act unconstitutional). An 1879 law declaring interracial marriages illegal was passed over the vocal opposition of a number of white legislators who thought it wrong. That, however, was the extent of the state's regulation of black-white interaction until 1895.[35]

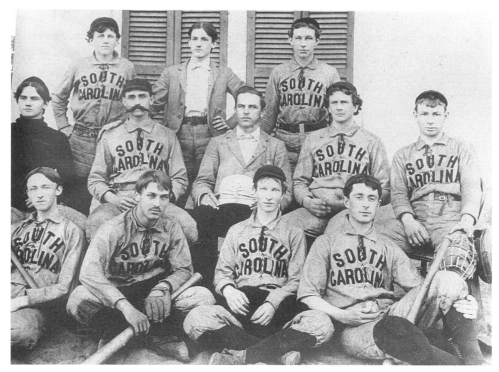

The University of South Carolina baseball team, 1896. Courtesy, University of South Carolina Archives.

Although blacks had chosen to withdraw from contact with whites in many phases of everyday life and in most South Carolina communities, that was not the case in Columbia and Charleston. In those cities restaurants, streetcars, theaters, and ice cream parlors were open to all. In 1880 the New Orleans Jubilee Singers gave a benefit performance in Columbia for Howard School before an integrated audience. An out-of-state visitor commented in 1877 that blacks' riding in first-class railway coaches and on streetcars was "now so common as hardly to provoke remark." An 1891 bill to introduce segregated railway coaches failed to pass the General Assembly. Residential neighborhoods across the state (especially in Charleston and Beaufort) were racially mixed. Black attorneys practiced law in Manning and Sumter, and black merchants prospered in St. Matthews, but rumors that there might be a black typesetter on the staff of the *Abbeville Press and Banner* caused quite a stir.[36]

The color line had already been drawn at white parlor doors, but it had not yet been drawn at the workroom door. However, by custom, it was drawn in a myriad of activities years before there was any Jim Crow legislation. Nowhere was that more apparent than in leisure-time pursuits, whether it was attending the circus, the fair, or playing baseball. Baseball, the national pastime, came to South Carolina with federal troops during Reconstruction. By the 1880s there were organized teams in almost every town. However, blacks and whites formed their own separate teams.[37]

In terms of community life, South Carolina in many ways was not much different from the rest of small-town America in the 1880s. Rare was the community that did not have churches, schools, and social and fraternal organizations. What made South Carolina's towns different, however, was that all such activities were divided by race. In some instances there were white and black chapters of the same organization: Knights of Pythias, Masons, or International Order of Odd Fellows. However, there were also organizations, many with religious overtones, that were unique to the black community, such as the Shekinah Society, Mary and Martha Society, Zion Travellers, Sons and Daughters of Elders of the Throne, Daughters of Meschech, Daughters of Noah, and Rising Sons and Daughters of Bethlehem Star. White-only groups included the Knights of Honor, American Legion of Honor, Knights of the Golden Rule, Good Templars, Order of Chosen Friends, and Knights and Ladies of Honor.[38]

Holidays, Sundays, and unusual events (the 1886 Charleston earthquake) were an excuse for excursions and picnics sponsored by lodges and fraternal, civic, and church groups. Because black and white Carolinians did not always celebrate the same holidays, there was seldom direct competition for excursion transportation. White Carolinians observed Confederate Memorial Day on 10 May (the anniversary of Stonewall Jackson's death) and Thanksgiving Day (fourth Thursday in November), but few remembered South Carolina Day (28 June, the anniversary of the Revolutionary War battle at Sullivan's Island), and almost none observed the Fourth of July. For black Carolinians, Independence Day was a major holiday, as were Decoration Day (30 May) and Emancipation Day (1 January).[39]

Christmas was one holiday celebrated with great joy by most South Carolinians. It was a time for family gatherings, gift giving, relaxation, and merrymaking. Unless Christmas happened to fall on a Sunday, the only churches that held services were those with a liturgical tradition (Episcopal, Lutheran, and Roman Catholic). After dark on Christmas Eve each year black Carolinians built a bonfire and spent the rest of the night in prayer and singing, awaiting the dawn and the birth of Christ. By the late 1870s Santa Claus, carols, Christmas trees, turkeys, stockings, eggnog, mistletoe, and fireworks were integral parts of the festivities. Benevolent organizations and churches hosted meals and community Christmas trees for the less fortunate. Old-timers grumbled about the commercialization of the holiday and all the noise, but the editor of the *Winnsboro News and Herald* expressed the feelings of most in 1879 when he asked: "Who would be without Christmas, a time when everybody can get young . . . and forget cares and troubles for one day in the year at least?"[40]

The Fourth of July was primarily a holiday for black Carolinians until well into the twentieth century. Photograph by Marion Post Wolcott (Farm Security Administration). Courtesy, Library of Congress.

Bringing the news of Christmas and serving as vehicles for its commercialization were newspapers, lots of them. There was at least one in every county, and some towns such as Marion and Newberry had two. Orangeburg in 1889 boasted three: *Times and Democrat, Spectator,* and the *Plain Speaker,* the latter a black-owned publication. Most of the 199 newspapers printed during the 1880s were weeklies, but there were dailies in Charleston (*News and Courier*), Columbia (*Daily Register*), and Greenville (*Daily News*). During the 1870s and 1880s the *News and Courier* had a statewide circulation and was, without question, the most important newspaper in South Carolina. Although the dailies covered politics, they and the weeklies gave a lot of space to local affairs, especially schools and churches.[41]

In 1882 there were 3,183 schools in South Carolina but only 3,413 teachers. Clearly, many of the schools were one-room schoolhouses. Of these, nearly one-third were still log structures; only 30 were brick. Towns considered it a mark of community pride when they had "graded schools." One of the major achievements of Reconstruction had been the constitutional provision for a public school system. The Bourbons, with their policy of toleration, provided for nearly equal funding for black and white children. In 1879–1880 the per pupil expenditure was $2.75 ($41.11) for whites and $2.51 ($37.52) for blacks. Gradually during the 1880s the funding was increased; however, in 1890 South Carolina provided an average of only $3.38 ($56.32) per child compared to the South Atlantic regional average of $7.63 ($127.13) and a national average of $17.22 ($286.95).[42]

Teacher training was minimal, pay meager, and supplies nonexistent. Teachers made blackboards out of boxes and copybooks from wrapping paper. Geography could be taught by drawing maps in a sandy schoolyard, and the alphabet by using newspaper headlines. In 1886, thanks to northern philanthropy, Winthrop Training School for teachers opened in Columbia. There were special summer institutes for teachers, but sometimes those for black teachers were canceled due to lack of funds.[43]

"What we want is education, good schools," wrote A. Smith Gibbes of Pendleton in 1880. Yet there were those who begrudged spending even the little that was appropriated. Between short-sighted carping and niggardly funding, it is a wonder that the state's schools were able to accomplish anything at all. Sometimes communities such as Cheraw sponsored adult education classes through a Chatauquan Circle. Nevertheless, despite the efforts of dedicated teachers and interested citizens, in 1880, 78.5 percent of the black population and 22 percent of the white were *totally illiterate*. Those destined for college frequently had to enroll in special preparatory classes such as those Wofford College offered through its Fitting School or Allen University through its high school program.[44]

Allen was sponsored by the African Methodist Episcopal Church, one of the branches of Methodism that flourished in the state after the war. By 1885, 91 percent of South Carolinians who had a religious affiliation belonged to either a Methodist or Baptist church. Churches might have been some of the most segregated places in South Carolina on Sunday mornings, but Sunday schools were sometimes run by white churches for black children (after the classes for whites were over).[45]

One of the few religious controversies during the 1870s and 1880s occurred in Greenville when civic-minded business leaders contributed toward the building of St. Mary's Roman Catholic Church. Their generosity aroused a brief Know-Nothing sort of flurry of speeches and letters to the editor from some upcountry Protestants who saw the church as a papist "fortification for the troops of an enemy."[46]

During the post-Civil War years a new religion emerged in South Carolina, one that may have been more deeply felt by its adherents than any traditional religious faith: the civil religion of the Lost Cause. White Carolinians, as did their southern contemporaries, wondered why the South had lost the war. There were all sorts of reasons, but in their hearts they searched for a deeper meaning of God's influence on the affairs of humankind. The Lost Cause as it emerged was not "a celebration of the Confederacy, but a monument to defeat."[47]

In 1862 Henry Timrod had penned "Carolina," a stirring call to duty. The concluding stanza exhorted Carolinians to "Fling down thy gauntlet to the Huns, / And roar the challenge from thy guns; / Then leave the future to thy sons, / Carolina!"

Confederate Memorial Day, 10 May 1900, Cheraw (Chesterfield County). The Cheraw monument (1867) is the oldest Confederate monument in the United States. Courtesy, Cheraw Visitors Bureau.

Four years later he composed an "Ode" (Sung on the Occasion of Decorating the Graves of the Confederate Dead, at Magnolia Cemetery, Charleston, SC, 1866). A generation of young white South Carolina males had made the supreme sacrifice for their state. The somber, defeated mood of the "Ode" was a marked contrast to the defiant challenge of "Carolina":

> Sleep sweetly in your humble graves,
> Sleep, martyrs of a fallen cause!—
> Though yet no marble column craves
> The pilgrim here to pause. . . .
>
> Stoop, angels, hither from the skies!
> There is no holier spot of ground,
> Than where defeated valor lies
> By mourning beauty crowned.

Historians generally trace the beginning of the cult of the Lost Cause to the dedication of the Stonewall Jackson monument in Richmond in October 1875. However, on Confederate Memorial Day 1871 the Reverend Dr. John L. Girardeau addressed those assembled to honor the reinterment of South Carolinians killed at Gettysburg. His remarks were a detailed guidebook for the Lost Cause and a justification for the overthrow of Reconstruction.[48]

Girardeau urged his listeners: "*Let us cling to our identity as a people!*" By so doing, white Carolinians would insure that the "precious blood" of those who died would not have been "spilt wholly in vain." The Radical influences in the state were a threat, but there were ways for the old Carolina to survive and, someday, reassert itself: wear mourning; accept the "trials which distinguish us from a people inflated with material prosperity"; refuse to participate in the Radical government in any way; institute "peculiar customs and organizations" which will perpetuate the past; set aside days of remembrance; form memorial associations; collect and publish "materials for our own history"; and educate our young "by making our nurseries, schools, and colleges channels for conveying from generation to generation our own type of thought, sentiment and opinion." Above all else, Girardeau said, Carolinians should remember that principle was more important than "material goods" and they should "tenaciously hold on to the fragments of a noble past." The heroes of Gettysburg had fought for a defeated but, prayed the good reverend, not a "wholly lost—Cause!"[49]

Although there were only several thousand who attended the service, obviously there were others of like mind in South Carolina. Within a decade Girardeau's outline had been implemented by white Carolinians everywhere. Like all white southerners, Carolinians used the war as a dividing line; events, individuals, and institutions from prewar days took on a special, almost religious, significance and should be venerated. Memories of the war years were sacred. Objects associated with the war became relics, and places shrines. In some ways living in the past was a way for Carolinians to cope with the unpleasant reality of the postwar world. An 1880 visitor to the state commented that "The true South Carolinian lives in the past." Sometimes an individual acted simply to preserve his or her family's heritage. Catherine Elizabeth Fitzsimons Hammond, for example, purchased Redcliffe (the Hammond estate in Aiken County) "to preserve it for my children." At the turn of the century, Elizabeth Allston Pringle, a woman rice planter in Georgetown County, struggled to pay property taxes on her family's land. In her diary she wrote that she was one of those South Carolinians "who live in the past so much." Others, in their capacities as civic, religious, and social leaders, influenced their communities and the state.[50]

Ellison Capers, a former Confederate general turned Episcopal priest, served as rector of Christ Church (Greenville) and Trinity Church (Columbia) before being elected bishop of the Diocese of South Carolina. Seldom was there an important Confederate observance of any kind in which the soldier-bishop did not participate. The sanctuary of Trinity Church, Capers's last parish, was just thirty years old when Reconstruction ended. However, thanks to Sherman's visit to Columbia, it was the oldest surviving church in the city—and the church of Wade Hampton and the Bourbon establishment. By the 1870s it was referred to as "Old Trinity" and "Dear Old Trinity." A late-nineteenth-century visitor described Trinity's churchyard as "green with creeping myrtle and grey with the tombs of aristocratic heroes."[51]

Every town in the state had its version of Trinity Church, a building that had survived the war and become a symbol of the resurrected old order in the 1870s and 1880s. It might be a church, such as First Baptist in Greenville, Bethesda Presbyterian in Camden, Trinity Episcopal in Edgefield, or St. David's Episcopal in Cheraw; a public building, such as the county courthouse in Walterboro, Kingstree, Lancaster, or Newberry; a college or school, such as Wofford in Spartanburg or Limestone in Gaffney; or a residence, such as the Burt House in Abbeville, Japonica Hall in Society Hill, the Jeter House in Union, or the White House in Rock Hill. Beaufort and Charleston were filled with such structures. John Ruskin wrote that the "greatest glory of a building is not in its stones, or in its gold. Its glory is in its Age." Carolinians agreed, up to a point. Surviving the war (not the four or five centuries Ruskin decreed) was enough to confer instant heritage on a building, and if it were associated with an individual or event from the war, it was likely to become hallowed.[52]

Charleston, already truly venerable, became the Holy City, its landscape a monument to the state's past. However, many of its social and cultural organizations had fallen on hard times; some had ceased to function. Gradually those closely identified with the city's antebellum world revived: St. Andrew's Society, St. George's Society, South Carolina Jockey Club, Charleston Club, Charleston Library Society, and Carolina Art Association. Among the individuals who worked diligently to re-create and promote the institutions of antebellum Charleston were Edward McCrady Jr. and Joseph W. Barnwell. McCrady, through speeches and articles, wrote unceasingly of the glories of antebellum South Carolina. Barnwell was active in a number of organizations, but it was as a member of the board of managers and president of the St. Cecilia Society that he shaped the social structure of the port city and made the St. Cecilia Society the innermost citadel of the old order.[53]

The South Carolina College, however, was "the cornerstone of *our* system," declared John Bratton. Most Bourbons would have agreed with him. Nothing had dismayed them more than the integration of the college in 1873. Hampton and his legislative allies closed the "Radical University" in 1877. When it reopened in 1880 as the new College of Agriculture and Mechanic Arts, the school hardly resembled the elite antebellum college. In 1882 the institution was reorganized along more traditional lines as the South Carolina College. Whatever its name, it supporters hoped that the school, like its antebellum predecessor, would inculcate in its students the old order's "notions of personal honor and truth."[54]

Nowhere were those notions more eloquently expressed than on the Confederate monument that was unveiled on the State House grounds on 13 May 1879. William H. Trescot's words on the monument captured the essence of the Bourbon worldview. In communities across the state committees and groups formed to raise funds to erect their own monuments to honor the Lost Cause. The most expensive and visible monument in the state honored the old order, not the Confederacy. In 1887 the Ladies' Calhoun Monument Association dedicated a $44,000 ($700,000) statue in Charleston honoring John C. Calhoun. The inscription on the base was particularly interesting. There were two lines about the greatness of Calhoun but four detailing the heroism of the association's leader, Mary Amarinthia Yates Snowden, during the war.[55]

On 21 December 1886, in Boston, Henry W. Grady, the editor of the *Atlanta Constitution,* announced the birth of the New South. A few South Carolinians such as Daniel A. Tompkins, the Edgefield County-born editor of the *Charlotte Daily Observer,* and Francis Dawson of Charleston might have been paying attention, but few others were. The men who controlled the state were not interested in a New South. They had expended what little vitality they had left in reviving the old.[56]

Charleston's *News and Courier* is often cited as a New South newspaper. Its editor Francis Dawson was forever plugging new schemes and recommending that his readers let the past be past and work to build a new South Carolina. If a newspaper's importance can be reflected in how its community responds, then the *News and Courier* had virtually no impact on Charleston. If ever there were a place that rejected the New South, it was the port city. It does not take much imagination to visualize how Dawson's suggestion that Charleston needed "about five hundred Yankees of the right stripe" (preferably a hybrid of Boston and Chicago) to "put a new face on affairs and make the whole place throb with life and vivid force" was received south of Broad Street.[57]

Charleston was the largest city in South Carolina, but its regional and national importance had been in decline since the early nineteenth century. In 1800 it was the fourth largest city in the United States; by 1890 it had fallen to sixty-eighth. Within the South, over the same time period, it had gone from being the largest city to sixth. The reasons for the city's decline were many. Some were external and beyond its control, such as the collapse of the lowcountry economy and northern-owned railroads' siphoning off traffic to New York. The main reason for Charleston's stagnation, though, was its lack of leadership.[58]

When the Bourbons took over the city government in 1879, they did exactly what their peers were doing at the state level. They slashed public expenditures, reduced the size of the police force and fire department, and refused to make capital improvements. The result was a shabby city with unpaved streets, open sewers, and polluted drinking water. The city had no central water or sewer system. More than seven thousand privies leaked one hundred thousand pounds of human waste a day and contaminated private wells, the main source of water. The only money spent on the city's infrastructure came from the outside. In 1878 the federal government built jetties to harness the tides to deepen the shipping channel, and the following year northern capital financed the state's first telephone exchange.[59]

In the 1880s Charleston's business community was dominated by the same men who had been in charge in 1860. These older men did not cotton to new ideas or new men. Energetic young men were not honored; they were ignored as the old political and economic elite refused to open its ranks to newcomers. The old, relaxed

Repairing St. Michael's Church, Charleston, after the 1886 earthquake. Courtesy, Calhoun County Museum.

style of doing business (going to work at 10:30 A.M., a full dinner at 3:00 P.M., and back to the office to close up) was pleasant but noncompetitive. Efforts to create efficient rivals to the "ancient Chamber of Commerce" foundered. When the country's oldest chamber of commerce celebrated its centennial in 1884, it looked to the glories of the past rather than the promises of the future. As a result, talented young men sought opportunities elsewhere. Charlestonians, old and new (including the city's mayor, William A. Courtenay), invested in upcountry textile mills and Birmingham coal and iron companies.[60]

The lack of vision and energy by the city's business community was compounded by outside forces. By 1881 the South Carolina Railroad, the "child of Charleston capital," was controlled by New Yorkers. On 25 August 1885 a category 3 hurricane with 125 mph winds and a tidal surge struck the city. The storm damaged or destroyed 90 percent of the homes in the city and killed 21. Property losses were set at $2 million ($31.3 million). A year later, on 31 August 1886, before it had fully recovered from the effects of the hurricane, Charleston was rocked by an earthquake that registered 6.6 on the Richter scale. Some two thousand buildings were destroyed and thousands more damaged; 110 Charlestonians died either in the rubble or from injuries and disease related to the disaster. Property damage was estimated at $6 million ($96.4 million), one-fourth the total assessed value. Nearly $1 million ($16 million) in relief was distributed by a local committee, much of it contributed by sympathetic northerners. Between the onslaught of nature and the actions of northern financiers, Charleston seemed to be at the mercy of events beyond its control. Yet, like a proper grande dame of the old order who had fallen on hard times, the city wore its cloak of stagnation and despair with pride.[61]

There were some outbreaks of New South boosterism in the upstate, especially in Anderson, Greenville, and Spartanburg Counties. However, in the 1870s and 1880s they were mild, for the most part contained, and not overly contagious.

Railroads continued to extend their steel tentacles into all sections of the state. It was accepted as gospel that towns such as Walterboro prospered because they had good railway connections and others such as Abbeville declined because they did not. The development of trunk lines by the Southern Railway and Seaboard Airline Railroad through the upper piedmont gave impetus to the growth of Rock Hill, Spartanburg, and Greenville. In 1860 none of these towns had been major cotton markets, but by 1880 all three were. During the decade of the 1880s Rock Hill's population tripled and Spartanburg, with sixteen textile mills (two hundred thousand spindles), billed itself as "the manufacturing centre of the state."[62]

Textile mills were as much a symbol of the New South as the Calhoun Monument was of the Old South. Yet much of the development that took place was not the result of entrepreneurship by brash new men on the make. Rather, almost all of the state's early mills were financed by local capital from individuals with connections to the prewar elite. Charlestonians such as Ellison A. Smyth and Francis J. Pelzer invested heavily in the growing upstate instead of their stagnant hometown. The Newberry and Winnsboro cotton mills were built by local enterprise, and farmers in Oconee County financed the Westminster cotton mill. The most successful textile capitalists were those associated with the Spartanburg firm of Walker, Fleming and Company, which developed a number of mills including Pacolet Manufacturing Company and Spartan Mills.[63]

Other "home boys" with strong community ties, especially to farming, were successful businessmen. John C. and Patrick Calhoun, grandsons of the statesman, sat on the boards of directors of railroads and helped engineer the merger of a number of local lines throughout the region. W. J. and W. L. Roddey were York County planters who got involved with the development of Rock Hill and prospered as cotton merchants. In Anderson the town's leading business and professional men all claimed kinship to an eighteenth-century settler, Edward Vandiver. Thus, while upcountry residents did not shy away from business, neither were they divorced from the agricultural community or the prewar elite. Those town merchants who made money in the 1870s and 1880s were just as much Bourbons as Wade Hampton.[64]

Prosperity, however, was something unknown to the vast majority of South Carolinians. It made little difference if one were a former planter or a former slave. Per capita wealth increased from $295 ($3,413) in 1870 to $297 ($4,386) in 1880 but represented only a fraction of the wealth held before the Civil War. In 1860 South Carolina's per capita wealth (with slaves included as part of the population) had been $864 ($15,693), well above the national average of $608 ($11,043). In 1880 the national per capita wealth was $870 ($12,847), nearly three times the state average.[65]

The state's economy was a shambles. Daughters of the old elite were happy to earn $4.22 ($67.24) for a six-day week in Charleston shops. Their daily wages (70¢ [$11.21]) were only a little more than what their grandfathers had paid a field hand to chop cotton on his day off. The Palmers of South Santee were one of the old planting families fallen on hard times. The big house at their Lenud's Ferry plantation fell into disrepair because they could not afford to keep it up. Eventually some of them sold the land and family furniture and moved away. Janie Watkins Palmer of Mount Pleasant took in sewing from white and black customers to help augment her family's income. Her family's monthly budget was $21 ($315). After setting aside $12 ($180) for rent, $5 ($75) for washing, $2 ($30) for help, and $2 ($30) for fuel, she noted that "there was little left each month to live on." One wonders how Elsie, "the help," got by on $2 ($30) a month. In 1890 sharecroppers probably made $50 ($833) for a year's hard work. And more than likely, at year's end they were paid either in kind or in scrip to be redeemed at the landlord's store.[66]

Increased cotton production, the abandoning of food crops, and abuse of the land all led to troubles in the state's agricultural sector. In 1860 South Carolina produced 353,412 bales of cotton. The figure had risen to 522,548 by 1880 and a decade later to 747,190. The figures for Anderson County are illustrative of the growth in cotton production. From less than 5,000 bales in 1860, the county's output rose to 20,000 in 1880 and 40,000 in 1890. Even Greenville County became part of the cotton belt. Increased production was the result of putting marginal lands under cultivation and the heavy use of fertilizers. The constant turnover of tenants and sharecroppers and the frantic effort to make the land yield ever more cotton in a vain attempt to pay off liens led to land butchery on a massive scale.[67]

Planting more cotton meant that farmers were devoting fewer acres to food crops. In 1880 the state's corn harvest was less than one-half what it had been before the war. Not until the turn of the century would corn and sweet potato production reach 1860 levels. Wheat production declined steadily. Between 1 January and 15 May 1886 the upcountry town of Greenwood imported 57 carloads of bacon, 9,560 bushels of cornmeal, 2,391 barrels of flour, and 445 barrels of molasses. "No wonder times are hard!" commented the *Winnsboro News and Herald*. South Carolinians should have been growing their own food. The *Sumter Watchman and Southron* echoed that sentiment and added a complaint of its own: "Planting all cotton and keeping one's smokehouse and corncrib in the West is bad enough, but cannot compare in evil with buying on credit."[68]

In 1885 the *Carolina Spartan* (Spartanburg) published an article, "Does Farming Pay?" Farming, the newspaper informed its readers, was the economic backbone of the county; without farming the "banks, factories, stores, and professions would all go under." Although farming may have been the "grand motive power" in Spartanburg and the rest of the state's counties, most who tilled the soil had a difficult time making ends meet. Overproduction led to lower prices. In 1873 cotton was

14.1¢($1.78) a pound, but by 1880 it had dropped to 9.8¢ ($1.45) a pound. That meant that a cotton farmer had to work longer to get the same return as he did seven years earlier. Six consecutive years (1881–1886) of falling prices, droughts, army worms, and bad harvests bedeviled the struggling farmers.[69]

For those who depended upon rice, the picture was just as grim. Worldwide rice production soared. The opening of the Suez Canal gave Asian rice growers easy access to European markets. During the 1880s Lower Burma exported more rice to Europe annually than the United States produced in the entire decade. In this country the mechanization of rice production and economies of scale shifted growing from the Carolinas and Georgia to Louisiana, Texas, and Arkansas. South Carolina's 1880 yield was 52 million pounds, less than one-half what it had been in 1860. In 1890 the state's production declined to 30 million pounds. In 1860 the state had produced 64 percent of the country's rice; in 1880 it was still the leading rice-producing state, but ten years later it had fallen far behind Louisiana.[70]

The Bourbon governors, with the exception of Hugh S. Thompson, were all farmers. Yet their comments concerning the plight of the state's agricultural community were out of touch with reality. In 1882 Johnson Hagood said in his report to the General Assembly that state government was "well-ordered, smooth-working, and economic" and that the people of South Carolina were "happy and prosperous." Such remarks must have seemed callous to the farmers who had endured a drought in 1881 and an infestation of army worms in 1882, and to the people of Mechanicsville (Sumter County) who were "in actual want of bread" and petitioned the General Assembly for state aid in 1882. After four more years of insufficient rainfall and crop failures, Gov. John P. Richardson said: "All over our fair & lovely State, with few exceptional localities, the sun of prosperity seems once again to have arisen from the dark clouds that have for so many years been obscuring its rays to shed abroad fresh & invigorated life." Elected to resurrect the old order, the Bourbons thought their mission complete once they had made South Carolina safe for white man's democracy. They had no leadership, no ideas, no vision. They were men of reaction, not action. After 1882 their main purpose seemed to be simply to remain in office. It was their due. It would also be their political downfall.[71]

By the mid 1880s white Carolinians had heeded Girardeau's admonition to cling to their identity as a people. Actually, they had done more than just hang onto "the fragments of a noble past." In following his advice (almost to the letter), they, like their counterparts in Victorian England and Scotland, not only preserved the past but sometimes invented it. The genteel world of Bourbon South Carolina—a place where family mattered more than money; where blacks were subordinated to whites and marginalized politically; where the past was celebrated and the present ignored as much as possible—was the result. Whether based upon real or invented traditions, the South Carolina that the Bourbons created during the late nineteenth century was durable enough to survive (with some modifications) the challenges of Ben Tillman, the New South, and most of the twentieth century.[72]

Chapter Nineteen

TILLMAN

We feel the dire necessity of a change in our present system of managing our lands, in which as a rule the anomaly is presented of men claiming to be sensible, ruining their farms and impoverishing themselves to raise cotton, while buying their supplies. . . . A majority of our people are now mere "hewers of wood and drawers of water."
> Edgefield Agricultural and Mechanical Society, 8 October 1884

The Farmers' Movement, for the farmers, of the farmers, and by the farmers, has been twisted into a Tillman movement, for Tillman, and by Tillman.
> *Greenville Daily News,* 29 March 1890

*D*URING THE DECADE of the 1880s things went from bad to worse for the state's farmers. Wedded to cotton through ignorance or necessity, they suffered. Drought, army worms, and crop failures followed one another like the plagues of ancient Egypt. When crops did come in, prices dropped. Caught in a vicious cycle by the crop lien system, thousands lost their farms. In 1886 some 954,000 acres and the next year another 100,000 acres were forfeited because their owners could not pay their taxes. In just two years almost 8 percent of all farmland in the state went on the auction block. With the state's leaders telling them that the economy was robust and that those who complained did not know what they were talking about, it was no wonder that farmers decided they had to take matters into their own hands.[1]

The Patrons of Husbandry, or the Grange, first appeared in the state in Charleston in 1871. By 1875 there were 342 local chapters, or granges, and ten thousand white members in such places as Manchester (Sumter County), Pomaria (Newberry), and Pear Ridge (Union), as well as Charleston and Greenville. D. Wyatt Aiken, a planter from Cokesbury (Abbeville County), was a national officer of the Grange and largely responsible for the rapid growth in the state. However, within five years membership declined even more quickly than it had grown because the Grange was not able to accomplish much and was rigidly apolitical. By the mid 1880s what was left of the organization had combined forces with the Bourbon-

Frank and Carrie Smith Rushton, Saluda County. Courtesy, Saluda County Historical Society.

controlled State Agricultural and Mechanical Society. The Patrons of Husbandry were, however, responsible for the creation of the Agricultural Bureau (1879) and for educating farmers to look to the government for assistance.[2]

More durable and more widespread was another organization, the Farmers' Alliance. Actually, there were two: the Southern Farmers' Alliance for whites and the Colored Farmers' Alliance for blacks. Both groups entered the state in the late 1880s and, because of the trying conditions in the agricultural sector, spread with the rapidity of a summer wildfire. The first chapter, or sub-alliance, of the Southern Farmers' Alliance was formed in Marion County in 1887. By 1890 there were sixty thousand Alliance members. The Chesterfield County Alliance had thirty sub-alliances, and those in Spartanburg and Marion Counties had twenty-four. The Spartanburg Alliance operated a cooperative store. For several years the state headquarters was in Greenville where the county alliance owned a commodity warehouse. The *Cotton Plant,* the organization's official newsletter, appeared first in Marion. It was then published in Greenville until the early twentieth century when it merged with the *Progressive Farmer.*[3]

Not all Alliance members were farmers, but most were. In 1889 nearly 86 percent of those on the rolls were real farmers, but only 55 percent owned their own land. The rest were either tenants or sharecroppers. Of the nonfarming members, about 3 percent were mechanics and the rest were professionals. Spartanburg County's "Alliance Senator" in the General Assembly in 1890 was a physician and town resident, not a farmer.[4]

Almost to a person the members of the Colored Farmers' Alliance were farmers. T. E. Pratt of Cheraw was one of the group's early leaders. Among the early sub-alliances were those at Cedar Creek in Lancaster County and Gadsden, Mill Creek, and Congaree in Richland. Like its white counterpart, the Colored Farmers' Alliance grew rapidly. There were twelve sub-alliances in Union County, and when the Sumter Colored Farmers' Alliance held a barbecue in 1889, more than one thousand attended and listened intently to a parade of speakers. By 1891 the state organization claimed forty thousand members.[5]

Farmers wanted action and, after a fashion, the state government responded. The Agricultural Bureau, funded by a 25¢ ($3.88) per ton tax on fertilizer, functioned very much like the modern farm extension service (except there were no county agents). It served as a clearinghouse for information on new seeds, fertilizers, and methods of cultivation; inspected and analyzed fertilizers to insure quality; maintained meteorological records; and provided some veterinary services. The state also provided a subsidy for the South Carolina Agricultural and Mechanical Society, which helped defray the costs of its annual meeting with the State Grange. In 1887 the General Assembly reorganized the South Carolina College as the University of South Carolina with an agricultural department. While these efforts might seem minimal, they were major steps for a state that had done nothing for its agricultural sector since the early 1800s.[6]

County farmers' associations, modeled after the South Carolina Agricultural and Mechanical Association, were sometimes little more than debating societies or promoters of county fairs. Talk was cheap and hot air did not bring rain, raise cotton prices, eradicate army worms, stop soil erosion, or pay off liens. Ironically, though, it was a county association and the 1885 annual meeting of the South Carolina Agricultural and Mechanical Association that provided platforms for a politician who would reshape South Carolina politics.[7]

An Edgefield County farmer, Benjamin Ryan Tillman, chafed at the inaction of the government in Columbia. Although he was proud to call himself a "dirt farmer," Tillman was anything but that. Had it not been for the intervention of the Civil War, the Tillmans with their one hundred slaves and large landholdings would have moved into the state's elite. As it was, they survived the war with their lands intact and Ben, through hard work and thrift, added to his inheritance. By 1881 he owned twenty-two hundred acres and operated a "thirty plow farm," which meant that he employed thirty men in agricultural labor. According to the standards of the day, he was a prosperous farmer. Then he overextended himself in the early 1880s and got caught in the series of droughts and crop failures that bedeviled the state. Although he did not lose his lands, he saw the need for diversification and agricultural education.[8]

In 1885 Tillman was one of the founders of the Edgefield Agricultural Society. His high-handed behavior soon drove off one-half the original sixty members, but those who remained became true believers in Tillman's cause of agricultural reform. In a June 1885 address to the society, Tillman said that among the farmers' prob-

Benjamin Ryan Tillman (1847–1918).
Courtesy, South Caroliniana Library.

lems was not "keeping abreast of the times" and their "butchery" of the land by "renting to ignorant lazy negroes." Two months later in Bennettsville he electrified those in attendance at the annual meeting of the Grange and South Carolina Agricultural and Mechanical Association with similar comments.[9]

The Bennettsville speech began with a vicious attack on the Bourbon regime, saying that the people had "been hoodwinked by demagogues and lawyers in the pay of finance." Every initiative, from the Agricultural Bureau to the agricultural department at the South Carolina College, were dismissed as "sops" and "bribes." He said that the state society to which he was speaking numbered "disreputable politicians" among its members. Then he proposed that the association pass five resolutions to promote agricultural education. His remarks were received coolly by the state's agricultural establishment, but the hundreds of farmers in the audience responded, as if on cue, to every biting comment. A century before spin doctors and politicians used sound bites to grab headlines Tillman was a master of the technique. Four of the five resolutions went down to defeat; only his call for a state experimental farm passed. But N. G. Gonzales, a reporter for the *News and Courier,* observed: "Mr. Tillman defended his resolutions in a speech full of hard sense, keen satire, and good-humored bandiage."[10]

The editor of the *News and Courier,* Francis W. Dawson, was impressed by Tillman's forthrightness and call for reform. For years the newspaperman had been trying unsuccessfully to get Charleston's urbane Bourbons to do something other than moon over the way it used to be. Now here was a bright, energetic farmer trying to shake up the state's lethargic agricultural community. Privately Dawson counseled Tillman to moderate his views so that they would be more palatable to a wider audience, but the Reformer, as he now styled himself, knew the public far better than the erudite editor and refused to pull in his verbal horns. Beginning in November 1885 the *News and Courier* published a series of letters from the Edgefield farmer. Full of bombast, innuendo, and insinuation, Tillman's words blamed all the state's woes on those in office. The "ring" that controlled the state was comprised of men who were lazy, stupid, and over-the-hill. As long as those who had no vision for the state were in office, things could not get better for the average white Carolinian. Later Dawson became one of Tillman's bitterest opponents, but had it not been for the *News and Courier* in 1885, it is probable that Ben Tillman would have remained nothing but an unhappy upcountry farmer. The Charleston newspaper, with its statewide circulation, gave him a forum and credibility.[11]

In March 1886 Tillman announced that a farmers' convention would meet in Columbia the following month. On 29 April more than three hundred delegates, representing thirty of the state's thirty-four counties, assembled in the capital city. Needless to say, it was Tillman who gave the keynote address. He continued his relentless attack on the inept politicians who were more devoted to the memory of the Confederacy than they were to the men who labored in the fields, voted, and paid taxes. Anyone who supported him was a "farmer," and all who opposed him were "little greedy men, office-seekers and their satellites." The body politic was infected with a "political leprosy" that needed to be expunged so that South Carolina could once again be clean and pure. Among the resolutions adopted by the convention were a call for the closing of the Citadel, with its buildings to house an industrial college for girls; an agricultural college (separate from the department at the university) funded by a special tax on fertilizer; an experimental station; reform of the Agricultural Bureau; and a reduction in government expenditures. Before they adjourned, the delegates agreed to meet annually every November.[12]

The Conservatives, as the establishment soon labeled themselves, were placed on the defensive by Tillman's Reformers. All, however, were members of the Democratic Party. At the party's convention Tillman tried unsuccessfully to get John G. Sheppard of Edgefield the nomination for governor. Even though Sheppard rejected many of the farmers' programs and thereby lost their official endorsement, he lost by only twenty-seven votes. That should have sent a message to the Conservative leadership, but in dealing with Tillman they truly were, like the Bourbons of France, oblivious to the sea change in the state's political climate.[13]

When the Farmers' Convention met in November 1886, even the most casual observer could see that it was not just a forum for agricultural reform; it was being molded into a political machine to further the ambitions of Ben Tillman. Its resolutions and its leader's unrelenting attacks on the establishment kept him on the front pages of the state's newspapers. The General Assembly authorized two agricultural experimental stations and reorganized the University of South Carolina with a strong agricultural department. The 1888 party convention rejected Tillman's plan for primaries to replace conventions as the means for nominating candidates for office. Alleging that the state needed to save money, the legislature amended the constitution to put off reapportionment until 1891. Upcountry legislators (many of them Reformers) mounted an all-out but unsuccessful attempt for reapportionment. By 1888 the Conservatives believed that they had buried Tillmanism politically with their maneuvers. They had; however, they did not count on the heirs of John C. Calhoun undermining their order.[14]

On 2 April 1888 Thomas Green Clemson, the late statesman's son-in-law, died. In his will he bequeathed 814 acres of the Calhoun plantation, Fort Hill, and an $80,000 ($1.27 million) endowment to the state for the creation of an agricultural college. Although something of a quarrelsome old man, Clemson was an ardent supporter of agricultural education. He also believed that South Carolina needed "an institution that vandal hands could not pollute" (his response to the desegregation of the South Carolina College). Immediately there was opposition from the Conservatives, who rightly viewed the Clemson bequest as a threat to their beloved University of South Carolina. They raised all sorts of roadblocks, not the least of which was that Clemson's granddaughter sued the estate, claiming that Fort Hill was rightfully hers.[15]

For more than a year there was a tremendous debate across the state over the issue of an agricultural college. Tillman was in his element, never missing an opportunity to speak. In November 1889, after the courts had dismissed the suit against the estate, Governor Richardson signed the bill creating Clemson College. (Although clearly tied into state politics, the establishment of Clemson coincided with a regional trend as Alabama, Georgia, North Carolina, Texas, and Virginia also opened "practical" colleges in the 1870s and 1880s.) The state agreed to Clemson's stipulation that there be a thirteen-member board of trustees, seven of whom were life trustees named in his will. That group would be self-perpetuating and thus a state-supported institution could not be controlled by the state. Benjamin Ryan Tillman of Edgefield County was one of the original life trustees.[16]

The Reformer was on a roll. One had to be living in a cave not to understand that the acceptance of the Clemson bequest was a personal victory for him. He had failed in the 1888 Democratic Convention to have primaries select candidates, but the delegates had decreed that in 1890 candidates would have to debate the issues at country stump meetings. It was a forum tailor-made for Tillman. He and his allies wasted little time in cranking up what was now a well-oiled machine, the Farmers' Convention.

In January 1890 G. Wash Shell of Laurens County, the president of the convention, published the "Shell Manifesto." In this widely circulated document he called for a special Farmers' Convention in March 1890 to select candidates for statewide office that it would "recommend" to the Democratic Party convention. It was a bold political ploy and succeeded only because of the skulduggery of Tillman's lieutenants, J. L. M. Irby of Laurens and W. Jasper Talbert of Edgefield. When the farmers met, the motion to recommend candidates was defeated, but Irby and others created distractions on the floor and Shell baldly announced in a recount that the motion had carried. Then a slate was chosen and, to no one's surprise, Ben Tillman was recommended for governor.[17]

There was considerable opposition to the politicization of the farmers' movement and the dread that the recommendation of candidates might split the state's white minority. The *Greenville News,* long a Tillman supporter, condemned his naked political ambitions now exposed for all to see. And the *News* was not alone. When the scales dropped from the eyes of disillusioned Reformers, they saw not a tribune of the people but just another greedy man, an office seeker.[18]

The 1890 canvass was no contest. The same party machinery that made it easy to eliminate black voters assured that the Reformers would win. From across the state nervous Conservatives reported that they had lost control of local clubs and county conventions. When the first state convention met in August, the Reformers were in control. In a desperate move, the Conservatives tried to change the rules and use primaries to select candidates. The Reformers had no intention of letting victory escape their grasp and defeated the effort to democratize the party. When the second convention was held in August, Tillman and his entire slate was nominated.[19]

A group of die-hard Conservatives, led by A. C. Haskell of Richland County, bolted the party and ran as independents. Calling themselves the "Straightout Democracy," this rump group openly appealed to the state's remaining black voters. It was a quixotic campaign. Few signed on, and most Conservatives agreed with the editor of the *Greenville Enterprise and Mountaineer* that "the Democratic Party will stand together as a unit." In 1882 Wade Hampton had declared that anyone who did not support the Democratic Party or was an independent was a Radical—with all the pejorative Reconstruction connotations the term carried. Now, here was Haskell, one of the organizers of the 1876 campaign, running for governor as an independent. Hampton reluctantly announced that he intended to vote for Tillman, but he refused to denounce Haskell.[20]

Stump meetings before and after the conventions were near riots and drunken brawls. There was little debate because Tillmanites howled down Conservative speakers. In Aiken even the venerated Wade Hampton was shouted down. In the few counties where Conservatives were strong (Charleston, Richland, and Sumter), their supporters returned the favor. For the most part, though, the Conservatives were so poorly organized that the county meetings turned into a triumphal parade for Tillman, reminiscent of Hampton's in 1876. The old Bourbons/Conservatives could not understand what was happening. For two decades they had relied on their Confederate service as a sure ticket to election; now, waving battle flags and empty sleeves no longer resonated with the voters. The Shell Manifesto had set the tone when it said that farmers could ill-afford to leave state government in the hands of those who were "wedded to ante-bellum ideas."[21]

Tillman was relentless. He blamed the Bourbon establishment for everything: the drought, low cotton prices, extravagant government, and lack of vision. About the only things he did not lay at their doorstep were the 1885 hurricane and the 1886 Charleston earthquake. He was adept at pushing voters' emotional buttons. They hooted and hollered when he denounced the "greedy old city of Charleston" and its "dude factory," the Citadel; the "niggerdom of Beaufort"; and "the seedbed of the aristocracy," the University of South Carolina. He openly sneered at the "broken-down aristocrats" who viewed the world "through antebellum spectacles" and "marched backwards when they marched at all." Although it was far from the truth, he dressed simply and proclaimed that he was nothing but "a plain simple farmer" taking on the "ring" that ran the state.[22]

The opposition was confounded. They were as ill-prepared for the rough-and-tumble of stump meeting debates as some twentieth-century politicians were for television. Tillman did have a nine-point platform, but his major goal—an agricultural college—had already been achieved. Everything else was more or less rhetoric. What he really wanted was power and office. Just as voters believed all the bad things he said about the Bourbons, so many believed that he was the Moses who would lower interest rates and raise cotton prices. He would lead his people to the promised land.[23]

When the results were tallied, Tillman had trounced Haskell four to one (sixty thousand to fifteen thousand). He swept thirty-two of thirty-four counties and won 95 percent or more of the votes in Abbeville, Edgefield, Greenville, Laurens, Lexington, Pickens, and York Counties. The Reform ticket lost only Beaufort and Berkeley Counties, both of which had large numbers of black voters.[24]

What did the election of 1890 mean? Who voted for Tillman? The winner considered his victory a revolution. It was not. He did not bring any new white voters to the polls in the poorer counties. There was no groundswell of debtors and poor whites backing the Reform ticket. Rather, the white minority (no matter how some may have felt about Tillman personally) voted for the Democratic Party candidate to forestall any possibility of allowing blacks to decide the contest between two white men.[25]

Incumbents were ousted, but no revolutionary program was proposed or implemented. Embittered Bourbons, such as Harry Hammond of Edgefield County, interpreted his neighbor's win as a narrow class triumph, a win for "the old non-Slaveholders against the old Slaveholders and the Negroes." Sentiments such as Hammond's and the endorsement of the Farmers' Alliance have led some historians to interpret the 1890 election as a class struggle, a political and social revolution, but it was not. Tillman had sought the Alliance endorsement, but the organization was not the key to his win. And the Bourbons, a combination of the old antebellum elite and upper middle class, were tossed out of office, but Tillman did so with the assistance of some members of the elite and a goodly portion of the state's upper middle class.[26]

The leaders of the farmers movement (and Tillman himself) were anything but dirt farmers. Of the twenty-five men identified as leaders of the Reform movement, eleven were lawyers, seven were planters, four were farmers, and three were professionals. More than 60 percent were college educated, but only a handful were graduates of the South Carolina College. Irby, for example, was the wealthy descendant of a distinguished South Carolina family and had been educated at Princeton and the University of Virginia. John Gary Evans of Aiken County, who would be Tillman's chosen successor, was another well-educated member of the state's elite. Tillman's chief lieutenant in Greenville County, Sen. Milton L. Donaldson, was connected with the leadership of the town of Greenville. His brother, a former state senator, was an avid promoter of textile mills, banks, and railroads. All seven of the upcountry senators elected in 1890 had some association with one or more agricultural organizations (the Grange, the Alliance, or the Farmers' Convention), but that did not mean that they were radicals. Two were attorneys, one was a physician, one a prosperous planter, one a professional civil engineer, and one a teacher; just one was a farmer. Except for Joseph L. Keitt of Newberry County, who supported the Populist Party in 1892, all remained within the folds of the South Carolina Democratic Party.[27]

Ben Tillman was an expert manipulator of crowds. Depending upon where he was speaking, he tended to pit the poor against the rich, tenant against landowner, hireling against employer, country against town, all of South Carolina against Charleston and Columbia, upcountry against lowcountry, white against black, do-somethings against do-nothings, and outs against those in power. By appealing to the darker side of mens' natures, he could rile them up and then appear as their champion, their Moses.[28]

Tillmanism was a political machine, not a social or political revolution. The Conservative opposition was aged, disorganized, inept and had done little or nothing while in office. *Tillman promised to do something.* The election of 1890 was a personal triumph for Ben Tillman, but it was also a triumph of superior organization. His followers had taken over the Democratic Party, the party of order. White unity and the fear of the black majority were as responsible for Tillman's election as any other factor. The state's white minority, no matter what their misgivings might be about Tillman and Reform, were not going to vote for an independent, especially one with black supporters. They voted for the Democratic Party's candidate, Ben Tillman.[29]

In his inaugural address the newly elected governor did not disappoint the thousands that thronged Columbia for the festivities. "The whites," he thundered, "have absolute control of the State government, and we intend at any and all hazards to retain it." He interpreted his win as a "triumph of democracy and white supremacy over mongrelism and anarchy, of civilization over barbarism."[30]

One of the first orders of business for the new administration was the humiliation of Sen. Wade Hampton. With clear majorities in both houses of the General

Assembly, the result was a foregone conclusion. Hampton, despite the urging of friends, refused to go to the State House and beg for reelection. He was decisively defeated by Tillman's chief of political tricks, J. L. M. Irby, an habitual drunk and accused murderer. Even former Confederate veterans deserted their old general and voted as Tillman wanted. At the age of seventy-two Hampton, ill and penniless, the man who had symbolized South Carolina for a generation, was forced to live off the charity of friends and admirers. Columbia Conservatives ostracized the Tillman family. Men ignored the governor on the street, and women refused to call on the first lady.[31]

Two months after Tillman became governor, the first issue of his most dedicated opponent, *The State* newspaper, appeared in Columbia. Founded by determined anti-Tillmanites (including A. C. Haskell, John P. Richardson, David R. Coker, and A. P. Butler) and ably edited by N. G. Gonzales, *The State* was unrelenting in its attempts to discredit the governor, his allies, and his program. While Gonzales was an excellent journalist, he was unabashedly anti-Tillman. The governor fumed, but *The State* in print did to him what he did to others on the stump. When a Greenville newspaper defended Reform, *The State* dismissed it as *The Reedy River Gnat* and regularly referred to the official Tillman newspaper, the *Piedmont Headlight* of Spartanburg, as the *Lighthead*. With its sometimes pompous and almost always preaching prose, the Columbia newspaper was a perfect foil for the earthy Tillman.[32]

In truth, once in office the Reformers were not nearly as revolutionary as they had appeared on the campaign trail. Agricultural education was *the* issue. Clemson was already a reality, but Tillman dismantled the University of South Carolina, reorganizing it as a liberal arts college. However, he did not close it or the Citadel as he had promised to do. Winthrop Normal School in Columbia was moved to Rock Hill where it became the state college for women; however, it was a more traditional liberal arts school than the industrial arts college he had envisioned. Corporate taxes were raised and the phosphate industry's agreements with the state renegotiated. Reapportionment, long overdue, resulted in a net loss of four seats for the lowcountry and a net gain of four for the upcountry.[33]

Tillman's first term was not a complete success. His strong-arm tactics backfired, and the legislature balked at passing railroad reform legislation. He never introduced any measure to modify or repeal the lien law. Because the Reformers had talked so much about reducing the cost of government, they were forced to cut already meager appropriations and thus made it more difficult for state government to serve the people. The completion of Clemson was delayed and state subsidies for fairs withheld. Even so, at the close of Tillman's first year in office he had spent more money than his Bourbon predecessors had averaged during the previous ten years. The governor always had a scapegoat. It was not his fault but that of the "driftwood" legislature. In December 1891 he announced his campaign for reelection and asked the people to defeat "driftwood" legislators who by opposing him had disregarded the will of the people.[34]

Joseph H. Earle of Greenville urged his fellow Conservatives to let Tillman be nominated and elected unopposed. Expressing the old fear that white division might lead to the resurrection of Reconstruction and black rule, he said, "Give me a Tillman a thousand times before a Scott or a Moses." Ignoring Earle's advice, a group of unrepentant Conservatives and disenchanted Tillmanites met in Columbia at what they called the Peace and Harmony Convention. Among those present were former governors Hampton, Richardson, and Sheppard. They rallied behind Sheppard as their candidate for governor and James L. Orr Jr., a Greenville textile manufacturer, for lieutenant governor.[35]

The county stump meetings of 1892 were so unruly that they made those of 1890 seem like Sunday school picnics. Thousands attended the meetings, which sometimes disintegrated into near riots. At Helena in Newberry County bloodshed was narrowly averted. The Conservatives were better organized this time and carried several counties they had lost in 1890. For example, in Sumter County 95 percent of the registered voters went to the polls; the Conservative slate won by 84 votes out of 2,606 cast. In others, such as Newberry, one of Tillman's strongholds, Conservatives cut into his margin considerably. The newspaper war was just as vitriolic as the stump meetings. *The State* attacked Tillmanism with bitingly clever satire, the "Chronicles of Zeracchaboam." The opening lines of the first chronicle let readers know that the governor was in for some roughing up: "Now in the fullness of time arose one Benjamin, a man haughty of spirit and subtle of heart, who greatly deceived the people. The same was spoken of by the Prophet, saying 'A one-eyed man shall be king among the blind.'"[36]

Nothing stopped the Tillman express. He entered the nominating convention with 83 percent of the delegates pledged to him. The Tillman platform, calling for the free coinage of silver, the issuance of paper currency, and the abolition of national banks, reflected the influence of the Alliance. But it was so mild that most Conservatives found it palatable. Although opposed to the nomination of Grover Cleveland for president, he refused to agree to bolt the Democratic Party if Cleveland were nominated. Cleveland handily carried South Carolina. His victory and Tillman's triumph ended the Alliance as a major force in state politics. The governor also carried into office on his coattails enough senators and representatives to give him complete control of the General Assembly. After the "driftwood" was cast out, 28 out of 36 senators and 102 of 124 house members were Tillmanites. In addition, five of the state's seven congressmen were allied with the governor.[37]

One of those who was not was Republican George Washington Murray. In a close race Murray was declared the winner over the Conservative Edwin W. Moise of Sumter by the Tillman-dominated board of elections. Murray was a member of the Colored Farmers Alliance and supported the free coinage of silver; Moise was a Conservative and a Cleveland Democrat. Therefore, the black Republican was more acceptable to the governor.[38]

During his second administration Tillman succeeded in getting bills passed authorizing a new railroad commission with the power to regulate rates; limiting the textile industry to a sixty-six-hour, six-day workweek; refunding the state debt at lower interest; and cutting state salaries by 10 percent. With the legislature filled with yes-men, he launched an assault on the independence of the state's judiciary. His most controversial action, though, was the creation of the state liquor monopoly, the Dispensary.[39]

In 1880 the General Assembly had outlawed the sale of liquor in rural areas. Organizations such as the Women's Christian Temperance Union, Sons of Temperance, and Good Templars promoted temperance, and by 1891, through local option, seventy-eight communities were dry. In 1892 the voters of the state, by a considerable majority, had approved a statewide referendum favoring Prohibition. The house passed a Prohibition bill and sent it to the senate. In the closing days of the legislative session, Tillman (who believed that Prohibition was impractical and the state should make money off men's indulgences) drafted an amendment that eliminated Prohibition and substituted for it the Dispensary. No other action better indicated his dictatorial nature. No matter that the people wanted Prohibition and so did a majority of the legislature; he did not. Bewildered Prohibitionists were ordered by the governor to vote for his bill. They did. On the last day of June 1893 towns across the state resembled a Roman bacchanal as stores and saloons sold off their stocks to all-too-willing buyers.[40]

On 1 July 1893 the Dispensary became the only legal source of alcohol in South Carolina. The State Dispensary Board (governor, comptroller general, and attorney general) appointed county boards, which chose one dispenser in each county seat to sell liquor (Columbia and Charleston could have more). If communities wanted a dispenser, they could petition the county board. Any county or community that was dry was unaffected. The law authorized Dispensary constables to enforce the law, and they did so with a zeal and arrogance that alienated independence-loving South Carolinians. Armed with warrants, they searched private homes on the slightest pretext and spied on their neighbors. They were quick to use their guns and even killed several citizens, but they were promptly pardoned by the governor.[41]

Citizens who were normally law-abiding took pride in resisting the tyranny of the Dispensary and the actions of its spies and goons. In Greenville the mayor and the sheriff supported the citizens who prevented constables from searching their homes. Charlestonians defiantly flouted the law, and blind tigers (illicit saloons) operated openly. One of the city's most notorious bootleggers, Vincent Chicco, was a member of city council. Efforts by the Tillmanite mayor to enforce the law resulted in his being defeated for reelection. In smaller towns, such as Florence, blind tigers cut into the county Dispensary revenues so heavily that it barely broke even.[42]

In March 1894 the so-called "Dispensary War" broke out in Darlington County. A group of constables had gone to Darlington to seize illegal liquor. They had ac-

A Dispensary bottle, featuring the palmetto tree. Courtesy, Calhoun County Museum.

complished their task and were waiting at the railroad station when an altercation broke out between two youths. A constable took sides, and in the ensuing fray a constable pulled his gun and killed a local resident. When everyone then drew their weapons, the altercation became a gunfight at the Darlington Railroad Station. When it was over, two Darlingtonians and one constable were dead and many were wounded (most of them local citizens).

The constables telegraphed the governor that they were under assault and there was no local law enforcement (which was not true). The governor declared Florence and Darlington Counties to be in a state of rebellion, seized control of the telegraph lines out of Darlington, and called out the militia. Companies from Columbia, Charleston, Manning, Newberry, and Sumter refused to respond. An enterprising reporter from *The State* tapped the line and sent dispatches from the "war zone." The *Greenville News* and the *News and Courier* joined *The State* in running sensational stories that fanned public discontent. Upcountry militia units responded to the governor's call and poured into Columbia. Some were sent to Darlington, but there was really no need as local officials had the situation well in hand. Tillman said that the opposition to him and his pet, the Dispensary, was "simply because the minority will not let the majority govern." The event was blown all out of proportion by the governor and his opponents, but nothing better illustrates the emotionalism of the day. Citizens who were otherwise well-meaning were blinded by partisanship. Even children got into the act; in Darlington, tots taunted Tillman militiamen with the rhyme "Tillman Spies / Eat Flies / And Tell Lies."[43]

Less than a month after the trouble in Darlington, the state supreme court (by a 2–1 vote) declared the Dispensary an illegal monopoly. However, Tillman was prepared. A new bill had already been passed by the General Assembly, and when the two Conservative judges' tenures were up, they were replaced by Reformers. The Dispensary was unassailable. It also made money for the state of South Carolina. By 1899 the Dispensary's profits of $414,000 ($7.5 million) equaled nearly one-half the state's total tax revenues.[44]

In 1894 Tillman set his sights on the United States Senate. At a stump meeting in Winnsboro he declared that President Cleveland was nothing but "an old bag of beef." Tillman said, "I am going to Washington with a pitchfork, and prod him in his old fat ribs." The incumbent, Matthew C. Butler, did not give up easily or gracefully and traded insult for insult, accusing the governor of being "a coward, a bulldozer, a liar, and a bribe-taker." He might as well have been spitting in the wind. Loyal Tillmanites believed none of the charges (although there was some truth in all of them), and the last of Hampton's lieutenants went down to defeat.[45]

With John Gary Evans, his handpicked successor, in the governor's office, Tillman still maintained a grip on the political life of the state. He had one item left on his agenda: the elimination of black Carolinians from the political process. The registration laws and the Eight Box Law had reduced black voting strength to fewer than fourteen thousand votes. Still, the threat posed by Haskell's 1890 campaign (appealing to black voters to hold the key to a white man's election) could not be allowed to recur. Tillman's answer was a constitutional convention that would not only eliminate black voters but also the 1868 Reconstruction constitution. Thereby, the white minority could finally be secure in its new order. In June 1895 an Edgefield County mob declared: "We have got the negro down, and, by God, we are going to keep him down." South Carolina became the second state (after Mississippi), to take steps to disenfranchise its black population (see Map 19).[46]

In 1894, by a narrow margin (31,402–29,523), the voters approved a call for a convention to meet in Columbia in the fall of 1895. The upcountry generally favored the convention, and the lowcountry opposed it. Initially Tillman held out an olive branch to the Conservatives because their faction contained the best legal minds in the state. Although a deal was negotiated with several Conservative leaders to split delegations between Reformers and Conservatives, the rank and file in both factions disavowed it. Nonetheless, the Tillman stronghold of Edgefield County allotted one-third of its seats to Conservatives. In Conservative-controlled Sumter and

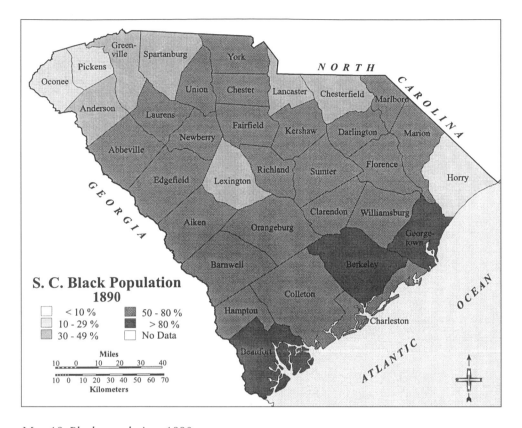

Map 19: Black population, 1890

Richland Counties, seats were given to Reformers. Six members of the convention were black (all five of the Beaufort delegation and one from Georgetown). However, seven out of every ten delegates were Tillmanites. There was no doubt that this was Ben Tillman's convention and he ruled it with an iron fist. It made no difference if the issue were the naming of a county (Saluda) or suffrage.[47]

The question of suffrage generated considerable debate. John Pendleton Kennedy Bryan of Charleston devised the suffrage clause so as to disenfranchise black voters without running afoul of federal authorities. Conservatives tried unsuccessfully to drive a wedge in Reformer ranks by asserting that the literacy provisions would disenfranchise poor whites as well as blacks. The literacy qualification was watered down by allowing that anyone who could "understand and explain" a section of the state constitution "when read to them by the registration officer, shall be entitled to register and become electors." Interestingly, this loophole for illiterate whites was only temporary. After 1898 a potential voter was expected to be able to "both read and write any Section of the Constitution submitted to him by the registration officer" or own and have paid taxes on property assessed at $300 ($5,400) or more. Individuals guilty of "burglary, arson . . . , perjury, forgery, robbery, bribery, adultery, bigamy, wife-beating . . . , fornication, sodomy, incest . . . , miscegenation, larceny, or crimes against the election laws" were disqualified. Convicted embezzlers and murderers, however, were not![48]

Black delegates, especially Thomas E. Miller, William J. Whipper, and Robert Smalls, tried their best to derail the disenfranchisement express. In a stirring address Miller recounted the contributions of black men to the history of the state and nation, showing that black Carolinians had "purchased this land of ours by our past deeds." Yet they were to be denied the right to vote because they were "an alien race." He pled for the banishment of "caste prejudice and hatred of one man towards another." In a sad irony, he understood the future better than his white detractors and that preoccupation with race would keep them from using "their energies . . . in a better cause."[49]

Because of the national media attention focused on the debates, Tillman took the floor and delivered a scathing speech in which he linked every ill facing the state to the corrupt black Reconstruction regime (his remarks were printed in the *Journal* of the convention, the only ones that were). It was a vintage Tillman performance, filled with half-truths and innuendos. Later, on the floor of the United States Senate, he said: "We of the South have never recognized the right of the negro to govern white men, and we never will."[50]

During the convention several woman's rights issues were raised. Cora S. Lott presented a memorial asking for woman suffrage, saying that if women could vote they would clean up the fraud and corruption that male voters could not. A petition from a group of Marion County women stated that "since true democracy maintains that every individual is born with an equal right to the protection and consideration of the law," women should be granted the right to vote. It was received as information but not forwarded to the suffrage committee. The constitution did grant women full control of their property and the right of contract with no restrictions. In one of the rare instances that Tillman did not get his way at the convention, the delegates rejected his proposal to legalize divorce in South Carolina.[51]

Because black disenfranchisement was the primary goal of the new constitution, the neutering of local government has often been overlooked. The 1868 Constitution had created, for the first time in two centuries, meaningful local government; however, some of the most severe criticism of financial misdeeds had been leveled at local officials in the 1880s, not the Reconstruction regime. Several counties had gone overboard in their support of railroads and other civic improvements. This angered taxpayers, and in 1890 the Bourbons pushed through an amendment repealing home rule. The constitutional convention reestablished centralized state control with a vengeance.[52]

The constitution was quite specific in limiting local governments and in detailing what authority the General Assembly could grant them. Counties and townships could not levy taxes or issue bonds except for "educational purposes, to build and repair public roads, buildings, and bridges, to maintain and support prisoners, pay jurors, County officers, and for litigation, quarantine, and court expenses, and for ordinary County purposes, to support paupers and pay past indebtedness." It was a constitutional provision looking to the past, not the future.[53]

Because counties were restricted in what they could do, it became necessary over time to create special-purpose districts to provide needed services. For example, since sanitation was not on the list of services that local governments could provide, special sanitation districts had to be created to build and maintain sewers. Local governments could quarantine yellow fever and cholera victims, but they could not do anything to prevent the diseases. Hospitals were legal only if counties or towns owned the buildings because the constitution did permit them to build and repair public buildings (in the eyes of the law, a hospital was just another "public building"). The fragmented system of local governments that bedeviled twentieth-century Carolinians was one of the most enduring legacies of Tillmanism.[54]

Under the 1895 constitution, power in South Carolina trickled down from state government to the people; it did not flow upward as it should have in a democracy. Because the constitution did not establish local governments as had the 1868 constitution, the General Assembly arrogated that power to itself. For counties, that meant that the legislative delegation was the local government. Annual supply bills for each county had to be approved by each delegation, and it was not an unknown practice for them to shift expenditures to pet projects once the bills were law. Even when the people of a county wanted change, their will could be (and often was) thwarted by the delegation in Columbia. There was only one senator per county, and because of senatorial courtesy, he had to approve all legislation concerning his county. South Carolina had as many little Ben Tillmans as it had counties. George Tillman, the senator's older brother, likened the state's centralized government to that of Chinese mandarins. And these mandarins spent more time dealing with local legislation than they did with governing the state of South Carolina (as late as 1940 some 86 percent of the laws passed by the General Assembly were local bills).[55]

When the convention completed its business in November 1895, the constitution went into effect; it was not submitted to the people for ratification. Before the convention there had been thirty-five counties. Saluda County was created under the constitution to make thirty-six. Within twenty years another ten were added because the constitution made it relatively easy to do so (see Map 20). There were a num-

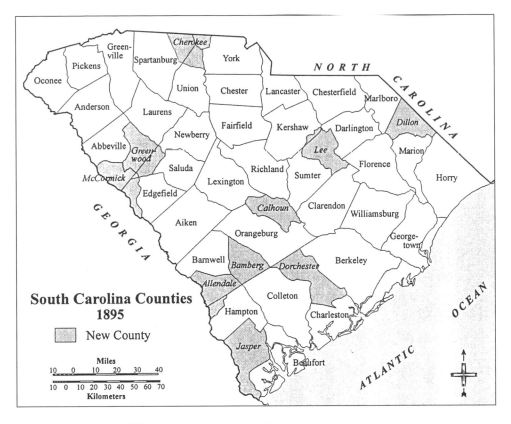

Map 20: Counties, 1895. Based on Edgar, *Biographical Directory*

ber of sound reasons for creating new, smaller counties, such as more efficient/effective law enforcement and reducing the distance citizens had to travel to the county seat. There were also those who favored the creation of more counties so as to render Charleston as politically impotent as possible.[56]

Charleston County, after two centuries of dominating South Carolina, was now just one of many. Its representatives and senator were often ignored in legislative deliberations. At least, though, white Charlestonians could still vote. They had some representation. That was no longer true for more than one hundred thousand black Carolinians who under the 1868 constitution would have been eligible to vote but now were disenfranchised.[57]

If the laws were not enough to limit black participation in politics, fraud and violence were acceptable. Lt. Gov. James Tillman (Ben's nephew) publicly said it was "no crime" for a county election supervisor to refuse to issue a voting certificate to a black man. In 1898 in Greenwood County, black and white Republicans challenged the suffrage restrictions of the constitution. The result was the Phoenix riot, which left seven blacks and one white dead. At the turn of the century there might have been about ten thousand registered black voters, but only two thousand to three thousand bothered—or dared—to vote in what was now the meaningless general election. For those few who could vote, the Democratic Party made participation as difficult as possible. Only blacks who had voted for Wade Hampton in 1876 (a dying number) could participate in the party's primary, which replaced the convention as the means of nominating candidates. The Democratic primary became the real election in South Carolina and by the early twentieth century was for whites only.[58]

The 1895 constitution laid the groundwork for the Jim Crow world that developed in South Carolina. If there were to be segregation, who was black? When one overenthusiastic delegate in the convention argued that one drop of black blood was sufficient, the Tillman brothers argued that too many black Carolinians had passed for white to use a standard that rigid. When the debate ended, a black person was defined by law as anyone having "one eighth or more negro blood." Everyone else was white.[59]

Separate schools for black and white children were mandated by the constitution, and Tillman's superintendents of education made no attempt to provide approximately equal funding as had their Bourbon predecessors. In 1896 Thomas E. Miller introduced a bill to create a separate black state-supported college in Orangeburg, the Colored Normal, Industrial, Agricultural and Mechanical College of South Carolina. Shortly thereafter the all-white board of trustees elected him the college's first president.[60]

When the U.S. Supreme Court in *Plessy* v. *Ferguson* pronounced the doctrine of "separate but equal" to be the law of the land in 1896, white South Carolinians were ready to act. In 1897, when Charleston installed its electric streetcars, they were segregated (much to the annoyance of the *News and Courier*). Gradually the legislature enacted statutes that introduced legal segregation to South Carolina: on railroad coaches (1898), on trolleys (1904), and in textile mills (1915). After 1902 only qualified voters could serve as jurors, which meant that few blacks would be called for jury duty.[61]

In 1898 the *News and Courier* opposed Jim Crow legislation, arguing that black and white Carolinians had gotten along "fairly well for a third of a century, including a long period of reconstruction," without the need for segregating the races in public places. The newspaper then derided the proposed law by saying that if railroad cars were to be segregated, why not every aspect of daily life in South Carolina where black and whites currently mingled peaceably? By World War I

The home of a black farmer near Beaufort. Photograph by Marion Post Wolcott (Farm Security Administration). Courtesy, Library of Congress.

everything that the *News and Courier* had scorned as silly had become law.[62]

Within a generation virtually all white Carolinians had forgotten that the old antebellum elite had considered squeamishness at coming into contact with blacks as a lower-class white attitude. The "better sort" might denounce lynching, but they quietly accepted segregation. "White only" and "colored only" signs sprouted on everything imaginable: stairways, water fountains, pay windows, and waiting rooms.[63]

What was not segregated by law was segregated by custom. South Carolinians, black and white, had to learn an intricate social minuet. Life became an elaborate ritual of do's and don'ts. For whites, a misstep could be socially embarrassing; for blacks, it could be fatal. In rural Bamberg County blacks were only supposed to shop in town on Saturdays. In Charleston a black woman could push a white baby around Colonial Lake but could not sit on any of its benches. Except on the Fourth of July, the Battery was normally off-limits to the city's black citizens. Blacks were expected to go to back doors and to address whites as "Massa, Master, Miss, or Boss." Had they used "Mr." or "Mrs.," they would have been considered impudent. Whites tried to avoid using "Mr." or "Mrs." when addressing blacks, even in legal situations. Regardless of age, whites addressed black people by their first names. If a courtesy title were used, it would likely be "uncle, daddy, aunty, or mauma." In Charleston, "Maum" was used by white families for favored black female employees. White children learned not to use the terms "lady" or "gentleman" when referring to black people. Public equality was dead.[64]

Black Carolinians remonstrated against the loss of civil and political rights they had enjoyed for a generation. One daring group of black Columbians actually requested and had an audience with Governor Tillman. A protest meeting in Sumter passed a resolution that condemned the proposed suffrage provisions of the 1895 constitution as a "badge of infamy . . . and a vile surrender of the commonwealth . . . to despotic demagogues." In 1897 former representative George W. Murray presented a memorial to Congress protesting counting the state's electoral votes because so many voters had been disenfranchised. The protests got nowhere. Black Carolinians were on their own. Thanks to the institutions they had developed during Reconstruction, black Carolinians were able to survive and in some areas, such as education and business, to continue moving forward. However, Jim Crow laws made everyday life for black Carolinians difficult. In 1899, after visiting Charleston, North Carolina journalist Walter Hines Page wrote that he would "rather be an imp in Hades than a Negro in South Carolina."[65]

In 1861 James H. Hammond had written about "the greatest problem of the ages," that of the relationship of blacks and whites. "On its solution," he concluded, "rests our all." Five years later William H. Talley of Columbia, a white man, addressed a black gathering in the capital city. He said that both races were "parts of the same society, inhabiting the same land, under the same sun, breathing the same atmosphere. And if the lessons of history taught anything, they taught that, under such circumstances, the two races must prosper or perish together." White South Carolinians, during the 1890s, ignored the lessons of history and abandoned the paternalistic white supremacy and limited racial accommodation of Wade Hampton for the Negrophobia and segregation of Ben Tillman.[66]

After the constitutional convention, Tillman began to devote more of his time to national affairs and less to South Carolina. He chose weak men to succeed him, and they let the Reform movement drift. His attempts to influence senatorial elections failed in 1896 and 1897. Tillmanites sought the support of *The State* and the *News and Courier* to insure their elections. The Dispensary, while making money for the state treasury, became the "most profound, insidious, and widespread agency of corruption" in South Carolina history. Rampant nepotism and office-seeking made a mockery of rotation in office. Tillman himself was guilty of accepting favors and gifts while governor. Local Reformer officials went on a stealing spree that rivaled the days of the Moses administration.[67]

For the state's farmers, support of whom was the reason the Reform movement had come into being, life was little better for all of Tillman's promises. The size of farms continued to decline. In 1880 the average farm was 143 acres; in 1890 it was 115 acres; by 1900 it was 90 acres. Smaller farms resulted in more intense cultivation and more land butchery. The percentage of farmers owning their own land declined from roughly half the farms in 1880 to 38 percent in 1900. That meant that six of every ten farmers in the state were either tenants or sharecroppers (41 percent white farmers; 78 percent black farmers). At the turn of the century the lowcountry probably "was the poorest part of the poorest census region in the United States." Tenants and sharecroppers had to pay a special fertilizer tax to fund Clemson, but only farmers with money could afford to send their sons there. Taxes were slightly higher in 1900 than they had been a decade earlier. Tillman's promises had "proven like Dead Sea apples, but ashes in the mouths of the people."[68]

In truth, many in the state were tired of the divisiveness caused by the Reformer-Conservative struggle. Families and friends had parted ways; schools, churches, and clubs had splintered. By the turn of the century some of the wounds of the past fifteen years were beginning to heal. Even Tillman reached out to his old enemies and they to him. In 1899 he was the guest of honor at a banquet in Columbia where the city's leaders thanked him for obtaining federal funds for the Congaree River. Five years earlier, during the Dispensary War, the local militia had literally turned their backs on him.[69]

After a decade of Reformer rule, Conservatives realized that South Carolina had not been revolutionized. With the exception of his attack on the phosphate industry (which he admitted was a mistake), Tillman had not done anything to harm business and industry. The textile legislation creating the sixty-six-hour workweek had been drawn up in consultation with the state's textile leaders. The crop lien law had not been modified, much to the joy of landlords and merchants. The Bourbon/Conservative strongholds of the Citadel and South Carolina College were not closed, but the state now had five, instead of two, institutions of higher education to support with limited funds. Although Conservatives opposed suffrage based upon race (they preferred education and/or property) and the implementation of Jim Crow laws, they acquiesced without much complaint. Only in politics had there been any significant changes.[70]

Since 1810 South Carolina had had universal white male suffrage; however, voters generally deferred to the leading men of their communities when it came to political decisions. Tillman raised the political consciousness of the state's white voters. He made them aware of their numbers and their power and encouraged them to look to state government to solve problems. Politics, no longer the preserve of the state's elite, were more rough-and-tumble, more like politics in the rest of the country. Those Conservatives who chose not to adjust to the new politics either lost to Reformers or withdrew from public life. Consequently, early-twentieth-century historians saw a reduction in the caliber of public officials. One went so far as to say that neither George Washington nor Robert E. Lee would have been able to win in a South Carolina Democratic primary. But by placing so much emphasis on class, Tillman's detractors and his defenders ignored the fact that his movement was not egalitarian. Tenants, sharecroppers, and mill operatives may have supplied the votes for Reform victories, but those they elected to statewide office had backgrounds not much different from their Conservative opponents'.[71]

Bourbon politicians may have been defeated at the polls, but the South Carolina that they created was more lasting. No one questioned the need for the Democratic Party and white supremacy, the tales of the evils of black Reconstruction, or the justice of the Lost Cause. Tillman and his Reformers wrought some changes in South Carolina; however, they did not tinker with the basic tenets of the Bourbon worldview. After a decade of "revolution," there was something of a new order, a revised version of the resurrected Old Order of Wade Hampton and his friends. This modified Bourbonism was more open to innovation and change. Despite (and because of) Benjamin Ryan Tillman, South Carolina was better prepared to deal with the new century and the New South.[72]

Chapter Twenty

SOUTH CAROLINA AND THE FIRST NEW SOUTH

In my opinion, compulsory education in the hands of the State means disrupting the
home, for it dethrones the authority of the parents and places paid agents of the State in
control of the children, and destroys family government.

    Coleman Livingston Blease, 17 January 1911

The time has come when we have to meet new conditions. We are progressive Democrats
and we must have the courage to do justly to each and every class of our citizens even if
this requires legislation hitherto untried by us.

    Richard Irvine Manning, 19 January 1915

*T*HE NEW SOUTH. The term has quite a ring to it. For more than a century,
since Henry Grady of Atlanta trumpeted the arrival of the "New South," southerners have been chasing a will-o'-the-wisp. Grady's New South was a region that was
trying its hardest to be just like the North, especially the Northeast. Industry was
the panacea for the South's ills and would enable it to catch up with the rest of the
country. Some South Carolinians, like their contemporaries in the states of the old
Confederacy, bought into the idea of industrialization and progress. However, as it
always seemed to be in South Carolina, there were differences.[1]

Historians have tended to focus on the upcountry as the center of New South activity; however, there was evidence of New South boosterism all across South Carolina. In Dillon and Florence enterprising young men created new businesses and
promoted civic pride. However, the one town in the state that best fit the New South
model was Georgetown. Its business and civic leadership during the 1880s and
1890s was comprised almost entirely of young men who were not sons of the
county's prewar rice-planting elite. They promoted the development of new economic ventures such as naval stores (especially turpentine) and lumber and welcomed northern interests that financed commercial fisheries.[2]

In Lexington County, Washington Bartow Rast was the embodiment of the en-
trepreneurial spirit of the New South. At the age of twenty-five, after clerking with
relatives in a Columbia hardware store, he and his brother opened their own general

The Georgetown waterfront (circa 1900). Courtesy, Morgan-Trenholm Photograph Collection, Georgetown Public Library.

store in Swansea. The new town, only a few miles from his birthplace, was a stop on the main line of the Seaboard Airline Railroad. In 1896 he established the Swansea Veneer & Basket Works, which manufactured wooden crates and baskets for the state's developing truck and fruit crops. By 1920 he was shipping his products all over the eastern seaboard and into Canada. He farmed on a large scale and operated three cotton gins. A national credit-rating firm noted that he paid his bills promptly. "Charitable and public-spirited," he was an organizer and director of the Bank of Swansea, trustee of the local schools, and intendant of the town. He was active in the local Methodist church and was an ardent Democrat. In towns all over the state there were hundreds of people like Rast who identified themselves with their communities and strove to improve them through economic development and civic responsibility.[3]

In the years after the Civil War, railroads had been the chief enterprise of most town boosters. As the nation's railroads consolidated during the late nineteenth century, South Carolina merchants began to deal directly with wholesalers and exporters in northern cities such as Baltimore, Philadelphia, or New York. Greenville and Spartanburg were on the main line of the Southern Railroad that linked them with Charlotte, Atlanta, and other cities. By the turn of the century Columbia, with eleven separate rail lines, was a regional hub served by 144 daily trains. Local

The railroad yard at Florence. Courtesy, South Caroliniana Library.

brochures boasted of travelers being able to get from Columbia to anywhere in South Carolina in just three hours and thirty-three minutes. Train schedules made it possible for *The State* newspaper to live up to its name and be in most South Carolina towns by breakfast; by 1910 the Columbia newspaper's circulation surpassed that of the *News and Courier*. In small towns, such as Blacksville, merchants remained open at night until the last passenger train arrived, about 8:30 P.M.[4]

Trains made Carolinians more aware of time. Because of schedules, railroads had to run on time, but which time? Each railroad maintained its own clocks and schedules. There were three different "standard" times in South Carolina. When it was 8:00 in Columbia, it was 8:04 in Charleston and 8:17 in Greenville. On 19 November 1883 the entire country adopted modern time zones and all of South Carolina was on Eastern Standard Time.[5]

The number of rail lines serving a community was grist for the local booster's mill. So, too, was anything else deemed progressive and modern: banks, hospitals, schools, parks, skyscrapers, colleges, churches, and hotels. A catchy motto was absolutely essential. Spartanburg tried half a dozen, including "The City of Smokestacks and Education," "Hub City of the Piedmont," and "City of Wideawakes." None really caught on. Nearby Greenville was the "Pearl of the Piedmont."[6]

Charleston, despite the exhortations of the *News and Courier*, did not indulge in such New South antics; however, after Atlanta and Nashville hosted successful expositions, a few Charleston businessmen decided that their city should have one too. In 1901–1902 the South Carolina Interstate and West Indian Exposition attracted 650,000 visitors to the 250 acres of gardens and exhibits built on the site of the old Washington Race Course. Financial support for the enterprise came from city and state governments, but only a few local businessmen were willing to put up their own money, so the exposition was a financial disaster. Everything that could go wrong did: a boycott by the black community (in protest over an offensive statue); unseasonably cold weather (which damaged Charleston's reputation as a tourist destination); and competition from another exposition in Buffalo, New York. The "Ivory City," as it was hailed in the press, closed in May 1902, and its buildings were sold for scrap to pay off the exposition's debts.[7]

In 1915 there was another exposition in South Carolina, but this one was quite different. Greenville's business leaders mounted the Southern Textile Exposition to celebrate the industry and serve as a trade fair for the Southern Textile Association. It was a rousing success, and Greenville became the permanent home of the biennial event housed in its own building, Textile Hall. The exposition was a tribute to the New South booster spirit of Greenville and a recognition that South Carolina was the South's leading textile-producing state.[8]

It took little more than a generation for cotton textiles to change the face of the Carolina upcountry. In 1880 the state had only fourteen mills (fewer than in 1860) that employed about two thousand operatives (as mill workers were called). During the 1880s mills opened in Anderson, Greenville, and Spartanburg Counties, but beginning in 1895 the state underwent a textile boom (see Maps 21, 22, 23).[9]

Between 1895 and 1907 businessmen built 61 mills and expanded older ones. The Columbia engineering firm headed by W. B. Smith Whaley was responsible for introducing architectural and technological innovations. The 21 mills the firm designed during this period accounted for about 20 percent of the new spindleage. The newer mills were quite different from the pre-1880 ones that had only about 6,000 spindles and produced either yarn or gray goods (unfinished material). The new mills, modeled after those in New England, averaged 25,000 spindles, and most produced finished cloth. Some of the mills were huge. The F. W. Poe Manufacturing Company in Greenville had 60,000 spindles and employed between 900 and 1,000 operatives. In Lancaster, Leroy Springs, who had already made a fortune as a cotton broker, began what would become Springs Mills. During the first decade of the twentieth century, John T. Woodside and Lewis W. Parker of Greenville built textile empires. Woodside was probably the wealthiest man in the upstate. Parker's company, capitalized at $15 million ($239 million), operated more than 1 million spindles in 16 mills in Greenville, Greer, and Columbia. In 1910 South Carolina was home to 167 mills that employed 47,000 operatives and ranked second only to Massachusetts as a textile-producing state. Although local investors continued to provide much of the capital, by 1916 northern interests controlled 28 percent of the outstanding stock in South Carolina mills (twice the regional average).[10]

South Carolinians invested in cotton textile mills primarily because they seemed like a good way to make money (early annual reports citing returns of 20 percent were not unusual). Secondarily, as town boosters, they saw the mills as sources of

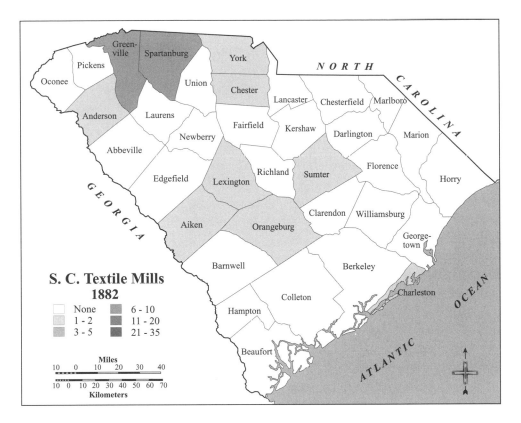

Map 21: Textile mills, 1882

jobs and community growth. What they had not taken into account, in their rush to build mills, were the consequences of industrialization. Before the 1890s towns-folk viewed black Carolinians as the only threat to their order; however, with the coming of the mills, there was now the "mill problem." For a generation (1895–1920), Carolinians wrestled with and responded to the social and political ramifications of the New South they had created.[11]

For South Carolinians with roots deep in the Old South, there were memories of the opposition of the state's antebellum leadership to industrialization. In his poem *The Hireling and the Slave,* Beaufort planter William J. Grayson had contrasted the plight of modern industrial workers toiling "in doubt and fear" with that of carefree slaves. Carolinians were well aware of the conditions in New England mills and did

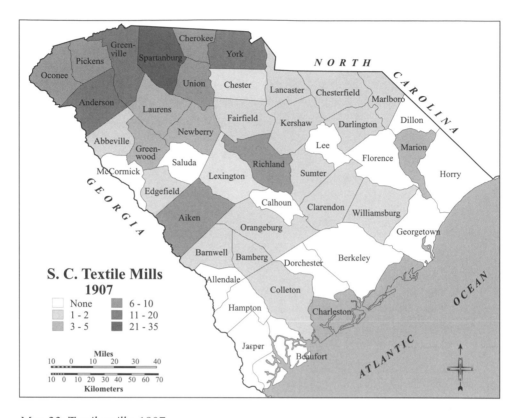

Map 22: Textile mills, 1907

not want to create a proletariat in their own state. Yet that is precisely what they did.[12]

The mill boom occurred in the upcountry where the population was rural, dispersed throughout the countryside. Mills had to recruit workers, and after they had gotten all they could from the upstate, they sent agents into the hills of North Carolina, northern Georgia, and eastern Tennessee. The white males that moved to the mills were not particularly well suited for their new jobs. Proud, independent, and not used to taking orders or being regimented, they sometimes resented their employers.[13]

They certainly resented the way they were treated by the town residents who regarded them as lesser folk. Prejudice abounded. Mill operatives fell into one of three

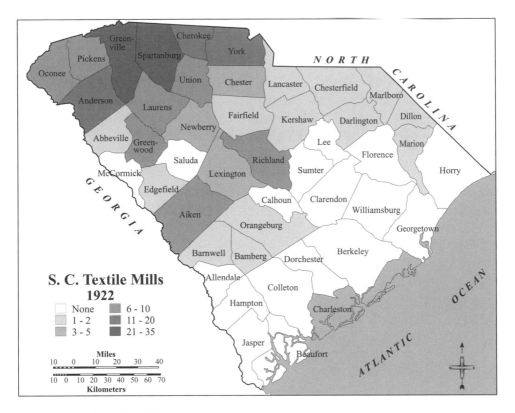

Map 23: Textile mills, 1922

stereotypes: yeoman farmers fallen on hard times (probably through their own fault), landless whites (sharecroppers or tenants), or mountaineers. Edna Holliday Burnette, daughter of a well-to-do Greenwood farmer, recalled that "it was a disgrace to work in the mill." In Greenville operatives noted that people crossed the street so as not to have to share the sidewalk with "lintheads" and "bobbin-dodgers." The social fissures that Hugh Wilson, editor of the *Abbeville Press and Banner*, had warned against in 1889 were a reality by the turn of the century. As he had predicted, the mills and their villages created a "caste between our own race." White supremacy did not mean white equality.[14]

The decision to leave the land was not an easy one for some. In *Red Hills and Cotton* upcountryman Ben Robertson described the agonizing conversation that

Tom Rampey, a tenant, had with Robertson's family. In the end, many of those who went agreed with Rampey, who decided to leave the land: "I want to improve my condition. . . . I want to educate my children, I want them to have things better than I have had." And they did: his eldest son graduated from college. Others, however, jumped at the opportunity to abandon hardscrabble farming for a regular pay-check.[15]

The smaller, older mill villages were primitive. "The typical mill village [of the 1880s]," said one former mill worker, "was a sun-baked collection of hovels on a hillside" where families lived amid an "atmosphere of flies, dirt, and foul odors." Some newer ones, such as Olympia and Granby in Columbia, were unhealthy places. In 1903 the Columbia mill villages were the subjects of a muckraking exposé, *The Woman Who Toils,* endorsed by President Theodore Roosevelt.[16]

Pelzer, in Anderson County, was one of the first modern upstate villages. Its residential area of 150 neat houses (four to six rooms) lined streets off a central square. Wells supplied drinking water. In 1895, when the mill converted from water power to electricity, the entire village, including operatives' houses, was wired. The company provided a school, paid the town marshal, and rented four stores to independent merchants (there was no company store). The Pelzers built a union church that was used alternately by Baptist, Methodist, and Presbyterian congregations. Among the regulations governing the village was one forbidding operatives to own dogs. Operatives signed a contract that required their children between the ages of five and twelve to attend the village school. Once a child reached twelve, he or she had to work in the mill unless excused by the mill superintendent. Any violation of these stipulations resulted in termination of employment.[17]

Rents were modest, 25¢ ($4) or 50¢ ($8) to $1.00 ($16) a room per month. In 1887 a four-room cottage in Graniteville rented for $4.00 ($64). Some mill villages had running water, but one of Greenville's largest, Woodside Mill, had neither running water nor sewers until the 1930s. When electricity was available, it was not unusual for mills to supply power to operatives' houses. At Camperdown in Greenville County, the company turned electricity on at 7:00 P.M. and off at 7:00 A.M. On Wednesdays it was turned on during the day and that became "ironing day."[18]

Workers generally were paid in cash, but some mills issued brass coins (called "looneys") that could only be redeemed at the mill store. Adult males earned $4.50 to $5.50 ($81 to $99) a week at the turn of the century. On the eve of World War I, some mills paid $7.00 ($105) for a sixty-hour week. Women and children earned less. On the average, South Carolina's textile workers received 60 percent less for their labor than did workers in other parts of the country. And the cost of living was not that much lower in the South than it was in New England. However, mill families generally had at least two incomes and, depending upon the age of their children, sometimes more.[19]

The blast of the mill whistle or the tolling of a bell roused operatives an hour before the start of the workday. At 6:00 A.M. the whistle or bell signaled the start of the shift. In Graniteville, if you were not inside the gates when the shift bell tolled at six, you were locked out and your salary docked. In the 1880s operatives worked until 6:30 P.M. (a twelve-hour day with thirty minutes off for lunch) five days a week and nine hours on Saturday. The workweek was reduced to sixty-six hours during Tillman's administration and to sixty in 1907.[20]

Mill villages might be separated from the rest of town by a street (as in Union) or the railroad tracks and city limits (as in Columbia), but the bells and whistles that regulated operatives' lives began to regulate those of nonoperatives as well. In Spartanburg the whistle could be heard for fifteen miles and became the standard time for the entire community.[21]

If mill villages were filled with good Anglo-Saxon rural folk, why was there a mill problem? Because the many operatives tended to be rowdy and crude; they were poor, uneducated, and unhealthy. All of a sudden middle-class merchants and professionals realized that the operatives they had so eagerly recruited could be threats to the order so carefully crafted in the generation since the end of Reconstruction.[22]

In addition, there was the possibility of violence with the appearance of labor unions. During the 1880s the Knights of Labor tried unsuccessfully to unionize mills in Anderson and Greenville Counties. The swift reaction of management in the firing of organizers crushed the movement. By the late 1890s, however, a shortage of labor coupled with steep increases in the cost of living led to brief union successes in Aiken and Richland Counties. Interestingly, middle-class town residents were not opposed to unions. If "farmers, lawyers, bankers, merchants, dentists, drummers, manufacturers, editors, all have their organized societies," queried a 1901 Columbia Labor Day orator, "then why not the operatives of our factories?" However, unions failed to make any real progress in the state until the 1930s. What order-loving townspeople did not want was disorder, whether the instigator were labor or management.[23]

For the most part, mill owners enjoyed the support of middle-class Carolinians. A representative of the National Child Labor Committee working in South Carolina reported that state government did not hesitate to investigate "New York insurance companies" or the railroads, "but to appoint an inspector to look into conditions in our mill villages is thought to be a reflection upon the word and character of good men." Owners and New South boosters, such as Daniel Tompkins, went into hysterics at the idea of regulating child labor. Tompkins compared those who favored regulation to antebellum abolitionists, and one mill owner said they were the hired shills of New England textile manufacturers trying to destroy the state's source of cheap labor. Not all of the attacks on child labor came from outsiders. The *Abbeville Press and Banner* denounced the mills for destroying family life. "Child Slavery in Our Mills" screamed a headline in *The State,* one of the most outspoken proponents of child labor legislation.[24]

The State and other advocates had plenty of ammunition. Lola Derrick Byars was eight when she went to work at the Granby Mill in Columbia and at twelve was considered as "experienced worker." Columbia's community Christmas tree for poor children had to be postponed from Christmas Eve 1896 until 26 December because most of the recipients were operatives and could not get off from work.[25]

As more and more town residents became aware of life in the state's mill villages, they saw problems that few mill owners were willing to address. One who did improve conditions was Thomas F. Parker, president of Monaghan Mill in Greenville. In 1905 he hired L. Peter Hollis as secretary of the Monaghan Mill village YMCA. Through his training with national youth organizations, Hollis introduced basketball and the Boy Scouts into South Carolina. He organized clubs, evening classes, and sports teams. After Parker's cousin Lewis formed the Parker Cotton Mill Company, he named Hollis to head the corporation's employee welfare program for sixteen mills. In addition, the company paved the streets of Columbia's Olympia mill village, installed sewers, and opened what was probably the city's first kindergarten classes. Thomas Parker was a firm believer in corporate welfare. If he took care of his workers, then they would be favorably disposed toward management and reject the blandishments of union organizers.[26]

Parker was not the only owner who practiced corporate welfare, but townspeople found that all too often owners did little or nothing to correct the social problems generated by their operatives. "An industry . . . does not need coddling at the expense of degrading our citizenship," editorialized *The State.* If owners refused to act, then concerned, progressive citizens would help those in need. At the same time they would protect the order and harmony of their communities.[27]

On the national level, the Progressive movement was a crusade for social and political reform that would correct the evils that beset early-twentieth-century America: political corruption, illiteracy, disease, and poverty. In South Carolina, Progressives were careful not to align themselves with any national reform effort (such as the National Child Labor Committee) because their opponents were itching for the chance to tar them with being influenced by "foreign" ideas. The Progressive impulse was also tempered by the reality of one-party politics. There was only so much that could be accomplished, and despite Tillman and the Reformers, the conservative legacy of the Bourbons was still strong. South Carolina Progressives were a cautious lot.[28]

Many trace the beginnings of the state's Progressive era to 1903 when a bill limiting child labor passed the General Assembly. Since 1898 *The State* had championed such a measure. The measure succeeded in 1903 after a group of Columbia women convinced Richland County senator J. Q. Marshall, an old Bourbon and chair of the committee on commerce and manufactures, to be the bill's sponsor. Despite intense lobbying by the textile industry, it became law. After 1 May 1903 no child under ten could be employed in a factory, mine, or mill; the age went up to eleven in 1904 and to twelve in 1905.[29]

The passage of the state's child labor law was proof that dedicated citizens, in concert with political leaders and the media, could do something to correct a social problem. Over the next decade concerned women and men in communities across South Carolina worked to improve schools, build libraries and hospitals, create parks and playgrounds, fund water and sewer systems, and reform local governments. They were determined to make their communities better and more orderly places in which to live.

Education was an area of great concern. The state's public schools were underfunded and understaffed. Illiteracy was a scandal. In 1890 some 361,000 Carolinians (45 percent of the state's population over the age of ten) could neither read nor write. Yet a majority of children attended school fewer than ninety days, and thousands attended fewer than thirty days. By 1900 illiteracy had declined somewhat, but only one-third of the state's children were in school. For those who were, though, the school year was longer and 65 percent were in class for at least four months a year. The credit must be given to dedicated teachers and local support because after 1900 state funding (which was based in part upon Dispensary revenues) was beginning to dry up.[30]

Higher education was not much better. There were nineteen institutions of "recognized college grade" and six more with "college" in their names. When the Southern Association of Secondary Schools and Colleges was formed in 1895, only six schools in the region (none from South Carolina) met the criteria for accreditation. In 1917 the University of South Carolina became the first college in the state (public or private) to be accredited. At publicly supported colleges tuition was free to all those who claimed financial hardship, but the system was much abused. In 1916, after proof of need was required, a majority of the state's public college students paid tuition.[31]

For the most part, higher education was on its own. The public was more concerned with primary and secondary schools. A 1910 report by William H. Hand grabbed their attention. After examining the curricula and personnel of the state's 166 high schools, he concluded that only 13 were "proper high schools": Abbeville, North Augusta, Anderson, Bamberg, Charleston (2), Darlington, Summerville, Johnston, Winnsboro, Marion, Mullins, and Bennettsville. There were only 250 seniors in those 13 schools.[32]

During the first two decades of the twentieth century, Progressives pushed for new school buildings and better-qualified teachers. Newspapers in Orangeburg and

Young mill operatives. Courtesy, South Caroliniana Library.

Columbia argued that good schools attracted and produced good citizens and that schools were as important to a community as a new factory or another rail line. The *Anderson Intelligencer,* in urging the building of a new school, said that it would be a magnet for "people who buy and improve property and contribute to the permanent advancement of the city." Columbia built six schools (including two high schools) in ten years. Spartanburg County boasted in 1906 that it had more school buildings (165), teachers (3,010), and pupils (16,232) than any other county. Dillon County increased its tax rate to fund schools, but the distribution per pupil ($22.50 [$337.75] white vs. $1.79 [$26.87] black) reflected the unequal opportunity afforded black children. The improvement of public education was left to individual communities and counties. There was strong opposition to compulsory education from rural and mill areas where children were needed to help support their families.[33]

By 1920 a number of districts had improved their schools. Spartanburg County alone had seven accredited high schools and the best-funded schools in the state. The school year had lengthened everywhere. Calhoun County's white town schools had the longest (180 days). Horry County's 136-day school year was the shortest but still a significant increase over state averages at the turn of the century. For white country schools Charleston County required 159 days, but Cherokee's 90-day term was a reminder of the way things used to be. With so little attention given to education, it was not surprising that Cherokee County had the highest percentage of illiterate voters in the state.[34]

In 1914, when all voters were required to reregister, 29 percent of those in Cherokee County could not sign their names. Even in Spartanburg, with its fine school system, one out of four voters could only make his mark at the registrar's office. In 1919, recognizing that unschooled adults wanted to learn, the State Department of Education established an adult school program. Wil Lou Gray was appointed to supervise the program, and she went to work with a zeal that brought immediate results. Within a year more than 11,000 adults (45 percent of them black) were attending evening classes. Gray was indefatigable in promoting adult education, which made a difference in the lives of thousands of South Carolinians.[35]

Only recently have women been given credit for their role in the Progressive movement. A typical southern Progressive was described as "a city professional man or businessman." Except for local equivalents of a chamber of commerce, the state's men were late in organizing civic associations. Greenville's Rotary (1916) and Kiwanis (1920) clubs were among the first. In South Carolina it was women who often provided the impetus, organizational skills, and money for Progressive causes. One of the earliest efforts was the Women's Exchange for Women's Work in Charleston, where women could sell their handiwork to provide income for their families. Women's efforts were not limited to women's projects. The Dillon County Federation of Women's Clubs successfully lobbied the county delegation to establish the office of county public health nurse. Two women's organizations in Florence sponsored the first Pee Dee Fair; after three successful years a group of businessmen took it over and created a separate sponsoring corporation. The Newberry Library Association and Darlington Civic League built public libraries in their towns. In the late 1920s the Darlington League disbanded, "leaving to the men the civic part of their program."[36]

City planning and beautification were important to every progressive community. Greenville's Municipal League funded a study that proposed the redevelopment of downtown. Newberry's Civic League was interested primarily in beautification. In Columbia the Civic Improvement League hired a landscape architect who prepared a master plan for the city, which resulted in a Tree and Park Commission, a boys' City Beautiful Club, and four new parks. Progress could sometimes go awry, though, as Columbia's city council, at the behest of business leaders, destroyed two parks for commercial development.[37]

Public parks provided an opportunity to honor the Confederacy. Celebrating the Old South was good business for the New South. Of the forty-eight Confederate or Civil War monuments erected before 1920, more than one-half went up between 1900 and 1920. In Fort Mill, Leroy Springs used profits from his new mills to pay for statues honoring the soldiers, women, and faithful slaves of the Confederacy. Civil War monuments, in addition to honoring the Lost Cause, were seen as a means to instruct lower-class whites to emulate the obedience, duty, respect, and loyalty of Confederate heroes and to be good citizens. Women, especially members of the United Daughters of the Confederacy, were often instrumental in raising money for memorials to the Lost Cause.[38]

All who called themselves Progressives were concerned with public health issues, but women were particularly active in this area. Women's church groups were key to the success of the temperance movement and in the campaigns for hospitals. In both Columbia and Greenville women raised the money for hospitals and then turned them over to male physicians to administer. In Columbia the women of Trinity Episcopal Church established the state's first tuberculosis treatment center.[39]

During the Spanish-American War, one of three South Carolina volunteers was rejected for service as medically unfit. In Greenville and Newberry Counties 45 percent of the volunteers were turned away for medical reasons. In 1900 the State Board of Health declared that mill villages were "pest holes for the corruption of the whole State." When operatives in Union literally fought public health officials' attempts to inoculate their children for smallpox, management supported them. Consequently, the disease reached epidemic proportions and spread to other communities. Less serious outbreaks of measles and typhoid were also traced to mill villages.[40]

Charleston, the state's oldest and largest city, was also a pesthole. Pigs and buzzards still foraged for garbage in the city's streets. Cows were kept in backyards or vacant lots and their unpasteurized milk sold to the poor. After early-twentieth-century outbreaks of typhoid and yellow fever, Charlestonians began to clean up their city. Thirty-five miles of central sewer system replaced most of the twelve thousand leaking privies that polluted the city's groundwater. Streets and sidewalks were paved and farm animals banned.[41]

Towns everywhere considered central sewers, water systems, and paved streets and sidewalks to be visible signs of a progressive community. Spartanburg and Greenville had municipal water and sewer service in the 1890s and Union in the early 1900s. Columbia had constructed a waterworks in the early nineteenth century, but its streets remained unpaved until 1907. Three years later Florence installed sixteen miles of sewers and began paving its streets and sidewalks. In 1914 and 1915 Sumter followed suit.[42]

Technological advances—trolleys, telephones, and electric lights—were other indications that a town was progressive. In 1893 Columbia's trolley line began to replace its horse-drawn cars with electric ones. By World War I the system included twenty-five miles of track and one hundred trolleys that linked the downtown business district with suburbs to the north, east, and south. The systems in Spartanburg and Greenville each had about fifteen miles of track and connected the surrounding mills and mill villages with their hub cities.[43]

The telephone was patented in 1876, and within three years Charleston had a telephone exchange. The Columbia exchange opened in 1880 and those in Newberry and Greenville in 1882. From Greenville lines soon ran to Piedmont, Travelers Rest, Batesville, Chick Springs, and Greer so that textile executives living in Greenville could communicate immediately with mill personnel in outlying communities. Sumter went on-line in 1891 and Florence in 1894. Lou Washington Floyd of Newberry created an upstate system that included Clinton, Greenville, Greenwood, Newberry, Prosperity, Spartanburg, and Union, which he sold to Southern Bell in 1903. By 1909 in Newberry County there were more telephones in rural homes (819) than there were in the county seat (382). Whether they lived on a farm or in town, Carolinians liked the telephone. But it changed the way people did business. Personal interaction, so much a part of the state's culture, was diminished.[44]

The first electric generating facility in the state supplied power to the State House in 1884. The city of Columbia, though, did not convert from gas to electric street lights until 1887. Then, in rapid succession, the towns of the middle and upcountry either built municipal power plants or granted franchises to local businessmen: Greenville (1888), Sumter (1889), Spartanburg (1890), Darlington (1894), Anderson (1895), and Union (1896). Virtually all of the early electrification was either for street lighting or industrial use. The electrification of smaller towns produced some interesting contrasts. Sumter's streets, for example, were better lighted than those in Charleston or Columbia. In Union the plant was shut down on Sundays; not until 1913 was electric power available there on the Sabbath. Some of the first private residences to have electric lights were those in Pelzer. When the mill converted to electricity in 1895, it supplied power to operatives' homes. It was after 1900 that electricity was generally available to Columbia residents.[45]

While infrastructure was important, so were morality and good government. Progressives believed that good citizens could solve almost any problem and improve their communities. They supported any venture that would improve the quality of life in their towns.

In 1892 the state's voters overwhelmingly endorsed prohibition; instead, they got the Dispensary, which even its supporters admitted resulted in more, not less, drinking. In 1898 prohibitionists, angry at Tillman and his Reform movement, tried to elect as governor Claudius C. Featherstone of Greenwood, a dedicated dry. William H. Ellerbe, the incumbent governor, was so fearful the liquor issue would defeat him that he made a deal with *The State* (which favored local option, not prohibition) for its support. Even with the backing of the Tillman machine and *The State*, Ellerbe won renomination by only about twenty-six hundred votes. In counties that favored prohibition, eighteen thousand voters scratched Senator Tillman's name from their ballots.[46]

Martin F. Ansel of Greenville, was elected governor in 1906. As a good progressive and supporter of local option, Ansel proposed that the Dispensary, which had become synonymous with graft and corruption, be abolished. In February 1907 the General Assembly closed the Dispensary, and counties were permitted to operate their own or enact prohibition. Two years later only six counties remained wet: Aiken, Beaufort, Charleston, Florence, Georgetown, and Richland. (Interestingly, the year after local option became law, the South Carolina Bar Association began its annual banquet with cocktails.) In 1915 South Carolinians voted overwhelmingly (35,000–15,000) to prohibit the sale of alcoholic beverages.[47]

If progressives thought that prohibition would reduce the violence that wracked South Carolina society, they were mistaken. Murder and lynching, legacies of Reconstruction, seemed out of control and threatened social stability. In 1897 the General Assembly amended the state's concealed weapons law, reducing the penalties for violating it. A state judge denounced the "deplorable custom of carrying pistols, a custom carried to such an extent, that our State may be regarded as an armed camp in times of peace." Public officials were not good role models. Four members of the state's congressional delegation in the 1890s had killed someone. As a result, "young men and boys, black and white, rich and poor" considered pistols a necessary part of their outfits. The results were lethal. During the first decade of the twentieth century the national homicide rate was 7.2 per 100,000. Memphis was the nation's murder capital, but Charleston was second. There were twice as many murders in South Carolina in 1906 as there were in Chicago, which had a larger population.[48]

When accused murderers were brought to trial, they were rarely convicted. In 1903 Lt. Gov. James Tillman shot N. G. Gonzales, editor of *The State,* in broad daylight. There were witnesses and Gonzales was unarmed, but a Lexington County jury acquitted Tillman. In courthouses across the state juries rendered similar verdicts in less celebrated cases.

Reformers had more success in trying to curb mob violence, especially lynching. Although apologists claimed that lynching generally was directed at southern blacks accused of rape, fewer than one-sixth of the region's lynching victims were accused of that crime. After the 1890 lynching of Willie Leaphart in Lexington County, responsible white citizens condemned lynchings. *The State* and the *News and Courier* were persistent and powerful foes of lynching and mob violence. The South Carolina Bar Association joined in the fight to curtail lynching and the rule of "the mob and pocket pistol." For a while progressives seemed to be winning the battle of public opinion in support of law and order. Then Cole Blease became governor (1911–1915) and openly endorsed lynching as "necessary and good." While blacks were the primary objects of his invective, he declared he would pardon any mill operative who killed a physician for giving his daughter a physical examination without parental consent. The governor's comments frightened law-abiding white middle-class Carolinians. "Today the negro," said the *Southern Christian Advocate,* "tomorrow the prominent attorney."[49]

Race was a blind spot for most white progressives. Although newspapers increasingly condemned lynching as a threat to law and order, there was little sympathy for lynch mobs' black victims. For the most part, whites ignored black protests against discrimination or racially charged entertainment, such as the movie *Birth of a Nation.* They did provide nominal support for black-initiated uplift efforts, such as the Reverend Daniel J. Jenkins's orphanage in Charleston or the Reverend Richard Carroll's South Carolina Industrial Home for Negroes in Columbia. Some whites even participated in Carroll's annual Conference of Race Relations (1907–1919). However white Carolinians, regardless of political persuasion, believed in white supremacy. The more enlightened ones, sometimes called "accommodationists," were willing to recognize blacks as an integral part of society as long as they were in a subordinate role. This paternalistic progressivism treated blacks (and mill workers) as "unfortunates" and "children" in need of moral and spiritual guidance from their social betters. Through the public schools, mill children would be taught "habits of regularity, neatness, kindness, obedience, and self-control."[50]

Many historians have long believed that progressivism was for whites only. The state's black majority was excluded from meaningful political power, but that did not mean that black Carolinians were not progressives. In Columbia, Dr. Mathilda Evans established Taylor Lane Hospital, trained black women as nurses, and founded the Negro Health Association. There was a Colored Civic League in Charleston. Black women were especially active and formed clubs and leagues not only in the larger cities, but also in Abbeville and Orangeburg. Within the sphere of the black community, these women's organizations promoted self-improvement, education, public health, and uplift—like progressive women's groups elsewhere in the country. The motto of the South Carolina Federation of Colored Women's Clubs, organized in 1909, was "Lifting as We Climb." The federation took on as its state project the creation of a facility for orphaned, abused, or delinquent girls (because state government did not think it had a responsibility to do so). The Fairwold Home, located near Columbia, was the result of these efforts. Black progressives had to cope with the reality of a Jim Crow society. Black women were doubly handicapped because they were frequently portrayed as sinful, immoral Delilahs. Yet they persevered and, within the bounds of their segregated communities, made a difference.[51]

When it came to such issues as government reform, white progressives ignored black Carolinians because they were of no consequence politically. Mill operatives, however, were quite another matter. Their conduct and their voting power were disconcerting to middle-class Carolinians, who, through a series of local election law revisions, tried to dilute the votes of working-class whites.

In 1904 the *Edgefield Chronicle* complained that the recent primaries were "the dirtiest ever held in South Carolina." If there were not a change, then good men would "steadfastly refuse to submit to such an ordeal to serve their State." In 1896 Carolinians held the first direct statewide primary (seven years before the first ones were held in the Midwest). By letting the voters, not a convention, select candidates, it was thought that politics would be more democratic. Unfortunately, democracy

The Tuesday Afternoon Club, Columbia, was typical of literary and cultural organizations formed all over the state at the turn of the century by blacks and whites, males and females. Courtesy, South Caroliniana Library.

and Ben Tillman's new form of campaigning coincided. The *Chronicle* reported that in the 1904 Edgefield primary, "more dirty, malicious falsehoods were distributed to defeat men than ever before." Democracy did not necessarily mean good government.[52]

In a number of communities the voting power of operatives was too large to suit town voters. How could the mill vote be diminished without violating the law? In Union the county registrar (as the sole judge of a voter's qualifications under the 1895 constitution) refused to register a large number of operatives. Columbia annexed residential suburbs to counterbalance the growing mill vote. When that did not reduce the influence of mill voters as significantly as planned, the city's aldermanic form of government was abolished in favor of a city commission. Instead of voting for aldermen by wards (much like today's single member districts), commissioners were elected by all the voters. No longer did the mill portions of the city have their own aldermen; instead, they were outvoted by the town residents, who were then in complete control of city government. Spartanburg went to a city commission form of government for the same reasons as Columbia. The at-large method of election that was so common in South Carolina municipalities until the 1980s can be traced to the progressives. They were determined that unenlightened mill operatives, whom they viewed as threats to order and progress, would have as little voice as possible in local government.[53]

Control of city government sometimes led to actions that were patently unfair. Self-interest took precedence over the uplift of mill children. In 1916 Columbia's mill wards provided the necessary ballots for additional school taxes and supported a bond issue. Yet the city's affluent residential areas got new schools while those in the mill village were "desperately crowded for room."[54]

Although women were increasingly active in community affairs and men were willing to listen to them on many reform issues, woman suffrage was not an issue that drew men's sympathy. Women who were active in the Women's Christian Temperance Union also debated suffrage issues, and in 1892 Virgina Durant Young of Fairfax (Greenville County) organized the South Carolina Equal Rights Association with members in places such as Frogmore (Beaufort County) as well as in larger cities such as Columbia and Charleston. In 1912 a group of Spartanburg women established the New Era Club specifically to promote the cause of women's suffrage. Within a few years there were suffragist organizations in Abbeville, Charleston, Greenville, and Columbia. In 1915 these groups formed the South Carolina Equal Suffrage League, and within four years there were twenty-five local leagues. Eulalie Chaffee Salley of Aiken and Susan Pringle Frost of Charleston were among the group's leaders. Although characterized as a middle-class movement, working-class women were also interested in the vote. A suffragist meeting in one of Columbia's mill villages attracted 350 persons. Black women, however, were excluded.[55]

In 1919 Congress passed the Nineteenth Amendment and sent it to the states for ratification. In January 1920 the South Carolina General Assembly considered the amendment. The house rejected it 93–21 and the senate 32–3. Individual members from several delegations voted for the amendment, but only Union County's delegation was united in its support. South Carolina's rejection of the amendment did not keep it from becoming law. In August 1920, after Tennessee became the thirty-sixth state to ratify it, the Nineteenth Amendment went into force (South Carolina, in a symbolic gesture, formally ratified the amendment in 1969).[56]

South Carolina's men did not accept the verdict gracefully. After the nation ratified the Nineteenth Amendment, the General Assembly passed a law giving women the right to vote. Simultaneously it passed another statute excluding women from jury duty. Legislators thought "respectable women had no real desire to be jurors" and that it was their duty to "protect" the weaker sex from "the unpleasantness of jury duty." In Williamsburg County woman suffrage was still such a hot issue in 1922 that not a single candidate for public office would endorse the idea of letting women join local Democratic Party clubs. The women of the county would not be deterred. The male candidates for office might not want to talk about it, but some three hundred women registered to vote, joined the clubs, and voted.[57]

Eulalie Chaffee Salley (1883–1975). Courtesy, Julian B. Salley, Aiken, South Carolina.

White, female South Carolinians as a group may have responded more favorably to the ideals of human progress and uplift than any other segment of the population. Because the causes they espoused most vocally (child labor, public education, and public health) were directed primarily at operatives and their families, women progressives became the targets of antireform politicians. They were accused of neglecting their homes and children and *"running around, 'doing society,' playing cards for prizes, etc."* While such criticism might be unfair, it was warmly applauded by mill villagers, who resented "stuck-up" women bent on making them good citizens.[58]

There was a negative side to progressive reform. Working-class whites, struggling to maintain some control over their lives, disliked being patronized by middle-class "do-gooders." It made little difference what the issue was: inoculations, medical examinations, child labor, or compulsory education. The operatives, heirs to a long tradition of republican independence, did not want anyone telling them what they could and could not do. They were especially offended by initiatives, such as child labor, that had the state making what had customarily been families' decisions. Another sore point was the progressives' blaming them for all the problems in the villages while absolving mill owners of any responsibility. Even when operatives did not want to be helped, progressives insisted that they should be—for their own good and for the greater good of the community. Progressives meant well, but all too often they were callously insensitive to the feelings of those whose lives they were determined to improve.[59]

The simmering resentment in the mill villages needed only a leader to bring the state's politics to a rolling boil. The man who emerged as the champion of the operatives was Coleman Livingston Blease of Newberry County. Early on, Blease, one of Tillman's original supporters, realized that the operatives made up an important block of voters. Tillman had little use for those he dismissed as the "damned factory class," but Blease cultivated them. He said what the operatives were either unable or afraid to say. He attacked the "do-gooders" who told them they could not send their children to school unless they got smallpox inoculations or who accused them of being "tin bucket toters" (deadbeat fathers who forced their children into the mills and lived off their paychecks). It was a raw class message, but one that resonated among the state's blue-collar workers.[60]

Whereas Tillman's 1890 campaign, despite the rhetoric, had not been a class struggle, Blease's 1910 one was. He blatantly appealed to the prejudices and emotions of working-class whites who were being relegated to the margins of South Carolina society. "Coley," as his devoted followers called him, is one of the most misunderstood figures in South Carolina history. He has been dismissed as a racist demagogue who claimed to be the operatives' friend and then blocked legislation aimed at making their lot better. What Blease's critics ignored, or failed to comprehend, is that the operatives did not want a women's club, a civic improvement league, or the state of South Carolina acting in their best interests. "These people," he said, "are our people; they are our kindred; they are our friends, and, in my opinion they should be let alone, and allowed to manage their own children and allowed to manage their own affairs." That one sentence explains why he was the operatives' hero. It was a restatement of the antebellum republican ideal, a world in which all white men were equal. It was also a direct challenge to the progressives and their drive to reorder South Carolina society.[61]

Blease had a program: no more government regulation. Tillman had been elected on the basis of promising to get government to do something for the state's farmers. Progressives had acted on the premise that it was the responsibility of government to improve the lives of its citizens. Blease promised to halt governmental intrusion into the daily lives of ordinary people. He may not have known anything about the naturalist school of American literature, but he spoke for those who could have populated the novels of Theodore Dreiser or Frank Norris. Caught in the maelstrom of industrialization and powerful impersonal forces over which they had no control, men and women struggled for personal dignity and survival. Many failed because they had to fight their battles alone. In South Carolina those who struggled had a voice, a champion. If earlier observers had been honest, they would have reported that Blease, not Tillman, deserved comparison to the biblical Moses. Blease really did strive to set his people free—to restore to them the individualism, the dignity, and the sense of worth they had lost when they deserted their farms for the mills.

In 1910, after two unsuccessful statewide races, Blease won the governorship with 57 percent of the mill vote and a strong showing in Charleston. In the port city

Coleman Livingston Blease (1868–1942).
Courtesy, South Caroliniana Library.

his laissez faire attitude toward prostitution, drinking, and gambling was immensely popular. If a man wanted to sin, that was his own business, not the state's.[62]

From his inaugural address in January 1911 until he resigned the governorship in 1915, Blease did not disappoint his supporters. The state's leading newspapers and reformers went after him with a vengeance. Even Tillman turned on his old lieutenant, condemning his "blind-tiger record, his race-track gambling record, his whore-house record," and demanded he be impeached. Nothing seemed to faze Blease. If anything, he gloried in taunting his opponents. His relationship with the General Assembly (where his friends were a minority) was rocky. He vetoed any legislation he considered likely to interfere with parents' rights to rear their children. His enemies accused him of betraying the interests of his followers, but the governor's vetoes were popular in mill villages. He issued pardons by the hundreds and countenanced mob violence. His intemperate and often crude language offended the sensibilities of the "better sort." On at least one occasion the legislature refused to print a veto message because it contained abusive language. For the same reason, newspapers omitted portions of Blease's speeches and messages so as not to expose their readers to the governor's obscenities. For middle-class townspeople, those who cherished social order, the Blease years were their worst nightmare come to life.[63]

Regardless of what people thought about Cole Blease, his presence in a race guaranteed a large number of voters. In his 1910 gubernatorial campaign, the voter turnout was 64 percent; two years later when he successfully ran for reelection, the figure was 80 percent. Blease was loved by his followers (unlike Tillman, who was feared) and he returned that devotion by trying to protect the working people from governmental interference in their lives. He so despised progressives that five days before his second term was up, he resigned as governor rather than have to meet with his successor, the progressive Richard I. Manning.[64]

Blease may have been governor, but progressives controlled the General Assembly and most of the major towns. As candidates for the 1912 presidential election began to jockey for position, James C. Hemphill, editor of the *News and Courier,* was one of several influential southern newspapermen to tout the merits of the governor of New Jersey, Woodrow Wilson. Although Hemphill later disavowed Wilson because he was too progressive, South Carolina was one of only two southern states where there was no organized opposition to Wilson's candidacy. At the Democratic convention the state's delegation remained loyal through forty-six ballots and Wilson's successful nomination.[65]

Carolinians claimed Wilson as one of their own because he had lived in Columbia during his formative teenage years. Narciso Gonzales of *The State* and former governor Martin Ansel were prominent Wilson supporters. When Wilson won, southerners were back in power in Washington after fifty years in the wilderness. Among those receiving federal appointments was Gonzales, who served as the country's minister to Cuba and ambassador to Peru. In Congress, with the Democrats in control of the House of Representatives, Asbury F. Lever of Lexington County was chairman of the powerful agriculture committee. He co-authored the Smith-Lever Act (1914) that provided grants-in-aid for county agents to operate under the direction of a state's land grant college. He convinced the president to modify the Federal Farm Loan Act (1916) so that the federal government provided capital for the twelve regional Federal Farm Loan Banks authorized by the legislation. One of those regional banks was located in Columbia.[66]

In June 1912 *The State* reported that "progressivism . . . has become a veritable tidal wave." The newspaper, however, had not counted on Blease's winning the Democratic primary. In November, South Carolinians voted overwhelmingly for an anti-progressive governor and a progressive president. Two years later Richard I. Manning swept into office. *The State*'s tidal wave finally came ashore.[67]

Manning was a product of the adjustments that had been taking place in state politics since the late 1890s. He was a descendant of the antebellum elite and numbered six former governors among his kin. His antecedents might have been Bourbon, but his political philosophy called for governmental action, not reaction. With Manning's able leadership (1915–1919) and large progressive majorities in both houses of the General Assembly, progressivism in South Carolina reached its zenith. According to one admiring twentieth-century historian, "No South Carolina Governor ever secured better coöperation with the legislature, or saw so many of his recommendations adopted." At the end of the twentieth century, that assessment remains valid.[68]

In four years Manning pushed through more than a dozen major pieces of legis-

Richard Irvine Manning (1859–1931). Courtesy, South Caroliniana Library.

lation that brought South Carolina into the twentieth century. An overhaul of the state's tax structure resulted in equalized assessments, the tracking down of cheaters, and a reduction in the common levy. Educational reform included increased funding and a compulsory education law (with local option). For the benefit of labor, there was the Board of Arbitration to mediate disputes with management and there was the outlawing of payment in kind at company stores. In the area of social services, the state hospital and prison came under the supervision of the Board of Charities and Corrections, child labor under the age of fourteen was outlawed, and schools were established for the mentally ill and delinquent white females. Improved farm markets and agricultural education benefited farmers. A state highway commission implemented a program of paving. And, for government reformers, the secret ballot was instituted for primaries. It was an impressive list of accomplishments, but more than that, Manning's progressivism was inclusive. It demonstrated to all segments of the white community (including Bleaseites) that state government could benefit them. It is hard to imagine what the progressives might have been able to accomplish had the country not entered World War I.[69]

On 6 April 1917 the United States declared war on the Central Powers. Governor Manning moved swiftly to make sure that South Carolina did its part, but support for the war was not unanimous. In Lexington, Newberry, Orangeburg, and Charleston Counties there was strong antiwar sentiment among those of German and Irish descent. The week before war was declared, there were a preparedness parade in Columbia and an antiwar rally at the Lexington County courthouse. Federal authorities jailed the editor of the *Abbeville Scimitar* for questioning Wilson's motives for going to war and briefly banned the *Charleston American* from the mails for allegedly subversive comments. Cole Blease condemned the war and in a biting speech compared Manning to the Reconstruction governors. "Dick Manning is the worst governor the State ever had," he said, "worse than Scott, Chamberlain or Moses, because they only stole money and he is trying to steal the souls and bodies of your boys." Although he later recanted and supported the war, he had made a political blunder of the first order.[70]

The State Council of Defense published a *South Carolina Handbook on the War* that reflected the zeal with which Americans went to war to overthrow "the barbarous rule of brutal Prussia." Either support the war or be labeled a traitor. There could be no middle ground: "Those who are not for us are against us." A corps of 200 business and civic leaders (called "Four Minute Men") were prepared to speak anywhere, anytime. The speakers' bureau, like much of the material in the pamphlet, was part of a coordinated national campaign to mobilize the home front. Carolinians, white and black, rallied to the flag, but because of Jim Crow all war support activities (Red Cross, bond drives, victory gardens) were segregated. Some 307,000 young men registered for the draft; of these, 54,000 were drafted. Patriotic fund drives raised nearly $100 million ($1 billion). On a per capita basis, the state's financial support of the war effort was among the highest in the nation. And after a half century white Carolinians once more celebrated the Fourth of July.[71]

The onset of war made civic leaders anxious to have military bases located near their towns. Greenville and Columbia had learned during the Spanish-American War how much money military installations could pump into a community. A combination of local initiative and the state's political influence with the Wilson administration resulted in the authorization for army training bases at Camp Jackson (Columbia), Camp Sevier (Greenville), and Camp Wadsworth (Spartanburg). The Marine Corps facility at Parris Island and the Charleston Navy Yard bustled with increased activity. Concern for servicemen's health led to federal pressure that closed down heretofore tolerated red-light districts in Charleston and Columbia.[72]

The state's national guard units were incorporated into the 30th (Old Hickory) Division that trained at Camp Sevier. Many Carolinians were members of the 81st (Wildcat) and the 371st Regiment, 93d (Negro) divisions that trained at Camp Jackson. All these units saw action in France, the 81st and 93d along the Hindenburg Line near Bellincourt. The state's servicemen distinguished themselves on the battlefield. Of the seventy-nine Medals of Honor awarded for conduct "above and beyond the call of duty," seven went to South Carolinians. Among the heroes were James Dozier of Rock Hill, who later served as the state's adjutant general for thirty-three years, and Freddy Stowers of Sandy Springs, who was the only black American to receive the medal in either world war.[73]

On the home front there were food and fuel shortages. Mondays became "heatless days," and stores and mills closed. The winter of 1917–1918 was one of the

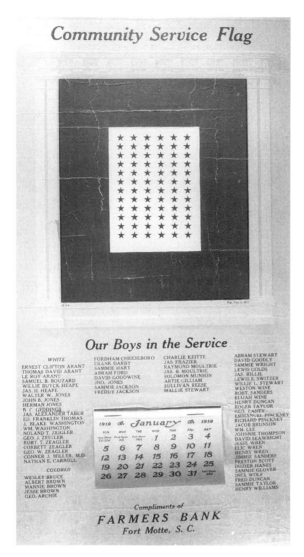

Community Service Flag

Our Boys in the Service

Jim Crow customs dictated the segregation of the names of young men in uniform fighting to "make the world safe for democracy." Courtesy, Calhoun County Museum.

coldest in years, which made everyone more miserable. Under the Lever Food Act (1917), the federal government regulated the prices of food, fuel, and fertilizer. Wheat was controlled, but through the efforts of southern congressmen, cotton was not. As a result, the Democrats lost seats in the grain-producing states (and control of Congress), but for South Carolina farmers, war-inflated prices meant good times.[74]

Since 1900 South Carolina's economy had been on a roller coaster. During the first decade of the new century, urban and rural property values rose as much as 50 percent. "The landlord, whether he have one hundred acres or two thousand," wrote William Watts Ball in 1911, "is contented and prosperous." But the prosperity was limited to the 39 percent of the farmers who owned their own land.[75]

Soldiers in training at Camp Sevier, Greenville. Courtesy, South Caroliniana Library.

In the lowcountry and middlecountry counties adjacent to North Carolina, to-bacco became a cash crop. In 1890 Frank M. Rogers of Florence introduced bright leaf tobacco into the state. In that year tobacco farmers produced only 223,000 pounds, but by 1900 the figure was an astounding 20 million pounds. Profits were just as amazing. A tobacco farmer in 1895 could net $150 ($2,700) to $200 ($3,600) an acre compared to a cotton farmer's $10 ($180). However, as produc-tion increased, prices and profits declined. In 1908 a tobacco farmer's proceeds per acre were still three times those of a cotton farmer; two years later tobacco farmers averaged $54 ($859) per acre and cotton farmers $37 ($589). (By way of compari-son, in 1995 the average cash receipts per acre were $3,778 for tobacco and $416 for cotton.)[76]

Because of soil and climate conditions, the bright leaf tobacco belt was limited to the counties of the Pee Dee. Elsewhere in the lowcountry rice production contin-ued to decline. Western competition, a new generation of black labor unfamiliar with rice cultivation, and a series of seven hurricanes within twenty years (two in 1893 and one each in 1894, 1898, 1906, 1910, and 1911) brought an end to the production of "Carolina gold." In 1927 Theodore Ravenel, the state's last commercial rice planter, sold his Combahee River plantation to E. F. Hutton of New York. Some lowcountry farmers turned to truck crops, but without rice the low-country reverted to what it had been two hundred years earlier, a semitropical wilderness. In the upcountry a few pioneering farmers began planting peaches, and by 1924 there were enough to form the South Carolina Peach Growers' Associa-tion.[77]

The sale of bright leaf tobacco, Dixie Warehouse, Florence. Courtesy, South Caroliniana Library.

Everywhere else farmers grew cotton. The widespread use of fertilizers and the development of improved seeds by David R. Coker of Hartsville boosted yields. In 1890 the cotton harvest was 747,000 bales; in 1900 it was 881,000; and in 1910 it was 1,280,000. South Carolina, in 1910 the smallest of the cotton-growing states, was the third largest producer behind Georgia and Texas. Cotton accounted for nearly 70 percent of the cash value of all crops in the state. Happily for farmers, prices rose with production.[78]

In July 1914 cotton stood at 13¢ ($1.82) a pound and a record crop was whitening in the fields. Then came war in Europe. Export markets disappeared and prices plummeted. Cotton exchanges across the South remained closed for three months. If farmers could find buyers, the price was 6 1/2¢–7¢ (91¢–98¢) a pound. A major difficulty facing cotton producers was a lack of storage facilities. What were they going to do with their cotton? In October 1914 Governor Blease called a special session of the General Assembly to deal with the crisis. South Carolina created a system of state warehouses that controlled the storing, grading, and marketing of the crop. When a farmer placed his cotton in a state facility, he received a certificate of deposit. Farmers with certificates usually could renew their loans at local banks. Bankers had little choice since all farmers had was cotton, not cash. To reduce the supply of cotton, the legislature passed a law forbidding a farmer to plant in cotton more than one-third of the total acreage he had planted (in any crop) in 1914. In

Washington, Congressman Lever sponsored the administration's Cotton Warehouse Act, which passed without much difficulty.[79]

Prices began to rise in 1915, and when the United States entered the war in 1917, prices soared. Everyone was making money: landowners, bankers, merchants, tenants, and sharecroppers. Cotton acreage expanded. For the first time in memory, tenants and sharecroppers had real disposable income and "engaged in a perfect orgy of spending" on machinery, barns, housing, and consumer products. The end of the war did not mean the end of high cotton prices. In the spring of 1920 cotton reached 40¢ ($3.03) a pound.[80]

Within six months after the war ended, South Carolina's men in uniform began returning home. In Spartanburg the 30th Division (nine thousand strong) paraded through town, and in Columbia the 371st Regiment was cheered by thousands of residents, white and black.[81]

Black World War I veterans who fought "to make the world safe for democracy" expected their own country to live up to its slogan. They were bitterly disappointed. In January 1919 a statewide Negro Convention protested against voting barriers and segregation and asked for better schools and representation on school boards. In May there was a race riot in Charleston sparked by white sailors' attacks on black citizens. By the time order was restored, three black Charlestonians were dead. There was considerable apprehension that racial disturbances would erupt in Columbia and elsewhere, but none occurred. During the height of the tense summer of 1919, Congressman James F. Byrnes spoke for almost all white Carolinians when he said, "the war has in no way changed the attitude of the white man toward the social and political equality of the negro." At the height of racial tensions in 1919, a group of white Columbians formed the South Carolina Constructive League to promote "the just treatment of the negro and the cultivation of harmony between the races" as long as it was understood that the "state shall be dominated by its white citizens." Once the crisis passed, the organization faded away.[82]

By 1920 most Americans seemed to have had enough of progressivism. They wanted a respite, a return to normalcy. South Carolina, in 1920, was out of step with the rest of the country. Buoyed by prosperity and peace in Europe, voters re-elected Robert A. Cooper governor. His progressive agenda called for raising taxes to improve education, public health, and highways. Cooper was unopposed—a good indicator of public sentiment. The high tide of progressivism in South Carolina that had risen in 1914 was still flowing strong. Then in 1921 it turned. Cooper's ambitious program came a cropper when farm prices collapsed.[83]

For the first six months of 1921 cotton prices were near or above 40¢ ($3.39) per pound; then they began to drop. By December cotton was 13 1/2 ¢ ($1.15) a pound. The state commissioner of agriculture estimated that farmers spent $250 million ($2.1 billion) planting a crop that would bring them only $140 million ($1.2

billion). Bright leaf tobacco fell from 40¢ ($3.51) a pound in 1919 to 21.1¢ ($1.60) in 1920. Sagging farm prices marked the beginning of a rural depression that affected the entire state.[84]

But economic problems were not enough to shake the new social and political order that had emerged by 1920. The thirty years of political turmoil that had begun with Tillmanism ended with Reformers and Bourbons making their peace with one another. Rejecting Coleman L. Blease's plea for a "poor government," Carolinians embraced a paternalistic progressivism. They concurred with Richard I. Manning's call for the state to enact "legislation hitherto untried by us." Government, historically considered a threat to individual liberty, was now seen as a means for solving the ills of the body politic. Through government, a new and more orderly South Carolina came into being. It was a middle-class world in which blacks were disenfranchised and working-class whites were politically neutralized (at least at the local level). The resulting power structure, centered in the county seats, would remain in control of South Carolina until the 1960s.

Chapter Twenty-one

THE DRAINING YEARS

All of us knew we were losing, that we were slipping, and how long any of us could with-hold depended finally on time alone. As our assets in the struggle we had only ourselves and the land we lived on and our climate, our long growing season, together with a for-midable list of intangibles. . . . We had our love of family, our love of history, our resis-tance to change that was both for and against us.

Ben Robertson, *Red Hills and Cotton*

WHILE MUCH OF the rest of the country began a decade-long party in 1920, South Carolinians tried to cope with economic distress, modernization, and progress. Many did not like the new morality of the Jazz Age that challenged long-cherished traditional values. All over the South men and women transformed the re-form impulse of progressivism into a movement for moral and spiritual revival.[1]

With the passage of the Eighteenth Amendment making it illegal to manufacture and sell alcoholic beverages, Prohibitionists thought they had eliminated demon rum as a threat to the American family. To keep society safe from the evils of liquor, church leaders, especially Baptists and Methodists, advised their members to vote against any candidate who favored the repeal of Prohibition.[2]

Prohibition was as big a failure in South Carolina as it was everywhere else. Nor-mally law-abiding citizens flouted the law. Charleston throughout Prohibition was "wringing, sopping, dripping wet," and city officials took payoffs from bootleggers. Somewhere between twenty-five and forty thousand Carolinians made a living as bootleggers, moonshiners, and rumrunners. The *News and Courier,* normally a sup-porter of law and order, complained that Prohibition had ruined Charlestonians' tastes. Because they could not obtain imported Madeira and brandy, they willingly guzzled "Hell Hole Swamp 'corn.'" In Greenville County, where whiskey was $2.50 ($22) a pint, moonshiners did a brisk business.[3]

When John G. Richards of Kershaw County was inaugurated as governor in 1927, he vowed that his administration would have "one great purpose . . . to place South Carolina upon a pedestal where she can be proclaimed by the world as a leader in righteousness." He had little luck suppressing illegal liquor, but with the support of the General Assembly he was able to stamp out gambling. He also announced that the state's blue laws would be strictly enforced. Businesses were supposed to be closed on Sundays—period. Police arrested golfers in Aiken, Camden, Greenville, Hartsville, and Sumter. The governor twice vetoed efforts by the legislature (reflecting the will of a majority of South Carolinians) to modify the state's blue laws. The press and business leaders criticized the governor, but he was not alone in his desire to see a return to old-fashioned decency.[4]

In Greenville a couple was sentenced to $11 ($95) in fines or thirty days in jail for "kissing while in an automobile on a principal street." A Saluda County judge declared that swimming pools were "tools of the devil." Furthermore, he attributed the drought and boll weevil infestation plaguing the state's farmers to divine retribution for the existence of swimming pools within the state's boundaries. In 1924 Florence passed some of the most stringent blue laws in the state.[5]

The state's fundamentalist and evangelical churches were in the vanguard of the efforts to protect traditional values. Not even fellow churchmen were spared. A visiting evangelist touched off a nasty controversy in Greenville when he condemned modernism at Furman University and the religious writings of the director of the YMCA. Fundamentalists and evangelicals attacked the curricula in high schools and colleges as biblically unsound. However, two years after the Scopes Trial in Tennessee, an effort to ban the teaching of evolution failed in the General Assembly.[6]

In the upstate churches had an unsavory ally in the drive to preserve traditional values: the revived Ku Klux Klan. Reborn in Atlanta in 1915, the Klan spread rapidly across the South and Midwest and was against anything it deemed not 100 percent American. In the South that meant blacks, Jews, and Roman Catholics. In Florence and Greenville there were indications that local law enforcement officials and the Klan were in cahoots. In Greenville the Klan paraded openly, terrorized black neighborhoods, and hosted community picnics. Congressman J. J. McSwain and local Baptist clergy addressed Klan rallies. In Columbia, John K. Hamblin of Union County, Speaker of the South Carolina House of Representatives, threw a barbecue for members of the General Assembly at the local Klan headquarters building. Evidently a number of politicians joined the Klan, some clandestinely. One who adamantly refused, much to the embarrassment of the Klan, was James F. Byrnes. Byrnes's refusal may have contributed to his loss to Cole Blease in the 1924 U.S. Senate race.[7]

The state's economic distress contributed to the overall climate of unease. Farmers, complained David R. Coker, should have set aside some of their profits during the heady years when cotton prices were on the rise. Rare was the man who did. Just before the cotton market crashed, Edward Rembert of Rembert (Sumter County) demanded his brokers pay him in gold for his bumper crop and they complied. He invested his profits in government securities and never farmed again. Almost everyone else went on a spending spree. Consequently, few farmers had the resources to tide them over the rough years of the 1920s.[8]

The collapse of cotton and tobacco prices in 1920 was the result of overproduction and the loss of overseas markets. Then a series of droughts and boll weevils hammered the cotton crop. For years the boll weevil had been moving northeastward from Mexico. Although first detected in the state in 1917, it was not until several years later that the pest made its presence felt. In 1921 the sea island cotton crop was wiped out, a blow from which that crop never recovered. By the 1930s, like rice, sea island cotton production was history.[9]

In 1922 the short staple crop was hit hard. In Williamsburg County production dropped from 37,000 bales in 1920 to 2,700 in 1922. A McCormick County farmer who produced 65 bales in 1921 made only 6 in 1922. It is estimated that in some years the boll weevil destroyed one-half the crop. About the same time the boll weevil struck, so did drought. In 1922 South Carolina farmers produced fewer than one-third the number of bales (500,000) produced just two years earlier. Between 1910 and 1920 annual average yield was 1,365,000 bales; during the 1920s it dropped to 801,000. Prices rose somewhat in the latter part of the decade, but not enough to make a difference. A common refrain heard everywhere was "Ten cent cotton and forty cent meat / How in hell can a poor man eat." Food costs in South Carolina were relatively higher because so much had to be imported. In 1935 the state's population was three times what it had been in 1850, but the amount of food produced was about the same. Consequently, poorer Carolinians subsisting on a diet of pork, cornbread, and molasses were more susceptible to disease. During the 1920s there was a marked increase in pellagra—a direct result of inadequate diet.[10]

By 1930, after nearly a decade of difficulties, South Carolina agriculture was about to go under. Farmland and buildings had lost more than one-half their value. One-third of the state's farms were mortgaged, and 70 percent of the state's farmers survived on borrowed money. The land itself was also in bad shape. The farming of marginal lands and improper farming methods caused major erosion problems. Gullies rived the land, especially the red clay hills of the upcountry. In 1934 eight million of the state's nineteen million acres were so badly worn out that they were declared "destroyed."[11]

"Those were the draining years on the cotton farms," wrote Ben Robertson. "Nearly all of the strongest tenant families left the cotton fields. Only the old and the young and the determined stayed on." Rural Carolinians had been leaving the state since the 1890s, but the agricultural collapse of the 1920s spurred a mass exodus. In an eight-month period following the disastrous 1922 harvest, more than fifty thousand black farmers gave up and left the state. So, too, did many whites. Between 1920 and 1930 twenty-four of the state's forty-six counties lost population; during the next decade eleven did. Hardest hit were Abbeville, Allendale, Edgefield, McCormick, and Saluda, which lost more than 15 percent of their population.[12]

White Carolinians were genuinely alarmed about white outmigration but ambivalent about blacks' leaving. Some welcomed it, but others were anxious over losing a source of cheap labor. In several rural counties white landowners were

Soil erosion in the Carolina upcountry. Photograph by the U.S. Forestry Service. Courtesy, South Caroliniana Library.

convinced that outside agitators were responsible for luring away blacks. Some communities passed ordinances making it expensive or illegal for anyone to be a labor recruiting agent. When a black man in McCormick County was apprehended with three railroad tickets in his possession, he was subject to being jailed for up to two years or fined from $1,000 ($8,900) to $5,000 ($44,500) because he did not have an immigration agent license. Both the *Greenville News* and *The State* blamed the threat of racial violence for blacks' leaving. There were bad memories for some, but they were counterbalanced by happy ones. For many who left, it was simply a matter of survival. They saw no future on the farms and left without bitterness. They would have agreed with Kelly Miller, an earlier Carolinian in exile, who still felt "an attachment for the old state that time and distance cannot destroy. After all, we love to be known as a South Carolinian."[13]

Poor, rural migrants were not alone in seeking better opportunities elsewhere. By 1939 many of the state's high school and college graduates also were looking for job opportunities outside the state. South Carolinians migrated to literally every state in the union. Black Carolinians went north, and white Carolinians went south and west. In 1930 there were more Carolinians living in Buffalo, Chicago, Cleveland, Detroit, and Pittsburgh than there were in Abbeville, Beaufort, Bennettsville, Conway, or Lancaster. By World War II nearly one-fourth of the 2,266,000 people born in South Carolina lived outside the state. Among the consequences of this out-

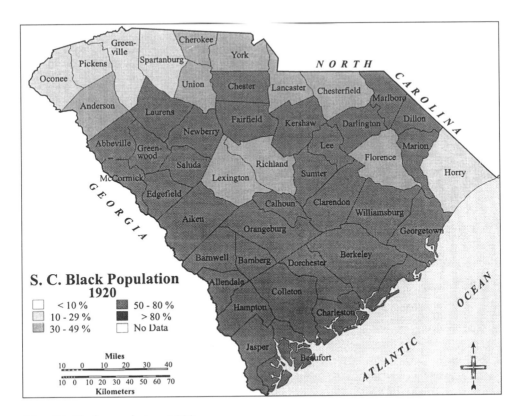

Map 24: Black population, 1920

migration were the loss of talent and resources (especially in the black community), a population with the youngest median age in the country (22.2 years), and a white majority (for the first time in a century) (see Map 24).[14]

Not all those who fled their farms left the state. Some moved to the cities and towns. Whites sought work in the mills, but blacks had fewer opportunities. About thirty thousand whites found jobs in the textile industry. South Carolina workers had the shortest workweek in the South (fifty-five hours set by state law), but they had the lowest wages in the industry. Life in mill villages, although still controlled by the mills, improved materially. During the 1920s most mills modernized their villages and installed running water, electricity, and indoor plumbing—something that many residents of Charleston and Columbia lacked. Organized recreational activities, such as baseball, became common. Mill owners, however, still believed that their mills had a social responsibility. "Our mills shall be run not only to make cotton cloth," said industrialist Ben Geer, "but to make the right kind of men and women as well." The corporate paternalism of the mills impinged on almost every facet of workers' lives, but operatives had few options open to them.[15]

During the 1920s the textile industry expanded, and by 1925 South Carolina led the nation in the production of cotton goods. The expansion created a false image of prosperity. Except in the years 1923 and 1927, most firms were only marginally profitable or lost money. Wartime demand generated huge profits, which, in turn, attracted northern investors. In 1923 a Boston firm purchased Pelzer Manufacturing Company, and in 1927 Deering-Milliken bought its third South Carolina plant, Judson Mill in Greenville. Some investors purchased locally owned mills at inflated prices and then saw competition and overproduction drive down prices. In an attempt to restore profitability, managers tried a variety of strategies. Some, such as the Union-Buffalo Mill, resorted to part-time rather than full-time employees. Others, such as American Spinning in Greenville, reduced their workweek. A few, such as Hamilton-Carhartt in Rock Hill, shut down for weeks at a time. The most widely used methods of reducing labor costs and improving profits were the "speed-up" and "stretch-out." Machinery was set at faster speeds, and workers were given a greater number of machines to tend. Although those still on the job got small raises, overall payroll expenses dropped because fewer workers were needed.[16]

Changes in the workplace, especially the speed-up and stretch-out, led to labor unrest in 1929. While there was violence in neighboring North Carolina and Tennessee, South Carolina's protests were relatively peaceful. Workers made it clear they did not want out-of-state assistance. Those mills that were managed by locals fared best. In virtually every instance in those mills, after operatives met with management, the hated speed-up or stretch-out was modified. In 1929 the House of Representatives launched an investigation of the problems and blamed the recent strikes on management for "putting more work on the employees than they can do."[17]

While the legislature was critical of management, it could do little to improve the health of an ailing industry. Overproduction in 1928 and 1929 led to low prices. By 1929 mills had begun to curtail production. Some operated only three days a week and others on alternate weeks. A reduced workweek meant a smaller paycheck. Operatives and their families now found themselves in the same subsistence struggle as tenant farmers and sharecroppers. Less money meant a poorer diet, and pellagra appeared in the mill villages. Women and children seemed to be particularly susceptible.[18]

No one—neither sharecroppers, tenants, landlords, operatives, nor mill owners—had any ready cash. In Rock Hill the Anderson Motor Car Company went out of business because there was no market for its beautiful but expensive automobiles. Employment at the Charleston Navy Yard declined to five hundred. Some families tried to make a go of it with two incomes. In 1920 one-third of the women in South Carolina worked outside the home.[19]

In small towns merchants, bankers, and ginners found themselves with uncollectible debts and fewer customers. When cotton and tobacco were high, credit was easy and people overextended themselves. "Almost overnight, our people were reduced from a riotous spree of making and spending," said Lt. Gov. E. B. Jackson in 1926, "to the stern reality of poverty staring them in the face." Debtors were no longer able to meet their installment payments. "The country is simply broke," wrote a Sumter County merchant. The president of the Bank of Laurens was concerned that "Nobody seems to have any money to spend or to pay debts." In 1929 the Greenville Chamber of Commerce could not meet the payments on its fancy high-rise building. Small businesses were forced to operate strictly on a cash-and-carry basis.[20]

Cash became more difficult to come by during the 1920s as banks failed. In 1919 there were 78 national and 387 state-chartered banks in South Carolina. Before Frankin D. Roosevelt was inaugurated in 1933, two-thirds of them (34 national and 273 state) closed their doors. A considerable number folded before the stock market crash of 1929, due to local economic conditions. In the fall of 1928, in the space of six weeks, 5 of the 8 banks in Darlington County and 7 of the 8 in Chesterfield failed. In Greenville and Newberry several staved off failure by merging or reorganizing only to go under in the Depression. While a few banks closed because of fraud and malfeasance, most did so because of undercapitalization, bad loans, and crop failures.[21]

Bankers, farmers, and operatives were not the only Carolinians with money problems. By 1925, because of the weak economy, the state faced a $2 million ($17.3 million) deficit. Six years later the deficit was nearly $5 million ($49.9 million). A state property tax was the primary source of revenue, and farmers paid a disproportionate share of taxes. Not only was it difficult for individuals to meet their tax obligations, but the property tax stifled capital investment. In order to raise money, the General Assembly adopted the concept of indirect taxes. Legislators took such a shine to what they called "painless" taxation that one critic sarcastically remarked: "South Carolina has put a tax on everything from bow legs to cuspidors." Among the items subject to a "luxury" tax were tobacco, playing cards, ammunition, certain candies, and soft drinks. Eventually property taxes were reduced somewhat, but at the end of the 1920s the state had a crazy-quilt of thirty different kinds of taxes.[22]

The new taxes helped fund education and highways. In 1920 South Carolina had the lowest per pupil expenditure not only in the South but also in the United States. At the urging of business, civic, and educational leaders, the General Assembly passed the "6–0–1" Act in 1924 to insure that all white children would have a minimum of seven months' schooling. The state would pay for the cost of six months ("6"), and local school districts were required to pay for one ("1"). The "0" was

Table 21.1

NUMBER OF HIGH SCHOOL GRADUATES, 1920–1940

Year	White Diplomas Awarded	Black Diplomas Awarded	Total Diplomas Awarded
1920	745	0	745
1925	3,716	0	3,716
1930	5,542	104	5,646
1935	7,974	303	8,277
1940	10,717	1,009	11,726

Daniel, "Public Education," 189–90.

for county appropriations, which were encouraged but not required. The act also established minimum standards and salaries for teachers. As a result of increased funding, more young Carolinians had the opportunity to obtain a real high school education. Even though there were several excellent black high schools, such as Booker T. Washington in Columbia, no young black man or woman received a diploma until 1930 when three black high schools were recognized by the State Department of Education.[23]

In terms of higher education, in 1940 South Carolina ranked eighteenth in the nation in percentage of citizens who had attended four or more years of college. Given the high illiteracy rate and the denial of educational opportunities to blacks and poor whites, that was an amazing statistic. The state still struggled, though, to fund six institutions of higher education (The Citadel; Clemson; Colored Normal, Industrial, Agricultural and Mechanical College; State Medical College; University of South Carolina; and Winthrop). There were eleven four-year private or denominational colleges for whites (Charleston, Coker, Columbia, Converse, Erskine, Furman, Lander, Limestone, Newberry, Presbyterian, and Wofford) and four for blacks (Allen, Benedict, Claflin, and Morris). The big news in higher education was Furman's being named a beneficiary of the Duke Endowment. The gift was bestowed because of the school's academic excellence and its energetic leadership.[24]

In some ways Furman's leadership was typical of that still found in most up-country counties in the early 1920s. In Greenville, Spartanburg, and Anderson Counties community leaders pushed local officials to create the infrastructure for a modern industrial society: electric power, water systems, and paved roads. All of these were paid for with local rather than state money. Consequently, when out-of-state businessmen investigated potential plant sites, they usually looked upstate. They certainly did not consider the lowcountry where "thousands of acres of . . . once fertile fields" lay "idle and forgotten save perhaps by a few sportsmen, by waterfowl and swamp game."[25]

The upcountry was taking care of itself while the lowcountry was letting the "march of progress and civilization" pass it by. A group of lowcountry legislators, headed by state senators Richard M. Jefferies of Colleton County and Edgar A. Brown of Barnwell, decided that the state should fund the lowcountry's infrastructure. In 1929, despite the state's shaky financial condition, Jefferies and his allies proposed that the state authorize a $65 million ($576 million) bond issue for highway construction. South Carolina certainly needed better roads. One editor likened the state's highways to "the condition described in the first chapter of Genesis: 'without form or void.'" In 1925 the state had 170,000 registered trucks and automobiles, but only 225 of 4,740 miles of roads were hard-surfaced. There were no bridges over the Santee or Savannah Rivers. Upcountry legislators opposed the measure because their constituents had already paid for their roads through county taxes; nevertheless, the measure passed and Governor Richards signed it.[26]

Opponents immediately went to court to challenge the constitutionality of the act. The 1895 constitution mandated a referendum (with two-thirds' approval by the voters) to increase the debt of the state. The constitution also required that any constitutional issue be decided unanimously by the state supreme court. When the court divided over the issue, a special court of the state's circuit judges ruled the bond act constitutional. The public, particularly in the upstate, was outraged. "The Constitution," thundered the *Anderson Independent,* "was raped by the legislature, the Governor and the judiciary to put through that road bond issue." The bond bill was the first show of power by a coterie of lowcountry legislators who, through seniority and parliamentary skills, used state government for the benefit of their poor, rural counties. These men, whose power was based in black-majority counties where few blacks could vote, would dominate the General Assembly until the 1960s.[27]

The highway bond bill and the "6–0–1" Act for schools were about the only signs of life in the State House during the 1920s. According to a contemporary historian, state politics in the 1920s were a "vacuity." Legislators were all too aware of the plight of those in their counties. In 1926 Lieutenant Governor Jackson mused that it was a problem to legislate for people facing poverty and a loss of morale. The following year *The State* lamented the loss of spirit in the midlands, where there was a great deal of talk but not much action. In June 1929 a speaker in Greenville challenged the local Kiwanis Club to revive "the old time spirit" that had disappeared from one of the bastions of progressivism. The years after 1925 were draining years for all Carolinians, not just those on the farms.[28]

There were feeble attempts at boosterism, but the energy of the early twentieth century was missing. In 1923 Gov. Thomas G. McLeod convened a statewide con-

Folly Beach (circa 1938). Courtesy, Calhoun County Museum.

The Ocean Forest Hotel, Myrtle Beach. Courtesy, South Caroliniana Library.

ference of civic leaders to devise a strategy for promoting the state. The "Boost South Carolina" conference was a bust, but several towns made efforts to attract tourists. Columbia sponsored the Palmafesta, something of a combination automobile show and straitlaced imitation of Mardi Gras. Folly Beach sponsored a beauty pageant in which "contestants were judged on the basis of complexion, hair, teeth, figures, and personality." Elsewhere along the coast, Greenville businessman John T. Woodside built the Ocean Forest Hotel (1926) and laid out the streets of Myrtle Beach. The year 1926 was a banner one for coastal developers as the secretary of state issued charters for Edisto Beach, Floral Beach (Garden City), and Sea Island Homes of Beaufort.[29]

Tourism was not a new idea in the 1920s. Since the 1880s Aiken, Camden, and Summerville had been frequented by wealthy northerners—either as destinations or as stops en route to Florida. In 1912 Charleston produced a *New Guide to Modern Charleston* to publicize the charms of "the city of destiny." As the economy worsened during the 1920s, city officials increasingly turned to tourism as a solution. Unfortunately, there was no place for visitors to stay. The city's older hotels were little more than flophouses. To remedy the situation, the city donated land on the historic Battery for the Fort Sumter Hotel (1923), and the following year the Francis Marion opened on Citadel Square. For the first time in nearly a century, "America's most historic city" had modern accommodations for visitors.[30]

By the thousands tourists flocked to linger in the city's "streets and lanes and gardens and enter a few shadowy interiors beyond the deep verandahs that turn to the South." By 1929 some forty-seven thousand visitors spent nearly $4 million ($35.4 million) annually. City officials were elated, but the curmudgeonly editor of the *News and Courier* confided to a friend that "nothing is more dreadful than tourists, whether grasshoppers, boll weevils, or money-bagged bipeds. They will make Charleston rich and ruin her." The Depression ended tourism for a while, but in the years before World War II, Charleston was inundated by as many as three hundred thousand visitors a year. They were lured by the city's historic district.[31]

There are few blessings of poverty in the United States; however, in twentieth-century South Carolina one was that neither individuals nor government had the money to replace the physical legacy inherited from previous generations. It was accepted as gospel that Sherman laid waste to Columbia and twenty-one other towns, but in reality his forces left a considerable number of antebellum buildings unharmed. For example, about two-thirds of the capital city's pre–Civil War structures remained after the state's first experiment with urban renewal. In Beaufort, Camden, and Charleston colonial and antebellum buildings survived, albeit a little worse for wear. Along country roads and in dusty courthouse towns, reminders of the Old South Carolina still stood.[32]

Whether the grandchildren of planters, upcountry farmers, or slaves, South Carolinians had pride in family and pride in a sense of place. Individuals understood and appreciated their heritage. In Charleston black grandparents described the intricately carved ceiling of Centenary Church: "Slaves did that wonderful work. . . . Fine people. But in slavery days they were relegated to the balcony. The white folks prayed to God downstairs." In the upcountry Ben Robertson began his memoir with the sentence: "By the grace of God, my kinfolks and I are Carolinians." There was a qualifier, however. When he used the term *Carolinian,* he, like his grandmother, meant *South* Carolina. "North Carolina to her, and to all the rest of my kinfolks," he wrote, "was hardly more than West Virginia." And the WPA guide to the state noted, "South Carolinians are among the rare folk in the South with no secret envy of Virginians." Occasionally a newspaper editor inveighed against paying too much attention to the past, but such comments were rare and, when made, ignored. The past was everywhere present; the material presence of "a world that has been ruined . . . a civilization that has passed" reinforced personal remembrances.[33]

In the decades between world wars, South Carolinians evidenced a growing concern in preserving their state's past. In 1917 Alice Ravenel Huger Smith and Daniel Elliott Huger Smith wrote *The Dwelling Houses of Charleston,* a pioneering work that described the architectural treasures of the port city. Three years later Susan Pringle Frost was the driving force behind the founding of Charleston's Society for the Preservation of Old Dwellings. At the society's insistence, the city passed a zoning ordinance that became a model for the country's historic preservationists. Because of the ordinance, the support of city government, and the society's promotional efforts, much of Charleston's architectural heritage would be protected from the bulldozer and wrecker's ball of "progress."[34]

The Charleston effort was just one of many in the state. Near Clemson the Old Stone Church and Cemetery Association (1921) preserved that historic structure, and in Columbia the American Legion Auxiliary saved Woodrow Wilson's Boyhood Home (1929). After Greenville boosters demolished the old courthouse and removed the Confederate Monument from Main Street to make way for civic improvements, a group of citizens formed the Upper South Carolina Historical Society (1928) to raise public awareness of the community's past. The South Carolina Historical Association (1930) encouraged the study of history, and the South Caroliniana Society (1937) collected manuscripts and historical materials.[35]

Preserving the state's past took on other forms as well. The etchings and paintings of Elizabeth O'Neill Verner and Alfred Hutty did much to create the ambience of a Charleston at peace with the past. Music faculty at Allen University collected spirituals; so, too, did lowcountry whites. When Charleston's first radio station, WCSC, went on the air in 1930, one of its initial programs was a presentation by the Society for the Preservation of Spirituals. It was as if Carolinians were responding with a vengeance to an essay in the *Nation* that had charged them with "letting their civilization perish without resistance."[36]

But it was in written form that the most significant efforts were made to capture

89, 91 Church Street, "Catfish Row." Courtesy, South Carolina Historical Society.

the past. Folklore was in its infancy, but Ambrose E. Gonzales and Edward C. L. Adams published Gullah tales and Chapman Milling wrote about the state's Indians. A torrent of histories, anthologies, articles, pamphlets, and essays appeared. There were more than three hundred major histories and nonfiction works about South Carolina. Even more important than the volume was the quality. Many of them have stood the test of time and historical revision.[37]

While some of the books are what we today would call local history, they were first-rate and so were their publishers. The country's best university and commercial presses eagerly sought South Carolina material. Among the works that have become standards are Alston Deas's *The Early Ironwork of Charleston*; Asa Gordon's *Sketches of Negro Life and History in South Carolina*; Duncan Clinch Heyward's *Seed from Madagascar*; Broadus Mitchell's *William Gregg: Factory Master of the Old South*; Elizabeth W. A. Pringle's *Chronicles of Chicora Wood*; Anna Wells Rutledge's *Artists in the Life of Charleston*; Samuel Gaillard Stoney's *Plantations of the Carolina Lowcountry*; Albert Simons and Samuel Lapham Jr.'s *Charleston, South Carolina*; and Leah Townsend's *South Carolina Baptists*. Although local historians were busy all over the state, lowcountry themes and titles predominated.[38]

Of the many cultural organizations that developed during the 1920s and 1930s,

The oak avenue, Tomotley plantation, Beaufort County. The oaks were planted about 1820 by Patience Wise Blackett Izard. Courtesy, South Caroliniana Library.

the most significant was the Poetry Society of South Carolina. Founded in 1920, the society was in the forefront of the Southern Literary Renaissance, but its influence was not limited to the promotion of poetry and creative writing. The group acted as both catalyst and nexus for the poets, novelists, essayists, artists, architects, folklorists, and historians who were its members.[39]

The South-bashing that was popular in northern intellectual circles provided the impetus for the founding of the society. Especially painful was H. L. Mencken's essay "The Sahara of the Bozart," in which he described the area between Virginia and Georgia as "a vast plain of mediocrity, stupidity, lethargy, almost of dead silence." His use of a poem by Columbia versifier J. Gordon Coogler made the humiliation complete: "Alas! for the South, her books have grown fewer— / She never was much given to literature." Unfortunately, there was some truth in Mencken's charge. The state's last two major nineteenth-century literary figures, Mary Chesnut and Paul Hamilton Hayne, had both died in 1886. With the exception of Edward McCrady's superb histories of colonial and revolutionary South Carolina, the cultural scene was pretty desolate until the 1920s.[40]

With the publication of its first yearbook in 1921, the Poetry Society picked up Mencken's gauntlet and set out to prove that "culture in the South is not merely an *antebellum tradition*." Almost immediately the society achieved national prominence and became a model for similar groups in other southern cities. In 1922 the editor of

Julia Mood Peterkin (1880–1961).
Courtesy, Calhoun County Museum.

Poetry turned over an entire issue of the magazine to the society (and not the Fugitives of Nashville) for "a Southern number." In a review of the 1922 *Yearbook,* the *New York Times* said it was "a real achievement not only in poetry but in all the sister arts." And Mencken, in another essay, "Violets in the Sahara," commented positively on the society's activities. Society members published in major periodicals on both sides of the Atlantic. Among them were Hervey Allen, John Bennett, DuBose Heyward, Julia Peterkin, Josephine Pinckney, and Archibald Rutledge. Heyward and Peterkin achieved national acclaim for their representations of black life but found that their efforts were not always appreciated back home.[41]

Initially, white Carolinians reacted unfavorably to Peterkin's novels. University of South Carolina history professor Yates Snowden dismissed them with the comment: "no Southern lady should be concerned with the Negro's fornications." In 1929 Peterkin's *Scarlet Sister Mary* won the Pulitzer Prize for Literature, but the Gaffney Public Library banned it as obscene. The *Cherokee Times* (Gaffney) evaded local censors and printed the novel in serial form.[42]

Whites were not any more comfortable with Heyward's *Porgy* or *Mamba's Daughters.* The latter has some unsettling passages in which the white protagonist considers using "Mr." when addressing a black man and the black heroine sings the black national anthem, "Lift Every Voice and Sing." It is a story about the New Negro, who, ironically, did not care for Heyward's portrayal of blacks in *Porgy.* The novel was a national sensation, and its characters became the best known in southern fiction of the 1920s. In collaboration with George Gershwin, Heyward transformed *Porgy* into the opera *Porgy and Bess,* which was not performed in South Carolina until 1970. If the cast accurately reflected the story line, it would have to include blacks and whites on the stage at the same time—and that was not permissible under Jim Crow.[43]

Black Carolinians hoped that after the war their condition would improve. After all, they had loyally supported the war effort at home and black Carolinians had served valiantly overseas. They found out quickly that being a good citizen did not translate into being able to enjoy the rights of citizenship. If anything were going to be done to improve the condition of black Carolinians, they would have to do it themselves. Occasionally whites provided some financial support for black organizations such as the Phillis Wheatley Association in Greenville or for special projects such as the Federation of Colored Women's Club's Fairwold Home.[44]

The National Association for the Advancement of Colored People (NAACP) established chapters in South Carolina, and the Charleston chapter successfully lobbied for replacing white teachers in black schools with black teachers. The Columbia chapter campaigned for and obtained a YWCA and a branch of the public library. In Greenville the chapter was not organized until 1930 but within a decade initiated a voter registration drive. Except in Greenville where the KKK tried unsuccessfully to intimidate black voters, there was not much white objection to these black endeavors because none were seen as challenges to white supremacy. Older black Carolinians tended to accept the status quo, but younger blacks such as Mamie Garvin Fields and Septima Poinsette Clark in Charleston and Mary Modjeska Monteith Simkins in Columbia were laying the groundwork for the civil rights movement of the 1960s.[45]

One of those questioning the established order was Benjamin Mays, a native of Rambo (Epworth) in Greenwood County and a professor at the Colored Normal, Industrial, Agricultural, and Mechanical College of South Carolina. He reported a conversation between two South Carolina black men: "I know my place and stay in it," said the older of the two. The younger replied that he found it difficult to know what his place was, given the confusing arrangement of Jim Crow laws and customs: "On the train . . . it is in the front; on the ship it is below; on the streetcar it is in the rear; and in the theater it is above." These men, Mays said, were both "born and reared in South Carolina" but lived in "two different worlds."[46]

On social issues there may have been divisions within the black community and there certainly was a wall between black and white Carolinians. However, the Great Depression of 1929 was color-blind.

The stock market was the last thing many Carolinians had on their minds on 24 October 1929. It was Big Thursday, the annual clash between Clemson College and the University of South Carolina. Coming into the game Clemson was undefeated and Carolina had only one loss, and both teams were solid contenders for the

Southern Conference championship. Fourteen thousand fans jammed the old wooden stadium at the State Fairgrounds in Columbia to see Clemson break a tie and win 21–14.[47]

It took a few days for the news from New York to sink in, but when it did, Big Thursday also happened to be Black Thursday. If Carolinians thought things could not get worse after the economic crisis of the early 1920s, they were mistaken. By June 1932 cotton dropped to 4.6¢(51¢) a pound, its lowest price since 1894. It climbed back up to 6¢(70¢) in early 1933, but there were few buyers. John T. Woodside's business empire collapsed, and his mills and resort developments were purchased for a fraction of their worth. Woodside, once one of the richest men in the state, lost everything he had, including his home. The per capita income of South Carolinians dropped from $261 ($2,313) in 1929 to $151 ($1,672) in 1933.[48]

Bank failures were nothing new, but now major financial institutions began to go under. On 31 December 1931 People's State Bank, with forty-four branches, closed. Bank examiners announced that patrons might be able to recover 18 percent of their savings. Frantic depositors, fearing the loss of their funds, began runs on otherwise sound banks. South Carolina National Bank was kept solvent in January 1932 by having $500,000 ($5.6 million) flown in from Charlotte. In Walterboro two armed men broke into a closed bank and took the amount of money they had on deposit. They buried the cash in a safe place and then turned themselves in to the sheriff. When brought to trial, the jury refused to convict them and they became folk heroes.[49]

Government at the state and local levels seemed unable or unwilling to act. By 1931 Charleston was on the brink of bankruptcy, and when the People's State Bank folded, it took with it the city payroll account. Greenville trimmed expenses and cut taxes. Florence reduced the budget and eliminated jobs. Columbia's mayor said in 1930 that there was no economic crisis and blocked the establishment of a municipal employment agency. State government, with its "clumsy, irresponsible administrative structure," did nothing. The one agency that might have at least tried to do something, the Board of Public Welfare, ceased to exist when Governor Richards vetoed its appropriation in 1926. Everyone seemed to be waiting to see what Uncle Sam would do. Gov. Ibra Blackwood's 1933 State of the State Address could have been ghost-written by Herbert Hoover. Balancing the budget and slashing expenditures were its main features. State salaries were reduced and employees paid in state scrip. City governments in Charleston and Columbia and the Greenville school districts also resorted to scrip.[50]

There was no social safety net. Opponents of social legislation blocked it on the grounds that the state's constitution permitted assistance only for Confederate veterans, their widows, and faithful slaves. By 1936 South Carolina was one of six states without old-age pensions, one of fourteen without assistance for the blind, and one of two with no aid for dependent children. After a referendum, in which voters by a 10–1 margin approved amending the constitution, the General Assembly

The Port of Charleston (circa 1938). Courtesy, Calhoun County Museum.

enacted public assistance for old-age pensioners, the blind, and dependent children. Until then the only relief for the poor and the homeless were county almshouses or poor farms.[51]

Local agencies could not cope with the magnitude of the worsening crisis. Seventeen counties (Allendale, Bamberg, Beaufort, Berkeley, Calhoun, Chesterfield, Colleton, Dorchester, Fairfield, Georgetown, Hampton, Jasper, Kershaw, McCormick, Oconee, Richland) had an unemployment rate of greater than 30 percent. By 1932 Columbia charities were serving more than seven hundred thousand free meals a year to destitute residents. In rural South Carolina individuals were literally dying from hunger, and in Columbia many were "on the verge of starvation."[52]

Hunger and *starvation* were terms that South Carolinians associated with the masses in Africa and Asia. Something needed to be done, and it was clear, even before the days of instant polling, that the Democrats would win the presidential election of 1932. But who would be the party's nominee? As early as 1928 key state officials had begun to back the candidacy of Franklin Delano Roosevelt, the governor of New York. In 1928 U.S. senatorial hopeful James F. Byrnes renewed his friendship with FDR. Two years later Claud N. Sapp, chair of the state Democratic Executive Committee, helped organize Roosevelt Southern Clubs. In 1931 state senators Dick Jefferies and Edgar Brown and Gov. Ibra Blackwood announced for Roosevelt. These men provided FDR with a solid base of support in the state, and at the nominating convention in Chicago they actively campaigned for their candidate. Byrnes, now a U.S. senator, was particularly effective in backroom negotiations leading up to the nomination.[53]

Roosevelt was a popular choice. Pickens County farmers rejoiced at the chance to vote for someone who opposed the godless corporations and banks of Wall Street. Rural newspapers mocked Hoover's slogan, "Prosperity is just around the corner." The *Lexington Dispatch News* suggested that perhaps the country should "abolish corners. Then prosperity will show itself." "From where we are standing," commented Camden's *Wateree Messenger,* "it is as dark as the inside of a bull frog's belly and sounds just as doleful." South Carolina's voters needed little prompting, giving FDR his widest margin of victory of any state (98 percent).[54]

When Congress met in special session in 1933, three members of the South Carolina congressional delegation emerged as champions of the New Deal: Reps. Hampton P. Fulmer of Orangeburg and John J. McSwain of Greenville, and Sen. James F. Byrnes of Spartanburg. In the senate it soon became clear that Byrnes was one of the administration's point men on legislation and the liaison between the administration and southern senators. He was the state's most influential senator since Calhoun and, like Calhoun, harbored presidential ambitions.[55]

During the first "100 Days" of the New Deal, Congress enacted legislation confirming the views of Ben Robertson's grandfather that the first duty of a nation was to "put people's security before its riches." Given the scope of economic distress in South Carolina, almost all New Deal legislation had an impact on the lives of its citizens.[56]

In May 1933 the Federal Emergency Relief Administration provided grants to the states for food, clothing, and work relief. By the end of the summer one-fourth of all Carolinians were on relief. The South Carolina Emergency Relief Administration (SCERA) was an "administrative nightmare." In some counties favoritism, nepotism, racism, and incompetence tainted relief efforts. One of the problems was the absence of either a state agency or any local relief or welfare program on which to build. Having to create overnight a program to serve 403,000 Carolinians (219,000 black; 184,000 white) was no easy task. Despite its difficulties, the SCERA literally saved thousands of Carolinians from starvation. And in a program that was administered at the county level, South Carolina was the only state in which black aid recipients outnumbered whites. The school lunch program made a big difference in the lives of children whose families could not feed them every day: "[My brother] Jim and me have to take turns at home; one morning he has breakfast and the next morning I eat. But like I told Jim this morning; he won't have to go hungry long cause at 12 o'clock he'll get a bowl of hot soup."[57]

The Civilian Conservation Corps (CCC) was as popular as the SCERA was unpopular. The state's senior U.S. senator, Ellison D. "Cotton Ed" Smith, who was less than enthusiastic about most New Deal legislation, declared that the CCC was "the most marvelous piece of legislation that has ever been enacted during this Administration or any preceding Administration." Young men between the ages of seventeen and twenty-five were eligible to participate in the program for six-month stints

Canning vegetables in the yard, Manning (Clarendon County). Photograph by Marion Post Wolcott (Farm Security Administration). Courtesy, Library of Congress.

for up to two years. For their labors the youths received $30 ($352) a month, $22 ($258) of which went home to their parents. By 1939 nearly fifty thousand Carolinians had been employed in thirty camps scattered across the state. Much of the work they did was conservation-oriented, and the state park system developed out of CCC projects (including Hunting Island, Paris Mountain, Myrtle Beach, and Poinsett State Parks).[58]

The Works Progress Administration (WPA) and the Public Works Administration (PWA) transformed the built landscape of South Carolina. The agencies employed local workers to build highways, bridges, schools, water and sewer systems, libraries, courthouses, and airports. Greenville got a new airport, post office, and high school. The PWA saved Charleston's Navy Yard, and the WPA transformed the decrepit Planters' Hotel into the Dock Street Theater. After a federal study revealed that Charleston had some of the worst housing in the nation, the PWA built two multi-million-dollar housing projects, one for blacks and one for whites. In Columbia there were three housing projects, a new courthouse, and dormitories at the University of South Carolina. The South Carolina Writers' Project of the WPA produced a history of Spartanburg County and *South Carolina: The WPA Guide to the Palmetto State*. And the WPA's Historical Project and Historic Records Survey copied historical records, conducted oral histories, and inventoried public records. More than 150,000 pages of materials were deposited in the University of South Carolina's South Caroliniana Library.[59]

Construction of the lock and dam at Pinopolis, the Santee Cooper Project. Courtesy, Calhoun County Museum.

The largest single New Deal project in the state, and one of the largest in the country, was Santee Cooper. In 1934 the General Assembly created the South Carolina Public Service Authority (Santee Cooper) with the power to produce and sell electricity; develop inland navigation along the Santee, Cooper, and Congaree Rivers; reclaim swamps; and reforest watersheds. After intensive lobbying by South Carolinians, especially by Senator Byrnes, Governor Blackwood, and Charleston mayor Burnet R. Maybank, FDR approved the project in 1935. Legal challenges in South Carolina delayed construction until May 1939. Then, in less than three years, some 171,000 acres of land were cleared, 200 million feet of timber cut, 42 million cubic feet of earth excavated, and 3.1 million cubic yards of concrete poured. Dams blocked the Santee and Cooper Rivers, which were connected by a six-mile-long canal. The Santee Cooper project was an incredible feat of engineering that was completed in record time and within budget. The hydroelectric plant at Pinopolis generated electricity for war industries in Charleston; flooding along the Santee was eliminated; and, for later generations, Lakes Marion and Moultrie would provide some of the country's finest sport fishing.[60]

In South Carolina in 1934 there was little electric power outside the cities and larger towns. Only 2 percent of the state's 168,000 farms had electricity. "In the country," remembered Mamie Garvin Fields, "there were no lights anywhere." When it got dark, rural residents went to bed with the chickens. The Rural Electrification Act (REA) provided low-cost loans for rural electric cooperatives. The New-berry Electric Cooperative took full advantage of the opportunity, and within a few years more than 150 miles of electric lines were providing inexpensive power to the county's farmers. By 1940 the number of farms with electricity had surged to 14.5 percent.[61]

Not as visible as power poles and lines but affecting more people was the Agri-cultural Adjustment Act (AAA). "Cotton Ed" Smith, chaired the senate Agriculture Committee and reluctantly went along with the AAA. In the house Rep. Hampton Fulmer of Orangeburg was chair of the Agriculture Committee and an enthusiastic backer of the AAA.[62]

The AAA was a program by which farmers who signed agreements with the fed-eral government to reduce the production of certain farm commodities (including cotton and tobacco) would receive government payments for their idle land. They also received a subsidy that would guarantee them parity (the equivalent purchas-ing power of cotton prices between 1909 and 1914 and tobacco between 1919 and 1929). Allotments for cotton were not new to South Carolina. During the Blease administration, in an attempt to raise cotton prices, the General Assembly passed legislation to reduce the amount of land in production. Cotton farmers were so en-thusiastic about the prospect of higher prices that they voluntarily ploughed up five hundred thousand acres. The week of 26 June–1 July 1933 was "Cotton Acreage Reduction Week." Night riders visited those who had not signed up and in some in-stances destroyed growing crops. The AAA and other farm programs such as the Soil Conservation Service improved production methods and stabilized agriculture. Under the New Deal farmers were better off than they had been earlier, but few were as prosperous as they had been before World War I, or even in 1929. For them, prosperity was as elusive in 1940 as it had been in 1932: it was still just around the corner.[63]

Textile workers and manufacturers were in almost as bad shape as cotton farm-ers. Low demand and overproduction resulted in a steady decline in prices and wages. The intent of the National Industrial Recovery Act (NIRA) was to increase wages and profits, stimulate employment, reduce hours, and safeguard labor's right to bargain. Under the supervision of the National Recovery Administration (NRA), every major industry developed its own code. The southern textile industry wel-comed the NRA, and Greenville executives Thomas M. Marchant, Robert E. Henry, and Harry R. Stephenson served on the committee that drafted the NRA code. Production in all southern mills was limited to 80 hours a week. Wages were increased, but the number of employees decreased. At a mill in Easley the operating hours declined from 128 to 80; the payroll increased 15 percent; and the number of employees dropped from 1,399 to 1,036. For those who had jobs, though, the pay was better.[64]

The NRA applied to all businesses. In Barnwell, Bishopville, Cheraw, Columbia, Florence, Greenville, and Laurens retailers unanimously agreed to the 40-hour week, and placards with the NRA's blue eagle symbol (indicating compliance) appeared in store windows. In August 1933 Columbia and Greenville held parades to highlight the NRA. Although the U.S. Supreme Court eventually overturned the NRA, many of its key provisions, such as the 40-hour week, 30¢ ($3.52) minimum wage, and prohibition of child labor, survived.[65]

While the NRA code for textiles specified hours and wages, it did not guarantee workers a 40-hour week. Manufacturers were allowed to reclassify positions and thereby reduce wages. Speed-ups and stretch-outs were not outlawed, and compliance with the code was uneven. Mill operatives were bitter and restless. In Winnsboro workers sang "The Winnsboro Cotton Mill Blues" in which they attacked the avarice of one of their supervisors: "Old Man Sargent, sittin' at the desk, / The Damned old fool won't give us no rest; / He'd take the nickels off a dead man's eyes / To buy a Coca Cola and an Eskimo Pie." Even though mill operatives had not been receptive to unions before, by 1934 nearly one-half belonged to the United Textile Workers (UTW). On 3 September they went out on strike. Nonmembers joined, and within a week two-thirds of the state's mill workers were participating in the General Textile Strike. From Alabama to Maine operatives walked off the job during what was the largest strike in American history.[66]

Picket lines went up at mills. Governor Blackwood called out the National Guard, and they patrolled the streets of most mill villages except those in Columbia. However, the strike was so widespread that the governor had to resort to commissioning "constables without compensation" to reply to demands for assistance from sheriffs and mill owners. There were occasional confrontations between pickets and strikebreakers, and the mood on both sides was such that sooner or later violence was inevitable. On 6 September a squadron of workers arrived in Honea Path to support the pickets at Chiquola Mills. A scuffle broke out between strikebreakers and union members, and special deputies opened fire on the crowd. Six strikers were killed and fifteen seriously wounded (another died later). The national media ran headlines such as "Textile War Zone." It was the worst violence of the General Textile Strike, and ten thousand sympathetic mourners from all over the country attended the mass funeral. By the end of the third week, the strike began to falter. President Roosevelt appealed to the workers to return to their jobs and let an impartial board resolve the issue. Workers agreed to end the strike, but a number of mill owners refused to reopen right away. Of the twenty-six mills in the country cited for not rehiring workers, fifteen were in South Carolina. Despite the UTW's claims of victory, the strike was a failure.[67]

The end of the General Textile Strike resulted in the collapse of the UTW in South Carolina, but labor unrest continued. The stretch-out remained a major issue and in 1936 led to a strike in Newberry that divided the town and left lasting scars. In 1937 the Congress of Industrial Organizations (CIO) created a textile workers' organizing committee and successfully organized mills in McColl and Bennettsville. However, unions had only limited success. Gaffney, with machine gun emplacements

Main Street, Piedmont Mill Village (1938). Courtesy, Pendleton District Commission.

outside mills, was considered one of the most antiunion towns in the country (yet by 1942 the union was established and textile workers controlled the legislative delegation and elected their candidate for sheriff). Although not prounion, Senator Byrnes was an outspoken critic of the stretch-out and of mill villages, which he condemned as un-American.[68]

James F. Byrnes was one of an interesting cast of characters on the South Carolina political stage between world wars. In 1924 he lost a close senate race to Cole Blease, but he won the 1930 rematch. Then Byrnes hitched his star to Franklin D. Roosevelt, which paid off handsomely for him and for the state. By 1939 he was considered the second most powerful man in the U.S. Senate. The state's senior senator, Ellison D. "Cotton Ed" Smith from Lee County, resented being upstaged and did what he could to discomfit the administration. Back home at stump meetings his voice could be heard extolling the virtues of his "sweetheart, Miss Cotton." *Time* magazine labeled Smith a "conscientious objector to the twentieth century," but the voters elected him to the senate for six terms. The same voters who returned Smith to Washington (in 1932 and 1938) also elected Byrnes (1930 and 1936) and two New Deal governors, Olin D. Johnston (1934) and Burnet R. Maybank (1938).[69]

Johnston was a self-made man proud of his mill village roots. As governor he presided over a mini–New Deal in South Carolina: workmen's compensation, compulsory education (for ages seven to sixteen), reduced fees for license plates, an eight-month school year, a forty-hour week for textile workers (fifty-six hours for all others), and social security. As governor he ran afoul of the lowcountry legislative leadership when he tried to take over the Highway Department. Like many up-country legislators, he had opposed the 1929 highway bond bill. In 1935, after the General Assembly refused to remove highway commissioners appointed by previous governors, Johnston unilaterally declared their terms over. The recalcitrant commissioners (with the support of Senators Brown and Jefferies) refused to leave the offices to which they had been legally appointed. The governor then declared the commissioners in "rebellion, insurrection, and insurgency." He declared martial law and ordered the National Guard to occupy the Highway Department. The courts ruled against the governor, and he had to back down. Unfortunately, his two-year confrontation with the Highway Department delayed a number of PWA road projects and contributed to the state's unemployment woes.[70]

In personality and background Burnet Rhett Maybank was the antithesis of Olin D. Johnston. Whereas Johnston was something of an antiestablishment political loner in the tradition of Tillman and Blease, Maybank was very much an establishment figure. He was one of Byrnes's protégés and political allies. With his unswerving loyalty to Byrnes and strong support of the New Deal, federal funds flowed into Charleston. In 1938 Maybank shattered the myth that a Charlestonian could not be elected governor. On the stump his strong Charleston brogue, rapid-fire delivery, and unnerving habit of changing subject in midsentence made his speeches virtually unintelligible to voters more than forty miles from the coast. However, his exuberance, sincerity, charisma, and firm control of Charleston's political machinery assured his win.[71]

Supporting the New Deal boosted the careers of Byrnes, Johnston, and Maybank. Opposing it ended those of Blease and Thomas Stoney, the former mayor of Charleston. Smith eventually turned on the administration but was reelected because of FDR's meddling in South Carolina politics.

Since 1933 Smith had chafed at having to play second fiddle to Byrnes. The 1936 National Democratic Convention in Philadelphia gave him the opportunity to spit in the face of the administration and win plaudits from his constituents. Smith and other southern delegates were shocked to see black delegates in the convention hall, and when a black clergyman gave the invocation, Smith stalked out. His performance attracted national attention and gave rise to what voters back home called the "Philadelphia Story." At rallies and stump meetings citizens were not interested in issues; they wanted to hear the Philadelphia Story—and he was more than happy to oblige: "And he started praying and I started walking. And as I . . . walked across that vast rotunda, it seemed to me that old John Calhoun leaned down from his mansion in the sky and whispered in my ear, 'You did right, Ed.'"[72]

Smith was not up for reelection in 1936, but Byrnes was. His opponents in the primary, Thomas P. Stoney and William C. Harllee, made race and the New Deal the issues. Byrnes refused to "out-nigger" his opponents and concentrated on what

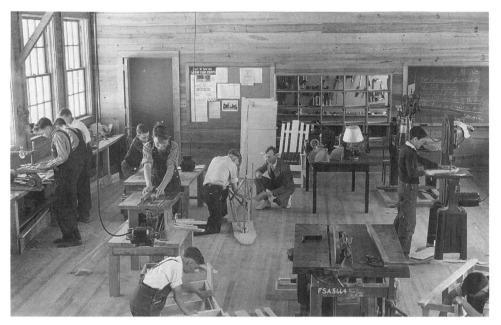

The Ashwood Resettlement Project of the WPA, Lee County (1939). Photograph by Marion Post Wolcott (Farm Security Administration). Courtesy, Library of Congress.

the New Deal had done for South Carolina. Since 1933 the state had sent only $10 million ($112.6 million) in tax dollars to Washington but had received $240 million ($2.7 billion) in return. Voters got the message and knew who was responsible for much of the federal largesse. Byrnes won 87 percent of the vote and trounced Stoney, the former mayor of Charleston, on his own turf (thanks to the Maybank machine).[73]

The ease of Byrnes's victory and Roosevelt's overwhelming vote (113,791 to 1,646) in 1936 masked the discontent that some white Carolinians were beginning to have with the New Deal (see Map 25). Those with radios (seventy-six out of every one thousand) hovered around them to listen to the president's fireside chats over stations WIS (Columbia), WSPA (Spartanburg), and WCSC (Charleston), but the print media, especially the *News and Courier,* were increasingly hostile. No sooner were the "100 Days" over than W. W. Ball, the paper's editor, declared there was no need for any federal programs. He and like-minded individuals thought that the solution to hunger was to ship all unemployed town residents to the countryside to grow their own food and fend for themselves. His disdain for Roosevelt and federal programs was shared by the editors of the *Horry Herald* (Conway), *Dispatch News* (Lexington), and *Calhoun Times* (St. Matthews).[74]

While some of the opposition was based on states' rights, much of it was based on race. The New Deal coalition included northern urban blacks who began to

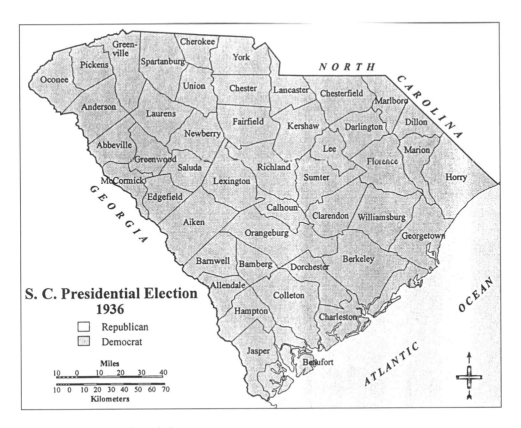

**S. C. Presidential Election
1936**

☐ Republican
▨ Democrat

Map 25: 1936 presidential election

switch from the party of Lincoln to the party of FDR. "Cotton Ed" Smith was not the only white Carolinian concerned about having blacks in the party. (What many white Carolinians did not know was that the black man charged with recruiting northern black voters was Julian D. Rainey, the son of Reconstruction-era congressman Joseph Rainey.) Blacks were beginning to register in small numbers in South Carolina, and they were registering as Democrats. When asked why, they cited FDR as the reason for joining the party. The administration's support of the Fair Labor Act and northern congressional Democrats' efforts to pass antilynching legislation further alienated white voters.[75]

In 1938 the president decided to purge congressmen who opposed his policies.

High on the list was "Cotton Ed" Smith, but in this instance FDR overreached himself. Not even his loyal lieutenants Byrnes and Maybank would go along. For their own political purposes, both secretly threw their support to Smith. Later Edgar Brown, who was also a candidate in the 1938 senatorial primary, reminisced: "Either Olin [D. Johnston] or I could have handled Ed on the race issue, but we were both licked the day Roosevelt came out against him." South Carolinians did not appreciate any outsider's meddling in their internal affairs.[76]

By the late 1930s an increasing number of white Carolinians viewed FDR and the New Deal with concern. Since the turn of the century the county elites had run the state without any interference. Between the disenfranchisement of black voters and the general acceptance of white supremacy and white unity, there was little chance of change from within. However, the New Deal was beginning to undermine the power base of the local elites. Whereas they had been the sole source of employment, financing, and credit, now government agencies bypassed the small town bankers, landlords, and county officials. The social safety net provided by various New Deal programs freed mill operatives, tenant farmers, and sharecroppers from total dependence on their old bosses.[77]

As at so many other junctures in South Carolina history, racism reared its ugly head. Businessmen who had willingly adopted the NRA standards for hours and wages wanted them to apply only to whites. They saw no need to raise wages for black labor. The appointment of blacks to prominent positions in Washington, such as Mayesville native Mary McLeod Bethune as director of the Negro Division of the National Youth Administration, implied an equality that whites were not willing to accept. When a white Laurens farmer-legislator was treated like everyone else, he was irate: "I had to stand in line behind a free nigger to get my ginning tags." The *News and Courier* warned its readers that blacks were taking over the Democratic Party.[78]

Disenchantment with the New Deal did not mean that whites would vote for a Republican presidential candidate. When Roosevelt ran for his third term in 1940, he garnered 95 percent of the vote in South Carolina. It was a landslide, but down from the 98+ percent totals he had received in 1932 and 1936.[79]

As the possibility of war in Europe grew, Byrnes and others rallied to the president. Smith was the only southern senator who balked at supporting the draft and other preparedness measures. Military bases in South Carolina reopened. Camp Jackson was reactivated as Fort Jackson in 1939 and, after the passage of a selective service act in 1940, became the home to thousands of military trainees. Army air bases opened in Lexington and Sumter Counties. The Charleston Navy Yard was directed to increase production and during 1941 launched twelve new destroyers. In January 1941 Byrnes successfully guided the Lend-Lease Act through the senate. In June the president nominated him to a vacancy on the Supreme Court. Within eight minutes after receiving Byrnes's nomination, the senate confirmed it; however, in less than twelve months the nation was at war, and Byrnes resigned from the court to become director of war mobilization.[80]

Most Carolinians remembered where they were when they learned the Japanese had bombed Pearl Harbor. In the hills of Pickens County, Ben Robertson recalled that 7 December was a bright, windy day. When he and his kinfolk heard the news, they gathered as a family: "We were in trouble and our country was in trouble, and as always whenever there was trouble, we found that automatically we had come together. . . . My cousin Billy said he was ready to go. So did my cousin George. So did J. B., Mary's nephew. We went alone to the cotton fields. There before us stood the hills. . . . The hills were eternal. Always, they gave us strength." A year later Ben Robertson, a reporter for the *New York Herald Tribune*, died in a plane crash in Lisbon, Portugal. He did not live to see the forces unleashed by the New Deal and World War II irrevocably alter the South Carolina he knew.[81]

Chapter Twenty-two

ALL IN ONE LIFETIME

It is frequently the case that a State might gain a momentary respite from the pressures of events by the simple expedience of shutting the gates to the outside world. But in the words of Mr. Justice Cardozo: "The Constitution was framed under the dominion of a political philosophy less parochial in range. It was framed upon the theory that the peoples of the several States must sink or swim together, and that in the long run prosperity and salvation are in union and not division."

James F. Byrnes, *Edwards v. California* (1942)

*I*N 1958 James F. Byrnes, former congressman, U.S. senator, U.S. Supreme Court justice, "assistant president," and governor, published his memoirs, *All in One Lifetime*. While he was concerned with telling his own story, he also related a more comprehensive story, that of a changing South Carolina. Byrnes did not like much of what was happening in the state in the 1950s, but as U.S. senator and New Dealer, he had helped set in motion the forces that were altering South Carolina's traditional society. The South Carolina of 1975 was a very different place from the South Carolina of 1945. Anyone who lived through the birth pangs of what historians now call modern South Carolina could also wonder at all that had occurred in his or her lifetime.[1]

In 1940 the modified Bourbon world of county elites, Jim Crow, and mill village paternalism seemed as if it would last forever. "I do not see that we shall make any radical change in this community—and this is the south," wrote James McBride Dabbs of Mayesville, "in generations, perhaps centuries." His contemporary Harry S. Ashmore of Greenville more or less agreed. However, if there were to be any change at all, Ashmore believed "the impetus would have to be initiated from outside the region."[2]

Rural South Carolina still looked as Julia Peterkin described in *Green Thursday:*

The main road on the plantation divides. One straggling, rain-rutted fork runs along the edge of a field to a cluster of low, weather-beaten houses grouped among giant red-oak trees. The Quarters, where most of the black people live.

The other fork bends with a swift, smooth curve and glides into a grove of cedars and live-oaks and magnolias, whose dense evergreen branches hide all beyond them but slight glimpses of white columns and red brick chimneys.

Right where the two roads meet is a sycamore tree. Its milk-white branches reach up to the sky. Its pale, silken leaves glisten and whisper incomplete cadences in the hot summer sun. . . .

There is hardly a sign of the black, twisted roots. There is not a trace to be seen of their silent, tense struggle as they grope deep down in the earth. There is nothing to show how they reach and grapple and hold, or how in the darkness down among the worms they work out mysterious chemistries that change damp clay into beauty.

More than three-fourths of the population was rural and lived either in the country or in towns smaller than 2,500. Only Arkansas, Mississippi, and North Dakota had larger rural populations. No other state had a smaller number of foreign-born residents. The 4,915 nonnatives came primarily from Greece, Germany, Russia, and Palestine-Syria, and, according to a recent study, even those from the southern and eastern Mediterranean were welcomed because they were "almost white."[3]

The New Deal altered the dependence of farmers, sharecroppers, and tenants on landlords, country stores, and local banks. Mill workers turned to the government, not management, to set minimum wages and hours. The war, however, did what the New Deal could not do. It brought full employment. The Japanese attack on Pearl Harbor accelerated the military buildup that had begun in 1940. The secretary of the army approved plans for Greenville Army Air Base (later renamed Donaldson Field) on 11 December. South Carolina firms (especially Daniel Construction and Poe Hardware and Supply of Greenville) became major government contractors.[4]

By the end of the war more than 184,000 men and women were in uniform. Some men were drafted and others volunteered. In Columbia's mill villages one young man "storied about his age to join" and escape the mill. And he was not alone. Thousands more might have served, but more than one-half of eligible black males and one-third of white males were declared unfit due to either illiteracy or poor health. These rejection rates were among the highest in the nation and an indication of the poverty in which the majority of all Carolinians lived.[5]

With so many able-bodied men in uniform, there was a shortage of labor for farms and factories. Textile mills operated in three shifts around the clock. In Charleston employment at the Navy Yard jumped from six thousand in 1941 to twenty-eight thousand in 1943. Another seventy-two thousand workers found employment at defense-related firms in the area. The flood of workers taxed local resources. The number of passengers on city buses doubled, and so did retail sales. Local merchants and landlords, however, saw no reason to expand their facilities or services. They believed that after the war the workers would leave. Price gouging, especially for housing, was common. Many workers commuted fifty to seventy miles one way every day. Others paid exorbitant prices for "hot beds," where they slept in shifts.[6]

A Navy Department investigation determined that the housing shortage and sub-

Home on leave, World War II. Sgt. John Riley and friends, Bowman (Orangeburg County). Photograph by Jack Delano. Courtesy, Library of Congress.

standard housing hindered productivity, costing the navy at least one destroyer a month. As a result, the U.S. Housing Administration subsidized the building of five thousand housing units and opened a rent-control office. When local landlords balked, the agency threatened to commandeer private housing. When city officials winked at brothels, the army declared Charleston off-limits. The houses were closed, but the women simply freelanced all over the city. Charleston was one of fifteen U.S. cities with a red letter for unsatisfactory vice control. Although there was a lot of grousing, these seemingly heavy-handed actions were deemed necessary to support the war effort.[7]

While the growth of Charleston proper was modest, the metropolitan area exploded to 225,000. During the war Charleston County's population increased 41 percent. Five other counties also gained new residents (Beaufort, Dorchester, Greenville, Kershaw, and Richland). The remaining forty counties lost population;

two of them, Lancaster (33 percent) and Union (21 percent) suffered significant population losses. As a result of losing workers to the armed forces and better-paying jobs in mills and defense industries, farmers were shorthanded. In an attempt to maintain and increase production, they worked longer hours and employed women and children in the fields more often. German and Italian prisoners of war at twenty-eight camps scattered throughout the state labored in nondefense factories and on farms.[8]

South Carolina farmers did produce bumper crops, but that did not necessarily result in more food for the civilian population. Rationing became an accepted part of everyday life. Sometimes ration cards and the various point systems assigned to seasonal produce were confusing, but housewives learned to cope. The federal government rationed more than two hundred commercially processed foods as well as sugar, red meat, and coffee. Butter, tea, and chocolate were scarce. "One to a customer" signs appeared in grocery windows. Shoes, tires, and gasoline were also rationed, but electricity was not. Even so, at night coastal towns were dark. With German submarines lurking off Charleston harbor, coastal blackouts were mandatory. Inland towns practiced blackouts and air-raid drills but discontinued them after D Day.[9]

Organized athletic events such as professional baseball and the Carolina Cup at Camden ceased, but the state fairs (one for blacks and one for whites) continued. The war did not mean much change for black Carolinians, but they loyally held their own Red Cross drives and operated USOs for black servicemen. When V-E Day came, there were even separate victory celebrations in Greenville.[10]

Not all black and white Carolinians were willing to accept the racial status quo. In 1941 a group of black teachers asked the state to pay them the same wages as white teachers with the same certificates. State bureaucrats stonewalled, lost paperwork, and tried to revoke certification. Getting no satisfaction, in 1944 the teachers filed suit, and Judge Waties Waring of Charleston ruled in their favor. In July 1942 Claude Evans, a young assistant minister at Columbia's Washington Street Methodist Church, preached a sermon, "This Conflict of Race" that startled not only his white congregation but also radio listeners over Columbia radio station WIS. The church's stewards, some saying he had "desecrated" the pulpit, voted 87–3 to bar him from preaching in the church again.[11]

In 1942 a group of prominent Columbia whites determined they would try to get black voters on the rolls, but the Democratic Party forbade blacks to vote unless they had cast their ballots for Wade Hampton in 1876. In 1944 the U.S. Supreme Court ruled that blacks could not be kept from voting in the Texas Democratic primary. South Carolina was the first southern state to respond to this threat to the all-white primary. In April 1944 when the General Assembly convened in special session, legislators introduced 147 bills to repeal all existing legislation concerning primaries. "The South Carolina Plan" was based on the premise that if the state let political parties hold primaries as private organizations, then the primaries would be beyond the reach of federal courts. With a speed that amazed even veteran legislative observers, the lawmakers enacted all 147 bills in six days. The following November the voters approved the necessary constitutional amendments to make political primaries private affairs. Although America was fighting against tyranny and for democracy, South Carolina was one of only two states that did not permit absentee voting for its men and women in uniform. In 1944 Albert D. Hutto, a young white soldier, wrote an angry letter to the editor of *The State:* "It seems to me that the average [white] South Carolinian is so afraid that the negro will get ahead that he is willing to sacrifice his own rights just to make sure that the negro won't have any." After the war veterans (white and black) would be in the forefront pressing for change.[12]

When Germany was defeated, there were organized festivities in Greenville, but reactions in Charleston and Columbia were more subdued. After Japan's surrender, Carolinians everywhere took to the streets in a raucous celebration of the end of World War II. In 1944 the state had begun making plans for its returning veterans. Of special concern was having the workforce of 700,000 increase by 184,000 (26 percent). The Research, Planning and Development Board (the precursor to the modern State Development Board) sent out sixty-five hundred questionnaires to a random selection of Carolinians in uniform (without regard to race or gender). The responses received gave an interesting glimpse of the aspirations of returning veterans.[13]

The survey confirmed that Carolinians had an attachment to place. Nine out of ten soldiers surveyed intended to return to their home counties. Nearly one-half wanted assistance in improving their educations, whether with vocational training, a high school diploma, or a college degree. "Good schools for country children, white and colored sorely needed," wrote one GI. In a sad commentary on the state's colleges, 40 percent of those desiring a college education indicated that they wanted to go to an out-of-state school.[14]

Even with specific information, the state's colleges did little to prepare for the wave of veterans. Enrollment at the University of South Carolina, for example, jumped from 2,244 in 1945 to 4,072 in 1948. There were more veterans on campus (2,374) in 1948 than there had been students in 1945. The school's leadership refused to spend funds appropriated by the General Assembly. Students were crammed four to a single room, and classes were taught in basements and attics. At the high school level there was supposed to be at least one school per county with special programs for veterans; however, since schools were segregated, if there were only one school in a county, it was for whites only.[15]

Specific comments on several surveys served notice that black GIs had no intention of quietly resuming their prewar roles. "Make definite plans to give the Negro soldier or veteran *equal opportunity,*" wrote one respondent. Another proposed that "South Carolina compose a bigger and better system for both white and colored, through which the race problem can be settled."[16]

Regardless of race, returning veterans had big plans. While 90 percent of them wanted to return home, not that many wanted to resume their old jobs. More than one-half of those who had worked in textile mills and nearly one-third of those in agriculture before the war wanted to pursue other occupations. For those who either were going back to farming or who wanted to enter agriculture (and a surprising number did), most hoped to own their own farms. They intended to utilize the GI Bill as much as they could, and so did the forty-nine thousand returning servicemen and women who wanted to own their own businesses. In Newberry County veterans founded a number of successful businesses. In the words of the county's historian, they desired "to make something of themselves." And they did. Similarly, in Allendale County veterans started new businesses and formed the nucleus of the county's industry-recruiting effort. Impatient with the do-nothing attitude at the University of South Carolina, veterans were among the administration's most vocal critics. Their persistent calls for change eventually resulted in the construction of much-needed new buildings and a legislative investigation of the university's leadership.[17]

Enthusiastic young veterans wanted to change South Carolina, but they faced the opposition of the county elites who preferred the status quo. In the 1946 campaign for governor, the Barnwell ring, the epitome of county elites, became the major issue of the campaign. There were ten candidates, including: Ransome J. Williams of Marion County, the incumbent who had succeeded to the governorship when Olin D. Johnston was elected to the U.S. Senate; Dr. James McLeod of Florence County, a conservative physician and favorite of the state's old-line politicians; and J. Strom Thurmond of Edgefield County, decorated war hero, former state senator, and judge. In announcing his candidacy, Thurmond said, "We need a progressive outlook, a progressive program, a progressive leadership. We must face the future with confidence and with enthusiasm." It was just the sort of go-get-'em attitude that would appeal to veterans and their families.[18]

The candidates still had to speak at stump meetings in every county. Race was not much of an issue, but who admired FDR the most was. All proclaimed their admiration for the man whose programs had saved the state from economic and social collapse. At the first stump meeting in Fairfield County, Thurmond attacked the ring. It was a "matter of common knowledge," he said, "that the government of South Carolina is under the domination of a small ring of cunning conniving men." The leaders of the ring, Sen. Edgar Brown and Speaker of the House Solomon Blatt, denounced Thurmond's charges and threw their support to McLeod. Despite the efforts of the establishment, the man they perceived as a liberal reformer led the ticket in the primary and swamped McLeod in the runoff. Blatt announced that he would not seek the Speakership, and Thurmond's handpicked man, C. Bruce Littlejohn of Spartanburg County, defeated another returning veteran, Thomas H. Pope of Newberry, for the post.[19]

During the four years of Thurmond's governorship, he prompted the General Assembly to pass a number of pieces of reform legislation. The State Probation, Parole, and Pardon Board supplanted the sometimes corrupt gubernatorial pardoning power. The State Ports Authority was given the necessary funding to begin modernizing the port of Charleston. The school year was extended to nine months for all children and the twelfth grade added to high schools. Voters approved constitutional amendments repealing the poll tax as a qualification for voting and legalizing divorce (South Carolina was the last state to forbid divorce). State finances were centralized in the Budget and Control Board (governor, treasurer, comptroller, and the chairs of the House Ways and Means Committee and the Senate Finance Committee), which became the single most powerful agency in state government. The General Assembly amended the Public Welfare Act to provide aid to dependent children under eighteen who were still in school.[20]

As impressive as was the list of legislative accomplishments, it was Thurmond's decisive handling of the Willie Earle lynching that stamped his administration as "liberal without being radical." On 16 February 1947 a young black man from Pickens County was arrested and charged with the murder of Thomas Brown, a white Greenville taxicab driver. The next day a mob broke into the Pickens County jail, seized Earle, and then shot, stabbed, and beat him to death on the outskirts of town. The FBI and the State Law Enforcement Division launched intensive investigations that led to thirty-one arrests. The governor urged the vigorous prosecution of those accused of the lynching, but after a highly publicized trial, the jury acquitted them. The presiding judge, J. Robert Martin, was so incensed that he left the courtroom without thanking the jury.[21]

The trial attracted national media attention—not, however, because it was a gruesome murder or because the jury returned a verdict of not guilty. The trial of the twenty-one white men in Greenville was a media sensation simply because it took place. In a Deep South state authorities had arrested and prosecuted individuals for what some white southerners had heretofore considered a justifiable action. The defendants were forced to listen to their cowardly crime described in open court. The governor's prompt and determined action brought thanks from the leaders of the black community.[22]

Black Carolinians were no longer willing to accept a subordinate place. The Earle case and the beating and blinding of Isaac Woodard, a black army sergeant, by a Batesburg policeman spurred the Truman administration to take a strong stand on civil rights. They also increased the determination of black Carolinians. Between

In 1948 black Columbians stood in lines for hours to exercise their newly won right to vote. Courtesy, South Caroliniana Library.

1939 and 1948 the membership of the South Carolina NAACP increased from eight hundred to fourteen thousand and individuals chapters united to form a statewide organization. Teachers demanded equal pay for equal work. Osceola McKaine and John McCray were among the founders of the Progressive Democratic Party (PDP), which began attending Democratic conventions in 1944 and embarrassing the state's white power structure.[23]

In July 1947 George Elmore of Richland County challenged the all-white private primary. Judge J. Waties Waring, an eighth-generation Charlestonian, heard the case. In a sharply worded decision, he chided his fellow Carolinians for denying blacks the opportunity of voting in primaries. "It is time," he said, "for South Carolina to rejoin the Union." The state party executive committee promptly required all who voted in primaries to take an oath stating that they would "support the social, religious, and educational separation of the races." In Richland and Marlboro Counties local party officials ignored the oath and allowed blacks to register. In July 1948 Judge Waring threw out the oath and the white primary was no more. The next

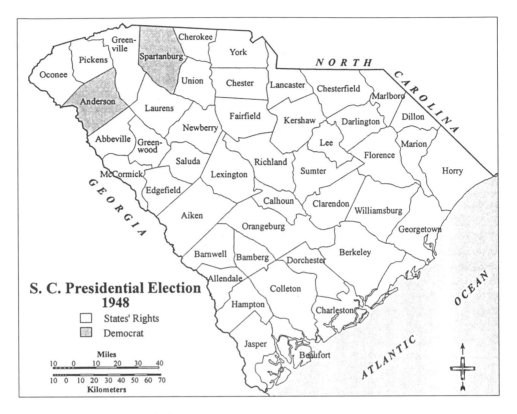

Map 26: 1948 presidential election

month some thirty-five thousand black Carolinians voted in the Democratic primary.[24]

The South Carolina establishment, like their peers in other southern states, felt besieged. Black Carolinians were no longer quiescent. The national Democratic Party and especially President Harry Truman advocated new civil rights legislation. For generations the Democratic Party had needed the votes of the solid South and ignored civil rights. By the 1940s that situation had changed. Votes of northern blacks were more crucial in local and presidential elections than southern white votes. Labor and civil rights leaders blocked James F. Byrnes's nomination as vice president in 1944. The old economic liberalism of the New Deal was abandoned for a moral liberalism that had only one issue: race.[25]

Gov. Strom Thurmond and his wife Jean Crouch Thurmond flew to Houston, Texas, for him to accept the Dixiecrat nomination for the presidency (August 1948). Courtesy, Special Collections, Clemson University Libraries, Clemson, South Carolina.

Southerners at the 1948 Democratic convention had not been so isolated since the fateful convention of 1860. They stood alone in opposing the civil rights planks in the party's platform and in supporting the candidacy of Richard B. Russell Jr. of Georgia. Disgruntled Democrats met in Birmingham and nominated Strom Thurmond and Gov. Fielding Wright of Mississippi as the candidates for president and vice president of the States' Rights Democrats Party (Dixiecrats). As a presidential candidate, Thurmond generally eschewed any overtly racist remarks; however, he made it clear where he stood on the question of civil rights: It was a matter that should be left to the states. In South Carolina, Alabama, Mississippi, and Louisiana, Dixiecrats seized control of the Democratic Party machinery. Elsewhere most conservative southerners chose to fight their battles within the party. In November the Thurmond-Wright ticket polled more than one million votes and garnered thirty-nine electoral votes in South Carolina and the other three states where Dixiecrats controlled the party apparatus. The Dixiecrat revolt against the possibility of civil rights legislation was a portent of what might be expected when, and if, such legislation were passed (see Map 26).[26]

The next challenge to the southern establishment would come from rural Clarendon County, South Carolina. In 1947 there were 8,906 children (6,531 black; 2,375 white) in the county's schools. Thirty buses transported any white students who needed rides. There were no buses for black schoolchildren. In Scott's Branch School (Clarendon District 26) some children had to walk nine miles one way to get to their school, which was heated by a wood stove, lighted by kerosene lamps, and had neither indoor plumbing nor running water. The Reverend Joseph A. DeLaine, an AME pastor and schoolteacher, encouraged black residents of the school district to speak up for themselves and their children. A group did petition the school board for buses. R. W. Elliott, the chairman of the school board, replied: "We ain't got no money to buy a bus for your nigger children." The parents of Scott's Branch somehow raised the funds to buy a used bus, but the school district refused to pay for gasoline or repairs. In 1948 one of the parents filed suit to obtain school buses. Under the *Plessy* doctrine of "separate but equal," buses should have been provided. On a technicality, the suit was dismissed and the plaintiff found he could not obtain credit at any store in the county.[27]

In 1949 DeLaine met with NAACP officials in Columbia, and Thurgood Marshall was there. The upshot of that meeting was that on 20 December 1950 Harry Briggs, a navy veteran, and twenty-four other Clarendon County residents filed suit against the Summerton School District (Clarendon District 22). *Briggs* v. *Elliott* was the first legal challenge to school segregation to originate in the twentieth-century South. In May 1951 the case came to trial in federal district court in Charleston. The state's legal counsel, Robert M. Figg of Charleston, stole the plaintiffs' thunder by admitting that the schools in question were unequal; however, he argued that the state had just begun a $124 million ($726.5 million) program to create a school system that was equal as well as separate. The court ruled 2–1 against the plaintiffs, but in a dissenting opinion Judge Waring said: "Segregation in education can never produce equality. . . . *Segregation is per se inequality.*" The plaintiffs appealed to the U.S. Supreme Court. There, thanks to some behind-the-scenes maneuvering by Governor Byrnes, the deciding case, *Brown* v. *Board of Education of Topeka,* would not be a southern one. The court took two years to make its decision. In the meantime, Byrnes was doing his best to buttress the state's insistence that schools for blacks and whites were equal.[28]

Byrnes had resigned as secretary of state and returned to South Carolina in 1946. After thirty-five years of public life, he chafed at retirement. Supposedly at the encouragement of Solomon Blatt, he agreed to stand for governor in 1950. Whether it was from boredom or a vision of himself as a twentieth-century Calhoun unifying the South to defy the North, Byrnes eagerly announced his candidacy. It was not much of a campaign. It was a triumphal procession, much like those of Hampton in 1876 and Tillman in 1890. Shortly after his inauguration in 1951, the new governor addressed the General Assembly: "It is our duty to provide for the races substantial equality in school facilities. We should do it because it is right. For me, that is sufficient reason. If any person wants an additional reason, I say it is wise." *Briggs v. Elliott* was pending in the federal courts.[29]

The legislators responded to the governor's initiative and passed the state's first sales tax (3 percent) to provide increased funding for public education. Between 1951 and 1956 the governor's school program spent $124 million ($726.5 million) on new construction and buses. About two-thirds of that sum went to black schools even though black children comprised only 40 percent of the school population. In Clarendon District 22 the state spent $894,000 ($5.1 million) for black school construction and only $103,000 ($587,000) for whites. In some communities black facilities were superior to those of whites. However, the sudden influx of dollars could not make up for three generations of neglect.[30]

New buildings were only one aspect of what the governor termed his "Educational Revolution." The other major component, school consolidation, reduced the number of school districts from 1,002 to 102. In 1951 there were 82 school districts in Greenville County, 76 in Horry, and 51 in Pickens; by 1954 there was one each in Greenville and Horry and two in Pickens. There was some consolidation later, but the 1951 plan created most of the districts that existed in the 1970s (see Maps 27, 28). Antiquated one- and two-room schoolhouses were abandoned and their students transferred to consolidated schools. Although Byrnes acknowledged that schools were the social and civic centers of many rural communities, he determinedly pushed consolidation. In three years 824 schools closed. Consolidation meant that children attended schools further from their homes, perhaps in the next town or the county seat. In 1951 only 142,000 children rode school buses; by 1955 the number had risen to 241,000.[31]

Taking its lead from the governor, the General Assembly did not stop with its attempt to provide equal facilities for black and white children (see Map 29). It was determined to maintain segregation at all costs. In 1951 the legislature created a special fifteen-man committee, chaired by Sen. Marion Gressette of Calhoun County. The Gressette Committee, as it was called, was charged with recommending measures to prevent desegregation. Its first proposal was to call for a referendum deleting the constitutional provision that the state provide public schools. Over the objections of educators and civic leaders, it passed overwhelmingly. The legislature also passed a statute providing for the withholding of state funds for any school to which courts had ordered a student transferred.[32]

Governor Byrnes, long familiar with the Washington political scene, was not willing to let the matter rest. He hired the best appellate lawyer in the country, John W. Davis of New York City, to represent South Carolina in *Briggs* v. *Elliott* before the Supreme Court. He lobbied members of the court with whom he had served. He discussed the matter with President Dwight D. Eisenhower, his political ally, and urged him not to be bound by President Truman's support of desegregation. The doctrine

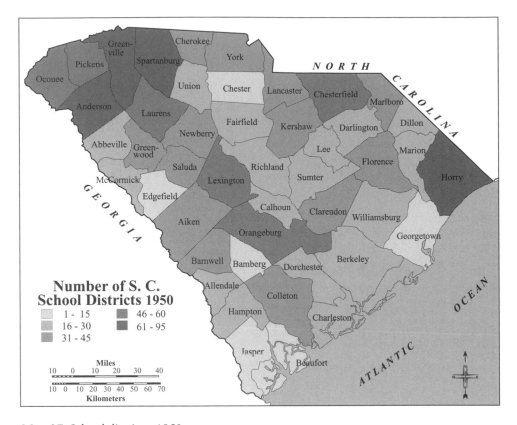

Map 27: School districts, 1950

of "separate but equal," he told the president, was legally sound. And, in a resurrection of states' rights, he advised Ike that segregated schools clearly were within the police powers of the state "to promote education and to prevent disorders." On 17 May 1954 the court unanimously ruled that "separate but equal" was unconstitutional.[33]

Shock, disbelief, anger, rage—any of these words could have been used to describe the reaction of most white Carolinians to the decision. The "Committee of 52," a group of respected white businessmen, authors, clergy, and politicians, published a declaration affirming the necessity of separate schools to preserve "public education and domestic tranquility." They called for the state to "interpose the sovereignty of the State of South Carolina between Federal Courts and local school of-

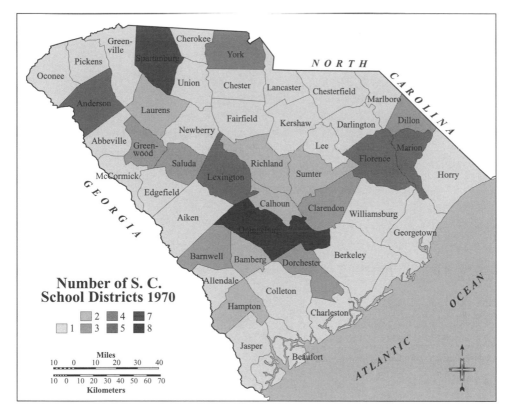

Map 28: School districts, 1970

ficials" and vowed to resist the "clear and present danger" to state sovereignty "without resort to physical strife, but without surrender of our position." Within weeks white supremacist groups emerged, trying to stir up trouble. The Ku Klux Klan resurfaced but found it was not welcome. State officials considered it a terrorist organization, and newspapers derided Klansmen as "bedsheeters" and "hotheads, crackpots, and bullies."[34]

As he left office, Byrnes—forgetting his comments in *Edwards* v. *California* that a state could not shut its gates to the outside world—championed massive resistance to the Brown decision. Few white Carolinians needed much encouragement. In 1955 White Citizens Councils appeared everywhere. They were especially strong in the old black-belt counties of the middle- and lowcountry. Council literature defended

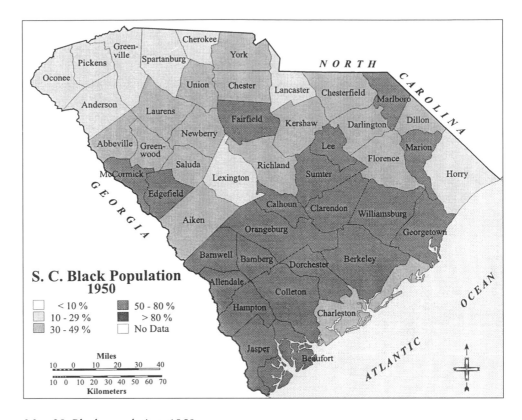

Map 29: Black population, 1950

the traditional community mores of a dying rural society in which white supremacy really meant white male supremacy. In promoting massive resistance, the councils worked closely with civic and patriotic organizations to spread their message. The emerging new metropolitan elites of business and professional men in Greenville and Columbia did not challenge the councils because they were uneasy about the question of equality.[35]

The councils did everything they could to undermine efforts to desegregate the schools. One of their favorite tactics was applying the squeeze to those who signed petitions or participated in court cases. The squeeze was not illegal, but it could have a chilling effect on rural blacks. Petitioners might suddenly find that they had no jobs, no credit, nowhere to live, or nowhere to gin their cotton. For example, in

Clarendon County, Harry and Liza Briggs lost their jobs, as did Joseph DeLaine, his wife, and their nieces. When whites in Orangeburg applied economic pressure to blacks who petitioned for the desegregation of the city's schools, the black community retaliated in kind. Supported by a $50,000 ($284,000) boycott fund deposited in Columbia's Victory Savings Bank, blacks in Orangeburg showed whites that the color of money was neither black nor white; it was green. After several months of boycott and counterboycott, a compromise was finally reached and tensions eased.[36]

The citizens' councils treated any whites who supported the decision as traitors. Social ostracism, economic boycott, and political pressure were all employed to force politically correct views. Anyone who did not disagree with the *Brown* decision was automatically assumed to be in favor of communism, atheism, and mongrelization. Chester C. Travelstead, dean of the University of South Carolina's College of Education, advocated peaceful compliance with the decision in public speeches and was fired. In his books and essays, James McBride Dabbs urged his fellow white Carolinians to obey the law of the land. Dabbs was the only prominent native southern critic of Jim Crow who saw more positives than negatives in the heritage of the American South. But one of his conclusions was that segregation rendered meaningless the definition of community. However, it is doubtful that many read his thought-provoking books, *The Southern Heritage* (1958) and *Who Speaks for the South* (1964). Lots of residents in the Pee Dee area read Jack O'Dowd's editorials in the *Florence Morning News* and did not like his advising them to accept the *Brown* decision with grace. After two years of harassment, he stepped down and left the state. In his farewell editorial, "Retreat from Reason," he restated his position in obeying the law and said he was not a "pro-integrationist" but an "anti-prosegregationist."[37]

The state's politicians denounced the Supreme Court and the NAACP at every opportunity. Such comments, remarked O'Dowd, had replaced "home, mother, God, and country in South Carolina political circles." Citizens' councils regularly asked candidates for office such questions as "Do you here and now promise not to seek the Negro vote directly or indirectly?" Politicians did not hesitate to say that they would rather close schools than integrate them. An alarming number of white parents agreed that segregation was more important than education. (It made little difference that nearly 20 percent of the white population was illiterate.) The Federation of South Carolina Women's Clubs bravely argued that "the abandonment of a system of public schools would set back the cause of education for all our people 100 years."[38]

In Washington, Strom Thurmond, now a U.S. senator (after besting the establishment again by winning his seat as a write-in candidate), led the fight against the *Brown* decision. In March 1956 he was the principal author of a "Declaration of Southern Principles" (sometimes called the "Southern Manifesto") which attacked the Supreme Court and commended the "motives of those states which have declared their intention to resist integration by any lawful means." The document condemned the court and "outside agitators" for "destroying the amicable relations" between blacks and whites. When published, the document was signed by 19 of 22 southern senators and 82 of 106 representatives. A year later Thurmond filibustered for a record 24 hours, 18 minutes in an unsuccessful effort to block passage of civil rights legislation.[39]

The 1956 General Assembly was so preoccupied with circumventing integration that *News and Courier* reporter W. D. Workman Jr. dubbed it the "Segregation Session." Although the legislature passed a resolution approving of the doctrine of interposition, it never followed Calhoun's doctrine and declared the *Brown* decision to be null and void (as did the legislatures of Alabama, Florida, Georgia, and Mississippi). Among the spate of laws passed were one closing Edisto State Park and another making it illegal for any public employee in South Carolina to belong to the NAACP. As a result of the latter, Charleston civil rights activist Septima P. Clark lost her job and her state retirement pension.[40]

Gov. George Bell Timmerman Jr. (1955–1959) was determined to do everything in his power to preserve the status quo. Clemson had to reject a $350,000 ($1.9 million) grant from the Atomic Energy Commission because the agency required that recipients not bar any student on the basis of race, color, creed, or religion. When twelve laypersons issued *South Carolinians Speak: A Moderate Approach to Race Relations* (1957), the governor denounced them. He forced Billy Graham to move a crusade rally from the State House grounds to Fort Jackson because of the evangelist's "endorsement of racial mixing." He pressured the administration of South Carolina State College to fire faculty who supported desegregation, and then he went after the faculty at two private black colleges in Columbia, Allen University and Benedict College. He was able to get the State Department of Education to withdraw its accreditation for Allen's education program. However, his heavy-handed tactics against Benedict only succeeded in rallying the black community and angering conservative white Columbians who supported the college's administration. Also, by having Allen's accreditation revoked, he gave black students a legal reason to apply to the educational program at the University of South Carolina.[41]

Since 1945 South Carolina had maintained a separate law school at South Carolina State College and paid tuition for black students to attend professional programs out-of-state. It was expensive, but state officials were determined that segregation be maintained at any cost. In 1954, when Dean Samuel L. Prince of the University of South Carolina Law School testified before a legislative committee, he was asked why it cost $100 ($566) per semester hour to educate black law students versus $17 ($96) for whites. His reply got right to the heart of the matter: "Gentlemen, well I'll tell you. The price of prejudice is very high."[42]

Despite expensive separate programs, resolutions, laws, and citizens' councils, nothing the white establishment did could preserve Jim Crow. In the fall of 1954 St. Anne's Roman Catholic School in Rock Hill and the Lutheran Theological Seminary in Columbia desegregated. After President Truman's executive order in 1948, facilities at the state's many military installations were open to all service personnel. Black baseball players for the Columbia Reds (including Frank Robinson) attracted huge crowds. White fans did not seem to care about a player's color "so long as he can hit that ball!" In 1955 the Annual Conference of South Carolina Methodists condemned the citizens' councils. The Christian Action Council had black and white members and received funding from both black and white denominations. The South Carolina Council on Human Relations had chapters in a half dozen cities, including Sumter and Rock Hill. Alice Buck Norwood Spearman of Columbia was one of the group's most visible members. More than nineteen thousand copies of *South Carolinians Speak* were sold at newsstands and, for the most part, were favorably received. Individual clergy preached that segregation and white supremacy were wrong and not justified by Holy Scripture. The U.S. Supreme Court in 1956 ruled that Columbia's city buses could not be segregated, but the South Carolina Public Service Commission said that state law was supreme. When the bus company in Rock Hill refused to permit passengers to sit wherever they chose, blacks instituted a boycott. The company retaliated by serving only white areas, but within six months it went out of business.[43]

Without exception, the daily newspapers continued to assure their readers that black Carolinians favored the status quo and that any trouble was the result of outside agitators and a few local troublemakers. The carefully reasoned pamphlet *South Carolinians Speak* was damned as "A Moderate Approach to Integration." For those who supported segregation, there was no such thing as moderation or compromise. In 1960 when Clemson professor Ernest M. Lander Jr. published a contemporary South Carolina history, the reviewer in Charleston's *News and Courier* reported that Lander had used the word *Negro* some 500 times in 245 pages and concluded: "This book seems to lean too heavily on the Negro theme." Lander's book simply attempted to tell the story of South Carolina. The reviewer, like many other South Carolina whites, did not know his state's true history. They wanted nothing to alter the South Carolina that had been created at the turn of the century.[44]

The old South Carolina, a world of small towns in which everyone knew one another and everyone knew his or her place, was dying. It made little difference if the town were a rural market town or a mill village. Mills had begun to sell off their mill houses before the war, and that continued. In Newberry workers bought the houses and the mills gave the streets and utilities to the town. By the 1950s there were few mill-owned houses left in the state. Good roads made it easier for farmers to purchase goods and market their crops in larger towns. In 1935 two-thirds of the six thousand miles of roads and highways were paved; fifteen years later there were twenty thousand miles of road in South Carolina (eleven thousand paved). Between 1946 and 1950 some fifty-three hundred miles of highways were built and forty-one hundred miles of farm-to-market roads paved. And the rural exodus continued.[45]

During the 1950s some 150,000 farm workers moved from the countryside to Charleston, Columbia, and Greenville and the state's urban areas grew rapidly. However, in 1960, even after its most rapid urban growth in history, South Carolina did not have a city with a population of 100,000. Some small towns such as Irmo, Lexington, Mauldin, and Mount Pleasant burgeoned as bedroom communities for nearby urban centers, but other rural communities declined as people moved away. In addition to the loss of residents, institutions began to disappear and with them the glue that helped bind communities. Between 1935 and 1965 more than 150 towns lost their post offices. Governor Byrnes's consolidation program closed 824 schools in the early 1950s. Rural congregations dissolved or merged with others. However, the loss of these institutions (continuing a trend that had begun with the rural exodus of the 1920s) gave people less reason to remain in the countryside. For example, Stoney Creek Church (Hampton County), from whose pulpit George Whitefield had preached in the eighteenth century, became an inactive congregation, although the building was maintained. Some former communities that are only names on old maps are Pulaski (Oconee County), Red Point (Union), and Barker (Berkeley).[46]

Changing agricultural patterns resulted in reduced job opportunities and were another factor in the depopulation of the countryside. Much has been made of the three hundred thousand black Carolinians who left the state between 1920 and 1940; however, between 1950 and 1970 another four hundred thousand moved away. In the thirty years after World War II, tens of thousands of jobs disappeared as mechanization, the soil bank, hard times, forestation, and a decline in cotton production reduced the number of acres being farmed. In upcountry counties, on average, the number of acres under cultivation decreased 75 percent, while in McCormick and Fairfield Counties they dropped 92 percent.[47]

As late as 1955 agricultural officials still used terms more appropriate to 1855: "*Cotton* . . . is also the King of crops and should anything happen to dethrone this King everybody in America will feel the effects." Within a year tobacco had displaced cotton as the state's leading money crop. In one respect, though, the demise of King Cotton contributed to the loss of farm jobs. In 1950 farmers harvested 1.2 million acres and used hand labor to pick 1.1 million acres; by the end of the decade they harvested only 453,000 acres and used hand labor to pick 236,000. In less than a decade 864,000 acres requiring intensive hand labor were put to other uses. In the Pee Dee bulk metal tobacco barns and mechanical harvesters reduced labor needs by 70 percent. Sharecroppers, wage laborers, and tenants moved away. No longer could a person operate a farm with a mule, a plow, and credit from the country store. It took considerable capital to purchase modern farm machinery. In the mid 1970s an Allendale County farmer paid $61,342 ($173,278) for his tractor. Perhaps one of the more telling illustrations of the changing agricultural scene appeared in the commissioner of agriculture's 1971 annual report to the General Assembly. Consumer protection got more notice than crops and livestock. For those rural communities that remained, there appeared to be dangers everywhere. There was, of course, "the Negro problem," which would not go away. Then there was the influx of new industries and businesses from the North.[48]

During the decade after the war the state experienced rapid industrial growth. Much of it was due to local boosters or simply luck. Not until 1954 did the modern State Development Board, charged with recruiting industry, come into being. Under the leadership of Francis M. Hipp of Greenville and J. Bratton Davis of Columbia, the State Development Board became an effective tool for bringing in new industries and new jobs. The State Ports Authority replaced the antiquated facilities in Charleston with up-to-date ones. In 1945 the old seaport was near the bottom of American ports in terms of tonnage handled; by the 1950s it ranked as one of the nation's busiest. At the same time, Georgetown and Port Royal developed into important secondary ports. South Carolina invested $21 million ($110 million) in its port system in 1959 and several years later began construction of containerized freight facilities.[49]

"South Carolina's government . . . is friendly toward industry," wrote James F. Byrnes. "Our government, our communities, and our people want industry and—want to see that it is prosperous and happy. No state and no people can offer more." Governors, beginning with Thurmond and Byrnes, put out the welcome mat for corporate executives. The General Assembly was also willing to do its part. In 1954, seven years after the passage of the Taft-Hartley Act, the assembly passed a right-to-work law without much opposition. Two years later, in a special session, legislators amended the state's alien ownership law so that non-Americans (including corporations) could own up to five hundred thousand acres of land. Previously the limit had been five hundred acres. State and municipal tax laws were amended to give tax breaks to new industries. The innovative technical education system (1961) with provisions for training workers specifically for a certain manufacturer attracted national attention and regional imitations. South Carolina was one of the most aggressive southern states when it came to industrial recruiting (see Maps 30, 31).[50]

The recruitment of multinational industries began in the early 1960s, and within a decade South Carolina was attracting 40 percent of the annual industrial development from overseas. There was more capital from the Federal Republic of Germany invested in South Carolina than anywhere except in West Germany itself. By

Table 22.1

CHANGING AGRICULTURAL PATTERNS

	1945	1974
Number of farms	148,000	32,000
Land in farms	11 million acres	6.3 million acres
Average farm size	75 acres	196 acres
Cropland harvested	4.1 million acres	2.1 million acres
Cropland in pasture	238,000 acres	717,000 acres
Cotton harvest	1 million acres	252,000 acres

Fairey, *Agricultural Land Use Change*, 6–7, 13.

1973 Spartanburg was home to twenty-four foreign corporations that employed four thousand workers. With so many European companies located on the strip of Interstate 85 between Gaffney and Greenville, locals nicknamed it the "auto-bahn."[51]

The only industries not welcome were those that hired union workers or who paid very high wages. Greenville businessman Charles Daniel was a one-person development board and recruited dozens of industries for the state. However, he told a Newberry civic club that he would not even consider enticing an industry to a county where there were unions until nonunion counties were surfeited. Newberry County, which had unionized textile plants, did not get any new out-of-state investment until 1964. When Michelin, the French tire maker, announced in 1973 that it was going to build two plants and hire eighteen hundred workers, there was immediate opposition. Textile manufacturers were upset that Michelin paid higher wages and would therefore either hire the better textile operatives or force textile companies to raise wages. Eventually the brouhaha died down and Michelin built the first of four plants. (The company later moved its American headquarters to Greenville.)[52]

The negative reaction to the possibility of having to pay higher wages was just one of many doubts that some natives had about recruiting outsiders. The *Columbia Record* was concerned that the majority of new businesses were not "South Carolina owned" (and hence outside the control of the old county elites). And what was worse, they were subsidiaries of *northern* corporations. A Cheraw businessman thought the local tax exemptions were "unfair to our own home-grown industries," which would then have to compete with them for labor. He concluded that "any industry that has to be paid to come into a community is not worth having." To a Charlestonian in the mid 1950s, new businesses did not necessarily mean more

The state's cotton crop was tilled and picked by hand from the 1790s until the 1950s. Photograph by Marion Post Wolcott (Farm Security Administration).
Courtesy, Library of Congress.

Until the 1960s tobacco still had to be harvested and tied by hand for curing as it had been since the 1890s. Photograph by Marion Post Wolcott (Farm Security Administration).
Courtesy, Library of Congress.

In 1959 the South Carolina Ports Authority modernized the state's antiquated facilities at Charleston. Courtesy, South Carolina Ports Authority.

money. It meant that he faced competition and had to work harder than he thought he should have to, simply to stay even. Heavens, he might even have to hustle like the newcomers in North Charleston. One small-town merchant and his friends were afraid that "industrialization would end their habit of closing up businesses to go fishing whenever they pleased."[53]

Those who feared that industrialization was a threat to the old order were correct; however, the threat was far more serious than changing the casual way business was conducted. By the late 1950s new leadership, a metropolitan elite (as opposed to the old county elite), emerged that was willing to discard the old ways. This new elite included individuals such as Greenville's Charles Daniel, whose business experiences in the 1930s and 1940s were not limited to the boundaries of his adopted city and county. He and others like him, primarily business and professional men in the metropolitan counties of Richland-Lexington and Greenville-Spartanburg-Anderson, were interested in bringing their communities into the mainstream of American life.[54]

As Donald S. Russell of Spartanburg, the successful gubernatorial candidate in 1962, said on the stump: "A job . . . that's the problem, that's the real campaign issue." In order to attract industries, the new metropolitan elites knew that they had to establish "a good political atmosphere" and show that they "had a real commit-

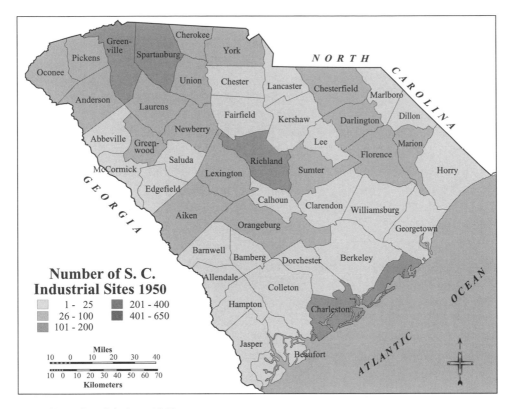

Map 30: Industrial sites, 1950

ment to economic growth." The state had demonstrated the latter, but official reaction to the *Brown* decision pointed to the possibility of social turmoil. Social disorder, encouraged by reactionary politicians, was not conducive to attracting outside capital. Events soon forced those who championed economic development to step forward.[55]

In November 1959 Jackie Robinson flew into Greenville to give a speech to the state conference of the NAACP. When leaving town, he was refused admittance to the white waiting room at the Greenville airport. On 1 January 1960 (Emancipation Day) a group of 350 black Carolinians staged a protest march from Springfield Baptist Church to the airport. The change in tactics by black Carolinians, from legal maneuvers through the courts to peaceful public protests, was the result of white intransigence. In early February 1960 a group of students staged a sit-in demon-

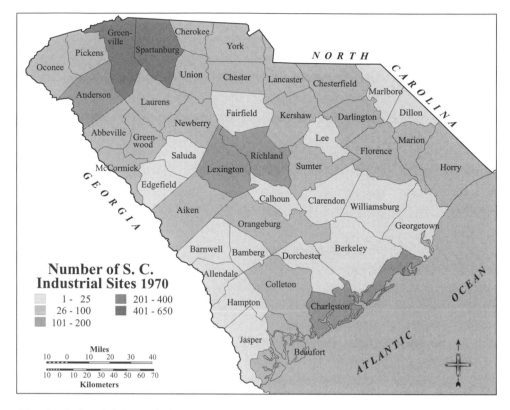

Map 31: Industrial sites, 1970

stration at a lunch counter in Greensboro, North Carolina. Within a few weeks there were sit-ins all over South Carolina and the rest of the South.[56]

There were demonstrations in Charleston, Columbia, Denmark, Greenville, Manning, Orangeburg, Rock Hill, Spartanburg, and Sumter. Once they began in 1960, they went on for nearly three years. Wherever they marched, demonstrators were likely to sing "We Shall Overcome," a Johns Island folksong that became the anthem of the American civil rights movement. They sang, clapped, and marched; they were orderly and well mannered. James McBride Dabbs could not resist saying that they were behaving as properly reared southerners should. Although most of the demonstrations were peaceful, in Greenville white and black gangs clashed. In Orangeburg law enforcement officials used tear gas and fire hoses and jailed hundreds

The Catawba plant of Bowaters Carolina Corporation was one of the largest capital invest-
ments in the state in the 1950s. Photograph by Lavoy Bauknight, Lavoy Studios, Lancaster,
South Carolina. Courtesy, Bowater Incorporated, Coated Paper & Pulp Division, Catawba,
South Carolina.

of protestors. The demonstrations, initiated by young black men and women (such
as Denmark native Cleveland Sellers), eventually were adopted by the state's more
traditional black leaders as they sought to maintain their constituents. Every march
and every sit-in belied the local media's message that black Carolinians accepted the
status quo.[57]

All the talk about massive resistance and interposition and acts of random violence were not good for the state's image. Nor were photographs and television shots
of sit-ins and street protests. The metropolitan elites had good reason to be concerned. They did not want the civil rights movement to derail industrial development. In 1957, before troubles over the desegregation of Central High School, eight
new plants opened in Little Rock, Arkansas. After the nationally televised confrontations between whites and blacks, it was four years before another outside corporation was willing to invest in the city. The entire state of Arkansas suffered. The
lesson was not lost on businessmen in Columbia, Greenville, and Spartanburg.[58]

In 1961 a group of Greenville business and community leaders (Charles E.
Daniel, Alester G. Furman Jr., L. P. Hollis, and the Reverend Thomas A. Roberts)
met and formed an advisory committee that decided segregation had to go. In July,
at the Hampton Watermelon Festival in the heart of the black belt, Daniel gave a
speech in which he said, "the desegregation issue cannot continue to be hidden be-

hind the door." He went on to say that South Carolina should treat its black citizens fairly and provide them with decent educational and employment opportunities. His remarks were the first public indication that men in positions of power were willing to abandon segregation. In 1962 Greenville's chamber of commerce formed a biracial committee that had the respect and support of the city's black and white leadership.[59]

In the midst of the civil rights movement, South Carolina and the nation celebrated the centennial of the American Civil War. In the late 1950s the state senate ordered the Confederate battle flag placed behind the rostrum of the senate chamber; the Confederate Home closed; and the General Assembly created the Confederate War Centennial Commission. During the four years of the observance there were parades, battle reenactments, and marker dedications. Somehow, though, the centennial never really caught on. Perhaps it was the times. Carolinians had other things on their minds. In 1965 a white mill worker dismissed the whole idea: "I don't believe in talking about all this Confederate business—this is America." The centennial did, however, have a lasting legacy. In February 1962 a concurrent resolution authorized the flying of the Confederate flag atop the State House dome. It is still there.[60]

The resolution to fly the flag came about six weeks after Harvey Gantt, a black Charlestonian, applied for admission to Clemson College. In off-the-record news conferences, Gov. Ernest F. Hollings (who had been elected as an outspoken segregationist) told reporters that they had better prepare their readers for desegregation. Behind-the-scenes Daniel, Hollings, Sen. Edgar Brown, textile lobbyist John Cauthen, Clemson president Robert Edwards, and *Greenville News* editor Wayne Freeman laid the groundwork for Gantt's peaceful admission.[61]

In the fall of 1962 there was bloody violence in Oxford, Mississippi, when the University of Mississippi was integrated. Several legislators demanded that Governor Hollings lead a motorcade to Mississippi to show support for Gov. Ross Barnett and segregation. He refused. On 9 January 1963, as the governor made his farewell address to the General Assembly, the Gantt case opened in the Fourth Circuit Court of Appeals. Hollings's calm, reasoned remarks were quite a contrast to the racist bombast coming from other southern governors: "As we meet, South Carolina is running out of courts. If and when every legal remedy has been exhausted, this General Assembly must make clear South Carolina's choice, a government of laws rather than a government of men. As determined as we are, we of today must realize the lesson of one hundred years ago, and move on for the good of South Carolina and our United States. This should be done with dignity. It must be done with law and order."[62]

The South Carolina Chamber of Commerce, the Bankers' Association, the Broadcasters' Association, and leading textile executives pledged their support for the

Black demonstrators (1963) in Columbia and other cities protested segregated facilities. Courtesy, South Caroliniana Library.

peaceful desegregation of Clemson and the preservation of law and order *before* a decision was reached in the Gantt case. On 16 January the court ruled that Gantt should be admitted. There were some last-ditch histrionics by a few die-hard segregationists in the legislature, but Marion Gressette spoke for the state's leadership when he said, "We have lost this battle but we are engaged in a war. But this war cannot be won by violence or by inflammatory speeches. I have preached peace and good order too long to change my thinking." A week later there were no disturbances when Harvey Gantt enrolled at Clemson College. The following fall the University of South Carolina also admitted black students without incident. By May 1965 all of the state's public colleges and twelve of its twenty-five private colleges agreed to admit qualified students without regard to race. Three years later 14 percent of black Carolinians attended formerly all-white institutions.[63]

Law and order; peace and good order—they were variations of a long-standing tradition in South Carolina, a tradition sometimes honored in the breach rather than the observance. But in 1963, when other southern communities were wracked with violence and bloodshed because their white establishments refused to abandon segregation, South Carolina began to dismantle Jim Crow. The political leadership of the state that was characterized by a northern reporter as "emotionally the deepest Deep South state of them all" did not behave as its peers did elsewhere in the South. Instead, it combined practical business decisions with the state's traditions and acted for the good order and harmony of the whole community. Edgar Brown described the behind-the-scenes actions of business, civic, and political leaders as a "conspiracy for peace." Some acted willingly, but most did so under increasing pressure from civil rights organizations.[64]

On 5 June 1963 the Reverend I. DeQuincey Newman of the state NAACP published a list of nine demands and announced that eight cities (Charleston, Columbia, Florence, Greenville, Orangeburg, Rock Hill, Spartanburg, and Sumter) were targeted for massive demonstrations unless progress were made in solving racial problems. Columbia, under the leadership of Mayor Lester Bates, responded, but slow progress resulted in a number of demonstrations. By the end of the year "White Only" and "Colored Only" signs disappeared from Main Street stores, restaurants, and theaters. Plans were made for the token desegregation of the city's schools in 1964. In contrast, Charleston witnessed rioting before city officials indicated a willingness to move forward, but change they did primarily because individuals on both sides of the racial divide knew one another. In Florence, Greenville, Rock Hill, and Spartanburg blacks and whites reached accommodation rather quickly, but in Orangeburg there was little communication between black and white leaders. A summer of escalating protests led to a hardening of attitudes by both blacks and whites—and to tensions that would explode in violence in 1968.[65]

Cities such as Anderson, Beaufort, Greenwood, and Newberry acted on their own volition. In Anderson the Chamber of Commerce, the Jaycees, the Merchants' Association, and the Ministerial Association supported a resolution calling for the repeal of the city's segregation ordinances. "We can solve these problems as grown men by mutual discussion," said chamber president John Holman, "or we can do nothing, allow these problems to deteriorate and end up with demonstrations, riots, and possibly bloodshed." On 10 June 1963 the council repealed the ordinances.[66]

Repealing laws and forming biracial committees could not change people's hearts and minds. During 1963 South Carolina made tremendous progress in eliminating legal racial barriers, but changes did not come easily. Looking back on the events of 1963, former Charleston mayor J. Palmer Gaillard said: "Our biggest problems were not with the blacks . . . but . . . with whites." Merchants who hired black employees or agreed to take down "Colored Only" signs sometimes found themselves subject to hate mail and white boycotts. Yet, as one modern state historian observed, "Whites . . . showed more flexibility than a historian might have anticipated." They certainly were less rigid in South Carolina than elsewhere in the states of the old Confederacy.[67]

Why? Part of the answer lies in the firm stand taken by state (and most local) officials on law and order. Another part lies in Harvey Gantt's often quoted remark, "If you can't appeal to the morals of a South Carolinian, you can appeal to his manners." Most white South Carolinians rejected mob violence in the 1960s just as they had rejected the Klan in the 1920s. And black Carolinians (who were very much a part of their communities and not outsiders) did not wish to destroy their towns over principle. They were less strident in their demands than activists elsewhere, and they were willing to work peacefully within the system to achieve their goals. South Carolina was still a small place in the 1960s, a place where, despite segregation, people knew one another across the racial divide. A tradition of civility combined with a determination to preserve law and order enabled South Carolina to undo three generations of segregation—with dignity.[68]

South Carolina in 1963 was different from other states of the Deep South, not only because of what did not occur, but also because of how the decisions were made. For example, in Birmingham, after the bloody confrontation between demonstrators and city police, it was the business community that negotiated the end to segregation. The business leaders then told the local politicians what to do, because in Birmingham the politicians were part of the problem, not the solution. "The matters were too critical," wrote a contemporary historian, "to entrust to politicians." In South Carolina politicians were involved in the process. They were part of the solution. When implemented, the various desegregation efforts were as much theirs as the metropolitan elites'.[69]

For the next five years there was relatively little racial unrest and some progress. In 1961 the textile industry began hiring black workers. Elsewhere in the manufacturing sector, more than one-half of all new jobs went to blacks. Charles Daniel's construction company led by example and opened up jobs in his company. Within a few years 26 percent of his employees were black. The employment of black women in manufacturing increased from 4 percent to 23 percent of the workforce. In 1964 there were only ten black students (.004 percent) in secondary classes with white students; three years later 6.4 percent were.[70]

The passage of the Voting Rights Act (1965) brought federal marshals into several counties in the state to oversee voter registration. The number of registered black voters mushroomed from 58,000 in 1958 to 220,000 in 1970. For the most part, blacks voted for Democrats and began to participate in party affairs. By 1968 their representation at the state convention was virtually proportional to their numbers in the total population. Democrats elected twelve black Carolinians to their delegation to the 1968 national convention. It was the only delegation from a Deep South state that did not have its credentials challenged. In 1970 Herbert U. Fielding of Charleston County and James L. Felder and I. S. Leevy Johnson of Richland became the first black Carolinians to serve in the General Assembly since the 1890s. By 1974 there were thirteen black legislators and a black caucus in the House of Representatives.[71]

In the late 1960s, however, the carefully crafted, fragile, racial peace almost came undone. In Orangeburg in February 1968 students at South Carolina State College began protesting the refusal of a bowling alley to admit black patrons. Within several days matters escalated and the highway patrol and National Guard were sent in to maintain order. On the evening of 8 February, students taunted the officers and pelted them with rocks and bottles. One officer was struck down, and his fellows thought he had been shot. In the darkness and uncertainty that followed, one of the patrolmen fired a carbine. Suddenly other officers opened fire on the students and three young men fell, mortally wounded. The beliefs of a number of black Carolinians in the moderation of South Carolina were shaken. Among them were the Reverend I. DeQuincy Newman and Allard Allston III. "Orangeburg," said Allston, "made the black middle class in South Carolina question what happened."[72]

In the aftermath of Orangeburg, a federal judge ordered the bowling alley desegregated. Interestingly, whites "continued bowling in the sixteen lane facility as though having Negroes bowl there had been an everyday occurrence." There were investigations and two trials. The highway patrolmen were acquitted, but only one person, black activist Cleveland Sellers, was tried for rioting. The state establishment stood solidly behind the patrolmen and law and order. Gov. Robert E. McNair and other state leaders worked diligently to restore trust and goodwill.[73]

A year after Orangeburg, a strike by predominantly black workers at several Charleston hospitals brought the national civil rights spotlight to the state. National media compared the situation in Charleston to that in Memphis a year earlier when Martin Luther King had been murdered. Outsiders flocked to the port city in support of the strikers. After one hundred days of demonstrations (and some disorder) the strike was settled, a curfew lifted, and calm returned to the city's streets. The *Charleston Evening Post* reported that many Charlestonians (and South Carolinians) had learned a number of lessons during the spring and summer. The most important of these lessons was that those who heretofore had been voiceless had "the power to disturb . . . institutions and customs which have remained on dead center for so long that most people have come to take them for granted."[74]

From without and within, the old order was under attack. One sally that caught the state's establishment off guard was U.S. senator Ernest Hollings's much-publicized poverty tour. Reacting to a physician's report on hunger in Beaufort County, Hollings led a tour of some of the poorest communities in the state. The nightly news flashed pictures of run-down shanties, filthy outhouses, and undernourished children. In *The Case Against Hunger* the senator made the case for food stamps and school breakfast programs. Some members of the establishment were furious, but state senator Rembert Dennis of Berkeley County agreed that the situation was serious and required remedial action.[75]

However, when it came to the dismantling of the state's dual school system, the county-seat elite fought a bitter rearguard action. In 1966 Solomon Blatt of Barnwell County, the Speaker of the house, took to the floor to oppose a bill reviving compulsory education. The bill failed, but the struggle to keep the public schools open was a real test of power between the county elites and the moderates in the metropolitan areas. The next year a compulsory education bill became law. The metropolitan elites carefully and forcefully supported public education, not desegregation.[76]

In 1968 the courts ruled that freedom-of-choice plans were unacceptable and that the next year all districts eliminate their dual school systems immediately. During the 1969–1970 school year the Fourth Circuit Court of Appeals ordered districts in Greenville and Darlington Counties desegregated. Taking their cue from civil rights activists, whites organized to protest the demise of freedom of choice. Carroll A. Campbell Jr. was spokesperson for the group and led a motorcade of protesters to Columbia. State officials, however, did not intervene in either district's case. When the U.S. Supreme Court refused to delay the desegregation order, Gov. Robert E. McNair appointed fifteen influential Carolinians to an ad hoc citizens' group, the South Carolina Education Advisory Committee. Chaired by Robert S. Davis, President of the R. L. Bryan Company of Columbia, the committee worked effectively with business and community leaders in making the transition from dual to unitary school systems.[77]

Governor McNair acted resolutely to head off racial confrontation that had brought violence to other southern communities. He went on television in Greenville and Columbia so that he could reach a majority of the students and parents affected by the court order. Segregationists and national news commentators were dumbfounded by his resolute stand: "I will oppose any attempt to close down public schools. The only way South Carolina is going to continue to grow is through its educational programs." And in advance he condemned anyone who might be inclined to cause trouble: "A society can't continue to operate without obedience of the law. When we run out of courts and time, we must adjust to the circumstances." The governor, a product of the old county elite culture, came down firmly on the side of the moderate metropolitan elite. Preserving public education was more important to South Carolina than maintaining segregation. The New South won this crucial contest.[78]

The governor's position was unpopular in some quarters. The state's two Republican congressmen, Sen. Strom Thurmond and Rep. Albert Watson, demanded that McNair disobey the federal government. Other southern governors bellowed interposition and defiance. In February 1970 four Deep South governors called a meeting to devise a strategy to thwart desegregation, but South Carolina's governor was not invited.[79]

In mid February 1970 the Greenville district complied with the court order. There

Sen. Ernest F. Hollings's 1969 "Hunger Tour" brought to public attention such rundown neighborhoods as Friday's Alley in Columbia. Courtesy, Bill Barley Papers, Modern Political Collections, South Caroliniana Library.

were some bomb threats and pickets, but the transition from a dual to a unitary school system for the district's fifty-eight thousand students went forward. The situation in Darlington County was more volatile. For several weeks three thousand white students boycotted the schools. In March a mob in Lamar overturned a school bus. Interestingly, federal marshals sat by in their cars while South Carolina highway patrolmen restored order. Later an all-white jury (using the same incitement to riot statute under which black activist Cleveland Sellers had been tried) convicted those who had attacked the bus.[80]

When schools opened in the fall of 1970, all districts operated unitary systems. The school year was marred by violence and school closings. Few communities were immune. Armed guards patrolled hallways, and bomb threats occurred with regularity. Individual scuffles between students often turned into racial incidents.[81]

How districts created their unitary systems was sometimes a factor in the unrest. In Columbia (Richland School District One), Booker T. Washington High School went from being all-black to 60 percent white. In Greenville three black high schools were closed and two others downgraded to junior highs. Blacks believed they "had to give up everything" they had in their former schools (mascots, team colors, yearbooks, school newspapers, and other extracurricular activities). In Spartanburg District Seven, where Carver High was merged with Spartanburg High, the students of the merged school chose a new school mascot and new names for the student newspaper and yearbook. In Orangeburg District Five, Orangeburg and Wilkinson High Schools were combined as Orangeburg-Wilkinson. And in suburban Richland District Two, white Dentsville High and black Hanberry High became middle schools and the district built Spring Valley, an entirely new high school. Other districts across the state opted for one or more of these solutions in creating unitary systems.[82]

Lost, somehow, in all of the desire for proper balances was the impact unitary systems had on communities, both black and white. In Richland District One, Olympia High (white) was closed and Webber High (black) became an elementary school. Both schools were more than just high schools; they were community centers as well. Both had proud athletic traditions. They were among a number of schools that graduated their last classes in June 1970: Schofield in Aiken, Riverside in Pendleton, Macedonia in Blackville, Haut Gap on Johns Island, Finley in Chester, Gallman in Newberry, and Bethune Memorial in Bowman.[83]

In spite of the efforts of the governor and the state's business leaders, thousands of whites abandoned the public schools. White parents kept their children in public schools so long as blacks were one-third or less of the student population. Once black enrollment passed one-third of a school's student body—and the school "tipped" black—whites withdrew their children and enrolled them in private academies.[84]

In 1956 there were only sixteen private or denominational schools in South Carolina. Between 1964, when the first racial barriers fell, and the mid 1970s nearly two hundred new schools appeared. Under the leadership of Dr. T. E. Wannamaker of Orangeburg and Dr. Charles Aimar of Beaufort, seventy of these schools formed the South Carolina Independent Schools Association (SCISA). In 1975 some 7.6 percent of the state's 672,000 schoolchildren were in private schools, a slightly larger percentage than the regional average.[85]

White reaction to the civil rights movement was not limited to the schools; it also took place in voting booths. In 1964 President Lyndon B. Johnson pushed through Congress the Civil Rights Act, which gave blacks another tool with which to attack discrimination. Sen. Barry Goldwater of Arizona, the Republican Party's nominee for president in 1964, opposed the measure. In September, Strom Thurmond went on statewide television and announced that he was switching parties. He then stumped the South for Goldwater, who ended his campaign with a regionally televised rally in Columbia. In November the Republicans carried South Carolina and four other states of the Deep South.[86]

Although other southern states had voted Republican in presidential elections, this was the first time since 1876 that South Carolina had done so. Between 1880 and 1944, in presidential elections, South Carolina was one of the nation's most solidly Democratic states. However, the state's love affair with the Democrats had begun to fade during FDR's second term. The push for antilynching laws and the attempt to purge "Cotton Ed" Smith did not go down well with voters. After the Dixiecrat revolt, the state was never a sure bet for the Democrats. In 1952 Governor Byrnes, who detested Harry Truman and his civil rights program, headed up "Democrats for Eisenhower." Although Adlai Stevenson carried the state, he got barely more than 50 percent of the vote. After the *Brown* decision, Byrnes fell out with the GOP, but his open support of a Republican made it acceptable for a white Carolinian to be something other than a Democrat (see Maps 32, 33, 34).[87]

Throughout the 1950s all state officials were white Democrats, but in the two decades after World War II, an increasing number of unhappy Carolinians joined the fledgling Republican Party. Some of them were, according to a northern Republican Party publication, just "mad Democrats." Perhaps so, but under the skilled guidance of David Dows of Aiken, W. W. Wannamaker Jr. of Orangeburg, J. Drake Edens of Columbia, and Mrs. A. Dabney Barnes of Greenville, a modern political party came into being. These new Republicans soon outnumbered old-line party regulars such as civil rights activist I. DeQuincy Newman. In 1962 W. D. Workman Jr. challenged Sen. Olin D. Johnston and won 43 percent of the vote; Lexington County representative Floyd Spence switched parties (the first sitting Democrat to do so); and Charles E. Boineau of Richland became the first white Republican member of the General Assembly in eighty years.[88]

The Goldwater campaign led to a reorientation of the southern political scene, including South Carolina's. While Thurmond's defection did not turn the state into a Republican stronghold overnight, it certainly gave the party a much-needed boost, and after a brief struggle his allies took control of the party machinery. In 1966, for the first time in the twentieth century, there were Republican candidates for major statewide offices. Only the senator won, but the others made respectable showings. In the General Assembly, Republicans won seventeen seats in the house and six in the senate. Although there would be reversals over the next few years, the number of Republicans in the General Assembly rose in the 1970s.[89]

Increasingly, South Carolina Republicans were involved with the national party. In 1968 Senator Thurmond met with Republican presidential hopeful Richard M. Nixon and agreed to support his quest for the nomination. In return, if elected, Nixon promised to appoint southern justices to the U.S. Supreme Court and to go slow on school desegregation. Thurmond and his aide, Harry Dent, became key members of the Nixon campaign team. The senator spoke in dozens of southern cities, urging voters to elect Nixon. One of the senator's main themes was that a vote for third-party candidate George C. Wallace was a wasted vote. Thurmond's efforts were crucial in South Carolina's going for Nixon.[90]

Once in the White House, Nixon fulfilled only a portion of the bargain he had

In 1952 Republican presidential candidate Dwight D. Eisenhower campaigned in Columbia with Democrat James F. Byrnes at his side. Courtesy, South Caroliniana Library.

made. He nominated federal judge Clement Haynsworth of Greenville for the supreme court, but the senate refused to confirm him because of his views on race and labor. Harry Dent became a White House counselor, and Spartanburg native Fred Dent became secretary of commerce. However, on the school desegregation question, the Nixon administration reneged. Instead of going more slowly, it pushed desegregation in order to further alienate white southerners from the Democratic Party, the party identified most closely with blacks and civil rights.[91]

In the 1970 gubernatorial election, state and national Republican Party officials found that there was a limit to playing the race card. Albert Watson, the party's gubernatorial candidate, ran the last racially oriented statewide campaign. The tactic backfired. R. Cooper White, the Republican mayor of Greenville, refused to endorse Watson, accusing him of "polarizing the races." *The State* and other newspapers that normally supported Republicans endorsed Democrat John C. West. Traditional voting patterns were skewed as suburban Republicans voted for West and moderation.[92]

In 1935 a South Carolina historian had discussed what he termed "that classic futility, 'a respectable Republican party' in South Carolina." The following year Gov. Olin D. Johnston had provoked much laughter among the delegates at the na-

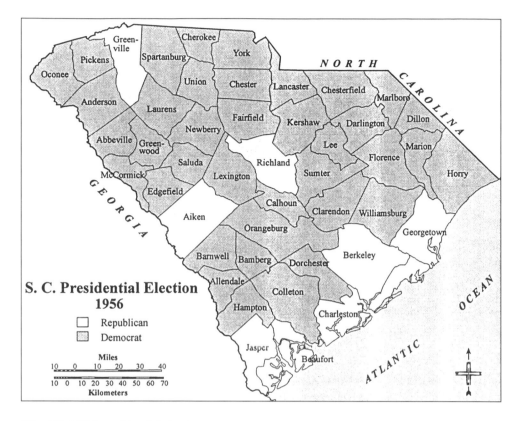

S. C. Presidential Election 1956

☐ Republican
▨ Democrat

Map 32: 1956 presidential election

tional Democratic convention when he said that most Carolinians would run from a Republican "if such a strange being wandered too close to their homes." Forty years later a lot of voters were running to, not from, the South Carolina Republican Party. And in 1974 James B. Edwards of Mount Pleasant was elected the state's first Republican governor in ninety-eight years. He was also the first Republican governor elected in a Deep South state in the twentieth century.[93]

The emergence of a viable two-party system was not the only political change taking place. The battle over schools and desegregation between the county elites and the metropolitan elites was the most visible manifestation of a power struggle to decide who would control South Carolina. In the General Assembly the old power structure was personified by Solomon Blatt of Barnwell County (Speaker of the

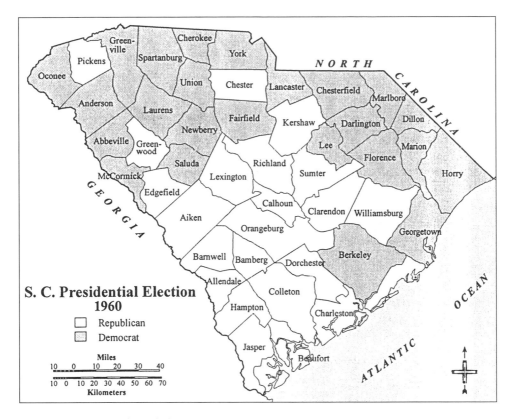

Map 33: 1960 presidential election

house), Edgar Brown of Barnwell (president pro tempore of the senate), and Marion Gressette of Calhoun (chair of the senate judiciary committee). Blatt sat in the house for fifty-three years (1933–1985) and served as Speaker for thirty-three years (1937–1946; 1951–1973). Brown, after representing Barnwell in the house (1921–1924), served as the county's senator for forty-four years (1929–1972). Gressette served three terms in the house (1925–1932) and was Calhoun County senator for forty-eight years (1937–1984). These men and their allies, mostly from rural lowcountry counties, controlled state government until the 1960s and, without much difficulty, were able to preserve the status quo.[94]

In 1963 the metropolitan elites of the middlecountry and upcountry won a major victory when South Carolina's leadership opted for desegregation with dignity. Three

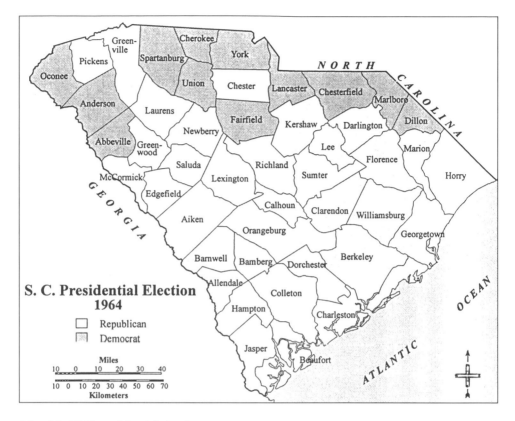

S. C. Presidential Election 1964

☐ Republican
▨ Democrat

Map 34: 1964 presidential election

years later reformers within the General Assembly succeeded in having a study committee formed to revise the 1895 constitution. The committee, named for its chair, Sen. John C. West of Kershaw County, made its report in 1969. It proposed seventeen new articles to replace those in the old constitution in order to streamline it and make government more effective. In 1971 and 1972 voters ratified twelve amendments. The judiciary article (Article V) was one of those, but since it called for a complete revamping of the state court system, its implementation was slow. Among the proposed reforms was the abolition of the county courts (which were virtually under the sway of individual senators). It took seven years before a new system of courts was in place and another five years before the General Assembly and the state supreme court could agree on whether the court or the legislature should make the rules governing practices and procedures in the state's courts. The last court reforms were not enacted until 1984—after the death of Marion Gressette and the mandatory retirement of Chief Justice J. Woodrow Lewis. In the end the reformers won.[95]

Federal courts, through reapportionment decisions, also chipped away at the power base of the county elites. In 1967 the legislature, unable to agree on a plan for reapportioning the forty-six seats in the senate, enlarged it to fifty seats. Subsequent court action approved that act temporarily but ruled that there should be no more than forty-six senators. In 1968 and 1972 the senate was reapportioned again. The 1972 reapportionment created sixteen election districts with forty-six seats; each seat was numbered, and candidates had to run for a specific seat. The courts eliminated an attempt to ensure a resident senator in smaller counties that were combined in districts with portions of larger ones. Although the senate was still a powerful body, somehow being the "Senator from District Thirteen" did not have quite the cachet as being the "Senator from Calhoun."[96]

Not until 1973 was the apportionment of the house questioned. In that year the U.S. Supreme Court in *Stevenson* v. *West* ruled that the distribution of 124 seats to 46 counties on the basis of population (but having at least 1 seat for each county) was a violation of the principle of "one man, one vote." Responding to the court's decision, in 1974 the legislature created 124 single-member districts for the house. Historical political boundaries were jettisoned for districts that were, as nearly as possible, 1/124 of the state's population.[97]

The redistricting of the senate and house made it difficult, if not impossible, for the old county-delegation system of government to work. In 1973 an amendment to the constitution authorized home rule for counties; it was implemented with the Local Government Act (1975), which gave counties limited home rule. County governments could enact ordinances, require licenses and permits of various sorts, and raise or lower property tax rates. They had the authority to enact only taxes specifically allowed by the General Assembly. Municipal and county governments still had to contend with special-purpose districts whose boundaries and functions defied logic. For example, in the Spartanburg County town of Pacolet, eight different "local governments"—Spartanburg County, Spartanburg Soil and Conservation District, Spartanburg School District Three, Pacolet Mills Rescue Squad, Pacolet Fire District, Spartanburg Sanitary Sewer District, Spartanburg Waterworks, and the City of Pacolet— provided services to the residents of the town.[98]

Initially there were five forms of government permitted under home rule: council, council-supervisor, council-administrator, council-manager, and commission. The commission form was declared unconstitutional. For the most part those counties that were growing and prospering chose one of the two reform types of government (council-administrator or council-manager), while those counties that were stagnant or declining opted for more traditional types (council or council-supervisor).[99]

Single-member districts reduced considerably the power of county elites in state government, and home rule eroded their authority back home. In 1972 Sen. Edgar Brown of Barnwell County chose not to stand for reelection. Across the State House lobby Rep. Solomon Blatt of Barnwell stepped down as Speaker in 1973 but remained a member of the house. It was the end of an era, but in the senate in 1975 a handful of the old guard remained: Rembert C. Dennis of Berkeley County, John W. Drummond of Greenwood, John Lindsay of Marlboro, John D. Long of Union, L. Marion Gressette of Calhoun, and James M. Waddell of Beaufort. They chaired the committees through which any meaningful legislation had to pass, and as the struggle for judicial reform illustrated, they would not relinquish their power without a battle.[100]

The county elites fought to preserve the status quo, but beginning in the 1940s they were on the defensive in a three-front war (economic, social, political). Outside forces, such as the New Deal, World War II, and federal courts, may have ignited the changes, but it was South Carolinians who effected those changes.

By 1975 the metropolitan elites had triumphed. In championing moderation and social stability, they made use of an old and venerated South Carolina tradition. They, not the county elites, stood for the good order and harmony of the whole community. At crucial junctures, especially in 1962–1963 and 1969–1971, key members of the old guard either stepped aside or supported the position of the metropolitan elites. Marion Gressette's remarks in 1963 that he had "preached peace and good order too long" to change his thinking were typical. Caught up in changing circumstances, they were willing to retreat from long-held positions for the good of all South Carolinians. The preservation of order and harmony was more important to them than the preservation of the status quo.

In 1940 James McBride Dabbs predicted that there would be no radical changes in the South for "generations, perhaps centuries." The changes that occurred between 1940 and 1975 were radical—and they all occurred in one lifetime.

By 1975 the Old South Carolina was giving way to a New South Carolina. However, this New South Carolina was not yet complete. There were too many unanswered questions. Should there be limits to industrialization? Would desegregation lead to better race relations and understanding? What impact would two-party politics and single-member districts have on the legislative state? What impact was the pursuit of materialism having on society? As our cities grew bigger and more modern, were we losing our sense of community? After a visit to South Carolina in 1974, a journalist wrote: "Time, for the South, is reduced to *now*. One generation. Twenty years." The New South Carolina would have to find answers to a lot of questions in one generation, a fraction of a lifetime.[101]

Chapter Twenty-three

ADJUSTING TO NEW CIRCUMSTANCES

I know that we have come a long way since 1960. Some have dragged their feet all the
way, but they have come. Some say there has been no progress, but they have forgotten
where we started. Some would stop here, for they cannot see how far we still have to go.

Charles Joyner, "The South as a Folk Culture" (1994)

*B*Y THE MID 1970s the days of the old rural barons were over. For three
decades the county elites had been under relentless attack from within and without.
Within South Carolina the emerging business-oriented metropolitan elites in Anderson, Columbia, Florence, Greenville, and Spartanburg pressed for a greater say-so
in state government. From without the state, federal courts and agencies hammered
away at these elites' bases of power.

Governors James B. Edwards of Mount Pleasant (1975–1979), Richard W. Riley
of Greenville (1979–1987), and Carroll A. Campbell Jr. of Greenville (1987–1995)
were all candidates whose moderate views on race and promotion of economic development coincided with those of the metropolitan elites. In the state senate the old
guard still occupied key positions, but younger senators no longer dropped reform
measures just because a venerable committee chair did not support them. In the
house a succession of four Speakers followed the record tenure of Solomon Blatt
and, with mixed results, presided over a legislative body that was increasingly frac-
tious. The metropolitan elites succeeded in destroying the power structure of the old
guard but failed to build anything to take its place.[1]

At the local level, though, the metropolitan elites were in complete control. In
Columbia, Mayor Kirkman Finlay Jr. used the city's bicentennial (1986) as a vehicle
for selling the community on the idea of revitalizing the downtown area and developing the long-ignored riverfront. In Greenville the Peace Center for the Performing Arts (1990) was a tribute to the cooperation of private philanthropy and local
government and a gleaming symbol of the New South Carolina. However, it was in
Charleston that local government had the greatest impact. First elected in 1975,
Mayor Joseph P. Riley Jr. led a city government that transformed the old port city.
The downtown area boomed. The Spoleto Festival USA, under local control, be-

came one of the country's finest cultural events. Private organizations and public funding revitalized old neighborhoods. For the first time in its history, Charleston became a livable city for most of its residents, not just those south of Broad Street. In 1995 an overwhelming majority of the city's voters (75 percent) rejected a partisan appeal and cast their ballots for the mayor.[2]

The metropolitan elites who brought about statewide political reform were also instrumental in promoting statewide civic improvement. There were differences, however, between the metropolitan elites of the 1980s and 1990s and the old progressives of the early 1900s. The most obvious difference was their willingness to reach across the racial divide and support endeavors that would benefit all segments of South Carolina society. Another difference was that, while their efforts might be centered in a particular city, their community was the state of South Carolina.

Two exemplars of this new statewide consciousness were John Stringer Rainey and Mary Rainey Belser. The children of Caroline Freeman Stringer and John Faulkner Rainey, M.D., of Anderson, since their college years this brother and sister were involved not only in their communities but also in the state's cultural and political activities. John Rainey, an attorney and businessman, was active in Republican Party politics and raised funds for both the Campbell and Beasley gubernatorial campaigns. He was chairman of Santee Cooper, Brookgreen Gardens, the Palmetto Economic Development Corporation, and the finance committee to raise the funds to erect the African American Monument on the State House grounds. He was also a trustee of the ETV Endowment of South Carolina, a member of the board of Spoleto Festival USA, and one of the group of prominent business leaders who filed a lawsuit to remove the Confederate battle flag from the State House. Mary Belser, recognized as one of Columbia's civic leaders, was a member of the board of trustees of Converse College, the State Museum Foundation, the South Carolina Governor's School for the Arts, and the South Carolina Orchestra Association. These two dedicated individuals, and others like them, worked diligently to improve the quality of life in South Carolina—not always an easy task.[3]

Promoting reform and civic improvement at the community level was one thing, but forging coalitions in the General Assembly for statewide efforts was another. After a great deal of difficulty, authorization and funding were obtained for a state museum, which finally opened in 1988. Among the obstacles to creating a state museum were parochial opposition to having a state museum at all that might compete with local museums and building it in Columbia. Similarly, there were struggles over the funding for and the location of the Governor's School of Science and Math and the Governor's School for the Performing Arts.[4]

Beginning in 1968 with the state-funded report *Opportunity and Growth in South Carolina, 1968–1985*, improving public education was a priority of a succession of governors. As a result of the report, Governor McNair pushed for a one-cent increase in the sales tax to fund a statewide kindergarten program to better prepare children for entering school.[5]

State funding, however, could only go so far in improving education. Students living in wealthy school districts had distinct advantages over those living in districts with small tax bases. It was an unfair system that Governor Edwards resolved to eradicate. In 1977 he appointed a task force to study the problem and make recommendations. The Education Finance Act of 1977 provided funds to school districts so that with equal tax effort the State Department of Education's "Defined Minimum Program" would be taught. In essence, the act authorized more money for poorer districts than it did for affluent ones. It did not, however, prevent school districts from taxing themselves to provide more than the state-mandated minimum. Consequently, students in larger, better-funded districts enjoyed opportunities not afforded others. The Education Finance Act and two other pieces of legislation, the Basic Skills Assessment Act (1978) and the Educator Improvement Act (1979), laid the foundation for what would be one of the most important pieces of education legislation ever passed in South Carolina.[6]

As a result of the legislation passed in the 1970s, the General Assembly did not see the need for doing anything else for the state's schools. In 1983 when Governor Riley proposed an Education Improvement Act (EIA), he received very little support from either the legislature or the business community. The governor then launched an intense lobbying effort and convinced business leaders that without a sound public school system their industry-recruiting efforts would be for naught. He shrewdly coupled more money for education with provisions for assessing classroom effectiveness. The state's business leadership signed on and joined parents, teachers, and students in what soon became a crusade for educational reform. Old hands around the State House swore they had seen nothing like the outpouring of support for the EIA. Citizen-lobbyists pushed legislators until they agreed to vote for the bill. The impact of single-member districts made this intense lobbying effort all the more effective.[7]

When Governor Riley signed the EIA in June 1984, he spoke for many Carolinians who placed the hopes for the state's future in a better-educated citizenry: "An old South Carolina is dying. A new South Carolina, strong and vital and very proud, is struggling to be born. We will not build the New South Carolina with bricks and mortar. We will build it with minds. The power of knowledge and skills is our hope for survival in this new age." The Education Improvement Act of 1984 was hailed in the national media and education circles as a model piece of legislation: "No state is more identified with education reform than South Carolina" (*Washington Post*); "Once near the bottom, [South Carolina] schools rank first in improvement" (*Chicago Tribune*); "South Carolina which enacted a one-cent sales tax increase in 1984 to pay for its widely acclaimed Education Improvement Act, stands as a paragon of reform" (*Wall Street Journal*). The penny sales tax provided $250 million ($365 million) in new funding for education.[8]

In the twelve years after the passage of the EIA, there were improvements in some areas. Student attendance was up; the percentage of high school seniors going to college increased from 41.9 percent to 54.7 percent; and the average Scholastic Aptitude Test scores rose forty-six points. More important, the interest that the business community expressed in 1984 was not just a passing fancy. In 1987 Governor Campbell appointed a special task force, headed by businessman Robert L. Thompson Jr. of Lancaster. The task force developed a master plan for public education to carry into the twenty-first century. Among the goals of Target 2000 (as the plan became known) were reducing the dropout rate, improving teacher training, and making arts education available in all schools. Also during the Campbell administration, state government and business teamed up to combat illiteracy and promote job training.[9]

While there was strong support for secondary education, higher education continued to be underfunded. During the 1960s and 1970s there had been money for higher education and the state's public colleges and universities expanded enrollments and programs. The legislature devised a formula for funding higher education but seldom honored it. By 1995 South Carolina had fifty-nine institutions of higher education (thirty-three public; twenty-six private), awarding nearly thirty-one thousand degrees. During the school year 1995–1996, 177,000 young men and women attended South Carolina colleges and universities (149,000 public; 28,000 private). Some 125,000 in-state students attended public colleges. Underfunding meant that at the three research institutions (Clemson, Medical University, and University of South Carolina) the state provided less than one-half of annual budgets. South Carolina's research universities had become state-assisted, not state-supported. The remainder of the budgets at the larger institutions came from grants, gifts, and student fees. South Carolina, with one of the lowest per capita incomes in the Southeast, had some of the highest public college fees. In 1992, though, the General Assembly allowed any four-year college (except the regional campuses of the University of South Carolina) to declare itself a university. Despite the obvious needs and the lobbying of students, administrators, and alumni, there seemed to be little interest in an EIA-type initiative for higher education.[10]

The 1984 campaign to improve public education succeeded because a determined governor used his office as a bully pulpit to rally the people and force the legislature to act. The very nature of the victory should have been a caution. In an earlier day a governor could have convinced one or two key legislative leaders of the merits of a program (for example, technical education) and it would have become law. However, by the 1980s the old legislative power brokers were no more. With single-member districts there was a diffusion of power—it was every representative and senator for him- or herself. Legislators only had to answer to the narrow constituency of their districts. There also appeared to be a changing, or narrowing, of the definition of the term *community* from state and county to district. The situation was ripe for corruption.[11]

In the spring and summer of 1990 South Carolina was rocked with a series of scandals involving public officials. In May the president of the University of South Carolina (after more than a year of public criticism, especially from the *Greenville News*) resigned amid charges that he misspent university funds. Two months later, on 18 July, the U.S. attorney for South Carolina announced that a federal grand jury was investigating a number of legislators for allegedly taking bribes or using drugs. The code name for the government's sting was, appropriately, "Operation Lost Trust."

Shortly thereafter the names of those under investigation were released. Even hardened politicians were stunned. Among the names were seventeen members of the General Assembly (including the Speaker pro tempore of the House of Representatives), a circuit judge, the chair of the State Development Board, a key aide to the governor, a top Clemson University administrator, six lobbyists, and a Spartanburg businessman. Those charged reflected the changed nature of South Carolina politics: black and white, Republican and Democrat, male and female. By October twenty of those indicted had pleaded guilty, six were convicted, and one was acquitted. In nonrelated scandals, the chief of the highway patrol and the head of the highway department resigned under pressure after accounts of alleged questionable activities became public; USC's president pleaded guilty to using his office for personal gain; and a Spartanburg senator pleaded guilty to defrauding investors in a development scheme. For a state that prided itself on honest public service, the ever-widening circle of corruption and malfeasance caused acute embarrassment. It also aroused a lethargic citizenry.[12]

Reaction to "Lost Trust" ranged from anger and disgust to calls for a serious look at reforming state government. Beginning with a series of opinion editorials in August 1990 and February 1991, *The State* newspaper called for more than reform; it urged that state government be restructured to respond more effectively to the needs of South Carolinians. The *Greenville News*, the *Charleston News and Courier*, and other newspapers also espoused a major overhaul of state government.[13]

In 1990 Carroll Campbell ran for reelection as governor on a platform calling for reform. So, too, did every other successful statewide candidate from lieutenant governor to state superintendent of education. All campaigned against the outmoded "horse and buggy constitution" that Tillman had forced on the state. In January 1991 Campbell appointed a group of thirty-eight citizens to the South Carolina Commission on Restructuring State Government. For eight months this panel held numerous public hearings and investigated constitutional reform in other states. In October it presented its 346-page report to the governor.[14]

The title of the commission's report, *Modernizing South Carolina State Govern-*

ment for the Twenty-first Century, captured the flavor of the document. It called for a streamlining of state government by reorganizing nearly all of the 145 state agencies, boards, and commissions into 15 cabinet departments. There were no sacred cows; every state agency was included in the report. The commission strongly recommended that this restructuring be done by constitutional amendment. Unfortunately, the plan was too audacious for legislators long used to having their own way, and the proposal for a referendum died in the General Assembly. Public opinion, however, would not let the issue rest, and in 1993 the legislature created a modified cabinet form of government. It was a step in the right direction, but it was government created by statute, not by constitutional amendment. What the General Assembly passed, it could also repeal.[15]

On 1 July 1993 South Carolina's new modified cabinet form of government went into effect. Thirteen new cabinet-level agencies replaced seventy-six. Eleven of the cabinet officers serve at the pleasure of the governor; the other two (the chief of the State Law Enforcement Division and the director of the Department of Public Safety) serve fixed terms and can be removed only for cause. For the first time in state history, a governor could be held responsible for the actions of the executive branch of government. The blame could not be shifted (as had been done in the past) to some faceless board or bureaucrat. Even though the realignment of agencies was not what the restructuring commission had recommended, it did provide for a more efficient and effective administration of government. One year after the new system had been in effect, even its most severe critics gave it high marks.[16]

The two major reform efforts of the 1980s and 1990s, education and government, occurred because public opinion made it difficult for legislators to oppose them. However, it took a tremendous effort to arouse the citizenry. And had it not been for "Lost Trust" and other governmental scandals, it is unlikely that there would have been any governmental reform.

South Carolina's government, even after reform, was still dominated by the General Assembly. The tradition of the legislative state could be traced to the eighteenth century when the Commons House of Assembly accrued power to itself at the expense of royal officials (see chapter 7). The 1895 constitution made governing more unwieldy by severely limiting the authority of county governments; creating numerous boards, commissions, and agencies; and authorizing special-purpose districts with overlapping boundaries and authority. It was quite a governmental jungle (see chapter 19).

As long as members of the county elites, with their many years of seniority and experience, controlled the General Assembly, the system worked. However, the metropolitan elites and the federal government dislodged the rural power brokers and destroyed the political framework that supported them. No new power structure was created. Single-member districts were a system, not a structure. The old order was gone, but to call the political system that replaced it a new order was a misnomer.

Individuals represented narrow constituencies and partisan interests. The days of someone saying, as Edgar Brown allegedly did, "It's my job to take care of the little people of South Carolina" were gone. Many reformers would shout hallelujah that someone with such an outmoded, patronizing, paternalistic outlook was no longer in public office. While Senator Brown may have been guilty of being patronizing and paternalistic, he and other county elites believed it was the duty of state government to help those who could not help themselves. It made little difference whether the origins of such a view came from the plantation or the church. What was important was that such people viewed state government as a gathering of community leaders. These leaders, in turn, then acted in what they thought were the best interests of the people of the state.[17]

Individuals elected on an at-large basis had to heed the interests of the various constituencies in their counties. There was something, therefore, of a consensus, and legislators responded accordingly. Single-member districts and partisan politics produced narrow, not broad, constituencies. For example, if the members of the Richland County house delegation were to run at large, they would have to win approval from voters drawn from the country's 285,720 residents; however, as representatives of single-member house districts, they were answerable to only about 28,000. As political scientist Blease Graham noted, "Single member districts are almost like we've gone from running a pasture to running row crops." Constituent service, not statewide issues, were more important.[18]

Complaints about partisanship and the lack of leadership in the General Assembly appeared regularly in the pages of the state's newspapers. Yet, it was many of these same newspapers that railed against the old county elites, helped bring them down, and promoted the creation of a viable two-party system. Partisan politics, however, were a contributing factor in the decline of the legislative state and the redefinition of community.[19]

The major story in southern politics after 1964 was the rise of the Republican Party. In South Carolina the party's growth at all levels has been phenomenal. In 1964 every member of the house was a Democrat; twelve years later nine of ten still were. However, beginning in 1976, with each successive election the number of Republicans in the house increased. After the 1994 election the Democrats still had a paper-thin majority, but several representatives switched parties and, for the first time since 1876, Republicans controlled the house. Under the Democrats the house had not been organized along party lines, but rather on a more or less "we're all South Carolinians" philosophy. The Republicans, on the other hand, organized the house strictly along party lines. Shell-shocked Democrats found themselves on the outside looking in.[20]

The growth of the Republican Party could be attributed to a number of factors. White Carolinians were basically conservative. After World War II they became increasingly disenchanted with the national Democratic Party's social and economic agendas. Within the state, many lived in urban areas whose leaders fought with the county elites for control of state government. As black Democrats became more active in the party, whites drifted away. The 1988 presidential candidacy of Greenville native Jesse Jackson accelerated the flight of white southerners from the Democratic Party (Jackson won South Carolina's Democratic preferential primary). In 1990 the Democrats nominated Theo W. Mitchell, a black attorney from Greenville, to run against the popular incumbent Republican, Carroll Campbell. Mitchell received only 30.5 percent of the vote (black voters represented about 26 percent of the electorate).[21]

During his eight years as governor, Campbell worked tirelessly and effectively to strengthen the party. He recruited Democrats and welcomed them into the party (despite some grumbling from old-time Republicans). His biggest catch was Rep. David Beasley of Darlington County, whom many thought the Democrats were grooming for the governorship.

In 1990 the Republicans made a tactical mistake they would not repeat. With Senator Thurmond and Governor Campbell at the head of a strong ticket and with a weak Democratic gubernatorial candidate, the party failed to challenge dozens of incumbent Democrats. Six years later Republicans contested 34 of 46 senate seats and 96 of 124 house seats. They held every constitutional office except that of comptroller general and 5 of the 8 seats in the congressional delegation. The only weakness the party showed was in the 1994 gubernatorial campaign when newly converted Republican David Beasley won a narrow victory over Lt. Gov. Nick Theodore. After eight years of Campbell's party building, a margin of 50.4 to 49.6 meant that the Democrats were still able to challenge Republicans in statewide contests.[22]

The Republicans were well organized down to the precinct level. Lexington County was one of the most partisan counties in the state, and its Republican wards made up the most dependable bloc vote in either party. Colleton County provided an excellent example of the speed with which the party developed. In 1988 there was no Republican Party, to speak of, in the county. Seven years later the sheriff, auditor, members of county council, and a majority of the members of the Walterboro city council were all Republicans.[23]

A 1995 survey of county party chairs (Democrat and Republican) revealed some startling information about how grassroots politicians viewed the political landscape. An overwhelming majority of Republicans (85 percent) believed that their county organization was improving and getting stronger, but only 42 percent of the Democrats believed theirs was. An equal number of Democrats thought that theirs was waning. When asked if the state were becoming increasingly Republican, every Republican said it was, and an astonishing number of Democrats (84 percent) concurred. Republicans (83 percent) were optimistic that they would be able to attract black Carolinians into the party, but most Democrats (80 percent) said this would never happen. In reply to a question on South Carolina's becoming a one-party (Republican) state, few thought it would occur. Instead, most county chairs predicted continued Republican gains at all levels.[24]

In many areas of the state the Democratic Party was in disarray. There were some counties, such as Allendale, that were as staunchly Democratic as Lexington was Republican. However, as a small rural county, Allendale, though loyal, could not supply the number of bloc votes that Lexington could (and regularly did) in statewide contests.[25]

On the statewide level, the Democrats were hard hit with desertions. Between 1993 and 1996 eighteen sitting Democratic legislators abandoned the party; fourteen became Republicans; and four declared themselves independents. Among those who switched parties were such key figures as Reps. John Felder of Calhoun County and William Boan of Kershaw, and Sen. Hugh Leatherman of Florence. And less than a year after being elected adjutant general as a Democrat, Stan Spears jumped to the GOP. The party switchers were "just being realistic," commented one observer. It was easier to get elected as a Republican than as a moderate Democrat. That difficulty probably accounted for the fact that Democrats fielded fewer legislative candidates than did the Republicans in 1996. The 1996 election confirmed the Republican majority in the house, but Democrats increased their majority in the senate.[26]

As the Republican Party increased in numbers, it began to suffer growing pains. There were divisions between economic and social conservatives, and between old-line regulars and new members, especially those associated with the Christian Coalition. For a while in the late 1970s there were two Republican factions in Greenville. They patched up their differences in 1980, but the fissures there and elsewhere ran deep. In Richland County, when Governor Beasley tried to oust local party officials, he and his backers were defeated by party stalwarts. In 1997 there was even talk of old-line Republicans' organizing committees to support the Democrats' candidate for governor, Jim Hodges.[27]

After 1968 the South Carolina Republican Party linked its fortunes with those of the national party. During the Nixon, Ford, and Reagan administrations, state party loyalists received federal appointments. Former governor James Edwards was Reagan's secretary of energy, and Columbia attorney Weston Adams served as ambassador to Malawi. Columbian Lee Atwater engineered George Bush's victory in 1988 and insured that Carolinians had another four years of access to the White House. After the election Atwater became chair of the Republican National Committee.[28]

Not as many South Carolina Democrats identified themselves with their national party; nonetheless, they were increasingly involved in national party affairs. Local officials campaigned for fellow southerner Jimmy Carter and helped him carry the state (the only Democrat to do so since 1960). One of the more memorable scenes from that campaign was Carter's making a lap at the Darlington 500 to the cheers of 70,000 stock-car-racing fans. After the election Carter named former governor John Carl West as ambassador to Saudi Arabia. During the Clinton administration former governor Richard Riley served as secretary of education; former state party chair Donald Fowler became chair of the Democrat Party, and businessman Philip Lader served as ambassador to Great Britain.[29]

The dominant figure on the state's political stage in the last three decades of the twentieth century was J. Strom Thurmond of Edgefield County, who as of 25 May 1997 had served in the U.S. Senate longer than any other individual (forty-one years and ten months). Thurmond first entered public life in 1928 when he was elected superintendent of education in Edgefield County. South Carolina and the South changed considerably over the next seventy years, and Thurmond changed with the times. In 1970 he was the first member of the state's congressional delegation to hire a black staff member. His service to constituents, regardless of race, was legendary. In his successful reelection campaigns of 1972, 1978, 1984, 1990, and 1996 he attracted an increasing number of black voters. During the 1972 campaign, black activist Victoria DeLee of Dorchester County supported the senator because he had helped obtain federal funding for poor, predominantly black, rural areas. "What a man was yesterday doesn't matter," said DeLee. "It's what he is today that counts."[30]

Strom Thurmond's willingness and ability to change and Victoria DeLee's comments were characteristic of the personal decisions that black and white South Carolinians made after the collapse of Jim Crow. The state and its people got through the civil rights years relatively unscathed. Orangeburg and Lamar were anomalies.

Publicly, South Carolina became an open society, but it was one in which racial identity, especially in politics, seemed ever present. In 1983 civil rights leader I. DeQuincey Newman became the first black senator since the 1880s, and he was elected from a district that was 64 percent white. In 1994 black Democrats joined forces with white Republicans in the General Assembly to create thirty-one black-majority districts in the house and eleven in the senate. However, in 1996 a federal court ruled that race could not be the determining factor in establishing districts and ordered new elections in twenty-one house and eight senate districts. The boundaries of the new black-majority Sixth Congressional District were similar to those of the black district created in 1882. In 1992 James Clyburn of Sumter was elected to represent the sixth, which covered most of the Pee Dee area but stretched from downtown Columbia to the coast. The creation of single-member districts with black

Chief Justice Ernest Adolphus Finney Jr. (b. 1931) of the South Carolina Supreme Court. Courtesy, the Hon. Ernest A. Finney Jr., Columbia, South Carolina.

majorities resulted in the election of thirty-four black legislators: twenty-six in the house and eight in the senate.[31]

In 1990 there were 322 black elected officials in South Carolina: mayors, school board members, and city and county council persons; in 1993 there were 450. On 11 May 1994 Ernest A. Finney Jr. of Sumter was elected chief justice of the South Carolina Supreme Court. In the 1990s, hundreds of other black Carolinians held appointed positions of public trust; among them were the police chiefs of Charleston and Columbia. In the 1990s Greenville County, which was more than 80 percent white, had a black county administrator and two black superintendents of education.[32]

In the 1960s and 1970s many of the black and white Carolinians involved in the civil rights movement believed that once segregation ended, South Carolina would develop a biracial society. That did not fully occur. Racial divisions were especially noticeable at the ballot box. The only thing approximating a biracial political action took place in 1976 when Jimmy Carter captured 44 percent of the state's white vote and almost all of the black vote when he carried the state. After that election whites increasingly voted Republican in national and local elections and blacks remained solidly Democratic (see Maps 35, 36, 37).[33]

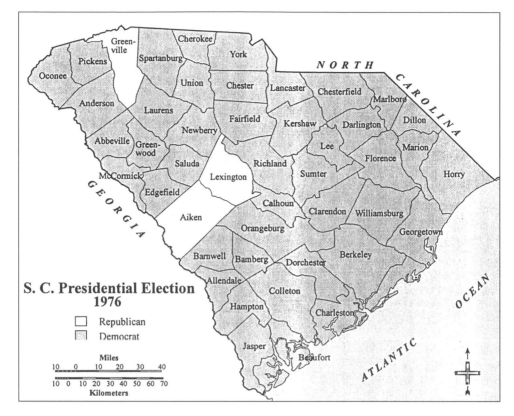

Map 35: 1976 presidential election

On a personal level, one had only to look around in 1997 to see evidence of a biracial society. In public schools and on playgrounds in larger towns, black and white children could be seen playing together. In bars and restaurants black and white patrons enjoyed their drinks and meals, sometimes separately, sometimes together. Even in pool halls and adult entertainment clubs, one could find black and white staff and patrons. Almost every grocery store in the state reflected the more than three hundred years of the exchange of foodways across racial lines. A black newcomer from Connecticut was astounded when he went into a grocery store in an upscale Columbia neighborhood and easily found what he considered soul food ingredients. "Back home," he commented, "food items were segregated by race and class. Down here, they weren't."[34]

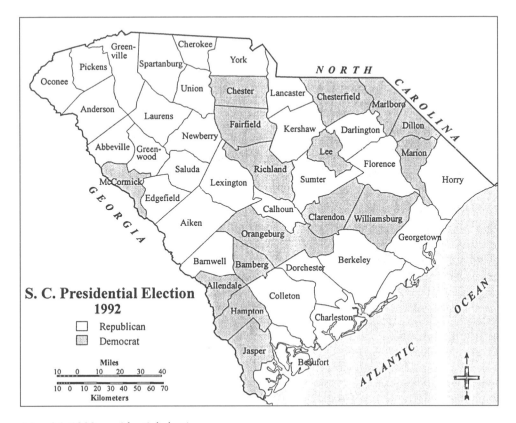

Map 36: 1992 presidential election

South Carolinians, in their quiet way, went about the business of dealing with people, not races. Several events from 1996 were illustrative. In Orangeburg the largest real estate company in town was Middleton and Associates, a black owned firm that had black and white employees (male and female). After attending a dinner where there were about an equal number of black and white guests, historian George C. Rogers Jr. penned a note describing the dinner as "the sign of a new age in South Carolina. Everybody present enjoyed being there. *They all wanted to be together.*" White Methodists in rural Calhoun, Orangeburg, and Lexington Counties welcomed their black female district superintendent, Angeline Simmons, into their churches. At the Calhoun County Museum's annual gala, the Jarvis Brothers (a black quartet from Orangeburg) performed a medley entitled "American Quilt,"

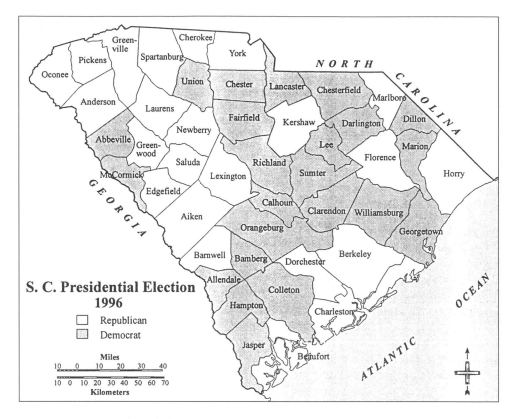

Map 37: 1996 presidential election

which included "Lift Every Voice and Sing" and "Dixie." Herbert Millette Jr., a white man born and reared in Clarendon County, selected a black friend, Albert Cooper, to be his head pallbearer. On his deathbed he remarked to his brother: "As far as we have come, most people won't even notice it."[35]

Many locals might not notice such things, but the casual, normal interaction of blacks and whites in a variety of settings were indications that South Carolina in the 1990s was a very different place than it had been in the 1960s. In 1992 John Edgar Wideman, a black man from Amherst, Massachusetts, and his elderly father traveled to their family's ancestral home in Greenwood County. As a child Wideman had declined to "go back home" with his grandfather because "going to South Carolina was about as appealing as going to Africa and living in the jungle." After a day or two in Greenwood and nearby Abbeville, he began to see that things were different in South Carolina. He especially noted the pleasant manners, the softness of speech, public access for all, and a black sheriff. He described a conversation with the desk clerks at the local Holiday Inn (a black male and a white female). He and his father wanted to go out for a drink. The joint reply was "There's black clubs and white clubs and mixed. No problem with youall going in just about any of them. Depends what youall looking for."[36]

Perhaps no one better symbolized the casual acceptance of personal relationships than the Columbia band Hootie and the Blowfish. Their album *Cracked Rear View* sold more than fifteen million copies. In its review of 1995, *Newsweek* described the group as follows: "An interracial band that made only passing mention of their racial identity, they became the most popular rock group in America, shaping the musical year in their image. In a year of intense racial polarization, highlighted by the Million Man March and the response to the O.J. verdict, their catchy, pedestrian songs and videos made just getting along feel downright commonplace." "Just getting along"—that was what most South Carolinians were trying to do.[37]

This did not mean that there were not racial difficulties. The press reported racial incidents: an Aiken restaurant refused to serve black customers (1989); an integrated youth group was turned away from a Saluda County pool (1989); an integrated softball team was not permitted to play in a charity tournament in Norway (1990); and KKK slogans were spray-painted on the dock of a black Charleston couple, warning them not to build a house in a predominantly white neighborhood (1996). Each of these events triggered immediate responses from government officials and the general public. Governor Campbell invited the Saluda youth group to the Governor's Mansion for a cookout and pool party. The attorney general succeeded in having the Aiken restaurant's liquor license revoked, and in 1990 the General Assembly passed a public accommodations law. In Norway apologies were issued almost as soon as word of the incident reached the media. In Charleston students, faculty, and alumni of the College of Charleston rallied to clean up the black couple's defaced property (the man was an alumnus).[38]

The incidents were disturbing because they recalled the 1950s, when the actions of individuals sometimes led to violence. The response to the events of the 1980s and 1990s was an encouraging sign that a great many Carolinians wanted to live in peace, to just get along. When individuals disturbed the harmony of the community, rather than ignore what happened, the public reaction was to reach out to victims and let it be known that such conduct was no longer acceptable. The laws had changed, but so had attitudes.

Racism had not disappeared, nor was it a one-way street. However, individual actions—bad and good—should be seen as just that, individual actions, not the deeds of a group. No one better understands this than Filbert native Dori Sanders,

Hootie and the Blowfish appeared live in concert on national television from the campus of their alma mater, the University of South Carolina (1996). Photograph by Jonathan Bové. Courtesy, University Publications, University of South Carolina.

whose novels *Clover* and *Her Own Place* deal with the reality of a biracial South Carolina. In *Her Own Place* Mae Lee, the black protagonist, observes that whites are "no better than colored people. . . . And no worse."[39]

Between January 1991 and December 1996 thirty-five churches in South Carolina burned (twenty-three black; twelve white). The majority of the church fires had nothing to do with race, but three did. In Walhalla (Oconee County), the State Law Enforcement Division labeled the burning of an Hispanic church a hate crime. Church fires in Clarendon and Williamsburg Counties were associated with Klan activity. After the torching of Mount Zion AME Church in Williamsburg County, Gov. David Beasley appointed a Commission on Race Relations. Charged with examining the state of race relations in South Carolina in the 1990s, the commission held a series of public hearings around the state. The religion subcommittee issued its report in January 1997 and recommended "gracefully transferring" the Confederate battle flag from atop the State House dome.[40]

No other issue in recent state history was as emotionally charged as the question of the flying of the Confederate battle flag. A proposed compromise in 1994, supported by Governor Campbell, failed. That same year the Republican Party had an advisory referendum on the issue in its primary, and three-fourths of those who voted said to keep it flying. In 1997 Governor Beasley proposed that the flag be taken down and placed on a pole by the Confederate monument on the State House grounds. Despite the strong support of business and religious leaders, the Republican-dominated house rejected the measure. Protest marches in Myrtle Beach and silent vigils in Columbia by those who wanted it taken down did little to persuade those who thought otherwise. Similarly, counterdemonstrations promoting "Heritage not Hate" made few converts. In the war of words over the flag, there were indications that for some the definition of community was narrow and that good order and harmony were unimportant. The debate was often heated, and some individuals on both sides of the issue damaged the state's reputation for civility and good manners.[41]

Ironically, while the racially tinged debate on the flag raged in the press (read the letters to the editor column in any newspaper from 1994 to 1997), the General Assembly authorized an African American monument on the State House grounds. In April 1997 a Citizens Advisory Committee on the African-American History Monument made its recommendations to a legislative commission. When completed as proposed, the monument would occupy a prominent position on the eastern portion of the State House grounds. Also, a bill making Martin Luther King's birthday and Confederate Memorial Day legal state holidays (not optional holidays) passed the senate, but did not become law.[42]

Even though black and white Carolinians shared strands of a common heritage, and even though they might get along individually, there were still divisions, separate worlds. Some were self-imposed. All one had to do was visit a school cafeteria or attend a professional meeting to discover the racial groupings that were noticeable even to the most casual observer. In the early 1990s the Allendale Cooter Festival, although promoted by the entire community, drew predominantly black crowds while the nearby Hampton Watermelon Festival attracted mostly white crowds. Barbershops, beauty salons, and funeral homes served clientele who were primarily of one race or another. Churches on Sunday mornings were still some of the most segregated places in the state. Except for Pentecostal churches that had had biracial congregations since the late nineteenth century, it was rare to find more than a handful of worshippers of either race in one another's churches.[43]

Church membership, regardless of race or class, remained an important part of people's lives. In 1990 more South Carolinians (62 percent) reported that they were church members than had been reported twenty years earlier (52 percent). Church growth cut across denominational lines. The largest denomination, as it had been since before the Civil War, was Southern Baptist, with 713,000 members—or one out of every three church members—in 1990. The fastest growing denominations, however, were the Roman Catholics and Church of God (Cleveland, Tennessee).

Former governors West, Campbell, McNair, and Edwards stood with Gov. David Beasley and supported his call for the removal of the Confederate battle flag from the State House dome. Photograph by Doug Gilmore. Courtesy, Office of the Governor of the State of South Carolina.

While mainline Protestant denominations lost membership nationally, South Carolina Episcopalians and United Methodists increased in numbers and Presbyterians remained virtually unchanged.[44]

Increased church membership did not necessarily mean that communities were more religious. Beginning in the 1960s, blue laws were repealed or ignored. At one time churches and their related activities (e.g., youth groups, women's circles, men's clubs) were the focal point of a good many Carolinians' lives. That changed. Two Greenville residents remembered when their city permitted movie theaters to open on Sunday afternoons: "On that night, South Carolina—the last pocket of resistance to secularity in the Western world—served notice that it would no longer be a prop for the church. . . . The Fox theater went head to head with the church over who would provide the world view for the young. That night in 1963, the Fox Theater won the opening skirmish." They skipped Methodist Youth Fellowship and went to the movies instead.[45]

In 1994 a referendum to permit video poker (county option) passed overwhelmingly statewide. Not only did South Carolina legalize video poker (which permits payoffs) and insist that it was not gambling, but the state imposed a minuscule (when compared with other states') sin tax. In the twelve counties where it was rejected, video machine operators immediately filed suit to get the people's votes reversed. Once, community pressure would have made such an action inconceivable. In 1996 the South Carolina Supreme Court ruled the county-by-county referendums on video poker unconstitutional. As a result, video poker was legal throughout the state.[46]

In smaller towns businesses remained closed on Sundays, but open stores in suburban malls tempted customers from rural areas to shop. In coastal resorts and the larger cities, bars opened on Sunday afternoons—if they paid a special license fee. It was a changing culture and one that caused a backlash from those who remembered, with passion, a seemingly more innocent South Carolina.

Religious organizations became involved in public debates, and sometimes the line of separation between church and state blurred. Since the 1950s black churches and clergy had been involved in politics; beginning in the 1980s white churches and clergy passed out voter information and supported or denounced candidates. Most notably, the state's Southern Baptists became more conservative and, breaking with historical Baptist tradition, more politically active.

As churches and church members got more involved in organized politics, they flocked to the Republican Party. These new Republicans soon outvoted longtime party regulars, and there were intraparty scuffles for control of the party in a number of counties. By 1997 supporters of the Christian Coalition claimed a majority of the seats on the state executive committee. Unlike the state's traditional middle-class and upper-middle-class Republicans, these newer party members tended to be less amenable to compromise. They took a particularly hard line on social issues.[47]

There were a variety of issues that were sure to attract a response from the newly active religious community, such as prayer in the public schools, sex education, and the role of women. The reaction to these issues reflected the changed and changing nature of South Carolina and American society. While desegregation was the major social change in the 1970s and 1980s, it was not the only one. Across the American South the woman's rights movement became the cause of the 1970s and 1980s. South Carolina was one of ten states that did not ratify the Equal Rights Amendment. However, out of necessity women had long been a part of the workforce in South Carolina. By 1990, 56 percent of women were employed outside the home. Two-family incomes were necessary in a state where in 1989 the average per capita income was $11,897 ($14,670), and many women were female heads of households (24 percent).[48]

Not only were more women in the workplace, but they began to fill leadership positions in government and business. Pansy Ridgeway became the mayor of Manning in 1969; Ferdinan Backer Stevenson of Charleston served as lieutenant governor (1979–1983); Gladys Elizabeth Johnston Patterson of Spartanburg represented the Fourth Congressional District for three terms (1987–1993); Jean Hoefer Toal of Columbia was elected to the state supreme court in 1988. Before her death in 1990, Jean Galloway Bissell of Due West (Abbeville County) had been vice chair of the board of directors of the South Carolina National Bank and later a member of the U.S. Court of Appeals. Women clergy were called to pulpits in churches of the major Protestant denominations. In 1997 there were nineteen women in the house (fourteen white; five black) and three in the senate (one black; two white). In 1997 Crandall Close Bowles of Fort Mill (York County) was CEO of one of the largest and oldest South Carolina–based firms, Springs Industries.[49]

South Carolina women were no different from other American women in wanting access to equal opportunity, especially education. In 1995 some 62 percent of undergraduate enrollment and 63 percent of graduate students at all colleges were female. In professional schools, such as the University of South Carolina's law and medical schools, 40 percent of the students were women. (Winthrop, formerly the state's women's college, had a male enrollment of 31 percent.) After a protracted and expensive legal battle, the Citadel, the Military College of South Carolina, was forced by federal courts to drop its all-male policy. The first woman admitted to the corps of cadets in 1995 quit after one week; however, two of the four women admitted in 1996, Petra Lovetinska of the Czech Republic and Nancy Mace of Goose Creek (Berkeley County), completed their "knob year" and were recognized as members of the corps of cadets in May 1997. Twenty-four women were accepted as members of the class of 2001.[50]

The changing role of women in South Carolina was just one of a number of indications that South Carolina was becoming more like the rest of the country. Nowhere was this more true than in the metropolitan areas. In 1980, for the first time in the state's history, more Carolinians (54 percent) lived in urban than rural areas. As of 1995 there were all or part of eight metropolitan statistical areas (MSA) in the state: Charleston–North Charleston (Charleston, Berkeley, and Dorchester), Columbia (Richland-Lexington), Florence (Florence), Myrtle Beach (Horry), Greenville-Spartanburg-Anderson (Greenville, Spartanburg, Anderson, Cherokee, and Pickens), and Sumter (Sumter). Aiken County was included in the Augusta, Georgia–Aiken MSA and York County in the North Carolina–centered Charlotte-Gastonia–Rock Hill MSA.[51]

The suburbs surrounding the central cities of these MSAs could just as easily have been Anywhere, USA. Some towns seemed to lose their sense of community and, if some boosters had had their way, would have lost their identity. In 1965 one Columbia businessman crowed that his home looked "as good as Toledo, Ohio." By the mid 1980s the capital city's civic, business, and political leaders were no longer

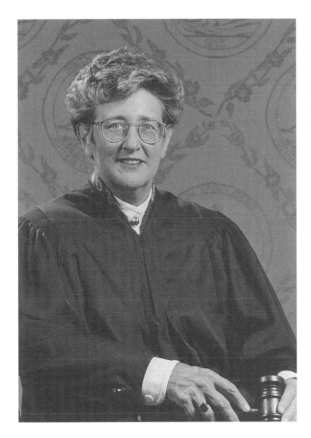

Justice Jean Hoefer Toal (b. 1943) of the South Carolina Supreme Court. Courtesy, the Hon. Jean H. Toal, Columbia, South Carolina.

interested in such a goal; they were trying to create an identity for the city by focusing on its long-neglected riverfront. They wanted Columbia to be special, not like somewhere else–especially Toledo, Ohio. Actually, all they really needed was to tell the world why poet James Dickey chose to live there: "Columbia," he wrote, "is an easygoing place, with some fine old houses, good local theater, and the most imaginative small zoo I have seen."[52]

As attractive as Columbia, Charleston, and Greenville were, a number of people chose to live in the countryside or smaller towns. The county seat towns of Abbeville, Newberry, and York underwent a revival. In Abbeville and Newberry restored turn-of-the-century opera houses became major cultural attractions. The five interstate highways that criss-crossed the state made commuting to jobs in the cities a breeze. This process of exurbanization and continued suburban sprawl undermined a traditional sense of community. It was not unusual for people to live in one town, shop and work in a second, and attend church in a third. The close-knit community in which many had grown up no longer existed.[53]

Part of the unease and even anger that some felt about life in the 1990s was the result of the loss of a sense of community and the feeling that things were not the way they used to be. Cookie-cutter suburbs and strip shopping centers built on plowed-under and paved-over cotton fields bore little resemblance to the tree-shaded residential areas and main streets of Abbeville, Cheraw, Edgefield, or Walterboro. Nor were the populations alike. Whereas older towns had a mix of classes and races who were born there and knew one another, suburbs tended to attract a population that was mostly white, individualistic, relatively affluent, and mobile. Mobility, individualism, and materialism eroded traditional values and were antithetical to the concept of community. People no longer sat on front porches or visited with neighbors. Air conditioning (considered a necessity, not a luxury, in South Carolina) helped doom front porches, and mobility made it difficult to keep up with one's neighbors—if one wanted to.[54]

The impact of urban sprawl on nearby small towns was captured by Josephine Humphreys in her novel *Rich in Love*:

> In the distance the highway appeared to flare suddenly into the air; that was the bridge to Charleston. But before the bridge, just beyond the television station, was an opening in the shopping strip and a nondescript road that cut back behind the import repair shop. That was my road. It led to my town, Mount Pleasant, which huddled secretly behind all this new development. In Latin class . . . I had studied the town of Herculaneum, buried by hot mud in the year 79 A.D. My town had been similarly engulfed, not by mud but by overflow from the city of Charleston, which had erupted and settled all around, leaving Mount Pleasant embedded in the middle.

Mount Pleasant managed to keep its independence and identity (at least in the old part of town), but other communities had difficulty doing so. Maintaining independence was one thing, but maintaining an identity was more difficult. Along the Grand Strand, from the U.S. Highway 17 bypass at Murrell's Inlet all the way to the North Carolina line, stretched an unbroken strip of urban development. If it were not for road signs, travelers would not know when they had crossed the border from Garden City to Surfside Beach to Myrtle Beach to North Myrtle Beach.[55]

The works of many post–World War II southern writers depict a South in which traditional themes such as family, community, and a sense of place were absent (just as they seemed to be in real life). This made much of the new southern writing quite different from that of the Southern Renaissance. The past was no longer sitting in judgment of the present. According to one literary critic, where communities were present, they were usually either black or female.[56]

South Carolina's contemporary authors have not exactly conformed to this general assessment, since community seems essential to their writing. In *Rich in Love* Humphreys wrote about a South Carolina in which there were two communities, one black and one white, but both female. Dori Sanders's *Clover* and *Her Own Place* were set in black female communities, but they were not isolated from the white world. Humphreys's *The Fireman's Fair*, however, was a more traditional southern community and, unlike her earlier works, had a male protagonist. In William Price Fox's short stories (*Southern Fried Plus Six*) and an early novel (*Moonshine Light, Moonshine Bright*), there were an old-fashioned sense of community and wonderfully lyrical descriptions of South Carolina in the 1940s and 1950s. Pat Conroy, a nonnative but sometime resident of Fripp Island, used the state as the locale for much of his writing. While readers might debate the community of Conroy's fiction and nonfiction, few Carolinians would disagree with his obvious love affair for the Carolina coast. The prologue to *The Prince of Tides* opens with the lines: "My wound is geography. It is also my anchorage, my port of call." That geography, that anchorage, was the South Carolina lowcountry.[57]

In the works of both Conroy and Humphreys the impact of development along the coast created a tension, a fear of what might be lost that quite a few Carolinians in real life shared. With Humphreys, it was the urban sprawl of Charleston engulfing the quiet community of Mount Pleasant and the hoards of tourists turning Charleston into a diesel-choked carnival (*Rich in Love*). With Conroy, it was the threat of modern civilization to the Gullah culture of Daufuskie Island (*The Water is Wide*), the effect of humankind on the fragile ecology of the coast (*Beach Music*), and the condemnation of wilderness areas for a government development—much like what had happened with the building of the Savannah River Plant (*Prince of Tides*).[58]

Until the late 1960s no one in the state questioned economic development. Any industry was sought as long as it brought jobs. Then in 1969 an unlikely coalition of white housewives, retirees, and professionals joined with black fishermen, the Audubon Society, Friends of the Earth, and Hilton Head developers to block the building of a petrochemical plant in Beaufort County. For nearly a year the State Development Board found itself involved in a struggle with Beaufort County residents, local and national politicians, and the secretary of the interior, who considered the plant and its effluent a threat to the environment. Eventually the company gave up. After the protracted public fight over the company and potential pollution problems, a poll revealed that Carolinians were concerned about pollution. However, they also wanted economic development, but they wanted their state government to be more selective in the industries it recruited.[59]

The confrontation in Beaufort between the environment and development was the first of many such battles that would be waged in the latter part of the twentieth century as more and more Carolinians decided that they did not want to sell their birthright for a mess of pottage. When citizens perceived that the state was not protecting them and their heritage, they organized to protest new industries or close down existing ones. The safeguarding of water and air cut across class, racial, and party lines. Irate Carolinians forced plants to close in Lexington and Pickens Counties and blocked new ones. In Sumter the local newspaper promoted rallies to oppose an industry it considered a threat to the environment. In most instances the issue was pollution, but in 1997 a Florence County couple refused to buckle under to pressure from government officials to sell their historic home as a plant location. Some of their neighbors were angry at them, but an equal number were furious with state officials.[60]

From 1971 until 1994 South Carolina waste management facilities took in nearly two-thirds of the nation's low-level nuclear waste. Much of it came from out of state; however, some was generated from within. The Savannah River Plant was a producer of nuclear weapons, and by the 1980s about one-half the state's electricity was generated by nuclear power. In 1986 Governor Riley initiated action that forced Congress to approve regional waste compacts. Three years later Governor Campbell issued an executive order limiting the amount of out-of-state hazardous waste that could be dumped in South Carolina, and the General Assembly supported his order with legislation. In 1994 the legislature voted to shut down the nuclear waste facility in Barnwell County. "'Enough,' Says America's No. 1 Nuclear Dump," ran the headline in a national newsmagazine; however, the story was a bit premature. In 1995 Governor Beasley and his allies in the legislature reversed the plan to shut down the facility and pledged that the fees from nuclear waste would go to education.[61]

While state development officials fretted about occasional opposition to new industries, they worried even more about the growth in South Carolina of its own version of the northern "Rust Belt." Employment in textile manufacturing, once the backbone of South Carolina's industrial sector, peaked in 1973 at 161,000; by 1995 it had declined to 86,000. Plant modernization and mechanization made older mills obsolete. For example, at Pacific Mill in Columbia (before it closed in 1996), 196 new looms did the work of 600 operatives and the company used only one floor of the mill instead of two. Even though Wilt Browning left the Easley mill village in 1955, the closing of the Easley Mill in 1990 was an emotional experience: "There is a lump in my throat, an emptiness in the pit of my stomach, neither of which I can satisfactorily explain." For eighty-nine years the Easley Mill had been a mainstay of the local economy. Its closing was wrenching to many residents who had grown up in its shadow. Easley, in the booming Greenville-Spartanburg-Anderson MSA, had a diversified economic base and was able to handle the loss of the mill. Other communities were not as fortunate.[62]

For small towns such as Iva (Anderson County), Woodruff (Spartanburg), and Lockhart (Union), the closing of a mill meant not only the loss of jobs but often financial ruin for local businesses. For example, in Iva one of four residents worked in the mills. It was not easy for a community to see its unemployment rate shoot up into double digits. In Lockhart the mill had been the economic heart of the town since the 1890s. When it closed, the county chamber of commerce was concerned about being able to attract new businesses because Lockhart was "in a poor location for industry."[63]

Another economic concern for towns was the merger mania that occurred in the 1980s. After nearly a century of striving for economic independence, South Carolina saw its locally owned corporations gobbled up by outsiders. Especially hard hit was the banking industry. Within a year after the approval of interstate banking, in 1985 Banker's Trust, Citizens & Southern National Bank, and Southern National Bank either merged or were acquired by out-of-state banks; six years later South Carolina National Bank, the state's oldest and largest bank, ceased to be. When the banking mergers ended, South Carolinians found that their major financial institutions were now based in North Carolina: NationsBank and First Union of Charlotte and Wachovia of Winston-Salem. One of the country's largest banks was Nations-Bank, headed by Bennettsville (Marlboro County) native Hugh McColl.[64]

Locally owned banks were not the only corporations that were acquired by out-of-state interests. Graniteville, one of South Carolina's pioneering textile firms, lost a hostile takeover bid from a Florida company. A California company purchased Daniel Construction of Greenville, and the new company, Fluor-Daniel, became the nation's second-largest construction company. In Columbia, Colonial Life Insurance Company and Columbia Newspapers, Inc., were purchased by out-of-state firms. So, too, was Multimedia, Inc., of Greenville. After Columbia Newspapers (*The State* and *Columbia Record*) and Multimedia (*Greenville News*) were sold, that meant that in the three largest newspaper markets, only the *Charleston News and Courier* (renamed the *Post and Courier* in 1992) remained in local hands.[65]

The loss of locally owned firms was not only demoralizing to communities, but mergers and buyouts usually meant downsizing, transfers, closings, and a loss of jobs. Sometimes it resulted in less corporate support for community activities—both in terms of contributions and personnel. In a state where personal relationships had always meant a great deal, corporate transfer policies resulted in management personnel being in a town for only two or three years before moving elsewhere. For example, beginning in the late 1980s three successive presidents of Columbia's chamber of commerce failed to complete a full term in office because of corporate relocations.[66]

Not all the economic news was gloomy. Bucking the downward trend in textiles, Delta Woodside Industries (a locally owned firm) grew from one plant in 1984 to twenty-three in four states by 1987. In Spartanburg, Wofford College graduate Jerry Richardson turned one of the original Hardee's franchises into Flagstar (which for a few years in the 1990s was one of the largest publicly held corporations in the state) and ownership of a National Football League franchise in nearby Charlotte, North Carolina.[67]

Capital investment seemed to set records almost every year. In 1995 and 1996

The BMW plant in Spartanburg was one of the best-known of the many foreign corporations that located in South Carolina. Courtesy, BMW Corporation, Spartanburg, South Carolina.

businesses committed more than $5 billion each year for new or expanded facilities. One-third of the 1995 total was foreign capital as overseas corporations continued to invest in South Carolina. During the 1990s the selection of South Carolina locations by Hoffman-LaRoche (Florence County), BMW (Spartanburg), and Honda (Florence) were international news. In particular, the successful wooing of the giant German automobile maker BMW caught the attention of industry recruiters everywhere. Various incentives, including the building of infrastructure and tax exemptions, helped land BMW and other foreign companies. By 1991 South Carolina had a larger percentage of its workforce on foreign payrolls than any other state and foreign corporations were major employers in two dozen communities.[68]

South Carolina (along with Alabama and Mississippi) had the lowest corporate tax rate in the country. Not everyone was happy with the state's "buying" industries, but gripes about incentives and the tax structure were muted. One of the primary reasons for the small number of complaints was that industries brought jobs. Nonagricultural employment increased from 322,000 in 1960 to 451,000 in 1970. Twenty years later the figure was 1.5 million. In 1990 South Carolina ranked twenty-fourth in the value of its manufactured products. While per capita income was still below the national average, Carolinians earned $11,897 ($14,670), more than two times as much in current dollars as the $1,379 ($7,075) they earned in

1960. They were better off economically than their parents and grandparents had been. Industrialization had made a difference.[69]

South Carolina by the 1980s had developed a modern economy, one based primarily on manufacturing (see Map 38). In little more than a generation the state had gone from an agricultural-based economy to an industrial one. Agriculture did not, however, disappear, but it was no longer the vassal of King Cotton. For example, in Newberry County by 1975 there were only four acres of cotton. The county was the state's leading producer of chickens and eggs, number two in dairy production, and number four in cattle. Peaches remained a major crop in Edgefield and Spartanburg Counties—and each county produced more of the fruit than did the entire state of Georgia, the "Peach State." In the 1990s the harvesting of pine trees for the paper industry was the state's number one cash crop. During the early 1990s trees brought in more money than tobacco, soybeans, and cotton combined. However, cotton was not dead. While in 1980 farmers planted only 97,000 acres, fifteen years later increased demand led to the planting of 345,000 acres. Cotton and other row crops such as tobacco, soybeans, and vegetables were grown mostly in the low-country.[70]

Although agriculture was still important in the lowcountry, particularly in the counties of the inner coastal plain, tourism was the region's most important industry. In this respect the lowcountry, the area of old rice and indigo plantations, shared something in common with the islands of the Caribbean from whence had come a goodly portion of its original population. Like Barbados, Jamaica, and St. Kitts, the lowcountry in the 1990s depended upon limited agriculture and tourism for economic survival.[71]

Until the 1960s mostly locals used the South Carolina beaches, and the ever-present threat of hurricanes kept development to a minimum. Prior to 1968 most beach houses were comfortable, modest cottages whose owners were willing to take a loss if a hurricane swept them away. All of that changed with the Housing and Urban Development Act of 1968 (as amended in 1969 and 1972), which made federal flood insurance available to homeowners and developers. Soon expensive resorts and hotels began to spring up all along the coast. Million-dollar "beach houses" became a familiar sight. By 1996, with the exception of private nature preserves and state parks, the entire coast was being intensely developed.

The concept of "going to the beach" changed. Natives, seeking to enjoy their traditional laid-back, casual vacations, abandoned their old haunts at Myrtle Beach, Cherry Grove (part of North Myrtle Beach), and Garden City for the elite enclaves of Debordieu, Hilton Head, and Kiawah; others preferred the "arrogant shabbiness" of Pawley's Island or the down-home feel of Edisto Beach.

For out-of-state tourists, the actual beach was no longer important. Myrtle Beach successfully marketed itself as a destination site with golf courses (more than one

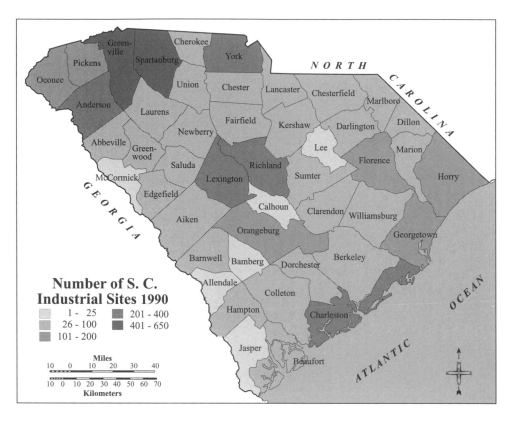

Map 38: Industrial sites, 1990

hundred), dinner theaters, music venues, and factory outlet malls. By the millions (twelve million annually by 1996) northern and foreign tourists jammed the greater Myrtle Beach area. Thousands never went near the ocean. The Grand Strand of the 1990s was no longer a slightly down-at-the-heels family resort. It had almost as much glitz and glamour and neon as Las Vegas.[72]

Tourism was big business for the entire state. In 1995 nearly thirty-two million tourists visited South Carolina and spent $13.2 billion. The industry directly employed three hundred thousand, had a payroll in excess of $4 billion, and paid $466 million in state and local taxes.[73]

Overdevelopment, however, was already a problem by the late 1980s. Shellfishing in Murrell's Inlet, one of the state's richest oyster and clam areas, was closed peri-

Mechanization on the farms spurred rural out-migration, leaving abandoned tenant houses along country roads. Courtesy, South Caroliniana Library.

odically because of pollution. Pollution and overfishing by out-of-state crabbers led to a decline in the blue crab population. The water supplies of Horry and Beaufort Counties became more saline as freshwater was drawn down and saltwater intruded into the underground aquifers. Beach erosion was a serious problem at Seabrook Island, Hilton Head, and Folly Beach.[74]

In 1988, responding to the need to do something about the untrammeled development, the General Assembly passed the Beachfront Management Act. Uncontrolled development along the coast, spurred by the liberal federal flood insurance program, had eradicated miles of protective dunes and threatened to destroy the very beaches that attracted many tourists. The premise of the bill was that it was "economically unwise and ecologically irresponsible to develop the coast in ways that . . . obliterate storm buffering dunes, and impair the natural processes that create and maintain wide, attractive beaches." However, after the initiation of a lawsuit (*Lucas* v. *South Carolina Coastal Management Council*) the council, in 1990, lifted its prohibition of new construction seaward of its established baseline. Instead, the council concentrated on stopping the construction of seawalls and hard erosion control structures.[75]

The necessity for controlling coastal development was underscored by Hurricane Hugo. Just before midnight on 21 September 1989, the eye of Hugo, a category-

The Colonial Cup, begun during the state's tricentennial celebration (1970), had by the 1990s become a national steeplechase event with corporate sponsors. In 1995 Lonesome Glory fought off Rowdy Irishman to win the $100,000 Marion duPont Scott Colonial Cup. Courtesy, Carolina Cup Racing Association, Inc.

The Darlington 500, the premier event on the NASCAR stock car racing circuit. Courtesy of Darlington Raceway.

four hurricane, crossed the coast twenty miles north of Charleston. A twenty-foot storm surge and sustained winds of 135 miles per hour pounded coastal communities from Charleston to North Myrtle Beach. Destructive winds caused major damage more than two hundred miles inland. Damage to property, including timber losses, exceeded $5 billion ($6.1 billion). Thanks to the leadership of Charleston mayor Joe Riley and Gov. Carroll Campbell, only seventeen lives were lost. The task of rebuilding began immediately. Within three weeks Grand Strand promoters launched a publicity campaign advertising that sixty-two golf courses and eleven thousand motel rooms were back in operation. Recovery elsewhere took a little longer; however, by 1992 almost all traces of storm damage were gone.[76]

Tourism and industrialization reshaped South Carolina in ways that, perhaps, those who promoted them had not anticipated. Both attracted new, permanent residents. During the decade of the 1970s the state grew more rapidly than it had in 150 years. Part of the growth was attributable to fewer Carolinians' leaving, but in addition thousands of newcomers moved here. Among the fastest growing counties were Beaufort, Berkeley, Dorchester, and Lexington. By 1990 more than one-half the population of Aiken and Beaufort Counties was nonnative, as were approximately 40 percent of the residents of Berkeley, Dorchester, and Horry Counties.[77]

In 1940 almost all of the state's population (91.9 percent) was native-born. Fifty years later nearly one-third (31.6 percent) of the state's 3,486,703 residents were born somewhere else. A majority of the nonnatives came from other southern states, but about 11 percent came from the Northeast and Midwest. Elected officials reflected the changed South Carolina. Although the governor and lieutenant governor could trace their families back for generations, three of the seven constitutional officers and at least twenty-three members of the 1997 General Assembly were nonnatives.[78]

For more than three hundred years historians told the story of South Carolina in terms of black and white, African and western European (see Map 39). And the assumption was that almost all were natives. By 1995 there were increasing numbers of Asian and Hispanic residents, and in the public schools each ethnic group comprised about 1 percent of the school-age population. Given the mobility of American society, the composition of a community could change almost overnight. In 1995 a Greenwood meat-packing company contracted with a labor firm to hire two hundred Hispanic migrant workers. Within two years there were twenty-eight hundred persons of Hispanic origin living in the town of twenty-one thousand. When *The State* announced its "South Carolina All-State Academic Team" in 1995 and 1996, eight were Asian Americans. The 1985 National Teacher of the Year was Terry Dozier of Irmo High School (Lexington County), a native of Vietnam.[79]

In *South Carolina: The WPA Guide to the Palmetto State* (1941), the first essay was "Who Is the South Carolinian?" The answer then was that a Carolinian was a native from the upcountry, the lowcountry, or the middlecountry. "South Carolini-

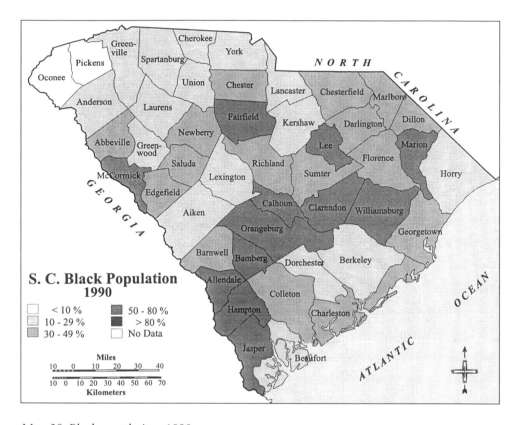

Map 39: Black population, 1990

ans," noted the *WPA Guide*, "are among the rare folk in the South who have no secret envy of Virginians. They have a love for their own State which is a phalanx
against attacks of whatever order." Although within the state race, class, and gender
made a difference, when facing the outside world a Carolinian was a Carolinian was
a Carolinian.[80]

At the end of the twentieth century there were many ways to answer the question "Who is a South Carolinian?" But one thing should be understood. Whether
descended from a first family of South Carolina (black, white, or native American)
or newly arrived from one of eighty-four different countries (according to the 1990
census), all who lived in South Carolina chose to do so. The newest Carolinians
were following in a tradition that stretched back over three centuries to when the

Lords Proprietors first laid plans for this land we call South Carolina. The proprietors, for a variety of reasons, wanted as many settlers as possible. Some came voluntarily: English, French, Germans, Irish, Jews, Scots, Swedes, Welsh, and Yamassee; some came in chains: Angolans, Bambaras, Calibars, Coromantees, Fantees, Ibos, Mandingos, Popos, and Sombas. They found already in Carolina: Catawba, Cherokee, Edisto, Etiwan, Santee, Savannah, Wateree, Waxhaw, and Westo.

Those who came in the 1990s might be new arrivals from different parts of the world, but in choosing to live in this "little triangle on the map known as South Carolina," they become part of the continuum of its history. The South Carolina at the end of the twentieth century was vastly different from the South Carolina of 1960, or even 1975. Things had changed, and for the most part they had changed for the better as successive generations acted in what they thought were the best interests of "the good order and the harmony of the whole community." As Myrtle Beach native Charles Joyner said: "Some say there has been no progress, but they have forgotten where we started. Some would stop here, for they cannot see how far we still have to go."

NOTES

PREFACE

1. Benjamin Brawley, "The Southern Tradition," *North American Review,* 226 (1928): 309.

2. Kelly Miller, "These 'Colored' United States: South Carolina," *Messenger* 7, no. 11 (Dec. 1925): 376.

3. An examination of the indexes of standard American history texts such as *The Growth of the American Republic* by Samuel Eliot Morison, Henry Steele Commager, and William E. Leuchtenburg (6th ed., 2 vols., New York: Oxford University Press, 1969) and George Brown Tindall, *America: A Narrative History* (New York: W. W. Norton, 1984) will bear this out. For example, in *The Growth of the American Republic* there are more references pre-1877 to South Carolina than there are to Massachusetts, New York, and Pennsylvania. After 1877 there is only a single reference to the Palmetto State. In *America: A Narrative History* there are three (all nineteenth century).

4. United States Bureau of the Census, *Statistical Abstract of the United States: 1995* (Washington, D.C.: Government Printing Office, 1995), 454.

5. Pat Conroy, *Beach Music* (New York: Nan A. Talese Doubleday, 1995), 422.

6. George C. Rogers Jr., "List of Lectures, No. 2." History 341: History of South Carolina to 1865. Fall 1976.

7. For discussions on the creation of a uniquely South Carolina culture, see James McBride Dabbs, *The Southern Heritage* (New York: Alfred A. Knopf, 1959). Dabbs, in discussing the relationships between black and white Carolinians, came to the conclusion that "through the process of history and the Grace of God, we have been made one people." In the thirty-seven years since he wrote that statement, the population of South Carolina has changed significantly. No longer is South Carolina history written in terms of black and white. As of the 1990 census, there were significant pockets of Asian, Hispanic, and Native American peoples. United States Bureau of the Census, *1990 Census of Population, Social & Economic Characteristics: South Carolina* (Washington, D.C.: Government Printing Office, 1993), 49.

8. "An Act to Establish a College at Columbia," 19 Dec. 1801, in Thomas Cooper and David J. McCord, *The Statues at Large of South Carolina [1682–1838]* (10 vols., Columbia: A. S. Johnston, 1838–1841), 5: 403 (hereinafter cited as Cooper and McCord, *Statutes*).

CHAPTER 1: THE LAND CALLED CHICORA

1. From its founding in 1670 until its incorporation in 1783, South Carolina's seaport, capital, and major town was called Charles Town. When the city was incorporated, its name was changed to Charleston. In this work the modern spelling will be used.

William S. Powell, *North Carolina Through Four Centuries* (Chapel Hill & London: University of North Carolina Press, 1989), 55.

2. "Instructions for Collonell Phillipp Ludwell Governor of That Part of Our Province of Carolina That Lyes North and East of Cape Feare" and "Instructions for Coll. Philip Ludwell Governor of Carolina," in *Colonial Records of North Carolina,* edited by William L. Saunders, 10 vols.(Raleigh: P. M. Hale, 1886–1890), 1: 362, 373–80.

3. Edward McCrady, *The History of South Carolina Under the Proprietary Government, 1670–1719* (New York: Macmillan, 1897), 236 (hereinafter cited as *Proprietary South Carolina*); A. S. Salley Jr., ed., *Journals of the Commons House of Assembly, September 20, 1692–October 15, 1692* (Columbia: State Printing Company, 1907); "Instructions for Collonell Phillipp Ludwell," 376–78. In his *History of the*

British Empire in America John Oldmixon, in describing Carolina, wrote: "'Tis very well known, that the Province of Carolina has been a long time divided into two separate Governments, the one being call'd North Carolina, and the other South Carolina; but the latter being the more populous, goes generally under the Denomination of Carolina." The term "South Carolina" appeared in a land grant as early as 1685, and in 1689 the term "North Carolina" occurred in Virginia records. Both turn up intermittently throughout the remainder of the proprietary period and probably were in common use. However, until 1719 the "official" term was "the southwest part of the province of Carolina." "From the History of the British Empire in America, by John Oldmixon, 1708," in Alexander S. Salley Jr., *Narratives of Early Carolina*, Original Narratives of Early American History, J. Franklin Jameson, gen. ed. (1911; New York: Barnes & Noble, 1967), 360. David Duncan Wallace, *The History of South Carolina*, 4 vols. (New York: American Historical Society, 1934), 1: 123–24. Powell, *North Carolina*, 75.

4. Wallace, *History of South Carolina*, 1: 360.

5. Philip M. Hamer, George C. Rogers Jr., C. James Taylor, and David R. Chesnutt, eds., and Peggy J. Clark, ed. asst., *The Papers of Henry Laurens*, 15 vols. (Columbia: University of South Carolina Press, 1972–1998), 3: 404n (hereinafter cited as Rogers et al., *Laurens Papers*). Wallace, *History of South Carolina*, 2: 47. *Journal* (Atlanta), 5 Sept. 1985. *Constitution* (Atlanta), 31 Mar. 1989. *State* (Columbia), 31 Mar. 1989, 8 Jan. 1990, 9 Jan. 1990, 26 June 1990, 11 July 1990.

6. Among Atlantic coastal rivers, the Santee's discharge is second only to the Susquehanna. Henry Savage Jr., *River of the Carolinas: The Santee*, Rivers of America Series, ed. Carl Carmer (New York: Rinehart & Company, 1956), 19. Charles F. Kovacik and John J. Winberry, *South Carolina: A Geography* (Boulder, Colo.: Westview Press, 1987), 23, 27. Suzanne Cameron Linder, "A River in Time: A Cultural Study of the Yadkin/Pee Dee River System to 1825," diss., University of South Carolina, 1993, pp. 8–11. Suzanne Cameron Linder, *Historical Atlas of the Rice Plantations of the ACE River Basin—1860* (Columbia: South Carolina Department of Archives and History, 1995), iii–iv, vii.

7. The coastal zone includes portions of Horry, Georgetown, Berkeley, Charleston, Dorchester, Colleton, Beaufort, and Jasper counties.

8. Stanley South, *The Discovery of Santa Elena*, Research Manuscript Series 165 (Columbia: Institute of Archaeology and Anthropology, University of South Carolina, 1980), 81.

9. William Hilton, "A Relation of a Discovery," in Salley, *Narratives of Early Carolina*, 44–45. Robert Sandford agreed with Hilton's description of the land as "rich fatt soyle." Robert Sandford, "A Relation of a Voyage on the Coast of the Province of Carolina," in Salley, *Narratives of Early Carolina*, 88.

10. John M. Barry, *Natural Vegetation of South Carolina* (Columbia: University of South Carolina Press, 1980), 175–90.

11. Mrs. A[ugusta] M[ansfield] French, *Slavery in South Carolina and the Ex-Slaves; or the Port Royal Mission* (New York: Winchell & French, 1862), 14. George Washington, *The Diaries of George Washington*, vol. 6, Jan. 1790–Dec. 1799, eds. Donald Jackson and Dorothy Twohig (Charlottesville: University Press of Virginia, 1979), 123. "Charleston, SC, in 1774 as Described by an English Traveller," in *The Colonial South Carolina Scene: Contemporary Views, 1697–1774*, edited by H. Roy Merrens (Columbia: University of South Carolina Press, 1977), 281, 287. *Agriculture, Geology, and Society in Antebellum South Carolina: The Private Diary of Edmund Ruffin, 1843*, edited by William M. Mathew (Athens: University of Georgia Press, 1992), 62, 63n, 69. Timothy Silver, *A New Face on the Countryside: Indians, Colonials and Slaves in South Atlantic Forests, 1500–1800* (New York: Cambridge University Press, 1990), 15–16.

12. The coastal plain includes all or part of twenty-six of the state's forty-six counties: Aiken, Allendale, Bamberg, Barnwell, Beaufort, Berkeley, Calhoun, Charleston, Clarendon, Colleton, Darlington, Dillon, Dorchester, Florence, Georgetown, Hampton, Horry, Jasper, Lee, Lexington, Marion, Marlboro, Orangeburg, Richland, Sumter, and Williamsburg.

13. Linder, "River in Time," 12.

14. Savage, *River of the Carolinas*, 29–30. Kovacik and Winberry, *South Carolina*, 21–22. Linder, "River in Time," 14.

15. Kovacik and Winberry, *South Carolina*, 32, 35, 41. A. S. Salley, *The History of Orangeburg County, South Carolina* (Orangeburg: R. Lewis Berry, 1898), 219.

16. Alexander Mackay, *The Western World; or, Travels in the United States in 1846–47* (1849; New York: Negro University Press, 1968), 199. Washington, *Diaries,* 6: 127, 145. Pelatiah Webster, "Journal of a Voiage from Philadelphia to Charlestown in So. Carolina, begun May 15, 1765," in Merrens, *Colonial South Carolina,* 221. Kovacik and Winberry, *South Carolina,* 45. Barry, *Natural Vegetation,* 158, passim. Silver, *New Face on the Countryside,* 179–80.

17. The sandhills includes all or portions of six counties: Aiken, Chesterfield, Kershaw, Lexington, Richland, and Sumter. There are other theories as to the origins of the sandhills, but the ancient seashore is the most widely accepted. Barry, *Natural Vegetation,* 97–98.

18. The piedmont contains all or portions of twenty-two counties: Abbeville, Anderson, Cherokee, Chester, Chesterfield, Edgefield, Fairfield, Greenville, Greenwood, Kershaw, Lancaster, Laurens, Lexington, McCormick, Newberry, Oconee, Pickens, Richland, Saluda, Spartanburg, Union, and York.

Kovacik and Winberry, *South Carolina,* 40. Writers' Program of the Work Projects Administration, *South Carolina: The WPA Guide to the Palmetto State,* with a new introduction by Walter B. Edgar (1941; Columbia: University of South Carolina Press, 1988), 8 (hereinafter cited as WPA, *South Carolina*).

19. Ben H. Robertson, *Red Hills and Cotton: An Upcountry Memory,* with a new introduction by Lacy K. Ford (1942; Columbia: University of South Carolina Press, 1991), 6. Barry, *Natural Vegetation,* 72. Silver, *New Face on the Countryside,* 179–80. Kovacik and Winberry, *South Carolina,* 43.

20. Barry, *Natural Vegetation,* 19, 23. Kovacik and Winberry, *South Carolina,* 32, 35, 42.

21. Granite was being quarried early in the nineteenth century. Gold was first mined in Lancaster County in 1829; phosphates for fertilizer along the coast by 1870; and tin in Cherokee County in 1937. Wallace, *History of South Carolina,* 1: 3–4; 3: 284–85. WPA, *South Carolina,* 11–14. Walter B. Edgar, "A Letter from South Carolina," *Journal of the Royal Society for the Encouragement of Arts Manufactures and Commerce,* 122 (1973–1974), 172.

22. See "Laudonnäire's Account of Ribaut's Settlement at Port Royal, 1562," in *South Carolina: A Documentary Profile of the Palmetto State,* edited by Elmer D. Johnson and Kathleen Lewis Sloan (Columbia: University of South Carolina Press, 1971), 7. See also: Hilton, "Relation of a Discovery," 44–45, 47–48; Sandford, "Relation of a Voyage," 88–91; and Thomas Ashe, "Carolina, or a Description of the Present State of that Country," in Salley, *Narratives of Early Carolina,* 141–56.

23. Stewart L. Udall, *The Quiet Crisis* (New York: Holt, Rinehart & Winston, 1963), 55. Trees were not the only source of amazement, for "in Carolina there are found far more plant species than in all of Europe, and more than in any other comparable area of America." Savage, *River of the Carolinas,* 29.

24. Samuel Wilson, "An Account of the Province of Carolina," in Salley, *Narratives of Early Carolina,* 170.

25. Hilton, "Relation of a Discovery," 44, 47. Robert Horne, "A Brief Description of the Province of Carolina," in Salley, *Narratives of Early Carolina,* 68.

26. Ashe, "Carolina," 150. Silver, *New Face on the Countryside,* 26, 100. Hilton, "Relation of a Discovery," 44. Horne, "Brief Description," 68–69. Ashe, "Carolina," 150–51. Wilson, "Account," 171. WPA, *South Carolina,* 16–17. Alexander Sprunt Jr. and E. Burnham Chamberlain, *South Carolina Bird Life,* rev. ed. (Columbia: University of South Carolina Press, 1970), 1, 292–94.

27. Ashe, "Carolina," 152. Hilton, "Relation of a Discovery," 45. Horne, "Brief Description," 69. Ashe, "Carolina," 152. Wilson, "Account," 171. Captain Martin, "A Description of Charles Town, in 1769," South Caroliniana Library, University of South Carolina, Columbia (hereinafter referred to as SCL).

28. WPA, *South Carolina,* 17–18. Ashe, "Carolina," 152–53. During the Spanish occupation of Santa Elena, a soldier hooked a "large fish" that pulled him into the water and he drowned. South, *Discovery of Santa Elena,* 21. Sprunt and Chamberlain, *South Carolina Bird Life,* 1. Silver, *New Face on the Countryside,* 30–31, 149. Horne, "Brief Description," 68. Ashe, "Carolina," 151.

29. John Archdale, "A New Description of that Fertile and Pleasant Province of Carolina, 1707," in Salley, *Narratives of Early Carolina,* 295.

30. Other monthly average temperatures in degrees Fahrenheit for the state are as follows: February (47°), March (54°), April (63°), May (71°), June (77°), July (80°), August (80°), September (74°), October (63°), November (54°), December (47°). The extreme records for the state are 19° below zero and 111°.

On 5 February 1899 the high was 78°; one week later the high was 16°. On 19 January 1996 a high of 70° Fahrenheit was recorded; the next day the high was 42°. Weather statistics supplied by Wes Tyler, assistant state climatologist, South Carolina Department of Natural Resources.

James Glen, "A Description of South Carolina," in *Colonial South Carolina: Two Contemporary Descriptions*, edited by Chapman J. Milling (Columbia: University of South Carolina Press, 1951), 11. Martin, "Description of Charles Town." Ashe, "Carolina," 141.

31. David M. Ludlum, *Early American Hurricanes, 1492–1870* (Boston: American Meteorological Society, 1963), 44–47. Kovacik and Winberry, *South Carolina*, 38–39.

32. Archdale, "New Description," 290. William H. McNeill, *Plagues and Peoples* (New York: Anchor Press, 1976), 199ff. Silver, *New Face on the Countryside*, 74–76, 156–58, 161–63. Tom Hatley, *The Dividing Paths: Cherokees and South Carolinians Through the Era of Revolution* (New York: Oxford University Press, 1993), 3–8, 16. Joseph I. Waring, M.D., *A History of Medicine in South Carolina, 1670–1825* (Columbia: South Carolina Medical Association, 1964), 18.

"Chicora" was the name that early Spanish explorers gave to the coast of what is now South Carolina. The word may be a derivation of the Catawba term *Yuchi-kerÇ*, which means "Yuchi are there" or "Yuchi over there," references to the location of a coastal tribe, the Yuchi. James Mooney, *The Siouan Tribes of the East* (1894; reprint, St. Clair Shores, Mich.: Scholarly Press, 1970), 86.

33. Kovacik and Winberry, *South Carolina*, 52–54. Lawrence S. Rowland, Alexander Moore, and George C. Rogers Jr., *The History of Beaufort County, South Carolina, Volume 1, 1514–1861* (Columbia: University of South Carolina Press, 1996), 7 (hereinafter cited as Rowland et al., *Beaufort County*).

34. Kovacik and Winberry, *South Carolina*, 54–56.

35. Kovacik and Winberry, *South Carolina*, 53–56, 57. Rowland et al., *Beaufort County*, 8–9.

36. Kovacik and Winberry, *South Carolina*, 54–56. Rowland et al., *Beaufort County*, 8–9.

37. Kovacik and Winberry, *South Carolina*, 56.

38. Kovacik and Winberry, *South Carolina*, 56–59. James H. Merrell, *The Indians' New World: Catawbas and Their Neighbors from European Contact through the Era of Removal*, published for the Institute of Early American History and Culture, Williamsburg, Va. (Chapel Hill: University of North Carolina Press, 1989), 10–18.

39. Rowland et al., *Beaufort County*, 9–11. Kovacik and Winberry, *South Carolina*, 56–59. Linder, "River in Time," 22.

40. Chapman J. Milling, *Red Carolinians*, 2d. ed. (Columbia: University of South Carolina Press, 1969), 232, passim. Kovacik and Winberry, *South Carolina*, 60. Mooney, *Siouan Tribes of the East*, 82–86. Charles M. Hudson, *The Catawba Nation* (Athens: University of Georgia Press, 1970), 8–17, 23, 28. Charles M. Hudson, ed., *Four Centuries of Southern Indians* (Athens: University of Georgia Press, 1975), 3–4. Gene Waddell, *Indians of the South Carolina Lowcountry, 1562–1751* (Columbia: Southern Studies Program, University of South Carolina, 1980), 16–22. Leland Ferguson, "First Carolinians," *South Carolina Wildlife*, 21:5 (1974): 23.

41. Some questions have been raised about the Catawbas being Siouan because, in the mid eighteenth century, twenty different dialects and languages were spoken in the Catawba nation. Hudson, *Catawba Nation*, 28. Waddell, *Indians of the Lowcountry*, 23–33. James H. Merrell, *The Catawbas*, Indians of North America Series, ed. Frank W. Porter III (New York: Chelsea House, 1989), 22–23. Charles M. Hudson, *The Southeastern Indians*, (Knoxville: University of Tennessee Press, 1976), 23–24.

42. For a listing of the traditional classification of the Indian nations of South Carolina, see Wallace, *History of South Carolina*, 1: 24–25.

Waddell, *Indians of the Lowcountry*, 4. Russell Thornton, *The Cherokees: A Population History* (Lincoln & London: University of Nebraska Press, 1990), 7–8. Theda Perdue, *The Cherokee*, Indians of North America Series, ed. Frank W. Porter III (New York: Chelsea House, 1989), 13. Theda Perdue, "Red and Black in the Southern Appalachians," *Southern Exposure*, 12 (1984): 17. Mooney, *Siouan Tribes of the East*, 83. Waddell, *Indians of the Lowcountry*, 369. Milling, *Red Carolinians*, 213.

43. Silver, *New Face on the Countryside*, 71. The exact location of San Miguel has not been ascertained; however, at least two sites have been suggested: Winyah Bay and near the mouth of the Savannah River. Lawrence S. Rowland, *Window on the Atlantic: The Rise and Fall of Santa Elena, South Caro-

lina's Spanish City (Columbia: South Carolina Department of Archives and History, 1990), 4. Linder, "River in Time," 30–31. Rowland et al., *Beaufort County,* 18.

There is some disagreement on the so-called Cussabo Confederacy. However, Gene Waddell makes a convincing argument that it did not exist. Hudson, *Catawba Nation,* 23. Waddell, *Indians of the Lowcountry,* xiii, 15–22.

Kovacik and Winberry, *South Carolina,* 60. Waddell, *Indians of the Lowcountry,* 15. Wallace, *History of South Carolina,* 1: 202. Silver, *New Face on the Countryside,* 39n. Peter H. Wood, "The Changing Population of the Colonial South: An Overview by Race and Region, 1685–1790," in *Powhatan's Mantle: Indians in the Colonial Southeast,* edited by Peter H. Wood, Gregory A. Waselkov, and M. Thomas Hatley (Lincoln: University of Nebraska Press, 1989), 61–65. Merrell, *Indians' New World,* 18–21.

44. Charles M. Hudson, "The Catawba Indians of South Carolina: A Question of Ethnic Survival," in Walter L. Williams, *Southeastern Indians Since the Removal Era* (Athens: University of Georgia Press, 1979), 120. Hudson, *Catawba Nation,* 11, 26–29. Mooney, *Siouan Tribes of the East,* 60. Merrell, *Catawbas,* 25–26, 37, 52–53. Merrell, *Indians' New World,* 112–22.

45. Merrell, *Indians' New World,* 92–143.

46. Hudson, *Catawba Nation,* 13–14, 28. Thornton, *Cherokees,* 9–10. John Phillip Reid, "The Cherokee Thought: An Apparatus of Primitive Law," in *Ethnology of the Southeastern Indians: A Source Book,* edited by Charles M. Hudson (New York: Garland Publishing, Inc., 1985), 285–87, 292. Perdue, *Cherokee,* 13, 21–25, 27, 49–50. Hatley, *Dividing Paths,* 6.

47. Hudson, *Catawba Nation,* 8, 9, 15. Waddell, *Indians of the Lowcountry,* 25–26, 75. Hudson, *Four Centuries of Southern Indians,* 3.

48. Silver, *New Face on the Countryside,* 39–42. Waddell, *Indians of the Lowcountry,* 65–57.

49. James Mooney, *Myths of the Cherokee* (1900; New York: Johnson Reprint Corporation, 1970), 240–42.

50. Quotation from Mark Catesby, *The Natural History of Carolina, Florida, and the Bahama Islands,* in Waddell, *Indians of the Lowcountry,* 42. Silver, *New Face on the Countryside,* 59–64. Waddell, *Indians of the Lowcountry,* 36–43, 46, 56, 65. John Witthoft, "Green Corn Ceremonialism," in Hudson, *Ethnology of the Southeastern Indians,* 58–61. Mooney, *Siouan Tribes of the East,* 75.

For a contemporary description of a perpetual fire, see Sandford, "Relation of a Voyage," 91.

51. Hudson, *Catawba Nation,* 20. Sandford, "Relation of a Voyage," 101. Waddell, *Indians of the Lowcountry,* 46–49, 431. Hatley, *Dividing Paths,* 13. Silver, *New Face on the Countryside,* 50.

52. Sandford, "Relation of a Voyage," 91. Mooney, *Siouan Tribes of the East,* 63, 75. Silver, *New Face on the Countryside,* 50, 56–57. Waddell, *Indians of the Lowcountry,* 44–49. Milling, *Red Carolinians,* 12–13. Merrell, *Indians' New World,* 125.

53. Thornton, *Cherokees,* 24. Wallace, *History of South Carolina* 1: 202. Waddell, *Indians of the Lowcountry,* 46–47.

54. Milling, *Red Carolinians,* 31–32. Waddell, *Indians of the Lowcountry,* 72–74. Hatley, *Dividing Paths,* 58–59.

55. Milling, *Red Carolinians,* 10–11, 207. Waddell, *Indians of the Lowcountry,* 43–44. "Letters of Early Colonists, 1670," Salley, *Narratives of Early Carolina,* 117. Merrell, *Indians' New World,* 125–26.

56. Silver, *New Face on the Countryside,* 41, 44–45. Waddell, *Indians of the Lowcountry,* 37–42, 75. Milling, *Red Carolinians,* 14–17. Hatley, *Dividing Paths,* 8–9.

57. Hudson, *Catawba Nation,* 21. Waddell, *Indians of the Lowcountry,* 38–40. Silver, *New Face on the Countryside,* 44–46, 52–53. Merrell, *Indians' New World,* 126–33.

58. Quotation from John Lawson, "A Description of North Carolina [1709]," in Waddell, *Indians of the Lowcountry,* 7. Mooney, *Siouan Tribes of the East,* 68, 71, 74–75.

The Iroquois Confederacy labeled the Catawba "Flat Heads," but there is no evidence that they or any other nation in the Catawba Confederacy, other than the Waxhaw, pursued the practice. Hudson, *Catawba Nation,* 26–27. Mooney, *Myths of the Cherokee,* 397–99.

59. Witthoft, "Green Corn Ceremonialism," 42–44, 50. Perdue, *Cherokee,* 22, 28–29. Waddell, *Indians of the Lowcountry,* 65, 68–72.

60. Rowland, *Window on the Atlantic,* 5–6. Mooney, *Siouan Tribes of the East,* 80. "The Narrative of the Expedition of Hernando De Soto, by the Gentleman of Elvas" in *Spanish Explorers in the Southern United States, 1528–1543* edited by Frederick W. Hodge and Theodore H. Lewis (1907; New York: Barnes & Noble, 1967), 172–74, 176–78, 180, 188, 224, 270–71. Perdue, "Red and Black," 17–18. Reid, "Cherokee Thought," 288–89. Waddell, *Indians of the Lowcountry,* 59, 75. Milling, *Red Carolinians,* 59. Hudson, *Southeastern Indians,* 204–5. Hatley, *Dividing Paths,* 8, 54–58, 148–52. Merrell, *Indians' New World,* 110.

61. Waddell, *Indians of the Lowcountry,* 58–60. Perdue, *Cherokee,* 16–17, 21–25. Reid, "Cherokee Thought," 287–89, 298–300. Hatley, *Dividing Paths,* 10–13.

Apparently the chieftain of the Santee had absolute authority, including that of life or death over the members of his nation. Mooney, *Siouan Tribes of the East,* 79. Merrell, *Catawbas,* 26–33, 46–47.

62. Hudson, *Catawba Nation,* 22. Merrell, *The Catawbas,* 46–47, 52–53. Waddell, *Indians of the Lowcountry,* 60–65, 386–87. Ferguson, "First Carolinians," 24.

CHAPTER 2: SPANISH SOUTH CAROLINA

1. Chicora's description of "lizard" people was similar to the twentieth-century one given for the "Lizardman" of Lee County: "It was green wetlike about seven feet tall and had three fingers, red eyes, skin like a lizard, [and] snakelike scales." *State* (Columbia), 19 July 1988.

Goncalo Fernández de Oviedo, *Natural History of the West Indies,* and Pietro Martiere d'Anghiera, *The Eight Decades of Peter Martyr.* Rowland, *Window on the Atlantic,* 3. Paul E. Hoffman, *The New Andalucia and a Way to the Orient: The American Southeast During the Sixteenth Century* (Baton Rouge: Louisiana State University Press, 1990), 34–39. Rowland et al., *Beaufort County,* 16–17.

During the sixteenth century "Florida" referred to the peninsula and "La Florida" to all of the Southeast. Hoffman, *New Andalucia,* xi.

2. There is disagreement over the location of San Miguel de Gualdape. Traditionally it has been sited on Winyah Bay. Some archaeologists, however, believe that it was on the Sapelo River in Georgia. Hoffman, *New Andalucia,* 67–71. Because of the recent determination of the site of Cofitachequi, it appears fairly certain that San Miguel de Gualdape would have to be located in South Carolina. Interview with Chester B. DePratter, 13 June 1996.

3. Rowland et al., *Beaufort County,* 18–19.

4. The traditional route of the Soto expedition located Cofitachiqui at Silver Bluff on the Savannah River. From there Soto traveled northwest into the Blue Ridge Mountains. A reexamination of the documentary evidence revealed a new route, the one described here. Charles M. Hudson, Marvin T. Smith, and Chester B. DePratter, "The Hernando DeSoto Expedition: From Apalachee to Chiaha," *Southeastern Archeology,* 3:1 (1984): 71–74.

5. *Narrative of the Expedition of Hernando De Soto,* 176. Hudson et al., "Hernando DeSoto Expedition," 71–74.

6. Silver, *New Face on the Countryside,* 39, 71. Wood, "Changing Population of the Colonial South," 61–65. Rowland, *Window on the Atlantic,* 5–6.

7. Eugene Lyon, *The Enterprise of Florida: Pedro Menéndez de Avilés and the Spanish Conquest of 1565–1568* (Gainesville: University Presses of Florida, 1976), 43, 61. Hoffman, *New Andalucia,* 119, 121, 208, 234.

8. Hoffman, *New Andalucia,* 169–71.

9. Rowland, *Window on the Atlantic,* 8.

10. Until 1996 the exact location of Charlesfort was a matter of controversy. Although there is a twentieth-century stone marker on Parris Island, most historians and archaeologists thought that the French fort had been built somewhere else. The recent identification of sixteenth-century French artifacts on Parris Island confirmed the exact location of Charlesfort. Chester B. DePratter and Stanley South, with a contribution by Bruce F. Thompson, *Charlesfort: The 1989 Search Project* (Columbia: University of South Carolina Institute for Archaeology and Anthropology, 1990). "USC Archaeologists Uncover Early French Fort off S.C. Coast," Office of Marketing and Media Relations, University of South Carolina, 6 June 1996. "A French Fort, Long Lost, Is Found in South Carolina," *New York Times,* 6 June 1996, A1.

Rowland, *Window on the Atlantic,* 8. There have been varying interpretations of the fort's dimensions, most of them smaller. Wallace, *History of South Carolina,* 1: 36. However, the larger dimensions are now those generally used. Interview with Chester B. DePratter, Columbia, S.C., 13 June 1996.

Although the exact location of the column is not known, most historians believe it was Dawes Island, although Lemon Island has sometimes been suggested. Wallace, *History of South Carolina,* 1: 36. Rowland, *Window on the Atlantic,* 8.

11. Eugene Lyon, *Santa Elena: A Brief History of the Colony, 1566–1587* (Columbia: University of South Carolina Institute of Archaeology and Anthropology, 1984), 1. Rowland, *Window on the Atlantic,* 12–13. Hoffman, *New Andalucia,* 226. Rowland et al., *Beaufort County,* 22–28.

12. Rowland, *Window on the Atlantic,* 16–17. Lyon, *Santa Elena,* 2. Rowland et al., *Beaufort County,* 29–31.

13. Even after Pardo's explorations revealed that Mexico was much further away, Menéndez only revised his distances to place the mines at 500 leagues (about 1,725 miles) beyond the mountains. Lyon, *Santa Elena,* 1, 3.

Rowland, *Window on the Atlantic,* 17–19. Rowland et al., *Beaufort County,* 31–33. For a detailed account of Pardo's expeditions and the building of the forts, see Charles Hudson, *The Juan Pardo Expeditions: Explorations of the Carolinas and Tennessee, 1566–1568* (Washington, D.C.: Smithsonian Institution Press, 1990), 23–50, 146–52.

Although there are several different measurements for a Spanish league, the 3.45 miles per league is one that is most often used. Interview with Chester DePratter, Columbia, S.C., 28 Aug. 1997.

14. Lyon, *Santa Elena,* 3–6, 16.

15. Lyon, *Santa Elena,* 4, 7. Among the furnishings listed for the church was a gilt image of Santa Clara.

16. Jeanette Thurber Connor, ed., *Colonial Records of Spanish Florida,* 2 vols. (Deland: Florida State Historical Society, 1925, 1930), 1: 85, 147–61. Lyon, *Santa Elena,* 2, 7, 10. Hoffman, *New Andalucia,* 231, 267.

17. Las Alvas's leadership ability was also questioned in an inquiry in Madrid. Connor, *Colonial Records of Spanish Florida,* 1: 293–321.

18. The Guale nation was located south of the Savannah River on the present-day Georgia coast. Rowland, *Window on the Atlantic,* 21–22.

19. Lyon, *Santa Elena,* 11.

20. Connor, *Colonial Records of Spanish Florida,* 1: 253. Rowland et al., *Beaufort County,* 37–39.

21. Rowland et al., *Beaufort County,* 40–43.

22. Lyon, *Santa Elena,* 11. Rowland, *Window on the Atlantic,* 22–23. Connor, *Colonial Records of Spanish Florida,* 2: 87, 273.

23. When Marqués Menéndez tried to find the survivors of the first settlement in Cuba, he reported that most had "passed on to New Spain or other parts." He found only four households, consisting of "four old and useless men burdened with daughters." Therefore, he opted to leave them alone. Connor, *Colonial Records of Spanish Florida,* 1: 205, 259. Thus, it appears that most of the colonists in the second Santa Elena were new settlers.

Lyon, *Santa Elena,* 12.

24. One of the substantial dwellings measured 18 by 20 feet. The huts measured 12 feet across. South, *Discovery of Santa Elena,* 9–13, 44. Stanley South, *Archeology at Santa Elena: Doorway to the Past* (Columbia: South Carolina Institute of Archeology and Anthropology, 1991), 21–22. Chester B. DePratter and Stanley South, with contributions by James B. Legg, Dennis G. Graham Jr., and Lisa R. Hudgins, *Discovery at Santa Elena: Boundary Survey* (Columbia: South Carolina Institute of Archeology and Anthropology, 1995), 88. Interview with Stanley South, Chester B. DePratter, and James B. Legg, Columbia, S.C., 13 June 1996.

In 1578 an inspector noted that the soldiers suffered "great discomfort" because of the lack of adequate housing. To remedy the situation, he recommended that Fort San Marcos be expanded. Connor, *Colonial Records of Spanish Florida,* 2: 187.

25. South, *Discovery of Santa Elena,* 21–39. "Inventory of the kiln at Santa Elena" (unpub. ms., South Carolina Institute of Archeology and Anthropology, Columbia, S.C.).

26. Interview with DePratter, 13 June 1996. There were a total of nineteen to twenty individuals in

the four households that Pedro Menéndez found in Cuba. Martin Diez, a farmer and former colonist, testified in Madrid that he had lived in Santa Elena with his wife and children. Soldiers as well as farmers brought their families to the colony. Connor, *Colonial Records of Spanish Florida*, 1: 83, 93, 163–69, 181–87, 259.

27. Lyon, *Santa Elena*, 13. Hoffman, *New Andalucia*, 267.

28. Lyon, *Santa Elena*, 15–16. Hoffman, *New Andalucia*, 205. Rowland et al., *Beaufort County*, 44–46.

29. Lyon, *Santa Elena*, 16. Rowland et al., *Beaufort County*, 44–46.

30. "When Sir Francis Drake burned St. Augustine in 1586, the weakened Spaniards were forced late in 1587 to draw in their garrison at Port Royal. The first blow had been struck by the rugged people who by the same rough means were in the generations following to wrest from Spain all her vast possessions north of the Rio Grande." Wallace, *History of South Carolina*, 1: 54.

CHAPTER 3: THE COLONY OF A COLONY

1. Powell, *North Carolina*, 46–52. Robert M. Weir, *Colonial South Carolina: A History* (Millwood, N.Y.: KTO Press, 1983), 46–47.

2. Jack P. Greene, "Colonial South Carolina and the Caribbean Connection," *South Carolina Historical Magazine*, 88 (1987): 192–210.

3. Neighboring North Carolina sprang primarily from the Chesapeake cultural model, although its Cape Fear region was really a cultural extension of South Carolina. So, too, were the colonies of Georgia and East and West Florida. Greene, "Colonial South Carolina and the Caribbean Connection," 192–93.

4. In 1559 France and Spain established the line. In the seventeenth century England joined in the contest for empire in the Caribbean and signed treaties that made her a party to the concept of the line. Richard S. Dunn, *Sugar and Slaves: The Rise of the Planter Class in the English West Indies, 1624–1713* (New York: W. W. Norton, 1973), 11–12. Carl Bridenbaugh and Roberta Bridenbaugh, *No Peace Beyond the Line: The English in the Caribbean, 1624–1690* (New York: Oxford University Press, 1972), 3–5, 35, 139–42, 393–95.

5. Dunn, *Sugar and Slaves*, 50–57, 68–72, 87–89, 226–29. Gary A. Puckrein, *Little England: Plantation Society and Anglo-Barbadian Politics, 1627–1700* (New York: New York University Press, 1984), 31–32, 40.

Similarly, in Virginia a white indentured servant in the seventeenth century "became for a number of years a thing, a commodity with a price." Edmund S. Morgan, *American Slavery American Freedom: The Ordeal of Colonial Virginia* (New York: W. W. Norton, 1975), 123–30.

6. Dunn, *Sugar and Slaves*, 59–74. Puckrein, *Little England*, 56–61. Bridenbaugh and Bridenbaugh, *No Peace Beyond the Line*, 69–100.

7. Puckrein, *Little England*, 11. Dunn, *Sugar and Slaves*, 84, 334. Bridenbaugh and Bridenbaugh, *No Peace Beyond the Line*, 3–4.

8. Dunn, *Sugar and Slaves*, 71–74, 83, 225. Puckrein, *Little England*, 30–32, 70–71. However, as Dunn points out, race would later be used to defend the institution.

9. The total population in 1638 was six thousand; in 1652 it was thirty-eight thousand. Puckrein, *Little England*, 31–32, 71–72.

The 1661 slave code of Barbados was later amended several times. The code was copied by Jamaica (1664), South Carolina (1696), and Antigua (1702). Dunn, *Sugar and Slaves*, 239.

10. Puckrein, *Little England*, 23.

11. Antoine Biât, *Voyage de la France Çquinoxiale en l'isle de Cayenne entrepois pas les franáais en l'annÇe MDCLII* quoted in Bridenbaugh and Bridenbaugh, *No Peace Beyond the Line*, 35. The population ratios in Barbados would increase, and in other English islands it would be as high as eleven, twelve, and fifteen to one. Greene, "Colonial South Carolina and the Caribbean Connection," 203. Interestingly, in 1860 South Carolina would have the same 60–40 black-white ratio as Barbados in 1670.

Greene, "Colonial South Carolina and the Caribbean Connection," 195. Bridenbaugh and Bridenbaugh, *No Peace Beyond the Line*, 129–64.

12. Puckrein, *Little England*, xvi.

13. The account of the obtaining of the Carolina charter is taken from: Weir, *Colonial South Carolina,* 47–53; M. Eugene Sirmans, *Colonial South Carolina: A Political History, 1663–1763* (Chapel Hill: Published for the Institute of Early American History and Culture, Williamsburg, Va., by the University of North Carolina Press, 1966), 3–16. Powell, *North Carolina,* 47–53.

14. "The second charter granted by King Charles II to the proprietors of Carolina" and "Fundamental Constitutions," in *Historical Collections of South Carolina; Embracing Many Rare and Valuable Pamphlets and Other Documents, Relating to the History of That State, From its First Discovery to its Independence in the Year 1776,* edited by B. R. Carroll, 2 vols. (New York: Harper & Brothers, 1836), 2: 41–42, 387. Sirmans, *Colonial South Carolina,* 6.

15. The account of the early attempts at settlement in North Carolina are from Powell, *North Carolina,* 51–60.

16. Sandford, "Relation of a Voyage," 77–84, 108. Powell, *North Carolina,* 56–57. Weir, *Colonial South Carolina,* 50–51.

17. A. S. Salley Jr., ed., *Records in the British Public Record Office Relating to South Carolina, 1663–1684,* Historical Commission of South Carolina (Atlanta: Foote & Davies Company, 1928), 6–10 (hereinafter referred to as *BPRO*).

The 1663 charter had boundaries of all lands from the 31° to the 36° parallel between the Atlantic and the Pacific. The 1665 charter had boundaries of 35°30' and 29°.

18. Weir, *Colonial South Carolina,* 47–53. Sirmans, *Colonial South Carolina,* 3–16.

19. John Alexander Moore, "Royalizing South Carolina: The Revolution of 1719 and the Evolution of Early South Carolina Government," diss., University of South Carolina, 1991, 74–82. Sirmans, *Colonial South Carolina,* 7. Weir, *Colonial South Carolina,* 53.

20. Using conversion formulas and tables devised by John J. McCusker in "How Much Is That in Real Money? A Historical Price Index for Use as a Deflator of Money Values in the Economy of the United States," *Proceedings of the American Antiquarian Society,* 101, pt. 2 (Oct. 1991): 297–373, it is possible to convert pounds sterling, colonial currencies, and earlier dollars into 1991 dollars. McCusker's tables, based upon a historical price index, stop in 1991. Between 1991 and December 1996 there has been an 11.5 percent inflation factor in the consumer price index. *Economic Report of the President Transmitted to the Congress, February 1997* (Washington, D.C.: Government Printing Office, 1997), 365. To account for that inflation, all figures resulting from McCusker's formulas and tables have been increased 11.5 percent.

All monetary figures in this history, with the exception of those in direct quotations, will be given in contemporary values, e.g., pounds sterling (£75 sterling), colonial currency (£75), or dollars ($75). They will be followed by the amount in 1996 dollars in parentheses, e.g., £75 sterling ($4,600). With the exception of commodity prices and wages, all figures will be rounded off. When the original figures are carried out to dollars and cents, the converted figures will be too, e.g., $61,342 ($173,278).

Monetary conversions, as McCusker notes, should be considered as "hypothetical rather than as definitive." The purpose of using contemporary dollars, based upon price indexes, is to provide contemporary readers with an approximate idea of what an item or service might have cost in 1690 or 1810 or 1920. Peter Coclanis suggested the use of McCusker's tables as the most reliable way to convert earlier monetary values into contemporary dollars. Conversation with Peter Coclanis, Chapel Hill, N.C., 30 June 1997.

21. Barbara Arneil, *John Locke and America: The Defence of English Colonialism* (New York: Oxford University Press, 1996), 118–31. Salley, *Records . . . Relating to South Carolina,* 5.

22. Arneil, *John Locke and America,* 88–91. Sirmans, *Colonial South Carolina,* 9. Weir, *Colonial South Carolina,* 54.

23. McCrady, *Proprietary South Carolina,* 109. Wallace, *History of South Carolina,* 1: 63. Weir, *Colonial South Carolina,* 10, 54.

The revised versions of the Fundamental Constitutions were approved by the Lords Proprietors on 1 Mar. 1670, 12 Jan. 1682, 17 Aug. 1682, and 11 Apr. 1698. Even though adopted by the proprietors, under the charter the Fundamental Constitutions had to be ratified by the freemen of the province. That never occurred. The first draft had 120 articles. Subsequent revisions had as many as 125 and as few as 41.

Ashley, to Maurice Mathews, 20 June 1672, in *The Shaftsbury Papers and Other Records Relating to the Carolina . . . prior to the Year 1676,* edited by Langdon Cheves, in *South Carolina Historical Society Collections,* 5 (1897): 399.

24. Weir, *Colonial South Carolina,* 54.

25. Articles xcv, xcvi, cix, cxviii. Fundamental Constitutions, Carroll, *Historical Collections of South Carolina,* 2: 384, 387, 389. Sirmans, *Colonial South Carolina,* 15.

26. Robert K. Ackerman, *South Carolina Colonial Land Policies,* Tricentennial Studies Number 9 (Columbia: University of South Carolina Press, 1977), 24. Articles xvii, xxvi, "Fundamental Constitutions," 2: 367, 368. Dunn, *Sugar and Slaves,* 67. Puckrein, *Little England,* 65–67.

27. Weir, *Colonial South Carolina,* 54–55.

28. Sirmans, *Colonial South Carolina,* 15–16.

29. Sirmans, *Colonial South Carolina,* 10–12. Weir, *Colonial South Carolina,* 55.

In 1692, when elections were called for the first Commons House of Assembly, there were four counties: Colleton (between the Stono and Combahee Rivers), Berkeley (from the Stono River to Seewee Bay), Craven (from Seewee Bay to the Roanoke River in North Carolina), and Albemarle (from the Roanoke River to the southern boundary of Virginia). Later in South Carolina, Craven County's boundary stopped at the southern boundary of North Carolina and a fourth county, Granville, was created for the territory south of the Combahee River to the Savannah.

30. Sirmans, *Colonial South Carolina,* 13.

The idea of votes by order, or required agreement among various interests within the colony, is remarkably similar to the ideas behind South Carolina's "Great Compromise of 1808" and John C. Calhoun's theory of the concurrent majority. Weir, *Colonial South Carolina,* 72.

31. Article LXXX. There were other negative references to the legal profession. See also article LXX. "Fundamental Constitutions," 2: 379, 382. Weir, *Colonial South Carolina,* 54–57.

32. Preamble, "Fundamental Constitutions," 2: 362. Sirmans, *Colonial South Carolina,* 15. Weir, *Colonial South Carolina,* 54–55.

33. Ashley, to Maurice Mathews, 20 June 1672, 5: 399.

CHAPTER 4: PEOPLING THE PROVINCE

1. Joseph I. Waring, *The First Voyage and Settlement at Charles Town, 1670–1680,* Tricentennial Booklet Number 4 (Columbia: University of South Carolina Press, 1970), 22–25.

2. Greene, "Colonial South Carolina and the Caribbean Connection," 197. Michael Craton and Gail Saunders, *Islanders in the Stream: A History of the Bahamian People* (Athens: University of Georgia Press, 1992), 69–80, 89–100. Moore, "Royalizing South Carolina," 73–86. Rowland et al., *Beaufort County,* 63–65.

Some recent scholars have tried to minimize the Barbadian connection with South Carolina and base their arguments primarily on the lack of surviving documentation in Barbados. Frankly, that is a weak reed upon which to base a case. See Kinloch Bull, "Barbadian Settlers in Early Carolina: Historiographical Notes," *SCHM,* 96 (Oct. 1995): 327–39. What is ironic is that Bull, who digs through others' references for proof positive, has himself relied on "family legend." Kinloch Bull Jr., *The Oligarchs in Colonial and Revolutionary South Charleston: Lieutenant Governor William Bull II and His Family* (Columbia: University of South Carolina Press, 1991), 241.

What is important is that seventeenth- and early-eighteenth-century Carolinians characterized themselves and others as "Barbadians." Perceptions and actions speak volumes.

3. Agnes Leland Baldwin, *First Settlers of South Carolina,* Tricentennial Booklet Number 1 (Columbia: University of South Carolina Press, 1969). McCrady, *Proprietary South Carolina,* 327n, 328n. Richard Waterhouse, *A New World Gentry: The Making of a Merchant and Planter Class in South Carolina, 1670–1770* (New York: Garland, 1989), 15–16. George C. Rogers Jr., *Charleston in the Age of the Pinckneys* (Norman: University of Oklahoma Press, 1969), 4–5.

From the other English islands came Sayle and Norwood of Bermuda and Trott of the Bahamas.

4. Commissary Gideon Johnston described early-eighteenth-century South Carolina society in a less than flattering light but in a fashion that clearly indicates that some of the less admirable traits of Barba-

dian culture had taken root here. Commissary Francis LeJau noted that "Mamon has hitherto got too many Worshippers." Quoted in Peter H. Wood, *Black Majority: Negroes in Colonial South Carolina from 1670 through the Stono Rebellion* (New York: Alfred A. Knopf, 1974), 133n, 134n.

Waterhouse, *New World Gentry,* 6–13. A big planter owned more than 60 slaves and a middling planter 20–59. There were 175 big planters and 190 middling planters. Dunn, *Sugar and Slaves,* 91. Thus, representatives of 10 percent of the largest slaveholding families and 17 percent of the next rank obtained grants in South Carolina.

5. Meghan N. Duff, "Imbibing Information at the Carolina Coffee House: Emigration and the Dynamics of Promotion of a Proprietary Colony" (International Seminar on the History of the Atlantic World, 1500–1800, Harvard University: Working Paper No. 96-18), 1, 3–5, 10–13, 23. Bertrand Van Ruymbeke, "A 'Best Poor Huguenot's Country'?: The Carolina Proprietors and the Recruitment of French Protestants" (International Seminar on the History of the Atlantic World, 1500–1800, Harvard University: Working Paper No. 96-20), 2, 6–11.

6. South Carolina's Jewish population lived primarily in Charleston. In 1790 there were probably 225–250 Jews in the city and 600 by 1800, which meant that it had a larger Jewish population than any other American city. That was still true in 1820. James William Hagy, *This Happy Land: The Jews of Colonial and Antebellum Charleston* (Tuscaloosa: University of Alabama Press, 1993), 14–16.

7. Quoted in David Ramsay, *History of South Carolina, From its First Settlement in 1670 to the Year 1808* (1809; 2 vols. in 1, Newberry, S.C.: W. J. Duffie, 1858), 1: 3n–4n.

8. Jon Butler, *The Huguenots in America: A Refugee People in a New World Society* (Cambridge, Mass.: Harvard University Press, 1983), 91–143. Arthur Henry Hirsch, *The Huguenots of Colonial South Carolina* (1928; Hamden, Conn.: Archon Books, 1962), 90–102. Amy E. Friedlander, "Carolina Huguenots: A Study in Colonial Pluralism," diss., Emory University, 1979, 292–321. Wallace, *History of South Carolina,* 1: 155.

9. McCrady, *Proprietary South Carolina,* 319. This list is only a sampling of Huguenot names. For others, see: Hirsch, *Huguenots,* passim; Friedlander, "Carolina Huguenots," 322–27; and the *Transactions of the Huguenot Society of South Carolina.*

10. Alexander Hewatt, "An Historical Account of the Rise and Progress of the Colonies of South Carolina and Georgia," in Carroll, *Historical Collections of South Carolina,* 1: 102–3. Wallace, *History of South Carolina,* 1: 124–25.

11. Walter B. Edgar, ed., *Biographical Directory of the South Carolina House of Representatives: Volume I: Sessions Lists, 1692–1973* (Columbia: University of South Carolina Press, 1974), 21–23. Walter B. Edgar and N. Louise Bailey, *Biographical Directory of the South Carolina House of Representatives: Volume II: The Commons House of Assembly, 1692–1775* (Columbia: University of South Carolina Press, 1977), 401–2.

12. Thomas Cooper and David J. McCord, *The Statutes at Large of South Carolina [1682–1838],* 10 vols. (Columbia: A. S. Johnston, 1838–1841), 2: 131.

13. Chapman J. Milling, *Exile Without an End* (Columbia: Bostick & Thornley, 1943). Marguerite B. Hamer, "The Fate of the Exiled Acadians in South Carolina," *Journal of Southern History,* 4 (1938), 199–208. George C. Rogers Jr., *The History of Georgetown County, South Carolina* (Columbia: University of South Carolina Press, 1970), 74–75. Warren B. Smith, *White Servitude in Colonial South Carolina* (1961; Columbia: University of South Carolina Press, 1970), 36–37.

14. Butler, *Huguenots in America,* 120–30. Hirsch, *Huguenots,* 44.

15. Robert L. Meriwether, *The Expansion of South Carolina, 1729–1765* (Kingsport, Tenn.: Southern Publishers, 1940), 19. South Carolina, Commons House Journals, 10 Oct. 1710–7 June 1712, 303, South Carolina Department of Archives and History, Columbia (hereinafter cited as SCDAH).

16. Weir, *Colonial South Carolina,* 208. Meriwether, *Expansion of South Carolina,* 259n. Ackerman, *South Carolina Colonial Land Policies,* 94–97.

17. There were also supposed to be townships on the Altamaha River in the debatable land along the Florida frontier, but they were never surveyed before the colony of Georgia came into existence. Weir, *Colonial South Carolina,* 208.

18. Hirsch, *Huguenots,* 28–34. Meriwether, *Expansion of South Carolina,* 33–36, 154.

19. Hirsch, *Huguenots,* 39–44. Wallace, *History of South Carolina,* 2: 46.

20. Wallace, *History of South Carolina,* 2: 45. Cooper and McCord, *Statutes,* 4: 209. Smith, *White Servitude,* 65–66.

21. Smith, *White Servitude,* 48–49.

22. Meriwether, *Expansion of South Carolina,* 29, 66–69, 255.

23. Meriwether, *Expansion of South Carolina,* 29, 43–48, 50, 61, 255–56. For further names see: Salley, *Orangeburg County;* George J. Gongaware, *The History of the German Friendly Society of Charleston, South Carolina, 1766–1916* (Richmond: Garrett & Massie, 1935); and Edward McCrady, *The History of South Carolina Under the Royal Government, 1719–1776* (New York: Macmillan, 1901), 131–32 (hereinafter cited as *Royal South Carolina*).

For an account of nineteenth-century German immigration see Ellis Reed-Hill Lesemann, "General Johann Andreas Wagener: A German Mechanic for Southern Problems," honors thesis, University of South Carolina, 1994.

24. The route of Interstate 81 from western North Carolina into Pennsylvania follows a great portion of the Great Wagon Road.

25. Richard J. Hooker, ed., *The Carolina Backcountry on the Eve of the Revolution: The Journal and Other Writings of Charles Woodmason, Anglican Itinerant* (Chapel Hill: Published for the Institute of Early American History and Culture at Williamsburg, Va., by University of North Carolina Press, 1953), 13–14.

26. George A. Howe, *History of the Presbyterian Church in South Carolina,* 2 vols. (1870–1883; reprint ed., Columbia: Synod of South Carolina, 1965), 1: 215. Meriwether, *Expansion of South Carolina,* 84, 87.

27. For other Scots-Irish names, see McCrady, *Royal South Carolina,* 133n, 134n, 317n, 318n.

28. Verner W. Crane, *The Southern Frontier, 1670–1732* (Ann Arbor: University of Michigan Press, 1929), 26, 28, 30–31, 162, 211. Weir, *Colonial South Carolina,* 62–64. Rowland et al., *Beaufort County,* 67–75.

29. Edward Cashin, *Lachlan MacGillivray, Indian Trader* (Athens: University of Georgia Press, 1992), 6–7. David Dobson, *Directory of Scots in the Carolinas, 1680–1830* (Baltimore: Genealogical Publishing Company, 1986), 156–57. Robert Pringle, for example, maintained ties with Edinburgh and had a picture of the Battle of Culloden. Walter B. Edgar, "Robert Pringle's World," *SCHM,* 76 (1975): 8–9. For other Scottish families see J. H. Easterby, *History of the St. Andrew's Society of Charleston, South Carolina, 1729–1929* (Charleston: Saint Andrew's Society, 1929).

30. McCrady, *Royal South Carolina,* 133–34.

31. For example, see the case of the immigrants on the ship *Pearl.* Less than half of those supposedly "free poor Protestants" were certified for the bounty. Rogers et al., *Laurens Papers,* 5: 504–5.

32. Rogers et al., *Laurens Papers,* 6: 149–50.

33. Smith, *White Servitude,* 65–66.

34. Weir, *Colonial South Carolina,* 210. Meriwether, *Expansion of South Carolina,* 103–4. For further information on the Quakers in South Carolina see Jo Anne McCormick, "The Quakers of Colonial South Carolina, 1670–1807," diss., University of South Carolina, 1984.

35. Forrest McDonald and Ellen Shapiro McDonald, "The Ethnic Origins of the American People, 1790." *William and Mary Quarterly,* 3d series, 37 (Apr. 1980): 198 (hereinafter cited as *WMQ*), 183–86.

36. Meriwether, *Expansion of South Carolina,* 90–98. Leah Townsend, *South Carolina Baptists, 1670–1805* (Florence, S.C.: Florence Printing, 1935), 61–77.

37. For additional names of families in the Welsh Tract, see McCrady, *Royal South Carolina,* 136n, 137n.

38. Smith, *White Servitude,* 47. Bradford L. Rauschenburg, "Charleston Furniture, 1690–1820: the Cabinetmakers" (unpub. ms. in progress, Museum of Early Southern Decorative Arts, Winston-Salem, N.C.), 88 (hereinafter referred to as MESDA).

39. Wallace, *History of South Carolina,* 1: 406n. McCrady, *Royal South Carolina,* 145. Edgar and Bailey, *Biographical Directory,* 2: 554–56.

40. Hagy, *This Happy Land,* 5–18.

41. Ibid., 9–11, 14–16.

42. Butler, *Huguenots in America*, 134–40.

43. Butler, *Huguenots in America*, 132–34.

In tracing one's roots in South Carolina, an individual is likely to find a variety of ethnic origins. After all, if a person is descended from someone who came over in 1670 in the first fleet, that is more than thirteen generations ago (allowing twenty-five years per generation). That descendant in 1998 would have at least 8,192 direct forebears.

44. McDonald and McDonald, "Ethnic Origins," 199. Weir, *Colonial South Carolina*, 209.

CHAPTER 5: MORE LIKE A NEGRO COUNTRY

1. Greene, "Colonial South Carolina and the Caribbean Connection," 197. Weir, *Colonial South Carolina*, 175, 197. Wood, *Black Majority*, 45, 131.

2. Daniel C. Littlefield, *Rice and Slaves: Ethnicity and the Slave Trade in Colonial South Carolina* (Urbana: University of Illinois Press, 1991), 8–13, 31–32, 54, 115 16.

3. Ibid., 21, 24–25, 111–13, 175.

4. Littlefield, *Rice and Slaves*, 8, 20–21, 74–113. Wood, *Black Majority*, 55–62. Weir, *Colonial South Carolina*, 178–79.

5. Littlefield, *Rice and Slaves*, 13.

6. Rogers et al., *Laurens Papers*, 4: 558.

7. Littlefield, *Rice and Slaves*, 58.

8. Clarence L. Ver Steeg, *Origins of a Southern Mosaic: Studies of Early Carolina and Georgia*, Mercer University Lamar Memorial Lectures No. 17 (Athens: University of Georgia Press, 1975), 117–21. Converse D. Clowse, *Economic Beginnings in Colonial South Carolina, 1670–1730*, Tricentennial Studies Number 3 (Columbia: University of South Carolina Press, 1971), 62–63, 172–78, 234–35. Weir, *Colonial South Carolina*, 174. Wood, *Black Majority*, 130n.

9. Littlefield, *Rice and Slaves*, 26.

10. Wood, *Black Majority*, xiv.

In 1760 the Charleston firm of Austin, Laurens, & Appleby announced a shipboard sale, and in 1768 Francis Stuart advertised one for Thomas Nightingale's tavern. Rogers et al., *Laurens Papers*, 3: 35–36. *South Carolina Gazette*, 11 Apr. 1768 (hereinafter cited as *Gazette*). Edmund L. Drago, *Broke By the War: Letters of a Slave Trader* (Columbia: University of South Carolina Press, 1991), 1.

11. Francis Varnod to secretary, 13 Jan. 1724, Society for the Propagation of the Gospel in Foreign Parts Archives, London quoted in Littlefield, *Rice and Slaves*, 75. Weir, *Colonial South Carolina*, 177–78. Littlefield, *Rice and Slaves*, 74–76.

12. Leland Ferguson, *Uncommon Ground: Archeology and Early African America, 1650–1800* (Washington, D.C.: Smithsonian Institution Press, 1992), 114–15.

13. Charles Joyner, "The Cultural Triangle: Creolization of African Culture in South Carolina and the Caribbean" (paper presented 19 July 1996 at the annual meeting of the Society for the Historians of the Early Republic, Nashville, Tenn.),6.

14. Littlefield, *Rice and Slaves*, 78.

15. Wood, *Black Majority*, 95–130.

16. Dunn, *Sugar and Slaves*, 239.

17. Wood, *Black Majority*, 144–47. "A Report of the Governor and Council, 1708," in Merrens, *Colonial South Carolina*, 32.

The black to white ratio in Barbados in the eighteenth century was three to one. Bridenbaugh and Bridenbaugh, *No Peace Beyond the Line*, 226–27.

18. Commons House Journals, 10 Oct. 1710–7 June 1713, 303.

19. Cooper and McCord, *Statutes*, 7: 347–49. Wood, *Black Majority*, 125–30. Weir, *Colonial South Carolina*, 195–97. Rogers et al., *Laurens Papers*, 5: 16.

20. *South Carolina and American General Gazette*, 31 July 1769 (hereinafter cited as *General Gazette*). Rogers et al., *Laurens Papers*, 2: 204.

21. Joyner, "Cultural Triangle," 2–5. Ferguson, *Uncommon Ground*, 118.

22. Joyner, "Cultural Triangle," passim. Weir, *Colonial South Carolina*, 178–80. Littlefield, *Rice and Slaves*, 62.

23. Ferguson, *Uncommon Ground*, 118–19. Joyner, "Cultural Triangle," passim.

24. Gentleman Planters of London, Journal of the Lords of Trade, 8 Oct. 1680, *Calendar of State Papers, Colonial Series, America and West Indies* (hereinafter cited as *CSP, Colonial Series*) quoted in Wood, *Black Majority*, 180. Patricia Nichols, "Language Diversity in the Waccamaw Region" (unpub. manuscript, 1981), 3–4.

25. Nichols, "Language Diversity," 3–4.

26. Ibid., 4–5.

27. American Bible Society, *De Good Nyews Bout Jedus Christ Wa Luke Write* (New York: American Bible Society, 1995), preface, 9.

28. Wood, *Black Majority*, 185–91.

29. Littlefield, *Rice and Slaves*, 160–61.

30. Meriwether, *Expansion of South Carolina*, 95. Littlefield, *Rice and Slaves*, 165–66. Rowland et al., *Beaufort County*, 128–32. Hatley, *Dividing Paths*, 74.

31. Littlefield, *Rice and Slaves*, 126–33.

32. Moore, "Royalizing South Carolina," 375–79.

33. Ibid., 376–78.

34. Board of Trade to George II, 8 Sept. 1721, *CSP, Colonial Series* quoted in Moore, "Royalizing South Carolina," 381. Wood, *Black Majority*, 298–307.

35. Wood, *Black Majority*, 308–12; quotation, 311.

36. Walter B. Edgar, ed., *The Letterbook of Robert Pringle*, 2 vols. (Columbia: University of South Carolina Press, 1972), 1: 69, 122 (hereinafter cited as Edgar, *Pringle Letterbook*). Wood, *Black Majority*, 312.

37. Wood, *Black Majority*, 312–14.

38. Ibid., 314–16.

39. Ibid., 315–19.

40. Ibid.

41. Littlefield, *Rice and Slaves*, 176. The figures given for white deaths range from twenty to forty and for blacks from twenty to perhaps as many as sixty. Wood, *Black Majority*, 317–19.

42. Wood, *Black Majority*, 319–23. Wallace, *History of South Carolina*, 1: 373.

43. Edgar, *Pringle Letterbook*, 1: 163. Sirmans, *Colonial South Carolina*, 211–14. Rowland et al., *Beaufort County*, 128–32.

44. Slaves were selling in the Charleston market in 1741 at an average of £15 sterling ($1,329). Edgar, *Pringle Letterbook*, 1: 284. Littlefield, *Rice and Slaves*, 116. Cooper and McCord, *Statutes*, 3: 556–68. Weir, *Colonial South Carolina*, 194. Wood, *Black Majority*, 325.

45. Cooper and McCord, *Statutes*, 7: 397–417.

46. Cooper and McCord, *Statutes*, 7: 397–417. Rogers et al., *Laurens Papers*, 4: 342n.

47. Cooper and McCord, *Statutes*, 7: 416–17.

48. Littlefield, *Rice and Slaves*, 116. Weir, *Colonial South Carolina*, 188.

49. Weir, *Colonial South Carolina*, 198.

50. Littlefield, *Rice and Slaves*, 62–64. Weir, *Colonial South Carolina*, 180.

51. Edgar, *Pringle Letterbook*, 1: 247–48.

52. Philip D. Morgan, "Work and Culture: The Task System and the World of Lowcountry Blacks, 1700 to 1880," *WMQ*, 3d series, 39 (Oct. 1982): 563–99. Ferguson, *Uncommon Ground*, 119. Weir, *Colonial South Carolina*, 180–85.

53. Littlefield, *Rice and Slaves*, 162–63. Weir, *Colonial South Carolina*, 188–90.

54. Littlefield, *Rice and Slaves*, 167. Weir, *Colonial South Carolina*, 180, 188–90.

55. Littlefield, *Rice and Slaves*, 67–68. Weir, *Colonial South Carolina*, 177.

56. Littlefield, *Rice and Slaves*, 66–70. Edward Copeland, "Jane Austen and the Consumer Revolution," in *The Jane Austen Handbook with a Dictionary of Jane Austen's Life and Works*, edited by J. David Guy; Brian Southam and A. Walton Litz, consultants (London: Athlone Press, 1986), 80–88.

In *Sense and Sensibility* (1811) the figure used for a respectable household with servants was £500. Using McCusker's tables, the 1811 pound sterling converts to £12,495 in 1989 pounds. The exchange rate for pounds to dollars in 1989 was 1.6382. There was a 12.6 percent inflation rate from 1989 to 1996. *Economic Report of the President, 1997, 385. Economic Report of the President Transmitted to the Congress February 1996* (Washington, D.C.: Government Printing Office, 1996), 400.

57. Rogers et al., *Laurens Papers,* 2: 378–80. Littlefield, *Rice and Slaves,* 176–77.

CHAPTER 6: THE PROPRIETARY REGIME

1. Sirmans, *Colonial South Carolina,* 37–38, 67, 72–73. Weir, *Colonial South Carolina,* 66–73. Ver Steeg, *Origins of a Southern Mosaic,* 12–21.

2. Weir, *Colonial South Carolina,* 71–73. Ver Steeg, *Origins of a Southern Mosaic,* 12–21.

3. Weir, *Colonial South Carolina,* 59–60. McCrady, *Proprietary South Carolina,* 140–41, 192, 227.

4. McCrady, *Proprietary South Carolina,* 120.

5. Sirmans, *Colonial South Carolina,* 17–100. McCrady, *Proprietary South Carolina,* 202, 719–20. Wallace, *History of South Carolina,* 3: 495–96.

6. McCrady, *Proprietary South Carolina,* 719–20. Wallace, *History of South Carolina,* 3: 495–96.

7. Sirmans, *Colonial South Carolina,* 28–32. Weir, *Colonial South Carolina,* 59–61.

8. Weir, *Colonial South Carolina,* 59–61. Sirmans, *Colonial South Carolina,* 28–32. Quotation from Ashley to Colleton, 27 Nov. 1672, Cheves, *Shaftsbury Papers,* 416, in Sirmans, *Colonial South Carolina,* 28.

9. McCrady, *Proprietary South Carolina,* 404.

10. Sirmans, *Colonial South Carolina,* 35–43. Mabel L. Webber, comp., "Grimball of Edisto Island," *SCHM,* 23 (1922): 101.

11. Sirmans, *Colonial South Carolina,* 29–34.

12. Weir, *Colonial South Carolina,* 61.

13. David H. Corkran, *The Carolina Indian Frontier,* Tricentennial Booklet Number 6 (Columbia: University of South Carolina Press, 1970), 5. Waddell, *Indians of the Lowcountry,* 9, 10, 12. Crane, *Southern Frontier,* 16–17.

14. Crane, *Southern Frontier,* 17–20. Corkran, *Carolina Indian Frontier,* 5–6. Sirmans, *Colonial South Carolina,* 22–23. Rowland et al., *Beaufort County,* 66.

15. Crane, *Southern Frontier,* 21, 30, 33–36, 37.

16. Crane, *Southern Frontier,* 25–26. Corkran, *Carolina Indian Frontier,* 7.

17. Corkran, *Carolina Indian Frontier,* 7–9.

18. Duff, "Imbibing Information," 1–17.

19. Sirmans, *Colonial South Carolina,* 17–54.

20. McCrady, *Proprietary South Carolina,* 329–30. Sirmans, *Colonial South Carolina,* 17–54.

21. Weir, *Colonial South Carolina,* 64–65. McCrady, *Proprietary South Carolina,* 717–18.

22. "Fundamental Constitutions," 2: 362. Edgar, *Biographical Directory,* 1: 14. Edgar and Bailey, *Biographical Directory,* 2: 37–38, 335–36. Sirmans, *Colonial South Carolina,* 43–44.

23. Daniel Defoe, "Party Tyranny: or an Occasional Bill in Miniature; as now practiced in Carolina" in Salley, *Narratives of Early Carolina,* 224–64. For example, in McCrady, *Proprietary South Carolina* and Sirmans, *Colonial South Carolina,* the Goose Creek Men are the unscrupulous troublemakers and the Dissenters the noble champions of truth and justice.

24. Sirmans, *Colonial South Carolina,* 39–43. Weir, *Colonial South Carolina,* 70–71.

25. Defoe, "Party Tyranny," 250–52. Edward Randolph to Board of Trade, 27 May 1700, *Records in the British Public Records Office Relating to South Carolina* (hereinafter cited as BPRO) quoted in Moore, "Royalizing South Carolina," 150. Moore, "Royalizing South Carolina," 145–62.

26. Edward Randolph, *Letters and Official Papers* quoted in Moore, "Royalizing South Carolina," 151.

27. Sirmans, *Colonial South Carolina,* 38–45. McCrady, *Proprietary South Carolina,* 199–210, 224–25, 719–20. Weir, *Colonial South Carolina,* 65–66. Charles H. Lesser, *South Carolina Begins: The Records of a Proprietary Colony, 1663–1721* (Columbia: South Carolina Department of Archives and History, 1995), 169.

28. Sirmans, *Colonial South Carolina*, 44–46. Proprietors to Philip Ludwell, 12 Apr. 1693, *BPRO* quoted in Sirmans, *Colonial South Carolina*, 45. McCrady, *Proprietary South Carolina*, 218–31. Weir, *Colonial South Carolina*, 66–67.

29. McCrady, *Proprietary South Carolina*, 226–29. Sirmans, *Colonial South Carolina*, 45–49, 52. Weir, *Colonial South Carolina*, 66–67.

30. Sirmans, *Colonial South Carolina*, 61–67. McCrady, *Proprietary South Carolina*, 279–86. Friedlander, "Carolina Huguenots," 123–31.

31. "The Representation and Address of several of the Members of this present Assembly return'd for Colleton County," in Rivers, *History of South Carolina*, 455.

32. Moore, "Royalizing South Carolina," 152–63. McCrady, *Proprietary South Carolina*, 407. Weir, *Colonial South Carolina*, 76–77.

33. McCrady, *Proprietary South Carolina*, 403–4. Weir, *Colonial South Carolina*, 75–76.

34. Edgar and Bailey, *Biographical Directory*, 2: 466–68. Sirmans, *Colonial South Carolina*, 52–53, 70–71, 76, 78.

35. Sirmans, *Colonial South Carolina*, 49, 52–53, 76. McCrady, *Proprietary South Carolina*, 373–74. "Proprietors to the Governor & Our Deputies at Ashley River in Carolina," in Rivers, *History of South Carolina*, 439.

36. "Representation and Address of several of the Members," 454. Sirmans, *Colonial South Carolina*, 76. McCrady, *Proprietary South Carolina*, 373–74.

37. David K. Eliades, "The Indian Policy of Colonial South Carolina, 1670–1763," diss., University of South Carolina, 1981, 88. McCrady, *Proprietary South Carolina*, 377–78. Sirmans, *Colonial South Carolina*, 84–87.

38. Eliades, "Indian Policy," 91–92.

39. Weir, *Colonial South Carolina*, 78. McCrady, *Proprietary South Carolina*, 394, 405–6.

40. "Fundamental Constitutions," 2: 384. Powell, *North Carolina*, 123.

41. Defoe, "Party Tyranny," 237–38. McCrady, *Proprietary South Carolina*, 369.

42. Weir, *Colonial South Carolina*, 76–78. S. Charles Bolton, *Southern Anglicanism: The Church of England in Colonial South Carolina*, Contributions to the Study of Religion, Number 5 (Westport, Conn.: Greenwood Press, 1982), 16–27.

43. McCrady, *Proprietary South Carolina*, 415–22. Weir, *Colonial South Carolina*, 76–78. Bolton, *Southern Anglicanism*, 25–27.

44. Moore, "Royalizing South Carolina," 232–55. Weir, *Colonial South Carolina*, 77–80. Sirmans, *Colonial South Carolina*, 87–89. McCrady, *Proprietary South Carolina*, 441–46.

45. Defoe, "Party Tyranny," 259. Moore, "Royalizing South Carolina," 232–55. Weir, *Colonial South Carolina*, 77–80. Sirmans, *Colonial South Carolina*, 87–89. McCrady, *Proprietary South Carolina*, 441–46.

46. Defoe, "Party Tyranny," 239, 245–46, 257.

47. Moore, "Royalizing South Carolina," 232–55. Weir, *Colonial South Carolina*, 77–80. McCrady, *Proprietary South Carolina*, 441–46. Sirmans, *Colonial South Carolina*, 87–89.

48. McCrady, *Proprietary South Carolina*, 441–46. Bolton, *Southern Anglicanism*, 25–27,

49. Weir, *Colonial South Carolina*, 80. Bolton, *Southern Anglicanism*, 25–28.
The parishes were Christ Church, St. Andrew's, St. James', St. John's, St. Phillip's, and St. Thomas'. Later South Carolina parishes would also have Barbadian antecedents, St. Michael's and St. Peter's. Puckrein, *Little England*, 4.

50. Moore, "Royalizing South Carolina," 272. Sirmans, *Colonial South Carolina*, 95.

51. Sirmans, *Colonial South Carolina*, 95. Edgar, *Biographical Directory*, 1: 30–39. Moore, "Royalizing South Carolina," 277.

52. Moore, "Royalizing South Carolina," 278–79. Sirmans, *Colonial South Carolina*, 96, 100. Weir, *Colonial South Carolina*, 71.

53. Sirmans, *Colonial South Carolina*, 86, 87, 108–9, 205. Weir, *Colonial South Carolina*, 94–97, 99, 100, 108–11.

54. Petition of the Council and Assembly of the Settlements in South Carolina to the King. Great Britain. *Calendar of State Papers. Colonial Series, America and West Indies,* 44 vols. (London: His Majesty's Stationery Office, 1933), 31: 334.

55. In Barnwell's troop there were 527 men, 495 of whom were Indians. Moore's larger force of 850 contained only 33 whites. Eliades, "Indian Policy," 97–101. Crane, *Southern Frontier,* 158–61.

The South Carolina pound was one of the most stable of the colonial paper currencies. Its value fluctuated initially but settled at seven pounds South Carolina currency to one pound sterling. Sirmans, *Colonial South Carolina,* 206.

56. Sirmans, *Colonial South Carolina,* 40–41. Eliades, "Indian Policy," 74–82.

57. Eliades, "Indian Policy," 82–83.

58. Eliades, "Indian Policy," 81–85. Weir, *Colonial South Carolina,* 82–83. Sirmans, *Colonial South Carolina,* 72, 78.

59. Eliades, "Indian Policy," 93–94. Crane, *Southern Frontier,* 149.

60. Eliades, "Indian Policy," 85, 101–2, 110–11. Wallace, *History of South Carolina,* 1: 203–5. Weir, *Colonial South Carolina,* 82–83. Edgar and Bailey, *Biographical Directory,* 2: 102–6, 491–92.

61. Eliades, "Indian Policy," 103–17. Rowland et al., *Beaufort County,* 12–13, 81–84, 91, 95–111. Edgar and Bailey, *Biographical Directory,* 2: 491–92.

62. Eliades, "Indian Policy," 103–17. Rowland et al., *Beaufort County,* 12–13, 81–84, 91, 95–111. Merrell, *Indians' New World,* 75–79.

63. Corkran, *Carolina Indian Frontier,* 20–34. Eliades, "Indian Policy," 103–17. Rowland et al., *Beaufort County,* 12–13, 81–84, 91, 95–111. Merrell, *Indians' New World,* 66–80, 75, 119, 144.

64. Hatley, *Dividing Paths,* 23–31.

65. Ibid., 23–31.

66. Weir, *Colonial South Carolina,* 85. Between 1718 and 1722 the mean of South Carolina's exports was £54,180 ($5.4 million) and its imports £19,050 ($1.9 million). Peter A. Coclanis, *The Shadow of a Dream: Economic Life and Death in the South Carolina Low Country, 1670–1920* (New York: Oxford University Press, 1989), 72, 73.

67. Eliades, "Indian Policy," 119–21. Moore, "Royalizing South Carolina," 289–86.

68. Moore, "Royalizing South Carolina," 288–90.

69. McCrady, *Proprietary South Carolina,* 589–623. Weir, *Colonial South Carolina,* 86–87.

70. McCrady, *Proprietary South Carolina,* 589–623. Weir, *Colonial South Carolina,* 86–87.

71. Parris to [Francis Yonge?], 30 Oct. 1719, in "Extracts of Sundry Letters," Privy Council Records quoted in Moore, "Royalizing South Carolina," 327.

72. Moore, "Royalizing South Carolina," 306–12.

73. Moore, "Royalizing South Carolina," 318–19. Weir, *Colonial South Carolina,* 99. Sirmans, *Colonial South Carolina,* 122–23. Arneil, *John Locke and America,* 128.

74. Moore, "Royalizing South Carolina," 318–20. Weir, *Colonial South Carolina,* 99. Sirmans, *Colonial South Carolina,* 124–35.

75. Moore, "Royalizing South Carolina," 320–25. Weir, *Colonial South Carolina,* 99–100. Sirmans, *Colonial South Carolina,* 125–28. Petition of the Council and Assembly, 338.

76. Moore, "Royalizing South Carolina," 325. Weir, *Colonial South Carolina,* 99–100. Sirmans, *Colonial South Carolina,* 125–28.

77. Weir, *Colonial South Carolina,* 100–103. Sirmans, *Colonial South Carolina,* 125–28.

78. Francis Yonge, "A Narrative of the Proceedings of the People of South-Carolina, In the Year 1719," in Carroll, *Historical Collections of South Carolina,* 2: 166. Moore, "Royalizing South Carolina," 325. Sirmans, *Colonial South Carolina,* 125–28.

79. Moore, "Royalizing South Carolina," 325–38. Weir, *Colonial South Carolina,* 104–5. Sirmans, *Colonial South Carolina,* 127–28.

80. Moore, "Royalizing South Carolina, 325–38.

South Carolina's rebels of 1719 were Arthur Middleton, Alexander Skene, George Logan, Christopher Wilkinson, John Fenwicke, Richard Beresford, Joseph Morton, George Chicken, Benjamin Schenckingh, Daniel Huger, Walter Izard, William Dry, Thomas Hepworth, Andrew Allen, Jonathan Drake, John Williams, John Godfrey, Paul Hamilton, Richard Smith, William Elliott, William Watkins, Samuel Jones, John Gendron, John Raven, Richard Harris, and Thomas Lynch. Moore, "Royalizing South Carolina," 336.

81. Convention to James Moore, 19 Dec. 1719, Miscellaneous Papers of the South Carolina Commons House of Assembly quoted in Moore, "Royalizing South Carolina," 338.

82. Sirmans, *Colonial South Carolina,* 127–28. Moore, "Royalizing South Carolina," 338–41.

83. Petition of the Council and Assembly, 541. James Moore to [James Craggs], Principal Secretary of State, 24 Dec. 1719, Privy Council Records quoted in Moore, "Royalizing South Carolina," 107. Moore, "Royalizing South Carolina," 342–55. Weir, *Colonial South Carolina,* 102–3.

84. McCrady, *Proprietary South Carolina,* 714–16.

85. Crane, *Southern Frontier,* 14. Arneil, *John Locke and America,* 118–31.

86. Edward Randolph to the Lords of Trade, 16 Mar. 1699. Rivers, *History of South Carolina,* 445.

87. Petition of the Council and Assembly, 335.

88. William Rhett to Commissioners of Customs, London, 21 Dec. 1719, Privy Council Records quoted in Moore, "Royalizing South Carolina," 341.

CHAPTER 7: TRYING ROYAL GOVERNMENT

1. Moore, "Royalizing South Carolina," 344–49.

2. Ibid., 356–65.

3. Ibid., 352–54, 359–60, 372–81.

4. Ibid., 382–87.

5. Ibid., 355, 387–91.

6. Moore, "Royalizing South Carolina," 391–93. Sirmans, *Colonial South Carolina,* 130–31.

7. "Edward Randolph to the Earl of Bridgewater," 22 Mar. 1699, in Rivers, *History of South Carolina,* 447–49. Weir, *Colonial South Carolina,* 102–3.

8. Moore, "Royalizing South Carolina," 394–98.

9. Ibid., 407–11.

10. Weir, *Colonial South Carolina,* 109–10.

11. Ibid., 108–9.

12. Moore, "Royalizing South Carolina," 411–13.

13. Edgar, *Biographical Directory,* 1: 55–69. Weir, *Colonial South Carolina,* 110–11.

14. An Act for establishing an Agreement with seven of the Lords Proprietors of Carolina, for the Surrender of their Title and Interest in that Province to His Majesty," in Cooper and McCord, *Statutes,* 1: 60–71.

15. Clowse, *Economic Beginnings in Colonial South Carolina,* 195–98, 238–40, 246–47. Weir, *Colonial South Carolina,* 108–11. W. Roy Smith, *South Carolina as a Royal Province* (New York: Macmillan, 1903), 228–75.

There were slight variations. McCusker places the exchange rate at £7.0624 currency to £1 sterling between 1725 and 1738 and £6.9716 currency to £1 sterling between 1766 and 1772. McCusker, "How Much is That in Real Money," 333.

16. For contemporary descriptions of South Carolina's governmental structure, see: Glen, "Description of South Carolina," 39–42. "Governor William Bull's Representation of the Colony, 1770," in Merrens, *Colonial South Carolina,* 256–60.

17. Glen, "Description of South Carolina," 40. Jack P. Greene, "The Jamaica Privilege Controversy," in Jack P. Greene, *Negotiated Authorities: Essays in Colonial Political and Constitutional History* (Charlottesville: University Press of Virginia, 1994), 358. Sirmans, *Colonial South Carolina,* 234. Weir, *Colonial South Carolina,* 106, 131.

18. Smith, *South Carolina as a Royal Province,* 74–77. Jack P. Greene, "The Gadsden Election Controversy and the Revolutionary Movement in South Carolina," in Greene, *Negotiated Authorities,* 346–47.

The increased cost of goods and services in 1760 (as compared to 1740) reduced the purchasing power of the governor's salary. In 1760 the stipend of the royal governor was £1,500 sterling ($126,000).

In 1996 the governor of South Carolina was paid $106,000. South Carolina, FY96–97 Appropriations Act, *Statutes at Large, 1996,* 458.

19. The dates for the governors reflect the time they were actually in South Carolina, not the original date of appointment. Glen, for example, was appointed governor in 1738 but did not arrive in South Carolina until 1743.

Sirmans, *Colonial South Carolina,* 195, 308–9. Moore, "Royalizing South Carolina," 432. Greene, "Gadsden Election Controversy," 329. Rogers, *Charleston,* xi. Wallace, *History of South Carolina,* 2: 123. W. Stitt Robinson, *James Glen: From Scottish Provost to Royal Governor of South Carolina,* Contributions in American History, Number 165, ed. Jon L. Wakelyn (Westport, Conn.: Greenwood Press, 1996), 14.

20. Edgar and Bailey, *Biographical Directory,* 2: 103–6, 120–26.

21. Lloyd to Temple Stanyan, 28 May 1725, *BPROC* quoted in Sirmans, *Colonial South Carolina,* 139. Edgar and Bailey, *Biographical Directory,* 2: 405–6. Smith, *South Carolina as a Royal Province,* 86.

22. These figures are averages only for those members of the council for which inventories and other records were available. Sirmans, *Colonial South Carolina,* 236–38.

23. Sirmans, *Colonial South Carolina,* 236–38, 312–13. Weir, *Colonial South Carolina,* 267–68.

24. George C. Rogers Jr., *Evolution of a Federalist: William Loughton Smith of Charleston (1758–1812)* (Columbia: University of South Carolina Press, 1962), 38–39. Weir, *Colonial South Carolina,* 127. Sirmans, *Colonial South Carolina,* 139, 202, 205, 223.

25. Hewatt, "Historical Account," 277.

26. Weir, *Colonial South Carolina,* 126–27. Sirmans, *Colonial South Carolina,* 201–4.

27. Resolution of the Commons House, 28 Nov. 1739, James H. Easterby, ed., *Commons House Journals, 1739–1741* quoted in Sirmans, *Colonial South Carolina,* 204.

28. Sirmans, *Colonial South Carolina,* 202–6. Weir, *Colonial South Carolina,* 126–27. Rogers, *Evolution of a Federalist,* 39.

29. Sirmans, *Colonial South Carolina,* 301–13. Weir, *Colonial South Carolina,* 266–67.

30. Sirmans, *Colonial South Carolina,* 301–13. Weir, *Colonial South Carolina,* 266–67.

31. Hewatt, "Historical Account," 277. Rogers, *Evolution of a Federalist,* 38–39. Rogers et al., *Laurens Papers,* 4: 467.

32. Rogers, *Evolution of a Federalist,* 39. Rogers et al., *Laurens Papers,* 4: 467n.

33. Edgar, *Biographical Directory,* 1: 117.

34. Waterhouse, *New World Gentry,* 16–17. Greene, "Colonial South Carolina and the Caribbean Connection," 204, 207–8. Sirmans, *Colonial South Carolina,* 239–40.

35. Weir, *Colonial South Carolina,* 132–34.

36. Weir, *Colonial South Carolina,* 135–38. Robert M. Weir, "'The Harmony We Were Famous For': An Interpretation of Pre-Revolutionary South Carolina Politics," *WMQ,* 3d series, 26 (Oct. 1969): 473–501.

37. Warren Alleyne and Henry Fraser, *The Barbados-Carolina Connection* (Basingstoke, U.K.: Macmillan Caribbean, 1988), 22. Yonge, "Narrative of the Proceedings," 2: 149.

38. Sirmans, *Colonial South Carolina,* 240.

39. Ibid., 235–36.

40. See, for example: Sirmans, *Colonial South Carolina,* 245–47. Richard Hofstadter, *America at 1750: A Social Portrait* (1971; New York: Vintage Books, 1973), 166. Carl Bridenbaugh, *Myths and Realities: Societies of the Colonial South* (1963; New York: Atheneum, 1968), 113, 117.

41. Weir, *Colonial South Carolina,* 122. Jack P. Greene, "Legislative Turnover in British Colonial America, 1696 to 1775: A Quantitative Analysis," in Greene, *Negotiated Authorities,* 218–19, 227–28.

42. Weir, *Colonial South Carolina,* 130. Sirmans, *Colonial South Carolina,* 241.

43. Weir, *Colonial South Carolina,* 130.

44. Weir, *Colonial South Carolina,* 131, 138–40. Sirmans, *Colonial South Carolina,* 243.

45. Waterhouse, *New World Gentry,* 175. Greene, "Colonial South Carolina and the Caribbean Connection," 204.

46. Edgar and Bailey, *Biographical Directory,* 2: 4–5, 747.

47. Waterhouse, *New World Gentry,* 170–74.

48. Edgar, *Biographical Directory,* 1: 146–48. Edgar and Bailey, *Biographical Directory,* 2: 5, 85–86, 97–100, 166, 171–73, 189–90, 232, 287, 291–94, 327–28, 415–18, 471, 548–49, 582, 616–17, 690–91.

49. Waterhouse, *New World Gentry,* 160–61, 182–83, 189. Weir, *Colonial South Carolina,* 135–39. Jack P. Greene, "The Role of the Lower Houses of Assembly in Eighteenth-Century Politics," in Greene, *Negotiated Authorities,* 167.

50. Waterhouse, *New World Gentry,* 124–28. See for example: Bridenbaugh, *Myths and Realities,* 75, 117. Sirmans, *Colonial South Carolina,* 250–52.

51. Alleyne and Fraser, *Barbados-Carolina Connection,* 22. Bolton, *Southern Anglicanism,* 151–52.

52. Edgar, *Pringle Letterbook,* 1: 211. In an examination of ten parishes in which there were 294 elections for churchwarden, there were only 12 declinations (4.08 percent). Waterhouse, *New World Gentry,* 134, 138. Bolton, *Southern Anglicanism,* 140–53.

53. Weir, *Colonial South Carolina,* 107.

54. Waterhouse, *New World Gentry,* 140. Rogers, *Charleston,* 20–22.

55. Cooper and McCord, *Statutes,* 2: 161–62; 9: 8–11; 4: 106–9.

56. J. W. G. DeBrahm, "Diary of a Journey Through the Carolinas," *Transactions of the American Philosophical Society* quoted in Waterhouse, *New World Gentry,* 144.

57. Cooper and McCord, *Statutes,* 3: 529; 4: 56; 9: 49–57. *Gazette,* 23 Apr. 1750. Quoted in Smith, *South Carolina as a Royal Province,* 82.

58. Waterhouse, *New World Gentry,* 126–28. *Gazette,* 2 Apr. 1737, 4 Nov. 1756.

59. Cooper and McCord, *Statutes,* 3: 529; 4: 56; 9: 131–56. Waterhouse, *New World Gentry,* 128–43.

60. Sirmans, *Colonial South Carolina,* 250–51. Jack P. Greene, *The Quest for Power: The Lower Houses of Assembly in the Southern Royal Colonies, 1689–1776* (1963; New York: W. W. Norton, 1972), 252–53. Waterhouse, *New World Gentry,* 144–45.

61. Waterhouse, *New World Gentry,* 189.

62. Rogers et al., *Laurens Papers,* 4: 671–72.

63. Jerome S. Handler, "Father Antoine Biet's Visit to Barbados in 1654," *Journal of the Barbados Museum and Historical Society* quoted in Puckrein, *Little England,* 13.

CHAPTER 8: THE RICHES OF THE PROVINCE

1. Coclanis, *Shadow of a Dream,* 21–23, 50–51. For an excellent example of early-eighteenth-century enterprise, see Alexander Moore, "Daniel Axtell's Account Book and the Economy of Early South Carolina," *SCHM,* 95 (Oct. 1994): 280–301.

2. "Coppy of Instruccons for Mr. West about our Plantacon," in Rivers, *History of South Carolina,* 343–44.

3. Ibid., 344.

4. Coclanis, *Shadow of a Dream,* 50–53.

5. "Coppy of Instruccons for Mr. West," 344. "Captain Halsted's Instructions," 1 May 1671, in Rivers, *History of South Carolina,* 359–61.

6. Sirmans, *Colonial South Carolina,* 29. Weir, *Colonial South Carolina,* 60. McCrady, *Proprietary South Carolina,* 165. Baldwin, *First Settlers,* passim.

7. Puckrein, *Little England,* 11. Coclanis, *Shadow of a Dream,* 56–57.

8. Wilson, "Account," 171. [Thomas Nairne], *A Letter from South Carolina; Giving an Account of the Soil, Air, Product, Trade, Government, Laws, Religion, People, Military Strength, &c. of the Province* (2d. ed., London: R. Smith, 1718), 12.

9. Ver Steeg, *Origins of a Southern Mosaic,* 114–16. Wood, *Black Majority,* 28–34. Cattle Brands Book, South Carolina Department of Archives and History (hereinafter cited as SCDAH). Cooper and McCord, *Statutes,* 2: 106–8.

10. Wilson, "Account," 171–72. Coclanis, *Shadow of a Dream,* 57–58.

11. Wood, *Black Majority,* 31, 144. Ver Steeg, *Origins of a Southern Mosaic,* 106, 114–16.

12. Coclanis, *Shadow of a Dream,* 57–58, 60–61, 81. Ver Steeg, *Origins of a Southern Mosaic,* 115–16.

13. Alexander Moore, ed., *Nairne's Muskhogean Journals: The 1708 Expedition to the Mississippi River* (Jackson: University Press of Mississippi, 1988), 50–51. Crane, *Southern Frontier,* 109. Eliades, "Indian Policy," 74–76.

14. John Lawson, *History* (1718) quoted in Crane, *Southern Frontier,* 110. Rowland et al., *Beaufort County,* 62, 72, 81.

15. Mooney, *Siouan Tribes of the East,* 78–79.

16. Crane, *Southern Frontier,* 115–17. Hatley, *Dividing Paths,* 10, 17–21, 44–47, 163. Merrell, *Indians' New World,* 5, 29–43, 60.

17. Sirmans, *Colonial South Carolina,* 72.

18. Crane, *Southern Frontier,* 109–11. S.P.G. MSS A, II, no. 156 quoted in Crane, *Southern Frontier,* 110.

19. Ver Steeg, *Origins of a Southern Mosaic,* 109–10. Sirmans, *Colonial South Carolina,* 194–95. Silver, *New Face on the Countryside,* 92–93.

20. "Temporary Laws to be added to the former," in Rivers, *History of South Carolina,* 353.

21. Crane, *Southern Frontier,* 109, 113. Eliades, "Indian Policy," 57. Silver, *New Face on the Countryside,* 74. Ferguson, *Uncommon Ground,* 60. Russell D. Menard, "Financing the Lowcountry Export Boom: Capital and Growth in Early South Carolina," *WMQ,* 3d series, 51 (Oct. 1994): 660. Merrell, *Indians' New World,* 36.

22. Moore, *Nairne's Muskhogean Journals,* 47–48. Hudson, *Catawba Nation,* 22.

23. Sirmans, *Colonial South Carolina,* 41–43. Rivers, *History of South Carolina,* 139. Defoe, *Party-Tyranny,* 240–41. Edgar and Bailey, *Biographical Directory,* 2: 491–92.

24. Rivers, *History of South Carolina,* 146. Weir, *Colonial South Carolina,* 66.

25. Rivers, *History of South Carolina,* 146–47. Weir, *Colonial South Carolina,* 62, 66, 71, 86. Sirmans, *Colonial South Carolina,* 39–43, 50, 54, 58. Ramsay, *History of South Carolina,* 1: 113–18.

26. Ver Steeg, *Origins of a Southern Mosaic,* 117–19.

27. Moore, "Daniel Axtell's Account Book," 289–92. Ver Steeg, *Origins of a Southern Mosaic,* 120–24.

28. Ver Steeg, *Origins of a Southern Mosaic,* 120–22. Linder, "River in Time," 75.

29. Linder, "River in Time," 76. Ver Steeg, *Origins of a Southern Mosaic,* 122. For an excellent description of the process of rendering tar, pitch, and turpentine, see Linder, "River in Time," 75–78.

30. Ver Steeg, *Origins of a Southern Mosaic,* 122–29. Linder, "River in Time," 75. As South Carolina's naval stores industry declined, that in North Carolina expanded as South Carolinians, such as Maurice and Roger Moore (sons of the first Governor James Moore and brother of the second Governor James Moore), moved into the Cape Fear area. Land was cheaper in North Carolina and yellow pine plentiful. By the late colonial period nearly 60 percent of the naval stores produced in North America came from North Carolina. Powell, *North Carolina,* 81–84, 135–36.

31. Edgar, "Letter from South Carolina," 97.

32. Glen, "Description of South Carolina," 95.

33. Duncan Clinch Heyward, *Seed from Madagascar* (Chapel Hill: University of North Carolina Press, 1937), 4–5. Glen, "Description of South Carolina," 102–3. Wood, *Black Majority,* 27, 35–37. Littlefield, *Rice and Slaves,* 98–102, 108.

34. Joyce E. Chaplin, "Tidal Rice Cultivation and the Problem of Slavery in South Carolina and Georgia, 1760–1815," *WMQ,* 3d series, 49 (Jan. 1992): 31–39.

35. Milligen-Johnston, "Short Description of the Province," 119, 135–36.

36. Wood, *Black Majority,* 151.

37. Littlefield, *Rice and Slaves,* 74–114. Wood, *Black Majority,* 55–62. Weir, *Colonial South Carolina,* 178–79.

38. Littlefield, *Rice and Slaves,* 92–98, 105–9. Judith Carney and Richard Porcher, "Geographies of the Past: Rice, Slaves and Technological Transfer in South Carolina," *Southeastern Geographer,* 33 (Nov. 1993): 127–47.

39. Ver Steeg, *Origins of a Southern Mosaic,* 130. Littlefield, *Rice and Slaves,* 109. Wood, *Black Majority,* 119–24.

40. Coclanis, *Shadow of a Dream,* 96–99.

41. [Nairne], *Letter from South Carolina,* 48–49. Coclanis, *Shadow of a Dream,* 98. Edgar and Bailey, *Biographical Directory,* 2: 26–27, 225–26, 360–61.

42. Joyce E. Chaplin, *Anxious Pursuit: Agricultural Innovation & Modernity in the Lower South, 1730–1815* (Chapel Hill: Published for the Institute of Early American History and Culture at Williamsburg, Va., by University of North Carolina Press, 1993), 85–87. Coclanis, *Shadow of a Dream,* 97.

43. Coclanis, *Shadow of a Dream,* 96–97. Littlefield, *Rice and Slaves,* 69–70.

44. Littlefield, *Rice and Slaves,* 67. [Nairne], *Letter from South Carolina,* 48–49. Russell R. Menard, "Financing the Lowcountry Export Boom: Capital and Growth in Early Carolina, 1700–1740" (unpub. paper presented to the Social Science History Association, Chicago, 1988), 20, Table 7.

45. Coclanis, *Shadow of a Dream,* 99–102. Littlefield, *Rice and Slaves,* 69.

46. Rogers, *Charleston,* 21. Walter J. Fraser Jr., *Charleston! Charleston!: The History of a Southern City* (Columbia: University of South Carolina Press, 1989), 115. Coclanis, *Shadow of a Dream,* 99.

47. Edgar, *Pringle Letterbook,* 1: 269, 287, 290; 2: 523, 534, 774, 811. Coclanis, *Shadow of a Dream,* 83, 106.

48. Edgar, *Pringle Letterbook,* 2: 774. David H. Rembert Jr., "The Indigo of Commerce in Colonial North America" (unpub. paper, 1978), 9. John J. Winberry, "Indigo in South Carolina: A Historical Geography," *Southeastern Geographer,* 29 (Nov. 1979): 91–92. John J. Winberry, "Reputation of Carolina Indigo," *SCHM,* 80 (1979): 242–50.

49. "A Letter from Eliza Lucas Pinckney, 1785," in Merreins, *Colonial South Carolina Scene,* 145–46. Wallace, *History of South Carolina,* 1: 384–85. Winberry, "Indigo in South Carolina," 92–93.

50. Winberry, "Reputation of Carolina Indigo," 243.

51. Ibid., 244–45.

52. "Method of Manufacturing Indigo," *Gentleman's Magazine,* 25 (1755): 256. "Observations on the Production of Indigo, 1747," in Merrens, *Colonial South Carolina,* 148–49, 156–59. For a description of the production of indigo from planting to market, see Winberry, "Indigo in South Carolina," 94–96

53. Winberry, "Reputation of Carolina Indigo," 246–47. "Observations on the Production of Indigo, 1747," 150, 152. Edgar and Bailey, *Biographical Directory,* 2: 68–69, 310–11, 586–87, 659–60. Winberry, "Indigo in South Carolina," 93.

54. Chaplin, *Anxious Pursuit,* 138–39. Laurens to John Ettwein, 7 Apr. 1762. Rogers et al., *Laurens Papers,* 3: 92–95.

55. Chaplin, *Anxious Pursuit,* 158–65. Edgar, "Letter from South Carolina," 97–98.

56. Edgar, "Letter from South Carolina," 171–72. Rogers et al., *Laurens Papers,* 7: 179.

57. Edgar, *Pringle Letterbook,* 2: 731–32. Edgar, "Letter from South Carolina," 95–98, 171–72, 231–33. Chaplain, *Anxious Pursuit,* 134–40.

58. John Bivins and Forsyth Alexander, *The Regional Arts of the Early South: A Sampling from the Collection of the Museum of Early Southern Decorative Arts* (Winston-Salem, N.C.: Museum of Early Southern Decorative Arts, 1991), 135. Artisans' Lists, MESDA.

59. Coclanis, *Shadow of a Dream,* 91–92. Ver Steeg, *Origins of a Southern Mosaic,* 128.

60. Edgar, *Pringle Letterbook,* vols. 1 & 2. Rogers et al., *Laurens Papers,* vols. 1–4. Rogers, *Charleston,* 11–12. Coclanis, *Shadow of a Dream,* 102, 104.

61. Kenneth Morgan, "The Organization of the Colonial American Rice Trade," *WMQ,* 3d series, 52 (July 1995): 433–52. Thomas J. Little, "The Influence of Slavery of the West Indies Upon Slavery in Colonial South Carolina, 1670–1738," thesis, University of South Carolina, 1989, p. 128. Coclanis, *Shadow of a Dream,* 26. James Glen to the Board of Trade, Mar. 1751. BPRO, 24 (1750–1751): 317.

62. Coclanis, *Shadow of a Dream,* 74–77, 106–7. Ver Steeg, *Origins of a Southern Mosaic,* 129.

63. Menard, "Financing the Lowcountry Export Boom," 2, 10, 24. Rogers, *Charleston,* 14–15. Coclanis, *Shadow of a Dream,* 96, 104–6. Edgar and Bailey, *Biographical Directory,* 2: 454–56.

64. James Glen to the Board of Trade, Mar. 1751, 318–19. Ramsay, *History of South Carolina,* 1: 66.

65. [Nairne], *Letter from South Carolina,* 47–48. Edgar and Bailey, *Biographical Directory,* 2: 321–23.

66. Rogers et al., *Laurens Papers,* 7: 176, 179.

67. Alice Hanson Jones, *Wealth of a Nation To Be: The American Colonies on the Eve of the Revolution* (New York: Columbia University Press, 1980), 10, 170–71, 377–79. Coclanis, *Shadow of a Dream*, 26, 90–91.

Jones converted 1774 pounds sterling to 1978 dollars at the rate of £1 = $54.26. Using that calculation, the estate values would be much higher (the South Carolina average, for example, would be $126,844 in 1978 dollars; adjusted for inflation, the average would be over $300,000). In this study, for consistency, Jones's estate values in pounds sterling have been converted using McCusker's formulas and tables.

68. Jones, *Wealth of a Nation To Be*, 170–71.

69. Jones, *Wealth of a Nation To Be*, 171. Fraser, *Charleston! Charleston!*, 102–3. Weir, *Colonial South Carolina*, 214, 222–23.

70. Rogers, *Charleston*, 9, 14–15, 24–25. Fraser, *Charleston! Charleston!*, 110–11.

CHAPTER 9: EVERYDAY LIFE IN COLONIAL SOUTH CAROLINA

1. "Journal of a Visit to Charleston, 1765," in Merrens, *Colonial South Carolina*, 219. Coclanis, *Shadow of a Dream*, 64–66.

2. Coclanis, *Shadow of a Dream*, 64–65.

3. Weir, *Colonial South Carolina*, 206–7. Robert Stockton, "Documents Relating to Birth and Death in South Carolina, 1670–1800" (seminar paper, University of South Carolina, 1978), 43–44.

4. Archdale, "New Description," 290–91. "From Oldmixon's History of the British Empire" in Salley, *Narratives of Early Carolina*, 368. Silver, *New Face on the Countryside*, 153–63.

5. Waring, *History of Medicine*, 371–72. St. Julien Ravenel Childs, *Malaria and Colonization in the Carolina Low Country, 1526–1696* (Baltimore: Johns Hopkins University Press, 1940), quoted in Stockton, "Documents Relating to Birth and Death," 16.

6. George D. Terry, "'Champaign Country': A Social History of an Eighteenth Century Lowcountry Parish in South Carolina, St. Johns Berkeley," diss., University of South Carolina, 1981, p. 92. Coclanis, *Shadow of a Dream*, 42–44. Weir, *Colonial South Carolina*, 206–7.

7. Louisa Susannah [Wells] Aikman, *The Journal of a Voyage from Charlestown, S.C. to London Undertaken During the American Revolution By a Daughter of an Eminent Loyalist in the Year 1778, and Written from Memory only in 1779* (New York: New York Historical Society, 1906), 77. Terry, "'Champaign Country,'" 93, 99.

8. Coclanis, *Shadow of a Dream*, 44. Wood, *Black Majority*, 88–91. Silver, *New Face on the Countryside*, 162–63.

9. Edgar and Bailey, *Biographical Directory*, 2: 466–68. Archdale, "New Description," 291.

10. Waring, *History of Medicine*, 74–77. Merrell, *Indians' New World*, 136, 192–97.

11. Rogers et al., *Laurens Papers*, 6: 119. Edgar and Bailey, *Biographical Directory*, 2: 393. Hooker, *Carolina Backcountry*, 39.

12. Terry, "'Champaign Country,'" 94–98. Alexander S. Salley Jr., *Death Notices in the South-Carolina Gazette, 1732–1775* (Columbia: Historical Commission of South Carolina, 1917), 8. Stockton, "Documents Relating to Birth and Death," 14.

13. Hooker, *Carolina Backcountry*, 85. Martha Elizabeth Ivey, "Women Publicans," senior thesis, University of South Carolina, 1975, p. 7. Edgar and Bailey, *Biographical Directory*, 2: 95–97.

14. WPA Transcripts of Charleston County Wills, SCDAH., QQ (1760–1767), 116 (hereinafter cited as Wills). Ivey, "Women Publicans," 19. Wills, 19 (1780–1783), 149–50. Stockton, "Documents Relating to Birth and Death," 14–15.

15. Wills, QQ (1760–1767), 191. Ivey, "Women Publicans," 10. "Charleston in 1774," in Merrens, *Colonial South Carolina*, 285. Weir, *Colonial South Carolina*, 203. John Christian Kolbe, "Thomas Elfe, Eighteenth Century Charleston Cabinetmaker," thesis, University of South Carolina, 1980, pp. 133–35. Stockton, "Documents Relating to Birth and Death," 34–36.

16. Salley, *Death Notices*, 8. "Journal of a Visit to Charleston, 1765," 223. Stockton, "Documents Relating to Birth and Death," 30–31, 37–39. Charles Joyner, *Down By the Riverside: A South Carolina Slave Community* (Urbana: University of Illinois Press, 1984), 138.

17. Cooper and McCord, *Statutes*, 7: 77. Chaplain, *Anxious Pursuit*, 271–73.

18. "Governor William Bull's Representation," 269. "Journal of a Visit to Charleston, 1765," 221–23. Hooker, *Carolina Backcountry*, 5.

19. Rogers, *History of Georgetown County*, 333–34. Winberry, "Indigo in South Carolina," 95.

20. Milligen-Johnston, "Short Description of South-Carolina," 128–30. Fraser, *Charleston! Charleston!*, 11, 16, 44, 83–85. Coclanis, *Shadow of a Dream*, 6.

21. Edgar, *Pringle Letterbook*, 1: 282. Glen, "Description of South Carolina," 36.

22. McCrady, *Proprietary South Carolina*, 6–7. Rogers, *Charleston*, 3–25. Bridenbaugh, *Myths and Realities*, 59–60, 76–94. Susan Quincy, ed., *Memoir of the Life of Josiah Quincy, Junior of Massachusetts: 1744–1775. By His Son, Josiah Quincy*, 2d. ed. (Boston: John Wilson and Son, 1874), 72–73. Jones, *Wealth of a Nation To Be*, 377–79. Jack P. Greene, *Pursuits of Happiness: The Social Development of Early Modern British Colonies and the Formation of American Culture* (Chapel Hill: University of North Carolina Press, 1988), 146–47.

23. Rogers, *Charleston*, 55–62. Fraser, *Charleston! Charleston!*, 6–9. Coclanis, *Shadow of a Dream*, 3–5.

24. Rogers, *Charleston*, 61.

25. Edgar, *Pringle Letterbook*, 1: 275, 282, 282n, 283n; 2: 478, 478n. One hundred thousand pounds sterling in 1740 corresponds to approximately $12.2 million in 1996 dollars.

26. Hewatt, "Historical Account," 501. Alexander Gregg, *History of the Old Cheraws* (New York: Richardson, 1867), 104, 118–19. Everett B. Wilson, *Early Southern Towns* (New York: Castle Books, 1967), 135. Joseph A. Ernst and H. Roy Merrens, "'Camden's Turrets pierce the skies!': The Urban Process in the Southern Colonies during the Eighteenth Century," *WMQ*, 30 (1973): 563. Salley, *Orangeburg County*, 60–63. Daniel Culler Marchant, *Orangeburgh District, 1768–1868: History and Records* (Spartanburg, S.C.: Reprint Company, 1995). William Gilmore Simms, *The Forayers* (New York: Redfield, 1857), 263–64.

27. Rogers, *History of Georgetown County*, 30–36.

28. Rowland et al., *Beaufort County*, 175–94, 196.

29. Ernst and Merrens, "'Camden's Turrets pierce the skies!,'" 558–63. W. S. Alexander and I. W. Corbett, *A Descriptive Sketch of Camden, S.C.* (Charleston: Walker, Evans & Cogswell, 1888), 7. Thomas J. Kirkland and Robert M. Kennedy, *Historic Camden, Part One: Colonial and Revolutionary* (1905; Camden, S.C.: Kershaw County Historical Society, 1968), 9–15.

30. Terry, "'Champaign Country,'" 186, 212–20.

31. Quoted in Terry, "'Champaign Country,'" 186. "Charleston in 1774," 283. Hooker, *Carolina Backcountry*, 5.

32. "Charleston in 1774," 283. Charleston Artisans, MESDA files, item 9085. Rogers et al., *Laurens Papers*, 3: 458.

33. Terry, "'Champaign Country,'" 205. Linder, "River in Time," 61–62.

34. Rogers, *History of Georgetown County*, 44. Rogers, *Charleston*, 4. *Gazette*, 14 Sept. 1767. Richard Maxwell Brown, *The South Carolina Regulators* (Cambridge, Mass.: Belknap Press of Harvard University Press, 1963), 16. Rogers et al., *Laurens Papers*, 3: 92–95.

35. Helen Cohen, *The South Carolina Gazette, 1732–1775* (Columbia: University of South Carolina Press, 1953), 3–5. Sidney Korbe, *The Development of the Colonial Newspaper* (Pittsburgh: Colonial Press, 1944), 147–48. Mark M. Boatner III, "Population," in *Encyclopedia of the American Revolution* (New York: David McKay, 1975), 882.

36. Lila Mills Hawes, ed., *The Letterbook of Thomas Rasberry, 1758–1761, Volume XIII, Collections of the Georgia Historical Society* (Savannah: Georgia Historical Society, 1959), 81, 91, 133–37.

37. Edgar, *Pringle Letterbook*, 2: 544, 690.

38. John William Gerhard De Brahm, *Philosophico-Hydrography of South Carolina* quoted in Waterhouse, *New World Gentry*, 125.

39. Rogers, *History of Georgetown County*, 105. Thomas H. Pope, *The History of Newberry County, South Carolina*, 2 vols. (Columbia: University of South Carolina Press, 1973, 1992), 1: 32–33.

40. Wood, *Black Majority*, 169. Littlefield, *Rice and Slaves*, 134.

41. Wood, *Black Majority*, 314.

42. Cooper and McCord, *Statutes,* 7: 410. Roger D. Abrahams, *Singing the Master* (New York: Pantheon, 1992), xix–xxi, 18, 21, 83–96, 112–32. Joyner, "Cultural Triangle," 10. Weir, *Colonial South Carolina,* 177–78, 190.

43. Coclanis, *Shadow of a Dream,* 71–76. Edgar and Bailey, *Biographical Directory,* 2: 374–77, 380–82. Milligen-Johnston, "Description of South Carolina," 134. Hofstadter, *America at 1750,* 164.

44. Artisan Lists, MESDA. Mabel L. Webber, ed., "Abstracts of Records of the Proceedings in the Court of Ordinary, 1764–1771," *SCHM,* 22 (1921): 95, 96, 128; 23 (1922): 77. Elizabeth H. Jervey, ed., "Abstracts from the Records of the Court of Ordinary, 1764–1771," *SCHM,* 43 (1942): 119, 180; 44 (1943): 45, 46, 112, 175. *South Carolina and American General Gazette,* 25 July 1766 (hereinafter cited as *General Gazette*).

45. Commons House Journals, 37, part 1 (28 Oct. 1765–28 May 1767): 260, 265, 329–36; 37, part 2 (3 Nov. 1767–19 Nov. 1768): 500–501, 505–6, 527, 577, 582; 38, part 1 (14 Mar. 1769–7 Nov. 1769): 58–59, 96–97, 100–101.

46. Commons House Journals, 37, part 1: 330, 331; 37, part 2: 577.

47. *Gazette,* 28 Sept. 1734, 5 Nov. 1763. *South Carolina Gazette and Country Journal,* 15 Sept. 1767 (hereinafter cited as *Country Journal*). Littlefield, *Rice and Slaves,* 136–37. Wood, *Black Majority,* 196–200. Richard Walsh, *Charleston's Sons of Liberty: A Study of the Artisans, 1763–1789* (1959; Columbia: University of South Carolina Press, 1968), 49. E. Milby Burton, *South Carolina Silversmiths, 1690–1860* (Rutland, Vt.: Charles E. Tuttle Company, 1968), 208.

48. Bridenbaugh, *Myths and Realities,* 85.

49. Mary Roberts Parramore, "'For Her Sole and Separate Use': Feme Sole Trader Status in Early South Carolina," thesis, University of South Carolina, 1991, 91–97, 104.

50. Weir, *Colonial South Carolina,* 230–33. Parramore, "'For Her Sole and Separate Use,'" 3–32.

51. Weir, *Colonial South Carolina,* 230. Edgar, *Pringle Letterbook,* 1: xv. A. S. Salley Jr., ed., *Marriage Notices in The South-Carolina Gazette; and Country Journal (1765–1775) and in The Charlestown Gazette (1778–1780)* (Charleston: Walker, Evans & Cogswell Co., 1904), 1, 8–9, 13, 22.

52. Salley, *Marriage Notices,* passim. Edgar and Bailey, *Biographical Directory,* 2: 25–26, 117, 201–2, 542–43.

53. Webber, "Abstracts of Records," 22: 124, 126; 23: 77, 79, 179, 180. Jervey, "Abstracts from the Records," 43: 119–20, 177; 45: 49. Commons House Journals, 37, part 2: 505, 582. *The Journal and Letters of Eliza Lucas* quoted in Stockton, "Documents Relating to Birth and Death," 20–21.

54. Cohen, *South Carolina Gazette,* 4, 238–41. *South Carolina Gazette,* 4 Jan. 1739. Julia Cherry Spruill, *Women's Life and Work in the Southern Colonies* (1938; New York: W. W. Norton, 1972), 263–64.

55. Hudson, *Southeastern Indians,* 269. Edgar, *Pringle Letterbook,* 1: 271–73. Rogers et al., *Laurens Papers,* 5: 703–4. Hatley, *Dividing Paths,* 8–9, 148–52.

56. Edgar, *Pringle Letterbook,* 1: 205–7. Rogers et al., *Laurens Papers,* 7: 300. Salley, *Marriage Notices,* 21.

57. *Gazette,* 15, 22 Aug. 1743. Parramore, "'For Her Sole and Separate Use,'" passim.

58. *Gazette,* 21 Nov. 1743. Weir, *Colonial South Carolina,* 231.

59. Hofstadter, *America at 1750,* 164–66.

60. Rogers, *Charleston,* 12–13. Rogers, *History of Georgetown County,* 95–96. Ivey, "Women Publicans," 12. *General Gazette,* 16 Jan. 1767; 22 Jan. 1768; 5 Feb. 1768. Quincy, *Memoir,* 83.

In Virginia the tidewater elite controlled both sports as patrons and organizers. Rhys Isaac, *The Transformation of Virginia* (Chapel Hill: Published for the Institute of Early American History and Culture, Williamsburg, Va., by University of North Carolina Press, 1982), 98–104, 132.

61. Bridenbaugh, *Myths and Realities,* 87–88. Milligen-Johnston, *Short Description of South-Carolina,* 135.

62. Milligen-Johnston, "Short Description of South-Carolina," 134. Walter B. Edgar, "The Libraries of Colonial South Carolina," diss., University of South Carolina, 1969, 114.

63. Fraser, *Charleston! Charleston!,* 60. Bridenbaugh, *Myths and Realities,* 89–91. *General Gazette,* 14 Oct. 1768.

64. Eola Willis, *The Charleston Stage in the XVIII Century* (Columbia: State Company, 1924), 14.

65. Fraser, *Charleston! Charleston!*, 59–60. Rogers, *Charleston*, 110. Bridenbaugh, *Myths and Realities*, 92–93. Walsh, *Charleston's Sons of Liberty*, 144–45. Willis, *Charleston Stage*, 24, 66, 91.

66. Ivey, "Women Publicans," passim. South Carolina, Commons House Journals, 37, part 1: 261; 38, part 1: 96.

67. Elfe was Backhouse's largest creditor and, as such, ended up as administrator of his estate. The description of items in the inventory are similar to those in Elfe's account books. Ivey, "Women Publicans," 4–8.

68. Ivey, "Women Publicans," 2–3. *South Carolina Gazette and Country Journal*, 2 Feb. 1768.

69. Ivey, "Women Publicans," 3. Quincy, *Memoir*, 81, 83. Fraser, *Charleston! Charleston!*, 56, 58–59. Cohen, *South Carolina Gazette*, 17–24.

70. Josiah Quincy Jr., "Journal of Josiah Quincy, Jr.," Mark Anthony DeWolfe Howe, ed., Massachusetts Historical Society *Proceedings*, 49 (1915–1916): 455. Hooker, *Carolina Backcountry*, 47.

71. Wood, *Black Majority*, 271–72. Quincy, "Journal," 455. Weir, *Colonial South Carolina*, 190.

72. Weir, *Colonial South Carolina*, 190.

73. Salley, *Death Notices*, 7. *Country Journal*, 12 June 1769.

74. Milligen-Johnston, *Short Description of South-Carolina*, 135.

75. Brooke Hindle, *The Pursuit of Science in Revolutionary America, 1735–1789* (Chapel Hill: Published for the Institute of Early American History and Culture at Williamsburg, Va., by University of North Carolina Press, 1956), 50–51. Quincy, *Memoir*, 75, 81.

76. Bernard Bailyn, *Education in the Forming of American Society: Needs and Opportunities for Study* (Chapel Hill: Published for the Institute of Early American History and Culture, Williamsburg, Va., by University of North Carolina Press, 1960), 93–94. Lawrence A. Cremin, *American Education: The Colonial Experience, 1607–1783* (New York: Harper & Row, 1970), 542–43. Wallace, *History of South Carolina*, 1: 193–95, 403–4. Linder, "River in Time," 110–11.

In 1890, 44 percent of South Carolina's population was totally illiterate. Walter B. Edgar, *South Carolina in the Modern Age* (Columbia: University of South Carolina Press, 1992), 19.

77. Wallace, *History of South Carolina*, 1: 193–95, 403–4. Weir, *Colonial South Carolina*, 248.

78. Wallace, *History of South Carolina*, 1: 193–95. Linder, "River in Time," 110–11. Hooker, *Carolina Backcountry*, 44–45.

79. Edgar, "Libraries of Colonial South Carolina," 70–80.

80. Judith R. Joyner, *Beginnings: Education in Colonial South Carolina* (Columbia: Museum of Education, McKissick Museum, 1985), 3–51.

81. Weir, *Colonial South Carolina*, 248–52. Rogers, *Charleston*, 97–98. "Governor William Bull's Representation," 264. Cohen, *South Carolina Gazette*, 25–39. Hooker, *Carolina Backcountry*, 72. Bridenbaugh, *Myths and Realities*, 84. Joyner, *Beginnings*, 33–58.

82. Rogers et al., *Laurens Papers*, 8: 140–42. Walsh, *Charleston's Sons of Liberty*, 22–23, 29–30. E. Milby Burton, *Charleston Furniture, 1720–1825* (1955; Columbia: University of South Carolina Press, 1970), 10–11. Burton, *South Carolina Silversmiths*, 207–9. Weir, *Colonial South Carolina*, 252. Joyner, *Beginnings*, 34–37.

83. Wallace, *History of South Carolina*, 194. Weir, *Colonial South Carolina*, 194. Joyner, *Beginnings*, 37–43.

84. Wood, *Black Majority*, 181–85. John C. Inscoe, "Carolina Slave Names: An Index to Acculturation," *Journal of Southern History*, 49 (Nov. 1983): 527–54 (hereinafter cited as *JSH*).

85. Joyner, "Cultural Triangle," 10–11.

86. Rogers et al., *Laurens Papers*, 6: 139–41, 425; 7: 585–87; 8: 30–32. Rogers, *Charleston*, 99.

87. Waring, *History of Medicine*, 182, 255, 336–37. George C. Rogers Jr., *Generations of Lawyers: A History of the South Carolina Bar* (Columbia: South Carolina Bar Foundation, 1992), 4. Rogers, *Charleston*, 99. Weir, *Colonial South Carolina*, 251.

88. "Governor William Bull's Representation," 263. Rogers et al., *Laurens Papers*, 7: 585–87; 8: 30–32.

89. Milligen-Johnston, "Short Description of South-Carolina," 147–48. Rogers, *Charleston*, 99. Edgar, "Libraries of Colonial South Carolina," 88, 90, 93. Wallace, *History of South Carolina*, 1: 404.

90. Greene, *Quest for Power,* 402–16. Wallace, *History of South Carolina,* 2: 106–7. Rogers, *Charleston,* 98–101. Bridenbaugh, *Myths and Realities,* 104. Rogers et al., *Laurens Papers,* 7: 585–87; 8: 30–32.

91. Wallace, *History of South Carolina,* 3: 50. Rogers, *Charleston,* 96–97. Marion B. Smith, "South Carolina and *The Gentleman's Magazine,*" *SCHM,* 95 (Apr. 1994): 102–29.

92. Raymond Phineas Stearns, *Science in the British Colonies* (Urbana: University of Illinois Press, 1970), 294–96, 315–21. Wallace, *History of South Carolina,* 1: 408. Edgar and Bailey, *Biographical Directory,* 2: 231–32.

93. *Gazette,* 10 Nov. 1766. *General Gazette,* 6 Mar. 1769. Steve Bender and Felder Rushing, *Passalong Plants* (Chapel Hill & London: University of North Carolina Press, 1993), 8, 13, 26, 46, 77, 107, 131. George C. Rogers Jr., "Gardens and Landscapes in Eighteenth-Century South Carolina" in *British and American Gardens in the Eighteenth Century* (Williamsburg, Va.: Colonial Williamsburg Foundation, 1984), 148–53. Sterns, *Science in America,* 317.

94. Waring, *History of Medicine,* 79, 204. Stearns, *Science in the British Colonies,* 594–98.

95. Hindle, *Pursuit of Science,* 37, 50–56. Stearns, *Science in the British Colonies,* 519, 596, 599–619. Waring, *History of Medicine,* 221–34. Edmund Berkeley and Dorothy Smith Berkeley, *Doctor Alexander Garden of Charles Town* (Chapel Hill: University of North Carolina Press, 1969), 47–48, 56, 158–62, 168–69, 178–79, 216–17, 317, 325–33. Rogers, *Charleston,* 96. Rogers, "Gardens and Landscapes," 148–52. Edgar, "Letter from South Carolina," 95–98, 171–74, 231–33. Wood, *Black Majority,* 117, 119–23, 289. Edgar and Bailey, *Biographical Directory,* 2: 65–66.

96. Edgar, "Libraries of Colonial South Carolina," 64–66. Cohen, *South Carolina Gazette,* 157–80. Christopher Gould, "Robert Wells, Colonial Charleston Printer," *SCHM,* 79 (Jan. 1978): 23–49.

97. Edgar, "Libraries of Colonial South Carolina," 64–66. Cohen, *South Carolina Gazette,* 157–80.

98. Rogers, *History of Georgetown County,* 87–88. Edgar, "Libraries of Colonial South Carolina," 33–34, 50–52, 55–64, 81–83. Weir, *Colonial South Carolina,* 240–42.

99. The most widely owned books, by title, in colonial South Carolina were, in order: *The Spectator;* one of Nathan Bailey's two dictionaries; William Burkitt, *Expository Notes, with Practical Observation on the New Testament; The Guardian; The Tatler;* Richard Allestree, *The Whole Duty of Man;* Paul de Rapin-Thoyras, *The History of England;* the works of Virgil; the works of William Shakespeare; Flavius Josephus, *The History of the Jews;* the works of Alexander Pope; one of Abel Boyer's dictionaries; Giovanni Marana, *The Turkish Spy;* James Hervey, *Meditations and Contemplations;* the works of John Tillotson; the works of Jonathan Swift; John Milton, *Paradise Lost;* and Samuel Butler, *Hudibras.* Walter B. Edgar, "Some Popular Books in Colonial South Carolina," *SCHM,* 72 (1971): 174–78. Richard Beale Davis, *A Colonial Southern Bookshelf: Reading in the Eighteenth Century* (Athens: University of Georgia Press, 1979), 96, 114–15.

100. Davis, *Colonial Southern Bookshelf,* 35–36, 40–41, 107–10. Edgar, "Some Popular Books," 174–78.

101. Davis, *Colonial Southern Bookshelf,* 8, 68, 74–75, 78–81, 89. Edgar, "Libraries of Colonial South Carolina," 24, 27, 236.

102. Hooker, *Carolina Backcountry,* 74, 75. Wallace, *History of South Carolina,* 1: 418.

103. Edgar and Bailey, *Biographical Directory,* 2: 5. Wallace, *History of South Carolina,* 1: 419. Hooker, *Carolina Backcountry,* 74. Weir, *Colonial South Carolina,* 122–23.

104. "Governor William Bull's Representation," 255.

105. Hooker, *Carolina Backcountry,* 8. "Governor William Bull's Representation," 254–55.

106. "Governor William Bull's Representation," 254–55. Wallace, *History of South Carolina,* 1: 418, 420–21.

107. Weir, *Colonial South Carolina,* 23. Wallace, *History of South Carolina,* 1: 418, 420–21. Hooker, *Carolina Backcountry,* 11, 20, 30–31, 42, 45–47, 62, 75, 93, 108, passim.

108. Weir, *Colonial South Carolina,* 210. Wallace, *History of South Carolina,* 1: 419. History of Synod Committee, eds., *A History of the Lutheran Church in South Carolina* (Columbia: South Carolina Synod of the Lutheran Church in America, 1971), 38–40. Townsend, *South Carolina Baptists,* 61–110, 122–75. Howe, *History of the Presbyterian Church,* 1: 285–99, 363. McCormick, "Quakers," 127–37.

109. Brown, *South Carolina Regulators*, 20–22.

110. Brown, *South Carolina Regulators*, 20–22. Townsend, *South Carolina Baptists*, 272–73.

111. Brown, *South Carolina Regulators*, 20–22.

112. Weir, *Colonial South Carolina*, 210.

113. Hooker, *Carolina Backcountry*, 73–74, 241.

114. Wallace, *History of South Carolina*, 1: 428.

115. Wallace, *History of South Carolina*, 1: 428–29. Weir, *Colonial South Carolina*, 220–21. George Whitefield, *Journals* (London: Banner of Truth Trust, 1960), 381–89, 437–51. Joseph Tracy, *The Great Awakening* (Boston: Tappan & Dennet, 1842), 55–56. Edgar, "Libraries of Colonial South Carolina," 180. Bolton, *Southern Anglicanism*, 50–53.

116. Edgar, "Libraries of Colonial South Carolina," 25–27. Howe, *History of the Presbyterian Church*, 1: 240–46. Edgar and Bailey, *Biographical Directory*, 2: 108–9. Weir, *Colonial South Carolina*, 220–21. Harvey H. Jackson, "Hugh Bryan and the Evangelical Movement in Colonial South Carolina," *WMQ*, 34 (Oct. 1986): 608–10. Rowland et al., *Beaufort County*, 34–36. Bolton, *Southern Anglicanism*, 53–56.

117. Weir, *Colonial South Carolina*, 185–86.

118. Joyner, "Cultural Triangle," 5–7.

Of course, black Carolinians were not alone in their belief in the supernatural. In 1706 a woman was accused of witchcraft and sentenced to fifteen months in jail. In arguing for her conviction, Justice Nicholas Trott informed the jury that witches existed and how to detect them. Six years later one of the English statutes incorporated into South Carolina law was "An Acte against Conjuration, Witchcraft, and dealinge with Evill and Wicked Spirits." When many English statutes were repealed in 1734, this one remained on the books. Cooper and McCord, *Statutes*, 2: 509–10, 739. Wallace, *History of South Carolina*, 1: 177, 414–15.

119. Joyner, "Cultural Triangle," 7–9. Rogers et al., *Laurens Papers*, 7: 126.

For other examples see: Elise Pinckney, ed., *The Letterbook of Eliza Lucas Pinckney* (Chapel Hill: University of North Carolina Press, 1972), 94–95. Weir, *Colonial South Carolina*, 237–38.

120. Bridenbaugh, *Myths and Realities*, 97–98. Edgar, "Libraries of Colonial South Carolina," 174–79. Samuel Quincy, *Twenty Sermons* (Boston: John Draper, 1750). Rogers, *Evolution of a Federalist*, 32.

121. "A Gentleman's Travels, 1733–34," in Merrens, *Colonial South Carolina*, 119. "Journal of a Visit to Charleston, 1765," 218, 222. Weir, *Colonial South Carolina*, 123, 219. Rogers et al., *Laurens Papers*, 7: 166–68.

122. Hooker, *Carolina Backcountry*, 1, 6, 11, 31, 34.

123. Ibid., 6, 99–100.

124. Bridenbaugh and Bridenbaugh, *No Peace Beyond the Line*, 393–94. Weir, *Colonial South Carolina*, 260. Bridenbaugh, *Myths and Realities*, 73–74. Hewatt, "Historical Account," 501. "Journal of a Visit to Charleston, 1765," 225. Milligen-Johnston, "Short Description of South Carolina," 139. Hatley, *Dividing Paths*, 48–50.

125. Bridenbaugh and Bridenbaugh, *No Peace Beyond the Line*, 393–94. *Gazette*, 6 Apr. 1769. Hooker, *Carolina Backcountry*, 47, 89n.

126. Hooker, *Carolina Backcountry*, 88–89.

127. Ibid., 6, 15, 99–100.

128. Daniel C. Littlefield, "Abundance of Negroes of That Nation: The Significance of African Ethnicity in Colonial South Carolina," in *The Meaning of South Carolina History: Essays in Honor of George C. Rogers, Jr.*, edited by David R. Chesnutt and Clyde N. Wilson (Columbia: University of South Carolina Press, 1991), 31–32. Littlefield, *Rice and Slaves*, 61, 64–65, 71. John W. Blassingame, *The Slave Community: Plantation Life in the Antebellum South* (1972; New York: Oxford University Press, 1975), 85–87. Joyner, *Down By the Riverside*, 136–38.

129. Littlefield, *Rice and Slaves*, 169–70. Winthrop D. Jordan, *White Over Black: American Attitudes Toward the Negro, 1550–1812* (Chapel Hill: Published for the Institute of Early American Culture at Williamsburg, Va., by University of North Carolina Press, 1968), 146–47.

130. Wood, *Black Majority*, 233–36. Littlefield, *Rice and Slaves*, 169. Jordan, *White Over Black*, 146.

131. Josiah Quincy Jr., "The Journal of Josiah Quincy, Junior, 1773," *Massachusetts Historical Society Proceedings* quoted in Littlefield, *Rice and Slaves,* 170–71.

132. Works Progress Administration, Will Transcripts of Charleston County, 24 (1786–1793), 1100–1101. Wood, *Black Majority,* 100. Larry Darnell Watson, "The Quest for Order: Enforcing Slave Codes in Revolutionary South Carolina, 1760–1800," diss., University of South Carolina, 1980, 171–76.

133. Wood, *Black Majority,* 100–101. Jordan, *White Over Black,* 148. Laurens to William Drayton, 15 Feb. 1783 quoted in Jordan, *White Over Black,* 173. Rachel N. Klein, *Unification of a Slave State: The Rise of the Planter Class in the South Carolina Backcountry, 1760–1808* (Chapel Hill: Published for the Institute of Early American History and Culture, Williamsburg, Va., by University of North Carolina Press, 1990), 71. Weir, *Colonial South Carolina,* 199. Hooker, *Carolina Backcountry,* 99.

134. Littlefield, "Abundance of Negroes," 31–32. "Governor William Bull's Representation," 268–69.

135. *Country Journal,* 10 Oct. 1769. Weir, *Colonial South Carolina,* 233. Edgar and Bailey, *Biographical Directory,* 2: 161–62.

136. South Carolina, Judgment Rolls of the Court of Common Pleas, 1761: 166A. *Country Journal,* 30 June 1767; 5 Sept., 10 Oct. 1769.

137. Hooker, *Carolina Backcountry,* 61.

138. Linder, "River in Time," 64. *Gazette,* 11 Oct. 1770, quoted in Brown, *South Carolina Regulators,* 31. Hooker, *Carolina Backcountry,* 31–33, 61.

139. Wood, *Black Majority,* 210, 232–33. Rogers et al., *Laurens Papers,* 1: 71, 205; 2: 381. Edgar, *Pringle Letterbook,* 1: 31.

140. Edgar, *Pringle Letterbook,* 1: 31. Walsh, *Charleston's Sons of Liberty,* 8. Rogers et al., *Laurens Papers,* 1: 275; 2: 524n. Moore, "Daniel Axtell's Account Book," 288–89.

141. Quoted in Weir, *Colonial South Carolina,* 222. Milligen-Johnston, *Short Description of South-Carolina,* 134. Spruill, *Women's Life and Work,* 113.

142. Spruill, *Women's Life and Work,* 116–22.

143. Ivey, "Women Publicans," 9–10.

144. "Visitors from Philadelphia, 1770–1774," in Merrens, *Colonial South Carolina,* 277. Ivey, "Women Publicans," 9. Quincy, *Memoir,* 74.

145. Walsh, *Charleston's Sons of Liberty,* 7, 15. Edgar, *Pringle Letterbook,* 1: 57–58, 63–64, 188; 2: 706–7, 834. Rogers et al., *Laurens Papers,* 1: 195.

146. Dunn, *Sugar and Slaves,* 285–86. Archdale, "New Description," 290–91.

147. Dunn, *Sugar and Slaves,* 279–83. Quincy, *Memoir,* 74, 75, 77, 79, 80, 86. Rogers, *Charleston,* 81–82. Wood, *Black Majority,* 210. "Governor James Glen's Valuation, 1751," in Merrens, *Colonial South Carolina,* 184. "Governor William Bull's Representation," 255.

148. Greene, *Pursuits of Happiness,* 150. Wood, *Black Majority,* 210. Milligen-Johnston, "Short Description of South-Carolina," 138–39. Ferguson, *Uncommon Ground,* 94.

149. Ivey, "Women Publicans," 4. Hewatt, "Historical Account," 506. Rogers et al., *Laurens Papers,* 1 & 2: passim. Edgar, *Pringle Letterbook,* passim. "Journal of a Visit to Charleston, 1765," 221, 223.

150. Walsh, *Charleston's Sons of Liberty,* 6, 9. *General Gazette,* 28 Oct. 1768; supplement, 12 Dec. 1768.

151. Cooper and McCord, *Statutes,* 3: 715–18. *Gazette,* 5 July, 4 Oct. 1760; 8 Dec. 1768. Walsh, *Charleston's Sons of Liberty,* 144–45.

The daily subsistence allowance was four shillings, currency. A half crown was two shillings, sixpence. In today's dollars the subsistence allowance in 1760 was about $2.40 and the cost of a loaf of bread was approximately $1.50. Whereas the standard loaf of bread today is about twenty ounces, the weight of a colonial loaf varied depending upon the price and quality of flour. In February 1760 weights ranged from thirty nine to fifty-eight ounces. *Gazette,* 23 Feb. 1760. The five-pound loaf in 1768 cost $1.35.

152. Joyner, "Cultural Triangle," 11. Ferguson, *Uncommon Ground,* 90, 93–107. Joyner, *Down By the Riverside,* 94–97. Karen Hess, *The Carolina Rice Kitchen: The African Connection* (Columbia: University of South Carolina Press, 1992), 21, 111–13. Hatley, *Dividing Paths,* 8–9. Merrell, *Indians' New*

World, 210–11.

153. Anna Wells Rutledge, ed., *The Carolina Housewife, or House and Home: By a Lady of Charleston* (1847; Columbia: University of South Carolina Press, 1979), v, 14–27, 45, 93, 101, 120, 121, 126, 129, 138, 141, 142, 191, 195–96, 210–12. Hess, *Carolina Rice Kitchen,* 35–83, 92–110.

154. Hooker, *Carolina Backcountry,* 13, 34, 39, 52, 196. "A Gentleman's Travels, 1733–34," 114.

155. Joyner, *Down By the Riverside,* 44, 78, 91, 96–97. Ferguson, *Uncommon Ground,* 98–100.

156. Hooker, *Carolina Backcountry,* 39. Rogers, *Charleston,* 81.

157. Ferguson, *Uncommon Ground,* 22–32, 36, 82–92. Joyner, *Down By the Riverside,* 75. Merrell, *Indians' New World,* 210–11.

158. Dale Rosengarten, *Row Upon Row: Sea Grass Baskets of the South Carolina Lowcountry* (Columbia: McKissick Museum, 1986), 5–8, 14–16. Joyner, *Down By the Riverside,* 75–76. Ferguson, *Uncommon Ground,* 32.

Today's "sweetgrass" baskets are made from different materials and have different forms and uses than their eighteenth-century predecessors. Coiling has not changed, but the makers have. Women have become the keepers of this three-hundred-year-old African–South Carolina tradition. Rosengarten, *Row Upon Row,* 5–6, 29–32.

159. Carl Bridenbaugh, *Cities in Revolt: Urban Life in America, 1743–1776* (1955; New York: Oxford University Press, 1971), 274.

160. Bivins and Alexander, *Regional Arts,* 67. Bradford Rauschenburg and John Bivins, "Charleston Furniture" (unpub. ms. in progress, MESDA), 734–36. Burton, *Charleston Furniture,* 7–8. Interview with Brad Rauschenburg and John Bivins, Winston-Salem, N.C., 26 June 1996. Artisan Lists, MESDA. Bridenbaugh, *Cities in Revolt,* 274. Bridenbaugh, *Myths and Realities,* 59–60.

161. Burton, *Charleston Furniture,* 87–88. Rauschenburg and Bivins, "Charleston Furniture," 90–99. Kolbe, "Thomas Elfe," 99–157.

162. *General Gazette,* 18 July 1766. Bivins and Alexander, *Regional Arts,* 80–81. Rauschenburg and Bivins, "Charleston Furniture," 2: 94.

163. Bivins and Alexander, *Regional Arts,* 90, 94. Coclanis, *Shadow of a Dream,* 106. The dollar value of the library bookcase illustrates the hypothetical nature of monetary conversions. John Bivins believes that the value of the bookcase should be more than fifteen times the assigned dollar value. Bivins to the author, 8 July 1997.

164. Quincy, *Memoir,* 77. "Charleston in 1774," 277. Hooker, *Carolina Backcountry,* 70–72.

165. Burton, *South Carolina Silversmiths,* 146-49, 203-6. Bivins and Alexander, *Regional Arts,* 73, 83, 88, 89.

166. Burton, *South Carolina Silversmiths,* 5, 210, 235.

167. "Governor William Bull's Representation," 264. Jack P. Greene, "Search for Identity: An Interpretation of the Meaning of Selected Patterns of Response in Eighteenth Century America," *Journal of Social History,* 3 (1970): 208–9.

168. "Governor William Bull's Representation," 264. "Charleston in 1774," 282.

169. Albert Simons and Samuel L. Lapham Jr., eds., *The Early Architecture of Charleston,* 2d ed. (Columbia: University of South Carolina Press, 1970), 22.

170. Alleyne and Fraser, *Barbados-Carolina Connection,* 47–52. Coclanis, *Shadow of a Dream,* 8–11. Joyner, "Cultural Triangle," 12. Bishop Roberts, "View of Charles Town," Carolina Art Association, Charleston, S.C.

171. Simons and Lapham, *Early Architecture of Charleston,* 19–23.

172. John Bivins and J. Thomas Savage, "The Miles Brewton House, Charleston, South Carolina," *Magazine Antiques* (Feb. 1993): 294–307. Bivins and Alexander, *Regional Arts,* 68. Caroline Wyche Dixon, "The Miles Brewton House: Ezra Waite's Architectural Books and Other Possible Design Sources," *SCHM,* 82 (Apr. 1981): 118–42.

173. Rauschenburg and Bivins, "Charleston Furniture," 2: 91–92.

174. Simons and Lapham, *Early Architecture of Charleston,* 20. Kolbe, "Thomas Elfe," 39.

175. Samuel Gilliard Stoney, *The Plantations of the Carolina Lowcountry* (Charleston: Carolina Art Association, 1938), 27, 54–55, 58–59, 61–62, 64, 76. Edgar and Bailey, *Biographical Directory,* 2:

428–31. Rogers, *Charleston,* 23. Quincy, *Memoir,* 86. Rogers, *History of Georgetown County,* 99. John Michael Vlach, *Back of the Big House: The Architecture of Plantation Slavery,* Fred W. Morrison Series in Southern Studies (Chapel Hill: University of North Carolina Press, 1993), 4.

176. E. T. H. Shafer, *Carolina Gardens* (New York: Devin-Adair, 1963), 27–46.

177. Ferguson, *Uncommon Ground,* 37, 62, 64–73, 77, 79. Richard Westmacott, *African-American Gardens and Yards in the Rural South* (Knoxville: University of Tennessee Press, 1992), 16–18. Vlach, *Back of the Big House,* 155–56, 163–66.

178. Linder, "River in Time," 96–98. Ramsay, *History of South Carolina* (1809 ed.), 2: 246–50. Hooker, *Carolina Backcountry,* 7, 32, 33. Merrell, *Indians' New World,* 173.

179. Greene, "Search for Identity," 190–91, 198–200.

180. Greene, "Search for Identity," 207–14. Weir, *Colonial South Carolina,* 217, 240–41. Bridenbaugh, *Myths and Realities,* 95. Waterhouse, *New World Gentry,* 109–10.

181. Bivins and Alexander, *Regional Arts,* 94. Rauschenburg and Bivins, "Charleston Furniture," 2: 191–93, 211, 226–38.

182. Rogers, *Charleston,* 79.

183. Greene, "Search for Identity," 200. Waterhouse, *New World Gentry,* 109–10.

184. Mabel L. Webber, ed., "Peter Manigault's Letters," *SCHM,* 32 (1931): 178. Weir, *Colonial South Carolina,* 141, 217, 263. Edgar and Bailey, *Biographical Directory,* 2: 431–34.

CHAPTER 10: THREATS

1. "A Journal of the Voyage to South Carolina in the Year 1767," in Merrens, *Colonial South Carolina,* 241. Weir, *Colonial South Carolina,* 281.

2. Brown, *South Carolina Regulators,* 14. Klein, *Unification of a Slave State,* 10, 14, 36. Hooker, *Carolina Backcountry,* 215.

3. Brown, *South Carolina Regulators,* 13–23. Klein, *Unification of a Slave State,* 38. Weir, *Colonial South Carolina,* 281–83.

4. Peter J. Hamilton, *Colonial Mobile,* ed. Charles G. Summersell (rev. ed. 1910; University: University of Alabama Press, 1976), 195–217. Corkran, *Carolina Indian Frontier,* 47–53. Hatley, *Dividing Paths,* 81–91, 98–115.

5. Corkran, *Carolina Indian Frontier,* 53–58. Weir, *Colonial South Carolina,* 268–70. Brown, *South Carolina Regulators,* 4–8. Hatley, *Dividing Paths,* 108–19. Cashin, *Lachlan McGillivray,* 190–93.

6. Corkran, *Carolina Indian Frontier,* 58–61. Brown, *South Carolina Regulators,* 4–8. Cashin, *Lachlan McGillivray,* 200–201. Weir, *Colonial South Carolina,* 270.

One hundred guineas converts to $8,800.

7. Brown, *South Carolina Regulators,* 9–11.

8. Hatley, *Dividing Paths,* 119–40. Cashin, *Lachlan McGillivray,* 200–202. Weir, *Colonial South Carolina,* 267–68. Brown, *South Carolina Regulators,* 9–11.

9. Cashin, *Lachlan McGillivray,* 202. Weir, *Colonial South Carolina,* 272–73. Wallace, *History of South Carolina,* 2: 31–35.

10. Klein, *Unification of a Slave State,* 38.

11. Greene, "Gadsden Election Controversy," 328–33.

12. Ibid., 332–34.

13. Ibid., 334–38, 347.

14. Wallace, *History of South Carolina,* 2: 32–33. Weir, *Colonial South Carolina,* 265–67, 288–93.

15. Weir, *Colonial South Carolina,* 270.

16. Merrell, *Indians' New World,* 143–202.

17. Weir, *Colonial South Carolina,* 291–92.

18. Walsh, *Charleston's Sons of Liberty,* 35.

19. Wells to Unknown, 13 Aug. 1765 quoted in Robert M. Weir, "Liberty and Property, and No Stamps: South Carolina and the Stamp Act Crisis," diss., Western Reserve University, 1966, p. 431. Weir, *Colonial South Carolina,* 287.

20. Walsh, *Charleston's Sons of Liberty,* 35–38. Rogers et al., *Laurens Papers,* 5: 26–28, 29–32. Wal-

lace, *History of South Carolina*, 2: 66–67. Edmund S. and Helen M. Morgan, *The Stamp Act Crisis: Prologue to Revolution* (1953; new rev. ed., New York: Collier Books, 1963), 201–2, 232–33.

21. Rogers, *Evolution of a Federalist*, 44–45. Weir, *Colonial South Carolina*, 296. Richard Walsh, ed., *The Writings of Christopher Gadsden* (Columbia: University of South Carolina Press, 1966), 65–68. Wallace, *History of South Carolina*, 2: 69–70.

22. Rogers, *Evolution of a Federalist*, 43–47. Wallace, *History of South Carolina*, 2: 70–73.

23. Wallace, *History of South Carolina*, 2: 73. Weir, *Colonial South Carolina*, 298. *Gazette*, 18 Aug. 1766.

24. Walsh, *Charleston's Sons of Liberty*, 41–45.

25. Hooker, *Carolina Backcountry*, 10, 86, 171. Klein, *Unification of a Slave State*, 39–41. Weir, *Colonial South Carolina*, 281.

26. Brown, *South Carolina Regulators*, 28–30. Cashin, *Lachlan McGillivray*, 213–30.

27. Brown, *South Carolina Regulators*, 28–34.

28. Ibid., 34–37.

29. Hooker, *Carolina Backcountry*, 215. Brown, *South Carolina Regulators*, 38. Weir, *Colonial South Carolina*, 275.

30. Brown, *South Carolina Regulators*, 1, 24–27, 40–41, 113–17. Klein, *Unification of a Slave State*, 68–69.

31. Brown, *South Carolina Regulators*, 43–47.

32. Hooker, *Carolina Backcountry*, 227. *Gazette*, 2 Sept. 1768. Brown, *South Carolina Regulators*, 47–52.

33. Brown, *South Carolina Regulators*, 47–52.

34. Ibid., 53–60, 83–89.

35. Klein, *Unification of a Slave State*, 48. Brown, *South Carolina Regulators*, 60–63. Commons House Journals, 17 Nov. 1768, SCDAH quoted in Brown, *South Carolina Regulators*, 62.

36. Brown, *South Carolina Regulators*, 59–60, 96–103. Edgar, *Biographical Directory*, 1: 134–35. Weir, *Colonial South Carolina*, 279–80.

37. Brown, *South Carolina Regulators*, 83–90.

38. Ibid., 90–95.

39. Klein, *Unification of a Slave State*, 51, 62–68. Hatley, *Dividing Paths*, 182–83.

40. Rogers et al., *Laurens Papers*, 5: xvii–xx; 6: 251–55. Weir, *Colonial South Carolina*, 301.

41. Weir, *Colonial South Carolina*, 303–4.

42. Jack P. Greene, "Bridge to Revolution: The Wilkes Fund Controversy in South Carolina," in Greene, *Negotiated Authorities*, 394–407.

43. Greene, "Bridge to Revolution," 407–22. Rowland et al., *Beaufort County*, 195–201.

44. Greene, "Bridge to Revolution," 394, 428.

45. Commons House Journals, 29 Aug. 1770, quoted in Greene, "Bridge to Revolution," 404. Greene, "Bridge to Revolution," 428.

46. Wallace, *History of South Carolina*, 2: 109.

47. Edgar and Bailey, *Biographical Directory*, 2: 259–63, 420–22, 458–60, 573–76, 577–81.

48. Weir, *Colonial South Carolina*, 315–16.

49. Walsh, *Charleston's Sons of Liberty*, 64. Peter Force, *American Archives*, 6th ser., 5 vols. (Washington, D.C.: M. St. Clair Clarke and Peter Force, 1835), 1: 526–27. Edgar and Bailey, *Biographical Directory*, 2: 95–97, 189–90, 331–33, 356, 552, 616, 635–37. N. Louise Bailey and Elizabeth Ivey Cooper, *Biographical Directory of the South Carolina House of Representatives, Volume III: 1775–1790* (Columbia: University of South Carolina Press, 1981), 296–98.

50. Edgar, *Biographical Directory*, 1: 151.

51. Ramsay, *History of South Carolina*, 1: 132. Wallace, *History of South Carolina*, 2: 119–20.

52. Robert A. Olwell, "'Domestick Enemies': Slavery and Political Independence in South Carolina, May 1775–March 1776," *JSH*, 55 (1989): 33–34. Weir, *Colonial South Carolina*, 200–203.

53. Robert Stansbury Lambert, *South Carolina Loyalists in the American Revolution* (Columbia: University of South Carolina Press, 1987), 34.

54. Fletchell to Henry Laurens, 23 July 1775, in Robert Wilson Gibbes, *Documentary History of the*

American Revolution quoted in Lambert, *South Carolina Loyalists,* 36. Lambert, *South Carolina Loyalists,* 34–38.

55. Lambert, *South Carolina Loyalists,* 38–42.

56. Rogers, *Charleston in the Age of the Pinckneys,* xi–xiii, 44.

CHAPTER 11: THE AMERICAN REVOLUTION

1. Lambert, *South Carolina Loyalists,* 40–42.

2. Lambert, *South Carolina Loyalists,* 45–46. Hatley, *Dividing Paths,* 186–90.

3. James Lowell Underwood, *The Constitution of South Carolina,* 4 vols. (Columbia: University of South Carolina Press, 1986–1994), 1: 85.

4. Henry Lumpkin, *From Savannah to Yorktown: The American Revolution in the South* (Columbia: University of South Carolina Press, 1981), 280–81.

Americans suffered twelve killed and twenty or so wounded, the British more than one hundred killed and sixty to seventy wounded. Lumpkin, *From Savannah to Yorktown,* 16. Among the casualties was Lord William Campbell, who died of wounds sustained during the battle.

5. There are many myths surrounding the state flag of South Carolina. The indigo blue flag with crescent moon was a militia flag. Not until 1861 did South Carolina, as an independent state, adopt a state flag: the white palmetto tree and crescent moon on an indigo blue field. Wylma Ann Wates, *A Flag Worthy of Your State and People: The History of the South Carolina State Flag* (Columbia: South Carolina Department of Archives and History, 1990), 1–2, 6–11.

6. Lambert, *South Carolina Loyalists,* 51–54. James H. O'Donnell III, "Indians in the War for American Independence" in Hudson, *Four Centuries of Southern Indians,* 55–56. Hatley, *Dividing Paths,* 191–97. Merrell, *Indians' New World,* 215–25.

7. Edward McCrady, *The History of South Carolina in the Revolution,* 2 vols. (New York: Macmillan, 1901–1902), 178–82 (hereinafter cited as *Revolutionary South Carolina*). Weir, *Colonial South Carolina,* 332. Henry Laurens quotation from the *Collections of the Historical Society of South Carolina* quoted in McCrady, *Revolutionary South Carolina,* 1: 179.

8. Wallace, *History of South Carolina,* 2: 168.

9. Walsh, *Writings of Christopher Gadsden,* 189. Bolton, *Southern Anglicanism,* 82–83.

10. Walter B. Edgar, "The Glorious Fourth of July in South Carolina," *News & Courier* (Charleston), 13 July 1979, B1. *General Gazette,* 9 July 1779.

11. Cooper and McCord, *Statutes,* 1: 147. McCrady, *Revolutionary South Carolina,* 1: 266–76.

12. Wallace, *History of South Carolina,* 2: 176–80. Cooper and McCord, *Statutes,* 4: 410–13, 513–14.

13. Don Higginbotham, *The War for Independence: Military Attitudes, Policies, and Practice, 1763–1789* (New York: Macmillan, 1971), 16–17. Charles Pinckney quoted in Asa H. Gordon, *Sketches of Negro Life and History in South Carolina* (1929; 2d. ed., Columbia: University of South Carolina Press, 1971), 40–41. Wallace, *History of South Carolina,* 2: 294. Bobby Gilmer Moss, *The Patriots at Cowpens* (Greenville, S.C.: A Press, 1985), 24, 29, 83, 248. Bobby Gilmer Moss, *The Patriots at King's Mountain* (Blacksburg, S.C.: Scotia-Hibernia, 1990), 98, 132–33, 234, 238, 244. George Fenwicke Jones, "The Black Hessians: Negroes Recruited By the Hessians in South Carolina and Other Colonies," *SCHM,* 83 (Oct. 1982): 287–302. M. Foster Farley, "The South Carolina Negro in the American Revolution, 1775–1783," *SCHM,* 79 (Apr. 1980): 75–86.

The Black Carolina Corps was transferred to Jamaica in 1781 and exists there still. Its official aire, or march, is "South Carolina is a Sultry Clime." Lewis P. Jones, *South Carolina, One of the Fifty States* (Orangeburg, S.C.: Sandlapper, 1985), 309–10.

14. Wallace, *History of South Carolina,* 2: 193. Ramsay, *History of South Carolina,* 1: 178–79.

15. McCrady, *Revolutionary South Carolina,* 1: 415–16. Wallace, *History of South Carolina,* 2: 200. Edgar and Bailey, *Biographical Directory,* 2: 248–51.

16. McCrady, *Revolutionary South Carolina,* 1: 432. There has been a great deal of debate about the authority granted Rutledge. Ramsay and McCrady say it was dictatorial, while Wallace dismisses that as "romantic" and contrary to the mood of the General Assembly. George Rogers, in the most recent analysis of the issue, stated that Rutledge was given "absolute power." Rogers, *Generations of*

Lawyers, 6.

Wallace, *History of South Carolina*, 2: 194–201. McCrady, *Revolutionary South Carolina*, 1: 445–510. Lumpkin, *From Savannah to Yorktown*, 248.

17. *New York Royal Gazette*, 21 June 1789 quoted in George Smith McCowen Jr., *The British Occupation of Charleston, 1780–1782* (Columbia: University of South Carolina Press, 1972), 11. Johnson and Sloan, *South Carolina*, 205.

18. Cornwallis to Lt. Col. John Cruger, 18 Aug. 1780, in Charles Ross, ed., *Correspondence of Charles, First Marquis Cornwallis* quoted in John Morgan Dederer, *Making Bricks Without Straw: Nathanael Greene's Southern Campaign and Mao Tse-Tung's Mobile War* (Manhattan, Kans.: Sunflower University Press, 1983), 32. Weigley, *Partisan War*, 12–13, 21–22. Dederer, *Making Bricks Without Straw*, 32. Lumpkin, *From Savannah to Yorktown*, 250. Peter Paret and John W. Shy, *Guerrillas in the 1960s* quoted in Russell F. Weigley, *The Partisan War: The South Carolina Campaign of 1780–1782* (Columbia: University of South Carolina Press, 1970), 10.

19. Weigley, *Partisan War*, 65.

20. For a list of Revolutionary War battles in South Carolina by counties (as of 1901), see: McCrady, *Revolutionary South Carolina*, 2: 744–53. Weigley, *Partisan War*, 21.

21. Dederer, *Making Bricks Without Straw*, 31. Weigley, *Partisan War*, 23. Rowland et al., *Beaufort County*, 232–36. Mao Tse-Tung, *On Guerrilla Warfare*, trans., with an introduction, by Samuel B. Griffith (New York: Praeger, 1961), 46.

22. Tarleton quotation from Weigley, *Partisan War*, 23. Cornwallis to Clinton, 3 Dec. 1780, in K. G. Davies, ed., *Documents of the American Revolution* quoted in Dederer, *Making Bricks Without Straw*, 33.

23. Weigley, *Partisan War*, 25. "Tarleton's Quarter" drew its name from an event of 29 May 1780 in the Waxhaws. A British force under Lt. Col. Banastre Tarleton captured a group of Continental soldiers. After they had surrendered and laid down their arms, Tarleton's men massacred them. "Tarleton's Quarter" became synonymous with unspeakable cruelty. In the backcountry both Whig and Tory units resorted to it.

24. Dederer, *Making Bricks Without Straw*, 14–17, 21, 32.

25. Dederer, *Making Bricks Without Straw*, 42. Weigley, *Partisan War*, 27–33.

26. Weigley, *Partisan War*, 26–33. Dederer, *Making Bricks Without Straw*, 48.

27. Weigley, *Partisan War*, 33–45. Dederer, *Making Bricks Without Straw*, 48–54.

28. Greene quotation from Weigley, *Partisan War*, 45. Weigley, *Partisan War*, 47.

29. Dederer, *Making Bricks Without Straw*, 55. Weigley, *Partisan War*, 67–68.

30. Weigley, *Partisan War*, 72. McCrady, *Revolutionary South Carolina*, 2: 750.

31. McCowen, *British Occupation of Charleston*, 13–42.

32. For a list of those exiled to St. Augustine, see McCowen, *British Occupation of Charleston*, 151–52. For a list of those whose property was sequestered, see McCowen, *British Occupation of Charleston*, 153–54.

33. McCowen, *British Occupation of Charleston*, 30. Bailey and Cooper, *Biographical Directory*, 3: 258–61. Caroline Gilman, ed., *Letters of Eliza Wilkinson During the Invasion and Possession of Charleston, S.C., by the British in the Revolutionary War* quoted in McCowen, *British Occupation of Charleston*, 64.

34. David K. Bowden, *The Execution of Isaac Hayne* (Lexington, S.C.: Sandlapper Store, 1977), 15, 47–53.

35. McCowen, *British Occupation of Charleston*, 44–52.

36. Kathy Roe Coker, "The Punishment of Revolutionary War Loyalists in South Carolina," diss., University of South Carolina, 1987, 11–13. Lambert, *South Carolina Loyalists*, 238–41, 281, 286–96. McCrady, *Revolutionary South Carolina*, 2: 582–85. Aedanus Burke, *An Address to the Freemen of South Carolina* quoted in John C. Meleney, *The Public Life of Aedanus Burke: Revolutionary Republican in Post-Revolutionary South Carolina* (Columbia: University of South Carolina Press, 1989), 80. Meleney, *Public Life of Aedanus Burke*, 66–67, 79–80.

For lists of those whose estates were either confiscated or amerced, see Cooper and McCord, *Statutes*, 4: 516–25.

37. According to Lambert, about 20 percent of the white population in 1775 were loyalists. Population estimates for that year range from sixty thousand to seventy thousand. Lambert, *South Carolina Loyalists,* 306. Wallace, *History of South Carolina,* 3: Appendix IV.

Transcripts of the manuscript books and papers of the Commission of Enquiry into Losses & Services of the American Loyalists, BPRO, microfilm of original from the New York Public Library, SCDAH, 55: 483–85. Lambert, *South Carolina Loyalists,* 111, 189–91, 269, 274, 281, 306.

38. Lambert, *South Carolina Loyalists,* 254, 259–81. McCrady, *Revolutionary South Carolina,* 2: 673. Craton and Saunders, *Islanders in the Stream,* 169–71, 184, 188–90. Rowland et al., *Beaufort County,* 242–48.

39. McCrady, *Revolutionary South Carolina,* 2: 704–38. Dederer, *Making Bricks Without Straw,* 57–59. Don Higginbotham, *War and Society in Revolutionary America: The Wider Dimensions of Conflict* (Columbia: University of South Carolina Press, 1988), 100. Russell F. Weigley, *The American Way of War: A History of United States Military Strategy and Policy* (New York: Macmillan, 1973), 29–30, 36–37.

40. Ted Robert Gurr, *Why Men Rebel* (Princeton, N.J.: Princeton University Press, 1970), 3–143, passim. See Weir, *Colonial South Carolina,* 268, 284–87.

The state did honor Greene by naming a town on the Pee Dee River and an upcountry county for him; also, the General Assembly made a gift of land to Mrs. Greene. However, if the streets of the new capital city were to be used as a guide to the state's Revolutionary War heroes, Greene was conspicuous by his absence. Archie Vernon Huff Jr., *Greenville: The History of the City and County in the South Carolina Piedmont* (Columbia: University of South Carolina Press, 1995), 48–49.

Thomas Sumter was the chair of the commission given the task of naming the streets of the new capital city. Therefore, it is no surprise that Greene's name was omitted. In 1976, on the occasion of the bicentenary of the American Revolution, the city of Columbia changed the name of Green Street to Greene Street in honor of Nathanael Greene.

41. Moss, *Patriots at Cowpens,* 1, 81, 104–5, 107, 246–47. Gurr, *Why Men Rebel,* 300. Klein, *Unification of a Slave State,* 136. William Moultrie's *Memoirs of the American Revolution* quoted in McCrady, *Revolutionary South Carolina,* 2: 353.

42. Lambert, *South Carolina Loyalists,* 230, 279. Coker, "Punishment of Revolutionary War Loyalists," 403–4. Wallace, *History of South Carolina,* 2: 278n. E. C. McCants, *History and Legends of South Carolina* (Dallas: Southern Publishing Company, 1927), 251–52, 258, 281. James Wood Davidson, *School History of South Carolina,* rev. ed. (Columbia: W. J. Duffie, 1869), 187–88. Charles E. Thomas, "Rebecca Couturier, Heroine of the Revolution," *News & Courier* (Charleston), 30 Sept. 1956, B10. John J. Dargan, *School History of South Carolina* (Columbia: State Company, 1906), 68–69. Bailey and Cooper, *Biographical Directory,* 3: 88–89.

43. Moss, *Patriots at Cowpens,* 69. Pope, *History of Newberry County,* 1: 50–51. R. W. Gibbes, *Documentary History of the American Revolution: Consisting of Letters and Papers Relating to the Contest for Liberty, Chiefly in South Carolina, From Originals in the Possession of the Editor, and Other Sources,* 3 vols. (1857; reprint ed., Spartanburg, S.C.: Reprint Company, 1972), 2: 138. Weigley, *Partisan War,* 65, 72–73.

44. Lambert, *South Carolina Loyalists,* 268, 189–90, 293, 296–97.

45. McCrady, *Revolutionary South Carolina,* 1: 303–4. Wallace, *History of South Carolina,* 2: 315–16. Jacob E. Cooke, ed., *The Reports of Alexander Hamilton,* Harper Torchbooks, University Library (New York: Harper & Row, 1964), 21.

46. Francisco de Miranda, *The New Democracy in America: Travels of Francisco de Miranda in the United States, 1783–1784,* trans. Judson P. Wood, ed. John S. Ezell (Norman: University of Oklahoma Press, 1963), 24. Burke to Guerard, 14 Dec. 1784, Records of the General Assembly, Governors' Messages, reprinted in Michael E. Stevens, "The Hanging of Matthew Love," *SCHM* quoted in Meleney, *Public Life of Aedanus Burke,* 248–49.

Chapter 12: The Quest for Order

1. Klein, *Unification of a Slave State,* 115. Petitions to the General Assembly, SCDAH, and *State Gazette of South Carolina,* 7 Feb. 1788 quoted in Jerome J. Nadelhaft, *The Disorders of War: The Rev-*

olution in South Carolina (Orono: University of Maine at Orono Press, 1981), 193, 214.

2. Meleney, *Public Life of Aedanus Burke,* 247.

3. Nadelhaft, *Disorders of War,* 156–57. Mark D. Kaplanoff, "How Federalist Was South Carolina in 1787–88?," in Chesnutt and Wilson, *Meaning of South Carolina History,* 70–71.

4. Nadelhaft, *Disorders of War,* 156–57. Laurens to James Bourdieu, 9 June 1785, South Carolina and Miscellaneous Bancroft Transcripts, New York Public Library and [Aedanus Burke], *A Few Salutory Hints* quoted in Nadelhaft, *Disorders of War,* 157, 161.

5. Nadelhaft, *Disorders of War,* 156–57. Rogers, *Evolution of a Federalist,* 136.

6. John A. Hall, "Quieting the Storm: The Establishment of Order in Post-Revolutionary South Carolina," D.Phil. thesis, Oxford University, 1989, 321–29. Nadelhaft, *Disorders of War,* 195. Klein, *Unification of a Slave State,* 137. Meleney, *Public Life of Aedanus Burke,* 245.

7. Hall, "Quieting the Storm," 74–82. Lambert, *South Carolina Loyalists,* 289–93. Walsh, *Charleston's Sons of Liberty,* 114–19. Rogers, *Evolution of a Federalist,* 97–111, 137.

8. Hall, "Quieting the Storm," 92–97, 256–65. Meleney, *Public Life of Aedanus Burke,* 247. Walsh, *Charleston's Sons of Liberty,* 117, 123.

9. Klein, *Unification of a Slave State,* 130, 179. John Drayton, *A View of South-Carolina, as respects her Natural and Civil Concerns* (Charleston: W. P. Young, 1802), 189–90.

Although the amount still outstanding was nearly 60 percent of the original amount issued, the dollar value was lower in 1800 than in 1785.

10. Nadelhaft, *Disorders of War,* 171–72.

11. A. S. Salley, "Origin and Early Development," in Helen Kohn Hennig, *Columbia: Capital City of South Carolina, 1786–1936* (Columbia: Columbia SesquiCentennial Commission, 1936), 3.

Given the strong centralization of South Carolina government throughout the state's history, perhaps Washington would have been a more appropriate name.

12. Klein, *Unification of a Slave State,* 129. Ramsay, *History of South Carolina,* 2: 238.

13. Clinton Rossiter, *1787: The Grand Convention,* A Mentor Book (1966; New York: New American Library, 1968), 113. George Bancroft, *History of the United States From the Discovery of the Continent,* author's last edition, 6 vols. (New York: D. Appleton & Co., 1891–1893), 6: 188.

14. Rogers, *Evolution of a Federalist,* 145. Rossiter, *1787,* 111.

The lowcountry elite has often been termed a vast cousinage. That certainly was true of the state's delegation in Philadelphia. The Pinckneys were cousins. Charles Pinckney married Laurens's daughter, and Rutledge's daughter married Laurens's son. C. C. Pinckney and Butler both married into the Middleton family (as did Rutledge's brother).

15. Catherine Drinker Bowen, *Miracle at Philadelphia: The Story of the Constitutional Convention, May to September 1787* (1966; New York: Bantam Books, 1968), 42, 70–73; C. C. Pinckney quotation, 73. Rossiter, *1787,* 149, 183.

16. Rossiter, *1787,* 114; C. C. Pinckney from Max Farrand, ed., *The Records of the Federal Convention of 1787* quoted in Rossiter, *1787,* 231. Rogers, *Evolution of a Federalist,* 145. Bowen, *Miracle at Philadelphia,* 192–96; C. C. Pinckney quotation, 195.

17. Rogers, *Evolution of a Federalist,* 147.

18. Rossiter, *1787,* 213–19. Bowen, *Miracle at Philadelphia,* 217. William F. Stierer Jr., "Four South Carolinians at Philadelphia: historians view the convention," in *With Liberty and Justice . . . Essays on the Ratification of the Constitution in South Carolina* (Columbia: United States Constitution Bicentennial Commission of South Carolina and South Carolina Department of Archives and History, 1989), 41–54.

19. Burke to John Lamb, 23 June 1788, Lamb Papers, New York Historical Society quoted in Rogers, *Evolution of a Federalist,* 156. Meleney, *Public Life of Aedanus Burke,* 141.

20. Carl J. Vipperman, *The Rise of Rawlins Lowndes, 1721–1800* (Columbia: University of South Carolina Press, 1978), 242–43. Rogers, *Evolution of a Federalist,* 153.

21. Kaplanoff, "How Federalist Was South Carolina?," 69–71, 76.

22. Rogers, *Evolution of a Federalist,* 151–58. Kaplanoff, "How Federalist Was South Carolina?," 75, 81–82. Meleney, *Public Life of Aedanus Burke,* 150.

23. Kaplanoff, "How Federalist Was South Carolina?," 82–84. Rogers, *Evolution of a Federalist,* 154. Meleney, *Public Life of Aedanus Burke,* 143–44.

24. Meleney, *Public Life of Aedanus Burke,* 149–50. Rogers, *Evolution of a Federalist,* 156–57; quotations, 157. Robertson, *Red Hills and Cotton,* 295.

25. Merrell Jensen et al., eds., *Documentary History of the First Federal Elections* quoted in Meleney, *Public Life of Aedanus Burke,* 154–55. Bailey and Cooper, *Biographical Directory,* 3: 725–26.

Although Tucker represented an upcountry district where he owned land, he was a Federalist from St. George Dorchester Parish. However, he had had a political disagreement with Ralph Izard, one of the Federalist Party's power brokers, that resulted in a duel.

26. Meleney, *Public Life of Aedanus Burke,* 187–97, 198; quotation, 188.

27. Rogers, *Evolution of a Federalist,* 159–305.

28. Ibid., 183, 188.

29. Rogers, *Evolution of a Federalist,* 184–86, 348–51. Klein, *Unification of a Slave State,* 202–18. Mark D. Kaplanoff, "Charles Pinckney and the American Republican Tradition," in *Intellectual Life in Antebellum Charleston,* edited by Michael O'Brien and David Moltke-Hansen (Knoxville: University Press of Tennessee, 1986), 111 14; William Reed to Jacob Reed, 10 Sept. 1795, Reed Family Papers, SCHS quoted, 113. Henry Adams, *The United States in 1800* (1955; Ithaca, N.Y.: Cornell University Press, 1971), 109.

30. Rogers, *Evolution of a Federalist,* 269–82. Meleney, *Public Life of Aedanus Burke,* 220–22. Klein, *Unification of a Slave State,* 218–21.

31. Lacy K. Ford, *Origins of Southern Radicalism: The South Carolina Upcountry, 1800–1860* (New York: Oxford University Press, 1988), 104.

32. Rogers, *Evolution of a Federalist,* 350–55; quotation, 351. Klein, *Unification of a Slave State,* 257–62.

33. Klein, *Unification of a Slave State,* 144–45. Nadelhaft, *Disorders of War,* 136–38.

34. Klein, *Unification of a Slave State,* 145–53. J. M. Lesesne, ed., *Basic Documents of South Carolina History: The Constitution of 1790* (Columbia: Historical Commission of South Carolina, 1952), 1.

35. Drayton, *View of South-Carolina,* 185. Rutledge's remarks from *Morning Post and Daily Advertiser* (Charleston), 11 Mar. 1786 quoted in Nadelhaft, *Disorders of War,* 136.

36. Klein, *Unification of a Slave State,* 144–48.

37. Klein, *Unification of a Slave State,* 221–22. Wallace, *History of South Carolina,* 2: 367.

38. Appius [Robert Goodloe Harper], *An Address to the People of South-Carolina, by the General Committee of the Representative Reform Association at Columbia* (Columbia, 1792), 5–12.

Charleston District consisted of the parishes of St. Philip's, St. Michael's, St. Bartholomew's, St. John's Berkeley, St. George Dorchester, St. Stephen's, St. James' Santee, St. Thomas & St. Denis, Christ Church, St. James' Goose Creek, St. John's Colleton, St. Andrew's, and St. Paul's.

39. [Harper], *Address to the People of South Carolina,* 21–22.

40. Ibid., 31–34.

41. Klein, *Unification of a Slave State,* 224–28.

42. Klein, *Unification of a Slave State,* 217–30. Charles Cotesworth Pinckney to Ralph Izard, 20 Dec. 1794, Charles Cotesworth Pinckney Papers, Manuscripts Department, Perkins Library, Duke University quoted in William A. Schaper, *Sectionalism and Representation in South Carolina* (1901; New York: Da Capo Press, 1968), 187.

43. Rogers, *Evolution of a Federalist,* 245–50; quotation, 249. Klein, *Unification of a Slave State,* 202–18, 230–34.

44. Ford, *Origins of Southern Radicalism,* 22–24. McCormick, "Quakers," 170–99. James Oscar Farmer Jr., *The Metaphysical Confederacy: James Henley Thornwell and the Synthesis of Southern Values,* The Frank S. and Elizabeth D. Brewer Prize Essay of the American Society of Church History (Macon, Ga.: Mercer University Press, 1986), 203.

For a discussion of the evangelical churches in the American South and their challenge to the established order, see Christine Leigh Heyrman, *Southern Cross: The Beginnings of the Bible Belt* (New York: Alfred A. Knopf, 1997), especially 3–27, 46–49, 68–69, 92–94, 120–25, 138, 141–52, 155, 217–25.

45. Klein, *Unification of a Slave State,* 147–48, 204–12, 250, 260–62. Kaplanoff, "Charles Pinckney," 114–15. Ford, *Origins of Southern Radicalism,* 103–4. Daniel W. Hollis, *University of South Carolina,* 2 vols. (Columbia: University of South Carolina Press, 1951, 1956), 1: 3–21; DeSaussure's remarks

from John Belton O'Neall, *Biographical Sketches of the Bench and Bar of South Carolina* quoted, 17.

46. Hollis, *University of South Carolina,* 1: 5, 18–21; Drayton remarks, *House Journals,* 23 Nov. 1801 quoted, 18.

In 1799 the term "county" was abolished, and in its stead the term "district" was used until 1868. The change was in name only. The boundaries remained the same until 1854 when Pendleton District was divided into Pickens and Anderson districts.

47. Hollis, *University of South Carolina,* 1: 255–70; *Daily Courier* (Charleston), 6 Dec. 1854 quoted, 4.

48. Klein, *Unification of a Slave State,* 214–17. Pierce Butler to Thomas Sumter, 11 Sept. 1791, Thomas Sumter Papers, II, Library of Congress quoted, 215.

49. Klein, *Unification of a Slave State,* 251–68. Heyrman, *Southern Cross,* 223–25, 253–60. Farmer, *Metaphysical Confederacy,* 203. Shaper, *Sectionalism in South Carolina,* 189. Rogers, *History of Georgetown County,* 192–94. Ford, *Origins of Southern Radicalism,* 22–24. McCormick, "Quakers," 193–99, 202–3.

50. Schaper, *Sectionalism in South Carolina,* 195–201.

51. Ford, *Origins of Southern Radicalism,* 106–8.

52. N. Louise Bailey, Mary L. Morgan, and Carolyn R. Taylor, *Biographical Directory of the South Carolina Senate, 1776–1985,* 3 vols. (Columbia: University of South Carolina Press, 1986), 3: 1836–37, 1846–47, 1856–57, 1866–67, 1876–77, 1886–87 (hereinafter cited as Bailey et al., *Biographical Directory, Senate.* Edgar, *Biographical Directory,* 1: 227. *Aggregate Amount of Persons Within the United States in the Year 1810, Book I, Third Census of the United States* (1811; New York: Luther M. Cornwall, Co., n.d.), 79. Clerk of the U.S. House of Representatives, *Abstract of the Returns of the Fifth Census, Book II; Fifth Census of the United States* (1832; New York: Luther M. Cornwall, n.d.), 21. J. D. B. DeBow, *Statistical View of the United States* (Washington: Beverley Tucker, 1854), 302–3. Wallace, *History of South Carolina,* 2: 374; 3: 504.

53. Bailey et al., *Biographical Directory, Senate,* 3: 1836–37, 1846–47, 1856–57, 1866–67, 1876–77, 1886–87. Edgar, *Biographical Directory,* 1: 227. *Aggregate Amount of Persons . . . in the Year 1810,* 79. Clerk of the U.S. House of Representatives, *Abstract of the Returns of the Fifth Census,* 21. DeBow, *Statistical View of the United States,* 302–3. Wallace, *History of South Carolina,* 2: 374; 3: 504. Klein, *Unification of a Slave State,* 266. Schaper, *Sectionalism in South Carolina,* 195–201.

54. Ford, *Origins of Southern Radicalism,* 102–8.

55. Ibid., 106.

56. Hollis, *University of South Carolina,* 1: 269.

57. Klein, *Unification of a Slave State,* 246–57. Ford, *Origins of Southern Radicalism,* 1–19.

58. Rogers, *Evolution of a Federalist,* 369–74. Meleney, *Public Life of Aedanus Burke,* 280–82.

59. *Columbian Herald* (Charleston), 29 Oct. 1795 quoted in Shaper, *Sectionalism in South Carolina,* 187.

CHAPTER 13: TO RAISE SOMETHING FOR SALE

1. Chaplin, *Anxious Pursuit,* 1–10. Laurens to Edward Bridgen, 23 Sept. 1784, photocopy in the Papers of Henry Laurens, University of South Carolina, Columbia.

2. Chaplin, *Anxious Pursuit,* 1–10, 277–78.

3. Winberry, "Reputation of Carolina Indigo," 248–50.

4. Chaplin, *Anxious Pursuit,* 228–32.

5. Chaplin, *Anxious Pursuit,* 228–51. William Dusinberre, *Them Dark Days: Slavery in the American Rice Swamps* (New York: Oxford University Press, 1996), 31–35.

6. Chaplin, *Anxious Pursuit,* 243–47. Mathew, *Agriculture, Geology, and Society,* 61–62, 78; quotation, 78.

7. Chaplin, *Anxious Pursuit,* 228–33. Mathew, *Agriculture, Geology, and Society,* 156–57.

8. Mathew, *Agriculture, Geology, and Society,* 63.

9. Joyner, *Down By the Riverside,* 45–48.

10. Joyner, *Down By the Riverside,* 48–49. Chaplin, *Anxious Pursuit,* 251–62.

11. Rogers, *History of Georgetown County,* 252–303. Dusinberre, *Them Dark Days,* 285–301.

12. Wallace, *History of South Carolina*, 3: 5. Coclanis, *Shadow of a Dream*, 112–17.

13. Coclanis, *Shadow of a Dream*, 133–42.

14. Coclanis, *Shadow of a Dream*, 133–37. "Ranking—1860—Per Capita Wealth—Free Population," a table compiled by Lacy K. Ford and Peter A. Coclanis.

15. Chaplin, *Anxious Pursuit*, 293–97. Ford, *Origins of Southern Radicalism*, 6–7.

16. Drayton, *View of South-Carolina*, 127–28. Chaplin, *Anxious Pursuit*, 210–15.

17. Charles F. Kovacik, "Plantations and the Low Country Landscape," in D. Gordon Bennett, *Snapshots of the Carolinas: Landscapes and Cultures* (Washington: Association of American Geographers, 1996), 4. Chaplin, *Anxious Pursuit*, 220–25. Wallace, *History of South Carolina*, 2: 379–80.

18. Chaplin, *Anxious Pursuit*, 307–19.

19. Ford, *Origins of Southern Radicalism*, 10–12, 84–88. Ford and Coclanis, "South Carolina Economy," 97–98. Chaplin, *Anxious Pursuit*, 298–319.

20. Ford and Coclanis, "South Carolina Economy," 97. Ford, *Origins of Southern Radicalism*, 8–12. Huff, *Greenville*, 53.

The production for Greenville District in 1840 was 275 bags. In neighboring Spartanburg District a bag of cotton weighed 420 pounds. Philip N. Racine, ed., *Piedmont Farmer: The Journals of David Golightly Harris, 1855–1870* (Knoxville: University of Tennessee Press, 1990), 159.

In 1744 Eliza Lucas had produced 17 pounds of the dye; the colony exported 138,000 pounds three years later and by 1775 one million pounds.

21. Ford and Coclanis, "South Carolina Economy," 97–98.

22. Ford, *Origins of Southern Radicalism*, 8–12. N. Louise Bailey, *Biographical Directory of the South Carolina House of Representatives, Volume IV: 1791–1815* (Columbia: University of South Carolina Press, 1984), 260–61, 440–41, 475–77, 585. United States Department of Commerce and Labor, Bureau of the Census, *Heads of Families, First Census of the United States: 1790, State of South Carolina* (Washington, D.C.: Government Printing Office, 1908), 29, 46, 102 (hereinafter cited as *Census: 1790*).

23. Michael P. Johnson and James L. Roark, *Black Masters: A Free Family of Color in the Old South* (New York: W. W. Norton, 1984), 65–81, 340. James L. Roark, "New Finds, New History: William Ellison and South Carolina's Free People of Color," in *Fiftieth Annual Meeting* (Columbia: University South Caroliniana Society, 1986), 3. Larry Koger, *Black Slaveowners: Free Black Masters in South Carolina, 1790–1860* (1985; Columbia: University of South Carolina Press, 1995), 144–45.

Another wealthy black slave owner was Reuben Robertson of Turkey Creek (Greenwood County). Lowrey Ware, "Reuben Robertson of Turkey Creek: The Story of a Wealthy Black Slaveholder and His Family, White and Black," *SCHM*, 89 (Oct. 1990): 260–67.

24. John Hammond Moore, *Columbia & Richland County: A South Carolina Community, 1740–1990* (Columbia: University of South Carolina Press, 1993), 138–46. Ford, *Origins of Southern Radicalism*, 61–62.

25. Moore, *Columbia & Richland County*, 93. Ford, *Origins of Southern Radicalism*, 14–16; quotation, 15.

26. Carol Bleser, ed., *Secret and Sacred: The Diaries of James Henry Hammond, a Southern Slaveholder* (New York: Oxford University Press, 1988), 62–63. Wallace, *History of South Carolina*, 2: 481–82. Ford, *Origins of Southern Radicalism*, 37–38, 53 55.

27. Donald B. Dodd and Wynelle S. Dodd, *Historical Statistics of the South, 1790–1970* (University: University of Alabama Press, 1973), 48. Ford, *Origins of Southern Radicalism*, 43, 250–51.

The size of a bale had changed over time. In the 1790s a bale was 230 pounds. By 1803 it was 300 pounds. Shortly thereafter 500 pounds became the standard size. Wallace, *History of South Carolina*, 2: 38.

28. Dodd and Dodd, *Historical Statistics*, 4, 8, 16, 20, 28, 36, 40, 48, 52, 56, 60.

29. Drayton, *View of South-Carolina*, 112–13. Wright, *Old South, New South*, 29–31. Mathew, *Agriculture, Geology, and Society*, passim.

30. Ford, *Origins of Southern Radicalism*, 40–43.

31. Ford, *Origins of Southern Radicalism*, 52–60, 84–88, 244–55. Moore, *Columbia & Richland County*, 174.

32. Bleser, *Secret and Sacred*, 25, 59, 62, 66–67, 191. John B. Edmunds Jr., *Francis W. Pickens and*

the Politics of Destruction (Chapel Hill: University of North Carolina Press, 1986), 7. Drew Gilpin Faust, *James Henry Hammond and the Old South: A Design for Mastery* (Baton Rouge: Louisiana State University Press, 1982), 108–11. Bailey and Cooper, *Biographical Directory,* 3: 308–11; Bailey, *Biographical Directory,* 4: 441–42. Bailey et al., *Biographical Directory, Senate,* 1: 654–55. Moore, *Columbia & Richland County,* 67. William W. Freehling, *The Road to Disunion: Secessionists at Bay, 1776–1854* (New York: Oxford University Press, 1990), 221.

33. Quoted in Julian J. Petty, *The Growth and Distribution of Population in South Carolina: Bulletin #11, Prepared for the State Planning Board* (Columbia: Industrial Development Committee of the State Council for Defense, 1943), 141. Moore, *Columbia & Richland County,* 94, 100–106. William Gregg, *Essays on Domestic Industry* (Charleston: Burges & James, 1845), 6. Alfred Glaze Smith Jr., *Economic Readjustment of an Old Cotton State: South Carolina, 1820–1860* (Columbia: University of South Carolina Press, 1958), 29–44. William W. Freehling, *Prelude to Civil War: The Nullification Controversy in South Carolina, 1816–1836,* Harper Torchbooks (1965; New York: Harper & Row, 1968), 258.

34. Smith, *Economic Readjustment of an Old Cotton State,* 24–29. John Barnwell, *Love of Order: South Carolina's First Secession Crisis* (Chapel Hill: University of North Carolina Press, 1982), 11–12. Ford, *Origins of Southern Radicalism,* 38–39. Wallace, *History of South Carolina,* 2: 418–19; 3: 2, 504. Coclanis and Ford, "South Carolina Economy," 98. Bailey, *Biographical Directory,* 4: 28, 67–68, 107–8, 189, 206–7, 255–56, 421–22, 427–28, 451–52, 535, 611–12.

35. Petty, *Growth and Distribution of Population,* 141. Smith, *Economic Readjustment of an Old Cotton State,* 26–29. Barnwell, *Love of Order,* 8. Wallace, *History of South Carolina,* 3: 504.

36. Coclanis, *Shadow of a Dream,* 111–15. Moore, *Columbia & Richland County,* 174. Ford, *Origins of Southern Radicalism,* 38–40.

37. Dodd and Dodd, *Historical Statistics,* 2, 6, 14, 18, 26, 34, 46.

38. Wallace, *History of South Carolina,* 2: 376. Donna Roper, "'To Promote and Improve Agriculture': A Study of Four Antebellum South Carolina Farmers' Societies," paper on file in the Pendleton District Agricultural Museum, 1–7.

39. Mathew, *Agriculture, Geology, and Society,* 5–23. Roper, "'To Promote and Improve Agriculture,'" 11–13.

40. Roper, "'To Promote and Improve Agriculture,'" passim; quotation, 9. Mathew, *Agriculture, Geology, and Society,* 165, passim.

41. Coclanis and Ford, "South Carolina Economy," 100. Moore, *Columbia & Richland County,* 146–47. Ford, *Origins of Southern Radicalism,* 270–71.

42. Ford, *Origins of Southern Radicalism,* 267–71. Moore, *Columbia & Richland County,* 146. Huff, *Greenville,* 119. Cinda K. Baldwin, *Great & Noble Jar: Traditional Stoneware of South Carolina,* Published for the McKissick Museum of the University of South Carolina (Athens: University of Georgia Press, 1993), 25–77.

In the 1990s collectors drove up the price of Edgefield pottery. At a 1996 auction in Lexington County, a Japanese collector paid $17,000 for "a plain piece." In 1997 an Atlanta museum paid $200,000 for an elaborately decorated pot. In June 1997, at a South Carolina auction, a decorated Edgefield pot went for $36,000. Interview with Horace Harmon, 16 July 1996. "Auction Yields pricey piece of Southern past," *State* (Columbia), 28 June 1997, B1.

43. Fraser, *Charleston! Charleston!,* 232–33. Coclanis, *Shadow of a Dream,* 118–19.

44. Ernest M. Lander Jr., *The Textile Industry in Antebellum South Carolina* (Baton Rouge: Louisiana State University Press, 1969), 10–11, 19–22, 63–80.

45. Lander, *Textile Industry in Antebellum South Carolina,* 80, 109–11.

46. Ford, *Origins of Southern Radicalism,* 272–77. Smith, *Economic Readjustment of an Old Cotton State,* 124–26. John McCardell, *The Idea of a Southern Nation: Southern Nationalists and Southern Nationalism, 1830–1860* (New York: W. W. Norton, 1979), 103–6.

47. Huff, *Greenville,* 85–86.

48. Wright, *Old South, New South,* 127–28. Ford, *Origins of Southern Radicalism,* 272–77.

49. Wallace, *History of South Carolina,* 3: 11–17. Lander, *Textile Industry in Antebellum South Carolina,* 52–55. McCardell, *Idea of a Southern Nation,* 100–106. Gregg, *Essays on Domestic Industry,* 19, 29–36, 39–44.

50. Lander, *Textile Industry in Antebellum South Carolina,* 55–56. Broadus Mitchell, *William Gregg, Factory Master of the Old South* (Chapel Hill: University of North Carolina Press, 1928), 33–40.

51. Klein, *Unification of a Slave State,* 245. Ralph Izard to Edward Rutledge, 9 Nov. 1791, Ralph Izard Papers, legal-sized documents folder, SCL. Ford, *Origins of Southern Radicalism,* 16. Wallace, *History of South Carolina,* 2: 398–400. Walter B. Edgar, *History of Santee Cooper, 1934–1984* (Columbia: R. L. Bryan Company, 1984), 3–4.

52. Huff, *Greenville,* 63–65.

53. Ford, *Origins of Southern Radicalism,* 16. Daniel W. Hollis, "Costly Delusion: Inland Navigation in the South Carolina Piedmont," *Proceedings of the South Carolina Historical Association* (1968): 29–43.

Today a remnant of the state's canal system can be seen in Lancaster County at Landsford Canal State Park.

54. Robert Mills, *Internal Improvements of South Carolina, Particularly Adopted to the Low Country* (Columbia: State Gazette Office, 1822). Robert Mills, *Inland Navigation: Plan for a Great Canal Between Charleston and Columbia, And for Connecting Our Waters with those of the Western Country* (Columbia: Telescope Press, 1821). Rhodri Windsor Liscombe, *Altogether American: Robert Mills, Architect and Engineer, 1781–1855* (New York: Oxford University Press, 1994), 108–10.

55. Wallace, *History of South Carolina,* 2: 401–2.

56. Ford, *Origins of Southern Radicalism,* 15–18, 220, 220n. Samuel Melanchthon Derrick, *Centennial History of the South Carolina Railroad* (Columbia: State Company, 1930), illus. between 84–85.

57. Wright, *Old South, New South,* 22. Ford, *Origins of Southern Radicalism,* 219–35.

58. Derrick, *Centennial History,* 17–18. Ford, *Origins of Southern Radicalism,* 234–38, 270–71. Fraser, *Charleston! Charleston!,* 233. Coclanis, *Shadow of a Dream,* 119. Wallace, *History of South Carolina,* 3: 5. Moore, *Columbia & Richland County,* 136–39, 146.

59. J. Mauldin Lesesne, *The Bank of the State of South Carolina: A General and Political History,* Tricentennial Studies Number 2 (Columbia: University of South Carolina Press, 1970), 101–37, 186. Ford, *Origins of Southern Radicalism,* 242. Coclanis and Ford, "South Carolina Economy," 99. Wallace, *History of South Carolina,* 2: 396–98. Coclanis, *Shadow of a Dream,* 148.

60. Lesesne, *Bank of the State of South Carolina,* 136–52. Coclanis, *Shadow of a Dream,* 148. Ford, *Origins of Southern Radicalism,* 242–43. Moore, *Columbia & Richland County,* 145–46.

61. Coclanis, *Shadow of a Dream,* 115–20.

62. Mathew, *Agriculture, Geology, and Society,* 61, 78, 92, passim. Coclanis, *Shadow of a Dream,* 111–58.

63. Coclanis and Ford, "South Carolina Economy," 98–99. Ford and Coclanis, "Ranking—1860 . . . Free Population. Per Capita Wealth." "Ranking—1860—SC—Per Capita Wealth—Total Population," a table compiled by Lacy K. Ford and Peter A. Coclanis.

64. Wright, *Old South, New South,* 19–20. Coclanis, *Shadow of a Dream,* 126–27.

CHAPTER 14: A VISIT TO ANTEBELLUM SOUTH CAROLINA

1. For a listing of travelers' accounts, see Thomas D. Clark, ed., *South Carolina: The Grand Tour, 1780–1865,* Tricentennial edition, Number 5 (Columbia: University of South Carolina Press, 1973), 319–28 (hereinafter cited as *Grand Tour*).

2. Thornwell, "Slavery and the Religious Instruction of the Coloured Population," *Southern Presbyterian Review* quoted in Stephanie McCurry, *Masters of Small Worlds: Yeoman Households, Gender Relations, and the Political Culture of the Antebellum South Carolina Low Country* (New York: Oxford University Press, 1995), 210. Farmer, *Metaphysical Confederacy,* 174–233.

3. "A Northern Farmer's View of South Carolina Plantation Country on the Eve of Secession, 1854," "An English Scientist Views South Carolina," and "Visiting South Carolina Style, 1857," in Clark, *Grand Tour,* 227–28, 261, 291–92. Wright, *Old South, New South,* 24. Elizabeth Fox-Genovese, *Within the Plantation Household: Black and White Women of the Old South* (Chapel Hill: University of North Carolina Press, 1988), 78. Pope, *History of Newberry County,* 1: 105–6. *Population of the United States in 1860; Compiled from the Original Returns of the Eighth Census* (Washington, D.C.: Government Printing Office, 1864), 452.

4. John Hammond Moore, *South Carolina Newspapers* (Columbia: University of South Carolina Press, 1988), 201, 202, 214, 215, 216. Moore, *Columbia & Richland County,* 136–58.

5. Faust, *James Henry Hammond,* 209. Blesser, *Secret and Sacred,* 16, 21. Bertram Wyatt-Brown, *Honor and Violence in the Old South* (New York: Oxford University Press, 1986), 88.

6. Hennig, *Columbia,* 134–52, 383–84. Moore, *Columbia & Richland County,* 122–26, 134.

7. Peter McCandless, *Moonlight, Magnolias, & Madness: Insanity in South Carolina from the Colonial Period to the Progressive Era* (Chapel Hill: University of North Carolina Press, 1996), 5–9. Clark, *Grand Tour,* 97.

8. Hollis, *University of South Carolina,* 1: 133–36. Rowland et al., *Beaufort County,* 406. John Morrill Bryan, *An Architectural History of the South Carolina College, 1801–1855* (Columbia: University of South Carolina Press, 1976), 3–58.

9. "A German Aristocrat Views an American Aristocracy, 1825" and "South Carolina, a State in Dissent," in Clark, *Grand Tour,* 90–91, 93; quotation, 252. Charles Ball, *Fifty Years in Chains* (1836; New York: Dover Publications, 1970), 125. Moore, *Columbia & Richland County,* 87, 163, 286, 316. Fraser, *Charleston! Charleston!,* 239–40.

10. Coclanis, *Shadow of a Dream,* 115–21. Bernard E. Powers Jr., *Black Charlestonians: A Social History, 1822–1885* (Fayetteville: University of Arkansas Press, 1994), 267. Barbara L. Bellows, *Benevolence Among Slaveholders: Assisting the Poor in Charleston, 1670–1860* (Baton Rouge: Louisiana State University Press, 1993), 103–7, 162–63, 175, 189; Simms quotation cited in Kenneth M. Severens, *Charleston: Antebellum Architecture and Civic Destiny* (Knoxville: University of Tennessee Press, 1988), 255–56.

11. "An Illustrator's View, 1828" and "A German Aristocrat Views American Aristocracy," in Clark, *Grand Tour,* 100, 122. "Guest of the Republic" in Clark, *Grand Tour,* 82.

12. Rogers, *Charleston,* 70–71, 163–64. Simons and Lapham, *Early Architecture of Charleston,* 102–4, 173–76. Alston Deas, *The Early Ironwork of Charleston* (Columbia: Bostick & Thornley, 1941), passim.

13. *This is Charleston: An Architectural Survey of a Unique American City* (3d ed., 1964; Charleston: Carolina Art Association, Historic Charleston Foundation, and The Preservation Society of Charleston, 1970), 17, 38, 73, 80.

14. Kenneth W. Severens, "Architectural Taste in Ante-Bellum Charleston" and Gene Waddell, "The Introduction of Greek Revival Architecture in Charleston," in *Art in the Lives of South Carolinians: Nineteenth Century Chapters,* edited by David Moltke-Hansen (Charleston: Carolina Art Association, 1979), GWa: 5–7; KS: 1–11. Liscombe, *Altogether American,* 89–93, 114, 116–19. *This is Charleston,* 58. Rogers, *Charleston,* 163–64.

15. Bellows, *Benevolence Among Slaveholders,* 25. Klein, *Unification of a Slave State,* 276–83. Ford, *Origins of Southern Radicalism,* 19–32.

16. Huff, *Greenville,* 67–70. Ford, *Origins of Southern Radicalism,* 19–29. Pope, *History of Newberry County,* 1: 231.

17. Albert S. Thomas, "Protestant Episcopal Society for the Advancement of Christianity," *Historical Magazine of the Protestant Episcopal Church,* 21 (Dec. 1952): 447–60. Charles Kershaw, "An Episcopal Church to be built in Columbia, So. Carolina," ms, SCL.

18. Wallace, *History of South Carolina,* 2: 504–6. Pope, *History of Newberry County,* 1: 93–98, 231. Huff, *Greenville,* 95–97. Rowland et al., *Beaufort County,* 409–10.

19. Janet Duitsman Cornelius, *When I Can Read My Title Clear: Literacy, Slavery, and Religion in the Antebellum South* (1991; Columbia: University of South Carolina Press, 1992), 37–58. Powers, *Black Charlestonians,* 17. Fraser, *Charleston! Charleston!,* 228. Wallace, *History of South Carolina,* 2: 505–6. Henry DeSaussure Bull, *All Saints' Church, Waccamaw: The Parish, The Place, The People, 1739–1968* (Georgetown, S.C.: Winyah Press, 1968), 19–39. Robert Nicholas Olsberg, "A Government of Class and Race: William Henry Trescot and the South Carolina Chivalry, 1860–1865," diss., University of South Carolina, 149–51.

20. McCurry, *Masters of Small Worlds,* 158–70. Wallace, *History of South Carolina,* 2: 504–6. Bull, *All Saints' Church,* 29.

Of the 440 "great" planters in 1860 (as defined in *The Last Foray*), 235 were Episcopalians. Chalmers Gaston Davidson, *The Last Foray, The South Carolina Planters of 1860: A Sociological Study* (Columbia: University of South Carolina Press, 1971), 5, 89–109, 170–267.

21. Ford, *Origins of Southern Radicalism,* 22–24. Pope, *History of Newberry County,* 1: 83–84, 112. McCormick, "Quakers," 194–200. Farmer, *Metaphysical Confederacy,* 203.

22. McCurry, *Masters of Small Worlds,* 208–25. Farmer, *Metaphysical Confederacy,* 174–233. Fraser, *Charleston! Charleston!,* 241. Bellows, *Benevolence Among Slaveholders,* 107–8. Rowland et al., *Beaufort County,* 411–12.

23. McCurry, *Masters of Small Worlds,* 208–76; quotations, 211.

24. Fox-Genovese, *Within the Plantation Household,* 242–56; Louisa McCord, "Woman and Her Needs" quoted, 256. Richard C. Lounsbury, with an introduction by Michael O'Brien, *Louisa S. McCord, Political and Social Essays,* 2 vols. (Charlottesville: University Press of Virginia, 1995), 1: 1–11, et passim.

25. Fox-Genovese, *Within the Plantation Household,* 243–46. Stephen M. Stowe, "City, Country, and the Feminine Voice," in O'Brien and Moltke-Hansen, *Intellectual Life in Antebellum Charleston,* 302–8.

26. "An Illustrator's View," 126–27. "Silver, Muslin, and Tinsel," in Clark, *Grand Tour,* 140, 143. Fraser, *Charleston! Charleston!,* 244. Carol K. Bleser, "Southern Planter Wives and Slavery," in Chesnutt and Wilson, *Meaning of South Carolina History,* 104–20. Fox-Genovese, *Within the Plantation Household,* 334–71.

27. Bellows, *Benevolence Among Slaveholders,* 119, 166–67. Parramore, "'For Her Sole and Separate Use,'" 100–116.

28. Bellows, *Benevolence Among Slaveholders,* 32, 40–49. "Guest of the Republic," 86. Robert Mills, *Statistics of South Carolina, Including a View of Its Natural, Civil, and Military History, General and Particular* (1826; Spartanburg, S.C.: Reprint Company, 1972), 428–35.

29. Bellows, *Benevolence Among Slaveholders,* 90–96. Ball, *Fifty Years in Chains,* 108.

Thus, in 1996 dollars, for a twelve-hour day a working woman earned 37¢ an hour and a field hand 82.5¢; the minimum wage in 1997 was $5.25 an hour.

30. "An Aristocrat Views American Aristocracy," 108. "An Illustrator's View," 127. Bellows, *Benevolence Among Slaveholders,* 84, 85.

31. Bellows, *Benevolence Among Slaveholders,* 27–28, 69, 120–59. "An Aristocrat Views American Aristocracy," 105–8. "Bad Roads, Loose Morals, Sadism, and Race Track Discipline, 1830," in Clark, *Grand Tour,* 158. Fraser, *Charleston! Charleston!,* 237–38.

32. Bellows, *Benevolence Among Slaveholders,* 98–105.

33. Rowland et al., *Beaufort County,* 381. Rogers, *History of Georgetown County,* 205–6. "Visiting South Carolina Style, 1857," in Clark, *Grand Tour,* 296. McCurry, *Masters of Small Worlds,* 110–11, 123–26, 142, 188–90.

34. Charles S. Sydnor, *The Development of Southern Sectionalism, 1819–1848* (Baton Rouge: Louisiana State University Press, 1948), 62. Rogers, *History of Georgetown County,* 213–16. Coclanis, *Shadow of a Dream,* 149. Wallace, *History of South Carolina,* 3: 37. Moore, *Columbia & Richland County,* 113–14.

35. Moore, *Columbia & Richland County,* 113–14. Pope, *History of Newberry County,* 1: 220. Rogers, *History of Georgetown County,* 213–16.

36. Louis P. Towles, ed., *A World Turned Upside Down: The Palmers of South Santee, 1818–1881* (Columbia: University of South Carolina Press, 1996), 5–6.

37. "Visiting South Carolina Style," 294–95. Wallace, *History of South Carolina,* 3: 24–27, 37. Moore, *Columbia & Richland County,* 111–15. Pope, *History of Newberry County,* 1: 213–21. Rogers, *History of Georgetown County,* 215–16. Huff, *Greenville,* 94–96. Rowland et al., *Beaufort County,* 1: 287–88. Horace Fraser Rudisill, ed., *Minutes of Saint David's Society (1777–1835)* (Florence, S.C.: Saint David's Society, 1986), i–iv. Jack Allen Meyer, "The Mount Sion Society of Charleston and Winnsboro, South Carolina, 1777–1825" (seminar paper, University of South Carolina, 1977). John Livingston, *Portraits of Eminent Americans* (New York: R. Craighead, 1854), 205.

38. O'Brien and Moltke-Hansen, *Intellectual Life in Antebellum Charleston,* 298–300, 308, 314. Margaret L. Coit, *John C. Calhoun: American Portrait* (1950; Columbia: University of South Carolina Press, 1991), 14–16. Wallace, *History of South Carolina,* 3: 24–27. Fraser, *Charleston! Charleston!,* 215.

39. Drew Gilpin Faust, *A Sacred Circle: The Dilemma of the Intellectual in the Old South, 1840–1860* (Baltimore: Johns Hopkins University Press, 1977), 104. Faust, *James Henry Hammond,* 240, 270–71, 322–23. "A Dour Scottish View of Slavery, 1856–1857," in Clark, *Grand Tour,* 277.

40. Bellows, *Benevolence Among Slaveholders,* 157–59. Fraser, *Charleston! Charleston!,* 236. Wallace, *History of South Carolina,* 3: 32–37.

41. Cornelius, *When I Can Read My Title Clear,* 37–58. Powers, *Black Charlestonians,* 52–55; quotation, 54. Joel Williamson, *After Slavery: The Negro In South Carolina During Reconstruction, 1861–1877* (1965; Hanover, N.H.: Wesleyan University Press/University Press of New England, 1990), 209–10.

42. Cornelius, *When I Can Read My Title Clear,* 37–58; quotation from John Belton O'Neall, "Slave Laws of the South," 54. Jacob Stroyer, *My Life in the South* (new & enlarged ed.; Salem, Mass.: Newcomb & Gauss, 1898), 30–32, 34–35. C. Vann Woodward, *Mary Chesnut's Civil War* (New Haven: Yale University Press, 1981), 251, 263, 464. Baldwin, *Great & Noble Jar,* 76. Williamson, *After Slavery,* 210.

43. Faust, *Sacred Circle,* 8–9, 104. Hollis, *University of South Carolina,* 1: 142–76, 206–11, 255–70.

44. Hollis, *University of South Carolina,* 1: 17. Rowland et al., *Beaufort County,* 284–86. Fraser, *Charleston! Charleston!,* 215.

45. Hollis, *University of South Carolina,* 1: 74–118.

46. Hollis, *University of South Carolina,* 1: 117–18, 160–76. Huff, *Greenville,* 124–25. Wallace, *History of South Carolina,* 3: 40–47. Rowland et al., *Beaufort County,* 396. *Erskine College Bulletin, 1965–1966* (Due West, S.C.: Erskine College, 1964), 19.

47. "Guest of the Republic," 79. "A German Aristocrat Views American Aristocracy," 93–96. "An Illustrator's View," 116. Faust, *Sacred Circle,* 83. Rodger Stroup, "UpCountry Patrons: Wade Hampton II and His Family"; Anna Wells Rutledge, "Beyond the Smell of the Salt: Artists in Up-Country South Carolina Before 1865"; and Letitia D. Allen, "Wade Hampton II's Patronage of Edward Troye," in Moltke-Hansen, *Art in the Lives of South Carolinians,* ARa: 1–10, RSb: 1–13, LA: 1–27.

48. Bleser, *Secret and Sacred,* 36–37. Faust, *James Henry Hammond,* 195–96. Walter Edgar, "Robert Wilson Gibbes: Columbia Patron and Collector," in *From Artist to Patron: The Fraser Collection of Engravings Presented to Dr. Robert Gibbes,* edited by Lynn Robertson Myers (Columbia: McKissick Museum and Institute for Southern Studies, 1985), 1–10.

49. Faust, *Sacred Circle,* 2–4, 10–11, 37–45, passim. Paul Hamilton Hayne, "Ante-Bellum Charleston," *Southern Bivouac,* new series, 1 (Oct. 1885): 257–68.

50. David Moltke-Hansen, "The Expansion of Intellectual Life: A Prospectus," in O'Brien and Moltke-Hansen, *Intellectual Life in Antebellum Charleston,* 38–44.

51. *Ballou's Pictorial,* 10 (21 June 1856): 385. Mary Ann Wimsatt, "William Gilmore Simms," in Louis D. Rubin Jr., Blayden Jackson, Rayburn S. Moore, Lewis P. Simpson, and Thomas Daniel Young, eds., *The History of Southern Literature* (Baton Rouge: Louisiana State University Press, 1985), 108–17.

52. Lacy K. Ford, "James Louis Petigru: The Last South Carolina Federalist" and John McCardell, "Poetry and the Practical: William Gilmore Simms," in O'Brien and Moltke-Hansen, *Intellectual Life in Antebellum Charleston,* 155, 176–77, 208. Moltke-Hanson, "The Expansion of Intellectual Life," 10, 14, 18, 34–38. Richard J. Calhoun, "Literary Magazines in the Old South," in Rubin et al., *History of Southern Literature,* 157–63.

53. Moltke-Hansen, "The Expansion of Intellectual Life," 18–21, 28. "A German Aristocrat Views American Aristocracy," 101–2. Olsberg, "Government of Class & Race," 164–67.

54. Wallace, *History of South Carolina,* 3: 58. Rogers, *History of Georgetown County,* 260. Moltke-Hansen, "The Expansion of Intellectual Life," 22, 27. Jared B. Flagg, *Washington Allston* (New York: Benjamin Blom, 1892), 32–36. Liscombe, *Altogether American,* 103–57. Gary Phillip Zola, *Isaac Harby of Charleston: 1788–1828: Jewish Reformer and Intellectual* (Tuscaloosa: University of Alabama Press, 1994), 150–68.

55. Faust, *Sacred Circle,* 74–75. Zola, *Isaac Harby,* 150–52. Bellows, *Benevolence Among Slaveholders,* 175–76. Paul Hamilton Hayne, "Ante-Bellum Charleston" in Edwin Mims, "Paul Hamilton

Hayne" in *The Library of Southern Literature* edited by Edwin Anderson Alderman, Joel Chandler Harris, and Charles William Kent, 16 vols. (New Orleans: Martin & Hoyt Company, 1907), 5: 2277.

56. Rogers, *Charleston*, 165. Jay B. Hubbell, *The South in American Literature, 1607–1900* (Durham, N.C.: Duke University Press, 1954), 366–69; quotation, 367.

57. Moltke-Hansen, "The Expansion of Intellectual Life," 40–42. William J. Grayson, *Witness to Sorrow: The Antebellum Autobiography of William J. Grayson*, ed. Richard J. Calhoun (Columbia: University of South Carolina Press, 1990), 8–10. Rogers, *Charleston*, 165. Rowland et al., *Beaufort County*, 402–3.

58. Ronald S. Numbers and Janet S. Numbers, "Science in the Old South: A Reappraisal," *JSH*, 48 (May 1982): 163–84. Fraser, *Charleston! Charleston!*, 211, 226–27. Moltke-Hansen, "The Expansion of Intellectual Life," 6–7. Lester D. Stevens, *Joseph LeConte: Gentle Prophet of Evolution* (Baton Rouge: Louisiana State University Press, 1982), 3–4, 8–11.

59. Sprunt and Chamberlain, *South Carolina Bird Life*, 5–6. Moltke-Hansen, "The Expansion of Intellectual Life," 6–7. Rowland et al., *Beaufort County*, 1: 404–5.

60. William Elliott, *Carolina Sports by Land and Water* with an introduction by Theodore Rosengarten, (1859; Columbia: University of South Carolina Press, 1994), xiii–xvi, xxv–xxvi. Sprunt and Chamberlain, *South Carolina Bird Life*, 6. Racine, *Piedmond Farmer*, passim.

61. Fraser, *Charleston! Charleston!*, 179–81, 196. Letitia D. Allen, "Wade Hampton II's Patronage of Edward Troye," in Moltke-Hansen, *Art in the Lives of South Carolinians*, LA: 1–27. Clark, *Grand Tour*, 125–26, 140–43, 153, 159–60. Randy J. Sparks, "Gentleman's Sport: Horse Racing in Antebellum Charleston," *SCHM*, 93 (Jan. 1992): 15–30.

62. Klein, *Unification of a Slave State*, 162. Ford, *Origins of Southern Radicalism*, 110–13, 164–65. Hubbell, *South in American Literature*, 439. Racine, *Piedmont Farmer*, 145.

63. John C. Roberson, "The Foundations of Southern Nationalism: Charleston and the Lowcountry, 1847–1861," diss., University of South Carolina, 1991, 675–82. John K. Mahon, *History of the Militia and the National Guard*, The Macmillan Wars of the United States, ed. Louis Morton (New York: Macmillan, 1983), 83.

64. Moore, *Columbia & Richland County*, 149. Bellows, *Benevolence Among Slaveholders*, 114–15. Huff, *Greenville*, 95–97.

65. Moore, *Columbia & Richland County*, 150. Clark, *Grand Tour*, 79, 92–93, 119, 126–27, 140, 146.

66. Barnwell, *Love of Order*, 26–31. Ford, *Origins of Southern Radicalism*, 110–13, 372–73. Orville Vernon Burton, *In My Father's House Are Many Mansions: Family and Community in Edgefield, South Carolina* (Chapel Hill: University of North Carolina Press, 1985), 75–80.

67. Barnwell, *Love of Order*, 26–31. Fox-Genovese, *Within the Plantation Household*, 224. McCurry, *Masters of Small Worlds*, 123–26. Bellows, *Benevolence Among Slaveholders*, 94–95, 181.

68. Rowland et al., *Beaufort County*, 432–34.

69. Jack K. Williams, *Dueling in the Old South: Vignettes of Social History* (College Station: Texas A&M University Press, 1980), preface, 4–8. Wallace, *History of South Carolina*, 3: 90–97. Hollis, *University of South Carolina*, 1: 92–93. Freehling, *Prelude to Civil War*, 150. Wyatt-Brown, *Honor and Violence*, 143. Burton, *In My Father's House*, 73.

70. "An Illustrator's View," 126. Wyatt-Brown, *Honor and Violence*, 31, 41, 49.

71. Wyatt-Brown, *Honor and Violence*, 98, 101. Burton, *In My Father's House*, 136–42. Bellows, *Benevolence Among Slaveholders*, 135–37. Fraser, *Charleston! Charleston!*, 212. Moore, *Columbia & Richland County*, 141.

72. Burton, *In My Father's House*, 136–42. McCurry, *Masters of Small Worlds*, 130–37; Gum Branch Baptist Church, Darlington District, Minutes, May 1854, SCL, quoted, 131.

73. Bleser, *Secret and Sacred*, 18–19. Woodward, *Mary Chesnut's Civil War*, 29, 31, 71–72, 168–69, 276, 348. "A German Aristocrat Views American Aristocracy," 99. "Bad Roads, Loose Morals," 156–57. Burton, *In My Father's House*, 185–89, 204–5. Stroyer, *My Life in the South*, 28.

There were occasionally relationships between white women and black men. In St. Peter's Parish, Ellender Horton took up with a free man of color. McCurry, *Masters of Small Worlds*, 89.

74. Johnson and Roark, *Black Masters*, 35–36, 45–46. Wyatt-Brown, *Honor and Violence*, 107–8.

Burton, *In My Father's House*, 185–89. Bleser, *Secret and Sacred*, xi, xvi, 17–18, 19, 212–14, 231, 234. Fox-Genovese, *Within the Plantation Household*, 192–93, 294, 297, 299, 315, 325–26. Faust, *James Henry Hammond*, 86–88; James Henry Hammond to Harry Hammond, 19 Feb. 1856, James Henry Hammond Papers, SCL quoted, 87. Cynthia Kennedy-Haflett, "'Moral Marriage': A Mixed-Race Relationship in Nineteenth-Century Charleston, South Carolina," *SCHM*, 97 (July 1996): 206–26.

75. Powers, *Black Charlestonians*, 56, 267. Chesnutt and Wilson, *Meaning of South Carolina History*, 126–27. Klein, *Unification of a Slave State*, 71. Wallace, *History of South Carolina*, 2: 506–7; 3: 504. Marina Wikramanayake, *A World in Shadow: The Free Black in Antebellum South Carolina*, published for the South Carolina Tricentennial Commission (Columbia: University of South Carolina Press, 1973), 42–45. Fraser, *Charleston! Charleston!*, 199–200. Burton, *In My Father's House*, 203–22.

76. Wikramanayake, *World in Shadow*, 42–45. Fraser, *Charleston! Charleston!*, 242. Johnson and Roark, *Black Masters*, 43–47. Powers, *Black Charlestonians*, 38–40.

The poll or capitation tax went into force in 1792. The amount remained at two dollars. The 1996 dollar conversion used in this example is based upon 1860 dollars.

77. Koger, *Black Slaveowners*, 18–30, 227–30. Wikramanayake, *World in Shadow*, 45. Johnson and Roark, *Black Masters*, 63–64, 111–12, 280. Powers, *Black Charlestonians*, 47–50. Manuscript Census for South Carolina, 1860, SCDAH. John W. Blassingame, ed., *Slave Testimony: Two Centuries of Letters, Speeches, Interviews, and Autobiographies* (Baton Rouge: Louisiana State University Press, 1977), 618.

There is some discrepancy in sources, but the $1.5 million figure is reasonable. Powers reports that free blacks owned real estate worth $759,870 ($13,801,785). Slave property was valued in excess of $300,000 ($5,449,000).

78. Johnson and Roark, *Black Masters*, 3–96, 127–29. Wallace, *History of South Carolina*, 3: 501.

79. Koger, *Black Slaveowners*, 18–141. Powers, *Black Charlestonians*, 49.

80. Powers, *Black Charlestonians*, 36–72. Fraser, *Charleston! Charleston!*, 199–200, 244. Koger, *Black Slaveowners*, 165–72. Michael P. Johnson and James L. Roark, *No Chariot Let Down: Charleston's Free People of Color on the Eve of the Civil War* (Chapel Hill: University of North Carolina Press, 1984), 3–84. Johnson and Roark, *Black Masters*, 281–95; Memorial of Free Negroes to His Excellency Gov. Francis W. Pickens, 10 Jan. 1861, Francis Wilkins Pickens Papers, Manuscript, Library of Congress quoted, 293. Leon F. Litwack, *Been in the Storm So Long: The Aftermath of Slavery* (New York: Alfred A. Knopf, 1980), 17.

81. Fraser, *Charleston! Charleston!*, 242–43. "A German Aristocrat Views American Aristocracy," 102. "Bad Roads, Loose Morals," 164–65. Johnson and Roark, *No Chariot Let Down*, 85–149. Johnson and Roark, *Black Masters*, 233–95.

82. Johnson and Roark, *Black Masters*, 274–82.

83. Barnwell, *Love of Order*, 11. Schaper, *Sectionalism and Representation*, 155. Wallace, *History of South Carolina*, 3: 501. Rowland et al., *Beaufort County*, 378–79. Rogers, *History of Georgetown County*, 259. Manuscript Census for South Carolina, 1860, SCDAH. Inter-University Consortium for Political and Social Research, Study 00003: Historical, Demographic, Economic, and Social Data: U.S., 1790–1970. Ann Arbor: ICPSR.

The total number of slaves owned by a single individual may have been undercounted, as holdings in different districts were not consolidated. Dusinberre, *Them Dark Days*, 391–95.

84. Davidson, *Last Foray*, 170–267. Rowland et al., *Beaufort County*, 297–312. McCurry, *Masters of Small Worlds*, 53.

85. Drago, *Broke By the War*, 43, 44, 46, passim. Ball, *Fifty Years in Chains*, 71–85. Chaplain, *Anxious Pursuit*, 279–90. Belinda Hurmence, ed., *Before Freedom: 48 Oral Histories of Former North and South Carolina Slaves* (New York: A Mentor Book, 1990), 191.

86. Weir, *Colonial South Carolina*, 188. Joyner, *Down By the Riverside*, 127–30. Rowland et al., *Beaufort County*, 351–52, 362–63. Morgan, "Work and Culture," 563–99.

87. Chaplin, *Anxious Pursuit*, 268–70; Pinckney to Izard, 26 Dec. 1794, Manigault Family Papers, SCHS quoted, 268. Joyner, *Down By the Riverside*, 65–70. Littlefield, *Rice and Slaves*, 141. "An Illustrator's View," 132–34. "Silver, Muslin, and Tinsel," 148–53. Rawick, *American Slave*, vol. 3, South Carolina Narratives, part 3: 49, 56. Olsberg, "Government of Class & Race," 136–39. Blassingame, *Slave Testimony*, 636.

88. Chaplin, *Anxious Pursuit*, 279–90, 321–27.

89. In addition to the 63,590 slaves on farms where there were fewer than nine, there were between 60,000 and 80,000 on small plantations of 10–19 slaves. Inter-University Consortium for Political and Social Research, Study 00003. Kenneth M. Stampp, *The Peculiar Institution: Slavery in the Antebellum South* (New York: Vintage Books, A Division of Random House, 1956), 30–35. Racine, *Piedmont Farmer*, 56, 65, 126–27, 134, 141, 156–60.

90. Mark M. Smith, "Time, Slavery and Plantation Capitalism in the Ante-Bellum American South," *Past & Present: A Journal of Historical Studies*, No. 150 (Feb. 1996): 142–68. Mark M. Smith, "Old South Time in Comparative Perspective," *American Historical Review*, 101 (Dec. 1996): 1453–64. Rawick, *American Slave*, vol. 3, South Carolina Narratives, part 3: 113, 271. Ball, *Fifty Years in Chains*, 145. Morgan, "Work and Culture," 586–88.

91. Ball, *Fifty Years in Chains*, 106–8. Amelia Wallace Vernon, *African Americans at Mars Bluff, South Carolina* (Baton Rouge: Louisiana State University Press, 1993), 29–30. Hurmence, *Before Freedom*, 106–7. Blassingame, *Slave Testimony*, 380, 512, 698.

92. Joyner, *Down By the Riverside*, 127. Rawick, *American Slave*, vol. 3, South Carolina Narratives, part 3: 38, 49, 56, 58, 127–28, 192, 271, 277, 285. Ball, *Fifty Years in Chains*, 145, 150. Rowland et al., *Beaufort County*, 364. Faust, *James Henry Hammond*, 85. Stroyer, *My Life in the South*, 37–38, 44–47. Racine, *Piedmont Farmer*, 40, 67, 94–95, 168.

93. Rawick, *American Slave*, vol. 3, South Carolina Narratives, part 3: 49, 56, 118, 172. Ball, *Fifty Years in Chains*, 106–8, 148–50, 209–10. "An Illustrator's View," 133. Vernon, *African Americans at Mars Bluff*, 29. Blassingame, *Slave Testimony*, 380, 512, 698.

94. Ferguson, *Uncommon Ground*, 62–82. Joyner, *Down By the Riverside*, 117–26. Ball, *Fifty Years in Chains*, 137–39. Westmacott, *African-American Gardens*, 16–18, 21, 26–30, 40–43, 79–82.

95. Hurmence, *Before Freedom*, 95–96, 114–15, 131–32, 167–68, 180–82, 191–93. Rawick, *American Slave*, vol. 3, South Carolina Narratives, part 3: 14, 112, 185, 227. "An Illustrator's View," 133. "A Northern Farmer's View of South Carolina Plantation Country on the Eve of Secession, 1854," in Clark, *Grand Tour*, 262.

96. Burton, *In My Father's House*, 148–51. Joyner, *Down By the Riverside*, 136–37. Fox-Genovese, *Within the Plantation Household*, 294–95. Faust, *James Henry Hammond*, 84–86. John W. Blassingame, *The Slave Community: Plantation Life in the Antebellum South* (New York: Oxford University Press, 1972), 77–103. Olsberg, "Government of Class & Race," 152–55.

97. Burton, *In My Father's House*, 148–52. Fox-Genovese, *Within the Plantation Household*, 296–99. Faust, *James Henry Hammond*, 84–86. Blassingame, *Slave Community*, 77–103. Olsberg, "Government of Class & Race," 152–55. Stroyer, *My Life in the South*, 17–18, 20–22, 24–25.

98. Joyner, *Down By the Riverside*, 230–31. Thomas D. Russell, "The Antebellum Courthouse as Creditors' Domain: Trial-Court Activity in South Carolina and the Concomitance of Lending and Litigation," *American Journal of Legal History*, 40 (July 1996): 331–64. Thomas D. Russell, "Articles Sell Best Singly: The Disruption of Slave Families at Court Sales," *Utah Law Review*, vol. 1996, no. 4, 1161–1209; Coggeshall to Becca Coggeshall, 30 May 1824, Coggeshall Family Papers, SCL quoted, 1193. Dusinberre, *Them Dark Days*, 305, 368–70. Blassingame, *Slave Testimony*, 512–13, 698.

99. Joyner, *Down By the Riverside*, 230–35; "An Englishman in South Carolina," *Continental Monthly* quoted, 230. William J. Grayson, *The Hireling and the Slave* (Charleston: J. Russell, 1854). Lounsbury, *Louisa S. McCord*, 1: 280.

100. Ball, *Fifty Years in Chains*, 158–62. Joyner, *Down By the Riverside*, 53–57. Fraser, *Charleston! Charleston!*, 199. Bellows, *Benevolence Among Slaveholders*, 44–47. Rawick, *American Slave*, vol. 3, South Carolina Narratives, part 3: 49, 277. Rowland et al., *Beaufort County*, 362. Faust, *James Henry Hammond*, 72–73, 100. Stroyer, *My Life in the South*, 17–25, 29–34. Dusinberre, *Them Dark Days*, 305–18. Blassingame, *Slave Testimony*, 380–81, 512–13, 687, 698.

101. Laura Jervey Hopkins, ed., *The Diary of Keziah Goodwyn Hopkins Brevard (1860–1861)* (n.p., n.d.), 19, 31–32, 36, 42. Rowland et al., *Beaufort County*, 437–40. Olsberg, "Government of Class & Race," 125–31. Steven A. Channing, *Crisis of Fear: Secession in South Carolina* (New York: W. W. Norton, 1970), 21–23. Stroyer, *My Life in the South*, 39–42.

102. Moore, *Columbia & Richland County*, 160–61. Walter B. Edgar, *A Training Guide for Kens-*

ington (Columbia: Union Camp Corp., 1985), 6–7, 28–34. Vlach, *Back of the Big House,* 36–37.

103. Edgar, *Training Guide for Kensington,* 6–7, 28–34.

104. Ethel Wylly Sweet, Robert M. Smith, and Henry D. Boykin II, *Camden: Homes & Heritage* (Camden, S.C.: Kershaw County Historical Society, 1978), 22–25, 70, 75–77. "A German Aristocrat Views American Aristocracy," 90–91, 98. "A Yankee View, 1843," in Clark, *Grand Tour,* 211. "A Northern Farmer's View," 261–62. Hurmence, *Before Freedom,* 191–93. Ball, *Fifty Years in Chains,* 85. Burton, *In My Father's House,* 38–40. McCurry, *Masters of Small Worlds,* 72–75. Harriet Ferguson Thogersen, "The Log Cabin Era of Lexington County, South Carolina, 1750–1830: A Discussion of Lifestyles and Aspirations of German Colonists," M.A. thesis, University of South Carolina, 1980, 24–70. Grady McWhinney, *Cracker Culture: Celtic Ways in the Old South* (Tuscaloosa: University of Alabama Press, 1988), 227–40. David Hackett Fisher, *Albion's Seed: Four British Folkways in America* (New York: Oxford University Press, 1989), 655–62.

105. Fred Kniffen, "Folk Housing: Key to Diffusion," *Annals of American Geographers,* 55 (Dec. 1965): 549–77. Virginia McAlester and Lee McAlester, *A Field Guide to American Houses* (New York: Alfred A. Knopf, 1984), 80–83, 96–97.

Sometimes architectural historians refer to this type of folk housing as "I houses" (because they were first identified in Indiana, although they were clearly built earlier along the eastern seaboard). Michael Southern, "The I-House as a Carrier of Style in Three Counties of the Northeastern Piedmont," in Doug Swain, ed., *Carolina Dwelling* (Raleigh: Student Publication of the School of Design: Vol. 26, North Carolina State University, 1978), 70–83. Sweet et al., *Camden,* 36, 76.

106. Edgar, *Training Guide for Kensington,* 28–31. Joyner, *Down By the Riverside,* 70–74. Mamie Garvin Fields, with Karen Fields, *Lemon Swamp and Other Places: A South Carolina Memoir* (New York: Free Press, a Division of Macmillan, Inc., 1983), 36.

107. "An Illustrator's View," 121. "A Northern Farmer's View," 269. Joseph I. Waring, *History of Medicine in South Carolina: 1825–1900* (Charleston: South Carolina Medical Association, 1967), 35–39, 41–54, 62, 65. Waring, *History of Medicine, 1607–1825,* 157. Rowland et al., *Beaufort County,* 401. Fraser, *Charleston! Charleston!,* 211, 217. Sally McMillen, "Mother's Sacred Duty: Breast-feeding Patterns among Middle- and Upper-Class Women in the Antebellum South," *JSH,* 51 (Aug. 1985): 341.

108. "A German Aristocrat Views American Aristocracy," 103, "Bad Roads, Loose Morals," 163–64. "An Eminent English Scientist Views South Carolina, 1845–46," in Clark, *Grand Tour,* 227–28. Mathew, *Agriculture, Geology, and Society,* 110. Rogers, *History of Georgetown County,* 312–23. Rowland et al., *Beaufort County,* 379–81. Huff, *Greenville,* 89–94. Towles, *World Turned Upside Down,* 2–3. Waring, *History of Medicine: 1825–1900,* 39. Grayson, *Witness to Sorrow,* 101–2. Percivel Reniers, *The Springs of Virginia: Life, Love, and Death at the Waters, 1775–1900* (Chapel Hill: University of North Carolina Press, 1941), 44–45, 48–66, 114–37.

109. Sarah Heron, "Glenn Springs: The Hotel and Its Miraculous Waters" (seminar paper, University of South Carolina, 1977), 1–7.

110. Moore, *Columbia & Richland County,* 139. Derrick, *Centennial History,* 187–219. Smith, "Time, Slavery and Plantation Capitalism," 142–68. Smith, "Old South Time," 1453–64. "Silver, Muslin, and Tinsel," 150–51. "Bad Roads, Loose Morals," 161. "Visiting, South Carolina Style," 286–91. Eugene Alvarez, *Travel on Southern Antebellum Railroads, 1828–1860* (Tuscaloosa: University of Alabama Press, 1974), 155.

111. Moore, *Columbia & Richland County,* 144, 154. Burton, *In My Father's House,* 140. "A German Aristocrat Views American Aristocracy," 105. "An Illustrator's View," 123. Fraser, *Charleston! Charleston!,* 227. Huff, *Greenville,* 138. Fox-Genovese, *Within the Plantation Household,* 109. John Hammond Moore, ed., *South Carolina Newspapers* (Columbia: University of South Carolina Press, 1988), passim. *Daily South Carolinian* (Columbia), 11, 25 Dec. 1856; 18 Dec. 1860. Racine, *Piedmont Farmer,* 46, 74, 100, 181, 220.

112. Coclanis, *Shadow of a Dream,* 128. Ford, *Origins of Southern Radicalism,* 31–40. Schaper, *Sectionalism and Representation,* 157–58. Bellows, *Benevolence Among Slaveholders,* 130.

113. Schaper, *Sectionalism and Representation,* 157. Bellows, *Benevolence Among Slaveholders,* 103–7, 130, 162–63, 189.

114. Preston quoted in Moore, *Columbia and Richland County,* 151.

CHAPTER 15: CALCULATING THE VALUE OF THE UNION

1. Smith, *Economic Readjustment of an Old Cotton State*, 220.

2. "Diary of Edward Hooker, 1805–1808," J. Franklin Jameson, ed., *Annual Report, American Historical Association, 1896* quoted in Meleney, *Public Life of Aedanus Burke*, 279. *Richmond Enquirer* quotation from Charles H. Ambler, *Sectionalism in Virginia from 1776–1861* quoted in Irving H. Bartlett, *John C. Calhoun, A Biography* (New York: W. W. Norton, 1993), 119.

3. Coit, *John C. Calhoun*, 105–19; quotation, 119.

4. Wallace, *History of South Carolina*, 2: 420–23; quotation, 421.

5. Bartlett, *John C. Calhoun*, 111–20.

6. Freehling, *Prelude to Civil War*, 97–105. Bartlett, *John C. Calhoun*, 105–20, 138.

7. Bartlett, *John C. Calhoun*, 111–20.

8. *Congressional Globe, 28 Congress* quoted in McCardell, *Idea of a Southern Nation*, 231.

9. Freehling, *Prelude to Civil War*, 108–9; *Annals of Congress*, 16th Cong. quoted, 109. McCardell, *Idea of a Southern Nation*, 22–23; Calhoun to John Ewing Colhoun, 8 Jan. 1821, in J. Franklin Jameson, ed., *Correspondence of John C. Calhoun* quoted, 23. Bartlett, *John C. Calhoun*, 109. Coit, *John C. Calhoun*, 146–47. Wallace, *History of South Carolina*, 2: 414–15.

10. Wallace, *History of South Carolina*, 2: 415.

11. Freehling, *Prelude to Civil War*, 53–61.

12. Lionel H. Kennedy and Thomas Parker, *An Official Report of the Trials of Sundry Negroes Charged with an Attempt to Raise an Insurrection in the State of South Carolina* (Charleston: James R. Schenck, 1822), 66–67.

13. Powers, *Black Charlestonians*, 30–32. John Lofton, *Insurrection in South Carolina: The Turbulent World of Denmark Vesey* (Yellow Springs, Ohio: Antioch Press, 1964), 155–81.

14. Lofton, *Insurrection in South Carolina*, 158–62; Kennedy and Parker, *An Official Report of the Trials of Sundry Negroes* quoted, 161.

15. Lofton, *Insurrection in South Carolina*, 163–67; John Potter to Langdon Cheves, 29 June 1822, Cheves Papers, SCHS quoted, 166, 173. Richard C. Wade, "The Vesey Plot: A Reconsideration," *Journal of Southern History*, 30 (1964): 143–61. Rogers, *Charleston*, 144–45.

16. Powers, *Black Charlestonians*, 21. Cooper and McCord, *Statutes*, 7: 461–66. Freehling, *Prelude to Civil War*, 111–15.

17. Freehling, *Prelude to Civil War*, 61–63, 116–17, 134–35, 140–41, 196–97. Wallace, *History of South Carolina*, 2: 425. Rogers, *History of Georgetown County*, 236–37.

One hundred thousand dollars in 1826 converts to approximately $1.53 million in 1996 dollars.

18. "Whitemarsh Seabrook on the Danger to Slavery, 1825," in William W. Freehling, ed., *The Nullification Era: A Documentary Record*, Harper Torchbooks/The University Library (New York: Harper & Row, 1967), 10–19. Freehling, *Prelude to Civil War*, 60–64, 250–51. McCardell, *Idea of a Southern Nation*, 4–5.

19. Ford, *Origins of Southern Radicalism*, 125. Edmunds, *Francis W. Pickens*, 13. Freehling, *Prelude to Civil War*, 201–5, 254–59; Calhoun to Virgil Maxcy, 11 Sept. 1830, Galloway-Maxcy-Markoe Papers quoted, 257. McCardell, *Idea of a Southern Nation*, 37. "James Hamilton, Jr., on the Slavery Issue and Nullification, September 1830," in Freehling, *Nullification Era*, 100–101. Coit, *John C. Calhoun*, 146. Rogers, *History of Georgetown County*, 238.

20. Freehling, *Prelude to Civil War*, 192–96.

21. Ford, *Origins of Southern Radicalism*, 116–19; James Black to Stephen D. Miller, 15 Feb. 1830, Chesnut-Miller-Manning Papers, SCHS quoted, 126.

22. Freehling, *Prelude to Civil War*, 140–41; *Register of Debates*, 19 Cong. quoted, 141. "Whitemarsh Seabrook," 10–19. Wallace, *History of South Carolina*, 2: 450.

23. "Robert J. Turnbull's 'The Crisis,' 1827," in Freehling, *Nullification Era*, 26–47. Bartlett, *John C. Calhoun*, 139–43. Wallace, *History of South Carolina*, 2: 425–26.

24. Bartlett, *John C. Calhoun*, 144–46. Freehling, *Prelude to Civil War*, 134–37; quotation, 137.

25. Bartlett, *John C. Calhoun*, 139–52. Coit, *John C. Calhoun*, 181–87. Freehling, *Prelude to Civil War*, 158, 167–68.

26. Bartlett, *John C. Calhoun*, 148–52. Robert E. Lee Meriwether, W. Edwin Hemphill, and Clyde N.

Wilson, eds., *The Papers of John C. Calhoun*, 23 vols. (Columbia: University of South Carolina Press, 1959–1997), 10: 444–534. Richard K. Cralle, *The Works of John C. Calhoun*, 6 vols. (New York: D. Appleton, 1883), 6: 1–59.

27. Freehling, *Prelude to Civil War*, 173–76.

28. Bartlett, *John C. Calhoun*, 139–61.

29. Bartlett, *John C. Calhoun*, 161–66. Coit, *John C. Calhoun*, 192–202.

30. Bartlett, *John C. Calhoun*, 166–68. Freehling, *Prelude to Civil War*, 183–86. Coit, *John C. Calhoun*, 209–12.

31. Bartlett, *John C. Calhoun*, 169–76. Coit, *John C. Calhoun*, 213–218.

32. Freehling, *Prelude to Civil War*, 201–218; I. W. Hayne to James H. Hammond, 29 June 1830, Hammond Papers, Library of Congress quoted, 201.

33. Grayson, *Witness to Sorrow*, 109–20. Ford, *Origins of Southern Radicalism*, 127–41. Freehling, *Prelude to Civil War*, 219–59.

34. Grayson, *Witness to Sorrow*, 109–20. Ford, *Origins of Southern Radicalism*, 127–41. Freehling, *Prelude to Civil War*, 219–59. Wallace, *History of South Carolina*, 2: 437–38. McCardell, *Idea of a Southern Nation*, 36–48; Petigru to James Chesnut, 9 Dec. 1834, Williams-Chesnut-Manning Papers, SCL, quoted, 36. Bartlett, *John C. Calhoun*, 188.

For a more complete listing of leaders of both factions see Wallace, *History of South Carolina*, 2: 437–38.

35. Freehling, *Prelude to Civil War*, 219–28. Bartlett, *John C. Calhoun*, 177–86.

36. Bartlett, *John C. Calhoun*, 183–89; Calhoun to Waddy Thompson, 8 July 1832 quoted, 186. Freehling, *Prelude to Civil War*, 219–59. Faust, *James Henry Hammond*, 43–57, 137–41. Ford, *Origins of Southern Radicalism*, 131–41. Wallace, *History of South Carolina*, 2: 436–39.

37. Bartlett, *John C. Calhoun*, 186–89. Freehling, *Prelude to Civil War*, 219–59.

38. "The Ordinance of Nullification, November 23, 1832," in Freehling, *Nullification Era*, 150–52.

39. Freehling, *Prelude to Civil War*, 111–16, 232–35, 348. Bartlett, *John C. Calhoun*, 191–92. "Andrew Jackson's Nullification Proclamation, December 10, 1832," in Freehling, *Nullification Era*, 153–63.

40. Freehling, *Prelude to Civil War*, 275–86. Bartlett, *John C. Calhoun*, 193–96; *Correspondence of James Polk* quoted, 194. "Mississippi on the Reaction of Other Southerners to Nullification," in Freehling, *Nullification Era*, 172–77.

41. Bartlett, *John C. Calhoun*, 194–201. Freehling, *Prelude to Civil War*, 284–94. "John C. Calhoun Urges Suspending the Ordinance," in Freehling, *Nullification Era*, 181–82.

There were twenty-four states (forty-eight senators) in 1833. The senate vote was 32–1 with John Tyler of Virginia voting nay. The remainder (including Henry Clay) abstained.

42. "James Hamilton, Jr., on the Nullifiers' Triumph" and "Robert Barnwell Rhett on the Nullifiers' Defeat," in Freehling, *Nullification Era*, 181–90. Bartlett, *John C. Calhoun*, 201.

43. Barnwell, *Love of Order*, 47–49, 84–85; Hamilton remarks from William L. Barney, *The Road to Secession* quoted, 47; "Report of General Wallace," Whitemarsh Benjamin Papers, Library of Congress quoted, 85 (hereinafter cited as LC). Ford, *Origins of Southern Radicalism*, 120. Grayson, *Witness to Sorrow*, 116. Wallace, *History of South Carolina*, 2: 476–79.

44. Pauline Maier, "The Road Not Taken: Nullification, John C. Calhoun, and the Revolutionary Tradition in South Carolina," *SCHM*, 82 (1981): 12. Bartlett, *John C. Calhoun*, 209. Cooper and McCord, *Statutes*, 6: 513. Freehling, *Prelude to Civil War*, 268–70, 309–23.

45. Rogers, *Charleston*, 145–50, 161–63. Wallace, *History of South Carolina*, 2: 451–53, 473–76. Underwood, *Constitution of South Carolina*, 1: 38–39. Barnwell, *Love of Order*, 31–49; John Berkeley Grimball Diary, Southern Historical Collection, University of North Carolina at Chapel Hill quoted, 34 (hereinafter cited as SHC). Bartlett, *John C. Calhoun*, 186.

46. Ford, *Origins of Southern Radicalism*, 145–46, 155–63, 172–77, 191. Bartlett, *John C. Calhoun*, 209, 230, 243–47, 317, 328–34. Coit, *John C. Calhoun*, 416–17. McCardell, *Idea of a Southern Nation*, 65. Edmunds, *Francis W. Pickens*, 10, 25, 39, 42–43, 48–58, 95–111, 119; Perry, *Reminiscences of Public Men* quoted, 103. Grayson, *Witness to Sorrow*, 131–32. Freehling, *Prelude to Civil War*, 351–55. Wallace, *History of South Carolina*, 2: 453. Rowland et al., *Beaufort County*, 420–23.

47. Bartlett, *John C. Calhoun*, 190–91, 229, 244–45, 248–49, 288, 361–62. Ford, *Origins of South-*

ern Radicalism, 145–46, 160–74, 194, 281–307. James M. Banner Jr., "The Problem of South Carolina," in *The Hofstadter Aegis: A Memorial,* edited by Stanley Elkins and Eric McKitrick (New York: Alfred A. Knopf, 1974), 60–93. Edmunds, *Francis W. Pickens,* 108. William J. Cooper and Thomas E. Terrill, *The American South: A History,* 2 vols. (New York: Knopf, 1990), 1: 170.

48. Barnwell, *Love of Order,* 20–25. Bleser, *Secret and Sacred,* 219–21. Edmunds, *Francis W. Pickens,* 55–57. Wallace, *History of South Carolina,* 2: 472–79. Ford, *Origins of Southern Radicalism,* 143–44, 154–57.

49. Wallace, *History of South Carolina,* 2: 417, 472, 496–98. Freehling, *Prelude to Civil War,* 302–3, 327–33. Ford, *Origins of Southern Radicalism,* 154–57. Rogers, *Charleston,* 141–66. Bartlett, *John C. Calhoun,* 230.

50. Rogers, *Charleston,* 149. A. E. Grimké, *Appeal to the Christian Women of the South* (New Jersey, 1836), 24. Sarah M. Grimké, *An Epistle to the Clergy of the Southern States* (New York, 1836).

51. Wallace, *History of South Carolina,* 2: 493–510; 3: 27; Cheves to *Mercury* (Charleston), Sept. 1844 quoted, 2: 495. Bartlett, *John C. Calhoun,* 227–28. Rogers, *Charleston,* 147. Moore, *Columbia & Richland County,* 115.

52. McCardell, *Idea of a Southern Nation,* 230–36. Bartlett, *John C. Calhoun,* 306–34. Ernest McPherson Lander Jr., *Reluctant Imperialists: Calhoun, The South Carolinians, and the Mexican War* (Baton Rouge: Louisiana State University Press, 1980), 1–12. James M. McPherson, *Battle Cry of Freedom: The Civil War Era,* Oxford History of the United States, C. Vann Woodward, gen. ed. (New York: Oxford University Press, 1988), 47–77.

53. McCardell, *Idea of a Southern Nation,* 231–35. Bartlett, *John C. Calhoun,* 325–49. Barnwell, *Love of Order,* 53–85; James W. Gettys Jr., "'To Conquer a Peace': Carolina and the Mexican War" quoted, 63. Ford, *Origins of Southern Radicalism,* 188.

54. Lander, *Reluctant Imperialists,* 80–150, 173. Jack Meyer, *South Carolina in the Mexican War: A History of the Palmetto Regiment of Volunteers, 1846–1917* (Columbia: South Carolina Department of Archives and History, 1996), ii. Wates, *Flag Worthy of Your State,* 4–5.

Of the 1,048 men who enlisted in the Palmetto Regiment, 441 died, 134 were discharged for disability, and 43 deserted. Only 430 returned home reasonably unscathed. Meyer, *South Carolina in the Mexican War,* ii.

55. Lander, *Reluctant Imperialists,* 80–150, 173. Barnwell, *Love of Order,* 53–85; Benjamin Franklin Perry Scrapbook, SHC quoted, 77–78. Ford, *Origins of Southern Radicalism,* 183–88. Bartlett, *John C. Calhoun,* 339–45.

56. Edmunds, *Francis W. Pickens,* 112–14. Ford, *Origins of Southern Radicalism,* 186–88. Barnwell, *Love of Order,* 81–82.

57. Bartlett, *John C. Calhoun,* 364–68.

58. Bartlett, *John C. Calhoun,* 350–75. Coit, *John C. Calhoun,* 487–94.

59. Bartlett, *John C. Calhoun,* 350–75. Lacy K. Ford, "Calhoun, South Carolina, and the Constitution," *SCHM,* 89 (1988): 153. Cralle, *Works of Calhoun,* 1: *A Disquisition on Government* and *A Discourse on the Constitution and Government of the United States.*

60. Bartlett, *John C. Calhoun,* 364–70. Ford, *Origins of Southern Radicalism,* 184–91. McCardell, *Idea of a Southern Nation,* 288–306. Edmunds, *Francis W. Pickens,* 119.

61. Barnwell, *Love of Order,* 103–6. Wallace, *History of South Carolina,* 126–27. Edmunds, *Francis W. Pickens,* 114–21. McCardell, *Idea of a Southern Nation,* 295–96. Faust, *James Henry Hammond,* 297–300.

62. Barnwell, *Love of Order,* 90–95, 112–20; Hammond to Calhoun in J. Franklin Jameson, ed., *Correspondence of John C. Calhoun* quoted, 93; David Outlaw to Emily Outlaw, 25 July 1850, David Outlaw Papers, SHC, quoted, 117. Ford, *Origins of Southern Radicalism,* 184, 193; *Herald* (Laurensville) quoted, 193. McCardell, *Idea of a Southern Nation,* 293–306. Wallace, *History of South Carolina,* 3: 126–27; Bryan remarks from Philip M. Hamer, *The Secession Movement in South Carolina, 1847–1852* quoted, 127. Bailey et al., *Biographical Directory, Senate,* 1: 213–24.

63. Barnwell, *Love of Order,* 131–48. Ford, *Origins of Southern Radicalism,* 193–214.

64. Ford, *Origins of Southern Radicalism,* 195, 311–13. Barnwell, *Love of Order,* 136. Wallace, *History of South Carolina,* 3: 128–29.

65. Barnwell, *Love of Order,* 141–48; *Republican* (Savannah), 19 Nov. 1848 quoted, 79. Wallace, *History of South Carolina,* 3: 128–29. Edmunds, *Francis W. Pickens,* 120–22. Faust, *James Henry Hammond,* 332–35.

66. Rowland et al., *Beaufort County,* 428–33; *Charleston Courier,* 16 Nov. 1850 quoted, 430. Barnwell, *Love of Order,* 154–66.

67. Barnwell, *Love of Order,* 157–90. Edmunds, *Francis W. Pickens,* 120–22. Faust, *James Henry Hammond,* 331–34.

68. Wallace, *History of South Carolina,* 3: 127–32; Rhett remarks from Hamer, *Secession Movement in South Carolina* quoted, 131. Faust, *James Henry Hammond,* 331–34; Hammond Diary, SCL, quoted 331. *Southern Standard* (Charleston), 14 July 1851 quoted in Barnwell, *Love of Order,* 168.

69. Barnwell, *Love of Order,* 166–91. Wallace, *History of South Carolina,* 3: 127–31; *Southern Patriot* (Greenville), 9 May 1851, in Chauncey S. Boucher, *Secession and Cooperation in South Carolina* quoted, 130. Edmunds, *Francis W. Pickens,* 120–21.

70. Ford, *Origins of Southern Radicalism,* 204–12. Barnwell, *Love of Order,* 177–81.

71. Barnwell, *Love of Order,* 181–90. Wallace, *History of South Carolina,* 3: 131–32.

72. Barnwell, *Love of Order,* 181–90; James Jones to James Henry Hammond, 26 Oct. 1851, Hammond Papers, LC quoted, 181. Wallace, *History of South Carolina,* 3: 131–32. Edmunds, *Francis W. Pickens,* 121–26. Ford, *Origins of Southern Radicalism,* 193–214.

73. Ford, *Origins of Southern Radicalism,* 281–307. Wallace, *History of South Carolina,* 3: 133–38.

74. Edmunds, *Francis W. Pickens,* 126–27. Charles Edward Cauthen, *South Carolina Goes to War, 1860–1865,* James Sprunt Studies in History and Political Science, vol. 32, Published under the direction of the Departments of History and Political Science of the University of North Carolina, Albert Ray Newsome, et al., eds. (Chapel Hill: University of North Carolina Press, 1950), 1–6.

75. Ford, *Origins of Southern Radicalism,* 343–49. Eliza Cowan Ervin and Horace Fraser Rudisill, *Darlingtoniana: A History of People, Places and Events in Darlington County, South Carolina,* 175. Anne King Gregorie, *History of Sumter County* (Sumter, S.C.: Library Board of Sumter County, 1954), 235–40. Rowland et al., *Beaufort County,* 435–36. Wallace, *History of South Carolina,* 3: 139–40. McPherson, *Battle Cry of Freedom,* 145–69.

76. John C. Roberson, "The Reaction of South Carolina to the Brooks-Sumner Affair" (seminar paper, University of South Carolina, 1989), 1–3; *Congressional Globe,* 34 Cong. quoted, 1. Edmunds, *Francis W. Pickens,* 131–32. Ford, *Origins of Southern Radicalism,* 348–49. Wallace, *History of South Carolina,* 3: 139–40. McPherson, *Battle Cry of Freedom,* 149–52.

77. Roberson, "Reaction of South Carolina," 7–28, 37–58; *Advertiser* (Edgefield), 28 May 1856 quoted, 10. "Preston Brooks on the Caning of Charles Sumner," ed. Robert L. Meriwether, *SCHM,* 52 (1951): 7. Wallace, *History of South Carolina,* 3: 139–40. McPherson, *Battle Cry of Freedom,* 149–52.

78. Roberson, "Reaction of South Carolina," 28–37; *Sumter Watchman,* from Elmer D. Herd, "Chapters From the Life of a Southern Chevalier: Laurence Masillon Keitt's Congressional Years, 1853–1860," M.A. thesis, University of South Carolina, 1958, quoted, 40–41.

79. Edmunds, *Francis W. Pickens,* 128–32; Francis W. Pickens to A. Burt, Burt Papers, Duke University Library quoted, 132. Ford, *Origins of Southern Radicalism,* 213–14. Wallace, *History of South Carolina,* 3: 140–43. Hammond's remarks from Hammond Papers, LC quoted in Faust, *James Henry Hammond,* 353. Cauthen, *South Carolina Goes to War,* 7–11.

80. Faust, *James Henry Hammond,* 344–48; *Congressional Globe,* 35th Cong. quoted, 346. McPherson, *Battle Cry of Freedom,* 170–201. Wallace, *History of South Carolina,* 3: 143–47.

81. Channing, *Crisis of Fear,* 20–57, 94–98; quotation, 96. Ford, *Origins of Southern Radicalism,* 367. McPherson, *Battle Cry of Freedom,* 202–13. Huff, *Greenville,* 130–31. Cauthen, *South Carolina Goes to War,* 11–13.

82. Channing, *Crisis of Fear,* 17–57. Pope, *History of Newberry County,* 1: 108–9. Huff, *Greenville,* 131.

83. Olsberg, "Government of Class & Race," 219–22. Wallace, *History of South Carolina,* 3: 149–50. Channing, *Crisis of Fear,* 195–226. Cauthen, *South Carolina Goes to War,* 14–25.

84. Channing, *Crisis of Fear*, 241–85. Rogers, *Generations of Lawyers*, 41–45. Olsberg, "Government of Class & Race," 213–72. Faust, *James Henry Hammond*, 356–59. Pope, *History of Newberry County*, 1: 205–12. Huff, *Greenville*, 127–35. Wallace, *History of South Carolina*, 3: 151–61. Walter B. Edgar, "W. W. Boyce," in *Encyclopedia of the Confederacy*, 4 vols., edited by Richard N. Current (New York: Simon & Schuster, A Paramount Communications Company, 1993), 1: 199–201. Emory Thomas, *The Confederacy as a Revolutionary Experience* (1971; Columbia: University of South Carolina Press, 1991), 1–2.

85. Ford, *Origins of Southern Radicalism*, 366–69; *Mercury*, 6 July 1857 and *Herald* (Laurensville), 25 June 1858 quoted, 366. Channing, *Crisis of Fear*, 286–93; *Spartan* (Spartanburg), 22 Nov. 1860 quoted, 287. McPherson, *Battle Cry of Freedom*, 221–33. Wallace, *History of South Carolina*, 3: 156.

86. Olsberg, "Government of Class & Race," 254–67. Channing, *Crisis of Fear*, 252–61; *Keeowee Courier*, 3 Nov. 1860 and *Weekly Journal* (Camden), 6 Nov. 1860 quoted, 256. Hopkins, *Diary*, 27–29. Rowland et al., *Beaufort County*, 387–91, 437–40. Cauthen, *South Carolina Goes to War*, 31–48.

87. Olsberg, "Government of Class & Race," 240–42. Wallace, *History of South Carolina*, 3: 151–52.

88. Wallace, *History of South Carolina*, 3: 153–61. Olsberg, "Government of Class & Race," 272–95. Channing, *Crisis of Fear*, 282–93. Moore, *Columbia & Richland County*, 183. John Amasa May and Joan Reynolds Faunt, *South Carolina Secedes* (Columbia: University of South Carolina Press, 1960), 5–16. Cauthen, *South Carolina Goes to War*, 68–78.

89. Louis Grimball to Elizabeth Grimball, 27 Nov. 1860, Grimball Papers, SHC and Arthur P. Hayne to James Buchanan, 22 Dec. 1860, James Buchanan Papers, Pennsylvania Historical Society quoted in Channing, *Crisis of Fear*, 291.

90. Channing, *Crisis of Fear*, 58–93. Wallace, *History of South Carolina*, 3: 151–61. McPherson, *Battle Cry of Freedom*, 221–46. Rowland et al., *Beaufort County*, 437–40. Stampp, *Peculiar Institution*, 33. Ford, *Origins of Southern Radicalism*, 371–72. Huff, *Greenville*, 133–34.

91. "G. W. Featherstonhaugh Describes Columbia in the Postnullification Period," in Freehling, *Nullification Era*, 190–94.

CHAPTER 16: THE CIVIL WAR, PART I

1. Vera Brodsky Lawrence, *Music for Patriots, Politicians, and Presidents: Harmonies and Discords of the First Hundred Years* (New York: Macmillan, 1975), 346. McPherson, *Battle Cry of Freedom*, 234–38.

2. Ford, "James Louis Petigru," 182–85; Sally Edwards, *The Man Who Said No* quoted, 182. Huff, *Greenville*, 133–35. Lillian A. Kibler, *Benjamin F. Perry, South Carolina Unionist* quoted, 135. Wallace, *History of South Carolina*, 3: 151–61. Rowland et al., *Beaufort County*, 450–52. Cauthen, *South Carolina Goes to War*, 74–78.

3. Cauthen, *South Carolina Goes to War*, 73–75; *Journal of the Convention of the People of South Carolina* quoted, 74. May and Faunt, *South Carolina Secedes*, 76–92. Rogers, *Generations of Lawyers*, 42–45.

4. Rogers, *Generations of Lawyers*, 44–45. Edmunds, *Francis W. Pickens*, 148–53; D. L. Wardlaw to Samuel McGowan Papers, 3 Dec. 1860, McGowan Papers, SCL quoted, 152. Woodward, *Mary Chesnut's Civil War*, 40. Faust, *James Henry Hammond*, 340–59. Wallace, *History of South Carolina*, 3: 168–69.

5. Cauthen, *South Carolina Goes to War*, 97–102.

6. Olsberg, "Government of Class & Race," 231–33, 274–97. Cauthen, *South Carolina Goes to War*, 97–102.

7. Cauthen, *South Carolina Goes to War*, 97–102. Walter B. Edgar, "Robert W. Barnwell," in Current, *Encyclopedia of the Confederacy*, 1: 133. McPherson, *Battle Cry of Freedom*, 262–67. Fraser, *Charleston! Charleston!*, 244–46; *Courier* quoted, 246.

8. Cauthen, *South Carolina Goes to War*, 85–88. Edgar, "Barnwell," 133. Emory Thomas, *The Confederate Nation, 1861–1865*, New American Nation Series, ed. Henry Steele Commager and Richard B. Morris (New York: Harper & Row, 1979), 72–73. Wallace, *History of South Carolina*, 3: 168–69.

Thomas, *Confederacy as a Revolutionary Experience,* 38–42.

9. Cauthen, *South Carolina Goes to War,* 87–91. Thomas, *Confederate Nation,* 62–65, 307–22. May and Faunt, *South Carolina Secedes,* 37–40. Wallace, *History of South Carolina,* 3: 167–69.

10. Among the South Carolinians who used the term *civil war* to describe the conflict that would ensue (if secession were not peaceful) were Mary Boykin Miller Chesnut, Caroline Howard Gilman, James Hamilton Jr., Sally Baxter Hampton, Emma Holmes, David G. Harris, Benjamin F. Perry, Joel R. Poinsett, and William H. Trescot. The *Charleston Courier* also used it. Channing, *Crisis of Fear,* 280. Racine, *Piedmont Farmer,* 182. Barnwell, *Love of Order,* 132. Olsberg, "Government of Class & Race," 10–11. Huff, *Greenville,* 129–30. Wallace, *History of South Carolina,* 3: 126. Ann Fripp Hampton, ed., *A Divided Heart: The Letters of Sally Baxter Hampton, 1853–1862* (1980; Columbia: Phantom Press, 1994), 118. Fraser, *Charleston! Charleston!,* 246–47. Woodward, *Mary Chesnut's Civil War,* 50. John F. Marszalek, ed., *The Diary of Miss Emma Holmes, 1861–1866* (Baton Rouge: Louisiana State University Press, 1979), 24.

11. Woodward, *Mary Chesnut's Civil War,* 51. Fraser, *Charleston! Charleston!,* 251.

12. Cauthen, *South Carolina Goes to War,* 113–15, 146–47. Rogers, *History of Georgetown County,* 387. Wallace, *History of South Carolina,* 3: 172–73. Racine, *Piedmont Farmer,* 171, 236, 266. Huff, *Greenville,* 135–36.

13. Wallace, *History of South Carolina,* 3: 186–89. Cauthen, *South Carolina Goes to War,* 146–47, 164–77. Racine, *Piedmont Farmer,* 313.

14. Robert Hartman, "The Civil War Experience in Lancaster County, 1861–1865," senior thesis, University of South Carolina, 1991, pp. 5–16.

15. Wallace, *History of South Carolina,* 3: 176–221. Huff, *Greenville,* 135–44. Moore, *Columbia & Richland County,* 183–207. Racine, *Piedmont Farmer,* 302, 330. Woodward, *Mary Chesnut's Civil War,* 63–78, 189–382, 670–714. Cheryl Watson, "Letters Home: The Civil War Correspondence of Three South Carolina Women" (seminar paper, University of South Carolina, 1991), passim.

16. Rowland et al., *Beaufort County,* 443–45. Rogers, *History of Georgetown County,* 387–92. Milby Burton, *The Siege of Charleston* (Columbia: University of South Carolina Press, 1970), 84–98.

17. Rowland et al., *Beaufort County,* 443–56.

18. Rowland et al., *Beaufort County,* 455–58. Woodward, *Mary Chesnut's Civil War,* 228–57. Hampton, *Divided Heart,* 118. Willie Lee Rose, *Rehearsal for Reconstruction: The Port Royal Experiment* (1964; New York: Oxford University Press, 1976), 3–16, 104–6. Olsberg, "Government of Class & Race," 315–28.

19. Emory Thomas, *Robert E. Lee, A Biography* (New York: W. W. Norton, 1995), 211–17. Woodward, *Mary Chesnut's Civil War,* 237. Cauthen, *South Carolina Goes to War,* 137–38. Olsberg, "Government of Class & Race," 310–15, 342–43. Fraser, *Charleston! Charleston!,* 252. Rosengarten, *Row Upon Row,* 19–20. Williamson, *After Slavery,* 1–6.

20. Edmunds, *Francis W. Pickens,* 164–72. Fraser, *Charleston! Charleston!,* 253–55.

21. May and Faunt, *South Carolina Secedes,* 48–51, 190–91. Cauthen, *South Carolina Goes to War,* 139–51.

22. Towles, *World Turned Upside Down,* 319.

23. Thomas, *Confederacy as a Revolutionary Experience,* passim; especially, 58–78. Cauthen, *South Carolina Goes to War,* 152–77. Olsberg, "Government of Class & Race," 365–66.

24. Woodward, *Mary Chesnut's Civil War,* 301.

25. Cauthen, *South Carolina Goes to War,* 152–63. Wallace, *History of South Carolina,* 3: 172–73.

26. Cauthen, *South Carolina Goes to War,* 152–63. Wallace, *History of South Carolina,* 3: 172–73. Edmunds, *Francis W. Pickens,* 162–72.

27. Cauthen, *South Carolina Goes to War,* 139–63. Wallace, *History of South Carolina,* 3: 172–73. Moore, *Columbia & Richland County,* 191. Towles, *World Turned Upside Down,* 319.

28. Thomas, *Confederacy as a Revolutionary Experience,* 58–71. Faust, *Sacred Circle,* 142–43; Hammond to William Gilmore Simms, Hammond Papers, LC quoted, 142. Cauthen, *South Carolina Goes to War,* 201–16. Thomas, *Confederate Nation,* 140–42.

29. Edgar, "Boyce," 199–201; Walter B. Edgar, "Lawrence Keitt," in *Encyclopedia of the Confederacy,* 2: 876–78. Edgar, "Barnwell," 133. Cauthen, *South Carolina Goes to War,* 208–23. Woodward,

Mary Chesnut's Civil War, 79, 121, 138–39, 142, 154, 204, 215, 219–20, 246, 352, 368, 436. Thomas, *Confederate Nation,* 139–41; Hammond's remarks from Bell I. Wiley, *Road to Appomattox* quoted, 140.

30. Olsberg, "Government of Class & Race," 359–61. Hartman, "Civil War Experience in Lancaster County," 12–16. Cauthen, *South Carolina Goes to War,* 172–77. Huff, *Greenville,* 136, 142–43. Wallace, *History of South Carolina,* 3: 188–89.

31. Thomas, *Confederacy as a Revolutionary Experience,* 65–68. Faust, *Sacred Circle,* 142–43. Faust, *James Henry Hammond,* 360–75. Cauthen, *South Carolina Goes to War,* 148, 184–87. Olsberg, "Government of Class & Race," 362–64. Rast Family Papers (private collection), Columbia, S.C. Racine, *Piedmont Farmer,* 308, 329.

32. Rogers, *History of Georgetown County,* 398–415; *Official Records of the Rebellion* quoted, 401. Olsberg, "Government of Class & Race," 338–40. Dusinberre, *Them Dark Days,* 303–5, 373–84.

33. Burton, *Siege of Charleston,* 97–112. Powers, *Black Charlestonians,* 67. Wallace, *History of South Carolina,* 3: 174–76. Fraser, *Charleston! Charleston!,* 258–61; James Petigru Carson, *Life, Letters and Speeches of James Louis Petigru* quoted, 259. Williamson, *After Slavery,* 6–7. Okon Edet Uya, *From Slavery to Public Service: Robert Smalls, 1839–1915* (New York: Oxford University Press, 1971), 11–17. Edward A. Miller, *Gullah Statesman: Robert Smalls, from Slavery to Congress, 1839–1915* (Columbia: University of South Carolina Press, 1995), 20–21.

34. Stephen R. Wise, *Gate of Hell: Campaign for Charleston Harbor, 1863* (Columbia: University of South Carolina Press, 1994), passim. Rose, *Rehearsal for Reconstruction,* 248–52, 255–60, 262–64. Burton, *Siege of Charleston,* 151–82. Wallace, *History of South Carolina,* 3: 183–86. Edgar, "Keitt," 876–78. Fraser, *Charleston! Charleston!,* 262–64.

35. Stephen R. Wise, *Lifeline of the Confederacy: Blockade Running During the Civil War* (Columbia: University of South Carolina Press, 1988), 121–26, 233–59. Fraser, *Charleston! Charleston!,* 257–58. Wallace, *History of South Carolina,* 3: 185–86. Rose, *Rehearsal for Reconstruction,* 244–47.

36. Fraser, *Charleston! Charleston!,* 257–58, 264–65. Towles, *World Turned Upside Down,* 379–80, 405–8.

37. Rose, *Rehearsal for Reconstruction,* 104–10. Olsberg, "Government of Class & Race," 310–17.

38. Rose, *Rehearsal for Reconstruction,* 15–39; quotation, 35.

39. Rose, *Rehearsal for Reconstruction,* 199–235. Wallace, *History of South Carolina,* 3: 171–72. Gordon, *Sketches of Negro Life and History,* 99–100. Etrulia P. Dozier, "Black Union Soldiers: Who Were the Civil War Black Soldiers?" (unpub. compilation of rosters compiled from official records, 1982, 1983). Williamson, *After Slavery,* 8–20.

40. Rose, *Rehearsal for Reconstruction,* 146–68, 200–202, 212–14, 239–96. Chuck Holland, "Letters Home From South Carolina" (directed research paper, University of South Carolina, 1995), passim.

41. Rose, *Rehearsal for Reconstruction,* 169–98, 229–38. Rowland et al., *Beaufort County,* 416–17. Rogers, *History of Georgetown County,* 406–22. Litwack, *Been in the Storm So Long,* 3–63. Powers, *Black Charlestonians,* 66–72. Stroyer, *My Life in the South,* 36–38, 98–100. Williamson, *After Slavery,* 4–5. Philip Jackson, "Potter's Raid in Sumter County," senior thesis, University of South Carolina, 1975, p. 29. Olsberg, "Government of Class & Race," 430–31. Royster, *Destructive War,* 20–21, 33. Blassingame, *Slave Testimony,* 449–54, 701.

42. Litwack, *Been in the Storm So Long,* 3–63. Olsberg, "Government of Class & Race," 325–41. Woodward, *Mary Chesnut's Civil War,* 60, 78, 114, 233, 309, 374–75, 464, 641, 699. Fraser, *Charleston! Charleston!,* 255. Thomas, *Confederacy as a Revolutionary Experience,* 120–27. Randall C. Jimerson, *The Private Civil War* (Baton Rouge: Louisiana State University Press, 1988), 50–85.

43. Racine, *Piedmont Farmer,* 357–58, 364–65. Olsberg, "Government of Class & Race," 364–82; quotation, 371–72. Thomas, *Confederacy as a Revolutionary Experience,* 120–27. Watson, "Letters Home," 13–26.

44. Olsberg, "Government of Class & Race," 364–87.

45. Fraser, *Charleston! Charleston!,* 252, 265–66. Wise, *Lifeline of the Confederacy,* 121–26. Mary Elizabeth Massey, *Ersatz in the Confederacy: Shortages and Substitutes on the Southern Homefront,* with an Introduction by Barbara Bellows, (1952; Columbia: University of South Carolina Press, 1993), 141–42.

46. Earl Schenck Miers, *When the World Ended: The Diary of Emma LeConte* (New York: Oxford

University Press, 1957), 4, 16, 40. Fraser, *Charleston! Charleston!*, 261–62. Moore, *Columbia & Richland County,* 196–97. Massey, *Ersatz in the Confederacy,* passim. Frances M. Burroughs, "The Confederate Receipt Book: The Study of Food Substitution in the American Civil War," *SCHM,* 93 (Jan. 1992): 31–50.

47. Bellows, *Benevolence Among Slaveholders,* 191. Hartman, "Civil War Experience in Lancaster County," 4, 22–27. Fraser, *Charleston! Charleston!*, 260–61, 265. Communion Alms Book, Trinity Episcopal Church, Columbia, S.C., passim.

48. Miers, *When the World Ended,* 3–17. Hartman, "Civil War Experience in Lancaster County," 4, 22–27. Cauthen, *South Carolina Goes to War,* 176, 193–94. Huff, *Greenville,* 143.

49. Racine, *Piedmont Farmer,* 308. Cauthen, *South Carolina Goes to War,* 223. Wallace, *History of South Carolina,* 3: 193. Thomas, *Confederacy as a Revolutionary Experience,* 120. J. G. Randall and David Donald, *The Civil War and Reconstruction,* 2d ed. (Boston: D. C. Heath and Company, 1961), 262–63. Communion Alms Book, Trinity Episcopal Church, passim. Woodward, *Mary Chesnut's Civil War,* 643. Olsberg, "Government of Class & Race," 388–89, 395. Moore, *Columbia & Richland County,* 190–91. Fraser, *Charleston! Charleston!*, 265. Huff, *Greenville,* 139–43.

During the war prices in the Confederacy skyrocketed. By April 1865 the general price index was ninety-two times that of January 1861. In January 1861 prices in the Confederacy and the Union were equal. Inflated Confederate dollars were converted to 1996 dollars, based upon tables complied by Eugene M. Lerner in combination with those of McCusker cited earlier. Eugene M. Lerner, "Money, Prices and Wages in the Confederacy, 1861–65," in Ralph Adreano, ed., *The Economic Impact of the American Civil War* (Cambridge, Mass.: Schenckman, 1962), 11–40. Interview with James Bradley, Department of Economics, University of South Carolina, 28 Aug. 1997.

50. *Report of the South Carolina Hospital Aid Association in Virginia, 1861–1862* (Richmond: MacFarlane & Fergusson, 1862), passim. United Daughters of the Confederacy: South Carolina Division, Mrs. Thomas Taylor et al., eds., *South Carolina Women in the Confederacy,* 2 vols. (Columbia: State Printing Company, 1903, 1907), 1: 21, 92, 154–55; 2: 88, 93, 119–20. Marion Brunson Lucas, *Sherman and the Burning of Columbia* (College Station: Texas A&M University Press, 1976), 24–25.

51. Fraser, *Charleston! Charleston!*, 258. Huff, *Greenville,* 138–39. Wallace, *History of South Carolina,* 3: 190–93. Racine, *Piedmont Farmer,* 207. G. Wayne King, *Rise Up So Early: A History of Florence County, South Carolina,* Published for the Florence County Historical Commission (Spartanburg, S.C.: Reprint Company, 1981), 48 (hereinafter cited as *Florence County*). Moore, *Columbia & Richland County,* 186–87. Mrs. Campbell Bryce, *Reminiscences of the Hospitals in Columbia, S.C.* (Philadelphia: J. B. Lippincott, 1897), 14, 29–30. Drew Gilpin Faust, *Mothers of Invention: Women of the Slaveholding South in the American Civil War,* Fred W. Morrison Series in Southern Studies (Chapel Hill: University of North Carolina Press, 1996), 24, 25, 93, 99–100, 106, 108–12, 206.

52. Towles, *World Turned Upside Down,* 326, 328, 341–48, 396–99. Woodward, *Mary Chesnut's Civil War,* 397–98, 451–53, 628. Huff, *Greenville,* 138–40.

53. J. Tracy Power, "From the Wilderness to Appomattox: Life in Lee's Army of Northern Virginia, May 1864–April 1865," diss., University of South Carolina, 1993, pp. 28, 55, 59, 130, 133, 144, 163; Francis Asbury Wayne Jr. to his mother, 17 May 1864, Mrs. E. K. Atkinson Collection, SHC quoted, 59; Private William C. Leak . . . to his wife and children, 25 May 1864, William Leak Papers, Petersburg National Battlefield, Petersburg, Va., quoted, 163. Racine, *Piedmont Farmer,* 273, 329, 358.

54. McPherson, *Battle Cry of Freedom,* 626–65. Wallace, *History of South Carolina,* 3: 180–96. Fraser, *Charleston! Charleston!*, 240, 253, 255–58; William Garland to "My Dear Father," William Garland Papers, SHC quoted 262. Woodward, *Mary Chesnut's Civil War,* 64–65. Cauthen, *South Carolina Goes to War,* 164–87, 228–30. Moore, *Columbia & Richland County,* 191–97. Thomas, *Confederacy as a Revolutionary Experience,* 117–18. Miers, *When the World Ended,* 3–5.

55. Olsberg, "Government of Class & Race," 359–61. Cauthen, *South Carolina Goes to War,* 217–23. Thomas, *Confederate Nation,* 287–306. Wallace, *History of South Carolina,* 3:186–87. Moore, *Columbia & Richland County,* 196–97, 200–201. Woodward, *Mary Chesnut's Civil War,* 678. Fraser, *Charleston! Charleston!*, 266–67. Edgar, "Boyce," 199–201. Faust, *Mothers of Invention,* 38–39, 91–92.

The value of the $11.00 in 1996 dollars was $197.81 in January 1861 but only $3.43 in January 1865.

56. Cauthen, *South Carolina Goes to War,* 224–30. Edward McCrady to Louisa Rebecca McCrady, 20 Dec. 1864, McCrady Papers, SCL. Olsberg, "Government of Class & Race," 418–20.

57. Charles Royster, *The Destructive War: William Tecumseh Sherman, Stonewall Jackson, and the Americans* (1991; New York: Vintage Civil War Books, A Division of Random House, Inc., 1993), 3–4. Wallace, *History of South Carolina,* 3: 204–5. Robert Major Richardson, "From Savannah to Columbia: Sherman's March Through the South Carolina Lowcountry," senior thesis, University of South Carolina, 1987, 10–11, 13, 15–16, 20–22, 24, 25. Katharine M. Jones, *When Sherman Came: Southern Women and the "Great March"* (Indianapolis: Bobbs-Merrill, 1964), 109–48. Edward G. Longacre, ed., "We Left a Black Track in South Carolina: Letters of Corporal Eli S. Ricker, 1865," *SCHM,* 82 (July 1981): 210–24. David B. Cheeseborough, "'There Goes Your Damned Gospel Shop!' The Churches and Clergy as Victims of Sherman's March Through South Carolina," *SCHM,* 92 (Jan. 1991): 15–23.

58. Royster, *Destructive War,* 5–6. Lucas, *Sherman and the Burning of Columbia,* 19–50.

59. Royster, *Destructive War,* 9–16. Lucas, *Sherman and the Burning of Columbia,* 50–71. Moore, *Columbia & Richland County,* 200–201.

60. William Gilmore Simms, *The Sack and Destruction of City of Columbia, S.C.* (Columbia: Power Press, 1865), 18. Royster, *Destructive War,* 15–33. Lucas, *Sherman and the Burning of Columbia,* 83–128. McPherson, *Battle Cry of Freedom,* 825–30. Jones, *When Sherman Came,* 149–256.

61. Fraser, *Charleston! Charleston!,* 269–70. Wallace, *History of South Carolina,* 3: 215. Powers, *Black Charlestonians,* 66–72. Williamson, *After Slavery,* 22–23.

62. Rogers, *History of Georgetown County,* 416–22. Jackson, "Potter's Raid," 1–2, 27–29. Williamson, *After Slavery,* 24–25.

63. Power, "From the Wilderness to Appomattox," 560–61. Racine, *Piedmont Farmer,* 370–71.

64. Fraser, *Charleston! Charleston!,* 164–69. Henry Timrod, "Carolina," in Richard James Calhoun and John Caldwell Guilds, eds., *A Tricentennial Anthology of South Carolina Literature, 1670–1970* (Columbia: University of South Carolina Press, 1971), 299–301. Miers, *When the World Ended,* 4. Jimerson, *Private Civil War,* 140–44. Faust, *Mothers of Invention,* 201.

Such memories die hard. In a 1984 publication Jimmie Childs Fort Rast referred to the destruction of the family home "at the hands of Sherman the Goth." *Pelion South Carolina: The Community and its People* (Pelion, S.C.: Pelion History Committee, 1984), 49.

65. An average value of $720 per slave was placed on the 412,320 slaves in South Carolina. The value of slave property is based upon figures and tables in Roger Ransom and Richard Sutch, "'Capitalists Without Capital': The Burden of Slavery and the Impact of Emancipation," *Agricultural History,* 62, no. 3 (1988): 133–60. This places the value of slave property ($296,870,400) at 70 percent of personal property in 1860—a bit higher than the 60–66 percent of personal property ($422,774,636) that other historians have used to estimate the investment in human capital. Wright, *Old South, New South,* 19–20. Coclanis, *Shadow of a Dream,* 126–27. Inter University Consortium for Political and Social Research, Study 00003.

In looking at the percentage of total wealth, Ransom and Sutch examined five cotton states (including South Carolina) and determined that 45.8 percent of the total wealth was in slave property. With its larger slave ownership, the 48.8 percent figure for South Carolina is not at all out of line. Roger L. Ransom and Richard Sutch, *One Kind of Freedom: The Economic Consequences of Emancipation* (Cambridge: Cambridge University Press, 1977), 51–55.

Earlier studies, citing the *Charleston Daily News,* place the loss of slave property at $200 million, but total property values at $400 million (which was considerably less than the $608 million reported in the census); however, the newspaper's figure for loss in human capital was 50 percent of what it reported as total wealth. Francis Butler Simkins and Robert Hilliard Woody, *South Carolina During Reconstruction* (1932; Gloucester, Mass.: Peter Smith, 1966), 10–12.

James L. Sellers, "The Economic Incidence of the Civil War in the South," in Adreano, *The Economic Impact of the American Civil War,* 79–90.

William J. Grayson, *James Louis Petigru,* quoted in Channing, *Crisis of Fear,* 281. Cauthen, *South Carolina Goes to War,* 189–200.

66. McPherson, *Battle Cry of Freedom,* 238, 854. Wallace, *History of South Carolina,* 3: 504. U.S. Navy, *State Summary of War Casualties [SC]* (N.p., 1946), 1. War Department, *World War II Honor*

List of Dead and Missing: State of South Carolina (n.p., 1946), iii. United States Bureau of Census, *16th Census of the U.S.: 1940, Population, vol. 4, Characteristics by Age, pt. 4, Ohio-Wyoming* (Washington, D.C.: Government Printing Office, 1943), 345.

67. Cauthen, *South Carolina Goes to War,* 177. Wallace, *History of South Carolina,* 3: 218–19. Hartman, "Civil War Experience in Lancaster County," 5. Ervin and Rudisill, *Darlingtoniana,* 130–31. Randolph W. Kirkland Jr., *Broken Fortunes: South Carolina Soldiers, Sailors & Citizens who Died in the Service of their Country and State in the War for Southern Independence, 1861–1865* (Charleston: South Carolina Historical Society, 1995), xiv, 192.

68. Edmunds, *Francis W. Pickens,* 152. McPherson, *Battle Cry of Freedom,* 238. For every killed or mortally wounded Confederate soldier in battle, another 2.5 were wounded. Thomas L. Livermore, *Numbers and Losses in the Civil War in America: 1861–1865* (Bloomington: Indiana University Press, 1957), 63–64. The loss of limbs was enough that Northern firms advertised prosthetic devices in Columbia newspapers in 1865. *Daily Phoenix* (Columbia), 1–31 Dec 1865, passim.

69. Faust, *James Henry Hammond,* 360–74. Olsberg, "Government of Class & Race," 381–82, 386–87, 395–401; Trescot quotation, 382. Thomas, *Confederacy as a Revolutionary Experience,* 37–42, 58–78, 133–38. Thomas, *Confederate Nation,* 287–306. Poinsett's remarks from Hamer, *Secession Movement in South Carolina* quoted in Wallace, *History of South Carolina,* 3: 126.

CHAPTER 17: THE CIVIL WAR, PART II

1. Richard Zuczek, *State of Rebellion: Reconstruction in South Carolina* (Columbia: University of South Carolina Press, 1996), ix–x, 1–6. In current United States military doctrine, an insurgency is sometimes styled a low intensity conflict (LIC) operation other than war (OOTW), or military operation other than war (MOOTW). John T. Fishel, "Little Wars, Small Wars, LIC, OOTW, The GAP, and Things that Go Bump in the Night," *Low Intensity Conflict & Law Enforcement,* 4 (Winter 1995): 372–98. A number of studies of guerrilla war and insurgencies have produced various principles of what are required to overthrow a government. See, for example, Mao Tse-Tung, *On Guerrilla Warfare,* 43 and Zuczek, *State of Rebellion,* 189. For effective tactics used by insurgents, see Kimbra L. Thompson Krueger, "The Destabilization of Republican Regimes: The Effects of Terrorism on Democratic Societies," *Low Intensity Conflict & Law Enforcement,* 5 (Autumn 1996): 253–54. Insurgencies generate counterinsurgencies by the government in power. In most instances a friendly power provides support for the threatened government and there are checklists for that as well. See Max G. Manwaring and John T. Fishel, "Insurgency and Counter-Insurgency: Toward a New Analytical Approach," *Small Wars & Insurgencies,* 3 (Winter 1992): 274.

2. Cauthen, *South Carolina Goes to War,* 228–29. Moore, *Columbia & Richland County,* 206–7.

3. Charles Edward Cauthen, "Confederacy and Reconstruction," in Hennig, *Columbia,* 41–44. Moore, *Columbia & Richland County,* 206–7. Lawrence, *Music for Patriots,* 349. Fraser, *Charleston! Charleston!,* 273.

4. Miers, *When the World Ended,* 98, 111. George F. McKay to Peter Johnson Shand, 11 June 1865, Shand to Edward McCrady, 12 July 1865, Bishop Thomas Davis to Shand, 19 June 1865, Peter Johnson Shand Papers, SCL. Fraser, *Charleston! Charleston!,* 270–71.

5. Robert W. Shand to Peter J. Shand, 28 May 1865, P. J. Shand Papers. Williamson, *After Slavery,* 71–72; Pickens to B. F. Perry, Benjamin Franklin Perry Papers, DUL, quoted, 71.

6. Williamson, *After Slavery,* 32–33. Bailey et al., *Biographical Directory, Senate,* 2: 1272–75. Racine, *Piedmont Farmer,* 378–89.

7. Williamson, *After Slavery,* 33–63, 106–11; Johnson's remarks from William Watts Ball, *The State That Forgot* quoted, 33. Fraser, *Charleston! Charleston!,* 270, 274. Moore, *Columbia & Richland County,* 217. Huff, *Greenville,* 159. Coclanis, *Shadow of a Dream,* 115. Powers, *Black Charlestonians,* 254–60. Eric Foner, *Reconstruction: America's Unfinished Revolution, 1863–1877* (New York: Harper & Row, 1988), 288–89, 431.

8. Williamson, *After Slavery,* 33–63, 106–11. Heyward, *Seed from Madagascar,* 141–42.

9. Marszalek, *Diary of Miss Emma Holmes,* 444–45, 466–67, 469–70, 479, 483, 487. Fraser, *Charleston! Charleston!,* 283. Malvina Gist (Waring) in Katharine M. Jones, ed., *Heroines of Dixie: Winter of Desperation* quoted in Faust, *Mothers of Invention,* 78.

10. Jimerson, *Private Civil War,* 82–85; Taveau's remarks, Manigault Papers, SHC from Eugene Genovese, *Roll, Jordon Roll* quoted, 83. Marszalek, *Diary of Miss Emma Holmes,* 441.

11. Williamson, *After Slavery,* 46–49, 254–55, 284, 304. Gordon, *Sketches of Negro Life and History,* 102. Marszalek, *Diary of Miss Emma Holmes,* 428, 440.

12. Williamson, *After Slavery,* 34–35, 64–125, 241–73; "Wife" (probably Mrs. Robert Pelot) to her husband, 11 Mar. 1866, Lalla Pelot Papers, DUL, quoted, 96.

13. Williamson, *After Slavery,* 126–63. Julie Saville, *The Work of Reconstruction: From Slave to Wage Laborer in South Carolina, 1860–1870* (Cambridge: Cambridge University Press, 1994), 110–21. Morgan, "Work and Culture," 584–99. Edward L. Ayers, *The Promise of the New South: Life After Reconstruction* (New York: Oxford University Press, 1992), 109.

14. Marszalek, *Diary of Miss Emma Holmes,* 483. Williamson, *After Slavery,* 100–105. Theodore Rosengarten, *Tombee: Portrait of a Planter with the Journal of Thomas B. Chaplin (1822–1890),* ed. with Susan W. Walker (New York: William Morrow, 1986), 270–82.

15. Williamson, *After Slavery,* 39–40, 246–60; Grace B. Elmore Diary, SHC quoted, 246. John Richard Dennett, *The South As It Is, 1865–1866,* ed. Henry M. Christman (1965; Baton Rouge: Louisiana State University Press, 1995), 190–95. Saville, *Work of Reconstruction,* 105–6, 143–51.

16. Marszalek, *Diary of Miss Emma Holmes,* 485. Racine, *Piedmont Farmer,* 389. Williamson, *After Slavery,* 274–99.

17. Williamson, *After Slavery,* 274–99. Fraser, *Charleston! Charleston!,* 280.

18. Williamson, *After Slavery,* 180–208. Erskine Clark, *Our Southern Zion: A History of Calvinism in the South Carolina Low Country, 1690–1990* (Tuscaloosa: University of Alabama Press, 1996), 225–28, 232–36. Ayers, *Promise of the New South,* 160–61.

19. Williamson, *After Slavery,* 180–208. George Brown Tindall, *South Carolina Negroes, 1877–1900* (1952; Columbia: University of South Carolina Press, 1970), 186–208. Powers, *Black Charlestonians,* 189–225. For AME (Zion) figures, see James Walker Hood, *One Hundred Years of the African Methodist Episcopal Zion Church; or the Centennial of African Methodism* (New York: Zion Book Concern, 1895), 625.

20. Ervin and Rudisill, *Darlingtoniana,* 71. Huff, *Greenville,* 171–74. Pope, *History of Newberry County,* 2: 289–93. Walter B. Edgar, "The Redeemers and Race: Segregating the Episcopal Church in South Carolina" (paper delivered at The Citadel Conference on the South, Apr. 1985). Powers, *Black Charlestonians,* 189–225. Lyon G. Tyler, "Drawing the Color Line in the Episcopal Diocese of South Carolina, 1876 to 1890: The Role of Edward McCrady, Father and Son," *SCHM,* 91 (Apr. 1990): 107–24.

21. Williamson, *After Slavery,* 204–7, 274–79.

22. Zuczek, *State of Rebellion,* 10–16. Underwood, *Constitution of South Carolina,* 4: 2–6; Constitution of 1868 quoted, 6.

23. Underwood, *Constitution of South Carolina,* 4: 2–6. John S. Reynolds, *Reconstruction in South Carolina, 1865–1877* (1905; New York: Negro Universities Press, 1969), 18–19.

24. Reynolds, *Reconstruction in South Carolina,* 16–17, 20–24. Huff, *Greenville,* 155.

25. Underwood, *Constitution of South Carolina,* 4: 6–7. Reynolds, *Reconstruction in South Carolina,* 27–34. Zuczek, *State of Rebellion,* 15–16.

26. Williamson, *After Slavery,* 72–79, 240–46; quotation, 76. Simkins and Woody, *South Carolina During Reconstruction,* 51–52.

27. Williamson, *After Slavery,* 76–79. Simkins and Woody, *South Carolina During Reconstruction,* 51–63. Powers, *Black Charlestonians,* 81, 84–85. Zuczek, *State of Rebellion,* 32–34. Foner, *Reconstruction,* 261–71.

28. Williamson, *After Slavery,* 76–79. Foner, *Reconstruction,* 268–69. Simkins and Woody, *South Carolina During Reconstruction,* 52–59; quotation, 53.

29. Zuczek, *State of Rebellion,* 32–37; quotation, 37. Williamson, *After Slavery,* 76–79. Foner, *Reconstruction,* 268–69. Simkins and Woody, *South Carolina During Reconstruction,* 52–63.

30. Williamson, *After Slavery,* 329, 343–46. Zuczek, *State of Rebellion,* 38–42. Simkins and Woody, *South Carolina During Reconstruction,* 70–71.

31. Zuczek, *State of Rebellion,* 47–49.

32. Zuczek, *State of Rebellion*, 47–50. Underwood, *Constitution of South Carolina*, 3: 11–34; *Proceedings of the Constitutional Convention . . . 1868* quoted, 22. Hollis, *University of South Carolina*, 2: 44–45.

33. Underwood, *Constitution of South Carolina*, 2: 47–67.

34. Zuczek, *State of Rebellion*, 47–51, 127; Henry D. Green in the *Edgefield Advertiser* quoted, 48 (emphasis in original). Reynolds, *Reconstruction in South Carolina*, 93–94. Thomas Holt, *Black Over White: Negro Political Leadership in South Carolina during Reconstruction* (Urbana: University of Illinois Press, 1977), 95. Manwaring and Fishel, "Insurgency and Counter-Insurgency," 272–74. May and Faunt, *South Carolina Secedes*, 152.

35. Zuczek, *State of Rebellion*, 50. Thomas C. Holt, "Negro Legislators in South Carolina," in *Southern Black Leaders in the Reconstruction Era*, edited by Howard N. Rabinowitz (Urbana: University of Illinois Press, 1982), 228. Holt, *Black Over White*, 225–42.

36. Williamson, *After Slavery*, 356–65. Walter B. Edgar, "South Carolina" and Raymond W. Smock, "Black Members: Nineteenth Century," in Donald C. Bacon, Roger H. Davidson, and Morton Keller, *The Encyclopedia of the United States Congress*, 4 vols. (New York: Simon & Schuster, A Paramount Communications Company, 1995), 1: 170–73; 4: 1852–53. Underwood, *Constitution of South Carolina*, 4: 24–25. Peggy Lamson, *Glorious Failure: Black Congressman Robert Brown Elliott and the Reconstruction in South Carolina* (New York: W. W. Norton, 1973), 153–71. Holt, "Negro Legislators," 223–46. Holt, *Black Over White*, 95–121.

The black Carolinians in Congress were Richard Cain (1873–1875), Robert C. DeLarge (1871–1873), Robert B. Elliott (1871–1874), Joseph H. Rainey (1870–1879), Alonzo J. Ransier (1873–1875), and Robert Smalls (1875–1877). After Reconstruction, Thomas E. Miller and George W. Murray were elected in the 1890s. Smock, "Black Members," 1: 170–73.

Statewide black officeholders were Alonzo J. Ransier, lieutenant governor (1870–1872); Richard H. Gleaves, lieutenant governor (1872–1877); Francis L. Cardozo, secretary of state (1868–1872) and state treasurer (1872–1877); Henry E. Hayne, secretary of state (1872–1877); and Henry W. Purvis, adjutant general (1870–1877). Holt, *Black Over White*, 225–41.

37. Holt, *Black Over White*, 96. Holt, "Negro Legislators," 229–30. Bailey et al., *Biographical Directory, Senate*, 4: 1898, 1900, 1902.

38. Holt, *Black Over White*, 95–96; *News & Courier*, 24 Dec. 1875 quoted, 96. Williamson, *After Slavery*, 254–55. Zuczek, *State of Rebellion*, 48–50, 127; *Advertiser* (Edgefield), 30 May 1868 quoted, 48. Edward King, *The Great South* edited by W. Magruder Drake and Robert R. Jones (Baton Rouge: Louisiana State University Press, 1972), 422–65. James S. Pike, *The Prostrate State: South Carolina Under Negro Government*, ed. Robert F. Durden (1874; New York: Harper Torchbooks, Harper & Row, 1968).

39. Holt, *Black Over White*, 36–40, 54. Holt, "Negro Legislators," 230–34. Simkins and Woody, *South Carolina During Reconstruction*, 116–17. Reynolds, *Reconstruction in South Carolina*, 87. Powers, *Black Charlestonians*, 83, 90, 149–50, 216. Williamson, *After Slavery*, 160–63.

40. Ford, *Origins of Southern Radicalism*, 112–13. Holt, "Negro Legislators," 233–34.

41. Williamson, *After Slavery*, 274–99. Underwood, *Constitution of South Carolina*, 4: 22.

42. Williamson, *After Slavery*, 274–99; *Daily Republican* (Charleston), 24 June 1870 quoted, 279; *Congressional Record*, 43d Cong. quoted, 280. Powers, *Black Charlestonians*, 241–46. Channing, *Crisis of Fear*, 287. Simkins and Woody, *South Carolina During Reconstruction*, 368–70. Moore, *South Carolina Newspapers*, passim.

The five Rollin sisters (Frances Ann, Katherine, Charlotte, Marie Louise, and Florence), children of free persons of color, were natives of Charleston. Willard B. Gatewood Jr., "The Remarkable Misses Rollin: Black Women in Reconstruction in South Carolina," *SCHM*, 92 (July 1991): 172–88.

43. Channing, *Crisis of Fear*, 65–67, 286–93; James Dunwoody Brownson DeBow, *The Interest in Slavery of the Southern Non-Slaveholder* quoted, 66.

44. Williamson, *After Slavery*, 209–24. Moore, *Columbia & Richland County*, 257. Holt, *Black Over White*, 241–42.

45. Gordon, *Sketches of Negro Life and History*, 92–100. Williamson, *After Slavery*, 187–88, 206, 230–33, 238.

46. Hollis, *University of South Carolina*, 2: 19–79. Williamson, *After Slavery*, 232–39. Tindall, *South Carolina Negroes*, 223–26. Henry Fulmer, "Richard T. Greener and the Radical University Library," in *Ex Libris* (Columbia: University of South Carolina Division of Libraries and Information Systems, 1995), 34–37.

47. Williamson, *After Slavery*, 279–87. Fraser, *Charleston! Charleston!*, 284–85. Moore, *Columbia & Richland County*, 220.

48. Williamson, *After Slavery*, 279–87. Moore, *Columbia & Richland County*, 287. Fraser, *Charleston! Charleston!*, 289. Powers, *Black Charlestonians*, 226–40.

49. Williamson, *After Slavery*, 287–99.

50. Williamson, *After Slavery*, 287–99, 341–54, 381–82; quotation, 288. Moore, *Columbia & Richland County*, 221. Zuczek, *State of Rebellion*, 62–63, 75–78, 81–83, 142–47.

51. Williamson, *After Slavery*, 287–99.

52. Ibid., 140–55, 393.

53. Zuczek, *State of Rebellion*, 135–37. Williamson, *After Slavery*, 381–87. Gordon, *Sketches of Negro Life and History*, 63. Lamson, *Glorious Failure*, 133–73.

54. Richard N. Current, *Those Terrible Carpetbaggers*, (New York: Oxford University Press, 1988), 214–35. Williamson, *After Slavery*, 331–35. Simkins and Woody, *South Carolina During Reconstruction*, 126–27.

55. Zuczek, *State of Rebellion*, 135–36. Reynolds, *Reconstruction in South Carolina*, 473–74. Williamson, *After Slavery*, 387–93.

56. Foner, *Reconstruction*, 387–88. Holt, *Black Over White*, 195–96. Williamson, *After Slavery*, 157–59, 381–87.

57. Moore, *Columbia & Richland County*, 222–27, 267. Fraser, *Charleston! Charleston!*, 282–83, 291–99. Williamson, *After Slavery*, 381–87.

58. Williamson, *After Slavery*, 223–29. Zuczek, *State of Rebellion*, 71–80.

59. Williamson, *After Slavery*, 54–63, 142–48. Carol K. Rothrock Bleser, *The Promised Land: The History of the South Carolina Land Commission, 1869–1890* (Columbia: University of South Carolina Press, 1969). Huff, *Greenville*, 167. Foner, *Reconstruction*, 375.

60. Martin Linton Abbott, "The Freedmen's Bureau in South Carolina, 1865–1872," diss., Emory University, Atlanta, Ga., 76–80, 232–35. Marszalek, *Diary of Miss Emma Holmes*, 440. Fraser, *Charleston! Charleston!*, 269–71, 274. Moore, *Columbia & Richland County*, 217. Huff, *Greenville*, 159. Williamson, *After Slavery*, 65–67.

61. Fraser, *Charleston! Charleston!*, 275, 291. Huff, *Greenville*, 152–54. Johnson and Roark, *Black Masters*, 310–25.

62. Sellers, "Economic Incidence of the Civil War in the South," 82–83. Dodd and Dodd, *Historical Statistics*, 46–49.

63. Fraser, *Charleston! Charleston!*, 291–95. Charles Hosmer, *From Williamsburg to the National Trust, 1926–1929*, 2 vols. (Charlottesville: Published for the Preservation Press by the University of Virginia Press, 1981), 1: 232–36, 273–74. John J. Duffy, "Charleston Politics in the Progressive Era," diss., University of South Carolina, 1963, pp. 3–4, 41.

64. Williamson, *After Slavery*, 174–75. Lacy K. Ford, "Rednecks and Merchants: Economic Development and Social Tensions in the South Carolina Upcountry, 1865–1900," *Journal of American History*, 71 (Sept. 1984): 309.

65. Holt, *Black Over White*, 195–96. Gordon, *Sketches of Negro Life and History*, 61–63.

66. Kreuger, "Destabilization of Republican Regimes," 253. Zuczek, *State of Rebellion*, 200. Burton, *In My Father's House*, 297–98; John Tuialy to Br. Major S. Walker, 9 Mar. 1866, in Letters and Reports Received, Records of the Bureau of Refugees, Freedmen, and Abandoned Lands, National Archives, quoted, 297.

67. Zuczek, *State of Rebellion*, 48–49, 118–30. Krueger, "Destabilization of Republican Regimes," 253–55. Manwaring and Fishel, "Insurgency and Counter-Insurgency," 272–73.

68. Williamson, *After Slavery*, 291. Krueger, "Destabilization of Republican Regimes," 253–54. Huff, *Greenville*, 168. Moore, *Columbia & Richland County*, 225. Zuczek, *State of Rebellion*, 50–61. Allen

W. Trelease, *White Terror: The Ku Klux Klan Conspiracy and Southern Reconstruction* (1971; Baton Rouge: Louisiana State University Press, 1995), 349–83.

69. Zuczek, *State of Rebellion*, 50–63. Fraser, *Charleston! Charleston!*, 286–87. Trelease, *White Terror*, 115–17. Edgar, *Biographical Directory*, 1: 407–11. Bailey et al., *Biographical Directory, Senate*, 2: 1335–36. Williamson, *After Slavery*, 260–67.

70. Zuczek, *State of Rebellion*, 50–75. Kreuger, "Destabilization of Republican Regimes," 270–71. Trelease, *White Terror*, 359–61.

71. Zuczek, *State of Rebellion*, 55–61.

72. Zuczek, *State of Rebellion*, 55–75. Wallace, *History of South Carolina*, 3: 269, 272–75.

73. Manwaring and Fishel, "Insurgency and Counter-Insurgency," 287. Kreuger, "Destabilization of Republican Regimes," 255–57. Zuczek, *State of Rebellion*, 92–93, 106, 141–42, 148, 163, 170, 176–77. Williamson, *After Slavery*, 260–67.

74. Zuczek, *State of Rebellion*, 75–108; quotation, 78. Trelease, *White Terror*, 349–80.

75. Zuczek, *State of Rebellion*, 88–93.

76. Zuczek, *State of Rebellion*, 93–97.

One of the tests of a patron nation in support of its client state is the willingness to intervene militarily, to shed the blood of its soldiers to defend the legitimacy of its client. During Reconstruction the federal government violated every principle of counterinsurgency in its response to the insurgency in South Carolina. Manwaring and Fishel, "Insurgency and Counter-Insurgency," 274.

77. Zuczek, *State of Rebellion*, 96–99, 106–8.

78. Zuczek, *State of Rebellion*, 98–106, 118–22. Trelease, *White Terror*, 407–8. Lou Faulkner Williams, *The Great Ku Klux Klan Trials*, Studies in the Legal History of the South, ed. Paul Finkelman and Kermit L. Hall (Athens: University of Georgia Press, 1996), 40–59, 85–130.

79. Zuczek, *State of Rebellion*, 106–8, 118–29.

80. Zuczek, *State of Rebellion*, 127–58; Hampton's remarks in *Advertiser* quoted, 127. *New York Herald* quoted in Trelease, *White Terror*, 379. Williamson, *After Slavery*, 414–17. Foner, *Reconstruction*, illustrations opposite 387.

81. Reynolds, *Reconstruction in South Carolina*, 245–61. Zuczek, *State of Rebellion*, 127–30.

82. Current, *Those Terrible Carpetbaggers*, 328–66. Foner, *Reconstruction*, 542–43. Zuczek, *State of Rebellion*, 148–53. Holt, "Negro Legislators," 242–43.

83. Zuczek, *State of Rebellion*, 150–53. Fraser, *Charleston! Charleston!*, 297–99.

84. Williamson, *After Slavery*, 349–52, 402–12. Hampton M. Jarrell, *Wade Hampton and the Negro: The Road Not Taken* (Columbia: University of South Carolina Press, 1949), 58–62. Zuczek, *State of Rebellion*, 159–72. Fraser, *Charleston! Charleston!*, 299.

85. Zuczek, *State of Rebellion*, 159–72. Williamson, *After Slavery*, 268–73. "Hamburg massacre" was the term that conservative nineteenth-century whites used to describe the confrontation. Carol Bleser, ed., *The Hammonds of Redcliffe* (New York: Oxford University Press, 1981), 272.

86. Zuczek, *State of Rebellion*, 167–73. Jarrell, *Wade Hampton and the Negro*, 63–85. William J. Cooper Jr., *The Conservative Regime: South Carolina, 1877–1890* (Baltimore: Johns Hopkins University Press, 1968), 22.

87. Zuczek, *State of Rebellion*, 172–80. Burton, *In My Father's House*, 289–91.

88. Zuczek, *State of Rebellion*, 172–74.

89. Foner, *Reconstruction*, 570–75. Williamson, *After Slavery*, 271–72. Zuczek, *State of Rebellion*, 166. Cooper, *Conservative Regime*, 22.

90. Zuczek, *State of Rebellion*, 188–93. Simkins and Woody, *South Carolina During Reconstruction*, 514–22.

91. Zuczek, *State of Rebellion*, 192–97. Simkins and Woody, *South Carolina During Reconstruction*, 514–27. Wallace, *History of South Carolina*, 3: 312–15.

92. Simkins and Woody, *South Carolina During Reconstruction*, 529–35; Hampton's remarks in *News & Courier* (Charleston) quoted, 529–30. Wallace, *History of South Carolina*, 3: 315–20.

93. Simkins and Woody, *South Carolina During Reconstruction*, 529–35. Wallace, *History of South Carolina*, 3: 315–20. Jarrell, *Wade Hampton and the Negro*, 112–13. Zuczek, *State of Rebellion*, 197–99. Williamson, *After Slavery*, 158–59, 291. Rogers, *Generations of Lawyers*, 67.

94. Zuczek, *State of Rebellion,* 197–201; quotation, 198. C. Vann Woodward, *Origins of the New South,* vol. IX in A History of the South, Wendell Holmes Stephenson and E. Merton Coulter, eds., The Littlefield Fund for Southern History of the University of Texas (Baton Rouge: Louisiana State University Press, 1951), 23–44.

95. Williamson, *After Slavery,* 417. Zuczek, *State of Rebellion,* 200–201.

CHAPTER 18: RETURN OF THE OLD ORDER

1. Zuczek, *State of Rebellion,* 179–80. Cooper, *Conservative Regime,* 18–19, 39–44.

2. Cooper, *Conservative Regime,* 16–19, 23, 43, 130, 208–10. Lewis Pinckney Jones, *Stormy Petrel: N. G. Gonzales and His State* (Columbia: University of South Carolina Press, 1973), 60–65. A. V. Huff Jr., "Urbane Bourbon: Joseph W. Barnwell and the Search for a New Aristocracy," *Proceedings of the South Carolina Historical Association* (1981): 136. Rogers, *Generations of Lawyers,* 96–99. Wallace, *History of South Carolina,* 3: 232. Clement Eaton, *The Waning of the Old South Civilization, 1860–1880s* (Athens, Ga.: Mercer University Lamar Memorial Lectures, No. 10, University of Georgia Press, 1968), 139–45. William Arthur Sheppard, *Red Shirts Remembered: Southern Brigadiers of the Reconstruction Period* (Atlanta: Ruralist Press, 1940), 86–87.

3. Cooper, *Conservative Regime,* 16–17. Woodward, *Origins of the New South,* 1–5, 14, 19, 75. Jones, *Stormy Petrel,* 60–61. Jones, *South Carolina,* 193–204, 211–13.

In *Origins of the New South* (1951) C. Vann Woodward dismisses the term "Bourbon" as out-of-date; however, in *The Conservative Regime* (1968) William J. Cooper makes an excellent case for South Carolina's post-Reconstruction leadership being different from that in other southern states. Lewis P. Jones in *South Carolina: A Synoptic History for Laymen* (rev. ed., Orangeburg, S.C.: Sandlapper, 1978) also uses the term. My own research supports both Cooper and Jones. The term "Bourbon" is appropriate and applicable to the men who ousted the Reconstruction regime in 1876–1877 and who governed South Carolina until 1890.

4. Towles, *World Turned Upside Down,* 802–3. Jones, *Stormy Petrel,* 64–65.

5. Cooper, *Conservative Regime,* 25. Tindall, *South Carolina Negroes,* 17.

6. Cooper, *Conservative Regime,* 24–25. Wallace, *History of South Carolina,* 3: 325–26. Tindall, *South Carolina Negroes,* 16–17.

7. Cooper, *Conservative Regime,* 26–27. Tindall, *South Carolina Negroes,* 17–18.

8. Williamson, *After Slavery,* 416–17. Cooper, *Conservative Regime,* 29–32. Tindall, *South Carolina Negroes,* 18–19. Gordon, *Sketches of Negro Life and History,* 55–79. Alfred B. Williams, *Hampton and His Red Shirts: South Carolina's Deliverance in 1876* (Charleston: Walker, Evans & Cogswell, 1935), 22–35.

9. Cooper, *Conservative Regime,* 45–50. Wallace, *History of South Carolina,* 3: 325–27.

10. Ford, "Rednecks and Merchants," 307–10.

11. Allan D. Charles, *The Narrative History of Union County, South Carolina,* Published for the Union County Historical Commission and Arthur State Bank (Spartanburg, S.C.: Reprint Company, 1987), 252–53. Wallace, *History of South Carolina,* 3: 328.

12. Woodward, *Origins of the New South,* 116–18. Cooper, *Conservative Regime,* 18, 120, 126–29.

13. Cooper, *Conservative Regime,* 50–53, 88, 112–15. Woodward, *Origins of the New South,* 79–80.

14. Tindall, *South Carolina Negroes,* 27, 63–64. Fraser, *Charleston! Charleston!,* 295–301. Huff, "Urbane Bourbon," 136–37.

15. Rogers, *History of Georgetown County,* 474–77, 480–84. Cooper, *Conservative Regime,* 84–88; *News & Courier,* 12 July 1881 quoted, 88.

16. Cooper, *Conservative Regime,* 53–65. Wallace, *History of South Carolina,* 3: 326–30; Gary's remarks quoted, 326. Ernest McPherson Lander Jr., *A History of South Carolina, 1865–1960* (Chapel Hill: University of North Carolina Press, 1960), 24–28.

17. Jones, *Stormy Petrel,* 77–78. Cooper, *Conservative Regime,* 80–93. Lander, *History of South Carolina,* 24–28. Jarrell, *Wade Hampton and the Negro,* 157–59.

18. Gregorie, *History of Sumter County,* 357. Jarrell, *Wade Hampton and the Negro,* 121–55. Cooper, *Conservative Regime,* 94–97.

19. Holt, "Negro Legislators," 244. Wallace, *History of South Carolina,* 3: 504.

The black population of the white counties was as follows:

Anderson (44 percent), Chesterfield (42 percent), Greenville (39 percent), Horry (32 percent), Lexington (40 percent), Oconee (26 percent), Pickens (26 percent), and Spartanburg (35 percent). Wallace, *History of South Carolina*, 3: 504.

20. Wallace, *History of South Carolina*, 3: 323. Towles, *World Turned Upside Down,* 802. Williamson, *After Slavery,* 361–62.

21. Cooper, *Conservative Regime,* 34–39, 84–93. Gregorie, *History of Sumter County,* 354. Wallace, *History of South Carolina,* 3: 336.

22. Cooper, *Conservative Regime,* 89–93.

23. Cooper, *Conservative Regime,* 98–103. Tindall, *South Carolina Negroes,* 68–73. Richard M. Gergel, "Wade Hampton and the Rise of One Party Racial Orthodoxy in South Carolina," *Proceedings of the South Carolina Historical Association* (1977): 13. Jarrell, *Wade Hampton and the Negro,* 158–60. Edward McCrady Jr., *The Necessity of Raising the Standard of Citizenship* (Charleston: Walker, Evans & Cogswell, 1881), 14. Edward McCrady Jr., *The Registration of Electors* (Charleston, n.d.), passim.

24. Tindall, *South Carolina Negroes,* 68–73. Cooper, *Conservative Regime,* 216. William Watts Ball, *The State That Forgot: South Carolina's Surrender to Democracy* (Indianapolis: Bobbs-Merrill, 1932), 169.

25. Cooper, *Conservative Regime,* 108–9. William Willis Boddie, *History of Williamsburg: Something about the People of Williamsburg County, South Carolina, from the First Settlement by Europeans about 1705 until 1923* (1923; Spartanburg, S.C.: Reprint Company, 1980), 461. Tindall, *South Carolina Negroes,* 73, 310.

26. Cooper, *Conservative Regime,* 103–8. South Carolina, *Statutes at Large,* 17: 1169–71. Tindall, *South Carolina Negroes,* 56–58, 73.

27. Williamson, *After Slavery,* 361–62. Tindall, *South Carolina Negroes,* 64–67, 310.

28. Thomas D. Clark, *The Southern Country Editor* (1948; Columbia: University of South Carolina Press, 1991), 236, 238, 241. Tindall, *South Carolina Negroes,* 238.

29. Towles, *World Turned Upside Down,* 846. Tindall, *South Carolina Negroes,* 233–51; *News & Courier,* 29 Dec. 1889 quoted, 240. Holt, *Black Over White,* 401–5.

30. Tindall, *South Carolina Negroes,* 240–47. Clark, *Southern Country Editor,* 241.

31. Charles, *Union County,* 252–53. Clark, *Southern Country Editor,* 36, 255–57. Fraser, *Charleston! Charleston!,* 321–22. Jones, *Stormy Petrel,* 124.

32. Lander, *History of South Carolina,* 29–30. Wallace, *History of South Carolina,* 3: 331–33. Towles, *World Turned Upside Down,* 838.

33. Woodward, *Origins of the New South,* 158–60.

34. Tindall, *South Carolina Negroes,* 233–51. Bolt, *Black Over White,* 419–22. Wallace, *History of South Carolina,* 3: 324. B. H. Liddel Hart, *Strategy,* quoted in Weigley, *Partisan War,* 69.

35. Williamson, *After Slavery,* 274–99. Tindall, *South Carolina Negroes,* 296–98. Cooper, *Conservative Regime,* 109, 113. Lorena Denise Land, "A Call to Service: Marion Birnie Wilkinson and the South Carolina Federated Club Movement," senior thesis, University of South Carolina, 1995, p. 4.

36. Woodward, *Origins of the New South,* 210. Tindall, *South Carolina Negroes,* 294–97. John Hammond Moore, ed., *South Carolina in the 1880s: A Gazetter* (Orangeburg, S.C.: Sandlapper, 1989), 180, 234, 277. Doyle, *New Men, New Cities, New South,* 301. Powers, *Black Charlestonians,* 246–52. Huff, *Greenville,* 232.

37. Clark, *Southern Country Editor,* 152–54, 204. Tindall, *South Carolina Negroes,* 117–20, 291. Moore, *Columbia & Richland County,* 235, 239. Fraser, *Charleston! Charleston!,* 284. Charles, *Union County,* 274.

38. Tindall, *South Carolina Negroes,* 284–85. Moore, *South Carolina in the 1880s,* 44, 71, 98, 101, 117, 126, 139–40. King, *Florence County,* 192–93.

39. Tindall, *South Carolina Negroes,* 282–83, 288–90. Elizabeth Allston Pringle, *A Woman Rice Planter,* with an introduction by Charles Joyner (1913, 1961; Columbia: University of South Carolina Press, 1992), 128. Charles, *Union County,* 254.

40. Tindall, *South Carolina Negroes,* 290. *Daily Register* (Columbia), 25 Dec. 1881. *Democrat* (Orangeburg), 5, 12, 19, 26 Dec. 1879. *Weekly News* (Charleston), 24 Dec. 1879. *News and Herald* (Winns-

boro), 23, 25 Dec. 1879. *Herald* (Laurensville), 19 Dec. 1879. *Enquirer* (Yorkville), 18 Dec. 1879. *Keowee Courier* (Walhalla), 18 Dec. 1879. *Journal* (Camden), 4, 25 Dec. 1879. *Kershaw Gazette* (Camden), 18, 25 Dec. 1879. August Kohn and Lewis Berry, *A Descriptive Sketch of Orangeburg* (Orangeburg, S.C.: R. L. Berry, 1888), passim. Pringle, *Woman Rice Planter,* 139–40, 271–75, 437.

41. Moore, *South Carolina in the 1880s,* 143, 184, 192, 198. Moore, *South Carolina Newspapers,* passim. Jones, *Stormy Petrel,* 67–69, 94.

42. Lewis Pinckney Jones, "50th Annual Meeting Address," South Caroliniana Society, Columbia, S.C., 30 May 1986 (Columbia: University South Caroliniana Society, 1987), 7. Cooper, *Conservative Regime,* 112–15. Woodward, *Origins of the New South,* 62. Boddie, *Williamsburg County,* 466–67. Moore, *South Carolina in the 1880s,* passim. King, *Florence County,* 118. Charles, *Union County,* 290.

43. Tindall, *South Carolina Negroes,* 219–20. Moore, *Columbia & Richland County,* 245.

44. Tindall, *South Carolina Negroes,* 219–20. Moore, *Columbia & Richland County,* 245. Lewis P. Jones, *A Synoptic History for Laymen* (rev. ed.; Orangeburg, S.C.: Sandlapper Publishing, Inc., 1978), 200. Moore, *South Carolina in the 1880s,* 66, 251. Gordon, *Sketches of Negro Life and History,* 94. Towles, *World Turned Upside Down,* 838.

45. Woodward, *Origins of the New South,* 170. Towles, *World Turned Upside Down,* 805–6.

46. Huff, *Greenville,* 205.

47. Charles Regan Wilson, *Baptized in the Blood: The Religion of the Lost Cause, 1865–1900* (1980; Athens: University of Georgia Press, 1983), 1–18. Thomas L. Connelly and Barbara L. Bellows, *God and General Longstreet: The Lost Cause and the Southern Mind* (Baton Rouge: Louisiana State University Press, 1982), 1–38, 119.

48. Wilson, *Baptized in the Blood,* 25–27. *Confederate Memorial Day at Charleston, S.C. . . . Address of Rev. Dr. Girardeau, Odes, &c.* (Charleston: William G. Mazyck, Printers, 1871), 8–9, 16–22.

49. *Confederate Memorial Day,* 8–9, 16–22.

50. *News & Courier,* 11 May 1871. Eaton, *Waning of the Old South Civilization,* 139. Cooper, *Conservative Regime,* 39–40; Edward Hogan, "South Carolina To-Day," *International Review* quoted, 39. Pringle, *Woman Rice Planter,* 423. Bleser, *Hammonds of Redcliffe,* 170. Wallace, *History of South Carolina,* 3: 324–25. Mary Reynolds Forbes, "Society," in Hennig, *Columbia,* 259. F. W. McMaster, *Address Before the Eighth Annual Meeting of the Survivors' Association of Ex-Confederate Surgeons* (Yorkville, S.C.: Tidings from the Craft, Job. Print, 1895), 13–16. Wilson, *Baptized in the Blood,* 12, 25–36.

51. William B. Capers, *The Soldier-Bishop: Ellison Capers* (New York: Neale, 1912), 164–77, 191–98. Walter B. Edgar, "Dear Old Trinity" (unpub. ms., Trinity Cathedral Archives, Columbia, S.C.), 1–2, 25–27. John Andrew Rice, *I Came Out of the Eighteenth Century* (New York: Harper & Brothers, 1942), 43.

52. WPA, *South Carolina,* 169–76, 181, 184–211, 256, 278, 288, 294, 305, 310, 315, 321, 339, 349. Walter B. Edgar, *South Carolina in the Modern Age* (Columbia: University of South Carolina Press, 1992), 57–62. John Ruskin, *The Seven Lamps of Architecture* (1849; London: Dent, 1963), 190, 198.

53. Fraser, *Charleston! Charleston!,* 314. Huff, "Urbane Bourbon," 133–41. Doyle, *New Men, New Cities, New South,* 238–44. Howard N. Rabinowitz, "Continuity and Change: Southern Urban Development, 1860–1900," in *The City in Southern History: The Growth of Urban Civilization in the South,* edited by Blaine A. Brownell and David R. Goldfield (Port Washington, N.Y.: National University Publishers, Kennikat Press, 1977), 88. Barbara L. Bellows, "At Peace With the Past: Charleston, 1900–1950," in *Mirror of Time: Elizabeth O'Neill Verner's Charleston,* edited by Lynn Robertson Myers (Columbia: McKissick Museum, 1983), 1–5. Rogers, *Generations of Lawyers,* 116–17.

54. Cooper, *Conservative Regime,* 42–44; Bratton to J. L. Weber, 11 Apr. 1891, SCL and Charles H. Simonton to W. P. Miles, 25 May 1877, Miles Papers, SHC quoted, 43. Hollis, *University of South Carolina,* 2: 80–97.

55. Huff, *Greenville,* 207–8. Thomas J. Brown, "Reconstructing Calhoun: the Charleston Monuments" (paper presented at the annual meeting of the Southern Historical Association, Little Rock, Ark., Oct. 1996), 15–18. Ralph W. Widener, *Confederate Monuments: Enduring Symbols of the South and the War Between the States* (Washington: Andromeda Associates, 1982), 171–89.

56. Cooper, *Conservative Regime,* 18–20. Thomas, *Confederacy as a Revolutionary Experience,* 135–38. Wallace, *History of South Carolina,* 3: 324–25. Woodward, *Origins of the New South,* 144–48.

57. Jones, *Stormy Petrel*, 68. Clark, *Southern Country Editor*, 28–29. David L. Carlton, *Mill and Town in South Carolina, 1880–1920* (Baton Rouge: Louisiana State University Press, 1982), 74. Dawson's remarks from the *News & Courier*, quoted in Woodward, *Origins of the New South*, 146. Doyle, *New Men, New Cities, New South*, 111.

58. Rabinowitz, "Continuity and Change," 93. Coclanis, *Shadow of a Dream*, 111–15, 146–47. Doyle, *New Men, New Cities, New South*, 62–75.

59. Fraser, *Charleston! Charleston!*, 302–10. Doyle, *New Men, New Cities, New South*, 58–60.

60. Doyle, *New Men, New Cities, New South*, 61–74, 111–18, 159–71. Fraser, *Charleston! Charleston!*, 328.

61. Fraser, *Charleston! Charleston!*, 314–18. Doyle, *New Men, New Cities, New South*, 74–76, 159. Wallace, *History of South Carolina*, 3: 334. Carlton, *Mill and Town*, 73–74.

62. Moore, *South Carolina in the 1880s*, 1–8, 60–73, 135–49, 220–30, 238–53, 288–90. King, *Florence County*, 115. Huff, *Greenville*, 181–84. Ford, "Rednecks and Merchants," 311. Carlton, *Mill and Town*, 48–49. Moore, *Columbia & Richland County*, 214.

63. Carlton, *Mill and Town*, 42–55, 66. Pope, *History of Newberry County*, 2: 89. Lewis J. Bellardo Jr., "A Social and Economic History of Fairfield County, South Carolina, 1865–1871," diss., University of Kentucky, 1979, 133. William L. Watkins, *Anderson County: South Carolina, The Things That Made It Happen* (Anderson, S.C.: Printer, 1995), 55.
Among the individuals associated with Walker, Fleming and Company were John B. Cleveland, Joseph Walker, C. E. Fleming, John H. Montgomery, and J. H. Sloan. Carlton, *Mill and Town*, 53–54.

64. Woodward, *Origins of the New South*, 121–22. Huff, *Greenville*, 198. Carlton, *Mill and Town*, 29, 51–53. Ford, "Rednecks and Merchants," 317–18. Jones, *South Carolina*, 201. Bellardo, "Social and Economic History of Fairfield County," 133–38. Ralph D. Werner, "'New South' Carolina: Ben Tillman and the Rise of Bourgeois Politics, 1880–1893," in Winfred B. Moore Jr., Joseph F. Tripp, and Lyon G. Tyler Jr., *Developing Dixie: Modernization in a Traditional Society* (New York: Greenwood Press, 1988), 150–52.

65. Woodward, *Origins of the New South*, 111. Fletcher W. Hewes and Henry Gannett, *Scribner's Statistical Atlas of the United States: Showing By Graphic Methods Their Present Condition* (New York: Charles Scribner's Sons, 1883), plate 70.

66. Towles, *World Turned Upside Down*, 799–803, 809, 812, 834, 847, 870–72, 891, 905, 921–22. Elizabeth Muhlenfeld, *Mary Boykin Chesnut: A Biography* (Baton Rouge: Louisiana State University Press, 1981), 130–223. Woodward, *Origins of the New South*, 207, 226.

67. Dodd and Dodd, *Historical Statistics*, 48. Ford, "Rednecks and Merchants," 306–7. Carlton, *Mill and Town*, 20, 24. Huff, *Greenville*, 178. Kovacik and Winberry, *South Carolina*, 106–12. Clark, *Southern Country Editor*, 279.

68. Dodd and Dodd, *Historical Statistics*, 48. Kovacik and Winberry, *South Carolina*, 111–12. *News & Herald* quoted in Clark, *Southern Country Editor*, 270. *Watchman and Southron* quoted in Gregorie, *History of Sumter County*, 361.

69. *Carolina Spartan* quoted in Spartanburg Unit of the Writers' Program of Works Projects Administration, *A History of Spartanburg County* (1940; Spartanburg, S.C.: Reprint Company, 1976), 186 (hereinafter cited as WPA, *Spartanburg County*). Francis Butler Simkins, *Pitchfork Ben Tillman, South Carolinian* (1944; Gloucester, Mass.: Peter Smith, 1964), 89. Cooper, *Conservative Regime*, 135. Gregorie, *History of Sumter County*, 359. Woodward, *Origins of the New South*, 185–86.

70. Coclanis, *Shadow of a Dream*, 136–37, 142. Woodward, *Origins of the New South*, 119–20. Kovacik and Winberry, *South Carolina*, 110.

71. *Daily Register* (Columbia), 6 Dec. 1882. *News & Courier*, 23 Nov. 1887. Cooper, *Conservative Regime*, 139–42. Gregorie, *History of Sumter County*, 359. Wallace, *History of South Carolina*, 3: 340–44.

72. Eric Hobsbawm, "Introduction: Inventing Tradition"; Hugh Trevor-Roper, "The Invention of Tradition: The Highland Tradition of Scotland"; David Cannadine, "The Context, Performance and Meaning of Ritual: The British Monarchy and the 'Invention of Tradition,' c. 1820–1977"; Eric Hobsbawm, "Mass-Producing Traditions: Europe, 1870–1914"; in *The Invention of Tradition*, edited by Eric

Hobsbawm and Terence Ranger (1983; Cambridge: Cambridge University Press, 1994), 1–42, 101–64, 263–307. Cooper, *Conservative Regime,* 13–20, 207. Huff, "Urbane Bourbon," 133–41. Doyle, *New Men, New Cities, New South,* 117–29, 227–45. Huff, *Greenville,* 198. Woodward, *Origins of the New South,* 160. Wallace, *History of South Carolina,* 3: 324–25. Mary Reynolds Forbes, "Society," in Hennig, *Columbia,* 246–53. Moore, *Columbia & Richland County,* 230, 248–49. Rogers, *Generations of Lawyers,* 99–100.

CHAPTER 19: TILLMAN

1. Wallace, *History of South Carolina,* 3: 337.

2. Simkins, *Pitchfork Ben Tillman,* 76–77. Cooper, *Conservative Regime,* 138–40, 146. Huff, *Greenville,* 222–23. Pope, *History of Newberry County,* 2: 81–82. WPA, *Spartanburg County,* 188–91. Charles, *Union County,* 248–49. Gregorie, *History of Sumter County,* 359. Williamson, *After Slavery,* 293. Woodward, *Origins of the New South,* 82.

3. WPA, *Spartanburg County,* 192. Pope, *History of Newberry County,* 2: 82–83. Huff, *Greenville,* 224. Moore, *South Carolina in the 1880s,* 252. Gregorie, *History of Sumter County,* 366. Charles, *Union County,* 248–49. Durwood T. Stokes, *The History of Dillon County, South Carolina* (Columbia: University of South Carolina Press, 1978), 156.

4. Woodward, *Origins of the New South,* 193. Bailey et al., *Biographical Directory, Senate,* 3: 1506–7. WPA, *Spartanburg County,* 193–94.

5. Charles, *Union County,* 249. Gregorie, *History of Sumter County,* 366. Moore, *Columbia & Richland County,* 269. Tindall, *South Carolina Negroes,* 57, 117–19.

6. Cooper, *Conservative Regime,* 139–42, 160–62. Hollis, *University of South Carolina,* 2: 139–51. When initiated in 1879, the 25¢ per ton tax would have been equivalent to $3.78; between 1879 and 1890 its average equivalent would have been $3.88.

7. Simkins, *Pitchfork Ben Tillman,* 90–91. Pope, *History of Newberry County,* 2: 81–82. Huff, *Greenville,* 222–23. Werner, "'New South' Carolina," 153.

8. Simkins, *Pitchfork Ben Tillman,* 23–56, 82–91.

9. Simkins, *Pitchfork Ben Tillman,* 90–91. Tillman's remarks in *Edgefield Chronicle,* 1 July 1885 quoted in Werner, "'New South' Carolina," 154.

10. Quoted in Jones, *Stormy Petrel,* 114. Simkins, *Pitchfork Ben Tillman,* 92–96. Cooper, *Conservative Regime,* 144–45.

11. Simkins, *Pitchfork Ben Tillman,* 97–103. Werner, "'New South' Carolina," 155. Jones, *Stormy Petrel,* 116–20.

12. Cooper, *Conservative Regime,* 147–60. Simkins, *Pitchfork Ben Tillman,* 100–105; quotation, 103.

13. Simkins, *Pitchfork Ben Tillman,* 105–9.

14. Cooper, *Conservative Regime,* 75–80, 160–63, 174–85. Simkins, *Pitchfork Ben Tillman,* 106–19, 124–25. Jones, *Stormy Petrel,* 123. Wallace, *History of South Carolina,* 3: 341.

15. Brown, "Resconstructing Calhoun," 13. Ernest M. Lander Jr., *The Calhoun Family and Thomas Green Clemson: Decline of a Southern Patriarchy* (Columbia: University of South Carolina Press, 1983), 132–35, 233–60. Simkins, *Pitchfork Ben Tillman,* 120–33.

16. Lander, *Calhoun Family and Thomas Green Clemson,* 245–60. Simkins, *Pitchfork Ben Tillman,* 120–37. Hollis, *University of South Carolina,* 2: 148–58. Cooper, *Conservative Regime,* 162–66. Ayers, *Promise of the New South,* 420–22.

17. Cooper, *Conservative Regime,* 166–68, 185–95. Simkins, *Pitchfork Ben Tillman,* 138–46. Jones, *South Carolina,* 210–11. Lander, *History of South Carolina,* 32–33.

18. Huff, *Greenville,* 225. Cooper, *Conservative Regime,* 185–95. Simkins, *Pitchfork Ben Tillman,* 138–46. Jones, *South Carolina,* 210–11.

19. Cooper, *Conservative Regime,* 162–68, 181–203. Simkins, *Pitchfork Ben Tillman,* 162–65. D. D. Wallace asserted that the primary was simply a political ploy, not a deeply held belief for Tillman—just as state sovereignty had been for Calhoun. Wallace, *History of South Carolina,* 3: 347.

20. Huff, *Greenville,* 228. Simkins, *Pitchfork Ben Tillman,* 163–66. Cooper, *Conservative Regime,*

71. Jones, *South Carolina,* 212–13. Jones, *Stormy Petrel,* 130–31. Jarrell, *Wade Hampton and the Negro,* 153. Brooks Miles Barnes, "Southern Independents: South Carolina, 1882," *SCHM,* 96 (July 1995): 230–51.

21. Cooper, *Conservative Regime,* 20, 195–98, 206–7; excerpt from the Shell Manifesto in *News & Courier,* 23 Jan. 1890 quoted, 167. Simkins, *Pitchfork Ben Tillman,* 153–60. Jones, *Stormy Petrel,* 62, 127–35. Lander, *History of South Carolina,* 36–37. Wallace, *History of South Carolina,* 3: 304–5, 343–44, 347–52. Huff, *Greenville,* 227–28.

22. Simkins, *Pitchfork Ben Tillman,* 70–81, 128, 153. Cooper, *Conservative Regime,* 205–6. Wallace, *History of South Carolina,* 3: 340, 344–45.

23. Wallace, *History of South Carolina,* 3: 351. Cooper, *Conservative Regime,* 17, 168–74. Simkins, *Pitchfork Ben Tillman,* 152–53. Jones, *South Carolina,* 206–8.

24. Simkins, *Pitchfork Ben Tillman,* 168. Wallace, *History of South Carolina,* 3: 349–50. Gregorie, *History of Sumter County,* 369. South Carolina, "Supplementary Report of the Secretary of State to the General Assembly of South Carolina: Election Returns," in *Reports and Resolutions of the General Assembly of the State of South Carolina* (Columbia: James H. Woodrow, State Printer, 1891), 1: 604.

25. William J. Cooper Jr., "Economics or Race: An Analysis of the Gubernatorial Election of 1890 in South Carolina," *SCHM,* 73 (Oct. 1972): 209–19.

26. Bleser, *Hammonds of Redcliffe,* 272. Jones, *South Carolina,* 206–8. Wallace, *History of South Carolina,* 3: 351–52. Simkins, *Pitchfork Ben Tillman,* 147–48. Ford, "Rednecks and Merchants," 315–18. Woodward, *Origins of the New South,* 204, 237–38. Carlton, *Mill and Town,* 65–66. V. O. Key Jr., with the assistance of Alexander Heard, *Southern Politics in State and Nation* (1949; new ed., Knoxville: University of Tennessee Press, 1984), 136–37, 142–45.

27. Cooper, *Conservative Regime,* 17, 203–13. Jones, *South Carolina,* 206, 212, 222–23. Ford, "Rednecks and Merchants," 315–17. Bailey et al., *Biographical Directory, Senate,* 1: 575–76, 710–11; 2: 857–58, 980–81, 1210–11, 1245–46; 3: 1555–56. Huff, *Greenville,* 226, 228. Wallace, *History of South Carolina,* 3: 350–52.

28. Simkins, *Pitchfork Ben Tillman,* 196. WPA, *Spartanburg County,* 198.

29. Jones, *South Carolina,* 206. Simkins, *Pitchfork Ben Tillman,* 78–81, 168. Werner, "'New South' Carolina," 155–57. Cooper, *Conservative Regime,* 80–83. Towles, *World Turned Upside Down,* 802–3.

30. Excerpts from Tillman's inaugural speech from *House Journal, 1890* quoted in Simkins, *Pitchfork Ben Tillman,* 171.

31. Wallace, *History of South Carolina,* 3: 350–51. Simkins, *Pitchfork Ben Tillman,* 185–88.

32. Jones, *Stormy Petrel,* 136–43, 186–241. Simkins, *Pitchfork Ben Tillman,* 201–3. Jones, *South Carolina,* 213–15. Wallace, *History of South Carolina,* 3: 379.

33. Simkins, *Pitchfork Ben Tillman,* 169–94. Jones, *South Carolina,* 206–8. Woodward, *Origins of the New South,* 237–38. Jones, *Stormy Petrel,* 187–88. Wallace, *History of South Carolina,* 3: 353–54. Simkins, *Pitchfork Ben Tillman,* 182. Edgar, *Biographical Directory,* 1: 405.

Some historians credit Reformers with reapportioning the legislature; however, that was mandated by a constitutional amendment in 1886. Six counties lost representation and nine gained. The counties that lost seats were Aiken, Colleton, Hampton, Kershaw, and Richland one seat each and Charleston, five. Eight counties gained one seat: Anderson, Beaufort, Berkeley, Clarendon, Florence, Greenville, Marlboro, and Sumter; Spartanburg gained two. Not all of the seats went to the upcountry, as has usually been reported. The lowcountry had a net loss of four seats and the upcountry a gain of four. The middlecountry representation remained the same. Edgar, *Biographical Directory,* 1: 405.

34. Cooper, *Conservative Regime,* 138–40. Simkins, *Pitchfork Ben Tillman,* 169–98.

35. Simkins, *Pitchfork Ben Tillman,* 197–98. Gregorie, *History of Sumter County,* 371–72.

36. Simkins, *Pitchfork Ben Tillman,* 209–15. Wallace, *History of South Carolina,* 3: 363–65. Pope, *History of Newberry County,* 2: 94–95. Jones, *South Carolina,* 215. WPA, *Spartanburg County,* 196–97. Gregorie, *History of Sumter County,* 374–75. Helen Tillman Nicholson Milliken, "Chronicles of Zeracchaboam," M.A. thesis, University of South Carolina, 1991, 1. Jones, *Stormy Petrel,* 195–201.

37. Wallace, *History of South Carolina,* 3: 363–64. Simkins, *Pitchfork Ben Tillman,* 216–17. Gregorie, *History of Sumter County,* 372–73. Ayers, *Promise of the New South,* 230, 275.

38. Gregorie, *History of Sumter County,* 375. Tindall, *South Carolina Negroes,* 56–58.

39. Simkins, *Pitchfork Ben Tillman*, 216–38. Wallace, *History of South Carolina*, 3: 358–59. Huff, *Greenville*, 229–30. Rogers, *Generations of Lawyers*, 104, 108–9. Jones, *Stormy Petrel*, 201–2.

40. Simkins, *Pitchfork Ben Tillman*, 234–46. Huff, *Greenville*, 230–32. Lander, *History of South Carolina*, 35–36. Gregorie, *History of Sumter County*, 377–78.

41. Wallace, *History of South Carolina*, 3: 359–60. Simkins, *Pitchfork Ben Tillman*, 238–50.

42. Huff, *Greenville*, 230–32. Fraser, *Charleston! Charleston!*, 325–26. King, *Florence County*, 221–23. Gregorie, *History of Sumter County*, 378–82.

43. Simkins, *Pitchfork Ben Tillman*, 247–61. Jones, *Stormy Petrel*, 204–9; Tillman remarks in the *State* (Columbia), 4 Apr. 1894 quoted, 207. Wallace, *History of South Carolina*, 3: 361–63. Lander, *History of South Carolina*, 38–39. Gregorie, *History of Sumter County*, 378–82. Pope, *History of Newberry County*, 2: 95. Eliza C. Ervin, "Recollections of the Darlington Riot," in Ervin and Rudisill, *Darlingtoniana*, 216–29. Jones, *South Carolina*, 217.

44. Simkins, *Pitchfork Ben Tillman*, 257–61. Rogers, *Generations of Lawyers*, 107–9. "Report of the Comptroller General . . . for the Fiscal Year 1899," in *Reports and Resolutions of the General Assembly* (Columbia: Bryan Printing Company, State Printers, 1900), 1: 422–27.

45. Simkins, *Pitchfork Ben Tillman*, 262–72; Tillman's remarks in *News & Courier*, 23 July 1894 quoted, 315, and Butler's remarks in *News & Courier*, 21 June 1894 quoted, 268.

46. Tindall, *South Carolina Negroes*, 73. Rogers, *Generations of Lawyers*, 110–15. *News & Courier*, 28 June 1895 quoted in Simkins, *Pitchfork Ben Tillman*, 291. Tindall, *South Carolina Negroes*, 81. Cole Blease Graham Jr. and William V. Moore, *South Carolina Politics and Government* (Lincoln: University of Nebraska Press, 1994), 38–39. Woodward, *Origins of the New South*, 321–23, 337.

47. Jones, *South Carolina*, 220. Rogers, *Generations of Lawyers*, 110–12. Gregorie, *History of Sumter County*, 384–87. Simkins, *Pitchfork Ben Tillman*, 286–309. Wallace, *History of South Carolina*, 3: 367–74.

48. Underwood, *Constitution of South Carolina*, 4: 58–157; excerpts from the Constitution of 1895 quoted, 60, 61, 62. Wallace, *History of South Carolina*, 3: 369–73. Jones, *South Carolina*, 221. Rogers, *Generations of Lawyers*, 112.

49. Rogers, *Generations of Lawyers*, 112–15; [Mary J. Miller], *The Suffrage: Speeches by Negroes in the Constitutional Convention* quoted, 113, 114. Simkins, *Pitchfork Ben Tillman*, 299–301. Tindall, *South Carolina Negroes*, 83–85, 91.

50. Simkins, *Pitchfork Ben Tillman*, 299–302. Tindall, *South Carolina Negroes*, 85–87; quotation, 88. Rogers, *Generations of Lawyers*, 112–15.

51. Wallace, *History of South Carolina*, 3: 374. Underwood, *Constitution of South Carolina*, 4: 66–68, 80–82.

52. Underwood, *Constitution of South Carolina*, 2: 47–67.

53. Underwood, *Constitution of South Carolina*, 2: 68–104; excerpt from the Constitution of 1895 quoted, 82.

54. Underwood, *Constitution of South Carolina*, 2: 78–88. George R. Sherrill, "State Governmental Organization," in *South Carolina: Economic and Social Conditions in 1944* (Columbia: University of South Carolina Press, 1945), 145, 154–55.

55. Underwood, *Constitution of South Carolina*, 2: 73, 92–96. Graham and Moore, *South Carolina Politics*, 39. Huff, *Greenville*, 233. Jones, *South Carolina*, 264.

56. Underwood, *Constitution of South Carolina*, 2: 71–74. Counties created under the 1895 constitution were Allendale, Bamberg, Calhoun, Cherokee, Dillon, Dorchester, Greenwood, Jasper, Lee, and McCormick. Four were lowcountry counties, three middle-country, and three upcountry. Edgar, *Biographical Directory*, 1: 464.

57. Simkins, *Pitchfork Ben Tillman*, 295.

58. Huff, *Greenville*, 233. Lander, *History of South Carolina*, 42. Jones, *South Carolina*, 222. Rogers, *Generations of Lawyers*, 130. Tindall, *South Carolina Negroes*, 256–59.

59. Simkins, *Pitchfork Ben Tillman*, 303–5. Land, "Call to Service," 6–7.

60. Tindall, *South Carolina Negroes*, 216, 221–23, 230. Huff, *Greenville*, 233. William E. Hine, "Thomas E. Miller and the Early Years of South Carolina State," *Carologue*, 12 (Winter 1996): 8–12. Gordon, *Sketches of Negro Life and History*, 109–10.

61. Tindall, *South Carolina Negroes,* 264. Edgar, *South Carolina in the Modern Age,* 25–29. Fraser, *Charleston! Charleston!,* 332, 336–38.

62. C. Vann Woodward, *The Strange Career of Jim Crow,* 2d rev. ed. (New York: Oxford University Press, 1966), 67–69. Edgar, *South Carolina in the Modern Age,* 25–29.

63. Tindall, *South Carolina Negroes,* 299–302. Fraser, *Charleston! Charleston!,* 332, 336–38. Edgar, *South Carolina in the Modern Age,* 29. Harry S. Ashmore, *Hearts and Minds: A Personal Chronicle of Race in America* (Cabin John, Md.: Seven Locks Press, A Calvin Kytle Book, 1988), 10–11, 16.

64. Tindall, *South Carolina Negroes,* 291–302. DuBose Heyward, *Mamba's Daughters: A Novel of Charleston* (Garden City, N.J.: Crowell, 1928), passim. Fields, *Lemon Swamp,* 10, 46–50, 55–56, 64–65, 71–72. Katharine DuPre Lumpkin, *The Making of a Southerner* (New York: Alfred A. Knopf, 1947), 130–51. Ayers, *Promise of the New South,* 132–36. Hylan Lewis, *Blackways of Kent,* vol. 2, Field Studies in the Modern Culture of the South prepared under the direction of John Gillin (Chapel Hill: University of North Carolina Press, 1955), 172–222.

65. Moore, *Columbia & Richland County,* 269. Underwood, *Constitution of South Carolina,* 4: 77–78; Sumter resolution quoted, 78. Tindall, *South Carolina Negroes,* 90; Page quotation from *The Training of An American: The Earlier Life and Letters of Walter H. Page* quoted, 303. Powers, *Black Charlestonians,* 265–66. Williamson, *After Slavery,* 176–79. Edgar, *South Carolina in the Modern Age,* 29. Lewis, *Blackways of Kent,* 172–222.

66. Hammond to F. A. Allen, 2 Feb. 1861, Hammond Papers, LC quoted in Channing, *Crisis of Fear,* 293. Tally's remarks in *Daily Phoenix* (Columbia) quoted in Moore, *Columbia & Richland County,* 219. Doyle, *New Men, New Cities, New South,* 308. "Thomas E. Miller on Reconstruction," *Carologue,* 12 (Winter 1996): 13.

67. Wallace, *History of South Carolina,* 3: 356, 365, 375–77, 391–93. Jones, *South Carolina,* 223. King, *Florence County,* 162–64. Milliken, "Chronicles of Zeracchaboam," 43–45. Jones, *Stormy Petrel,* 228–41. Gregorie, *Sumter County,* 370–71. Simkins, *Pitchfork Ben Tillman,* 187–93, 226. Boddie, *Williamsburg County,* 458–59.

68. Kovačik and Winberry, *South Carolina,* 112. Dodd and Dodd, *Historical Statistics,* 46–47. Cooper, *Conservative Regime,* 133n. Woodward, *Origins of the New South,* 407–8. Coclanis and Ford, "South Carolina Economy," 102. Simkins, *Pitchfork Ben Tillman,* 223–24. Jones, *South Carolina,* 225. WPA, *Spartanburg County,* 198–99; editorial from *Piedmont Headlight* (Greenville), June 1901 quoted, 199. Wallace, *History of South Carolina,* 3: 384. United States, *Twelfth Census of the United States: Agriculture, Part I* (Washington: United States Census Office, 1902), 118–19.

69. Pope, *History of Newberry County,* 2: 94–95. Fraser, *Charleston! Charleston!,* 323–24. Stokes, *History of Dillon County,* 145. WPA, *Spartanburg County,* 199. Jones, *Stormy Petrel,* 235. Rogers, *Generations of Lawyers,* 119–22.

70. Huff, *Greenville,* 229–30. Simkins, *Pitchfork Ben Tillman,* 182–83. Hollis, *University of South Carolina,* 2: 158, 339–40. Jones, *South Carolina,* 214. WPA, *Spartanburg County,* 202–3.

71. Wallace, *History of South Carolina,* 3: 491–93. Boddie, *Williamsburg County,* 458–59. Carlton, *Mill and Town,* 4–5. Simkins, *Pitchfork Ben Tillman,* 215, 547–55. Cooper, *Conservative Regime,* 208–13.

72. Cooper, *Conservative Regime,* 15. Jones, *South Carolina,* 205. Simkins, *Pitchfork Ben Tillman,* 547–55. Werner, "'New South' Carolina," 155–57. Woodward, *Origins of the New South,* 393. Ashmore, *Hearts and Minds,* 10.

CHAPTER 20: SOUTH CAROLINA AND THE FIRST NEW SOUTH

1. George B. Tindall, "1986: The South's Double Centennial," in Moore et al., *Developing Dixie,* 327–36.

2. Ford, "Red Necks & Merchants," 294–318. Carlton, *Mill & Town,* 13–39. Rogers, *Georgetown County,* 464–73, 498–99. Kovacik & Winberry, *South Carolina,* 116–17. Moore, *South Carolina in the 1880s,* 128–34. Stokes, *Dillon County,* 122–41. King, *Florence County,* 271–93. Woodward, *Origins of the New South,* 144.

3. Wallace, *History of South Carolina,* 4: 832–33. The Merchants Mercantile Agency, *The Credit Experience Guide* (Pittsburgh: Merchants Mercantile Agency, 1913), 440. Carlton, *Mill and Town,* 9.

Woodward, *Origins of the New South*, 150–51.

4. Moore, *Columbia & Richland County*, 292, 296–97. Jones, *Stormy Petrel*, 157, 252, 282. King, *Florence County*, 165–66. Carlton, *Mill and Town*, 48–49. Bellardo, "Social and Economic History of Fairfield County," 139. Kovacik and Winberry, *South Carolina*, 119–20. John K. Cauthen, *Speaker Blatt: His Challenges Were Greater* (Columbia: University of South Carolina Press, 1965), 24–25.

5. Moore, *Columbia & Richland County*, 236.

6. Moore, *Columbia & Richland County*, 295–97. WPA, *Spartanburg County*, 218–19. Huff, *Greenville*, 211, 258.

7. Doyle, *New Men, New Cities, New South*, 182–85, 309–12. Fraser, *Charleston! Charleston!*, 339–41.

8. George Brown Tindall, *The Emergence of the New South, 1913–1945*, vol. X in *A History of the South*, Wendell Holmes Stephenson and E. Merton Coulter, eds. (Baton Rouge: Louisiana State University Press and the Littlefield Fund for Southern History of the University of Texas, 1967), 97. Huff, *Greenville*, 275–76.

9. Huff, *Greenville*, 188–89. Kovacik and Winberry, *South Carolina*, 114. Carlton, *Mill and Town*, 40–72.

10. Tindall, *Emergence of the New South*, 76. J. Tracey Power, "'The Brightest of the Lot': W. B. Smith Whaley and the Rise of the South Carolina Textile Industry, 1893–1903," *SCHM*, 93 (Apr. 1992): 126–42. Moore, *Columbia & Richland County*, 305–8. Carlton, *Mill and Town*, 40–41, 133–34. Huff, *Greenville*, 235–39. Moore, *Columbia & Richland County*, 305–8. James A. Dunlap III, "Changing Symbols of Success: Economic Development in Twentieth Century Greenville, South Carolina," diss., University of South Carolina, 1994, 18–25. Edgar, *South Carolina in the Modern Age*, 70. Mary Katherine Davis Cann, "The Morning After: South Carolina in the Jazz Age," diss., University of South Carolina, 1984, 93–94. Louise Pettus, *The Springs Story: Our First Hundred Years* (Fort Mill, S.C.: Springs Industries, 1987), 22, 46–53.

11. Pope, *History of Newberry County*, 2: 113. Moore, *Columbia & Richland County*, 305–8. Carlton, *Mill and Town*, 37, 59–63, 128–33. Bryant Simon, "The Appeal of Cole Blease of South Carolina: Race, Class, and Sex in the New South," *JSH*, 62 (Feb. 1996): 64–66.

12. Carlton, *Mill and Town*, 83–87.

13. Huff, *Greenville*, 239–44. Carlton, *Mill and Town*, 5–8, 14. Wright, *Old South, New South*, 137. W. E. Woodward, "A Cotton Mill Village in the 1880's," in *Perspectives in South Carolina History: The First Three Hundred Years*, Ernest M. Lander Jr. and Robert K. Ackerman, eds. (Columbia: University of South Carolina Press, 1973), 264–65. William A. Link, *The Paradox of Southern Progressivism, 1880–1930*, Fred W. Morrison Series in Southern Studies (Chapel Hill: University of North Carolina Press, 1992), 170.

14. Huff, *Greenville*, 239–44, 247. Carlton, *Mill and Town*, 5–8, 11, 14, 112–17, 122–24, 135, 154–58; *Abbeville Press & Banner*, 1883, quoted 124. Cann, "Morning After," 80–81; interview with Edna Holliday Burnette, Greenwood, S.C., 27 July 1982 quoted 80.

The prejudice of townspeople toward mill operatives and their families continued throughout the twentieth century. John Kenneth Morland, *Millways of Kent*, vol. 3 in the Field Studies in the Modern Culture of the South, prepared under the direction of John Gillin (Chapel Hill: University of North Carolina Press, 1958), 73–74, 96–104, 174–84.

15. Robertson, *Red Hills and Cotton*, 274–78. Wright, *Old South, New South*, 125, 138–46. Woodward, "Cotton Mill Village," 264–65.

16. Huff, *Greenville*, 242–43. Woodward, "Cotton Mill Village," 255. Mrs. John Van Vorst and Marie Van Vorst, *The Woman Who Toils: Being the Experiences of Two Ladies as Factory Girls* (New York: Doubleday, Page & Co., 1903), vii–ix, 3–5, 217–303.

17. Carlton, *Mill and Town*, 91–92. Watkins, *Anderson County*, 57–58.

18. Huff, *Greenville*, 242–48. Woodward, "Cotton Mill Village," 255–58.

19. Wright, *Old South, New South*, 67. Huff, *Greenville*, 239–44. Moore, *Columbia & Richland County*, 305.

20. Huff, *Greenville*, 241. Woodward, "Cotton Mill Village," 259. Edgar, *South Carolina in the Modern Age*, 31. Carlton, *Mill and Town*, 175. Moore, *Columbia & Richland County*, 305.

21. Carlton, *Mill and Town*, 69, 135. Robertson, *Red Hills and Cotton*, 274–77.

22. Carlton, *Mill and Town*, 83, 127. Moore, *Columbia & Richland County*, 310. Simon, "Appeal of Cole Blease of South Carolina," 64–66.

For every operative employed in the mills, there were 1.33 dependents. Thus, in 1890, when there were 8,000 operatives in the state, there were probably 18,600 residents of mill villages. In 1920 there were 47,000 operatives and one-sixth of the state's white population were either operatives or had operatives in their families. Carlton, *Mill and Town*, 7, 127.

23. Huff, *Greenville*, 190–99. Carlton, *Mill and Town*, 138–42; *State* (Columbia), 3 Sept. 1901 quoted, 139. Moore, *Columbia & Richland County*, 311–12. Woodward, *Origins of the New South*, 421–22. Wright, *Old South, New South*, 137, 218–19. Duffy, "Charleston Politics," 126–27.

24. Tindall, *Emergence of the New South*, 6–7; W. H. Swift, "Why It Is Hard to Get Good Child Labor Laws in the South, in *Child Labor Bulletin* quoted, 7. Woodward, *Origins of the New South*, 418. Jones, *Stormy Petrel*, 253–56. Carlton, *Mill and Town*, 123–24, 131–32.

25. Carlton, *Mill and Town*, 135–36. Moore, *Columbia & Richland County*, 309. "WPA Interviews, South Carolina Writers' Project: Textile Worker," in *Columbia Reader*, 125.

26. Huff, *Greenville*, 245–48. Moore, *Columbia & Richland County*, 310–13. Carlton, *Mill and Town*, 89–90, 129–37.

27. Carlton, *Mill and Town*, 129–214. Jones, *Stormy Petrel*, 253–56; *State* (Columbia), 29 Jan. 1900 quoted, 255.

28. Carlton, *Mill and Town*, 180–81. Duffy, "Charleston Politics," 1–2. Woodward, *Origins of the New South*, 371–73.

29. Jones, *Stormy Petrel*, 254–56. Bailey et al., *Biographical Directory, Senate*, 2: 1058–60. Carlton, *Mill and Town*, 130–32, 141, 169–70, 180–84. Huff, *Greenville*, 253–54. Fraser, *Charleston! Charleston!*, 341–46.

30. Moore, *Columbia & Richland County*, 325. Lander, *History of South Carolina*, 126–32. U.S. Census Office, *Abstract of the Eleventh Census, 1890*, 64–67, 74. U.S. Census Office, *Abstract of the Twelfth Census, 1900*, 70–75, 79.

By race, 18 percent of the white and 64 percent of the black population were illiterate. U.S. Census Office, *Abstract of the Eleventh Census, 1890*, 64–67, 74.

31. Lander, *History of South Carolina*, 142. Woodward, *Origins of the New South*, 439. Hollis, *University of South Carolina*, 2: 177, 267, 269–70. Wallace, *History of South Carolina*, 3: 486.

32. William H. Hand, "The Sad State of the High Schools in 1910," in Lander and Ackerman, *Perspectives*, 305–15. South Carolina, "42d Annual Report of the State Superintendent of Education, 1910," in *Reports and Resolutions, 1911* (Columbia: Gonzales & Bryan, 1911), 3: 951.

33. Moore, *Columbia & Richland County*, 352–54. WPA, *Spartanburg County*, 202. Stokes, *Dillon County*, 301–3, 305. Carlton, *Mill and Town*, 36–37, 174–78, 234–35; Anderson *Intelligencer*, 11 June 1902 quoted, 37.

34. WPA, *Spartanburg County*, 280. Stokes, *Dillon County*, 305. Wallace, *History of South Carolina*, 3: 433–34.

35. Cann, "Morning After," 294. Lander, *History of South Carolina*, 136–37. Wallace, *History of South Carolina*, 3: 433–34. "WPA Interviews, South Carolina Writers' Project: Textile Worker," 127–29. Link, *Paradox of Southern Progressivism*, 140, 233.

36. Woodward, *Origins of the New South*, 371. Carlton, *Mill & Town*, 169–70. Ayers, *Promise of the New South*, 77–78. Huff, *Greenville*, 257–58. Stokes, *Dillon County*, 326–30. Ervin & Rudisill, *Darlingtoniana*, 234–35. King, *Florence County*, 290. Wallace, *History of South Carolina*, 3: 423

37. Huff, *Greenville*, 260–61. Moore, *Columbia & Richland County*, 298, 313–18. Fraser, *Charleston! Charleston!*, 362. Pope, *History of Newberry County*, 2: 117.

Beautifying and Improving Greenville, S.C., the 1907 study prepared for Greenville by Kelsey and Guild of Boston, contained several references to the community's waking up to the New South.

38. Widener, *Confederate Monuments*, 171–89. Woodward, *Origins of the New South*, 154–57. Carlton, *Mill and Town*, 70. Gaines M. Foster, *Ghosts of the Confederacy: Defeat, The Lost Cause, and the Emergence of the New South 1865 to 1913* (New York: Oxford University Press, 1987), 3–8, 123–44,

194–95. Charles, *Union County,* 347.

39. Huff, *Greenville,* 200. Robert E. Seibels, "Medicine and Hospitals," in Hennig, *Columbia,* 157–58. Board of Directors, Richland County Anti-Tuberculosis Association, *Second Annual Report* (Columbia: DuPre, 1918), 3–4; *Fourth Annual Report* (Columbia: Gary, 1921), 3–4.

40. Wallace, *History of South Carolina,* 3: 386. Carlton, *Mill and Town,* 153–56. Woodward, *Origins of the New South,* 420, 425–28. Edward H. Beardsley, *A History of Neglect: Blacks and Mill Workers in the Twentieth Century South* (Knoxville: University of Tennessee Press, 1987), 42–74.

41. Fraser, *Charleston! Charleston!,* 341–46, 351, 353–58. Duffy, "Charleston Politics," 47–53.

42. WPA, *Spartanburg County,* 208–9. Charles, *Union County,* 342–44. Gregorie, *History of Sumter County,* 408–9. King, *Florence County,* 256–60. Huff, *Greenville,* 196. Walter B. Edgar and Deborah K. Woolley, *Columbia: Portrait of a City* (Norfolk, Va.: Donning Company, 1986), 58–59. George A. Buchanan Jr., "Government: Municipal, State and Federal," in Hennig, *Columbia,* 74–75, 81–82.

43. Moore, *Columbia & Richland County,* 284–86. WPA, *Spartanburg County,* 211. Huff, *Greenville,* 269.

44. Huff, *Greenville,* 195. Fraser, *Charleston! Charleston!,* 302–3. King, *Florence County,* 190. Moore, *Columbia & Richland County,* 241. Pope, *History of Newberry County,* 2: 117–18. Rogers, *Generations of Lawyers,* 138.

45. Moore, *Columbia & Richland County,* 241. Huff, *Greenville,* 197. Gregorie, *History of Sumter County,* 483–84. Moore, *South Carolina in the 1880s,* 269–78. WPA, *Spartanburg County,* 209. Ervin and Rudisill, *Darlingtoniana,* 218–19. Carlton, *Mill and Town,* 91. Charles, *Union County,* 342–44. Watkins, *Anderson County,* 57. Boddie, *Williamsburg County,* 518–19.

46. Wallace, *History of South Carolina,* 3: 392. Jones, *Stormy Petrel,* 231–32.

47. Huff, *Greenville,* 276–77. Jones, *Stormy Petrel,* 233–34. Wallace, *History of South Carolina,* 3:422–23. Rogers, *Generations of Lawyers,* 133–36.

48. Duffy, "Charleston Politics," 25. Tindall, *South Carolina Negroes,* 233–38; *News & Courier,* 3 Apr. 1900 quoted, 236. Carlton, *Mill and Town,* 145–46. David R. Goldfield, *Cotton Fields and Skyscrapers: Southern City and Region, 1607–1980* (Baton Rouge: Louisiana State University Press, 1982), 93.

49. Tindall, *Emergence of the New South,* 173. Wallace, *History of South Carolina,* 3: 400n. Tindall, *South Carolina Negroes,* 239–59. Carlton, *Mill and Town,* 246–49; *Southern Christian Advocate,* 1908 quoted, 246. Rogers, *Generations of Lawyers,* 127–32; Charles A. Woods, "Lawlessness and Patriotism," in *Transactions* of the 10th meeting (1903) of the South Carolina Bar Association, quoted, 128.

50. Moore, *Columbia & Richland County,* 328, 372–78. Fraser, *Charleston! Charleston!,* 334, 354–55, 359–61. Carlton, *Mill and Town,* 177–85, 242–48; quotation, 183. Edgar, *South Carolina in the Modern Age,* 41. Cann, "Morning After," 260–70. Simon, "Appeal of Cole Blease of South Carolina," 58–59.

The lack of concern for lynch-mob victims continued into the 1940s. Kari Frederickson, "'The Slowest State' and 'Most Backward Community': Racial Violence in South Carolina and Federal Civil-Rights Legislation, 1946–1948," *SCHM,* 98 (Apr. 1997): 188–93.

51. Woodward, *Origins of the New South,* 369–95. Moore, *Columbia & Richland County,* 370–81. Fraser, *Charleston! Charleston!,* 359. Fields, *Lemon Swamp,* 189–91, 197–99. Land, "Call to Service," 3–16. Anne Firor Scott, "Most Invisible of All: Black Women's Voluntary Associations," *JSH,* 61 (Feb. 1990): 3–22. Cann, "Morning After," 264–66. Darlene Clark Hine, Elsa Barkley Brown, and Rosalyn Terborg-Penn, eds., *Black Women in America: An Historical Encyclopedia,* 2 vols. (Bloomington: University of Indiana Press, 1993), 1: 249–52, 401–2, 426–28; 2: 1032–35.

52. *Edgefield Chronicle* quoted in Clark, *Southern Country Editor,* 302. Woodward, *Origins of the New South,* 372–73.

53. Carlton, *Mill and Town,* 163–65, 226–32. Moore, *Columbia & Richland County,* 278–84, 310.

54. William Augustus Shealy to Patterson Wardlaw, 15 May 1916, in *A Columbia Reader* (Columbia: Institute for Southern Studies and South Caroliniana Library, 1986), 117–18.

55. Moore, *Columbia & Richland County,* 313. Huff, *Greenville,* 262–64. King, *Florence County,*

219–20. Paula Giddings, *When and Where I Enter: The Impact of Black Women on Race and Sex in America* (New York: William Morrow, 1984), 120–30. Eliza Herndon, "Women's Suffrage in South Carolina, 1872–1920," M.A. thesis, University of South Carolina, 1953, 37–61. Link, *Paradox of Southern Progressivism,* 119, 185, 187–89, 196. Antoinette Elizabeth Taylor, "South Carolina and the Enfranchisement of Women: The Early Years," *SCHM,* 77 (Apr. 1976): 115–26. Ayers, *Promise of the New South,* 319–20.

56. South Carolina, *Journal of the House of Representatives, 1920* (Columbia: Gonzales & Bryan, 1920), 1044–45. South Carolina, *Journal of the Senate, 1920* (Columbia: Gonzales & Bryan, 1920), 111–12.

The House vote is reported as 93–21, but only twenty members' names are listed in the roll call vote. (No vote is recorded for Edward C. Dennis of Darlington.) Individual representatives from the following counties voted in favor of the amendment: Anderson, Beaufort, Charleston, Chester, Darlington, Edgefield, Georgetown, Greenville, Lancaster, Marion, Sumter, Williamsburg, and York. All house members from Dillon and Union voted in favor. The three senators voting for the amendment were from Georgetown, Oconee, and Union. *Journal of the House of Representatives, 1920,* 1042–47, 1134, 2107–8. *Journal of the Senate, 1920,* 13, 66, 88–89, 111–12. Edgar, *Biographical Directory,* 1: 511–14.

57. Boddie, *Williamsburg County,* 465–66. Arnold Shankman, "A Jury of Her Peers: The South Carolina Woman and Her Campaign for Jury Service," *SCHM,* 81 (Apr. 1980): 102–21. Cann, "Morning After," 247–54.

58. Grace Lumpkin, *The Wedding* (1939; Carbondale: Southern Illinois University Press, 1976), 188. Huff, *Greenville,* 277–79. Carlton, *Mill and Town,* 179, 238–39; quotation, 39 [emphasis in original].

59. Carlton, *Mill and Town,* 10, 171–214, 244–48. Van Vorst and Van Vorst, *Woman Who Toils,* 223–24. Link, *Paradox of Southern Progressivism,* 307–10. Ayers, *Promise of the New South,* 416–17. Simon, "Appeal of Cole Blease of South Carolina," 66–72.

60. Carlton, *Mill and Town,* 161–62, 196, 221–23. Judith T. Bainbridge, "Judson" (unpublished paper, Furman University, 1996), 3. Simon, "Appeal of Cole Blease of South Carolina," 76–82.

61. Huff, *Greenville,* 277–79. South Carolina, *Journal of the House of Representatives . . . 1911* (Columbia: Gonzales & Bryan, 1911), 95. Simkins, *Pitchfork Ben Tillman,* 485–504. Woodward, *Origins of the New South,* 392–94. Wallace, *History of South Carolina,* 3: 424–30. Carlton, *Mill and Town,* 223–25, 235–39.

62. Carlton, *Mill and Town,* 215–21. Huff, *Greenville,* 277–79. Wallace, *History of South Carolina,* 3: 424–26, 430. Fraser, *Charleston! Charleston!,* 352.

63. Simkins, *Pitchfork Ben Tillman,* 491–501. Pope, *History of Newberry County,* 2: 105–8, 111. Wallace, *History of South Carolina,* 3: 424–30. Carlton, *Mill and Town,* 235–39. Simon, "Appeal of Cole Blease of South Carolina," 59–61, 86.

64. Carlton, *Mill and Town,* 215–17.

65. Woodward, *Origins of the New South,* 470–78.

66. Woodward, *Origins of the New South,* 456–81. Huff, *Greenville,* 276–77. Tindall, *Emergence of the New South,* 1–32. Lander, *History of South Carolina,* 80n, 116. Moore, *Columbia & Richland County,* 326, 348.

67. Tindall, *Emergence of the New South,* 4–5; quotation, 5.

68. Wallace, *History of South Carolina,* 3: 438–44.

69. Robert Milton Burts, *Richard Irvine Manning and the Progressive Movement in South Carolina* (Columbia: University of South Carolina Press, 1974), 83–158, 180–203. Tindall, *Emergence of the New South,* 21–22, 31–32. Wallace, *History of South Carolina,* 3: 438–44. Carlton, *Mill and Town,* 258–60.

70. Burts, *Richard Irvine Manning,* 158–79. Tindall, *Emergence of the New South,* 42, 49–52. Moore, *Columbia & Richland County,* 326–28. Wallace, *History of South Carolina,* 3: 445–49; quotation, 447.

71. Tindall, *Emergence of the New South,* 49. Burts, *Richard Irvine Manning,* 165–66. Wallace, *History of South Carolina,* 3: 456. Huff, *Greenville,* 280–84. Moore, *Columbia & Richland County,* 327–28. Boddie, *Williamsburg County,* 512–13. Idus A. Newby, *Black Carolinians: A History of Blacks in South Carolina from 1895 to 1968* (Columbia: University of South Carolina Press, 1973), 188. *The*

South Carolina Handbook of the War (Columbia: South Carolina State Council of Defense, 1917), 7–60, 69, 87.

72. Lander, *History of South Carolina,* 44. Moore, *Columbia & Richland County,* 282, 317–21, 377. Huff, *Greenville,* 254. Wallace, *History of South Carolina,* 3: 449. Fraser, *Charleston! Charleston!,* 357, 359–61. Duffy, "Charleston Politics," 97. WPA, *Spartanburg County,* 236–59. John Hammond Moore, "Charleston in World War I," *SCHM,* 86 (1985): 41–42.

73. Newby, *Black Carolinians,* 188–89. Wallace, *History of South Carolina,* 4: 684–85. "WWI Vet Gets Overdue Medal," *Soldiers,* June 1991, 3. "General Dozier Retires," *Palmetto Guardsman,* 2 (Jan. 1959): 1–5.

Stowers's medal (the seventy-ninth for WWI) was awarded posthumously in 1991. In a ceremony in the East Room of the White House, President George Bush presented the medal to Stowers's sisters. *State* (Columbia), 24 Apr. 1991, B1.

74. Huff, *Greenville,* 382–86. Moore, *Columbia & Richland County,* 27. Tindall, *Emergence of the New South,* 66 67.

75. Woodward, *Origins of the New South,* 406–7; quotation, 407. Fraser, *Charleston! Charleston!,* 343–44. *Abstract of the Twelfth Census (1900),* 225–27.

76. Lander, *History of South Carolina,* 115. King, *Florence County,* 168–78. Dodd and Dodd, *Historical Statistics,* 49. Nannie May Tilley, *The Bright-Tobacco Industry, 1860–1929* (Chapel Hill: University of North Carolina Press, 1948), 144–46. "Seventh Annual Report of the Commissioner of Agriculture, Commerce and Industries of the State of South Carolina, 1910," in *Reports and Resolutions of the General Assembly, 1911* (Columbia: Gonzales & Bryan, State Printers, 1911), 160. Information from the S.C. Agricultural Statistics Service, 1996.

77. Rogers, *History of Georgetown County,* 488. Coclanis, *Shadow of a Dream,* 142, 155. Robert Cuthbert, "Combahee River Plantations," *Carologue,* 11 (Spring 1996): 15–19. Linder, *Historical Atlas,* 160, 479–80, 515. Heyward, *Seed from Madagascar,* 211–48. Huff, *Greenville,* 224–25. Tindall, *South Carolina Negroes,* 93. Henry C. Dethloff, *A History of American Rice Industry, 1686–1985,* (College Station: Texas A&M University Press), 46–94.

78. Dodd and Dodd, *Historical Statistics,* 47. Department of Commerce and Labor, Bureau of Census, *Thirteenth Census of the United States Taken in the Year 1910: Abstracts of the Census* (Washington, D.C.: Government Printing Office, 1913), 404, 412, 615, 628–31. Tindall, *Emergence of the New South,* 33. Kovacik and Winberry, *South Carolina,* 110. Lander, *History of South Carolina,* 118. George Lee Simpson Jr., *The Cokers of Carolina: A Social Biography of a Family* (Chapel Hill: University of North Carolina Press, 1956), 132–53. James A. Rogers and Larry E. Nelson, *Mr. D.R.: A Biography of David R. Coker* (Hartsville, S.C.: Coker College Press, 1994), 39–43.

79. Burts, *Richard Irvine Manning,* 80–81. Tindall, *Emergence of the New South,* 33–37.

80. Tindall, *Emergence of the New South,* 60–61; David R. Coker, "Open Letter to Farmers," in Simpson, *Cokers of Carolina* quoted, 61. Lander, *History of South Carolina,* 67. Jones, *South Carolina,* 244. Cann, "Morning After," 11–12.

At adjusted 1920 prices, a 1995 cotton farmer in South Carolina with an average yield of 547 pounds per acre would have averaged $3,550 instead of $416.

81. Huff, *Greenville,* 286. WPA, *Spartanburg County,* 263, 269. W. J. Megginson, *Black Soldiers in World War I: Anderson, Pickens and Oconee Counties, South Carolina* (Seneca, S.C.: Oconee County Historical Society, 1994), 14–17. Moore, *Columbia & Richland County,* 379.

82. Fraser, *Charleston! Charleston!,* 363–64. Cann, "Morning After," 258. Kirkman G. Finlay, *A Collection of Sermons, Notes and Clippings,* ed. Augustus T. Graydon (Columbia, 1965), 75–91. Moore, *Columbia & Richland County,* 379–80; South Carolina Constructive League goals from James Heyward Gibbes Papers, SCL quoted, 380. Pope, *History of Newberry County,* 2: 109. Cann, "Morning After," 257–58. Winfred B. Moore, "'Soul of the South': James F. Byrnes and the Racial Issue in American Politics, 1911–1941," *Proceedings of the South Carolina Historical Association* (1978): 41–45; *Cong. Record,* 66th Cong. quoted, 43–44. Daniel W. Hollis, "Cole Blease and the Senatorial Campaign of 1924," *Proceedings of the South Carolina Historical Association* (1978): 55. Link, *Paradox of Southern Progressivism,* 259.

83. Wallace, *History of South Carolina,* 3: 461–62. Lander, *History of South Carolina,* 67. Tindall, *Emergence of the New South,* 68–69.

84. Tindall, *Emergence of the New South,* 111–12. Cann, "Morning After," 11–14. Jones, *South Carolina,* 244.

CHAPTER 21: THE DRAINING YEARS

1. Tindall, *Emergence of the New South,* 219. Cann, "Morning After," 1–6.

2. Cann, "Morning After," 378–80. Tindall, *Emergence of the New South,* 246–51.

3. Tindall, *Emergence of the New South,* 219–21. Fraser, *Charleston! Charleston!,* 361, 370–71. Huff, *Greenville,* 321–22. Edgar, *South Carolina in the Modern Age,* 43. Jack Irby Hayes, "South Carolina and the New Deal, 1932–1938," diss., University of South Carolina, 1972, 26.

4. Cann, "Morning After," 359–79. Huff, *Greenville,* 321–22. S. R. Anderson, "Governor John G. Richards and the Blue Laws," thesis, University of South Carolina, 1983, 32–79.

5. Cann, "Morning After," 361–62. King, *Florence County,* 329, 346.

6. Huff, *Greenville,* 325–27.

7. Tindall, *Emergence of the New South,* 187–95. Huff, *Greenville,* 323–25, 356–57. King, *Florence County,* 331–32. Moore, *Columbia & Richland County,* 361–62. Moore, "'Soul of the South,'" 44–45. Lander, *History of South Carolina,* 68–69. David Robertson, *Sly and Able: A Political Biography of James F. Byrnes* (New York: W. W. Norton, 1994), 91–92.

8. Robertson, *Red Hills and Cotton,* 157. Interview with David H. Rembert of Columbia, S.C., great-nephew of Edward Rembert, 28 Apr. 1997. Tindall, *Emergence of the New South,* 112–13.

9. Tindall, *Emergence of the New South,* 121–22.

10. Cann, "Morning After," 25. Lander, *History of South Carolina,* 117, 120–21. Wallace, *History of South Carolina,* 3: 479. S. M. Derrick, "Manufacturing Industries," in *South Carolina: Economic and Social Conditions in 1944* (University of South Carolina Press, 1945), 51–52. Ashmore, *Hearts and Minds,* 12–14; quotation, 12. South Carolina, Board of Health, *61st Annual Report* (1940), 98. Beardsley, *History of Neglect,* 54–58, 197–204. Wallace, *History of South Carolina,* 3: 477–78. Moore, *Columbia & Richland County,* 329. Pope, *History of Newberry County,* 2: 124.

11. Cann, "Morning After," 8–9, 54, 66–67. Hayes, "South Carolina and the New Deal," 410. Wallace, *History of South Carolina,* 3: 478. WPA, *South Carolina,* 60, 64. Kovacik and Winberry, *South Carolina,* 112.

12. Robertson, *Red Hills and Cotton,* 278. Newby, *Black Carolinians,* 200–201. Petty, *Growth and Distribution of Population,* 99–104. Julian J. Petty, "Population," in *South Carolina: Economic and Social Conditions,* 28–40. Pope, *History of Newberry County,* 2: 124. Cann, "Morning After," 68–73. Elizabeth Rauh Bethel, *Promiseland: A Century of Life in a Negro Community* (Philadelphia: Temple University Press, 1981), 171–94.

13. Cann, "Morning After," 71–73. Tindall, *Emergence of the New South,* 147–49. Fields, *Lemon Swamp,* 200–203. Newby, *Black Carolinians,* 193–96, 200. Huff, *Greenville,* 312–15. Miller, "These 'Colored' United States," 377, 400. South Carolina Department of Agriculture, Commerce and Industries and Clemson College, *South Carolina, A Handbook* (Columbia: Department of Agriculture, Commerce and Industries, 1927), 20–21 (hereinafter cited as *South Carolina Handbook, 1927*). Bethel, *Promiseland,* 223–28, 238–55.

14. Julian J. Petty, *Twentieth Century Changes in South Carolina Population: A Study for the State Organization for Associated Research* (Columbia: Bureau of Economic Research, School of Business Administration, University of South Carolina, 1962), 160, 180. Newby, *Black Carolinians,* 200–201. Edgar, *History of Santee Cooper,* 4. Petty, *Growth and Distribution of Population,* 32, 35, 156–60, 168. Petty, "Population," 35–45. *South Carolina Handbook, 1927,* 20–21.

15. Fraser, *Charleston! Charleston!,* 381. Cann, "Morning After," 109–17, 124–38; Geer's remarks in *Index-Journal* (Greenwood), 15 July 1922 quoted, 129. Hayes, "South Carolina and the New Deal," 279. "WPA Interviews, South Carolina Writers' Project: Textile Worker," 125–29. Huff, *Greenville,* 294, 299–301, 312–13. Wilt Browning, *Linthead: Growing Up in a Carolina Cotton Mill Village* (Asheboro, N.C.: Down Home Press, 1990), 11–22. Alvin W. Byars, *Olympia Pacific: The Way It Was, 1895–1970*

(n.p.: Progressional Printers, Ltd., 1981), 87–185.

16. Wallace, *History of South Carolina,* 3: 481. WPA, *South Carolina,* 70. Huff, *Greenville,* 295, 301–2. Cann, "Morning After," 80–120. Tindall, *Emergence of the New South,* 76–78, 161–64.

17. Tindall, *Emergence of the New South,* 324, 349–50; *Journal of the House of Representatives, 1930* quoted, 350. Huff, *Greenville,* 334. Cann, "Morning After," 138–58.

18. Huff, *Greenville,* 334. Cann, "Morning After," 110–15. Beardsley, *History of Neglect,* 54, 57.

19. Tindall, *Emergence of the New South,* 323. Cann, "Morning After," 52, 85. Fraser, *Charleston! Charleston!,* 370. J. Edward Lee and Ron Chepesiuk, "Mr. Anderson's Automobile," *Carologue,* 12 (Autumn 1996): 8–13.

20. Pope, *History of Newberry County,* 2: 124. Cann, "Morning After," 19–23, 179–82; *Journal of the Senate, 1926* quoted introductory epigraph; D. R. Coker to Sue Wilkinson, 5 Feb. 1925, David R. Coker Papers, SCL quoted 21; J. J. Adams to W. W. Ball, W. W. Ball Papers, DU quoted, 22. Wallace, *History of South Carolina,* 3: 458. Huff, *Greenville,* 334.

21. Wallace, *History of South Carolina,* 3: 479. Tindall, *Emergence of the New South,* 354. Pope, *History of Newberry County,* 2: 124. Huff, *Greenville,* 333–34. Watkins, *Anderson County,* 75–76. Hayes, "South Carolina and the New Deal", 4, 152. Cann, "Morning After," 164–70. John G. Sproat and Larry Schweikart, *Making Change: South Carolina Banking in the Twentieth Century* (Columbia: South Carolina Bankers Association, 1990), 19–102.

22. Cann, "Morning After," 274–87; *Anderson Daily Mail,* in *Index-Journal* quoted, 278. Wallace, *History of South Carolina,* 3: 472–74.

23. Tindall, *Emergence of the New South,* 231. Wallace, *History of South Carolina,* 3: 482–86. J. McT. Daniel, "Public Education," in *South Carolina: Economic and Social Conditions,* 188–205.

During the decade South Carolina had the largest increase in per pupil expenditure in the nation (149.6 percent). In 1920 the state spent $16.02 ($121.24); in 1930 the figure was $39.98 ($363.08). In 1920 South Carolina was last in the South; in 1930 it ranked seventh. United States Office of Education, *Biennial Survey of Education in the United States, 1928–1930,* 2 vols. (Washington, D.C.: Government Printing Office, 1932), 2: 28–29.

24. Tindall, *Emergence of the New South,* 266. Daniel, "Public Education," 203–4. Hollis, *University of South Carolina,* 2: 296–338. Alfred Sandlin Reid, *Furman University: Toward a New Identity 1925–1975* (Durham: Duke University Press, 1976), 40–42, 49–51, 82–83, 154–55.

25. David L. Carlton, "Unbalanced Growth and Industrialization: The Case of South Carolina," in Moore et al., *Developing Dixie,* 119–22. Huff, *Greenville,* 270. WPA, *Spartanburg County,* 273. Watkins, *Anderson County,* 69–71. Edgar, *History of Santee Cooper,* 4–5; quotation, 5.

26. Edgar, *History of Santee Cooper,* 4–5; Harry Ashmore in the *Piedmont* (Greenville), Santee Cooper scrapbooks, Santee Cooper Archives, Monks Corner, S.C., quoted, 5. Lander, *History of South Carolina,* 103–5; *Record* (Columbia), 8 Dec. 1918, in Robert M. Burts, "The Public Career of Richard I. Manning" quoted, 103. John Hammond Moore, *The South Carolina Highway Department, 1917–1987* (Columbia: University of South Carolina Press, 1987), 74–100.

27. Lander, *History of South Carolina,* 69–72. Wallace, *History of South Carolina,* 3: 465–70; *Independent* (Anderson) reprinted in *Herald* (Spartanburg), May 1930 quoted, 468. Carlton, "Unbalanced Growth and Industrialization," 121–26. Key, *Southern Politics,* 150–55. Graham and Moore, *South Carolina Politics,* 119–27. Ashmore, *Hearts and Minds,* 25–26. Cauthen, *Speaker Blatt,* 125–27. W. D. Workman Jr., "The Ring That Isn't," in Lander and Ackerman, *Perspectives,* 393–407. Nadine Cohodas, *Strom Thurmond & the Politics of Southern Change* (1993; Macon, Ga.: Mercer University Press, 1994), 86–90. Moore, *South Carolina Highway Department,* 74–100. Marvin Cann, "Burnet Maybank and Charleston Politics in the New Deal Era," in *Proceedings of the South Carolina Historical Association, 1970,* 39–48. David R. Goldfield, *Promised Land: The South Since 1945,* American History Series, ed. John Hope Franklin and Abraham S. Eisenstadt (Arlington Heights, Ill.: Harlan Davidson, 1987), 36–37. Bryant Simon, "The Devaluation of the Vote: Legislative Apportionment and Inequalities in South Carolina, 1890–1962," *SCHM,* 97 (July 1996): 235–45.

28. Wallace, *History of South Carolina,* 3: 465. Cann, "Morning After," introductory epigraph. Moore, *Columbia & Richland County,* 331–34. Huff, *Greenville,* 333. Robertson, *Red Hills and Cot-*

ton, 278.

29. Cann, "Morning After," 401–7; quotation, 404. Moore, *Columbia & Richland County,* 333. Huff, *Greenville,* 306–12. South Carolina, Secretary of State, Records, Secretary of State, SCDAH: Charter Private Companies, 14200–14999, charter nos. 14706, 14733, 14737, 14774, 14807.

30. Coclanis, *Shadow of a Dream,* 156. Cann. "Morning After," 401–7. Fraser, *Charleston! Charleston!,* 354, 368, 373–74, 381–83. Moore, *South Carolina in the 1880s,* 9–14, 38–45, 264–69. Tindall, *Emergence of the New South,* 103.

31. Ludwig Lewisohn, "South Carolina: A Lingering Fragrance of the Past," *Nation,* 115 (12 July 1922): 36–38. Fraser, *Charleston! Charleston!,* 373–74, 376, 381–83, 386; quotation, 374.

32. Lucas, *Sherman and the Burning of Columbia,* 128. WPA, *South Carolina,* 157–468.

33. Fields, *Lemon Swamp,* xvii. Gordon, *Sketches of Negro Life and History,* 94–99. Newby, *Black Carolinians,* 103–5, 224–27. Septima Poinsette Clark, with LeGette Blythe, *Echo in My Soul* (New York: E. P. Dutton & Co., 1962), 14, 29–31. Robertson, *Red Hills and Cotton,* 3–30, passim. WPA, *South Carolina,* 3. Cann, "Morning After," 1, 212. Archibald Rutledge, *My Colonel and His Lady* (Indianapolis: Bobbs-Merrill, 1937), 128–29.

34. Charles B. Hosmer, *Preservation Comes of Age: From Williamsburg to the National Trust, 1926–1949,* 2 vols. (Charlottesville: Published for the Preservation Press of the National Trust for Historic Preservation in the United States by the University Press of Virginia, 1981), 1: 234–74. Sidney R. Bland, "Transcending the Expectations of a Culture: Susan Pringle Frost, A New South Charleston Woman," in Moore et al., *Developing Dixie,* 245–59. Fraser, *Charleston! Charleston!,* 374–77.

For an intriguing account of the early restoration efforts of individual Charlestonians, see Robert Preston Stockton, "The Evolution of Rainbow Row," thesis, University of South Carolina, 1979.

35. Huff, *Greenville,* 310, 364. Cann, "Morning After," 3.

36. Bellows, "At Peace With the Past," 1–5. Boyd Saunders and Ann McAden, *Alfred Hutty and the Charleston Renaissance* (Orangeburg, S.C.: Sandlapper, 1990), 43–56. Cann, "Morning After," 206. WPA, *South Carolina,* 122. Fraser, *Charleston! Charleston!,* 377. Allen University Quartet Suggested Melodies, "Hand Me Down De Silver Trumpet" (Chicago: Rodeheaver, 1923). Lewisohn, "South Carolina," 36.

37. Tindall, *Emergence of the New South,* 308. J. H. Easterby, *Guide to the Study and Reading of South Carolina History: A General Classified Bibliography* (Columbia: Historical Commission of South Carolina, 1950).

Easterby's *Guide* contains only works he classified as "history" and therefore is not inclusive. For example, works on architecture are included, but those on folklore are not.

38. Tindall, *Emergence of the New South,* 307–8. See Easterby, *Guide to . . . South Carolina.*

Virtually every major commercial press of the 1920s and 1930s is listed. Southern university presses, especially the University of North Carolina Press, also appear frequently.

39. Tindall, *Emergence of the New South,* 291–93. Walter B. Edgar, "The Circle of the Charleston Poetry Society and the Creation of the Image of the Carolina Lowcountry," in *Rewriting the South: History and Fiction,* edited by Lothar Hönnighausen and Valeria Gennero Lerda, in collaboration with Christoph Irmscher and Simon Ward (Tübingen, Germany: Francke Verlag, 1993), 199–209.

40. Ashmore, *Hearts and Minds,* 1–3, 35–36. Tindall, *Emergence of the New South,* 184–218. Thomas L. Johnson, "Henry Bellaman and His Columbia Connection," *Record* (Columbia), 6 May 1982, A18.

When the state celebrated its tricentennial in 1970, it published an anthology of South Carolina literature. The last nineteenth-century writer featured was Paul Hamilton Hayne and the first twentieth-century writer was Julia Peterkin, whose works first appeared in the 1920s. Calhoun and Guilds, *Tricentennial Anthology of South Carolina Literature,* ix–x.

Technically, Coogler was from Doko (Blythewood) in upper Richland County; however, he lived and worked in Columbia. Claude Henry Neuffer and Rene LaBorde, introduction to reprint edition, J. Gordon Coogler, *Purely Original Verse* (1897; Columbia: Vogue Press, 1974).

41. "The Worm Turns: Being in Some Sort A Reply to Mr. H. L. Mencken," in *The Year Book of the Poetry Society of South Carolina, 1921* (Charleston: Poetry Society of South Carolina, 1921), 41–42.

"Members' publications," in *The Yearbook of the Poetry Society of South Carolina* (Charleston: State Company, 1923–1925), 1923: 90–98; 1924, 78–82; 1925, 55–59. Tindall, *Emergence of the New South,* 291–93. Louise Cowan, *The Fugitives: A Literary History* (Baton Rouge: Louisiana State University Press, 1959), 114–16. *New York Times,* 28 Jan. 1923, II: 6. H. L. Mencken, "Violets in The Sahara," *Evening Sun* (Baltimore), 15 May 1922.

42. Cann, "Morning After," 207–10.

43. Don H. Doyle, Introduction to DuBose Heyward, *Mamba's Daughters* (1928; Columbia: University of South Carolina Press, 1995), vii–xxiii. Tindall, *Emergence of the New South,* 309. Bellows, "At Peace With the Past," 5. Tindall, *Emergence of the New South,* 159–60. Fields, *Lemon Swamp,* 184–86.

44. Fields, *Lemon Swamp,* 189–96. Graydon, *Collection of Sermons,* passim. Huff, *Greenville,* 312–15. Land, "Call to Service," 11–12.

45. Clark, *Echo in My Soul,* 27–48. Tindall, *Emergence of the New South,* 569–70. Fields, *Lemon Swamp,* 185–86, 203. Moore, *Columbia & Richland County,* 381–82. Huff, *Greenville,* 312–15, 355–58. Newby, *Black Carolinians,* 232–34. Paul Lofton, "A Social and Economic History of Columbia, South Carolina During the Great Depression, 1929–1940," diss., University of Texas at Austin, 1977, 218–43.

46. Benjamin E. Mays, "The New Negro Challenges the Old Order," in Gordon, *Sketches of Negro Life and History,* 192–212. Newby, *Black Carolinians,* 232–33; Moore, *Columbia & Richland County,* 384–85. Lofton, "Social and Economic History of Columbia," 218–43.

47. Lofton, "Social and Economic History of Columbia," 1–2. Don Barton, *The Clemson-Carolina Game, 1896–1966* (Columbia: State Printing Company, 1966), 120–25.

48. Fields, *Lemon Swamp,* 223–24. Cann, "Morning After," 19, 36. Hayes, "South Carolina and the New Deal," 406. Dunlap, "Changing Symbols of Success," 18–30. Huff, *Greenville,* 335. Jones, "50th Annual Meeting," 10.

49. Pope, *History of Newberry County,* 2: 124. Huff, *Greenville,* 333–34. Sproat and Schweikart, *Making Change,* 84–85. Hayes, "South Carolina and the New Deal," 5. Robertson, *Red Hills and Cotton,* 282. Lander, *History of South Carolina,* 73.

50. Fraser, *Charleston! Charleston!,* 378–79. Huff, *Greenville,* 335–39. King, *Florence County,* 342. Moore, *Columbia & Richland County,* 338–40. Sherrill, "State Governmental Organization," 141, 163–65. G. Croft Williams, "Public Welfare," in *South Carolina: Economic & Social Conditions,* 207. Hayes, "South Carolina and the New Deal," 218–21, 528–29.

51. Williams, "Public Welfare," 209–13. Hayes, "South Carolina and the New Deal," 218–21. Lofton, "Social and Economic History of Columbia," 151–54. Huff, *Greenville,* 333–38.

52. Hayes, "South Carolina and the New Deal," 5–6, 173–78. Lofton, "Social and Economic History of Columbia," 32, 60, 71–74. Huff, *Greenville,* 333–38. Harvard Sitkoff, *A New Deal for Blacks: The Emergence of a Civil Rights Crusade as a National Issue, Volume I: The Depression Decade* (New York: Oxford University Press, 1978), 45.

In 1930 the population of Columbia was approximately 51,000 and that of Richland County 88,000. Thus, the 700,000 meals represent the feeding of a sizeable percentage of the population. Hennig, *Columbia,* 397. Wallace, *History of South Carolina,* 3: 504.

53. James F. Byrnes, *All in One Lifetime* (New York: Harper & Brothers, 1958), 59–66. Hayes, "South Carolina and the New Deal," 7, 10–26. Robertson, *Sly and Able,* 98, 121–44.

54. Robertson, *Red Hills and Cotton,* 272–74. *Wateree Messenger* (Camden), 22 Mar. 1932 and *Dispatch News* (Lexington), 11 May 1932 quoted in Hayes, "South Carolina and the New Deal," 33. Lander, *History of South Carolina,* 73n.

55. Robertson, *Sly and Able,* 145–56. Dewey W. Grantham, *The South in Modern America: A Region at Odds,* New American Nation Series, ed. Henry Steele Commager and Richard B. Morris (New York: HarperCollins, 1994), 122. Tindall, *Emergence of the New South,* 610–11. Hayes, "South Carolina and the New Deal," 48–151.

56. Robertson, *Red Hills and Cotton,* 273–74.

57. Tindall, *Emergence of the New South,* 546–47. Hayes, "South Carolina and the New Deal,"

173–99; quotation, 188. Cann, "Morning After," 231–32. Wallace, *History of South Carolina*, 3: 502. Anthony J. Badger, *The New Deal: The Depression Years, 1933–1940*, American Century Series (New York: Hill & Wang, 1989), 194, 212.

58. Hayes, "South Carolina and the New Deal," 176–77, 264–69. Perry H. Merrill, *Roosevelt's Forest Army: A History of the Civilian Conservation Corps, 1933–1942* (Montpelier, Vt.: Perry H. Merrill, 1981), 172–74. Huff, *Greenville*, 346–49. Smith quoted in Badger, *New Deal*, 174.

59. Huff, *Greenville*, 346–49, 367. Moore, *Columbia & Richland County*, 341–42. Fraser, *Charleston! Charleston!*, 380–81. WPA, *South Carolina*, v–xx. Lofton, "Social and Economic History of Columbia," 149–50. Pope, *History of Newberry County*, 131–32. Jones, "50th Annual Meeting," 11–12. Hayes, "South Carolina and the New Deal," 244–46, 260–62, 274–87.

60. Robertson, *Sly and Able*, 201–45. Edgar, *History of Santee Cooper*, 5–11, 21, 67–94, 112–20.

61. Hayes, "South Carolina and the New Deal," 449–52. Pope, *History of Newberry County*, 2: 132. Fields, *Lemon Swamp*, 112. Jones, "50th Annual Meeting, 13."

62. Hayes, "South Carolina and the New Deal," 57–61.

63. Hayes, "South Carolina and the New Deal," 406–54. Tindall, *Emergence of the New South*, 392–93. Huff, *Greenville*, 344–35. Harry Herbert Lesesne, "Opposition to the New Deal in South Carolina, 1933–1936," M.A. thesis, University of South Carolina, 1995, 31–33.

64. Hayes, "South Carolina and the New Deal," 310–52. Jones, "50th Annual Meeting," 11. Huff, *Greenville*, 345–46.

65. Hayes, "South Carolina and the New Deal," 312–17. Huff, *Greenville*, 349–50. Jones, "50th Annual Meeting," 11. Tindall, *Emergence of the New South*, 434–36, 532. Thomas E. Terrill, "'No Union for Me': Southern Textile Workers and Organized Labor," in Chesnutt and Wilson, *Meaning of South Carolina History*, 207–8.

66. Terrill, "'No Union for Me,'" 207–8. Hayes, "South Carolina and the New Deal," 320–54; quotation, 324. Tindall, *Emergence of the New South*, 509–11. Lander, *History of South Carolina*, 93. Robertson, *Sly and Able*, 161–70.

67. Hayes, "South Carolina and the New Deal," 355–65. Lander, *History of South Carolina*, 93. Tindall, *Emergence of the New South*, 509–12. Lofton, "Social and Economic History of Columbia," 184. Robertson, *Sly and Able*, 171–83.

68. Tindall, *Emergence of the New South*, 509–11, 517–24. Pope, *History of Newberry County*, 2: 132–33. Hayes, "South Carolina and the New Deal," 365–405. Huff, *Greenville*, 350–55.

69. Tindall, *Emergence of the New South*, 610–11. Ashmore, *Hearts and Minds*, 24. Daniel W. Hollis, "'Cotton Ed' Smith—Statesman or Showman," *SCHM*, 71 (Oct. 1970): 235–56. Wallace, *History of South Carolina*, 3: 423, 435.

70. Tindall, *Emergence of the New South*, 643–44. Hayes, "South Carolina and the New Deal," 275–76, 530–36. Jones, *South Carolina*, 249. Anthony Barry Miller, "Palmetto Politician: The Early Political Career of Olin D. Johnston, 1896–1945," diss., University of North Carolina at Chapel Hill, 1976, 74–263. Moore, *South Carolina Highway Department*, 101–58.

71. Marvin L. Cann, "The End of the Political Myth: The South Carolina Gubernatorial Campaign of 1938," *SCHM*, 72 (July 1971): 139–49. Robertson, *Sly and Able*, 187, 222, 248, 271, 279, 298. Fraser, *Charleston! Charleston!*, 380–85.

72. Hollis, "'Cotton Ed' Smith," 249–51. Tindall, *Emergence of the New South*, 556–57. Ashmore, *Hearts and Minds*, 20–22. Robertson, *Sly and Able*, 186–96. Harry S. Ashmore, *An Epitaph for Dixie* (New York: W. W. Norton, 1958), 101. Sitkoff, *New Deal for Blacks*, 93–94, 115–16.

73. Robertson, *Sly and Able*, 196–200. "'Palmetto Stump'—Thirties Style," in Lander and Ackerman, *Perspectives*, 349–53.

74. Fraser, *Charleston! Charleston!*, 377. Cann, "Morning After," 188. Lesesne, "Opposition to the New Deal," 20–26. Tindall, *Emergence of the New South*, 371. Hayes, "South Carolina and the New Deal," 492.

75. Tindall, *Emergence of the New South*, 551–53, 556–57. Byrnes, *All in One Lifetime*, 96–107. Hayes, "South Carolina and the New Deal," 499–503. Robertson, *Sly and Able*, 246–66, 282–87. Sitkoff, *New Deal for Blacks*, 98, 104–10, 287–88.

76. Ashmore, *Hearts and Minds,* 21–22; Robertson, *Sly and Able,* 267–87. Lander, *History of South Carolina,* 77–80. Tindall, *Emergence of the New South,* 628–29. Hayes, "South Carolina and the New Deal," 510–22.

77. Tindall, *Emergence of the New South,* 618–19. Ashmore, *Hearts and Minds,* 10. Lesesne, "Opposition to the New Deal," 97–98. Wright, *Old South, New South,* 216–38.

78. Huff, *Greenville,* 349–50. Hayes, "South Carolina and the New Deal," 177–78, 543–45, 502–3; Carroll Nance's remarks in *State* (Columbia), 25 Apr. 1935 quoted, 432. Lesesne, "Opposition to the New Deal," 71. Sitkoff, *New Deal for Blacks,* 79–82.

79. Hayes, "South Carolina and the New Deal," 506–8, 522.

80. Robertson, *Sly and Able,* 288–319. Tindall, *Emergence of the New South,* 687–94. Hayes, "South Carolina and the New Deal," 522. Gregorie, *History of Sumter County,* 489. Robertson, *Red Hills and Cotton,* 293–94. Fraser, *Charleston! Charleston!,* 386–87. Moore, *Columbia & Richland County,* 393–95.

81. Robertson, *Red Hills and Cotton,* 294–95.

Chapter 22: All in One Lifetime

1. Tindall, *Emergence of the New South,* 689–31. Numan V. Bartley, *The New South, 1945–1980,* vol. XI in A History of the South, ed. Wendell Holmes Stephenson and E. Merton Coulter (Baton Rouge: Louisiana State University Press, 1995), 1–37. Huff, *Greenville,* 343, 374–88. Fraser, *Charleston! Charleston!,* 394–427. Moore, *Columbia & Richland County,* 389–431. Pope, *History of Newberry County,* 2: 138. Edgar, *South Carolina in the Modern Age,* 81–114.

2. Bartley, *New South,* 1–4; James McBride Dabbs, "Is a Christian Community Possible in the South?," *Christian Century,* 57 (10 July 1940): 4. Ashmore, *Hearts and Minds,* 1–30.

3. Paula Marie Stathakis, "Almost White: Greek and Lebanese-Syrian Immigrants in North and South Carolina," diss., University of South Carolina, 1996, 22–74. Petty, *Growth and Distribution of Population,* 110, 115, 117. Jack Temple Kirby, *Rural Worlds Lost: The American South, 1920–1960* (Baton Rouge: Louisiana State University Press, 1987), 275.

North Carolina had a slightly smaller percentage of foreign-born residents than did South Carolina, but the latter had the smallest number. Petty, *Growth and Distribution of Population,* 115.

4. Lesesne, "Opposition to the New Deal," 97. Huff, *Greenville,* 378–80. Hayes, "South Carolina and the New Deal," 176–77. Dunlap, "Changing Symbols of Success," 151–55.

5. Eric L. Cooper, "Coopers on the Mill Hill: One Midlands Family's Experience in South Carolina's Cotton Mills (seminar paper, University of South Carolina, 1991), 23–25. Newby, *Black Carolinians,* 275. South Carolina State Development Board, *South Carolina Servicemen After the War* (n.p., 1945), 7–8, 14–15 (hereinafter cited as *South Carolina Servicemen*). Moreland, *Millways of Kent,* 214–18. Lewis, *Blackways of Kent,* 12–14.

6. Fraser, *Charleston! Charleston!,* 387–88. Enid Ewing, "Charleston Contra Munda," *Nation,* 157 (20 Nov. 1943): 579–81. Lander, *History of South Carolina,* 209.

7. Ewing, "Charleston Contra Munda," 579–81. Fraser, *Charleston! Charleston!,* 387–91.

8. Fraser, *Charleston! Charleston!,* 387–88. Petty, "Population," 41–42. John Hammond Moore, "Nazi Troopers in South Carolina," *SCHM,* 81 (Oct. 1980): 306–15. Andrew H. Myers, "Black, White, and Olive Drab: Military-Social Relations During the Civil Rights Movement in Columbia and at Fort Jackson, South Carolina," diss. in progress, University of Virginia, chap. 2, 30–31.

9. Huff, *Greenville,* 381–82. Fraser, *Charleston! Charleston!,* 389–90. Moore, *Columbia & Richland County,* 396, 399. Browning, *Linthead,* 23–38.

10. Moore, *Columbia & Richland County,* 397, 415. Huff, *Greenville,* 382, 384. Fraser, *Charleston! Charleston!,* 388.

11. Miles S. Richards, "Osceola E. McKaine and the Struggle for Black Civil Rights: 1917–1946," diss., University of South Carolina, 1994, 103–5, 115–16, 121–24, 130–48. Moore, *Columbia & Richland County,* 415–16. Personal files of Rhett Jackson, Columbia, S.C.

12. Sitkoff, *New Deal for Blacks,* 98. Tindall, *Emergence of the New South,* 716, 726–27. "Killbillies," *Newsweek,* 23 (1 May 1944): 3. Richards, "Osceola E. McKaine," 163–67. Key, *Southern Poli-*

tics, 626–27. Lander, *History of South Carolina,* 169–71. Moore, *Columbia & Richland County,* 416. Bartley, *New South,* 135. Albert D. Hutto to the editor of *State* (Columbia), 5 Aug. 1944. Copy in Dr. Wil Lou Gray Papers, South Caroliniana Library. Bethel, *Promiseland,* 224–37. Lewis, *Blackways of Kent,* 40–41, 173, 187, 198. Brad Warthen, "Where are those who will lead South Carolina?," *State* (Columbia), 11 Mar. 1997, A8.

13. Huff, *Greenville,* 385. Moore, *Columbia & Richland County,* 400. Fraser, *Charleston! Charleston!,* 392. *South Carolina Servicemen,* 7–9.

14. *South Carolina Servicemen,* 17, 22–25, 28.

15. Hollis, *University of South Carolina,* 2: 340–43. South Carolina Department of Agriculture, *Report, 1945–1946,* 25.

16. Newby, *Black Carolinians,* 229. *South Carolina Servicemen,* 30, 31; emphasis supplied. Lewis, *Blackways of Kent,* 40–41, 173, 187, 198.

17. *South Carolina Servicemen,* 12–17. Pope, *History of Newberry County,* 2: 138–43. Files of *State* (Columbia), "Industry General" (Workman), *Record* (Columbia), 19 Dec. 1945. *Gamecock* (University of South Carolina), 12 Oct., 10 Dec. 1946. *State* (Columbia), 20 Jan., 6 Feb., 7 Feb. 1947.

18. Pope, *History of Newberry County,* 2: 138. Bartley, *New South,* 31–34, 135. *South Carolina Servicemen,* 26–31. Cohodas, *Strom Thurmond,* 83–84; quotation, 84. Warthen, "Where are those who will lead South Carolina?," A8.

19. Cohodas, *Strom Thurmond,* 84–91, 98–99; quotation, 86. Ashmore, *Hearts and Minds,* 125–26. Key, *Southern Politics,* 133, 147–50. Lander, *History of South Carolina,* 196–201. *The State* (Columbia), 6 Feb. 1947. *Gamecock* (University of South Carolina), 10 Dec. 1946. Bruce Littlejohn, *Littlejohn's Political Memoirs: 1934–1988* (Spartanburg, S.C.: Bruce Littlejohn, 1989), 33–40.

20. *Annual Message of J. Strom Thurmond, Governor of South Carolina to the General Assembly* (Columbia, 1951), 11–16. Lander, *History of South Carolina,* 200. Fraser, *Charleston! Charleston!,* 393, 408. Underwood, *Constitution of South Carolina,* 3: 310–11; 4: 202. Rogers, *Generations of Lawyers,* 189–90. Graham and Moore, *South Carolina Politics,* 145–48.

21. John Egerton, *Speak Now Against the Day: The Generation Before the Civil Rights Movement in the South* (New York: Alfred A. Knopf, 1994), 371–73; quotation, 372.

22. Huff, *Greenville,* 399–401. Cohodas, *Strom Thurmond,* 99–101, 111–12. Rebecca West, "Opera in Greenville," in Lander and Ackerman, *Perspectives,* 360–69. Dunlap, "Changing Symbols of Success," 153–54, 180–84.

23. Richards, "Osceola E. McKaine," 107–8, 167–88. Bartley, *New South,* 29. Tindall, *Emergence of the New South,* 716. Newby, *Black Carolinians,* 229, 256–57. Moore, *Columbia & Richland County,* 417. Egerton, *Speak Now Against the Day,* 496–97. Cohodas, *Strom Thurmond,* 107–12. Frederickson, "'Slowest State,'" 177–202.

24. Newby, *Black Carolinians,* 284–89. Key, *Southern Politics,* 628. Samuel Grafton, "Lonesomest Man in Town," *Collier's* (29 Apr. 1950): 50. Fraser, *Charleston! Charleston!,* 394–98. Lander, *History of South Carolina,* 174. Cohodas, *Strom Thurmond,* 101–4, 114–18, 149–50, 152.

25. Bartley, *New South,* 37–38, 73–78, 85–86, 208, 458–61. Badger, *New Deal,* 8. Earl Black and Merle Black, *The Vital South: How Presidents Are Elected* (Cambridge, Mass.: Harvard University Press, 1992), 93–94. Robertson, *Sly and Able,* 332–64.

26. Black and Black, *Vital South,* 94–99, 142–49. Cohodas, *Strom Thurmond,* 175–93. Bartley, *New South,* 87–95. Egerton, *Speak Now Against the Day,* 499–501, 510.

27. Goldfield, *Promised Land,* 44–45. Egerton, *Speak Now Against the Day,* 589–90. Ashmore, *Hearts and Minds,* 180–81.

28. Egerton, *Speak Now Against the Day,* 589–97; quotation (with emphasis), 596. Bartley, *New South,* 158–59. Ashmore, *Hearts and Minds,* 180–90. Robertson, *Sly and Able,* 505–20. Moore, *Columbia & Richland County,* 414–18.

For a detailed account of *Briggs v. Elliott,* see Richard Kluger, *Simple Justice: The History of Brown v. Board of Education and Black America's Struggle for Equality* (1975; New York: Vintage Books, a Division of Random House, 1977), passim.

29. Robertson, *Sly and Able,* 492–505. Byrnes, *All in One Lifetime,* 407.

30. Bartley, *New South,* 147–50. Goldfield, *Promised Land,* 45–46. Howard H. Quint, *Profile in Black and White: A Frank Portrait of South Carolina* (Washington: Public Affairs Press, 1958), 15–16, 93. Byrnes, *All in One Lifetime,* 408.

31. *South Carolina's Educational Revolution* (n.p., n.d.), passim. Byrnes, *All in One Lifetime,* 408–9, 418.

32. Byrnes, *All in One Lifetime,* 419–20. Bartley, *New South,* 162–63. Ashmore, *Hearts and Minds,* 186. Harry S. Ashmore, *Civil Rights and Wrongs: A Memoir of Race and Politics, 1944–1994* (New York: A Cornelia & Michael Bessie Book, Pantheon Books, 1994), 98. Quint, *Profile in Black and White,* 16–17.

33. Robertson, *Sly and Able,* 507–9. Byrnes, *All in One Lifetime,* 418.

34. William D. Workman, *The Case for the South* (New York: Devin-Adair, 1960), 18–22, 279–81; quotation, 280. Quint, *Profile in Black and White,* 25–27, 38–42. Bartley, *New South,* 202. Egerton, *Speak Now Against the Day,* 609. John G. Sproat, "'Firm Flexibility': Perspectives on Desegregation in South Carolina," in *New Perspectives on Race and Slavery in America,* eds. Robert H. Abzug and Stephen E. Malish (Lexington: University Press of Kentucky, 1986), 173–74.

35. Robertson, *Sly and Able,* 519–25. Egerton, *Speak Now Against the Day,* 577–78, 593. Bartley, *New South,* 187, 199–202. Moore, *Columbia & Richland County,* 420. Quint, *Profile in Black and White,* 38. Huff, *Greenville,* 401–3. Sproat, "'Firm Flexibility,'" 166–69.

36. Julian Scheer, "The White Folks Fight Back," *New Republic,* 31 (Oct. 1955): 9–12. Robertson, *Sly and Able,* 513. Cohodas, *Strom Thurmond,* 219–21. Newby, *Black Carolinians,* 320. Quint, *Profile in Black and White,* 32, 48–57.

37. Bartley, *New South,* 205. Egerton, *Speak Now Against the Day,* 550–52. Quint, *Profile in Black and White,* 175–79. Workman, *Case for the South,* 7. Herbert Ravenel Sass, "Mixed Schools and Mixed Blood," *Atlantic Monthly,* 198 (Nov. 1957): 45–49. Lander, *History of South Carolina,* 203. Joyner, "'One People,'" in Chesnutt and Wilson, *Meaning of South Carolina History,* 230. Fred Hobson, *Tell About the South: The Southern Rage to Explain* (Baton Rouge: Louisiana State University Press, 1983), 341–42, 351.

38. Quint, *Profile in Black and White,* 98–99, 111; quotations, 99, 111. Scheer, "White Folks Fight Back," 10, 12. Newby, *Black Carolinians,* 308.

39. Bartley, *New South,* 198–99, 235; "Declaration of Constitutional Principles," *Southern School News,* Apr. 1956 quoted, 198. Ashmore, *Hearts and Minds,* 231–32. Egerton, *Speak Now Against the Day,* 621–23. Cohodas, *Strom Thurmond,* 255–67, 294–97. Alberta Lachicotte, *Rebel Senator: Strom Thurmond of South Carolina* (New York: Devin-Adair, 1966), 131–38.

40. Lander, *History of South Carolina,* 202. Fraser, *Charleston! Charleston!,* 409. Clark, *Echo in My Soul,* 111–18. Quint, *Profile in Black and White,* 110. Bartley, *New South,* 194–95. Joyner, "'One People,'" 227.

41. Quint, *Profile in Black and White,* 102–3, 116–24. *State* (Columbia), 23 Oct. 1958, A1. Moore, *Columbia & Richland County,* 421–22. Lewis P. Jones, "Religion in South Carolina: An Overview" and Robert M. Calhoon, "Religion Confronts the Social Order," in *Religion in South Carolina,* ed. Charles H. Lippy (Columbia: University of South Carolina Press, 1993), 15–17, 179–80.

42. Interview with Augustus T. Graydon, 10 July 1991. Conversation with Hallie Bacote Perry and Matthew J. Perry Jr., 5 Feb. 1996. Rogers, *Generations of Lawyers,* 186–88, 203. Newby, *Black Carolinians,* 280, 351. Quint, *Profile in Black and White,* 11.

43. Moore, *Columbia & Richland County,* 419–20. Quint, *Profile in Black and White,* 56–57, 63–64, 167–80. Bartley, *New South,* 176, 181. Jones, "Religion in South Carolina," 16. Kevin Lewis, "Religion Addresses the Public Order," in Lippy, *Religion in South Carolina,* 186–87. Newby, *Black Carolinians,* 317–18. Joyner, "'One People,'" 230.

44. Quint, *Profile in Black and White,* passim. Huff, *Greenville,* 401–3. John D. Stark, *Damned Upcountryman: William Watts Ball, A Study in American Conservatism,* (Durham, N.C.: Duke University Press, 1968), 198–235. S. L. Latimer Jr., *Almost Four Score: The Story of The State, 1891–1969 and the Gonzales Brothers* (Columbia: State Printing Company, 1970), 231–36. Review of Lander, *History of South Carolina,* in *News & Courier,* 25 Sept. 1960, C11. Workman, *Case for the South,* 270–84.

45. Pope, *History of Newberry County,* 2: 129, 139. Dunlap, "Changing Symbols of Success," 55, 60–63. Moore, *South Carolina Highway Department,* 198. *Annual Message of J. Strom Thurmond,* 12, 14. Bartley, *New South,* 108–13, 122–26. Jones, *South Carolina,* 275–76. Watkins, *Anderson County,* 90–91. Kirby, *Rural Worlds Lost,* 123–24, 115–54, 354–55.

46. Goldfield, *Promised Land,* 142–43. Newby, *Black Carolinians,* 294. Bartley, *New South,* 113, 116–18, 122–26. Petty, *Twentieth Century Changes in South Carolina Population,* 24. Elias B. Bull, "Community and Neighborhood Names in Berkeley County, Part III," in Claude Henry Neuffer, ed., *Names in South Carolina,* 13 (Nov. 1966): 37. John A. Bigham, "Discontinued Post Offices in South Carolina," in Neuffer, *Names in South Carolina,* 15 (Nov. 1968): 62–63. Byrnes, *All in One Lifetime,* 408. *State* (Columbia), 3 June 1997, B1. George Frederick Hayne, "The Distribution of Churches and Church Membership in South Carolina," thesis, University of South Carolina, 1966, 60–63. Clark, *Our Southern Zion,* 275, 283. Kirby, *Rural Worlds Lost,* 181–85. *Street Atlas USA,* a CD-ROM (Freeport, Maine: DeLorme, 1995).

47. Kovacik and Winberry, *South Carolina,* 134–39. Daniel A. Fairey, *Agricultural Land Use Change in South Carolina, 1945–1974: A Review* (Columbia: Soils and Resource Development Division, South Carolina Land Resources Conservation Commission, 1978), 8–10, 25–26, 35–39. Bartley, *New South,* 287. Kirby, *Rural Worlds Lost,* 334–60.

48. South Carolina Department of Agriculture, *Report of the Department of Agriculture, 1955–1956* (Columbia: Department of Agriculture, 1956), 55; *Report of the Department of Agriculture, 1970–1971* (Columbia: Department of Agriculture, 1971), 3, 11, 30. Fairey, *Agricultural Land Use Change,* 30–39, 60. John Carl West, "South Carolina Looks to the Future," in Lander and Ackerman, *Perspectives,* 408. Kovacik and Winberry, *South Carolina,* 150, 159–60, 166. South Carolina State Budget and Control Board, *Economic Report, The State of South Carolina, 1972* (Columbia: State Budget & Control Board, 1973), 92–94. Wright, *Old South, New South,* 245–46. Newby, *Black Carolinians,* 295. Lander, *History of South Carolina,* 225.

49. Lander, *History of South Carolina,* 211. Jones, *South Carolina,* 274. Fraser, *Charleston! Charleston!,* 393. South Carolina State Ports Authority, *Port News,* Dec. 1951, 7; Nov. 1955, 11; Dec. 1959, 3, 7; Jan. 1960, 8–9; Jan. 1966, 12. Files of *State* (Columbia), "Industry: General (W. D. Workman)," 1954–1956, 1956–1961, 28 Aug. 1947 and "Industry: General (W. D. Workman)," *Record* (Columbia), 19 Dec. 1945. South Carolina State Development Board, *Annual Report, 1948–1949,* 25. idem., *South Carolina on the March: 1943–1953, Ten Years of Progress* (Columbia: South Carolina Development Board, 1954), 31, and *South Carolina News,* Sept. 1962, passim.

50. Grantham, *South in Modern America,* 267. James C. Cobb, *The Selling of the South: The Southern Crusade for Industrial Development, 1936–1980* (Baton Rouge: Louisiana State University Press, 1982), 166–67, 169, 230. Files of the *State* (Columbia), "Industry: General (Workman)," 24 Aug. 1955, 17 May 1959; from *News & Courier,* 14 May 1958 and "Industry: South Carolina Development Board (1955–1983)," 22 Jan. 1967. South Carolina State Development Board, *Annual Report, 1950–1951* (Columbia: State Budget & Control Board, 1951), 7, 11–13, 17–18, 24–29, 32–34, 79–80. idem., "Technical Training in South Carolina" (n.p., [c. 1968]), 4–5, 8–9. James C. Cobb, *Industrialization and Southern Society* (Lexington: University Press of Kentucky, 1984), 106. Dunlap, "Changing Symbols of Success," 159–72.

51. Cobb, *Selling of the South,* 189, 191–92. Grantham, *South in Modern America,* 267. Cobb, *Industrialization and Southern Society,* 58. Norman J. Glickman and Douglas P. Woodward, *The New Competitors: How Foreign Investors Are Changing the U.S. Economy* (New York: Basic Books, 1989), 193, 202–3, 205, 208.

52. Pope, *History of Newberry County,* 2: 138. Huff, *Greenville,* 390–91. Glickman and Woodward, *New Competitors,* 203–5. "Michelin Go Home," *New Republic,* 168 (19 May 1973): 8. Dunlap, "Changing Symbols of Success," 159–70.

53. Files of the *State* (Columbia), "Industry: General (Workman)," 19 Dec. 1945, 2 Aug. 1947, 30 Aug. 1947. Donald Davidson, *Still Rebels, Still Yankees and Other Essays* (Baton Rouge: Louisiana State University Press, 1957), 219–20.

54. Bartley, *New South,* 293–97. "The South: Into a New Century," *Newsweek* (3 May 1965): 27. Kovacik and Winberry, *South Carolina,* 146–47. Dunlap, "Changing Symbols of Success," 153–54,

180–85, 191–92, 195.

The struggle of the metropolitan elites to displace county elites is one of the major themes of Numan Bartley's *New South,* 293–97, passim. For a study of the triumph of metropolitan elites in South Carolina, see Maxie Myron Cox Jr., "1963—The Year of Decision: Desegregation in South Carolina," diss., University of South Carolina, 1996.

55. Bartley, *New South,* 293–97. "The South: Into a New Century," *Newsweek* (3 May 1965): 27. Quotation, Cobb, *Selling of the South,* 141. Goldfield, *Cottonfields and Skyscrapers,* 190–91; quotation, 191. Kovacik and Winberry, *South Carolina,* 146–47.

56. Bartley, *New South,* 298–306. Newby, *Black Carolinians,* 314–28.

It is ironic that black Greenvillians chose Emancipation Day for their protest march because in other upstate black communities Emancipation Day celebrations had been "long-abandoned." Lewis, *Blackways of Kent,* 162.

57. Huff, *Greenville,* 402–3. Newby, *Black Carolinians,* 314–28. Bartley, *New South,* 298–306. Cleveland Sellers, with Robert Terrell, *River of No Return: The Autobiography of a Black Militant and the Life and Death of SNCC* (Jackson: University Press of Mississippi, 1990), 18–32. Paul S. Lofton Jr., "Calm and Exemplary: Desegregation in Columbia, South Carolina," in Elizabeth Jacoway and David R. Colburn, *Southern Businessmen and Desegregation* (Baton Rouge: Louisiana State University Press, 1982), 77–76. Goldfield, *Promised Land,* 96, 100. Charles Joyner, *Folk Song in South Carolina,* Tricentennial Booklet No. 9 (Columbia: University of South Carolina Press, 1971), 107–8. Guy Carawan and Candie Carawan, recorders and eds., *Ain't you got a right to the Tree of Life?: The People of Johns Island, South Carolina—Their Faces, Their Words, and Their Songs,* rev. and exp. ed. (Athens: University of Georgia Press, 1989), 195, 208.

58. Bartley, *New South,* 213. Jones, *South Carolina,* 278–80. Wright, *Old South, New South,* 265–68. Cox, "1963," 346–466, 471. Jones, *South Carolina,* 278–80. Sproat, "'Firm Flexibility,'" 170–73.

59. Bartley, *New South,* 293–97, 305–6. Huff, *Greenville,* 401–4. George McMillan, "Integration With Dignity," in Lander and Ackerman, *Perspectives,* 382–83. Dunlap, "Changing Symbols of Success," 185–91.

60. South Carolina Confederate War Centennial Commission, *South Carolina Commemorates the Confederate War Centennial* (n.p., n.d.). Supplement to Confederate Monuments and Markers in South Carolina, a manuscript in the Confederate Relic Room, Columbia, S.C. "The South: Into a New Century," 32. South Carolina, *Journal of the House of Representatives, 1962* (Columbia: State Budget & Control Board), 458, 962. idem., *Journal of the Senate, 1962* (Columbia: State Budget & Control Board), 316–17, 671, 721.

61. McMillan, "Integration With Dignity," 381–84. Cox, "1963," 14–26.

62. Goldfield, *Promised Land,* 71, 100. McMillan, "Integration With Dignity," 381–91. Sproat and Schweikart, *Making Change,* 155–58. South Carolina, *Journal of the House of Representatives, 1963* (Columbia: State Budget & Control Board, 1963), 38.

63. McMillan, "Integration With Dignity," 381–91. Cox, "1963," 14–143. Newby, *Black Carolinians,* 332. Sproat, "'Firm Flexibility,'" 171–73, 177–80.

64. McMillan, "Integration With Dignity," 16. Cox, "1963," 346–51, 467–74. Jones, *South Carolina,* 278–80, 285–86. Newby, *Black Carolinians,* 274–360. Jack Bass and Walter DeVries, *The Transformation of Southern Politics* (New York: Basic Books, 1976), 248–49, 257–59. Joyner, "'One People,'" 234.

65. Cox, "1963," 346–461. Moore, *Columbia & Richland County,* 423, 428–29, 436. Huff, *Greenville,* 403–4. Fraser, *Charleston! Charleston!,* 413–18. William D. Smyth, "Segregation in Charleston in the 1950s: A Decade of Transition," *SCHM,* 92 (Apr. 1991): 99–123. William C. Hine, "Civil Rights and Campus Wrongs: South Carolina State College Students Protest, 1955–1968," *SCHM,* 97 (Oct. 1996): 310–31.

66. Cox, "1963," 462–66; Holman in *Daily Mail,* 11 June 1963 quoted, 462.

67. Fraser, *Charleston! Charleston!,* 401–3, 413–18. Jones, *South Carolina,* 286–86. Cox, "1963," 465–66.

68. Jack Bass, *Porgy Comes Home: South Carolina . . . After Three Hundred Years* (Columbia: R. L.

Bryan Company, 1972), 3–8; quotation, 8. Jones, *South Carolina*, 285–86. Cox, "1963," 467–80. Newby, *Black Carolinians*, 279–80, 330–45. Lofton, "Calm and Exemplary," 81. Sellers, *River of No Return*, 10, 16.

69. Bartley, *New South*, 335–37.

70. Cobb, *Industrialization and Southern Society*, 86. Newby, *Black Carolinians*, 330–39. Wright, *Old South, New South*, 268. Sproat, "'Firm Flexibility,'" 178.

71. Bass and DeVries, *Transformation of Southern Politics*, 260, 274–75. Edgar, *Biographical Directory*, 1: 617–20. Orville Vernon Burton, "South Carolina," in *The Quiet Revolution: The Impact of the Voting Rights Act in the South, 1965–1990*, eds. by Chandler Davidson and Bernard Grofman (Princeton: Princeton University Press, 1994), 191–232, 420–32. *Report of the South Carolina State Election Commission for the Period Ending June 30, 1973* (Columbia: State Budget & Control Board, 1974), 3: 301. "Report of the Secretary of State, Fiscal Year 1957–58," in *Reports & Resolutions 1959*, vol. 1.

72. Jack Nelson and Jack Bass, *The Orangeburg Massacre* (New York: World Publishing, 1970), 18–98, 222–38. Sellers, *River of No Return*, 206–19. Newby, *Black Carolinians*, 336, 357–60. Interview with Philip Grose, Columbia, S.C., 8 Aug. 1997.

The U.S. Department of Justice investigated the matter and compiled a massive file but wrote no formal report. As of this writing, access to these files had not yet been gained.

The Federal Bureau of Investigation also did an investigation, but the material, as released (much of it was blacked out), provided no new insight into the matter. Interview with William Hine, Orangeburg, S.C., 8 Aug. 1997.

73. Nelson and Bass, *Orangeburg Massacre*, 99–124, 164–221. Bass and DeVries, *Transformation of Southern Politics*, 259–60.

Sellers was charged with three counts of rioting and inciting to riot, but Judge John Grimball dismissed two of the charges. Sellers was convicted on one charge, sentenced to one year in prison, and fined $250 ($980). Sellers, *River of No Return*, 269–71. Nelson and Bass, *Orangeburg Massacre*, 138–46.

74. Fraser, *Charleston! Charleston!*, 421–23; *Evening Post* (Charleston), 21 July 1969 quoted, 423. *Time* (25 Apr. 1969): 23.

75. Goldfield, *Promised Land*, 142–44. Bass and DeVries, *Transformation of Southern Politics*, 261. Grantham, *South in Modern America*, 288. Robert Sherrill, "The Education of a Conservative," *Nation*, 213 (16 Aug. 1971): 105–10. "US Letter: Columbia," *New Yorker*, 43 (25 Nov. 1967): 208–16. *New Republic*, 160 (11 Jan. 1969): 32–33. David Nolan, "The 'Movement' Finally Arrives," *Nation*, 208 (26 May 1969): 654–56.

76. Jack Bass, foreword to Cauthen, *Speaker Blatt*, xvi–xvii. Bartley, *New South*, 254, 261–66.

77. Huff, *Greenville*, 404–6. *News* (Greenville), 28 Jan. 1970. *Piedmont* (Greenville), 26 Jan. 1970 in Scrapbooks, Robert Evander McNair Papers, Institute for Southern Studies, University of South Carolina, Columbia. Newby, *Black Carolinians*, 331. C. Blease Graham, Interview with Robert S. Davis, 25 Sept. 1979 (transcript, SCDAH: Robert E. McNair Oral History Project), 14–25.

78. Bass and DeVries, *Transformation of Southern Politics*, 260. Neal R. Pierce, *The Deep South States of America: People, Politics, and Power in the Seven Deep South States* (New York: W. W. Norton, 1974), 395–96. *Piedmont* (Greenville), 28 Jan. 1970; *News* (Greenville), 28 Jan. 1970; *Record* (Columbia), 21 Jan. 1970; *Evening Post*, 21 Jan. 1970 in Scrapbooks, McNair Papers. Sproat, "'Firm Flexibility,'" 171–73.

79. Bass and DeVries, *Transformation of Southern Politics*, 260. *State* (Columbia), 9, 18 Feb. 1970. *News* (Greenville), 23 Jan. 1970, Scrapbooks, McNair Papers.

80. *Observer* (Charlotte, N.C.), 9 Mar. 1970, *News* (Greenville), 18 Mar. 1970, *State* (Columbia), 9, 21 Feb. 1970 in Scrapbooks, McNair Papers. Pierce, *Deep South States*, 396. Bass and DeVries, *Transformation of Southern Politics*, 262. Conversation with Robert E. McNair, 1 Oct. 1996.

81. Huff, *Greenville*, 404–6. Bass and DeVries, *Transformation of Southern Politics*, 262. *State* (Columbia), 17 Oct. 1970, in Scrapbooks, McNair Papers. Watkins, *Anderson County*, 99.

82. Moore, *Columbia & Richland County*, 427. Huff, *Greenville*, 404–6. Henry H. Lesesne, "With Common Courtesy and Effort From Everyone": Desegregation at Spartanburg High School" (seminar paper, University of South Carolina, 1996), passim. Ella Poats, *The First Ninety-Eight Years, 1884–1982*:

Spartanburg County School District Seven (Columbia: R. L. Bryan Company, 1982), 93. "All Desegregation Orders Obeyed—Then School Chaos in Greenville, S.C.," *U.S. News & World Report*, 7 Dec. 1970, 26–28.

83. South Carolina High School League, *Palmetto's Finest* (Columbia, 1989), 48–52. South Carolina State Department of Education, *School Directory of South Carolina, 1955–1956, 1969–1970, 1970–1971, 1988–1989. Record* (Columbia), 17 Mar. 1971.

84. John Egerton, *The Americanization of Dixie: The Southernization of America* (New York: Harper's Magazine Press, 1974), 151–71. Bartley, *New South*, 417–22. *Newsweek* (27 Nov. 1972), 109–10. Fraser, *Charleston! Charleston!*, 423–24.

85. Robert J. Steeley, "A History of Independent Education in South Carolina," diss., University of South Carolina, 1979, 91, 97, 111–12, passim. Huff, *Greenville*, 404–6. Bartley, *New South*, 417–22. State Superintendent of Education, *Annual Report, South Carolina 1975–1976* (Columbia: State Budget & Control Board), 253, 265.

86. Black and Black, *Vital South*, 149–58, 169–75. Cohodas, *Strom Thurmond*, 355–62. Bartley, *New South*, 383–97. John C. Topping Jr., John R. Lazarek, and William H. Linder, *Southern Republicanism and the New South* (Cambridge, Mass., 1966), 10–11. Fowler, *Presidential Voting in South Carolina*, 35–51. Bartley, *New South*, 380. Harrison Jenkins, "On the Record," *State* (Columbia), 3 Apr. 1968, A14. Westbrook, "One Party State?," 14, 21–25. Grantham, *South in Modern America*, 203.

87. Fowler, *Presidential Voting*, 1–6. Thadeous H. Westbrook III, "A One Party State?: The Rising Tide of the Republican Party in South Carolina," honors thesis, University of South Carolina, 1996, 9–13, 17. Robertson, *Sly and Able*, 510–12. Bartley, *New South*, 100. Huff, *Greenville*, 407–10.

88. Fowler, *Presidential Voting in South Carolina*, 7–13. Topping et al., *Southern Republicanism*, 91–92, 96. Lachicotte, *Rebel Senator*, 253. Bass and DeVries, *Transformation of Southern Politics*, 254–55. Edgar, *Biographical Directory*, 1: 598–601. Westbrook, "One Party State?," 35.

89. Bartley, *New South*, 383–97. Westbrook, "One Party State?," 23. Cohodas, *Strom Thurmond*, 380. Topping et al., *Southern Republicanism*, 92–99. Bass and DeVries, *Transformation of Southern Politics*, 255.

90. Cohodas, *Strom Thurmond*, 396–400. Egerton, *Americanization of Dixie*, 128–31. Black and Black, *Vital South*, 166, 298–303. Goldfield, *Promised Land*, 187. Dan T. Carter, *The Politics of Rage: George Wallace, The Origins of the New Conservatism, and the Transformation of American Politics* (New York: Simon & Schuster, 1995), 328–30, 332.

91. Cohodas, *Strom Thurmond*, 405–7. Huff, *Greenville*, 410. Goldfield, *Promised Land*, 187. Bartley, *New South*, 407–13.

92. Graham and Moore, *South Carolina Politics*, 89, 92–93. Topping et al., *Southern Republicanism*, 25–28. Bartley, *New South*, 399–400. Cohodas, *Strom Thurmond*, 410–12. Billy B. Hathorn, "The Changing Politics of Race: Congressman Albert William Watson and the South Carolina Republican Party, 1965–1970," *SCHM*, 89 (Oct. 1990): 227–41. Bass and DeVries, *Transformation of Southern Politics*, 262–63. *State* (Columbia), 8 Sept. 1970, 6 Nov. 1970, 27 May 1971, in Scrapbooks, McNair Papers.

93. Wallace, *History of South Carolina*, 3: 367. Johnston's remarks in John E. Huss, *Senator for the South: A Biography of Olin D. Johnston* quoted in Hayes, "South Carolina and the New Deal," 486. Fowler, *Presidential Voting*, 52–78. Graham and Moore, *South Carolina Politics*, 93–94. Westbrook, "One Party State?," 24–25.

94. Edgar, *Biographical Directory*, 1: 548–624. Bailey et al., *Biographical Directory, Senate*, 1: 201–5, 612–15. Ashmore, *Hearts and Minds*, 24–28. Graham and Moore, *South Carolina Politics*, 121–27. Goldfield, *Promised Land*, 37.

95. Graham and Moore, *South Carolina Politics*, 40–45. Underwood, *Constitution of South Carolina*, 1: 59–82. Jean H. Toal, "The Illusion of Judicial Independence—Influence of the South Carolina General Assembly on the Structure, Powers and Selection of the State's Judiciary" (paper presented to the Kosmos Club, Columbia, S.C., 18 Mar. 1997), passim.

96. Bailey et al., *Biographical Directory, Senate*, 1: 6–7. Underwood, *Constitution of South Carolina*, 4: 270–96.

97. Underwood, *Constitution of South Carolina,* 4: 270–96.

98. Graham, "South Carolina Counties" and Charlie B. Tyer, "The Special Purpose District in South Carolina," in *Charlie B. Tyer and Cole Blease Graham, Jr., Local Government in South Carolina, vol. I: The Governmental Landscape* (Columbia: Bureau of Governmental Research and Service, University of South Carolina, 1984), 65–70, 75–89.

99. Graham, "South Carolina Counties," 51–64.

100. Graham and Moore, *South Carolina Politics,* 132–34.

101. West, "South Carolina Looks to the Future," 409–14. Egerton, *Americanization of Dixie,* 171. Bartley, *New South,* 132, 261–66.

CHAPTER 23: ADJUSTING TO NEW CIRCUMSTANCES

1. Graham and Moore, *South Carolina Politics,* 132–34.

2. Edgar and Woolley, *Columbia,* 172. Huff, *Greenville,* 413. Fraser, *Charleston! Charleston!,* 428–38. Westbrook, "One Party State?," 51. David Broder, "Riley has turned Charleston landscape into his master work," *State* (Columbia), 9 Mar. 1997, D2. Michael Shnayerson, "Southern Revival," *Condé Nast Traveler* (Aug. 1997): 94–101, 126–27. "Where are those who will lead South Carolina?," *State* (Columbia), 11 Mar. 1997, A8.

3. "Monument urged to honor blacks," *Post & Courier,* 24 May 1995, A8. "Rainey takes helm of utility," *Coastal Observer* (Pawley's Island), 21 Dec. 1989, 13. "Rainey appointed chairman of Santee Cooper Board," *Summerville Journal-Scene,* 29 Dec. 1989, B1. "Brookgreen taps Wall successor," *Sun News* (Myrtle Beach), 27 Mar. 1997. "Utility chief to lead Brookgreen board, *State* (Columbia), 28 Mar. 1997, B2. "An unavoidable issue," *State* (Columbia), 28 Apr. 1996, D2. Biographical Sketch of John Stringer Rainey provided by Santee Cooper, Monck's Corner, S.C. Biographical Sketch of Mary Rainey Belser provided by Heathwood Hall Episcopal School, Columbia, S.C. "Silver Fox Award," *Impact* (Junior League of Columbia, S.C.), Nov. 1992, 19.

4. *State* (Columbia), 23 Nov. 1979, A16; 3 June 1981, C2; 21 Aug. 1987, A24; 30 Oct. 1988, A1.

5. Moody's Investors Service, *Opportunity and Growth in South Carolina, 1967–1985* (New York: Moody's Investors Service, Inc. 1968).

6. "An Act to Establish the South Carolina Education Finance Program," in South Carolina, *Acts & Joint Resolutions of the General Assembly, Regular Session, 1977* (Columbia, 1977), 365–78. "An Act to Provide for the Establishment of a Basic Skills Assessment Program," in ibid., *1978,* 1807–13. "An Act to Provide the Training, Employment and Evaluation of Public Educators," in ibid., *1979,* 415–26.

7. Interview with William R. McKinney Jr., Governor Riley's press secretary, 8 Mar. 1990.

8. Richard Wilson Riley, 28 June 1984, quoted in Edgar, *South Carolina in the Modern Age,* 115. South Carolina State Department of Education, *EIA V: A Report on the Education Improvement Act of 1984 and South Carolina's Continuing Quest for Quality Public School Education* (Columbia, 1989).

9. Graham and Moore, *South Carolina Politics,* 167–69. South Carolina Department of Education, *Educational Trends in South Carolina, February 1984* (Columbia: Office of Research, 1984), 10. *Idem., Annual Report, 1984–1985* (Columbia: State Budget & Control Board, 1985), 217. *Idem., Annual Report, 1993–1994* (Columbia: State Budget & Control Board, 1994), 72.

10. South Carolina, *Acts and Joint Resolutions of the General Assembly, 1995* (Columbia: State Budget & Control Board, 1995), 2: 1193. South Carolina Commission on Higher Education, *Higher Education Statistical Abstracts, 1996* (Columbia: Division of Finance & Statistical Services, 1996), 20–21, 44–47.

11. Bass and DeVries, *Transformation of Southern Politics,* 250–51.

12. "S.C. still 'stinging' year later," *Observer,* 14 July 1991, A1. "Scandals Cloud Life in South Carolina," *New York Times,* 12 May 1991, Y11. "Embarrassing Success," *State* (Columbia), 14 May 1991, A8. "Other sting indictments," *State* (Columbia), 20 June 1991, A15. "South Carolina: Tammany Hall, South," *Economist* (18 Aug. 1990): 21. "The Funbelt State," *Economist* (13 Apr. 1991): 26.

13. "Legislature has been dominant throughout S.C. history," *State* (Columbia), 26 Aug. 1990, D2. "State's administrative authority hopelessly fragmented," *State* (Columbia), 10 Feb. 1991, D2. "Cabinet form of government more responsive," *State* (Columbia), 11 Feb. 1991, A12. "Initiative, referendum, re-

call useful tools of government," *State* (Columbia), 12 Feb. 1991, A8. A series of special investigative and editorial reports entitled "Power Failure" in the "Impact" section, *State* (Columbia), 5, 12, 19, 26 May 1991. Edgar, *South Carolina in the Modern Age,* 119–21. "Two sting casualties," *State* (Columbia), 19 Aug. 1990, D2. "FBI Sting Tactics," *News & Courier,* 19 Aug. 1990, A16. "Ruling underscores low ethical standard," *News,* 20 Aug. 1990, A4. "Playing a Little Poker," *News,* 19 Aug. 1990, E2. "A thoughtful public must seize the reins," *State* (Columbia), 26 Aug. 1990, D2.

14. "Governor names restructuring panel," *State* (Columbia), 23 Feb. 1991, B3. South Carolina Commission on Government Restructuring, *Modernizing South Carolina State Government for the Twenty-first Century* (Columbia, 1991).

15. Graham and Moore, *South Carolina Politics,* 179–80. South Carolina Commission on Government Restructuring, *Modernizing South Carolina State Government,* 56–330, 339–40.

16. Graham and Moore, *South Carolina Politics,* 176–81. "In ways large and small, new government starts today," *State* (Columbia), 1 July 1993, A1, 14. "Reform Wins," *State* (Columbia), 2 July 1994, A1. "Restructuring a bend in the road of state history," *Post & Courier,* 13 Jul. 1993, A1, 17.

17. Graham and Moore, *South Carolina Politics,* 121–27. Burton, "South Carolina," passim. Interview with William R. McKinney Jr., Columbia, S.C., 27 June 1997.

18. "For 300 years, a Legislative State," *State* (Columbia), 5 May 1991, D8–9. "Drawing S.C. into a corner," *State* (Columbia), 12 May 1991, D1–7; quotation, D5. Graham and Moore, *South Carolina Politics,* 121.

19. "Where are those who will lead South Carolina?" A8. "Supreme Court Showdown," *Times and Democrat* (Orangeburg), 19 June 1996, B4. "Campbell takes lead on battle flag issue," *News,* 3 July 1994, G2. "History shows leadership key to civil change in S.C.," *State* (Columbia), 24 Nov. 1996, D2. "Confederate flag's future is in hands of legislative leaders," *State* (Columbia), 4 Feb. 1997, A9. "Negro Block Voting," *News & Courier,* 16 Oct. 1964, A6. "Democratic Mess," *News & Courier,* 17 Oct. 1964, A6. "Arm-Twisting," *News & Courier,* 19 Oct. 1964, A10. "The Humphrey Position," *News & Courier,* 17 Oct. 1968, A12. "A Footnote to History," *News & Courier,* 21 Oct. 1968, A8. "The Chief Issue," *News & Courier,* 25 Oct. 1968, A10. "Voting in the General Election," *News,* 8 Oct. 1964, 4. "Some Dare Call It Blackmail," *News,* 13 Oct. 1964, 4.

20. Graham and Moore, *South Carolina Politics,* 67. Westbrook, "One Party State?," 3–8, 93.

21. Graham and Moore, *South Carolina Politics,* 69–74. Burton, "South Carolina," 15. Fowler, *Presidential Voting in South Carolina,* 35–98. Grantham, *South in Modern America,* 297–98, 303. Jack W. Germond and Jules Witcover, "GOP gains as blacks seek high office," *State* (Columbia), 29 May 1990, A6. Westbrook, "One Party State?," 43–48.

22. Westbrook, "One Party State?," 50–51, 66–72.

23. Ibid., 64–66.

24. Ibid., 43–48, 60–63, 72–76.

25. Westbrook, "One Party State?," 64–66. Edgar, *South Carolina in the Modern Age,* 122.

26. Westbrook, "One Party State?," 34–39, 49–51, 66–72. "GOP tide ebbing, poll hints," *State* (Columbia), 15 Sept. 1996, A1, 11. "State Legislature," *State* (Columbia), 7 Nov. 1996, B4.

27. Huff, *Greenville,* 407–10. "If It's Inglis vs. Condon, Hollings Wins," *State* (Columbia), 20 Apr. 1997, D4. "Coalition's Kingdom Has Come," *State* (Columbia), 21 Apr. 1996, D4. "Bad Blood Boils In Senate Race," *State* (Columbia), 6 May 1996, B1. "Jilted GOP might dance with Hodges," *State* (Columbia), 17 Aug. 1997, D4.

28. Black and Black, *Vital South,* 281–87, 299–325. Graham and Moore, *South Carolina Politics,* 77–78, 83–86.

Atwater was not a native South Carolinian, but he grew up and attended high school and college in the state. John Brady, *Bad Boy: The Life and Politics of Lee Atwater* (Reading, Mass.: Addison Wesley Publishing Company, 1997), 1–43.

29. Black and Black, *Vital South,* 331–37. Graham and Moore, *South Carolina Politics,* 83–84.

30. Cohodas, *Strom Thurmond,* passim; quotation, 427. "Thurmond Shows the Way," *State* (Columbia), 31 May 1996, A10; "Gala Toasts Thurmond," *State* (Columbia), 31 May 1997, A1. "The lionized Dixiecrat," *U.S. News & World Report* (16 June 1997): 33.

Thurmond himself said that his public service career began in 1923 when he started teaching school in McCormick County. "Floor Statement in response to tribute to Senator Thurmond," 3 June 1997 (ms. copy in author's possession).

31. Bailey et al., *Biographical Directory, Senate,* 2: 1197–99. Goldfield, *Promised Land,* 113. Westbrook, "One Party State?," 58–60. "Judge calls remap legal," *State* (Columbia), 1 Nov. 1996, B3; "Run Again, Judges Tell Senators," *State* (Columbia), 29 May 1997, A1. "The races are on," *State* (Columbia), 17 June 1997, B3. Sandra K. McKinney, ed., *1997 Legislative Manual,* 78th ed. (n.p., 1997).

32. Edgar, *South Carolina in the Modern Age,* 121. *Black Elected Officials: A National Roster,* 21st ed. (Washington: Joint Center for Political and Economic Studies, 1994), 377–96. McKinney, *1997 Legislative Manual,* 316. Interview with James Hammond, Columbia, S.C., 14 July 1997.

33. Black and Black, *Vital South,* 327, 331, 335, passim. Westbrook, "One Party State?," 57–72. Charles Joyner, "The South as Folk Culture" (paper presented at the Institute for Southern Studies, University of South Carolina, 24 June 1994), 5–8.

34. Conversation with James Miller, Columbia, S.C., 23 Jan. 1997. Walter B. Edgar, "Beyond the Tumult and the Shouting: Black and White in South Carolina in the 1990s" (paper presented at the Southern Studies Forum, 22 Aug. 1997, Odense University, Denmark).

35. "Orangeburg business has cut across racial lines," *State* (Columbia), 3 May 1992, G1. "Funeral told the story of changes in a lifetime," 30 Apr. 1996, A9. Calhoun County Museum, St. Matthews, S.C., 5 May 1996. George C. Rogers Jr. to author, 5 Feb. 1996 (emphasis supplied). Interview with Elizabeth Rast Giles, Swansea, S.C., 16 Apr. 1997. Edgar, "Beyond the Tumult and the Shouting," passim.

36. John Edgar Wideman, *Fatheralong: A Meditation on Fathers and Sons, Race and Society* (1994; New York: Vintage Books, A Division of Random House, 1995), 17, 87–116.

37. John Leland, "Crossover Culture: Goodbye Gangstas, Hello Hootie," *Newsweek* (25 Dec. 1995–1 Jan. 1996): 126, 128. "Hootie's Story is also Columbia's," *State* (Columbia), 22 June 1997, F4. Edgar, "Beyond the Tumult and the Shouting," passim.

38. Edgar, *South Carolina in the Modern Age,* 135–36. "Responding to Racism," *State* (Columbia), 5 May 1996, A8.

39. Wideman, *Fatheralong,* 109–12. Dori Sanders, *Her Own Place* (Chapel Hill: Algonquin Books, 1993), 164. Aimee Berry, "An Extended Essay" (honors seminar paper, University of South Carolina, 1996), 1–4.

40. Of the thirty-four fires, only one was labeled a hate crime and two were linked to the Ku Klux Klan. The causes of the others included thrill crime, vandalism, revenge, and covering up other crimes. "Recent S.C. church fires," *State* (Columbia), 15 Dec. 1996, D5. Peter Applebome, *Dixie Rising: How the South is Shaping American Values, Politics and Culture* (New York: Times Books Random House, 1996), 139.

"Wildfire" and "The State didn't add fuel to fires," *State* (Columbia), 15 Dec. 1996, D1, 5. "A triumph from the ashes," *State* (Columbia), 7 June 1997, A1, 7. "Flag shades proceedings of race panel," *State* (Columbia), 14 Dec. 1996, B3. E-mail message from the Very Rev. Samuel G. Candler, a member of the Race Relations Commission, to author, 23 June 1997.

41. "Flagging effort," *Independent-Mail* (Anderson), 17 May 1995, A6. "NAACP action against state may be postponed," *News* (Greenville), 24 June 1994, C1. "Campbell could call for flag session," *State* (Columbia), 25 June 1994, A1. "For Business, Flag Debate Mars Image of New South," *Wall Street Journal,* 23 Nov. 1994, S1. "Business takes on Confederate flag," *U.S. News & World Report* (5 Dec. 1994), 57. "A War of Words," *State* (Columbia), 28 May 1995, D1. "The center must hold," *Observer* (Charlotte), 22 Sep. 1994, A13. "Beasley 'not discouraged' by backlash to flag proposal," *State* (Columbia), 19 Nov. 1996, A1. "Debating the flag: 3 views" and "Who's for moving flag? Our state's true leaders," *State* (Columbia), 1 Dec. 1996, D2, D4. "Banner divides House," *State* (Columbia), 4 Dec. 1996, A1, 6. "Confederate flag's future is in the hands of Legislature's leaders," *State* (Columbia), 4 Feb. 1997, A4. "'Let all old wars die out,'" *State* (Columbia), 13 Dec. 1996, A1. "House unravels on flag," *State* (Columbia), 4 Apr. 1997, A1, 10. "Battle flag issue comes down to manners," *Sun News* (Myrtle Beach), 23 June 1996, D5. "Governor seeks to move Confederate flag," *Washington Post,* 27 Nov. 1996, A3. "Flag fight takes odd twists," *Journal and Constitution* (Atlanta), 19 Mar. 1995, A3. "S. Carolina's bat-

tle over its Confederate flag is a '90s-style civilized war," *Tribune* (Chicago), Evening-2. "Gov. Beasley's Courage," *Globe* (Boston), 5 Dec. 1996, A22. "Time to Lower Rebel Flag, A Southern Governor Says," *New York Times,* 27 Nov. 1996, A16.

42. The bill passed the senate but did not pass in the house before the 1997 legislative session ended. "Confederacy," *State* (Columbia), 1 May 1997, A1. Interview with Sen. John Courson of Richland County, 23 June 1997.

43. Clarke, *New Zion,* 287–88. Interview with Lorena D. Land, Columbia, S.C., 15 July 1997. Interview with Rhett Jackson, Columbia, S.C., 21 July 1997.

The United Methodist Church had a black bishop, Joseph Benjamin Bethea (1988–1995) and, beginning in June 1990, assigned black pastors to white churches and white pastors to black ones. Interview with Charles Johnson, Columbia, S.C., 22 July 1997. Trinity Episcopal Cathedral (Columbia) in 1997 had a black vestryperson and a black priest on its clergy staff.

44. Between 1970 and 1990 membership increased in the Episcopal Church 8.6 percent and in the United Methodist Church 7.5 percent. Nationally both denominations suffered significant declines in membership during the same twenty years. Roman Catholics increased by 68 percent and Church of God (Cleveland, Tenn.) by 59 percent. Douglas W. Johnson, Paul R. Picard, and Bernard Quinn, *Churches and Church Membership in the United States: An Enumeration by Region, State and County* (Washington: Glenmary Research Center, 1974), 1–2, 178–81. Martin B. Bradley, Norman M. Green Jr., Dale E. Jones, Mac Lynn, and Lou McNeil, *Churches and Church Membership in the United States 1990: An Enumeration by Region, State and County Based on Data Reported for 133 Church Groupings* (Atlanta: Glenmary Research Center, 1992), 1–2, 343–49. Donald A. Luidens, "Fighting 'decline': Mainline churches and the tyranny of aggregate data," *Christian Century,* 113 (6 Nov. 1996): 1075–79. "Church Attendance on the Decline," *Christian Century,* 113 (11 Sept. 1996): 843–44.

45. Stanley Hauerwas and William H. Willimon, *Resident Aliens* quoted in Loren B. Mead, *The Once and Future Church: Reinventing the Congregation for a New Mission Frontier* (Washington: Alban Institute, 1991), 23.

46. "Payouts Go Up in Smoke: Gamblers Lose Bet in 11 Counties," *State* (Columbia), 10 Nov. 1994, B1. There were another twenty-four articles dealing with the subject of video gambling in the *State;* see video gambling entries on the CyberState: (http://www.thestate.com). "High Court Decision Plugs in Video Poker: Games of Chance Now Legal in All S.C. Counties," *State* (Columbia), 10 Dec. 1996.

The twelve counties that voted to ban video poker were Abbeville, Aiken, Anderson, Cherokee, Chester, Chesterfield, Greenwood, Lancaster, Oconee, Pickens, Union, and York. South Carolina Department of Revenue.

47. Interview with Lee Bandy, Columbia, S.C., 29 Aug. 1997.

48. South Carolina Budget & Control Board, *South Carolina Statistical Abstract, 1992* (Columbia: Office of Research & Statistics, 1997), 136, 239, 289.

49. Sproat and Schweikart, *Making Change,* 175. Bartley, *New South,* 423–27, 451–52. Graham and Moore, *South Carolina Politics,* 91–92. *Biographical Directory, Senate,* 2: 1242–43. "List of top female executives shrinks," *State* (Columbia), "Palmetto 50" (special section): 7. "Judge Jean G. Bissell dies of cancer at 53," *State* (Columbia), 2 May 1990, B1. McKinney, *1997 Legislative Manual.*

50. "Male Cadet Accused of Hazing Leaves Citadel," *State* (Columbia), 31 Jan. 1997, A1. "Female Cadets Say Year Fair, Challenging," *State* (Columbia), 24 May 1997, A1. Female enrollment statistics supplied by admissions personnel at Medical University of South Carolina, USC Medical School, USC Law School, and Winthrop University. South Carolina Commission on Higher Education, *Higher Education Statistical Abstracts, 1996,* 30–33, 36–37.

51. Kovacik and Winberry, *South Carolina,* 142–49.

52. "The South: Into a New Century," 27. Edgar and Woolley, *Columbia,* 168–72. James Dickey, *The Starry Place Between the Antlers: Why I Live in South Carolina* (Bloomfield Hills, Mich.: Bruccoli Clark, 1981), 12.

"Ohio bashing" has a long and rich tradition in southern fiction. Fred Hobson, *The Southern Writer in the Postmodern World,* Mercer University Lamar Memorial Lecture No. 33 (Athens: University of Georgia Press, 1991), 40, 59–60.

53. Kovacik and Winberry, *South Carolina,* 152–53.

54. Bartley, *New South,* 132, 261–66, 448–51, 455–57. Berry, "Extended Essay," 4–7. Browning, *Linthead,* 174–76.

55. Josephine Humphreys, *Rich in Love* (1987; New York: Penguin Books, 1992), 11. Jan Nordby Gretlund, "Citified Carolina: Josephine Humphreys' Fiction," in *Southern Landscapes,* eds. Tony Badger, Walter Edgar, and Jan Nordby Gretlund, with Lothar Hönnighausen and Christoph Irmscher (Tåbingen, Germany: Stauffenburg Verlag, 1996), 254–61.

56. Bartley, *New South,* 453. Hobson, *Southern Writer in the Postmodern World,* 1–10, 58–72.

57. Hobson, *Southern Writer in the Postmodern World,* 58–72. "Storytelling from the Heart," *State* (Columbia), 11 Aug. 1996, E3. Gretlund, "Citified Fiction," 254–65. Martha E. Cook, "Old Ways and New Ways, in Rubin et al., *History of Southern Literature,* 532. Dannye Powell, interviews, and Jill Krementz, photographs, *Parting the Curtains: Interviews with Southern Writers* (Winston-Salem, N.C.: John F. Blair, 1994), 48, 183–85, 190–91, 271–77, 280–81. William Price Fox, *Southern Fried Plus Six* (Philadelphia: J. B. Lippincott, 1968). idem., *Moonshine Light, Moonshine Bright* (1967; New York: Bantam Books, 1970). idem., *Ruby Red* (1971; New York: Bantam Books, 1973). Pat Conroy, *The Prince of Tides* (1986; New York: Bantam Books, 1987), 1. idem., *The Great Santini* (1976; New York: Avon Books, 1977). idem., *Beach Music* (New York: Nan A. Talese, Doubleday, 1995). idem., *The Lords of Discipline* (Boston: Houghton Mifflin, 1980). idem., *The Water Is Wide* (Boston: Houghton Mifflin, 1972). *South Today,* 2 (Dec. 1970): 1, 2, 9, 10. *Life,* 72 (2 June 1972): 3, 4, 55–72. "Passion and power imbue life's work," *State* (Columbia), 25 June 1995, A1. "High Tide in the Low Country," *San Francisco Examiner Magazine,* 16 July 1995, 11, 22–25, 27. "Growing Literature," *Post-Herald* (Birmingham, Ala.), 8 Mar. 1995, D1. "The Booklist Interview: Dori Sanders," *Booklist,* 89 (15 Feb. 1993): 1–2. "Becoming a writer, remaining a farmer," *New York Times,* 3 May 1993, C11. "Fox on His Writing," *State* (Columbia), 1 Jan. 1978, E1.

58. Drew Stewart, "Yankees Annex Myrtle Beach," typescript of column prepared for *Gamecock* (University of South Carolina), 2 Mar. 1995 issue. "South Carolina: 'Out of Season Every Season,'" broadside (n.p., [c. 1996]).

59. Marshall Frady, *Southerners: A Journalist's Odyssey* (New York: New American Library, 1980), 286–301. Cobb, *Selling of the South,* 238, 240–42, 248–50. Goldfield, *Promised Land,* 197. "The Showdown at Hilton Head," *Business Week* (17 Apr. 1971): 102. "Environment Fight at Hilton Head," *Newsweek* (13 Apr. 1970): 71–75. "Industry Grows Up in South Carolina," *Business Week* (2 Sept. 1972): 36–37.

60. *Progressive,* 53 (June 1989): 12–13. Edgar, *South Carolina in the Modern Age,* 132–34. "Pee Dee history, progress collide," *State* (Columbia), 5 Mar. 1997, A1; *State* (Columbia), 3 June 1997, B3. Interview with Winona B. Vernberg, dean of the College of Public Health, University of South Carolina, 15 May 1990. "SC Chamber Wrong," "Come out Nov. 14 to oppose GSX," "Thanks for taking our waste," *Daily Item* (Sumter), 9 Nov. 1988, A11. "2,000 protest GSX," *Daily Item,* 15 Nov. 1988, A1. "'10 years of frustration,'" *Daily Item,* 15 Nov. 1988, A6.

61. Goldfield, *Promised Land,* 204–5. Files of *State,* "GSX," *Record* (Columbia), 18 Mar. 1986. "'Enough,' Says America's No. 1 Nuclear Dump," *U.S. News & World Report* (11 July 1994): 18.

62. Browning, *Linthead,* 1–19. Files of *State,* "Textiles," *State* (Columbia), 22 Feb. 1987. "With mills' closing, neighborhood starts new era," *State* (Columbia), 30 June 1996, A1, 16. Ford and Coclanis, "South Carolina Economy," 106.

63. "Mill's closing hits Iva in heart," *State* (Columbia), 16 Dec. 1995, A1, 10; "Rural Upstate towns cope with life after textiles," *State* (Columbia), 27 May 1996, B6. "With mills' closing, neighborhood starts new era," *State* (Columbia), 30 June 1996, A1, 16.

64. Sproat and Schweikart, *Making Change,* 166–81, 235–36. "Carolina's NationsBank eyed," *Observer* (Charlotte), 24 Sept. 1994, D1.

65. Files of the *State,* "Industry," *State* (Columbia), 25 July 1983; *Record,* 18 May 1977. Huff, *Greenville,* 391.

66. "Keeping Fed Center only makes sense," *State* (Columbia), 8 June 1997, G1. Interview with Fred Monk, Columbia, S.C., 9 June 1997.

67. Files of the *State,* "Industries," *State* (Columbia), 10 Aug. 1987. "The Caretaker," *State* (Columbia), 12 Jan. 1997, S4.

Flagstar had the largest revenue. Interview with Fred Monk, Columbia, S.C., 21 July 1997.

68. "Accent on German in South Carolina," *Los Angeles Times,* 30 Nov. 1994, A5. "Business South Carolina," *State* (Columbia), 27 Sept. 1993, special section. "Industry investments soar," *State* (Columbia), 19 Jan. 1996, A1, 6. "S.C. hails a 'home run' year," *State* (Columbia), 17 Jan. 1997, A1, 12. "Tax breaks help win Honda," *State* (Columbia), 6 May 1997, A1, 6. "*Carolinas?*," *Observer,* 16 May 1993, D7, 10. "S.C. rolls out the welcome mat," *State* (Columbia), 22 Sept. 1991, G1, 4. Glickman and Woodward, *New Competitors,* 193.

69. "Accent on German in South Carolina," *Times* (Los Angeles) A5. "King Paper," *State* (Columbia), 24 July 1994, A9. 30 Nov. 1994, A5. *State* (Columbia), 24 July 1994, A9. Coclanis and Ford, "South Carolina Economy," 103–6. *S.C. Statistical Abstract, 1972,* 31, 43; *1992,* 253; *1993,* 158, 169. Bureau of the Census, *Statistical Abstract of the United States, 1996* (Washington, D.C.: Government Printing Office, 1996), 741.

70. Pope, *History of Newberry County,* 2: 155–69. Kovacik and Winberry, *South Carolina,* 162, 172. A1, 8. Ag Econ home page (http:\\cherokee.agecon.clemson.edu/crops.html), *South Carolina Agricultural Statistics Service, 1996. Crops: Acreage, Yield and Production, 1994 and 1995.*

71. Coclanis, *Shadow of a Dream,* 155–56. "2 military towns on alert," *State* (Columbia), 1 June 1997, A10.

72. Stewart, "Yankees Annex Myrtle Beach." "Where the Buys Are," *Washington Post,* 18 Dec. 1996, D9. "Grand Strand Booms," *State* (Columbia), 30 June 1996, G1, 4. Applebome, *Dixie Rising,* 9.

73. Fraser, *Charleston! Charleston!,* 425. "Riding tourism's big wave," *State* (Columbia), 8 Feb. 1996, B1, 12.

74. Interview with Winona B. Vernberg, Columbia, S.C., 15 May 1990. Edgar, *South Carolina in the Modern Age,* 133–35. "Small haul has Lowcountry blue crab fishermen worried," *State* (Columbia), 14 Jan. 1996, B4. "Crew helps nature restore beach," *State* (Columbia), 3 Apr. 1996, B1. "Report gives beaches thumbs-up," *State* (Columbia), 15 June 1997, B7.

75. Robert L. Janiskee, "Storm of the Century: Hurricane Hugo and the Impact on South Carolina," *Southeastern Geographer* (30 May 1990): 66. Wade Graham, "Beachless," *New Yorker* (16 Dec. 1996): 58–67. Interview with Wayne Beam, South Carolina Coastal Council, 24 June 1997. James Kilpatrick, "When is a 'taking' not a 'taking'?," *State* (Columbia), 3 Feb. 1992, A6.

76. Janiskee, "Storm of the Century," 63–66.

A 1996 poll of coastal county residents revealed that only about one half had any recollection of Hugo, just seven years earlier. "S.C. hopes to duck sucker punch this hurricane season," *State* (Columbia), 17 June 1997, D1.

77. Bureau of the Census, *1990 Census of Population & Housing: Social, Economic, and Housing Characteristics: South Carolina* (Washington, D.C.: U.S. Bureau of Census, 1993), 2–11. George C. Rogers Jr., "Who Is a South Carolinian?," *SCHM,* 89 (Jan. 1988): 11–12. Kovacik and Winberry, *South Carolina,* 133–35. *State* (Columbia), 7 June 1992, A1, 12.

78. Petty, *Twentieth Century Changes in South Carolina Population,* 168. McKinney, *1997 SC Legislative Manual,* passim.

There were thirty-five other members of the General Assembly who did not list a place of birth in their biographies, although all attended South Carolina high schools. McKinney, *1997 SC Legislative Manual,* passim.

79. "1995 South Carolina All-State Academic Team" and "1996 South Carolina All-State Academic Team," *State* (Columbia), special sections. Interview with Deborah K. Woolley, South Carolina Chamber of Commerce, 15 May 1997. Interview with Jackie Asbury, State Department of Education, 25 June 1997.

80. WPA, *South Carolina,* 3–7.

SELECTED BIBLIOGRAPHY

Although there are South Carolina manuscript collections out of state, the richest are those in the South Carolina Department of Archives and History, the South Caroliniana Library at the University of South Carolina, and the South Carolina Historical Society. Both the South Carolina Historical Society and the South Caroliniana Library have published guides and established WEB sites on the internet. The *South Carolina Historical Magazine* and the *Proceedings of the South Carolina Historical Association* contain numerous articles cited in the text.

This selected bibliography contains works that will enable the reader to investigate more fully particular areas of the state's history. All of the books deal specifically with South Carolina or South Carolina–related topics. With the exception of a few older works (e.g., Wallace's *The History of South Carolina* and Simkins's *Pitchfork Ben Tillman*), almost all of them are the result of recent scholarship. Most are available in university and public libraries. A number of them are still in print, and many of those are in paperback editions.

The bibliography is divided into topics that cut across time periods: General Works, Local Histories, Race and Ethnicity, Economics, Military, Politics and Government, and Everyday Life.

GENERAL WORKS

Barry, John M. *Natural Vegetation of South Carolina.* Columbia: University of South Carolina Press, 1980.

Chesnutt, David R., and Clyde N. Wilson, eds. *The Meaning of South Carolina History: Essays in Honor of George C. Rogers, Jr.* Columbia: University of South Carolina Press, 1991.

Edgar, Walter B. *South Carolina in the Modern Age.* Columbia: University of South Carolina Press, 1992.

Graham, Cole Blease Jr., and William V. Moore. *South Carolina Politics and Government.* Lincoln: University of Nebraska Press, 1994.

Jones, Lewis P. *South Carolina; A Synoptic History for Laymen.* Rev. ed. Orangeburg, S.C.: Sandlapper Press, 1978.

Kovacik, Charles F., and John J. Winberry. *South Carolina: A Geography.* Columbia: University of South Carolina Press, 1989.

Lander, Ernest M. Jr., and Robert K. Ackerman, eds. *Perspectives in South Carolina History: The First Three Hundred Years.* Columbia: University of South Carolina Press, 1973.

Rogers, George C. Jr. *Generations of Lawyers: A History of the South Carolina Bar.* Columbia: South Carolina Bar Foundation, 1992.

Underwood, James Lowell. *The Constitution of South Carolina.* 4 vols. Columbia: University of South Carolina Press, 1986–1994.

Wallace, David Duncan. *The History of South Carolina.* 4 vols. New York: American Historical Society, Inc., 1934.

Writers' Program of the Works Projects Administration. Introduction by Walter B. Edgar. *South Carolina: The WPA Guide to the Palmetto State.* Columbia: University of South Carolina Press, 1988.

LOCAL HISTORIES

Bethel, Elizabeth Rauh. *Promiseland: A Century of Life in a Negro Community.* Columbia: University of South Carolina Press, 1997.

Burton, Orville Vernon. *In My Father's House Are Many Mansions: Family and Community in Edgefield, South Carolina.* Chapel Hill: University of North Carolina Press, 1985.

Charles, Allan D. *The Narrative History of Union County, South Carolina.* Spartanburg, S.C.: Reprint Company, 1987.

Fraser, Walter J. Jr. *Charleston! Charleston!: The History of a Southern City.* Columbia: University of South Carolina Press, 1989.

Gregorie, Anne King. *History of Sumter County.* Sumter, S.C.: Library Board of Sumter County, 1954.

Huff, Archie Vernon Jr. *Greenville: The History of the City and County in the South Carolina Piedmont.* Columbia: University of South Carolina Press, 1995.

Joyner, Charles. *Down by the Riverside: A South Carolina Slave Community.* Urbana: University of Illinois Press, 1984.

King, G. Wayne. *Rise Up So Early: A History of Florence County, South Carolina.* Published for the Florence County Historical Commission. Spartanburg, S.C.: Reprint Company Publishers, 1981.

Linder, Suzanne Cameron. *Historical Atlas of the Rice Plantations of the ACE River Basin—1860.* Columbia: South Carolina Department of Archives and History, 1995.

Moore, John Hammond. *Columbia & Richland County: A South Carolina Community, 1740–1990.* Columbia: University of South Carolina Press, 1993.

Pope, Thomas H. *The History of Newberry County, South Carolina.* 2 vols. Columbia: University of South Carolina Press, 1973, 1992.

Powers, Bernard E. Jr. *Black Charlestonians: A Social History, 1822–1885.* Fayetteville: University of Arkansas Press, 1994.

Rogers, George C. Jr. *Charleston in the Age of the Pinckneys.* Columbia: University of South Carolina Press, 1984.

———. *The History of Georgetown County, South Carolina.* Columbia: University of South Carolina Press, 1970.

Rosen, Robert. *A Short History of Charleston.* Columbia: University of South Carolina Press, 1997.

Rowland, Lawrence S., Alexander Moore, and George C. Rogers Jr. *The History of Beaufort County, South Carolina, Volume 1: 1514–1861.* Columbia: University of South Carolina Press, 1996.

Stokes, Durwood T. *The History of Dillon County, South Carolina.* Columbia: University of South Carolina Press, 1978.

Vernon, Amelia Wallace. *African Americans at Mars Bluff, South Carolina*. Columbia: University of South Carolina Press, 1995.

RACE AND ETHNICITY

Alleyne, Warren, and Henry Fraser. *The Barbados-Carolina Connection*. Basingstoke, U.K.: Macmillan Caribbean, 1988.

Bridenbaugh, Carl, and Roberta Bridenbaugh. *No Peace beyond the Line: The English in the Caribbean, 1624–1690*. New York: Oxford University Press, 1972.

Conroy, Pat. *The Water Is Wide*. New York: Bantam Books, 1987.

Dunn, Richard S. *Sugar and Slaves: The Rise of the Planter Class in the English West Indies, 1624–1713*. Published for the Institute of Early American History and Culture, Williamsburg, Va. New York: Norton Library, W. W. Norton & Company, Inc., 1973.

Dusinberre, William. *Them Dark Days: Slavery in the American Rice Swamps*. New York: Oxford University Press, 1996.

Gordon, Asa H. *Sketches of Negro Life and History in South Carolina*. 2d ed. Columbia: University of South Carolina Press, 1971.

Hagy, James W. *This Happy Land: The Jews of Colonial and Antebellum Charleston*. Tuscaloosa: University of Alabama Press, 1993.

Hatley, Tom. *The Dividing Paths: Cherokees and South Carolinians Through the Era of Revolution*. New York: Oxford University Press, 1993.

Hoffman, Paul E. *The New Andalucia and a Way to the Orient: The American Southeast During the Sixteenth Century*. Baton Rouge: Louisiana State University Press, 1990.

Hudson, Charles. *The Juan Pardo Expeditions: Explorations of the Carolinas and Tennessee, 1566–1568*. Washington, D.C.: Smithsonian Institution Press, 1990.

Littlefield, Daniel C. *Rice and Slaves: Ethnicity and the Slave Trade in Colonial South Carolina*. Urbana: University of Illinois Press, 1991.

Lofton, John. *Insurrection in South Carolina: The Turbulent World of Denmark Vesey*. Yellow Springs, Ohio: Antioch Press, 1964.

Lyon, Eugene. *The Enterprise of Florida: Pedro Menéndez de Avilés and the Spanish Conquest of 1565–1568*. Gainesville: University Presses of Florida, 1976.

Meriwether, Robert L. *The Expansion of South Carolina, 1729–1765*. Kingsport, Tenn.: Southern Publishers, Inc., 1940.

Merrell, James H. *The Indians' New World: Catawbas and Their Neighbors from European Contact through the Era of Removal*. Published for the Institute of Early American History and Culture, Williamsburg, Va. Chapel Hill: University of North Carolina Press, 1989.

Nelson, Jack, and Jack Bass. *The Orangeburg Massacre*. New York: World Publishing Company, 1970.

Newby, Idus A. *Black Carolinians: A History of Blacks in South Carolina from 1895 to 1968*. Tricentennial Studies, No. 6, published for the South Carolina Tricentennial Commission. Columbia: University of South Carolina Press, 1973.

Puckrein, Gary A. *Little England: Plantation Society and Anglo-Barbadian Politics, 1627–1700*. New York: New York University Press, 1984.

Sellers, Cleveland, with Robert Terrell. *The River of No Return: The Autobiography of a Black Militant and the Life and Death of SNCC*. Jackson: University Press of Mississippi, 1990.

Silver, Timothy. *New Face on the Countryside: Indians, Colonials and Slaves in South Atlantic Forests, 1500–1800*. New York: Cambridge University Press, 1990.

Tindall, George Brown. *South Carolina Negroes, 1877–1900*. Columbia: University of South Carolina Press, 1952.

Waddell, Gene. *Indians of the South Carolina Lowcountry, 1562–1751*. Columbia: Southern Studies Program, University of South Carolina, 1980.

Wideman, John Edgar. *Fatheralong: A Meditation on Fathers and Sons, Race and Society*. New York: Vintage Books, A Division of Random House, Inc., 1994.

Williamson, Joel. *After Slavery: The Negro in South Carolina During Reconstruction, 1861–1877*. Hanover, N.H.: Wesleyan University Press, University Press of New England, 1990.

Wood, Peter H. *Black Majority: Negroes in Colonial South Carolina from 1670 through the Stono Rebellion*. New York: Alfred A. Knopf, 1974.

ECONOMICS

Carlton, David L. *Mill and Town in South Carolina, 1880–1920*. Baton Rouge: Louisiana State University Press, 1982.

Chaplin, Joyce E. *Anxious Pursuit: Agricultural Innovation & Modernity in the Lower South, 1730–1815*. Published for the Institute of Early American History and Culture, Williamsburg, Va. Chapel Hill: University of North Carolina Press, 1993.

Coclanis, Peter A. *The Shadow of a Dream: Economic Life and Death in the South Carolina Low Country, 1670–1920*. New York: Oxford University Press, 1989.

Johnson, Michael P., and James L. Roark. *Black Masters: A Free Family of Color in the Old South*. New York: W. W. Norton & Company, 1984.

Koger, Larry. *Black Slaveowners: Free Black Masters in South Carolina, 1790–1860*. Columbia: University of South Carolina Press, 1995.

Lander, Ernest M. Jr. *The Textile Industry in Antebellum South Carolina*. Baton Rouge: Louisiana State University Press, 1969.

Ver Steeg, Clarence L. *Origins of a Southern Mosaic: Studies of Early Carolina and Georgia*. Mercer University Lamar Lectures, No. 17. Athens: University of Georgia Press, 1975.

MILITARY

Dederer, John Morgan. *Making Bricks Without Straw: Nathanael Greene's Southern Campaign and Mao Tse-Tung's Mobile War*. Manhattan, Kans.: Sunflower University Press, 1983.

Lambert, Robert Stansbury. *South Carolina Loyalists in the American Revolution*. Columbia: University of South Carolina Press, 1987.

Lander, Ernest McPherson Jr., *Reluctant Imperialists: Calhoun, The South Carolinians, and the Mexican War*. Baton Rouge: Louisiana State University Press, 1980.

Lucas, Marion Brunson. *Sherman and the Burning of Columbia*. College Station: Texas A&M University Press, 1976.

Lumpkin, Henry. *From Savannah to Yorktown: The American Revolution in the South*. Columbia: University of South Carolina Press, 1981.

Wise, Stephen R. *Gate of Hell: Campaign for Charleston Harbor, 1863*. Columbia: University of South Carolina Press, 1994.

POLITICS AND GOVERNMENT

Barnwell, John. *Love of Order: South Carolina's First Secession Crisis*. Chapel Hill: University of North Carolina Press, 1982.

Bartlett, Irving H. *John C. Calhoun, A Biography*. New York: W. W. Norton & Company, 1993.

Burts, Robert Milton. *Richard Irvine Manning and the Progressive Movement in South Carolina*. Columbia: University of South Carolina Press, 1974.

Cauthen, Charles Edward. *South Carolina Goes to War, 1860–1865*. The James Sprunt Studies in History and Political Science, No. 32, Albert Ray Newsome et al., eds. Chapel Hill: University of North Carolina Press, 1950.

Channing, Steven A. *Crisis of Fear: Secession in South Carolina*. New York: Norton Library, W. W. Norton & Company, Inc., 1970.

Cohodas, Nadine. *Strom Thurmond & the Politics of Southern Change*. Macon, Ga.: Mercer University Press, 1993.

Coit, Margaret L. *John C. Calhoun: American Portrait*. Introduction by Clyde N. Wilson. Columbia: University of South Carolina Press, 1991.

Cooper, William J. Jr. *The Conservative Regime: South Carolina, 1877–1890*. Baltimore: Johns Hopkins University Press, 1968.

Edmunds, John B. Jr. *Francis W. Pickens and the Politics of Destruction*. Chapel Hill: University of North Carolina Press, 1986.

Faust, Drew Gilpin. *James Henry Hammond and the Old South: A Design for Mastery*. Baton Rouge: Louisiana State University Press, 1982.

Ford, Lacy K. Jr. *Origins of Southern Radicalism: The South Carolina Upcountry, 1800–1860*. New York: Oxford University Press, 1988.

Freehling, William W. *Prelude to Civil War: The Nullification Controversy in South Carolina, 1816–1836*. New York: Harper Torchbooks, Harper & Row, 1968.

Holt, Thomas. *Black Over White: Negro Political Leadership in South Carolina during Reconstruction*. Urbana: University of Illinois Press, 1977.

Jones, Lewis Pinckney. *Stormy Petrel: N. G. Gonzales and His State*. Tricentennial Studies, No. 8, published for the South Carolina Tricentennial Commission. Columbia: University of South Carolina Press, 1973.

Klein, Rachel N. *Unification of a Slave State: The Rise of the Planter Class in the South Carolina Backcountry, 1760–1808*. Published for the Institute of Early American History and Culture, Williamsburg, Va. Chapel Hill: University of North Carolina Press, 1990.

Lamson, Peggy. *Glorious Failure: Black Congressman Robert Brown Elliott and the Reconstruction in South Carolina*. New York: W. W. Norton & Company, Inc., 1973.

Meleney, John C. *The Public Life of Aedanus Burke: Revolutionary Republicanism in Post-Revolutionary South Carolina*. Columbia: University of South Carolina Press, 1989.

Miller, Edward A. *Gullah Statesman: Robert Smalls, from Slavery to Congress, 1839–1915*. Columbia: University of South Carolina Press, 1995.

Nadelhaft, Jerome J. *The Disorders of War: The Revolution in South Carolina*. Orono: University of Maine at Orono Press, 1981.

Robertson, David. *Sly and Able: A Political Biography of James F. Byrnes*. New York: W. W. Norton & Company, 1994.

Rogers, George C. Jr. *Evolution of a Federalist: William Loughton Smith of Charleston*

(1758–1812). Columbia: University of South Carolina Press, 1962.

Simkins, Francis Butler. *Pitchfork Ben Tillman, South Carolinian*. Reprint ed. Gloucester, Mass.: Peter Smith, 1964.

Sirmans, M. Eugene. *Colonial South Carolina: A Political History, 1663–1763*. Published for the Institute of Early American History and Culture, Williamsburg, Va. Chapel Hill: University of North Carolina Press, 1966.

Waterhouse, Richard. *A New World Gentry: The Making of a Merchant and Planter Class in South Carolina, 1670–1770*. New York: Garland Publishing Company, 1989.

Weir, Robert M. *Colonial South Carolina: A History*. Millwood, N.Y.: KTO Press, a Division of Kraus-Thomson Organization, Limited, 1983.

Williams, Lou Faulkner. *The Great Ku Klux Klan Trials*. "Studies in the Legal History of the South", edited by Paul Finkelman and Kermit L. Hall. Athens: University of Georgia Press, 1996.

Zuczek, Richard. *State of Rebellion: Reconstruction in South Carolina*. Columbia: University of South Carolina Press, 1996.

EVERYDAY LIFE

Bellows, Barbara L. *Benevolence Among Slaveholders: Assisting the Poor in Charleston, 1670–1860*. Baton Rouge: Louisiana State University Press, 1993.

Bolton, S. Charles. *Southern Anglicanism: The Church of England in Colonial South Carolina*. Contributions to the Study of Religion, No. 5. Westport, Conn.: Greenwood Press, 1982.

Browning, Wilt. *Linthead: Growing Up in a Carolina Cotton Mill Village*. Asheboro, N.C.: Down Home Press, 1990.

Clark, Erskine. *Our Southern Zion: A History of Calvinism in the South Carolina Low Country, 1690–1990*. Tuscaloosa: University of Alabama Press, 1996.

Farmer, James Oscar Jr. *The Metaphysical Confederacy: James Henley Thornwell and the Synthesis of Southern Values*. The Frank S. and Elizabeth D. Brewer Prize Essay of the American Society of Church History. Macon, Ga.: Mercer University Press, 1986.

Fields, Mamie Garvin, with Karen Fields. *Lemon Swamp and Other Places: A South Carolina Memoir*. New York: Free Press, 1983.

Fox, William Price. *Moonshine Light, Moonshine Bright*. New York: Bantam Books, 1970.

Hollis, Daniel W. *University of South Carolina*. 2 vols. Columbia: University of South Carolina Press, 1951, 1956.

Humphreys, Josephine. *Rich in Love*. New York: Penguin Books, 1992.

Lippy, Charles H., ed. *Religion in South Carolina*. Columbia: University of South Carolina Press, 1993.

McCandless, Peter. *Moonlight, Magnolias, & Madness: Insanity in South Carolina from the Colonial Period to the Progressive Era*. Chapel Hill: University of North Carolina Press, 1996.

McCurry, Stephanie. *Masters of Small Worlds: Yeoman Households, Gender Relations, and the Political Culture of the Antebellum South Carolina Low Country*. New York: Oxford University Press, 1995.

O'Brien, Michael, and David Moltke-Hansen, eds. *Intellectual Life in Antebellum Charleston*. Knoxville: University of Tennessee Press, 1986.

Rice, John Andrew. *I Came Out of the Eighteenth Century.* New York: Harper and Brothers, 1942.

Robertson, Ben H. *Red Hills and Cotton: An Upcountry Memory.* Introduction by Lacy K. Ford. Columbia: University of South Carolina Press, 1991.

Sanders, Dori. *Her Own Place.* Chapel Hill, N.C.: Algonquin Books of Chapel Hill, 1993.

Townsend, Leah. *South Carolina Baptists, 1670–1805.* Florence, S.C.: Florence Printing, 1935.

Walsh, Richard. *Charleston's Sons of Liberty: A Study of the Artisans, 1763–1789.* Columbia: University of South Carolina Press, 1968.

Woodward, C. Vann. *Mary Chesnut's Civil War.* New Haven: Yale University Press, 1981.

INDEX